GALLETTI'S
TELUGU DICTIONARY
A DICTIONARY OF CURRENT TELUGU

GALLETTI'S
TELUGU DICTIONARY
A DICTIONARY OF CURRENT TELUGU

BY

A. GALLETTI DI CADILHAC, I.C.S.
SOMETIME SCHOLAR OF TRINITY COLLEGE, OXFORD
CAVALIERE DELLA CORONA D'ITALIA
CORRESPONDING MEMBER OF THE ROYAL BATAVIA SOCIETY

Author of Sahacarula Parapati Sanghamulu, Vimala Gnyan' opadesamulu, The Dutch in Malabar, Translation of K. Viresalingam's Vinodha Tarangani, &c.

Verborum Vetus Interit Aetas
Et Juvenum ritu Florent modo nata Vigentque

Introduction By

R. Galletti, I.C.S.

GYAN

Published by

Gyan Publishing House
5, Ansari Road
Daryaganj, New Delhi-110002
Phone: 011-47034999, 9811692060
E-mail: books@gyanbooks.com

Distribution Network
gyanbooks.com
India, USA, Canada, UK, Australia, France

ISBN : 978-81-212-3067-4 (PB)
First Published, 1935

2nd Impression 2020

Printed at: Gyan Press, Delhi.

Galletti's
Telugu Dictionary A Dictionary of Current Telugu
Author: A. Galletti Di Cadilhac

GALLETTI'S TELUGU DICTIONARY

A DICTIONARY OF CURRENT TELUGU

By

A. GALLETTI DI CADILHAC, I.C.S.

SOMETIME SCHOLAR OF TRINITY COLLEGE, OXFORD

CAVALIERE DELLA CORONA D'ITALIA

CORRESPONDING MEMBER OF THE ROYAL BATAVIA SOCIETY

Author of *Sahacārula Parapati Sanghamulu, Vimala Gnyān' ōpadēṣamulu, The Dutch in Malabar*, translation of K. Vīrēṣalingam's *Vinōdha Tarangani, &c.*

Verborum vetus interit aetas
Et juvenum ritu florent modo nata vigentque

INTRODUCTION BY

R. GALLETTI, I.C.S.

OXFORD UNIVERSITY PRESS

LONDON : HUMPHREY MILFORD

1935

Photo. Vandyk, London

THE RAJA OF BOBBILI

of a Telugu family once famous in war, now devoted to civil administration. He is our present Chief Minister and Chief Patron of this work. His grandfather was the first Indian Member of the Executive Council of the Presidency.

Í vyávahárica bhásha dicshanari vidya vyápimpa galad ani nammi Prathama Mantri v'unna ṢRÍ BOBBILI RÁJAGÁRULA *pádapadmamula samukhamucu samarpinchinánu cánuca.*

Trusting that this dictionary of current Telugu will conduce to the diffusion of knowledge I lay it at the feet of the Honourable the RAJA OF BOBBILI, Chief Minister.

LIST OF PATRONS AND SUBSCRIBERS

CHIEF PATRON

DEDICATED BY PERMISSION TO

THE HONOURABLE THE RAJA OF BOBBILI

Chief Minister to the Madras Government and Pro-Chancellor of the Andhra University

OTHER PATRONS

SIR GEORGE FORBES

Emeritus Member of Council, Madras

S. H. SLATER, ESQUIRE, I.C.S., C.M.G.

THE DISTRICT BOARD, ANANTAPUR

THE ZAMINDAR OF MUNAGALA

THE DISTRICT BOARD, CHITTOOR

THE DISTRICT BOARD, WEST GODAVARI

THE DISTRICT BOARD, CUDDAPAH

THE DISTRICT BOARD, VIZAGAPATAM

SUBSCRIBERS

THE HONBLE. SIR KURMA VENKATREDDI, *Member of Council, Madras.*
THE HONBLE. MR. KUMARASWAMI REDDIAR, *Minister of Education, Madras.*
THE DIRECTOR OF PUBLIC INSTRUCTION, MADRAS.
THE DIRECTOR OF PUBLIC INSTRUCTION, MYSORE.
THE ANDHRA UNIVERSITY.
THE OSMANIA UNIVERSITY COLLEGE, HYDERABAD.
THE CENTRAL COLLEGE, BANGALORE.
THE KERN INSTITUTE, LEYDEN.
TRINITY COLLEGE, OXFORD.
THE CEDED DISTRICTS COLLEGE.
RAJAHMUNDRY COLLEGE.
THE MAHARAJA'S COLLEGE, VIZIANAGARAM.
THE GOVERNMENT TRAINING SCHOOL, VIZAGAPATAM.
THE NATIONAL GIRLS' HIGH SCHOOL, MYLAPORE.
THE LORD BISHOP OF MADRAS.
THE RAJA OF KHALLIKOTE.
THE ZAMINDAR OF SINGAMPATTI.
THE HONBLE. MR. M. RÁMACHANDRA RAO.
MR. GOPALASWAMI MUDALIAR, M.L.C.
A. S. OWEN, ESQUIRE, *Fellow of Keble College, Oxford.*
C. F. BRACKENBURY, ESQUIRE, I.C.S.
P. MACQUEEN, ESQUIRE, I.C.S.
V. PANDURANGA RAO, ESQUIRE, I.C.S.
A. F. W. DIXON, ESQUIRE, I.C.S.
SRIMAN D. MAHANTY MAHASAYO.
K. NAGESWARA RAO, ESQUIRE.
DOCTOR G. SALVADORI.
MESSRS. GRINDLAY AND CO.
THE MADANAPALLE COLLEGE.
THE GIRLS' HIGH SCHOOL, NELLORE.
DIWAN BAHADUR V. N. VISWANATHA RAO.
MR. PATHIKONDA BALASUBBA CHETTI, HOSPET.
MR. MULA VENKATASWAMI, HOSPET.
THE ADYAR LIBRARY.
THE DISTRICT BOARD, BELLARY.
THE RAJA OF JEYPORE.
THE MUNICIPAL COUNCILS, HINDUPUR, KURNOOL, TADPATRI AND ANANTAPUR.
G. T. BOAG, ESQUIRE, I.C.S.
C. R. REDDI, ESQUIRE, *sometime Vice-Chancellor, Andhra University.*
JANAB ROSHAN HUSSAIN, *Sahib Bahadur of Adoni.*
THE IMPERIAL LIBRARY, CALCUTTA.
THE HIGH COMMISSIONER FOR INDIA.
THE POLIGAR OF KOSGI.
RAO SAHIB B. TAMI REDDI, KOWTALAM, BELLARY DISTRICT.
MR. K. R. RACHA REDDI, KOWTALAM, BELLARY DISTRICT.
M. R. RY. B. KRISHNA RAO AVERGAL.
M. M. RAHMATULLAH SAHIB.
M. R. RY. C. PEDDA RANGA REDDI GARU.
I. HAJEE PEERA SAHIB.
M. R. RY. B. SOMI REDDI GARU.
B. H. HUSSAIN SAHIB.
A. P. ABDUL KHADER SAHIB.
DONGRE SAHIB.
Y. GOUSE MOHIDEEN SAHIB.
R. SABDAR HUSSAIN SAHIB.
K. AHMAD ALI SAHIB.
REV. R. E. SMITH.

PREFACE

I WROTE this dictionary *ad usum delphini* when my son was sent to me as Assistant Collector. I publish it in the hope it may be useful to other Assistant Collectors, young officials, missionaries, and business men, and to Telugu boys learning English. There is no other Telugu dictionary in the least like it. I have for one thing used Roman characters, and for another left out all words that are not in common use. I do not conceal from myself that a common verdict of the Telugus will be: 'Idi ye dicshanari? dicshanari, gicshanari'; that is, this is no dictionary at all. It is perfectly true that it is not a dictionary in the ordinary sense, but rather a manual for young people learning Telugu or English, and it aims at educating, edifying, or even amusing them when they look up words.

A. GALLETTI.

Scr. in villa prope
IGUVIUM,
A.D. 1933, *men. sext.*

ILLUSTRATIONS

INTRODUCTION

THOUGH speech may have been given to express our thoughts, writing was intended, according to the Telugu practice, to obscure them. There is a most serious estrangement between spoken and written Telugu; at one time it threatened at least a *decree nisi*, till the necessity of earning his daily rice compelled the educated Telugu to write in a manner intelligible to more than one in a hundred of his countrymen. Even now the leading articles of every newspaper and the more pretentious works of the learned are mere gibberish to half the number of literate Telugus and mean nothing at all to the illiterate. But the news is reported in colloquial language, and magazines are published in which stories told with simple force jostle poems and articles enervated by pedantry.

The pedantry of 'grammatical' Telugu is tragically absurd. Beginning with the false premiss that grammatical correctness and elegance of diction must be based on the usage of past centuries, and continuing with mistaken formulations of that usage, the pundits had reached a stage when every one of them found the style of every other one contaminated and abominable, before a few sensible scholars were at last found to explode their whole theory and practice. The new school pointed out that grammar is not a fixed unchanging scheme but a body of rules deduced from usage; as usage changes, so must grammar change; and when you have the perfect, perpetual, immutable grammar, the language is dead. A new approach to writing was demanded. Instead of paralysing elegances and affected intricacies of style, which made the writing of Telugu an exercise of mystification and the reading of it the solution of innumerable puzzles, to the joy of the pundits and the scorn of their adversaries, there was to be the natural, easy, nervous expression of the writer's meaning in the words and the constructions which the writer would use in conversation with his friends. Though the pundits denounced the vulgarity, the 'village' origin, of the new vocabulary and the new grammar, these were bound to prevail if anybody had any meaning he really wished to express. They have not yet conquered all along the front, but they have established themselves in modern Telugu prose.

It now remains to see what can be made of the new prose. So far it has lacked a great exponent. The most eminent figure in modern Telugu literature halted midway between the camps. In many of his works he used the *gramyamu*, the common dialect, freely and unashamedly, and the popular appeal of his village comedies was enormously increased by their adaptation to the popular ear. But in his more exalted flights he entered the kingdom of the pundits and wandered in the cloudy realm of Sanskrit compounds and archaic survivals. In many of his works you may observe the remarkable (but still not uncommon) practice of explaining the 'Telugu' word by an English word. The English word is used in ordinary parlance; but it would be blasphemy in the pundit not to prefer the Sanskrit compound, newly coined and wholly incomprehensible to all save himself and the very few of the elect. The vicious practice of drawing upon Sanskrit for new compounds, even when another word is in common use, seems almost ineradicable. It is one of the causes of the needless obscurity of newspaper leaders, scientific articles, and treatises on matters removed from everyday life; even though the writer makes no display of grammatical elegance and writes as it were in conversational vein he will be thwarted in his attempt to make his meaning clear if he refuses to use the words in which he frames his thoughts.

Now it may be a pity, but it is a fact, that on nearly all matters except those of domestic and personal concern the educated Telugu learns to think and to express himself, not in Telugu, but in English. The abstract terms which he can really handle are English. Whether he is talking of politics, of economics, of medicine, of agricultural science, of law, of education, the odds are that he has imbibed his information in English, that his concepts are founded on the English words, and that he could express himself with greater accuracy, fluency, and force in English than in the vernacular. This state of affairs, be its causes and its defects what they may, has a curious dominance in modern Telugu. It brings it about that a writer, so soon as he leaves the spheres in which he is accustomed to use the vernacular as his daily medium of expression, begins as it were to translate his thoughts into Telugu rather than to compose in Telugu. All who have had occasion to study the official translations of Government publications and of Acts of the legislature will know the consequence that generally follows: the language is thrown out of its stride and becomes a curious hybrid, with no style of any kind. Just as the English schoolboy writes dog-Latin in trying to put English into Latin without reconstructing the meaning in a Latin form, so does the Telugu graduate write dog-Telugu because his thought was born in English and resists transmigration. When he tries to reincarnate it in a language not even his own, that is in the Sanskritized and obsolescent dialect of the pundits, the infant becomes a monster. Nobody who knows English at all will ever make use of the versions prepared by Government translators—better a foreign language than a distortion of language.

It does not follow that English is in any way likely to oust Telugu. Telugu is a living language because millions speak it in the villages, and the Telugu of the villages will go its own course in spite of the graduates. It is very hospitable to the foreign word: in time past it adopted Urdu words to supplement its own stock where it was poor; from time immemorial to this day it has been taking Sanskrit words to its bosom with various degrees of change; and it has no difficulty in entertaining the English word. *Róḍḍu* has practically supplanted all other words in talking of highways: *pólísu*, *stéshanu*, *suparindentu*, *mā̄ilu*, *mótáru*, *rélu*, and many others are good modern Telugu words for which there are no substitutes. Men of education import words and the villager uses them without question. When his betters use such phrases as *ná wátch slógá v'undi*, *í lā̄in márc chési*, *instrüment level lédu*, *ácṭu páss ā̄inadi*—and would be hard put to it to express the same meaning in words of indigenous growth—it is no wonder that the villager, when he has to do with the things of a novel civilization, borrows the terms of an unknown language. It is obvious that a nation's vocabulary reflects a nation's life: translators constantly find themselves stumped by words denoting things familiar to one people but not found at all amongst the other; and this dictionary in explaining words has incidentally become a manual of practices and manners. As the life of a Madras village begins to embrace the novelties of the brave inventive new world the village language picks up counters to pass current for them. Since English is now the language of the administration, the courts, the marts, and the colleges—in short, of every manifestation of the new activity—the vernacular naturally enriches itself from the English. But should the period of English dominance end to-morrow and the Andhras form their own government, they must make an attempt to conduct their own affairs in their own language. There can never be any hope of changing the language of the mass of the people, and a nation's government, however despotic, cannot use a foreigner's tongue with a good grace.

It is, however, hardly conceivable that Telugu as it now is can meet the future demands of the Andhra people. The colloquial Telugu of to-day is a simple tongue, sufficient for the wants of a simple life. But as a people comes to maturity, and its range of thought and feeling widens, words must be found to express the whole gamut of meaning. At the same time political organization proceeds; the village gives place to the district and the district to the province as the microcosm of communal life; and the province calls for a standard speech. Telugu as the tongue of an independent and advancing people must be enriched and modelled to a form which can everywhere prevail over discrepant dialects.

At present there is a great difference between the Telugu of different districts. In the schools a certain uniformity of pronunciation and grammar has been compassed, but so far is this from being carried into current speech that an experiment which was made at Madras of allowing the candidates for certain examinations to write in the colloquial vernacular of their own region failed because the examiners could not cope with the immense variety of vocabulary thus let loose. Indeed Telugu is now in the condition attributed to the 'lingua del sí' by Dante in his treatise *De Vulgari Eloquio*. If history should only repeat itself, it may develop as that language in its many dialects developed, and achieving a greater uniformity, dignity, and harmony, truly earn the title of 'the Italian of the East'.

As yet it hardly deserves the title. Some pronunciations of Telugu are in the highest degree clear, mellifluous, harmonious. On the stage, when actors give each vowel a precise sound and each consonant its true character, Telugu can be a fascinating language. In the bazaars, where counterfeit too often passes current and clipped coin is the rule, Telugu can be as strident, raucous, and mumble-mouthed as any language in the world, and can in no way compare with the Italian of provincial piazzas. The consonants are generally slovenly. Hard *d* for one requires too much effort for the mechanic herd; in such words as *ḍḍutáru* it becomes very like *r* (*ḍrtáru*) and elsewhere is barely distinguishable from English *d*. The distinction between *s*, *ṣ*, and *sh* is neglected. The Sanskrit aspirates lose their aspiration. The sounds *ts* and *ch*, *dz* and *j*, are confounded—sometimes, however, to advantage, as when the sibilant *tsúṭsutsu* is improved into *tsúchutu* and so into the usual form *tsúṣtu*. Vowels are very unstable. Short *a* is as often as not indefinite, approximating sometimes to *e* rather than to *a*. Long *a* varies with its place in the word and the stress upon it. Such words as *vastárá* are pronounced *vastără* because the stress is on the first and last syllables. Short *u* varies according to the sounds preceding and following; it sometimes approximates to *o*, sometimes to *a*. Final short *u* is hardly ever pronounced at all, so that though written Telugu is full of *u*, spoken Telugu is dominated by *i* and *a*. Other final vowels are either elided or quietly dropped whenever possible. The same fate befalls many a whole final syllable, especially the inflected endings of verbs: *nu, vu, ḍu, du, mu, ru, vi, ri* are all apt to vanish away. *Ikkaḍ'lé* for *ikkaḍa lédu* is normal; for *nuvvu pó, nénu vastánu* you may hear *nuppó, né vastá*. From plays in the colloquial dialect may be culled such mutilations as *á máṭac'osté* for *á máṭacu vasté*, *yaracca* for *yerugaca*, *nác'em cávâli* for *nácu yémi cávalayunu*, *sacchăn rá* for *tsachchinánu rá*, *appanitrá* for *appanu yeṭlu rá*, *láccó* for *lágucó*, *tíscochchănu* for *tísuconi vachchinánu*. Yet in these literary productions a limit is set to vulgarisms; the speech of ryots and shopkeepers is even harsher and more curtailed. It is not altogether at fault, since Telugu words are unduly long; but as the mutilations have not yet been reduced to rule, and as different contractions are in vogue in different districts, the colloquial forms are not all suited to a universal literary language. First a norm must be set up on the foundation of some chosen usage.

As every district with equal vehemence maintains its own title to be the home of the true, the ancient, the perfect Telugu, the choice is invidious. The opinion of the learned is not entirely agreed. Some favour the region of Guntur and Nellore and some the region of Godavari and Kistna. The author of this dictionary is among the latter; the vocabulary he has compiled consists of the words in common use from Cocanada to Bezwada. In so defining his limits and purging his language he has taken one step towards the King's Telugu.

Greater steps remain for Telugu writers to take. A foreigner may be permitted to point out a vocabulary suited to the reformed language of the future: but who is to create a literature in it? The literary languages of modern Europe owe their foundation to some man or group of men. When Luther translated the Bible into pure and simple German he made it a model for the generations to come. The Elizabethans gave English a norm. Italian owns Dante as a foster-father. Yet Dante was in some degree a pedant and had the same exaggerated respect for Latin that Telugu pundits have for Sanskrit and Sanskritized Telugu. The first book of his *Convito* might well be cited on either side of the controversy between pundits and reformers. Dante would not use Latin for that work from two sets of motives. The first is worthy of the pundits: Latin was too noble, excellent, and beautiful for a commentary on verses in the vulgar tongue; too noble, because eternal and incorruptible; too excellent, as expressing concepts more perfectly than Italian; too beautiful, as following art instead of usage in its harmony and construction. The reply to Dante and the pundits is the same. Neither Latin nor Sanskrit nor Sanskritized Telugu is eternal and incorruptible; Dante's own Latin was very different from Cicero's and equally different from that of Erasmus; the pundit's Telugu fails by its own canons. Neither Latin nor Sanskrit nor Sanskritized Telugu is better adapted to expressing thought than a modern tongue used with genius or even with skill. Neither Latin nor Sanskrit nor Sanskritized Telugu is freer from usage or more capable of art than their living derivatives. The notion that the Latin gloss might have been too good for the Italian verses was purely fantastical. The verses still live. So will Telugu verses in the colloquial.

Dante's other set of motives was first, liberality, and second, love of his native speech. In order to make largess of his knowledge to the multitude of his countrymen, he must use their language; nor was he averse, because he had a natural affection for it. These are exactly the motives of the reformers. But from among them has arisen as yet no Dante. There is now no figure in the Telugu literary world so outstanding as the late Veerasalingam Pantulu; and even that giant of the last generation was not of so great a stature. His works exploded the notion that elegance and beauty in Telugu prose consisted of overwrought descriptions of natural and erotic scenes composed throughout of indigestible Sanskrit epithets and unpronounceable Sanskrit nouns. But he left no work meet to thrill the millions and open their eyes to the imaginative universe.

Among other peoples and in other eras the great ages of literature have begun with song. The Andhra nation sings naturally, constantly, melodiously—though the matter of the songs that cartmen and porters sing as they move in file down the road is not always worthy of their singing. But Telugu literature has ignored and despised Telugu song; it has imported an alien prosody, in which the language moves uneasily, as though constricted by borrowed garments. The author of this dictionary holds the opinion that a quantitative prosody on the Greek pattern would best suit the genius of the language and has rendered two verses of Homer (*Od.* xv. 54–5) into very passable Telugu hexameters:

Gnyapti y'athidci marí y'untunnadi rózulu y'anni
Satcáram Ṣri Rája samastam chésina y'andu.

The experiment might be worth continuing; anyhow it is for the modern Telugu to fashion himself a measure in which he can readily wield his own language and be understood by the many. A Telugu poem of to-day is understood only by the learned; the words, the constructions, the inflectional forms are all strange and incomprehensible to the vulgar.

Poetical diction has run so wild that the common word is wholly inadmissible; prosodical necessity is so overbearing that every word is distorted. Other nations have won beauty out of imported forms: Latin poets enslaved themselves to Greek to their profit: English poetry adapted the Italian verse and gained sweetness. But to all seeming Telugu verse is now only a kind of jig-saw puzzle, and the picture that emerges is too often cheap and nasty. Vicious canons of composition have made shoddy panegyrics and erotic rhapsodies the common matter of poetry; such things are not worthy of a self-respecting people.

It might appear that Telugu is not naturally a poetical language. It is somewhat deficient in metaphorical expressions and shy even of similes. It avoids epithet and is richer in nouns than in adjectives. It is remarkably concrete in expression: the figurative and the abstract are rare in comparison with the bald statement of sensible fact (or nonsensical superstition). But all this might have been said of Latin when Ennius began to wield it and even after Lucretius had carved philosophy into poetry with it. *Vires acquirit eundo.* A language is a great poet's garden, and the flowers spring up as he goes about it.

Not otherwise the great orator and the great thinker develop a language in wielding it. The Greek of Solon and the Latin of the Gracchi were hardly richer than modern Telugu. They too loved the concrete expression, fled the abstract; they too were terse rather than florid; they too preferred the personal turn and the active mood. The work of the dramatists, the historians, the orators, the poets, the philosophers, from Aeschylus to Plato, gave Greek every instrument it lacked, till it could discourse on everything in earth and heaven. Lucretius and Virgil and Cicero between them did the same service for Latin. The old words were enriched with new shades, new depths, new discriminations, new subtleties of meaning. New words were minted as they were wanted. There was little need to borrow; the old speech was capable of both variety and precision in the hands of the masters.

So is Telugu. For oratory in particular it is eminently suited. Its precise structure, giving weight to the essential words and emphasis to words abnormally placed, has the same advantages as Latin's. Its inflectional nature affords every opportunity for ellipse, balance, and symmetry; its very want of conjunctions forces on it the rhetorical devices of the ancients. The peculiar Dravidian form of the relative clause tightens the texture of the sentence. If the Andhra orators only studied the proverbs of their people and imitated their compact energetic expression, their speeches might engender conviction by their very form. The turgid longevity of the sentences they are wont to deliver may fascinate the unfortunate listener but lets the point escape. In the narrative style a similar fault prevails. The old principle, the longer a sentence the better, still has many adherents. The flowing spineless sentences have no relation to the articulations of the sense. It is not so in common speech, where the sentences are in comparison as live kraits to dead pythons. In truth the illiterate villager often has more sense of style than the product of the colleges: the common petition-writer sometimes has a sure touch in ordering his facts and putting them out in few and telling words, though his writing is often more intelligible than legible.

He has indeed to cope with an unmanageable alphabet. It is less absurd than the Tamil, Kanarese, and Malayalam, but not by much. It is syllabic and consequently difficult to read even in print. Where the last vowel of a word is elided, that word undeservedly gets saddled with the first vowel of the next, which equally undeservedly loses its head. The letters are pretty, but untidy in combination. In cursive writing the untidiness becomes a welter. The claim that the alphabet is strictly phonetic is not well founded. One letter does duty for the two sounds *ts* and *ch*, another for both *z* and *j*, and a third for both aspirate *ph* and *f*. There are entirely unnecessary symbols for a hard *r* and hard *n* which are never used in speech. In some books an obsolete symbol still appears for an imaginary nasal sound of indeterminate character alleged to be present in many words. The same sound *ts* is sometimes written as one letter and sometimes as two. The six long vowels, six short vowels, and two diphthongs for which there are characters by no means exhaust the range of vowel sounds used in speaking. For instance, the modified long *a* in such contractions as *pilchäru* or such borrowed words as *bäncu* has to be represented by the same symbol as ordinary long *a*. Modified long *e* is found in the usual pronunciation of such words as *lĕca*, *mĕta*, but is not to be distinguished in writing. A Telugu can apparently discriminate between the various pronunciations of long *a* in *gunḍá* when it represents (1) *gunḍa+á*, (2) *gunḍi+á*, (3) *gunḍu+á*, (4) *gunḍe+á*, and in *cótá* when it represents (1) *cóta+á*, (2) *cótu+á*, (3) *cóti+á*, or of short *u* in *méc'undi* according as it is (1) *méca undi*, and (2) *mécu undi*. But the difference does not appear in writing. The Telugus are proud of their alphabet in spite of its defects; but the author of this dictionary may be excused for thinking that his work will both be easier to read and more phonetically correct in its dress of Roman letters with appropriate diacritical marks.

The International Phonetic Alphabet would in some ways be even better, but its correctness does not compensate for its unfamiliarity to any but trained phoneticians. The professors of phonetics have hitherto neglected Telugu; yet there is much to interest them in a language whose system of vowel harmony has a natural origin in the speech habits of the people and a completeness very remarkable in so natural a growth. In inflected forms the vowel modification extends even to a change from *u* to *i* or from *a* to *u*, while in all words the common pronunciation assimilates neighbouring vowels as far as possible to each other or modifies them to go with neighbouring consonants. Even the use of the euphonic interpellatives *v* and *y* is phonetically regular.

The phoneticians have the advantage that their principles require them to study the prevailing usage; the dictionary spelling has for them no unassailable sanctity. The author of this dictionary has to reckon with the bogey of India, *mámúl*, established custom, in the form of recognized spellings, though he can add notes on the usual pronunciation. Telugu spelling is fortunately very sound in the main. It is in accidence and syntax that the opinion of the learned and the practice of the vulgar are at loggerheads. A reconciliation is to be effected by discarding obsolete doctrine and examining the speech of educated men all over the Andhra country to see what usages are admissible and what must be regarded as solecisms. So may be compiled a Dictionary of Modern Telugu Usage which will do for grammar what this work attempts for vocabulary, establishing a norm and encouraging the men of genius to use the tools most fitted for their work. Perhaps inspiration will be lacking while the Telugu nation is in tutelage; but when the noble and puissant nation mewe its mighty youth, when the full tide of inspiration begins to flood the land, it is surely the common people, the people of the villages, who should hear and applaud. It is their language that must be used; therefore to its study this work is devoted.

R. GALLETTI.

TELUGU DICTIONARY

-A. No equivalent suffix. 'Oh' or 'My' prefixed.

The classical languages of course have a vocative. The modern European languages do without, prefixing 'Oh' sometimes or to express strong emotion 'My'.

The vocative suffix, lengthened to *á!* and in the plural *ára!* Thus a high official opens a cattle show, making a speech which is translated as he goes on. He begins: 'Ryots'. The translator translates 'ryots' at somewhat greater length: *chennapaṭnapu pedda boarḍ membaru iccaḍacu daya chési tsálá dúram nunchi vacchi cheppinadi yémanṭé: raituláral!* From Madras the great Board Member having deigned to come here from a great distance what he says is: 'Ryots!' Or in the Telugu hymn-book published by the Lutherans you will find 'O Lamb of God', translated *Gorre-pilla Dévuḍa!*, i.e. O son of a sheep, God! This is not recommended as a good example. Christian Telugu is a language apart.

-a. No equivalent suffix. In Indian English it is translated 'only'. In English 'indeed', 'self', or by circumlocution. Tamil *tán*. Emphatic suffix: more commonly *-é*: *Antá níva yeṟuguduvu*, you know it perfectly well; don't pretend you do not.

a-, un-, in-, less, dis-. Negative prefix. *In-*, Latin, Italian, French; *a-*, *an-*, Greek; *a*, *an*, *na-*, Skt.; *un-*, German. *a-jírṇamu*, indigestion; *a-jágrata*, careless; *a-námicá*, nameless; *a-y-ishṭamu*, disfavour; *a-n-ádaraṇa*, unkindness.

abaddhamaina, false. Composed of *a-baddhamu-aina*.

abaddhamu, falsehood, lie. Tamil: *poi*; *pachchi abaddhamu*, barefaced lie. *asatyam*, the Sanskrit word, is also commonly used in all the Dravidian languages, just as the words derived from Latin (*falso*, *faux*, *falsch*) are used in all the European languages. *oca abaddhamu cammaḍánici veyyi abaddhálu cávalenu*, a thousand lies are wanted to cover one; *chésévi Śiva pújalu chéppévi abaddhálu*, what he does is pūjas to Siva, what he says are lies; *dévuni y'eduṭa antá nizam chepputánu, abaddham ḍḍanu* is the form of oath in law-courts.

abaddhapu, false (e.g. witness).

a-balamu, weak. *abala*, the weak thing, is commonly used in books for 'woman'.

abba, father. Same in Hebrew. *tannina tarváta ní abbató cheppucó*, when he has kicked you, go and tell your father; *pórá, ní abbató cheppucórá!*

abba! what a wonder!

abba! ayyó! exclamation of grief and pain.

abbabba! an interjection of disgust. *abbabba! yenta gáḍida v'ai póyávu*, Lord, what an ass you are!

abbáyi, my boy (to a junior); **abbi,** my good fellow (to an inferior). Forms of address such as *abbáyi*, *abbi*, *ammáyi*, *oré*, *bábu*, *yémói* are in English and other languages names: 'I say, John!' 'Do you know, Mrs. Smith?' 'Mary, run away and play', &c. *abbáyi, chinnaváḍavu, nic émí teliyadu*,—'Boy! you are young, you know nothing'. The commonest substitute for the name as form of address is the relationship, as *anna*, elder brother; *tammuḍu*, younger brother; *talli*, mother. By a curious inversion a mother will call her daughter *talli*, and so on.

abbé! good God! dear me! Exclamation of surprise or indignation. **abbé,** no, no; *abbé yémi lédu*, no, no, it is nothing. **abburamu, abramu,** wonder; **abburapáṭu,** wonderment. *y'enducu inta abburapáṭutó tsústávu?* why are you so amazed?

abbuṭa, to be obtained or acquired, grow on one (as habits). *bógamdánni v'untsucóvaḍam valla durmárgulató sahavásam abbutundi*, by keeping a dancing girl one gets into the habit of bad company.

abhamu-şubhamu, good and evil. *abhamu-şubhamu y'eragani amdyacuḍu,* a simpleton not knowing good from evil.

abhaya-hastamu, promise of protection; from Skt. *a-bhaya,* fearless, and *hastamu,* hand.

abhayamu, security. *várini racshinchedam ani abhaya-hastam ivva valenu,* you must promise them your protection. In the old plays some one or other is always seeking the protection of one God or hero against another.

abhásu, abhásamu, coarse. *abhásapu Telugu,* coarse and low dialect of Telugu, as *cúcó* for *cúrtsó,* sit; *yellu* for *veḷḷu,* go.

abhicáramu, ghee. Skt. *abhi-gáram.* The Telugu for ghee is *neyyi.* This is one of those Sanskrit words which, though not used in common talk, is understood because of its connexion with religious rites. Thus in England chalice is not now the word for cup, but most people know what a chalice is.

abhicáramu, the sprinkling of ghee upon food before the beginning of a dinner. *abhicáramu cániyyanḍi,* sprinkle ghee that we may begin dinner.

abhignyánamu, intelligence; from Skt. The Telugu is *telivi,* but for intelligence, opinion, &c., Sanskrit words are in quite common use, and are at any rate easily understood, just as the corresponding words used in English are of Latin origin.

abhilásha, strong desire, love. *Telugu nértsucuné abhilásható v'unnánu,* I have a strong desire to learn Telugu. *abhilashintsuṭa,* to desire, Skt.

abhimatamu, desire, wish, opinion, inclination. Skt. *véré rájadháni cáválani Teluguvári abhimatamu,* the Telugus desire a separate province.

abhimánamu, love. Skt. The common words are *áşa, córica, préma,* but this is common at any rate in books. *ná manasşuló v'unna abhilásha pracárangá,* according to the wish in my heart; *nácu vidya anṭé mahá abhilásha,* I have much love of knowledge; *sárthaca paḍa valayun ani ná y'abhimatam,* I wish to profit. *désábhimánamu* is the combination by which patriotism, once an unknown emotion, is now translated.

abhimukhamu, facing, favouring; from *mukhamu,* face.

abhinandintsuṭa, to rejoice; from *ánandam,* joy.

abhinava, modern, new. The component parts are Sanskrit; the Telugu for new is *cotta,* but *nava* is commonly understood, and English *new* and *novel,* German *neu,* Italian *nuovo,* French *neuf,* Spanish *nuevo,* Dutch *nieuw,* Latin *novus,* Greek *neos* are all the same word—one of the most diffused of all words. *abhinava brühaspatul aina y'í mantrula mantra balam chéta,* by means of the sorcery of those modern Brühaspatis.

abhinayamu, expression of sentiment by actors, especially by gesture and posture. Skt.

abhinayintsuṭa, the corresponding verb of the preceding word. Skt. The modern European languages have no word for this; mimic action is perhaps the nearest English. *páḍédáni abhinayam bágá tsúḍa modalú peṭṭináḍu,* he began to observe closely the action of the songstress.

abhinivéşamu, zeal; a Sanskrit word used in books; the Telugu is *paṭṭu. váḍu manchi abhinivéşamutó pani chéstáḍu,* he works with tremendous zeal.

abhipráyamu, opinion. Skt., but one of the commonest of Telugu words. *abhipráya-bhédamu,* difference of opinion.

abhipráyapaḍuṭa, to be of opinion.

abhiruchi, taste, relish (for non-material things). Skt. *ruchi,* however, is the common Telugu for taste (of things to eat); *abhiruchi* is used for music, &c. *sangítam andali abhiruchi,* taste for singing; *anduló ná émí abhiruchi lédu,* I do not care for that at all.

abhishécamu, anointing (at coronation, &c.). A sacerdotal word from the Sanskrit. *bindeḍu níḷḷu netti mída abhishécam chésináḍu,* anointed his head with a potful of water.

abhivrüddhi, increase, progress. Skt. Frequently used for progress and increase in newspapers but unusual in common conversation. *andarú santánam caligi janam abhivrüddhi autú v'unṭe y'í bhúmi mída panḍé panṭa váḷḷa tinḍici tsáladu,* if every one had children the population would so increase that there would not be enough food on earth to feed them all.

abhíshṭamu, wish. Skt. *ní abhíshṭamu síghramugáné neravérutundi,* your wish will soon be fulfilled; *mana abhishṭamu púrṇamugá saphalam autundi,* our desire will soon be fulfilled.

abhracamu, mica. Skt.

abhyantaramu, objection. Skt.; very common in Telugu. *ná abhyantaramu léḍu,* I have no objection; *ańdu chétané y'í abhyantaram,* that is why we object.

abhyasintsuṭa, to practise, study.

abhyásamu, practice. Skt. *nívu y' incá yóg' ábhyásamló modaṭi avasthalóné v'unnávu,* you are still in the first stage of Yoga practice; *abhyásam cúsu vidya,* practice makes perfect; *vyácaraṇa ṣástramu abhyasintsuṭa,* to study grammar.

acalancamu, spotless. Skt.

acasmáttuga, suddenly. Skt.

acaṭa, alas; more commonly *ayyó!*

acáryamu, evil. Skt. *iṭuvanṭi acárya cáraṇam zarigina taruváta váḷḷanu veli veyyacunḍá v'unṭé y'incá matam yémiṭ anḍi?* if you don't excommunicate them for so evil an act, what becomes of religion?

acca, elder sister; also used as a form of address when there is no relationship; also *appa.* It is a Dravidian word. Tamil *accai*; Can. *acca-accachellellu,* sisters. *ammal-accalu,* of women generally; his sisters, and his cousins, and his aunts.

accaḍa, there. Dravidian *á-cáḍa,* that place; Tamil *ange*; Can. *alli.*

accara, need, necessity. *accara* is hardly ever used by itself, *avasaram, agatyam,* &c., being commonly used for necessity.

accara lédu, don't want, no thanks, no. One of the commonest expressions in Telugu and in other Dravidian languages; Tamil *vénḍam,* usually pronounced *váná, vénḍá.*

accaracu-vatstsuṭa, to come to (female) maturity, to be useful; and with negative verb (*rávaḍam*) to be useful. *accaracu ráca póté manaváḷḷu bógam váḷḷanu yenducu chésináru?* if they were not useful, why did our ancestors introduce dancing girls?

accassu, anger. *nácu nizamgá pichchi y'ettin aṭṭ aité í páṭici ní talacáya renḍu checcalu chési ná accassu anta tírtsucónú?* if I were really mad, would I not by this time have split your head in two and satisfied my anger?

achchi-vatstsuṭa, to prosper, to suffice. *achchi vachchina bhúmi aḍug-eḍé tsálunu,* in land quality before quantity.

acramamu, wrong. Skt. *ninnaṭi míṭinguló y'émi acramam zarigindi?* what injustice was done at yesterday's meeting?

acsha-mála, rosary. Skt.

acsharamu, letter or, rather, syllable. Skt. word 'imperishable'. In Telugu it means either a vowel or a combination of consonant and vowel and thus two English letters.

acshatalu, acshintalu, raw rice with saffron on it. *acshatalu* is the Sanskrit form; *acshintalu* more usual. *acshintalu vésuconuṭa,* to sprinkle *acshintalu.*

acshi-acshuḍu, eye. Skt. The Telugu for eye is *cannu,* plural *canḍlu. acshi* is recognized because *acshuḍu* is used as a suffix in combinations while *cannu* is not. Thus *hiraṇyácshuḍu,* golden-eyed.

acṭu, Act (of the legislature); English.

aḍa-catti or **aḍa-cottu,** betel-nippers; from *aḍḍamu* and *catti,* cross-knife. In an inventory: *ittaḍi aḍacottu, y'ittaḍi sunnapu cáyi, manchi addamu,* brass betel-nippers, a brass box for the lime eaten with betel and areca nut; *aḍacattulóni póca,* the areca nut between the pincers, i.e. caught in a vice or in a dilemma.

aḍacuva, aḍagintsuṭa, aḍaguṭa, humility, to humble, to be humbled, to lower.

aḍalintsuṭa, to rebuke.

aḍaluṭa, to grieve.

adamáyintsuṭa, to rebuke. *nén émi ninnu ágnya peḍutáná? adamáyistáná?* do I ever give you orders or scold you?

adanangá, in abundance, exceedingly, in excess.
aḍangal, the most important of the village accounts prepared by the karnam; also known as the No. 2 Account. Tamil, *aḍangal*. From *aḍangu*, to be contained; so called as it originally contained accounts of the whole village.
adanu, season, opportunity.
aḍaru, fear. Telugu word, but *bhayamu* is more common. *adari-paḍuṭa*, *adari-páṭu*, are said of pride, not fear; from the idea of quivering or capering in pride. *bhúmi adaruts'unnadi*, the earth has a tremor.
aḍatsuṭa, to humble; causative of *aḍaguṭa*.
aḍavi (n.), jungle. Skt. *aṭavi*. *aḍavi cáchina vennela*, moonlight in the wilds, i.e. wasted moonlight; *hindú vitantuvula bratucu aḍavi cáchina vennela*, the life of a Hindu widow is moonlight in the jungle, i.e. no good to any one.
aḍavi (adj.), wild. Usually translated forest, but this is incorrect; Indian jungle or uncultivated, wild country often has no trees to speak of in it. As an adjective the word is the usual one for wild as opposed to tame. *aḍavi cóḍi*, the jungle fowl; *aḍavi bátu*, the wild duck; a tame duck being *pempuḍu bátu*.
aḍavipandi, wild boar.
aḍáttugá, suddenly, properly. *haṭháttugá* (Skt.).
aḍávuḍi, hubbub.
adbhutamu, wonder, wondrous; subst. and adj. from the Sanskrit.
aḍḍa-caṭṭa, dam; from *aḍḍamu*, across, and *caṭṭuṭa*, build.
aḍḍa-dári, short cut; from *aḍḍamu*, across, and *dári*, way. Tamil *curucavali*.
aḍḍa-diḍḍamugá, irrelevant. *aḍḍadiḍḍamugá máṭláḍacu*, don't speak irrelevantly; *aḍḍadiḍḍapu pani*, an idle job.
aḍḍa-góḍa, party wall; from *aḍḍamu*, across, and *góḍa*, wall. *aḍḍa-góḍa mída pilli*, a cat on a party wall, i.e. sitting on the fence.
aḍḍamaina, what comes to hand; from *aḍḍamu*, across, what meets you. *aḍḍamaina tiṭlu tiṭṭináḍu*, he called me all the names he could think of.
aḍḍam-póvuṭa, to obstruct.
aḍḍamu, across, in the way; one of the words in Telugu with innumerable applications. *conḍa mingé-vánici gópuramu aḍḍamá*, a man who can swallow a temple tower in his stride; *cussancalu chési, aḍḍalu peṭṭi pótundémó ani má pillanu nénu garalsu scúlucu pampinánu cánu*, I did not send my girl to school, thinking that if I did she might become disobedient (make difficulties and objections).
addamu, looking-glass. *cótici addamu tsúpinaṭlu*, showing a monkey a looking-glass (unappreciated gift).
aḍḍamugá, in the way.
aḍḍamu-vatstsuṭa, (1) to come in useful; (2) to be in the way. *andánici peṭṭina sommu ápadacu aḍḍam vastundi*, jewellery put on for ornament will be useful in misfortune.
aḍḍa-saválu, cross-examination.
adde, rent (of house). *i bangáḷá nénu addecu putstsucunṭánu*, I will take this bungalow on rent.
aḍḍigalu, neck-jewel (female).
addira! bravo! Interjection. *addira! bábu!* well done, my lad. **addirapáṭu,** amazement. *níc inta addirapáṭ enducu rávàli?* why are you so much amazed?
aḍḍuchepputa, to contradict. *aḍḍu cheppa pócu* (*bócu*), do not contradict me.
adduṭa, to press, to blot. *sirá addumu*, blot your paper.
ad-ém-anṭé, if you ask why, viz.
adhairyamu, want of courage. *iṭuvanṭi váḍi y'eduṭa nívu adhairyamu y'entamátramú canaparatsa cúḍadu*, you must not show any sort of fear before such a man.
adhairyapaḍuṭa, to be afraid.
adhamamu, at least, at lowest. *mana v'úḷḷó adhamam aidu vandalainá tsandá cáca pótundá*, we cannot get less than 500 rupees subscription in our village.
adharmamu, injustice.
adháttuga, suddenly; properly *haṭháttuga*; from the Sanskrit. *mému adháttugá chevuḍu vachchind anucun-*

námu, we thought you had suddenly gone deaf; *adháttugá vachina piḍugu*, a bolt from the blue.

adhicamaina, additional.

adhicamu, superiority. Skt.

adhicangá, additionally.

adhicaprasangamu, impertinence; talking too much. Skt. Tamil has the same expression for impertinence. *ní adhicaprasangam tsálintsu*, hold your tongue; *nívu mahá adhicaprasangam chéstú v' unnávu*, you are talking very insolently.

adhicáramu, authority. Skt. *adhicáram chéyuṭa, itstsuṭa*, to exercise, give authority.

adhicári, ruler, authority, owner. Skt. *adhicárlu* is the usual expression for the Government, the authorities; thus *pólisu adhicárlu* is the police authorities. *adhicáritó viródhamu cá rádu*, keep on good terms with the authorities; *púrṇ' ádhicári*, having full powers.

adhicshépamu, to blame, to ridicule. *yí y'inglishu tsaduvulu tsadivi nannu adhicshépintsaḍánici vastává?* how dare you ridicule me who have had a foreign (English) education.

adhipati, ruler. Skt., from *pati*, Lord. More general term than *adhicári*.

adhínamu, possession. Skt. Much the same as *adhicáramu* but less general.

adhínata, control, charge. Skt. *adi ná adhínamuló lédu*, she is not under my control.

adhógati, a ruined state; perdition; utter destruction. Skt. *svárdhaparáyaṇula valla y'í déṣamu adhógati pálu ainadi*, this country is ruined by self-seekers; *vitantuvuni peḷḷi chésuconi adhógati pálu avutávu*, you will go to perdition by marrying a widow.

adhvaryuḍu, Brahmin officiant at sacrifice. Skt.

adhyacshata, chairmanship; in Sanskrit it means superintendence.

adhyacshuḍu, president. Skt. Commonly used in newspapers of chairmanship of a meeting, e.g. *áhvánasangh' ádhyacshuḍu*, chairman of reception committee.

adhyátmalu, spiritual songs. *adhyátmalu páḍé vánici ácali y'eccuva*, the chanting of hymns does not appease hunger (i.e. does all the more intensify hunger).

adhyátmamu, spiritual or scriptural philosophy. Skt. Rarely used.

adhyáyamu, chapter. Skt. Extensively used.

adi, she; also used as a form of address to one's wife. *inṭidi* (*inṭi*+*adi*, the thing in the house) is a wife; and somewhat contemptuous, so that it is doubtful whether it is composed of *adi*, she, or *adi*, it.

adi, it, that, that time. *adi modalu*, from that time; *adi varacu*, up to that; *adi gáca*, besides; *adigó!* behold! French *voilá*.

adigáca, moreover; also *adigácunḍá*.

aḍigiconuṭa, to ask; from *aḍuguṭa*; also *aḍuguconuṭa*, a very common colloquial form.

adrüshtahínuḍu, a luckless man.

adrüshṭamu, luck. Skt.

adrüshṭavantuḍu, a lucky man.

adugó, lo, behold, look there; 'lo' and 'behold' are book English, *adugó* and *idugó* are colloquial. French *voilà* and *voici*, Italian *ecco*. *idugó pul 'anṭe, adugó tóca annaṭṭu*, one said, 'Look, there is a tiger there'; the other, 'Yes, I see its tail.'

aḍugu, step, beginning, bottom, foot (measure), line (verse). *conḍa aḍuguna*, at the bottom of a mountain; *aḍugula záḍa paṭṭuconuṭa*, trace footsteps; *aḍug-aḍugunacu*, step by step.

aḍugu peṭṭuṭa, place one's foot. *y'eppuḍú gummam dáṭi vídhuló aḍugu peṭṭaḍu*, he won't step out into the street.

aḍugunabaḍuṭa, aḍuccu-povuṭa, to sink; colloquial forms of *aḍuguta*.

aḍuguṭa, ask. *aḍugagáné*, on demand. *adigévánici cheppévádu lócuva*, It is easier to ask questions than to answer them (the answerer is inferior to the asker).

adumuconuṭa, to press, to squeeze.

aduruṭa, to tremble. *venuca Condalrávu Pantulu Gáru Ṣaristádári chésin appuḍu garbhálaló pinḍálu adiri póyévi*, when Kondala Rau Pantulu Garu was Sharishtadar the foetuses used to tremble in the womb.

aḍusu, mire. *aḍusuló nátina sthambhamu,* a post fixed in the mire (said of a time-server as it swings to and fro).

advaitamu, monism. Skt.

advaiti, Monist. Skt. The Hindus have three principal sects divided according to the three possible views of ultimate reality: the Monists, the Dualists, and the Mixed; and the three main divisions of the Brahmin caste are based on this philosophic disagreement. The Monists follow Śankarácharya.

afísu, office. English.

agaḍta, moat. Used in historical novels.

agamyamu, inaccessible. Skt. Used in colloquial language, with another word, *agócharamu,* which means imperceptible, dissolved into its atoms. *tsávuci teginchi agamya-gócharamgá póvdlani cúni chéṣáḍu,* he committed the murder at the risk of his own dissolution.

agapaḍuṭa, to appear. Used commonly when we use 'to see'; the subject is the thing seen; instead of saying 'I see a snipe', one says, 'A snipe appears to me'. *nácu canḍlu agapaḍavu* means 'my eyes don't see', literally 'I can't see my eyes'.

agatyamu, necessity.

agáramu, house. Skt. Used in books.

aggi, fire.

aggi-rámuḍu, a nickname applied to an angry person. *pillal 'antá pérlu peṭṭi pilustú v'unté váḍu vidhiló paravaḷḷu toccutú y'élá aggi-rámuḍu ai póyáḍó tsúḍu,* when the mischievous children are after him calling him names he shows himself in a fury and dances on the road.

aghóramu, terrible. Skt.

aghórintsuṭa, to grieve. Skt.

agni, fire. Skt.; Latin, *ignis.* The Telugu is *nippu,* but *agni* is common enough.

agnicanamu, spark.

agni-hótramu, fire.

agniparvatamu, volcano.

agnyána daṣa, age of innocence. Skt. *agnyánadaṣaló viváham chésté tsúḍaḍánici bahu mutstsaṭagá v'unṭundi,* it is very pretty to see a marriage in the age of innocence.

agnyánamu, ignorance. Skt., *a* privative and *gnyánamu,* knowledge. *víru agnyán 'ándhacáramuló munigi v'unna janulu,* people steeped in ignorance.

agnyáni, ignorant person.

agra-, chief, end. A Sanskrit word used in compounds in Telugu.

agraculamu, chief caste, i.e. Brahmin. *taccuva culamváru agraculamváritó cúḍá cúrtsóvaḍánici córité,* if a lower caste man ever wishes to sit with a high caste man.

agragaṇyuḍu, leader.

agrahúramu, Brahmin street or village. Skt., from *agra* and *háramu,* row; the part of a village or town set apart for Brahmins.

agramu, top. Skt. *ámúl-ágramugá,* from top to bottom; completely. *parvatágramu varacu,* to the top of the hill.

agrasthánamu, chief seat. Skt., *agra* and *sthánamu,* place. *agra-sthánam 'andu nénu cúrtsónu,* I won't take the chief seat; so also *agrásanásinuḍu, agrásanádhipati, agrastuḍu,* person taking the chair; *agrásanádhipatyamu,* chairmanship.

agrésaruḍu, leader. Skt.

agugáca, would that, so be it. *gáca* for *cáca,* euphonic.

aguṭa or **auṭa,** to become. Like common verbs in all languages extremely irregular; the root is *cá*; *cádu,* the negative 3rd person, is one of the forms of 'no'; *ai,* the past participle, is used as a suffix to form adjectives, *cá-valenu* means it is wanted; *cávintsuṭa,* the causal used in the high-flown leader-writing of newspapers instead of *chéyuṭa,* to do. *váḍu y'ém aindáḍu?* what has become of him? *á pani aunu, cáca póvunu,* that work may or may not be done; *pani sighramugá cávalenu,* work must be done soon; *bhójanam 'aindi,* dinner is over; *Mahátmá Gándhi darṣanam 'aindi,* I got a sight of Mahátmá Gándhi; *artham aindá?* do you understand? *tirpu cá lédu,* judgement has not yet been pronounced; *iccaḍa vari cádu,* rice does not grow here; *váḍu nic'emi* *autáḍu?* what relation is he of yours? *vibhágálu ai vér' inṭi cápuramu chést' unnáru*, the (joint) family divided up and occupy separate houses; *Barmáló modaṭi nunḍiyu tagin'anta bala prayógamu gávimpaca* (*cávimpaca*) *unḍuṭa ché*, through not having used enough force in Burma to start with.

aham-, my, I. Used only as a prefix in Telugu. Skt. for 'I'; Latin *ego*.

ahambhávamu, egotism, pride. Skt. *aham* and *bhávamu*.

ahamcáramu, conceit, arrogance. Skt. *aham* and *cáramu*, doing. *guru ṣuṣrúsha prabhávam chepputánu vinu, dánivalla vidyárthulu ahancára virahitulunu vijiténdriyulunu autáru*, I will explain to you the glory of serving your guru; the disciples become modest and temperate.

aharmukhamu, morning. Skt., from *aham*, day, used in novels in descriptive passages; not in colloquial use.

ahimsa, harmlessness. Skt. *ahimsa parama dharmamu*, harmlessness is the chief virtue (blessed are the meek), is the commonest of all Hindu religious maxims.

ahituḍu, evildoer.

ahó! oh, indeed; good! Skt.

ahórintsuṭa, to be upset; also *aghórintsuṭa*. *y'émí tótsacunḍá ahóristú v'unṭé*, while I am much upset and don't know what to do.

ai, suffix used to form adjectives and adverbs; 'like', 'about'. It is the past participle of *aguṭa*, become. *mán ai nilachenu*, he stood like a tree (in terror or surprise); *á vishayam-ai*, about that matter; *bhayam-ai*, frightened.

ai, having become, being; past participle of *aguṭa*, become. *cheṭṭu ai vanganidi mánu ai vangund?* if it won't bend when it is a shrub, will it bend when it is a tree?

aica-, Skt.; adjectival form from *éca*, one, used in compounds in Telugu.

aicacanṭhyamuga, with one voice. Skt.

aicamatyamu, being of one mind, co-operation, unanimity. Skt. *aicamatyamunacu mand' édi? dṣa vadaluṭa*, the only way to harmony is to get rid of desire. This Hindu maxim is a counsel of despair. Hindus are so naturally fissiparous that only those who renounce their will can be persuaded to agree about anything.

aicyaparatsuṭa, to consolidate. Skt.

aicya-vácyamu, unanimous, with one voice. Skt., from *aicya*, one, and *vácyamu*, voice.

aidava, fifth.

aidótanamu, being a wife, female wedlock; from *aiduva*, matron. *ávida aidótanamu tinnagá v'unṭé mí vaidyam rácané pónu*, if the marriage were a success, your doctoring would not be wanted (attributing a man's death to the ill-luck of his wife).

aidu, five.

aiduguru, aidumandi, five persons.

aiduva, matron.

aihicamu, of this world. Skt., adjectival form from *iham*.

-aina, suffix forming an adjective by simple addition to any noun; past participle of *auṭa*, having become. *nác-aina manishi*, my friend; *nác-aina*, who is to me, my; *andam aina*, handsome; *dhaniculaina*, rich.

aina, being, having accumulated; past participle of *auṭa*. *aina vaḍḍi*, the accumulated interest.

aina, past; past participle of *auṭa*. *aina panici chintinchéváḍu alpa buddhi galaváḍu*, he is a fool who grieves over the past.

-aina, suffix meaning 'ever'; past participle of *auṭa* emphasized. *eccaḍaina*, wherever; *evvaḍaina*, whoever; *vaaḍaina viḍaina*, whether it is this man or that.

ainanu, though, even. *nác-ainanu*, even to me.

ainappaṭici (ni), nevertheless, even when it is so; from *aina* and *appuḍu*, when.

ainaṭṭaité, if it is; from *aina*, being, *aṭṭu*, like, and *aité*, which also comes from *auṭa*, if. *mídi ainaṭṭaité*, supposing it is yours.

aipóvuṭa, to be finished; from *auṭa* and *póvuṭa*, go, to be gone, become. *aipóyindi* is the usual expression for 'finished'.

aiṣvaryamu, wealth. Skt., from *íṣvara*, god, adjectival form.

aité, if it is, even if it is, but, then;

from *auṭa*, become, and *té*, if; usually post-fixed to *aṭṭu*, as if, and the past participle of a verb; at the beginning of a sentence it means 'if it comes', 'succeeds'; opposite *cácunṭe*. *váḍu vachchin' aṭṭ aité*, if he comes; *aité y'emi?* what if? *aité áruga, cácunṭé candi*, we shall get either *candi* (red gram) or *áruga* (millet), i.e. if we sow both together; *mícu tondaragá v'unn' aṭṭ aité*, if you are in a hurry; *nénu cheppina pracáram nívu zarigistú v'unnaṭṭ aité*, if you do as I tell you; *aité ná peḷḷám sangati nuvvu yeragav ánna máṭa*, then you don't know my wife.

aivázugá, in exchange. Hindustani.

ajágrata, carelessness; from *a* privative and *jágrata*, care.

ajírṇamu, indigestion; from *a* privative and *jírṇamu*, digestion.

ajírti, indigestion.

akhanḍamu, entire, abounding. Skt., from *a* privative and *khanḍamu*, piece. *nívu akhanḍa ṣacti galaváḍavu*, you have abundant power; *akhanḍa Cáveri*, the undivided Cauvery, i.e. the river before it splits up into the delta.

ala, wave.

alabhyamu, unobtainable. Skt., from *a* privative and *labhyamu*, obtainable.

alacshyamu, carelessness. Skt., from *a* privative and *lacshyamu*, regard.

alacshyapu, careless. *iṭuvanṭi alacshyapu manishi peḷḷáḍaḍam nácu y'enta mátramunnu y'ishṭam lédu*, I do not care at all to marry so casual a person.

alancarintsuṭa, to adorn. Skt. *á píṭhamu alancarintsanḍi*, adorn that seat, i.e. polite way of saying 'Take a seat'.

alancáramu, ornament. Skt. *nácu peṭṭina alancáramulan annițini ná déham nochchéṭ aṭṭu balavantamgá tempi vési*, pulling all the ornaments off my person so as to hurt me.

alancára ṣástramu, rhetoric. Skt. *vyácaranamu, tarcamu, alancára-ṣástramu cúḍá telusunu*, he knows grammar, logic, and rhetoric too.

alancrütamu, adorned. Skt.

alanghyamu, out of reach. Skt., from *a* privative and *langhyamu*, reachable.

alaráruṭa, to shine. A word used in novels of a brilliant city, &c.

alasaṭa, weariness. *alasaṭa chéta nácu nóru y'enḍucu pótú unnadi*, my mouth is dry through weariness.

alasinadi, tired. The verb is *alayuṭa*. *Alasinadi* is the part in common use. *ná gurram tsála alasinadi*, my horse is very tired.

alasüḍu, lazy.

alavaḍuṭa, to be acquired, of a habit. *mí ṣishyulacu cúḍá sadguṇamul' alavaḍinavi*, your disciples also have acquired good habits.

alaváṭu, habit.

alaváṭu paḍuṭa, to be accustomed. *aité paḍutsuntanamuló v'unḍaḍam chétanu alaváṭu paḍaḍam chétanu vaca paṭṭuna mána lécunḍá v'unnámu*, we can't suddenly stop, being young and having acquired the habit.

alavi cádu, not possible.

aláhida, separate. Hindustani.

allacallólamu, hubbub.

allamu, ginger (green); dry ginger is *ṣonṭhi*.

allari, tumult, row. *nannu allari pilla cáyalu vidhilo géli chési*, rowdy boys mocking me in the street; *niṣchcáraṇamgá allari cheyyacanḍi*, do not make a row for no reason.

allari chéyuṭa, to make a row.

-allá, suffix meaning all. This most common word will not be found in other dictionaries; the dictionaries give *-ella*, but *-alla* is the common form, even in books. *nénu y'eccaḍacu veḷité accadic' allá tóca lágu venṭa tirugutú v'unṭáv émi?* why do you follow me about everywhere like my shadow? *dínici v'unna lópam allá*, the only drawback to this; *udyógasthulalón-allá*, among all the officials.

alláḍuṭa, to wander, to toss about, to be in want; *cúṭici alláḍutáḍu*, he is in want of food.

allica, netting. *allica pani nácu ćnṭuc' unnadi*, network is cleaving to me.

allintsuṭa, to get plaited.

alluḍu, son-in-law; plural *alluru*. *ménalluḍu* is a nephew by the female side. *angaṭló anní v'unnavi, alluḍu nóṭló ṣani v'unnadi*, everything in the shop and misfortune in the mouth of the son-in-law. This is a proverb which means though there be excellent opportunities, fate always deters a person from taking advantage of them.

alluṭa, to plait. *tsápa allinaṭlu,* plaited like a mat.

almáru, wardrobe. Hindustani.

alpa (mu), small, trifling. Skt. *alpagnyánulu chésé máyópáyálu y'ilágantivi,* tricks of small minds; *á y'adbhutamunu nívu alpa cálamulóné tsúḍa galavu,* you can see that wonder in a short time; *aina panici chintinchéváḍu alpa buddhi galaváḍu,* he is a fool who grieves over the past.

alpáchamánamu, urine. Skt. *tellavárugaṭla chícaṭlo alpáchamánánici léchi,* getting up in the dark before dawn to make water; *vacca céca vésté v'úḷḷó vaḷḷ' antá gaḍa-gaḍa vaḍaci baṭṭalaló alpáchamánam chésucunéváru,* if he just raised his voice there was not a dry dhoty in the village; *méghálu samudramlóci veḷḷi niḷḷu táguṭ' anéculu tsúchinúru; álá niḷḷu tági vachchi alpáchamánam chésté, á níru varsha rúpangá bhúmi míḍa paḍutundi,* (Hindu explanation of rain) the clouds drink water out of the sea and then discharge it; *góvu alpáchamánam chéstú v'unḍagá veḷḷi tócató netti míḍa tsalluconi panchitam múḍu puḍisiḷḷu lópalici putstsucunṭé marí puṇyam,* (Hindu recipe for gaining virtue) when a cow is making urine shake its tail over your head, take three handfuls of its sacred urine (*panchitam*) and drink.

alpuḍu, rotter, worthless fellow. Skt. *oré! alpuḍá!* wretch!

aluca, alca, wrath, anger. *alluni aluca,* the wrath of a son-in-law which is a common feature of Indian household technique. *aluca viḍuva bócu,* never put away your wrath, is considered to be a sound maxim with sons-in-law if they want to profit and prosper. *aluca pánpu míḍa v'unna alluḍu,* the wrathful son-in-law in the bedchamber is an essential feature in marriage functions.

alucu, fear.

alucuṭa, smear, e.g. the floor with cow-dung.

aluguṭa, to be angry.

amadalu, twins.

amaladáruḍu, amildar, officer of rank of tahsildar, under a subedar. Hindustani.

amalamu, pure. Skt.; *a* privative and *malam,* dirt.

amaluló, in force, in authority. Hindustani. *álágaṇṭi áctu cúḍá vacaṭi amaluló v'unḍédá?* was such an Act in force? *ménéjarú, mémú, ṣániṭari y'inaspecṭarú y'écamai idivaracu iṭuvanṭi rijalyúshanlu lacsha amalu zaragacundá ápi vésinámu,* the Manager, we, the Sanitary Inspector have between us stopped 100,000 such resolutions coming into force.

amandamu, great. Skt., *a* privative and *mandamu,* little.

amangaḷamu, unpropitious. Skt., *a* privative and *mangalam,* propitious.

amaracamu, lease. *bhúmulanu y' énúru rúpáyalacu amaracam chésinámu,* we have leased our land for 500 rupees.

amartsuṭa, to fit, prepare, supply. *iravai lacshala y'écaramula nélacu jalamu amartsabaḍinadi,* water was supplied to two million acres.

amaryáda, disrespect. Skt., from *a* privative and *maryáda,* respect.

amavásya, new moon day; common for Skt. *amavasya.*

amánatu, deposit. Hindustani. A common treasury term for money not placed in the strong room but deposited temporarily outside.

amáni, departmentally managed. Hindustani. When renting or other systems of land revenue failed in Muhammadan times the tax was collected direct by the officials, and this was called *amáni.*

amánushamu, inhuman, supernatural. Skt.; *a* privative and *mánusham,* human.

amáyacuḍu, innocent. *abhamu ṣubhamu y'eragani amáyacuḍu,* an innocent man knowing neither good nor evil.

ambali, gruel.

ambaramu, sky; for *ácáṣamu,* Skt. Used only in books and compounds. *digambaruḍu,* sky-surrounded, is the usual word for 'naked'.

ambaru, amber.

ambá y'anuṭa, to low.

ambáramu, a heap of grain; also the

share of a crop due to Government or landholder.

ambudhi, sea. Skt. Used in books; the common word is *samudramu.*

ambuvu, water. Skt. Used in books only.

amitamu, boundless. Skt., *a* privative and *mitam,* bound, limit.

amínu, process-server. Hindustani. Now we use the word only of our head process-server; formerly it was applied to lower and even the higher courts; the Court of Sudder Amin was the highest Indian Judge under the Company.

amíru, baron. Hindustani. *náḍu v'unṭé navábu sáyébu, annamu v'unṭé amíru sáyébu,* if he has territory a Muhammadan is a Nawab Sahib; if he has enough to eat he is an Amir Sahib.

amma, mother, especially in address; used also in addressing any older woman: a housewife; a woman. Telugu; but connected with words in all languages (onomatopoeic *ma* for 'mother'). *amma grüha pravéṣamu ayya ṣmaṣána pravéṣam,* the housewife entered the house and its master left it a corpse (sudden and unexpected calamity); *caḍuputó v'unn amma canaca mánuná, vanḍin amma tinaca mánuná?* will not the pregnant woman bring forth her child? will the woman who has cooked abstain from eating? (the inevitable result).

amma-caḍupucálá! a common kind of abuse. *víḍi amma caḍupucálá! Ná mídaná nóru chésuconṭáḍu?* let him and his mother's womb perish! How dare he direct his tongue against me?

ammacamu, sale.

ammaḍu, applied to a girl or daughter in the Northern Districts; same as *ammáyi.*

ammalaccalu, mothers and sisters; his sisters and their cousins and his aunts; the women gossips. *ammalu,* mothers, combined with *accalu,* elder sisters. *irugu porugu ammalaccalu cheppututunnáru,* the womenfolk in the houses round about say.

ammamma, mother's mother, grandmother.

ammavári jáḍyamu, smallpox, supposed to be due to a goddess. *v'úḷḷó ammavári jáḍyálu ilága v'unn appuḍu manam ammavárini naḍi vídhiló nilupan' accara lédá?* when smallpox is in the village should we not set the village goddess up in the middle of the street? (Hindu notions of hygiene).

ammaváru, goddess, especially of the village.

ammá! exclamation of pain, love, surprise.

ammáyi, little girl; used also as form of address. *má ammáyini y'ichchi á canyá dána phalamu nénu daccintsu cunṭánu.* I will give him my little girl and earn the merit of the bestower of a virgin.

ammi, form of address to girl.

ammuḍu, sale. *ammuḍu pócunḍá nilava v'unna sarucu,* old stock.

ammuṭa, to sell. *amma póté aḍavi, cona póté corivi,* jungle when he went to sell, firebrand when he went to buy; *cammara vídhiló súdulu ammi-naṭṭu,* like selling needles in Blacksmith street.

amóghamaina (adj.), infallible, **amóghamu** (n.), irrefutable, **amóghamgá** (adv.), inevitably. Skt., *a* privative and *mógham,* fallible. *amógha nidarṣanálu v'unnavi,* there are irrefutable proofs; *amóghamaina vádamu,* irrefutable argument; *tama córica amóghamgá siddhistundi,* your wish will inevitably be fulfilled; *áyana anna máṭa y'amóghamu sumá,* his prophecy will inevitably come true.

ampuṭa, to send, especially in compounds; more usually *pampintsuṭa. ságan'ampuṭa,* to send off; *piluvanampuṭa,* to send for.

amrütamu, nectar. Skt. *oca ginneḍu pánacamu nénu y'ippuḍu amrütamgá y'entsucunṭánu,* the tiniest drink would be like a drop of nectar to me just now.

amṣamu, subject, particular. Skt. *rendó amṣam,* the second subject; *váḍu anni amṣamulu telisinaváḍu,* he knows all particulars.

amúlyamu, priceless. Skt., *a* privative and *múlyamu,* price. *amúlya parimaḷamu,* a priceless scent.

anacaṭṭu, dam; from *caṭṭuṭa,* to build; *ánacaṭṭu* is commoner.

anada, anátha, one who is forlorn or destitute.

anagá, namely; from *anuṭa,* to say. *anagá anagá oca rázu,* one day a king, is the way stories begin.

anaguṭa, to yield to; to obey; also *aṇuguta. ápada vacchinappuḍu aṇagi v'unḍáli,* in misfortune show a humble and a contrite heart.

anantamu, endless. Skt., *a* privative and *antam,* end.

anantaramu, afterwards. Skt., *a* privative and *antaram,* interval.

anapacáya, a commonly grown bean. The botanical name of the plant is *dolichos catjang*; it is grown as a field crop, see **anumulu.**

anarhamu, unfit. Skt., *a* privative and *arham,* fit.

anarhata, unfitness, disability.

anarhuḍu, unfit person.

anarthamu, harm. Skt., *a* privative and *artham,* meaning. *bógamu váḷḷanu viváhádi subhacáryamulalónu, v'utstsaválónu, pilichi gauravintsaḍamu chéta tsálá anarthálu calugutú v'unnavi,* much harm comes from calling dancing girls to marriage and other festivals and religious functions and giving them honour; *ṣástra viṣvásamu cheḍina pacshamuna déṣamuna y'eṭṭi anarthamul aina sampráptamul' agunu,* if faith in Sastras is destroyed, any number of evils come over the land.

anati, not much. Skt., *a* privative and *ati,* very much. *anati dúramu,* not so far.

aṇatsuṭa, to suppress, to reduce. *cúrṭuló cúḍá vyájyálu véyinchi váḍi pogaru aṇatsanḍi,* bring some cases against him in Court too and reduce his pride; *ippudu elágainá y'í panḍituḍi garvam aṇatsa valenu,* now by any means we must reduce the pride of this pandit. Used in books. The colloquial form is *aṇutsuṭa.*

anavaratamu, perpetual. Skt.

anácári, ugly person. Skt., *a* privative and *ácáramu,* form. *inṭló dánitó nénu pagalu máṭláḍaḍánic anná valla cádu; anté cácunḍá adi anácári,* I may not even talk by day to the thing in my house (my wife); besides she is ugly.

anácháramu, want of good customs. Skt., *a* privative and *ácháramu,* custom. *dacshiṇádi váḷḷacu bottigá maḍi lédu, á déṣamuló ṣuddha anácháram,* the Southerners don't dress for dinner at all; they have no proper observances.

anáchára partsuṭa, to defile.

anádarana, contempt, neglect. Skt., *a* privative and *ádaraṇa,* respectful treatment. *ní vale nannu áyana anádaraṇa cheyyaḍu,* he does not despise me like you.

anádi nunchi, anádigá, from time immemorial. Skt., from *a* privative and *ádi,* beginning. *anádi biḍu,* immemorial waste land; *anádigá zarugutú v'unna ácháram,* an immemorial custom.

análóchitamu, thoughtless, imprudent.

anámica, nameless, the fourth finger. Skt., *a* privative and *náma,* name. There are two series of words for the fingers and thumb, Sanskrit and Telugu. The Telugu for the fourth finger is *ungarapu vélu,* the ring finger.

anása, pine-apple.

anátha, destitute. Skt., *a* privative and *nátha,* lord, protector.

anáthalaina, destitute.

anátha ṣaraṇ-álayamu, orphanage.

anávrüshṭi, drought. Skt.

ance, figure (numbers). *sunnálacu viluva y'élágu vastundi? mundu ancelu chéristé sari,* how do you give value to noughts? by putting figures before them.

anche, the post. This post, a relay of runners, is now obsolete; the word still survives in the *anchal,* or local post, of the Travancore State which exists side by side with the British post office.

ancili, obstruction.

ancitamu, dedication. Skt.

ancuramu, germ. Skt.

ancurintsuṭa, to sprout. Skt., often used metaphorically of thoughts, &c.

ancuritamu, sprouted, emanated.

ancuṣamu, elephant goad.

andacatte, pretty girl, from *andamu,*

beauty. *í chinnadi andacatte*, this girl is pretty.

andagáḍu, handsome fellow. *nívu mátram máha andagáḍavá y'émiṭi? nallagá cóti lágu v'unnávu*, are you so good-looking? you are black and like a monkey.

andalamu, palanquin. *andaru andalamu y'eccité mósévâru y'evaru?* if all go in their palanquins, who will carry them?

andali, on, adjective, from *andu*. *crama cramamugá sangítam andali abhiruchi adhicamai*, his love for song gradually growing.

andamu, beauty. *andamunacu peṭṭina sommu ápadacu aḍḍam vastundi*, jewellery put on for beauty comes in useful in bad times (this is why Hindus bank their money in their women's jewellery).

andamu, way, manner.

and-andu, here and there.

andaru, all (people). *andaru andalamu y'eccité mósévâru y'evaru?* if all go in their palanquins, who will carry them? *caliginavárici andaru tsúṭṭále*, all are relations to the rich.

andáca, so far; from *anta* and *dáca*.

andelu, anklets worn by women, usually silver.

andhacáramu, darkness. Skt. Commonly used metaphorically, the Telugu for darkness is *chicaṭi*. *víru agnyán ándhacáramuló munigi v'unna janula cannulu vippi gnyána súryódayam caluga chéstú v'unnáru*, opening the eyes of persons plunged in the darkness of ignorance they make them see the dawn of knowledge.

anḍi, sir; honorific affix. *y'ém'anḍi*, sir; *aṭlu cheppac'anḍi*, do not say so, sir; *yenduc-anḍi amma tiḍatáru*, why do you scold me, madam?

andintsuṭa, to cause to reach, to hand; causative from *anduṭa*, to reach. *miṭháyi v'unḍalu y'í chinnadánici andintsu*, hand the sweets to this girl.

andu, there, that. *anducu, andalucu*, for that; *anduló*, in that; *andu nimittam*, because of that; *andu chéta*, by means of that; *andu midaṭa*, after that; *andu valla*, by that; *unn' anducu*, because it is; *indun'andu*, here and there, i.e. in this life and the next; *andu cósaram*, for that reason.

-andu, suffix meaning 'on', 'at'. *ní y'andu nammacam unchi*, placing reliance on you.

andubaḍi, to hand; in legal language service of a process; from *anduṭa*, to reach. *adi andubaḍi aina tarváṯa*, after it had come to hand.

anducani, as it is so; also *andunacani*.

anduconuṭa, reach with the hand.

anducu, for it; also *andunacu*.

anduṭa, to reach; intransitive. *andani púlu dévunici arpaṇa*, offering flowers out of reach to the God; *tama zábu nácu anda lédu*, Your Honour's letter did not reach me; *adi nác andadu*, it is out of reach; *rayilu andaca*, missing the train.

ané, anédi, that which is, namely, which; relative pronoun from *anuṭa*, to say. *cávalen ané manasu*, a mind to have.

anéca, many. Skt., from *a* privative and *éca*, one.

anécamandi, many persons.

ané-cábólu, perhaps it is so.

anémó, perhaps it is so; from *ani* and *émó*, I don't know what.

anésarici, when it is said. *nénu á máṭa anésarici manḍi paḍḍáḍu*, when I told him so he lashed himself into a fury.

anga, stride.

angabalamu, strength; from *angam*, limb. *manac angabalam taccuvagá v'unnadi*, we are too weak.

angaḍi, shop, bazaar. *angiṭló bellamu guḷló Lingánici naivédyamu*, offering the bazaar jaggery to the God.

angahínamu, mutilated; from *angam*, limb, and *hínam*, short of.

angalártsuṭa, to grieve.

angamola, naked; from *angamu*, limb, and *mola*, waist.

angamu, limb, department. Skt. *rájyángamulu* are the Departments of Government. *chaturangamulu* are the four limbs of the army which are *rathamulu* (chariots), *énugulu* (elephants), *gurramulu* (horses), *banṭulu* (foot). *sáshṭánga namascáramu* is salutation with the eight limbs (prostrate).

angaracá, coat. Hindustani. *cóṭu* is the commoner. *nénu lópalici póyi* *págá, angaracá vési y'ippuḍé vastánu,* I will go inside, put on my turban and coat, and come at once.

angavastramu, upper cloth.

angavéyuṭa, to stride.

-angi, limbed; used in compounds. *sundarángi,* beautifully limbed; *latángi,* slender limbed, from *lata,* twig.

angili, palate. *angiṭa bellamu átmaló vishamu,* sugar on the lips, poison in the soul; *angiṭa vishamu, munnálicanu tiyyadanamu,* poison on the palate, sweetness on the tip of the tongue.

angicarintsuṭa, to consent. Skt.

angícáramu, consent. Skt.

angóstramu, upper cloth. Skt. *angavastramu. angóstramu conguna,* in the border of one's upper cloth.

angulamu, inch. From Skt. for thumb.

angustán, thimble. Hindustani.

angusthamu, thumb, big toe. Skt. Both a Sanskrit and a Telugu series is used for fingers and thumbs; the Telugu for thumb and big toe is *boṭana vrélu. angushṭa mátram,* thumb-size.

ani, having said, participle of *anuṭa.*

ani, aniyu, that, to; the past participle of *anuṭa. nannu pomm' ani cheppéḍu,* he told me to go; *váru accaḍa unḍinár ani annáḍu,* he said that they were there; *antarátmalu léné lévani bódhintámu,* we will preach that the soul does not exist at all.

-ani, suffix added to onomatopoeic expressions. *bussum'ani,* hissing; *guṭuccum'ani,* gulping; *usúrum'ani,* sighing; *cangu-cangum'ani,* tinkling; *minucu-minucum'ani,* twinkling.

anipintsuṭa, to cause to say; causative from *anuṭa. inṭló v'unḍinni léd' anipinchi,* pretending you have nothing in the house when you have.

anipótárani, lest it should be said.

anitya, impermanence, used esp. in philosophy; Skt. from *a-,* privative, and *nitya,* permanent.

anjali, folded hands. Skt. *váḍu anjali chésináḍu,* he saluted with folded hands.

anjanamu, lamp-black. This is used in magic, you are made to look into a drop of lamp-black and see visions.

anna, having said; past participle of *anuṭa. y'ém anná saré,* it does not matter what they say.

anna, elder brother; also used as a form of address to older men.

annadammulu, brothers; from *anna* and *tammuḍu. ávalintacu annadammul' unnáru gáni tummucu tammuḍ ainá léḍu,* yawning is infectious, sneezing is not.

annamu, rice, food; only used of cooked rice, uncooked is *biyyamu. náḍu v'unṭé naváhu sáyébu, annamu v'unṭé amíru sáyébu,* if he has territory a Muhammadan is a Nawab Sahib; if he has enough to eat he is an Amir Sahib.

annasatramu, choultry, restaurant; from *annamu* and *satramu,* choultry or an eating-house.

annavastramulu, food and clothes; from *annamu* and *vastramulu,* clothing. *áyana nácu anna vastrálacu y'émi lópam léc'unḍá tagina ádháramu chési póyinár,* he has given us suitable maintenance—food and clothes without stint.

anná, a corrupted form of *ainá,* even. *máṭlaḍuṭac'anná,* even to talk.

anni, annitini, all. *nácu peṭṭina alancáramulan annitini balavantangá tempi vési,* forcibly cutting off all my ornaments; *annitici tammuné nammi y'unnánu,* I trust you in everything.

anrütamu, false. *dévunni árádhintsadam máni vési, nénu y'érparachina bommala púja chéstú, prazalu múḍhul autú v'unnáru, satyam vadali peṭṭi anrütavádul autú v'unnáru,* people abandoning God's worship and taking to the service of idols which I have set up are becoming stupid, and abandoning truth are becoming false.

-anta, suffix meaning 'whole'. The final *a* is lengthened, in talk. *déṣamantá,* the whole country.

anta, then; in plural, times. *antaló,* meanwhile; *múḍ'antalu,* three times (as much); *anta-dáca,* till then (*andáca* in talk).

anta, that. *anta canṭe,* than that; *anta maṭṭucu,* up to that; *anta mátram,* so much; *antacu mundu,* before that.

anta, as much as, such, so much, as far as. *ácali acáṣam anta, gontuca súdi bezzam anta,* biting off more than one can chew; *góranta v'unṭe conḍanta chéstáḍu,* making a mountain of a molehill.

anṭa, till, to, close to; from *anṭuṭa*, touch. *télucu pettanam isté, tellavárlu anṭa poḍichindaṭa*, when power was given to the scorpion it stung till dawn, so they say; *modal anṭa cóyuṭa*, to eradicate; *ventrucalanu modal anṭa cattirinchinḍḍu*, he cropped his hair close.

anṭa, to say; contracted from *anuṭa*.

antacantacu, by degrees; from *anta*, then.

antach-, prefix meaning in; the *ch* is pronounced as in loch. Skt.

antachcaraṇamu, the mind, heart, the inner sense. Skt. *itanu manchi antachcaraṇa calaváḍu*, he has a very good heart.

antachpuramu, the inner rooms, i.e. the zenana, seraglio. Skt.

antadáca, till then; from *anta*, then, and *dáca*, until. *andáca* in talk.

anṭagaṭṭuṭa, to join, foist; from *anṭuṭa* and *caṭṭuṭa*. *nácu panici ráni mótáru banḍini Rámayyacu anṭa gaṭṭénu*, I foisted my useless car on Ramayya.

antagá, so much, very much. *ninnu antagá aḍigité*, however much he may ask you; *antagá cá valen'anṭé*, if he wants very much.

antamandi, so many people.

anta maṭṭucu, so far, *pro tanto* (in law).

antamu, end. Skt. *áṣacu antamu lédu*, desire has no limit.

antamu lécunḍá, *ad infinitum*.

antantagá, so — so.

antaramu, space, difference, disparity, other. Skt. *vári y'antaramu émi ní y'antaramu émi*, consider their rank and yours. Used particularly in compounds: *bháshántaramu*, translation; *sthal'ántaram'andu*, in another place; *granthántharam' andu*, in another book; *déṣántaramu póyináḍu*, he went to another country; *matántaramu*, another religion; *dvípántara-vásamu*, transportation (law).

antarangamu, mind, heart. Skt., *antach*, inner, and *rangam*, scene. *nénu áyanacu antaranga snéhituṇṇi*, I am his bosom friend.

antarátma, soul. Skt. *yevarici antarátmalu léné lév ani bódhintámu*, we will teach that souls do not exist at all.

antardhánamu, disappearance. Skt., from *antaramu*. *antardhánam' aipótámu*, we shall disappear.

antargica sabha, newspaper word for Privy Council.

antaricshamu, sky. Skt., from *anta* and *ricshamu*, what is seen in the middle. Used in books.

antarintsuṭa, to cross. Skt.

antastu, story. *Bombáyiló padi antastula méḍal anécamulu v'unnavi*, there are many 10-storied buildings in Bombay.

antaṭa, there; from *anta*.

antaṭa, in combination means self, by one's own. *evari-antaṭa-váru póyináru*, each went his own way; *tan-antaṭa táné léchi rá valenu*, he must get up by himself and come.

anté, just so much; from *anta*, more emphatic. *í v'úrici á v'úr entó, á v'úrici í v'úr'anté*, it is just as far from A to B as from B to A, i.e. six of one and half-dozen of the other.

anṭé, if one says or asks; if you want to know. Conditional form of *anuṭa*. *áyana cheppin' adi y'ém anṭé*, if you want to know what he said, i.e. he spoke as follows; *í rózu varjyamu y'eppuḍ anṭé pagalu múḍu ganṭalacu*, if you want to know when unlucky time is to-day it is at 3 p.m.; *enduc' anṭé*, if you ask why, because.

anṭintsatagina, adhesive (of a stamp); from *anṭintsuṭa* and *taguṭa*, fit.

anṭintsuṭa, to stick; causative form *anṭuṭa*.

anṭlu, ceremonial impurity, filth in general; from *anṭuṭa*, infect. *anṭlu tómu conuṭa*, to clean up filth.

antsaná, estimate, used especially of crop estimates.

antsu, hem, border, brim, bank. *y'éṭi antsu*, bank of a river; *ginne antsu*, brim of a cup; *cuṭṭina antsu*, a sewn hem.

antsuna, on the edge, margin, brim. *úri antsuna*, on the edge of the village.

antu, end.

anṭu, dirt, contagion.

anṭu, close-fitting.

anṭuconuṭa, to stick (intransitive), to catch fire, to catch a disease. *agnini tagilinchi dari colpina tarváta adi anṭuconi manḍutú v'unṭé maḷḷi árpi* *veyyaḍam sádhyam cádu*, when fire has once kindled and flamed it is difficult to quench.

anṭuḍu, contagious; from *anṭuṭa*, to infect.

anṭu mámiḍi, graft mango.

anṭupógulu, close-fitting ear-rings used by males; from *anṭuṭa*, stick close, and *pógu*, ear-ring.

anṭuṭa, to stick, touch (intransitive), infect. *dáni rógamu vánici anṭinadi*, he caught her disease from her.

antyamu, last. Skt. *antya nishṭhuramu canna ádi nishṭhuramé mélu*, it is better that a man should be cruel to you in the beginning than at the end.

anu, prefix meaning with, under. Skt.; corresponds with Latin *con-*, *sub-*.

anubandhamu, tie, bond. Skt., from *anu* and *bandham*. *prémánubandhamu*, the bond of love.

anubhavamu, experience. Skt., from *anu-*, under, and *bhavam*, being. *nénu mí andari canṭé yeccuva anubhavam galaváḍini*, I have more experience than any of you. As revenue term, enjoyment (of lands, &c.).

anubhavaṣáli, man of experience. Skt., from *anu-bhavam* and *ṣáli*, possessed of. *anubhavaṣálul aina váru cheppinadi vinna taruváta*, after hearing what experienced men have to say.

anubhávamu, dignity, grandeur. Skt. from *anu-*, under, and *bhávam*, mind, nature.

anubhógamu, enjoyment. Skt., from *anu-*, under, and *bhógam*, enjoyment.

anubhóga bádhyata, easement, right of enjoyment. A legal term.

anucampa, pity. Skt. A literary word. *záli* or *daya* are commoner.

anucarintsuṭa, to imitate. Skt., used in newspapers.

anucáramu, imitation. Skt.

anuchitamu, unsuitable. Skt., from *a* privative and *uchitam*, fit.

anuconuṭa, to think, reflexive from *anuṭa*, the ordinary word for 'to think', 'suppose'. *gáḍída coḍucu Brahma Dévuḍu áḍaváḷḷacu inta anyáyam chéstáḍ'ani nénu calalóní anucó lédu*, I never supposed in my dreams that the beast Brahma would do such injustice to women.

anucúlamu, suitable, favourable, convenience. Skt., from *anu-*, under, and *cúlam*, fit. *anucúla cálamu*, suitable time; *daivánucúlamu valla*, by God's grace.

anucúlangá, favourably, according to. Skt. The opposite is *praticúlangá*. *tamaru má prayatnánici anucúlangá chepputárá? praticúlangá chepputárá?* will you speak for or against our proposal?

anugnya, order, command. Skt.

anugrahamu, favour. Skt.

anugrahintsuṭa, to favour. Skt. *dévuḍu mícu anugrahintsa valen ani ná manasphúrtigá prárthistú v'unnánu*, I heartily pray God to favour you; *má inṭi dácá anugrahist'unnárá?* will you favour me with a visit?

anuguṇamugá, conformably. Skt. Also *anuguṇangá*. *tad'anuguṇangá*, according to that.

anumati, consent. Skt. *míru anumati y'ichché dácá páṇigrahaṇam cheyyaḍánici nén'angicarintsa lédu*, I do not agree to marry till you give your consent; *mí anumatini pondi*, getting your consent.

anumatintsuṭa, to consent. Skt.

anumánamu, suspicion. Skt. *anumánáspadamaina manushyulu*, suspicious characters.

anumánintsuṭa, to suspect. Skt. *míru á vishayamló anumánintsac'anḍi*, have no suspicion about that.

aṇumátramu, small as an atom. Skt., from *aṇuvu*, atom, and *mátram*, measure.

anumulu, an edible pulse, *dolichos catjang*, a bean that grows in the fields; used in the plural of the seeds or beans as in case of other food crops.

anuracti, love. Skt.

anurágamu, love. Skt.

anusarintsuṭa, to follow. Skt.

anusáramugá, according to.

anushangamu, love, accompaniment, concomitant. Skt. Used only in books.

anushṭhánamu, observance (religious). Skt.

anushṭhíntsuṭa, to observe. Skt.

anuṭa, to say, think. The commonest word for 'to say' is *chepputa*, but this also is very common, especially where it is more euphonic. *ramm'anu*, tell him to come, is used rather than *ramm'ani cheppu*. The meaning 'think' is usually expressed by the middle voice, *anuconuṭa*. The past participle *ani* is the ordinary word for 'that'; *ané, anédi* are the ordinary words for 'which'; the mind which desires is *cá valenu ané manasu*; the conditional form *anṭé* is the ordinary way of introducing an explanation in the combinations *yémanṭé* and *yenducanṭé*, if you ask what, if you want to know why.

anutápamu, sorrow. Skt. There are about 40 words for grief in Telugu; this is one of the common ones; the commonest of all is *duhkhamu* (Skt.).

aṇutsuṭa, to suppress. *iṭuvanṭi póciri vállanu aṇichi veyyaḍánici manam émainá chésténé cáni bottigá bágá v'unnadi cádu*, it is our clear duty to try to suppress such rogues.

anuvartana, following, obedience. Skt., *anu-* and *vartana*, conduct. *garvamu lénidí, anuvartana caladí ai v'unn'aṭṭ'aité*, if she is humble and obedient.

anuvartintsuṭa, to serve, follow, court. Skt.

anuvádamu, translation.

aṇuvu, atom. Skt.

anuvu, suitableness. *anuvugáni tsóṭu*, an improper place.

anvéshaṇamu, investigation. Skt. Used also as a suffix, in such words as *varánvéshaṇamu*, search after a bridegroom; *satyanvéshaṇamu*, search after truth; *Gándhí gáru satyánvéshaṇa parul anṭáru*, people say that Gandhi is in quest of truth.

anvéshintsuṭa, to search for. Skt.

anya-, prefix meaning other, alien, foreign. Skt. *anya matamu*, foreign religion, such as Christianity; *anya déṣamu*, foreign country; *anya déṣapu*, foreign; *anya déṣasthulu*, foreigners.

anyáyamu, injustice. Skt., from *a* privative and *nyáyamu*, justice.

anyáyamugá, unjustly.

anyónyamu, mutuality, attachment. Skt., reduplicated.

anyónyangá, mutually (attachment); from *anya*, other. *Satyavatí, moguḍú yenta anyónyangá v'unḍi prati vishayamlónú y'aicavácyangá v'unṭáró tsúchinárá?* have you not seen how Satyavati and her husband are full of mutual attachment and always of one mind?

anyuḍu, other person, stranger. *nácu tappa anyulacu teliyadu*, it is not known to any one except me.

apa-, prefix meaning away from. Skt. The Latin *ab-*, Greek *apo*, English *ab-*, *av-*.

apabhramṣamu, vulgar (of words, language), colloquial. Skt. Vulgar Telugu, of which this is a dictionary, is also known as *grámyam*, village language; it is, however, much to be preferred to the dog-Sanskrit used in books.

apacáramu, injury, sin. Skt., from *apa-* and *cáram*, deed. *vacari y'andu cárpaṇyamu vahinchi várici apacáram cheyyaḍánici tsúḍaḍam*, bearing malice against some one and seeking to do him an injury.

apacáramaina, defamatory (in law). Skt.

apacári, one who has injured you. Skt. *apacáric'aina v'upacáramé cheyya valenu*, do good even to him who has done you evil; this maxim is just as much Hindu as Christian or Jewish (Proverbs xxv. 21).

apacháramu, incivility. Skt.

apacírti, ill fame. Skt., from *apa* and *círti*, fame. *apacírti chéta crúngi póyi*, crushed by bad repute; *vál̤la manchi péru cheḍa coṭṭi apacírti vachchéṭ'aṭlu chétámu*, destroying their good name we shall bring bad repute on them; *iṭuvanṭi acárya caraṇánici púnucunṭé míru apacírti pálai pótáru*, if you venture on such an improper course you will fall into ill repute.

apaharintsuṭa, to carry off, to plunder. Skt.

apaháramu, carrying off, misappropriation, robbery. Skt. *néramugala apahāramu* is the way our official translators translate criminal misappropriation.

apajayamu, defeat. Skt., from *apa-* and *jayamu*, victory.

apakhyáti, disgrace. Skt., from *apa-* and *khyáti*, renown. *nénu paniló nunḍi círti sampádistú v'unṭé ná chellelu y'inṭa apakhyáti testú v'unnadá?* when I have got such a good reputation by my work, is my younger sister to bring disgrace upon me?

apamánamu, dishonour. Skt., from *apa-* and *mánam*, honour.

apanammacamu, distrust. *ippuḍu aṭuvanṭi apanammacam yémi lédu cáni,* though there is no suspicion of the sort now.

apanepamu, false or unjust accusation.

apaninda, slander.

apapádi, injustice.

apaprayógamu, misapplication of a word or an idiom.

apara, prefix meaning other, last, behind. Skt.

aparabuddhi, want of sense; *apara-*, behind, loitering, and *buddhi*, sense. *aḍadáni buddhi aparabuddhi,* female sense is sense that lags behind.

aparacriyalu, last, i.e. funeral rites.

aparádhamu, fault, fine. Skt. In common use; also *zulmáná*.

aparádhi, delinquent.

aparáhṇamu, afternoon. Skt., from *apara-*, after, and *áhṇam* (*ahamu*), day. *má tanḍri gáru má v'uḷḷó aparahṇamu tirigiténé cáni bhójanánici vachchéváré cáru,* my father used not to come to dinner till after his afternoon stroll in the village.

aparálu, mixed beans, grains.

aparávatáramu, reincarnation. Skt., from *apara-*, after, and *avatáram*, incarnation. *míru iddaru Dhanvantari yocca aparávatárálu,* you are two reincarnations of Aesculapius.

aparimitam, boundless. Skt., from *a* privative and *parimitam*, boundary.

aparúpamu, ugly. Skt., from *apa-* and *rúpam,* form.

aparúpamugá tsútsuṭa is colloquially used in the sense of being strangely fond. *váḍu pillaváḍini bahu aparúpamugá tsústaḍu,* he is inordinately fond of the child.

apaṣacunamu, ill-omened. Skt., from *apa-* and *ṣacunam*, omen. *aṭuvanṭi apaṣacunam aina taruváta yédi yémainá prayáṇamu cheyya cúḍadu,* no journey should be undertaken after such a bad omen.

apasatyamu, perjury.

apasavyamu, contrary, on the wrong side, perverse. *váḍu vaṭṭi apasavyapu manishi*, he is a most perverse person.

apasvaramu, false note. Skt., *apa-* and *svaram*, note. *apasvarálu cavitvamu cheppina várivi cáni, dánivi cávu,* she has not made any false notes, they are the composer's.

apaṿádamu, libel. Skt., from *apa-* and *vádamu*, speech. *úriló intamandi y'unḍagá y'í apavádamu ní mídaci vachchinadi y'émayyá?* why should you be singled out for calumny in the whole village?

apayaṣamu, infamy.

apángtéyuḍu, an unfashionable man, an outcaste. Skt. Used in Telugu as a term of abuse. *vitantuvuni peḷḷi chésu conna apángtéyapu gáḍida coḍucu viḍici yenta pogaru vachchinadi?* look at the swank of this wretch who has married a widow.

apáramu, boundless. Skt., from *a* privative and *páram*, opposite shore. *ná manassulóní santósham apárangá pongi porli pótú v'unnadi,* boundless joy is bubbling over in my heart.

apárthamu, misinterpretation. Skt., from *apa-* and *artham*, meaning. *ṣástramu telisinaváḍini nénu v'unṭú v'unḍagáné, ná mundara paḍḍálici iṭuvanṭi apárthálu chéstú v'unnávu,* you dare make such misinterpretations of words before me when I, who know the Shastras, am present; *ná máṭalacu apárthálu cheyyacu,* do not misinterpret my words.

apátramu, unworthy. Skt., from *a* privative and *pátram*, worthy.

apátravyamu, unworthiness. *nénu vaṭṭi apátravyam yenducu cheyya valenu?* why should I be guilty of utter unworthiness?

apáyacaramu, dangerous. Skt.

apáyamu, danger. Skt.

apécsha, desire. Skt. *í y'indriya sukhápécsha nunchi ná hrúdayamu maḷḷunu gáca!* may my heart be turned from this sensual desire!

apécshintsuṭa, to desire. Skt.

apílu, appeal. English. *apílucórṭu*, court of appeal; *apíludáru*, appellant; also *appílu*.
apóhamu, wrong suspicion, false inference. Skt., from *apa-* and *úha*, thought, suspicion. *Jánaci mída apóha paḍi dánni tsampaḍánici prayatnam chésináḍu*, having a false suspicion of Jánaci he tried to murder her.
appa, father. Hebrew *abba*, Italian *babbo*.
-appa, suffix added to names to show respect. *Rámappa*, Mr. Rama.
appa, elder sister; more commonly *acca*.
appaḍamu, fried flour flakes, eaten with curry by Europeans.
appaginta, handing over; also *oppaginta* or *vappaginta*.
appagintsuṭa, to hand over; also *oppagintsuṭa* or *vappagintsuṭa*.
appamu, a sweet cake.
appaṭici, by that time; from *appuḍu*, then.
appaṭicini, even then.
appaṭi nunchi, from that time.
appaṭlo, at that time.
appílu, English; same as *apílu*.
appitstsuṭa, to lend; from *appu*, loan, and *itstsuṭa*, give.
appó soppó, some debt or other; alliterative reduplication. *yé appó soppó chési*, having made some debt or other.
appu, loan. *appu muppu*, debt is a misfortune; *appu léca póté uppu ganjé mélu*, it is better to live on rice-water and salt than to get into debt.
appu putsuconuṭa, to take a loan.
appuḍappuḍu, from time to time.
appuḍé, at that moment.
appuḍu, then, when; when post-fixed to a past participle it must be translated 'when'. *chésin'appuḍu*, when he had done.
apratishṭha, bad name, dishonour. Skt., from *a* privative and *pratishṭha*, fame, consecration. *ippuḍu bógamdánni v'untsucóvaḍamé pratishṭha gánu, v'untsucóca póvaḍamu apratishṭha gánu y'entsa baḍutú v'unnadi*, nowadays it is honourable to keep a dancing girl, dishonourable not to keep one.
apratishṭha-néramu, defamation; a legal term. *itaḍu ní mída techchina apratishṭha-néramu púrtigá ruzuvu paḍḍadi*, the defamation case he brought against you has been fully proved.
apriyamu, unpleasant. Skt., from *a* privative and *priyam*, love.
apsarasa, apsara-strí, heavenly courtesan. Skt. These heavenly harlots have names, Rambha, &c.; they provide one of the pleasures of heaven for those who have been virtuous on earth (Hindu religion). *í lócamló apsara strílu léca póyiná á lópam lécunḍá v'úr'úrá cávalasinantamandi apsara strílu, véṣya stríl'unnáru; váḷḷu lécunḍá y'í lócamló dévatalacu yevarici v'utstsaválu zarugavu*, as there are no heavenly courtesans on this earth, to cure that defect there are in every village as many dancing girls as necessary; without them no God's procession can take place.
aputruḍu, sonless; from *a* privative and *putruḍu*, son.
apúrvamu, strange. Skt., from *a* privative and *púrvam*, previous. *idi yédó apúrva panḍita lacshaṇam cáni samányamaindi cádu*, that is an unusual, not a common, characteristic of pundits.
ara, half, adjective; the noun is *arthamu* or *sagamu*.
araca, plough complete with bullocks.
aracálu, sole of foot; also *aricálu*.
aracheyyi, palm of hand; also *arachéyi*. *arachétilóni addamu*, a very clear thing. An idiom. *adi arachétiló addamu lágu telustúné v'undi*, it is quite clear.
aradanḍa, handcuff.
araguṭa, to wear away. *aragatíyuṭa* is to grate.
aramara, hesitation. *manaló manacu v'unna púrvapu snéhánni baṭṭi yémí aramara lécunḍá aḍugutú v'unnánu*, I ask without hesitation in view of our old friendship.
aramóḍutsuṭa, to half-close.
aramómu, profile. *aramómu chéyuṭa*, to turn away the face, to disregard.
araṇamu, dowry. Skt. *suguṇa sampadayé goppa araṇam*, virtue is a great dowry; *á chinnadi y'iravai véla rúpá-*

yalu aranam tisucu vastundi, that girl has a dowry of Rs. 20,000.

araṇyamu, wilderness, jungle. Skt. Often translated 'forest', but wrongly. *araṇya ṣunacamu*, a wolf; *araṇyaróda-namu*, a cry in the wilderness.

araṇyaródanamu, a voice crying in the wilderness, vain lamentations. Skt., from *araṇyam* and *ródanam*, weeping. *réṭlanu taggintsa valen ani araṇya ródanamul'ainavi*, a vain cry for reduction of rates.

arapa, field platform.

arapu, cry, roar; from *aratsuṭa*, roar; usually the roar of a beast or of a man in a temper. *céca* is the usual human cry, *cûta* the cry of a bird or a beast.

araṭáculu, plantain leaves.

araṭi-cáyalu, green plantains.

araṭi-cheṭṭu, plantain tree.

araṭi-panḍu, plantain fruit. *araṭipanḍ' olichi chétici itsuṭa*, to simplify. An idiom. *y'í pustacamu araṭipanḍ'olichi chétici ichchin'aṭlu Telugu bháshanu bódha chéstundi*, this book makes the teaching of Telugu as simple as peeling a potato.

aratsuṭa, to roar, of men and various animals. *araché cucca carava néradu*, a barking dog does not bite; *nivu v'úricé aravaca nóru músucó*, hold your tongue and do not make a silly noise. Bleating and barking and roaring may be *aratsutsunnadi*, but barking is usually *morugutsunnadi*, and roaring, *garjintsutsunnadi*.

aravai, 60.

aravaimandi, 60 people.

aravamu, Tamil.

aravindamu, lotus. Skt. There are at least 20 words for lotus with which they make play in descriptions in books; this is one of the three or four common words. *padma* is perhaps the commonest. Both *aravinda* and *padma* are female names.

arayuṭa, to inquire. *yógacshémamulu arayuṭa*, inquire about one's health.

archacuḍu, priest. Skt.

archana, worship. Skt.

archintsuṭa, to worship. Skt.

arhamaina, fitting. Skt. *mí goppa-tanánici y'idi yentamátramu arhamai-nadi cád'ani nácu telusunu, gáni ná bhactini baṭṭi mír'idi angicarintstsa valenu*, please accept this in token of my devotion, though I know it is unworthy of your greatness.

arhata, fitness. Skt.

arhuḍu, worthy. *nén'arhunnaina san-gati mícu telusunu*, you know I am a fit man.

aricálu, sole of the foot. *aricálu manṭa nettici vastundi*, an idiom for angry. *váḍini tsústé nácu aricáli manṭa nettici vastundi*, when I look upon him bad blood flows in me from head to foot.

arise, sweet fried rice cake.

arishṭamu, calamity. Skt.

arjí, petition. Hindustani. Arjís begin *A tálúká B grámam cápurasthuḍu C vrásuconna arjí yémanṭé* and end up with the prayer introduced by *ganuca*; some officers tell their clerks to start from *ganuca* when they have petitions read to them.

arjídáru, petitioner.

arpana, offering. Skt. *andani púlu dévunici arpaṇa*, offering God flowers out of reach.

arpintsuṭa, to offer. Skt.

arpitamu, offered. Skt. *grámamu samudrárpitam ainadi*, the village became the sea's prey (was eroded).

arthamu, half. Skt. *artha gaḍiya bhógam'áru nelala rógam*, half an hour's enjoyment and six months' disease.

arthamu, meaning. Skt. *nícu artha-mu ainadá?* do you understand?

arthamu, wealth. Skt.

-arthamu, suffix meaning on account of. Skt. *racshaṇarthamai pó*, go to save.

arthamu chéyuṭa, construe.

artharátri, midnight. Skt.

arthaṣástramu, political economy. Skt., from *artham*, wealth, and *ṣás-tram*, science.

arthángícáramu, half consent. *váḍu arthángícáramutó Telugu tsaduvut un-náḍu*, he studies Telugu rather unwillingly.

arthántaramu, another meaning. Skt., from *artham*, meaning, and *anta-ram*, other.

arudentsuṭa, to go; combination of

arugu and *tentsuṭa* which both mean 'to go' in books. In books the Telugus dislike using common words like *póvuṭa* (go) or *chéyuṭa* (do); so for 'to go' *arudentsuṭa*, *étentsuṭa*, *tsanuṭa*, *tsanudentsuṭa*, &c., are used and for 'to do' *onartsuṭa*, *cávintsuṭa*, &c. They do this even in newspapers; the same feeling makes our clerks write 'proceed' instead of 'go' in English, and 'commence' instead of 'begin'.

arudu, rare.

arugu, pial (Anglo-Indian), stoep (Dutch), tinnai (Tamil). There does not seem to be an English word for this raised platform or verandah outside a house. *ippuḍu y'í arugula vishayamuló nácu yémi istáru?* (municipal councillor speaking) now what will you give me in the matter of these pials? (Pials are the commonest form of encroachments on streets, and municipal councillors are commonly supposed to wink at them for a consideration.)

arugudentsuṭa, to go, in books, from *aruguṭa*, to go, and *tentsuṭa*, to go. *arugudentsuṭa* is sometimes used in the sense of *dayachéyuṭa*, deigning to come. *chacravarti gáru y'í déṣamunacu renḍu sárlu arugudenchindru*, the King Emperor has deigned to come twice to this country.

aruguṭa, to be digested. *nácu yenta tinná arugutundi, nénu rálḷu tini jírṇamu chésucó galanu*, however much I eat it will be digested, even stones.

aruguṭa, to go.

arulumarulu, dotage; an onomatopoeic word.

aruṇódayamu, dawn. Skt., from *arunuḍu*, sun, and *udayam*, rising. Commonly used in novels and descriptive passages. Telugu novelists all think they must describe at least one sunrise and one sunset in dog-Sanskrit.

aṛupu, a roar; from *aratsuṭa*, to roar.

aruvadi, 60; more commonly *aravai*.

aruvu, loan in kind, grain, &c., given on credit. *bazáruló v'uppú chintapanḍú y'ichché láguna dinici aruvu béramu lédu; roccamu cummarintsa valenu*, it is not like getting salt and tamarind on credit in the bazaar; cash must pour out.

aṣacti, aṣactata, weakness. Skt., from *a* privative, *ṣacti*, strength, vigour.

aṣactuḍu, a weak man. Skt. *nívu aṣactuḍavu ganuca y'itarula saháyamu lécunḍá yémi cheyya lévu*, because you are weak you can do nothing without the help of others; *aṣactadurjanatvamu*, wickedness born of incompetency.

asaháyaṣúruḍu, single-handed hero. Skt., from *a* privative, *saháyam*, help, and *ṣúra*, hero. *mí vanṭi asaháyaṣúrulu cheyya valenu gáni má chéta yémí cádu*, we can do nothing, it is for knight-errants like you to do it.

asahyamu, loathsome. Sktic., from *a* privative and *sahintsuṭa*, to bear.

asahyintsuṭa, to loathe. Sktic.

asalu, to begin with, really. Hindustani; adverb. *vaca cágitam mída vrási asalu nícu vráta vachchin aṭṭu canaparatsu*, put it on paper and show that you can really write; *mícu tanḍri asalé léḍá?* have you really no father?

asalu, original. Hindustani; adjective. *asalu vádi*, the original plaintiff.

asalu, principal, capital. Hindustani; short for *asalu-mottam*, the original sum.

asamarthata, incapacity. Skt., from *a* privative and *samartham*, capacity.

asamarthuḍu, incompetent man.

asamayamu, unreasonable, untimely. Skt., from *a* privative and *samayam*, occasion.

asambandhamu, disconnected. Sktic., from *a* privative and *sambandham*, connexion.

asambhavamu, unlikely. Sktic., from *a* privative and *sambhavintsuṭa*, happen.

asammati, disapprobation. Skt., from *a* privative and *sammati*, consent.

asampúrti, incomplete. Skt., from *a* privative, *sam*, with, and *púrti*, complete.

aṣanamu, boiled rice, food. Skt. for Telugu *annam*. Used chiefly in compounds. Thus a meat-eater is *mámsáṣanuḍu*, a term of contempt in brahmin mouths.

asandarbhamu, inconvenience. Skt., *a* privative and *sandarbham*, circumstance. *puṭṭillu daggira v'úru cávaḍam chéta y'i asandarbham vastú v'unṭundi*, this inconvenience occurs because the town is near (my wife's) parents' home.

asantushṭi, dissatisfaction. Skt., *a* privative and *santushṭi*, joy.

asatyamu, untruthfulness. Skt., *a* privative and *satyam*, truth. *zúdamú, pánamú, asatyamú modalaina dushcáryamulu*, gambling, drink, lying, and other vices.

aṣauchamu, uncleanness. Skt., from *a* privative and *ṣuchi*, purity; adjectival form.

asádháraṇamu, uncommon. Skt., *a* privative and *sádháraṇamu*, ordinary. *vaḍiló asádháraṇam aina yógyata v'unnadi*, he is a man of uncommon merit.

asádhyamu, impossible. Skt. *Ocaḍu: Í lócamló asádhyam anédi yédí lédu. Snéhituḍu: Aité ná peḷḷám sangati nuvvu yeragav anna máṭa.* A Hindu: There is nothing impossible in this world. Friend: Then you don't know my wife.

asádhyata, impossibility.

asádhyuḍu, extraordinary person. *itanu yeccaḍi váḍó asádhyuḍu lág' unnáḍu, ábharaṇam tsancaló v'unna sangati cúḍá grahinchináḍu*, he seems to have some sort of extraordinary gift, he has guessed that I have the jewellery in my armpit.

asámányamu, extraordinary. Skt., from *a* privative and *sámányam*, ordinary.

asámányuḍu, extraordinary person.

asesaru, assessor (in Sessions Court). English.

aṣéshamu, whole. Skt., from *a* privative and *ṣésham*, remainder. *í paṭṭaṇamló aṣesha janam santóshinchinıáru*, the whole population of this town rejoiced; *úr' aṣéshamumú pilichináru*, they invited the whole village; *mana grámamu aṣéshamu*, the whole of our village.

ashṭami, 8th day after full moon or new moon; from Skt. for 8.

asmat-, prefix meaning my. Skt. Used in composition with Sanskrit words in books only. *asmaddágamanamu*, my arrival.

aspashṭamu, indistinct. Skt., from *a* privative and *spashṭam*, distinct.

asprüṣyuḍu, untouchable. Skt., from *a* privative and *sprüṣa*, touch. *déválayamu n'andu asprüṣyulu pravéṣintsuṭacu svéchcha y'osaga valenu*, freedom must be given to untouchables to enter temples. (The Hindu religion does not allow pariahs to enter temples; the removal of untouchability is part of the Congress platform. But when in the no-tax campaign at Guntur in 1922 a pariah was taken to a temple the local Vaiṣyas made a bonfire of khaddar cloth to show their disgust and severed their connexion with the Congress.)

aṣraddha, negligence. Skt., from *a* privative and *ṣraddha*, concentration. *bahu-aṣraddha* is a legal term for gross negligence.

aṣruvu, tear. Skt. The Telugu is *can-níru*, eye-water.

astamánamu, all day long. Skt. In Sanskrit it means 'sunset', 'evening'. *mí nóṭici astamánamu 'ose osé' anna máṭacu visugu lédu*, you do not tire of girling me my good girl all day; *mícu astamánamu nannu áḍipósucóvaḍamtóné sari pótundi*, you keep scolding me all day long.

asthi, asthica, bone. Skt.

asthi-panjaramu, skeleton. From Skt., *asthi*, bone, and *panjaramu*, cage.

asthiramu, unstable, transient. Skt.

asti-násti, doubtful, partly true and partly false. Skt.

astramu, missile. Skt.

aṣuchi, impurity. Skt., from *a* privative and *ṣuchi*, pure.

aṣuddhamu, impurity, filth. Skt., from *a* privative and *ṣuddham*, pure.

aṣuddha paratsuṭa, to foul.

asura, demon. Skt., supposed to be derived from Assyrian. *Rávaṇa* is an *asura*.

asúya (ta), disgust. Skt.; in Sanskrit it means 'envy'. *asúyató mogamu trippuconṭ'unnáḍu*, twists his face in disgust; *doralacu mana míḍa asúyata puṭṭistáru*, they will make the gentlemen (Europeans) disgusted with us.

aṣvamu, horse. Skt. Used only in books and compounds. Telugu, *gurramu*.

aşvaddha, holy fig-tree. Skt. In Telugu, *rávi cheṭṭu*.

aşvamédhamu, horse-sacrifice. *aşva-radhamu*, horse chariot; *aşva-şástra-mu*, veterinary science; *aşvavaid-yuḍu*, veterinary doctor, *aşvarúḍhuḍu*, mounted on a horse; *aşvaşála*, stable.

asvasthata, ill-health. Skt.

-aṭa, suffix meaning 'he says', 'so they say'; very common, the speaker takes no responsibility for the accuracy of the statement; from *anuṭa*, to say. H.E. the Governor having come and failed to shoot a bear, says he will come again and shoot one; this being translated to the beaters would be *maḷḷí vastár'aṭa, elugubanṭini coṭṭutár' aṭa*, he says he will come again and says he will shoot a bear.

aṭa, there. *aṭacu pó*, go there; *aṭu-nunchi*, from there.

aṭa, that. *aṭamunnu*, before that.

aṭaca, lift, shelf. *aṭaca mída gummaḍi cáyalu tsálá v'unnavi*, there are many pumpkins on the shelf.

aṭacáyintsuṭa, to obstruct. Hindu-stani, *aṭacáná*.

ataḍu, he.

atagáḍu, he, contemptuous.

atanu, he.

aṭé, form of address to a woman.

ati, prefix meaning great, excessive. Skt.

aticintsuṭa, to solder, fit.

aticramamu, transgression. Skt., from *ati-*, beyond, and *cramam*, line.

aticramintsuṭa, to transgress.

atidírghamu, prolix. Skt., from *ati-*, beyond, and *dírgham*, long.

atimútramu, diabetes (excess of urine). Skt.

atirécamu, excess. Skt., from *ati-*, beyond, and *récam* line. *yauvanam'an-du javaránḍru cámátirécamu chéta cashṭa-sughamulan' entsaca péru pra-tishṭala páṭimpaca yentaṭi sáhasa crütyamun'ainá chéyuṭacu sáhasinturu*, young women stirred by excess of lust in youth, will venture on any daring deed without considering comfort or discomfort, name or fame.

atisamípa, nearest, very near. Skt., from *ati-* and *samípam*, near. *atisa-mípa gnyáti*, nearest of kin.

atişayamu, excess. Skt.

atişayintsuṭa, to surpass. Skt.

atişayócti, exaggeration. Skt.

atisáramu, diarrhoea, dysentery. Skt.

atithi, guest. Skt., from *a* privative and *tithi*, day. *intamandi grühasthu-lanu tsúchinánu gáni mícu vale atithici inta şraddhábhactulató svayamgá v'upa-cháram chésé várini nénu y'eccaḍá tsúḍa lédu*, I have seen many hosts but never one who himself served his guest with such devotion and atten-tion as you;

> *Gnyapti y'atithci marí y'unṭunnadi rózulu y'anni*
> *Satcáram Sri Rája samastam chési-na y'andu.*

The guest will remember all his days the hospitality of the Raja. (It will be noted that these lines of Telugu are hexameters. They are a translation of two lines of Homer which I wrote in a Raja's Visitors' Book. Colloquial Telugu runs easily into hexameters and this is the metre which I recom-mend to the Telugus for translation of Homer, the *Rámáyaṇa*, &c.)

atithi-satcáramu, hospitality. Skt.

ativádi, an extremist, usually applied to a Congress propagandist.

ativáguḍu, excessive talk; *váguḍu*, sounding, noise. *ní ativáguḍu caṭṭi peṭṭu*, hold your tongue, make no more noise; *y'í déşamuló ativáguḍu-váḷḷa gaḍabiḍa zórugá v'unnadi*, the extremists are making much noise in this country.

ativáguláḍu, chatterbox; from Skt. *ati-*, excessive, and Telugu *váguṭa*, chatter.

ativrüshṭi, excess of rain. Skt., from *ati-* and *vrüshṭi*, rain.

aṭla, aṭlá, aṭlé, aṭlu, so, in that way, that way. *aṭlé* is emphatic. *aṭlá chep-pinḍḍu*, he said so; *eppaṭiyaṭla*, as usual; *aṭlá pó*, go there; *aṭlá v'úrici pó-vatstsuná?* does that road lead to the village?

atrüpti, dissatisfaction. Skt., from *a* privative and *trüpti*, satisfaction.

atstsu, print, mould. *magaváḷḷ'antá vaccaṭé atstsu*, males are all made in one mould; *váḍu tandri atstsu*, his father's image.

atstsu véyuṭa, to print.
atta, attagáru, mother-in-law. *atta tsasté cóḍalu y'édchin'aṭlu,* like a daughter-in-law weeping at her mother-in-law's death, crocodile tears; *attá vacar' inṭi cóḍalé,* the mother-in-law was daughter-in-law once in some one's house; *attaléni cóḍalu v'uttamurálu, cóḍalu léni atta guṇavanturálu,* where there is no mother-in-law the daughter-in-law is excellent, where there is no daughter-in-law the mother-in-law has all good qualities.
attamu, bunch of plantains.
attaru, attar (of roses or fragrant flowers).
aṭṭé, there (emphatic), so (emphatic), as it is, precisely then or there, as before. *aṭṭé unḍan'i,* leave it where it is, just there; *noppi aṭṭé unnadi,* the pain is no better; *áṭṭé póyináḍu,* he went at once, that moment.
atti, atti-mánu, Indian fig tree; *Ficus glomerata. attimánu púchinaṭṭu,* like the *atti* tree flowering (it never flowers); milk from a stone. The fruit is *atticáya* or *attipanḍu. attipanḍu tsúḍan' anḍamai y'unḍunu poṭṭa vichchi tsúḍa purugul'unḍu,* the fig is handsome, but there is a worm inside (All that glitters is not gold). These are oft-quoted lines from Vémana, a most popular poet. His poetry has the authority of proverbs in literate as well as illiterate mouths in Telugu.
aṭṭi, such. Contraction of *aṭuvanṭi. praccanu naḍachi póvun aṭṭiváru,* passers-by.
aṭṭu, sort of cake.
aṭṭu, like, as, that, to. *énuguni tsúchi cuccalu morigin 'aṭṭu,* like dogs barking at an elephant; *nénu cheppin'aṭṭu chésináḍu,* he did as I said; *ataḍu vachchéṭaṭṭu vrásinánu,* I wrote him a letter to come; *aṭṭé v'unn'aṭṭ'aité,* if it were as it was.
aṭu, that, then. *aṭupúrvamu,* before that; *aṭuvalené,* in the same way; *éṭici aṭu pacca,* on the other side of the river.
atucu, joint. *atuculabonta,* a patched-up rug; *atuculabonta cápuramu,* an embarrassed life; *atucula-bratucu,* living without a job, on some one's bounty.
aṭuculu, parched rice. *i rátri conchem aṭuculu phalahárамu tappa yémi tina cúḍadu,* you must eat nothing to-night except a light meal of parched rice.
atucuṭa, to fit, be soldered, be suitable. *bangáránici ṭancam poḍi vésin aṭṭugá yenta nizamainá madhya nálugu abaddhálu vésténẽ cãni atacadu,* you must use a few lies as alloy for truth, otherwise it won't be solid.
atushṭi, dissatisfaction. Skt., from *a* privative and *tushṭi,* satisfaction.
aṭuvanṭi, such; from *aṭu,* that, and *vanṭi,* like.
atyanta, very great. Skt., from *ati-,* beyond, and *antam,* end.
atyavasaramu, very necessary; emergency; from *ati* and *avasaram,* necessary.
atyáṣa, avarice. Skt., from *ati-,* excessive, and *áṣa,* desire.
au, also spelt *ávu,* cow.
auchityamu, propriety; adjectival form of *uchitamu,* proper. Skt.
audáryamu, liberality; adjectival form of *udáramu.* Skt. *mi audáryamu nácu y'idi varacé telisindi, míru nácu chésina gauravá́laló y'idi vacaṭi,* your liberality is known to me of old; this is one of the honours you have done me.
auddhatyamu, rudeness; adjectival form of *uddhati.* Skt.
auḍu, the under lip. *auḍu caratsuṭa,* to bite the lips in anger.
aunu, yes; from *auṭa,* it may become. *aunu* is sometimes used in its proper sense, *adi ná chétan'aunu,* I can do this; more usually it means 'yes'. *auná cádá?* yes or no?
aupanishada, belonging to the Upanishads; adjectival form of Sanskrit *Upanishat.*
aura! oh! *aura, yenta mósam!* oh, what a swindle!
auru, bulrush.
aushathamu, medicine; adjectival form of Skt. *óshadhi. mandu* is the Telugu word but *aushatham* is also exceedingly common.
auṭa, become; another form of *aguṭa* and *avuṭa*; the root is *cá* as in *nácu cá valenu,* I want. Common uses of the parts of this verb are *aunu,* yes; *aindi,* it is finished; *aité,* if. The opposite

to *aunu* is *cádu*; the opposite to *aina*, being, is *cáni*, not being. *ainavánḍlunnu cánivánḍlunnu*, friends and enemies; *auná cádá?* yes or no? *váḍu mic'émi autáḍu* means what relation is he of yours? *vánici mému yémi cámu*, we are no relations of his. *ai póyinadi* means it is finished, as of work or money. *samvatstsaram ainadi*, a year is past. *artham'ainadá?* do you understand? The causal *cávintsuṭa* is used for 'to do'. *cá lédu* means it has not been done or come out, as *tírpu cá lédu*, judgement has not been delivered. *cá valasina váru* means relations. In fact *auṭa* with its negative *cádu*, its root *cá*, its causative *cávintsuṭa*, its past participle *ai*, its conditional *aité*, and so on, is the most useful word in the language. *Óristé Órugallu paṭnam autundi*, 'Patience and Orugallu (Warangal) will become a city' is a common proverb.

ava, prefix meaning bad, untoward. Skt. *avalacshaṇamu*, bad trait.

avacatavaca, absurd, untoward. *ní avacatavaca prasangam mánaca póyinaṭṭ aité y'ippuḍu nálugu tanni ninnu inṭló nunchi avatalici ságan' amputánu*, if you don't stop your nonsense, I shall kick you out of the house; *iṭuvanṭi váḷḷacu ṣástrálaló y'év ainá avacatavaca praṣnalu veyya valenu*, with such people the only thing to do is to ask some nonsense questions out of the Shastras; *anduló yém'aina avacatavaca zarigité*, if anything untoward happens.

avacáṣamu, opportunity. Skt. *chicci v'unna chilucala vale svéchchá vihára-munac' avacáṣamu léca*, without opportunity for free exercise like caged parrots.

avaḍamu, become. A colloquial form of *aguṭa*.

avaḍamuchéta, as it came to that.

avadhánamu, attention. Skt. *avadháni*, person skilled in Shastras; postfixed in compounds, as *ashṭávadhání*, a versatile man who can attend to eight things simultaneously. *ṣatávadhání*, a poet who can solve a hundred poetic riddles at one and the same time. They are also given as titles to poets that have attained literary eminence and precede their names as *ashṭávadhání Dómá Vencaṭaswámi Gupta*, and *ṣatávadhání Tirupati Ṣástri*. For an account of *ashṭávadhánamu* performed by Mr. K. Viresalingam Pantulu see his *Autobiography*, vol. i.

avadhánuḍu, person skilled in the Vedas, a priestly title, Skt.

avagáhamu, comprehension. Skt. *sura yocca mahima suralac'ainá duravagáhamé*, the splendour of nectar is difficult even for the immortals to comprehend.

avagnyata, contempt. Skt. *ati parichaya avagnyata*, familiarity breeds contempt.

avalacshaṇamu, bad omen, dishonour. Skt. *udyógam purusha lacshaṇam, adi póté avalacshaṇam*, office is the mark of a man, its loss dishonour.

avalambintsuṭa, to profess (a creed, opinion). Skt.

avalílagá, easily. Skt.

avalócanamu, sight, looking. Skt.

avalócintsuṭa, to see. Skt. Connected with English 'look', a word used only in books for *tsútsuṭa*.

avamánamu, disgrace, shame. *áṣa bódhist'unnadi avamánamu bádhist' unnadi*, desire incites, shame repels; *avamána paratsaḍam*, to insult.

avamánintsuṭa, to dishonour.

avaródhamu, obstruction. Skt. *várici márgávaródhamu calagacunḍun'aṭlu*, to prevent their way being obstructed.

avaródhintsuṭa, to obstruct. Skt. *saukhyamunacu márgamu avaródhinchi*, having obstructed the way to happiness.

avasaramu, necessity. Skt. *avasaram'ain'appuḍu*, when it is necessary.

avasarapaḍuṭa, be in a hurry; be in need.

avasánamu, end. Skt. Commonest in the compound *paryavasánam*, result. *avasána cálamun'andu*, on his death-bed.

avaṣishṭamu, remainder. Skt. *práṇávaṣishṭamugá*, with just life left, half dead.

avastha, state, condition. Skt. *bályávastha,* childhood; *várdhacyávastha,* old age; *míru y'incá yógábhyásamló modaṭi avasthalóné v'unnáru,* you are still in the first stage of Yoga.

avaṣyacatvamu, necessity.

avaṣyamu, necessity. Skt.

avaṣyangá, necessarily.

avatala, beyond, on the other side. The opposite is *ivatala,* on this side.

avatali, next, further. *avatali Sómaváramu,* next Monday; *avatali taṭṭu,* the other side; *avatali vainamulu,* further particulars.

avatali-váḷḷu, men on the other side.

avatarintsuṭa, to become incarnate. Skt., meaning 'to come down'. *Krüshṇuḍugá avatarinchenu,* he was incarnated as Krishna.

avatáramu, incarnation. *Vishṇuvu y'ettina daṣavatáramulu,* the ten incarnations of Vishnu.

avayavamu, limb. Skt.

avi, those things. *avi yevarivi?* whose are those?

avibhactamu, undivided. Skt., from *a* privative and *vibhactam,* divided. *avibhacta cuṭumbamu* is a joint or undivided family; *míru vibhactulá, avibhactulá?* have you divided your family property, or haven't you?

avichchinnamu, uninterrupted. Skt., from *a* privative and *vichchit,* parting. *iṭuvanṭi aicamatyam manaló v'unnadi ganuca Méru parvatamu vale sustirangá v'unḍi yentamátram cheḍacunḍá néṭi varacu avichchinnangá ságutú v'unnadi,* Hindu unanimity stands like a rock and goes on uninterruptedly and uninjured (this is ironic, the Hindus being notoriously fissiparous); *mí lantsálacu y'ellacálamú avichchinnangá sági rávaḍánici pani chésinárá?* did you manage to get your bribes uninterruptedly all the time?

avidhéyata, disobedience. Skt. *avidhéyata mukhyangá pógoṭṭa valenu,* you must specially drive out disobedience; *itanu y'ikha yeppuḍú peddala yeḍa avidhéyatagá pravartintsaḍu,* in future he will never behave disobediently to grown-ups.

avisi, flax.

avivécamu, folly. Skt., from *a* privative and *vivécam,* wisdom. *inṭi vóccyamu y'entamátram caluga chésucócunḍá vachchina váritóṭ'allá máṭláḍutú v'unḍaḍamé pedda avivécamu,* it is a great folly in him to pay no attention to his household affairs and to talk to every one who comes along.

avuḍu, underlip; also *auḍu.*

avura! oh! also *aura!*

avuṭa, become; one of the colloquial forms of *aguṭa.*

avuṭa-valla, as it has come to it.

avvâ, grandmother; also form of address to any old woman.

avyacta, unevolved (philosophy). Skt., from *a-*, privative, and *vyacta,* evolved.

avyactapu, stupid, ignorant. Skt. *iṭuvanṭi avyactapu prasangam y'enducu chéstáru?* why this stupid talk?

ayidu, five; same as *aidu. ayidu padi chéyuṭa,* to bow in humility; bringing the fingers of your hands together so as to make them ten after the Indian fashion of salutation.

ayina, past; another way of spelling *aina,* past participle of *auṭa. ayina panici chintinchéváḍu alpa buddhi galaváḍu,* only a fool grieves over what is past.

ayiná, even. Also past participle of *auṭa* but means 'although'. *chinna pámu-n-ainá pedda carrató coṭṭa valenu,* though it be a small snake, hit it with a big stick.

ayiri, an emphatic but peculiar form of the verb *aguṭa,* become; in spelling it is exactly similar to its 3rd person plural but it is used in a different sense. *enta ahórinchiná váḍu nátó cheppaḍ'ayiri,* however I importune him he does not tell me; *mana bhédhamulu manamu sadducó lém ayiri,* whatever we do we cannot compound our differences.

ayishṭamu, displeasure. Skt., from *a* privative and *ishṭamu,* pleasure.

ayógyamu, unworthy. Skt.

ayógyuḍu, a worthless man. Skt. *ayógyulu manaváḷḷ ainá, váḷḷanu chéran' iyyacu,* do not allow worthless people to come near you even if they are our own people.

ayuctamu, wrong. Skt., from *a* privative and *yuctam*, right. *yuctá'yuctamulu teliyaca*, not knowing right from wrong.

ayya, master, sir, father. *yémayyá?* what, sir? *musalayya*, old gentleman; *amma grühapravéşamu ayya smaşána pravéşamu*, the bride in the house and the master in the tomb (unexpected calamity).

ayya, ayyamma, lady's maid or children's nurse; used in English as *áyah*.

ayyaváru, teacher.

ayyó! alas!

azmoish, inspection of crops. Hindustani. A revenue term for the annual crop inspection made by revenue officers; the word properly means experiment, trial.

Á

Á? Interrogative affix; to express interrogation in Telugu and other Dravidian languages you merely add *-á* to the last word of the sentence; to express doubt you add *-ó*; *-é* is the corresponding emphatic. At tennis *out-á?* means is it out?; *outó*, it may be out; *outé*, it *is* out.

-á, vocative; affix; lengthened form of *-a*.

á, yes; same as *aunu*; spoken with a half-nasal sound. *paina doricéd'edó adé udyógam ani gharáná manushyula úha. í paina doracaḍam anédi mahá gaḍusu mucca. dánné condaru téliggá' á lantsam anṭáru*, some important people are of opinion that the dignity of an office depends upon the amount of surplus earnings (extraordinary gain) which it can enjoy. This 'surplus earnings' is a most cunning term. Some people don't admit it and lightly say, 'O, yes, it is a bribe'.

á, that, those, adjectival; pronoun is *adi*, singular, *avi*, plural. *á* is both plural and singular; *í*, this, these, is also plural and singular; *é?* is the interrogative, which is also both plural and singular. *á cathalu*, those stories; *á venuca*, after that; *á tanḍrici coḍucu cáḍá?* is he not his father's son?

á-, prefix meaning up to. Skt. Used only in compounds. *áchandratárácamu*, as long as the sun and the moon and the stars endure, used in grants of jaghirs, &c., which were as a matter of fact valid only for the life of the granter or grantee; if that (Hindu legal fictions).

á—á, various. Also *áyá*. *á—á inḍlaló*, in the various houses.

ábcári, tax on liquor. Hindustani. The *ábcári* department is also called the *uppu* or Salt department because the same establishment at one time collected the liquor and salt taxes; it is a department proverbially administered harshly, the men not being trusted by their superiors. *tappuléni-vánni v'uppuló veyyum annáḍ'aṭa*, put him in the salt, he said, as there is nothing against him (enemy speaking).

ábharaṇamu, ornament, especially jewellery. Skt.

ábhásamu, corruption. Skt.

ábiḍa, she; extensively used south of Bezwada. Also *áviḍa, áme*.

ábótu, bull, especially a bull allowed loose for the common service of the village cows and not worked; from *áu* and *pótu*, the cow's male. Commonly *ámbótu*.

ácali, hunger. *ácali ácáşam anta, gontuca súdi bezzam anta*, his hunger is as great as the sky, his throat the size of a needle's eye (great ambition, small abilities); *ácali ruchi y'erugadu, nidra sukham' erugadu, valapu sigg' erugadu*, hunger needs no sauce, sleepiness no comfort, lust has no shame; *telivi taccuva, ácali y'eccuva*, the less the sense, the greater the greed; *vánici ácali cá lédá?* is he not hungry? *ácali tírtsuṭa*, to satisfy hunger; *ácali conuṭa* or *áconuṭa*, to be hungry.

ácarshamu, attraction. Skt. Also *ácarshaṇamu*.

ácarshintsuṭa, to attract. Skt. *ní rúpamu yauvana purushulanu vivádhánic ácarshinché láguné v'unnadi*, your beauty is such as to attract young men to marriage.

ácáramu, form, shape. Skt.

ácári, a well-formed, handsome man. So in Latin *formosus*, from *forma*, means handsome.

ácasmicamugá, suddenly. Skt. *ácasmicamugá nannu iccaḍacu y'iḍtsucuni vachchi paḍavésinàru*, they suddenly dragged me here and left me.

ácasmicamaina, unexpected, casual. *í anugraham nénu yentamátramunnú y'eduru tsúḍanidinní ácasmicamainadinní*, I neither hoped for nor expected this favour in any respect (note the clumsy length of Telugu words).

ácáṣamu, sky; in composition fanciful, non-existent. Skt. *ácali ácáṣam' anta, gontuca súdi bezzam anta*, a man who bites off more than he can chew; *ácáṣánici nichchena vésévāḍu*, a man who plants a ladder against the sky (an ambitious man). In philosophy, space.

ácáṣa-panchángamu, sky calendar, pack of nonsense.

ácáṣa-Rámanna, Ramanna from the sky, i.e. non-existent. This is the common signature to frankly anonymous petitions. The pseudonymous petition-writer will use a real name.

ácáṣa vartacuḍu, impostor.

ácáṣa-váni, 'sky-speaking' as the voice of an angel or invisible being.

áchandratáracamu, as long as the sun and the moon and the stars endure. Skt., from *á-*, till, *chandra*, moon, and *tára*, star. Used in deeds and grants of land, but never taken seriously by indigenous governments. The grant would be revoked at the death of either the granter or the grantee; our Government took the expression seriously in some cases and misguidedly confirmed grants in perpetuity.

ácharintsuṭa, to do habitually, observe (ceremonies). Skt.

ácháramu, observance, custom, especially religious, religiosity. Skt. *ácháránici antamu lédu, anáchárànici ádi lédu*, we are all born with original sin and can never attain the full observance of religion; *pilavacunḍá vachchina vállacu vindu cheyyaḍam nácu áchàram lédu*, I am not accustomed to feast uninvited guests.

Áchári, caste title (1) of Vaishnavite Brahmins, (2) of goldsmiths and blacksmiths. These people ridiculously write themselves in Roman characters Mr. Gopala chari or Mr. Venkata chari instead of Gópál Áchári, Venkaṭ Áchári. This is because they have the prejudice, derived from their primitive syllabic alphabet, that a word cannot end with a consonant. There is no such word or title as Chári.

Áchàryuḍu, a kind of Brahmin. Skt. This is the Brahmin who invests a Brahmin boy with the sacrificial thread and then instructs him in religion. *áchāryunni talachi nippuló cheyyi peṭṭité cáladá?* is a proverb laughing at the pretensions of these people; put your hand in the fire with your mind full of your teacher and you will find it will burn just the same.

ácramamu, encroachment. Skt.

ácramintsuṭa, to encroach. A very common word and fact; Hindus think it laudable to try to add to their field or their house-site by encroachment, and we have not in a century of government with other ideas been able to give them another angle of vision; the Telugus have even a proverb commending this, in their view, admirable conduct. *chénuló chénu calasiná, jágáló jágá calasiná pón ivva cúḍadu*, never lose a chance of mixing a bit of field with your field or a bit of house-site with your house-site; *míru sarcáru sthalam ácramintsucunnáru*, you encroached on Government land.

ácrüti, form, shape. Skt.

ácshépaṇa, objection. Skt.

ácshépintsuṭa, to object. Skt.

ácṭu, act (of the legislature). English.

ácu, leaf, leaf of young rice; as prefix 'green'.

ácuchilaca, green butterfly, green parrot.

ácucúralu, green vegetables.

ácumaḍi, rice nursery, seed-bed.

ácupatstsa, sap-green.

ácuráyi, file.
ácuṭillu, leaf hut; from *ácu*, leaf, and *illu*, house.
ácutóṭa, plant garden, betel garden.
áda, grief.
áḍa, female.
áḍabiḍḍa, unmarried daughter, from *áḍa*, female, and *biḍḍa*, child; the daughter of the house. *áḍa pettanamu Tambali doratanamu*, the monstrous regiment of women and of the Tamilian. The daughter of the house is supposed to join her mother in giving a bad time to the *cóḍalu*, or daughter-in-law. The unmarried or widowed sister-in-law is the natural enemy of the daughter-in-law.
áḍadi, a female; a male is *mogaváḍu*. Inflected form *áḍadáni*, plural *áḍaváḷḷu*. *áḍadáni chéti arthamú, mogaváni chéti biḍḍa bratacadu*, a child in male keeping, and property in female keeping are soon ruined; *áḍadáni buddhi apara buddhi*, woman's sense is nonsense; *áḍadáni máṭa niḷḷa múṭa*, 'la donna è mobile'; *áḍadi boncité góḍa peṭṭin aṭṭu, mógaváḍu boncité taḍica caṭṭin aṭṭu*, a woman's lie is built up like a wall, a man's lie is a mat partition.
áḍamanishi, woman; from *áḍa*, female, and *manishi*, human being.
ádamarachi, soundly; from *áda*, grief, and *marutsuṭa*, forget. *ádamarachi nidra póvuṭa*, sleep soundly. Corrupted into *adamarachi* in talk.
áḍambaramu, pomp.
áḍangi, womanish. *áḍangi máṭalu*, womanish talk; *á munḍá-coḍucu vaṭṭi áḍangi máṭalu péltáḍu*, that wretch glories in womanish prattle; *áḍangi abbanna*, a girlish fop.
áḍangulu, women, only in the plural, the singular *áḍangi* is not used.
ádaramu, ádaraṇa, kindnesses done. Skt. *chésina ádaraṇacu santóshinchi*, grateful for the kindness shown; *míru chésina ádaraṇa nénu bratici v'unn anta cálamú marichi pónu*, I shall not forget your kindness as long as I live.
ádarintsuṭa, to do kindnesses. Skt. *parul ainá cáni yogyul aité váḷḷanu ádarinchi chétan aina sahdyam cheyyi*, do kindnesses to and help good people even if they are strangers.

ádarṣamu, ideal; from a Skt. word meaning mirror, pattern, model.
ádáyamu, income. *nelacu renḍu vandala rúpáyilu áddyam vastundi*, an income of Rs.200 a month.
ádháramu, support, what a man, or thing, or case depends on. *jal ádháramu*, water support, means the water source on which irrigated land depends; *jal ádháramu léni bhúmi* is unirrigated land; *dastavézula ádháramu*, documentary support of a case.
ádhicyamu, superiority. Skt.; adjectival form of *adhicam*. *Bráhmaṇa varṇamunacu ádhicyam yém unnadi?* what superiority has the Brahmin caste? *ad antá Bráhmalu tama ádhicyam niluvaḍḍnici pannina pannugaḍa*, that is all a trick of the Brahmins to maintain their superiority; *pámarulu v'upayóginché sámánya máṭalé v'upayógisté má pánḍityamú má ádhicyamú yémiṭ anḍi?* if we use the ordinary words of common folk what becomes of our scholarship, of our superiority?
ádhipatyamu, dominion, rule. Skt.; from *adhicam*, great, and *pati*, lord.
ádhínamu, possession. Skt. *adiná ádhínamló v'unnadi*, that is in my possession or charge.
-ádhyamu, affix meaning that which has. Skt. *váḍu baláḍhyuḍu*, he is a man of pith.
-áḍi, suffix meaning woman. *rancul' áḍi*, a debauched woman; *vagal'áḍi*, a coquette, belle; *boncul'áḍi*, a woman who tells lies.
ádi, beginning. Skt. *antya nishṭhuramu canná ádi nishṭhuramé mélu*, it is better to be harsh at the beginning than the end; *ádyantamulu*, first and last.
-ádi, suffix meaning etcetera, or merely adjectival. Skt. *anécamandi bráhmalu prati dinamú má vadda brándi, jinnú, modalaina sárálu buḍládi paṭṭucu veḷḷutú v'unṭáru*, many brahmins will come to me every day and take away bottles full of brandy, gin, &c.; *dacshiṇádi saruculu*, goods from the south; *uttarádi vánḍlu*, people from the north.
áḍintsuṭa, to cause to play, dance to one's tune. Causative from *áḍuṭa*.

ikha nénu itanini manasu vachchin attu ádintsa valenu, I shall have to let him pull the strings for me; *atuvanti násticulanu pattuconi sicshinchévâru léru; púrvam vale ráti gánugalaló petti ádinché rázul unté villu y'itlá antár andi?* There is no one now to punish such atheists; if there were kings as in the old days who would squeeze them in oil-presses, would they speak so?

ádipósiconuta, vilify, scold; a common word with women. *ástamánam nannu ádipósicóvadam*, scolding me all day long; *eppudú míru nannu ádipósicóvadamtóte saripótundi?* when will you be tired of scolding me?

áditappani vádu, man who does not break his word. *Harischandrudu áditappanivád ani váduca*, Harischandra had the reputation of keeping his word.

Ádiváramu, Sunday. Skt., from *áditya*, sun, and *váram*, day. *aité Ádiváram cácunté Sómaváram*, if it is not Sunday it will be Monday, any day will do.

-ádu, suffix meaning man. *andacádu*, a handsome man; *vagal-ádu*, a gallant.

ádudi, ádubidda, &c., are also used for the more common *ádadi, ádabidda*, &c.

áduta, to play; in compounds it merely verbalizes the noun and in this use it is very common; and in general it means not only to play but to move, to do, to tell or almost anything else according to the context. *mátladuta*, use words, is the ordinary word for to talk; *mudduláduta*, give kisses, is to kiss; *bonculáduta*, is to tell lies; *reccaláduta*, use wings, fly; *pótláduta*, to fight; *pelláduta*, is to marry; *tagaváladuta*, to quarrel. *cancanamula cheyyi ádité cadiyamula cheyyi ádunu*, if the arm that wears the bangle moves, the arm that wears the (man's) bracelet moves too; *vádu ádinadi áta pádinadi páta*, all he does or says is right (in his opinion).

ádyantálu, beginning and end. Skt., from *ádi*, beginning, and *antamu*, end.

ágnya, order, command. Skt.

ágnyápintsuta, to order.

ágrahamu, anger. Skt. The common word is *cópam*; *ágraham* is hardly used except in books. *nishcáranamgá ná mida doragárici y'i pracáramgá ágraham rávadánicí cáranam ém andi?* what is the reason the Collector has got so angry with me without cause?

águta, to stay, stop, usually intransitive, the transitive being *áputa, ápivéyuta*. *idi lénidi nácu ágadu*, I can't get on without it.

áha! interjection, same meaning as in all other languages.

áháramu, food. Skt. *áháram'andú. vyavaháram'andú siggu pada cúdadu*, modesty is misplaced in eating and business.

áhó! alas!

áhuti, offering. Skt.; what is offered by fire to the God.

áhvána, welcome, invitation; adjectival form of *áhvánam*. *áhvána patricalu* are invitation cards; *áhvána sanghádhyacshudu* is the newspaper translation of Chairman, Reception Committee.

áhvánamu, welcome, invitation. Skt. *satramuló digi y'unna yógini mír áhvánamu chésinárá?* have you invited the yogi who has put up at the choultry?

ájánubáhudu, longimanus (one whose arms reach to his knees, a sign of greatness, Sir T. Munro was in popular legend such a one).

ájyamu, ghee. Skt. *agniló ájyam pósin attu*, pouring oil on the flames. The Telugu word is *neyyi*.

ákharu, last, final. Hindustani. *ná dabbu nívu putstsucovadánici y'idé ákharu sári*, this is the last time you get my money.

ákharucu, ákharuna, finally, lastly. Also *ákharici. ákharucu scúlu méstarla vadda rijaltu gránțuló cúdá núțici padi rúpáyalu tsoppuna camishan putsucónidí sommu y'ivvaru*, finally they won't pay the schoolmasters' result grants unless they get 10 per cent. commission.

álacintsuta, to listen. A book-word for *vinuta* but also used in petitions. *dínulam aina má mora álacinchi*, hear our humble prayer.

álasyamu, delay. Skt. *inta álasyamu*

chésindv émayyá? what do you mean by keeping me waiting?

álayamu, abode, especially a deity's. Skt. *dévālayamu* is a common word for temple. *Himálayamu*, the Himalayas, is the abode of snow.

álá, álágu, that way.

álágaṇṭi, such.

áli, must; short for *valenu.*

álinganamu, embrace. Skt.

álintsuṭa, to listen; even more literary and less common than *álacintsuṭa*. The common word is *vinuṭa.*

álóchana, thought, idea. Skt. *í álóchana divyangá v'unnadi*, that is a very good idea.

álóchintsuṭa, to think.

álóna, meanwhile.

álu, wife. *álu cádu, adi vrálu*, ill-mated ill-fated (not a wife but the writing on the forehead); *várthaca daṣaló viváhamu chésuconnavárici pátl' eccaḍanu y'ilágunané y'unḍunu, álu cádu adi vrál anna sámeta nác ippuḍu anubhavamunacu vachchinadi*, men who marry in their old age will always suffer like this; the proverb ill-mated, ill-fated has come home to me by experience; *álini ollanivánici cúraló uppu y'eccuv'ainad aṭa*, as the saying goes the man who does not get on with his wife complains of too much salt in the vegetables.

Áḷváru, Vaishnavite name for Saint; they have 12 Álvars.

ámaḍa, 8 miles. *ámaḍa* and *cósu* (2 miles) are the Telugu measures of distance. *ámaḍalu dúram aité antachcaraṇálu dúramá?* love at a distance.

áme, she, declined *ámecu, ámenu.*

áminu, bailiff. Hindustani. Now used only of the Court bailiffs sent out to distrain, &c.; under Muhammadan rule and in our early times an *amín* was a judge, the Sudder Amin was the High Court.

ámódintsuṭa, to agree. Skt., from *módam*, joy. *mému andaramú ámódinchinámu*, we all agree; *andarú ámódinchinárá?* do all agree? (in putting a resolution to a meeting).

ámu, kiln; same as *ávamu.*

ámudamu, castor oil.

ámudapu cheṭṭu, the castor-oil plant.

ámudálu, castor-oil seeds.

ámúlamu, radical. Skt., from *múlam*, root. *ámúlangá*, radically; *ámúlágramugá*, root and branch.

ána, *anno domini*; from Latin *anno.*

ánacaṭṭu, dam, anicut. *ánacaṭṭulu caṭṭi, cálavalu travvinchináru ganuca désam antá níru pravahinchéṭaṭṭu dvadaṣa varsha-cshámálú gimálú cúḍá haḍili pári pótáyi*, now that they have built anicuts, dug canals, and made water flow over the whole country your twelve lean and fat years is so much idle chatter.

ánandamu, joy, bliss; **ánandintsuṭa,** rejoice. Skt. *púrṇánandam*, complete bliss, also used as a name. *ánanda báshpamulu*, tears of joy; *mícu iṭuvanṭi manchi bhárya doricin anducu nénu ánandist'unnánu*, I am glad you have found such a good wife.

ánatitsuṭa, to give order, but more usually a word for 'to say' like *selavitsuṭa*, which is literally 'give leave'. *Brahmacu nálugu mukhálu yé pracárangá v'unṭavó ánat' ichchedará?* will you explain how Brahma has four faces?

ánaválu, identification mark; the ordinary words used in courts when a person or thing has to be identified. *mí misálu tsúḍaḍamtoṭé ánaválu paṭṭinánu*, I recognized you as soon as I saw your moustache; *yé ánaváḷḷú lénidi*, unidentifiable.

ánaválu paṭṭuṭa, recognize.

áncshapatrica, letter of excommunication. Skt., *áncsha*, properly custody, and *patrica*, paper. *tana cúturuni pannenḍ éḷḷu vachchina dácá viváham cheyyacunḍá aṭṭé v'unchin anducu áncshapatrica pampistám ani Svámulaváru cheppináru*, His Holiness said he would send him an excommunication letter for keeping his 12-year-old daughter unmarried (Hindu social customs).

Ándhra, Telugu. The Skt. word for Telugu; a more distinguished word. *ándhra rájyam* was the old Telugu Kingdom of Vijayanagaram of which the Telugus are proud; the agitation for a separate Telugu province has always been called the Andhra movement. The early Andhras ruled the ancient Kingdom of Māgadha (now Bihar), at the beginning of the Christian Era. Their language was Andhra-Prakrit, the root language of Modern Telugu. *Ádi Ándhrulu*, the untouchable castes of Andhra Desa, so called as they claim to be the original inhabitants of the country.

ándóḷanamu, agitation, swinging. Skt. The ordinary word used in newspapers for political agitation. *ándóḷitam aina manassu*, an agitated mind.

ánḍru, plural of *álu*, wives, women; a book-word.

Ángla, English.

ánuconuṭa, to lean against, to border on. *aḍavini ánuconna chénulu*, fields adjoining the jungle.

ánucúlyamu, convenience. Skt.

ánuṭa, to rest on, to be contiguous to. In books only *ánuṭa* is used for *táguṭa*, to drink.

ápada, misfortune, bad times. Skt., a form *ápattu* is also used in books. *ándánici peṭṭina sommu ápadacu aḍḍam vastundi*, jewellery worn for ornament comes in useful in bad times (Hindu economic notions); *ápat'cálamuna mocculu, sampat'cálamuna bútulu*, vows when times are bad, blasphemy when they are good (when the devil was ill the devil a monk would be, when the devil was well, the devil a monk was he); *nác émó ápada vachchinad ani úhinchi*, thinking some misfortune had happened to me.

ápe, she. *áme* is common.

ápí-véyuṭa, to stop. *pancá ápei*, stop the punkah.

áptamu, intimate. Skt. *ápta bandhuvuḍu*, close relation.

áptuḍu, ápturálu, an intimate friend or relation.

ápuṭa, to stop, transitive. Commonly not used by itself but with the auxiliary verb *véyuṭa*. Stop the punkah is *pancá ápivei* or even, reduplicated, *áp'és'ei*.

-ára, vocative plural affix. *annalára!* brothers! *raitulára!* ryots!

-ára, suffix meaning fully, clearly, one's own. *ataṇṇi nénu caḷḷárá tsúchinánu*, I saw him clearly (*canḍlu*, eyes, and *ára*). *caḍupára bhójanamu chésinánu*, I ate my bellyful; *chétulára*, with my own hands; *vínul'ára vinnánu*, listened with my own ears.

áracshuḍu, watchman. Skt., from *racsham*, protection, used in books; commonly *cápalávádu*.

áragintsuṭa, to eat. *tinuṭa* is commoner. *áragintsagá lénidi aḍigité vastunnadá?* if it is not there to eat, is it any good to ask for it?

árambhamu, beginning. Skt.

árambhintsuṭa, to begin. Skt.

ára peṭṭuṭa, árapóyuṭa, ára véyuṭa, to put to dry.

árava, 6th; from *áru*, 6.

árayuṭa, to inquire.

árádhanamu, worship, adoration. Skt.

árádhintsuṭa, to worship. Skt. *dévuṇṇi árádhintsaḍam máni vési nénu y'erparachina bommala púja chéstú prazalu múḍhul autú v'unnáru*, people have given up worshipping God and stupidly taken to adoring the idols I have set up.

árádhyuḍu, reverend. *lócárádhyulu*, adored by all the world; the Lingáyats are particularly fond of this title.

árámamu, grove. Skt.

áráṭamu, grief. Skt.

árbháṭamu, uproar; bustle. Skt.

** áriga, áruga,** or **árica,** an inferior sort of millet. Latin name, *paspalum scrobiculatum*. *áruga cósina muhúrtam n'andé candi cúḍá cósin aṭlu*, reaping the good pulse with the bad millet (i.e. in too much haste); *aité árica cácunṭé candi*, if ariga fails there will be red-gram (i.e. if you sow both together); *árica tsallina Reḍḍici álumogalacu ocaṭé chira*, if the Reddi sows *ariga* he will have to do with one cloth for himself and his wife.

árjintsuṭa, earn, acquire. Skt.

árjitamu, acquired. Skt. *pitrárjitam*, acquired by one's ancestors; *cashṭárjitam*, acquired by toil; *svárjitam*, self-acquired.

árógyamu, health. Skt.

árópintsuṭa, to impute. Skt. *má má-*

magári mída nívu nishcáraṇamgá léni dóshálu árópistú v'unnávu, you are imputing non-existent faults to my father-in-law without cause.

árpintsuṭa, to have something put out, quenched.

árpuṭa, put out, quench, usually not by itself but with the auxiliary *véyuṭa*; put the lamp out is *dípam árpéi*. *manassuló conchem cámágnini tagilinchi daricolpina taruváta adi anṭucuni manḍutú v'unṭé, maḷḷi árpiveyyaḍam sádhyam cádu sumá*, when the flame of passion has once got a start it is impossible to quench it.

árthica, economic. Skt., from *arthamu*, wealth.

árti, grief. Skt. Used only in books.

ártsuṭa, to quench.

ártsuṭa, to comfort; more commonly *óddártsuṭa*. *árchéváré gáni, tírchéváru léru*, there will be comforters but not helpers, i.e. people to help with words but not with deeds.

ártsuṭa, braying. *árché gáḍida vachchi mésé gáḍidanu cheripinaṭlu*, a busybody disturbing an earnestly occupied person; loquacious diversion from business.

áru, 6.

áru-'múdu, everything in confusion. *pani áru-'múd'aipóyinadi*, the work is all in confusion, at sixes and sevens.

-áru, -árina, -áruta, suffix meaning to teem with or simply to be. *veyyáru* means a full thousand and not 1,006; *chennárina*, beautiful; *sompárina*, blooming; *alaráruṭa*, to bloom, and other such compounds are commonly used in books to describe cities and countries.

áruṭa, to dry; intransitive.

árutsuṭa, to roar. Also *arutsuṭa*.

árya, sir. Skt. for Telugu *ayya* used in books; also *áryavarya*, good sir.

Áryuḍu, Aryan.

áṣa, desire, hope, avarice. Skt. *áṣacu antamu lédu*, desire has no limit; *áṣa píḍimpagá*, desire tormenting; *áṣá bhangamu*, breach of hope, i.e. disappointment; *aicamatyamunacu mand édi? áṣa vadaluṭa*, harmony cannot be attained except by giving up desire.

áṣa paḍuṭa, to desire, to hope.

ásacti, wish. Skt. *áyana nácu végiram viváham cheyya valen ani ásacti caligi v'unḍuṭa chéta*, because he wants to marry me quickly.

ásanamu, sitting. Skt. Common in books.

ásara, support, prop. Skt. *carra chétic' ásará y'ichchi léva tísinánu*, I gave him a stick in his hand as a prop and raised him. Also used in the same sense as *ádhárامu*.

áṣauchamu, pollution. Skt., *a* privative and *ṣuchi*, purity. *aṣauchamu* is commoner.

ásavamu, toddy. Skt. A Sanskrit word used only in books for Telugu *callu*, toddy.

áṣayamu, opinion, harbour, source, mind, rest. Different words which have no connexion whatever are understood by this single word; does immense service to public speakers and news-editors. *í vishama sthitiló í tsaṭṭamu pyásu chéyuṭa valana Sarcáruvári aṣayamu gócharam cácunḍá v'unnadi*, we don't know what the Government mean by promulgating such a law, at this critical juncture. *Ándhra Mahájanul'andaru occaṭé áṣayamtó pani chésté véré ráshṭramu avalilagá vastundi*, if the Andhras work with a single-minded purpose they will get a separate province in no time.

ásámi, individual. Hindustani.

áṣápátacuḍu, a covetous man; from *áṣa*, avarice, and *pátacuḍu*, sinner. *duráṣá pátacuḍu*, an extremely covetous or rapacious man.

áṣcharyamu, astonishment. *aruvadi y'énḍlu daṭi samastam telisina mí vanṭi peddalu sahitamu penḍli chésiconi sukha paḍa córutsunḍagá vayasuló n'unna bála vidhavalu cáma ćhádacu lóbaḍuṭa áṣcharyamá?* when experienced sexagenarians like you marry to satisfy their senses, is it strange that young widows half-way through life should yield to lust?

áshádhamu, a month, June–July. Skt.

ásínulai, seated. Skt., from *ásanam*. Common in books.

áṣírvachanamu, áṣírvádamu, blessing. Skt. *mí áṣírvachana prabhávam valla neravéra valenu*, it must be accomplished by the power of your blessing.

áṣírvadintsuṭa, to bless. Skt.

áspadamu, basis. Skt., used chiefly as a suffix. *sandéháspadamaina*, doubtful; *vyájyáspadamaina*, subject of litigation; *hasyáspadamaina*, ridiculous.

áspatri, hospital. English. The common word; there is also the Skt. *vaidyaṣála*.

áṣramamu, hermitage. Skt. Mahátma Gándhi professes to live in an aṣramam but he is very far from being alone; there are about 50 other persons in it.

áṣrayintsuṭa, to take refuge with, to court. Skt. *ippuḍu matácháryula máṭa vinévár'evaru? matácháryulu cúḍa pedda manushyulanu áṣrayisténé cáni, várici bhicshalu zaragavu*, who cares now for religious heads? If they don't court big men they won't get their alms (these religious heads of different sects are given titles of Holiness and *svámula váru* and go about in state with elephants and a large train collecting large sums of money in every village).

áṣrituḍu, dependant. Skt., from *áṣrayintsuṭa*. *áṣrituṇṇi marichi pócanḍi*, do not forget your dependant (a humble way of taking leave, keep favour).

ásthánamu, court. Skt. *ásthána cavi*, court poet.

ásti, property. Skt. *sthirásti* is immovable property, *charásti* movable.

ásu, ace (in cards). English.

áṣvayujamu, the seventh month, say October. Skt. The month of the Dasara festival.

áṭa, play. The same meanings as the English word, including stage-play and gambling.

áṭacatte, actress.

áṭacáḍu, actor.

átaḍu, átagáḍu, he, less common than *ataḍu, atagáḍu*.

áṭancamu, hindrance. Skt.

áṭanca paratsuṭa, hinder.

áṭáḍuṭa, to play in a play.

átithyamu, hospitality. Skt., from **atithi**, guest.

átma, soul. Skt.

átma-, prefix meaning my, own. Skt. *átmacáryamulu*, private affairs.

átmagatamuna, mentally, aside (in plays).

átmahatya, self-murder, suicide. Skt., from *átma-*, own, and *hatya*, murder.

átmaja, own daughter. Skt.

átmajuḍu, own son. Skt.

átmaracshaṇamu, self-defence. Skt., from *átma-*, own, and *racshaṇam*, defence.

átmastuti, self-praise. Skt., from *átma-*, own, and *stuti*, praise.

átmavanchanamu, self-delusion. Skt., from *átma-*, own, and *vanchanam*, deceit.

átmíyamu, one's own. *tanadi* is commoner.

átmíyuḍu, one's own fellow. *cávalasinaváḍu* is commoner.

átsóci, trace; also written *átsúci*. A common word in police inquiries.

áṭṭe, any more (nonsense). *áṭṭe tega ságaca naḍuv*, get out, no more nonsense.

áturamu, eager. Skt. *cám'áturalainaváru*, persons eager with lust.

átura-paḍuṭa, to be eager.

áturata, eagerness. Skt.

áva, mustard, plural *áválu*. *áválu mudda chésinaṭṭu*, like making mustard seeds into a ball (a thing which can't be done).

ávaginza, mustard seed, particle; from *áva*, mustard, and *ginza*, seed. *ávaginz'ant'aina sandéham lédu*, no possible, probable shadow of doubt.

ávahintsuṭa, to possess (of devils). *itaṇṇi y'ippuḍu deyyam sampúrṇangá ávahinchi v'unnadi*, the devil now possesses him completely.

ávala, that side, beyond.

ávalinta, a yawn. *ávalintacu annadammul'unnáru gáni, tummucu tammuḍ'aind lédu*, yawns have elder and younger brothers, sneezes not even a younger brother.

ávalintsuṭa, to yawn.

ávamu, kiln; also *ámu*. *iṭucámu*, brick-kiln; *pencámu*, tile-kiln.

ávaraṇa, enclosure, precincts. Skt.

ávaraṇapu góḍa, compound wall.

ávarzá, ledger. Hindustani. The *chiṭṭá*, day-book, and the *ávarzá* or *cáta*, ledger, are the two accounts usually kept by Telugu money-lenders and merchants.

ávaṣyamu, necessity. Skt.

ávaṣyamugá, necessarily.

ávéṣamu, possession, inspiration. Skt. Used chiefly in compounds. *cópá-véṣam*, anger.

áviḍa, she, that woman. The ordinary word for 'she' is *áme*. *inṭ'áviḍa*, the mistress of the house, corresponding with *inṭi áyana*, the master.

áviri, steam.

áviribalamu, steam power.

-ávrütamu, suffix meaning surrounded by. Skt.

ávu, cow, also spelt *áu*; plural *ávulu*, *áulu*, *álu*. *ávu chénuló méste dúḍa gaṭṭuna méstundá?* if the cow grazes in the field, will the calf graze on the bank? *aravai áru pinḍivanṭalu ávu tsanṭilón'unnáyi*, there are 66 sweetmeats in the cow's udder; *ávula tolu tsúru, gédelu malu tsúru*, a cow's first calf and a buffalo's second; *dúḍa cuḍisténé cáni áu chépadu*, unless the calf sucks, the cow won't give milk.

áyacaṭṭu, the area contained in e.g. a village or under a tank. The original meaning is a yard and *áyamu* also means income and *áyacaṭṭu*, measure of income, but its common use is in land-revenue accounts where it is a collective noun for fields in an area or under a tank.

áyana, he, more respectful than *átaḍu*. *inṭi áyana*, the master of the house; the mistress is *inṭáviḍa*.

áyá, áyamma, lady's-maid or children's nurse. Hindustani.

áyá, this and that, various; *á*, that, reduplicated (*á*, *á*).

áyásamu, fatigue, vexation, trouble. *ná nimittam mic i áyásam antá yenducu?* why take so much trouble for me? It is too good of you.

áyenu, was done.

áyiri, an emphatic form of the verb *aguṭa*, to become. Also *ayiri*.

áyudhamu, weapon. Skt. *yudhamuló mí áyudhamul émiṭi?* what will be your weapons in the fight? *áyudha-púja*, the worship of tools, which is done once a year by every one (in the Dasara festival); e.g. the Collector's peons worship his pens and ink. *áyudhamulu míruṭa*, getting ready, equipping; *vádaprativádamulacu áyudhamulu míruts unnáḍu*, he is getting ready for the controversy.

áyudhópajívi, one who lives by his sword, a warrior. *Hindú-deṣamuló Ángléyulu Áyudhópajívul'aiyunḍina bahu játulanu ṣánticaram'aina nirváhamuna bratucun'aṭlu chésináru*, the English have made a number of warrior-tribes turn to peaceful pursuits of life.

áyurárógyaiṣvaryamulu, long life and health and wealth. Skt., blessing, from *áyuvu*, life, *árógyam*, health, and *aiṣvaryam*, wealth.

áyuvu, áyussu, life. Skt.

áyurvédamu, medicine, medical science. Skt., from *áyuvu*, life, and *védamu*, science. The Ayurvedic system of medicine is one of great antiquity; its drugs and herbs are of some value and it is being brought up to date and encouraged by Government; its anatomy and physiology are primitive and can only be discarded.

ázmáyishi, field-inspection. Hindustani. Properly it means 'trial', but is only used as a revenue term for the inspection of fields by revenue officers to see whether water has been taken, whether one or two crops have been grown, the state of the crops, &c.

B

bacáyi, arrears. Hindustani.

bacca, thin. *mí vanṭi peddal antá catti caṭṭuconi nilavabaḍutu v'unḍagá má vanṭi baccaváḷḷu yémi cheyya galaru?* when you big people all stand with knives drawn, what can we lean ones do?

bacíru, information, report.

baḍa-baḍa, onomatopoeic, for a gurgling noise.

badaláintsuṭa, to transfer; official term from *badalu,* exchange, used especially of transfers of officials.

badali, substitute.

baḍalica, fatigue.

badari, jujube tree. Skt.

baḍáyi, boasting. Hindustani.

badda, piece, especially of wood. *cávaṭibadda,* the yoke of a *cávaḍi.*

baddacamu, weariness, tiresome. *nácu pani anṭé baddacam,* I find work tiresome; also *badhacamu.*

baddalaipóvuṭa, to go to pieces; from *badda,* piece. *cécalu vésivési gontuca baddalaipóyinadi,* my throat has gone to pieces with shouting.

baddalavuṭa, to go to pieces.

baddalu coṭṭuṭa, coṭṭuconuṭa, to knock to pieces. *talacáyalu baddalu coṭṭucunṭáru,* they will knock their heads to pieces; *nénu y'ippuḍu y'í talupu baddalu coṭṭutánu,* I will now knock this door to pieces.

baddhuḍu, bound, tied. Skt. *nénu y'eppuḍú mí selavucu baddhunní, míru selaviyyanḍi,* I am bound to obey you, command me! more often as a suffix. *carmabaddhuḍu,* fate-ridden, predestined; *agnyábaddhuḍu,* obedient.

baḍi, school; *scúlu* is more common, and *páṭhaṣála* is a more distinguished word.

badili, substitute; especially in an office. *áfísuló Góvindaráu Pantulucu badili cávaḍamtóné Padmanábhayya gáru vachchi,* as soon as *Padamanábhayya* came to the office in place of *Govindaráu Pantulu*; also *badali.*

baḍinadi, baḍináḍu, the form of the verb *paḍuṭa,* to become, which is used to turn a verb into the passive aorist; in composition the *p* usually becomes *b. coṭṭabaḍináḍu,* he was beaten; *tsúḍabaḍinadi,* she was seen; *adi baiṭabaḍinadi,* this came to light.

baḍita, thick stick. *baḍita bája,* corporal punishment.

badramu, careful; from Skt. *bhadram.* Coolies will go along with heavy loads saying '*badram, badram*', and a British soldier with them said, 'I will teach them to say, "bother him, bother him".'

badulu, exchange, transfer (official).

badulu, loan. *chétibadulu,* hand loan, is a common expression for a loan given without security; also *chébadulu.*

baduluchepputa, to reply.

badulugá, in exchange, instead of.

badulumáṭa, a reply.

bahirangamu, public; from Skt. *bahich,* outer. *bahirangamu chéyuṭa,* to publish; *bahirangamaina vélamu,* public auction; *bahirangamaina néla,* public land.

bahirangamugá, publicly.

bahirbhúmi, latrine-ground; from Skt., *bahich,* outer, and *bhúmi,* land; any public land is used as latrine-ground by Hindus.

bahishcarintsuṭa, to excommunicate, to put out of caste. Skt. Same as *velivéyuṭa,* which is the Telugu expression.

bahishcáramu, excommunication. *bahishcára patrica,* letter of excommunication, same as *áncsha patrica.*

bahu, much, very. Skt. The Telugu is *tsálá. bahu cálamu,* long time; *bahu bágá,* very nice; *bahu aṣraddha,* legal term for gross negligence; *bahu náyacam, bála náyacam, strí náyacam,* the rule of many, of children, of women (is bad); *á máṭa vinaḍam chéta nácu bahu santóshangá v'unnadi,* I am very glad to hear that; *bahu buddhimantuḍu,* very clever; *bahu dharmátmuḍu,* very charitable.

bahumánamu, present. Skt. *idigó ní bahumánam ani renḍ anál itstsutsunnáḍu,* 'here is your tip', he said, giving him two annas.

bahumútramu, diabetes; from *bahu,* excess of, and *mútram,* urine.

bahusha, probably. *mari yeccaḍacu veḷatávu? bahusha cheraṣálalóci,* where will you be going? probably to jail.

bahutvamu, plurality. Skt. *bahuvachanamu,* the plural (in grammar). Skt., from *bahu,* many, and *vachanam,* speech.

bailicipovuṭa, to go to the latrine-ground, to evacuate the bowels.

bailu, open space, outside; also *bayalu.*

bailudéruṭa, to go out, to start. *iyanacu y'inṭi nunḍi baildérin appuḍu y'inta mattu lédu,* he was not so drunk when he started from his house; also *bayaludéruṭa.*

bailupaḍuṭa, bailuvatstsuṭa, bailicivatstsuṭa, to come out, to transpire. *yenta pani chésiná péru bailici rácunḍá v'unnadi,* however much work he does for me I won't let his name appear.

bairági, religious beggar, ascetic. Skt., *vairági,* adjectival form of *virági,* which is compounded of *vi-,* without, and *rágamu,* desire.

baiṭa, out, outside; inflexion of *bailu. baiṭa veḷlináḍu,* he went out; *inṭló y'igapuli, baiṭa peddapuli,* at home a spider, abroad a tiger.

bala-bala, more and more, bit by bit; onomatopoeic. *baḷabaḷa tellavárinadi,* it got more and more light; also *baḷa-baḷa.*

balahínamu, weak. Skt., from *balam,* strength, and *hínam,* defect.

balahínata, weakness. Skt.

balamu, strength. Skt. *santósham sagam balamu,* cheerfulness is half one's strength.

balaparatsuṭa, to strengthen. *ippuḍu manam venṭané jágrata paḍi punádi balaparisténé cáni antá cheḍi pótundi,* unless we at once carefully strengthen the foundations all will go to ruin.

Balarámuḍu, Krishna's brother.

balavantamu, violence.

balavantamugá, forcibly.

balavantuḍu, a strong or powerful or violent man. *balavantulató viródhamu cá rádu,* don't incur the enmity of the powerful. It is a common complaint that so-and-so are *balavantulu,* by which the complainer means that they are both powerful and unscrupulous.

balátcarintsuṭa, to force. Skt.

balátcáramu, force. Skt.

bali, offering (sacrificial) victim. Skt. *viváhamu ané misha mída pillanu bali peṭṭi,* sacrificing the child on the plea of marriage; *víḷlu nácu baṭṭalú, puvvulú alancarinchi yédó dévatacu bali peḍutáru cabólunu,* I suppose they are decking me out with fine clothes and flowers to sacrifice me to some god.

balipintsuṭa, to fatten, to get fat; from *balamu,* strength. *végiramu accaracu rávalen ani tallidanḍrulu tama cúturni balipistú v'unḍéváru,* the parents were feeding up their daughter in the hope that she would soon mature.

balisina, stout, fat.

baliyuṭa, to get strong, to get fat; derived from *balamu,* strength. The antiquated idea that fat and strength go together appears also in the English *stout,* the Italian *forte,* and the German *stark.*

balla, plank, table.

ballacaṭṭu, flat-bottomed boat used on ferries; from *balla,* plank, and *caṭṭuṭa,* to construct, to tie. It is the same combination of words as Tamil *caṭṭamaran,* but the cattamaran is a surf raft of logs rather than planks tied together.

ballemu, spear; also *íṭe.*

balli, lizard. *pálaló paḍḍa balli láguna,* like a lizard that has fallen into a pot of milk (embarrassment); *vanṭa chésucunṭú v'unḍagá balli mída paḍi vaca máṭunnú, súdraváḷla máṭa vinabaḍi vaca máṭunnú renḍu snánálu chésinánu,* once while I was cooking a lizard fell on me, and once I heard a Sudra talking, so I had to take two baths (Brahmin woman's scrupulousness about pollution).

balṭi, also *palṭi,* somersault. Hindustani, *pallaṭi.*

baluvaina, heavy. Skt., from *balamu,* strength.

baluvu, weight.

baluvugá, heavily, ill. *atanici v'oḷlu baluvugá n'unnadi,* he is seriously ill.

banátu, tweed. Hindustani.

bancamannu, clay.

banḍa, indecent; from *banḍa,* rock, which is commonly used only in the combination, *banḍa-ráyi.*

banḍabútulu, foul language.

banḍacunca, slut, term of abuse both of males and females, like *vedhava*, widow.

banḍamunḍácoḍucu, scoundrel, term of abuse meaning son of a slut. *banḍamunḍácoḍucu y'ivvaca póté nén émi cheyyan'anḍi?* what am I to do if that son of a whore won't give it?

banḍapani, drudgery. *gumástá lécunḍá y'i banḍapani nénu chéstáná?* am I to do this drudgery without a clerk to help me?

banḍaráyi, rock, from *banḍa*, rock or block, and *ráyi*, stone.

Bandaru, Masulipatam; the word originally meant port. *Bandarucu Bezaváḍa sarigá paḍamara,* Bezwada is due west of Masulipatam.

banḍaváḍu, sturdy rogue. (They go about with a big stone with which they say they will beat out their brains if alms are not given.)

bandeladoḍḍi, cattle pound; from Skt. *bandham*, binding, and *doḍḍi*, yard. *má doḍḍeḍu paṣuvulanu cáluva gaṭṭu toccinav'ani vanca peṭṭi y'í nelaló múḍu máṭlu bandeladoḍló peṭṭinchináḍu,* he had my farm cattle impounded three times this month, pretending that they had trespassed on the canal bank.

bandhamu, binding; used in compounds. Skt. *ippuḍu nácu bandhavimóchanam caliginadi,* I am now rid of my bonds.

bandhintsuṭa, to bind. Skt.

bandhutvamu, relationship.

bandhuvargamu, kith and kin.

bandhuvu, relative.

banḍi, conveyance. *banḍi chésuconi,* having engaged a conveyance; *banḍi bóltá paḍḍadi,* the cart upset; *nácu zóḍu gurramula banḍi v'unnadi,* I have a carriage and pair.

bandipóṭu, gang-robbery, dacoity.

banḍladoḍḍi, cart-stand.

bandóbastu, arrangements. Hindustani. *bandóbastu chési banḍi y'ecci baildérinámu,* we made our arrangements, got into a cart, and set out.

bandu, hinge; connected with Skt. *bandham*, binding.

banḍubútulu, obscene language, from *banḍu*, obscene, and *bútu*, foul language. *banḍabútulu* is commoner.

banganabayalu, an open plain.

Bangálamu, Bengal; also *Vangadéṣamu*.

bangáḷá, bungalow. Hindustani.

bangáramu, gold. *talli bangáram 'ainá camsálíváḍu dongilintsaca mánaḍu,* a goldsmith will steal even his mother's gold.

bangáramugá, rare. *nícu máṭáḍuṭé bangáramugá n'unnadi?* are your words so precious?

bangaru, golden. *bangáru chinnaváḷḷu,* golden lads and lasses (a term of endearment).

bangáru-pichchica, yellow-hammer; also *bangáru-pitstsuca*.

bangáru-púta, gilding.

bangáru-tígalu, a fine variety of sugar-cane.

banti, ball; e.g. tennis-balls are *bantulu*. *bantul'áṭa*, playing at ball.

banti, line; corrupted from Skt. *pancti*. *banti-cuḍupu,* a dinner-party, because Hindus sit in a line at meals and the server passes up and down the line. *vaḍḍinchéváḍu tanaváḍu aité caḍa bantini cúrtsunná vacaṭé,* if the server is your friend, it does not matter if you are sitting at the end of the line.

-banṭi, affix meaning 'up to'. *molabanṭi,* waist-high; *mócálibanṭi,* knee-deep.

banṭrótu, menial attached to revenue officers, peon, dalayat; derived from *banṭu*, foot-soldier, and *rautu*, horseman. *evaró banṭrótu vachchi ninnu pilutsunnáḍu,* some peon has come and is calling you.

banṭu, foot-soldier, hero; from Skt. *bhaṭa*. *míru y'iddarú gunḍelu tísina banṭulu,* you are both warriors without a heart-beat in danger (quite heedless of danger); *crama-cramamugá bógamváḷlacu inṭi-banṭulu autáru,* little by little they become domestic soldiers of courtesans.

banṭutanamu, soldierly behaviour, bravery.

banzaru-(bhúmi), waste (land). Hindustani. A revenue term. *anádi banzaru* is immemorial waste.

baratarapu, dismissal. Hindustani,

bartarf. yémí cáraṇam lécuṇḍá paiváḷḷu mátram vúricé baratarapu chéstárá? will the superior authorities dismiss a man without any reason at all?

barátamu, *huṇḍí,* i.e. a draft or cheque. Hindustani.

barice, a small stick. *chinta-barice,* a small tamarind stick with which village schoolmasters used to inflict corporal punishment. Children still fear it.

bariṇe, small box. *ittaḍi cuncuma-bariṇe,* a brass cosmetic box; *poḍi bariṇe,* a snuff-box.

barre, female buffalo, also *géde. ˆénugacu vaca síma, gurránici vaca v'úru, barrecu vaca bánisa,* it takes a district to keep an elephant, a village to keep a horse, the she-buffalo only requires a maid; *tallini tsúchi pillanu, páḍini tsúchi barrenu tísucó-valenu,* take the daughter after seeing the mother, the she-buffalo after seeing the yield of milk.

barucuṭa, to scratch. *Canacángi cinda paḍi yéḍustú léchi Visvacarma mokham antá baricindi,* Canacangi fell down and got up crying and scratched Visvacarma all over his face.

baruvu, weight. *evari paiguḍḍa várici baruvé,* every one feels the weight of his own clothing; *mósévárici telusunu cáviṭi baruvu,* it is the man who carries the yoke that knows its weight.

baruvuga, heavy. *idi yenta baruvugá v'unnadi?* how heavy is this? *tsápa tsuṭṭa yenta láginanu ráca baruvagá canabaḍutsunnadi,* the mat roll seems heavy, it won't move however much it is pulled.

basa, place where one puts up. French, *pied-à-terre*; no exact English equivalent, 'quarters' is nearest. *nénu répu mí basacu vastánu,* I shall go to your place to-morrow; *basalu lév'ani cheppi nalabhaimandini avatalici pampi vésinánu,* saying I had no room I turned forty people away; *áyana basaló léru,* he is not at home.

bastá, bag, sack, bale. Hindustani.

bastí, town. Hindustani.

batimáluconuṭa, to entreat, also *bratimáluconuṭa. nénu yenta bratimálucanná y'itaḍu putstsucócuṇḍá v'unnáḍu,* however much I begged him he would not take it; *chétulu zóḍintsuconi batimáluconnáḍu,* he clasped his hands and prayed.

baṭṭa, cloth. *taḍi baṭṭató gontuca cóyuṭa,* cut the throat by slow torture (with a wet cloth)—applied to any cunning piece of roguery; *baṭṭ'appu, poṭṭ'appu nilavadu,* debts for food and clothing cannot be left unpaid.

baṭṭa, bald. *baṭṭa talalacú mócáḷḷacu muḍi vésin aṭlu,* like tying bald heads and knees in a knot (a difficult operation).

baṭṭabayalu, open plain; reduplicated form of *bayalu.*

battemu, subsistence, allowance, *batta.* Hindustani, probably from Skt. *bhrüti,* maintenance, the usual word for the daily camp allowance of peons and servants.

baṭṭí, lime-kiln. *iṭuc'ámulunnu, penc' ámulunnu, sunnapu baṭṭílunnu,* brick-, tile-, and lime-kilns.

batucuṭa, to live; *bratucuṭa* is more usual.

baṭuvu, a thin ring.

baṭvádá, disbursement. Hindustani. *baṭváḍá* or *baṭṭuváḍa chéyuṭa,* to disburse.

batyamu, same as *bhatyamu, battemu,* allowance. Hindustani. *jítamu, batyamu lécuṇḍá tóḍélu mécalu cástán'ann' aṭṭu,* like the wolf offering to guard the sheep without wages or batta.

bayalu, open space; same as *bailu.*

bayaludéruṭa, to set out; same as *bailudéruṭa,* so also *bayalupaḍuṭa, bayalicipóvuṭa,* &c.

bazáru, market, bazaar. Arabic.

bazáru-dhara, market value.

bazáru-máṭa, bazaar rumour.

bábatu, item. Hindustani, *bápat. municipal naucarla jítálalónu, y'iṭuca ámulalónu, pencámulalónu, y'incá iṭuvanṭi lacsha bábatulaló micú máců y'émí y'ivvaḍam lécuṇḍá,* without giving you and me anything from the municipal servants' wages, brick- and tile-kilns, and a lakh of other items.

bábu, father.

bábú, form of address, friend! sir! used by inferiors to superiors usually; if used by superiors, it is contemptuous; my good friend!

bácí, debt. Hindustani. *bácí unnáḍu,* he is in debt.

bácídáruḍu, debtor.

bádamu, bádamucáya, almond. Hindustani. *bádamu cáyalu baddalucoḍité pappu canipintsunu,* if you split almond nuts, the kernel appears.

báḍe, báḍi, mud; also *burada.*

bádha, pain. Skt. *bála vidhavalu cámabádhacu lóbaḍuṭa áścharyamá?* Is it strange that young widows should yield to the pain of desire?

bádhacamu, obstacle, prejudice. Skt.

bádhapaḍuṭa, to be in pain.

bádhintsuṭa, to pain, to hinder. *áṣa bódhist'unnadi, avamánamu bádhist' unnadi,* desire incites, shame repels.

bádhyamu, responsibility, connected with. Skt.

bádhyata, responsibility, heirship, right, claim. *bádhyata* and *bádhyamu* are extensively used in courts. *bádhyatalu* is sometimes used for vakil's charges, *bádhyata* being any liability as well as any claim. They are in fact vague legal words which indicate any sort of connexion with a case.

báḍiga, hire, rent. *báḍiga bassu,* bus for hire, will be found on the ordinary motor-buses in the Telugu country.

báḍisa, adze; also *baḍita.*

báḍita, adze. *nácu sutti accaralédu, nénu báḍitató pani chésucunṭánu,* I don't want a hammer, I will do the work with an adze.

bágá, well. The Telugus say, *bágá lédu,* it is not well, where we say 'it is not good', e.g. *í baṭṭa bágá lédu,* this is not a good cloth; *chinnadi bágá unnadi,* does not mean the girl is well but the girl is suitable or pretty; *bágáné unnadi,* all right. For 'he is well' the Telugus usually say *vánici bágá unnadi,* it is well with him, but can also say *váḍu bágáné unnáḍu,* he is quite well.

bágu, well-being, health, use, interest, good. Noun form of *bágá. idantá ní bágucósamé cáni mari vacaṭi cádu sumá,* it is all for your good (as the father said when he thrashed the child); *áṭla chésté yémi bágu?* what is the good of that?

bágu-bágu, well done; often used as an interjection of ridicule. *bágu-bágu, y'enta doḍḍa váḍavu,* oh! you are such an upright man!

báguchéyuṭa, to set right. The ordinary word for mending, repairing, &c.

bágupaḍuṭa, to be or get right. The ordinary word for 'to prosper', 'to recover', &c.

báhátangá, openly; from Skt. *bahich,* outside. *intamandi pitstsaváḷḷu báhátangá tirugutú v'unṭé paṭṭucócunḍá pólisuváḷḷu yémi chéstú v'unnáru?* what are the police doing leaving so many lunatics to wander about in public? *báháṭamugá paṭṭapagalé padimandini venṭapeṭṭuconi mari véṣyala y'inṭici veḷḷutú v'unnáru,* they will openly go in company in full daylight to the house of the courtesans.

báhuvu, arm. Skt. Used chiefly in compounds. The Telugu is *cheyyi.*

báhyamu, outer, external. Skt. *manamu báhyártham vichárintsa rádu, váru cheppé máṭalacu anniṭici gúḍhártham unṭundi,* we must not inquire about the exoteric meaning, there is an esoteric meaning in all they say.

báhyamu, any place which lies outside a house, or the outskirts of a village or town.

báhyamunacu póvuṭa, to stir out of a house for the purpose of evacuating the bowels. Public grounds, fields, and waste lands are used as latrine-grounds in India.

bájá, music, especially drum beating. Hindustani. *bájá bhajantrílu,* band; *bájá váḷḷacu ḍappula váḷḷacu ayyé khartsu,* the expenses of the musicians and drummers.

bála, young. Skt. *bahu náyacamu, bálanáyacamu, stríla náyacamu,* bad is rule by too many, by the too young, by women.

bálica, girl. *bógam méḷam v'unna tsoṭici támu veḷḷacunḍá v'unḍaḍánicinní mana bálicalu vidyató páṭu sangítamu cúḍá cheppintsaḍánicinní rijalyúshanu cheyyavalen'ani nénu propózu chéstú v'unnánu,* I propose a resolution that we won't go to nautch parties and that we teach our girls singing as part of their education.

bálintarálu, woman in childbed.

báluḍu, boy. Skt.
bályamu, childhood, youth. Skt.
bámu, grief. One of the numerous words for grief, common only in books.
bána, pot.
báṇamu, arrow, rocket. Skt., in common use of fireworks.
báṇásanchi, báṇásantsu, fireworks. From *báṇam*, rocket, and *sanchi*, bag. Commonest in the plural, *báṇásantsulu*.
bándhavyamu, relationship, from *bandhuvu*, relative; also *bandhutvamu*.
bánisa, female slave; also *dási*. *énugacu vaca síma, gurránici vaca v'úru, barrecu vaca bánisa,* for the support of an elephant a district, of a horse a village, of a she-buffalo a maid.
bánisatvamu, slavery; also *dásyamu*.
bánisíḍu, male slave; also *bánisaváḍu*, or *dásuḍu*.
bápanacca, Brahmin woman; **bápana,** (adj.); **bápanayya, bápanáḍu,** Brahmin. These words are not used by Brahmins, but by other castes, somewhat contemptuously, in speaking of Brahmins.
bápanicamu, Brahminhood; contemptuous.
bápanidi, Brahmin woman.
bápat, item. Hindustani. A common revenue term; thus *bápat wet* or other item wet is wet land other than registered wet land.
bápata, Brahmin woman. Used in books.
bára, fathom, 6 feet (the length of the two arms extended). *bára tsátsu,* to extend the arms so as to embrace; *padi báralu naḍachi*, stepping out 20 yards.
báru, a line, row. *chímala báru,* a line of ants; *báru tíri,* standing in a line.
báru chéyuṭa, peṭṭuṭa, to load (a gun); English. To put the bar (English word) as was done in the old muzzle-loaders.
básachéyuṭa, to promise, to swear. *bása* is a corrupt form of Skt. *bhásha*, language.
báshpamu, tear. Skt., common in books only; the Telugu is *canníru*, eye water.
báṭa, road. *pedda báṭaló v'unna satram tísi véyinchi pátra sámánu diváṇamlóci teppinchináru,* they have abolished the choultry on the main road and taken the cooking vessels to the Diwan's office.
báṭasári, wayfarer. *nénu vachchina báṭasárlacu chésé v'upacháramló yémi lópam cheyyanu,* there will be nothing to find fault with in my attendance on travellers.
bátu, duck. Hindustani. *pedda bátu* is goose and *gúḍa bátu*, pelican.
báva, male relation older than oneself on the female side; e.g. sister's husband, cousin on the mother's or father's sister's side.
bávamaradi, brother-in-law.
bávi, well. In the Circars they say *nuyyi*, elsewhere usually *bávi*.
bávuconuṭa, to swallow, to gobble. Used also metaphorically. *á mahábhágyam antayu nén eppuḍu bávucondunú ani nóṭiló vrélu peṭṭuconi guṭacalu mringutsú dinam oca calpangá gaḍuputsu nénu tondara paḍina coladini pilladi y'iḍéruṭa venucacé póvutsu vachchenu,* I daily gloated on the thought of the sweet morsel in store for me, and in anticipation of hymeneal joys I would lay my fingers on my lips and gulp and quaff; the swifter the current of my passion the more time seemed to drag, lingering in centuries and cycles, till she budded into womanhood.
bedaracoṭṭuṭa, to frighten.
bedarimpu, threat. *á bedarimpul' anní caṭṭi peṭṭanḍi,* a truce to your threats.
bedarintsuṭa, to frighten.
bedari póvuṭa, to take fright. *chícaṭló veḷḷi bedari póyináḍu,* he went into the dark and was frightened.
bedaru-peṭṭuṭa, to intimidate, to threaten. Used in the Ceded Districts, not in the Circars.
bedaruṭa, to take alarm. *gurramu bedarinadi,* the horse has taken fright.
beḍḍa, small stone or clod. *rátri curra mundá coḍuculu y'evaḷḷó má y'inṭi mída beḍḍalu vésináru,* in the night some wretched boys threw pebbles at my house (a favourite method in India of baiting unpopular people).
bellamu, jaggery, molasses. The usual

form in which sugar is taken in India, also used as an offering. *angaṭi bellamu guḷḷó lingánici naivédyam*, offering the shopkeeper's jaggery to the god; *angiṭa bellam átmaló visham*, jaggery in the mouth, poison in the heart.

beḷucu, glitter. *taḷucu-beḷuculu*, foppish airs.

beṇacu, sprain; also *beṇucu*.

beṇacuta, to be sprained; also *beṇucuṭa*.

benḍacáya, ladies' fingers, a vegetable. *vancáya, bíracáya, benḍacáya*, brinjal, cucumber, and ladies' fingers are the common Indian vegetables eaten with rice.

benga, anxiety. *nácu bengagá v'unnadi*, I am in anxiety.

benga peṭṭuconuṭa, to be anxious, to be dejected. *íme mí cósam benga peṭṭuconi tinnagá annam tina lédu*, she could not eat her meals properly out of anxiety for you; *tánu chira cálamu cashṭa paḍi chésina grandhamulu póyinav'anna duhkhamu chéta bengapeṭṭuconnáḍu*, he was dejected at the loss of manuscripts over the composition of which he had spent much labour.

beraḍu, bark.

bestaváḍu, fisherman, plural *bestaváḷḷu, bestalu*, a caste name.

bettamu, cane; *pépa-bettamu*, rattan.

beṭṭina, for *peṭṭina*, put, placed, in composition. *cúḍa beṭṭina dhanamu*, hoarded wealth.

bezzamu, hole; *randhram* is also 'hole' but *bezzamu* is smaller than *randhram*. *ácali ácáşam anta, gontuca súdi bezzam anta*, his appetite is as big as the sky, his gullet the size of a needle's eye; he bites off more than he can chew.

bébácí, balance nil; from Hindustani *bé-* privative and *bácí*, debt. Chiefly a revenue term meaning that the whole tax demand of a village has been collected and that the balance is consequently nil.

béḍa, 2-anna bit, one-eighth rupee. The four-anna bit is called *pávalá*, quarter (from *pávu*).

bédi, purging, for Skt. *bhédi*.

bédimandu, purgative; also *bhédimandu*, from *bhédi*, purge, and *mandu*, medicine.

bégi, quickly. Hindustani, probably with some confusion with the Skt. derivative *végirangá*, which is also used. *bégi* and *tvaragá* are the common words for 'quickly'.

bémarammatu, out of repair. Hindustani, from *bé-* privative and *marammat*, repair.

bépana, vulgar for *bápana*, Brahmin, which itself is colloquial for *bráhmaṇuḍu*.

béramáḍuṭa, to clinch a bargain. *i rátri béram áḍuconi sommu chétiló paḍavéyintsucondi*, clinch the bargain and see that we get the money to-night.

béramu, bargain, contract. Perhaps from Skt. *viháram*. Purchasing on credit is *aruvu béramu*, loan bargain.

béramu chéyuṭa, to make a contract.

bérízu, total of the account. Hindustani. Chiefly used as a revenue term meaning the whole revenue of a village, but may mean the total of any account. *indáca véré cágitamu mída bérízu vési tsústé aravaiyéḍu véla rúpáyala paḍi anḍala enimidi paisalu aindi*, I wrote the total down on a slip of paper, it is Rs. 67,000-10-8.

béshu, well done! good! Also *bhéshu*. Hindustani.

bétáḷamu, ghost. A *bétáḷamu* is supposed to inhabit a corpse, not necessarily its own body, when alive, and to make it move and dance.

bétáḷuḍu, a demon (servant of Yama). Also the vampire of the Indian folklore—a demon supposed to be ruled by canons of righteousness and to terrorize the wicked.

bévárasu, without an heir or successor. Hindustani from *bé-* privative and *várasu*, heir. *peṭishanarlú míru y'écamai sarcáru sthalálú bévársu sthalálú dobbi vésinavi yenni v'unnavi?* how many government and ownerless sites have you and the petitioners stolen, conspiring together?

bézarúru, not urgent, unnecessary, irrelevant. Hindustani from *bé-* privative and *zarúr*, urgent. *iṭuvanṭi bézarúru saváḷḷu veyyaca y'itarula máṭa vadili peṭṭi mí máṭa míru tsútsucondi*, stop putting irrelevant questions and talking about other people, and consider your own case.

bézáru, fatigue, weariness, annoyance. Hindustani. *bézár'aguṭa, bézáru paḍuṭa,* to become fatigued, or disgusted; *bézáru chéyuṭa,* to tease or torment.

bhacshaṇamu, eating. Skt.

bhacshintsuṭa, to eat. Skt.; the Telugu is *tinuṭa. canṭhachpúrtigá bhacshintsuṭa,* to eat one's throatful (bellyful).

bhacti, devotion. Skt. The commonest of religious terms; used also for devotion to persons or institutions. *prabhu-bhacti,* loyalty. The opposite is *dróhamu,* treachery. *déṣabhacti* is patriotism while *déṣadróhamu* or *rája-dróhamu* is generally understood as sedition. *uḍatacu uḍata-bhacti,* the squirrel has its own form of devotion (the squirrels helped Rama to build the Rameswaram causeway); *ná y'eduṭa bhacti tsúpi pati-púja cheyutsun-naṭṭu paic'ainá naṭistú rávé,* please make some show of dutifulness and make believe at least that you are a devoted wife.

bhactuḍu, devotee. *bhayabhactulu,* respect and reverence.

bhadramugá, carefully. Skt., *bhadram,* prosperity.

bhadrata, safety. Skt., *sarira bhadrata,* personal safety. *paṭṭa bhadruḍu,* a crowned head, the lord of the land.

bhagabhaga, blazing, of flames and of anger, onomatopoeic.

bhagavad, pertaining to God. Skt., *bhagavat,* adorable, worshipful.

Bhagavadgíta, the Divine Song. Skt. The famous interlude in the *Mahábhárata* containing a discourse on duty.

Bhagavantuḍu, God. *lanjala chéta bútupáṭalu páḍisténé cáni Bhagavad vishayamaina gánamu chéyisté bágá v'unḍadá?* would it not be well to have music about God, instead of having obscene songs sung by courtesans?

bhagavati, respectable woman.

Bhagavánuḍu, Almighty God.

bhagguna, ablaze, onomatopoeic. *bógam vrütti manchidi cád'anéváḷḷanu tsústé ná vaḷḷu bhagguna manḍuconi pótundi,* I am all ablaze with rage when I see people who say the nautch girls' profession is not a good one.

bhagíratha prayatnamulu, herculean labours, from *Bhagíratha,* an ancient king said to have brought the Ganges from the celestial regions to India.

bhajana, musical worship, party to sing hymns. Skt. *Ráma-bhajana,* singing hymns to Ráma.

bhajantrílu, musicians conducting *bhajana.*

bhajintsuṭa, to adore. Skt.

bhaḷí, bhaḷirá, well done, bravo!

bhallúcamu, bear. Skt. word; the Telugu word is *elugubanṭi.*

bhallúcapu paṭṭu, bear-hug.

bhangacaramaina, disappointing, from Skt. *bhanga,* breaking.

bhangamu, breaking. Skt. *prajá ṣántici bhangamu,* breach of public peace; *nidrábhangamu,* broken sleep or sleeplessness; *manam bógam vrüttici bhangam caluga chéyyaḍánici prayatnam chéstú v'unnámu,* we are trying to break the courtesans' trade. *mána-bhangamu,* disgrace, dishonour; if applied to a woman it means outrage of chastity.

bhangaparatsuṭa, to disappoint.

bhangapáṭu, disappointment, disgrace.

bhangapeṭṭuṭa, to disgrace.

bhangi, manner, mode, used in books. *é-bbhangi,* how?

bhanguramu, perishable, fleeting. *bratucu cshaṇa-bhanguramu,* life is transitory.

bharaṇamu, maintenance. Skt.

Bharata-khanḍamu, India. Literally the land of *Bharata.* Skt. The newspapers have adopted this term from the ancient Indian Epics. *Bharata-khanḍa* is properly the kingdom of *Bharata,* who only ruled over a part of Northern India. There is no Telugu word for India or Indians, *Bharata-khanḍamu* and *Bháratíyulu* both being Skt. The term *Hindú* is Persian through Skt. *Sindhu,* the Indus.

bharintsuṭa, to bear, to maintain. Skt. root *brü.*

-bharitamu, suffix meaning 'filled with'. Skt. *-púritamu* has the same meaning; both are used in Skt. compound adjectives. *ánanda bharituḍu*, full of joy.

bharmamu, gold. Skt.; used in Skt. compounds in books.

Bharmádéṣamu, Burma. Skt., the land of gold; used in books. Telugus have now adopted *Burma* in speaking.

bharta, husband; from Skt. root *brü*, bear. Common, but the Telugu *magaḍu* and *penimiṭi* are commoner; *bhárya*, wife, is from the same root *brü*, maintain; the *bharta* maintains the *bhárya*.

bhartí-chéyuṭa, to fill up a deficiency.

bhartrü-, husband in compounds; from *bharta*, husband.

bhasmamu, ashes. Skt. The common Telugu word is *búḍida*.

bhasmícarintsuṭa, to reduce to ashes.

bhaṭuḍu, servant. Skt. The common Telugu words are *panivádu* and *naucaru*, *bhaṭuḍu* is a book-word; *racshaca bhaṭulu* are policemen. *bhaṭulanu cávali y'istánu*, I will give you servants as guards.

bhautica, elementary, natural; adjectival form of Skt., *bhútamu*, element. *pancha bhauticamu*, composed of the five elements.

bhavad-, prefix meaning your. Skt., used in composition with Skt. words. Letters close with *bhavad vidhéyuḍu*, yours obediently.

bhavadíyamu, yours.

bhavamu, existence, life. Skt., a theological term. *bhavamócshaṇamu*, is release from this fleshly coil; *bhavaduhkhamulu*, the sorrows of existence.

bhavanamu, mansion. Skt. *sentral jailu tappacunḍá rája bhavanamé*, the Central Jail is undoubtedly a nobleman's mansion (a colossal structure).

bhavanti, pavilion, house with a court in the middle. *lópali bhavantilóné sarducuni, y'idi vara ḍácá nénu paḍucuné tóṭaló y'í mundara bhavanti cáḷi chési addecu y'ivvaḍánici siddham chésinánu*, making shift with the inner pavilion I vacated the outer pavilion in the garden, in which I used to sleep, and made it ready to be let.

-bhavinchi, suffix meaning getting or becoming. Skt. *múrtibhavinchi*, getting shape, assuming a visible form; *uḍbhavinchi*, being born, produced.

bhavish-, prefix meaning future. Skt. *bhavishyatcálamu*, the future tense in grammar.

bhayabhactulu, respect and reverence; from *bhayam*, fear, and *bhacti*, devotion. *y'í v'úḷḷó scúlu curraváḷḷu mahá pogar' ecci v'unnáru; bhayamú bhactí lécunḍá ná mundara penci zavábulú savádḷú véstáru*, the schoolboys in this village are very insolent, they bandy saucy questions and answers before me without fear or respect.

bhayamu, fear. Skt. *nácu tupáci tsústé bhayamu véstundi*, I am frightened at sight of a gun; *nácu chinn'appuḍu samétú chicaṭ' anṭé bhayamu*, I have been afraid of the dark from my childhood.

bhayancaramaina, fearful.

bhayancarangá, frightfully. *míru bhayancarangá cana paḍa valenu*, you must look frightful.

bhayapaḍuṭa, to be afraid. *bhayapaḍa cúḍadu, dhairyangá niluva valenu*, don't be afraid, stand your ground courageously.

bhayaparatsuṭa, to intimidate.

bhayapeṭṭuṭa, to frighten.

bhayasthuḍu, a timorous or timid man; *bhayasthurálu*, a timid woman.

bhádrapadamu, the 6th month, August–September. Skt.

bhágahláramu, division in arithmetic. Skt., from *bhágam*, part, and *háram*, taking.

bhágamu, part. Skt.

bhágasthuḍu, sharer, partner.

Bhágavatamu, the Krishna epic; from *Bhagaván*, the Lord.

bhágavatuḍu, an adept in religious discourses.

bhágárintsuṭa, to divide. Skt.

bhágyamu, luck, happiness. Skt. *penḍli ainadi modaluconi pilladi y'edigi yeppuḍu cápuramunacu vatstsuná á mahá bhágyamu eppuḍá y'ani*, impatient for the great pleasure of my young wife coming to live with me after she had grown up.

bhágya rékha, the line of luck on the hand.

bhágyaşáli, a fortunate man; from *bhágyamu*, luck.

bhágyavantuḍu, happy man, but more often rich man; in its common use the ordinary word for a well-to-do man; feminine *bhágyavati*.

bhánchót, Muhammadan term of abuse, sodomite. Hindustani. *oré bhánchót! má zólici nícu yenducu v'öi?* why are you interfering with me, you sodomite? The Hindu expressions are *lanje coḍucu*, son of a whore, and *vedhava*, widow, which is applied also to things and to males.

Bhánuḍu, Phoebus. Skt. A name of the Sun God; used in descriptions of sunrise and sunset in novels.

bháramu, burden. Skt. *andu valla bhúbháramu conta taggutundi*, the earth's burden will be slightly reduced thereby.

Bhárata Déşamu, India; a newspaper word. *Bhárata Máta*, Mother India; also *Bharata-khanḍamu*.

Bháratamu, the poem *Mahábhárata*. Skt.

Bháratíyulu, Indians; newspaper word. *Bháratíya Criceṭṭu Jaṭṭu*, the Indian Test Team.

bhárya, wife. Skt. root *brü*, maintain. *penḍlámu, inṭidi* (the thing in the house) are other words for wife.

bhásha, language. Skt.; *déşabhásha* is the vernacular. *déşa-bháshal'andu Telugu lessa*, Telugu is the finest of the Indian vernaculars. This is an oft-quoted line from a Telugu work of Krishna Déva Ráya, one of the greatest of South Indian monarchs, who ruled at Hampi-Vijayanagar, now in ruins, in the Bellary District.

bháshaṇamu, speech. Skt. *vacra bháshaṇamu*, irrelevant speech.

bháshántaramu, translation. Skt., from *bhásha*, speech, and *antaramu*, other.

bháshintsuṭa, to converse. Skt.

bháshíyamu, idiom. Skt.

bháshyamu, commentary, dictionary. Skt.

bhávamu, mind. Skt. *bhédabhávamu*, difference of opinion. Some poetic riddles in Telugu close with *díni bhávam'émi Tirumal'éşa*, what meaning does it convey, O Lord of Tirumala! which is a challenge to the reader to understand the meaning of a piece of poetry or solve a riddle.

bhávintsuṭa, to think. Skt. *nénu buddhimantuṇṇi, nann'andarú nútana Brühaspati y'ani bhávistáru*, I am a wise man, every one considers me a modern *Brühaspati*.

bhávyamu, fit. Skt. *nícu álágé tóchina taruváta ikha mító maṭláḍaḍam bhávyam cádu*, if those are your ideas, it is not proper to talk to you any more; *hásyam péru peṭṭi nannu anta máṭa anaḍam mícu bhávyam éná?* is it proper to speak so, calling it a joke?

bhédamu, difference. Skt.

bhédi, purge. Skt.

bhédimandu, purgative.

bhédintsuṭa, to split. Skt. *vári manasu bhédinchinadi*, there has been a split between them.

bhéri, kettledrum. Skt. *ghóra sarpam vachchi paṭṭucunnad'ani bhérilu váyinchi ganṭalu coṭṭi dánní bedaracoṭṭaḍánic'ai pedda dhvani chéstáru*, they think a terrible serpent has come to catch (the sun or moon at an eclipse) and beat drums and gongs and make a big noise to frighten it away (Hindu Science); *mí cáryam sádhinchi chivaracu jayabhéri véstáru*, you will succeed and beat the drum of victory.

bhicsha, bhicshamu, alms. Skt. *turaca vídhiló sanyáşi bhicsha*, a Hindu religious mendicant begging in a Muhammadan street; *yágabhicsha cósam vacca sári déşa sanchárам chési vattund?* shall I go out for once and wander about for alms to perform a sacrifice? *patibhicsha*, prayer for restoration of husband.

bhinnamu, broken, separate, different. Skt. roots *bhit* and *bhéd*. *bhinna grühamulu*, separate houses; *bhinna cálamulu*, different times; *bhinnabhinna bháshalu*, different languages.

bhinnamugá, separately.

bhícarangá, terrible. Skt. root *bhí*, same as *bhayancarangá*.

Bhíshma, *Bhíshma* in the *Mahábhárata*. Skt. *bhíshmintsuṭa* is to protest like *Bhíshma*, to assert forcibly, as *Bhíshma* did in the story of the *Mahábhárata*.

bhíti, fear. Skt. *pápa bhíti viḍichi*, having lost all fear of sin.

bhógamu, enjoyment, fortune; also *bógamu*. Skt. The Telugus enumerate eight kinds of enjoyment: *grühamu* or *annamu*, *ṣayya*, *vastramu*, *ábharaṇamu*, *strí*, *pushpamu*, *gandhamu*, *támbúlamu*, house or food, bed, clothes, jewellery, woman, flower, scent, betel. *écabhógamu*, undivided possession; *sambhógamu*, coitus; *pálibhógamu*, separate possession; *bhóga grühamu*, bedroom; *ṣilá bhógamu*, *sthala bhógamu*, *nara bhógamu cána rávu*, you cannot say what will happen to a stone, a place, or a man.

bhógamudi, courtesan, nautch girl. Skt., also *bógamudi*.

bhógastrí, courtesan, nautch girl; also *bógastrí*, plural *bhógamvánḍlu*, *bhógamváḷḷu*; also *bhógamudi*, *véṣya*. *bhógamvrütti*, profession of a courtesan.

bhógyamu, usufruct, a legal term. *bhógyapatramu* is a deed of mortgage with possession.

bhójanamu, food, a meal. Skt. *bhójanamu chéyuṭa*, to take a meal, is almost always contracted to *bhónchéyuṭa*.

bhónchéyuṭa, to take a meal, contracted from *bhójanamu chéyuṭa*; very common.

bhrama, confusion, hallucination.

bhramaconuṭa or **bhramagonuṭa,** to be confused. *mému grühamunacu póyé dári teliyaca bhramagoni nilichi y'unnámu*, not knowing the way to the house we are standing perplexed.

bhramapaḍuṭa, to be mistaken. *nívu bhramapaḍutú v'unnávu*, you are labouring under a mistake.

bhramapartsuṭa, to mislead.

bhramapeṭṭuṭa, to confuse. *nannu v'úricé praṣnalu vési bhrama peṭṭacanḍi*, do not confuse me by idly asking questions.

bhramaramu, big black bee. Skt. *bhramara nádamu*, the hum of the bee. The bee is a favourite topic in descriptive passages. See also *bhrüngamu*.

bhramintsuṭa, to be confused.

bhrashṭamu, fallen, lost, depraved. Skt. *mí tammuḍu bhrashṭ'ai póvutsunnáḍu*, your brother is going to the dogs.

bhrashṭuḍu, fallen person. Skt. *cula bhrashṭuḍu*, an outcast. *bhrashṭasya cává gati?* what refuge is there for an outcast? (The answer is an emphatic 'none'. He will sink lower and lower.) This is a well-known Skt. precept which has gained an enormous currency in spoken Telugu. *déṣa-bhrashṭuḍu*, one who is driven from his country; *mata-bhrashṭuḍu*, one who is excommunicated; *nítibhrashṭuḍu*, a depraved man.

bhrashṭulai, fallen from caste.

bhrátrü, prefix meaning belonging to a brother; used in Skt. compounds, *bhrátrü-snéhamu*, brotherly love.

bhrüngamu, big black bee. Skt., used in books only. See also *bhramaramu*.

Bhrüngi, Ṣiva's griffin. Skt. This attendant of Ṣiva's has three legs or a head and two legs only; he will be found carved on Ṣiva's temples.

bhrütyuḍu, servant. Skt. Used in books for *naucaru*, *panivádu*. *paici mahá bhrütyuḍu lágu naṭistáḍu*, he affects outward servility.

bhuctamu, enjoyment, possession. Skt.

bhucti, food. *bhucti-mucti*, enjoyment of this world and salvation in the next; *ná-bhuctamló n'unḍé chénu*, the field in my possession; *bidaváḍu bhuctici zaragaca*, poor and starving (not able to keep going for want of food).

bhujintsuṭa, to eat, enjoy.

bhúcampamu, earthquake. Skt. root *bhú*, earth.

Bhúdévi, Mother Earth. Skt.

Bhúdévuḍu, God on earth, i.e. a Brahmin. Skt. Also *bhúsuruḍu*, *bhúsuróttamuḍu*, illustrates the arrogance of the Indian Brahmin.

bhúlócamu, earth, world. Skt.

bhúmi, earth, land. Skt. The usual word for the earth and also for landed possessions. *nícu yenta bhúmi?* how much land have you? *núr'ecaramula bhúmi*, 100 acres of land.

bhúmikhámandu, landowner.

bhúmisistu, land-tax.

bhúsandu, isthmus.

bhúsáramu, fertility.
bhúshaṇamu, ornament. Skt.
bhúshitamu, adorned. Skt.
bhúsuruḍu, brahmin. Skt.
bhúsvámi, landowner.
bhútacálamu, the past tense in verbs.
bhútaci, an ogress.
bhúta-daya, kindness to animals.
bhúta-dhátri, the nurse of animal life, the earth.
bhútamu, element, being. Skt. *pancha bhútamulu* are the five elements; *bhútadaya* is elementary or natural kindness.
bhútamu, ghost. Skt. *atanu mícu cávalasin' anni bhúta préta pisách' ádula cathalu cheputáḍu,* he will tell you any number of ghost and spirit and demon stories. *bhútavaidyamu* is the art of exorcism (Hindu medicine); *bhúta vaidyuḍu,* one who drives away spirits.
bhútávéṣamu, possession by spirits.
-bhútuḍu, suffix meaning who has become. Skt. *saháyabhútuḍu,* an ally; *hétubhútuḍu,* causer; *ádhárabhútam' ainavi ádhára mulu,* evidence in support of the fact (legal). *bhútuḍu* usually adds nothing to the meaning.
bicári, beggar; from Skt. *bhicsham. másina baṭṭalu caṭṭuconi bicári vésham vési,* putting on dirty clothes and disguising oneself as a beggar.
bicháná, bedding. Hindustani.
biḍáyintsuṭa, to fold up. Hindustani, e.g. a letter. *talupulu biḍáyinchi,* shutting the doors.
biḍḍa, child. *goppa y'inṭi biḍḍa,* child of a great house.
biḍḍatanamu, childhood. *áḍadáni chéti arthamú mogaváni chéti biḍḍá bratacadu,* do not trust money to a woman, or a child to a man; *caḍupuló biḍḍa caḍupulóné v'unḍagá coḍucu péru Sómalingam annaṭṭu,* naming the child before it is born (counting one's chickens before they are hatched).
biḍiyamu, shyness, shame. *váḷḷacu siggú biḍiyamú, paruvú pratishṭhá yémí lédu,* they have no sense of shame or of honour.
biga, tight. *úpiri biga paṭṭi,* holding one's breath.
biga-paṭṭuconuṭa, to hold tight. *práṇamulu bigapaṭṭuconi máṭáḍaca,* holding his breath and not saying anything.
biggaragá, loudly, the usual word for loud. *biggaragá máṭáḍacu,* do not talk loud.
bigintsuṭa, to tighten.
bigiya, tightly; same as *biga.*
bigutu, tightness. *ungaramu bigutu chéta canḍalónici tósuconi póyinadi,* the ring has eaten into the flesh.
biguvu, tight. *á ungaramu ná vélici paṭṭadu, vaddu, biguvu,* that ring won't fit my finger; I do not want it, it is tight.
biḷḷa, disk, dish, in fact anything round and flat. *banṭrótu biḷḷa,* the badge peons wear on their scarves; *venḍi biḷḷa,* a silver dish. *molabiḷḷa,* the female infant's modesty disk that is hung in front of its private parts, from *mola,* the waist.
binámi, in the name of another. Hindustani. It is common to bid or to purchase or put property in the name of another to obtain some legal or fiscal advantage, and is not regarded by Hindus as immoral.
binde, large metal vessel with narrow neck, water-pot. *Góddávarici veḷḷi snánam chési binde y'ettucuni vastú baṭṭalu v'utuccuné váḷḷa niḷḷu paḍḍaṭṭu tóchi maḷḷí veḷḷi munigindnu,* I was coming from the Godavari after my bath carrying my pot when I thought I had been sprinkled by the water of the people washing clothes, so I went back and had another dip (Hindu notions of ceremonial impurity).
binduvu, a drop. The letter *n* not followed by a vowel, which is written as a small circle (also known as *púrṇánusvdramu,* the complete nasal); there is also *boṭṭu,* which often means the round mark on the forehead.
birabira, quickly, onomatopoeic.
biraḍá, cork.
birudu, title. *nívu tsúpina pánḍityánici tagina birudu péru ṣáṣvitangá labhinchinadi,* you have acquired a suitable title for ever for the scholarship you have shown.
birusu, rough.
bitstsagáḍu, beggar; from Skt. *bhicsham. ataḍu caṭica daridruḍu, púṭa-*

cúṭici gati lédu, vaṭṭi bitstsagáḍugá v'unnáḍu, he is a miserable pauper and beggar.

bitstsamu, alms. *bitstsamettuconuṭa,* to beg.

biyyamu, rice; this is husked rice, Italian, *riso,* rice in the husk. Italian *risone* is *vaḍlu*; England not being a rice-growing country the English language does not make the distinction.

bídapaḍuṭa, to be poor. Skt. *bhiti. náḍu v'unṭé Navábusáyebu, annamu v'unṭé Amírusáyebu, bídapaḍité Facirusáyebu,* if a Muhammadan has land he is a Nawab, if he has enough to eat, an Amir, if he is poor he is Mr. Fakir.

bídaricamu, poverty.

bídatanamu, poverty.

bídaváḍu, poor man. *nénu bídaváṇṇi, pillalu galaváṇṇi,* I am poor and have children, is the favourite preface to a petition.

bíḍu, fallow land. It is usually translated meadow, but this is wrong; there are no meadows in South India; cattle are left to pick up what they can from jungle and fallows.

bígamu, padlock; the key is *chevi* (ear).

bíjamu, seed. Skt. *ginza* is the Telugu word; another Skt. word, *vittu, vittanam,* is also in common use. *bíjam* also means a testicle.

bímá, insurance. Hindustani; also *bhímá.*

bíracáya, a sharp-angled cucumber called the ribbed gourd. *vancáya,* brinjal, *bíracáya,* cucumber, and *benḍacáya,* ladies' fingers, are the vegetables commonly eaten with rice.

bíruva, chest of drawers. From French *bureau* through the English, but the meaning has changed; in the French it means an office desk, whence bureaucratic and bureaucracy, desk rule.

bíṭa, a crack.

bobba, pustule, blister. *véḍi niḷḷu paḍi áme vréḷḷu bobbal'eccinavi,* hot water fell on her fingers and raised pustules on them.

bocca, hole (a big one), loss in business. *gaṭṭucu bocca peṭṭi,* breaching the bund; *nénu é boccaló dúrutánu?* where shall I hide my head?

boccasamu, money-bag.

boccesa, bundle.

boḍḍu, navel, whirlpool.

boḍḍucongu, central knot of man's cloth. Money is often kept in the *boḍḍucongu. ná boḍḍucongu rúpáyalu,* the rupees tied up in my cloth. The navel-stone (*boḍḍu rái* or *manṭapamu*) of a village is a platform placed at the centre.

bogada, golden ear-knob, any knob. *gubba* also means a knob or bub; these words for protuberance are, like the English 'bub', onomatopoeic. The fitting of sound to sense is one of the characteristics of pure Telugu.

boggu, charcoal. *síma-boggu,* coal.

boma, eyebrow. Skt. *brahma. bomalu paic'etti chintintsu muddu mogamu,* the sweet face musing with raised eyebrows.

bomma, image, puppet, doll, picture.

bommaḍu, brahmin, for *bráhmaṇuḍu.*

bommaláṭa, puppet-show; from *bomma,* puppet, and *áṭa,* play.

bommaramu, a top.

bommarillu, doll's house; from *bomma,* doll, and *illu,* house.

boncari, liar.

boncu, lie.

boncuṭa, to lie. *áḍadi boncité góḍa peṭṭinaṭṭu, mogaváḍu boncité taḍica caṭṭinaṭṭu,* a woman's lies are an impenetrable wall, a man's a mat partition that you can see through; *práṇa vitta mána bhangam' andu bonca vatstsu,* you may lie in defence of your life, property, and honour (Hindu ethics).

bonḍacoyya, stocks. The punishment of the stocks is one that village magistrates were once expressly authorized to inflict.

bonḍaló véyuṭa, to confine to the stocks.

bondi, body; the Skt. *ṣaríram* and another Telugu word *oḍalu* (usually *voḷḷu*) are commoner than *bondi.*

bongaramu, top. *bongaramu trippa galavá?* can you spin a top?

bongu, giant bamboo stick. *bongu buzána vaichi coni póvadam'etstsaṭic' aina,* let us go a-begging with a yoke on our shoulders.

bonta, quilt.

bont'araṭi, kind of large plantain, banana.

boppi, bump; onomatopoeic.

boṭaboṭa, splash-splash; onomatopoeic of tears falling, &c.

boṭanavrélu, thumb, great toe; this is the Telugu word. The Skt. *angushṭham* is also used.

botstsu, wool; usually of sheep, but a horse's coat is also called his *botstsu*.

bottámu, button. English. The Telugu is *gunḍi*, round thing.

bottigá, altogether. *mana bráhmaṇyamu bottigá cheḍi póvutsunnadi*, our brahminhood is going altogether to the dogs.

boṭṭu, drop, castemark on the forehead, round bit of gold, the round form of *n* and *m*. *táḷi boṭṭu* is the bit of gold that is tied round a girl's neck at marriage and corresponds with our wedding-ring.

boṭṭucaṭṭuṭa, to marry, to tie the *táḷi boṭṭu*.

boṭṭudáramu, string by which the *táḷiboṭṭu* is suspended; also called *mangalasûtram*.

bozza, belly. *Rázugáru oca chétitó misamu vaḍi véyutsû rendava chétitó bozza nimuru conutsû pravéṣintsutsunnáru*, the zamindar comes in twisting his moustaches with one hand and rubbing his belly with the other (characteristics of Hindu nobility).

bozzaváḍu, fat man.

bócu, don't; for *pócu* from *póvuṭa*. *callal'áḍa bócu*, don't tell lies.

bóde, trunk of a tree.

bóde, small channel.

bódha, teaching, persuasion. *mana matam bódha chéyistû v'unḍa valenu*, we must be teaching our religion.

bódhachéyuṭa, to teach.

bódhapaḍuṭa, to be persuaded. *ippuḍu bódhapaḍḍadi*, now I understand.

bódhaparatsuṭa, to teach. *véṣyala vrütti valla caligé nashṭálu janulacu bódha parichi*, preaching about the evils that come from the dancing girls' trade.

bódhintsuṭa, persuade, induce. Skt. *dṣa bódhistunnadi avamánamu bádhistunnadi*, desire applies the spur, shame the rein.

bóḍi, bald, shaven; used not only of bald men but of shaven women, i.e. widows, and so abusively as an expletive.

bógaḍu, man of dancing-girl caste.

bógamméḷamu, band of dancing girls.

bógamu, belonging to the dancing-girl caste; from Skt. *bhógam*, enjoyment. *viváhádi ṣubhacáryálaló bógam méḷam pilipintsaḍam máni vési purushula chéta páḍintsaḍánici y'í sabhaváru rejalyúshan cheyya valen ani nénu propózu chéstunnánu*, I propose a resolution that we should not engage nautch parties in future for our marriage and other festivities but should have the singing done by men.

bógamudi, dancing girl. The plural is *bógamvánḍlu*, *bógamváḷḷu*; the accusative is *bógamdáni*; another common word for dancing girl is *véṣya*.

bógamváḍu, a male member of the dancing-girls' community.

bógamvrütti, dancing girl's profession.

bógandi, bógastrí, dancing girl; *samsára strí* or *culastrí* is the opposite, respectable woman, family woman.

bóle, bowl, pot. *bóleḍu* is a potful.

bónacatte, female cook; *bón* is short for *bhójanamu*, meal.

bónchéyuṭa, to eat, short for *bhójanamu chéyuṭa*; the short expression is the one commonly used.

bónu, trap. *ill'anaḍam canṭe dínni manushyula bón anṭé bágá v'unṭundi*, this should be called a man-trap rather than a house.

bóragilapaḍuṭa, to fall face downwards.

bóragilaparunḍuṭa, to lie on one's breast.

bórlapaḍuṭa, to be upset.

bórlatóyuṭa, to upset.

bórlintsuṭa, to upset.

bósháṇamu, a large chest. Hindustani. It is a chest used specially for keeping safe valuable cloths and jewellery.

-bótu (-pótu), an affix meaning male. *tágubótu*, drunkard.

bóyaváḍu, a man of the *bóya* caste, palanquin bearer, plural *bóyílu*. The

PLATE I

The Honourable Diwan Bahadur S. Kumaraswami Reddiar,
Minister for Education, Madras, a Telugu by origin

The Zamindar of Munagala
(Photo. M. Doss and Bros., Madras)

Anglo-Indian 'boy' for servant is supposed to be derived from this.

Brahma, God the creator. Skt. *yevaḷḷú v'untsucón accara léca póté lócamló bógamváḷḷanu Brahma Dévuḍu yenducu puṭṭinchináḍu?* if no one need keep dancing girls why did the Creator put them into the world?

brahmacharyamu, bachelorhood. Skt.

brahmachári, bachelor, celibate. Skt.

brahmahatya, killing a brahmin. Skt., from *bráhmaṇuḍu*, brahmin, and *hatya*, killing. *egatisté brahmahatya, digatisté góhatya,* if I pull one way it is brahmin murder, the other, it is cow-murder (of a witness in a cattle trespass complaint by a brahmin). These are the two most atrocious forms of murder (Hindu religion).

brahmarácási cheṭṭu, aloe, used as a hedge or fence, especially by the railways.

brahmasútramu, brahmin's sacred thread. Skt.; also precepts from the Vedas.

brahma-taram cádu, quite impossible. Skt., from *brahma* and *taram*, possible. *váḷḷanu maḷḷintsaḍḍánici brahma taram cádu,* God himself could not turn them back

bramayuṭa, to be perplexed; from Skt. *bhrama*, confusion.

brahmánandamu, bliss. Skt., from *brahma* and *ánandam*, joy. *nácu brahmánandamgá v'unnadi, idigó mí bahumánamu núru rúpáyalu,* I am in the seventh heaven of delight, here is your honorarium, Rs. 100 (to a singer).

brahmánḍamu, the universe, a fuss. Skt. *vaca púṭa bhójanam léca póté y'inta brahmánḍam chéstú v'unnávú!* what a fuss about missing one meal!

braticintsuṭa, to bring to life.

bratimáluconuṭa, to entreat; also *batimáluconuṭa*.

bratucu, life, livelihood; also *batucu*. *aṭuvanṭi váḷḷa bratuc'enducu? vedhava bratucu?* what is the good of a life like that, a rotten life? *í bhúmi má bratucu,* we live on this bit of land, it is all we have.

bratucuṭa, to live. *váḍu bratici y'unḍagáné tólu valchi vésináru,* they flayed him alive; *aḍadáni chéti arthamú, magaváni chéti biḍḍá bratacadu,* a child will not live in a man's hands nor money in a woman's.

bráhmaṇuḍu, brahmin. Skt., from *brahma*; feminine is *bráhmaṇi*. *cappacu cáṭu, bráhmaṇunici póṭu lédu,* frogs cannot bite, brahmins cannot fight. Plural, *bráhmaṇulu, bráhmalu.*

bráhmaṇyamu, brahminhood. Skt. *mana bráhmaṇyamu bottigá cheḍi póvutsunnadi,* our brahminhood is going altogether to the dogs.

brándí, brandy. English. *brándí, jinnú modalaina sárálu,* brandy, gin, and other spirits.

Brühaspati, the priest of the Gods, wisdom personified. Skt. *má váḷḷu nann' andarú nútana Brühaspatigá bhávistáru,* my people all think me a new Solon; *buddhi y'andu tamaru Brühaspatini minchinaváru,* you are wiser than Brühaspati.

bründamu, crowd, band. Skt. *mitrabründamu,* a band of friends.

buccá, scent powder. *paḷḷem ninḍá buccá,* a tray full of scent powder, extensively used on the fifth day of the marriage.

buḍama, a kind of paddy grown in the Circars.

budbulamu, bubbling; onomatopoeic.

buddhi, sense. Skt. *aina panici chintinchéváḍu alpa buddhi galaváḍu,* it shows little sense to cry over spilt milk; *buddhi y'andu tamaru Brühaspatini minchinaváru,* you surpass *Brühaspati* in wisdom; *cheppina buddhi caṭṭina tsaddi nilavadu,* advice and food soon get stale.

buddhi chepputa, to give advice, to reprimand. Skt.

buddhihínata, folly. Skt.

buddhihínuḍu, fool. Skt. *inta buddhihínuṇṇi y'í lócamló nénu y'eccaḍá tsúḍa lédu,* I have never seen such a born fool; *lócamló buddhimantulu taccuvagánu, buddhihínulu eccuvagánu v'unṭáru,* there are more fools than wise men in this world.

buddhipúrvacamugá, on purpose. Skt. *idi buddhipúrvacamaina pani cádu,* I did not do it on purpose.

buddhiṣáli, sensible man. Skt.

buddhi-svásthyamu, soundness of mind. Skt. The term which is used in the law courts (or would be if they ever spoke Telugu there).

Buddhuḍu, the Buddha.

buḍḍi, bottle, plural *buḍlu*. *sárábuḍḍi tsútsucunéṭ'appaṭici vaṭṭi buḍḍi v'unnadi,* when I looked for my rum bottle I found it empty.

budhavára mu, Wednesday. Skt., from *budhuḍu,* Mercury; the days of the week being called after the planets.

bugga, cheek. *váḍu dáni bugga ṅalipináḍu,* he pinched her cheek.

bugulubugulumanuṭa, to pitpat; onomatopoeic.

buláci, nose-ring, the one worn by women not the one worn by men. Hindustani, from Būlāq, suburb of Cairo; also a flower-basket or a tray.

buracá, cloth cover. Hindustani.

burada, mud. *inglíshu tsaduvuconna váḷḷu nadiló burada niḷḷ'ani núti niḷḷaló munugutáru,* those who have studied English will bathe in well water, saying the river water is muddy; *burada guṇṭaló pandi,* a pig in a mud pit; *ná baṭṭalu burada ainavi,* my clothes got muddy.

burra, head; properly speaking, 'nut', but in English also 'nut' is used for 'head'. *burracu vaca guṇamu, jivhacu vaca ruchi,* tastes differ and no two heads are made alike; *róṭló burra peṭṭi rócaṭi debbacu zaḍisin'aṭṭu,* putting your head in the mortar and then fearing the blow of the pestle (you should think of the danger first before putting your head in the lion's mouth).

burruna, rustling; onomatopoeic. *burruna tsápa tsuṭṭinaṭṭu,* the sound of a mat being rolled up.

buruzu, bastion. Hindustani.

busabusal'ani, puffing; onomatopoeic. Cobras and elephants say *busa, busa.*

bussum'ani, hissing; onomatopoeic, of snakes, &c.

buṭṭa, basket.

buvva, food. *naucari mánucunṭé nicu nagalú, buvvá yeccaḍa nunchi vastáyi?* if I leave service where will your jewels and food come from? *míru techché jítamu buvvacunu, guḍḍalacunu saripóvuts unnadi,* the pay you get is just enough for food and clothes.

buzamu, shoulder; from Skt. *bhujam.*

buzzagintsuṭa, to coax. *váṇṇi mellagá manchi máṭalató buzzaginchi,* wheedling him with soft words.

búchi, ogre; derived from Bussy, the French general; used to scare children. *búchiváḍu y'ettucu pótáḍu,* the ogre will come and carry you away.

búḍida, ashes. *búḍidaló pósina panníru* rosewater thrown on ashes (pearls before swine).

búḍidavanne, ash-coloured, grey.

búṭacamu, trick. *id antá vaṭṭi búṭacamu,* that is all a trick.

bútu, obscenity. *bútulu tiṭṭutáḍu,* he uses foul language.

bútupáṭalu, obscene songs. *lanjala chéta bútupáṭalu páḍisténé cáni Bhagavad vishayam'aina gánamu chéyisté bágá v'unḍadá?* would not sacred music be better than coarse songs sung by courtesans?

búzu, mildew. *baṭṭalú nagalú peṭṭe ninḍá búzu paḍutú v'unnavi,* I have a boxful of clothes and ornaments getting mouldy for want of use. *búzu paṭṭi v'unna Puráṇa pustacamu,* a mildewed *Purána* book.

búzupaḍuṭa, búzupaṭṭuṭa, to get mildewed.

byánci, bank (money). English.

byáncinoṭu, bank-note. English.

C

cabaḷamu, mouthful, morsel. Skt. *á crúra rácshasunici néṭi sáyancála bhójanamunacu néné pradhama cabaḷam' agudun ani tóchi,* thinking I would provide the cruel giant with the first morsel for to-night's supper; *cabaḷintsuṭa,* to swallow, devour.

cabbamu, an original poem; used in books.

cabélá, deed of grant. Hindustani; a revenue term applied to grants of land.

cabódi, a blind man.

caburu, word, enquiry, information. Hindustani. *nénu pustacamu coracu caburu pampinánu,* I sent word for the book; *vídhiló nilutsuni canuccuni váḷḷu lópala lér'ani caburu telisina taruváta veḷḷi póyináḍu,* he stood in the street and enquired and after ascertaining that they were not at home, went away.

cabúliyatu, counter agreement. Hindustani. The *cabúliyat* is the agreement signed by a zamindar at the permanent settlement in exchange for the *sanad.* The derivation is from Hindustani, *cabúl,* acceptance.

caccu, tooth of saw, dent, notch. *coḍavali cacculu cósináḍu,* he has jagged his sickle.

caccu, vomit; also *craccu.*

caccu, noise; onomatopoeic. Also *carucu,* of sawing, whooping, &c.

caccuconuṭa, to vomit; also *craccuconuṭa. pilla annamu caccucunnadi,* the child brought up its dinner.

caccus, latrine; from Dutch *caakhuis.* The only Dutch word in Telugu. Extensively used in the Southern Districts; in the north, *páci-doḍḍi.*

caccuṭa, to vomit; also *craccuṭa. pilla guḍḍ'antá caccinadi,* the child was sick all over its clothes.

caccuváyi, whooping cough.

caccuriti or **caccúrti,** desire, caprice. *inta caccuriti paḍutávu.* you are so capricious. *bráhmalu ḍabbu cósam caccúrti paḍi mana şástrál'anní váḷḷacu cheppi páḍu chéstú v'unnáru,* brahmins have told them all that is in the shastras from a desire to make money and so spoil the shastras.

cachcha, rough, second-rate. Hindustani. Opposed to *pacca* (pukka).

cachchhapamu, tortoise. Skt. The Telugu is *tábélu. gaja cachchhapa póru tsandamu,* like a fight between an elephant and a tortoise.

cachéri, office. Hindustani. The old word for a Government office, now called *afísu. sivil córtucu yeduṭa má cachéri v'unnadi,* our office is opposite the civil court.

cacshi, party, faction.

cacshidáruḍu, member of a faction, party in a case. *idi nyáyasabha cádu, iccaḍa pliḍarla vádálatónú, sácshyálatónú, cacshidárla vivádálatóní yémí pani lédu,* this is not a law court, it is no question here of pleaders' arguments, witnesses and the disputes of parties.

-caḍa-, prefix or suffix meaning up to or very near, at a place, last; may also become *gaḍa,* in composition. *caḍatérá vinu,* listen to the end; *caḍasamípamu,* very near; *caṭṭacaḍa,* at the very end; *irugaḍa,* on both sides; *caḍasári,* the last time; *caḍatsúpu,* last look; *caḍavaracu,* to the end; *vaḍḍinchéváḍu tanaváḍu aité caḍabantini cúrtsunná vaccaṭé,* if the server of the food is your man it does not matter if you are sitting at the end of the line; *caḍapaḷḷu,* molars; *í pani caḍa canṭi vánici teliyacuṇḍá cheyyáli,* you should do this without letting it be known to either of your eyes. (Let not thy left hand know what the right hand does, to do a thing in much secrecy.)

-caḍa, an affix forming verbs into nouns; may become *gaḍa* in composition. *rácaḍa,* coming; *pócaḍa,* going; *manugaḍa,* maintenance; *talagaḍa,* pillow.

caḍabantini or **caḍapanctini,** at the end of the line (at a dinner party), the last or worst place. *vésucunna vistari vacanici viḍichi peṭṭi caḍapanctini cúrtsóvaḍam vyasanacarangá v'unnadi,* it is annoying to leave one's leaf-platter to another and go and sit at the bottom of the row.

caḍacu, at last.
caḍacu, to. *atani caḍacu vachchindru,* they came to him.
caḍagaḷḷu, afflictions; also *caḍagandlu.*
cadalamedalacunḍa, without moving or stirring; from *cadaluṭa,* to move, and *medaluṭa,* to stir. *saháyam tísuconi cshanamló vastánu, nívu cadalamedalacunḍá v'unḍu,* I shall be back in a moment with help, meanwhile don't stir an inch.
cadalintsuṭa, to move (transitive).
cadalipóvuṭa, to start.
cadaltsuṭa, cadalintsuṭa, to shake, to jog, to move or mention as a topic.
cadaluṭa, to move (intransitive). *caḍupuló pinḍamunacu práṇamu vatstsuṭatóné tallici pilla cadalutsunnad'ani teliyutsunnadi,* the mother knows she is quick with child as soon as she feels the child moving in the womb; *balla cadalacunḍá cinda ráḷḷu yettu peṭṭináḍu,* he put stones under the table to steady it; *cadalav'émi!* bestir yourself! ; *nénu iccaḍa nunchi cadalanu,* I shall not stir from here.
caḍama, rest, balance.
cadannamu, bad food. Skt., used in books.
caḍapa, gateway; also the town misspelt Cuddapah by the English.
caḍapaṭa, finally.
caḍapaṭiváḍu, the last one. *ná vamṣamló nénu caḍapaṭiváṇṇi ainánu,* the last of my race.
cadapá, bond. Hindustani.
cadapuṭa, to move (transitive); also *cadupuṭa.*
caḍatéra, to the end. *caḍatéra tsadavanḍi,* read to the end.
caḍatértsuṭa, to finish, make an end of. *ná paruvu caḍatérchináḍu,* he has destroyed my honour; *id antá bráhmalu janulanu telivitaccuvaváḷḷanu chési, váḷḷa ḍabbu caḍatértsaḍánici pannina yantram,* that is all a trick of brahmins, to get money out of fools.
caḍava, large pot. *perugu caḍava,* pot of curds.
cadá! indeed! more commonly *gadá!*
caddaru, khaddar, home spun cloth, the fetish of Indian protectionists; also *khaddaru.*
caddu, common form of *caladu,* it is, there is, it is usual. *aṭlá cheppaḍamu caddu,* it is usual to say so; *caddu léd'anaca,* saying neither yes nor no.
caḍiyamu, bracelet, especially one worn by men. *cancaṇamula cheyyi ḍḍité caḍiyamula cheyyi ḍḍunu,* the man follows where the woman leads.
caḍugu, water in which rice has been washed before cooking.
caḍuguṭa, to wash (transitive), but not to wash clothes, which is *utucuṭa;* thus Monkey Brand soap will *caḍuguṭa* but it will not *utucuṭa. í paḷḷemu caḍigi tísucu rá,* clear this plate and bring it here.
caduluṭa, to move (intransitive); also *cadaluṭa.*
cadumu, bruise.
caḍupu, belly (which is also the seat of the affections in Telugu; a cool belly is regarded as a blessing), the womb. *caḍupu cúṭici y'éḍisté coppu púlacu y'éḍchinaṭṭu,* the belly cried for food, the topknot for flowers; *caḍupu ninḍá gárelu tinṭé vanṭi ninḍá jvaram,* a bellyful of cakes and a bodyful of fever; *caḍupuninḍina béramu,* a rich man's bargain (will be a hard one); *caḍupulóni máṭa anṭé v'úr'antá autunnadi,* if you tell your secret it will be all over the village; *caḍupuló lénidi caugalintsuconṭé vastunḍá!* if you have no bowels of affection, affection won't come by embraces; *canṭici y'imp aité caḍupucu y'impu,* pleasant to the eye and pleasant to the taste; *váḍu caḍupuló tsalla cadalacunḍá v'unnḍḍu,* he lived at ease; *váru caḍupu ninḍá tinnáru,* they ate their full; *ámecu caḍupu póyinadi* or *diginadi,* she miscarried; *ámecu caḍupu chésinḍḍu,* he got her with child.
caḍupu dintsuṭa, to procure abortion.
caḍupunoppi, stomach-ache.
caduputa, to move (transitive); also *cadapuṭa, cadalintsuṭa.*
caḍuputónunḍuṭa, to be with child. *tudacu nénu caḍuputón' unnán' ani cheviló rahasyamugá cheppitini,* finally I whispered in his ear that I was with child.
caḍupu tsallagá, may the belly be cool, is an expression referring to the womb of the addressee's mother, and

is by way of being a good wish. *mí talli caḍupu tsallagá, míru véyéḷḷu vardhillavalenu,* blessings on your mother's womb, may you live 1,000 years.

caduru, spindle. *árdṭapu caduru yé ráṭána peṭṭiná bara bara,* the spindle will scream whatever wheel you attach it to (*árdṭapu* is a play on *rátnam,* spinning wheel, and *árdṭam,* grief).

caiconuṭa, to take, from *cai,* hand, in Tamil, and *conuṭa,* an auxiliary verb forming the middle tense; *putstsuconuṭa* is the usual word.

caicólu, agreement, acceptance.

caidí, prisoner. Hindustani. Also *khaidi.*

caidu, prison. Hindustani. English *jailu* is more common now.

caifíyatu, statement. Hindustani. Properly particulars, but used of a statement recorded by a tahsildar or magistrate.

cailásamu, Ṣiva's heaven.

caincaryamu, service, especially divine service. Skt., adjectival form of *cincarata,* service; used chiefly in books and among the Vaishnavite brahmins.

caivàramu, circumference.

cajána, treasury. Hindustani. Also *khajána.*

cajjá, quarrel. Hindustani. Also *khajjá.*

cala, dream. *calalóci rácundá v'undunu gáca,* I hope it will not come back to me in my dreams.

caḷa, brightness, air (of persons). Skt. *ní mogánici y'ippuḍu caḷa chérucunnadi,* a cheerful air has come back to your face.

-cala, affix meaning 'having', usually *gala;* participle of *calaguṭa,* very common in forming adjectives out of nouns. *budhigala,* sensible.

calabanda, aloe. *calabandaci yenḍú, cóḍalici cotta, lédu,* a daughter-in-law is no more new than an aloe is withered.

calaca, turbidity. *calaca,* to turn turbid; *canṭi calaca,* the disease called country sore eyes.

calacala, twittering; onomatopoeic. *calacala dhvanulu,* twittering noises; *calacala navvuṭa,* to laugh loud; *mogam yeppuḍú calacalal áḍutú v'unṭundi,* a continually laughing face.

calacanḍa, sugar candy.

caladu, there is, it is; from *caluguṭa,* usually shortened to *caddu.* The plural is *calavu.*

calaguṭa, to be disordered.

calagúra, mixed herbs (*olla podrida*), from *cala,* mixed, and *cúra,* vegetable.

calagúra-gampa, a mixture of all varieties (an *olla podrida*), from *calagúra,* mixed herbs, and *gampa,* basket. A whole section in the Telugu magazines is often styled *calagúra-gampa;* it will be an *olla podrida* containing odd bits of news gleanings, amusing anecdotes with topical interest, &c. *í másapu bhárati patricaló calagúra-gampa cinda manushyulacu tócalunḍé v'ani rámayaṇamló v'unna vánarulavanṭi manushyulu nizangá v'unḍévárani vrasinḍru tsúchindrá?* Have you seen the item in the miscellaneous part of this month's *Bharati* about the reality of the existence of the wild men in the Ramayana?

calahamu, dispute. Skt. *ṣushca calahálu,* subtle disputes; *í calahamunacu cáracuḍavu nívu,* you are at the bottom of the quarrel; *calahapriyuḍu,* delighting in disputes, firebrand, mischief-maker.

calamu, pen. Hindustani; Latin *calamus,* reed-pen, Italian *calamo,* reed, *calamaio,* inkstand. *nívu pustacamu vráyumu, calamu cágitamu nénu jágrata peḍutánu,* write the book, I will provide you with ink, pen, and paper; *calamu porabáṭu,* clerical error (slip of the pen).

calapa, timber.

calapuṭa, to join (transitive); causal of *calayuṭa,* to join (intransitive).

calará, cholera. English; *vántibhédi,* vomiting and purging, is the proper Telugu; *vishúchi* the Sanskrit, but *calará* is more generally used. *calará chéta padinṭic ocaḍu tsachchinaḍu,* one out of ten has died of cholera.

calata, trouble.

calatsuṭa, to trouble.

calavaramu, confusion.

calavarintsuṭa, to talk in one's sleep, be delirious, babble.

calayatsútsuṭa, to look all round.

calayuṭa, to mix (intransitive); also *caliyuṭa.*

caḷáyi, plating with tin, electroplate, &c. Hindustani.

calecṭaru, collector. English.

caḷébaramu, corpse. Skt.; *ṣavamu* and *pinugu* are commoner.

cali, the Iron Age. Skt. *caliyugamu* is commoner, also *calicálamu* or *ghóra-cali*, which means the frightful age of Cali, who in the Puranas is described as the presiding deity for everything unworthy and sinful. *ṣástrál anni tagalabaḍi varṇa sancaram aipótú v'un-nadi, y'entaṭi ghóra-cali vachchinadi!* The scriptures are destroyed, there is chaos in the structure of castes—what frightful things are committed in this age!

caligintsuṭa, cause to be, caused to happen; from *caluguṭa*.

calimi, being, having; from *caluguṭa*, to be. Comes to mean 'having', because 'being to you' = having. *calimi lémulu cávaṭi cunḍalu*, having and want are the two pots of the yoke, i.e. there are always ups and downs.

caḷinga, weir; the outlet weir of a tank. Weir and *caḷinga* are, however, distinguished here, a *caḷinga* being a weir with upright stones planted at distances on it; the spaces between the stones can then be filled up to raise the height of the weir and the level of the water in the tank.

calisiconuṭa, to meet; from *caliyuṭa*, to mix.

caliyabaḍuṭa, to engage; from *caliyuṭa*, mix, and *paḍuṭa*, fall. *caliyabaḍi coṭṭuconi debbaláḍináru*, they engaged, struck and dealt blows.

caliyugamu, the Iron Age in which we are supposed to live. Skt. *caliyugamu aidu véla samvatstsarálu cá vachchinadi*, we have had 5,000 years of the Iron Age.

caliyuṭa, to mix (intransitive), meet, be included. *atani bhúmiló calasinadi*, included in his land; *ródlu accaḍa caliyutsunnavi*, the roads join there; *musali bhartalacunu paḍutsu bháryalacunu manass eppuḍunú caliyadu*, old husbands and young wives will never be of the same mind.

calla, lie, false. *calla préma*, false love.

callaláḍuṭa, to lie.

caḷḷamu, caḷḷapu miṭṭa, thrashing-floor.

callari, marauder, bandit, called colleries in old English records, when marauding bands were one of the afflictions of South India; there are none now. *callaríḍu* in books.

caḷḷárá, with one's own eyes, plainly; short for *cannulu*, eyes, and *árá*, clearly. *ataṇṇi nénu caḷḷárá tsúchinánu* I saw him plainly. Also *canḍlárá*.

caḷḷemu, reins. *gurram digi paṭṭu-comm' ani gurram caḷḷem ná chétic ichchináḍu*, he got off his horse, told me to hold it, and gave me the reins.

callólamu, turmoil. Skt.

callu, toddy (palm beer). *callu gísuconi bratucutáḍu*, he lives by drawing toddy (from palms).

calludukháṇamu, toddy-shop; also *calluducáṇam*.

calmashamu, dirt. Skt.

calpamu, a religious rule. Skt.

calpamu, cycle of 4 million or so years. Skt. *nimisham oca calpamugá gaḍa-puts unḍiri*, a minute passed like an age.

calpana, fabrication. Skt. *adi vaṭṭi calpana*, that is a mere fabrication.

calpavrücshamu, the Wishing Tree. Skt. The tree is in the Hindu paradise.

calpintsuṭa, to fabricate, frame. Skt. *appaṭi rázu y'í tsaṭṭamulanu calpin-chinḍḍu*, the then king framed these laws.

calpitamu, fabricated, fictitious. Skt.

calti, mixture, adulteration; from *caliyuṭa*, to mix. Also *caltí*.

calugu, hole, cave.

caluguṭa, to be, to be able, to happen; changes to *galuguṭa* in composition. Telugu, like Spanish, has two words for 'to be', *unḍuṭa* (Spanish *ser*) and *caluguṭa* (Spanish *estar*). *caluguṭa* signifies something more than mere empty being; it is rather to happen or, implying a dative of possession, to have. *sommu galaváḍu* is a man who has money; *pillalu calaváḍu*, a man who has many children; *vráya galaváḍu*, one who has writing, i.e. can write; *chellintsa galavár amu*, we can pay; *telivi galaváḍu*, a sensible man; *caligin ayya gáde tíséṭ appaṭici péda vánici práṇam póyinadi*, by the time

Dives had made open his bin Lazarus was dead; *caligina várici andarú tsuṭṭalé*, everybody is related to the rich man.

calupu, weeds.

calushamaina, turbid. Skt.

calusuconuṭa, to meet; from *caliyuṭa*. *répu v'udayánna bhójanapu véḷacu tappacuṇḍá vachchi calusucuṇṭánu*, I will meet you without fail to-morrow morning at breakfast time.

caḷyáṇamu, marriage. Skt. *caḷyáṇótstsavamu* (*utstsavamu*) is the day of a god's marriage; *caḷyáṇa manṭapam*, the platform on which this ceremony is carried out.

camalamu, lotus. Skt. One of the commoner words for lotus, of which there are many. *camala* is a female name.

camatagánḍlu, farm servants. *á y' asámi vadda vanda mandi camatagánḍḷu v'unnáru*, that individual employs 100 labourers on his farm.

camatamu, landed property.

camánu, arch, spring of a carriage or a watch. Hindustani.

camánu, a march or military journey (from French *commander*). Has lost its original meaning and is used in the sense of going on circuit. *injaniyaru gáru yeppuḍu camánu pótáru?* when does the engineer go on circuit?

camáyishu, business. Hindustani.

cambaḷi, blanket. Skt.

cambaḷipurugu, hairy caterpillar; also *gongaḷi-purugu*, from *gongaḷi*, a hairy blanket.

cambu, a millet (*pennissetum typhoideum* or *spicatum*). The word used in the Circars is *sazzalu*; *cambu* is Tamil; the Hindustani is *bajra*. The millet with a head like a bulrush and smaller grains than *zonna* (*cholam, jawari*).

camchí, whip.

camiṭí, committee. English.

camízu, shirt. Portuguese. There is only one other Portuguese word in Telugu, *cusini*, kitchen.

camma, a large ear-ring.

camma, missive; used in books.

camma, sweet, fragrant. *camma* or *cammani távulu*, fragrant odours.

camma, the chief Telugu cultivating caste.

cammaramu, smiths' work. *cammara vidhiló súdulu ammin' aṭṭu*, like selling needles in Blacksmiths' Street (taking coals to Newcastle).

cammatamu, landed property; also *camatam*.

cammi, wire, bar; *mucammi* is a nose-ring.

cammi, concealment; from *cammuṭa*, to misappropriate. *tálúcá leccaḷḷó padi véla rúpáyala sommu cammi-chéyabaḍinadi*, there is misappropriation of accounts to the extent of Rs. 10,000 in the Sub-Treasury.

cammuconuṭa, cammuṭa, to hide, surround. *oca abaddhamu cammaḍánici veyyi abaddhamulu cávalenu*, 1,000 lies are required to hide one.

cammudala, concealment.

campa, thorn-bush.

campamu, tremor. *bhayam chéta campam y'etti vaḷḷ'antá chemaṭa pósinadi*, I trembled and sweated all over the body in fear; *bhúcampamu* is an earthquake.

campení, company; especially the East India Company. *inglish doralu tsúḍu, campenilu peṭṭi nyáyangá vyavaharisté vacaṭi renḍu saṁvatstsarálaló lacshala coḍḍi sommu yélá sampádistáró*, see how the English form companies, trade honestly, and make money by lakhs in one or two years.

campintsuṭa, quake. *bhúmi campinchinadi*, the earth quaked; *déhamu dipamu vale campimpa modalu peṭṭinadi*, my body began to tremble like the flame of a lamp.

campu, stench. *musali campu*, smell of old age.

campu coṭṭuṭa, or **campu goṭṭuṭa,** to stink, taste bad. *í níru chilumu campu coṭṭutsunnadi*, this water tastes of verdigris; *nácu pinugu campu goṭṭutsunnadi*, I smell a corpse.

camsálivánḍu, goldsmith. *talli bangáram ainá camsálivánḍu dongilintsaca mánaḍu*, a goldsmith will steal even his mother's gold; *mádiga maḷḷi camsáli y'elli*, the cobbler will say, 'come again', the goldsmith, 'to-morrow'.

camuzu, partridge. Also *canzu*.

canacamu, gold; a Sanskrit word used in composition as *canacángi*, golden haired.

caṇacaṇa, blazing; onomatopoeic.

canamu, particle. Skt. *agnicanamu* is a spark.

canapaḍuṭa, to appear; also *canupaḍuṭa*

canaparatsuṭa, to show. *pravartana valla yógyata canaparatsaḍánici nác' avacáṣam cheyyanḍi*, give me a chance to prove my value by my conduct; *ṣástramló v'unnadi nénu canaparustánu*, I will show what is in the shastras. Also *canuparatsuṭa*

caṇata, temple (of the head).

canálu, canal. English. *cáluva* is commoner.

cancaṇamu, marriage thread tied on the wrist at the beginning of the ceremony. Bracelet worn by women; *caḍiyamu*, bracelet worn by men. *cancaṇamula cheyyi áḍité caḍiyamula cheyyi áḍunu*, the hand that wears a *caḍiyamu* will follow the hand that wears a *cancaṇam*.

cancaṇamu caṭṭuconuṭa, tie the marriage thread, be wedded. Also metaphorically, *cancaṇamu caṭṭuconnáḍu*, he took up the work as if wedded to the idea of it.

cancara, gravel. Hindustani.

canche, hedge; also pasture.

cancherusumulu, pasture fees.

canci, ear of corn; also *vennu*.

canda, an esculent bulb (*amorphophallus campanolatus*).

canḍa, flesh. *ungaramu canḍalónici tósuconi póyinadi*, the ring has bitten into the flesh. Also flesh of fruit.

candacamu, ditch, trench.

canḍacávaramu, sensuality, from *canḍa*, flesh, and *cávaramu*, fat. *munḍalu tinḍi tini tinnagá unḍa léca canḍacávaramunacu lóbaḍi cánipanulu chéyuduru*, widows eat well and unable to keep straight yield to sensuality and commit sins.

canḍe, cob of millet or maize. *núlu canḍe* is a ball of thread.

candi, a pulse, red gram, *cajanus indicus*. The beans of this, *pappu* (dholl), are the most nutritious food eaten with rice by vegetarians.

candipappu, dholl.

candiríga, hornet; from *íga*, fly.

canḍlárá, with one's own eyes, plainly. Also *callárá*.

canḍlu, eyes; plural of *cannu*.

canḍlutiruguṭa, be giddy. *nácu canḍlutirugutsunnavi*, I am giddy.

canduṭa, be burned, grieve. *ní mukhamu candinadi*, your face is burnt; *manasu candinavḍḍai*, being grieved at heart.

canḍuvá, upper cloth; also *khanḍuvá*. *núru rúpáyala banárasu canḍuvá*, a Benares shoulder-cloth worth Rs. 100.

cangucangu, clanging; onomatopoeic. The sound of bells, &c.

cani, having seen clearly; from *canuṭa*. *canichepputa*, to speak clearly; the word is common in books, but in speaking you say *tsúchi*, not *cani*.

canicaramu, compassion.

canicarintsuṭa, to pity.

canipeṭṭuṭa, to find out, to discover. *anní canipeḍutú v'unṭáḍu*, he finds everything out; *vaca cotta sangati canipeṭṭinánu*, I have found out something new; *pracrúti ṣástragnyulu dinadinamu cotta sangatul'ennó canipeṭṭuts' unnáru*, the scientists are making new discoveries every day.

canipeṭṭuconuṭa, to wait. *canipeṭṭucom'anu*, tell him to wait; *ná cósamu canipeṭṭucó*, wait for me.

canipintsuṭa, to seem, to come out (as a disease), to find. *váḍu nácu canipintsa léḍu*, I could not find him.

canishṭa, little finger. Skt. The Telugu is *chiṭicina vélu* or *chiṭicina vrélu*.

canísamu, the least. Skt.

canna, who has begotten or given birth; from *canuṭa*, to give birth, common in the expressions *cannatalli, canna tanḍri*. *nalugurini canna tanḍri*, the father of four; *cann'ayya*, the natural father.

canna, prefix meaning 'any'; from *canuṭa*, to see. *cannatsóṭa*, anywhere; *cannaváḷḷu*, strangers; *cannacúḷḷu*, any food you can get.

canna, than; more usually *canṭé*. *antya nishṭ uramu canna ádi nishṭ uramé mélu*, annoyance at the end is worse than annoyance at the beginning.

cannabiḍḍa, natural as opposed to adoptive child; from *canuṭa*, to give

birth. *cánaca-cannabiḍḍa*, a child begotten after long years of waiting.
cannacanna, the first to come, any; from *canuṭa*, to see. *cannacannavāḷḷ' evar' ainá vyabhicharistú*, committing fornication with the first comer.
cannacóla, jemmy.
cannaḍa, Canarese.
cannaḍamu, the Canarese country, the Carnatic.
cannagáḍu, burglar.
cannamu, hole in mud wall, burglars' hole. Houses being mostly of mud, burglars do not get through a window as in England but make a hole at the bottom of the mud wall. *Cannayya* is a name given to a baby put through a hole in the wall from outside; this will prevent it dying if it is sickly, like *Kuppuswami*, the Tamil Ash Child.
cannamvéyuṭa, to make a burglars' hole. *cáryam chési vāḷḷu santóshinchi nálugu ḍabbulu y'isté putstsucunṭé yémi dóshamu? id yémi cannálu veyyaḍamá?* if a few coins are exchanged to oblige people and do something for them, what is wrong? is that committing burglaries? (ethics of bribery).
canne, virgin; *canya* or *canyaca* is commoner. *yógyuránḍraina cannelacu ituvanṭivi yémí teliyavu*, good girls know nothing of such things; *canne ichchitivó, cannu ichchitivó?* is it your daughter or your eye you will be giving? (When a large dowry is demanded.)
cannericamu, virginity. *áme cannericamu cheripináḍu*, he took her virginity; *cannericamu chéyuṭa*, enjoyment of a courtesan when she publicly takes up such a career.
canníru, tear; plural *canniḷḷu* from *can*, eye, and *nír*, water. The ordinary word. The Sanskrit *aṣruvu* and *báshpam* are used in preference in books.
cannu, eye. *oca cannu canní cádu, oca coḍucu coḍucú cáḍu*, eyes and sons should be in pairs; *canṭici imp'aité caḍupucu y'impu*, what pleases the eye will please the palate. The plural is *canḍlu* or *caḷḷu* or *cannulu*. *caḷḷárá* means plain to the eyes (*cannul-árá*). *canḍlu agapaḍavu*, he cannot see; this is the common word, the books prefer to use *nétramu*.
cannu, arch of a bridge; from the word for eye. But the eye of a needle is *bezzamu*. *cannulerrachéyuṭa*, to be angry (make your eyes red).
cannula nírupeṭṭuṭa, to cry (put water in the eyes).
cannulapanḍuga, a feast for the eyes.
canṭa, in the eye. *atani canṭa paḍacunḍá*, so as not to be seen by him; *paici canṭa taḍi peṭṭin'aṭṭu*, pretending to cry.
cantà, fissure, chink. *nénu lópalici póyi y'í talupu cantaló nunchi mi y'iddari charyalú canipeḍutú v'unṭánu*, I shall go inside and see through the chink in the door what you two are up to.
canṭe, a gold necklace worn by women.
canṭé, than; also *canna*, from *canuṭa*, to look, looking at, i.e. in comparison. *tsaddi canṭé v'úracáya ghanamu*, if you observe your cold rice the pickle is the best part of it; *váni canṭé véré manishi*, a different man from him.
canṭhamu, throat. Skt. *canṭham lótu niḷḷaló digináḍu*, he went into the water up to his throat.
canṭhapáṭhamu, rote. Skt. *conni manchi padyamulu canṭhapáṭhamu cheyya valenu*, you must learn some good verses by heart.
canṭhaṣóshaṇamu, throat-drying, i.e. waste of breath. Skt., from *canṭham*, throat, and *ṣósha*, drying; also *canṭhaṣosha*.
canṭhasvaramu, voice. Skt., from *canṭham*, throat, and *svaram*, sound. *ní canṭhasvaram nénu tarutsugá vinnadi lág'unnadi*, your voice sounds familiar.
canṭi, canṭiló, to the eye, in the eye; oblique of *cannu*, eye. *canṭiló nerasu*, particle in the eye. *caḍacanṭi*, ashance.
canti, boil. *í tailamu cantulu caragacoṭṭutsunnadi*, this oil dissolves boils; *vanṭi nindá cantulu bayaludérutú v'unnavi*, boils are breaking out all over the body.
canṭicalaca, sore eyes.
cantsamu, metal plate.
cantsaragáḍida, mule. *cantsaragáḍida gurramunacu gáḍidecu puṭṭinadi*, a mule is a cross between a horse and an ass.

cantsaraváḍu, coppersmith.

cantsu, bell metal.

canu, eye; usually *cannu*, except in composition, where *canu* is preferred.

canubomma, eye-brow.

canuca, therefore, but *ganuca* is almost always the form used; from *canuṭa*, to see; 'seeing that' is similarly used in English.

canucaṭṭu, legerdemain. *adi cévalam máya, vaṭṭi gáraḍi, ṣuddha indrajálamu; canucaṭṭu chéta canabaḍḍadé cáni nizam cádu*, that is simple illusion, mere juggling, pure conjuring; it appears to be by legerdemain but is not really.

canucconuṭa, to find out; also spelt *canugonuṭa*, but not so pronounced. *veḷḷi canuccó*, go and find out or enquire.

canuchícaṭi, twilight.

canudóyi, pair of eyes; used commonly in books.

canugantaláṭa, blind-man's buff.

canugoni, canungoni, having seen; used in books.

canuguḍḍu or **canugruḍḍu,** eye-ball.

canumúyuṭa, caḷḷumúyuṭa, to deceive. *nác enducu ilá caḷḷumuyyálani tsústávu?*, why do you try to deceive me?

canupaduṭa, to appear, seem. *canapaḍḍadé cáni nizamu cádu*, it seems but it is not. The common word for 'see', the Telugus preferring to say 'it appears' rather than 'I see'. *iccaḍa y'eduṭa vaca mantsamu canapaḍutú v'unnadi*, I see a bed there opposite; *á cheṭṭu mída cóti canabaḍutsunnadá?* do you see the monkey on yonder tree?

canuparutsuṭa, to show; also *canaparatsuṭa*.

canupaṭṭuṭa, to appear, come out, come to light.

canupápa, pupil of the eye; from *canu* and *pápa*, child, i.e. the small reflection seen in the pupil. (Latin *pupillus* has the same derivation, *pupus*, baby.)

canupu, joint, especially of the fingers and of a sugar-cane, knuckles.

canureppa, eyelid. *reppa* by itself also means an eyelid.

canureppapáṭu, the twinkling of an eye, a moment, instant; from *canureppa* and *páṭu*, fall.

canureppaventrucalu, eye-lashes; from *canureppa* and *venṭrucalu*, hairs. Also *canu-venṭrucalu*.

canuṭa, to see; *tsútsuṭa* and *canapaḍuta*, to appear, are more often used. *cané guḍḍi, viné chevuḍu*, blind though seeing, deaf though hearing (eyes have they but they see not, ears have they but they hear not).

canuṭa, to bring forth, bear, beget. *canna tanḍri, canna talli*, the father who begot you, the mother who bore you; *caḍuputó v'unn'amma canáca mánuná, vanḍin amma tinaca mánuná?* will the woman with child fail to bring it forth, will the woman who has cooked, fail to eat? *í pillanu nícu cannán anṭundi*, she fathers the child on you; *áme cané dinamulu*, she is near her time.

canuzu, sambhur deer (*cervus hippelaphus*), a large brown deer; distinguished from *camuzu*, which is partridge.

canya, canyaca, virgin. Skt.

canyádánamu, gift of a virgin. Skt. It is a meritorious act to give a daughter in marriage. *y'evarú pillan iyyaca póté má ammáyini y'ichchi á canyádána phalamunu nénu daccintsucunṭánu*, if no one will give a girl I will give mine and obtain the merit of the virgin gift.

canyáṣulcamu, selling a bride, i.e. demanding money from the bridegroom. Skt., from *canya*, virgin, and *ṣulcam*, tax. *ataḍu bálya vivóhálu canyáṣulcálu cúḍad ani vádistú v'unṭáḍu*, he argues against child-marriage and selling brides. *varaṣulcamu*, bridegroom money, is commoner; the price of graduates in the market is high; girls can only be sold to old men.

canyátvamu, virginity; also *canneri-camu*. Skt.

capaṭamu, deceit. Skt. *capaṭamléni máṭalu*, guileless words; *capaṭam viḍichi nizamu cheputánu vinanḍi*, I will lay aside deceit and tell you the truth.

capálamu, skull. *capála mócshamu*, deliverance through the head; the spirit in a body is supposed to burst out of the head when cremation takes place. Used figuratively it means to break a head. *capála mócsham ayyé-*

ṭaṭṭu burra pagulagoṭṭiná viḍici buddhi lédu, wisdom does not come down upon him though I broke his head.

caphamu, phlegm; a common word with Indian medical men.

capi, ape. Skt., used in books. The common word is *cóti*.

capile, water-lift (large leather bucket, a wheel, and bullocks).

capólamu, cheek. Skt. Used in books for *bugga*; commonly used in the compound. *svacapólacalpitamu*, one's own invention, the term for an original story in Telugu; *teluguló svacapólacalpitam'aina navalalu taccuva,* there are only a few original novels in Telugu.

capótamu, dove. Skt., used in books for *guvva*.

cappa, frog. *cappacu cáṭu bráhmaṇunici póṭu lédu,* frogs don't bite and brahmins don't fight; *cheruvu ninḍité cappalu chérutavi,* the frogs assemble when the tank fills.

cappabaḍuṭa, to be covered; from *cappuṭa* and *paḍuṭa*, *cheppulu toḍuguconnavánici lócam antá tólutó cappabaḍḍaṭṭu tóstundi*, the man who wears shoes thinks the whole earth is covered with leather, i.e. does not feel for the suffering of bare feet on red hot soil.

cappagantuláṭa, ducks and drakes; from *cappa*, frog, *gantulu*, jumps, and *áṭa*, play. *á pillacáyalu cappagantuláṭa áḍut' unnáru,* those boys are playing at ducks and drakes.

cappamu, tribute.

cappa-táḷamu, padlock.

cappi, pulley.

cappiputsuṭa, to hide. *ataḍu tinnagá vádam cheyya léca tana chétacánitanam cappiputsaḍánici cópam tetstsucunnáḍu,* not being able to argue he lost his temper to cover his weakness.

cappu, roof, covering. *paicappu*, *inṭicappu*, roof.

cappuṭa, cappuconuṭa, to cover.

cara, caraca, black. *caraca néla,* black soil; the usual word for black is *nalla*.

caracara, noise of grinding or chewing; onomatopoeic. *mícu caracaral' áḍutú ácali bágá véstú v'unnaṭṭ'unnadi,* from the noise of your chewing you seem to be really hungry.

caradúpamu, soot.

caragagoṭṭuṭa, melt (transitive); from *caraguṭa* and *coṭṭuṭa*. *i tailamu cantulanu caragagoṭṭutsunnadi,* this oil dissolves boils.

carigintsuṭa, to cause to melt.

caraguṭa, to melt (intransitive). *caṭhinamaina manassu núr agnihótrálu daricolpiná carigédi cádu,* 100 fires may blaze without melting a steadfast mind; *anducu váni manassu cariginadi,* his heart melted at that; *itani páṭa anṭé mrügálú, pacshulú santóshistavi, manúshyula manassulu caragaḍánic áşcharyam yémi v'unṭundi!* birds and beasts rejoice at his singing, what wonder that men's hearts melt.

caralághavamu, dexterity. Skt.

caramu, hand. Skt. A word used in books for *cheyyi*.

caramu, much. Sanskrit word used in books for *tsála*.

caraṇamu, village accountant. *úru mída núru paḍḍá caraṇam mída cásu paḍadu,* though the village has to pay a pound the karnam will not have to pay a penny.

caraṇamu, instrument. Skt. *acárya caraṇamu,* instrument of evil.

caratalamu, palm of the hand. Skt.

caratalámalacamugá, easily. Skt. Merely a book word; no one is so audacious as to use a word of that length in conversation; they say *sulabhamugá*, *avalílagá*, or *télicagá*, which are quite long enough.

caratsuṭa, to bite. *carraléni váṇṇi gorre ainá carastundi,* even a sheep will bite a man without a stick; *arachê cucca carava néradu,* a barking dog won't bite. (The Italians have the same proverb, *cane che abbaia non morde*.) *pálu pósi penchiná pámu caravaca mánadu,* feeding a snake with milk won't stop it biting; *cassum'ani cáṭla cuccalágu carava vachchédi,* she used to come at me growling like a dog as if to bite me.

caraválamu, sword. Skt. Used in books; colloquial is *catti*, knife.

caráru, agreement. Hindustani.

carárunáma, agreement in writing. Hindustani.

caráṭamu, small box for pills, rouge,

&c. *nic enni vastuvulu techchinánó! dantapu duvvena vacaṭi, vaca boṭṭu peṭṭe; y'ittaḍi cuncam bariṇe, y'ittaḍi caṭuca carḍṭam,* see what I have brought you, a toothbrush, a caste-mark paste-box, a brass rouge box, a brass eye-blacking box.

carcóṭacamu, cruelty. Skt.

carcóṭacuḍu, a cruel man. Skt. *váḷḷu nálugu dabbula sommu tini y'ainá paróbacaram cheyyaḍam y'eragaru, váḷḷu vaṭṭi carcóṭaculu,* they are cruel men who won't do a favour even when you have bribed them (ethics of bribery).

carmabaddhuḍu, Skt., from *carma,* duty, and *baddha,* bound.

carmabhúmi, pious India, just as the Yankees call the United States God's own country.

carmamu, duty, fate. Skt. A fundamental idea of Hindu religion; a man's *carma* is the fruit of good and evil actions in a previous existence.

carṇamu, ear. Skt. Book word for *chevi,* used chiefly in composition as *carṇacaṭhóramugá,* horrible to the ear.

carṇamu, village accountant; also *caraṇamu.*

carṇícamu, office of village accountant.

carṇótstsavamu, feast for the ear. Skt., from *carṇam,* ear, and *utstsavam,* festival. *carṇótstsavangá áyana páṭa vini,* hearing his singing with delight.

carpúramu, camphor.

carra, stick. *váḍu carran ánuconi y'unnáḍu,* he is leaning on a stick; *carra lénivánini gorre cúḍá carustundi,* even a sheep will bite a man without a stick.

carra, dark stain.

carri, black.

carru, plough-share, a stain. *carru y'erragá cálchi váta vési nippu cálutundó lédó tsúpistánu,* if I heat a plough-share red-hot and brand him we will see whether the fire burns him or not; *ní baṭṭalacu netturu carr enducu vachchinadi?* why are your clothes blood-stained?

-carta, suffix denoting agency. Skt. root, *crü,* to do. *grandhacarta,* author; *dharmacarta,* temple superintendent.

cartavyamu, what must be done. Skt., root *crü,* to do. *mícu cartavyam antá nénu v'upadéṣistánu,* I will explain what you have to do.

cartsu, expense. Hindustani. Also *khartsu. zama-cartsu* is credit and debit. *Yenta cartsu chésiná mícu lacshyam lédu,* you do not care how much you spend.

carucu, sawing noise; onomatopoeic.

caruṇa, mercy. Skt. *caruṇa máli,* devoid of pity.

caruṇintsuṭa, to pity, have mercy. Skt.

carutsuṭa, to bite; also *caratsuṭa.*

caruva, to bite; from *caratsuṭa. á cucca nannu caruva vachchinadi,* that dog came to bite me.

caruvu, famine. *caruvu mánpu panṭa miḍatala mánpu manṭa,* harvest stops scarcity, fire stops locusts; *panḍé panṭa tinḍici tsálaca caruvulu vastavi,* the harvest being insufficient for food famines come.

casaratu, exercise, gymnastics.

casaru, scolding.

casaruconuṭa, to speak sharply.

casaruṭa, to scold.

casavu, grass. *gaḍḍi* is commoner.

casáyi, butcher. Hindustani. *casáyi-vyápáram,* butcher's trade, used also metaphorically.

casbá, principal town in a district. Hindustani.

casháyamu, a decoction, any extract prepared by boiling or evaporation.

casháyi, the colour of holy men's garments—a dirty yellow or yellowish red. Skt. *sanyási casháyi vastramulanu dharintsuconi vachchináḍu,* the hermit came in his yellow robes.

cashṭamu, difficulty, work. Skt. *váni vráta tsaḍuvuṭa cashṭamu,* his writing is difficult to read; *váḍu cashṭamulón unnáḍu,* he is in difficulties. '*cashṭé phalí*' *y'ani n'aṭlu modaṭa ṣrama paḍuváru, venuca sukhamu chenduduru,* 'cashṭé phalí', as the saying goes, those who at first exert themselves will afterwards attain comfort.

cashṭapaḍuṭa, to be in difficulties, in want.

cashṭapaḍuṭa, to work. *bangáru golusulu vídhulaló doracuṭann appuḍu iccaḍa evvarunnú cashṭapaḍan accara lédu,* as gold chains are said to be found about in the streets no one need work (or be in want).

casi, spite. *ná casi tírtsu conṭánu*, I will vent my spite.

castúri, musk. Skt.

castúritilacamu, patch of musk put as a beauty-spot. A famous stanza on Krishna begins *castúritilacam laláṭa phalacé*, which means 'the lovely spot of musk on the forehead'.

caṣum ani, growling; onomatopoeic.

caṭacaṭa! alas!; also contracted to *caṭṭá!*

catamuna, because of. Used chiefly in books, the books will say *aṭṭicatamuna*, while people will say *andu cósam*.

caṭácshamu, favour.

caṭácshintsuṭa, to favour.

catha, story, riddle. *á catha savistaramugá cheppu*, tell that story from end to end.

cathanamu, telling.

caṭhinamu, hard, severe. Skt. *caṭhinahrūdayuḍ'aina*, hard-hearted.

caṭhinatvamu, harshness.

caṭhinuḍu, hard man.

caṭhóramu, severe, terrible. Skt. *carṇacaṭhóramugá*, terrible to the ear.

caṭica, downright. *caṭica chícaṭi*, pitch darkness; *caṭica munḍavḍḍu*, an utter scoundrel; *caṭica daridruḍu*, a very poor man.

caṭicaváḍu, butcher.

-caṭla, affix meaning 'at'. *tellaváru-caṭla*, at dawn; more usually *tellaváru-gaṭla*; *edurucaṭla*, in front.

caṭlapámu, Russell's viper.

caṭnamu, present, especially marriage present.

caṭṭa, bundle, sheaf; from *caṭṭuṭa*, to tie.

caṭṭa, embankment; from *caṭṭuṭa*, to build; more usually *gaṭṭu*.

caṭṭacaḍa, caṭṭacaḍapaṭa, at the very end; from *caḍa*, end, reduplicated.

caṭṭaḍamu, a building; from *caṭṭuṭa*, to build.

caṭṭe, scoundrel. *váḍu siggumálina caṭṭe*, he is a scoundrel lost to shame.

-catte, feminine affix. *panicatte*, maid; *chelicatte*, playmate.

caṭṭelu, firewood.

cattera, scissors; also *catteracóla*.

catti, knife, sword. *vitstsucatti*, drawn sword.

caṭṭintsuṭa, to get built; from *caṭṭuṭa*, to build.

caṭṭipeṭṭuṭa, to stop (transitive); from *caṭṭuṭa*, tie, and *peṭṭuṭa*. *á bedarimpulu anni caṭṭipeṭṭanḍi*, stop all those threats.

cattipiḍi, knife-handle.

cattirintsuṭa, to cut. *váḍu dorala tarahágá tala cattirintsu cunnáḍu*, he has cut his hair like a European; *vatti coḍi cattirintsu*, trim the wick.

caṭṭivéyuṭa, to class; from *caṭṭu*, bond. *mimmalni áḍadáni cinda caṭṭi véstáru*, they will class you as a woman.

caṭṭu, bond, knot, band, bund. *naḍi-caṭṭu*, waistband; *cóla léni peṭṭu, táḍu léni caṭṭu*, striking without a stick, tying without a rope, in fact, moral influence; *chénucu caṭṭu úrici caṭṭu v'unḍa valenu*, a field requires a bund and the village a bond.

caṭṭu, strike. *váru caṭṭu caṭṭináru*, they struck work.

caṭṭu, union. *vaca caṭṭugá*, unanimously.

caṭṭubaḍi, settlement of land tenure, articles of service. *caṭṭubaḍi* peons were feudal retainers who got inams in return for military service; *coḍucunu ná vadda caṭṭubaḍi naucarici v'unchináḍu*, he articled his son to me.

caṭṭubaṭṭalu, the clothes you stand up in; from *caṭṭuconuṭa*, to wear, and *baṭṭalu*, clothes. *caṭṭu baṭṭalató pári póyináḍu*, he ran away with nothing but the clothes on his back. Also *caṭṭuguḍḍalu*.

caṭṭuconuṭa, to wear, put on. *baṭṭa caṭṭuconuṭa*, to put on clothes.

caṭṭuconuṭa, to marry. *caṭṭuconna bhárya*, one's wedded wife; *áru samvatstsaramula pillanu caṭṭuconnánu*, I married a girl of six.

caṭṭuconuṭa, to take upon oneself, e.g., *appulu*, debts, *pápamu*, blame.

caṭṭupaḍuṭa, to be tied down, to be articled; more usually *caṭṭubaḍuṭa*.

caṭṭupáṭu, regulation, bye-law. Used in books to translate 'convention'.

caṭṭuṭa, to tie, harness, connect. *banḍi caṭṭu*, get the carriage ready; *naḍumu* *caṭṭu*, gird your loins; *gáyamu caṭṭu*, dress the wound; *catti caṭṭu*, put on your sword.

caṭṭuṭa, to pay. *pannu caṭṭu*, pay the tax; the ordinary word for to pay or levy taxes.

caṭṭuṭa, to assess, impose. *pannu caṭṭuṭa* means to impose a tax as well as to pay it.

caṭṭuṭa, to strike a total. *ipaddulu verasi caṭṭu*, strike the total of these items.

caṭṭuṭa, to restrain, stop. *dóva caṭṭi*, stopping the road; *caḍupu caṭṭu*, restrain your appetite.

caṭṭuṭa, to build. *ḍḍadi boncité góḍa peṭṭinaṭṭu, mogaváḍu boncité taḍica caṭṭinaṭṭu*, a woman's lies are built up like a wall, a man's like a mat partition. In the example it is easy to see how *caṭṭuṭa*, to tie, passes into *caṭṭuṭa*, to build. *caṭṭinavánici vaca y'illu, caṭṭani vánici veyyinḍlu*, a man who builds a house has one house, a man who does not build has 1,000 houses.

caugalintsuṭa, caugalintsuconuṭa, to embrace. *caugalintsuconi muddu peṭṭuconi*, embracing and kissing.

caugili, chest. *caugiṭa chértsu*, take to the chest, i.e. embrace.

caulu, agreement. Hindustani, especially an agreement with a cultivator to let him have land tax free for a period of years while he is bringing it under cultivation.

cauludáruḍu, a cultivator who holds land under cowle or *emphyteusis*.

caumáramu, bloom. Skt., from *cumára*, young.

cauṣalamu, skill. Skt., from *cuṣalata*, cleverness.

cauzu, partridge; also *camuzu*.

-cava, pair. Used in composition in the form *gava*, as *cannugava*, pair of eyes; *tsannugava*, pair of breasts.

cavachamu, armour.

cavalapillalu, twins; also *amaḍalu, amaḍabiḍḍalu, cavalalu, cavalavánḍlu*.

cavanamu, poetry, composition.

caváṭamu, door. Skt. Used in books for *talupu*.

cavi, poet. Skt. The Sanskrit word means 'a maker' like the English, which is derived from the Greek for 'to do', 'to make'.

cavisina, covered with; in composition *gavisina*. *nivuru gavisina nippu vale*, like fire under ashes, unappreciated talent.

cavitvamu, poetry.

caviyuṭa, to rush upon, fall upon.

cavíṣvaruḍu, prince of poets. Skt., from *cavi* and *iṣvara*, Lord.

cavvamu, churning-staff. *golladi cavvamutó chilucunu*, the shepherd-caste woman churns with a stick.

cazzúrapu cheṭṭu, date tree. This is the Arabian date tree; the Indian date tree, which yields no edible fruit, is *íta*. The Arabian date won't grow in India, it is not hot enough.

cazzúrapu panḍu, date.

-cá, affix forming adverbs. It is the root of *auṭa*, to become; becomes *gá* in composition. *sukhamu*, health; *sukhamugá*, healthily.

cábaṭṭi, therefore; from *cá*, becoming, *paṭṭi*, according to. Also *ganuca*, from the same root *cá*.

cábólu, cábólunu, I suppose; from *cá*, becoming, and *póluṭa*, to seem. *míru tsálá dúrámu nunchi vachchindru cábólunu*, I suppose you have come a long way.

cáca, hot; from *cáguṭa*, to be hot. *vánidi cáca ṣaríramu*, he is of a hot habit of body; *cáca curupulu*, heat boils; *cáca máṭalu*, hot words.

cáca, not being, without, besides; negative participle of *auṭa*, usually lengthened to *cácunḍá*.

cáca, not being able to stand, disliking; negative participle of *auṭa*. *ná mída cáca idi chésináḍu*, he did this because he could not stand me.

-cáca or **-gáca,** affix meaning 'besides'. Also from root *cá*. *idicáca* or *idigáca*, besides that.

-cáca or **-gáca,** affix meaning 'may you be'; optative from root *cá*. *cáca* is added to the second person. *sukhamugá unḍuvugáca*, may you be happy.

cácapóté, if it is not.

cácapóvuṭa, to fail; from *cáca*, negative of *auṭa*, to become, and *póvuṭa*, to go.

cáca yémi? why not?

cáci, crow; onomatopoeic. From the cawing sound, just as the Khond word for cat is *miau*. *cáci pilla cácici muddu*, the young crow is a darling to the crow; *cáci cávu cávum anuts unnadi*, the crow caws.

cácibangáramu, false gold, tinsel.

cácundá, without, besides; from root *cá* and *unduṭa*. *inté cácundá*, besides this.

cácunṭé, if not. *aité adiváramu cácunṭé sómaváramu*, if Sunday won't do Monday will.

cáḍa, at. *inṭicáḍa*, at home.

cáḍa, stalk.

cádá, is it not? *adi manchidi cádá?* is it good or is it not?

cáḍi, yoke; plural *cáṇḍlu, cáḷḷu. nícu y'enni cáḷḷa paṣuvul'unnavi?* how many pairs of cattle have you?

cáḍici, at the rate of. *padi rúpáyala cáḍici*, at the rate of Rs. 10.

cáḍinunchi, since. *modaṭi peḷḷi aina cáḍinunchi*, since his first marriage.

cádó, whether it is not. *idi tappidam aunó cádó micu bágá telusunu*, you know very well whether it is wrong or not.

cádu, no, not; negative 3rd person present of *auṭa*, to become. *álu cádu adi vrálu*, she is not his mate but his fate; in the masculine, *cáḍu ocar'iddarini tsampiténé cáni vaidyuḍu cáḍu*, a doctor is no doctor till he has killed one or two.

cádu, does not agree. *vánicí nácú cádu*, he and I do not get on.

cáḍu, funeral pyre, cemetery. *cáṭici cáḷḷu tsátsuconi*, one foot in the grave.

-cáḍu, affix meaning male person, usually inferior; becomes *gáḍu* in composition and talk. *atagáḍu* from *atanu*, he. *Rámigáḍu* will be a labourer while *Rámayya* will be a farmer; *véshagáḍu*, actor, impostor.

cáfí, coffee. English. *cáfí hoṭélu*, café.

cágaḍá, torch; from *cáguṭa* to be heated. *cunḍaló peṭṭina cágaḍá*, hiding one's light under a bushel.

cágá, by means of. *tamaru cágá idi ságinadi*, this has been accomplished under your auspices.

cágáné, as soon as it is done or becomes; from root *cá*. *rátri cágáné*, as soon as it became night, at nightfall; *penḍli cágáné*, as soon as the marriage was over.

cágitamu, paper. Hindustani, *cágaz*. *á cágitam incutsunnadi*, this is an absorbent paper.

cágu, pot used for boiling.

cáguṭa, to be hot, boil, be angry; *váḍu cági tsallárina pálu*, he has sown his wild oats.

cálacramamugá, periodically. Skt., from *cálam*, time, and *cramam*, order.

cálacshépamu, occupation, pastime, waste of time. Skt., from *cálam*, time, and *cshépam*, scattering. *manam i vrüdhá cálacshépam máni vési mana pani tsútsucunḍámu*, let us stop wasting time and get on with our work. *vidyá vishayica cálacshépamu*, literary pursuits.

cáladharmamu, a phrase for death. Skt., from *cálam*, time, and *dharmam*, duty owed. *cáladharmamun' onduṭa*, to pay the debt of nature.

cálaharaṇamu, waste of time. Skt., from *cálam*, time, and *haraṇa*, lapse. *úrice cálaharaṇam autú v'unnadi*, it is a simple waste of time; *cálamahima*, portent. Skt., from *cálam*, time, and *mahima*, greatness.

cálamu, time, season. Skt. *varshácálamu*, the rains; *sitacálam*, the cold weather; *enḍa cálam*, the hot weather; *eṭlá cálam zarupuconṭ'unnáru?* how do you pass the time? *cálam vrüdhágá gaḍupa vaddu*, time must not be frittered away; *gulábi puvvulu yella cálamú v'unṭavi*, roses are always in season; *vachché cálamu canná vachchina cálamu mélu* (*laudator temporis acti*), old times are the best.

cálamuchéyuṭa, to die.

cálapu, the adjective of *cálam*. *váná-cálapu tsaduvu valla vidya rá néradu*, you can't get an education by studying only in the rains.

cálayápanamu, waste of time. Skt., from *cálam*, time, and *yápanam*, passing. *vrüdhá cálayápanam*, simple waste of time.

cálá! an expletive, bother! damn!; from *cáluṭa*, to be hot. To wish a thing to be cold (*tsallagá*) is a blessing in Telugu, to be hot is a curse. This comes of living in the tropics; similarly *súryuḍu*, sun, is masculine in Telugu, but *Sonne*, the German word, is feminine, because in Germany the sun is weak and mild. *cálá* is used at the end of the phrase, *váni garvamu cálá!* curse his pride!

vádi y'amma caḍupu cálá! may he and his mother's womb perish!
cálárá, cholera. English.
cálávasánamu, death. Skt., from *cálam*, time, and *avasánam*, end.
cáldári, footpath; from *cál*, foot, and *dári*, way. *cáliḍonca* may also be said.
Cáḷi, the goddess *Káḷi*. Skt.
cálibanṭu, foot-soldier; from *cál*, foot, and *banṭu*, soldier.
cálimaḍama, heel.
cálivéḷḷu, toes; from *cál*, foot, and *vélu*, finger or toe.
cáḷí, vacancy. Hindustani; also *khálí*. The Collector's usual answer to applicants for appointments: *khálí lédu*, there is no vacancy.
cáḷḷu, legs, feet; plural of *cálu* or *cál*, leg, foot. *ná cáḷḷu buradaló chiccinavi*, my legs are stuck in the mud.
cálóchitamu, opportune. Skt., from *cálam*, time, and *uchitam*, fit. *manamu cálóchitamugá pó valenu*, we must be opportunists.
cálpintsuṭa, to have something burnt; causal of *cáltsuṭa*.
cálpu, a shot; from *cáltsuṭa*, to shoot.
cáltsuṭa, to burn (transitive), to smoke (a cigar), to fire (a gun). *teḍḍu v'unḍagá cheyyi cáltsu con'aṭṭu*, like burning your hand when you have a ladle (a silly thing to do); *pistólu paṭṭuconi cáltsutáḍ'émo?* will he take a pistol and shoot?
cálu, foot, leg. *cáli coddi*, up to your legs; *caligité cáḷḷu muyyi léca póté mócáḷḷu muyyi*, dress yourself down to your feet if you can afford it, down to your knees if you can't (cut your coat according to your cloth). Mahatma Gandhi can only afford to dress down to his knees. *cálu záruṭa* is to slip, lose one's footing.
cálu, quarter. *cálu taccuva éḍu ganṭalu* is 6.45 hours (quarter less seven). ¾ is *muccálu*.
cálubalamu, infantry; from *cálu*, foot, and *balam*, force.
cáluṭa, be hot, be cursed. *mívanṭi musalivánḍru múḍ'énḍla pillanu penḍli chésuconuts'unḍagá, vayasuló n'unn'appuḍu penḍli chési conaca y'unḍuṭacu stríla grahachâram émi cálinadi*, what a cursed fate is that of women in their prime who can't marry when old men like you marry children of three?
cáluva, channel, canal. *nannu vípu mída vésuconi cáluva dáṭinchináḍu*, he carried me across the canal on his back.
cámamu, lust. Skt. *naḍi vayasuló n'unna bála vidhavalu cáma bádhacu lóbaḍuṭa áscharyamá?* is it surprising if women widowed in their youth and still not past their prime should respond to the goad of their prurient instincts?
cámadhénuvu, the cow of plenty (in heaven). Skt., from *cáma*, desire, and *dhénuvu*, cow. The mythological cow that gives all you want.
cámandu, master. Hindustani. *bhúcámandu* is landowner.
cámágni, fire of lust. Skt., from *cámam*, desire, and *agni*, fire.
cámándhuḍu, blind with lust. Skt., from *cámam*, desire, and *andhuḍu*, blind.
cámerlu or **cámála rógamu,** jaundice.
cámintsuṭa, to desire (carnally). Skt. *nívu nannu cámintsaḍamú, nannu viváham chésucóvaḍamú cûḍá pariyáchicánicé cádu gadá?* was it only a joke that you loved me and wanted to marry me?
cámpu, delivery; from *canuṭa*, to give birth.
cámucuḍu, lover. *cámuculú vrásé v'uttarálu*, love letters; also *praṇayalékhalu*. Used in books.
cámuḍu, the god of love, Cupid. Skt. Also *cáma-dévuḍu*.
-cámuḍu, affix meaning 'desirous'. *círti cámuḍu*, desirous of fame, ambitious (cf. the Virgilian *laudis immensa cupido*).
cána, therefore. The more common form is *ganuca*; also *cávuna, cábaṭṭi*.
cánapaḍuṭa, to appear; also spelt *cánabaḍuṭa*, another form of *canapaḍuṭa*, which is commoner.
cánavatstsuṭa, to appear; *cánuṭa*, to perceive, and *vatstsuṭa*, to come.
cáncsha, wish. Skt.
cáncshintsuṭa, to desire. Skt.
cáncshitamu, desire. Skt. *cáncshitam' aina mélu*, the desired benefit.

cáṇḍru, tiger's roar.

cáni (gáni), though, but. *adi y'antayu mí y'upadéṣamunu baṭṭiyé cáni mari y'ocandu chéta gádu,* this all comes from your teaching and nothing else.

cáni, wrong (adj.); from root *cá* and *ni* the negative suffix (the thing which is not). *muṇḍalu tiṇḍi tini tinnagá v'uṇḍa léca caṇḍa cávaramunacu lóbaḍi cánipanulu chéyuduru,* widows who live on the fat of the land will grow randy and wanton and do wrong things.

cáni (gáni), (adv.) unless. *vasténé cáni,* unless he comes; *ocarini y'iddarini tsampiténé gáni vaiḍyuḍu cáḍu,* a doctor is no doctor till he has killed one or two.

cáni, not before. *répu cáni ráḍu,* he won't come before tomorrow.

cáni, besides. *inté cáni nén émi y'eruganu,* I know nothing more than this.

cáni, ¼ anna, 3 pies, a coin. Also *paisá* in Ganjam, *ḍabbu* in the Godavaries and *boṭṭu* in the Ceded Districts.

cáni, or not. *ayiná cáni,* whether it is or not.

cáni cálamu, one's bad time; from *cáni,* not, and *cálamu,* time. *cáni cálamucu carra pámu autundi,* in your evil hour your stick will become a snake to you.

cáni-cáni (gáni-gáni), either, or. *adi gáni, y'idi gáni,* either this or that.

cáni panulu, wrong acts; from *cáni,* not, and *pani,* act.

cánitanamu, enmity; from *cáni,* not; not being able to stand a person.

cání, let it be done, go ahead; from root *cá,* become, and *í,* the imperative of *itstsuṭa,* to give, allow. *dáni máṭa taruváta tsútsucundámu gáni mundugá manamu vachçhinapani cán' iyyanḍi,* we will see to that later, meanwhile let us get on with the work in hand; *dpani mundara cání,* let that work be done first.

cántá, fair one, fair lady. Skt., meaning 'a shining one'. A word for woman used in books, especially in addressing a lady. *ó cántá!* fair lady!

cánti, light, lustre, complexion. *enḍaló déha cánti cheḍunu,* exposure to the sun spoils the complexion; *nindá cántigala vajram,* a diamond of the finest water.

cántsuṭa, to bring forth; from *canuṭa,* which is commoner.

cánuca, present, especially one made to a superior and touched and remitted; from root *canu,* to see. It is a present which the superior casts his glance over.

cánupu, bringing forth, bearing; also *cámpu.*

cánuṭa, to see, foresee; another form of *canuṭa. ṣila bhógam, sthala bhógam, nara bhógam cána rávu,* the luck of a stone, of a place, of a man, cannot be foreseen (one may become a god's image, the other the site of a palace, the third a king).

cápari, watcher, herd; from *cátsuṭa,* to tend. *pandula cápari,* swineherd; also *cáparivádu* or *cápalávádu.*

cápaṭyamu, deceitfulness. Skt.; *capaṭamu* is commoner. *lócamlóni cápaṭyamu antayu múrtibhavinchi áyana rúpamuna avatarinchinadi,* an incarnation of all deceit.

cápáḍuṭa, cápáḍuconuṭa, to guard, to save. *véla coladi janula práṇamula cápáḍenu,* he saved lives by the thousand.

cápu, man of the chief cultivating caste and in general a peasant proprietor. The head-ryot in the village is often spoken of as *pedda-cápu.*

cápu, guarding. *canḍlacu reppalu cápugá v'unnavi,* the eye-lids guard the eyes.

cápuramu, residence, domicile, the husband's house. *í chinna pillal'edigi cápuramunacu ráru,* these small children will not grow up to live with their husbands; *á pilla y'incá maganitó cápuramu cheyya lédu,* that girl is not living with her husband yet.

cápurasthuḍu, inhabitant. The usual word in petitions, A. B, *cápurasthuḍu,* inhabitant, of village C, in Taluk D, prays. . . .

cápurasthurálu, female inhabitant.

-cáracamaina, suffix meaning 'causing'. Skt. Used in books. *duhkhacáracamaina,* causing grief.

cáracuḍu, cáraculu, causer, author. Skt. *dáni duravasthac'antacunu crüsh-*

ṇa ṣástri cáracuḍu, Krishna Shastri is the author of all her ills; *í calahamunacu cáracuḍavu nívu*, you are at the bottom of this quarrel; *á panic'antá nívé cáracurálavu*, you are at the bottom of it all.

cárágrühamu, prison. Skt.; also *cheraṣála* and *bandikháná*, but the English *jailu* is commoner than any of these words.

-cáramu, affix denoting making or doing. *zumcáramu*, humming.

cáramu, pungency.

cáraṇamu, cause. Skt. *cáraṇamu léca cáryamu puṭṭadu*, no effect without a cause.

cárchitstsu, forest fire.

cáremu, the hollowed palm which is the chief component part of a picottah or water-lift.

-cári, suffix meaning 'causing'. Skt. *dóshacári*, sinful; *árógyacári*, wholesome (health-giving).

cárizamu, liver.

cárkháná, factory, workshop. Hindustani.

cárpaṇyamu, spite. Skt.

cárticamu, the 8th month, about November. Skt. Also *cárticamu*.

cártsuṭa, to make to flow, as tears; causal of *cáruṭa*. *canníru cárchi*, letting eye-drops flow.

cáru, tongs; also *paṭacáru*. *sutte mundá cáru mundá?* which came first, hammer or tongs?

cáru, brackish, saline. *cáru níḷḷu*, brackish water; *cáru néla*, saline soil.

cáru, black, withered. *cár'ácu*, a withered leaf.

cáru, not; 3rd person plural, root *cá*. *váru vachchináru cáru*, they have not come = *váru rálédu*.

cárucálamu, harvest time.

cárucútalu, abuse. *pedda manushyula vishayamai y'iṭuvanṭi cárucútalu cúyacu*, do not use such language about respectable people.

cáruṭa, to flow. *cannula nunḍi níru cárinadi*, tears flowed from his eyes; *pípá cárutsunnadi*, the cask leaks, but 'the roof leaks' is *curiyutsunnadi*, from *curiyuṭa*, to rain.

cáruvásana, strong smell, often bad, as the smell of tar.

cáryacarta, agent, assign. Skt., a legal term.

cáryacramamulu, programme, proceedings. Skt., a legal term.

cáryadarṣuḍu, cáryadarṣi, secretary. Skt. Secretary of a society, &c. Used chiefly in newspapers; *secriṭari* would be used in speaking. *gaurava cáryadarṣi*, honorary secretary.

cáryamu, act, use, effect, anything which is done or ought to be done, business, success in business. Skt. *cáraṇamu léca cáryamu puṭṭadu*, no cause no effect; *Jánacini nindinchina cáryamu lédu*, it is no use blaming Janaci; *cáryácáryamulu teliyaca*, not knowing right from wrong; *nácu jayam calugutund' ani mícu nammacam v'unṭé cáryam ain' aṭṭe*, your confidence is equivalent to success.

cáryanirváhacuḍu, manager. Skt., from *cáryam*, business, and *nirváhamu*, management. *Cácinḍḍaló pedda médaló peṭṭina campenici míru cáryanirváhaculugá v'unḍa lédá?* are you not employed as manager of a company in a big building at Cocanada?

cáryaniyuctuḍu, person appointed, assign. Skt., from *cáryam*, business, and *niyuctam*, appointed. A legal term.

cáryasiddhi, success. Skt., from *cáryam*, affair, and *siddhi*, success.

cáryasthánamu, place of business. Skt., from *cáryam*, business, and *sthánam*, place.

cásamu, cough. Skt. The Telugu is *daggu*.

cásáramu, lake. Skt. Used in books.

cásepani, mason's work, brick-laying.

cásevádu, mason, bricklayer.

cáshṭhamu, funeral pyre. Skt. word for wood.

Cáṣi, Benares. Skt. *tana muḍḍi cáca póté Cáṣi dácá décam annáḍu*, he advised sliding to Benares on your hams, so long as it wasn't his own hams.

cáṣícóca, a strong girdle of narrow cloth made of muslin.

Cáṣmíramu, the Land of Cashmere.

cássépu, a little time; from *cásta*, little, and *sépu*, time. Also *contasépu*. *cássépu v'úrucó*, be quiet for a minute. *contasépu* would be a longer period.

cásta, cástalési, little.

cásu, a coin, especially the smallest, a pie; and the biggest, a gold sovereign. *úri mida núru paḍḍá caraṇamu mida cásu paḍadu,* if the village pays 100 rupees the *carṇam* won't pay even one pie of it; *dási coḍuc ainá cásu galaváḍu ráju,* though he be a slave-girl's son, the man with coin is king; *ná tsandugá peṭṭiló múḍu vandala cásul unnavi,* I have 300 sovereigns in my trunk; *cásula péru* is a necklace of gold coins; so is *cásula daṇḍa.*

cáṭacamu, famine; also *caruvu.*

cátá, ledger. Hindustani.

cáṭá, large scales; the large scales in the treasury are *cáṭá,* the small ones *trásu.*

cáṭhinyamu, severity. Skt., from *caṭhinam,* severe.

cáṭlacucca, biting dog; from *cáṭu,* bite, and *cucca,* dog. *cáṭlacucca lágu mana mida paḍutáḍu,* he attacks us like a mad dog.

cátsuconuṭa, to wait. *ná coracu cátsuconnáḍu,* he was waiting for me.

cátsuṭa, to boil (transitive).

cátsuṭa, to bear fruit. *cheṭṭu viraga cáchinadi,* the tree is in full bearing.

cátsuṭa, to shine. *aḍavi cáchina vennela,* moonlight in the jungle (wasted energy).

cátsuṭa, to watch. *jítamú batyamú lécunḍá tóḍélu mécalu cástán'annaṭṭu,* like the wolf offering to watch the goats without pay or perquisite.

cáṭu, bite. *cappacu cáṭu bráhmaṇunici póṭu lédu,* the frog has no bite, the brahmin no fight; *cáṭlacucca,* a fierce dog.

cáṭuca, lamp-black used for adornment of eyes by darkening around them. *cáṭuca cardáṭam* or *cáṭucabariṇe* is the little box a woman keeps her lamp-black in. Only the lamp-black of castor oil is used for such a purpose; kerosene is never used.

cávaḍi, the shoulder-yoke; also *cáviḍi.*

cávaḍibadda, the stick of the *cávaḍi* or shoulder-yoke for carrying 2 pots; from *cávaḍi* and *badda,* piece of thin wood.

cávalasina, what is wanted, necessary; from root *cá* and past participle of *valayuṭa,* the ordinary word for 'necessary'. There are also various Sanskrit words, *avasaram, agatyam,* &c., which will be found in English-Telugu dictionaries, while *cávalasina,* the ordinary word, is not given at all.

cávalasinanta, as far or as much as necessary.

cávalenu, it is wanted; from root *cá* and *valenu* for *valayunu* from *valayuṭa.* It is used with the dative: *nácu cávalenu,* I want; *nícu cávalenu* or *cáváli,* you want. In speaking it is usually shortened further to *cavála,* or *caváli.* Perhaps the commonest word in the language. Tamil, *vönḍum.* Although about the commonest word in the language it will not be found in the dictionaries.

cávalenu, belongs to, is related to. *Rámáyaṇam antá vini, Rámuḍici Síta yémi cá valenu ani aḍigín aṭṭu,* like asking what relation Sita was to Rama after hearing the whole of the Ramayana.

cávali, watch, custody; from *cátsuṭa,* to watch. *velupala pólisuvárini cávali peṭṭi vachchinámu,* we placed a watch of police outside before we came.

cávalilónuntsuṭa, place in custody; from *cávali,* guard, and *untsuṭa,* to place.

cávalisté, if necessary. This very common word will not be found in the dictionaries.

cávaramu, flesh, pride of flesh. Skt. Used in books in conjunction with *canḍa,* flesh. *canḍacávaramu,* concupiscence; *vayasu cávaramu,* the vigour of youth.

cávatstsunu, it may be, perhaps; root *cá* and *vatstsuṭa,* to come, often shortened to *cávatstsu.* One of the commonest words in the language; will not be found in the dictionaries.

cávála, cáváli, it is wanted; short for *cávalenu.*

Cávéri, the river Caveri in the south; also a feminine name.

cávéshamu, spite. Skt., also *cávéshi.*

cávi, a colour, russet or tawny.

cáviḍi, shoulder-yoke with 2 pots. Also *cávaḍi. calimi lémulu cávaṭi cunḍalu,* ups and downs are like the two pots of the yoke (i.e., they alternate); *canchi-*

cávaḍi, mendicants borne by men in a yoke. It was a custom with village schoolmasters to order a *canchi-cávaḍi* of defiant children refusing to attend school; the child will be made to lie down flat and will be carried by lifting up his limbs. It is rarely practised now, but its terrors still survive. Also *ganji-cávaḍi*.

cávintsuṭa, to do; causal from root *cá*. A word which the newspapers use to avoid writing anything so common as *chéyuṭa*.

cávu, cawing; onomatopoeic, pronounced *cáu*.

cávuna, therefore. *ganuca* and *cábaṭṭi* are commoner; they are all from *cá*, the root of *auṭa*, to become.

cávyamu, poetry. Skt., from *cavi*, poet.

cáya, green fruit, berry, nut, anything round. A fruit is either *panḍu*, such as an orange or ripe plantain, or a *cáya*, such as an unripe plantain, a coconut, or an onion (*ullicáya*).

-cáya, affix, adding nothing to the meaning. *talacáya*, head; *pillacáya*, child; *chempacáya*, slap; *gontuccáya*, throat.

cáyacátsuṭa, to harden (one's hands with work). *váḍi chétulu cáyalu cáchinavi*, he is a horny-handed son of toil.

cáyamu, body. Skt. Used chiefly in composition. *cáyapushṭi*, full habit of body; *cáyaclésamu*, asceticism.

cáyamu, tonic (usually administered to a woman in child-bed). *cáyamu-peṭṭi, lancaṇamulu caṭṭi*, giving a tonic and prescribing a fast.

cáyamu, permanent. Hindustani. *kháyamu* is commoner.

cáyasthuḍu, a man belonging to the writer's caste. Skt. The writer's caste, still called Cayastha in Bengal, corresponds to the karnams in Madras, who are, however, of different castes, usually brahmins in the Telugu country and Pillais in the Tamil.

cáyilágá, ill. Hindustani. *cáyilá*, illness. The commonest word for ill; the dictionaries do not give it at all.

cáyuṭa, to shine. *enḍa cástunnadi*, the sun shines.

cáyuṭa, tend. *toḍélini gorrela cáya peṭṭinaṭṭu*, like putting a wolf to tend sheep.

cem- or **cen-,** prefix meaning red. *cem-móvi*, rosy lip; *cen-dámara*, red lotus (amaranth); *cen-dúḷi*, red dust—all used in books.

cempu, ruby; from root *cen*, red.

cendámara, amaranth; from *cen*, red, and *támara*, lotus.

cenzáya, red complexion; from *cen*, red, and *cháya*, colour.

céca, cry, of human and animal cries; any loud and shrill cry, e.g. the peacock's. But the lion's roaring is *garjintsutsunnadi*, the wolf's howling is *cúyutsunnadi*, the dog's bark is *morugutsunnadi*, the horse's neighing is *sacilintsutsunnadi*. *cécalató inṭi mída nálugu penculu y'egiri póyinavi*, tiles flew off the roof with the noise they made; *cécalu véyuṭa*, to shout, scream; '*dongalu dongal' ani vidhiló cécalu véstánu*, I will shout 'thieves, thieves!'; *evaró nannu vidhi gummamuló cécalu véyutsunnáru*, someone is shouting to me from the street door.

célu, hand; literary for *cheyyi*.

céndra, central. Skt. Used in the newspapers in such expressions as *céndra prabhutvamu*, central government; *céndra ráshṭramulu*, Central Provinces.

cépumári, a rogue, a swindler. Tamil. *cépumári sámájacamu*, a fraternity of swindlers.

céraḷamu, the country called Malabar or *Malayáḷam* on the West Coast, including Travancore and Cochin.

céṣamulu, hair. Skt. Used in books for *venṭrucalu*.

césaramu, lion's mane; a filament. Skt.

cési, towards. *áme cési tsútsutsu*, looking towards her.

cétanamu, flag. Skt.

cétuvu, a mythological dragon, a flag. *dhúma cétuvu*, a comet, 'being smoke-tailed', i.e. having a trail of smoke.

cévalamu, simple, mere, altogether. Skt. *cévala máya*, simple illusion.

cévu, freight. Hindustani.

-ci, affix forming the dative; also *-cu*.

ciccirisi, crowded; also *criccirisi*.

cichchili cheṭṭu, orange-tree.

cichchili panḍu, orange. More commonly *nárinja panḍu*.

cifáyatu, profit. Hindustani. *nícu tsálá cifáyatu chéyistánu,* I will get you a big profit.

cilacila, sound of laughing, twittering, &c.; onomatopoeic. *cila-cila navvuṭa,* to laugh aloud.

cim, what. Skt. *cim anṭé cam ana léḍu,* he can't say boo to a goose.

cimmatu, price, value. Hindustani. *núru rúpáyila cimmatu chésé peraḍu,* a house-site worth Rs. 100.

cincaruḍu, slave. Skt. *yama cincarulü,* the emissaries of death.

cinda, under; also *crinḍa. atani chéti cinda,* in his power; *á cartsu cinda paḍi rúpáyilu vrásináḍu,* he wrote Rs. 10 under that expense.

cinda, below, on the ground. *cinda parunḍuṭa,* to lie on the ground.

cindaṭa, ago. *nela cindaṭa,* a month ago.

cindaṭi, last. *cindaṭi nela,* last month.

cindi, downward, following (adjective). *cindi tsúpu,* a downward look; *cindi prasna,* the following question.

cîndici, downward; also *crindacu. cindici póyináru,* they went downward.

cinnera, lute. *canṭham cévalamu cinnera svaramu,* his voice is really lute-like.

cintsa, chagrin. *manassuló cintsa paḍḍánu,* I felt chagrin.

cipáyatu, cipháyatu, profit. Hindustani. Same as *cifáyatu.*

ciraṇamu, ray. Skt. *súrya ciraṇamula véḍimi chéta samudramulónú, nadulalónú, maḍugulalónú, v'unḍé níru áviri rúpanga paici léchi, vaca tsóṭa cúḍuconi, paini gáliló méghamgá y'érpaḍunu,* the water in the sea, rivers, and lakes is heated by the sun's rays, goes up as steam, gathers together and forms clouds in the upper air.

Cirastáni, Ciristánu, Christian, English.

ciráta, cruel, wild.

cirátuḍu, a cruel man, a wild man of the forest. Skt. *ciráta crütyamulu,* cruel deeds; *dora vaṭṭi cirátuḍu,* the Collector is a very cruel man.

ciríṭamu, crown. Skt.

cirósin, the oil which is called kerosene in India and paraffin in England and petroleum everywhere else.

cirru-cirru, creaking; onomatopoeic. *ná cheppulu cirrucirrum'anutsunnavi,* my shoes are creaking.

cirrupurugu, cicada.

cistí, instalment of land revenue. Hindustani. These instalments are 3 to 4 in number, payable by the 10th of the months January to April or February to April after the harvest.

cistíbandí, list of instalments of the *kistí.* Hindustani.

citábu, title. Hindustani. The Telugu is *birudu.*

ciṭicí, window.

citsacitsa, squeaking, chirping noise made by person tickled; onomatopoeic. *citsacisalááḍuṭa* is used of a mouse, sparrow, monkey, and *citsacitsapeṭṭuṭa* is to tickle.

ciṭṭuṭa, to get on with. *ciṭṭanivár evaró,* some enemy. Also *giṭṭuṭa.*

cí-, prefix meaning under; from *cinda.*

cíḍu, evil. *cíḍ'enchi mél entsa valenu,* consider both sides of a question; *iṭuvanṭi dushcáryálaló pravéṣisté y'i cíḍu múḍacunḍá v'úrice pótunḍá yémiṭi?* if you get into such bad ways do you think you will get off without some misfortune?

cíḍu-méḷḷu, both sides of a question.

cíganti tsúpu, downcast looks, ogle.

cílu, a joint (of a thing of the body). *Pantulugárici cíḷḷ'anni noppulugá v'unnavi,* Mr. Pantulu has pains in all his joints.

cílubomma, puppet.

cílucatti, claspknife.

cílutsápa, tarpaulin. This is not from *cílu,* joint, but from *cílu,* a mixture of tar, &c., used for caulking boats.

cíníḍa, under-darkness, i.e., shade under a lamp, &c.; from *cinda,* below, and *níḍa,* shade. *ci* becomes lengthened to *cí*; also in *cíganṭi tsúpu,* downcast look.

círtana, hymn (song to the glory of God). Skt. *váḷḷu páḍé bútucútala canté haricírtanalu páḍisté bágá v'unḍada?* would it not be better if they sang hymns and canticles instead of bawdy songs?

círti, fame. Skt.

cíṭamu, worm; also *ciṭacamu.* Skt. In speaking you say *purugu*; this is used in books, especially figuratively, *manushya ciṭamulu,* we worms.

clésamu, affliction. Skt. One of the numerous words for grief of which *duhkhamu* is the most common. *cáya clésamu* is mortification of the body, asceticism.

clüptamu, contracted, abbreviated. Skt. *manam'ikha appu chéyaca clüptangá váḍucundámu,* in future we won't make debts but practise thrift.

cobbaricáya, coconut. *cótici cobbaricáya doricinaṭṭu,* a monkey with a coconut (no use to him but he won't give it up, dog in the manger); *cobbaricáya coṭṭa vaddu,* don't open the coconut.

cobbarichettu, coconut palm.

coccemu, buckle, hook.

coccu, bandicoot (big rat); also *pandicoccu* (*pandi,* pig), from which bandicoot is derived. *gáde cindi pandicoccu,* the bandicoot inhabiting a granary (a term of abuse applied to a parasite); *gáde cinda pandi-coccu láguna vár inṭló tega tini pogaru baṭṭi v'unnávu,* you have fed upon him and have grown impudent.

codava, the remainder, deficiency.

coḍavali, scythe, sickle. *chénú coḍavalí ní chétici y'ichchinánu,* I have given field and sickle (i.e., full title).

-coddi, affix meaning as much as, up to; also *coladi,* from *colutsuṭa,* to measure. *micu tóchina coddi,* as much as you think proper; *váni balamu coddí chesináḍu,* he did it as well as he could.

coddi, a few, a little. *coddi dinálacu,* in a few days; *váḍu coddiló antá tanḍri pólica,* he is just his father in miniature.

coddigá, slightly.

coddimandi, a few people.

coḍi, tip. *vatti coḍi cattirintsu,* snuff the candle.

coḍucu, son; the Telugu word. Sanskrit *cumáruḍu* is also common. *penḍli coḍucu* is a bridegroom; *álú lédu tsúlú lédu coḍucu péru Sómalingam,* counting your chickens before they are hatched; *oca cannu cannú cádu, vaca coḍucu coḍucú cádu,* eyes and sons should be in pairs; *váni coḍucunu ná vadda caṭṭubaḍi naucarici v'unchináḍu,* he articled his son to me.

cojjá, eunuch. Hindustani.

cola, measure.

colacarra, measuring rod.

coladi (ni), according to. *nénu tondara paḍina coladini,* in proportion to my haste.

colanu, lake; also *maḍugu, sarassu.*

colata, measurement.

colatavéyuṭa, to survey.

colici, loop. *cannu colici,* corner of the eye.

colimi, forge.

colimititti, forge bellows.

colipintsuṭa, to get measured; causal from *colutsuṭa.*

colla, pillage.

collaconuṭa, collacoṭṭuṭa, collapeṭṭuṭa, to plunder.

collapóvuṭa, to be plundered.

collari, bandit.

collu, plunder.

coluputa, to egg on, more usual in the compound *usicolputa. cuccalanu usicolipináru,* they set the dogs on.

colutsuṭa, to measure.

colutsuṭa, to serve. The noun is *coluvu.*

coluvu, service.

coluvuṣála, Durbar Hall.

coluvuṭa, to serve, especially God. *dévuṇṇi coluvacunḍá,* without serving God.

comma, branch. *mudi comma vangadu,* the old branch will not bend; *commanu téne tuṭṭe paṭṭinadi,* the bees swarmed on a branch. *paṭṭucomma* is used figuratively for a handle, something to take hold of.

commu, horn; also a musical horn. *pedda cécalu vési, commulu v'údi, ḍappulu váyinchi,* shouting loud, sounding horns, beating drums.

commuváḍu, trumpeter (a horn blower).

compa, our (their) miserable house (fortune). *lécapóté váḷḷu compa tísivéstunu,* otherwise I should have ruined them; *adi telisi v'unn' aṭṭ aité y'idi varacé ná compa munigédi,* if this had been known, I should have been ruined already; *compa gunḍam vésucu póyinadi,* the family is ruined; *compa cáltú v'unṭé nuyyi tavvin'aṭṭu,* digging a well when the house is on fire (unavailing exertion in distress).

cona, end, tip, top. *conachevi,* tip of

the ear; *tsanțicona*, nipple; *chețțucona*, top of tree; *pustacamuló cágitamula conalanu managa n'iyya vaddu*, do not dog's-ear the book.

conaconuța, to try.

concanacca, a small fox, an awkward figure.

concaravancara, twisted and twirled. *concaravancara-máța*, an awkward word.

conchemu, a little. *nénu conchem aité padé vádané*, I nearly fell.

conchemuconchemugá, little by little.

conḍa, hill. *conḍa tavvi yelucanu paṭṭi n'aṭṭu*, digging up a hill to catch a mouse; *dúrapu conḍalu nunupu*, distance lends enchantment to the view; *conḍ'anta áṣa*, great desire; *conḍanta chicaṭi*, mountainous darkness.

conḍachiluva, hill python.

conḍachíma, hill ant.

conḍa - mutstsu, the lion - tailed monkey; also an ugly person. *váḍu conḍa-mutstsu láguna v'unnáḍu*, he is like an ape.

conḍanáluca, uvula. *conḍanálucacu mandu vésté, unna náluca úḍi póyin aṭṭu*, like loosening your tongue to apply medicine to your uvula (the remedy worse than the disease).

condaru, a few people; contracted from *contavấru*, but always used in the contracted form.

conḍáḍuṭa, to praise; also *coniyáḍuṭa*.

conḍemulu, slanders.

conḍetanamu, back-biting.

conḍi, sting. *duradagonḍi*, stinging nettle; *télu conḍi*, scorpion's sting.

conéváḍu, customer; from *conuṭa*, to buy.

conga, heron and similar birds. *púconga* is a flamingo and *colléṭiconga* a pelican.

congu, end of cloth, used to tie up money, &c. *angóstramu conguna*, at the end of the upper cloth; *ná boḍḍu congu rúpáyalu*, the rupees in the knot of my cloth over my navel.

conipóvuṭa, to carry away; the full expression, *tísi coni póvuṭa*, is common.

coniyáḍuṭa, to praise.

connáḷḷu, a few days; from *coni* and *náḍu*, day. *chícaṭi connáḷḷu, vennela connáḷḷu*, moonlit and dark days (i.e. joy and sorrow) succeed one another.

conni, some (plural).

conta, some (singular). *contavaḍici, conta cálamunacu, conta sépaṭici, conta sépu*, for some time.

contamaṭṭucu, to some extent.

conṭe, mischievous, naughty. *i gurramu daggira conni conṭe chéshṭalu v'unnavi*, this horse has some bad tricks.

conṭe bommalu, obscene sculptures.

conṭe chéshṭalu, lewd tricks.

conṭecunca, lewd fellow.

conṭe-padigaṭṭu, a mischievous rogue.

conṭetanamu, naughtiness, mischief. *induló yédó conṭetanam unnadi, ná jágrata mída nénu v'unṭánu*, there is some mischief behind this, I will be on my guard.

conṭe-vrátalu, obscene writings.

conubaḍi, cost price. *nácu conubaḍi mída vanda rúpáyalu nashṭam vachchinadi*, I sustained a loss of Rs. 100 on the cost price.

conucconuṭa, to buy (for oneself). *váḍu tanacu paici baṭṭa léca póyiná saré gáni pustacamulu conucconṭé tsálun anuconnáḍu*, he denied himself clothes to buy books (contrast the length and clumsiness of the Telugu phrase with the brevity of the English).

conuṭa, to buy. *amma bóté aḍavi cona bóté coravi*, when he went to sell it was jungle, when he went to buy it was a firebrand (loss both ways; in proverbial expressions Telugu instead of being clumsy is pithy).

conuṭa, to take, to get; changes to *gonuṭa* in speech and in books. *ácali gonuṭa*, to be hungry; *daya gonuṭa*, to feel pity; *prabhuvu váru, má y'andu daya gona valenu*, your Honour, please show a little mercy.

-conuṭa, auxiliary verb forming the middle tense. *illu caṭṭináru*, they built a house; *illu caṭṭuconnáru*, they built a house for themselves. But this distinction is not always made and *-conuṭa* is often added to a verb as a matter of course, without altering the meaning. Thus *tísuconirá* (usually abbreviated to *tíscrá*) is 'bring' and more often 'bring for me' than 'bring for yourself'; the auxiliaries *véyuṭa* and *conuṭa* are both used in this way without adding anything to the meaning.

Thus you do not say *ápu*, stop, but *ápei* (*ápi-véyumu*) or even *ápései* (*ápi-vési-véyumu*). You do not usually say *conu*, buy, but *conuccó*. You do not say *peṭṭu*, put, but *peṭṭucó*. You do not say *paṭṭi*, having caught, but *paṭṭuconi*. *tetstsuconuṭa* is 'to get for oneself'; *váḍu práṇamula mídacu tetsuconnáḍu*, he endangered his own life; *váḍu ṭicálu véyintsu connáḍu*, he got himself vaccinated.

coṇuzu, a tick.

coṇuzu-chíma, a kind of anṭ that stings sharply.

copparamu, the hump of an ox.

coppu, female top-knot. *coppu mídanu rommu mídanu buccá pósi rudduṭa*, to rub powder on one's top-knot and back; *caḍupu cúṭici y'éḍisté coppu púlacu y'éḍchin' aṭṭu*, the hair cried for flowers when the belly cried for food (it is usual for women to put flowers in their hair when they dress up); *coppu paṭṭuconi pícináḍu*, he caught her by the topknot and pulled (the topknot is a convenient article to catch hold of in a quarrel; men also catch hold of one another's *zuṭṭu*, tuft).

cora, what remains, balance. *coray' úpiri*, the last breath.

cora-cantsu, a firebrand. *vaṭṭi cora cantsu nippatstsarápu mundácoḍucu*, the beast of a scoundrel, a cut-throat villain.

coracatstsu, firebrand. Same as *cora-cantsu*.

cora cora, anger, hate; onomatopoeic. *dánici y'eppuḍú cora cora*, she is always peevish.

coracoraláḍuṭa, sound of anger, gnashing teeth; onomatopoeic.

-coracu, affix meaning 'for', same as *cósamu*. *Lacshmi coracu y'eduru tsútsuts'unnánu*, I am expecting Lakshmi; *cóṭi vidyalú cúṭi coracé*, all arts are for getting your food; *Ándhrulu pratyéca ráshṭramu coracu prayatnam chéstunnáru*, the Andhras are trying to get a separate province.

coraḍá, whip. *camchí* is the commonest word for whip, but *coraḍá* is also common. *ninnu gurrapu coraḍátó vípu baddalu coṭṭutánu*, I will horsewhip you.

coraḍupóvuṭa, to be benumbed, to become callous; also *coraḍubári-póvuṭa*. *váḍu durnadata y'andu coraḍubári póyináḍu*, steeped in villainy he has grown callous.

coragámi, fruitlessness, unbecoming conduct. Used in books. *ná y'eduṭa nannu tsúchi navvuṭa vaṭṭi coragámi*, it is sheer impertinence to laugh at me.

coramálina, worthless.

coramánu, (*briedalia spinosa*), a large tree.

coramuṭlu, tools. *panimuṭlu* is commoner.

corapani coyya, a worthless wretch, a villain.

corapóvuṭa, to be choked, to swoon.

corata, defect, remainder, unfinished.

Coravalu, the Coravas, a tribe of hillmen.

coravanji, gipsy dance.

coravi, firebrand; also *corivi*. *váḍu compalu cálché corivi*, he is a disturber of domestic tranquillity; *ill ecci corivi tippin' aṭṭu*, like getting on the house (a thatched one) and waving a firebrand about (smoking in a powder magazine); *ammabóté áḍavi, conabóté coravi*, a wilderness when he sold, a firebrand when he bought.

corná or **cornási ganḍu,** the hyaena.

corralu, the Italian millet (*panicum italicum*).

corru, hook, spike, thorn.

corrupaṭṭina, torn. *í baṭṭa renḍu nelala cindaṭané corrupaṭṭiná, y'í cásta chinugú cuṭṭucón ainá cuṭṭucó lédu*, though this cloth has been torn for the last 2 months, I have not mended the small tear.

corucu, a venereal disease, syphilis.

corucuṭa, to gnash. *yémayyá álá paḷlu corici véstú v'unnávu? nannu coḍatává yémiṭi?* what sir, gnashing your teeth? are you thinking of assaulting me?

cotta, new, fresh. *cotta vintá, páta róta*, fresh news is rare to the ears, stale news excites disgust; *mangali páta, tsácali cotta*, stick to the old barber, choose a new washerman; *chépala ducánam mída 'cotta chépalu iccaḍa ammutáru' ani bórḍu caṭṭiri*, they placed a board over a fish-shop with the legend 'fresh fish are sold here'.

coṭṭamu, shed.

cottaníru, floods (new water).
cottaricamu, novelty, shortly after. *ní alluḍu póyina cottaricamuló*, shortly after your son-in-law died; *chérina cottaricamu*, shortly after arrival.
cottimíra, cottimiri, coriander grass used as a spice seasoning a dish made of vegetables; some call it *cottamalli*, from *cotta*, new, and *malli*, jasmine.
coṭṭintsuṭa, have (a person or thing) beaten; causative from *coṭṭuṭa*.
coṭṭivéyuṭa, strike off, e.g. to strike a case off the file or dismiss a petition; *nén anna máṭa coṭṭivéyacu*, don't disregard my advice.
coṭṭu, storehouse.
coṭṭu, cell, jail. *coṭló peṭṭuṭa*, put in jail.
coṭṭuconipóvuṭa, be carried away, drift.
coṭṭuconiveḷḷuṭa, to carry away, as a stream carries away a man.
coṭṭuconuṭa, to beat oneself, feel anxious, lament. *yémí teliyaca coṭṭuconutsunnánu*, I am perplexed.
coṭṭuṭa, to strike; also used as an auxiliary verb. Changes to *goṭṭuṭa* and *coḍuṭa* in composition and talk. *chinna pámun' ainá pedda carrató coṭṭa valenu*, even a small snake should be struck with a big stick; *í níru campu coṭṭutsunnadi*, this water stinks; *idi castúri vásana coṭṭutsunnadi*, this smells of musk; *ḍérá coṭṭuṭa*, to pitch a tent; *saicilu coṭṭu*, pump the bicycle; *atstsu coṭṭuṭa*, to print; *dongalu coṭṭinároo*, thieves robbed me; *úḍagoṭṭuṭa*, to loosen; *cheḍagoṭṭuṭa*, to spoil; *télagoṭṭuṭa*, to set afloat; *digagoṭṭuṭa*, to drive in; *íta coṭṭuṭa*, to swim; *pagalagoṭṭuṭa*, to break; *pógoṭṭuṭa*, to lose.
cotválu, police-officer. Hindustani; the old word. English words are now used.
covvu, fat, insolence.
covvuṭa, to grow fat, insolent. *peṭṭela ninḍá dhanam múlugutú covvi v'unnáru*, their boxes got filled with money and their bodies with pride.
coyya, wood (noun and adjective). *coyyacálu*, a wooden leg; *coyya pinuga*, no man but a block of wood devoid of pity.
-có, imperative affix from the auxiliary, *conuṭa*, short for *conumu*. *tísicó* is take; *músicó*, shut; *cheppucó*, guess and find out if you can.
cóca, woman's cloth. *caṭṭu cócató vachchinadi*, she came in the clothes she stood up in.
cócila, cuckoo.
cóḍalu, daughter-in-law. *atta tsasté cóḍalu y'eḍchinaṭṭu*, like the daughter-in-law who cried when the mother-in-law died (a strange phenomenon); *attá vacar' inṭi cóḍalé*, the mother-in-law was a daughter-in-law in someone's house (and is now getting her own back). There are many similar proverbs in Telugu, just as there are many jokes about mothers-in-law in the European languages; but in Europe it is the man's mother-in-law that is unpopular, in India the woman's. The woman living with her husband is referred to as '*attavár inṭi cóḍalu*', a very hard place indeed.
cóḍaricamu, daughter-in-law-ship.
cóḍi, fowl, hen; plural *cóḷḷu*, poultry. *nénu cóḍi cuyyagá bailudérinánu*, I started at cockcrow; *cóḍi có-có-có ani cúyunu*, the cock crows co-co-co.
cóḍicúta, crowing.
cóḍicúta-véḷa, dawn.
cóḍipilla, chicken.
cóḍipunzu, cock.
cóla, rod. *cóla léni peṭṭu, táḍu léni caṭṭu*, hitting without a rod, tying up without a cord, i.e. government by soul force.
cóláhalamu, uproar. *lópala cóláhalamu vini*, hearing an uproar inside.
cólátamu, dance in a ring with sticks which are struck together (*cóla*).
-cólu, affix turning verbs into nouns, from *conuṭa*; common in plural *cóḷḷu*. *moṭṭucóḷḷu*, lamentations; *véḍiconuṭa*, to pray; *véḍicólu*, prayer (plural, *véḍicóḷḷu*).
cóluconi-póvuṭa, to plunder. *collapeṭṭuṭa* and *dótsuconuṭa* are commoner.
cóluconuṭa, recover. *duhkham marachi póyi nela dinamulacu conchem cóluconnánu*, forgetting my grief I recovered to some extent in a month.
cólupaḍuṭa, to be lost, ruined. *dhanamu cólupóyi*, losing money.
cólupáṭu, loss, ruin.
cólupóvuṭa, to lose.
cómalamu, comely. *éḍenimidi éḷḷa cindaṭa nénu y'intacanṭé cómalangáné*

v'unnánu, 7 or 8 years ago I was even better looking.

cómaṭi, the merchant caste, merchant. *cómaṭi nizamu*, a merchant's truth; *cómaṭi viṣvásamu*, the faith of a merchant; *cómaṭi sácshyamu*, the evidence of a merchant, are all proverbial phrases indicating that in the opinion of the Telugus merchants are deceivers ever. They are also supposed to be cowards: *cómaṭi pirici coṭṭité v'urici*, the merchant is a coward, if you beat him he flees.

cóna, cóṇamu, corner.

cóṇangi, buffoon. *cóṇangi chéshṭalu*, the tricks of a buffoon.

cónéru, stone-faced tank with steps.

cópadrüshṭi, angry look. Skt., from *cópam* and *drüshṭi*, look.

cópagintsuṭa, to be angry.

cópamu, anger. Skt. *eccum' anṭé yedducu cópam, digum'anṭé cunṭiváḍici cópam*, if you say get up the bullock is angry, if you say get down the lame man is angry; *ní cópamunu aṇatsucó*, keep your temper.

cópapaḍuṭa, to be angry.

cópávéṣamu, heat of passion. Skt., from *cópam* and *dvéṣam*, passion. *cópávéṣam chéta voḷḷu teliyaca*, out of his mind with fury.

cópi, angry man. Often compounded with the word *muccu*, nose; *muccópi*, a man flinging himself into a passion without cause.

cópishṭi, angry man. *itanu vaṭṭi cópishṭi*, he is a churl.

córa, fang, tusk. *córa-pandi*, a boar with tusks.

córáḍuṭa, to purr.

córica, a wish, desire. *córica tírtsucóca*, not being able to satisfy one's desires; *gontemma córicalu*, castles in the air.

córṭu, court (law, tennis). English; the usual word for a law court. *nyáyasthánam* is an artificial word used only in books.

córu, share, especially of the crop. *sangóru* is half share, *irugóru* both shares, i.e. those of the landlord and of the tenant.

córuconuṭa, to request, beg. *cshamápaṇa córucunṭánu*, I will beg pardon.

córuṭa, to wish, choose, elect (to legislative council, &c.). *ocaḍu manacu yélá chéya valen ani córudumó manam ocarici álágé chéya valenu*, do as you would be done by.

cósamu, for. *dáni cósamu*, on that account.

cóṣamu, sheath, envelope. *svásacóṣamulu* are lungs; *annacóṣamu* is stomach.

cósaramu, for; not as common as *cósamu*.

cósu, 2 miles. Four *cós* make one *ámaḍa*, the usual way of reckoning distance before the English mile came in and still used.

cóṭa, fort. All the Dravidian languages have this word, Tamil *coṭṭai*, Can. *cóṭe*, Malayalam *coṭṭa*, and it occurs in the names of many famous towns, Palamcotta, Pudukotta, Samalkot.

cóta, cutting; from *cóyuṭa*.

cótacálamu, harvest.

cóti, monkey. *cótici addam tsúpin'aṭlu*, like putting a glass in front of a monkey; *cóti chéti púladanḍa*, a flower-garland in a monkey's paw; *cóti chéti pámu vale*, a snake in a monkey's paw. A monkey does not appreciate mirrors and flowers and is afraid of the snake but won't let it go. *tá cheḍḍa cóti vanam ella cherachina aṭlu*, like one bad monkey infecting the whole grove.

cóṭi, a crore, 10,000,000; 100 lakhs. Skt. *núṭici peṭṭi cóṭici goriginchéváḍu*, one who grinds down a crore of people to feed 100; *cóṭi vidyalú cúṭi coracé*, there are a crore of professions but the object of all is food; *váḍu cóṭici paḍagettináḍu*, he is a millionaire.

cóṭu, coat. English. *í cóṭucu anní cuṭṭle*, this coat is all seams.

cóvela, cóvila, temple. A word common to all the Dravidian languages and found in the form *coil* in the names of many towns and villages; in Telugu *gudi* or the Sanskrit *déválayam* are commoner.

Cóya, the Koyas are a hill tribe in the Godavari Agency.

Cóyadora, a Koya chieftain.

cóyila, cuckoo.

cóyuṭa, to cut, reap. *váḍu gontu cóséváḍu*, he is a cut-throat; *áme tóṭalo* *pushpamulu cóyutsunnadi*, she is picking flowers in the garden; *dunnaca tsallité coyyaca pandinadi*, the field sown without ploughing was harvested without reaping (i.e. there was no crop).

craccuṭa, to vomit; also *caccuṭa*.

cramacramangá, gradually.

cramamu, regularity, propriety, justice.

crammuṭa, to spread, swell. *sandhyachícaṭi crammutsunḍenu*, twilight spread.

crauryamu, cruelty. Skt., from *crúram*, cruel.

crayacuḍu, buyer. Skt. Used in books.

crayadhanamu, purchase money.

crayamu, a purchase, a price. Skt. *cálacrayamu*, the current price.

crayamu chéyuṭa, to sell, dispose of; more commonly *vicrayintsuṭa*.

crayapatrica, purchase deed.

crayavicrayamulu, buying and selling.

crayintsuṭa, to buy. Skt. The Telugu is *conuṭa*.

criccirisi, crowded; also *ciccirisi*.

crimi, animalcule. Skt. The word used to translate *bacillus*.

crinda (and derivatives), down, below, past, &c., are other forms of *cinda*, *cindaṭa*, *cindaṭi*. *crindala* or *crindutala*, head downwards; *talacrindala*.

criya, act. Skt.

criḍa, sport, play. Skt.

críḍintsuṭa, to sport. Skt.

críganṭi tsúpu, ogle, downcast look.

crotta, new; another form of *cotta*.

crovvu, fat, pride; another form of *covvu*.

cródhamu, anger. Skt. *cópamu* is the common word.

cróḍícarintsuṭa, to abridge. Skt. *dharmaṣástrál anni samagrangá tsadivi, cróḍícarinchi, sáram tísi*, having read all the Scriptures, abridged them, and drawn out the juice from them.

cruccuṭa, to stuff, cram.

crummaruṭa, to wander over. *Palnáḍu antayu crummaritini*, I wandered all over the Palnad.

crunguṭa, to bend (intransitive). *attagárini tsúchi nivvera paḍi lólóna crungenu*, seeing his mother-in-law he crouched in dismay; *í apacírti chéta crungi póyi*, bending under this disgrace.

crúramu, cruel. Skt. *á crúra rácshasuni náṭi sáyancála bhójanamunacu nénu pradhama cabaḷam agudun' aniyu tóchi*, thinking I would provide the cruel giant with his first morsel for the night's supper; *crúra crütyamulu*, cruel deeds.

crúratvamu, cruelty. Skt. *nívu y'ippuḍu crúratvam anédi áyanacu taginanta vivécam lécapóvaḍam valla taṭasṭham autú v'unnadi*, what you now call his cruelty results from want of sense.

crúruḍu, a cruel man. Skt.

crüshi, agriculture. Skt. *crüshitó násti durbhicsham, japató násti pátacam*, agriculture annuls famine, penance cancels sin.

crüshi, exertions. Skt. *bharta viyógam sambhavinchi ímé crüshi saphalam ainadi cádu*, as she had lost her husband her exertions were vain; *sangítamuló gaṭṭigá crüshi chési*, having worked hard at singing.

Crüshna, the river Krishna or Kistna named after the god who is *Crüshnuḍu*, *Crüshṇa* being the adjectival form. Skt. *Crüshṇacu varada vachchinadi*, the Kistna is in flood; *Crüshnuḍu Rádha yocca paiṭanu tolaginchináḍu*, Krishna removed Radha's breastcloth; *váḍu Crüshṇa véshamu vésináḍu*, he acted Krishna in the play.

crüṣintsuṭa, to pine away, grow thin. Skt. *lólópalané crüṣinchi*, inwardly pining; *á duhkhamutóṭé crüṣistu v'unḍagá*, pining away with that sorrow.

crütaghnata, ingratitude. Skt., from *crütam*, act, and *ghnata*, destroying.

crütaghnuḍu, ungrateful person.

crütagnyata, gratitude. Skt., from *crütam*, act, and *gnyata*, recognizing.

crütagnyuḍu, grateful person.

crütamu, act. Skt.

crütayugamu, the age of creation, the golden age. Skt., from *crütam*, act, and *yugam*, age. *crüta yugam náṭi nunchi vastú v'unna sadáchâram*, a good custom dating from the beginning of the world.

crütárthata, success. Skt. *M.A. paricshaló crütárthuḍ ai*, having come out successful in the M.A. examination.
crüti, dedication. Skt. *váḍu á cávyamunu rázucu crüti y' ichchináḍu*, he dedicated that poem to the king.
crütrima, false, fabricated. Skt. *máyalunnu, crütrim álóchanalunnu*, illusions and false ideas.
crütyamu, deed. Skt. *míru chésina ghóra crütyamunacu ná ṣaríramu pulacarintsutsunnadi*, I shudder at your cruel deed.
csh- is commonly pronounced *ṭsh-*, q.v.
cshama, patience. Skt.
cshamápaṇa, forgiveness. Skt. *nácu bahu vichárangá v' unnadi, nénu cshamápaṇa véḍucunṭánu*, I am very sorry, I beg pardon; *nénu chésina aparádham cheppinaṭṭ aité nénu venṭané ní cáḷḷa mída paḍi cshamápaṇa córuсunṭánu*, if you will tell me what I have done wrong I will at once fall at your feet and beg pardon.
cshamintsuṭa, to pardon. Skt. *cshamintsa valenu*, please forgive me.
cshaṇamu, instant. Skt. *nénu veḷḷi sahâyam tísuconi cshaṇamló vastánu*, I will go to fetch help and be back in an instant.
cshatamu, wound. Skt. Used in books for *gáyamu*.
cshatriya, the kshatriya or warrior caste. Skt., from verb for 'to strike'.
cshauramu, shaving; also spelt *cshavaramu*. The ordinary words for shaving are *pani chéyuṭa, goruguṭa*, but this also is common especially in a figurative sense. *nívu andariní svajanánni chéristé ní taruváta vachchinaváḍu váḷḷ andaricí cshavarálu chéstáḍu*, if you put in all your caste men the man who comes after you will shave them all.
cshayarógamu, consumption. Skt., from *cshayamu*, wasting away.
cshámamu, famine. Skt.; *caruvu* is the Telugu word.
csháнti, patience. Skt.
csháramu, salt. Skt. A book word for *uppu*.
cshátramu, Kshatriya's duty. Skt.
cshémamu, health, happiness. Skt.; ordinary word in enquiring after health, &c. *yógacshémamulu vichárintsuṭa* is to make such usual enquiries.
cshétragaṇitamu, geometry. Skt.
cshétramu, place of pilgrimage. Skt.
cshétramu, field. Skt. *cshétram erigi vittanamu, pátram erigi dánamu*, sow seed to suit the field, give charity to the deserving.
cshínamu, decline, decay. Skt. *cshína daṣaló 'n unnámu*, we are on a downhill course; *áyuch cshínamu*, the decline of age; *dhana cshínamu*, decrease of wealth.
cshíṇintsuṭa, to waste away. Skt. *benga peṭṭuconi adi á dinamu canna á dinam cshíṇinchi déham antá pálipóyi*, in her distress she wasted away day by day and grew pale.
cshíra, milk. Skt.; book word for *pálu*.
cshóbha, grief, trouble. Skt. One of the numerous words for grief; the shade of meaning is agitation. *sancshóbhamu*, agitation; *chittacshóbhamu*, trouble of mind; *jailuló yenta cshóbha paḍḍáḍu!* what distress he felt in jail! *cshóbhapeṭṭuṭa* is to distress, trouble; *chinnadánni nannu nishcáraṇangá y' ílágu cshóbha peṭṭaḍam canṭe crúra crütyam lócamló yédí v' unḍadu*, there is nothing more cruel in the world than to oppress a poor girl like me in this way.
cshóbhintsuṭa, to be distressed. Skt.
cshudha, hunger. Skt. Book word for *ácali*, used in compounds such as *cshudbádha*, pains of hunger.
cshudra, petty, low, trifling. Skt. *manam cshudrálu páṭigá paṭṭa rádu*, we should not pay attention to trifles.
cubjuḍu, hunchback.
cucca, dog. *araché cucca carava néradu*, barking dogs don't bite (Italian proverb, *cane che abbaia non morde*); *cucca vasté ráyi doracadu, ráyi doricité cucca rádu*, when the dog comes there is no stone, when you find the stone the dog isn't there; *chandruni tsúchi cuccalu y' édtsunu*, dogs bay at the moon; *incó janmánici mí y' inṭló cuccan ai puḍutánu*, I will be born as a dog in your house at a re-birth (gratitude); *moruguṭa* is to bark.
cuccuṭa, to crush. *amé pélu cuccutsun-*

nadi, she is cracking lice (a common occupation in India, where delousing is one of the arts of peace). The term *cuccina pénu* is often applied to a person eating humble pie.

cucshi, stomach. Skt. Book word for *caḍupu*, used especially in compounds. *váḍu niracsharacucshi*, he is an illiterate boor; *váḍu vaṭṭi cucshimbharuḍu*, he cares only for his personal comforts.

cuḍi, eating. Used in books.

cuḍi, right (hand). It is in vain that the motorist will say *cuḍi chétici tóla cúḍadu, y' eḍama chétici tól áli*, drive on the left, not the right; for the rule of the road is not observed in India.

cuḍichi, after eating. *cúḍu cuḍichi curtsó léca goppalu cheppucunṭáḍu*, he spends the leisure after dinner in blowing his own trumpet.

cudiripóvuṭa, be obtained. *áyanacu ná mída nammacamu cudiri póyindi*, he got faith in me.

cuḍuca, scale (of a balance).

cuḍupu, food.

cudurtsuṭa, to settle, cure. *á uttaramunácu chittu cudirchinánu*, I have settled the draft of that letter; *váru pitstsa cudirché vaidyulu*, they are doctors who cure madness.

cuduru, a garden bed.

cudurupaḍuṭa, to be settled.

cudurupáṭu, cure, settlement.

cuduruṭa, to recover; ordinary word for recovering from illness. *mícu cudirindá?* have you recovered?

cuduruṭa, to be arranged, settled, obtained; also, of handwriting, formed. *ná pedda cumártecu varuḍu cudirináḍu*, my eldest daughter is engaged (a bridegroom has been engaged for her); *vráta cuduruṭa*, forming the handwriting; *cudirina vráta*, a formed hand; *antá bágá cudirindi*, all has been settled.

cuduṭapaḍuṭa, to be settled.

cuḍutsuṭa, to feed. *dúḍá cuḍisténé cáni ávu chépadu*, if the calf is not fed the cow will not give milk.

cuḍutsuṭa, to eat, suck (of babies). *á pillacu tsannu cuḍutsuṭa mánpinúru*, they have weaned that child.

cuduva, pledge. *cuduva peṭṭuṭa*, to pledge, pawn.

cugrámamu, twopenny halfpenny village. Skt., from *cutstsitam*, vile.

cuhi-cuhi, whistling sound of reeds; onomatopoeic. *váni gontucaló cása rógam valla cuhi-cuhi y'ani dhvani avutú v'unnadi*, he is afflicted with a cough and whistles in his throat.

cuhuv-cuhuv, the cry of the cuckoo, which is a favourite theme of Indian poets; in books it is also known as *cuhút-cáram*.

culabhrashṭuḍu, expelled from caste. Skt., from *culam*, caste, and *bhrashṭam*, fallen. *maḷḷi peḷḷi chésuconi culabhrashṭulai*, expelled from caste for remarrying.

culadharmamu, caste observances. Skt.

culahínuḍu, of low caste. Skt.

culamu, caste. Skt. *culam erigi tsuṭṭamu, sthalam erigi vásamu*, marry into the caste you know and live in the place you know. (Italian proverb: *moglie e buoi dai paesi tuoi*, wife and oxen from your own place.)

culasthuḍu, member of a caste, fellow casteman. Skt.

culastrí, a good woman, family woman. Skt. *járiṇula y'odda sangítam v'unḍaḍam chéta culastríl adi nichangá y'enchi sangítam nértsucóru*, because music is practised by prostitutes respectable women look down on it and will not learn it.

culavrütti, the caste profession. Skt. *vyabhicháram viḷḷacu culavrütti*, fornication is their caste profession.

culácháramu, caste custom. Skt.

cuḷláyi, cap, wig. Hindustani.

cuḷḷipóyina, rotten.

cuḷḷu, rotten. *putstsu vancáyalú, tsatstsu biracáyalú, cuḷḷu araṭipanḍlú*, decayed brinjals, dead cucumbers, rotten plantains.

cumárte, daughter. Skt. The Telugu is *cúturu*.

cumáruḍu, son. Skt. The Telugu is *coḍucu*.

cumbhamu, pitcher. Skt. *cumbhapótagá* (or *cumbha vrüshṭigá*) *curiyutsunnadi*, it rains pitchers (cats and dogs).

cummarasána, potter's wheel.

cummari, potter. Skt. *cumhára*.

cummarintsuṭa, to pour out.
cummu, ashes. *adi dummu, idi cummu*, from the frying-pan into the fire (from dust to ashes).
cummucu chéyuṭa, to abet. Hindustani.
cummuláṭa, a fight.
cummuṭa, to butt.
cumpaṭi, stove, firepan.
cumpini, company, especially the East India Company. English.
cumuluṭa, to waste away. *lólópalané crüṣinchi cumulutsu*, pining and wasting away.
cuncuḍucheṭṭu, soap-nut tree. The soap-nuts are *cuncuḍucáyalu*.
cuncuma, the common cosmetic of women made chiefly of turmeric. *pasupú-cuncuma*, a woman's pin-money; *pasupú cuncam tinnagá v'unṭé*, if her saffron and rouge are provided for; *cuncam bariṇe*, rouge-box.
cuncuṭa, to set (of sun and moon); also *cruncuṭa* and *cúcuṭa*. *banḍacunca* is a term of abuse.
cunḍa, pot. *illálu guḍḍid aité y'inṭi cunḍalacu chéṭu*, if the housewife is blind it is ruin to the pots; *calimi lémulu cávaṭi cunḍalu*, life has its ups and downs.
-cunḍa, affix meaning 'without'. *viḍuvacunḍa*, without ceasing; *cácunḍa*, besides. *lécunḍa*, without.
cunḍalamu, ear-ring. *néné pillan iyyaca póté ná chevul' avi cunḍaldlu cávu, nénu tsaduvuconnadi ṣástramu cádu*, if I don't give the girl, what is in my ears are not ear-rings, what I have read is not Scripture; *cunḍaldla zóḍu chéyinchi véstánu*, I will have a pair of ear-rings made.
cundélu, hare. *cundéṭini cuccalu pasi paṭṭinavi*, the dogs are on the scent of the hare.
cunicipáṭu, cunucu, forty winks, a nap. *vacca cunucu póyi*, dropping off into a doze; *jadji vimarṣa chéséṭ' anta sépu balla mída cúrtsunḍi cunicipáṭlu paḍéváḍ'aṭa*, they say the judge was asleep all the time he was sitting on the bench holding trial; *cunicipáṭlu vastú v'unnavi*, I am getting sleepy.
cunṭa, pond.
cuntamulu, cuntalamulu, tresses. Skt. A book word for *venṭrucalu*, hair.
cunṭenacatte, procuress.
cunṭenagáḍu, pimp.
cunṭhlu, abuse.
cunṭhuḍu, a boor.
cunṭi, lame.
cunṭiváḍu, cunṭu, a lame man. *úḷḷó cunṭi aḍiviló léḍi*, lame in the village, a deer in the jungle; *eccum anṭé y'edducu cópam, digum' anṭé cunṭivánici cópam*, if you say get up the ox is angry, if you say get down the lame man is angry; *cunṭicálu*, a lame leg; *guḍḍiváḷḷacu, cunṭiváḷḷacu dánam chéyuṭa*, charity to the blind and lame.
cuntsamu, a grain measure, of which four go to one *túmu*.
cunṭuṭa, to limp. *cunṭu cunṭú vastú v' unnáḍu*, he comes limping.
cunucu, nap.
cunucuṭa, to nod.
cuppa, heap. *cuppaló máṇicyamu*, a diamond in a dunghill.
cuppateppalugá, abundantly.
curchí, chair. Hindustani. This word is spelt *curichí* in the dictionaries, but no one says *curichí*.
curiyuṭa, to rain, to leak. *vána curustóndi*, it is raining; *paicuppu curistundi*, the roof leaks; *varshálu curisiná curiyaca póyiná*, whether it rains or not.
curra, young, little.
curradi, girl.
curratanamu, childhood.
curraváḍu, boy. *curra munḍá coḍucul' antá bottigá páḍ'autú v' unnáru*, the present generation of boys are all going to the devil.
curulu, curls.
curupu, a boil. *curupu chiticinadi*, the boil has burst.
curúpamu, ugly. Skt.
curúpi, ugly person. Skt., from *cutstsa*, vile, and *rúpam*, form. *tala goriginchi curúpini chési*, shaving her head and making her ugly.
cusa-cusa, onomatopoeic of jolting. *yeguḍu diguḍu róḍla mída baḷḷu cusacusal áḍunu*, the carts jolt on the roads.
cuṣalamu, welfare. Skt. *cuṣala praṣnalu*, enquiries after health.
cuṣalata, ability. Skt. *míru mahá*

budhi cuṣalata galavàru, you are a very clever man.

cuṣamu, sacrificial grass. Skt.

cushṭharógamu, leprosy. Skt.

cuṣini, kitchen. Portuguese. There are only two Portuguese words in Telugu, this and *camízu*, shirt; and only one Dutch, *cáccus*, latrine, in spite of the long connexion of the Portuguese and Dutch with India.

cuṣinivàḍu, cook.

cuṣanca, cavil. Skt. *iṭuvanṭi cuṣancalu cheyyacu*, don't make such silly objections; *annínṭici cuṣancalu chési*, raising frivolousr objections to evey-thing.

cutica, gullet, throat; also *cutuca*.

cuṭíramu, hut, bower. Skt. *latá cuṭíramu*, arbour.

cutra, plot. Skt. In the 1922 No-tax campaign in Guntur a village headman observed, *idi bráhmaṇa cuṭra*, this is a brahmin plot.

cuṭrapuváḍu, tailor; from *cuṭṭuṭa*, to stitch.

cutstsitamu, vile. Skt.

cutstsu, tassel.

cutticáya, Adam's apple.

cuṭṭintsuṭa, to get something sewn; causal of *cuṭṭuṭa*.

cuṭṭu, seam, stitch, also a stitch in the side. *á cóṭucu anní cuṭṭlé*, that coat is all seams.

cuṭṭuṭa, to sew, pick. *panḍlu cuṭṭuconuṭa*, to pick the teeth; *cheppulu cuṭṭéváḍu*, a cobbler.

cutuca, throat; also *cutica*.

cuṭumbamu, family. Skt. *nénu pedda cuṭumbamu galavánni*, I have a large family to support, is a common phrase in petitions.

cuṭumbícuḍu, a man with a large family. A man of high family is *goppa vamṣasthuḍu*.

cutúhalamu, eagerness, curiosity. Skt. *yucṭul émaina vina valenani ná manassu miccili cutúhala paḍutsunnadi*, I am full of curiosity to hear any witty sayings.

cuyucti, fraud, a wicked device. Skt., from *cu-*, bad, and *yucti*, device. *mír anniyu cuyuctulu chepput'unnáru. nava nágaricula cuyuctula nammi, mír evvarunnu ṣúdrula vidyac angícarimpa cúḍadu*, you must not believe in the fallacies of the modernists and admit sudras to learning (the orthodox view is that learning must be confined to brahmins).

cúca, a cry, shout. Used in books.

cúcalu véyuṭa, to scold. *váḍu bháryanu cúcalu vésináḍu*, he scolded his wife.

cúcuṭa, to set (of sun and moon). *poddu cúcinadi*, the sun has set. Also *cuncinadi*, which is more common.

cúcuṭa, to sit down. Vulgar for *cúrtsunḍuṭa*, but very common; *cúcó*, sit down.

cúḍa, cúḍá, together; also, even, with. *atanitó cúḍá vachchináḍu*, he came with him; *níḷḷu cúḍá y' ivvaru*, they won't even give you water.

cúḍadu, mustn't. *níru peddalató hásyam chéya cúḍadu*, you mustn't joke with your elders; *rúṇa ṣésham, vraṇa ṣésham agni ṣésham v'untsa cúḍadu*, you should not keep the remains of debt, a sore, fire.

cúḍali, union, joining. A word used in newspapers to translate the English union (political union); also *sanghamu, sammeḷanamu*. *cúḍalidári* is four crossroads; *cúḍaliráyi*, corner-stone.

cúḍani, not fitting. *cúḍani máṭa*, an inappropriate expression.

cúḍapeṭṭuṭa, to put together, amass. *ná jitamló nunchi núru rúpáyalu cúḍa peṭṭinánu*, I put together Rs. 100 out of my pay.

cúḍánu, also. An emphatic form of *cúḍa*. *váḍu abaddham áḍéváḍu, paigá tágubótu cúḍánu*, he is a liar and a drunkard to boot.

cúḍu, food. *mála cúḍu*, foul (pariah) food; *vánici cúṭici lédu*, he is starving.

cúḍuṭa, to meet, fit, be able, collect, be connected, assemble. *induló cúḍina pani*, a connected matter; *dommi cúḍi vachchináru*, they came in a mob; *idi cúḍac' unṭe*, if this can't be done.

cújá, goglet. Hindustani.

cújitamu, the cries of birds. Used in books. *cúta* is commoner.

cúlapaḍuṭa or **cúlipóvuṭa,** to fall, collapse. *pedda yuddhamló modaṭa Austria tarvata Jarmaní cúlipóyinavi*, in the Great War first Austria then Germany collapsed.

cúlatróyuṭa or **cúlavéyuṭa,** to thrust down.
cúli, wages. *cúlici chéyuṭa,* to work for hire.
cúlimanishi, labourer, usually female.
cúlináli, drudgery.
cúliváḍu, labourer.
cúḷḷu, plural of *cúḍu,* food, victuals. *cannacúḷḷu,* any victuals available.
cúluṭa, to lie down. *cúli nidra paṭṭaca y'éḍchinadi,* she lay down sleepless and cried.
cúna, a young one, usually of animals, but may be used, like our kid, of human young. *pasicúnal eppuḍó y'edigi cápuram chéstú sukham paḍudur' ani manam santósha paḍa valasinadi,* our kids must grow up sometime, marry, be happy, and give us joy.
cúni, murder. Hindustani; also *khúni.*
cúpamu, pit, hole, vorago. Skt. *yamacúpamu* is hell. The word is a literary one; *randhram* is the usual word for hole and *goyyi* for pit.
cúralu or **cúragáyalu,** vegetables. *ácu cúralu* are leafy vegetables, *cúragáyalu* (*cáyalu*) those with *cáyalu* or pods. *talliléni pilla, v'ulli léni cúra,* a motherless child and onionless vegetables; *ná bhárya cúra poga tsúra peṭṭinadi,* my wife has smoked the curry.
-cúrchi, affix meaning 'about'; more usually spelt *-gúrchi,* and *-gurinchi* is commoner.
cúrpu, joining, seam, edition of a book, from *cúrtsuṭa,* to join.
cúrtsunḍa peṭṭuṭa, to give seats to.
cúrtsunḍuṭa, to sit. *tana talupu tísi porigintici peṭṭi, rátri antá cuccalu tólutú cúrtsunn' aṭṭu,* like the man who took his own door down to give to his neighbour and spent the night driving away the dogs; *parugétti pálu trágé canṭé, cúrtsoni níru trágité mélu,* better to sit and drink water than run for milk.
cúrtsuṭa, to join (transitive), to convene, to bring together.
cúrucu, dropping off to sleep. *vánici cúrucu paṭṭutsunnadi,* he is dropping off.
cúruṭa, to load (a gun), cram. *bráhmaṇulu penḍliló poṭṭa ninḍá cúrutáru,* brahmins cram their stomachs at weddings.
cúsamu, snake's slough.
cúsu, inferior. *abhyásamu cúsu vidya,* practice is an inferior sort of learning.
cúta, a cry, crow, bray, &c. *piṭṭa conchem, cúta ghanam,* small bird, big cry (of ambitious men); *í páṭa y'éḍisin'aṭṭé v'unnadi, gáḍida cúta lágu unnadi,* this singing is wretched, like a donkey braying; *nannu tiṭṭi aḍḍam' aina cáru cútalu cúsináḍu,* he abused me in any horrid language that occurred to him.
cúṭamu, meeting-hall; from *cúḍuṭa,* to assemble.
cúṭasácshi, false witness. Skt., from *cúṭam,* false. *váḷḷu cúṭasácshul ainaṭṭu spashṭam ainadi,* it became clear that they were false witnesses.
cúturu, daughter. *penḍlicúturu* is a bride.
cúyuṭa, to cry, crow, bray, hoot, quack, cackle or howl of cocks, geese, ducks, owls, donkeys, wolves.

Ch

chaccara, sugar; also *tsaccera, pantsadára.*
chacóramu, large partridge of North India. Skt. Used in books. *chandra chacóra nyáyamu,* great friends.
chacracéḷi, the sugar plantain. *chacracéḷi araṭi paḷḷu veyyacu, avi tsála priyam,* do not serve sugar plantains, they are very expensive.
chacramu, wheel. Skt. Vishṇu's wheel, i.e. his thunderbolt which he hurls like a quoit, is called *chacram.* A small copper coin still used in Travancore is also called a *chacram.*
chacravarti, emperor. Skt. The King Emperor of India; also *sárvabhaumuḍu.*
chacshuvu, eye. Skt. Used in books for Telugu *cannu.*
chaitramu, the 1st month, April-May.

Skt. *chaitra másamu Englishu nelaló Épriyalu-Mé nelalacu sari y'ainadi*, chaitra corresponds with the English April-May.

chalanamu, shaking. Skt. *chalachittuḍu*, a man of wandering mind.

chalámaṇi, current; from *chelluṭa*. *í náṇemulu ippuḍu chalámaṇi cávu*, these coins are not now current.

chaláná, memo., especially memo. of payment into a treasury. Hindustani. The memo. of payment is on a printed form in duplicate; one copy is retained by the payer and serves as a receipt.

chaláyintsuṭa, to make current or valid; same as *chellintsuṭa*.

chalintsuṭa, to shake, tremble. Skt.

chalitamu, trembling. Skt.

chamatcáramu, adroitness. Skt.

champacamu, chrysanthemum. Skt.

chanchalamu, trembling. Skt.

chanchalintsuṭa, to tremble. Skt.

chandanamu, sandal. Skt.

chanḍáluḍu, pariah. Skt. *parian* is the Tamil generic word, the Sanskrit word is used in Telugu; the particular pariah tribes in the Telugu country are *málas* and *mádigas* (leather-workers), now commonly classed as '*ádiándhras*'. *yeccaḍa léni chirácunu vachchi nannu chanḍáluni tsúchin' aṭlu tsútsunu*, he pulls a face of the utmost disgust and looks me up and down as if I were a pariah.

chandra-, prefix meaning 'moonlike'. Skt., from *chandra*, moon. *chandrahámu* is a necklace; *chandrahásamu*, the sword of *Rávaṇa*; *chandravanca*, a crescent worn in the hair; *chandraṣála*, a roof room; *chandramukhi*, a moon-faced woman; *chandracántapu ráyi*, moonstone.

chandródayamu, rising of the moon. Skt., from *chandra*, moon, and *udayam*, rising.

chandruḍu, moon. Skt. Moonlight (*vennela*) is a Dravidian word, but the Sanskrit word is used for the moon itself. *lacsha nacshatramul ainá vaca chandruḍu cádu*, 100,000 stars don't make one moon. The moon rising is *udayintsuṭa*, setting is *astamintsuṭa*.

chapalachittuḍu, a crack - brained man. Skt., from *chapala*, lightning.

chapalatvamu, whimsicality. Skt., from *chapala*, lightning.

charamu, moving, trembling. Skt.

charaṇamu, couplet. Skt., from *charaṇam*, foot.

charásti, moveable property. Skt., from *charam*, moveable, and *ásti*, property. *sthirásti* is immoveable property; these are the common legal terms.

charchintsuṭa, to discuss. Skt., from *charcha*, search.

charitártham, purpose. Skt., from *charita*, conduct, and *artham*, meaning. Commonly used to denote success. *charitárthurálu* is a woman who gains her ends.

charitramu, story, history.

-charituḍu, affix meaning 'conducting oneself'. Skt. *iṣvara bhacti gala y'udára charitulacu lócam antayu cuṭumbamé*, to pious persons of liberal conduct the whole world is their family.

charmamu, skin. Skt.

charya, procedure. Skt. root *char*, to move. *mí charyalu tsúste nácu sáhásam v'unḍacunḍá v'unnadi*, seeing the way you go on all my daring is oozing out of me; *mícu cópam vastú v'unnaṭṭu mí mukha charya valla canapaḍutú v'unnadi*, from your expression it looks as if you were getting angry. *charya* is also the legal translation of 'procedure'.

chatura, dexterous. Skt. *chaturulu*, trickish men.

chatur, chatush, four. Skt. Used in compounds as *chaturthi*, 4th day of the lunar month, *chaturdaṣi*, the 14th day of the lunar month. *chaturbhujuḍu*, four-armed, an epithet of Vishṇu; *chaturmukhuḍu*, four-faced, an epithet of Brahma; *chatushpáda jantuvulu*, four-footed creatures.

chavititalli, stepmother; corrupted from *savati-talli*. The derivation is from Skt. *sapatni*, co-wife.

chácirí, menial service. Hindustani *chácri*. *guruvulu ṣishyula chéta chácirí chéyintsu coni vastáru*, spiritual teachers have menial services done for them by their disciples; *aḍḍamaina veṭṭi chácirí chéstámu*, we do all kinds of unpaid drudgery.

chácu, pen-knife. Hindustani. *ná chácu truppu paṭṭinadi*, my pen-knife has rusted.
chádastamu, bigotry, ceremonialism. *ná cóḍalu cápuránici vachchina taruváta y'inṭló vaṭṭi mála cúḍu calustú v'unnadi, yémainá anṭé y'eduruc' eduru nácé chádastam anṭáru*, it is all pariah food since my daughter-in-law came to the house, if I say anything I am countered with accusations of bigotry.
chádastuḍu, a bigot, a person wedded to caste customs.
chámantipuvvu, chrysanthemum, an ornament in the form of a chrysanthemum; also *chémantipuvvu. péḷḷámu chámanti puvvu tácaṭṭu peṭṭi*, pledging his wife's chrysanthemum.
chánchalyamu, agitation. Skt., from *chanchalam. atanici conchem chitta chánchalyam*, he suffers a little from mental agitation.
chándini guḍḍa, awning, canopy. Hindustani.
chápalyamu, caprice. Skt., from *chapalam.*
cháru, pepper water. Always served with the last dish of rice. *renḍu púrilu tini miriyála cháru táganḍi*, eat a couple of wheat cakes and drink pepper water.
cháruḍu, spy. Skt.
cháya, colour. Skt.; also *chháya. bangáru pasimi cháya*, the yellow colour of gold.
che-, prefix meaning 'tender', 'pretty', short for *chennu.*
checca, piece, of wood, or of similar things. *póca checcalu*, pieces of areca nut. They are usually chewed with betel leaves and spices after dinner.
checcili, checcu, cheek.
checcuṭa, to engrave, pave, set (jewels). *checcuṭaddamu* is a framed looking-glass.
checumuci, flint. *checumuci ráyi*, flint-stone; *checumuci tupáci*, flint musket.
cheḍa, bad; more commonly spelt *cheḍḍa*. Compounded with verbs it intensifies rather than pejorizes. *cheḍatinuṭa* is to over-eat; *cheḍa tráguṭa* is to get drunk.
cheḍagoṭṭuṭa, to spoil; from *cheḍa* and *coṭṭuṭa.*
chedalu, white ants. In the singular and in compounds, *cheda. bongucu cheda paṭṭinadi*, the bamboo has been eaten by white ants.
cheḍapóruṭa, to fight violently. *cheḍa* is commonly used in such compounds; e.g. *cheḍa-aratsuṭa*, to cry aloud; *cheḍatinuṭa*, to over-eat. *nívu poṭṭa baddal' ayéṭ' aṭṭugá cheḍa-tinnávu*, you ate enough to burst your stomach.
cheḍaragoṭṭuṭa, to disperse, defeat; from *chedaruṭa*, to be scattered, and *coṭṭuṭa*, to beat.
chedaruṭa, to be scattered, (with *cannu*) to be dazzled. *cannu chedaru n'aṭṭugá occa sári núru cásulu tísiconi veḷḷi tahassiludáru gári bhárya chétiló pósi*, taking 100 sovereigns at once to dazzle her eyes and laying them in the hands of the tahsildar's wife.
cheḍḍa, bad, naughty; short for *cheḍina*, from *cheḍuṭa. manchi cheḍḍalu*, good and bad; *cheḍḍa pilla*, naughty child. Tamil and Canarese *ceṭṭa*, Malayalam *chítta.*
cheḍḍatanamu, wickedness.
cheḍuṭa, to be spoilt. *ní rúpam conchem márinḍ, andam cheḍa lédu*, though your features have changed a little, your beauty has not been spoilt; *mati cheḍi*, perplexed; *vánici mati cheḍi póyinadi*, he is crazy.
chelaguṭa, to frolic.
chelama, pit, spring, especially a pit dug in a dry river-bed for drinking-water.
cheli, chelicatte, cheliya, girl's female playmate.
chelicáḍu, male playmate, pal.
chelimi, friendship.
chellani, not current.
chellelu, chelli, younger sister.
chellintsuṭa, to pay.
chellubaḍi, authority.
chellubaḍicáni, inoperative, a legal term.
chelluṭa, to pass (as of money or time) (intransitive). *í rúpáyi paici manchidi lágé canapaḍutú v'unnadi, chellutundi gadá?* this rupee looks all right, is it a current one? *taruváta vayasu chelli bádha paḍéṭ' appuḍu*, when the ills of

old age are upon you; *á tsaṭṭam chelladu*, that law is not in force.

chemartsuṭa, to sweat.

chemaṭa, sweat. *vaḷl'antá chemaṭa pósinadi*, I sweated all over the body; *vaḷl' antá chemaṭa paṭṭéṭaṭṭugá parugettutú v'unnáḍu*, he is running so as to sweat all over the body; *mí mátalu vinṭé nácu vaḷlu chemaṭa paḍutú v'unnadi*, your words make me sweat. When we say 'I sweat', the Telugus say 'my body sweats'.

chemaṭacáyalu, prickly heat.

chembaḍiváḍu, fisherman.

chembu, the indispensable small metal water pot that everyone carries.

chemma, damp.

chemmabhúmi, marsh.

chempa, cheek, cheek of a mango.

chempacáya, slap on the cheek.

chenduṭa, to befall, be experienced. *chendina bhayamu*, the terror experienced.

chengávi, reddish; from *chennu*, slight, and *cávi*, tawny.

chengu, edge, border of cloth. *chengu paṭṭi aḍuguṭa*, to seize by the lappet of the coat and ask. The bride and bridegroom are tied together by the *chengus* of their cloth, so *á panici chengu vésináḍu* means he is wedded to that business.

chenguchenguna, suddenly.

Chennapaṭnam, Chennapuri, Madras. The Telugu name of Madras has always been *Chennapaṭnam*; in the old English records it is Madraspatnam or Madraspatam, from *paṭnam*, town. The Madras Presidency is sometimes called *Chennaráshṭramu*.

chennáruṭa, to be beautiful, bloom. This word is used in books of a smiling country or a fine town, &c. It is derived from *chennu*, beauty, and *áruṭa*, to teem with; *chennárina*, *sompárina*, *alarárina*, are synonyms.

chennu, beauty; a word used in books. *andamu*, *saundaryamu*, *rúpamu* are the common words.

chenta, by, near.

Chentsu, a hill tribe found in Kurnool, Cuddapah, Kistna, and Nellore. Their language is corrupt Telugu.

cheppintsuṭa, to get someone taught or to get something said; causal from *chepputa*. *vánici tsaduvu cheppinchinánu*, I got him educated; *vánici pani cheppinchinánu*, I got him a job.

cheppu, clog, sandal, slipper. *cucca cáṭucu cheppu debba mandu*, cure a dog's bite with a slap from a slipper (the dog here meaning a slanderer); *chittamu Ṣivuni mída, bhacti cheppula mída*, his mind on Siva but his real devotion to his slippers (left outside the temple); *váciṭiló cheppula tsappuḍ agutsunnadi*, I hear a noise of clogs on the threshold; *ninnu cheppu tísucuni coḍutánu*, I will take off my slipper and beat you with it (a most gross insult since leather pollutes); *cheppula zóḍu* is a pair of shoes; *cheppulu chinnavi ani cálu tega cósucó vatstsuná?* will you cut off your feet because your shoes are tight? *cheppulu toḍuguconna vánici lócam antá tólutó cappabaḍḍ' aṭṭu tóstundi*, the man who wears sandals thinks the whole earth is covered with leather (does not feel for others).

cheppuconuṭa, to say; middle form of *chepputa*. The meaning is the same practically; *cheppuconuṭa* is more commonly used; 'to speak' is *máṭláḍuṭa* (use words). *cheppuconnánu*, I said; *vánitó máṭláḍinánu*, I spoke to him.

chepputa, to say. *aḍigévánicí cheppéváḍu lócuva*, it is easier to ask questions than to answer them; *cheppina buddhi, caṭṭina tsaddi niluvadu*, the spoken advice and the tied up rice won't keep.

chera, captivity.

cheracu, sugar-cane; also *cherucu*.

cherapaṭṭuṭa, to capture, to rape; also *cheratsuṭa*.

cherapóvuṭa, to go to jail.

cheraṣála, jail.

cheratsuṭa, to spoil, rape.

cheri, prefix meaning 'each'. *cherisagamu*, half each; *cheri y'ocaṭi*, one each.

cheripivéyuṭa, to ruin. *vénucaṭi tahassildáru mammul andarini cheripivésináḍu*, the last tahsildar ruined us all.

cherucu, sugar-cane; also *cheracu*. *cherucu v'unḍe tsóṭici chimalu támé vastavi*, ants come of themselves where the sugar-cane is; *cherucu gaḍa*, the cane.

cheruguṭa, to winnow.

cherupu, ruin. *bápaḷḷa vyavasáyam bápaḷḷa cherupu,* brahmin tillage, brahmin ruin.

cherupuconuṭa, to spoil, to rub off. *cuḷam cherupucunṭárá?* will you spoil your caste?

cheruvu, tank, i.e. reservoir, artificial lake, not in the usual English sense of tank, i.e. an iron cistern, for which there is no precise word; *inupa toṭṭi*, iron tub, might be used. In India artificial reservoirs for irrigation and drinking are among the commonest features of the landscape; a small one is called *cunṭa* rather than *cheruvu*. Other words are *colanu*, which may also mean a natural lake, and *maḍugu*, which is rather a depression in the ground. *cheruvu ninḍité cappalu chérutavi*, the frogs assemble when the tank fills.

chetta, sweepings. *chettachedáramu*, trash and dirt.

cheṭṭa, by the hand. Used in books; from *cheyyi*, hand.

cheṭṭapaṭṭálu, **cheṭṭálu,** holding hands. *manam cheṭṭál vésucuni y'i tóṭaló tirugutú v' unḍaga*, while we were walking about the garden hand in hand.

cheṭṭapaṭṭuconuṭa, to take by the hand, shake hands.

cheṭṭapaṭṭuṭa, to marry. Used in books; *penḍli chésiconuṭa* is commoner.

cheṭṭu, shrub, tree; usually translated 'tree', but is used even oftener of shrubs. *cheṭṭu' ái vanganidi mánu ái vangunú?* if a plant won't bend when it is young, will it bend when it is a tree? *á cheṭṭu viraga cáchinadi*, that tree is in full bearing; *cheṭṭu cheḍa calánici cuccamúti pinde*, the dying shrub produces measly berries (by their fruits ye shall know them).

chevi, key. *táḷamchevi*, ear of the lock.

chevi, ear. *oca sári daggiracu vachchi, cheviló-máṭa cheppedanu, vini pó,* come here a minute and I will say a word in your ear and then you can go; *góḍalacu chevul unnavi*, walls have ears; *ná máṭalu chevin iḍucona lédu*, he did not listen to my advice.

cheviṭi, deaf; from *chevi* and *aviṭi*, crippled.

cheviṭi-múga, deaf-mute.

chevuḍu, deafness, deaf. *itanici chevuḍu rávaḍam tsústé záli vastú v' unnadi*, seeing he is deaf one pities him; *cané guḍḍi, viné chevuḍu*, eyes have they but they see not, ears have they but they hear not.

chevulapilli, hare; from *chevi*, ear, and *pilli*, cat.

chevulára, with all one's ears; *chevulára vinuṭa*, to listen with all one's ears.

chevvácu, ear-ring, ear-pendant.

cheyi, **cheyyi,** usually translated 'hand', but it just as often means 'arm', also 'sleeve'. *aracheyyi* is the palm, *muncheyi* the wrist, and *mócheyi* the elbow. The *e* is lengthened in the inflected forms: genitive *chéti*, locative *chéta*. *chéti sommu* is cash in hand; *chétipani*, handwork; *chévrálu*, handwriting (often signature). To feel the pulse is *cheyi tsútsuṭa*; *chéti cindi manishi* is a dependent servant. For 'he gave to me' the Telugus will usually say *ná chétici ichchináḍu*. There are various proverbs in which the word occurs: *áḍadáni chéti arthamú, mogaváni chéti biḍḍá bratacadu*, a child will not live in a man's hands or property in a woman's; *áchâryuni talachi nippuló chéyi peṭṭité cáladá?* thinking of your priest will not prevent your hand burning if you put it in the fire; *cóti chéti pámu vale*, a snake in a monkey's paw (afraid of it but won't let it go); *teḍḍu v'unḍagá cheyyi cáltsuconn'aṭṭu*, like burning your hand when you have a ladle (a silly thing to do); *chéyan ani chétiló chéyi véyyi*, give me your hand on it that you won't do it.

ché-, prefix, being an abbreviation of *cheyi*, hand.

chébadulu, unsecured loan.

chébiyyamu, rice that is cleaned by the hand; frequently applied to coarse rice. *boṭléruváḍu manam y'ichchina praśastham'aina sanna biyyam yeccaḍanó dáchi, yeccaḍivó mutaca chébiyyam vanḍi peṭṭi, doragáritó tahassiluḍáru iláganṭi pàḍu biyyam pampinchináḍ' ani cheppináḍ aṭa,* the butler hid our best quality fine rice somewhere, cooked and served some coarse rice and, so they say, told the Collector the tahsildar had sent bad rice.

chécatti, small knife but longer than a penknife, which is *chácu*.

chécaṭṭu, a particular kind of bracelets made of gold and coral beads alternately.

chéconuṭa, to accept, take.

chécúruṭa, to come to hand.

chéda, water-bucket. *chédubávi* is a draw-well, *chédeḍunillu* is a bucket of water; *chéda* is also the bucket-rope.

chédastamu, bigotry; also *chádastamu*. *míru chédastam chéta ivi tina cúḍad aní, avi tina cúḍad' aní mánutáru*, you abstain from this or that food out of bigotry.

chédastuḍu, bigot; also *chádastuḍu*. *y'í bráhmaḍu vaṭṭi chédastuḍu*, this brahmin is a dreadful bigot.

chédu, bitter. *adi cherucu pippéná? náluca chédugá v'unnaṭṭ'unnadi*, is this sugar-cane fool? it seems bitter to the taste.

chéduḍubávi, draw-well.

chéduṭa, to draw up hand over hand (as a bucket).

chémantipuvvu, chrysanthemum; also *chámantipuvvu*.

chémiri, sour milk used to curdle; also *tóḍu*.

chéntáḍu, chéntráḍu, (*chéda*+*táḍu*), well-rope.

chénu, field. *áu chénuló mésté dúḍa gaṭṭuna mésuná?* if the cow grazes in the field, will the calf graze on the bank? *chénú, coḍavalí ni chéta y'ichchinánu*, I have given you field and sickle (i.e., full powers). Another common word for field is **polam**.

chépa, fish. *chépa pillacu y'íta nérpa valená?* has a young fish got to be taught to swim?

chépaḍuṭa, to be caught.

chépalaváḍu, fisherman.

chépaṭṭuṭa, to marry (to take by the hand).

chépuṭa, to give milk. *dúḍa cuḍistiné cáni ávu chépadu*, the cow won't give milk unless you feed the calf.

chéra, hollow of the hand.

chéragilapaḍuṭa, falling back against; also *jérlapaḍuṭa*. *góḍacu chéragila páḍi cannulu músiconnáḍu*, he fell back against the wall and shut his eyes.

chérapaṭṭuṭa, to bring close.

chéreḍu, handful. *tsachchinaváḍi cannulu chér'eḍ'ési*, death widens the eyes.

chérica, union, familiarity. *aláganṭi pani cheyyaḍánici chérica v'unḍa valenu*, to carry through a thing like that you must be united among yourselves.

chértsuṭa, to join (transitive).

chérubaḍi, union, familiarity.

chéruconuṭa, to join (intransitive).

chérugaḍa, nearness.

chéruṭa, to reach, approach, be included, come under. *cáviḍi yenni vancalu pótén' émi y' illu chéríté sari*, however many bends the yoke may make, if it reaches the house that is enough; *bráhmalaló yevaru goppa v' udyógálalóci vachchiná váḷḷu tamavárine gáni manavárini yevarini áfísulò chéran'iyyaru*, if brahmins hold the high appointments they won't allow any of us, but only their own lot, into the office; *idi á tsaṭṭamló chéradu*, it does not fall under that rule; *Baḷḷárici chérinámu*, we arrived at Bellary.

chéruva, nearness.

chésaiga, sign, beckoning. *ramm' ani chésaiga chéyutsunnáḍu*, he is beckoning you to come.

chéshṭalu, pranks. *pillachéshṭalu*, childish behaviour; *marcaṭuchéshṭalu*, monkey tricks.

chésiconuṭa, to procure.

chésténécáni, unless you do.

chéta, by means of.

chéta, locative of *cheyi*, hand, used idiomatically for ability, possibility. *nic'i pani chétan'aun'émó cheppu*, say whether you can do this; *nác'í pani chéta cádu*, I can't do it.

chéta, deed; from *chéyuṭa*.

chéṭa, winnow (basket or fan).

chétacáni, impossible, useless, vile.

chétanaina, as far as possible. *ná chétan' ain' anta prayatnam chéstánu*, I will do my best.

chétanaité, if possible.

chétappu, clerical error; from *ché-*, hand, and *tappu*, mistake.

chétibadulu, loan without security.

chétibiḍḍa, baby.

chéticarra, walking stick.
chétiguḍḍa, handkerchief.
chétipani, handwork.
chétisommu, cash in hand.
chétráḍu, well-rope.
chéṭu, disaster. *illálu guḍḍid'aité inṭi cunḍalacu chéṭu,* if the housewife is blind disaster to the pots; *pagaṭi máṭalu panici chéṭu, rátri máṭalu nidracu chéṭu,* talking by day spoils business, talking by night spoils sleep.
chéṭucálamu, one's bad time, period of misfortune.
chéva, heart or core of a tree. *mudi mánu chéva,* heart of oak.
chévrálu, handwriting, signature.
chéyintsuṭa, to get done; causal from *chéyuṭa.*
chéyitsútsuṭa, to feel the pulse.
chéyuṭa, to do, to be worth, to make, to put. *béramu chéyuṭa,* to make a bargain; *appu chéyuṭa,* to make a debt; *svádhínamu chéyuṭa,* to put in charge; *vartacamu chéyuṭa,* to trade; *cá-chéyuṭa,* to misappropriate; *rúca lénivádu póca chéya léḍu,* a man without cash is not worth an areca nut; *vanṭa chéyuṭa,* to cook; *nannu áḍadánni chési,* looking upon me as a mere woman; *vánici zalubu chésinadi,* he caught a cold.
chhanḍáluḍu, pariah. Skt. Also written *chanḍáluḍu* and *chánḍáluḍu.*
chhágamu, goat. Skt. Used pedantically in books for *méca.* It amuses the authors of plays and even novels to write *chhágamu* instead of *méca* and *aṣvam,* Skt. for horse, instead of *gurram;* and the readers can understand just as English readers will understand 'equitation test' for 'riding test', and will usually know the derivation of Capricorn.
chhándasuḍu, ritualist, textualist. Skt. The more common word *chádastuḍu,* bigot, is a corruption of this.
chháya, colour. Skt.
chhédanamu, cutting up. Skt.
chhédintsuṭa, to cut up. Skt.
chhidramu, schism, fault. Skt. *chhidram,* hot. *grühachhidramu* is domestic scandal.
chiccintsuconuṭa, to obtain; causal middle from *chiccuṭa. chétiló chiccintsuconnánu,* I got it into my hands.
chiccu, tangled (adj.); from *chiccuṭa. chiccu zaḍalu,* tangled plaits of hair.
chiccu, perplexity, mess, troubles. *í pedda manishi yédó chicculó v'unnaṭṭu cana paḍutú v'unnáḍu,* this gentleman seems to be in some mess; *í chiccul' anní lécunḍá maharázu vale v'unḍi v'unḍuru,* you will be like a maharaja without all these troubles.
chiccuconuṭa, to involve, get entangled. *dáramu naḍuma chiccuconnadi,* the string got entangled between.
chiccuṭa, to become lean. *gurramu ná samsthánam valené chiccinadi,* my horse has got lean like my estate, as a dispossessed zamindar said as he came riding up on a scarecrow.
chiccuṭa, to be found, to be caught. *í v'utstsu y' itani chétulacu vési biginchinám' anṭé y' itaḍu manacu chiccinaṭṭé,* we have as good as got him if we get this noose round his hands; *váḷḷa chétiló chiccindi,* it has got into their hands.
chicilicaḷḷu, luring eyes.
chicitstsa, medical treatment. Skt. Though Sanskrit this is the usual word and very common.
chiḍimuḍi, peevishness.
chiḍumu, itch. *váḍici vaḷḷ' antá gajji chiḍumú paṭṭinadi,* he was smarting and itching all over.
chidumuṭa, to nip. *góṭa chiduma taginadi goḍḍanṭa narucuṭa,* taking an axe to cut what you could nip with the nail (breaking a butterfly on a wheel).
chigirintsuṭa, to spout.
chiguru, gum (of the teeth), quick (of the nail); plural *chiguḷḷu. váḍu ná góru chigur anṭa cósindáḍu,* he cut my nail to the quick.
chiguru, (adj.) tender. *chigur' ácu,* tender leaf.
chihnamu, sign, symptom, characteristic. Skt. *mukha chihnálanu baṭṭi tsústé,* judging by the symptoms in his face; *tamaru parácu paḍaḍamé dharmam' andi, adi maharázu chihnamu,* it is right for your Honour not to remember, that is a sign of nobility, as the diwan said to the zamindar when they were going through the accounts (*noblesse oublie*).

chilaca, parrot; also *chiluca.*

chillara, petty, retail, small change. *chillara ducáṇam* is a retail shop; *padi rúpáyilu pai chillara,* ten rupees odd; *ní daggira chillara undá?* have you any change? *mánéjaru veyyi rúpáyilu cáchéṣáḍu, pustacamló émani vrásédi? chillara khartsul ani ráyi,* 'The manager has misappropriated Rs. 1,000, under what head do I put it?' 'Petty expenses.'

chilli, hole.

chilligavva, a broken cowry (shell that was once used as money). Now used in such phrases as: *chinnáyanagáru tana ástilo nácu chilligavvainá y'ivvaru,* my uncle won't give me a penny; *í rátri bhójanánic ainá chilligavva lédu,* I haven't a farthing even for to-night's supper; *ḍabbucu venucá mundú tsúḍaca rúpáyi chilligavvagá khartsu chésinámu,* we spent a rupee as though it were a pie without caring for money.

chillipaḍuṭa, chillipóvuṭa, to go into holes.

chiluca, parrot. *palleṭúri nunchi vachchina sácshici bódha chéséṭ'appaṭici sácshyam antá vácita panjaramuló v'unna chilucacu cúḍá vachchinadi,* after he had instructed a rustic witness the parrot in its cage on the threshold had the whole evidence by heart.

chilucacoyya, peg.

chilucuṭa, to churn.

chilumu, verdigris, slang for money. *í níru chilumu campu coṭṭutsunnadi,* this water tastes of brass; *chilumu vadilité chhidramu vadulutundi,* no tin, no household broils.

chimiḍipóvuṭa, to over-boil (of rice). *í lógá annam chimiḍi póyindi,* meanwhile the rice got over-boiled.

chimmachícaṭi, pitch dark.

chimmana, pop! onomatopoeic.

chimmanagoṭṭamu, squirt.

chimmeṭa, moth.

chimpi, a tear, rag.

chimpuṭa, to tear; also *chintsuṭa, chimpivéyuṭa. viluva chiral ichchinanu marunáṭicé chimpivéyuduvu,* if I give you costly cloths next day you tear them.

chimuḍuṭa, to over-boil.

chindapóyuṭa, to spill (transitive).

chindulu toccuṭa, to dance.

chinduṭa, to be spilt, to spread.

chinna, small, young. *mukhamu chinnaputstsuconuṭa* or *chésuconuṭa,* to make your face small, means 'look ashamed'; *chinna tsúpu* is look of scorn; *chinna pámun' ainá pedda carrató coṭṭa valenu,* though the snake be small take a big stick to beat it.

chinnadi, girl.

chinnanáḍu, one's young days.

chinnapóvuṭa, to be out of countenance. *váni mukham chinna póyinadi,* he was out of countenance.

chinnaputstsuṭa, to make one look small.

chinnatalli, aunt, being mother's sister; composed of *chinna,* little, and *talli,* mother. Also *pinatalli,* and *chinni* for short.

chinnatanamu, disgrace. *álá chésté manac andarici bahu chinnatanam sumá,* if you do that we shall all be greatly dishonoured.

chinnatanamu, childhood.

chinnaváḍu, boy; also *curraváḍu.*

chinnáyana, uncle, being father's younger brother; also *pinatanḍri.*

chinta, grief. Skt. One of the numerous words for grief (the *nuance* is a musing or brooding grief). *mogani chinta chéta grámamu viḍichi léchi póyinadi,* brooding over her husband she left the village and went away.

chintacáya, tamarind in the shell.

chintacheṭṭu, tamarind tree.

chintanamu, reflection. Skt.

chintapanḍu, tamarind fruit, an indispensable ingredient in South Indian cookery.

chintácrántuḍu, overwhelmed with grief. Skt.

chintámaṇi, the wishing stone. Skt. from *chinta,* wish, and *maṇi,* gem. This was a ruby whose possession gave all one wished. It is also the name of a much advertised quack medicine. Skt.

chintintsuṭa, to grieve. Skt. *ayina panici chintinchéváḍu alpa buddhi galaváḍu,* grieving over spilt milk.

chintsuṭa, to tear.

chinucu, a drop.

chinuculu, drizzle.

chinuguṭa, to be torn.
chippa, earthenware saucer, shell, pan. *mócáli chippa* is the knee-pan; *tala chippa*, skull pan.
chira, long (of time). Skt.
chirachiraláḍuṭa, to be angry, sullen; onomatopoeic. *penimiṭini tsústé nívu álá chira chiral áḍutú v'unṭáv émi?* will you growl at your husband like that?
chiranjívi, long lived. Skt. Used especially in blessings on young people. It is prefixed to the names of young people in Telugu letters.
chirata, wedge. *chiratalu*, pincers.
chirácu, peevishness, disgust. *áme éḍupu mogamu paḍi yeccaḍaléni chirácunu vachchi, nannu chanḍáluni tsúchin' aṭlu tsútsunu*, making a crying face and looking me up and down with the utmost disgust as if I were a pariah.
chiri, small.
chiricappa, the small or chunam frog.
chirináluca, uvula (small tongue).
chirru, expression of anger; onomatopoeic. *musalitanam vachchi mati póyi prati dánici chirru-bussum-anṭú v'unṭé*, when you are old and mad and growl and grumble about everything.
chirugu, chirugula, torn. *chirugu tsápa vésináru, manchi tsápa lédá yémiṭi?* you have put a torn mat, haven't you a good one? *chirugula guḍḍalu*, torn clothes.
chiruguṭa, to tear.
chirunavvu, smile (small laugh). *chirunavvu navvi*, smiling.
chirunáma, address (on a letter). Hindustani; also *paivilásamu*. *í v'uttarálu tísuconi velli pai chirunámála pracáram yevarivi váric ichchi*, taking these letters and distributing them according to the addresses.
chirutapuli, panther, cheetah.
chirutinḍi, light refection.
chitacacoṭṭuṭa, to beat into a jelly; from *chitucuṭa*, to be smashed, and *coṭṭuṭa*.
chiṭachiṭamanuṭa, to crackle, to be vexed; onomatopoeic.
chiti, funeral pyre. Skt.
chiṭi, prefix meaning 'small.' *chiṭipoṭi*, trifling; *chiṭi tsápa*, small mat; *chiṭi vélu*, little finger.
chiṭica, snap or rap of the fingers, pinch of snuff. *nácu vaca chiṭica poḍumu véyi*, give me a pinch of snuff.
chiṭicinavélu, little finger. *pápishṭi télu yeccaḍanunchi vachchinadó cáni tsaṭuccuna chiṭicinavél anṭa poḍichinadi*, a beastly scorpion coming out from somewhere suddenly stung my little finger.
chiṭicipóvuṭa, to be smashed. *ráḷḷu veyyaḍam tsálá tappitam, iḷḷa mída penculu chitici pótavi*, it is wrong to throw stones (at houses), the tiles will be smashed.
chiṭlintsuṭa, to break, to frown. *mukhamu chiṭlintsuṭa* is to frown.
chitracáruḍu, painter. *rangulató likhintsuṭa* is to paint, *vráyuṭa* to draw.
chitramu, novelty, wonder (properly 'speckled'). Skt. *oca chitramu zarigindi, vinnárá?* a wonder has occurred, have you heard?
chitrapaṭamu, picture, drawing.
chitrapupratima, image. *manassu sthiraparichi téripára tsúchinán' anṭé yóganidra chéta chitrapu pratima lágu 'aipótáḍu*, I concentrate my mind, stare at him, and will put him into a hypnotic sleep until he is still as an image.
chitravastuvulu, curiosities. Skt., from *chitram*, curious, and *vastuvu*, thing. Hence *chitra-vastu-pradarşana-şála*, a very long word for museum, but people prefer to use the English word.
chitrica, carpenter's plane.
chitrintsuṭa, to paint (a picture), to limn. *vráyuṭa, bommalu véyuṭa* are more commonly used.
chitstsu, fire. Skt. *eluca mída cópána y'inṭici chitstsu peṭṭin'aṭṭu*, setting fire to one's house to spite a rat (biting off one's nose to spite one's own face). Also used of a fiery taste: *ī tsalla chitstsu*, this buttermilk is sharp to the taste.
chiṭṭachivaracu, at the very last, reduplication of *chivara*, end.
chittagintsuṭa, to attend, consider; from Skt. *chittam*, mind. It is a word used to superiors; thus 'yours respectfully' at the end of a letter is *chittagintsa valenu*. *aṭlu chittaginchináḍu*,

the Collector or other authority came to this decision (heard this prayer); *chittagintsa valenu* at the end of a petition means 'do me the favour to consider'.

chittamu, mind. Skt. *chittamu Ṣivuni mida, bhacti cheppula mida,* his mind is on Siva but he is really thinking of the shoes he left outside the temple; *chittachánchalyamu,* agitation of mind.

chittamu, yes, Sir (your pleasure). It is what your peons say when you give an order.

chittaruvu-vráyuṭa, to engrave, to paint. *ámenu panḍuconn' aṭlugá chittaruvu vrásinádu,* he painted her in a recumbent position.

chiṭṭá, account book. *chiṭṭá* is the daily cash-book, *ávarzá* the ledger; the two accounts that every merchant keeps.

chiṭṭeluca, mouse; from *chiru,* small, and *eluca,* rat.

chittu, draft. *á uttaramunacu chittu cudirchinánu,* I have prepared a draft of that letter.

chiṭṭu, bran; also *tauḍu.*

chiṭucu, chirrup, any soft sound; onomatopoeic. *chíma chiṭucum anṭé nidra munḍi léstáḍu,* he will wake up at the tread of an ant.

chitucuṭa, to be smashed, burst. *curupu chiticinadi,* the boil is burst.

chivara, end. *chiṭṭachivara* is 'the very end'; *úrichivara,* at the end of the village.

chiváluna, suddenly.

chíváṭlu, scolding (from *chí!* fie!). *rózú tahassildáru gáru andari mundará nannu chiváṭlu peṭṭutáru,* the tahsildar scolds me every day before every one.

chí! chí! fie! fie! *aṭṭé pélacu, naluguru chí! chí! anṭáru,* people will say 'fie! fie!' to such nonsense.

chícaṭi, darkness. *ippuḍu chícaṭi paḍutú v'unnadi,* it is getting dark now; *chícaṭi connáḷḷu, vennela connáḷḷu,* some days dark, some days light (i.e. there are ups and downs in life); *conḍanta chícaṭi,* pitch dark.

chícácu, disgust.

chícuṭa, suck, smack with the lips.

chíḍa, rot, blight.

chíḍapurugu, any grub or worm that rots fruit, &c.

chíduṭa, to blow one's nose.

chíla, linch pin.

chílamanḍa, ankle; also *manḍa* only.

chílica, splitting, a slice.

chíltsuṭa, to split (transitive).

chíluṭa, to split (intransitive).

chíma, ant. *cherucu v'unḍé tsóṭici chímalu támé vastávi,* ants will come by themselves to the place where there is a sugar-cane; *nívu chímalágu pácutávu,* you are crawling as slow as an ant (as a snail, we should say).

chímiḍi, snot of the nose.

chímu, pus.

chímupóyuṭa, to suppurate.

Chíná, China.

chípurugaṭṭa, a broom (*gaṭṭa* for *caṭṭa,* tied). *adigó Sómidévi chípurugaṭṭa paṭṭuconi tsávaḍilónici vatsutsutsunnadi,* see, Somadevi is coming into the hall with a broom in her hand.

chíra, a woman's cloth. *viluva chíral ichchinanú marunáṭicé chimpivéyuduvu,* if I give you costly cloths next day you tear them.

chíruṭa, to tear.

chíṭi, a note (letter), certificate, the Anglo-Indian chit.

chíṭlu, cards (playing).

chívállu, scolding; also *chiváṭlu. bahu vidhála chiváṭlu peṭṭi bádhimpagá,* troubling with all sorts of scoldings.

chódyamu, wonder. Skt.

chóri, theft. Skt. The Telugu word is *dongatanamu.* However, *chóri* is used in the official translation of the Penal Code and is familiar in police stations and law courts. *chórisottu* is stolen property; *chóruḍu* is never said for 'thief', it is always *donga.*

chúḍámaṇi, jewel worn on the head; figuratively any jewel. *íyane nigarva chúḍámaṇi,* he is a jewel of modesty. *chúḍa* is the peacock's crest (Skt. *maṇi,* jewel).

chúrnamu, powder. Skt.

D

daba-daba, audibly, soundly. *daba-daba coṭṭinḍḍu,* he beat him soundly (with audible blows).

ḍaba-ḍaba, noisily. *vádu ḍaba-ḍaba vágutáḍu, cáni vaṭṭi ṣunṭha,* an empty fool but he makes much noise (empty vessels make most noise).

ḍabbá, small box; also *ḍabbí. poḍi ḍabbá,* snuffbox.

ḍabbu, ¼ anna, money in general. *ḍabbu galavárici y'eppuḍunu y'é velu-lunu rávu,* there is no excommunication for people with money; *ḍabbucu vachchina cheyyi varahácu vastundi,* the hand that steals the penny will steal the pound; *ḍabbucu pránánici lance,* there is a link between money and life; *ḍabbu ivvanivádu mundu paḍava y'eccin'aṭṭu,* like the man who did not pay his fare but got first into the boat.

dabbuna, suddenly.

ḍabhai, 70; also *ḍebhai, ḍebbadi.*

daccintsuṭa, to preserve, secure. *illu tanacu daccintsuconnáḍu,* he secured the house for himself. *míru máṭa daccintsucó valenu,* you should get the credit of doing it.

daccuṭa, to be left or obtained, keep. *ásti antá manací daccutundi,* all the property will come to us; *ḍabbu cartsu cácunḍá péru mícu daccaḍánici vach-chinadi,* you have got the credit without spending a penny; *nívu mí y'inṭici veḷli pó, míru y'iccaḍa v'unṭé maryáda daccadu,* go home, you will lose respect if you stay; *ḍabbu khartsu cheyyaḍu cáni maṭa mátramu tanacu daccálani tsústáḍu,* though he does not spend anything over it he wants to secure the credit of doing it.

dacshata, protection. Skt. *má talli póvaḍam chéta y'inṭló áḍa dacshata léca,* deprived of female protection by my mother's death.

dacshiṇa, present to a priest. Skt.

dacshiṇamu, south; from Skt. *dacshi-ṇam,* right-hand side (which is *cuḍi* in Telugu), because the south is on your right when you face the east.

dacshuḍu, clever person. Skt.

daḍa, trembling. *lópala daḍa puṭṭi,* trembling inwardly; *vaḷḷu daḍa y'ettu-tóndi,* I tremble.

dadduru, weal.

dafá, a time. Hindustani. *oca dafá,* once.

ḍafédáru, head peon of an office. duffadar; a very important person in India, and a very common word which, curiously enough, will not be found in the Telugu dictionaries.

dagá, cheating. Hindustani. *mósamu* is the Telugu word but *dagá* is very common.

dagácheyuṭa, to cheat.

dagdhamu, burnt. Skt.

daggira, daggara, near, at, with. *ná daggira v'unnadi,* it is with me, the way Telugus mostly say, 'I have'; *vadda* is an equivalent; in fact 'to have' does not exist in Telugu. *inṭi daggira* is 'at home'; *dúrapu conḍalu nunupu; daggirici póté ráḷḷa gunḍlu,* distance lends enchantment to the view.

daggu, a cough.

dagguṭa, to cough. *tátacu dagga nérpa valená!* teach your grandmother to suck eggs; *vráyagá vráyagá caraṇamu, daggagá daggagá maraṇamu,* write and write you are karnam, cough and cough and you are a dead man.

dahanamu, burning. Skt. *ṣavamunu dahanam chéyintsuṭa,* to get a corpse burnt.

dahintsuṭa, to burn. Skt. *navami-náḍu puḍacató danta dhávanamu chési-naṭṭ aité, éḍava taramu varacunu culamunu dahintsu n' ani cheppabaḍi v' unḍagá inta pápacáryam yenducu chésináró cheppanḍi?* whereas it is written that if you clean you? teeth on the 9th day you destroy your caste to the 7th generation, why did you commit such a sin?

dainyamu, meanness, humiliation. Skt., adjectival from *dínam,* low.

daiva, prefix meaning 'of God'. Skt., adjective from *dévuḍu,* God. *daiva-dúshanam* is blasphemy; *daivádhínam* is providence; *daivavácyam,* the word of God; *daivagati*, act of God; *daiva-yatnamu*, decree of providence; *daiva-vaṣáttugá*, by the act of God, i.e. accidentally.

daivamu, God. Skt. *tsúḍa tsuṭṭamú, mocca daivamú léḍu*, no relation to visit, no God to pray to (i.e. complete destitution); *tán ocaṭi talachité, daivam ocaṭi talaché*, man proposes, God disposes.

daivatamu, a deity. Used in books for *dévata*, a god.

daivicamugá, by act of God; i.e. accidentally. *daivicamugá labhinchina samayamu*, a providential opportunity.

daḷamu, petal. Skt.

daḷamu, army.

daḷaváyi, a general; some families still have *daḷaváyi* as a hereditary title, e.g., the Dalavai Mudaliars of Tinnevelly.

dalálí, broker. Hindustani.

ḍaḷáyatu, peon. Hindustani. A more honourable word than peon, which comes from the Portuguese (foot-soldier) or *banṭrótu* (trooper); *daḷáyatu* probably does not come from *daḷamu*; it is also spelt *ḍhaḷáyatu*. *ḍhaḷáyatunu yenni mátulu tsúchi rammani pampinchiná dóragáru pani mída v'unnáru*, however often I sent the peon to see, the Collector was always busy.

dambhamu, cheating, insolence. Skt.

dambhamu, boast. *ní dambha vácyamulu vini mósapóyinánu*, I was deceived by your boasts; *váḍu vaṭṭi dambhála ráyuḍu*, he is a vain-glorious man.

dammiḍi, a pie, $\frac{1}{12}$ anna. *sommu chétuló padaḍamtóṭé vacca dammiḍí migultsucócunḍá yevaridi várici panchi peḍatáru*, as soon as he gets the money he will distribute it all to the last pie.

dammu, wet ploughing (in rice fields).

dammuchéyuṭa, to plough wet.

dammunágali, plough used to plough in water.

dampa ságubaḍi, wet cultivation.

dampatulu, man and wife, married couple. Skt., from *pati*, husband. The Telugu is *álumagulu*.

ḍancá, drum. *ḍancá mída debba coṭṭi cheppa galanu*, I can say it triumphantly.

danḍa, necklace, garland.

danḍamu, salutation, vulgarly *daṇṇam*; the usual salutation, hands folded before the breast. *dásari tappu danḍamutó sari*, a dásari's fault is wiped off with a salutation.

danḍamu, danḍanamu, danḍana, punishment. *danḍam daṣa guṇam bhavét*, there is a ten-fold merit in chastisement; *maraṇadanḍana*, capital punishment; *danḍanáyacuḍu*, a general (Skt., from *danḍu*, army, and *náyacuḍu*, leader).

danḍayátra, invasion. Skt., from *danḍu*, army, and *yátra*, expedition.

danḍádhipati, a general. Skt., from *danḍu*, army, and *adhipati*, commander. Also *danḍa-náyacuḍu*.

danḍárhuḍu, deserving of punishment. From *danḍamu*, punishment, and *arhuḍu*, fit.

danḍemu, clothes-line; vulgarly *daṇṇemu*.

danḍemulu-tíyuṭa, to do press-ups.

danḍettuṭa, to raise an army, invade; from *danḍu*, army, and *ettuṭa*, to raise; colloquially understood, to attack.

danḍintsuṭa, to punish. Skt., from *danḍana*.

danḍóra, proclamation by drum.

danḍórávéyuṭa, to proclaim.

danḍu, army. Skt. *púrvamu danḍuló coluvu chésina vrilddha bhaṭuḍu*, an old soldier who had served in the army.

danḍuga, loss, forfeit. *atani chétiló moṭṭamodaṭané nálugu rúpáyilú peṭṭin' aṭṭ aité y'i danḍugal anní tappév énd?* should we not have avoided all these losses if we had given him a small bribe to start with?

daniyálu, coriander; also *dhaniyálu*.

daṇṇamu, salutation; vulgar, but common, for *danḍamu*. *nícu daṇṇam peḍutánu*, I salute, i.e. beg, you; *á v' undráḷlu ná mundu peṭṭi, daṇṇam peṭṭi, dúrangá nilutsunḍi, bhacti canapartsu*, place the offerings before me, salute, stand at a distance and show devotion; *maháprabhó! mému máṭláḍam' anḍi, nícu daṇṇam peḍatámu*, my Lord! we will not speak, we will do obeisance to you.

daṇṇemu, vulgar for *danḍemu*, clothes-line.

dantadhávanamu, cleaning of teeth. Skt., from *dantam*, teeth, and *dhávanam*, cleaning.

dantamu, tooth, ivory. Skt. The Telugu is *paḷḷu* or *pannu*. *dantamu* in the sense of tooth is used only in compounds; *dantapu duvvena* is an ivory comb.

dantsuṭa, to pound (grain in a mortar); also metaphorically, to beat. *nénu 'donga donga' ani céca veyyaḍamtóṭe á gadiló v' unna dushṭuṇṇi velupalici y' íḍtsucuni vachchi mettagá dantsa valenu*, when I cry 'thief, thief' lug the scoundrel out of that room and pound him fine.

danuca, a book form of *dáca*, up to.

danujuḍu, demon, giant. Skt.

dappi, thirst. *nácu dappigá v' unnadi*, I am thirsty. The Skt. *dáhamu* is commoner.

ḍappu, drum. *ḍappu putstsuconi ṭámaṭamá vésé Mádigavâḍitó cheppu*, speak to the Madiga who takes the drum and makes tom-tom; *commulu v' údi ḍappulu váyinchi*, blowing horns and beating drums; *mácu ḍappula pani léca póvaḍam chéta callu-niḷḷaci léca tsachchi pótú v'unnámu*, as we (Madigas) have no drumming to do, we are dying for want of toddy.

dappuṭa, for *tappuṭa*, to fail. Used in print, not speech.

darakhástu, application. Hindustani. Used especially for an application for land.

darbáru, audience-chamber, government. Hindustani. To receive in darbar is to receive in public audience; the word comes to mean the audience itself and the person who grants the audience. It is sometimes applied to the rajah's ministers rather than to the rajah himself. *guḍḍi darbáru, naváb darbáru*, the rule of any administrative officer that is a benevolent despotism.

darbhalu, sacred grass used in sacrifices. Skt.

dari, shore, refuge, limit. *dari chéruṭa*, to reach the shore, means 'to die'.

darici, darigá darini, near. *darici chéracunḍá tarimi véstú*, not allowing to come near but driving away; *inṭi darini* is 'near the house'.

daricolpuṭa, to set on fire. The commoner word is *tagala peṭṭuṭa*; this is used metaphorically also. *manassuló cámágnini daricolpina taruváta, adi anṭuconi manḍutú v'unṭé, maḷḷí árpi veyyaḍamu sádhyamu cádu sumá*, after the fire of passion is kindled in the mind and has caught on and is flaming it is difficult to quench.

daridramu, poverty. Skt. *tamarini tsústé ná daridra vimóchanam autundi*, (a beggar speaking) you will remove my poverty; *daridradaṣa*, condition of poverty.

daridruḍu, a poor man. Skt. *ataḍu caṭica daridruḍu, púṭacúṭici gati lédu*, he is an absolute pauper without money for a meal.

darimilánu, afterward. Hindustani.

dariyáftu, enquiry. Hindustani; commonly used of administrative investigations. *dariyáftu cheyyagá atani nizam'aina péru Rámayya*, on enquiry his real name was found to be Ramayya; *nénu paigá dariyáftu chésinánu*, I made further enquiry.

darjí, tailor. Hindustani. *darjiváḍu cuṭṭin anducu cúli putstsucócunḍá v' unḍaḍu*, the tailor won't go without his stitching wages.

darpamu, pride. Skt. *darpam yerugaca*, having no proper pride; *atanici ḍábú darpamú yemi lédu*, he has no pomp or pride.

darṣanamu, sight, visit. Skt. Properly sight, but the common use is 'visit'; as we say 'to go and see a person'. It is used all over India; large crowds gather to get a *darṣan* of Mahatma Gandhi. *áyana darṣanam chéyistánu*, I will get you an interview with him; *áviḍe darṣanam manac eccaḍa aútundi?* where can we see her? *dúraṣravaṇa dúradarṣan' ádi ṣactulu*, powers of hearing and seeing, &c., at a distance.

daruvu, time in music. *daruvu véyuṭa*, to beat time; also *táḷamu véyuṭa*.

daṣa, condition, stage. Skt. *várdhaca daṣa*, old age; *báladaṣa*, childhood; *csháma daṣa*, famine time; *graha daṣa*, influence of the stars; *agnyána daṣa*, state of ignorance; *yógi rendava daṣaló sampúrṇa gnyánamu ponduṭáḍu, múḍava daṣaló y' indriya nigraham chési, chatur vargamulanu bhútamulanu jayistáḍu*, the adept gets full wisdom in the second stage, sense control in the third stage, and conquest of the elements in the fourth.

daṣabandha inámu, is a piece of land granted on favourable terms to a person who constructs an irrigation tank; the derivation is from Skt. *daṣa*, ten. The tax was $\frac{1}{10}$th the gross, which is much more than our usual tax; but the old ideas of a reasonable tax were very different from ours.

daṣami, the tenth day of the full moon or the new-moon day. Skt., from *daṣa*, 10.

daṣara, the ten-nights festival; from Skt. *daṣa*, ten, and *rátri*, night. The most important festival of the Hindu year in the Telugu country; it comes in October. One of the items is the *áyudha púja* or worship of the implements of one's trade; the Collector's peons do homage to the stationery on his office table, his driver decorates his car, and so on.

dascatu, signature. Hindustani; the Telugu is *chévrálu. ica mundu bógam méḷam tsúḍan' ani cágitam mída dascatu chésináḍ' aṭa*, he is said to have signed a paper declaring that he would never go to a nautch party again.

dastávézu, document. Hindustani.

dastramu, papers tied up in a cloth. Hindustani. *Baḍé Sáhébu ménéjaru gári peṭṭi tísucuni vastú v'unnáḍu; dastrálu vippi y'ica míru pani tsútsucunṭú v'unḍ anḍi*, (clerk speaking) Bade Sahib is coming with the manager's box; open your paper bundles and be at work.

dastu, money, especially Government cash collections. Hindustani. *púrvam nénu tahassiludáru vésham vési sarcáru grámamulalóné dastu vasúlu chésinánu*, before I personated a tahsildar and made cash collections in Government villages.

dastúri, hand-writing. Hindustani. *tícharu. ní dastúri bottigá bág' unḍa léḍu, bágá ráyaḍam nértsucó. báluḍú. bágá rásté mícu tappul anni canipistáy' anḍi*. Teacher. Your hand is bad. Learn to write. Boy. If I write well you will see all my mistakes.

daṭṭamaina, thick, coarse.

daṭṭamu, thickness, crowd.

dattata, dattu, adoption. Skt., to give (connected with Latin *dare*).

dattuchésiconuṭa, dattutísiconuṭa, to adopt.

dauḍa, davaḍa, jaw, cheek. *dauḍa panḍlu* are the grinders.

dauḍu, gallop, invasion. Hindustani.

dauhitruḍu, daughter's son. Skt., from *duhita*, which is the same word as English *daughter* and German *Tochter*.

ḍaulu, dowle, an old word for the Government revenue demand.

daurbalyamu, weakness. Skt., from *dur*, bad, and *balam*, strength. *váda daurbalyamu*, weakness of argument.

daurbhágyamu, misfortune. Skt., from *dur*, bad, and *bhága*, fortune.

daurbhágyuḍu, wretch; used as an expletive. *órí daurbhágyuḍá!* wretch! *á peḷḷi coḍucu vaṭṭi daurbhágyuḍu*, that bridegroom is worthless.

daurjanyamu, violence, rudeness. Skt., from *dur*, bad, and *jan*, produce. *nívu ica mundu iṭuvanṭi daurjanyam chésinávanṭé*, if I hear of your being so rude again; *iṭuvanṭi daurjanyam zarigina y'í miṭinguló pedda manishi ainaváḍu yevaḍú v'unḍa cúḍadu*, no gentleman can stay at this meeting after such hooliganism.

dautyamu, ambassadorship. Skt., from *dúta*, envoy.

daya, grace, favour, mercy. Skt. A word much used in polite conversation. *daya chéyanḍi*, do me the favour, means step this way or take a seat according to circumstances; *ná yandu daya chési pedda manushyul'antá daya chési v'unnáru*, all the gentlemen have done me the favour to come.

dayádácshiṇyamu, amiability. Skt., from *daya*, favour, and *dácshiṇyam*, kindness. *antaṭi buddhimanturálu y'í tsuṭṭupaṭla áḍaváḷḷaló mari yevvarú léru, á vinayam émi! á calisicaṭṭutanam émi! á dayádácshiṇyál émi!* there is no such sensible woman among the neighbours; such gentleness! such affability! such amiability!

dayárdrahrüdayuḍaina, tender-hearted; from *daya*, *árdramu*, which is 'moist' in Skt., and *hrüdayam*, heart.

dayáṣúnyuḍu, merciless. Skt., from *daya*, mercy, and *ṣúnya*, empty.

dayyamu, fiend; derived from *daivamu*, god. *dága póyina tsóṭa dayyálu paṭṭuconn' aṭṭu*, he went to hide and fell among devils; *dayyamu paṭṭina váni vale*, like a man possessed by devils. In books *dayyamu* is also used as a term for God: *dayyamu y'etticólu tudamuṭṭinadi*, the purpose of God is fulfilled.

ḍábu, pomp. *ḍábú darpamú*, pomp and pride.

dáca, up to, until. *endáca*, how far; *indáca*, up to this; *padi dáca*, up to ten; *indácaṭiváḍu*, the man who was here till now; *tellavárina dáca*, till it dawned.

dáchipeṭṭuṭa, to lay by.

dáconuṭa, to happen.

dácshiṇyamu, kindness. Skt. *dayá-dácshiṇyálu léni*, unkind, discourteous.

dácṭaru, doctor. English. Also *vaidyuḍu*.

dádápugá, almost, about. *dádápugá muppadi dinamul ainadi*, it is about 30 days ago.

dáḍi, beard. Hindustani. Also *gaḍḍamu*.

dádi, nurse.

dáḍi, invasion. Skt.

dáḍicheyyuṭa, to invade.

dádrütvamu, liberality. Skt., from *dá*, give; also spelt *dátrütvamu*. *nelacu renḍu vandala rúpáyalu tetstsuconi v' udyógasthulu cúḍá dádrütvamló mílo sahasráṃṣamainá pólaru*, even officials drawing Rs. 200 a month are not one-thousandth part as liberal as you. *audáryam* is another word for liberality.

dágali, anvil; from *calu*, stone, and *dáyi*, bench.

ḍágu, stain. *proddunné léchi nírucávi dhóvati caṭṭucunnánu, ad antá pénnilḷató ḍágulu paḍḍadi*, I put on a yellow cloth when I got up this morning, it was all stained with dung water (not everyone is convinced of the cleansing properties of dung water, the most purifying substance according to the orthodox Hindu).

dáguḍumútalu, blind man's buff; from *dáguṭa*, to hide.

dáguṭa, dágapóvuṭa, to hide. *dága póyi talári y' inṭló dúrinád' aṭa*, like the thief who hid in the policeman's house.

dáhamu, thirst. Skt. *énuga dáhamucu tsúru níllá?* will eaves-drops quench an elephant's thirst? *conchem pálu dáham putstsucunṭárá?* will you quench your thirst with a little milk? *méghamulu vachchi samudramuló dáham tírtsuconunu*, the clouds quench their thirst in the sea (Hindu physics); *áyanacu dáham mahá viṣéshangá v'unnadi, anta dáham nénu tírtsa lén anḍi*, he has got a great thirst (for bribes), I cannot satisfy so great a thirst; *dáhánici póyináḍu*, he has gone for a drink.

dákhalá, proof. Hindustani. *goppa dákhalá*, it is a clear proof.

dákhaluchéyuṭa, to produce, file. Hindustani. A legal and administrative term for filing or putting in a petition or application.

dáltsuṭa, to take; for *táltsuṭa*, in print not speech.

ḍálu, shield. *á debbanu De Brassey tana ḍálu ché aḍḍaginchenu*, De Brassey parried the blow with his shield.

dáḷvapanṭa, an irrigated crop.

dámáshámída, on an average, on apportionment. Hindustani.

dámbhicuḍu, hypocrite; also *ḍámbicuḍu*. *manchiváḷḷanu dámbhicul aninní asatyavádul aninní, pápátmul aninní, vantsacul aninní, crúrul aninní, nighantuló v'unna páḍu pérl anní peṭṭi*, calling the good hypocrites, liars, sinners, cheats, cruel and by all the bad names in the dictionary.

dámpatyamu, marriage. Skt., from *dampatulu*, man and wife.

dána, gift (in composition). Skt. root *dá*. *dánadharmamulu*, gifts and graces.

dánacarṇuḍu, liberal man. Skt. (as liberal as Carna in the Mahabharat). *míru mahá bhagavantul aninní, dánacarṇul aninní*, saying you were very rich and generous.

dánamu, gift. Skt. *cshétram erigi vittanamu, pátram erigi dánamu,* sow when you know the soil, give when you know the character.

dánapatramu, deed of gift. Skt.

dáni, genitive of *adi,* she, it.

dánici, to it, her.

dánimma, pomegranate. *dánimma cheṭṭu,* the tree; *dánimma panḍu,* the fruit.

dánini, accusative of *adi,* she, it.

dápuramu, nearness, coming into possession. *nácu capaṭa sishyuḍ ocaḍu dápuram ainádu,* a false disciple has thrust himself on me.

dára, wife. Skt. Book word for *penḍldmu, inṭidi.*

dárabandamu, door frame. Skt., also *dvárabandamu.*

dáramu, thread.

dárḍhyamu, vigour. Skt., from *drü-ḍham,* strong. *déhaddárḍhyamu,* bodily strength.

dári, way, road. *Baḷḷárici dári iṭlágá?* is this the way to Bellary? *iṭléná?* is it not the way to Bellary?

dáridryamu, poverty. Skt. *ítacu minchina lótú, góchici minchina dári-dryamu,* depth such that you have to swim, poverty reducing you to your drawers, there is nothing beyond that.

dáruṇamu, horrible. Skt. *Ṣiva dróha-mu valana dáruṇam'aina naracamunu pondutsunnáḍu,* there is a horrible hell in store for traitors to Siva.

dásari, Vishnu temple attendant. Skt. *dásari tappu danḍamutó sari,* a dásari's sin is atoned for by a salutation.

dásitanamu, slavery. Skt.; also *dasi-tanamu.*

dásiṭicamu, overbearing conduct. *dásṭicap-pantulu,* a nickname applied to any overbearing or cunning brahmin officer.

dásuḍu, slave, servant. Skt.; the feminine is *dási* or *dásidi. dási coḍuc ainá cásu galaváḍu rázu,* though he be the son of a slave girl he who has the chink is a king; *nénu yeppuḍú ní dásuṇṇé,* ever your obedient servant.

dásyamu, bondage, service. Skt. *cona-baḍinaváḍ ainá cáca póyiná ṣúdruḍu dásyamu chéya valenu, ataḍu bráhma-ṇuni dásyamu nimittamé brahmadévuḍi chéta srüjimpa baḍináḍu,* the sudra was created to be the brahmin's slave (Hindu religion and ethics).

dáṭintsuṭa, to pass over (transitive).

dáṭipóvuṭa, to pass. *appuḍé aidu ganṭalu dáṭipóyinadi,* it was already past 5.

dátrütvamu, liberality. Skt., from root *dá,* to give; also *dádrütvamu.*

dátsuconuṭa, to hide or spare oneself. *cashṭapaḍi voḷḷu dátsucócundá bágá páṭupaḍéváḍu,* he was a hardworking man who worked without sparing himself; *marmam dátsuconuṭa,* to hide a secret.

dátsuṭa, to hide (transitive).

dáṭuṭa, to cross, transgress.

dává, lawsuit, complaint. Hindustani; also *vyájyamu.*

dávádáruḍu, claimant, plaintiff.

dáyádi, related by the father's side. Skt. *dáyádi racta sambandhamu,* collateral consanguinity.

dáyáduḍu, paternal kinsman. Skt. It is the important relationship as property, primogeniture, and so on descend only in the male line; a widow inherits for life, but the ultimate heirs of the property are the *dáyádulu.*

dáyi, a giver. Skt.

dáyi, bench, anvil.

debba, a blow. *mandú mácú accara lécunḍá, nálugu lankhanḍlu chésté, vacca debbana padi rózula nátici vaḷḷu nimmaḷangá v'unḍunu,* take no medicine but do a few fasts and you will be well in ten days at one blow; *cucca cáṭucu cheppu debba mandu,* for a biting dog a blow with the slipper; *manchi vánici vaca máṭa, manchi goḍḍucu vaca debba,* one word for a good man, one blow for a good bullock; *debba dévendra lócamu,* spare the rod and spoil the child; a proverb much quoted by schoolmasters.

ḍebbadi, ḍebhai, 70; also *ḍabhai.*

debbalutinuṭa, to be beaten (to eat blows), to be wounded. The wounded are *debbalutininaváru*; if you wound a snipe, *debba tinindi* is the proper expression.

ḍecca, hoof, claw.

ḍendamu, heart.

deppu, taunt.

deppuṭa, to taunt.
deṣa, side, quarter, condition. Skt. *diṣa.*
décuṭa, to slide on the haunches.
ḍéga, hawk.
ḍéhacánti, déhachháya, complexion. *enḍaló déhacánti cheḍunu,* the sun spoils the complexion.
déhamu, body. Skt. The Telugu word is *voḷḷu* (*voḍalu*), but *déham* is also common. *déhamu manḍuṭa* is to be angry; *déham viḍutsuṭa* is to die; *bádha tsústé voccoccappuḍu déham viḍisté bágá v'unṭund'ani tóstundi,* in view of the pain I sometimes think it would be well to shuffle off this mortal coil; *déhamuló zabbu vatstsuṭa,* to fall ill; *déhamulu véru gáni, práṇamulu ocaṭé,* separate in body but one in soul.
déhaparityágamu, to shuffle off the mortal coil, death. Skt., from *déham,* body, and *tyágam,* renunciation.
déhasmrütti, consciousness. *déhasmrütti tappi póyinadi,* he lost consciousness.
déhaṣrama, bodily exercise. Skt., from *déham* and *ṣrama,* labour.
déni? of what? Inflected form of *édi?* which?
dénici? to what? Dative of *édi?* which?
dénini? which? Accusative of *édi?* which?
ḍérá, tent; also *ḍhérá. doragári ḍérá daggira vaḍigá máṭláḍutú v'unnárani banṭrótulanu peṭṭi coṭṭinchi pótáru,* they will set the peons on us and have us beaten for talking loud near the Collector's tent.
déṣabhásha, the vernacular. From *déṣam,* country, and *bhásha,* language.
déṣamu, country. *pradéṣamu* is a region, place.
déṣasthuḍu, inhabitant of a country, fellow-countryman.
déṣaváḷi, belonging to the country. *síma sárálu tágutámu cáni déṣaváḷi sárálu tágamu,* we drink foreign but not country liquor.
déṣácháramu, custom of the country; from *déṣam* and *ácháram,* custom.
déṣádhipati, king; from *déṣam* and *adhipati,* ruler.
déṣántaramu, foreign country; from *désam* and *antaramu,* other.
déṣántaramu póvuṭa, -veḷḷuṭa, to emigrate. *ducci-ṭ-eḍḍu déṣántaramu veḷḷi-n-aṭṭu,* the ox that was wanted for the plough was away; *déṣántaram léchi póṭánu,* I shall emigrate.
déṣántarayátra, emigration.
déṣántaruḍu, emigrant.
déṣáṭanamu, travelling.
déṣíyamu, provincialism (in speech).
déva, divine, of God. Skt.
Dévadattuḍu, Deodatus, God-given. Skt., used as a name, etc.
dévadáruvu, the deodar tree. Skt.
dévadási, dancing-girl. Skt., from *déva,* God, and *dási,* servant. These *dévadásis,* also called *véṣyalu* and *bhógastrílu,* are married to the god and thereafter promiscuous; *dévadási* inams or endowments in land are now being resumed and the practice of dedicating young girls has been made illegal.
dévadúta, angel. Skt., from *déva,* god, and *dúta,* messenger; hence the word is used by missionaries to translate angel.
dévara, a form of address used, e.g., by the Collector's peons to the Collector; it is literally 'O god!', like *swámi,* which is also used, but means no more than 'Sir'.
dévasthánamu, abode of God, temple. Skt. *tsadivédi rámáyaṇamu, paḍagoṭṭévi déva sthalálu,* what he reads is the Ramayana, what he knocks down are temples.
dévata, god, goddess. Skt. *gráma dévata* is the village goddess.
dévatárchana, divine service. Skt. *ní mída préma chéta dévatárchanac ani inṭinṭa tirigi nityamunu manchi puvvulu techchi istánu,* I go about from house to house all out of love of you collecting nosegays for the god's service, so I say, and give them to you. In brahmin phraseology *dévatárchana* is understood as dinner, as worship of the household deity is a necessary precedent to a good dinner. *míru má y'inṭló dévatárchanacu daya cheyya valenu,* please deign to take your dinner in our house. In the higher castes *dévatárchana* simply means filling one's stomach: *váḍu*

The Author as an undergraduate at Oxford (1896)

vaṭṭi dévatárchana priyuḍu, he is a glutton.

déválayamu, temple. Skt., from *déva* and *álayamu*, abode. *mana déválayálalónó mari yé bahiranga sthalamulónó váránici renḍu sárlu pillal andaru póg ayyé-ṭ-aṭṭu chési contamandi panḍitula chéta mana matam bódha chéyistú v'unḍa valenu*, all the boys should be collected in our temple or other public places and instructed in our religion by learned men twice a week.

dévendruḍu, Indra (*déva*+*Indruḍu*).

dévi, goddess, lady. Skt. *paṭṭapu dévi* is a crowned lady, queen.

dévuḍu, God. Skt. *andani púlu dévunici arpaṇa*, offering to God flowers out of reach; *dicculéni-vánici dévuḍé diccu*, God, help of the helpless; *dévuḍ' itstsuné gáni tinipintsuná?* God gives but does he put the food in your mouth? *dévuḍu varam ichchiná pújári varam ivvaḍu*, though God grant the boon, the priest will not; *níḷḷu pallam erugunu, nizam dévuḍ' erugunu*, water knows its level and God the truth; *dévuḍá!* O God!, a common exclamation; but the translation in a Christian hymn book of 'O Lamb of God' as *gorrepilla dévuḍá!* (O son of a sheep, God) has nothing to recommend it.

dévuláduṭa, to struggle, be in trouble.

dhagadhagamanuṭa, glittering, flashing; onomatopoeic.

dhairyamu, courage. Skt. *dhairyamuléni rázu yóchanaléni mantri*, to a courageless king a planless minister; *dhairyamu sarva sádhacamu*, through courage success.

dhairyamuchéyuṭa, to take courage.

dhairyamucheppuṭa, to cheer up (transitive).

dhairyaṣáli, a brave man. Skt., from *dhairyamu* and *ṣáli*, possessed of. *nívu mahá dhairyaṣálivigá v' unnávé!* you are very brave!

dhaláyatu, peon, especially the Collector's; also *dalayatu, banṭrótu. ḍhaláyatutó yenni máṭlu cheppiná veḷḷi tsúchi doragáru pani mida v' unnáru*, every time I asked a peon and he went to see, the Collector was at work.

dhanahínuḍu, poor. Skt., from *dhanam*, money, and *hínam*, lacking. *nénu dhanahínuṇṇi cáni sangati nícu telusunu gadá?* you know I am not a poor man?

dhanamu, money. Skt. *inṭló dhanam múlugutú v' unnadi*, the house is swimming in money; *stridhanam* is a woman's separate money, pin-money.

dhanavantuḍu, a rich man. Skt. *dhanavantul'ai garva paḍutú v'unṭáru*, they have become rich and proud.

dhanicuḍu, rich. Skt. *tsaduvuconnaváru, dhaniculu, chellubaḍi calaváru*, educated, rich, and respected persons.

dhaníyálu, coriander; also *daniyálu. dhaniyála játi*, the coriander race, are the komatis or merchants because you have to squeeze them to get anything out of them.

dhanuvu, dhanassu, bow. Skt. The Telugu is *villu. Indradhanassu*, Indra's bow, is the rainbow.

Dhanvantari, Aesculapius. Skt. The gods' physician.

dhanyuḍu, fortunate man. Skt. *nannu dhanyuṇṇi cheyyanḍi*, make me a fortunate man.

dhara, price; the usual word for rate, price of commodities, produce, &c., especially in the plural.

dhara, dharaṇi, earth. Skt. *tappu léniváru dharaṇiló léru*, there is none without fault on earth; *tallini namminavádu, dharaṇi namminavádu cheḍaḍu*, trust in your mother and trust to the earth (an agricultural proverb).

dharávatu, valuation, deposit; from *dhara*.

dharintsuṭa, to wear. *sanyáṣi cásháya vastramulanu dharintsuconi vachchináḍu*, the sanyasi came in his yellow robes.

dharma, nature of things, matter, phenomenon (philosophy). Skt.

dharmacarta, temple manager. Skt.

dharmamu, virtue, privilege, duty, or characteristic of a caste or profession, law of nature, rightness, custom, charity. Skt. *rázu yentó dharmam anté*, the people will be dutiful if the king is good; *lantsam pantsam tinaḍam v'udyóga dharmam*, bribe-taking is an official privilege; *zúḍam rázulacu dharmamé cádanḍi?* is not gambling a duty and privilege of rajás? *mí* *cóṣam srüshṭi dharmálu cottagá máravu,* the laws of nature will not be changed for you; *cáladharmam' onduṭa* is to pay nature's debt, to die; *dharmamá?* is it right? meaning it is very wrong; *culadharmamu* is the law of your caste; *dánadharmamulu,* gifts and graces.

dharmapatni, lawful wife. Skt. *mícu dharmapatni cávalen anṭé,* if you want a wife.

Dharmarázu, Plutus, the ruler of hell; also called Yama. Skt.

dharmaṣástramu, law. Skt., from *ṣástramu,* science, and *dharmam,* right.

dharmasatramu, rest-house for travellers or the poor. *satram,* choultry; *í grámamuló dharmasatram véyisté bágá v'unḍunu,* it will be a good thing if you build a choultry in this village.

dharmasúcshmamu, point of (religious) law. Skt., from *dharmam* in the sense of religious law and *súcshmam,* subtlety. *índuló y' incoca dharmasúcshmam cúḍá v' unnadi, nénu brahmaṇṇi, agra janma racshaṇam andu cúḍá bonca vatstsunu,* there is another doctrinal point here, I am a brahmin, and we may lie in defence of the highest-born.

dharmátmuḍu, a charitable man. Skt.

dharmishṭuḍu, charitable. Skt.

dhavaḷamu, white, bright. Skt. A word used in books for *tella.*

ḍháca, violence, onset. *indriyamula ḍhácac órtsuṭa,* to withstand the onset of the senses.

dhámantamu, provocative conduct. *buddhi málina dhámantamu chésináv anṭé mému sahinchédi lédu,* if you are foolish enough to provoke us we shall not stand it.

dhányámu, grain; especially rice in the husk. Skt. The various grains, wheat and gingelly are reckoned among the *dhányálu;* not so the millets.

dhára, stream, flow. Skt. *y'erra niṭi dháralu,* courses of red water, i.e., bleeding scratches; *dháradháragá,* pouring (of rain); *váḍu manchi vác dhára calaváḍu,* he has a good flow of words at his command.

-dhári, suffix forming adjectives. Skt. *vishadhári,* poisonous; *véshadhári,* a person in disguise, from *véshamu,* guise; *nivu capaṭa náṭacamu' aḍutú v' unna vaṭṭi véshadháriv ani nácu teliyad' anuconnává?* Do you think that I am not aware that you are playing a deceitful role?

dhárálamugá, Fluently, freely. Skt. *manasuló unnadi dhárálamugá cheppu,* speak freely what is in your mind.

dháṭi, an assault, an invasion.

dháṭí-cala, resolute, firm.

dháṭiga, spiritedly, firmly. *váḍu dháṭiga manchi upanyásál' istáḍu,* his speeches are forcible.

dhénuvu, cow. Used in books, especially of the mythological cow that gives unlimited milk; commonly known as *cámadhénuvu.*

ḍhérá, tent; also *ḍérá.*

dhiccarintsuṭa, to scorn. Skt. More commonly *tirascarintsuṭa.*

dhiccáramu, scorn. Skt. More commonly *tirascáramu. nénu y'iláganṭi praṣna aḍigéṭ'appaṭici guru dhiccáramu chésináv' ani nannu tiṭṭináḍu,* when I asked him such a question he scolded me for contempt of teacher.

dhímantamu, clever. Skt. *mana púrvula pólina dhímantalu,* clever people like our ancestors.

dhíruḍu, a brave man. Skt. *dhíruḍ' aina cá vale, dínuḍ'aina cá vale,* what is wanted is either courage or humility.

dhóraṇi, manner, tenor. Skt. *itani máṭala dhóraṇi tsústé yédó vintagá v'unnadi,* there is something curious about the tenor of his speech; *á aḍagaḍam dhóraṇi tsúchinává?* did you notice the way he asked? *mari yoca dhóraṇilóci rá,* change the conversation; *mí dhóraṇici aḍḍu vatstsutsunnánu,* I contradict you.

dhóvati, dhoty, being the cloth worn by men; also *dóvati.*

dhrüti, firmness, valour. Skt.

dhuni, river. Skt. Used in books for *nadi, éru.*

dhúḷi, dust. Skt. Used in books for *dummu.*

dhúmamu, smoke. Skt. Used in books for *poga.*

dhúpamu, incense. Skt.

dhvajamu, banner. Skt. *dhvajastambhamu* is the common post in front of temples with a symbolic flag made of wood at the top; *janḍá* is the common word for flag; *dhvajamu* is the word used metaphorically, e.g., *mana ṣatru-vula mida dhvajam etta valenu*, we must raise our banner against our foes.

dhvani, sound, noise. Skt. The Telugu is *tsappuḍu*, but *dhvani* is also used in speaking. *chinádéṣamuló cúḍá ghóra sarpamu vachchi paṭṭucunnad' ani bhérilu váyinchi ganṭalu coṭṭi dánni bedara coṭṭaḍánici pedda dhvani chés-tár' aṭa*, they are also said to think in China that eclipses are due to a terrible serpent coming and catching the sun or moon and they beat drums and ring bells and make a big noise to frighten it away.

dhvántamu, darkness. Skt. A book word for *chicaṭi*.

dhyánamu, meditation, especially by looking at your navel. Skt. *rátrim-pagaḷḷu nácu dini midané dhyánam*, my attention is fixed on that night and day; *mému vacca dévuné dhyánamu chéstámu*, we meditate on a single God.

dibba, mound, heap. *eruvu dibba*, manure heap; *Olanda dibba*, the Dutch mound, is all that is left of the Dutch factory at Nagulavamsa.

diccu, quarter, side, refuge. Skt. *dicculu* are the points of the compass; *dicculéni* or *diccumálina* are the common words for helpless.

dicculénivádu, helpless man. *diccu-léni várici Dévuḍé diccu*, God helps the helpless.

diccumálina, helpless, wretched; also as an expletive. *diccumálina vaidyuḍu*, the confounded doctor.

diccunna-tsóṭu, a place where one has any protection. *á sáhébu munḍá coḍucu vánni tsáva tanni diccunna tsóṭa cheppu cóm'annáḍu*, that beast of a sahib kicked him within an inch of his life and bade him report to his benefactors if he has any.

dicpáluḍu, a demi-god who rules one airt or point of the compass in the heavens; there are eight such rulers in the Hindu mythology.

ḍicshanari, dictionary. English. *í máṭa nácu y'inglíshu ḍicshanariló yec-caḍá tsúchin aṭṭu gnyápacam rá lédu*, I don't remember ever seeing this word in the English dictionary.

diddintsuṭa, to make one correct a mistake.

diddu, diddupáṭu, correction.

didduṭa, to correct.

diga, down. This word, rather than *cinda*, is used in compounds. *digapa-ḍuṭa*, to get down; *digapaṭṭuconuṭa*, to drag down.

digagoṭṭuṭa, to knock down; from *diga* and *coṭṭuṭa*.

digambaruḍu, naked. Skt., from *dic*, sky, and *ambaruḍu*, clothed; an epithet of Siva. *disamola* is commoner.

digantam, an end of the earth of the heavens. *diganta-cirti*, one whose reputation has penetrated to the end of the earth; also *diganta-khyáti*. *cirti* and *khyáti* are Skt. words for fame. *cinimá rangamuló Chárli Cháplin gárici diganta-khyáti v'unnadi*, in the film land Charlie Chaplin has attained a world-wide reputation.

digapaḍuṭa, to get down, bring down; from *diga* and *paḍuṭa*. *caḍupu diga baḍuṭa* is to procure abortion; *caḍupu digabaḍuṭac iyané mand ichchináḍu*, he is the man who gave the medicine to procure abortion.

digatíyuṭa, to pull down. *ega tísté brah-mahatya, diga tísté góhatya*, (witness in a case of a brahmin complaining of cattle-trespass) if I pull this way it is brahmin-murder, if I pull that way it is cow-murder (the two greatest sins in the Hindu law code).

digavéyuṭa, to weigh down. *monna monna chinna y' udyógamuló pravéṣin-chinavár andaru manasu vachchin'aṭṭu sampádinchi bháryalacunu biḍḍalacunu déhamu ninḍá nagalu digavéyutsunnáru*, men who have just entered service all pile up money as they like and load their wives and children with jewellery.

digbhramamu, stupor. Skt.

digmanḍalamu, the horizon. Skt.

digulupaḍuṭa, to be afraid.

digulupartsuṭa, to frighten.

digulupáṭu, fright.

digumati, importation; from *diga*, down (off the ship). *egumati* (up on to the ship) is exportation.

diguṭa, to come down, to get out at, take up a lodging. *eccum' anṭé y' edducu cópam, digum'anṭé cunṭivánici cópam,* if you say get up, the bull is cross, if you say get down the lame man is cross; *satramuló digi y' unna yógi,* the ascetic who has taken up a lodging at the choultry; in French and Italian also to descend at a hotel is used for going to a hotel after a journey.

diguva, below.

digvijayamu, world conquest. Skt.

dimmarintsuṭa, to pour over.

dimme, cone, stopple, bezel of a ring, nave of a wheel, stamen of a flower.

dimmu, giddiness. *tala dimmu paṭṭinadi,* I feel giddy.

dimpuṭa, to put down, unload; causal of *diguṭa. garbhamu* or *caḍupu dimpuṭa* is to cause abortion. *í rácshasini y' eṭlu sanmárgamunacu dimpa galugudunu?* how am I to turn this she-devil to ways of righteousness?

dinacharya, diary. Skt.

dinamu, day. Skt. *dina-dinamu,* daily; *dinamu viḍichi dinamu,* every other day; *váḍu dinam ella vrástunnáḍu,* he drives the pen all day long; *dinadina ganḍam veyy'énḍlu áyussu,* threatened men live long; *dinamu manchid' ani tellavárlú dongilin'aṭṭu,* like the thief who waited till dawn because he thought the day was a lucky one.

dinaváramu, funeral. Skt. *peddayya gárici vivâha mahótstsavamu canṭé dinavára mahótstsavam chésté bágá v'unṭundi,* it would be better to celebrate the old gentleman's funeral than his marriage.

dinḍu, pillow. *ná venucan unchina dinḍunacu chéragila paḍi nénu háyigá nidra póyinánu,* leaning back on the pillow behind me I went comfortably to sleep.

dintsuṭa, to put down, same as *dimpuṭa.*

dinusu, article, especially in a shop. Hindustani.

diruguṭa, to turn, for *tiruguṭa* in print, not speech.

disamola, nakedness. *disamolaváḍi daggara digambaruḍu baṭṭal' aḍigin' aṭṭu,* like the naked man trying to borrow clothes from the nude; *mantram v'upadéṣam aina taruváta disamolató veḷḷi puṭṭa mida v'unna jilléḍu cheṭṭu peḷḷaginchi dáni véru gandham vrásté y'eṭuvanṭi télu cuttiná pótundi,* if you say the charm and go naked and pull up a swallow-wort on an ant-hill and rub on the juice from its roots it will cure the sting of any scorpion (Hindu medicine).

dishṭi, the evil eye; corruption of Skt. *drúshṭi,* sight. *dishṭi tagulutundi,* the evil eye will fall on us.

diṭavu, courage.

diṭṭamu, stout, firm, thorough. *diṭṭamugá coṭṭuṭa,* to give a good thrashing; *nénu vánini diṭṭangá záḍinchinánu,* I gave him a good dressing down; *diṭṭangá bhójanálu chési,* taking big meals.

diṭṭaparatsuṭa, to regulate.

diṭṭatanamu, pluck, spirit, firmness; also *diṭṭaritanamu. sarcáru-váru paripálanam'ippuḍu manchi diṭṭatanamutó nirvahistú v'unnáru,* the Government is carrying on the administration with a firm hand.

divasamu, day. Skt. A book word for *dinamu, rózu.*

divála, insolvency. Hindustani.

diváláyettuṭa, divålátíyuṭa, to go bankrupt. *Bhimayya diválá tísi nivu sampádinchina somm antá harinchi manchi pani chésináḍá?* did Bhimayya act rightly when he went bankrupt and robbed you of all your savings?

divánamu, durbar hall of a raja, or a zamindar's palace. Hindustani. *pedda báṭaló v'unna satram tísi véyinchi pátra sámánu divánamulóci techchinánu,* I abolished the choultry on the high road and brought the cooking vessels to the palace.

divánu, dewan, raja or zamindar's chief minister. Hindustani.

diviṭí, torch. *diviṭí cinda dípamu,* a lamp under a torch (relatively insignificant); *tama méḷam v'unna taruváta yé méḷam yenducu? diviṭí cinda dípálu,* after your nautch party why another nautch party? It would be lamps beneath a torch (an anti-climax).

divve, lamp. Skt. *divve tísina gúḍu*

vale, like the lamp-niche without the lamp.

divyadrüshṭi, second sight. Skt., from *divyam* and *drüshṭi*, sight.

divyagnyánamu, divine or esoteric knowledge. Skt., from *divyamu* and *gnyánam*, knowledge. *mahátmul ácáṣa gamanamu chéta tama vaddacu vachchi máṭáḍi pótár' ani divyagnyána samájam váru anna máṭa*, the statement of the esoteric knowledge society that mahatmas come to them by way of the sky and speak and go (of theosophy).

divyamu, divine. Skt.

divyangá, divinely, excellently. *Désicácháryulavárini panḍitulanugá niyamisté bahu divyangá v'unṭundi*, it will be an excellent thing to appoint Desicachari as a teacher.

dícsha, vow. Skt. *dícsha chéyuṭa, dícsha paṭṭuṭa, dícsha vahintsuṭa*, to vow. *mácu cúḍu paḍagoṭṭi múlachchhédam cheyyaḍánici dícsha paṭṭaḍam valla mícu mah' ápratishṭha vastú v' unnadi*, you are greatly dishonoured by your vow to take our food from us and ruin us root and branch.

dínamu, low, wretched, humble. Skt. *dínam' aina ná mora álacinchi*, hearing my humble complaint, is a common phrase in petitions; also *dínamugá prárthintsutsunnánu*, I humbly pray.

dínatvamu, humility. Skt.

dínuḍu, a humble man. Skt. *dhíruḍ' ainá cávale dínuḍ' ainá cávale*, either courage or humility.

dípamu, dípica, lamp. Skt. *diviṭí cinda dípamu*, a lamp under a torch (sunlight puts out the fire); *ándhra dípica*, the lamp of Telugu, is the title of a dictionary.

dípávaḷi, the Dipavali festival. Skt., from *dípam*, lamp, and *ávaḷi*, row. The festival is held on the 14th day of the dark fortnight in *Áṣvayuja*, November; there is a great consumption of fireworks and squibs.

dírghamu, long, deep. Skt., used especially in compounds. *dírghadarṣanamu*, farsightedness; *dírghavichárana*, deep examination; *dírghálóchana*, deep thought.

dírgháyushmantuḍu, long - lived. Skt., from *dírgham* and *áyussu*, life, used in blessings. *míru dírgháyushmantul' ai sukhapaḍanḍi*, may you live long and be happy; *dírgháyushyamastu!* live long!

díruṭa, for *tíruṭa*, to finish, in print, not speech.

dívana, dívena, blessing. *míru mammalini vacca máṭu áṣirvadintsandi, y' idé nácu mí ákharu dívena*, just bless us once, that will be my last blessing.

dívi, island; *dvípamu* is commoner.

dívintsuṭa, to bless.

dobbuṭa, dobbivéyuṭa, to shove, to knock off (money, property), to ravish (a woman). *anna véḷacu lantsamu sommu dákhalu cheyya lécapóté monna vaca ḍeltá súparenḍenṭunu tísivéyinchi renḍu vandala rúpáyilu putstsuconi á pani marivacaḍici véyinchináḍu, í cottavánini cúḍá tíyinchi vési múḍu vandalu dobbi marivacanici véyinchináḍu*, recently a Delta Superintendent did not pay the bribe money on the date fixed and was dismissed for another man who gave Rs. 200, the new man was also dismissed and the post given to a third man for Rs. 300; *piṭishanarlú, mírú y'écamai sarcáru sthalálu bévársu sthalálu dobbivésinavi y'enni v'unnavi?* how many government and ownerless sites are there that you and the petitioners have not put your heads together to knock off?

ḍocca, flank. *ḍocca baddalu chéstánu*, I will break your flanks.

doḍḍa, nice. *í Cámayya bahu doḍḍa bráhmaḍu sumi*, this Kamayya is a very nice brahmin; *nívu mahá doḍḍa y'illálavu*, you are a very nice woman; *ná doḍḍatanam antá búḍidaló pósina pannír aipóyindi*, my goodness is like pouring scent into ashes, i.e., wasted (throwing pearls before swine).

doḍḍi, court or yard at the back of a house. *góḍalu dúci doḍló pravésinchi*, jumping over the wall and entering the backyard; *nénu má guruvu gári vadda tsaduvuconé-ṭ-appuḍu doḍḍi tavvi sanvatsaránici cávalasina cúralu panḍinchéváḍini*, when I was studying with my teacher I used to dig in his backyard and rear the year's supply of vegetables; *doḍḍ'eḍu goḍlanu don-*

galu tóluconi póté, goḍḍu géde Ṣrí Mahalacshmi ainadi, when thieves drove away the whole backyardful of cattle the barren buffalo became Mahalakshmi (the goddess of wealth).

doḍḍicáḷḷu, bandy legs.

dolaguṭa, for *tolaguṭa*, to retire; in print, not speech.

doḷḷuṭa, to roll over; more commonly *dorluṭa*. *ráyi conḍa mida nunchi crindici baḍabaḍam ani doḷḷutsunnadi*, the stone rolls rub-a-dub down the hill.

dommari, dommaraváḍu, mountebank (it is a caste name). *chéppévi ṣúranga* (or *ṣriranga*) *nitulu, chésévi mághasnánálu, dúrévi dommari guḍiṣelu*, what he says are moral sayings, what he does are ceremonial ablutions, what he enters are mountebanks' huts.

dommi, hubbub, mob. *bráhmalu lópala dúri dommi chéstú v'unnáru*, the brahmins have got inside and are making a hubbub; *dommi cúḍi vachchináru*, they have come in a mob.

dommuláḍuṭa, to riot, fight; also *dommí chéyuṭa*. *mí Vaḍaghali Tenghali khajjálu cálipónu, iccaḍa dommuláḍacanḍi*, confound your Vadagali and Tengali disputes and don't fight here (the Vadagalies and Tengalies, northerners and southerners in Tamil, are two sects of Vaishnavite Brahmins who have been quarrelling at Conjeevaram for 400 years about such important matters as whether a hymn should be recited in Sanskrit or in Tamil).

ḍonca, bramble.

ḍonca, cattle path.

donga, thief, rogue. *ínṭi donganu y'íṣvaruḍú paṭṭa lédu*, God himself cannot catch the household thief; *dongacu talupu tísi doranu lépináḍu*, he opened the door to the thief and then woke his master; *dongacu donga buddhi, doracu dora buddhi*, a thief has a thief's thoughts, a gentleman a gentleman's; *donganu télu cuṭṭin' aṭṭu*, as when a scorpion stings a thief (he will keep his mouth shut); *donganu donga y'erugunu*, thief knows thief; *dongalu tólina goḍḍu yé révuna dáṭiná vacaṭé*, it is all the same by what ford the thieves drove the stolen ox; *dongamu dongé paṭṭa valenu*, set a thief to catch a thief; *dongalacu guruvu*, thieves' attorney; *páta donga paṭṭupaḍaca mánaḍu*, the confirmed thief will be caught at last; *pontsunḍé donga*, eavesdropper.

donga, false. *donga máṭalu*, deceitful words; *donga firyádu*, false complaint; *donga dári*, a byeway; *donga bígamu*, a false key; *dongamunḍa*, a false jade.

dongatanamu, theft. *dongatanálu bayalu paḍacunḍá dáchi lantsálu putstsucunévállú condaru dhanavantul'ai garva paḍutú v'unṭáru*, some (police inspectors) have got rich and proud by taking bribes to prevent thefts coming out.

dongilintsuṭa, dongiluṭa, to steal. *talli bangáram' ainá camsáliváḍu dongilintsaca mánaḍu*, the goldsmith will steal even his mother's gold (when he is making it into jewellery).

donne, cup made of leaves. The *donne*, or cup of leaves, and *vistari*, or plate of leaves, are the simple table (but there is no table) apparatus of the Hindus.

dontara, donti, set or pile (of pots, cakes, &c.). *púrila dontara*, pile of cakes.

dora, doragáru, gentleman, especially a European, master. *nimishamló doranu jébuló vésuconnáḍu*, it did not take him a minute to put the Collector in his pocket; *doragáru ḍérá daggira vaḍigá máṭláḍutú v'unnár ani banṭrótulanu peṭṭi coṭṭinchi pótáru, pári póḍámu ranḍi*, let us run away before we are beaten by the peons for talking loud in front of the white man's tent. The Koyyas of the Godavari agency like to be called *conḍa doralu*, hill lords; zamindars also like to be called *doragáru*.

doracipóvuṭa, to be caught.

doracuṭa, to occur, be found, obtained. In Telugu you do not say you find anything, you say it turns up or occurs; another similar word is *chiccuṭa*. *doracanidi panici rádu*, what you don't get is no use (sour grapes); *cucca vasté ráyi doracadu, ráyi doricité cucca rádu*, if the dog comes you can't find the stone, if you find the stone the dog does not come; *tama darṣanam doracaḍam valla nácu bahu santóshangá v'unnadi*, I am delighted at your receiving me.

dorasáni, lady; the feminine of *doragáru*.

doratanamu, government.

doratanamuváru, the government, commonly used of the British Government.

dorlintsuṭa, to roll (transitive).

dorluṭa, to roll (intransitive). *rátri tellavárin ḍácá nidra paṭṭaca mantsam mída iṭú aṭú dorlutú*, all night till dawn sleepless and rolling about on his bed.

doruvu, a well near a tank. There are special rules for the charge for irrigation from *doruvu* wells.

dóchipeṭṭuṭa, to give for plunder. *ill' antayu várici dóchipeṭṭutsunnadi*, the whole house is given to them to plunder.

dóḍu, for *tóḍu*, with. In print, not speech.

dólanamu, swinging. Skt. *dólána mánasuḍai y' unnáḍu*, his mind is in a see-saw.

ḍólé, palanquin. Hindustani.

ḍólu, drum; also *bhéri, dhancá, maddela*.

dóma, mosquito.

dómatera, mosquito curtain.

dóne, a boat made out of a dug-out palm. *dóne caḍupu* is a pot-belly.

dópiḍi, dópu, robbery.

dóragilapeṭṭuṭa, to tilt up. *chevulu dóragilapeṭṭináḍu*, he pricked up his ears.

dósacáya, cucumber. The excellent melons of the Ceded Districts are also called *dósacáya*.

dóshacári, sinner.

dóshamu, sin. *cáladósham* (laches of time) is the legal term for prescription.

dóshi, guilty person.

dósili, handful, the hands held together to form a cup.

dótsuconuṭa, dótsuṭa, to plunder. *tálúcá antá dótsucunnáḍu*, he (the tahsildar) plundered the whole taluk; *dongalu lópala tsórapaḍi nannu nimishamló dótsuconi pó vatstsunu*, thieves may enter and plunder me in a minute.

dóva, way, path. *oca v'úrici veyyi dóvalu*, there are 1,000 ways to a village; *cásucu dóva lédu núṭici paravá lédu*, he did not see his way to a penny but did not mind spending a pound.

dóvati, dhoti (male lower cloth); also *dhóvati, pancha*.

dóyi, a pair; used in books in compounds. *cannudóyi*, pair of eyes; *tsanudóyi*, pair of breasts.

dravya, substance (philosophy). Skt.

dravyamu, money, property. Skt.

dravyasaháyamu, subvention, contribution. Skt., from *dravyam*, money, and *saháyam*, help.

drácshapanḍu, grape.

drácshasárá, wine.

drácshatíge, vine.

dressaru, dresser, doctor. English. The class of medical officers now known as sub-assistant surgeons were formerly called dressers and hospital assistants.

droccuṭa, for *troccuṭa*, tread. In print, not speech.

dróhamu, treachery. Skt. *rájadróhamu* is treason; *mému máṭláḍuconna dániló rájadróham yémí lédu*, there was no treason in what we said.

dróhi, traitor.

drücpathamu, point of view. Skt., from *drüṣ*, eye, and *patham*, path. A word used in newspapers. *prabhutva drücpathamu* is the point of view of the Government.

drüḍhamu, firm, strong. Skt. *má tanḍri gáru áṭṭé peddaváru cáru, mana andari canṭenu áyané drüḍhangá v'unnáru*, our father is not so old, he is stronger than any of us.

drüshṭamu, visible. Skt.

drüshṭántamu, example. Skt.

drüshṭi, look, evil eye. Skt. *yóga drüshṭitó tsúchi y' itanini tacshaṇam ṣánti parustánu*, I will quiet him by fixing him with a yogi's look; *cópa drüshṭitó*, with an angry look; *tana drüshṭici*, towards himself; *ántara drüshṭi*, inward vision.

drüshṭibommalu, scarecrows. *drüshṭi tagalacunḍá n' unḍuṭacu gánu chélaló drüshṭibommalu peṭṭutáru*, they place scarecrows in the fields to ward off the effects of the evil eye (not like us to scare the birds).

dubási, dubash, interpreter. Skt. *dvi*,

two, and *bhásha*, language. An old word scarcely in use now; in the old days the Company's dubashes were very important persons. Also *dvi-bháshi*.

dubbu, stubble.

ducáṇamu, shop. Hindustani. The Telugu is *angaḍi*. *chépala ducáṇamu mída 'crotta chépalu iccaḍa ammu-táru' ani bórḍu caṭṭináru*, over the fish-shop there was a board 'fresh fish sold here'. *shápu* (shop) is also used.

ducci, ploughing. *ducci v'unṭé diccu v'unnadi*, till well and all will be well.

duccipolamu, a ploughed field.

ducciṭeddu, a ploughing bullock. *ducci-ṭ-eddu déṣántaramu veḷḷinaṭṭu*, like the ploughing ox having left the country.

duḍḍu, money, originally the name of a coin. *duḍḍugalaváru*, rich people.

duḍḍucarra, cudgel.

duḍucu, rash, silly. *duḍucu máṭalu*, hasty words.

duḍucutanamu, rashness, silliness.

duḥkhamu, grief. Skt.

duḥkhintsuṭa, to grieve. Skt.

dulupuṭa, to dust. *á pustacál anniṭini Agnihótrunici samarpaṇa chésté nácu yentó santóshangá v' unṭundi, víṭi pu-rugulu dulupa léca tsachchipótú v' un-nánu*, I shall be very pleased if you offer all those books to Vulcan; I am half-killed dusting the vermin off them.

dumadumaláḍuṭa, to be angry; onomatopoeic.

dummu, dust. *adi dummu, idi cummu*, one is dust and one is ashes (from the frying-pan into the fire).

dummu, bone, more commonly *emuca*.

dummulagonḍi, hyaena (bone-eater).

dumpa, edible root. *dumpalanu pha-lálanu tinutsu*, eating roots and fruits; *penḍalapu dumpa* is a yam; *bangáḷá* or *síma dumpalu*, Bengal or foreign roots, are names for the potato, but *urlagaḍḍa* (the crumbling root) is more common.

dumucuṭa, to jump. *góḍa paic ecci gadilónici dumicenu*, he climbed the wall and leapt into the room.

dunḍagíḍu, blackguard; plural *dunḍa-gínḍru*.

dunga, block of wood.

dunnapótu, male buffalo, also used as term of abuse, from *dunnuṭa*, to plough, and *pótu*, male; also *enupótu*. *eddu enḍacu lága dunnapótu níḍacu lága*, the bullock was for pulling to-wards the sun, the buffalo towards the shade (bad yoke-fellows); *vaca clayin-ṭutó rahasyangá máṭláḍina máṭalu y'í dunnapótu vinnáḍu*, this buffalo eaves-dropped when I was conferring con-fidentially with a client.

dunnuṭa, to plough. *dunnaca tsallité coyyaca panḍinadi*, sowing without ploughing, no reaping at harvest (nothing is to be had without toil); *dunné rózulaló déṣamu mída póyi, cóta rózulaló coḍavali paṭṭuconi vachchi-náḍu*, in the ploughing days he wandered about the country, at har-vest he came with his sickle (reaping when you did not sow).

duppaṭi, cloth, sheet. *angaḍiváḍu: í duppaṭi conanḍi, oca purushántaramu varacu v'unṭundi. vrüddhuḍu: nác'anta manchidi accara lédu, nácu ippaṭici ḍebbai éḷḷu*. Shopkeeper: Buy this cloth, it will last a life-time. Old man: No, thank you, I am 70.

duppi, spotted deer (*cervus axis*). The common deer of South India are *duppi*, spotted deer, *caṇuzu*, sambhur; *léḍi* is the generic term.

dur-, dus-, (also **dush-**), prefix mean-ing 'bad'. Skt. The opposite prefix is *sa-, sat-*, good; almost any word may be combined with *dur-*; I give a few common combinations below *passim*.

durabhimánamu, arrogance. Skt.

durabhyásamu, bad habit. Skt.

duradagonḍi, stinging nettle; from *durada*, stinging. Also *dúlagonḍi*.

duradamu, itching, stinging. *manu-maḍu nértsuconn'aṭṭu avvacu durada tírin aṭlu*, like the grandmother who relieved her itching by making the child write his lesson on her back (killing two birds with one stone); *cheyyi duradagá unn'anduna gócucon-ṭini*, because my hand was itching I scratched.

duradrüshṭamu, misfortune. Skt.

durantamu, endless or bad end. Skt.

duravagáhamu, difficult to under-stand. Skt.

duravastha, ill fate. Skt.
durácháramu, bad custom. Skt.
durácháruḍu, backslider (in religion and custom). Skt.
durágatamu, ill-gotten. Skt. *ágatam*, obtained.
durálóchana, bad intent. Skt.
durátmuḍu, bad-hearted man. Skt. Also *dushṭátmuḍu*.
durbalamu, weak. Skt.
durbharamu, hard to bear. Skt. *durbhara hrüdayamu*, a heavy heart.
durbhágyamu, misfortune. Skt.
durbhágyuḍu, unhappy man. Skt.
durbhásha, abuse. Skt.
durbharamu, unbearable. Skt.
durbhicshamu, famine. Skt. *crüshitó násti durbhicshamu, japató násti páta-camu*, crop-failure, famine; prayer-failure, sin.
durbódha, bad advice. Skt.
durbuddhi, bad ideas, bad mind. Skt. *nícu yenta durbuddhi puṭṭinadé!* what an idea!
durdaṣa, ill-fate. Skt.
Durga, another name of Parvati.
durgamu, hill fort. Skt. Corrupted to 'drug' in English as in *Ramandrug*, *Rayadrug*.
durgandhamu, bad smell. Skt. The Telugu is *campu*, but *durgandham* is also common.
durgati, hell.
durghaṭamu, difficult. Skt.
durguṇamu, bad quality or nature. Skt.
durjanuḍu, a wicked man. Skt. *aṣacta durjanatvamu*, wickedness born of incompetency.
durjayamu, invincible. Skt.
durlabhamu, rare. Skt.
durmanascuḍu, evil-minded. Skt.
durmaraṇamu, a bad end. Skt.
durmárgamu, wickedness. Skt. *dur-márgamunacu tandri baddhacam*, idleness is the root of all evil; *nénu ni durmárgam antá baiṭa peḍutánu*, I will reveal all your misconduct.
durmárguḍu, blackguard. Skt. *dur-márgúlató sahavásam*, bad company.
durnaḍata, bad conduct. Skt.
durṇayamu, immorality. Skt.
durníti, bad morals. Skt. *durníti paṭṭucommalai véṣyala sthiti*, the condition of dancing girls that gives rise to bad morals.
duruddéṣamu, bad intention. Skt.
durusu, rough, stubborn. *níru y' indácá tsálá durusugá v'unnáru, ippuḍu nemmadi paḍḍáv anucunṭánu*, you have been very stubborn so far, now I think you will be quiet.
durúha, bad idea. Skt. *nícu yenta durbuddhi puṭṭinadé; ní manassuló yenta durúha v'unnadé!* what dreadful thoughts and ideas have entered your mind!
durvádamu, bad argument. Skt. *vaṭṭi durvádamuló digutáru*, they descend to fallacies.
durváramu, intolerable. Skt. *dur-vára vyádhula pálai*, a prey to intolerable diseases.
durvárta, bad news. Skt.
durviniyógamu, wrong use, misappropriation. Skt. Used as a legal term for the crime of misappropriation.
durvrütti, bad profession or life. Skt. *durvrüttiló pravéṣinchi*, falling into a bad way of life.
durvyayamu, extravagance. Skt.
duryógamu, misfortune. Skt.
duschéshṭalu, bad deeds. Skt.
dushcáryamu, vice. Skt. *zúdamu, pánamu, asatyamu, modalaina dush-cáryamulu*, gambling, drink, lying, and other vices.
dushcrütyamu, sin. Skt.
dushpravartanamu, bad conduct. Skt. *mana dushpravartanam antanu cálamu mída tróchi vaichi*, laying the blame for all our own bad conduct on the times.
dushprayatnamu, intrigue. Skt. *míru chésé dushprayatnálu yeppaṭicí cona ságavu*, your intrigues will never be successful.
dushṭátmuḍu, bad-hearted man. Skt. Also *durátmuḍu*.
dushṭuḍu, scoundrel. Skt. *írshyá-grastulaina dushṭulu*, scoundrels full of malice.
dusṣacunamu, bad omen. Skt.
dussvabhávamu, bad disposition. Skt.
dustaramu, difficult. Skt.
dustu, cloth, **dustulu,** clothes.
duvvena, comb.

duvvuṭa, to stroke, comb. *misálu duvvuṭa* is to stroke one's moustaches; *tala duvvuṭa*, to comb one's hair.
dúcuṭa, to leap over.
dúḍa, calf. *ávu chénuló mésté dúḍa gaṭṭuna méstundá?* if the cow grazes in the field, will the calf graze on the bank? *dúḍa cuḍisténé gáni ávu chépadu*, unless the calf drinks the cow won't give milk.
dúdécula, man of cotton-cleaning caste; they are converts to Muhammedanism. *turacalu léni v'úḷḷó dúdḙcula-váḍu sahib miyyá*, the dudecula is king in a village in which there are no genuine Muhammedans.
dúdi, cleaned cotton. Uncleaned cotton is *patti*, a cotton cloth is *núli baṭṭa*.
dúlagonḍi, nettle; also *duradagonḍi*.
dúlamu, a beam.
dúpamu, incense. Skt.
dúramu, far, distance. Skt. *dúra-déṣamu*, distant country; *ámaḍalu dúram aité, antachcaranḍlu dúramá?* though the leagues be long, will the hearts be far?
dúramugá, far (adverb). Skt.
dúrapu, far (adjective). Skt. *dúrapu conḍalu nunupu*, distant hills are smooth (distance lends enchantment to the view).
dúrintsuṭa, dúrtsuṭa, to make to enter, to entangle, introduce; causal of *dúruṭa*. *váḷḷanu cúḍa yé césulónó dúristán ani bedarinchi*, threatening to entangle them too in some criminal case; *á taruváta vachchina Khádar Sáhébu Niyyógul andarini mellagá ságanampi gaḍḍála Sáhébulanu afísuló dúrchináḍu*, Khadar Sahib who came after gradually got rid of all the Niyogi Brahmins and introduced bearded Muhammedans into the office.
dúripóvuṭa, dúruṭa, to enter, penetrate. *taḍacaléni y' inṭloci cucca dúrin aṭṭu*, as a dog enters an open door; *cheppévi nítulu, chésévi snánálu, dúrévi dommara guḍiselu*, what he says are morals, what he does are ablutions, what he goes into are mountebanks' huts.
dúshaṇamu, reviling, libel. Skt. *brahmaṇadúshaṇa*, reviling of brahmins (a great sin); *nénu lén' appuḍu tsáṭuna yémi cúsiná saripóyindi gáni, ná mogam yeduṭa cúḍá y'ilá dúshaṇá chéstú v'unṭé, nénu sahinchi v'úrucunṭán anucunnáru rá?* you may caw behind my back but do you think I am going to stand your reviling me to my face?
dúshintsuṭa, to revile. Skt. *strílu manchivaḷḷu cár ani dúshistú v'unná*, though you revile women; *práchína sadácháramulanu dúshistáru*, they revile age-old good customs.
dúsiconuṭa, dúyuṭa, to draw off (as a sword from its scabbard, but the Telugus think of the scabbard as drawn *off* the sword, not of the sword as drawn *out of* the scabbard; they say *ora dúsi*, drawing the scabbard, when we say 'drawing his sword').
dúta, messenger. *váyu dévuḍu dútagá vachchináḍu*, the wind god came as a messenger.
dvaitamu, dual. Skt. *dvaitamu* is the philosophy of dualism as opposed to *advaitamu*, monism.
dvandvamu, pair, couple, duality. Skt. *dvandvayudhamu* is a duel; *advaita sthiti vacca nimushamló autundí; appuḍu dvandválu yémí v' unḍavu*, monism will be brought in in a minute and then there will be no dualities; *míru vírabhaṭula vale á vachché y' iddaritóní dvandvayuddham cheyyanḍi*, do you two like heroes fight duels with these two who are coming.
dvádaṣi, the 12th lunar day. Skt., from *dvádaṣa*, 12th.
dvárabandhamu, door frame. Skt., from *dváramu*, door, and *bandham*, tying.
dváramu, door. Skt.
dvárá, by means of, through. *atani dvárá vinnánu*, I heard through him.
dvéshamu, enmity. Skt. *ní y' andu nácu manassuló yémí dvésham lédu*, I bear you no ill-will.
dvéshi, enemy. Skt.
dvéshintsuṭa, to hate. Skt.
dvibháshi, interpreter. Skt., from *dvi*, two, and *bhásha*, language. *dubash* in the old records.
dviguṇamu, double. *dhana dviguṇamulagá*, cent. per cent. on your money.
dvijanmuḍu, dvijuḍu, twice-born (i.e. a brahmin). The brahmins are

twice-born because they are born again when they first put on the sacred thread.

dvitíyamu, second. Skt. The Telugu is *rendava.*

dvípántaravásamu, transportation for life. Skt. A legal term, literally, removal to islands, i.e., to the Andamans.

dvípántarayánamu, journey to islands. Skt.

dyótacamulaina, illuminating. Skt., from *dyótam,* light.

E

Initial *e* in Telugu is like snakes in Ireland; there are really no words beginning with *e* because all words printed with initial *e* are pronounced with a euphonic *y* before them, and a few of the more common ones will be given again under *y*; thus the Telugu for 'why' is *yenducu,* though it is often printed *enducu*; the *y* is so much part of the word that I do not insert an apostrophe in printing in Roman characters. The *y* is always inserted after a vowel, but not always after a consonant.

ecaráru, confession. Hindustani; a law term. In speech people say *oppuconnáḍu,* he confessed.

eccaḍa, where? with negative 'nowhere'. *yeccaḍá doracani,* not to be found anywhere.

eccaḍacu, eccaḍi, whither? *pápam cheyyanivâḷḷu yeccaḍici pótáró nícu telusuná?* do you know where people go who commit no sins?

eccaḍaléni, unprecedented, monstrous. *peḷḷi rózunané nác í magaḍu vadd'ani yeccaḍaléni allari chési,* on the marriage day she made a monstrous noise crying that she did not want that husband.

eccaḍanó, in some place or other.

eccaḍanúlédu, nowhere.

eccaḍavó, something or other.

eccaḍi, of what place? what sort? nothing of the sort! of whatever place. *nív eccaḍiváḍavu?* where do you come from? *idi yeccaḍi sancaṭam!* what a trouble! (trouble coming from where); *dyanacu aravai yéḷḷu dáṭinavanḍi! yeccaḍ' anḍi! monnaṭi bhádrapada másánici yábhai nálugu sanvatsaramulu dáṭinavi,* he is over 60! Nothing of the sort! he was 54 last August; *í puvvulu nícu eccaḍivi?* where did you get those flowers from? *eccaḍivár accaḍici veḷḷipóyináru,* every one went home.

eccaṭi, single. *eccaṭi poru,* single-handed combat (duel).

eccili, hiccup. *abbáyici yecciḷḷu puṭṭinavi,* the boy has got hiccups.

eccintsuṭa, to raise, make to get up; causative of *eccuṭa. cheṭṭu yeccinchi nichchena tísin'aṭṭu,* like making a man climb a tree and then taking the ladder away; *cágitam mída vaca acsharam yeccintsa rádu,* do not put a word in writing.

eccirintsuṭa, to mock; for *veccirintsuṭa. guḍḍu vachchi pillanu yeccirinchinadi,* the egg came and mocked the chicken.

eccoṭṭuṭa, to rob, run away with; from *ega* and *coṭṭuṭa.*

eccuṭa, to go up, get on to. *vánici sárá talac eccinadi,* the spirits have gone to his head; *andarú andalamu yeccité mósévâru yevaru?* if every one gets into the palanquin, who is to carry it? *eccumanṭé yedducu cópam, digum'anṭé cunṭivánici cópam,* if you say get up the bullock is cross, if you say get down the lame man is cross; *conḍa mída yeccaḍánici daggira dári yédainá v'undá?* is there any short way up the hill? *pogar' ecci* means proud.

eccuva (*v* pronounced *w*), more, superiority. *telivi taccuva, ácali yeccuva,* least sense most appetite; *vári yeccuva yémiṭi?* in what is their superiority?

eccuvataccuva (*v* pronounced *w*), more or less. *eccuvataccuvagá núr rúpáyalu,* Rs. 100 more or less.

eḍa, space, interval. *eḍa lécunḍá,* without interval, continuously.
eḍa, towards, (of time) on. *ná yeḍa,* towards me; *chérun eḍa,* on arrival.
eḍa, young, tender.
eḍa, prefix meaning 'apart'.
eḍabáṭu, separation. *ná biḍḍa yeḍabáṭu nénu sahintsa lénu,* I cannot bear separation from my child.
eḍabáyuṭa, to separate from, abstain from.
eḍagilluṭa, to stand aside.
eḍala, suffix meaning 'if'. *balamu léni yeḍala,* if he has not strength.
eḍama, left. It will be in vain that the motorist will say to the waggoner *yeḍam chétici tólu,* drive on the left, for the rule of the road is ignored in South India.
eḍamu, space, room, opportunity. *yentamandi bandhuvul unnáró má y'inṭló tsúḍu, y'ippuḍu cálu peṭṭaḍánici yeḍam ledu,* come once to my house and see how many relations I have, there is not room to set foot in it.
eḍapa-daḍapa, now and then. *viluni baṭṭi yeḍapa-daḍapa vastú-pótú v'unḍu,* be coming as frequently as you can.
eḍapeṭṭuṭa, to put aside.
edaṭa, opposite; from *eduru.* Also *eduṭa. á y'inṭi yedaṭa,* opposite that house.
eḍategacunḍá, incessantly.
eḍatíyuṭa, to remove.
eḍári, desert.
eddu, bullock. *eccumanṭé yedducu cópam, digum'anṭé cunṭivánici cópam,* if you say get up the ox will be cross, if you say get down the lame man will be cross. Plural is *edlu. ducci yedlu,* ploughing bullocks; *eddu rance véyuts unnadi,* the ox bellows.
-eḍési, affix meaning by certain quantities; compounded of *eḍu,* full, and *ési,* at the rate of. *gampeḍési,* by basketfuls.
eḍlabanḍi, bullock-cart; from *eddu,* ox, and *banḍi,* cart. *cangu cangum'ani ganṭala mrótalató eḍlabanḍlu vatstsuts unḍenu,* bullock carts were coming with the clanging noise of bells; *gúḍubanḍi* is a covered cart; *cochíbanḍi,* from English coach, a particularly smart turn-out.
edirintsuṭa, to oppose, resist; from *eduru,* opposite. *garalscúluló tsaduvucunna múḍ éḷḷa munḍa ná peḷḷamu péḍa muṭṭucunṭé asahyam ani nannu yediristundi,* a chit of a girl who studies in the girls' school stands up to me and says it is disgusting for my wife to handle dung (a particularly pure article according to the Hindus).
-eḍu, affix denoting measure. *buḍḍeḍu,* bottleful; *doḍḍeḍu paṣuvulu,* a yardful of cattle; *mundu sanvatstsaram mámúluló vaca rúpáyi taccuva vachchinad' ani giddeḍu níru vadalipeṭṭinḍáḍu cáḍu,* because there was a rupee short in the usual bribe he did not let a pint of water into our fields.
eduguṭa, to grow. *nannu muṭṭucócu, paḍutsuváḷḷu yedigina áḍadánni muṭṭucó ráḍu,* do not touch me, young men must not touch a grown woman; *penḍli y'ainadi modaluconi pilladi yedigi yeppuḍu cápuramunacu vatstsuná, á mahábhágyam antayu nén eppuḍu bávucondunà ani nóṭiló vrélu peṭṭuconi guṭacalu mringutsu tondara paḍinánu,* from the time of my marriage I was gloating over the thought that the girl would grow up and live with me and give me that great happiness; *biḍḍa yedigité cunḍa yedugunu,* the pot grows with the child—the pot in which it takes its food.
eduru, opposite. *yeduru-gáli,* head wind. *yedurcólu,* the mutual advances of bride and bridegroom at the marriage ceremony; also, in general, meeting. *yeduráḍuṭa,* to speak against, to oppose, and so in numerous compounds.
eduruconuṭa, to meet, opposite; pronounced *yedurconuṭa.*
edurugunḍá, opposite; also *edaṭacu. yedurugunḍá rá* (come opposite) means simply come out or come here.
edurunacalu, counterfoil.
edurupaḍuṭa, to meet.
eduruṭa, to advance.
edurutsútsuṭa, to hope, expect. *nénu vrásina v'uttaránici zavábu nimittam yeduru tsústú v' unnánu,* I am hoping for an answer to my letter. The usual word for 'to hope'; 'hope' is *áṣa.*
eduruzavábu, answer, especially in contradiction. *nívu ikha mundu yeppuḍú pedda manushyulu máṭláḍutú*

v' unṭé yeduru zavábu cheppacu, in future when gentlemen talk to you don't answer them back.

eduṭa, opposite, in front of. *ná yeduṭa,* before me; *dévuni yeduṭa,* before God, the words with which the oath taken by witnesses in court begins; *dévuni yeduṭa nizam chepputánu, antá nizam chepputánu, abaddham cheppanu,* I will speak the truth, the whole truth, and nothing but the truth.

ega, prefix meaning 'up'; the opposite is *diga,* down. *ega tísté brahmahatya, diga tísté góhatya,* (witness in cattle trespass case by brahmin, to himself) if I pull one way it is brahmin-murder, if I pull the other way, it is cow-murder (the two worst sins—Hindu religion).

egapeṭṭuṭa, to misappropriate, knock off. *munupu ménéjarugáru padulu putstsucunná, núrulu putstsucunná eḍapá-daḍapá mana chétuló cuḍá renḍu rúpáyulu péṭṭéváḍu, y'ippuḍ aví yegapeṭṭináḍu,* formerly the manager when he got 10 rupees or a hundred used now and then to put two into our hands, now he makes away with these.

egaruṭa, to fly; also *eguruṭa.*

egasana, upwards.

egatáḷi, mockery. *míru yegatáḷi cheyyacanḍi,* do not mock me.

egatíyuṭa, to pull up.

egavu, flying; from *eguruṭa.*

eggu, harm.

egirintsuṭa, to make to fly; causal of *eguruṭa.*

egiripóvuṭa, to go flying.

eguḍudiguḍu, up and down. *í róḍḍu yeguḍudiguḍugá n' unnadi,* this road is all up and down; *yeguḍudiguḍu róḍla mída baḷḷu cusa cusal'áḍunu,* waggons jolt on rough roads.

egumati, export. Loading up on to ships is export; unloading, *digumati,* is import.

egumati chéyuṭa, to export.

eguruṭa, to fly. *ill 'egiri póyé-ṭ-aṭṭugá cécalu véyuṭa* is to scream the house down (but the Telugus say 'up'); *pacshi lágu yegaraḍánici nácu reccalu lévu,* I have not wings to fly like a bird; *nénu hiringu* (hearing) *chésé cálamandu córṭu yegiri póyinadi,* I set the court flying with my argument.

eguva, above. *ná vistari y' odda yeguvanu cúrtsónḍi,* take the higher seat.

ella, suffix meaning all. *lancaló puṭṭinavár-ellá rácshasulé,* the people born in Lanka are all demons; *váḍu dinam-ellá vrástú v'unḍenu,* he drove the pen all day; *mana púrvulu cheppinad'ellanu manchid'anu múrkha paṭṭunu máni, mana buddhi chéta n'álóchinchi y'ippaṭi sthitini baṭṭi cálánuguṇamul 'aina márpulanu chésiconutsu, lócamunacu sukhábhivrüddhi caluga chéyuts' unḍa valenu,* abandoning the stupid prejudice that all our ancestors said was right, we must use our own brains, making changes suited to the present day, and improve the world.

ellappuḍu, always; from *ella,* all, and *appuḍu,* then. *yellappuḍu* is the usual word for 'always'; *yeḍama chétici tól'áli yellapuḍu,* you must always drive on the left.

ellaváru, every one.

ellayeḍala, everywhere.

ellecshanu, election. English. *ellecshanuló yevaru tánu membarugá n'unḍa córi munducu vatstsunó, vánini 'cänḍiḍéṭ' anṭáru,* people who stand at elections are called candidates.

elli, to-morrow. Used in books for *répu. mádiga maḷḷi, camsáli yelli,* the cobbler says, 'come again', the goldsmith, 'come another day'. To-morrow is more commonly *répu,* yesterday is *ninna,* the day before yesterday is *monna.* Malli and Yelli are also women's names.

ellunḍi, the day after to-morrow; from *elli,* to-morrow, and *unḍi,* from.

eluca, rat. *yeluca tsávucu pilli múrchha póná?* will the cat faint at the rat's death? *yeluca mída cópána y'inṭici chitstsu peṭṭu conn'aṭṭu,* like setting your house on fire to kill a rat; *pillici chelagáṭámu, yelucacu práṇa sancaṭamu,* sport to the cat, death-throes to the rat; *conḍa tavvi yelucanu paṭṭin' aṭṭu,* digging away a hill to get at a rat; *yeluca citsa citsal áḍuts unnadi,* the rat squeaks.

elucabónu, rat-trap; also *elucala-bónu.*

elugu, voice. Used in books for *svaramu.*

elugubanṭi, elugugoḍḍu, bear. *pedda*

pulinó yelugubanṭinó tsúchin'aṭṭu bhayapaḍutu, frightened as if he had seen a tiger or a bear.
emuca, bone.
enabhai, eighty; also *enubadi*.
enamanḍuguru, eight persons.
enḍa, sunlight, sunheat. The Telugus, unlike us, distinguish the sun and the moon from their light, which is *enḍa* (also heat) of the sun, and *vennela* of the moon. *yeddu yenḍacu lága, dunnapótu nídacu lága*, the bullock pulling towards the sun, the buffalo towards the shade (an ill-matched pair); *'mápaṭi yénḍa*, evening sun; *yenḍamávulu*, mirage.
endáca ? how far? from *dáca*, up to.
enḍacálamu, the hot weather; from *enḍa*, sun's heat, and *cálamu*, time. This would be even more inadequately translated 'summer'; it is the Indian hot weather, inadequately described as the hot, when from the bazaars comes a din which, though often called music, is not.
enḍadebba, sunstroke.
enḍa peṭṭuṭa, to put to dry.
endaru ? how many persons?
enḍipóvuṭa, to dry up.
enḍipóyina, dry.
endó, somewhere.
endu ? what? where? *yendu gurinchi?* about what? *yendu póyináḍu?* where has he gone? Hence also *yenducu?* for what? why?
enḍu, dried up. *alasaṭa chéta nácu nóru yenḍucu pótunnadi*, my mouth is dry with fatigue. *enḍugaḍi, straw*.
enducanina, because; from *enducu*, why, and *anuṭa*, say; if you ask why. Also *enducanṭé*.
enducanṭé, because; composed of *enducu* and *anuṭa*, to say.
enduchéta ? why do you ask? *nuvvu śamudra prayáṇam chéṣává?* have you been to sea? *chéṣánu gáni nácu visugu puṭṭinadi*, I have, but got bored; *y'enduchéta?* why? *oca ala tsústé anni alalu aṭlágé v'undi, bhédam émí lédu*, if you have seen one wave, you have seen them all, there is no difference. *enduchétananṭé*, if you want to know; composed of *endu*, *chéta*, and *anuṭa*, to say. *uttara déṣam antá tirigávu gadá, Himavatparvatánni tsúṣává?* you have travelled all over the north, I suppose you have seen the Himalayas? *tsúḍa lédu, yenduchétananṭé accaḍa nilutsunṭé mana chinnatanamu baiṭa paḍutundi*, I have not and if you ask why not, because if you stand there our insignificance comes out.
enducó ? for what? *yenducurá indáca nunchi yéḍustunnávu?* why have you been crying all this time? *yenducó gnyápacamu lédu*, I can't remember what for.
enducu ? why? *mánamu póyina venuca práṇam enducu?* what is the good of life when honour is gone? *chitracárulu tama paṭála crinda santacam chéstáru yenducu? paṭánici modal édó chivar édó tsúchéváḷḷu telusucóḍánici*, why do painters sign their pictures? So that you may know which is the beginning and which is the end.
enducu ? for what? with negative, for nothing. *enducu panici ráni mibhágyuḍu*, a worthless wretch.
endulacu ? where to?
endunḍi ? whence? *eccaḍa nunḍi* is commoner.
endunu, everywhere.
endunú lédu, nowhere.
endu nunchi ? *endununḍi?* from where? *eccaḍa nunchi* is commoner.
enḍuṭa, to dry up. More commonly in the compound form *enḍipóvuṭa*.
engili, spittle, unclean. The spittle is regarded as particularly dirty; so *yengili* often means dirty. *mana yengili vistaḷḷu*, our dirty plates; *yémí teliyaca nálugu yengili y'ingilíshu muccalu tsaduvucóvaḍamtóṭe voḷl' erugaca púrv' ácháránni peddalini dúshistáru*, they know nothing but as soon as they have learnt four dirty English words not knowing what they are doing they abuse old customs and people.
enimidava, eighth.
enimidi, eight. *enimidinn'ara ganṭa* is half-past eight.
ennaḍó, some time or other; derived from *náḍu*, day. *ennaḍó zarigina sangati*, an event which has occurred in the past.
ennaḍú ? ever? *ṭícharu: pillulacu tsali yeṭlá veyyacundá v'unṭundi? av'émaind tsoccáyi tóḍuccunṭavá? baṭṭa cappu-*

cunṭavá? Teacher: How do cats escape cold? Do they wear coats? Do they put on clothes? *báluḍu: míru yennaḍu pillini tsúḍa léḍá?* Boy: Have you never seen a cat?

ennaḍu, always.

ennáḷḷu ? how many days? how long? *tummité poyyé muccu yennáḷḷu v'unḍunu?* if your nose goes when you sneeze, how long will it last? The usual word for 'how long'. 'How long is it since?' is *yennáḷḷ aindi?* with past participle.

enni ? how many? *peddamanishi: sanvatsaramló yenni rütuvul' unnavi?* Gentleman: How many seasons are there in the year? *vidyárthi: ṭennisurütuvu, phuṭbálu rütuvu, renḍu.* Schoolboy: Two, the tennis and the football seasons.

ennicalu, elections, but *ellecshanu* is commoner. So also *abhyarti, anvéshi* may be used for 'candidate', but every one says *cănḍiḍéṭu.*

enni-yó, however many; also *ennó. yéru yenni vancalu póyiná samudramulóné paḍa valenu,* however many twists the river makes it must fall into the sea (the weariest river winds safe at last to sea).

ennu, ear of corn; corruption from *vennu.* Many other words beginning with *v* are commonly pronounced with initial *y* instead, e.g., *vélam,* auction, is vulgarly *yálam, veḷḷuṭa,* to go, is vulgarly *yeḷḷuṭa.*

ennuṭa, to reckon, count.

enta ? how much? what? *yenta unnadi?* what is the price? *yenta anyáyamu?* what injustice? *adi yenta pani?* what is there in that? *yentamátram?* how much? *yentamátram cádu,* not at all; *nív'enta, áyana yenta?* what comparison is there between you two? *nív' enta nén'enta ani póṭláḍinátu,* they quarrelled about which was the bigger man; *grühasthu: bhárya v' unṭé yenta cashṭam vachchiná marachi pó vatstsunu. brahmachári: brahmacháriki asalu cashṭamé unḍadu.* Married man: If you have a wife however much trouble comes you can forget it. Bachelor: If you are a bachelor the trouble does not come at all.

enta y'ainá, however much.

entacu ? for how much? *y'entacu istunnáru?* or *y'entacu istávu?* for what will you sell it?

entamandi ? how many persons?

entamátramu ? how much; not in the least, not at all. *entamátramu v'oppuconnáḍu cádu. Entamátramu vallapaḍad' annáḍu,* he did not consent to it in the least or he said that it was not at all possible.

entamátramu léḍu, not at all; also with *cádu* or any negative verb. *mír adhairyamu yentamátramú cana paratsa cúḍadu,* you must not show any fear at all.

entasépaṭici ? how long after? *váḍu yenta sépaṭici vachchináḍu?* how long after did he come?

entasépu, all the while. *váḍu yentasépú tana goppalé cheppu conṭáḍu,* he blows his own trumpet all the while.

entasépu ? how long? *inṭici póvaḍániki yenta sépu paḍutundi?* how long will it take to get home? *enta sépú,* always; *enta sépú tana saukhyamé,* always his own comforts.

entaṭiváru ? what sort of persons?

entavaracu ? up to what? up to when?

entayu, greatly; also *entó.*

entayu léḍu, not at all, nothing; also *émí léḍu.*

entó, so much, such, great, whatever, however great; also *enta-yó. atanu yentó manchiváḍu,* he is such a nice man; *mí valla nácu yentó upacáram calugutundi,* you will be doing me a great favour; *í v'úriki á v'úr entó á v'úriki í v'úr anté,* whatever the distance between this village and that, the distance between that village and this is the same; *rázu yentó dharmam anté,* the virtue of the people will be proportionate to the greatness of the king (every government has the subjects it deserves). *Qualis rex talis grex.*

entsuṭa, to count, think. *cíḍ enchi mél entsa valenu,* count the loss and then profits.

enubadi, eighty; more commonly *yenabhai.*

enupótu, male buffalo; more commonly *dunnapótu.*

eppaṭi ? eppaṭici ? inflected form of

eppuḍu, when; with a negative, never. *vindu tsálá bágá zarigindi, nénu yeppaṭici marachi pónu*, the dinner-party went off very well, I shall never forget it; *yeppaṭi pani*, one's usual work.
eppaṭivale, as usual.
eppuḍainá ? ever? *yevarainá bádha paḍutunṭé míru válla cashṭam yeppuḍ' ainá tirchárá?* when any one was in trouble did you ever do anything to relieve them?
eppuḍó, some time or other.
eppuḍu ? when? *ninnu yeppuḍú tsúchin atḷu gnyápacamu lédé*, I do not remember when I saw you.
eppuḍú lédu, never.
eppuḍunu, always.
era, bait. *eranu tsúpi chépa paṭṭi n'aṭṭu*, showing the bait and catching the fish.
eravu, loan, bailment; also *eruvu*. *pustacamu eruvichchi*, having lent a book.
erigintsuṭa, to make known, enlighten, proclaim; causal of *eruguṭa*, to know.
erra, errani, erragá, red, red-hot, blond. *carru yerragá cálchi*, making the ploughshare red-hot; *mogam* (or *caḷḷu*) *yerrachési*, to be angry (making the face or eyes red); *yerraniváḷḷu*, blond people, as opposed to *nallaváḷḷu*, dark people; *yerrapárina*, bloodshot.
eruca, knowledge. *lóguṭṭu perumáḷḷacu yeruca*, God knows the secrets of the heart; *yeruca piḍicedu dhanamu*, acquaintance is worth a fistful of money.
erucachepppuṭa, fortune-telling.
erucaladi, gypsy woman, fortune-teller.
erucalaváḍu, gypsy man.
eruguṭa, to know. *ácali ruchi yerugadu, nidra sukham erugadu, valapu siggu yerugadu*, hunger has no palate, sleep demands no comfort, lust knows no shame; *donganu donga yerugunu*, one thief knows another; *yerigi chésináḍu*, he did it on purpose; *déham erugaca*, unconscious; *buddhi yerugaca munupé*, before the age of discretion; *cuḍi cheyyi yeḍama cheyyi yeruganiváramai*, as we do not even know our right hand from our left (we are ignorant people).
erupu, redness.
eruvu, manure.
eruvu, loan; also *eravu*. *yeruvu tetstsú coni*, taking a loan; *eruvu sommu paruvu chéṭu*, borrowed plumes (*sommu* means jewellery here) lower one's dignity.
eruvucaṭṭuṭa, to manure.
esaru, boiled cooking water. *poyyi mída yesaru peṭṭi dásídi tómi techchina gariṭe tolutsucó póyi dánini masi vadalan'anduna núti daggira snánam chésinánu*, the maid put the boiling water on the fire and rinsed the scraped ladle, and I, not escaping pollution, went to the well and had a bath.
eṭlá ? how? *ocaḍu: pani yeṭlá v' unnadi? incóḍu: tsálá bág unnadi, ná cinda aiduguru pani chést unnáru. ocaḍu: ad eṭlá? incóḍu: nénu méḍa mída pani chést unṭánu.* A: How's the work? B: First-rate, I have five men working under me. A: How's that? B: I work on the first floor; *i móṭáru cáru mícu yeṭlá vachchindi?* how did you get this car? *Ballárici póyé dári yeṭlá?* which is the way to Bellary?
eṭlágaina, somehow or other.
eṭlágó, how. *móṭáru banḍi cheḍi póté bágu cheyyaḍam yeṭlágó telipé pustacam coni tsaduvutunnánu*, I have bought and am reading a book which shows how to repair a motor car.
eṭlágu ? eṭlu ? of what sort?
etsaṭa ? where? also *yeccaḍa*.
etstsarica, hint, warning; more commonly *hetstsarica*.
etstsarintsuṭa, to warn, remind, rally; more commonly *hetstsarintsuṭa*.
etstsutaggu, difference (high and low); more commonly *hetstsutaggu*.
etstsutaggulugá, scornfully, insolently.
etticólu, endeavours.
etticonipóvuṭa, to take away, steal.
etticonivatstsuṭa, to fetch, bring.
etticonuṭa, to carry, raise.
eṭṭidi ? of what kind?
ettintsuṭa, to erect, raise; causal of *ettuṭa*, to raise (or open) a sluice.
ettipoḍupu máṭa, taunt.
ettipoḍutsuṭa, to taunt. *bógamváḷḷanu v'untsucóvaḍam chéta nácu santánam léd ani yettipoḍichináḍu*, he taunted

me with having no issue through keeping dancing girls.

ettivéyuṭa, to throw away, abolish.

ettu, height, move at chess or draughts and so figuratively. *dánici véré yettu v'unnadi,* she has another move up her sleeve.

ettuconipóvuṭa, to steal; also *etticonipóvuṭa. muddáyi: nénu ém' ettuconpóyinán ani míru anumána paḍut unnáru? pólísu inaspecṭaru: gurram, banḍi. muddáyi: aité nannu sarchi cheyyanḍi, nácu bhayam lédu.* Accused: What do you suspect me of having stolen? Inspector: A horse, a carriage. Accused: Then search me, I am not afraid.

ettuconivatstsuṭa, to bring; also *etticonivatstsuṭa.*

ettuconuṭa, to carry; also *etticonuṭa.*

ettuṭa, to raise. *danḍettuṭa,* to raise troops; *nórettuṭa,* to lift up the voice; *bicshamettuṭa,* to beg; *pérettuṭa,* to acquire a reputation; *máṭayettuṭa,* to mention; *yevaru ná pér'ettutú v'unnáru?* who is mentioning my name? *parug'ettuṭa* is the common word for 'to run', from *parugu,* pace, and *ettuṭa.*

eṭu, how; same as *eṭlu.*

eṭu, with negative, nothing. *eṭu tótsaca,* not knowing what to think.

eṭuvanṭi ? of what sort?

evaḍó, some one. *yevaḍó accaḍa cúrtsunnáḍu,* some one is sitting there.

evaḍu ? who? (singular masculine).

evanidi ? whose?

evarainá, any one. *yevar'aina bádha paḍutunṭé míru váḷḷa cashṭam yeppudainá tírchára?* did you ever relieve any one in trouble?

evari, every one's, genitive of *evaḍu.*

evaricaina ? to any one? '*mí afísuló gumástá pani khálí aind'ani vinnánu, nác ippistárá?*' '*álasyam aindi, valla cádu.*' '*yevaric'ainá ichchárá?*' 'I hear there is a vacancy of a clerk's post in your office; will you give it to me?' 'Too late, nothing doing.' 'Have you given it to any one?'

evarinipaṭṭitéváru, any one (whoever you may pitch upon).

evarinó, who I am. *nénu yevarinó nícu telusuná?* do you know who I am?

evari-váru, their own. *yevari mámúḷḷu váḷḷacu ivvacapóté,* if you don't give every one the baksheesh they expect.

evaró, who (relative). *mí pér evaró cheppanḍi,* tell me your name. The Telugus do not usually say 'What is your name?' but 'Who is your name?' *ní pér émi?* is, however, also used.

evaru ? who? (plural form, but also used for the singular). *upanydsacuḍu: prapanchamlóc' ellá goppa upanyásaculu yevaru? sabhicuḍu: nénu cheppută, gáni mí péru yevaró cheppanḍi.* Lecturer: Who is the greatest lecturer in all the world? Auditor: I will say, but first tell me your name; *andarú andalamu yeccité, mósévárú yevaru?* if all get into the palanquin, who is to carry it? *nívu yevaru?* what is your caste? *ní pér evaru?* what is your name?

evate ? who? (female).

evattainá, any woman.

evi ? which? more commonly *yévi.*

E

-é, emphatic affix. This becomes *né* after a vowel: *á rózuné,* on that very day, from *rózuna,* accusative of *rózu,* and *é.* At tennis *ouṭ-á?* is it out? *ouṭ-é,* it is indeed out. This emphatic *-é* (Tamil *tán*) is very common; clerks translate it 'only' and add 'only' grotesquely to many phrases in their drafts where 'myself', &c., would be correct. Thus they translate *néné chésitini,* I did it myself, by 'I only did it', or *ataḍé ná y'anna,* he only is my brother, instead of simply 'that is my brother'.

é- ? interrogative prefix; almost always *yé.*

é- followed sometimes by **-á,** whatever, any. *yé páṭu tappiná sá-páṭu tappadu,* you may miss anything but meals; *yé pillanu chésu códánici nénu ishṭa paḍa lédu*, I did not care to marry any girl.

é, followed by *-ainá*, any, whatever. *yé cheṭṭ ainá*, any tree whatever.

ébadi, 50; more commonly *yábhai*.

éca-, prefix meaning one. Skt.

écabhógamu, undivided possession. Skt., from *éca*, one, and *bhógam*, enjoyment.

écagarbhajanituḍu, uterine. Skt., from *éca*, one, *garbham*, womb, and *jan*, born.

écamai, écamugá, écangá, unitedly. *manam naluguramú calisi yécangá bhójanam cheyya vatstsunu*, we four may join and eat together; *andarú yécamai cheputú v'unṭé yenta manchiváḍ ainá vinṭáḍu*, if all say the same thing any man, however good, will believe them.

écamanasculai, with one mind. Skt., from *éca*, one, and *manasu*, mind.

écapacshamugá, *ex parte*, a legal term from *éca*, one, and *pacsham*, side.

écaputruḍu, only son. Skt.

écaramu, acre. English.

écarítigá, similarly. Skt., from *éca*, one, and *ríti*, way.

écaruvupeṭṭuṭa, to recite; from *éca*, one, and *ruvvu*, lesson. *cávalisté ilágantivi gucca tippacunḍá lacsha sangatulu yécaruvu peṭṭa galanu*, if necessary I can recite 100,000 things of this kind at one go.

écasamsáranugá, in a joint-family.

écatáḷamu, harmony; from *éca*, one, and *táḷamu*, time in music.

écatvamu, oneness. Skt.

écavachanamu, the singular. Skt., from *éca*, one, and *vachanam*, speech. *yécavachana prayógam* is using the singular instead of the plural in addressing a person or speaking of him. *guruvula vishayamló alá yécavachana prayógam cheyya vatstsuná?* can you use the singular in speaking of a spiritual teacher? (French: *tutoyer*).

écavácyamugá, écasvaramutó, with one voice. Skt., from *éca*, one, and *vácyam*, voice. *Satyavatí mogudú yenta anyónyamgá v'unḍi prati vishayamló yécavácyangá v' unṭáró tsúchindárá?* have you noticed how well Satyavati and her husband get on, and that in all matters they have only one voice? *sabhavár andarú yécavácyangá ámódinchinár ani rizalyúshan vrásinánu*, I have written down a resolution that the meeting has unanimously consented.

écádaṣi, eleventh day of the lunar month or after full moon. Skt. *vaicunṭha yécadaṣi* is the December fast.

écántamu, aside, solitary, secret. Skt. *écántamugá* is 'aside' in plays; *écánta sthalamu n'andu khaidu* is solitary confinement.

écintsuṭa, to make one clean cotton; causal of *écuṭa*.

écíbhavintsuṭa, to concur. *í vishayamuna manam écíbhavimpa tsálamu*, we cannot agree to this; *ní abhiprdyamutó nén écíbhavimpa tsálanu*, I cannot concur in your opinion.

écu, flock of cotton. *tala vaṇacutsú v' unnadi, netti yécula buṭṭa lágu ainadi*, his head shakes and the top of it has become like a basket of cotton; *ámudamló munchina yécu vale v'unnáḍu*, he is like a flock dipped in castor oil (a bit of chewed string).

écuṭa, to pick cotton, and so to pick to pieces (a character, &c.). *váḷḷacu ayishṭam puḍité péparlaló yéci doralacu mana mída asúyata puṭṭistáru*, if we offend them they will abuse us in the papers and get us disliked by Europeans.

édainá, any. *ocaḍu: í áfisu panulacu bádhyata galavár evaru? gumástá: nácu bágá teliyad anḍi, yédainá lópam vasté mátram nanné andaru tiṭṭutáru*, who is responsible for the work in this office? Clerk: I don't well know, only if anything goes wrong they all blame me.

éḍava, seventh.

éḍádi, year, longer form of *éḍu*.

édi? where? *railvé inspecṭaru: mí ṭicceṭu yédanḍi? jébuló vedaci Lacshmayya: ayyó canupintsa léd' anḍi. inspecṭaru: maḷḷí tsúḍanḍi canipistundi, mí vishayamai nácu bhayam lédu. Lacshmayya: mícu bhayam léd'émó gáni nácu bhayamgá v'undi, nén é sṭéshanuló dig'dlenó ṭicceṭu tsústé gáni *teliyadu*. Ticket Inspector: Where's your ticket? Lakshmayya (searching his pocket): Oh dear, I can't find it. Inspector: Look again, you will find it, I am not afraid. Lakshmayya: You aren't afraid, but I am; without seeing the ticket I don't know at what station to get out.

édi? which?

édicóla, plough-shaft.

édilédu, édinnílédu, nothing.

ẹ́disindi, ẹ́disinaṭṭé v'undi, it is lamentable; from *ẹ́ḍtsuṭa*, to weep. The commonest of all swear words. *nícu mátram mahá ṣástram telisi y'ẹ́disindilé*, damn your knowledge of the ṣastras; *y'ẹ́disinaṭṭé v'unnadi, nícu pani chéta cádu, yémi chéta cádu*, it is lamentable, you are no good at work or anything else; *mí tirpu yẹ́disinaṭṭé v'unnadi*, your judgement is lamentably bad.

édó, some. *nyáyádhipati: nuvvu iṭlá césulaló chiccucóvaḍam mí ammacu cashṭangá v'unḍadá? Yellamma: unḍadanḍi, má amma cúḍá yédó jayalucu póyi háyigá batucutundanḍi*. Judge: Is not your mother in difficulties when you are involved in criminal cases like this? Yellamma: No sir, my mother too will go to some jail and live happily, sir.

ẹ́ḍpuṭa, to cry, to cry for. *goḍḍuvádu goḍḍuc ẹ́disté, tóluvádu tóluc ẹ́ḍpinádu*, the owner cried for the beast, the cobbler for the hide (it is an ill wind that blows no one any good).

eḍtsuṭa, to weep. *atta tsasté cóḍalu yẹ́ḍchin' aṭṭu*, like a daughter-in-law weeping at her mother-in-law's death (crocodile tears); *talli ainá yẹ́ḍavanidí pál ivvadu*, even a mother won't give milk unless the child cries.

édu, seven.

ẹ́ḍu, year; plural *yẹ́ḷḷu* and *yenḍlu*. *sanvatsaram* is another common word.

éḍuguru, ẹ́ḍumandi, seven persons.

édumu, five tooms; from *é* short for *aidu*, and *túmu*.

édupandi, porcupine; also *munḍla-pandi*.

ẹ́ḍupu, crying; from *ẹ́ḍtsuṭa*, to weep. *dánic' ẹ́ḍupu mogamu paḍi*, looking as if she were going to cry.

éguṭa, to go, a word used in books for *póvuṭa* and *veḷḷuṭu*; it is thought distinguished to avoid such common words. *étentsuṭa, égudentsuṭa, zanuṭa, arudentsuṭa, arugudentsuṭa* are the other words commonly used in books for *póvuṭa*.

éhyamu, abominable. Skt.

éi, throw, put; also merely auxiliary. The imperative of *véyuṭa*, in books it will be written *véyumu*; 'pull the punkah' in speaking is *pancá lág'éi*, 'shut the door' is *talupu mús'éi*. This word, though it is one of the commonest in the language, has to wait for a colloquial dictionary to receive recognition.

élaculu, cardamoms; vulgarly pronounced *yálaculu*.

élamu, auction; vulgarly pronounced *yálam*.

élamuvéyuṭa, to sell by auction.

élá? how? why? A common expression is *véyéla?* why a thousand (words)?, in ending a paragraph in a book or newspaper. *yéla yẹ́ḍchedavu?* why are you crying?

élágaina, in any way.

élágu? in what way? how?

éláṭi? of what sort?

élinaváru, the rulers; from *éluṭa*, to rule. A Collector is often addressed in petitions as *yélinaváru*; in speaking, more often as *mapróbó* (*mahá prabhu*, great lord) or *dévará* (lord, god). *yélinaváru* is also applied to God as well as to Collectors; thus in the proverb, *yélina várici réyimpagalu vacaṭé*, the darkness and the light are both alike to Thee.

éḷḷu, years; plural of *ẹ́ḍu*. *nícu yenni yẹ́ḷḷu unṭavi?* which becomes in rapid speech *nícennẹ́ḷḷunṭai*, is the usual phrase for asking a person's age.

éḷḷu, rivers; plural of *éru*.

éluconuṭa, éluṭa, to govern.

émainá, anything. *bhárya: magavál-ḷaci yémainá cheviló cheppité, incó cheviló nunchi y'ivatalici vastundi. bharta: ḍḍadánici yémainá cheppité, renḍu chevulalóci póyi nóṭló nunchi baiṭici vastundi*. Wife: If you say anything in a man's ear it will come out at the other ear. Husband: If you say anything to a woman it will go in at both ears and come out at the mouth.

émaindi? what has happened to it? what has become of it? with the 'it' as subject in the nominative. *pustacam yémaindi?* what has happened to the book?

émanagá, émanṭé, if you want to know, that is to say; from *émi*, what, and *anuṭa*, to say. Very common expressions in introducing the prayer at the end of petitions and in general in introducing explanations. *Lacshmayya: ní bháryacu viṣránti cósam puṭṭinṭici pampävá? Vencayya: pampänu, nizam yémanṭé nácu viṣránti cávalisi aṭlá chéstánu.* Lakshmayya: Have you sent your wife to her parents' home for a rest? Venkayya: Yes, but to tell the truth I do it when I want a rest myself.

émani? what? *yémani aḍigáru?* what did he ask?

émarintsuṭa, to put a person off his guard, deceive. *rátriḷḷu yazamánulu yeragacunḍá yémarichi yettucu pótáru,* they rob at night deceiving the unsuspecting owners. In the above sentence there are three consecutive words which are supposed to begin with *e*, but really begin with euphonic *y*.

émariyunḍuṭa, to be taken off one's guard, to be deceived. *yellavárunu cheppucógá vini, nammi, yémari y'unnánu,* when every one said it, I listened, believed, and was deceived.

émarupáṭugá, émarupáṭuna, off his guard. *yémaripáṭuna vachchin anducu cshamintsanḍi,* excuse me for taking you off your guard.

émayyá! what, sir! *móṭáruváḍu: yémayyá, í róḍḍu antá nídé anuconi naḍustáv émayyá?* Motorist: Hullo, sir, what are you walking along for, sir, as if the whole road belonged to you?

émé! here, woman! also *ósí*.

émi? émiṭi? what? The commonest of the interrogatives, often shortened to *ém*. *iyyac ém?* supposing I don't give? *aité yém?* what if it be? *yém cheyyum anṭáru?* what do you want me to do? *aité níc émi cávale?* then what is it you want? *nícú Lacshmayyacú sambandham émiṭi? nác istán anna pillanu Lacshmayyac ichcháru.* What is your relationship with Lakshmayya? They gave Lakshmayya the girl they had promised to me; *nénu yém talatsucunṭunnánó cheppu,* read my thoughts; *id ém goppa cádu,* there is nothing remarkable about this; *mí manassuló yém' anucunṭunnadí nénu cheppa galanu,* I know what you are thinking, doctor; *nic ém bádha?* what is wrong with you? *aité nuvvu yém chéstávu?* what will you do next? *yémirá?* what sir? hullo! is a common form of address to inferiors.

émiṭicó, for something or other, for what.

émiṭó? what? why? *abaddhálu áḍutunnávu, inducu ṣicsha yémiṭó telusuná?* you are telling lies, do you know what the punishment for that is? *naṭuḍu: nénu náṭacamló tsachchipótú v'unn' appuḍu précshaculu yeṭlá yéḍtsáró tsúchává? snéhituḍu: dánici cáraṇam yémiṭó telesuná? naṭuḍu: yémiṭó nuvvu cheppu. snéhituḍu: nuvvu nizamgá tsáva léd ani.* Actor: When I was dying in the play did you see how the spectators cried? Friend: Do you know why? Actor: Tell me why. Friend: Because you did not really die.

émó, something or other, I don't know what, perhaps. *vachchináḍ émó,* perhaps he has come; *adi yémó cáni,* however that may be.

émói, the common form of address among equals (males). In starting a conversation or on meeting a person you begin with *yémói!* among equals; to inferiors you say *óri*, so spelt, but commonly pronounced *oré* or *oréi*. To superiors you say *yémanḍi*.

-éná? suffix meaning 'is it not?', an interrogative implying an answer in the affirmative. (Latin *nonne.*) A very common suffix. *Ballárici idi dáréná?* is not this the road to Bellary? *adi cherucu pippéná?* isn't this sugar-cane refuse? *nannu anta máṭa anaḍam mícu bhávyam éná?* is it proper to say such a word to me? (i.e., is it not improper?).

Énádi, a hill tribe. They are animists, not Hindus, and so are not untouchable and can be employed as servants and sweepers, for instance, on the Tirupati hill, without pollution to temples. When the sweepers of a municipality in the Ceded Districts went on strike, the strike was broken by importing Enadis. Pronounced *Yánádi.*

énḍlu, plural of *yéḍu*, year.

-éni, suffix meaning 'if'. *nívu nannu nammavéni*, if you won't believe me.

-éni . . . -éni, reduplicated *-éni* means 'whether . . . or'. *puṭṭenéni giṭṭenéni*, whether they are born or die.

énu, 5; in compounds for *aidu*.

énuga, énugu, elephant. *tinḍici yénugu, panici pínugu*, an elephant to eat, a corpse to work; *yénugu ghímcarintsuts unnadi*, the elephant screeches; *yénugacu vaca síma, gurránici vaca v'úru, barrecu vaca bánise*, it takes a barony to keep an elephant, a village to keep a horse, only a slave girl to keep a buffalo; *miṭṭanu v'unná yénugé, pallána v'unná yénugé*, an elephant is an elephant whether he stands on the ridge or in the pit. The castle at chess is *énuga*.

énugacálivádu, a man with elephant's legs, i.e. afflicted with elephantiasis.

énúru, 500.

épáruṭa, to bloom, flourish. A literary word from *épu*, increase, and *áruṭa*, to teem.

épu, excess. *í moccalu mahá yépugá periginavi*, these weeds have grown to excess.

érá ! hullo there! short for *émirá*.

éri ? where? *vár' éri?* where is he?

érpaḍuṭa, to settle (intr.); the causal form *érpartsuṭa,* to cause to be arranged, is commoner.

érparatsuṭa, to see to, arrange.

érpáṭu, arrangement. *érpaṭu chéyuṭa* is the common expression for making arrangements.

éru, river. *yéru yenni vancálu póyiná samudramulóné pada valenu,* even the weariest river winds safe to sea at last; *yéru dáṭi teppa tagala vésinaṭṭu,* like burning your ships (cross the river and burn your raft).

éruṭa, to glean, pick up, clean out. *tsúchináru cárá Góvindarárau Pantulucu budili cávaḍamtóné Padmanábh Ayya gáru vachchi, áfisuló purugu lécunḍa yélá yéri vésináḍo?* Did you not see how when Padmanabh Ayya took over charge from Govindarau Pantulu he cleaned the office right out? *accaḍá accaḍá tirigi nálugu ḍabbula sommu yérucu vachchéváru*, he used to wander here and there and pick up small sums; *váḷlacu nálugu ḍabbulu yérucóvaḍamú chéta cádu*, they can't put two coppers together; *idéruṭa*, to pick up one's age, is used of female puberty.

ésa, wild; commonly pronounced *y'ása*, just as *élam* becomes *yálam* and *énádi* becomes *yánádi.*

-ési, a suffix, meaning at the rate of, so many at a time, so *padési*, 10 at a time. *inta-l-ési*, so large.

ési, past participle of *véyuṭa*, the *v* being dropped; very common.

éṭaválu, slope, especially a slope in a canal bank for the passage of cattle and carts, but it is much commoner to call this *slópu*.

éṭá, yearly; from *éḍu*, year.

étámu, picottah. *samudránacu yétámu vésin' aṭṭu*, like fixing a picottah to the sea.

étentsuṭa, to go. A book word for *póvuṭa* or *veḷluṭa.*

éṭéṭa, year by year. *yéṭéṭa voccoccaḍu tsoppuna padimandi pillalu*, ten children at one a year.

éṭi, inflected form of *yéru*, river. *yéṭi voḍḍu chénu*, field on the river bank, a proverbial expression for a dangerous situation.

éṭi, inflected form of *yéḍu*, year.

éṭici ? why? not so common as *yenducu.*

éṭiciy'éḍádi, for a whole year. *pullalu maḷḷ í zamábandi vachchina dácá yéṭici yéḍádi saripótundi*, the fire-wood, &c. (supplied in the Jamabandi camp), will last (the hosts of the clerks) for a year till next Jamabandi.

étu, pride.

évagintsuṭa, to be disgusted.

évi ? which? out with it! *yévi rúpáyalu té,* out with the rupees; *níḷḷ évi?* where's the water?

évó, whatever (plural). *míc ém cá valenu ! yévó cheppite tondaragá istánu,* (shopman) What do you want, sir? Whatever you say, I will produce it quickly.

F

There is no *f* in Telugu. The following are a few Hindustani or English words in common use. There is also no *f* in Telugu script. The proper pronunciation of *ph* is as in 'uphill'. The Telugus find it difficult to pronounce *f* and usually mis-pronounce it *p*; thus they say 'pig-fruit' for 'fig' and 'pish' for 'fish'.

facíru, fakir. Hindustani. *nádu v'unṭé Navábu Sáyebu, annamu v'unṭé Amíru Sáyebu, bida paḍité Facíru Sáyebu, tsasté, Píru Sáyebu,* a landed Muhammedan is Mr. Nawab, one who has enough to eat, Mr. Amir, a poor one, Mr. Fakir, a dead one, Mr. Holy Peer.

factu, simply, only. Hindustani. *nénu piṭishanu vaccanṭici rúpáyi, arthá, pávalá tsoppuna putstsucunná, factu piṭishanlaló rózucu muppai rúpáyalacu taccuva lécunḍá caḷḷa tsúchévánṇi,* taking ¼, ½, or 1 rupee on each petition I used to see the colour of not less than Rs. 30 a day on petitions alone.

failauṭa, to fail in an examination. English.

fairu, brilliant. English, from *fire*. Frequently used in the compound word *aggi-fairu*, brilliance; also *aggi-fóru. vádu aggi-fóru gáḍani nácu telusu,* I know that he is a man of brilliant parts. *aggi-fóru* is also an interjection of praise; *aggi* itself is a term for fire, cf. *géṭu-gummamu,* a gateway, and *aggi-nippu,* fire.

faisalá, or **faisalu,** settled, decided. Hindustani. *faisal ainadi,* 'the Court has delivered judgement', is the answer to a petitioner who still protests after the Collector has rejected the petition.

farmána, firman. Hindustani. A royal decree or order, used especially of the decrees of the old Moghul and other emperors. Fort St. George was held on a firman of the Empire of Vijayanagar issued at Chandragiri; all the trading companies obtained firmans from the Great Moghul also as well as from inferior rulers.

fasal, adjective of *fasli*, the Muhammedan year. Hindustani *fasaljásti*, which means excess of the year, is a revenue term for second-crop charge; *tírvajásti,* which means excess of tax, is water-rate on dry land. A dufasal crop is a crop raised in two faslies.

fasali, Muhammedan year. Hindustani. It illustrates the conservatism of the administration that the Muhammedan year in Madras, 1st July to 30th June, is still used for revenue purposes. It is easy to remember the fasli corresponding to any year. Fasli 1340 ends in June 1930—deduct 590. This is for Madras only, in Bengal the calculation is different.

fáramu, form. English.

fárjari, forgery. English.

fáyidálu, profits. Hindustani.

firangí, European. English, from Frank, *feringhu,* i.e. the French.

firangí, cannon; from *firangí,* foreigner. *tupácí caḍupuna firangí puṭṭin aṭṭu,* like a cannon born in a musket's belly.

firyádi, complainant, plaintiff. Hindustani.

firyádu, complaint. Hindustani. The ordinary word for a complaint in criminal cases.

firyádu chéyuṭa, to complain. *pínal cóḍḍu cámmenṭarí tsúchi ḍífémêshan cinda firyádu tettámu,* this sentence is perfectly good Telugu but it will be noticed that it only contains three Telugu words; *nénu lántsam putstsucunṭán ani Hai Córṭu jadjílacu telusunu, ṣivil jadjíci telusunu, aind nénu yeppuḍú ḍoricévánṇi cánu; nálugú,* *múḍú lantsam yichchévāḷḷu firyádú chésucóru, firyádu chésucunná ruzuvu partsaḍam mahá cashṭam, yeduru firyádu chésinavāḍicé ṣicsha autundi,* that I take bribes is known to the judges of the High Court and to the district judge, but I have never been caught; people who have paid only three or four rupees won't complain; even if they do, proof is very difficult; a counter complaint will be brought and it is they who will be punished.

fitúri, raid. Hindustani. It is used figuratively of a false complaint, &c. *samayam tsúchi doragáritó yédaina fitúri chéstāru,* they will wait for an opportunity to make a false charge against us to the Collector.

fitúri, rebellion. *Rampa-fitúri,* the Rampa rebellion; disturbances in the Agency tracts are generally termed *fitúrilu. fitúri-dáru,* such an insurgent.

fízu, fees. English, especially of vakil's fees.

G

-ga, the adverbial suffix, more commonly *-gá*; from root *cá*, become.

gabagaba, hubbub, gabbling; onomatopoeic. *gabagaba tsadivi,* reading gabble gabble.

gabbilamu, bat. *gabbilamu ácáṣamuna paḍacunḍá paṭṭu contán anuconn aṭṭu,* like the bat which thought it was holding the sky up.

gabbu, stink.

gada, club. Skt.

gaḍa, stick. Telugu. *cherucugaḍa,* sugar-cane; *zonnagaḍa,* millet-stalk.

gaḍabiḍa, trouble, row; onomatopoeic. *á rózuna y'inṭló yémi gaḍabiḍa! yémi allari! cécalató y'inṭi mída penculu nálugú yegiri póyinavi,* that day what a row there was in the house! what a hubbub! with the screeching some tiles flew off the roof; *í gaḍabiḍa antá yémiti?* what's all this noise about? *mír í madhya bógamváḷḷa vishayamló cádá v'úḷḷó tsálá gaḍabiḍa chéstú vachchináru,* you have been making a big row in the village about the dancing-girls.

gaḍagaḍa, quickly, excitedly; onomatopoeic. *gaḍagaḍa chepputa,* to gabble; *gaḍagaḍa tinuṭa,* to gobble (in English as in Telugu the letter *g* denotes rapidity and excitement); *gaḍagaḍa vaḍacuṭa* or *gaḍagaḍa áḍuṭa,* to quiver; *venuca Condatráu Pantulugáru ṣirashtáddri chésin appuḍu garbhdló pinḍálu adiri poyévi, vacca céca vésté v'úḷḷóváḷḷ antá gaḍagaḍa vaḍaci battalaló alpáchamánamu chésucunévāru,* when Kondatrao Pantulu held the sheristadar's office the foetuses quivered in the womb; if he gave a shout the whole village fell a-trembling and there would not be a dry dhoty between them.

gaḍapa, gateway. *gummam dáté-ṭ-appuḍu jágratá, cálici debba tagulutundi, gaḍapa melligá dáṭanḍi,* careful over the threshold not to knock your feet, gently through the gate. Also *caḍapa,* whence Cuddapah town and district; it was the gate into the Nizam's territories.

gaḍapuṭa, to pass, get on; also *gaḍatsuṭa, gaḍupuṭa, gaḍutsuṭa. nimisham oca calpamugá gaḍaputs unḍiri,* they passed through an age in a minute; *idi lécunḍá nácu gaḍavadu,* I can't get on without it; *gaḍichi braticinaváru,* the survivors; *iccaḍa gaḍavan anduna deṣántaramunacu veḷḷináru,* they emigrated because they could not get on here; *vádu tana appulaváḷḷanu y'iváḷḷa (í véḷa) cádu, répu, répu cád ellunḍi y'ani cálamu gaḍipináḍu,* he temporized with his creditors. Note the Telugu preference for the concrete.

gadavu, term, the time fixed for a payment or expiry of a bill or an adjustment; also *gaḍuvu, gaḍuvunáḍu.*

gadá! indeed! This, one of the commonest words in the language, will not be found in any dictionary but this. It stands for *cádá?* is it not? which is also used for 'indeed'; but *gadá* is far commoner, and the Telugus, being fond of emphasis, say *gadá* much oftener than we say 'indeed', 'really', 'you don't say so', &c., though not perhaps oftener than the Germans say their equivalents *so! doch!* &c. Also shortened to *gá*.

gadda, kite; also *gedda*. *cáculanu coṭṭi gaddalacu vésin aṭṭu*, driving away the crows to feed the kites (robbing Peter to pay Paul).

gaḍḍa, clod, especially a hard one; tumour. It takes a *gaḍḍapára* or pick-axe to break a *gaḍḍa*, and *gaḍḍacaṭṭina* is used metaphorically of hardness of heart. *í Prabhuvugáru gaḍḍacaṭṭina consarvativulu*, this peer is a hide-bound conservative; *gaḍḍapoyyi* is a fire-place made of three clods fitted together.

gaḍḍamu, beard, chin; usually pronounced *geḍḍam*. *ocaḍu: conni sanvatsarála cindaṭa ní vale nácu gaḍḍam v'unḍédi, adi bágá v'unḍa léd ani canuconni dánni tísi véshánu. incóḍu: conni sanvatsarála cindaṭa ní vale nácu mukham unḍédi, adi bág unḍa léd ani canuconni dánni tísi véstán anṭé vílu léca póyinadi, andu cheta gaḍḍam penchänu.* Smith: A few years ago I had a beard like yours; not thinking it nice I took it off. Jones: A few years ago I had a face like yours; not thinking it nice, I wanted to take it off, but not being able to I grew a beard.

gaḍḍála, bearded. *á tarváta vachchina Khádar Sáhibu Niyyógul andariní mel-ligá ságan ampi, gaḍḍála Sáhébulanu andariní áfisuló dúrchináḍu*, Khadar Sahib, who came after him, gradually got rid of all the Niyogis and introduced nothing but bearded Muhammedans into the office.

gaḍḍapára, crowbar. *gaḍḍapáralu mingi sonṭhi casháyálu tágin aṭṭu*, like the man who took ginger potions after swallowing the crowbar.

gadde, throne.

gaḍḍi, grass. *varigaḍḍi* is rice straw; *patstsa gaḍḍi*, green grass, is used to distinguish the grass your horse eats from the *varigaḍḍi* or *yenḍu gaḍḍi* or *yenḍu casavu* he lies on. The word 'straw' is not known to Indians who speak English; they always call it hay. Hay does not exist. The Indian feeds his cattle on straw, not hay, and keeps only straw-stacks, not hay-stacks.

gaddinésina, thatched; from *gaḍḍi* and *néyuṭa*, to weave.

gaddintsuṭa, to chide.

gaḍḍiparaca, blade of grass or straw. *dánici para purushuḍ anṭé gaḍḍi paracató samánam*, she does not care a fig for any other man.

gaḍḍi tinuṭa, to be an ass or to be made an ass of; from *gaḍḍi* and *tinuṭa*, to eat. *í láguna gaḍḍi tináḍu*, so was he made a fool of.

gadgada svaramu, broken voice, fluttering accents. Skt. *murchillutsu gadgada svaramutó: ayyo! végiram vaidyunni pilipintsanḍi*, fainting, with a tremulous voice: 'O dear! Call the doctor quickly.'

gadi, room. *vanṭa gadi*, the cook-room, kitchen; *paḍacagadi*, bedroom; *áfisu-gadi*, office room; *í gadi nádi-róyi, ná gadiló nunchi y'ivatalici rá*, this is *my* room, GET OUT! *ná gadi nácu viḍichi peṭṭí vési nívu marivaca tsóṭa tsávu*, get out of my room, damn you!

gaḍintsuṭa, to earn, amass, acquire.

gaḍiya, the Telugu hour of 24 minutes. *gaḍiyacu oca máṭa cheppenu*, he changed his mind every 20 minutes.

gaḍiya, bolt. *nannu velupala peṭṭi, lópala talupu gaḍiya peṭṭucunnáḍu*, he turned me out and bolted the door inside.

gaḍiyáramu, watch, clock, hour-glass; from *gaḍiya*, hour. *Rámayya: ní cotta naucaru yeṭlá pani chést unnáḍu? Sómayya: ippaṭici nálugu chimní glásulu baddalu coṭṭáḍu, oca gaḍiyáram ákhar aindi, tsála cashṭa paḍi pani chéstáḍu.* Ramayya: How is your new servant doing? Somayya: So far he has broken four lamp chimneys and done for one clock; he is a very hard-working man; *peddamanishi: nannu cshamintsanḍi, ná gaḍiyáram yevaró yettuconi póyinár ani mícu ninna ripórṭu chésháiu, inṭici vellé-ṭ-appaṭici peṭṭelóné canipinchindi. polísu inspecṭaru: yém lábham? mému dong-anu paṭṭuconi coṭló peṭṭämé.* Gentleman: You must excuse me, I reported to you yesterday that some one had stolen my watch, but when I got home I found it in a box. Inspector: What's the good of that? We have arrested the thief and put him in the lock-up.

gadumuṭa, to rebuke.

gaḍupuṭa, to pass; also *gaḍatsuṭa, gaḍutsuṭa. á mahá bhágyam antayu nén eppuḍu bávuconḍuná ani dinam oca calpamugá gaḍuputsu,* a day passing like an age while I was looking forward to that great happiness.

gaḍusu, hard.

gaḍuvu, term; also *gaḍapu. Presiḍenṭu Húvaru Gáru Jarmanic oca sanvatsaramu gaḍapun osaga valayun ani niṣchayinchiri,* President Hoover has resolved to give Germany a year's moratorium; *álóchintsu conuṭacu níc áru ganṭala cálamu gaḍuv ichchinánu,* I give you six hours to think it over.

gadya, prose. Skt. *vachanamu* is commoner.

gai-, gairu-, negative prefix. Hindustani. *gaiházaru,* not present.

gairumanjúru, not approved, rejected (of petitions, &c.).

gajadonga, great rogue; from *gajam,* elephant.

gajamu, elephant. Skt. *gajam* is used in books and compounds; the common word is *énugu.* In compounds it often means great or long, as *gajapippali,* long pepper; *gaj ítagáḍu,* a great swimmer. *gaja cachchapu póru tsandamu,* like a fight between an elephant and a tortoise.

gajamu, yard. *gajamu vadda múḍu aḍugulu,* there are three feet to the yard. *gajamu* or *daṭṭinché gajamu* is also a ramrod.

gajje, small bell. *gajjegolusu* is a necklace made of little tinkling bells.

gajjecatte, dancing-girl.

gajji, itch, mange, scab. *váḍici vaḷḷ antá gajji chiḍumu paṭṭuconi vachchindi,* itching and smarting all over the body.

-gala, suffix meaning 'having'; for *cala,* participle of *caluguṭa.* This is one of the commonest words in the language, but is not given in the ordinary dictionaries; it is used to form adjectives. *ḍabbugala* is having money, rich; *ḍabbugalaváḍu* is a man of means.

galabili, confusion, noise; onomatopoeic.

galagala, twittering, tinkling, jingling, rattling; onomatopoeic. *galagalamanuṭa* is used of the sounds of birds, bells, rattles, &c.

galamu, throat. Skt. The ordinary word is *gontu.*

galamu, we can. *galanu* is 'I can', *galaḍu,* 'he can', *galavu,* 'you can', *galaru,* 'they can'. These words for 'can' are not to be found in the ordinary dictionaries in their alphabetical place; they would have to be looked for under *caluguṭa,* to have. 'I can say' is *nénu cheppa galanu.* 'Can you tell me?' is *cheppa galavá? Lacshmayya: nácu ninnaṭi nunchi zabbugá undi. Vencayya: vaidyuḍini pilichédá? Lacshmayya: jantu vaidyuḍini pilipintsu. Vencayya: yenducu? jantuvaidyuḍu yém canucó galaḍu? ḍácṭaru praṣna vésté jantuvulu zavábu cheppavu cádá? Lacshmayya: zavábu cheppavu cá baṭṭé jantuvaidyulu praṣnal aḍagacunḍá rógam canipeṭṭa galaru.* Smith: I have been ill since yesterday. Jones: Shall I call the doctor? Smith: Call the vet. Jones: Why? What can the vet find out? If a doctor asks a question the animals can't answer, can they? Smith: Just so, they don't answer, and the vet can diagnose the disease without asking questions.

galásu, glass. English.

galigina, having; for *caligina.* But this is the more usual form; so also *galuga* for *caluga* in the infinitive. *nác émi ibbandi galuga lédu,* I suffered no inconvenience.

gamaḷḷaváḍu, toddy-drawer (caste name); also *ídiga.* The feminine is *gamaḷḷadi. gamaḷḷa munḍá coḍucu mányam léca póté callu gitsuconi bratucutáḍu,* (unlike us brahmins) a whoreson gamalla can live by drawing toddy if he has no inam land.

gamanamu, going. Skt. *sahagamanamu,* going together (with a dead husband), means suttee. *mahátmul ácáṣa gamanamu,* mahatmas visiting heaven (those of the theosophists); *dhyánaṣacti chéta y'i déhamutó léchi váyuvuló téli ácáṣa gamanam cheyya galugudunu*, by force of meditation I can rise with this body and float to heaven on the wings of the wind.

gamanintsuṭa, to think. Skt. Used in books for the common words *anuconuṭa, tótsuṭa, álóchintsuṭa, entsuṭa*.

gambhíramu, solemn. Skt. *parihásam máni vési gambhíramugá máṭláḍa valenu*, stop joking and talk seriously; *gambhíramuga álóchints unnáv émi?* are you thinking profoundly?

gampa, basket. The most ordinary word for basket. *buṭṭa* is also common.

gamyamu, attainable. Skt. *gamyapradéṣamu* and *gamyasthánamu* are words for destination.

ganagana, fierce, glowing; onomatopoeic. *ganaganamanuṭa* is used of sparks, &c.; *ganagana nippulu*, glowing fires.

ganana, calculation. Skt.

Ganapati, the elephant god, *Ganéṣa*. Skt.

ganḍamu, danger. Skt. *dina ganḍamu veyy énḍlu ayussu*, threatened men live long; *pilla ganḍamu, talli ganḍamu v'unṭundi gáni, mantrasáni ganḍam yeccaḍá v' unḍadu*, the child may be in danger, the mother may be in danger, the midwife never is; *manam goppa ganḍam tappintsu cunnámu*, we have escaped a great danger.

gandaragóḷam, disorder, hubbub. *pillalu ná pustacamulu gandragóḷam chésináru*, the children have mixed up all my books; *commulu v'údi, dappulu váyinchi, bhúmi ácáṣamu cóláhala dhvani y'ichché-ṭ-aṭṭu gandaragóḷam chesi*, blowing horns, beating drums, and making hubbub enough to cause earth and sky to roar in unison; *á gandragóḷam yémiṭi?* what is all that noise about?

gandhacamu, sulphur. Skt.

gandhamu, sandal, scent, fragrance. Skt. *manchi gandhamú malle puvvulú teppintsu*, get sandal paste and jasmine flowers; *vidyá gandhamu*, fragrance of learning; *yedd émi yerugundá aṭucula tsavi, gáḍid émi yerugundá gandhi poḍi vásana?* throwing parched rice before bullocks or sandal paste before asses (pearls before swine).

gandhapu cheṭṭu, sandal-tree.

gandharvuḍu, cherub. Skt. *gándharva vivâham* is a marriage without ceremonies.

ganḍi, chink, pass, breach.

ganḍu, manliness, male of an animal. *cúna ai penchité, ganḍu ai carava vachchindi*, he brought up a kitten and it tried to bite him when it was a tom; *ganḍuchépa* is the carp; *ganḍupilli*, tom-cat; *ganḍuchíma*, the big black ant; *ganḍucóti*, the baboon.

Ganéṣa, the elephant god. Skt.

Ganga, the Ganges, also water in general. Skt., from root *-ga*, go. *Pancha Gangulu* are the five sacred rivers, Ganges, Godavari, Kistna, Cauvery, and Tungabhadra. *Gangaló munigina cáci hamsa autundá?* will a crow become a swan by dipping in the Ganges? *tá valaṣinadi Rambha, tá muniginadi Ganga*, all his geese are swans (the girl he loves is a Rambha, the river he bathes in the Ganges).

gangaḍólu, dewlap.

gangi, sacred, in the expressions *gangeddu*, the decorated bullock that beggars take about, and *gangi góvu*, sacred ox. *Cásici pógáné carri cucca gangi góvu auná?* will a black dog become a holy ox by going to Benares?

gangódacamu, Ganges water. Skt., from *Ganga* and *udacam*, water.

gani, having borne; for *cani*. *yevvaró pillanu gani, tsampi vési, rátri véḷa mana gummamunacu edurugá vídhiló páravésináru*, some one gave birth to a child, killed it, and exposed it at night in the street opposite our gate.

gani, mine. Skt. *Navvulagani* is the title of a humorous work. *ganiboggu*, coal.

ganima, ridge.

ganintsuṭa, to compute. Skt. *práṇam bág unṭé, sommu marivaca náṭici ganintsucó vatstsunu*, if you escape with your life, you may leave the computation of the pecuniary loss to another day.

ganipani, mining.

ganitamu, computed.

ganiváḍu, miner.

ganji, rice-water. This is regarded as

the simplest of food, just as we regard bread. Bread and water are for us the essentials, for the Telugus ganji and salt. *appu léca póté, v'uppu ganjé mélu*, it is better to live on bread and water than to get into debt; *ganji vártsuṭa* is to drain the ganji from the rice.

gannéru, oleander. *vásana léni cherucu puvvul ocaricini yógyamulu cávu, vásana gala gannéru puvvul andaricini yógyumul aunu gadá*, no one has any use for the scentless cane-flower, all are for the scented oleander.

ganṭa, gong, and so hour, the hour being beaten on a gong at taluk offices and such places. So *ganṭa coṭṭuṭa* is to beat the hour on the gong. *ippuḍu coṭṭinavi nálugu ganṭal éná?* wasn't it four that struck just now? *táginaváḍu: ippuḍu onṭi ganṭa ani nácu telusunu, gaḍiyáram varasagá áru sárlu occa ganṭa coṭṭindi, nácu teliyadaná?* Drunkard: I know it is one o'clock; didn't I notice that the clock struck one six times running? *méjisṭréṭu: nuvvu vantena mída ati tondaragá móṭáru pón istunnáv ani chhárji vachchindi, accaḍa ganṭacu padi maiḷḷa canna yeccuvagá pó cúḍad ani nótisu caṭṭäru, tsadava lédá? draivaru: ayyó, nénu muppadi maiḷḷa tsoppuna banḍi naḍuputú v'unṭé nótísu yeṭlá tsadava galan anḍi?* Magistrate: You are charged with driving a car at excessive speed over the bridge; there is a notice there that you are not to drive more than 10 miles an hour; didn't you read it? Driver: Oh dear! when I was driving 30 miles an hour how could I read the notice? *ḍácṭaru vind ichchenu, vindu samayamló tana rámachilaca canabaḍacunḍá téra aḍḍamu peṭṭenu, vachchina athidhulaló ocaru ganṭala coddi máṭláḍut unḍiri. áyana muginchina pimmaṭa chilaca teraló nunchi iṭlá anenu: 'mí náluca tsúpintsanḍi'*, a doctor was giving a dinner-party; he hid his parrot behind a curtain during the meal; one of the guests talked for hours on end. When he finished the parrot said: 'Please put your tongue out'.

ganta, pack-saddle. *gantacu tagina bonta*, like saddle, like quilt.

gantu, jump, step in dancing. *gantul iduṭa* and *gantulu véyuṭa* are expressions for 'to jump'; another word for 'to jump' is *dumucuṭa*. *bahu santóshanga v'unnadi ani gantalu vési áḍuts unnáḍu*, how delightful, said he, dancing up and down; *gaḍichi braticinám ani gantulu veyya rádu*, don't hulloo till you are out of the wood.

ganuca, therefore. It goes at the end, not as with us, at the beginning, as a rule. The derivation is from root *can-*, to see. *adi ganuca* is 'seeing that', i.e. for that reason. It means seeing all that comes before (therefore). *ninnu pad énḍla baṭṭi yerugudunu ganuca*, seeing that I have known you for ten years; *ocaḍu: nannu pad énḍla baṭṭi yeruguduvu gadá, padi rúpáyalu avasaram ainadi, badul istává? incóḍu: ivvanu. ocaḍu: yendu chéta? incóḍu: ninnu pad énḍla baṭṭi yerugudunu ganuca.* Smith: You have known me for ten years; I am in want of ten rupees, will you lend them me? Jones: No, I won't. Smith: Why not? Jones: Because I have known you for ten years. The prayer at the end of petitions always begins with *ganuca* and experienced collectors who only want to know what the request is, leave out the exordium about their own greatness and the misery of the petitioner, and start reading from *ganuca*.

ganzái, ganja. Drug made from the hemp plant; monopolized by Government.

ganzáicheṭṭu, hemp plant (*cannabis sativa*). *tulasi vanamuló ganzái mocca*, a ganja sprout in a basil plot (a black sheep in the flock).

garalsuscúlu, girls' school. English.

garbhadaridramu, great poverty. Skt., from *garbhamu*, womb, and *daridram*, poverty. *atanici pútacúṭici ṭicáná léd aṭa, garbhadaridram aṭa*, they say he is stony broke.

garbhádhánamu, nuptials (consummation ceremony). Skt., from *garbham*, womb, and *ádhánam*, keeping. *í munḍa nannu garbhádhánam nád ainá paini cheyyi veyyan ichchinadi cádu*, this whore did not allow me to lay hands on her even on the marriage day.

garbhagrühamu, the inside shrine, holy of holies. Skt.

garbham carigipóvuṭa, to miscarry. *ámecu garbham carigi póyindi,* her womb has melted, i.e. she has miscarried.

garbhamu, womb. Skt. Used metaphorically for the inside of anything.

garbhamu dharintsuṭa, to conceive.

garbhamu niltsuṭa, not to miscarry. *ámecu garbham nilchindi,* her womb has stood, i.e. she has not miscarried.

garbhamutó n'unḍuṭa, to be pregnant; more commonly *caḍuputó n'unḍuṭa.*

garbhani, a pregnant woman.

garbhaṣatruvu, a secret foe.

garbhasrávamu, abortion; from *srávamu,* oozing.

garbhavati, a pregnant woman. *balavantamugá mléchchula chéta tísuconi pó baḍi strí garbhavati aina pacshamuna, aṭuvanṭi strílu ṣuddhini córaru, á strí múḍu rátrulaló ṣuddhurál aguts unnadi,* if a woman is carried off forcibly by barbarians and becomes pregnant, such women do not require purification and that woman becomes a pure woman in three nights (Hindu ceremonial law).

garbhavichchitti, miscarriage. *vichchitti* is a Sanskrit word meaning separation.

garbhótpati, conception. Skt., from *utpati,* arising.

garise, garce. Originally the small round building used for storing grain; the grain measure of the old settlements. As a salt measure it was 424 mercals, as a grain measure 400 or 185 cu. ft., about 52 hecto-litres. A garce of land was land calculated to yield a garce of grain.

garishthamu, venerable. Skt.

gariṭe, ladle, spoon. *inṭici vachchina tarváta poyyi mída yesaru peṭṭi, dásidi tómi techchina gariṭe tolutsu có póyi, dánini masi vadalan anduna núti daggira maḷḷi snánam chésinánu,* when I got home I put the water to boil, rinsed the ladle the maid had scraped, and to remove the pollution went to the well and again bathed.

garja, garjanamu, a roar.

garjintsuṭa, to roar. *simhamu garjints unnadi* is 'the lion roars', but the elephant *ghímcarints unnadi.*

garu, bristling.

Garuḍadhvajuḍu, he of the eagle emblem, i.e. Vishnu.

garuḍa muccu, the eagle's beak; a Roman nose.

garuḍa pacshi, the eagle. Skt.

garuḍapárva, eagle glance.

garupoḍutsuṭa, to bristle. *nácu voḷḷu garupoḍust unnadi,* I bristle all over (in fear); *viri vishapu navvu tsúḍaḍamtóté ná vaḷḷu garupoḍichi, manassu nír autundi,* when I hear his poisonous laugh I bristle all over and my mind goes to water.

garutmantuḍu, eagle. Skt.

garvamu, pride. Skt. *vánici garvam eccinadi,* he has got above himself; his head is turned.

garvapótu, a proud man. *váḍu vaṭṭi garvapótu,* he puts on any amount of side.

garvi, garvishtuḍu, a proud, conceited man. *nívu yeppuḍú ní goppatanamé tsútsucuntávu, nívu garvishtivi,* you are always thinking what a great man you are, you are full of conceit.

garvintsuṭa, to be proud. The Telugus translate these words not by 'proud' but by 'haughty', which they pronounce 'hearty'; so if you hear a man described as 'very hearty' there is no reference to the effusiveness of his manner; what is meant is that he is, in the opinion of the speaker, a conceited ass.

gasagasálu, poppy seeds; from the Arabic *khash khash. gasagasála cheṭṭu* is the poppy plant; *khaskas* is the spelling in the old records. To be distinguished from the *khaskhas,* a Persian word for grass used in the familiar cuscus tatties or screens which are put over doors and windows in the hot weather and watered so that the wind coming through cools the room.

gasica, wedge.

gasti, patrol. Hindustani.

gastu, nasty smell; also *gabbu, gappu.*

gata, past, over. Skt. *gata cálam,* the past; *gata culam,* extinct family; *gata-*

jala, sétu bandhanamu, flood banks when the flood has gone past (shutting the stable door after the horse has been stolen); *sétuvu* (Skt.) is especially the Ramesvaram causeway, hence the Raja of Ramnad's hereditary title of *Sétupati*, Lord of the causeway.

gatamu, the past. Skt., from root *ga-*, to go. *gatamu gurinchi vicharintsaḍam prayójanam lédu*, no use grieving over spilt milk.

gati, way, fate. Skt., from root *ga-*, to go. *daivagati*, Divine Providence; *putruḍu lénivánici gati lédu*, the childless have no hope of heaven; *ná gati yémi?* what is to become of me?

gatiléni, forlorn (having no way to escape one's fate). *gatilén ammacu matiléni magaḍu*, to the forlorn woman the foolish husband.

gatstsu, lime, plaster. *í gatsts arugula y'ill evaridi oi?* whose is that house with the plaster pials?

gaṭṭeccintsuṭa, to muddle through, overcome trouble; from *gaṭṭu*, bank, and *eccintsuṭa*, to climb.

gaṭṭi, hard, clever, strong. *poṭṭi-gaṭṭi*, short and strong; *gaṭṭi paṭṭu*, a firm resolution; *induló manchi y'illálu tahassíluddárigári bhárya várini racshinchinadi. pedda manushyula vishayamló mariyoca vidhamugá zariginchina pacshamuna nútilo paḍed ani, áme gaṭṭi paṭṭu paṭṭa baṭṭi gáni, léni yedala*, that worthy matron, the tahsildar's wife, has saved her; by threatening to throw herself into the nearest well if he acted otherwise than she wished towards a respectable family, she got a hefty hold on him; *Lacshmayya: tallidanḍrula gundlu coḍuculacu sancramistav ani vamṣa páraparyapu siddhántmaló mícu nammacam unnadá? Vencayya: gaṭṭigá v'unnadi; ná ḍabbu antá aṭlágé vachchindi.* Smith: Do you believe in the heredity principle? Jones: Firmly, all my money came that way.

gaṭṭigá, harshly.

gaṭṭi lóhamu, hard metal, steel.

gaṭṭivádu, a clever man.

gaṭṭu, bank. *áu chéniló méste dúda gaṭṭuna méstundá?* if the cow grazes in the field, will the calf graze on the bank? (evil communications corrupt good manners; like father, like son).

gaṭṭuṭa, for *caṭṭuṭa*, to tie, build, &c.

gatucuṭa, to lap up.

gauravamu, respectability, honour. Skt. *ná gauravam nénú cápáḍu có valenu*, I must preserve my honour.

Gauri, Parvati. Skt., from *gauri*, maiden.

gavácshamu, window. Skt.

Gavernarugáru, His Excellency the Governor. *mana sangham Gavernarugári ḍaggirici ráyabáram pampints ále*, our association has to send a deputation to the Governor.

gavernmenṭuváru, the Government. *idi Ránigaru vinṭé, ní cáḷḷacu gaṭṭi lóhamtó andelú golusulú vési, Gavernmenṭuváru caṭṭinchina divya bhavanálaló cápuram unchi, sarcáru jíṭála mída v'unḍé bhatulanu cávali y'ichchi, yella cálamu anna vastrálu doratanamvári khartsu mídané y'istú, v'úru dáṭi veḷḷan accara lécundá, ninnu bahu ádarana chéstáru*, if Queen Victoria comes to hear of this, the Government will fit you up with nice steel fetters and chains, assign you one of their lovely palaces for a residence, give you a guard paid by themselves, be at the charge of your board and clothing for ever, and treat you with all hospitality without giving you the trouble of ever leaving the town.

gavva, cowry shell; formerly used as small change. *ácáṣamu nunḍi gavvala nacshatramul anniyu néla mída ráli unḍunu*, all the stars fell to the earth from the sky like a shower of cowries; *púrvam sampádinchinadi vacca guḍḍigavva lédu*, I haven't a farthing left of what I earned before; *míru gavvacu panici ráru*, you will be no use for anything.

gayáḷubhúmi, fallow, waste land.

gayyáḷi, shrew. *nívu panici málina gayyáḷivi*, you are a worthless shrew.

gazza, groin. *noppi gazzalóci yeccinadi*, the pain has mounted to the groin.

gáca, without, except, besides; for *cáca*, negative of *auṭa*, to become. *idi gáca*, besides this.

gáca, may it become (Latin *utinam*); for *cáca*, imperative of *auṭa*, to become.

It comes at the end of a sentence. *nívu sukhamugán unḍuvu gácá!* may you be happy!

gáde, large basket for storing grain. *caliginayya gáde tiseṭ appaṭici, pédavánici práṇam póyindi,* by the time Dives had opened his bin, Lazarus was dead.

gádhamu, deep, intense. Skt. *gádha nidra,* deep sleep; *gádhándhacáramu,* pitch darkness; *gádhálinganamu,* close embrace; *mimmalini y'iddaru paṭṭuconi cadipiná cáni mélacuva rán anta gádha nidra pó valenu,* you must get to sleep so soundly that you won't wake unless two persons catch hold of you and shake you.

gáḍi, trough, trench.

gáḍidacoḍucu, son of an ass, a term of abuse.

gáḍide, ass; also *gáḍida, gáḍede.* Also called *tsácali gurramu,* the dhoby's horse, because asses are chiefly used in India to carry washing. In the sense of fool as common as in English. *gáḍide punḍucu búḍide mandu,* mud is the medicine for a donkey's ulcer (not worth a more expensive medicine); *iddaru pillalu póṭláḍut unḍiri. peddamanishi: úrucondi, yenducu póṭláḍutáru? modaṭi pilla: ní cósamé. peddamanishi: ná cósam póṭláṭa yenducu? modaṭi pilla: nícu gáḍidi unna telivi ainá léd ani váḍ anṭé, nénu v'und annánu, andu chéta póṭláṭa vachchindi,* two boys were fighting and a gentleman said: Stop, what are you fighting about? First boy: About you. Gentleman: What about me? First boy: He said you hadn't even the brains of an ass, and I said you had. *ocaḍu: í conḍa mida yeccaḍánici daggira dári yédaina v'undá? grámasthuḍu: accaḍa canipinché ḍonca dári v'undi; gáḍidelu á dáriné conḍa yeccutai,* Tourist: Is there any short way up this hill? Native: See that way there? That is the one the donkeys go up; *cásici veḷḷi gáḍide guḍḍu techchin aṭṭu,* like going to Benares and bringing back an ass's egg (travellers' tales).

gáḍikhána, coach-house. Hindustani; from *gáḍi,* carriage.

gáḍpu, breeze.

gáḍu, not; for *cáḍu.*

-gáḍu, suffix of contempt. Just as *-gáru* is added to the names of respectable people, so *-gáḍu* is added to the names, caste-names, &c., of pariahs and other despised people.

gálamu, hook, especially a fishing hook.

gáli, wind, climate. There is no word for 'climate' in Telugu; they say the water of a place or the wind of a place is good or bad. *gáli vachchin appuḍu túrpára paṭṭu có valenu,* winnow when the wind comes (make hay while the sun shines); *yé gálici á tsápa yettin aṭṭu,* setting your sail to the wind; *gálici puṭṭi, dhúlici perigin aṭṭu,* born of the wind, reared of the dust (ingratitude). *gálintsuṭa* is to sift.

gáligópuram, the tower over a temple gate. *Hinduvulu viṣála gáligópuramulu aviṣvaníya y'itihása, padyacávya pustacamul ádhára pai nirmistáru,* the Hindus raise a vast superstructure on unbelievable books of stories and poetry.

gálipaṭamu, a paper kite.

gálivána, tempest (wind and rain).

gámbhíryamu, solemnity. Skt., from *gambhíram,* solemn.

gána, therefore. Used in books for *ganuca.*

gánamu, music; one of the eight *bhógamulu* or pleasures.

gándharva viváhamu, one of the forms of marriage in which all ceremonies are dispensed with. Used commonly of elopements and seductions; from *gandharvuḍu,* heavenly musician.

gánḍlaváḍu, turner of oil-mills (*gánuga*), a caste. The feminine is *gánḍladi.*

gáni, but, unless; from root *-cá,* become, negative form. It is attached, like *ganuca,* to the end of the preceding clause. One of the commonest of all words, but not to be found in the ordinary dictionaries in its alphabetical place. They show it under *cáni,* though it is usually both spelt and pronounced *gáni. archéváré gáni, tírchéváru léru,* consolers there are but not helpers (Job's comforters); *diválá tisté gáni,* unless I go bankrupt;

idi atani chéta gáni, mariyocani chéta cádu, he alone can do it; *atadu vasténé gáni, y'i pani cá néradu*, nothing will be done unless he comes.

gáni, singer, musician (female); from *gánamu*, music.

gántsuṭa, to see, bring forth; for *cántsuṭa*.

-gánu, for the purpose of. *vamanamu cácundán unduṭacu gánu támbúlamu vésucunnánu*, I took betel to stay my stomach.

-gánu, *-ga*, adverbial suffix, with *-nu* for repetition. *ippuḍu bógamdánni v'untsucóvaḍamé pratishṭhagánu, v'untsucóca póvaḍam apratishṭhagánu yentsa baḍutú v'unnadi*, nowadays it is thought respectable to keep a dancing-girl, not respectable not to keep one.

gánuḍu, singer, musician (male); from *gánamu*, music. More commonly *gáyacuḍu*.

gánuga, oil-mill, any press. *cherucu gánuga*, sugar-cane press; *púrvapu vale ráti gánugalaló peṭṭi, áḍinché rázul unṭé, viḷḷu iṭlá anṭár anḍi?* would they talk like this if we had the old kings who used to press the seditious in stone oil-mills?

gárábamu, affection.

gáraḍi, gáriḍi, conjuring. *adi cévala máya, vaṭṭi gáraḍi, ṣuddha indrajálamu*, that is pure deception, simple conjuring, just legerdemain; *ocaḍu: nénu gáraḍi chést unṭé tsúchéváḷḷu navváru. incóḍu: yenducu? ocaḍu: nénu cheppé máṭalu aravamlóci tarzumá cheyyaḍánici ocaḍini cudurtsucunṭé, váḍu á máṭalu tinnagá cheppaca, gáraḍi yeṭlá chéstánó cúḍá cheppaḍam modalu peṭṭáḍu; á sangati nácu chivaracu gáni teliya lédu*, Conjurer: Once when I was conjuring, the spectators laughed. Friend: Why did they laugh? Conjurer: I engaged a man to translate into Tamil; instead of translating properly he began to explain how I did the tricks. I did not find out till it was all over.

gáraḍiváḍu, juggler.

gárḍu, guard. English. *upádhyáyuḍu: ná salahá avalimbintsanḍi, míru anni vishayáḷḷó mundugá v'unṭé bágu paḍutáru. vidyárthi: ná nánna venuca v'unná pedda jitam tetsu cunṭ unnáḍ anḍi. upádhyáyuḍu: mí nánnac ém pani? vidyárthi: railvé gárḍu pani*, Teacher: Take my advice and always be forward in everything and you will prosper. Pupil: My father is always behind and draws good pay. Teacher: What is your father's job? Pupil: He is a railway guard.

gáre, round cake made of black gram flour. *caḍupu ninḍinaváríci gárelu chédu*, the full stomach scorns cake; *vanṭa bráhmanuḍu vanḍina gárelanu mundugá tinṭ unḍenu, intaló yazamáni vachchenu. yazamáni: ninnu tsústé áṣcharyamugá v'undi. vanṭa bráhmanuḍu: mimmunu tsústénu áṣcharyamugá v'undanḍi, míru iccaḍici vastár ani nénu anucó lédu*, the brahmin cook was sampling the cakes he had cooked when his mistress came along. Mistress: I am surprised at you. Cook: I am surprised, too; I never thought you would be coming into the kitchen.

-gáru, honorific affix added to names, designations, &c., Mr., Esq. The corresponding scornative is *-gáḍu*. In addressing a letter put M.R.Ry. (Mahárája Rája Shrí) before the name, and *gáru* after it. This is equivalent to Esquire. The Tamil corresponding affix is *avargal*. President Hoover will be *Presiḍenṭu Húvaru gáru. váru* is also used after designations and signifies even greater respect. Thus, a tahsildar being a high official, many people will say *tahassíluddáruváru* rather than *tahassíluddárugáru*. The plural *várulu* will be used of exalted personages like svámis and mahárájas. *gáru* means very little. Even your pariah boy will be *boṭléru* (butler) *gáru* to common people, though the brahmin karnam will allude to him as *boṭlérugáḍu*.

gá valenu, must; for the more common *cá valenu*.

gá vatstsunu, may; for the more common *cá vatstsunu*.

gávintsuṭa, to cause to become; for *cávintsuṭa*. A book and newspaper word for 'to do'; authors scorn *cheyyuṭa* as being too common. Similarly your camp clerk will announce that the Collector is proceeding to camp, not merely going, or will inform (not merely tell) the Collector that when he met a wild elephant on the path he receded (not merely went back).

gáyacuḍu, singer, musician; from *gánamu*, music.

gáyamu, wound. *gáyamu tagaluṭa* is to be wounded, with the dative; *ishnappucu gáyam tagilindi*, or simply *tagilindi*, you hit that snipe.

gáyatri, brahmin prayer to the sun. It is a Sanskrit prayer, which being interpreted, runs: Oh Earth! Heaven! Let us meditate on the supreme splendour of the divine sun, may he illuminate our minds.

gázu, glass bangle. *gázula béram bhójanánacu saré*, the glass bangle trade just gives you your food (because so many break; used of any risky trade); *nénu gázulu toḍigintsu cunṭé adi gázulu toḍigintsu cunṭundi*, if I wear glass bangles, so does she.

gázulaváḍu, bangle-seller.

gedda, kite (the bird); usually spelt *gadda*.

gela, bunch (of plantains, &c.).

gelpintsuṭa, to cause to win.

gelpu, victory.

geltsuṭa, to win. *yevaru gelchédi mícu viṣadam autundi*, you will see who will win; *zúdam áḍi rózucu nálugu rúpáyalu gelustáḍu*, he wins 4 rupees every night at cards; *iddariló abaddham yevaru tvaragá calpinchi chepputáró, váru pandem gelichéṭ aṭṭu Lacshmayya Vencayya nirnayinchiri. Lacshmayya: Chennapatnamló anagá anagá oca peddamanishi v'unḍéváḍu. . . . Vencayya: aité nuvvé pandem gelicháu, nénu inta canna abaddham cheppa lénu*, Lakshmayya and Venkayya had a bet as to who would make up a lie first. Lakshmayya: Once upon a time there was a gentleman in Madras . . . Vencayya: You win, I can't tell a bigger lie than that; *ocaḍu: ní césu yém aindi? vacílu: nyáyam gelichindi. ocaḍu: aité venṭané appílu cheyyanḍi*, Smith: What happened in your case? Vakil: Justice triumphed. Smith: Then appeal at once; *inṭa gelchi rátstsa gelava valenu*, command at home before you command the state (learn to walk before you run).

genṭintsuṭa, to have something pushed.

genṭivéyuṭa, to push away. *nálugu tanni vánni vidhilóci genṭi vésindnu*, I kicked him out into the street.

genṭuṭa, to push. *vánni avatalacu genṭu*, turn him out.

genusu, sweet potato (*dioscorea aculeata*).

gédé, she-buffalo. *góvu léni v'úḷḷó goḍḍu gédé Srí Mahalacshmi*, in a cattleless village the barren buffalo is Holy Lakshmi (the goddess of wealth).

géhamu, house. Skt. A word used in books for *illu*. Home is supposed to be etymologically connected with *géhamu*.

géli, ridicule. *allari pillacáyalu vídhiló nannu géli chési*, mischievous boys mocking me in the street.

géṭu, gate. English. *Rámuḍu: Lacshmayya gári illu idénâ? Dámuḍu: idi cádu. Rámuḍu: í vídhiló v'undá? Dámuḍu: undi. Rámuḍu: nambar émiṭó cheppanḍi. Dámuḍu: nambaru inṭi géṭu mída v'unṭundi, tsúḍanḍi*, Roe: Is this Mr. Smith's house? Doe: No. Roe: Is it in this street? Doe: Yes. Roe: What's the number? Doe: The number is on the gate, look and see.

ghallighallumanuṭa, to clang (of bells); onomatopoeic.

ghanacáryam, glorious deed. Skt.

ghanamu, honour, glory. Skt. *tsaddi canṭé v'úracáya ghanamu*, the pickle is the glory of the cold rice; *piṭṭa conchem, cúta ghanam*, small bird, big cry (much cry and little wool).

ghanata, greatness. Skt.

ghanavaiṣályamu, cubic contents. Skt.

ghaníbhavintsuṭa, to freeze. Skt.

ghanuḍu, great man. *víru paḍuguru Yélúruló ghanulu*, behold the bigwigs of Ellore.

gharána, respectable. *gharána sácshulu*, respectable witnesses; *íyana tsústé gharána manishi lágu canapaḍutú v'unnáḍu*, he looks like a respectable man; *nénu gharána manishi lágu naḍutsucunṭú v'unnánu gáni, chillara manishi lágu pravartintsaḍam lédu*, I am conducting myself like a man of weight and respectability, I am not behaving like a trifler.

ghaṭamu, body. Skt. Book word for *oḷḷu*. *ghaṭa visarjana*, shuffling off this mortal coil; *mana ghaṭálu ṣáṣvatálu cávu*, our bodies are not immortal.

ghaṭṭigá, severely; for *gaṭṭigá*. *peddatanamló peḷḷi chésucó vadd ani tandrigáritó ghaṭṭigá cheppa léca póyináva?* didn't you tell your father strictly that he should not marry in his old age?

ghaṭṭiváḍu, clever man; for *gaṭṭiváḍu*. *váḷḷu rana vaidyamló ghaṭṭiváḷḷu*, they (the I.M.S.) are clever army doctors.

ghátamu, blow, cruel act. Skt. *samsára ghátalu palacadánici nícu nór eṭlá vachchindi?* how could you disclose the skeleton in our cupboard?

ghátu, mountain pass, ghat, police station. Hindustani.

gháṭuca, gháṭaca, cruel, savage. Skt. *crúramaina gháṭuca mrügam*, a cruel, savage beast.

ghátucamu, cruelty, villainy, mischief. In law *néramugala viṣvása ghátucamu* is criminal breach of trust.

ghátucuḍu, cruel man, villain; feminine *gháṭucurálu*. *ósi ghátucurálá!* O cruel woman!

ghímcarintsuṭa, to screech, roar; especially of elephants.

ghóramu, horrible. Skt. *ghóramaina narahatya*, a horrible murder; *míru strílacu punar vivàhamulu cúdav andaru, avi léca pó baṭṭiyé cadá ghóra crütyamulu nityamunu mana strílaló zaruguts unnavi*, you say widows should not remarry, without that horrible things (i.e. abortions) occur daily among our women.

ghóruḍu, scoundrel. Skt.

ghósha, loud noise, proclamation. Skt. *ṣástramulu ghósha peṭṭuts unnavi*, the shastras proclaim; *pillala vaddá, peddala vaddá ghósha peṭṭinchi*, proclaiming to old and young; *samudrapu ghósha*, the roar of the sea; *jayaghóshamulu*, cries of triumph, cheers.

ghóshintsuṭa, ghósha peṭṭuṭa, to proclaim.

ghóshá, for the more common *góshá*. Hindustani.

ghrütamu, ghee. Skt. The book word for *neyyi*; *ghrutódadhi* is the mythological ocean of ghee.

-ghürnitam, suffix meaning rolling. Skt. Used in Sanskrit compounds in books.

gi-, gí- (if the syllable repeated is long), repetitive prefix denoting contempt or impatience. This is exceedingly common. You repeat a word substituting *-gi* for its first syllable by way of impatient contradiction of the last speaker. *anna ginna* is 'bother your brother'; *Vencanna gincanna* is 'Veñkanna be blowed!' *allari gillari*, noise and nonsense; *mogulu gigulu*, silly men; *dévaḍavu givuḍavu*, whether you are a god or a goose; *prámáṇálú gímánálú nácu yémi panici ráu*, I have no use for your vows and protestations; *musaliváḍú lédu gisaliváḍú lédu, vánni avatalici gențu!* I don't care if he is a Methuselah, shove him out! *yóga drüshṭi giga drüshṭi*, esoteric vision indeed, what next! *cshámálu, gímálu!* famine my foot! (what the Collector says to deputations of ryots who wail over a failure of crops and want famine relief); *ṣánti ginti!* funny kind of non-violence! (what the District Magistrate says when Congress boycotters come to him, and assert that their picketing is non-violent, after there has been a riot); *ṣakhanálu gikhunálu*, idiotic omens; *nagalú gigulú*, jewel me no jewels. This figure of repetition is not confined to *gi-*. A similar word or a made-up similar word is repeated. *lantsam pantsam!* bribe indeed! *répó mápó*, day or night; *pandugó pabbunó*, festival or not; *appó sappó*, some debt or other; *voncara tincara*, all up and down (of a bad handwriting, &c.); *voncara* stands for *vancara*, crooked. Repetition is also used in onomatopoeic formations such as *gabagaba*, gobbling; *vaḍavaḍa*, trembling; *gusagusa*, whispering; *ḍaḍa-ḍaḍa*, pit-pat. As the last example shows, we have the same figure—pit-a-pat, higgledy-piggledy, tut-tut, tinkle-tinkle, sighing and sobbing, seething and surging, weeping and wailing, but we do not use it so commonly, and we have nothing corresponding exactly with the scornative *gi-* syllable, which plays so large a part in Telugu back-chat. *ataḍici tana nyáyamunu giyamunu ṣighramugáné marachi póvunu lé*, he will soon forget about his rights and rubbish! *iddaru bráhmanulu pravéṣintsuts unnáru. pradhamuḍu: yevarayyá míru? dvitiyuḍu: mému bráhmanulu. dandac áranyamuló nunchi agastya bhrátagári áṣramamló nunchi vastú v'unnámu. pradh: yuddha vártal émainá telustunnáyyá? dviti: teliyac émi? yeppaṭi caburu appuḍé telustu v'undi. pradh: yeṭlá telustu v undi? mí mahá muni gáru divya drüshṭi valla canipeṭṭutu v'unnárá yémiṭi? dvití: má mahá munici divyadrüshṭi givyadrüshṭi yémi lédu. yeppaṭic appuḍu vánarulu vachchi chepputú v'unnáru. andu valla mác eppaṭi várta appuḍu teliyuts unnadi*, a forest monk said they heard all the war news in the forest. Friend: How so? By divine revelation to your abbot? Monk: Neither by revelation nor by drivelation of our abbot. The forest dwellers come and tell us from time to time; *ní cópamu gipamu ná vadda panici rádu*, your tears and tantrums cut no ice here; *ní cámulu gímulu dúrangá peṭṭu*, but me no buts.

gidda, a measure, ¼ sola, $\frac{1}{64}$ cuntsam.

giḍḍangi, warehouse; from Malay *gandong*. The Anglo-Indian godown and compound are two Malay words brought by the Dutch from Java. It is about all the Dutch have left except *cak-huis* (caccus), latrine, the sweet limes of Palcol, and a few tombs and an *olanda dibba* or two (Dutch mound) in Telugu tracts, where they once had numerous factories—Pulicat, Masulipatam, Draksharama, Palcol, Nagulavamsa, Bimlipatam, &c.

giḍḍi, cow.

giligili, tickling; onomatopoeic.

giligilintsuṭa, giligilipeṭṭuṭa, to tickle.

gillugillumanuṭa, to tinkle; onomatopoeic of bangles, bells, &c.

gilluṭa, to pinch.

ginguruṭa, to be deafened.

ginguretttuṭa, to make a deafening sound, to feel deaf. *í chevi ginguretttu v'unnadi*, as Lacshmayya said, turning his other ear to Vencayya, 'This ear has gone deaf'.

ginne, cup, bowl; not a china cup, a metal one. Crockery (*pingáni*) is not much used. *venḍi ginneló pálú púrilú y'ilá tiscrá*, bring milk and cake in a silver cup.

ginza, seed, stone. *chinta ginza* is a tamarind stone; *áva ginza*, mustard seed, is used in such phrases as *ávaginza sandéham lédu*, there is not a shadow of doubt.

ginzalu, grain, seeds. *cuncheḍu ginzalacu cúlici póté, túmeḍu ginzalu dúḍa tinnaṭṭu*, like the cooly woman who went to work for a pint of grain while the calf at home ate a bushel; *yeddu aḍuguló yéḍu ginzalu panḍité, panṭa palatsan aunu*, though seven seeds lie within the ox's foot-print the crop may be thin (don't sow too thick).

ginzuconuṭa, to twist, writhe, struggle. *cáḷḷunu chétulunu ginzuconutsu*, writhing with arms and legs; *úricé ginzucócu*, no use struggling.

giráci, dear (in price). Hindustani. The ordinary word. The opposite is *tsauca*, cheap. *priyam* is dear in all senses.

giri, mountain. Skt. Occurs only in place-names such as Venkatagiri and Skt. compounds such as *giricanya*, the mountain nymph Parvati.

girruna, giragira, round and round; onomatopoeic. *bongaram giragira tippuṭa*, to spin a top. *tala girruna tirigi pótunnadi*, my head is turning round.

gitta, a young bull.

giṭta, hoof.

giṭṭuṭa, to agree, to suit. *mana mída giṭṭaniváḷḷu*, people who don't get on with us, is a very common phrase for 'our enemies'; *nácu giṭṭadu*, it doesn't suit me; *dhara giṭṭaca*, not being able to agree on the price; *í tinḍi vánici giṭṭadu*, this food does not agree with him.

giṭṭuṭa, to die. *puṭtiréni giṭṭiréni*, what though they be born, what though they die, comes in the Vemana verses, the didactic verses which children have to learn by heart.

gizagizaláḍuṭa, flutter, writhe; onomatopoeic. Used, e.g., of a child stung by a scorpion; also *gaṣagaṣa*.

gícuṭa, to draw a line, scrape, scratch.

gíruṭa, to scrape, smooth the hair with the fingers.

gíta, line.

Gíta, the poem *Bhagavad Gita*. Skt. (the holy song).

gítsuṭa, to tap (the palm-tree, &c.), to draw a line. *callu gitsuconi bratucutáḍu*, he lives by tapping for toddy.

gíṭu, line; same as *gíta*.

gíyuṭa, to draw a line, to tap, to prune. *gisecatti* is a pruning or tapping knife.

glásu, glass. English. *ocaḍu: Lacshmayya caṭhinamaina manish alle unnáḍu. incóḍu: yeṭlá telisindi? ocaḍu: atani canḍlu tsústé telustundi; cuḍi cannutó atanu guḍḍu tippacunḍá nannu tsústé nácu bhayam (v)ésindi. incóḍu: cuḍi cannu glásu cannu, nizam cannu cádu*, Smith: Brown is a bit of a terror. Jones: How so? Smith: I go by his eyes; when he fixes me with his right eye I am terrified. Jones: It's a glass eye, not a real one.

gnyapti, memory. Skt. *gnyaptici rá lédu*, it did not come back to me.

gnyánamu, wisdom, spiritual meditation. Skt. *gnyána nidra* is the abstraction from the world of the sage in meditation; *gnyána márgamu* is the way of salvation; *gnyána ṣaríram* is the astral body.

gnyánuḍu, sage. Skt. *alpagnyánulu*, people with little wisdom.

gnyápacam peṭṭuconuṭa, to remember.

gnyápacamu, memory. Skt. *ocaḍu: mí ménamáma villu vrásin appuḍu ninnu gnyápacam peṭṭuconáḍá? incóḍu: peṭṭuconáḍu, anducané nác émi ichchi pó lédu*, Smith: Did your uncle remember you when he wrote his will? Jones: Yes, he remembered me all right and left me nothing; *á sangati mícu gnyápacam unnadá?* do you remember that? *ninnu yeppuḍú tsúchin aṭṭu gnyápacam lédu*, I don't remember ever seeing you before.

gnyátamu, known. Skt. *agnyáta vásam*, incognito.

gnyáti, agnate. Skt. A relation on the male side. Property descends that way in Hindu law. In Hindu society your paternal uncle's sons are your brothers, while your maternal uncle's daughter is no relation, and you may, and in fact, ought to, marry her, *ménaricamu*, marriage of cognates, being the best kind of marriage. *gnyáti gurru, arati carru vadalavu*, there is no cure for rot in plantains or sulks in relations.

gnéyamu, knowable, cognizable (philosophy). Skt.

-go, affix of indication. *adigó*, look there; *idigó*, look here.

goḍava, grief, trouble. *á goḍav antá yenducu?* what's all this grumbling about?

goḍḍali, axe. *góṭa chidumu taginadi goḍḍanṭa naracuṭa*, to fell with an axe what you could fillip with a fingernail (*góru*); *pápishṭa télu yeccaḍa nunchi vachchinadó cáni, tsatuccuna chiṭicina vél anta poḍichindi: ippaṭici cheyy antá veyyi goḍḍallató naricin aṭṭu baddalu vésuconi pótú v'unnadi*, a damned scorpion from heaven knows where suddenly stung me on my little finger; even now my whole hand feels as if it had been cut in little pieces by a thousand axes.

goḍḍu, cattle, a beast, an ox. *yelugu-goḍḍu* is a bear; *musali-goḍḍu* (of a man), poor old beast; *manchivánici vaca máṭa, manchi goḍḍucu vaca debba*, a word to a good man, a blow to a good beast; *dongalu tólina goḍḍu yé révuna dáṭiná saré*, it is all the same which ford the thieves took with the stolen ox; *utta goḍḍucu arupul eccuva*, much cry and little wool; *y'eccuva vela peṭṭi guḍḍanu, taccuva vela peṭṭi goḍlanu cona rádu*, don't buy dear cloth or cheap cattle.

goḍḍu, barren. *góvu léni v'úḷḷó goḍḍu gédé Srí Mahálacshmi*, the barren buffalo is a goddess in a village in which there are no cows.

godrálu, barren woman. *godrálici yémi telusunu biḍḍa noppulu?* what does a barren woman know of the pangs of child-birth?

goḍugu, umbrella. *ocaḍu: vána cáláníci conchem untsucó valenu. incóḍu: nénu untsucunṭánu. ocaḍu: yém untsu-*

cunnuiu? incóḍu: goḍugu. Smith: You must keep something for a rainy day. Jones: I do. Smith: What do you keep? Jones: My umbrella; *peddamanishi: ni daggira v'unna goḍugulalóci tsaucadi tsúpintsu. angadiváḍu: tsúpistánu, gáni avi tsála cálam nilavadanḍi. peddamanishi: railu mida vaca v'úrici veḷḷi rá vále; yeṭlágu accaḍa marachi póyi vadali peṭṭedi, cábaṭṭi tsaucadi iyyi,* Gentleman: Show me a cheap umbrella. Shopkeeper: They don't last long, but I can show you one. Gentleman: I am going on a railway journey and may lose it; so I want one cheap.

golusu, chain.

golusucaṭṭu, running hand (the letters being chained together).

gollaváḍu, shepherd caste man; feminine *golladi. gollaváḍá, gollaváḍá, dhányamu yeccaḍa v'unnad anṭé? gorre muḍḍiló y'unnad anṭáḍu,* shepherd, shepherd, where is grain to be had? In my sheeps' rumps, quoth he (alluding to their efficiency as manure producers).

goḷḷemu, bolt. *talupu lópala gollemu vési,* bolting the door from inside.

gollu, uproar. *golluna góla peṭṭuṭa,* to wail aloud.

gonaconuṭa, to try.

gonagonaláḍuṭa, to murmur; onomatopoeic.

gonḍlemu, bolt; same as *gollemu.*

gondi, lane.

-gonḍu, affix denoting a male person. *lantsagonḍulu,* bribe-takers.

gongali, blanket.

gongalipurugu, caterpillar.

gontemmacóricalu, castles in the air. *Gontemma* is a village goddess.

gontu, gontuca, throat. *gontu rásinadi,* I am hoarse; *gontu pundugá n'unnadi,* I have a sore throat; *ácali ácáṣam anta, gontuca sudi bezzam anta,* hunger as great as the sky, a throat the size of a needle's eye; *gontuca savarintsuconi,* clearing his throat; *ni gontuca páḍai pótú v'unnadi, svaram bágá rávaḍam lédu,* your throat is going, the voice is not coming out clear; *cécalu vési vési gontuca baddalai póyinadi,* I have burst my throat shouting; *vangi vangi salámu chéstu v'unná, lópala taḍi guḍḍató gontucalu cósi háni chéstáru,* outwardly they lick your boots, inwardly they are ready to cut your throat with a wet cloth; *gontuca varacu cópam,* anger up to your neck.

gonuconuṭa, gonuguṭa, to murmur; onomatopoeic. *yémó artham léni máṭalu gonucunṭú palavaristúné v'unnáḍu,* he is wandering in his mind and muttering some meaningless words.

goppa, big. *vaidhyuḍu: nénu y'í madhya goppa áparéshanu chéṣánu. snéhituḍi: dénici chéṣáru? vaidhyuḍu: oca úpiri tittini pégunu cósi veyya valasi vachchindi. snéhituḍu: rógi yeṭlá v'unnáḍu? vaidhyuḍu: yeṭlá v'unnadi yémiṭi? appuḍé tsachchi póyinḍḍu,* Doctor: I have just done a big operation. Friend: What part of the body? Doctor: Lung and gut. Friend: How is the patient? Doctor: What's that got to do with it? He died on the spot; *upanyásacuḍu: prapanchamlóc ella goppa upanyásaculu yevaru? sabhicuḍu: nénu chepputánu, gáni mí pér evaró cheppanḍi,* Lecturer: Who is the greatest lecturer in the world? Voice from the audience: Excuse me, I did not catch your name; *goppa vamṣaṣthuḍu,* a man of great family. A man with a big family is *pedda cuṭumbam galaváḍu. idi goppa cádu,* that is of no consequence.

goppa chepputa, to talk big. *Lacshmayya tánu chinn appuḍu yuddhamló tsúpina sahásam gurinchi upanyásamló goppagá chepput unḍenu. sabhicuḍu: yuddham antá míré chésté, migilina sainyam antá yém chésind anḍi?* Lakshmayya was boasting in a lecture of all the courage he had shown in the war when he was young. Voice from the audience: If you did everything, what was left for the rest of the army to do? *ná vadda ní goppa cheppa bócu,* don't boast before me.

goppa chéyuṭa, to flatter. *nannu goppa chési,* flattering me (making me out to be big).

goppatanamu, greatness, conceit. *rógi: idigó, mi bahumánam, núr rúpayalu. vaidhyuḍu (adbhuta paḍi): núr* *rúpáyalá? rógi (vinayamutó): mi goppatanánici y'idi yentamátramu arham ainadi cád ani nácu telusunu gáni, ná bhactini baṭṭi mír idi angícarintsa valenu,* Patient: Here is your fee, 100 rupees. Doctor (surprised): 100 rupees? Patient (respectfully): I know it is not worthy of your greatness, but you must take it in view of my devotion to you; *nívu yeppuḍu ní goppatanamé tsútsucunṭáu, nívu garvishṭhivi,* you are always showing conceit, you are a stuck-up fellow.

goppaváru, bigwigs.

gorigintsuconuṭa, to get oneself shaved; causative middle of *goruguṭa*. The usual expression is *pani chéyintsuṭa,* to get the work (of shaving) done.

gorigintsuṭa, to get shaved; causative of *goruguṭa*. Used metaphorically. *núṭici peṭṭi, cóṭici gorigincheváḍu,* he fleeces a 100,000 and gives in charity to 100.

goruguṭa, to shave. *itani tala goraga valenu,* we must shave his head (do him down); *cshavara pani* or simply *pani* is shaving; *mangalaváḍu* is a barber; *mangala catti,* barber's knife, is a razor.

gorre, sheep. *gorre troccina tsálunu,* it is enough if the sheep tread (the feet of the sheep are golden; sheep are largely kept for manure in the Telugu country); *carra léni vánici gorre aina carustundi,* even a sheep will bite a man without a stick; *tóḍélini gorrela cáya peṭṭin aṭṭu,* putting a wolf to watch the sheep.

goṭṭamu, tube, any long, hollow thing. *addapu goṭṭamu* is a telescope; *chimanna goṭṭamu,* a squirt; *núlu goṭṭamu,* a shuttle; *údu goṭṭamu,* a blow-pipe; *veduru goṭṭamu,* a hollow bamboo; *goṭtapu núyi,* a tube well; *goṭṭapu táḷam,* a hollow padlock; *tupáci goṭṭamu,* a gun barrel; *goṭṭapu nuyyi,* a tube well.

goṭṭuṭa, to strike, &c.; for *coṭṭuṭa*.

goyya (pandu), guava (fruit).

goyyi, pit. *mundarici vasté goyyi, venucacu póté nuyyi,* pit in front, well behind (Scylla and Charybdis); *yevaru travvucunna gótiló váré paḍutáru,* falling into your own trap, the engineer hoist with his own petard.

-gó, suffix meaning 'see! lo!' *idigó, adigó* are the French *voici, voilà*.

góvu, cow. Skt. Used chiefly in composition. *góhatya* is cow-murder, a mortal sin; *gómayamu* is cow-dung, a hygienic substance used to purify kitchens, floors, and interiors generally, including the interior of man.

gócharamu, manifest. Skt. *tsúpu méra dúram gócharam cá lédu,* he was out of sight.

gócharintsuṭa, to become manifest.

góchi, loin-cloth. *inupa góchi caṭṭináḍu,* he put on an iron loin-cloth (took a vow of chastity); *itacu minchina lótú, góchici minchina dáridrayamú lédu,* no poverty beyond the loin-cloth, no depth beyond out of your depth. Hence Mahatma Gandhi's loin-cloth is a double symbol of poverty and chastity. A loose loin-cloth (like wearing boots) is a sign of profligacy. *miváḍu vibhúti peṭṭaḍu, zárugóchi peḍutáḍu; monna búḍsala zóḍu toḍuconni, mukháni boṭṭu lécunḍá paṭṭa pagalu vídhiló nunchi veḷḷutú v'unṭé nénu caḷḷárá tsúchinánu,* your boy does not smear himself with cow-dung ash, he wears a loose loin-cloth; the other day I saw him with my own eyes walk down the street with boots on and without the patch on the forehead; *góchici pedda, angavastramucu chinna,* too big for a loin-cloth, too small for a body-cloth (too many for an embassy, too few for an army).

gócuṭa, to scratch. *cattitó gócuṭa,* to scratch out, erase; *cheyyi duradagá unn anduna gócu contini,* I scratched my hand because it was itching; *rahasyamugá Giriráunu góci,* nudging Girirau secretly. Also to scribble: *uttaram gócináḍu,* he scribbled a letter.

góda, ox; *goḍḍugóda,* cattle.

góḍa, wall. *góḍalacu chevul unnavi,* walls have ears; *áḍadi boncité góḍa peṭṭin aṭṭu, mogaváḍu boncité taḍaca caṭṭin aṭṭu,* a woman's lies are as difficult to see through as a wall, a man's as easy as a wicker screen.

Gódávari, the river Godavari, one of the five sacred rivers; considered to be a goddess. *akhanḍa Gódávariló snánamu chéyuṭa vallana pápamulu* *pariháram agunu*, if you bathe in the waters of the undivided Godavari (before it splits at the Delta) your sins will be washed away. This is specially the case at the Pushcaram, a great bathing festival held once in twelve years.

góḍu, one of the numerous words for grief. The Telugus are always lamenting. *nénu tupácul ainá, cattulac ainá v'ópa galanu, gáni Ándhraválla góllató v'ópa lénu*, I can stand guns and swords but not the wailings of the Telugus.

gódhumapinḍi, flour. *ati vistáramugá tinṭé gódhumapinḍi aragadu*, wheat-flour is indigestible in large quantities. Yet when the District Magistrate sent the Congress secretary to jail he asked to be put on wheat-flour instead of rice on the ground that his digestion was weak.

gódhumulu, wheat; the plural is used, as is customary for grains.

gódurucappa, bullfrog, toad. *góduru-* in composition, like our *bull-*, means anything big.

gógu, hemp (*cannabis sativa*). *síma* or foreign *gógu* is the roselle plant.

góhatya, cow-murder, a mortal sin. *yega tisté góhatya, diga tisté brahmahatya*, (a witness placed in the dilemma of accusing a cow of trespass in a brahmin's field, or giving evidence against a brahmin) one way vaccicide, the other way brahminicide.

góla, wail.

góḷamu, sphere.

gólapeṭṭuṭa, to wail, one of the unpleasant habits of the ryots of a distressful country. *polálu yenḍi póyi raitul andaru golluna góla peṭṭináru*, the crops withered and the ryots lifted up their voices and wept.

gólé, a marble. Hindustani; also *góḷi*.

gómayamu, cow-dung. Skt., from *góvu*, cow. A holy excrement. The excrements of sacred animals or saints are purificatory. Mahatma Gandhi has been offered large sums to deposit his excreta in the backyard of a devotee. *gómayam manacu vésténé cáni yédí ṣuddhi cádu gadá?* there is no purification without putting down cow-dung; *dévala smrütiló yerr áu mútramuna, tell áu gómayamu, patstsa áu pálunu, níli áu perugunu, nalla áu neyyiyu panchagavyam*, the Holy Scriptures tell us that the five purifying elements are (1) a red cow's urine, (2) a white cow's dung, (3) a green cow's milk, (4) a blue cow's curds, (5) a black cow's clarified butter (but the Holy Scriptures do not indicate how we are to come by the blue and green cows).

gómámsamu, beef (which it is mortal sin to eat).

gónesanchi, gunny-bag. Skt. *góna*, Hindustani *ganni*, whence our gunny, the sack made from jute fibre (*zanupanára*).

góngúra, a dish made from hemp leaves; from *gógu*, hemp, and *cúra*, curry.

gópagrühamu, shepherd's hut. Used only in books.

gópi, shepherdess. Skt. The Gopies are the shepherdesses Krishna made love to when he was a boy.

gópuramu, temple tower. Skt. *gópuram mída yetti peṭṭináḍu*, he placed him on a pinnacle of the temple; *conḍa mingévánici gópuram aḍḍamá?* a temple tower is a flea-bite to a man that can swallow a mountain.

gópyamu, secret. Skt. *gópyamugá unḍa valenu*, keep it quiet.

góranṭa or **gorinṭa,** henna (*acacia intsia*). *górinṭa cheṭlanu váni y'ácula nunḍi vatstsu rangu coracu pairu chéyuts unnáru*, henna is grown for the dye that comes from its leaves.

górinca, the common myna.

góru, finger-nail; plural *góḷḷu*. *ná góru chigur anta cosinánu*, I cut my nail to the quick; *gór anta v'unṭé, conḍ anta chéstáḍu*, he makes mountains out of mole-hills; also *górantalu conḍantalu chési*. *góṭa miṭité poyyé panici goḍḍali yenducu?* why use an axe for what can be done with a fillip of the nail?

góruṭa, to wish, choose; for *córuṭa*.

górutsuṭṭu, whitlow; from *góru*, nail. *górutsuṭṭu pai rócaṭi pótu*, the blow of a rice-pounder on a whitlow (blow upon blow, trouble upon trouble).

góruvanca, the common myna; more commonly *górinca*.

góruvetstsa, lukewarm.

gósáyi, friar. *aṭuvanti mandulu gósáyila vadda v'untavi,* friars keep such drugs.

góshá, gosha (seclusion of women). Hindustani; also *ghósha. míru vinnáró lédó cáni Áḍamalayáḷam ani yeccaḍanó v'unnad aṭa! accaḍ antá áḍaváḷḷa adhicáram. áḍaváḷḷu v'udyógálu chéstu v'unṭé mogaváḷḷu y'inṭló vanṭa chési peḍutú v'untár aṭa! á déṣamuló mogaváḷḷacu yeccaḍaléni góshá v'unnad aṭa!* you may or may not have heard of the Amazon country. There woman rules and holds all the offices and man cooks and serves food and is kept in the strictest gosha.

góshṭi, Skt., secret assembly of the initiated. In Telugu it means conversation or social function. *ishṭagóshṭi* is the newspaper word for viceregal garden-parties, &c.

góṭa, on or with the nail; oblique case of **góru.** *góṭa chidumuṭa,* to nip off with the finger-nail.

gótramu, family. Skt. The paternal family; the maternal family does not count.

gövu, cow. Skt.

góvumámsamu, gómámsamu, beef. Skt. *góvumámsamu tinéváru prabhutvánici vachchina tarváta y'ikha yélá autund anḍi? ippuḍu siḍulu póyinavi gadánḍi? sahaganamu cheyyan iyyaru gadá anḍi? ammavárini álóchintsacundá Gódávarini caṭṭi vésináru gadánḍi? dévatalané y'ílá chéséváḷḷacu manushyul anṭé lacshamé lédu,* now that eaters of beef are in power what will happen next? Hook-swinging has gone already. They won't allow suttee. They have dammed the Godavari regardless of the goddess. Will people who treat the gods so have any respect for men?

gradda, kite; usually written *gadda* and pronounced *gedda.*

grahacháramu, misfortune. Skt., from *graham,* what seizes, a devil. *ná grahachháram chétané,* to my misfortune; *id eccaḍi grahachháram!* what bad luck! *í grahachháramunacu tóḍu,* to add to my misfortunes; *jagattuló andaru áru nelalu vachchin appaṭi nunchi pillalacu annam peṭṭistú v'unṭé y'í paitu pósintsaḍapu grahachháram mana vaccuri y'inṭlóné vachchindi,* when all the world feeds babies on rice as soon as they are six months old, this unfortunate system of dieting them on milk has been introduced only in our house (Hindu notion of suitable baby-food).

grahamu, seizing, planet, devil. Skt. The usual meaning in Telugu is devil. *bhúcampálu modalainavi vasté, taccina panul anni máni vési, graha ṣántulu cheyya valenu,* if earthquakes or other calamities come we should give up all other work and appease the devils (earthquakes and epidemics being the work of devils, exorcism is the only remedy).

grahanamu, seizing, eclipse. Skt. An eclipse is the seizing of the sun or the moon by a devil (Hindu science). *ocaḍu: súryuḍici bhúmici madhya chandruḍu aḍḍam vasté súrya grahanam paḍutund antáru tellaváḷḷu. incóḍu: Ráma! Ráma! Ráma! yenta abaddhálu vrásinár ayyá! váḷḷacu vacaṭi teliyadu. ocaḍu: calacṭaru gáritó cheppi, mícu mányam ippistánu, gáni grahanála sangati yémiṭó nácu marmacamgá cheppanḍi. incóḍu: púrvam gáḍide coḍucu Ráhuvu gáḍu Dévatalaló cúrtsunḍi amrútam táginádu; á sangati Súryuḍú Chandruḍú veḷḷi cheppéṭ appaṭici, Ṣrí Vishṇumúrti Váru chacram dharinchi, váḍi tala renḍu vaccalú chési vésináru; amrútam tágaḍam chéta váḍu tsávaca, á rósham caḍupuló v'untsuconi, sarva dinálaló Súryunni Chandrunni mingi, sacala bádhalú peḍutú v'unṭáḍu,* First Hindu: The white people say that an eclipse of the sun comes through the moon getting between the earth and the sun. Second Hindu: Rama, Rama, Rama, what lies they write! they know nothing! First Hindu: I will tell the Collector and get you a free gift of land if you reveal the cause of eclipses in confidence. Second Hindu: Once upon a time that son of a gun Rahu was sitting drinking nectar with the gods and the Sun and the Moon went and sneaked to Vishnu and Vishnu took his disk and cut Rahu's head in two and because he had been drinking nectar he did not die and kept that grudge against the Sun and Moon and tries to swallow them and do them all kinds of mischief.

grahintsuṭa, to seize, grasp, understand. Skt. *miló miru chésucunna prasangam antá nénu bágá vini, mi v'uddéṣam púrnangá grahinchinánu,* I overheard your private conversation and have quite understood your intentions; *nivu dharma súcshmam yémi grahintsa lévu,* you are utterly unable to grasp the subtleties of religious law; *miru sangitamló sarasulu, dánni grahistáru; anduló nác émi abhiruchi lédu,* you are a musical expert and understand it; I have no taste for music; *rayilu cadala pót unḍenu, gárḍu prayánicuḍini yetti railulóci tósenu. tarváta stéshanuló gárḍu banḍi daggiraci vachchenu. gárḍu: micu nénu yenta upacáram chéṣánó grahinchárá? nénu yeccintsaca póté micu railu tappi póyédi, nácu bahumánam ippintsanḍi. prayánicuḍu: nénu rail eccaḍánici rá lédu, railuló uttaram veyyaḍánici vachchánu; miru railulóci toyyaḍam valla malli iccaḍa nunchi má v'úru veḷḷa valasi vachchindi, ḍabbu danḍuga ainadi,* the train was just starting and the guard pushed a passenger into the train and at the next station came to the carriage. Guard: You understand what I did for you? If I had not shoved you in, you would have lost the train. What about a tip? Passenger: I did not come to the station to take the train but to post a letter. I have now to get back home at much expense.

granthabhásha, book language. Skt., from *grantham,* book, and *bhásha,* language.

granthacarta, author. Skt., from *grantham,* book.

granthachauryamu, plagiarism. Skt., from *grantham,* book, and *chauryam,* theft.

granthamu, book. Skt.; the ordinary word is *pustacam. nénu madhyánam árambhinchina grantham púrti chésténé cáni paḍucóvaḍánici ránu,* I shan't come to bed till I have finished the book I began this afternoon; *oca Húna vachana prabandhacáruḍu tana grantha piṭhica y'andu cathanu vrási y'unnáḍu,* a Hun prose-writer told a story in the preface to his book (the Telugus call us by the name we applied to the Germans; Hun here means English).

granthálayamu, bookshop, library. Skt., from *grantham,* book, and *álayam,* place. *verrayya granthálayamlóci póyi oca pustacam tísuconi tsaduvutú, adé panigá navvut unḍenu. granthálayádhicári: yenduc ayya aṭlá navvut unnáu? verrayya: nénu tsadivé pustacamló oca bomma v'unnadi, oca báluḍini oca yeddu tarumacu vastu v'unn aṭṭu veṣáru. granthálayadhicári: aité navvu yenducu? verrayya: yenta sépu parigettiná yeddu anducuné lédu, inca yeppaṭi anducuntundó ani navvut unnánu,* a loony goes into a bookshop, takes up a book and laughs as he reads. Bookseller: What makes you laugh? Loony: There is a picture in the book of a bull chasing a boy. Bookseller: Is that so funny? Loony: However long the bull chases the boy it will never catch him; that's what makes me laugh.

granthálayádhicári, proprietor of a bookshop. Skt., from *grantham,* book, *álayam,* place, and *adhicári,* owner.

-grastudu, suffix meaning 'involved in', 'full of', 'swallowed up in'. Skt., from *grasintsuṭa,* to swallow. *vichára-grastuḍu,* full of woe; *cábaṭṭi ná y'andu daya v'unchi vichára grastuḍanai v'unna nannu santósha peṭṭa valen ani mari mari véḍucuntú v'unnánu,* again and again I pray you to smile on this poor wretch, who is plunged in grief (a lover writing); *írshyágrastulaina dushṭulu, pápánici bhaya paḍḍaca, nácu háni cheyyaḍánacu tsústú v'unnáru,* bad men full of venom with no fear of committing sins are looking out for an opportunity of harming me (an official describing the attitude of superior authority towards him).

gráchaca, subject (philosophy). Skt.

gráhya, object (philosophy). Skt.

grámacanṭhamu, village area, the area (pasture and fields) comprised in a revenue village. Skt., from *grámam,* village, and *canṭham,* vicinity.

grámadévata, village deity. Skt.

grámadévatulu are the special deities of village life. They are of Dravidian, not Aryan, origin and are mostly female and of ample proportions, and always maleficent. Their nature is to bring cholera, small-pox, and blight, and they have to be propitiated and bribed not to do so. Their names are peculiar; some of them are said to be Christian. Thus Mariamma or Maremma, who brings cholera, is said to be the Virgin Mary, and Agatamma, St. Agatha. *ammavári jádyam* is the ordinary term for small-pox. *Peddamma*, Big Mama, and *Yellamma* are other common names of village goddesses. *nannu moguḍ ani paṭṭuconi á grámadévata* is the Telugu translator's version of the Shakespearian 'the mountain of mad flesh that claims marriage of me'.

grámamu, village, town. Skt. *grámacáryamulu* is village affairs, parish pump politics; *grámalekha* is the village account of customary annual payments to magistrates, the police, irrigation, overseers, and other *dévatalu* who have to be propitiated; *Chennapaṭnam pedda grámam,* Madras is a large town (not 'a big village').

grámani, village headman. Skt. An old word; now the village headman is *munasabu,* from his title as village munsiff or judge, *reḍḍi* from the name of the caste from which many of them come, &c.

grámapálanamu, village rule. Skt., from *grámam,* village, and *pálanam,* rule. In Guntur, during the no-tax campaign, the organ of the revolutionaries was the *Grámapálanam,* published by a dismissed karnam, which maintained that all would be well with the world again (*prapancham ânta páḍai póyinadi*, the whole world has gone to the dogs), if the brahmin karnams were restored to their old influence and affluence and again ruled the country as they used to do before the advent of the Hun Government.

grámasthuḍu, villager. Skt. In the plural *grámasthulu,* the two village officers (munsiff and karnam); used by tahsildars in their takids or orders; as also *munasabu-carnúlu,* an idiomatic way of forming the plural which does not mean the munsiffs and karnams but the munsiff and the karnam. The village officers claim that the taluk office should use the honorific form of this and address them as *munasabu-carnálangárulu.* One of the alleged sins of the Hun Government is that it has dropped honorific forms, omits *gáru* in addresses, and no longer subscribes itself 'your most obedient, humble servant'.

grámádulu, villages; simply a form of the plural, though *ádulu* means etcetera by itself.

grámyamu, village (adjective), especially village or rustic speech. Skt. This is a dictionary of *grámyam.* *grámyam* is gradually coming into its own and is being used more and more in newspapers and novels. The difficulty of bringing *grámyam* into general use as a literary vehicle lies in the diversity of dialects. The solution is that of Dante and Luther: to stabilize a particular dialect. I use the *grámyam* of Rajahmundry as slightly refined and elevated by the late Kandukuri Viresilingam and others.

grámyadhármamu, the way of the village, i.e. sexual intercourse, the way of a man with a maid. Skt., from *grámam,* village, and *dhármam,* custom, duty. The reference is to the universality, not to the rusticity, of the custom.

grásapu paicam, a legal term for subsistence or maintenance allowance; from Skt. *grásam,* subsistence.

grásávásamulu, board and lodging. Skt., from *grásam*, board, and *vásam,* lodging.

gríshma rütuvu, the hot weather. Skt. Also and more commonly *vésavi.* The Telugus have six seasons, not four like us; they are (1) *vasantam,* spring, (2) *vésavi,* the hot weather, (3) *varsham,* the rains, (4) *ṣarattu,* the dews, (5) *hémantam,* the cold, (6) *tsali* or *ṣiṣiram,* the chill.

grucca, a gulp.

grucca conuṭa, to swallow.

grucciḷḷu, gulps.
gruḍḍi, guḍḍi, blind. *gruḍḍiló mella,* it is better to squint than to be blind (the lesser of two evils).
gruddu, blow; for the more usual *guddu.*
gruḍḍu, egg; for the more usual *guḍḍu.*
grutstsuṭa, to thrust; for the more usual *gutstsuṭa.*
grühachhidramu, domestic split. Skt., from *grüham,* house, and *chhidram,* cleft. *grühachhidram velladi chésucó rádu,* dirty linen should not be washed in public.
grühacrütyamulu, household affairs. Skt., from *grüham,* house, and *crütyam,* affair.
grühadhipati, grühapati, head of the family. Skt., from *grüham,* house, and *pati,* head.
grühapravéṣamu, house-entry (of a bride at marriage), house-warming. Skt., from *grüham,* house, and *pravéṣam,* entry. *crottagá grühapravéṣamunacu tísi coni vachchin appuḍu nannunu á chinnadánini tsúchi, yeruganivár andarunu nác adi manumarál anuconiri cáni, yevvarunu bhárya y'ani telisicó tsálaca póyiri,* (old man speaking) when she first crossed my threshold, strangers who saw her took her for my grand-daughter; it never entered their heads that she was my wife; *tarváta grühapravéṣa mahótsavam* (*mahá utsavam*), *dinavára mahótsavamu vacca sáré cá vatstsunu,* (of an old man's marriage) we can have the house-entry and funeral ceremonies on the same day; *amma grühapravéṣam, ayya smashána pravéṣam,* bride in the house, bridegroom in the tomb.
grühasthâṣramamu, the married state. Skt., from *grühastha,* householder, and *áṣramamu,* state.
grühasthuḍu, householder. Skt. A married man as opposed to *brahmachári,* a bachelor. *intamandi grühasthulanu tsúchinánu gáni, mícu valé atithici y'inta ṣraddhabhactulató svayamugá v'uppachâram chésévárini nénu yeccaḍa tsúḍa lédu,* I have seen many householders but never another so devoted to his guest as you.
grühini, mistress of the house.
gubagubalu, hubbub; onomatopoeic. *vár émó gubagubal áḍuts unnáru,* they are getting excited about something.
gubicígubicí, bang bang; onomatopoeic.
gucca, gulp, drawing in the breath. *guccedu panamu,* one gulp of a drink; *gucca tirugacunḍá,* without taking breath; *cávalisté iláganṭivi gucca tirugacunḍá lacsha sangutulu yécaruvu peṭṭa galanu,* if need be I can reel off a hundred thousand such things without taking breath.
guchchamu, cluster. Skt. A bunch of flowers, a cluster of fruit, &c.
gudagudalu, sobs, rattlings, &c.; onomatopoeic. The corresponding verbs are *gudagudaláḍuta* and *gudagudananuṭa.*
guḍáramu, tent. *ḍéra* is commoner.
guḍḍa, a cloth; the common word for cloth, garment. *míru techchédi jítamu buvvacunu guḍḍalucunu sari póvuts unnadi,* your pay is only just enough to provide us food and clothing (and not the jewellery which Indian women think equally necessary); *cúḍú guḍḍá aḍagaca póté, biḍḍanu sácin aṭṭu sácutánu annad aṭa,* if you don't ask me for food and clothes, I will bring you up like a child of my own (very generous); *cotta guḍḍac anṭin aṭṭu páta guḍḍac anṭadu,* old cloth (age) won't take impressions like new cloth (youth); *yeccuva vela peṭṭi guḍḍanu, taccuva vela peṭṭi goḍlanu, cona rádu,* don't buy dear cloth or cheap cattle.
guddali, hoe.
guḍḍi, blind. *illálu guḍḍid aité y'inṭi cunḍalacu chétu,* blind mistress, broken pots. *cani guḍḍi, vini chevuḍu,* eyes have they but they see not; they have ears but they hear not. *guḍḍiváḷḷacu cunṭiváḷḷacu dánam chésté "punyam vastund aṭa,* they (Europeans) say that charity to the halt and the blind is meritorious (whereas of course there is only one meritorious form of charity: squandering money on brahmins); *dora guḍḍiváḍu ganuca ṣirastádáru áḍin alla áṭa, páḍin alla páṭa ai, dinálu sági vastú v'unnavi,* the Collector is blind and whatever the sheristadar

does goes and so the days pass (what the sheristadar plays is play and what he sings is song, i.e. all dance to his tune); *guḍḍi canná mella mélu*, it is better to squint than to be blind; *léni báva canṭé guḍḍi báv ainá mélu*, a blind brother-in-law is better than none (Indians do not appreciate spinster sisters).

guḍḍidi, blind woman.

guḍḍigavva, something worthless. *gavva* is a shell (cowry) once used as small change; *guḍḍi* here means broken; a dud farthing. *nénu páṭha-śála peṭṭi, mimmaln andarini taribitu chésténé cáni, míru y'í lócamló guḍḍi gavvac ainá panici ráru*, unless I set up a school and train you all, you will be worth nothing in this world; *pani mánucuné varacu púrvam sampádin-chinadi vacca guḍḍigavva lédu*, I haven't a brass farthing left of what I earned in service.

guḍḍiváḍu, blind man.

guddu, blow. *gudduláṭa*, fisticuffs, boxing match.

guḍḍu, egg. *guḍḍu vachchi pillanu yeccirinchin aṭṭu*, like the egg making faces at the chicken (*cóḍipilla*).

guḍḍu, eyeball. *guḍḍu tippacunḍá tsútsuṭa*, to stare.

gudduláḍuṭa, to box, fight.

gudduṭa, to strike, knock. *upanyá-sacuni andaru nindist unḍiri. ata-ḍini samarthintsaḍánici ocaḍu léchenu. ocaḍu: upanyásacuḍu oca tsóṭa ich-china upanyásam incó tsóṭa ivvaḍu. incóḍu: iyyac ém? yeccaḍa cheppina ocaṭé upanyásam. ocaḍu: ainá oca tsóṭa guḍḍina balla incó tsóṭa guddaḍu*, every one was abusing the lecturer. Smith took up the cudgels for him. Smith: The lecturer never repeats himself. Jones: Oh doesn't he? it's the same lecture everywhere. Smith: Anyway it isn't the same table he thumps. *talupu gudduṭa* is to knock at a door; *cáḷḷu gudduṭa* is to massage the legs, an operation every good Hindu wife performs for her hus-band.

guḍi, temple. *calupu tíyani maḍi, dévuḍu léni guḍi*, an unweeded field is like a temple without the god; *angaṭló bellam guḷḷó lingánici naivéd-yam*, offering the sugar in the shop to the god in the temple (being liberal at the expense of others); *guḷḷó dévuḷ-lanu ráḷḷ anṭáru*, they (the English) call the gods in the temples stones; *guḍici mécapótu veḷḷin aṭṭugá*, a bull in a china shop.

guḍi, circle and circular things like the secondary form of the Telugu vowel i, a halo, a round bunch.

guḍicaṭṭu, area of revenue village, what-ever is included in its circumference.

guḍicálu, heel.

guḍintsuṭa, to multiply. Skt. More commonly *gunintsuṭa*. *pani chésina tarváta viṣránti cá valen ani máṭa y'í lócamló micu pratidinamu anubhavam-ló v'unnadi cádá? vacca janmamló cashṭa paḍḍa tarváta maḷḷi janmam yettaḍánici madhya yenimidi véla yéḷḷu viṣránti cá valenu; nálugu véla yenimidi vandala renḍu janmalanu viṣránti cálam aina, yenimidi véla chéta guḍisté, madhya janmálaló jívinché cálam gáca, nirvánam ponḍaḍánici múḍu cótla yen-abhai nálugu lacshala padaháru véla sanvatsarálu cá valenu*, daily experi-ence in this world shows that intervals of rest are required after work. After you have worked a whole lifetime an interval of 8,000 years rest is required before you take up life again; multi-plying the 4,802 lives by 8,000 you get 38,416,000 years, without counting the time spent on leading the lives, before you attain Nirvana.

guḍise, hut. *rája bhárya méḍa yeccité, cummaraváḍi cóḍalu guḍise yeccinadi*, when the king's wife went up to the terrace, the potter's daughter-in-law climbed the roof of the hut.

guḍiséṭidi, whore, dancing-girl; from *guḍise*, hut. *ocaḍu: véşyalu léca póté sangítam paḍi pótund ani míru gaṭṭigá váḍintsa valenu. incóḍu: mí manasu vachchin anta gaṭṭigá váḍistánu; sa-bhaló ná váḍamtó y'inti mída pencelu yegiri pó valenu, nénu y'intamandi bógamváḷḷanú guḍisáṭiváḷḷanú ádarin-tsaḍamé cáni, vocca náḍu váḷḷa páṭa mátram vini yeraganu sumandi, mítóḍu nizam chepputánu*, a Hindu: You must argue forcibly that without dancing-girls music would go to the dogs. Another Hindu: I will argue as forcibly as you like, I will argue so forcibly that the tiles fly off the roof, but to tell the truth I have been friends with dozens of dancing-girls and never troubled about their singing. (It will be observed that three words for dancing-girls are used in this short conversation; there are also others, nautches being a national recreation; for the same reason there are many words for horse in English and for bull in Spanish; and the argument that nautches improve music is like the argument that horse-racing or bull-fighting improves the breed of horses and bulls; it is a good argument as far as it goes, but the real object of racing is betting and the real use of dancing-girls is their nearer acquaintance.)

guḍitipputa, to lunge a horse, to make the horse go round in a circle (*guḍi*).

guḍlagúba, owl. *ataḍu tella póyi, ná cési guḍlagúba vale téri pára tsúchináḍu*, he turned pale and stared at me like an owl; *banḍi cósam vartamánam pampintsa pótu v'unṭé, guḍlagúba cúsindi*, I was just about to send word for a bullock-cart when an owl hooted (a bad omen which will deter a Hindu from starting on a journey).

gudurtsuṭa, to arrange; for *cudurtsuṭa*.

guggilamu, gum (resin).

guggiḷḷu, boiled horse-gram. Boiled *ulavulu*, a pulse (*dolichos biflor*), takes the place of oats as the staple food of horses in India. *gurránici guggiḷḷacu séru v'ulavulu tsálunu*, a pint of horse-gram is enough for the horse's cooked meal; *gurránici guggiḷḷu tina nérpa valená?* has a horse to be trained to eat oats?

guha, cave. Skt.

guhyamu, secret. Skt.

gujastá, past. Hindustani. *sálu gujastá* is last year.

gulaca, pebble. *gulaca régaḍa bhúmi* is gravelly black cotton soil.

guḷaguḷa, itching, shaking, crawling; onomatopoeic. *buḍḍiló niḷḷu pósi gulagulal áḍinchi caḍigináḍu*, he poured water into the bottle and shook it up and down to clean it; *punṭiló purugulu gulagulal aḍuts unnavi*, the worms are crawling over the wound.

gulábi, rose. Hindustani. *gulábirangu*, rose-colour.

gulimi, wax in the ear. *váḍu chevuló gulimi tísu cunṭ unnáḍu*, he is picking his ears.

gulla, shell, husk, gewgaws, trinkets. *mí bhárya vanṭanu v'unna gullalu tegan ammu*, take her trinkets off your wife and sell them; *nácu núru varahála gullal aina lévu*, I haven't even 100 pagodas worth of jewellery.

gullauṭa, to be emptied, *gulla chéyuṭa*, to empty; used of a house being made like a shell, i.e. emptied, plundered of all that is in it. *íláqu talacu minchina véshálu vésté tsúchinaváru navvutáru, íláganṭi véshálu ságan isté vacca rózuló ní y'illu gulla autundi*, every one who sees such extravagant finery on your wife will laugh, and if you let her go on you will be cleaned out of house and home.

gumastá, gumástá, clerk, agent, deputy. Hindustani. The ordinary word for an office clerk, a merchant's assistant, the deputy of a village officer. *ocaḍu: mí áffísuló gumastá pani kháḷi aind ani vinnánu, nác ippistárá? mánéjaru: álasyam aindi, valla cádu. ocaḍu: yevaricainá ichchárá? mánéjaru: iyya lédu, nuvvu iravai samvatsarála cindaṭa darakhástu peṭṭité ichchéváḍin émó, nícu vayasu mudirindi*, Aged applicant: I hear there is a clerk's vacancy in your office, will you get it for me? Manager: Too late, nothing doing. Applicant: Have you given it to any one else? Manager: No, you might have got it if you had applied twenty years ago, you are a bit too ripe.

gumi, crowd. *lacshala coladi janulu gumi cúḍi*, crowding in hundreds of thousands.

gummaḍicáya, pumpkin (*cucurbita maxima*), a common vegetable for curry. *aṭaca mída gummḍicáyalu tsála v'unnavi*, there are plenty of pumpkins in the loft; *gummaḍicáyalu donga anṭé, bhuzálu táne paṭṭi tsútsucun-*

nádu, when they spoke of the thief who stole the pumpkins he felt his own shoulders (and so let the cat out of the bag).

gummamu, door-way. *ammalárá! y'ilá randi, gummam dátét appudu jágrata, cálici debba tagulutundi*, ladies, this way, careful as you pass through the door not to knock your feet; *doddi gummamuna tótalóci vellutsun-nádu*, he is going into the garden by the back door.

gumpu, crowd, gang, flight of birds. *dongala gumpu náyacudu*, captain of a gang of robbers.

guna, modality of nature (philosophy). Skt. The three gunas (*triguna*) are *tamas*, darkness (chaos, ignorance), *rapas*, high light (half reality, action, and pain), *sattva*, full light (reality, purity, goodness).

gunacamu, the multiplier. Skt.

gunacáramu, multiplication. Skt. (*gunacáháramu*).

gunamu, quality, virtue, symptom (of a disease). *burracu vaca gunamu, jihvacu vaca ruchi*, no two heads are made alike and tastes differ; *talli-dandrula gunálu codulacu sancrami-stavi*, children inherit their parents' qualities; *andu valla yémi gunamu?* what is the use of it? *vántibédi gunamu*, symptoms of cholera; *tadanugunam-gáné* is 'accordingly' (*tad*, that).

-gunamu, -fold. Skt. *dvigunamu*, twofold; *trigunamu*, threefold; *sata-gunamu*, hundredfold. The Sanskrit, not Telugu, numeral must be prefixed.

gunasampanulaina, virtuous. Skt.

gunavantudu, a good man. Skt.

gunavati, a good woman. Skt. Also *gunavanturálu. tsaccani gunavanturá-laina padahár élla chinnadi*, a good and pretty girl of sixteen.

gunágunamulu, merits and demerits. Skt.

gundamu, pit, fire-pit.

-gundá, suffix meaning through; also for *-cundá*, without.

gunde, heart. The Telugu word. The Sanskrit, also commonly used, is *hrüdayamu. gundecáya*, the heart vessel, and *gundelu*, the plural, are also common. *gundelu pagulun attu parigettuta* is to run so as to break your heart; *rátigundevádu* is a stony-hearted man; *nícu gunde zabbu v'unté vaidyudini yenducu canuccó lédu?* if you have heart disease why didn't you see the doctor? *gundelu tatu tata cottucógá*, my heart beating pit-pat.

gundí, button. *ticharu: ní cótucu yenni gundíl unnai? báludu: aidu. ticharu: nénu nálugu tísucunté yém autundi? báludu: ná nánna tantádu.* Teacher: How many buttons are there on your coat? Boy: Five. Teacher: If I take four away, what then? Boy: My dad will kick.

gundramu, gundrani, round.

gundráyi, pestle; from *gundram*, round, and *ráyi*, stone; also *rócali. códi guddu pagala cotta gundráyi cá valená?* breaking eggs with a pestle.

gundu, bullet, lump. The plural is *gundlu* or *gullu. dúrapu condalu nunu-pu, daggira póté rálla gundlu*, distant hills are smooth; near they are boulder-stacks (distance lends enchantment to the view); *gulla báru pettuta*, to load a gun; *vatti mandu cúrutánu gundlu veyyanu*, I will only put powder in, not bullets; *donga: mí dabbu antá istárá, léca póté pistóluto cálustá? peddamanishi: pistólu isté dabb antá istá. donga: dabbu tísuconi pistól ichchenu. peddamanishi: ná dabbu nác istává, léca póté pistólató cálchedá? donga: dabb iyyanu, pistó-luló mandu gáni, gundu gáni lédu, nác ém bhayam lédu.* Thief: Give me all your money or I shoot. Gentleman: Give me the pistol and I will give you the money. The thief takes the money and hands over the pistol. Gentleman: Give me back my money or I shoot. Thief: Shan't; the pistol ain't loaded; I'm not afraid.

gundusúdi, pin.

gunintsuta, to multiply, calculate. Skt. *nénu panchángam guninchinánu*, I have calculated the calendar.

gunitamu, multiplication. Skt.

gunta, pond, pit. *gunta candlu* are hollow eyes.

guntaca, a harrow.

guntanacca, fox; also *concanacca*; also

used chaffingly of lean men. *nacca* is a jackal.
gunza, small post.
gunzuconuṭa, to draw out, extort. *paicam gunzuconuṭa* is to get money out of some one.
guptamu, hidden. Skt. *guptadánamu,* secret gift; *guptacéḷi,* secret pleasure.
guraca, snoring; onomatopoeic.
guracapeṭṭuṭa, to snore.
gurgurintsuṭa, to grunt (of pigs, &c.).
guri, mark, aim.
guri, respect, faith. *vaidyuḍi y'andu guri v'unṭé áyana mannu nalipi chetiló peṭṭiná yetuvanṭi rógálú nimushamló cudurutavi,* if you have faith in your doctor he will cure you of any disease in a minute by making mud into a pill and giving it you.
guriconuṭa, to aim.
gurinchi, about. *santána niródháni gurinchi upanyásam zarugutund aṭa,* they say there is going to be a lecture on birth-control.
guritappuṭa, to miss the mark.
gurram, horse; the knight at chess, the hammer of a gun. The Dravidian word, Tamil *cudirai*; Canarese *cudure*; Malayalam *cutira.* The common Hindustani word that every one knows is *ghóḍá.* In books various Sanskrit words: *aṣvam, turangam,* and so on, are used. *yênugacu vaca síma, gurránici vaca v'úru, barrecu vaca bánise,* to keep an elephant you want a district, a horse a village, a she-buffalo a slavey; *gurramu tócanu caḷḷemu peṭṭin aṭṭu,* like the man who put the bridle on the horse's tail; *zamíndári gurrálacu tinḍ eccuva, pani taccuva,* noblemen's horses are under-exercised and over-fed; *gurramu guḍḍid ainá, ulavulu taccuva v'unḍadu,* the blind horse does not eat less gram; *gurránici guggiḷḷu tina nérpa valená?* has a horse to be trained to eat gram? a horse neighs is *gurram sacilintsuts unnadi*; what he eats in India is *ulavulu,* horse-gram, which when boiled for him is called *guggiḷḷu*; *gurrapu gúḍu,* a mare's nest.
gurrapudanḍu, cavalry; from Skt. *danḍu,* troop.
gurrapurautu, cavalryman, trooper. *rahutu* is the Skt. for trooper. *yeccité gurrapurautu, digité cáli banṭu,* mounted he is a good trooper, dismounted a good foot soldier (useful anywhere).
gurrapuváḍu, horse-keeper, groom, syce.
gurru, grumble. *gnyáti gurru, arati carru, vadalavu,* there is no cure for cousins' rows or plantain-rot.
gurrupeṭṭuṭa, to snore; onomatopoeic. *gurrapeṭṭi paḍuconuṭa,* to lie snoring; also *gurrucoṭṭuṭa, gurrutiyuṭa.*
gurteruguṭa, to recognize, identify. A common word in courts for recognizing a person or identifying a thing; from *gurtu,* mark, and *eruguṭa,* to know. *anaválu peṭṭuṭa* is even commoner.
gurtintsuṭa, to distinguish. *Lacshmayya: ná daggira manchi cucca unḍédi, adi dongal evaró peddamanushyal evaró tsappuna gurtinchédi, dongalanu mátram carichédi. Vencayya: á cucca y'ippuḍ ém ainadi? Lacshmayya: nannu caravaḍam chéta inṭló nunchi veḷḷa goṭṭánu.* Lakshmayya: I had a very good dog which could tell thieves from honest men; it would only bite thieves. Venkayya: What has become of that dog? Lakshmayya: It bit me, so I drove it out of the house.
gurtu, mark of identification, sign. *yenta varacu tsadavinánó gurtu cósam cágitam peṭṭi v'unnánu,* I put a piece of paper in to mark my place.
gurtupaṭṭuṭa, to recognize. *nyáyádhipati: ṣicsha cheppaca mundu yémainá aḍugutává? muddáyi: nannu tsúchi pacca crinda dáccunnaváḍu nannu yeṭlá gurtupaṭṭa galaḍó cheppanḍi*; Judge: Have you anything to ask before I pass sentence? Accused: Say, how could he recognize me when he hid under the bed at the sight of me? In this example note the Telugu idiom. The Telugus, like the Italians, say 'before I don't pass sentence', not, as the English, 'before I pass sentence'. *dáccunnaváḍu* stands for *dátsuconi unnaváḍu,* which is much too long to say.
guru, gurudu, guruvu, preceptor, spiritual guide. Skt. *guruvucu tagga ṣishyuḍu,* a disciple worthy of his teacher (contemptuous); *nénu nd*

guruvuvárici vadda tsaduvuconéṭ appuḍu doḍḍi tavvi samvatsaránici cávalasina cúralu pandinchevádini; y'iddaru cúliváḷḷu moyya léni múṭalanu polamló nunchi paṭṭuconi vachchi y'inṭi cáḍa vappaginchevánni; y'inṭló panul anni néné chésévánni; áyana, anugraham vachchi, tírubaḍigá v'unn appuḍu renḍu muccalu cheppévádu; voccocca náḍu adi lédu, When I was studying with my guru, I used to dig in his back-yard and raise the year's supply of vegetables; I used to carry loads from the fields which two coolies could not have carried and bring them to the house; I used to do all the housework; when he had leisure he would condescend to teach me two texts; some days not even that (the Hindu institution of spiritual apprenticeship in its actual working); *dongalacu guruvu,* a Newgate attorney, an adviser of thieves.

gurutvamu, spiritual preceptorship. Skt. *ní gurutvamu yéḍisin aṭṭe v'unnadi, v'úrucó,* a fig for your priesthood, hold your tongue.

guruváramu, Thursday. Skt., from *guruvu,* preceptor, especially *Brühaspati,* preceptor to the gods.

gusagusaláḍuṭa, to whisper; onomatopoeic. *iccaḍa yémiṭó gusagusaláḍutú v'unn aṭṭu tsappuḍu vinabadutú v'unnadi,* I hear a sound as of whispering here.

gutstsuconuṭa, to prick oneself, to prick. A thorn pricked me is *nác oca mullu gutstsucunnadi.*

gutstsuṭa, to prick.

guṭaca, gulp. *nóṭiló vrélu peṭṭuconi, guṭaculu mringutsu,* putting his finger in his mouth and swallowing (in anticipation of dainties).

gutta, rent, contract; in the Ceded Districts it means land-revenue and the humble prayer of the ryot always is that the gutta should be remitted.

guṭṭa, hill, heap.

guṭṭa, bunch, cluster of flowers, fruit, &c.

guṭṭu, a secret. *mí guṭṭu baila peṭṭutánu,* I will expose you; *mí guṭṭu baila peṭṭacundá nénu dástánu,* I will shield you; *má inṭi guṭṭu baiṭa paḍ iyya vaddu,* don't reveal the skeleton in our cupboard; *guṭṭuga v'úrucó,* lie low; *lóguṭṭu Perumállacu yeruca,* God knoweth the secrets of the heart.

guṭṭucumumanuṭa, to gulp; onomatopoeic. *guṭṭucuna mringuṭa,* to devour at a gulp.

guvva, dove. A very common bird in India. Pigeon is *pauram* and, in books, *capótamu.*

guzzu, pulp.

gúba, drum of the ear.

gúḍa, with, for the commoner *cúḍa.*

gúḍabātu, pelican. *gúḍabátlu coṭṭa vaddu, avi grámam samracshistavi,* do not shoot pelicans, they protect the village.

gúḍadu, for *cúḍadu,* must not.

gúḍuṭa, for *cúḍuṭa,* to be able, &c.

gúḍemu, hamlet; especially a pariah hamlet. The pariahs are not allowed in the main village. They live in the *málagúḍem* or the *mádigagúḍem* and dhobies live in the *tsácaligúḍem.*

gúdhamu, secret. *gúdhamugá vyabhicharintsuts unnáru,* they are secretly committing adultery.

gúḍhárthamu, secret meaning. *íyana máṭalaló yenta gúḍhártham unnadó chittaginchinára?* did you observe what depth of meaning there is in his words?

gúḍu, nest, bird-cage, niche in the wall, waggon-hood, ship's hatchway, fly-proof cover, fowl-coop, spectacle-case; in fact anything more or less round and hollow. *gurrapu gúḍu* is a mare's nest; *divvena tisina gúḍu* is the lamp-niche without the lamp, the play without Hamlet, the bung-hole without the cask.

gúna, a big pot (*cunḍa* is a smaller one). *néti gúna chéta púni nichchena yeccin aṭṭu,* mounting a ladder with a jar of ghee in one's arms (not a safe thing to do).

gúniváḍu, a hunchback, dwarf. *gúniváḍu paḍucuné valla gúnivánicé telusunu,* the hunchback knows on which side to lie (every one knows best where his own shoe pinches).

gúnu, hump (crooked back).

gúrchi, about, concerning; for *gurinchi.*

gúrtsuṭa, to convene, &c.; for *cúrtsuṭa.*

H

haccu, a right. Hindustani.

haccudáruḍu, rightful owner, heir.

haddu, boundary. *haddu cheḍi pravartintsuṭa,* to kick over the traces; *pedda manushyul annavâré á pracáramgá vyabhicharistu v'unḍaḍam chéta pókhirilu bottigá haddu miri vitstsalaviḍigá tirugutú v'unnáru,* when so-called respectable people practise fornication lewd fellows of the baser sort naturally pass all bounds of licentiousness.

haddulanuyérparatsuṭa, to demarcate.

haimamu, golden; Skt., from *hémam,* gold.

hainyamu, baseness; Skt., from *hínam,* base.

haiscúlu, high school. English.

hallacallólamu, hullaballoo, tumult; onomatopoeic. *pedda gáli samudramu hallacallólamugá chéya tsochenu,* a gale began to lash the sea into a fury.

hamésha, always. Hindustani.

hamsa, swan. Skt. *gangaló munigité cáci hamsa autundá?* a crow won't become a swan by dipping in the Ganges (there is no making a silk purse out of a sow's ear).

hamsatúlicatalpamu, eiderdown. Skt., from **hamsa,** swan, *túlica,* down, and *talpam,* bedding.

hamsáyi, neighbour, neighbouring. Hindustani. *hamsáyi grámamu,* a neighbouring village.

hamṣamu, subject; for *amṣamu. miru sabhaló cheppa póyyé hamsam émiṭó selav iyyandi,* please tell me what subject you are going to talk about at the meeting.

hanta, murderer. Skt., from *han,* to kill; cf. *hatya,* murder.

hantacuḍu, murderer.

Hanumantuḍu, Hanumánuḍu, the monkey god who served Rama. *Rámuni vanṭi rázu v'unṭé, Hanumantuni vanṭi banṭu appuḍé v'untáḍu,* when there is again a king like Rama, then there will be a servant like Hanuman (like master like man).

harabbi, Arab, Arab horse. Hindustani.

haramu, taking, snatching. Skt.

haranamu, theft, rape, loss (of time). Skt. *miccili cálaharanam aindi,* there has been much loss of time; *sommu chellintsaḍḍnici cála haranamu chéstunnáḍu,* he is postponing payment.

harcárá, courier. Hindustani.

hari, horse. Skt. Only in books for *gurram*; *aṣvam, turangam,* are other words for horse.

Hari! Lord! Sanskrit; epithet of Vishnu, Yama, Indra, esp. Vishnu; *váḷḷu páḍé bútu cútula canṭé Hari cirtanalu páḍisté bágá v'unḍaḍá?* would it not be better to sing hymns instead of the obscene ribaldry that they (the nautch-girls) sing?

harinámasmarana, repetition of the name of the Lord. Skt., from *Hari,* Vishnu, *náma,* name, and *smarana,* recollection.

harintsuṭa, to seize, steal. Skt. *itani daggira dongatanamu lédu, parula sommu harintsaḍu,* there is no thievishness about him, he will not steal his neighbour's money.

harmyamu, palace, mansion. Skt. Used only in books.

harshacamu, delightful. Skt. A book word.

harshamu, joy. Skt. Used only in books for *santósham.*

harshintsuṭa, to rejoice. Skt. Used in books. *yevaḍaina vacaḍu á cálamló munḍanu v'untsu cunṭé, pedda manushyulu yevarú vánni maryáda cheyyaca póvaḍam chéta bhayam caligi, taccinaváḷḷ andarú níti galigi v'unḍéváru; y'ippuḍu pedda manushyulu tsúchi, harshinchi, v'úrucóvaḍam chétané cáḍá, prativáḍunu vitstsaláviḍigá bháryalanu vadili peṭṭi munḍalanu v'untsucunṭú v'unnáru,* in those days if any one kept a woman respectable people turned the cold shoulder and for fear of that the others all remained moral, but now respectable people look on quite satisfied and every one deserts his

The Author in an Indian snipe-ground (1930)

wife without fear and keeps a woman.

Harudu, Siva. Skt.

hastadóshamu, slip of the pen. Skt., from *hastam*, hand, and *dósham*, mistake.

hastalághavamu, sleight of hand. Skt., from *hastam*, hand, and *lághavam*, dexterity.

hastamu, hand. Skt. Telugu *chéyyi*; *hastam* is used chiefly in compounds but also in the proverb *ṣushca priyamulu, ṣúnya hastamulu*, vain endearments, empty hands (words not deeds).

hasti, elephant. Skt. *hastimaṣacántaram*, the difference between an elephant and a mosquito.

hastódacamu, (ceremonial) hand-washing. Skt., from *hastam*, hand, and *udacam*, washing. *yentó ṣrótriyulam ani cheppu conutsu, mívanṭi Sómayájula péḷḷavdré y'iṭuvanṭi rancu munḍala chéta lacsha vattula vrattamulu modalainavi chéyinchi sancóchimpaca, hastódacamulu putsisuconi, mundugá bhójanamunacu siddha paḍuduru*, for all your pretence of piety and your high-sounding ecclesiastical titles you are ready to perform for adulterous widows rites and ceremonies for the souls of their departed husbands and, without a moment's hesitation, let them lave your hands and place your repast before you.

hatamu, slain. Skt.

haṭháttugá, suddenly. Skt., also *adháttugá*.

hatti, elephant; from Skt. *hasti*. A word used all over India; the Telugu word is *yénugu*.

hatya, murder. Skt. The forms of murder, arranged in order of descending abomination, are *brahmahatya*, brahmin-murder, *góhatya*, vaccicide, *pitrühatya*, parricide, *narahatya*, homicide, *ṣiṣuhatya*, infanticide.

haudá, howdah. Hindustani.

havéli, palace. Hindustani.

hayamu, horse. Skt. One of the book words for *gurramu*.

hayámu, reign. Hindustani. Used commonly of an official reign, such as that of a Huzur Sheristadar—in the time of so-and-so—or even of that lesser luminary, a Collector. *venuca Richchhardu doragári hayámuló iṭuvanṭi arji vasté, valla cád ani selav ichchináru*, in Mr. Richard's time he ordered that if such petitions came in there was nothing doing.

há! alas!

háhá! oh!

hálu sálu, this year. Hindustani. *sálgujastá* is last year.

háni, harm. Skt. Very common.

hániçalugachéyuṭa, to harm.

hánicaramu, harmful. Skt.

háramu, necklace. Skt.

háramu, divisor, denominator. Skt., meaning 'taking'. Used in arithmetic.

hárati, wave-offering. Skt. *hárati-cárpúramu*, camphor offered to gods or at marriages; *háratipáṭalu*, songs sung during these ceremonies.

háryamu, dividend in arithmetic. Skt.

háṣcharyamu, astonishment. For the more usual *áṣcharyamu*. *monna Buchchirázu gári fórjarí cézuló sácshulanu taribítu chési, abaddham nizamgá canapadét aṭṭu chésináru; áyana ṣactici Jaḍjí gáru cúḍá háṣcharya paḍḍáru*, the other day in Buchchirazu's forgery case he turned the witnesses inside out and made the false look true, and the Judge too marvelled at his cleverness.

hásintsuṭa, to laugh. Skt. The Telugu is *navvuṭa*.

hásyacáḍu, buffoon. Skt.

hásyamu, good-tempered jesting as opposed to *véḷácóḷam*, mockery. Skt. *ocaḍu: ṣasturlugárú! namascáramandi; ṣástri: dírghayúshyamastu! vamṣábhivrüddhirastu! rájadváré rájabhavané sarvadá digvijayamastu! ocaḍu: appudé áṣirvachanam antá ai póyind anḍi? ikha mícu émi rávanḍi? ṣástri: í y'Inglishu tsaduvucuné váḷḷacu mammalni tsústé véḷácóḷamgá v'untundi; ocaḍu: véḷácóḷam cád anḍi, mícu tátagár autáru ganuca hásyánic annánu.* Hindu: My respects, Mr. Shastri; Rev. Mr. Shastri: The Lord grant thee length of days! the Lord grant thy seed increase! the Lord grant world-victory to my lord and king! Hindu: Is that all your blessings or don't you know any more? Rev. Mr. Shastri: You English-educated people mock us when you see us. Hindu: No mockery, you are a sort of grandfather to me and I just said it in fun.

hásyáspadamu, ridiculous. Skt., from *hásyam* and *áspadam*, basis.

háyigá, happily, comfortably. *háyigá nidra pótánu,* I will go comfortably to sleep; *yentó háyigá v'undédi,* how nice it would be.

házarauṭa, to be present.

házaru, present. Hindustani. Used in answering roll-calls, &c.

házaruparatsuṭa, to produce a person.

házarupaṭṭi, attendance register.

házaruzáminu, bail.

hetstsarica, warning, encouragement.

hetstsarintsuṭa, to warn, encourage.

hetstsintsuṭa, to increase (verb active).

hetstsu, much, great. *hetstsu svaramutó pilutsuts unnáḍu,* he is raising his voice and calling; *nácu conchem cópam hetstsu,* I am rather an angry man.

hetstsuṭa, to increase, grow.

hetstsutaggulugá, up and down, more or less; from *hetstsu,* much, and *taguṭa,* to diminish. *connáḷḷu hetstsutaggulugá,* a few days more or less.

héla, sport. Skt.

hélanamu, mockery. Skt.

hémamu, gold. Skt.; also *hiranyamu.* The common word is *bangáram; héma* is used in compounds like *hémapushpacam,* the golden champak, *hémahémilu,* millionaires—*Nellúri jilláló cápulu hémahémilugá v'unnáru,* the farmers of Nellore district are all made of gold.

hémanta rütuvu, late autumn. Skt. It is the fifth of the six Telugu seasons—(1) spring (*vasantam*), (2) hot weather (*vésavi*), (3) wet (*varsha*), (4) sultry (*ṣarattu*), (6) cold weather (*tsali*).

hésha, a neigh. Skt. Telugu, *sacilinta.*

héshintsuṭa, to neigh. Skt. The Telugu word is *sacilintsuṭa.*

hétubhútuḍu, causer. Skt.

hétuvu, cause. Skt., also *cáranamu.* Both these words are common. *strílu vidyaléni hétuvu chéta, yuct'áyuctamulu teliyaca, paṣutulyaráṇḍrai n'anduna gadá, purushulac ituvanṭi manóvyadhalu sambhavintsuts' unnavi,* it is because our women are uneducated and are like beasts not knowing right from wrong that we men are made to suffer these agonizing conflicts of the mind (dreadful consequences of the neglect of female education in Hindu society); *cópa paḍaḍḍánici y'induló nácu hétuv émó canapaḍaḍam lédu,* (if you object to my previous remark) I don't see what you have to be angry about.

héyamu, vile. Skt.

héyata, vileness. Skt.

himagiri, himálayamu, snow mountains. Skt., from *himam,* snow, and *giri,* mountain, *álayam,* place, abode; the Himalayas are the Abode of Snow.

himamu, snow, dew, frost. Skt. The Telugu is *mantsu.*

himsa, harm. Skt. *ahimsa,* harmlessness, is the highest virtue in Hindu religion—*ahimsa paramó dharma.*

himsintsuṭa, to harm. Skt. *nannu himsintsaḍánici má y'inṭicé vachchináwá?* have you come to my own house just to harm me?

Hindí, the Hindi language.

hinduvu, Hindu, from Skt. *Sindhu.*

hiranyagarbhamu, Golden Womb (ceremony). Skt. The ceremony is thus described by the Most Worshipful Dutch Governor Moens writing at Cochin in 1781: 'It is true that he (the king of Travancore) is not of noble birth, but he caused himself to be ennobled. This is called by the people of Malabar "to be reborn"; for that is the force of the word by which they express it. It is derived from the droll ceremony which the ennobled person goes through, viz., passing through a big cow made of gold; after which the golden cow is beaten to pieces and divided among the Nambudries or priests.' The ceremony was performed in many parts of India and was both a regenerative and a coronation ceremony. The king went in at the mouth of the golden cow, came out at the tail, and was received in the arms of his brahmin guru's wife, and he had to try and cry like a baby.

hiranyamu, gold. Skt. The common word is *bangáram*; *hiranya* is used chiefly in compounds; *hiranyácshuḍu*, golden-eyed (*acshi*, eye), *hiranyagarbhuḍu*, golden-bellied (epithet of Brahma). *hiranyagarbha*, the golden egg, the primeval germ of the universe.

hitabódha, good advice. Skt., from *hitam*, good, and *bódha*, advice.

hitamu, good, friendly. Skt. *míru mí anubhavam chéta samasta cashṭamulanú telusuconi, mácu hitam chepputú v'unnáru*, knowing all difficulties from your experience you give us advice for our good; *mí cshémamu córi hitam cheputú v'unnánu*, I am giving you good advice out of a wish for your welfare.

hitavu, hituḍu, friend. Skt. *snéhituḍu* is commoner.

hitópadéṣamu, friendly advice; Skt., from *hitam* and *upadéṣam*, teaching. There is a book on morals called the *Hitópadéṣam* or Advice of a Friend.

hizáru, trousers. Hindustani; also *izáru*.

hí-hí! an exclamation, not as with us, of merriment, but of sorrow, surprise, or scorn; also *ihihí!*

hínamu, vile, low. Skt. *hína daṣacu vatstsuṭa* is to come down in the world; *hínavrütti*, a mean occupation; *hínasvaramu*, a low voice; *hínajátiyaina*, of low caste; *hínajátiváru*, low caste people; *hínam ainadi, vaṭṭi siggula chéṭu*, it was a low, shameful thing to do.

-hínuḍu, affix meaning 'low', 'bereft of'. Skt. *culahínuḍu*, low or outcaste; *angahínuḍu*, crippled; *buddhihínuḍu*, foolish; *rúpahínuḍu*, ugly; *dhanahínuḍu*, penniless; *lazzáhínuḍu*, shameless.

híringu, hearing. English. The court's hearing; also used of the vakil's harangue.

hlódamu, joy. Skt. Used only in books for *santósham*.

hódá, office, title, designation. Hindustani. *míru bágá paḍḍa, mávanṭiváriní paḍimandini bágu chésiná, á hódá micé rá valenu*, you should get that office and you will do well out of it and will do good to lots of us.

hómamu, burnt offering. Skt.

hóra, hour. Skt.; also Latin, whence English *hour*, French *heure*, Italian *ora*. *á v'udyógam tamac aité tamadí álágaṇṭí hóre, nimishamló doranu jébuló vésucórá?* if you get that office (Huzur Sheristadar's) you will have an hour like that and in a moment put the Collector into your pocket.

hóta, hótri, priest who offers *hómam*. Skt.

hrüdayamu, heart. Skt. The Telugu is *gunḍe*, but this is common; *suhrüdayuḍu* is a good-hearted man. *hrüdayapúrvacamaina*, from the heart; *hrüdgatamu*, by heart. Skt. *á padyamu nácu hrüdgatamu cá lédu*, I don't know that verse by heart.

hrüshṭi, joy. Skt. A book word for *santósham*.

hucumu, order, command. Hindustani. Very common all over India; especially Collector's office orders. *tahassiluddáruḍu: yémi cáranam lécundá paiváḷḷu mátram v'úricé baratarapu chéstárá? gumástá: veticéváḷḷacu anní cárandlé cana paḍatavi; mí lágé áyana jamábandíló mámúḷḷu y'ivvaca póyéṭ appaṭici, á cópam manasuló v'untsuconi, accaḍa nunchi prati vishayamlónú chiváṭlu peḍutú hucumulu vrási, tálúcá ṣaristudáru dvárá iḷḷu caṭṭucóvaḍánici balavanta peṭṭi, iṭuca putstsuconnáḍ ani donga firyádu teppinchi, baratarafu chéyinchináru.* Tahsildar: Will the superior authorities dismiss you without cause? Clerk: Those who look for a cause will always find one; he, like you, did not give mamuls at Jamabandi, and they kept that grudge in their hearts, and they wrote censures and orders about everything from head-quarters, got up a false case that the tahsildar had obtained bricks by force through the taluk sheristadar to build a house, and got him dismissed.

humcarintsuṭa, to utter a menacing sound (of crowds, &c.). Skt.

hunḍi, hundi, the Indian banker's cheque or draft. Hindustani. *váḍu* *nácu vaca darṣana huṇḍi vrásináḍu*, he drew on me at sight.

huzúru, the Presence, Head-quarters, the Collector. Hindustani. The Huzur Sheristadar or Collector's Sheristadar or Sheristadar of the Presence is a very important person, so are the Huzur Gumastas; so are the clerks of even minor Presences such as the Executive Engineer. *manam váḷḷacu yélá lócuvó, paiváḷḷacu váḷḷí álágé lócuva; ippuḍu huzúruna yevaró ménéjaru v'unnáḍ aṭa, ataḍu Ḍeltá Súparenḍenṭi modalainaváḷḷa vadda lantsálu mahá dótsucunṭú v'unnáḍ aṭa! anna véḷacu lantsam sommu dákhalu cheyya léca póté, monna vaca Ḍeltá Súparenḍentunu tísi véyinchi, renḍu vandala rúpáyalu putstsuconi, á pani marivacaḍici véyinchináḍu*, village officer speaking: just as we are subordinate to revenue officials so the overseers have their superior authorities; they say there is a manager (Executive Engineer's office manager) at head-quarters; he is said to plunder the Delta Superintendents and others extensively; recently a Delta Superintendent did not pay his bribe to scheduled time and the manager got him dismissed and another man who paid him Rs. 200 appointed in his place.

hú! sound of a yawn; onomatopoeic.

hú-hú! expresses shivering; onomatopoeic.

húna, foreign, especially European; Skt. for Hun which was used of all light-skinned people; we applied the term specially to Germans, the Telugus specially to us; thus *húna páṭhaṣála* means a school maintained by the British Government; *húna prabhutvamu* is the British Government; it is not so disparaging as our Hun and does not connote cruelty, but only barbarism. We are of course barbarians to the orthodox Hindu; and some of them still think we have tails under our clothes.

húnuḍu, Hun, foreigner, European, Englishman, barbarian. *jantu-himsa chési, mámsabhacshanamu chéyu húnuḍu*, a Hun who kills animals and eats meat (it is of course the acme of barbarousness to be a flesh-eater; we are flesh-eating animal-slayers to the orthodox).

I

Initial *i* can hardly be said to exist because euphonic *y* is almost always prefixed to it; thus *illu*, house, is usually written and pronounced *yillu*, but it is not always so; hence I catalogue the words under *i* not *yi*. English words beginning with *s* and another consonant usually have euphonic *i* or *yi* prefixed to them; e.g. *yispéṭu*, spade, *yishnappu*, snipe; the same rule is followed in Italian, as the Italians also find a difficulty in pronouncing initial *s* followed by another consonant.

i, give; short imperative of *itstsuṭa*; more commonly *ichchéyi* or *immu* or *í*.

ibbaḍi, twice as much, from *inu baḍi* or *maḍi*; the full form *inumaḍi* is commoner.

ibbaḍintsuṭa, to double; for *inumaḍintsuṭa*.

ibbandi, straitness, inconvenience. *níḷḷucu ibbandigá n'unnadi*, it is difficult to get water.

ica, next, in future, further, longer; also *inca*. *i' sangati mír ica máṭáḍacanḍi*, no more of that; *ica lédu* is no longer.

icamídaṭa, icamundu, in future, again. *monna zarigina míṭinguló Vivécaráugári durbódha chéta támu icamundu bógam méḷam tsúḍan ani á chinnaváḍ émó cágitam mída dascatu chési vachchináḍ aṭa!* at the other day's meeting the boy is actually said to have signed a paper by the bad advice of Mr. Wiseman that he would not keep a dancing-girl in future!

(untoward results of social reform meetings which sap the foundations of many old and respected institutions); *méjisṭréṭu: maḷḷí vachchává? ná vadda ica mídaṭa rá vadd ani nénu cheppa lédá? donga: míru cheppär ani, cheppiná vinacunḍá polisuvāḷḷu nannu aresṭu chési tísucu vachchär anḍi.* Magistrate: Here again? Didn't I tell you never to come before me again? Thief: I told the police you said that, sir, but they would not listen and arrested me and brought me here.

iccaḍa, here; also *itstsaṭa*; for 'come here'; do not say *iccaḍa* (which in any case would be *iccaḍici*) *rá*, but *ilá rá*.

iccaṭṭu, difficulty; from *irucu*, narrow, and *caṭṭu*.

ichchha, love, propensity. Skt. More commonly *itstsa*.

ichcheyi, give; imperative of *ichchivéyuṭa*, to give; also *icheyyi* and *ichchiveyyi*.

ichchiputstsucólu, ichchiputstsucóvaḍálu, giving and taking; used of bargaining and of marriage; also *itstsaputstsucólu. y'itara deṣalaváritó sambandhálu chésté tallidanḍrulu tana cútullanu tarutsugá tsústú v'unḍar ani, itara déṣalaváritó y'ichchiputstsucóvaḍálu mánivésináru,* they gave up marrying their daughters to people in other countries because when they had these foreign marriages the parents could not see their daughters often. The Italians have a proverb 'donne e buoi dai paesi tuoi', women and oxen from your own parts.

icshuvu, sugar-cane. Skt. Used only in books and compounds. *icshuvudhanvuḍu*, the archer with the sweet bow, is Manmadha, Cupid.

iddaru, two, of persons. Two, of things, is *renḍu*. Two of persons is also *iruguru. iddarini rán iyya vaddu*, let neither of them come in; *vár iddaru* is they two; *ocarini y'iddarini tsampiténé cáni vaidyuḍu cáḍu*, a doctor is no doctor till he has killed one or two (I regret to have to record this Telugu view of the medical profession); *vár iddaru iddaré,* six of one and half a dozen of the other; *y'í sangati mana y'iddarilóné v'unḍa valenu sumí, váḍu tágubótu*, between you and me, he is a drunkard; *idduzóḍu*, a match, man and wife.

iddumu, a grain measure, 2 tooms; from *iru*, two, and *túmu*. A toom is 4 cuntsams and about equal to 15 bushels, an iddumu 30 bushels.

idi, this, pronoun not adjective. The adjective is *í*.

idigá, not the thing. *á naḍaṭa bahu y'idigá n'unnadi*, that conduct is not at all the thing; *í rózuna váḍ émó y'idigá n'unnáḍu*, he is a little out of sorts to-day.

idigó, idugó, lo, behold, but a common word like the French *voici*, not a book word like the English 'lo, behold'. *idigó puli anṭé, adigó tóca annaṭṭu*, There's a tiger, said A. Yes, look at his tail, said B. (and there never was a tiger there at all).

idivaracu, idivaradáca, up to now, before. *y'idivaradáca nénu paḍucuné ṭóṭaló v'unna y'í mundara bhavanti cáḷi chési, addecu y'ivvaḍánici siddham chésinánu*, I prepared to give on lease the pavilion in the garden in which I used to sleep before.

idivarac-unḍina, quondam. *idivaracunḍina snéhitulu*, quondam or former friends; also *idivaralónunḍina*.

idugó, same as *idigó*.

iḍuma, trouble. One of the numerous words for misfortune.

iḍuṭa, to give place. Used especially in compounds as *gantuliḍuṭa*, to jump; *aḍḍamiḍuṭa*, to obstruct; *pújaliḍuṭa*, to offer worship; *tácaṭṭiḍuṭa*, to pawn; *ṣabdamiḍuṭa*, to give tongue; *cheviniḍuṭa*, to give ear; *cécaliḍuṭa*, to scream.

igilinta, a grin.

igilintsuṭa, to grin. *paḷḷu y'igilintsuṭa*, to grin with the teeth, is also used.

igiripóvuṭa, to evaporate, go dry. *náluca y'igiri pótu v'unnadi*, my tongue is going dry; *poyi míḍi pulusu y'igiri póyinadi*, the sauce on the hearth evaporated away.

iguru, a sprout, young leaf. *ocanici y'iguru cúra y'ishṭamu, ocanici pulusucúra,* some like strongly flavoured curry, others don't (one man's meat is another man's poison).

iguru, gums.

igó, lo, behold: short for *idigó*.

ihalócamu, this world. Skt. The other world is *paralócam*.

ihamu, this side. Adjectival form *aihicamu*. *ihamandu* is on this side of the grave, the opposite is *paramandu*, on the other side of the grave.

ihaparamulu, the things of both worlds. Skt., from *iham*, this, and *param*, other. *bógamváḷla saḥásam mánivéstár ani miccili córutsunnánu, andu valla mícu ihaparamulu rendú calavu*, I beseech you to give up the company of nautch-girls and you will gain this world and the next; *játi, mata bhédam vichárintsacuṇḍá yógyata v'unn 'appuḍu, andariní samánamugá tsúḍa valasinadé cáni, vacari y'andu cárpanyamu vahinchi, várici apacáram cheyyaḍánici tsúḍaḍam, ihánici paránici cúḍá manchidi cádu*, we should not consider differences of caste and religion but where there is worth look on all alike, while bearing malice against any one or trying to do them harm is equally disastrous to our prospects in this world and the next (a counsel of perfection in fissiparous India, where communal and caste hatred is widely prevalent); *ihaparádulacu veraca*, having no fear of God or man.

ihihi! ha ha! onomatopoeic of laughter.

ikha, for *ica*, next, more. *ikha váḍitó máṭláḍa rádu*, don't talk to him any more.

ilacóḍi, cicada.

ilá, this way; for *ílá*. *idi márgamu, ilá ranḍi*, this is the path, come this way.

ilácá, connexion. Hindustani; a very common word with a wide range of uses; *má y'ilácáváḷlu* is my people (relations, caste men, &c.). *A tálucá ilácá B* (village), i.e. 'the village B in taluk A' occurs in the heading of every petition; *ilácá putstsuconuṭa* (with the genitive) is a common expression for 'to take account of', 'take into consideration'; *ilácá* is also used of a liaison with a woman or of making friends with a man; *ná vadine garitó snéham chési, má y'inṭló puráṇam cheppé ṣástrulató y'iláca chésinánu*, I chummed up with the priest who got friendly with my sister-in-law and recited puranas in our house; *á sommu tanacé vastundi gáni, dániló nác émi ilácá léd ani, sommu apaharinchi cheppinááu*, he cheated me out of the money saying it was due to him and I had nothing to do with it; *dániló nác ilácá lédu* is what the Collector says to petitioners who come to him about something which is not his business but the business of, say, the civil courts or the district board.

iláṭi, such.

iláyi, torch; also *iláyi-buḍḍi*.

ili, grain of rice. *ígacu y'ili, pámucu bali puṭṭadu*, no food for a fly, no sacrifice for a snake (a miser's house).

illaricamu, illatamu, living with one's father-in-law (of a male). *ippuḍu paṣcháttápam caligi, nizamugáné ní nadata tinna chésucuné-ṭ-aṭṭaité, ná cúturini nícu tappacuṇḍá y'ichchi, ninnu y'illaricam v'untsucunṭánu*, if you now repent and truly reform your conduct, you may take my word for it I will give you my daughter and you shall both live with me.

illálu, housewife. *illálu guḍḍid aité, y'inṭi cunḍalacu chéṭu*, if the housewife is blind it is disaster to the pots of the house; *nívu mahá doḍḍa y'illálu lágu*, you seem to be a first class housewife; *induló manchi y'illálu tahaṣṣíludárugári bhárya várini racshinchinadi*, that good woman, the tahsildar's wife, has saved them in this matter (by inducing her husband to take a bribe).

illáṭi, such; more commonly *iláṭi*.

illu, house; the genitive is *inṭi*, the plural *iḷḷu* or *inḍlu*; also spelt *ilu*, especially in compounds; *aṫtá vacar inṭi cóḍalé*, the mother-in-law was once a daughter-in-law in some one's house; *illú vácili*, lock, stock, and barrel; *ill egiri póvun aṭṭu allari*, noise enough to send the roof flying; *iḷḷu caṭṭi tsúḍu, penḍli chési tsúḍu*, think twice before you build or marry (look before you leap); *ill aluca gáné panḍuga y'aguná?* smearing the floor with cow-dung does not make a festival (unwarranted anticipation).

immu, give; imperative of *itstsuṭa*; also shortened to *i*; more commonly *ichchéyi* from *ichchi véyuṭa*.

impu, pleasingness. *canṭici y'imp aité, caḍupucu y'impu*, what pleases the eye pleases the stomach (food should be nicely served); *vasanta rütuvu y'impu*, spring is pleasant.

impugá, pleasing. *madhya coṭṭucóvaḍam peḍiténé cáni vinévāḷḷacu y'impugá v'unḍadu*, unless you put (into the press report) some beating (of the svarajists by the police) it won't tickle the ears of the groundlings. *iṭuvanti máṭalu vinuṭac entayu n'impugáné y'unḍunu*, it will be so pleasing to hear such words (e.g. of the beating of the svarajists by the police).

imuḍuṭa, to be contained in. *jébuló y'imiḍé rendu chinna vastuvulu*, two little objects that will fit into the pocket; *purushulacu samasta dharmamulu patní sévalóné y'immiḍi y'unnavi*, all man's duty is summed up in wife-devotion (this is a sarcasm; the usual saying is that devotion to her husband is the whole of a woman's duty).

inaspecṭaru, inspector, especially of police, but also sanitary inspector, &c.; English. *arugulu tíyinchi veyya valasinad ani hucum vrási, doragári santacam chéyinchi, ṣánitari inspecṭarucu pampinchin aṭṭu áfísu bucculó y'inṭaru chési, pampintsacunḍá v'úrucuntáḍu*, (if you bribe the municipal manager) he will write an order that the pials should be removed, get the gentleman's signature, note in the registers that it has been sent to the sanitary inspector, but never send it.

inámu, gift, especially gift-land. Hindustani; more usually *ínámu*.

incamūndu, hereafter. *incamundu jágratagá v'unḍu*, be careful in future.

incá, yet, further. *incá rá lédu*, he has not come yet; *incá tsúḍu*, look again.

inci, ink. English, more usually understood than the proper Telugu *sirá*, which is in derivation Hindustani; try *sirá* on your peons and you will see. *inci-buḍḍi* or *sirá-buḍḍi* is the ink-pot.

incoca, incó, another. *incó puráṇamló cheppin aṭṭu*, as it is written in another purana; *bhárya: magaváḷḷaci yémainá chevіló cheppité, incó chevuló nunchi ivatalici vastundi: bharta: áḍadánici yémaina cheppité, renḍu chevulalóci póyi nóṭiló nunchi baiṭici vastundi.* Wife: If you say anything into a man's ear it comes out at the other. Husband: If you say anything to a woman it goes in at both ears and comes out at the mouth; *incó janmánici mí y'inṭló cucca'n ai puḍatánu*, in another life I will be reborn as a dog in your house (to show my gratitude).

incocaḍu, incóḍu, another man.

incocate, another woman.

incocaṭi, another thing.

incuṭa, to dry up, sink. *cheruvuló nír incinadi*, the tank is dry; *í cágitam y'incutsunnadi*, this paper runs.

indandu, here and there; here and hereafter.

indaru, so many persons; *andaru* is all (persons).

indáca, up till now, so far; then.

indácaṭi, previous. *indácaṭi praṣna*, the previous question; *indácaṭiváḍu*, the man who was here just now.

indársmenṭu, endorsement. English. Used especially of the order on a petition. '*inḍársmenṭu rá lédu*', means I have received no orders; *nénu y'inḍársmenṭu putstsuconi mari pani árambham chésinánu*, I did not start building till I had got orders on my petition; *cávalisté inḍársumenṭu tsúḍanḍi*, look at the order if you want to.

Inḍiá, India. English. This is not a Telugu word; in fact there is no Telugu for India; but India, taken from the English, is commonly used in newspapers, &c. When the newspapers want to be pedantic they say *Bhárata déṣamu*.

Inḍiámantri, His Majesty's Secretary of State for India; from *mantri*, minister.

Indra, the god Indra. Skt.

indradhanassu, the rainbow (Indra's bow).

indrajálamu, juggling. *idi y'indrajálam lágu v'unnadi*, this is like magic; *adi cévalam máya, vaṭṭi gáriḍi, suddha* *indrajálam*, all conjuring, pure legerdemain, simple juggling; *aṭuvanṭi máyópáyálú indrajála mahéndrajálálu v'unnavi ganucané, yenta léd anná yévaréji mída rózucu nálug aidu rúpáyalacu taccuva lécunḍá yérutáḍu*, he has all these magic tricks at his finger-ends; so he will never fail to collect four or five rupees a day on an average (the foreigner need not be shocked by the association of magic with the God Indra; is not magic Mahá Vidya, the Great Knowledge?).

indralócamu, Indra's heaven.

indranílamu, sapphire.

indriyamu, organ of sense. Skt. *y'indriya vijéyamé nizamaina vijéyamu*, the conquest of the senses is the real victory; *gnyánéndriyamulu* are the organs of perception; *carméndriyamulu*, the organs of action; *antarindriyamulu*, the internal organs, organs of the mind; *panchéndriyamulu* are the five senses and *panchéndriyabaddhuḍu* is the sensual man; *indriyamu* is also used of semen.

indu, this, this place. *indu valla*, by means of this; *indu mída*, hereupon; *indu-n-andu lédu*, neither here nor there; *indulacu*, over this.

induṭa, be contained in; for *imuduṭa*.

ingitamu, idea, opinion. Skt. *Gándhi gáru y'ingitamu teliyacunḍá v'unnadi*, Mr. Gandhi's ideas are incomprehensible.

Inglishu, English. *y'Inglishu tsaduvuconnavá!!u vaṭṭi duráchárulu*, English educated people are all unprincipled; *nadiló burada níḷḷ ani, núti níḷḷalló munugutáru, snánamu cheyyaḍam vanṭi ṣubhram cósam aṭa!* they actually declare that bathing is for bodily cleanliness, and bathe in wells, saying river water is muddy; *vaṭṭi durvinítulu guḍḍiváḷḷacu cunṭiváḷḷacu dánam chésté punyam vastund aṭa!* they are so lost to all moral sense as to say you gain virtue by charity to the halt and the blind (instead of to brahmins which is true ethics); *práchí sadácháramulanu dúshistáru; y'í bógamváḷḷanu v'untsucóvaḍam yenta cálam nunchi vastú v'unna sadácháramu?* they revile good old customs; how long has not the good custom of keeping dancing-girls endured?

inguva, asafoetida.

inta, so much, this much. *intá antá*, with a phrase for 'it is impossible to say', is the Telugu substitute for our 'ineffable, inexpressible, unutterable, countless, innumerable, indefinable,' &c.' *brahmalacu dánálu dharmálu chésté, á punyamy'intá antá ani cheppan alavi cádu*, the merit of conferring gifts and graces on brahmins transcends all expression; *nénu paḍé bádha y'int' ant ani cheppa ṣacyamu cádu*, I am suffering unutterable pain. In the plural *-intalu*, -fold, *ṣatruvu chéyu ciḍunacu padintulugá nívu mélu chéya valenu*, for the harm done to you by your enemies return tenfold good.

-inṭa, at the rate of. *nálugiṇṭa gunintsuṭa*, to multiply by four; but *nálugintalu* with soft *t* is four times as much.

inṭa, in the house; locative of *illu*.

intacumundu, intacupúrvamu, before this.

intadáca, so far.

intaṭa, with this.

intaṭi, such.

intaṭiló, within this time.

inté, so much, just so much, no more; exactly, precisely, just so; a very common word, not to be found in the dictionaries.

inṭiáviḍa, wife, matron; from *illu*, house, and *áviḍa*, she; *nívu ná bharyanu tsúchináva? í y'inṭiáviḍanu tsúchi v'unṭávu*, do you know my wife? you probably know this matron.

inṭiáyana, husband, householder; from *illu*, house, and *áyana*, he.

inṭibanṭu, house-servant.

inṭicappu, roof.

inṭicápu, householder.

-inṭici, at the rate of; *aidinṭici*, by fives. *ocinṭici padi rúpayilu ichchiňánu*, I gave Rs. 5 for each; *gajam ocaṭinṭici yenta?* how much a yard?

inṭici, to the house; dative of *illu*, house.

inṭidána, inṭidi, the woman in the house, the thing in the house; this is the polite way in which Telugu men refer to the wives; it is of course a matter of some shame to allude at all to her; another very common way is to refer to her simply as 'the family'; if you ask a man how his family is or whether he is taking his family into camp, he takes you to mean his wife, not his wife and children. *má inṭi-dánici yábhai yéḷḷu ninda vachchinavi,* my wife (the person in my house) is full fifty years old.

inṭidonga, the thief in the house. *inṭi donganu y'íṣvaruḍú paṭṭa lédu,* the Lord God himself won't catch the household thief.

inṭigéṭu, the gate of the house. *Rámuḍu: Lacshmayya gári illu idéná? Dámuḍu: idi cádu. Rámuḍu: í vídhiló v'undá? Dámuḍu: undi. Rámuḍu: nambar émiṭó cheppanḍi. Dámuḍu: nambaru inṭi géṭu mida v'unṭundi tsúḍandi.* Ráma: Isn't this Mr. Lakshmayya's house? Dáma: No. Ráma: Is it in this street? Dáma: It is. Ráma: Tell me the number. Dáma: The number is on the gate, look and see.

inṭiguṭṭu, the skeleton in the cupboard (secret of the house). *má inṭi-guṭṭu baiṭa paḍ iyya vaddu,* do not reveal the skeleton in our cupboard.

inṭillipádi, the whole family; from *illu,* house, and *ella,* all. *má y'inṭilli-pádici dáni chéta biyyam colipinchi ippinchévánni,* I used to get her to measure out and distribute food to my whole family.

inṭinṭa, from house to house; in every house. *dévatárchanac ani y'inṭinṭa tirigi nityamunu puvvulu techchi,* I used to go from house to house daily collecting flowers on the pretext that I wanted them for divine service.

inṭipéru, surname. Just as we have a Christian and a surname so the Telugus have a house (or family) name and a personal name; but while we give importance to the surname and usually indicate the Christian name only by its initial and prefix it, the Telugus do just the contrary; the surname is a prefixed initial; in Telugu I should be G. Arthur instead of A. Galletti; then there is the caste title which comes last; so I should be G. Arthur Paramahamsa.

inṭitagavu, domestic broil. *inṭitagavu Íṣvaruḍ ainá tírpa lédu,* God Himself cannot settle household disputes.

idṭiváḍu, the man in the house (used by women in referring to their husbands).

inṭivenuca, backyard. *innáḷḷu bratici inṭivenuca tsachchin aṭṭu,* like a man who has had his day and is now dead in his backyard.

intsuca, a little, ever so little. *nén intsucayu samarthuḍanu gáca póyin-anu, manchiváḍanu,* though I am not at all clever, I am good; *nív intsuca taḍavu dúramugá n'unḍa valenu,* please stand aside for a bit.

intsumintsugá, more or less. *intsu-mintsugá janul andarú nácu bhactul ainâru,* all the people more or less adore me (I am a very popular Collector).

inu-, two, in compounds.

inucuṭa, to dry up; more usually *incuṭa.*

inumaḍi, double.

inumaḍintsuṭa, to double.

inumáru, twice.

inumu, iron (noun). *inumu virigité ataca vatstsunu gáni, manasu virigité ataca cúḍadu,* broken irons may be mended, but not broken friendship.

inupa, iron (adjective). *ráti cunḍacu y'inupa teḍḍu,* an iron ladle for a stone pot (i.e. if a mahatma is obstinate and defiant, send him to jail).

inupacatstsa, iron girdle; also continence, chastity, from the use of such iron girdles by ascetics.

inupadári, the iron way, i.e. the railway.

inupagugiḷḷu, iron grains, i.e. jaw-breakers. *í cávyamu inupa gugiḷḷu,* this poem is all jaw-breakers (Telugu poems usually are, the method of compilation being to turn to the Nighantuvu or dictionary of Sanskrit synonyms and excerpt jaw-breakers to put in your poem, which will then be described as chaste and elegant).

innúru, 200, from *inu,* two, and *núru,* hundred.

ippacheṭṭu, *mohwa* palm tree. *ippa púlacu vásana vetaca valená?* you have not got to smell out the *ippa* (it has a strong smell).

ippaṭi, of this time, adjective of *ippuḍu,*

now. *ippaṭi pani*, the present business; *ippaṭivándlu*, the moderns.

ippaṭici, till now. *y'i véḷa maṭṭucu y'ippaṭici padi snánálu chésinánu*, (bigot speaking) only to-day I have up to now taken 10 ceremonial baths (he would have to take one if, for example, he saw a European, to wash away the pollution).

ippáṭa, thus, so.

ippintsuṭa, to get given, procure; causal of *itstsuṭa*, to give. *váḷḷacu biyyam ippinchévánni*, I used to procure them food.

ippuḍu, now; also spelt with one *p*.

iracaṭamu, a narrow place; also *irucaṭamu*.

irasa, a grain measure—2 cuntsams or half a toom; from *iru*, two.

irasálmeṭṭu, insolvent. Corrupt form of the English word.

irsálnáma, memorandum of remittance. Hindustani. One of the prescribed village accounts.

irsálu, remittance. Hindustani. Used especially of remittances of the land-tax from the village to the *taluk* office.

iru-, two; in compounds. *irucelaculu*, both sides.

irucaṭamu, a narrow place; also *iracaṭamu*.

irucu, straits, narrowness. *iruculó paḍḍa cóti láguna coṭṭuconuts unnáḍu*, he is struggling like a monkey caught in a vice (of persons in a dilemma).

irucu, narrow.

irucuconuṭa, iruconnuṭa, be caught, entangled, in distress.

irucumánu, post in a gateway or hedge which lets men through and keeps cattle out.

irugaḍa, on both sides; from *iru*, two, and *caḍa*, side.

irugóru, both shares of the crop (the landlord's and the tenant's).

iruguporugulu, the neighbours. *y'iruguporugulu ammal accalu cheppuconutsunnáru*, the neighbouring sisters, cousins, and aunts say so.

iruguru, both persons, two persons.

irulu, darkness; not nearly as common as *chícaṭi*.

irupaccalu, both sides.

irusa, same as *irusu*, 2 cuntsams.

irusálu, same as *irsálu*, remittance.

irusu, axle.

iruvadaina, one 20th.

iruvadi, iruvai, 20.

ishṭadaivamu, one's favourite or patron god. Skt. *míc í buddhi v'unḍéṭ aṭṭu cheya valen ani ná y'ishṭa daivamunu nityamú prárthistú v'unṭánu*, I shall daily pray my patron saints to keep you of the same mind.

ishṭagóshṭhi, agreeable, comfortable, informal; in the last meaning common in the newspapers in describing parties and meetings; *ishṭagóshṭhi sabha* is an informal meeting.

ishṭamu, wish, pleasure. Skt. *mí ishṭamu*, as you please. The common word for pleasure, liking, wish. I should like to do a thing is *nácu ishṭam unnadi* with dative of verbal noun. Very pleased, I am sure, or thank you, I shall be very pleased to come, in accepting an invitation, is *tsála ishṭam* or *tsála santósham* (without any verb). *ishṭam putstsuconuṭa* with the genitive is to consult a person; *ishṭam vatstsuṭa* with dative of the subject is to feel pleasure, to like. *ishṭa pracáram* is according to one's wish, as one likes or wants to; as for instance when the village servant, unmindful of the fact that the Collector wears boots, tries to insist on the Collector's taking a roundabout way for the avoidance of thorns, the Collector remarks *ná ishṭa pracáram pótánu*, I shall pass where I please; *mana ishṭa putstsucócunḍá peddaváḷḷu svatantrinchi tama ishṭam vachchina váḷḷanu manacu caṭṭi peṭṭinánu*, our elders married us to those they chose off their own bat without consulting us; *ishṭam unna anta cálam*, as long as you like.

ishṭánusáram, according to one's pleasure, at one's option.

ishṭapaḍuṭa, to like.

ishṭuḍu, friend.

ispétu, spades in cards. English. Sometimes used for cards in general. *ispéṭáṭa* is a card game.

istimirári, perpetual. Hindustani. Used of the permanent settlement, grants in perpetuity and such things in treaties and deeds.

istiri, ironing. Hindustani. *istiri anagá baṭṭalu chinna inupa peṭṭeló nippu vési rátsaḍam,* ironing is putting fire into a little iron box and rubbing.

isuca, sand. *isucadibba* or *isucadinne* is a sand bank; *isucaparra,* a sandy waste.

isuḷḷu, winged ants.

ita, here. Skt. Used in books and compounds for *iccaḍa. itachparamu,* nothing more; *anté cáni itachparamu nácu teliyadu,* I know no more than this.

itaḍu, he.

itara, other; in compounds, other than. *bráhmanétarulu* is non-brahmins; *Purushétara Mahá Jana Sabha* is the Great Feminist (non-man) Conference (sarcastic).

itaruḍu, another man. *báluḍu: nánná manam í prapanchamuló ituralacu saháyam chéyaḍánicé v'unnám ani ṭícharu cheppāḍu. tandri: á sangati nizamé. báluḍu: aité itarul enduc unnáru?* Boy: Daddy, the teacher said we are in this world to help others. Father: That's true. Boy: Then what are the others here for?

iti. Skt. For Telugu *ani.* Takes the place of inverted commas.

ityádi. Skt. &c. (*iti* plus *adi*).

iṭica, brick. *vacca vidhini túmu caṭṭintsa valasi vasté, veyyi y'iṭicalu lekhaló vési, bazáruló ammédáni cante renḍu reṭlu yeccuva kharídu putstsuconi, tellavárét appaṭici vaccoca y'inṭi góḍalu léva tiyinchévánni,* (municipal contractor speaking) if a culvert had to be built in a street I would put 1,000 bricks in the bill at double the market value and get the money and go at dawn and collect the bricks out of people's walls.

iṭicámamu, brick-kiln; from *iṭica* and *ámam; y'ikha camishnarlató sambandhamu lécundá, íyana svantangá caḍi térchévi y'iṭic ámalú, penc ámalú, peḷḷi pandiḷḷú, modalainaváṭi bápaṭu cávalisin anta v'unṭundi,* apart from what he shares with the municipal commissioners he (the municipal manager) will get any amount under the head of licenses for brick and tile kilns, marriage pandals, and so on.

itihásamu, legend, myth, tradition. Skt.

iṭívala, lately, also later. The late king is *iṭívala n'unḍi póyina rázu*; the later operations is *iṭívali panulu*; subsequent particulars is *iṭívali vivaramulu.*

iṭlá, so, this way, as follows. 'Come here' is *iṭlá rá*; *oca pracaṭanaló y'iṭlá v'unḍenu,* a notice ran as follows.

iṭlágu, so, this way.

iṭláṭi, so, such like.

iṭlu, so, thus; also *iṭulu.*

itstsa, fancy. Skt. *itstsa tírpuṭa,* satisfy one's desire; *itstsa vachchin aṭṭu cheyya vatstsunu,* do as you like.

itstsâcamu, cajolery. *nív ippuḍu itstsacamulacai máya máṭal áḍuts unnáu,* you are now speaking falsely to cajole me.

itstsacálamari, flatterer, rogue.

itstsaṭa, here; also *iccaḍa.*

itstsuputstsucólu, givings and takings; also *ichchiputstsucólu.*

itstsuṭa, to give, to let or allow; the ordinary word; imperative *í, ichchéi, iyyamu, immu*; past *ichchánu,* future *istánu*; usual infinitive *ivva* as *ivva vatstsunu,* you may give; also *iyya*; causative *ippintsuṭa,* get something given. *ichchévánni tsústé tsachchéváḍainá létsunu,* even a dying man will rise if he sees some one who is going to give; *chéyan ichchiri,* they permitted it to be done; *pón'í,* go on; *tsúḍan'í,* let me see; *cán'í,* be it so; *nannu rán ichchináru cáru,* they would not let me come; *artham itstsuṭa* is to give a meaning, mean; *manas itstsuṭa* is to give one's mind, attend; *isté cheḍédi lédu, tsasté vachchédi lédu,* give and spend and God will send.

ittaḍi, brass. *jívaratnam y'ittaḍini podigité ratnánici yémi lópam?* if a fine gem is set in brass does that make it less a fine gem? (A real gem of a man will shine bright as a tahsildar or Deputy Collector if he is never set on a throne or translated to the Board of Revenue.)

ittamu, let us give.

iṭṭi, like this, thus.

iṭṭé, at once.

iṭu, thus, this way.

iṭuca, brick; same as *iṭica.*

iṭulu, so, thus; also *iṭlu.*

iṭunaṭu, this way and that; from *iṭu*

and *aṭu; iṭunaṭu tirugutsu*, turning this way and that.

iṭununchi, from or along this side. *vídhiló iṭununchi vaca banḍi, aṭununchi vaca banḍi vasté, yeṭununchi veḷḷaḍánici valla cáca, yenta ibbandi calugutundi*, if one cart comes on one side along the road and another the other side and there is no room to pass, what a nuisance! (as many a motorist has had to remark in this country where they will not follow the rule of the road and if you ask them don't know it, and some will say the rule is to keep to the north and others the rule is to keep to the south).

iṭuvanti, such.

ivaca, moisture, damp. *cheruvu daggira unḍuṭa valla y'í y'inṭi nela y'ivacaga unnadi*, the floor of this house is damp as it is near a tank.

ivatala, on this side; opposite to *avatala*, on that side, beyond.

ivataḷintsuṭa, to be cool. *vésavi cálamun andu cúḍá Nilagiri conḍala mída y'ivatalinchi y'unḍunu*, the Nilgiris are cool even in the hot weather.

ivi, these; plural of *idi*, this.

iyyacolupuṭa, persuade.

iyyaconuṭa, consent; also *íyaconuṭa*.

iyyacólu, consent; also *íyacólu*. The common word is *oppudala*.

iyyadi, this, for *idi*.

iyyamu, give; imperative of *itstsuṭa*. *Lacshmayya: Rangaḍu occa rúpáyi badulu iyyum anṭé ivvan annáḍu; inta canṭé níchulu unṭárá? Rámayya: nénu unnánu.* Smith: Jones refused to lend me a shilling when I asked him; could there be any one so base? Brown: Yes, myself.

izárá, farm, especially of the revenue or of a monopoly. Hindustani.

izárádáruḍu, farmer of the revenue or of a monopoly.

izáru, trousers. Hindustani.

Í

í, give, allow; imperative of *itstsuṭa*. *pón'í*, go on; *cán'í*, be it so; for 'give me something' *ichchéi* (*ichchi véyi*) is commoner.

í, this.

-í, final *i* is lengthened for emphasis; every final vowel can be lengthened for emphasis; especially *e, i, u*; *a* lengthened is usually interrogative; *o* lengthened dubitative; lengthening consecutive final *i* or *u* is the usual way of saying 'and'. *Satyavatici maḍimayilá snánamú sandhyá léni Inglishu tsaduvuconna mogaḍu doricináḍu ganuca, iddarici calisi póyinadi, váḷḷacu y'iddarici cúḍa bidiyamú parupú pratishṭhá yémi lédu; váḷḷu mogaḍú pellámú paṭṭa pagalu máṭáḍutár ani v'uḷḷó naluguru tsáṭuna váḷḷanu chí anṭú v'unnáru*, Satyavati having an English-educated husband who does not know purity from impurity and omits his baths and prayers, they naturally get on well together; they neither of them have any shame, pride or proper feeling; every one secretly says fie on them for a husband and wife talking together openly in full daylight. In the above example notice the emphatic final vowels, the copulative final vowels, the alliteration in *maḍimayilá, snánamú sandhyá, parupú pratishṭhá* and *paṭṭa pagalu*. It is a highly idiomatic example of colloquial Telugu.

íbiḍa, íbiḍe, she.

íca, íce, feather.

ícáḍici, to such a state; from *í* and *cáḍa*, near. *ní bágu cósamai nén enni vidhamulugánainá tanṭálu paḍi y'í cáḍici techchinánu*, I have got things so far suffering all kinds of trouble for your good; *váni y'illu í cáḍici vachchinadi*, to such a state is his family reduced.

íce, feather; same as *íca*.

íce, she; *íme* is commoner.

ícuṭa, to soak in; same as *incuṭa*.

íḍéruṭa, to mature (of girls), attain puberty; from *íḍu*, age, and *éruṭa*, to pick up. *pedda auṭa* is an even more common equivalent; also simply *yedigi*, having grown. *dinam oca calpamugá gaḍuputsu, nénu tondara paḍina coladini, pilladi y'íḍéruṭa venucacé póvutsu vachchenu*, time lingered in centuries and cycles till she budded into womanhood (old man waiting for his child wife to attain puberty).

ídértsuṭa, accomplish, effect. *í cashṭam ídértsutavá?* will you see me through?

íḍigaváḍu, toddy-drawer. *íḍiga* is the caste name; the derivation is from *íḍsuṭa*, to draw. *banṭrótuváḷḷu v'úri mída paḍi y'íḍigaváḷḷa illalónú, tsácaliváḷḷa y'iḷḷalónú dúri, cóḍi piṭṭalunú cúragáyalanú balavantamgá coṭṭi, láccu pótu v'unnáru*, the Collector's peons have fallen upon the village and invaded the houses of the toddy-drawers and the dhobies and robbed chickens and vegetables (a Collector should always try and see that his peons pay for supplies but as a matter of fact they *never* take money into camp and live on the country like bandits).

íḍpintsuṭa, to cause to draw; causative of *íḍuṭa*, to pull.

íḍsuṭa, to pull, draw; causative of *íḍuṭa*, to pull, in form; actually it simply means to draw, as toddy from a tree, to draw a cart, and so on.

íḍu, equal. *núru máṭalu vaca vráṭacu y'íḍu cávu*, 100 oral statements are not equal to one document.

íḍu, age. *íḍuvachchina* is full grown; *íḍuráni*, not full grown.

-íḍu, a suffix denoting a person (male); same as *-váḍu*. *sáliḍu*, a weaver or a spider; *cannaḍíḍu*, a Canarese man.

íḍuṭa, to draw, to milk.

íduṭa, to swim. *ocaḍu: nuvvu y'ída galavá? incóḍu: ída galanu. ocaḍu: poḍugu y'ída galavá? incóḍu: ída lénu. ocaḍu: vedalpu y'ída galavá? incóḍu: ída lénu. ocaḍu, aité, yémi y'íduṭáu? incóḍu: lótu.* Smith: Can you swim? Jones: Yes. Smith: Lengthwise? Jones: No. Smith: Breadthwise? Jones: No. Smith: Then how do you swim? Jones: Downwise. *ída póte tága níḷḷu lévu*, he wanted to go for a swim and found not even enough water to drink.

íga, fly. *téne v'unna tsóṭa y'ígalu pógavutavi*, where the honey is the flies collect; *inṭlo y'ígala móta, baiṭa savárila móta*, in the house buzzing of flies, outside the hum of lordly palanquins (all outward show).

ígapuli, spider; from *íga*, fly, and *puli*, tiger. Spider is also *sálepurugu*, the insect which is a weaver by caste (*sále*, weaver's caste); *inṭló y'ígapuli, baiṭa peddapuli*, at home a fly-tiger, abroad a real tiger (the bold ruffian who is hen-pecked by his wife).

íla, whistle.

ílavéyuṭa, to whistle.

ílá, ílágu, so, in this way.

íláganṭi, such.

íláṭi, such.

ílógá, meanwhile.

íme, she.

índradi, toddy-drawing woman.

índraváḍu, toddy-drawer. Same as *íḍigaváḍu*.

ínuṭa, to yield (as grain); to bear (young); to bring forth. *ínina puli*, a tigress with cubs, is applied to ferocious people.

ípaṭḷa, in this manner.

ípáṭi, now. *ípáṭi y'inṭici veḷuddámu*, now let's go home; *ípáṭi tsálintsu*, now shut up; *ípáṭi tsálunu*, that's enough.

ípáṭici, up to now. *ípáṭici vachchi y'unḍunu*, he will have come by now.

ípe, she. *íme* is commoner.

ípi, dung of flies. *ípipeṭṭina*, fly-blown.

ípsa, desire. Skt. Used in books.

íréḍu, 14; from *íru*, twice, and *éḍu*, 7. *íréḍu lócamulu* are the 14 worlds of Hindu mythology.

írshya, spite. Skt.

írshyagrastuḍaina, spiteful. Skt., from *írshya* and *-grastuḍu*. *írshyagrastulaina dushṭulu pápánici bhaya paḍaca mácu háni cheyyaḍánacu tsústú v'unnáru*, spiteful enemies are unscrupulously trying to harm us (a very common remark in petitions; if we are to believe the Telugus every man Jack of them has spiteful enemies).

ísadintsuṭa, to be angry.

Íṣvari, Parvati, wife of Siva.

Íṣvaruḍu, The Lord, i.e. Siva. *Íṣvara náma smaranamu chési*, repeating Siva, Siva. *inṭi donganu y'Íṣvaruḍú* *paṭṭa lédu*, God Himself cannot catch the thief in the house. In compounds *-íṣvaruḍu* means lord; *bhúmíṣvaruḍu*, lord of the earth, king; *mantríṣvaruḍu*, the lord minister.

íta, swimming. *ítacu minchina lótu, góchici minchina dáridryamu lédu*, out of depth is as deep as you can get, when you are reduced to your loin-cloth you are as poor as you can be; *chépa pillacu y'íta nérpa valená?* teaching a young fish to swim.

íta cheṭṭu, date-palm. *íta ginza y'ichchi, táṭi ginza lágéváḍu*, throwing in a sprat to catch a salmon (a date to get a palmyra fruit; the fruit of the Indian date-tree is worthless and the Arabian date-palm will not grow in India).

ítacáḍu, swimmer; also *ítagáḍu*.

ítala, here, on this side. *ítalan evaru léru*, there is no one here.

íte, dart, spear.

ítsóṭuna, at this place, here.

ívala, this side, since.

ívalávala, on this side and on that.

ívéḷa, this day; to-day is *néḍu*.

íví, liberality; from *itstsuṭa*, to give.

ívimánu, the fabulous tree that grants all wishes (Fortunatus' cap).

íviḍa, íviḍe, she; same as *ibiḍa, ibiḍe*.

íyaconuṭa, to consent; same as *iyyaconuṭa*.

íyacólu, consent, approval; same as *iyyacólu*.

íyadi, this. Used in books for *idi*.

íyama, she. Used in books for *íme*.

íyana, he, my husband, the master; honorific of *itaḍu*.

J

jaḍa, braid (of hair). *gaḍḍamu perigi, tala jaḍalu caṭṭi poté, vacca sárigá yógi n'ai póḍunu*, I will grow my beard, wear my hair in braids, and at one stroke become a yogi. Just as among us it is in fact, whatever the proverb may say to the contrary, the cowl that makes the monk, so in India the beard and hair and yellow dress make the sanyasi or yogi; *áme jaḍa vésucunnadi*, she plaits her hair.

jaḍji, judge. English.

jaḍuḍu, idiot. Skt.

jagach, jagad, jagan. Adjectival forms of *jagam*, world. Skt. *jagan móhini*, the world's sweetheart; *jagan nádhuḍu*, the lord of the world (the Puri Vishnu is so called); *jagachchacshuvu*, the eye of the world (the sun); *jagadbhícaramu*, frightful to the whole world; *jagatpráṇamu*, the world's life, i.e. the air; *jagatpráṇamucu yógya sthánam aina vellaḍi tsóṭlu*, the life-breathing open.

jagamu, jagattu, the world. Skt. *mana ṣástrálu bahu manchi ṣástrálu, váṭiló samánam ainavi jagattuló lévu*, our shastras are most excellent shastras; there is nothing to equal them in the world. Missionaries will do well to bear in mind that the Hindu places his Scriptures above the Bible; *jagattoló andarú áru nelalu vachchin appaṭi pillalacu annam peṭṭutáru*, all the world begins to feed children on rice as soon as they are six months old (it is common for every race to think its own customs universal); *dhana múlam idam jagat*, the world is founded on money (Skt. proverb).

jainamu, the Jain religion. Skt.

jainuḍu, a Jain.

jaitruḍu, victor. Skt., from *jayam*, victory.

jala, jalamu, water. Skt. *jalasútramu*, pump; *gata jala sétu bandhanamu*, making a causeway for water that has flowed away (shutting the stable door after the horse has been stolen).

jalabhádhacu póvuṭa, to go to make water, pumpship.

jaladári, aqueduct, water-way; from *jala*, water, and *dári*, way.

jambhamu, big word, boast. Corrupt form of Skt. *dambham*. *bahu jambhálu coḍutúv'unnáu*, you are using big words.

jambukháná, carpet. Hindustani. The usual Telugu word is *tivási.*

jambuvu (*eugenia jambos*). Skt. Also *jambu nérédu*. We eat the fruit of this.

-janacamu, creating. Skt. Used to form compounds. *hásajanacamu*, mirth-creating, and *santóshajanacamu*, joy-creating, are common; *vánitó máṭláḍuṭa nácu santóshajanacam*, it is a real pleasure to talk to him.

janacuḍu, procreator, father. Skt.

janamu, people. Skt. *jana pratinidhi sanghamu* means legislative council, parliament, representative assembly; *pratinidhi* is representative.

jananamu, birth. Skt. *jananatidhi*, date of birth.

janani, procreatrix, mother. Skt.

jananijanaculu, father and mother, parents. The plural refers to the two people, not more; a common use, cf. *tallidanḍrulu*, *annadammulu*.

janasámányamu, general public. *jana sámányamu yocca árógyamu* is newspaper Telugu for public health.

janábhá, population. Hindustani. The usual census word.

janábhádastu, poll-tax.

janábhálecca, census.

janábhásistu, poll-tax.

janáná, *zenana*, seraglio. Hindustani.

jangalamu, jungle. Skt. But the English idea that jungle means forest is wrong; it only means wild, uninhabited country.

jangamuḍu, a Jangam (sect of Siva devotees). *dásarivá jangamuvá anṭé, mundari v'úri coddí annáḍ aṭa*, when asked whether he was a Vaishnavite or a Saivite he said, 'that depends on the next village' (a time-server).

jangha, calf of the leg; same as *picca*.

janintsuṭa, to be born, arise. Skt.; same as *janmintsuṭa*.

janituḍu, born. Skt. *áyana nénu y'oca garbha janitulamu*, he and I were born of the same womb.

janmabhúmi, janmadeṣamu, native land. Skt.

janmadinamu, birthday. Skt.

janmamu, birth. Skt. *incó janmánici*, in another birth; *í dinamu ná janmam sáphalyam ainadi*, my life's purpose is to-day fulfilled; *agrajanma racshanam andu bonca vatstsunu*, it is permissible to lie to save a brahmin. (*agrajanmuḍu* is a person born on the apex of society, brahmin conceit).

janmapatrica, horoscope (birth-paper). Skt.

janmi, animal. Skt.

janmintsuṭa, to be born, arise. Skt., same as *janintsuṭa*.

jantramu, machine. Skt., more commonly *yantramu*.

jantuvadhaṣála, slaughter-house. Skt., from *jantuvu*, animal, *vadha*, slaughter, and *ṣála*, hall. The common people will not understand this Sanskrit compound, they say *sláṭer-hausu*.

jantuvaidyuḍu, veterinary doctor. Skt.

jantuvu, animal. Skt.

januḍu, a man. Skt., used nearly always in the plur. *janulu*, people.

japamu, silent prayer, meditative penance. Skt.; the original meaning is prayer, then silent prayer, meditation on God; not quite silent, but moving the lips in prayer; entirely silent meditation is *dhyánam*. *nánnagáru v'úricé japam pitstsaló paḍi póyináru, tinnagá véḷacu bhójanánic ainá rávaḍam lédu*, my dad has fallen into religious mania, he does not even come to meals regularly; *bráhmala chéta mahá mantrálu japam chéyisté, ṣatruvul antá vacca debbaló naṣinchi pór anḍi?* if you have charms recited and silent prayer performed by brahmins will not your enemies be destroyed at one blow? *japamála*, rosary.

japintsuṭa, to perform *japam*, to mutter prayers. *strí váṣyánici v'upadéṣamaina mantram japinchi, mantródacamu Bhimaraogári bhárya mída vidhíló veḷḷutú v'unḍagá tsallét appaṭici, áviḍa nannu paṭṭucuni cheḍa tiṭṭinadi*, I was muttering the charm that puts women in your power and sprinkled the charm-water on Mrs. Bhimarao as she was going along the street, but she caught hold of me and abused me furiously (to such base uses may Holy Japam be turned).

jara, old age, decrepitude. Skt.

jarimáná, a fine. Hindustani. More commonly *zulmáná*.

jaṭa, matted locks. Skt. One of the marks of an ascetic.

jaṭacábandi, jutka, a covered one-horse fly without seats.

jaṭharamu, the belly. Skt. *jaṭharayátana,* the plight of a child unborn (*yátana,* anguish; the expression implies a pessimistic view of the universe).

javabhérí, drum of victory (song of triumph), from *jayam,* victory, and *bhérí,* drum. *míru mí cáryam sádhinchi chivaracu jayabhéri veyyaṇḍi,* don't crow too soon.

javábu, answer. Hindustani. More commonly *zavábu*; *javábuddáruḍu,* surety; *javábunísu,* clerk.

javádi, civet. Skt.

javánu, peon, bailiff, constable. *japtíjavánu* is a bailiff; *japtíjavánu vóḷḷ antá chemaṭalu paṭṭéṭ aṭṭugá parugettutú v'unnáḍu,* the bailiff is running up sweating all over; *bhatuḍu* is also used for bailiff. *mejisṭreṭu: inspecṭarugáru! tamaru dánni máṭládacuṇḍá bandóbastu cheyya valenu. inspecṭaru: javán, á sarvadhicárini avatalici pampinchi veyyi.* Sub-Magistrate: Mr. Inspector! See that that woman is not allowed to speak. Inspector: Constable, remove the Congress Dictatrix.

javvanamu, youth; corrupt form of Sanskrit *yavvanam*; also *zavvanamu.*

javvani, damsel; bad Skt.

javvarándru, young women; bad Skt.

jayagóshamulu, cheers.

jayamu, victory, success. Skt. *oca ḍácṭaru: mí jayánic émi cáranam? renḍó ḍácṭaru: rógi yém córité á pracáram cheyyaḍánici vappucunṭánu.* 1st doctor: What is the secret of your success? 2nd doctor: I always order exactly what the patient wants.

jayanti, the anniversary of an incarnation, e.g. Krishna's birthday corresponding with Christmas.

jayilu, jail. English. *Ráma: Chennapaṭnamló tsurucaina vartaculu ocarú canipintsaru. Gópu: aṭlánṭi váḷḷu jayiluló v'unṭár anḍi, cávalisté accaḍa tsúḍa vatstsunu.* Smith: There don't seem to be any smart merchants about in Madras. Jones: There will be plenty in the Penitentiary. If you want them, look in there.

jayintsuṭa, to conquer. Skt.

jáci, the knave in cards; from English Jack.

jáḍyamu, disease. *anṭuḍu jáḍyam* is contagious disease; *cástá jáḍyam,* coast, foreign, i.e. venereal disease; *jáḍyam tagaluṭa* is to contract disease; *buddhi jáḍyam* is stupidity; *ammavári jáḍyamu* is small-pox; *sukhajáḍyamu,* venereal disease.

jága, place. Hindustani.

jána, clever.

jánatanamu, sagacity.

jánuḍu, a wit.

jágaramu, vigil. *répu yécadaṣi v'upavásam chési rátri jágaram cheyya valenu,* after the 11th day fast to-morrow we must keep vigil.

jágarúcata, vigilance. *tana cumártenu sévacula vaṣamuna viḍichi y'úracuṇḍaca, táné yentó jágarúcatató vichárintsuts unḍenu,* she did not leave the care of her daughter to servants, but saw vigilantly to everything herself.

jágarúcuḍu, a vigilant man.

jágíru, an estate held on feudal tenure. Jagirs are assignments made by the old Muhammedan rulers, usually for military service. The word itself is Hindustani. Many jagirs were confirmed by our Government without the condition of military service. sometimes a quit rent was imposed, more usually not. A large example of a jagir is Banganapalle, which has been converted into an Indian State with complete internal sovereignty and no tribute. There are also many jagirs consisting of a single village or even part of a village; and some grants of land-revenue without any land are also described as jagirs. Jagirs were granted 'as long as the sun and the moon endure', but this was a mere form of words; it was perfectly well understood that they lapsed (1) at the death of the granter, (2) at the death of the grantee. We confirmed them in perpetuity or for a fixed number of lives. Banganapalle used to be parcelled out into a number of sub-jagirs held by the Nawab's relations. During temporary administration by the Madras Government they were all resumed without compensation on the death of the Nawab.

jágrata, careful, carefulness, guard. *jágrata!* careful, look out! *vádu tana y'intló nácu sthalam ichchinádu gáni, bhójanamu mátramu ná antața néné jágrata chésucunnánu,* he put me up but I found for myself; *jágrata ní dummu duluputánu,* careful, or I will dust your jacket for you; *váni gati tsúchi nívu jágrata padu,* take warning by his fate; *ná jágrata mída nénu v'unțánu,* I will be on my guard.

jágratapaduța, to be careful.

jágratapeṭṭuṭa, to place in safety, put away, put by.

jálamu, multitude. Skt.

jálamu, deceit. Skt.

jápyamu, dawdling. *ica jápyam cheyya cúḍadu,* don't dawdle any more.

járastrí, harlot. Skt.

járatvamu, fornication, adultery. Skt. *ippuḍu samsárulé bógamváḷḷa canțé yeccuvagá járatvam chéstú v'unnáru,* now married women indulge in license worse than nautch-girls.

járavrüthi, prostitution. *járavrüthiló v'unnavárini mana illacu pilavaḍam valla tsálá nashṭálu calugutú v'unnavi,* much harm is done by calling prostitutes (nautch-girls) to our houses.

jári chéyuța, to issue, publish, put in force. Hindustani. Used of issuing an order and publishing a notification and putting a scheme in force; a common official word.

járuḍu, adulterer, fornicator. Skt.

jásti, extra. Hindustani. (You are asking) far too much is *tsála jásti.*

játacamu, horoscope. Skt. *má tanḍri ná játacam vrásinádu,* my father cast my nativity; *monna nénu játacam tsúpisté má v'úḷḷó jyótishcuḍu mic í sanvatsaramló dhana nashṭam vastund' ani cheppináḍu,* the other day I showed my horoscope to our village astrologer and he said that within a year I should suffer a money loss.

játamu, kind or class. Skt.

játi, kind or caste. Skt. *dhaniyála játi,* the coriander caste, the Chettis. Coriander is rubbed before it is sown and the Chetti has to be rubbed before he will part; *adi manchi játi gurramu,* a high-class horse. *yé játi?* what caste?

játíya, belonging to a tribe or caste, native. Skt. Used in the newspapers for 'national'; national government is *játíya prabhutvamu váru.*

játyamu, of good caste or family, high-class. Skt.

jáya, wife. Skt. A book word for *bhárya.*

jelaga, leech; also *zalaga. jelaga váni cheyyi gaṭṭigá paṭṭucunnadi,* a leech fastened on his hand. Dialogue between Vivécabhüshaṇuḍugáru (Mr. Wiseman) and Matihínaraopantulugáru (Mr. Senseless): *Vivécabhüshaṇuḍugáru: émayyá Matihínaraogárú! alá rágálu peḍutúv' unnáru?* Wiseman: Hullo, Mr. Senseless, what are you crying about? *Matihínaraogáru: mari yémi léd andi; yi Janavanchacácharlagárini télu mantram v'upadéṣintsam ani, nálugu nelala nunchi anusaristú v'unnánu; ná vadda nálugu rúpáyalu putstsuconi grahanam rán unn ani y'ippaṭi dácá zaripinádu; ninna rátri tírá v'upadéṣam chéstán ani, v'úri baiṭi cheruvulóci tísucuni veḷḷi, canṭham lótu niḷḷaló dimpinádu; ussi! abbabbá! gunḍelalóci pótlu póḍustú v'unnavi; cheyyi baddalu vésucu pótú v'unnadi.* Senseless: It is nothing, sir; I have been in attendance on this Rev. Mr. Humbug for the last 4 months receiving instruction in the scorpion charm; he took Rs. 4 from me and has gone on till now saying 'wait for the eclipse'; last night he said he would give me the last lesson and took me out of the village to the tank and dipped me up to the neck in the water; oh! ah! the pain in my heart! my hand is torn in pieces! *Vivécabhüshaṇuḍugáru: á cáli nindá nettur émiṭ ayya?* Mr. Wiseman: What is that bleeding leg of yours? *Matihínaraogáru: adé n'andi, manavi cheyya pótu v'unnánu; grahanam samayamló snánam chési canṭham lótu niḷḷaló nilutsunḍi mantram v'upadéṣam autú v'unḍagá diccumálina jelagalu vachchi, cáḷḷ anní pici, netturu collu chésinavi.* Mr. Senseless: That's it, I was going to tell you; during the eclipse while I was standing in the water up to my neck and receiving charm instruction the confounded leeches came and tore at my legs and plundered my blood. (I fear that almost all Telugus believe in scorpion charm and in all sorts of charms, not only for prevention but for cure; thus one of my servants was induced with much difficulty to have himself injected for malaria; the doctor used a particularly fine needle, because the man was so frightened; the needle broke and the doctor could not extract the broken part; the man left my service to go to his village and have the needle extracted by charms. My servants also employ charms to discover house-thieves, sometimes successfully, as the culprit gets frightened and confesses.)

jemuḍu, cactus, milk-hedge; this is the general word for all cactuses; the common big cactus is *bommajemuḍu*, corrupt for *brahmajemuḍu*. (Tip: when short of gum, go to the milk-hedge.)

jemuḍucáci, crow pheasant (*centropus sinensis*), a very common bird in the Telugu country; he is the cactus crow presumably because he often flies out of cactus hedges.

jenḍá, flag. Hindustani.

jeppuṭa, to say, for *cheppuṭa*.

jerri, centipede.

jeṭṭi, wrestler.

jeṭṭipaṭṭu, wrestling.

jeṭṭipóru, wrestling match.

jé! victory! a salutation; from *jayam*, victory; also *jéyi*.

jébu, pocket. *vaidyuḍu: gumpul unna tsóṭici pó vaddu, ní árógyam cheḍi pótundi. rógi: pócapóté ná vrütti sága-danḍi. vaidyuḍu: ní vrütti yémiṭi? rógi: jébu dongatanam.* Doctor: You must not go into crowds, you will lose your health. Patient: Can't help that, it is my trade. Doctor: What is your trade? Patient: Pickpocket. *váḍu ná jébulóni rúcalu dongalinchináḍu*, he picked my pocket of my cash; *jébuló vésucunnánu*, I put it in my pocket; *nimishamló doranu jébuló vésucórá?* can't you put the Collector into your pocket in a minute?

jéburumálu, pocket handkerchief.

jéjé, god or goddess; the Telugu word for Sanskrit *dévuḍu*, which is commoner.

jéma, guava; also *záma*.

jéna, span. About a foot. *jéneḍu*, span-long.

jépaṭṭuṭa, to catch hold of; for *ché-paṭṭuṭa*.

jérlapaḍuṭa, to fall back against; also *chéragila paḍuṭa*.

jérpuṭa, to join; for *chérpuṭa*.

jésina, done; for *chésina*.

jéyuṭa, to do; for *chéyuṭa*.

jhamja, wind; a literary word for *gáli*.

jharamu, torrent. Skt. *jharamu anagá conḍa nadi. jharam* means hill stream; as the child's primer has to explain, for it is not a colloquial word.

jhúṭá, false. Hindustani.

jhúṭácóruḍu, rogue; also *jhúṭácóru. nívu vaṭṭi jhúṭácóruv ani nénu yerugu-dunu*, I know you are an out and out dissembler.

jiḍḍu, grease. *mana v'úḷḷó vódhrulu múcalu múcalugá vachchi, murici guḍ-ḍalató mulagaḍam chéta, Gódávari jiḍḍu téri nallagá Yamuna nadi autú v'unnadi*, our village vodders (digging caste) come crowd upon crowd, bathe in the Godavari with their dirty clothes on, and turn it into a black Styx swimming in grease (brahmin intolerance; they think sacred waters should be preserved for brahmins; so also at the Courtallum falls).

jiddu, emnity.

jiguru, gum, glue.

jihva, tongue. Skt. for Telugu *náluca. burracu vaca gunamu, jihvacu vaca ruchi*, tastes differ and no two heads are made alike. *ná musali campu nícú vaddu, ní paḍutsu campu nácú vaddu, jihvacu y'impugá véḷacu mátram bhójanam peḍudú*, old man to young wife: you don't like the smell of old man, I don't like the smell of young girl; only give me tasty food every day.

jilacarra, cummin; also *jílacarra*; means also 'fiddlesticks', cummin not being appreciated by Telugus as it deserves.

jilajilamanuṭa, to tingle; onomato-poeic.

jilibili, nice.

jillá, district. Hindustani; also *zillá*; the old records use *zillá*.

jilladáruḍu, head of a district. Hindustani.

jillébi, a sweetmeat.

jilléḍu, a weed (*asclepias gigantea*), very common in the fields; its only use is medicinal. *téṭici jilléḍ éṭicin?* what's the good of the swallow-wort to the bee? (it being bitter to the taste); *jilléḍu cheṭṭu vellaginchi ḍáni véru gandham vrásté yeṭuvanṭi télu cuṭṭiná pótundi,* pull up a swallow-wort, smear juice from its root, and any scorpion's bite will go.

jinca, black-buck. The *jinca* is the *váhanam* of the Wind God; i.e. he rides an antelope.

jiráyati, cultivation. Hindustani. *jiráyati bhúmulu* are assessed lands as opposed to *inams* and *jiráyati rayitu* is the holder of such as opposed to *inamdar*; *má jiráyati* is simply our land.

jirru, the noise the cricket makes, loud chirp; onomatopoeic like the English chirp, chirrup.

jirruna, suddenly; onomatopoeic.

jitamu, conquered. Skt.

jiténdriyuḍu, self-controlled. Skt. From *jitam*, conquered, and *indriyam*, senses. *jiténdriyuḍai y'unnáḍu* means he controls his senses completely, he is entirely continent.

jittu, prank, trick; *láyarla jittulu,* lawyer's tricks.

jittulamári, trickster.

jíḍi, cashew; also *jíḍimámiḍi*. *jíḍimámiḍi cheṭṭu modaṭa Dacshiṇa América déṣamu nunḍi mana déṣamunacu té baḍinadi,* the cashew was introduced into India from South America.

jíḍipappu, cashew nut or kernel.

jílacarra, cummin, fiddlesticks; also *jílacarra*.

jínamu, namda, pad which is put under the saddle; *namdá,* which is the Hindustani, is the commoner word.

jínu, saddle. Hind. from Persian *zín*.

jíráḍuṭa, to sweep.

jírnamu, digestion, digested. Skt. *nénu ráḷḷu tini jírnam chésu có galanu,* I can digest stones; *mitangá tágité déhánici bahu manchidi; annam jírnam autundi; vanṭló khuldságá v'unṭundi,* moderate drinking is to be commended; it assists digestion and makes glad the heart of man (*c'est que le vin donne de la gaîté*; makes one feel jolly, bucks one up).

jírnamulaina, worn out. *ṣúdralacu yengili y'annamunu, chinigi baṭṭalunu, pollu dhányamunu, jírnamulaina dup-paṭulunu iyya valenu,* resurrection rice, torn clothes, empty ears, worn-out sheets are good enough for sudras (but if you give a present to a brahmin it must of course be of the best).

jírnintsuṭa, to be digested, wear away. *sukhajádyamulu vanṭini jírninchi v'un-ṭavi ganuca, bógamuváḷḷacu santánam élá calugutundi?* how can dancing-girls with bodies worn out by venereal disease produce children?

jíruṭa, to dangle.

jítagáḍu, hired man, wage-earner. *chinna jítagáḷḷu yenta cshóbha paḍu-táró, vandala coddi jitálu putstsuconé váḷḷacu mícu yémi telustundi?* what do you people with your salaries in hundreds understand of the sufferings of people on small pay?

jítamu, pay, salary. *jítamú batyamú lécunḍá tóḍélu mécalu cástán ann aṭṭu,* like the wolf saying he would guard the goats without pay or perquisite. *gumastá: nácu jítam tsállad anḍi! vartacuḍu: míc ippuḍu yém y'istun-námu? gumastá: yém iyyaḍam léd anḍi, mundugá paricsha chéstám anṭé úric á pani chéstunnán anḍi. varta-cuḍu: aité vachché nela nunchí renḍin-ṭalu chést álé.* Clerk: I want more pay, sir. The Boss: What are we giving you now? Clerk: Nothing, you said you would try me first and I am working for nothing. The Boss: That being so we must double your pay from next month; *jítamu léni naucaru, cópamu léni dora,* the master must keep his temper if he pays his servant no wages.

jíva-, live (in compounds). Skt. *jívadantamu,* solid ivory; *jívaratnamu,* gem of the first water.

jívamu, life. Skt. More usually

jívanamu. véyéla, vánini jívamutó vadalaru, in short they won't leave him alive.

jívanamu, life, livelihood, means of subsistence, profession. Skt. *adi ná jívanam*, that is what I live by, as the ryot objects to the Land Acquisition officer who is compulsorily acquiring part of his land; *váḍu ná jívanamu paḍa coṭṭináḍu*, he took away my bread.

jívanópádhi, livelihood. Skt., from *jívam*, life, and *upádhi*, means.

jívaratnamu, gem of the first water; from *jíva*, live, and *ratnam*, gem. *chícaṭló jívaratnam*, a light shining in the darkness; *jívaratnam y'ittaḍini podigité ratnánici yémi lópamu*, though this gem (of say, a Collector) is set in brass (by not being promoted to the silver setting of the Board or the gold setting of Council), it does not diminish his lustre.

jívarúpamu, the living image. *á biḍḍa tanḍri jívarúpamu*, that child is a living image of its father.

jíválu, cattle, live-stock (the same idea as English live-stock).

jívi, a living creature. Skt.

jívintsuṭa, to live. Skt.

jívitacálamu, life-time. Skt.

jívitacharitra, biography.

jívitamu, living, existence. Skt.

jívuḍu, alive. *jívan mrütuḍu, mrüta jívuḍu*, the good man still lives when dead, the bad man is dead alive.

jócyamu, concern. *induló nácu jócyamu lédu*, no concern of mine, as the Collector says when they petition him for a well (which is for the taluk board), or about a dispute (which is for the civil courts); also *zócyamu*.

júṭamu, matted hair such as is worn by hermits. Skt.

jvalanamu, burning. Skt. Used in books only.

jvalintsuṭa, to burn, shine. Skt. Used in books only.

jvaramu, fever. *tsalijvaramu* is malaria; the word used in the Village Officers' Manual, *mányapu jvaramu*, is a purely Northern Circars word and means the Agency fever; *y'í páḍu jvaramu múlamugá gáni*, but for this confounded fever.

jvála, flame. Skt.

jyéshṭha, first-born. Skt. Used in literature. (I excite much admiration for my scholarship by referring to my eldest son as *má jyéshṭha cumáruḍu. yémi pánḍityam! abbá!* Lord, what a scholar!)

jyéshṭha, a month; June-July. Skt. Ploughing begins on *jyéshṭhávadhi*.

jyóti, light, radiant light. Skt. *gnyánajóti*, the radiance of knowledge.

jyótishamu, astrology. Skt. From *jyóti*, light.

jyótishcuḍu, astrologer. Skt.

jyótsna, moonlight. Skt. A literary word; *jyótsni* is a moonlight night.

Kh

kha-, prefix meaning sky from the Skt. Used in compounds to coin scientific terms in astronomy as *khadyótamu*, celestial luminary.

-khachitamaina, suffix meaning set with, studded with, inlaid. Skt.

khachchitamu, emphatic, forcible. Skt. *khachchitamaina zavábu*, an emphatic answer.

khaddaru, khaddar, homespun. Mahatma Gandhi's specific for India's woes; more commonly *khádí* in Telugu.

khaḍgamrügamu, rhinoceros. Skt.

khaḍgamu, sword. Skt. *khaḍgavádamu*, the argument of the sword.

khajáná, treasury. Hindustani.

khajjá, quarrel. Hindustáni. Also *cajjá. mí vaḍaghali tenghali khajjálu cáli pónu*, confound your Vadagalai and Tengalai quarrels; as was remarked by the Collector of Chingleput when the Vadagalais and Tengalais of Conjeeveram, who had been disputing for 1000 years, and had had their case decided 500 times already, came and bothered him to decide it again.

khalamu, threshing floor. Skt. Also *callamu,* which is commoner.

khaluḍu, wretch. Skt. Only used in books.

khanḍamu, piece, chapter of a book, act of a play, district, country, continent. Skt., from *khan,* to cut; the word means anything separated. *í suvásana yocca mostaru tsústé y'idi yeccaḍidó paşchima khanḍam nunchi sísálaló digumati aina amúlya parimaḷangá tóstu v'unnadi gáni, mana déşapudigá tótsaḍam lédu,* from the nature of the fragrance I should say it was a precious scent imported in bottles from the west and not produced in our country. *bhúkhanḍamu* is the ordinary word for continent.

khanḍanamu, cutting, criticism. In English also criticism may be cutting.

khanḍinchi véyuṭa, to refute.

khanḍitamugá, clearly, forcibly. *khanḍitamugá chepputa* is to assert; *khanḍitangá béram áḍuconuṭa* is to make a clear bargain (*patti chiari, amici cari,* as the Italians say), a thing it is wise to do beforehand with gharry-wallahs and suchlike.

khandí, a candy, a measure often of 500 lb., but sometimes more or less; the usual cotton candy is a little less.

khandrica, part of village. Skt., from root *khan.* A severed portion of a village granted as *inam.*

khanḍuvá, upper cloth (male); also *canḍuvá. bandrasu khanḍuvá,* valuable Benares silk cloth for a man to wear over his shoulders.

khangu, clang; onomatopoeic. *khangumanuṭa,* to clang, sound of a bell.

khararáná, trustworthy. Hindustani.

khararáru, agreement, contract. Hindustani. *Dora: míló vivábam anagá yémiṭi? Míra Sahébu: peḷḷichésucunnavááḍú peḷḷichésucunnadí bratici v'unna anta cálamú vacarini vacaru míri tiragacunḍá v'unḍaḍánici chésucuné khararu. Dora: saré, mír annaṭṭugá adi vivábam chésucunévaru y'iddarú yáva jívamú vacarini míri vacaru tirugacunḍánú, vacari cashṭa-sukhamulacu, vacaru autú y'iddaru calisi, vaccarugá v'undéṭ aṭṭugánú chésucunna canṭrácṭu; aité canṭrácṭucu yémi mukhyangá v'unḍa valenó míru cheppa galará? Míra Sahébu: chésucunévááḷḷu y'iddarú sammatipaḍa valenu; álá sammati lécunḍá balavanta peṭṭi chésté yé khararu chelladu. Dora: vivábam náṭici áldganṭi sammati y'ivvaḍánici şacti caligi v'unḍaḍánici váru yucta vayassu vachchinavárugá cúdá v'unḍan accara lédá? Míra Sahébu: tappacunḍá v'unḍa valenu; álá léca póté vivábálé cávu. bhánchót! bráhmalaló chésé peḷḷiḷḷu yémi peḷḷiḷḷ andé? váṭi canté bommala peḷḷiḷḷ ainá manchivé.* Collector: How do you Muslims define marriage? Míra Sahib: A contract that bridegroom and bride will not transgress one against the other the whole of their lives. Collector: Yes, as you say, a contract that the contracting parties will not transgress against one another the whole of their lives, will share weal and woe, will be two in one; but can you say what is the most important element in a contract? Míra Sahib: The consent of both the contracting parties; a forcible contract made without such consent is void. Collector: In order to be able to give such consent on the marriage day must not the parties have reached the age of discretion? Míra Sahib: Of course; otherwise it is no marriage at all. Lord, what marriages are the brahmin marriages? Doll-marriages are better marriages.

khararáruṇáma, deed of contract. Hindustani. Common in the old records.

kharídu, price. Hindustani; the common word. The Telugu is *vela.*

kharjúram, date. Skt. *kharjúrapu cheṭṭu,* the date tree; *kharjúrapu panḍu,* date.

khartsu, expense, debit. Hindustani; the ordinary and common word. *váni sampádana váni khartsunacu sarigá saripaḍutundi,* he makes both ends meet.

khaskhas, cuscus; a grass screen or mat hung over doors and windows and wettened to keep the heat out in the weather inadequately described as the hot.

khádanamu, eating. Skt. Used in compounds as *mámsakhádi,* flesh-eater.

khádí, homespun; the khadder advocated by Mahatma Gandhi.

khálí, vacancy. Hindustani. The ordinary and common word for vacancy in a job or office, in a room or house, &c. *í coṭṭu kháli chéyinchi v'unchinánu,* I have kept this godown vacant; *cul abhimánam v'unḍaḍam vidháyacam ganuca, yélágainá y'ikha mundu khálílu vachchin appuḍu paṭṭu paṭṭi manaváḷḷacé y'ippistánu,* it being my duty to observe *esprit de caste* I shall see that vacancies go to our own people.

khámandu, master, owner. Hindustani. *bhúkhámandu* is land-owner.

khásá, servant. Hindustani.

khátá, ledger. Hindustani; also *cátá.*

kháyamu, settled. Hindustani.

kháyaparatsuṭa, to confirm.

khédamu, grief. Skt. One of the numerous words for grief; quite common.

khédintsuṭa, to grieve. Skt.

khéla, khélanamu, sport, dalliance. Skt. A book word.

khilamu, ruined, dilapidated. Skt. Used in books.

khillá, hill fort. Hindustani.

khilladárudu, officer commanding hill fort. Hindustani.

khinnamu, grief. Skt. A book word.

khudduna, personally. Hindustani. The Collector is often asked, in petitions and orally, to inspect *khudduna.*

khulásá, happiness. Hindustani. *álá khulásá paḍi pótávu?* why are you so jubilant?

khuláságá, comfortably, happily. Hindustani. *mitangá tágité déhánici bahu manchidi; annam jírnam autundi; vanṭló khuláságá v'unṭundi,* moderate drinking is very good for the body, it assists digestion and makes you feel comfortable.

khúni, murder. Hindustani.

khyáti, fame. Skt.; also *vikhyáti* and *prakhyáti. idi vara dácá tama khyáti vinṭú rávaḍamé cáni, yeppuḍú darṣanam cheyya lédu,* I have been often hearing of Your Honour's fame, but never paid you a visit before.

L

labalaba, labbuna, thud-thud, onomatopoeic; beating oneself on the mouth in distress, and so on; also means much. *v'úr antá góla yetti labbuna mottucunṭú v'unnáru,* the whole village (when the Collector's peons have been making a raid and collecting chickens, &c.) is wailing and beating its bosom and lamenting.

labdhamu, obtained, quotient. Skt. Also *labhyam*; in arithmetic these words mean the quotient in division, what is obtained, the result; 10 *inṭini chéta bhágimpagá vachchina labdhamu,* the quotient obtained by dividing by 10.

labdhamauṭa, to be obtained.

labdhi, gain.

labhintsuṭa, to happen, to be lucky enough to get. Skt. *daivicamugá labhinchina y'í samayam,* this God-given opportunity; *ní punyam chéta janma janmálacú nícu y'í bharté labhistáḍu,* by virtue you will gain this same husband again from life to life; *nívu tsúpina pánḍityánici tagina birudu péru nícu ṣáṣvitangá labhinchinadi,* for the scholarship you have shown you have obtained a suitable title of honour for ever; *mí darṣanam labhintsaḍam valla néḍu sudinam,* as we have been able to see you to-day, we shall mark the day with a white stone (as flatterers say to the Collector).

labhyamu, obtained. Skt.; same as *labdham. ná punyam chéta néḍu y'í ammáyi chéti vaḍḍana cúḍá nácu labhyam ainadi,* my virtue has had its reward to-day in the serving of food by this maiden.

lacca, wax, lac. Skt. *aṭuculacca,* shellac; *coyyalacca,* sticklac.

lacóṭa, envelope. Marathi. The peons, however, understand *cavaru* (cover) better.

lacsha, lakh, 100,000. Skt. *lacsha*

nacshtramul ainá vaca chanḍruḍu cádu, one moon gives more light than 100,000 stars; *saválacsha*, a lakh and a quarter (*sava*, quarter) is used in the phrase *savâlacsha granthamu*, which means an endless quarrel.

lacshanamaina, handsome. Skt.

lacshanamu, sign, quality. Skt. *varshalacshanamulu*, signs of rain; *jvaralacshanamulu*, symptoms of fever; *udyógam purusha lacshanam*, office makes the man; *vinayam panḍita lacshanamu*, modesty marks the scholar; *pichcha lacshanam yentamátramu canapaḍaḍam lédu*, he has none of the external marks of madness; *dhairyam purusha lacshanam*, courage is the mark of a man; *idéná mana nágaricatá lacshanamu?* is this a mark of our civilization? (e.g. to marry our daughters off at eight); *chinna cathalacu idi y'iṭl ani haddulu lacshanamulu vráyuṭacu vílu lédu*, it is impossible to lay down the limits and characteristics of the short story.

lacshanamu, prosody. Skt. *í cálamuló lacshanamu teliyac' unḍáné cávyálu vrás ést unnáru*, nowadays men who do not know the elements of prosody try to write verse.

lacshavattula, 100,000 candles. Skt., from *lacsha* and *vatti*, wick, candle. *lacshavattula vratamu* is a vow of 100,000 candles taken for the soul of a departed husband, &c. *mí vanṭi Sómayázula péḷḷavárė y'iṭuvanṭi rancu munḍala chéta lacsha vattula vratamulu modalainavi chéyinchi sancóchimpaca hastódacamulu putstsuconi mundugá bhójanamucu siddha paḍuduru*, for all your high-sounding ecclesiastical titles, you are ready to perform for adulterous widows rites and ceremonies for the souls of their departed husbands and, without a moment's hesitation, let them lave your hands and place your repast before you; also *lacshavattula nómu*.

lacshádhicári, possessor of *lakhs*, corresponding to our millionaire. *bhicshádhicári ainá cá vale, lacshádhicári ainá cá vale*, you must either be a master millionaire or a sturdy beggar.

Lacshmaṇuḍu, Rama's brother.

Lacshmí, Vishnu's wife, the goddess of wealth; also *Mahálacshmí*. *Lacshmí* is also a very common female name.

Lacshmípati, Lakshmi's husband, i.e. Vishnu.

lacshmívâramu, Thursday; also *guruvâramu*.

lacshyamu, mark, regard. Skt. *ná y'andu vánici lacshyamu lédu*, he does not mind me, he does not care for me; *tamac émi lacshyamu lédu*, you don't care a bit; *bottigá lacshyam lédu*, no attention at all.

lacshyamuchéyuṭa, lacshyamupeṭṭuṭa, to care for, esteem, respect, pay attention to. Skt.

laddi, dung of quadrupeds (horse, ass, elephant, and camel, but not horned animals). The general word for dung is *péḍa*. Skt. *gómayamu* is used for the sacred cow-dung.

laddipurugu, dung-beetle.

laḍḍu, a common sweetmeat.

lagga, escalade. *laggaleccuṭa*, to scale a fort; *cshanamu niluvacunḍá álaguna laggalacu yeccité yélágu?* how is it to be done if you are in such a devil of a hurry? (you can't take the fort by assault like that).

lagáyatu, from the beginning, since. Hindustani. *í rózu lagáyatu*, beginning from to-day.

laghuvu, light (in weight). Skt. The Telugu is *télica*.

lagnamu, rising of a constellation, auspicious time. Skt. The original meaning is 'contact', e.g. congress of the sun with a sign of the zodiac. *peḷḷi lagnam peṭṭuconnáru*, they fixed an auspicious time for the marriage.

lagnasamayamu, auspicious time. Skt., from *lagnam* and *samayamu*, time. *lagna samayamló vachchi vadhúvarulunu áṣírvadinchi pó valasinad ani prárthinchinánu*, I prayed that I might be present at the auspicious moment and bless the bride and bridegroom and then go.

laguvu, light. Skt., same as *laghuvu*.

lajja, shame. *í lajjá bharamunacu nénu tála tsálanu*, I cannot bear the burden of this shame; *purusha bhúshaṇamaina lajja viḍichi*, throwing off the shame which is the embellishment of a man (sarcasm; it is women that false modesty is supposed to embellish).

lajjahínuḍu, shameless man.

lalana, a fair damsel. Skt.

-laláma, a suffix meaning excellent, especially of women. Skt. *mani lalámamu,* peerless among women; *ramaníla lalámulu,* loveliest of women; *sádhvíla lalámamu,* the most virtuous of women; *bhúpála lalámuḍu,* the noblest of kings.

laláṭamu, forehead. Skt. *laláṭamula y'andu paṭṭe námamulanu peṭṭú conḍuró, á vaishnavulu lócamunu nimishamuló pavitramu chéyuduru,* Vaishnavites who put the Vaishnavite marks on their forehead (these represent the female organ of generation) in one minute purify the earth.

lalitamu, lovely. Skt. A book word.

lalitángi, woman with a lovely figure. Skt. A book word.

lambamu, long. Skt. A book word in compounds like *lambacarnamu,* the long-eared, i.e. a hare.

lambádi, gypsy; also brinjarries. Before there were roads or wheeled vehicles they used to keep large herds of pack-bullocks and conduct the salt trade, carry the baggage of armies and so on; they have now mostly settled down to agriculture combined with petty thieving; their women wear a picturesque costume.

lanca, island. Skt. *yéṭi y'ítacu lanca métacú sari,* the grazing on the island is hardly worth the swim across (the game is not worth the candle).

Lanca, The Island, i.e. mythological Ceylon. Skt. Modern Ceylon is *Simhaḷadvípamu. Lancaló puṭṭina vár ellá rácshasulé,* all are racshasas in Lanka.

lancanamu, fasting. Skt., from *langhanam.* In the maxim *langhanam param aushadham,* fasting is the best medicine, the word is written in the Sanskrit way, the proverb being a Sanskrit one; *nálugu lancanálu chésté vacca debbanu paḍi rózula náṭici vaḷḷu nimmaḷangá v'unḍunu,* do a few fasts and you will cure yourself at one blow in ten days.

lance, link. *vánici dudducu lance,* he and money are linked together; i.e. he is much attached to money; *ḍabbucú práṇamunacú lance,* money and life are linked; *cheruvulu lancelugá v'unnavi,* linked or connected tanks; *lancepíṭa,* a plank coupling bullocks.

lance peṭṭuṭa, lancintsuṭa, to link, couple, e.g. to yoke two bullocks together.

langaru, anchor. Hindustani. *váru langaru vésináru,* they cast anchor.

langhanamu, fasting. Skt. Same as *lancanam*; *langhanam param aushadham,* fasting is the best medicine.

langóṭi, loin-cloth. Hindustani. The Telugu is *góchi.*

lanja, lanje, whore, the common word; *lanja coḍucu,* whoreson, is the commonest of all terms of abuse; others are *gáḍidacoḍucu,* son of an ass; *cuccalacoḍucu,* son of a dog.

lanjaricamu, prostitution.

lanjecáḍu, whoremonger.

lanjecoḍucu, whoreson. *lanjecoḍucá! vaidyamu nimittamu vachchina gáḍida coḍucav aina pacshmuna, tsápa tsuṭṭaló dúra valasina pani níc émi vachchinadirá?* you son of a whore, even if you are a whoreson doctor come to attend on my wife, why should you burrow into a mat?

lantsagonḍi, bribe-taker.

lantsampantsam, bribes and perquisites; reduplicative of *lantsamu,* bribe; *lantsampantsam tinaḍam udyóga dharmam,* to take bribes and perquisites is part of one's official duty (this view is obsolete and was always contrary to regulations).

lantsamu, bribe; the common word for a common thing. *í vedhava vyavahára muló tahaṣṣíludárugáru lantsamu putstsuconnár ayyá?* and so the tahsildar has taken a bribe for a rotten thing like that?

lascaru, lascar. Hindustani. The original meaning is army and soldier; it is now used chiefly of the lascars or peons of the D.P.W. and of sailors.

lata, creeper. Skt. A book word for *tíga*; *latagrúhamu* is a leaf hut, *latángi* a slender-limbed girl.

laṭṭuva, cudgel; also *laṭṭu.*

laucicamu, secular. Skt., from *lócam*, world. *laucica vyavahāramulu* are secular matters.
laucicuḍu, a secular brahmin as opposed to *vaidicuḍu*, a clerical brahmin.
laucyamu, secular matters. Skt., from *lócam*, world. *laucyam yeriginavāru*, people who understand secular things.
lauhamu, metallic. Skt., from *lóham*, metal.
lavalėṣamu, minute. Skt. *ravanta lavalėṣamainanu yeruganivāḍu*, a complete ignoramus.
lavamu, particle. Skt.
lavaṇamu, salt. Skt. The Telugu is *uppu*; *lavaṇam* is used in compounds and chemistry manuals; *lavaṇadrāvacamu* is hydrochloric acid (*acidum muriaticum*).
lavangálu, cloves. Skt.
layamu, destruction. Skt. *pralaya* is the final destruction of the universe, cosmic regression.
lá, law. English. *lá pracáram álá cávalen émi?* does the law require that?
lábhacaramu, profitable. Skt. *mósálú, abaddhálú conta cálam lábhacarangá v'unná, caḍapaṭa satyamé jayistundi*, deceit and lies are profitable for a short time but honesty wins in the end (honesty is the best policy).
lábhamu, profit. Skt. *modaṭici mósamu, lábhánici guddulāṭa*, fighting for the profits after losing the capital.
lácconuṭa, to seize; from *láguṭa*, pull, and auxiliary *conuṭa*.
lácshanicuḍu, grammarian. Skt., from *lacshanam*.
láḍamu, horse-shoe. Hindustani.
láḍamucaṭṭuṭa, to shoe a horse.
lághavamu, lightness. Skt., from *laghuvu*.
lágintsuṭa, to cause to pull.
lágu, láguna, suffixes meaning like. *pánacāmló pulla lágu*, like a straw in one's drink; *ataḍu cheppina láguna*, as he said; *adi ayyé láguna*, to get this done; *éláguna*, like this; *áláguna*, like that; *yéláguna*, how?
láguṭa, to pull, extract. *ná cálamló nénu yenni vidhálanó ḍabbu lágédánni*, in my time I used to get money (corruptly) in every sort of way; *yeddu yenḍacu lága, dunnapótu nīḍacu lága*, the bullock pulled towards the sun, the buffalo towards the shade; *vánini pichchi vánini chési, ḍabb antá lági conáru*, they fooled him out of all his money.
lálana, coaxing. Skt.
lálintsuṭa, to wheedle. Skt.
lánṭaru, lantern. English. *lánṭaru paruvu cósam*, a (street) lantern for dignity (municipal councillors have such lamps put up opposite their houses).
látarí, lottery. English. *Lacshmayya: í mōṭáru cáru mīcu yeṭlá vachchinadi? Vencayya: láṭariló. Lacshmayya: mí nambaru gelichindi cábólu? Vencayya: nénu láṭariló ḍabbu peṭṭa lédu; láṭarí yérpáṭu chésindi néné.* Smith: How did you get that car? Jones: In a lottery. Smith: Did you draw the winning number? Jones: No, I did not buy a ticket; I ran the lottery.
láṭicarra, staff, especially the one used by the police to disperse meetings.
láu, thick, stout, stoutness, manure. *láu léni chénu, léga léni áu*, a field without manure, a cow without a calf.
láupiṭṭa, a sort of plover (*cursarius coromandelicus*).
láuváḍu, stout or fat man.
lávanyamu, beauty. Skt.
láyakhu, fit. Hindustani. Used as a revenue term—*ságu láyakh* means fit for cultivation.
láyamu, stable. English; from *lines* in which horses and their syces were kept.
láyaru, lawyer. English.
lecca, lekka, account. *angaḍiváḍu ná mída ból eḍu lecca pentsuconi cūrtsunnáḍu*, the shopkeeper has run up the devil of an account against me; *váḍu nácu lekhá pátramá?* what do I care for him? (has he account or bond against me?); *yémayyá, gumástágárú lekhal anni siddhangá v'unnavá?* ho, clerk, are all the accounts ready?
leccaléni, numberless.
leccapeṭṭuṭa, to count, esteem, regard, mind. *illu tsorabaḍi y'inṭi vásálu lecca peṭṭináḍ aṭa*, he got into the house and counted the rafters (preparatory to making a false claim to it); *dáni lecca peṭṭa valasina cád ayya*, never mind that.

leccatéltsuṭa, to balance the account.
leccatsútsuṭa, to look over the account, make out the account.
leccintsuṭa, to calculate.
lega-, prefix meaning up; from *létsuṭa*, to rise.
legatíyuṭa, to pull up. *khálilu vachchin appuḍu paṭṭupaṭṭi manavdḷḷacé y'ippinchi, váḷḷanu paici legatiyya valen ané v'unnadi*, when vacancies occur we must try hard and get them for our own caste people and give them a leg up.
leggoṭṭuṭa, to knock up, drive out.
lemmu, get up; imperative of *létsuṭa*.
lempa, cheek; also *chempa*.
lempacáya, slap.
lenḍi, get up, come along, of course, to be sure; imperative plural of *létsuṭa*. *míru cúḍá yevvaró stríla valaló paḍi, peḷḷi cávalen ani córé cálam vastundi, cáni ráca pódu lenḍi*, to be sure the time will come without fail when you will fall into the toils of women and want to be married; *veḷḷi pódâmu lenḍi*, come let us be going (a very common expression).
lessa, good, good health (a greeting, &c.). *déṣabhásħal andu telugu lessa*, of the vernaculars Telugu is the best (a line from Krishna Deva Raya); *Garuḍáya lessá anṭé, Ṣésháya lessa annaṭṭu*, how d'ye do? said Garuda, how d'ye do? replied Sesha; this is a proverb from a story about how Sesha, the snake, being on Siva's wrist, was impertinent to Vishnu's kite, Garuda; being in a safe place he wasn't afraid Garuda would carry him off to his larder.
lessagá, all right, well, soundly; *lessagá coṭṭuṭa* is to give a good thrashing.
-lé, emphatic suffix. *tsálulé v'úrucó*, come now, that will do, hold your tongue; *iccaḍa unnáru lé*, never mind, they are here; it can't be helped.
lé-, prefix meaning tender, young; short for *léta*; *lévayasu*, tender age; *lénaguvu*, slight laugh.
lé! get up! imperative of *létsuṭa*.
lé, not; short for *lédu*.
léca, without, unable, from root *lé*, not, negative verbal participle; *cúṭici léca* (in want of food), starving; *rá léca*, unable to come; *tsúḍa léca*, unable to bear the sight of it.
léca, or. *váḍu ásucavi léca nimisha cavi*, he is an improvisator or extempore poet.
lécaléca, at last. *lécaléca vánici oca coḍucu puṭṭináḍu*, at long last a son was born to him.
lécané, without (emphatic). *cáryamu lécané cáryamu puṭṭadu*, no effect without a cause.
lécapóté, if you have not, else, otherwise, if that is impossible; opposite of *caligité*, if you have; one of the commonest expressions in the language; the vulgar say *lácapóté* or *lácpóté*; also, redundantly, *lácpóté mánenu. appu lécapóté v'uppu ganjé mélu*, it is better to eat rice-water and salt than to be in debt; *caligité cáḷḷu muyyu, lécapóté mócáḷḷu muyyu*, wear a dress down to your feet if you can afford it, to your knees if you can't (cut your coat according to your cloth); *cheppévádici siggu lécapóté, vinéváḍic ainá vivécamu vaddá?* if the man who tells the story has no shame, should not the listener at least have some sense? (i.e. the sense to disbelieve it); *ná cóḍi cumpaṭi lécapóté yélágu tellavárut unnadi?* as the old woman said, how would the world go round without my cock and chafing-dish?
lécapóvuṭa, to be without, not to have, not to be.
lécapóyinanduna, because it didn't or wasn't.
lécari, writer. Skt., from *lékha*.
léchipóvuṭa, to go away; a very common word; *léchipó!* off with you!; from *létsuṭa*, to rise.
lécunḍa, without. *ataḍu lécunḍa* (he not being) *ná valla* (my possibility) *cádu*, I cannot do without him; *váḍu tala tóca lécunḍá máṭláḍuṭú unnáḍu*, his talk has no head or tail to it; *jítamu batyamú lécunḍá tóḍélu mécalu cástán ann aṭṭu*, as the wolf said, I will guard the goats without pay or perquisite.
lécunṭé, if it isn't or hasn't. *guḷḷó dévunici naivédyamu lécunṭé, pújári puḷihóracu yédchináḍ aṭa*, like the

priest who cried out for pulihora when the God hadn't even naivédyam; *tetstsuconṭé bhónchéyi, lécunṭé v'úracunḍu*, if you can get anything to eat, eat, if you can't, keep quiet.

lédanuṭa, to deny, to say no; from *lédu*, no, and *anuṭa*, to say.

lédá, or not. *auná lédá?* yes or no?

léḍi, antelope, deer. *úra cunṭu, aḍavi léḍi*, lame in the village, an antelope in the jungle (a man who prefers sport to work); *léḍici léchinadé prayánam*, the antelope is ready for the journey as soon as it rises.

lédu, not. *álú lédu, tsúlú lédu, coḍucu péru Sómalingam*, naming the boy Somalingam before you are wedded or bedded (counting your chickens before they are hatched); *manóvyádhici mandu lédu*, there is no medicine for a mind diseased.

léḍu, he is not. *anni telisinaváḍu léḍu, yémi teliyaniváḍu léḍu*, there is no one who knows everything and no one who knows nothing.

léḍu, he is not able. *anna tsoravé gáni, acshara tsorava léḍu*, he can get round his food all right but not his books.

léduṭrá? not, sirrah? (to an inferior); *lédu*, not, combined with *óri*, sirrah, contracted to *rá*; *accara léduṭrá?* is it not required?

léga, légadúḍa, a sucking calf. *áu oca léganu vésindi*, the cow has dropped a calf; *láu léni chénu, léga léni áu*, an unfattened field and a calfless cow; *légadúḍa podugu talató cummutsunnadi*, the calf butts the udder. The derivation is from root *lé-*, young, and root *can-*, to bring forth.

léhanamu, licking. Skt. To lick in Telugu is *nácuṭa*; *léhanam* is a book word.

lékha,* letter. Skt. A book word for *uttaram*.

lékhanamu, writing. Skt. The Telugu is *vráyuṭa* or *ráyuṭa*.

lémi, want, as opposed to *calimi*, having. *calimi lémulu cávaṭi cunḍalu*, having, not having, pots of the shoulder-yoke (the ups and downs of life); *varsham lémici urumulu yeccuva*, incessant thunder forebodes drought.

lému, we can't.

lénagavu, budding laugh, i.e. a smile; from *lé-*, tender, and *nagavu*, laugh.

lénappuḍu, when one is not there. *bharta: nuvvu úḷḷó lén appuḍu dongala tsappuḍu ainadi, parugettuconi meṭlu digi cindici vachchánu. bhárya: dongalanu paṭṭucunnárá? bharta: dongalu inṭi cappu mida nilutsunnáru, andu chéta vílu paḍa lédu.* Husband: Thieves came when you were away; I ran down the steps. Wife: Did you catch the thieves? Husband: No, I couldn't, they were on the roof.

lénaṭṭu, as if not. *ataḍu lén aṭṭu telisi*, hearing he was not there; *ataḍu lén aṭṭ unnadi*, it seems he is not there.

lénayya, master of nothing. *caliginayya caliginayyacé peṭṭunu, lénayya caliginayyacé peṭṭunu*, the rich and the poor will feast the rich but no one will feast the poor.

lénḍlu, deer; plural of *léḍi*.

-léni, devoid of, false. *teliviléni* and *buddhiléni* are the ordinary words for stupid; *tappuléni*, faultless; *nóruléni*, dumb; *dóvaléni aḍavi*, a pathless forest.

léni, not having, not being, poor, not being able. *léni v'udári canṭé caligina monḍi mélu*, better deal with a close-fisted Croesus than a lavish Lazarus; *vanḍa léni ammacu v'oppulu menḍu, té léni ayyacu tinḍi menḍu*, the woman who can't cook is all airs and graces, the man who can't earn anything is all appetite.

lénidi, what is not, what you have not got. *aragintsagá lénidi aḍigité vastunnadá?* no use asking for what isn't there to be eaten; *léniddánici póté y'unnadi úḍinadi*, losing what you have in trying to get what you haven't.

lénimáṭalu, slanders.

lénipóni, utterly false, what isn't there at all, absurd. *lénipóni saukhyamulu*, vain deluding joys; *lénipóni pani*, nonsense; *lénipóni sácu*, a false pretext. *hinduvulu lénipóni dévatalacu mroccutáru*, Hindus worship gods that aren't there at all; *lénipóni anumánamu*, absurd suspicion.

lénivádu, the man who is without or the absent man. *tappulénivánni v'uppuló veyyum anndḍ aṭa,* as they say, if you want to ruin the blameless man, put him in the Salt Department (where they treat subordinates badly).

léniyeḍala, in the alternative, if not, otherwise.

lénu, I can't; I can is *galanu. váḍu nannu bhójanamunacu pilichináḍu gáni, rá 'lén ani manavi chésucunnánu,* I excused myself from dining with him.

lépanamu, smearing. Skt. The Telugu is *púyaḍam.*

lépintsuṭa, to smear.

léputa, to rouse. *inṭivánni lépi, donga chétici carra ichchin aṭṭu,* rousing the master and handing the thief a stick (running with the hare and hunting with the hounds); *nidrapóyina vánini lépa vatstsunu gáni, mélucunna vánini lépa lému,* you can rouse sleepers but not those who are awake (none so blind as those that won't see).

léru, they aren't or can't. *tappuléni váru dharaṇiló léru,* there's no one without his faults.

léṣamu, a little. Skt. *léṣamaina lédu,* there isn't even a particle; *léṣamu nácu bhayam lédu,* I am not afraid at all; *atanici ná mída préma v'unn anducu léṣamú sandéham lédu,* there is no doubt he is in love with me.

-lési, suffix meaning 'however much' or 'little', 'at the rate of'; for *-ési,* the *l* being euphonic. *mantra mahima chéta n'enta lési vintal ainanu puṭṭa vatstsunu,* the force of charms can produce miracles of any magnitude; *cástalési váḷḷu biyyélu pyás ai, v'udyógálóci vachchi, v'udyógála vakharé cheḍa coṭṭi véstú v'unnáru,* however few graduates there may be in an office, one of them in an office is enough to spoil it (won't take bribes and objects to others taking them).

léta, young, tender, light, soft. *léta vanne,* a light tint; *léta yenḍa,* soft sunlight.

létatanamu, infancy, softness.

létsuṭa, to rise. *ichchevánni tsústé tsachchéváḍ ainá létsunu,* at sight of a giving man even a dying man will rise; *yenta proddu v'unḍagá léchiná tummagunṭa vaddané tellavárinadi,* however early he got up he was still at the tank at dawn; *tóca toccina pámu láguna léchináḍu,* he sprang up like a snake whose tail has been trodden on; *léḍici léchinadé prayánamu,* deer don't pack for a journey.

léva, to rise; infinitive of *létsuṭa. cúrtsunḍi léva lédu gáni, vangunḍi tírtham veḷḷután annáḍ aṭa,* he could not get up but said he would crawl to the holy water.

lévagoṭṭintsuṭa, to get driven out; also *leggoṭṭintsuṭa,* e.g. *inṭiló nunchi,* from a house.

lévagoṭṭuṭa, to drive out; also *leggoṭṭuṭa.*

lévanettuṭa, to lift up, help up. *vánni lévanettu,* help him up.

lévatíyuṭa, to take away.

lévayasu, infancy; from *lé,* tender, and *vayasu,* age.

léviḍi, disgrace. Hindustani. *mana pratipacshulanu léviḍi coṭṭistámu,* we will shame our adversaries.

lévu, there are not (of things).

likhintsuṭa, to write, draw. Skt. *rangulató likhintsuṭa* is to paint.

likhitamu, written, drawn. Skt. *likhita sácshyam* is written or documentary evidence.

likhitapúrvacamaina, written. Skt. A legal term, opposed to oral.

lingamu, mark, phallus, element in science, gender in grammar. Skt. It is especially the phallus which symbolizes Siva; *punlingam* is the masculine in grammar, *strílingam* the feminine; *angaṭló bellamu guḷḷó lingánici naivédyamu,* offering the bazaarman's jaggery to the phallus in the temple (generous at others' expense); *lingam caṭṭuconuṭa* is to wear a small phallus (usually in a small silver case, *linga cáya,* hung by a cord round the neck).

lipháphá, envelope. Hindustani; better say *cavaru* (cover).

lipi, written characters. Skt. *dévanágara lipi,* the Devanagara script; *sannani lipi canḍlacu zabbu,* small type injures the eyes.

líla, sport. Skt.

lílávati, a sportive girl. Skt. Also a female name.

loḍaloḍa, quickly, confusedly, loosely; onomatopoeic. *ní loḍaloḍa mánu*, stop your clack; *tsoccáyi chétiló cheyi dúristé loḍa loḍam ani y'unnadi*, the sleeve is loose.

loḍita, span.

loḍiteḍu, span long. *váḍu loḍiteḍu*, he is a dwarf.

loḍugu, weak, lean, wretched. *poṭṭi gaṭṭi, poḍugu loḍugu*, short and stout, tall and weak.

loḷḷu, barking, fierce growling, snarling; onomatopoeic. *cucca nóṭló carra peṭṭité loḷḷu m'antunnadi*, if you put a stick in a dog's mouth it will growl; *loḷḷ ani carava póyinadi*, snarling it rushed on him to bite.

longuṭa, to yield. *bágá ṣicshisténé cáni pillalu yeppuḍú longaru*, spare the rod and spoil the child.

loṭaloṭa, noise of a thud, gulp, &c.; onomatopoeic. *yénugacu velaccáyalu loṭaloṭa*, a wood-apple is one gulp to an elephant; *talupulu mingévánici appaḍálu loṭaloṭalu*, appadams are one gulp to a man who eats doors.

loṭipiṭṭa, camel.

loṭṭa, hollow (of eyes). *lécaléca Lócáya puṭṭité, Lócáya cannu loṭṭa póyinadi*, when at long last Locaya was born to them he was born with sunken eyes; *tsávu tappi cannu loṭṭa póyinadi*, he escaped with hollow eyes.

-ló, suffix meaning in, on, of, at. *dáriló*, on the road; *intló*, in the house; *vachchin antaló*, on his coming; *talaló pdgá tsuṭṭuconnáḍu*, he rolled the turban round his head; *inta rátriló*, so late at night; *véliló n'unḍe ungaramu*, the ring on his finger; *máló andaru*, all of us; *paniló máṭláḍuṭa*, to talk at work; *ataḍu ná chétiló cósináḍu*, he wounded me on the hand.

ló-, prefix meaning under, below, inner, sub. *lógadi*, an inner room; *lócápu*, sub-tenant; *lócheyyi*, palm of the hand; *lómanushyuḍu*, a reserved man.

lóbaḍi, subject; from *ló*, under, and *paḍuṭa*.

lóbaḍuṭa, to be subject, to submit; from *ló*, under, and *paḍuṭa*. *asatyamu modalaina dushcáryamulac anniṭicini lóbaḍa valasi vastundi*, you have to fall into untruth and every other kind of vice; *bála vidhavalu cáma bhádhacu lóbaḍuṭa áṣcharyamá?* is it a wonder that young widows yield to the sting of desire?

lóbarutsuconuṭa, to master; from *ló*, under, *parutsuṭa*, to effect, and *conuṭa*, auxiliary verb.

lóbhamu, avarice. Skt.

lóbhi, miser. Skt. *lóbhi sommu dongaváḍi pálu*, the miser's money falls to the thief.

lóbhintsuṭa, to covet. Skt.

lócabándhavuḍu, the universal kinsman, i.e. the sun.

lócamáta, the world's mother, i.e. Lakshmi.

lócamu, world. Skt. The worlds of the gods, or heavens, are also *lócams*; there are 3 and also 7 and also 14 worlds; *ihalócam* is the world on this side, the earth; *paralócam*, the world on the other side, heaven. *cheppulu toḍuguconnavánici lócam antá tólutó cappa baḍ aṭṭu tóstunnadi*, the whole earth seems to be covered with leather to the man who wears shoes (he does not realize that naked feet may be burnt or pricked); *debba dévendra lócamu*, the stick is the way to heaven (as the Telugu schoolmaster often says; spare the rod and spoil the child); *pichchivánici lócam antá pichchi*, to the mad the whole world is mad; *lócamu verachi*, fearing the world.

lócaprasiddhamu, famous throughout the world.

lócapravádamu, common report.

lócántaraghatuḍu, dead, from *lócam*, world, *antara*, other, and *ghatuḍu*, gone.

lócánubhavamu, worldly experience; from *anubhavamu*.

lócárádhyuḍu, the universally worshipped, from *árádhintsuṭa*, to worship; i.e. God.

lóchanamu, eye. Skt. The Telugu is *cannu*.

lócheyyi, palm; the inner hand.

lócócti, proverb; from *lócamu* and *yucti*, opinion. *sámeta* is commoner.

lócópacáramu, philanthropy, universally beneficial; from *upacáram*, help. *nénu lócópacáramaina mahá vishayamunu gúrchi y'upanyasimpa póvuts unnánu*, I am going to lecture on a subject of great importance and universal utility.

lócóttamu, best in the world; from *uttamu*, excellent.

lóculu, people. Skt. *lóka*; also *janulu*.

lócuva, subject. *aḍigévánici cheppé-váḍu lócuva*, it is easier to ask than to answer; *andarici nénu lócuva, nácu Nambi Rámayya lócuva*, no one so low that he has not some one below him (thus if you scold your butler, he passes it on to the matey, who passes it on to the chokra, who passes it on to the dog-boy, who passes it on to the sweeper, who passes it on to the dog); *manam váḷḷacu yélá lócuvó, paiváḷḷacu váḷḷú álágé lócuva*, just as we are subordinate to our superiors, so they are subordinate to theirs (there is no one in India who is not subordinate to some one else; even the Government of India is subordinate to the Secretary of State).

lógá, in the way. *Tirupati poyé lógá*, on the way to Tirupati.

lógada, interval, previous.

lógaṭi, former. *lógaṭi dinam*, the day before.

lógili, interior of house. *í lógiṭici nálugu meṭla varusal unnavi*, this interior contains four flights of steps.

lóguṭa, to yield.

lóguṭṭu, secret. *lóguṭṭu Perumáḷḷacu yeruca*, God knoweth the secrets of the heart.

lóhamu, metal. Skt.

lólópala, inwardly, right inside. *váḍu lólópala navvutunnáḍu*, he is laughing in his sleeve.

lóna, inside. *lóna vicáramu, baiṭa srüngáramu*, fair without, foul within (a whited sepulchre).

lónaguṭa, to be seduced, brought over.

lóni, internal.

lónici, into.

lónu, the inside, the mind.

lópala, inside, among, within. *inṭi lópala*, at home, *yéṭi lópala*, within a year.

lópali, inner.

lópamu, omission, defect, fault. Skt. *ocaḍu: í áfísu panulacu bádhyata galavár evarú? gumastá: nácu bágá teliyad anḍi, yédainá lópam vasté mátramnanné andaru tiṭṭutáru*. Smith: Who is responsible for the work of this office? Clerk: All I know is that if anything goes wrong they all blame me. *jívaratnamu ittaḍini podigité, ratnánici yémi lópamu?* an ill-set gem does not lose its natural lustre; *míru yenta lópam lécunḍá pani chéstú v'unná ṣirastáddáru gáru paṭṭu có valen anṭé, lópálu doracacunḍá mánavu*, however faultless your work is, faults will be discovered in it if the sheristadar has a down on you.

lópamugala, defective.

lópaicári, deputy, sub-contractor.

lópalici, (towards the) inside. *lópalici vastú chepputánu*, I dare you to come in.

lóparatsuconuṭa, to conquer; also spelt *lóbaratsuconuṭa*.

lóṭá, a small drinking vessel. Hindustani.

lóṭu, deficiency.

lóṭupóvuṭa, to be deficient.

lótu, depth. *ítacu minchina lótú, góchici minchina dáridryamú lédu*, once you have to swim it does not matter how much deeper the water is, when you are reduced to your loin-cloth you can't get poorer.

lóvainamu, former.

lóvi, a brass water pot.

lubdhatvamu, avarice. Skt.

lubdhuḍu, miser.

lucaluca, noise of insects boring, &c.; onomatopoeic.

lúṭi, loot. Hindustani.

lúṭichéyuṭa, to loot.

M

mabbu, cloud, dim, dark, drowsy. *idi vána vachché mabbu cádu*, this is not a cloud that will bring rain; *nidra mabbu*, drowsiness; *mabbu rangu*, a dark colour; *cannu mabbu*, dimness of sight.

mabbuconuṭa, to cloud over, to be tipsy.

mabbupartsuṭa, mabbupeṭṭuṭa, to cloud, conceal.

macámu, halting place. Hindustani. The Collector's camp is commonly called his *macám*.

Macca, Mecca.

maccuva, desire, especially sexual desire. *Vírabhadrarázu tana mída maccuva v'unnadá ani aḍigité máṭláḍaca v'úrucunnánu; ná manassuló v'unna córice cheppé-ṭ-aṭṭ aité, maccuva v'unnad'ani ventané cheppa valasindé; aité nácu atani mída móham v'unna sangati conta cálam dácá teliyacuṇḍá v'untsutánu*, when Virabhadrarazu asked me whether I was fond of him I was silent; if I had told the truth about the wish of my heart, I would have had to say yes at once, but I propose to keep my love for him a secret for some time yet.

machchica, tameness, fondness.

machchicapaḍuṭa, to become tame or fond of.

machilí, fish. Skt. Used in compounds such as *machilí-pannu*, fishing-tax. Masulipatam is *machilí-paṭnam*, the fish-town.

macila, dirt.

macilichéyuṭa, to soil, tarnish. *báḍi cálitó vachchi vanṭa y'illu macili chésinárú*, you have dirtied the kitchen with your muddy feet.

mactá, fixed tax on land; fixed rent for the occupation of land on lease. Hindustani. One of the old forms of land settlement; the land was given on lump sum tenure, no cesses being leviable.

maḍaca, plough with bullocks complete.

maḍacarra, stout stick, log for the fire.

maḍaguṭa, to be bent, folded, to be humble. *ápadaló aḍagi, maḍagi v'unḍa valenu*, be meek and humble in adversity.

maḍama, heel (*cálimaḍama*). *goḍḍalimaḍama* is the back of an axe; *tupácimaḍama* is the butt end of a gun.

madamu, pride, lust, rut. Skt., from word whose first meaning is fat. *vidya madamu*, pride of learning; *dhana madamu*, purse pride; *cula madamu*, pride of caste; *udyóga madamu*, pride of office; *strí madamu*, lust for women; *mada gajamu* or *madapu-ṭ-énugu*, elephant in rut.

madapitstsa, madapupitstsa, erotomania. *í pitstsaváḍu dínni caugalintsucóvaḍánici prayatnam chéstu v'unn aṭṭ unnáḍu; idi madapitstsa ai v'unṭundi*, the lunatic seems to be trying to embrace her; it may be erotomania.

maḍata, a fold, bundle (of papers), folded clothes, hood of a carriage. *marivaca cágitapu maḍatalo dúrinadi*, it got into another bundle of papers; *pillalanu pentsaḍam áḍaváḷḷa canṭé magaváḷḷacu mícu yeccuva telustundá yémiṭi? áḍaddáni chéti arthamú, magaváḍi chéti biḍḍa nilavad ani cheppina ṣástracáruḍu anta verriváḍ éná? mícu yémi teliyaca póvaḍam chétané pillaváḍi paccacu chinna guḍḍalu vésinán ani ácshépistú v'unnáru; paccaló v'utstsa pósé váḷḷacu murici baṭṭalú pélicalú cáca póté v'uticina tella maḍatalu pacca vésu cunṭárá?* do you think you know more about rearing babies than a woman? property in a woman's hand, a child in a man's, are ruined—was the seer who said this mad? it is only because of your utter ignorance that you object to my wrapping the child in small cloths; instead of using dirty cloths and rags for babies who let out urine, you would use clean folds of cloth, would you?

maḍatacóṭu, coat with an open collar (glad neck).

maḍatapeṭṭuṭa, to fold up.

maḍatoccuṭa, to pile palm-leaves and trample them flat (for thatching).

maḍatsuṭa, to fold.
maddatu, help. Hindustani.
maddela, drum. *áḍa néraca maddela mída tappu cheppin aṭṭu,* like finding fault with the drums if you can't dance (bad workmen find fault with their tools); *maddela tinnagá váyintsu,* beat the drum properly.
maddi, a tree (*terminalia alata*).
maḍḍi, another tree (*morinda citrifolia*), used for dying cloth red.
madhuramu, sweet, delicious. Skt. A literary word used of delicious breezes and such things.
madhuvu, spirits, honey. Skt. A literary word used for alcoholic beverages but also for the honey bees take from flowers and such things.
madhya, middle. Skt. *á madhya,* meanwhile; *í madhya,* lately; *madhya-madhya,* here and there. *ocaḍu: nénu railulóci yeccé-ṭ-appuḍu pramádam rácunḍá madhya banḍiló madhya sthánamló cúrtsunṭánu. incóḍu: aité daiva crūpacu yémí vadali peṭṭavá?* Smith: When I go by rail I sit in the middle seat of the middle carriage for safety. Jones: Then you leave nothing to God's grace. *talli: náṭacam yeṭlá v'unnadi? báluḍu: tsálá bág unnadi; dípálu, teralu adbhutangá v'unnavi. talli: mí nánna anta bág unḍa lédu; madhya madhya mátrame bág unnad annáré. báluḍu: nizamé, anducané cábólu, madhya madhya nánna baiṭacu póyi santóshistú lópalici vachchéváḍu.* Mother: How was the play? Boy: Excellent, the lamps and curtains were wonderful. Mother: Your father did not think so much of it, he said it was only good in parts. Boy: Just so, because, I suppose, he went out from time to time and was pleased only when he came inside.
madhyama, central, middle finger; also *naḍimi vélu,* which is Telugu, while *madhyama* is Sanskrit.
madhyamu, the middle; also the name of a note in music. Skt. *naḍumu* is the Telugu word.
madhyasthamu, arbitration. Skt.
madhyasthuḍu, arbitrator. Skt. *nénu y'induló madhyasthunni,* I am arbitrator in this case.
madhyavarti, arbitrator. Skt.
madhyavartitvamu, arbitration. Skt.
madhyáhnamu, afternoon. Skt. *prati dinamu madhyáhnam accaḍici póyi,* going there every afternoon. *ṭícharu: ninna madhyáhnam scúlucu rá léd ém? báluḍu: má nánnagáru sarcasucu tísucu pó valasinadi.* Teacher: Why did you not come to school yesterday afternoon? Boy: I had to take my father to the circus.
madi, mind; for Skt. *mati.* Used in books.
maḍi, small plot of wet land; the plot in which paddy seedlings are sown before transplantation is called *ácumaḍi* or *nárumaḍi. mányálú maḍulú,* ground and glebe; *maḍici gaṭṭu, inṭici guṭṭu,* ridge your field and ring your family; *chénici yeruvu, maḍici manḍa,* apply cattle manure to your dry land, leaf manure to your wet land.
maḍi, purity, a clean cloth; a Telugu word from *maḍaguṭa,* to fold. *maḍibaṭṭa* is the clean folded cloth brahmins put on before they sit down to eat; *maḍi-mayila,* purity and impurity. *prodduṭí nunchi maḍi caṭṭuconi cúrtsunn anduna caḍup ubbi, avatalacu pó valasi vachchi, ákharu snánamu chésinánu,* having sat in my dinner cloth from the morning my belly swelled and I had to go outside and I took my last bath; *lantsamulu putstsucóm ani, paici maḍi caṭṭuconn aṭṭu naṭinché goppa adhicárlé curáculacu sahitamu caccúrti paḍutú v'unṭáru,* even high officers who make outward show of purity will accept a bribe of a few vegetables.
-maḍi, suffix meaning -times, from *maḍuṭa,* to fold; *inumaḍi,* twice, two-fold.
**maḍigáḷḷu,* stilts; also *maragáḷḷu.*
maḍimayila, purity and impurity. *maḍimayila snánamú sandhyá léni inglishu tsaduvu connaváru,* English educated people who don't know purity from impurity or bathing or prayers.
madimpu, estimate. Skt., from *madi,* mind. Also *matimpu.*
madintsuṭa, to estimate; also *matintsuṭa.*
madira, toddy. Skt. A book word for *callu.*

madugu, maduvu, sluice; also *mar-ava*; but *sluis* is commoner.

maḍugu, a depression in the ground of large size; also for a tank when there is water in the depression. *súrya ciranamula védimi chéta samudramu-lónú nadulalónú maḍugulónú v'unḍéníru áviri rúpangá paici léchi, vaca tsóṭa cúḍuconi, paini gáliló mékhangá yér-paḍi, baruvu yecc ain appuḍu níru cinda paḍutundi, dánné varsham an-ṭáru,* the heat of the sun's rays falls on the sea, rivers, and lakes, and turns the water into steam; this rises and forms clouds in the upper air; when the clouds grow heavy, water falls, and this is rain.

maḍupucaṭṭi, clasp knife; from *ma-ḍuta*, to fold, and *caṭṭi*, knife.

maduru, coping. *maduru mídi pilli*, the cat on the coping (calculating the jump) is used for a calculating man.

madyamu, intoxicating drink. Skt. *madya pánamu mánumu*, give up drink.

maga, male; also *moga*. *maga póḍimi yeruganidi*, a girl who has not had intercourse; *muddula múta caṭṭi maga ṣiṣuvu puṭṭináḍu*, a boy who was a bundle of charms was born; *maga-páḍi*, manliness.

magadi, the male of any animal.

magaḍu, a male, husband; also *mo-gaḍu* and *mogáḍu* for *mogaváḍu*. *magaḍu vallan ammanu mári valladu*, plague spares the unloved wife; *ma-gaḍu póyina munḍa vale rátrimpagaḷḷu panipáṭalu léca y'illé paṭṭucuni vadala-vu*, you sit indoors everlastingly with your hands folded like a widow in mourning for her husband.

maganálu, a woman whose husband is alive.

magatanamu, manhood, manliness; also *mogatanamu*. *nívu ná manassu vachchina magaváḍavu, magatanam anṭé y'ilágu v'unḍa valenu*, you are a man after my own heart; that is what I call real manliness.

magaváḍu, a male, man. *tsaduvu nérchina áḍadánitónu, vanṭa nérchina magaváḍitónú, v'ópa ráḍu*, intolerable is a woman who has learnt to read or a man who has learnt to cook. *bhárya: magavállaci yémainá cheviló cheppité, incó cheviló nunchi ivatalici vastundi. bharta: áḍadánici yémainá cheppité renḍu chevulalóci póyi, nóṭló nunchi baiṭici vastundi.* Wife: Say anything to a man and it goes in at one ear and out at the other. Husband: Say any-thing to a woman and it goes in at both ears and out at the mouth. *magaváḍu cácunḍá, áḍadi cácunḍá*, neither fish nor fowl.

maggamu, loom; *maggamu peṭṭuṭa* is a phrase for to set to work (to arrange the loom); *ná maggamu cheḍa coṭṭi-náḍu*, he bashed up my work.

magguṭa, to turn mouldy; *mámiḍi maggité sazzalu panḍunu*, mouldy mangoes mean good millet (an agri-cultural proverb).

-magnuḍu, suffix meaning 'plunged in'. Skt.

maguduṭa, to return. Used in books for *maraluṭa*.

maguva, woman, wife. *maguva maga-nici oca mantri*, a wife is her husband's prime minister (the wife is the key of the house).

maha-, mahat-, great, much. Skt.

Mahalacshmí, Vishnu's wife Lakshmí or Shrí who came forth at the churn-ing of the waters. She is the goddess of fortune and beauty. *nívu má y'inṭici cévalamu mahalacshmívi*, you are the good angel of our house; *góvu-lé-v'úḷḷó goḍḍu géde ṣrí mahalacshmí*, in a cattle-less village a barren buffalo is a mahalakshmi, properly *mahálaxmi*.

mahamméru, mahámeru, the golden mountain on which Brahma sits sur-rounded by rishis. Skt. *manasu mahamméru dáṭutunnadi, cálu caḍapa dáṭa lédu*, you can ascend heaven in your mind without leaving your home.

mahaníyuḍu, a great man. Skt.

mahantu, abbot. Skt. A mahant is the head of a matt or monastery; the most famous mahant in South India is the Mahant of Tirupati who lives on the Tirumalai hill where pilgrims continually go to make vows and obtain favours from Venkatesvara. The Mahant's annual income from offerings and endowments is 12 lakhs or £90,000.

mahaprabhuvu, great lord. Skt. The Collector is commonly so addressed by petitioners and his peons, who pronounce the word *maprobó*.

maharshi, great saint. Skt., from *maha-*, great, and *rüshi*, rishi.

mahattu, glory, greatness. Skt. Also *mahatvamu*.

mahatyamu, great quality, miraculous power. Skt. *tama mantra ṣacti chéta lócánic antaṭicí santósham caluga chésévaru, bráhmala vadda alágaṇṭi mahatyamu v'unnadi*, brahmins used to be able to make it rain by uttering charms, such miraculous power had they; *id antá caliyuga mahatyam*, this is all the pressure of the iron age.

mahazaru, petition signed by many persons, round robin. Hindustani. e.g. when a man wants to be an honorary magistrate he gets his caste people to send a mahazar to the district magistrate.

mahá, great, much. Skt. *tanacu mahá telisin aṭṭu*, as if he knew a lot.

mahábhágyamu, great or highest good. Skt. *árógyamu mahábhágyamu*, health is the chief good; *mahábhágyuḍu*, an eminent man; *mahábhágyavantuḍu*, a very lucky or rich man. The fem. is *mahábhágyavati*.

mahábháratamu, the epic Mahabharata; also shortened to *bháratam*.

Mahácáḷi, Durga, Siva's wife, a very terrible goddess—and sometimes immoral. She is also called Parvati and Uma.

mahácáyuḍu, big-bodied. Sanskrit.

Mahádévuḍu, the Great God, i.e. Siva; there is a famous poem of Goethe's about how Mahadev came to earth and took up with a dancing-girl.

Mahálacshmí, Vishnu's wife; also *Mahalacshmí*; she is the goddess of prosperity.

mahálu, palace. Hindustani. There are famous old mahals still in existence; the Chandragiri Mahal, for instance, where the last of the Ráyulus signed the firman giving Madras to the East India Company, and the Lotus Mahal at Vijayanagaram (Hampi); both illustrated in this book.

mahámahópádhyayuḍu, great teacher. Skt.; compounded of *mahá*, *mahá*, and *upádhyayuḍu*. A title given by the Government of India to Sanskrit scholars.

Mahámári, another name of Mahácáḷi or Durga, goddess of small-pox, &c.

mahámeru, Brahma's mountain; also *mahamméru*.

mahánadi, the big river, name of the Cuttack river and other rivers in the Uriya country.

mahánandamu, great joy. Skt.

mahánubhávuḍu, great man, superior person, often used ironically. His Excellency Lord Curzon was regarded as a *mahánubhávuḍu*. *í dinamu á mahánubhávuḍi darṣanamu chési, áyana séva chési, carnótsavamgá áyana máṭa vini, paramánandam pondi, crütárthunni aindnu*, on the day I was received by that Great Personage (Lord Curzon) and paid my humble duty to him and heard the music of his words, I was in the seventh heaven of delight, and shall ever cherish the memory of that interview with the profoundest gratitude.

mahápraбhú, great lord, vocative of *mahápraбhuvu*. Skt. *grámamuna n-asésha janamunu í bráhmanuḍé biḍḍanu cannáḍ ani cheppuconutsunnáru, mahápraбhú!* your honour, every one in the village says this brahmin has given birth to a child.

maharáshṭramu, the great empire, i.e. the Mahratta country.

mahárázu, great raja; properly only of the major ruling chiefs, but applied to himself by every petty zamindar. *mahárázu vale vidhilóci póyi*, stir your stumps like a nobleman and go into the street.

maháṣúruḍu, great hero. Skt. *nénu dhairyangá v'unḍi maháṣúrunni ain aṭṭu canapartsa vatstsunu*, I may take courage and pose as a hero.

mahátma, great soul, applied especially to Kút Húmi and M. K. Gándhi.

mahátmyamu, greatness, glory. Skt.

maháttaramu, greater, from *maha*, great, and *taram*, sequence, sort.

mahátvamu, greatness, glory.

mahávádi, a great or extreme debater. Skt., from *vádamu*, argument. Used also of extremists in politics.

mahávidya, the great science, i.e. magic.

maháyugamu, the revolution of the ages, eternity. Skt.

mahéṣvaruḍu, the Great Lord, i.e. Siva. Skt., from *mahá* and *ísvaruḍu*, lord.

mahima, greatness, power. Skt. *yóga mahima cana paratsadánici y'ippuḍu manchi avacáṣam caliginadi*, a good opportunity to show the power of yogi; *yémi y'í cála mahima! ippuḍu bhárya maganitó máṭṭáḍuṭa ranc ainadi!* what times! if a wife talks to her husband it is regarded as immodesty!

mahishamu, buffalo. Skt. Used only in books; the Telugu is *dunnapótu*.

mahishaváhanuḍu, riding a buffalo, i.e. Yama, the God of Hell. Skt., from *mahisham*, buffalo, and *váhanam*, vehicle.

mahónnatamu, elevated, noble. Skt., from *mahá* and *unnatam*, high.

mahótsavamu, great festival. Skt., from *mahá* and *utsavam*, festivity, procession.

maicamu, intoxication.

maidánamu, maidan, plain, open ground.

maila, mayila, defiled, impure, dirty. Skt., from *malinam. maila vastramulu*, dirty clothes; *maḍimaila*, pure and impure; *monna má y'inṭici vaca dacshinádi bráhmaḍu vachchináḍu; tellagá puvvu lágu tsácalidi v'utici techchina baṭṭa caṭṭu coni, v'úr antá tirigi vachchi, á baṭṭató vistari daggira cúrtsunnáḍu; y'id ém anṭé tánu caṭṭu cunna taruváta viḍuva lédu, tanadi maḍi baṭṭa antáḍu; produnne Góḍávari v'onḍu niḷḷaló nunchi tetstsucunna ná panche tsúchi, ìávalisté nídi maila baṭṭa annáḍu*, the other day a southern brahmin came to my house; wearing a cloth fresh as a flower from the wash he wandered all over the town and sat down in it to food; I asked the meaning of it and he said he wasn't changing and his cloth was a pure one and, if anything, the cloth in which I had bathed in the morning in the muddy waters of the Godavari was an impure cloth.

mailaboṭṭu, mourning mark.

mailapaḍuṭa, be in defilement or mourning.

mailu, mile. English. *méjistréṭu: nuvvu vantena mída ati tondaragá móṭáru pón istunnáv ani chárji vachchindi; accaḍa ganṭacu padi maiḷḷa canná eccuvagá pó cúḍad ani nóṭísu caṭṭäru; tsadava léda? draivaru: ayyó, nénu muppadi maiḷḷu tsoppuna banḍi naḍuputu v'unṭé, nóṭísu yeṭlá tsadava galan anḍi?* Magistrate: You are charged with exceeding the speed limit on the bridge; there is a notice there 'speed limit 10 miles per hour'; can't you read? Driver: How could I read it when I was driving 30 miles an hour?

maimarutsuṭa, to swoon (to forget the body, *mai*; a word not used except in this compound).

mainamu, wax.

mainapuvatti, wax candle.

mainaru, minor. English. *mainaru veḷḷina*, of age.

maithunamu, sexual intercourse. Skt., from *mithunam*, a couple; *grámya dharmam*, village custom, is a decent expression for this.

maitri, friendship. Skt., from *mitra*.

majilí, stage in a journey. Hindustani.

majilíbangalá, travellers' bungalow.

majjiga, buttermilk. *mandi yeccuv aité majjiga palatsana*, the more the people the thinner the buttermilk.

makhamalu, velvet; also *mokhamal*. Hindustani.

malabacshacuḍu, eater of dirt. Skt., from *malam*, excreta, and *bacshacuḍu*, eater.

malamala, in pain; onomatopoeic. *pasi pillalu ácali chéta malamalan áḍutsu*, children tortured for want of food; *yenḍaló chímalu malamalan áḍutsunnavi*, the ants are suffering agony in the sun.

malamu, faeces. Skt.

malamútramulu, faeces and urine. Skt.

malatsuṭa, to chip.

malayamárutamu, fragrant breeze.

A book term, common in descriptive passages in novels.

Malayamu, Malabar.

malinamu, dirt. Skt. A book word.

malle, jasmine. Skt.; also *mallica*.

maḷḷi, again (short for *maralì*). *mádiga maḷḷi, camsáli yelli*, cobblers say 'come again', goldsmiths say 'to-morrow' (Malli and Yelli also happen to be common female names); *prastutam selavu putstsuconi maḷḷi darṣanam chéstánu* (the usual polite way of taking leave), I will take leave now and again call on you.

mallica, jasmine. Skt.; also *malle*.

maḷḷintsuṭa, to turn off, cure, bring back. *manóbalam chéta yetuvanṭi rógál ainá maḷḷintsa vatstsunu*, any disease can be cured by strength of mind; *cám ándhulai v'unna y'iddaru calusucunṭé, váḷḷanu maḷḷintsaḍánici brahma taram cádu*, God himself could not turn a couple of love-blinded lovers once they get together; *áulu maḷḷinchinaváḍu Arjunuḍu*, it was Arjuna brought the cows back. These were Virata's cows, and it is said of any one who gets the credit of a successful undertaking.

malluḍu, wrestler.

maḷḷuṭa, to wrestle, struggle, struggle out, turn. *váḷḷa valaló paḍḍa taruváta maḷḷaḍam cashṭam*, once caught in their net it is difficult to struggle out; *í y'indriya sukh ápécsha nunchi ná hrüdayamu maḷḷunu gáca!* may my heart turn from this sensual desire; *óda maḷḷinadi*, the ship went about.

malu-, prefix meaning other, second. *malucáru* is the second crop, *malutsúlu*, the second offspring; *ávulu tolu tsúlu, gédelu malu tsúlu*, the first calf of the cow, but the second of the she-buffalo (is best).

maluputa, to put out (a light), to twist. *ártsuṭa, árpu véyuṭa*, are commoner for putting out a light; *gontu malupu* is twist the neck (e.g. of a wounded bird; also *gontu pisugu*).

mammulanu, us.

mana, our, including those spoken to; *má* excludes these. *sabhádhipati: í rózu upanyásam ichché áyana Américá déṣasthuḍu; áyana tólu tellanid ainá, áyana hrüdayam mana valé nallanidé.* Chairman: To-day's lecturer is an American gentleman; though his skin is white, his heart is as black as ours.

managuṭa, to be bent, folded; same as *maḍaguṭa*.

manamaḍu, grandson. *manamaḍu nértsu conn aṭṭu, avvacu tírin aṭṭu*, the grandmother was relieved and the grandson learnt his lesson (when she made him write it on her back to relieve the itching); (killing two birds with one stone). *vrüddhuḍu: ná manamuḍu mí áfísuló pani chést unnáḍu, vánini míru yerugudurá? máné-jaru: yerugudunu, í madhyané míru tsachchi póyinár ani selavu putstsuconi veḷḷáḍu.* Old man: My grandson works in your office, do you know him? Manager: I know him, he has just taken leave on the ground that you had died.

manamarálu, granddaughter. (Old man with young wife) *andaru nác adi manamarál anuconiré cáni, yevvarunu bhárya y'ani telisi có tsálaca póyiri*, every one took her for my granddaughter, no one for my wife.

manamu, we, including, unlike *mému*, those addressed; thus in translating: We, Citizens of this Great Empire, use *manamu*, to include your Indian audience, and not *mému*, to exclude it.

manamu, mind. Skt.

manascarintsuṭa, to be pleased, accept. Skt. *manascarinchédi* is used in ending a letter, 'may it please you'; it is a complimentary word for which there is no exact English equivalent; the German *genehmigen* exactly translates it.

manascáramu, attention, meditation. Skt.

-manascuḍu, affix meaning minded. Skt. *sanmanascuḍu* is right-minded; *durmanascuḍu*, evil-minded.

manasphúrtigá, attentively, willingly, really, honestly. Skt. *ataḍu dhanyuḍ ani míru manasphúrtigá talustárá?* do you honestly think him rich? *ná manasphúrtigáné cheputu v'unnánu*, I am saying exactly what I think.

manassancaṭamu, agony of mind. Skt.

manassu, mind, but often to be translated heart, feelings. Skt. *vánici manassuló ocaṭi baiṭa ocaṭi*, one thing in his heart and another in his mouth; *í máṭa ní manassuló unḍan í*, keep it to yourself; *váni manassunu yenducu noppistáu?* why hurt his feelings? *manassu paṭṭuṭa*, to set one's heart on; *vánici manassu rá lédu*, he had not made up his mind; *mí manassu*, as you please; *manassu untsuṭa*, to pay attention; *idi chéyuṭacu manassu rán anduna*, not being able to find it in his heart to do it; *ná manassuna paṭṭinadi*, it was impressed on my mind; *tsaccagá tala duvvuconi, coppu peṭṭuconi, nálugu nagalú vanṭa peṭṭuconi, manchi chíra caṭṭuconi v'unḍagá, tsúda valen ani nác entó manassu véstundi*, how I should like to see you nicely combed, dressed, and bejewelled. *ocaḍu: mí manassuló yémi anucunṭunnadí nénu cheppa galanu. incóḍu: aité cshamintsanḍi. ocaḍu: yenduc ani? incóḍu: mimmunu gúrchi anucunṭunnaḍánici*. Smith: I can tell what is in your mind. Jones: Please pardon me, then. Smith: What for? Jones: For what was in my mind about you.

manastápamu, repentance, remorse, distress, vexation. Skt.

manastimitamu, balance or soundness of mind. Skt. *virici manastimitam lécunḍá v'unn aṭṭ unnadi*, he does not appear to be of sound mind.

manavi, request; the common word for the prayer in a petition. *adé má manavi*, it is this we request.

manchi, good; *manchi nidra*, sound sleep; *manchi debba*, a good hit; *manchi gáyamu*, a severe wound. *tandri: ninnu nénu yenducu coṭṭinánó telusuná? ní canṭé chinna pillaváḍini nuvvu coṭṭin anducu. báluḍu: ní canṭé chinnaváḍ ani gadá, nuvvu coṭṭaḍam manchid éná?* Father: Do you know why I thrashed you? Because you hit a boy smaller than yourself. Boy: Aren't I smaller than you? Was it right for you to hit me?

manchicheyi, the good hand, i.e. the right hand; the left hand is reserved for base uses.

manchidi, a good one. *angaḍiváḍu: í duppaṭi conanḍi, oca purushántaramu varacu unṭundi. vrüddhuḍu: nác anta manchidi accara lédu, nácu ippaṭici ḍebbai yéḷḷu*. Shopkeeper: Buy this cloth; it will last a generation. Old customer: I don't want so good a one, I am 70.

manchi níḷḷu, drinking water. *vána níḷḷu régaṭi néla paḍi manchi níḷḷ aunu, tsaviṭi néla paḍi uppu níḷḷ aunu*, rainwater will be drinkable if it falls on clay, it will be brackish if it falls on salt land.

manchitanamu, goodness.

manchiváḍu, a good person. *manchivánici máṭláḍanidé mandu*, silence is sufficient reproof to a good man (e.g. when the Collector is asked for a favour); *manchivánici maranamé sácshi*, the memory of the just is blessed; *manchivánici máṭé mandu*, a word to the wise; *manchivánici vaca máṭa, manchi goḍḍucu vaca debba*, a nod for a wise man, a rod for a fool; a variant is *múrkhunici vaca chéṭa*, for a fool a blow with the winnow-fan. Blows with winnow-fans and slippers are particularly insulting.

mancu, foolish, especially of stubborn folly.

mancutanamu, folly, stubbornness. *yédi cávalisté, ad ellá coni peṭṭi, pillalacu mancutanam nérputáru*, you only teach children stubbornness by giving them everything they ask for.

manda, herd, flock; *mandamandalugá*, in herds. *yeccaḍa caṭṭité-n-émi? mana mandaló íníté sari*, who cares what bull it was so long as the cow calves in our herd?

manda, dull. Skt. *nívu vaṭṭi manda mativi!* you are a bloody fool! *manda márutamu*, a gentle breeze (in books).

manḍa, ankle; usually *chílamanḍa*.

manḍa, twig with the leaves on. *chénici yeruvu, maḍici manḍa*, cattle manure for dry land, leaf manure for wet land.

manḍa, an expletive, from *manḍuṭa*, to burn. *váḍi moham manḍa!* damn him! (may his face burn!).

mandabuddhi, a dullard.

mandagintsuṭa, to become dull. Used also of the market being dull.

mandahásamu, smile. Skt. *á manda-*

hásam sogasu tsúchinává? observe the beauty of that smile.

mandalamu, disk, horizon. Skt. The orb of the sun or moon; any circumference but especially the horizon. *mukhamandalamu,* face-orb, is used in books for face.

mandalamu, district. Skt. Presumably a district was regarded as something rounded off; *mandalam* is a book word for district; the common words are *districtu,* English, and *jillá,* Hindustani: in books they use *mandala cáragrühi* for district collector and *mandala nyayádhipati* for district judge, but the people say *calectaru* and *jadji.*

mandalintsuta, to rebuke, remonstrate. *ná págá vaca pedda manishi muddi cinda naligi v'unnadi: 'yémayyá! ná págá mettagá vésucuni cúrtsovadam mícu dharmam éná?' ani nén á peddamanishini mandalinchinánu,* a gentleman sat on my turban; I remonstrated asking him whether it was right to use my turban as a cushion.

mandamu, thick, stout, stupid. Skt. *cáni mandam cóti duhkham,* a pennyworth of stupidity and a pound of sorrow.

mandamugá, gently. Skt.

mandapamu, pavilion, a platform with pillars on it. Skt. More commonly *mantapamu.*

mandasamu, big chest or box. Skt.

-mandi, suffix meaning several, many; attached to numerals when the reference is to persons. *aidumandi,* five persons; *contamandi,* a few persons; *sagamumandi,* half the people, *yentamandi?* how many persons? *padi padihénu mandi,* several people (10, 15 people); *mandi yeccuva y'aité majjiga palatsana,* the more people there are the more the butter-milk will be watered.

mandiramu, mansion. Skt.

-manditamu, suffix meaning decorated. Skt. Used in books.

mandu, medicine (the common word; *aushadhamu,* Skt., is also used); the Tamil is *marandu. perati chettu manducu rádu,* familiarity breeds contempt; *manchivárici máté mandu* (*verbum sat sapienti*); *manóvyádhici mandu lédu,* there is no cure for the heartache; *mandú mácú accara lécundá, nálugu lankhanálu chésté, vacca debbanu padi rózulu nátici vallu nimmalangá v'undunu;* fast a few times and you will be well in ten days without physic or pills (*mácú* is merely reduplicative and has no meaning by itself); *oca nádu vindu, oca nádu mandu;* feast one day, physic the next; *dáctaru: ní vrütti yémiti? rógi: nénu gharáná manishi n'andi. dáctaru: aité nén ichchina mandu panici rádu, incó mandu putstsucó váli.* Doctor: What is your profession? Patient: I am a man of standing. Doctor: Is that so? Then the medicine I prescribed won't do, I will prescribe another; *tiyyani rógamulú, cammani mandulú v'unnavá?* are there sweet illnesses and delicious medicines?

mandu, heat. *nácu vallu manducu pótu v'unnadi,* I am furious (heated).

mandu, gunpowder. *tupáciló mandu cúrutánu,* I will stuff the gun with powder.

mandudu, fool. Skt.

mandulamári, poisoner.

manduta, to burn (intransitive); also used as an expletive. *anni marricarralú, rávicarralú; v'úrice poga rávadamé cáni yémi mandavu,* they are all banyan or fig sticks, they smoke but don't burn. Used, very commonly, figuratively of anger; *déham mandi,* angry; *vánici vallu mandinadi,* his blood was up; *cadupu mandutsunnadi,* I am much grieved; *nácu vallu manduconi vastú v'untundi,* I am furious; *váni moham manda!* damn him! *yedati poyyi mandité, tana poyyiló nillu pósu conn attu,* like the man who poured water on his own hearth when his neighbour's hearth blazed (envy).

manduvá, courtyard.

mangala, prosperous, propitious. Skt. Used freely in Skt. compounds such as *mangalárati* (*mangala* plus *árati*), lamp waved before idol; *mangaláśásanamu,* benediction (*mangala* plus *śásanam*).

mangala, barber.

mangalacatti, razor; from *mangala,*

barber, and *catti*, knife; also *mangalicatti. mangalacatti techchinádu, gontuca cóstádá yémiti?* he has a razor, will he cut my throat?

mangalamu, earthenware dish used for roasting and frying. *dongila póté, mangalamu doricinadi,* the housebreaker got nothing but an earthen dish (disappointment); *condaru Turaca Sultánula hayámuló janulanu mangalamuló petti véchin atlu nána vidhamaina himsalanu pettiri,* under the rule of some of the Muhammedan Sultans, the people were roasted alive (figuratively).

mangalapani, shaving. *pani* by itself (work) is commonly used to mean shaving; *cshauramu* also means shaving.

mangaḷasútramu, the cord on which the marriage-symbol (*táḷi*) is fastened round a woman's neck. Skt., from *mangaḷa,* propitious, and *sútramu,* cord. *táḷi* in the south.

mangalaváḍu, barber; often pronounced *mangaláḍu.*

mangaḷaváramu, Tuesday; the day of Lakshmi, who is also known as *mangaḷadévata. lacshmiváramu* is, however, Thursday.

mangali, barber, same as *mangala. mangali páta, tsácali cotta,* an old barber, a new washerman (are best).

maṇi, gem. *maṇi maṇitó coyya valenu,* you must cut a gem with a gem; *nava maṇulu,* the nine gems, are diamond (*vajram*), pearl (*mutyam*), ruby (*mánicyam*), emerald (*maracatam*), sapphire (*nílam*), topaz (*pushyarágam*), coral (*pagaḍam*), onyx (*gómédhicam*), and cat's-eye (*vaidúryam*); *vipramaṇi,* best of brahmins; *sundarimaṇi,* gem among women; *dinamaṇi,* the sun (gem of day).

manicaṭṭu, wrist.

manishi, person, especially female person; also each person; also servant; the proper masculine is *manushyuḍu*; plural *manushulu,* people. *pólísu súparinṭendenṭu: aṭlá poyyé manishini pilu. cánsṭébilu: dyana manishi cád anḍi, sabinspecṭaru gár anḍi.* Police Superintendent: Call that man who is going along there. Constable: That's not a man, Sir, that is Mr. Sub-Inspector, Sir; *manishici oca rúpayi y'ichchináḍu,* he gave them a rupee each; *manishic oca máṭa cheppináḍu,* every man had his own opinion; *áme láuḍṭi manishi,* she is a stout woman; *manishivá paṣuvuvá?* are you a man or a brute? *ná manishini pamputánu,* I will send my servant; *á déṣapu manushulu,* the people of that country; *manishi cáṭucu mandu lédu,* there is no cure for a human bite (slander).

manjúru, sanctioned. Hindustani. An official term.

manjúruchéyuṭa, to sanction.

Manmathuḍu, Káma, Cupid. Skt. He has many names, e.g. *Icshudhanvuḍu,* the archer with the sweet bow; *Manmatha* is he who confuses the mind. *manmath agni chéta cáli tsávaḍam canṭé, tappacunḍá viváham áḍaḍamé v'uttamam,* it is better to marry than to burn.

mannana, favour, grace.

mannemu, the Godavari Agency; the word properly means highlands.

mannepu jvaramu, agency fever, i.e. malaria.

mannimpu, forgiveness. *vánici debbalu mannimpu chésináru,* they excused him the flogging.

mannintsuṭa, to forgive. *ná valla caligina apacháramu mannintsanḍi,* forgive my offence.

mannu, earth, soil, mud. *páti peṭṭi, paini mannu veyyinchináru,* they buried it and covered it with earth; *vári nóḷḷaló mannu vésinánu,* I put dust in their mouths, i.e. humbled them (made them lick the dust); *mannu minnu,* heaven and earth.

mannu, bison.

manóbhíshṭamu, desired by the mind. Skt., from *man,* mind, and *abhíshṭam,* desired. *ná manóbhíshṭa siddhi ayyé cálam samípinchinadi,* the time for the fulfilment of my desire approaches.

manóharamu, fascinating. Skt., from *man,* mind, and *har,* to seize. *strílu tsúḍaḍánici sambháshintsaḍánici manóharangáne v'unṭáru,* women are captivating to see and to talk to.

manójayamu, conquest of the mind.

manóniṣchayamu, determination.

manórathamu, wish. *ná manóratham púrnangá saphalam autundi,* my wish is completely fulfilled.

manóvarti, maintenance, alimony. Skt. (*manuvrütti*). *ná tammuḍi bháryá manóvartici ná mida vyájyam vésinadi,* my younger brother's wife has sued me for maintenance.

manóvédana, distress of mind. Skt., from *man,* mind, and *védana,* distress.

manóvyádhi, pain of mind. Skt., from *man,* mind, and *vyádhi,* pain. *manóvyádhici mandu lédu,* there is no balm for a wounded spirit; *strílu vidyaléni hétuvu chéta yuctáyuctamulu teliyaca, paṣu tulyuráṇḍr'ain anduna gaḍá, purushulac iṭuvanṭi manóvyádhulu sambhavintsuts unnavi,* we men suffer such tortures of the mind because our uneducated women do not know right from wrong and are like the beasts of the field.

manṭa, flame. *penṭa mída panṭa, manṭa mída vanṭa,* crops depend on manure, cooking on flames. *caruvu mánapu panṭa, miḍatalu mánapu manṭa,* a crop is the end of a famine, flame the end of locusts; *dánini tsústé nácu manṭa vast unnadi,* I am aflame at seeing that; *caḍupu manṭa,* envy, rage; *caḍupu manṭa tíra tiṭṭináḍu,* he swore till his rage was exhausted, till he had disgorged all his venom.

manṭi, earthen; from *mannu; manṭinúne,* earth-oil, petroleum.

mantrabalamu, force of charms. Skt. *y'i mantrula mantrabalam chéta yenta pani chésinánu,* what a success I have made by force of charms.

mantracáḍu, mantragáḍu, mantravádi, charm-teller, magician. *pámula mantragáḍu* is a snake-charmer.

mantramu, charm, incantation. Skt. *ní divya náma mantramu chéta,* by the force of thy blessed name; *mantramu cheppa Mallubhoṭlu, tinaḍḍánacu Yellubhoṭlu,* Mallubhotlu attended to the incantations while Yellubhotlu did the eating part.

mantrasáni, midwife. *mantrasáni mundara marmamu dáchin aṭṭu,* concealing the private parts from the midwife (false modesty); *pilla ganḍanicí, talli ganḍamú v'unṭundi gáni, mantrasáni ganḍamu yeccaḍá v'unḍadu,* the mother or the child may be in danger, but the midwife is in none.

mantri, minister. Skt. The queen in cards or chess. *dhairyamu léni rázu, yóchana léni mantri,* a king without courage has a minister without judgement.

mantrintsuṭa, to bewilder, to charm. Skt., from *mantramu.*

mantsamu, cot, bedstead. *oca cantsána tini, vaca mantsána paḍu conévúru,* they ate from one platter and lay in one bed (great intimacy). *donga mantsam cinda pácut unḍenu. bharta: (bháryató) yém év? nuvvá mantsam cinda savarist unnáu? donga: nénu donganu; mí bhárya vanṭimída nagalu y'idi varacé tísucunnánu; mantsam cinda peṭṭeló yém unnávó ani tsúst unnánu, paḍuconḍi,* a thief has crawled under the bed. Husband (to his wife): What's that? Are you tidying under the bed? Thief: I am a thief; I have already removed your wife's jewellery; I am looking to see what there is in the box under the bed; turn over and go to sleep; *donga vácita mantsam vésin aṭṭu,* like placing your bed in the thief's yard (outwitting the crafty).

mantsu, dew, snow, ice; the ordinary word for dew; there is no snow in the Telugu country, but *mantsuconḍa* means the Himalayas and *mantsugaḍḍa* is the Telugu for ice. *conḍa vale vachchi, mantsu vale télin aṭṭu,* coming like a mountain but melting like dew (difficulties melt away when they come near); *mantsu cammi y'unnadi,* there is dew; *mantsu curiyuts unnadi,* it is snowing; *mámiḷḷacu mantsu cherupu,* dew blights mangoes.

-mantuḍu, affix denoting a person, one who has. *buddhimantuḍu* is a sensible man; *ṣactimantuḍu,* an energetic person.

Manu, Manu; *Manusmrüti,* Scriptures of Manu.

manubótu, male bison; also *manupótu.*

manugaḍa, maintenance, way of life; same as *manuvrútti. níchapu manugaḍa,* a low way of life.

manugu, maund of 8 viss; varies, but is usually 25 to 28 lb.; the railway maund is 28 lb., 2 stone. *vipu mida vise guddulanu, managu guddulanu dabadaba varshamu láguna curipinchenu,* he rained blows upon his back. *ţicharu: vancáyalu vise aná aité, managu yém autundi? báluḍu: putstsu vancáyal autav anḍi.* Teacher: If brinjals are an anna a viss, what will a maund be? Boy: They will be rotten.

manuguḍupu, the last entertainment given by a bride's parents after marriage.

manujuḍu, man. *ducci gala bhûmi, diccu gala manujuḍu cheḍaḍu,* a well-turned field and a man who has friends to turn to will never come to grief.

manumaḍu, manumarálu, grandson, granddaughter. *bhûmi mída nívu incá yentamandi manumalanú manumaráḷḷanú yetta valenó?* how many more grandsons and granddaughters are you going to scatter over the earth?

manupenţi, female bison.

manupótu, male bison.

manushyamu, human. *manushya mátruḍ anu aina nácu,* to me, being of a human measure; *manushyamátrulacu alavi cádu,* beyond human powers.

manushyáşanudu, cannibal. Skt., from *manushya* and *aşanam,* food.

manushyuḍu, man. *manushyulu v'unḍaru gáni, máţalu v'unţunnavi* (*littera scripta manet*).

manyamu, fief, inam, land given to show respect, especially brahmin inams; for the more common *mányamu*; also the Godavari Agency (*mannemu*).

manzúru, confirmed, sanctioned. Hindustani; same as *manjúru.*

maprobhó, sir; corruption of Skt. *maha-prabhuvu,* great lord. The peons call you *maprobhó* if they don't call you *Dévara,* God.

mara, wooden; from Tamil *maram,* tree; *maracálu* is a wooden leg; also a stilt.

mara, screw, machine, mill. *maraló biyyam áḍintsacu rá,* go and get the rice pounded at the mill.

maraca, stain.

marachipóvuţa, to forget. *Gópu: ivváḷa ná goḍugunu renḍó sthalamló marachipóyin aţţugá tóstundi. Rámuḍu: oca véḷa modaţi sthalamlóné marachipóyinár émó? Gópu: lédu, modaţi sthalamló nácu y'í goḍugu modaţa doricindi,* Smith: I think I lost my umbrella to-day in the second place. Jones: Perhaps you lost it in the first. Smith: No, that's where I found it; *grühasthuḍu: bhárya v'unţé yenta cashţam vachchiná marichi pó vatstsunu. brahmachári: brahmacháricí asalu cashţamé unḍadu gá,* Married man: If you have a wife however great a trouble comes, you can forget it. Bachelor: Bachelors have no troubles.

maradalu, younger sister-in-law; under which is included a younger brother's wife and a wife's younger sister.

maradi, younger brother-in-law; under which is included a younger sister's husband and a husband's younger brother; also *bávamaridi.*

maragáḷḷu, stilts; also *maḍigáḷḷu.*

maraguţa, to be used to, addicted to, devoted to. *tágamaraginavádu,* a man addicted to drink; *dánini maraginádu,* he became devoted to her; *madhurasam ruchi maragité maḷḷi vadalí peţţutárá?* when you have got used to the taste of drink will you give it up again?

maraguzzu, dwarf; also *maruguzzu.*

marala, again. Book word for *maḷḷi.*

maralintsuţa, to turn away from. *durvyayamula nunḍi maralintsuţa,* to turn away from extravagance.

maraluţa, to turn, return.

marámatu, repair. Hindustani; also *marammatu,* figuratively redemption. *lóca marámatu cósam dévuḍé paḍi avatárálu yetti avastha paḍa valasi vachchindi,* God Himself was fated to go through a cycle of ten births for the redemption of the world.

maramécu, screw; also used figuratively like our screw, but of tyrants, not misers. *y'í ménéjaru anta maramécu gáḍini yeccaḍa tsúḍa lédu,* I have never known such a manager for putting the screw on his subordinates.

marammatu, repairs. Hindustani; also *marámatu.*

maraṇacaramaina, mortal. *maraṇacaramaina gáyamu* is a mortal wound.

maraṇadaṇḍa, capital punishment. Skt., from *maraṇam,* death, and *daṇḍam,* punishment.

maraṇamu, death. Skt. *mañchivárici maraṇamé sácshi,* death itself sets its seal on a good man's life; *nénu vánini maranávasta* (*avasta*) *y'andu tsúchinánu,* I saw him in the article of death; *vrayagá vrayagá caranamu, daggagá daggagá maraṇamu,* write and write and you will be a karnam, cough and cough and you will be a dead 'un.

maraṇaṣásanamu, a will. Skt. But people usually both say and write *villu.*

marasána, grindstone.

maratsuṭa, to forget; but it is more usual to use the compound *marachipóvuṭa. pustacam eccaḍanó peṭṭi marachinánu,* I have mislaid the book.

marava, sluice; but almost every one says *sluis.*

maravu, privacy; also *maruvu.*

Maráṭi, Mahratta.

marcaṭachéshṭalu, monkey tricks.

marcaṭamu, monkey. Skt. Book word for *cóti.*

mari, so, then, again. *marémi?* what else? *nénu mar eppuḍu vastánu?* then when shall I come? *mariyeṭlu?* then how? *mari* is constantly stuck in when we say nothing; one of the commonest words in the language.

mariconni, a few more.

maridi, younger brother-in-law; same as *maradi.*

mariḍijádyamu, cholera. *mariḍi* is the goddess of cholera; people mostly say *cálárá.*

marinta, all the more. *alacarintsu coni vachchi, dípamu veluturuna páḍutú v'unṭé, dáni mogam antacantacu marinta andamugá canupaduṭú v'unḍedi,* she looked all the prettier dressed up and singing before the footlights.

marivaoa, mariyoca, another.

marivacalágu, mariyocalágu, otherwise. *í vishayamló míru marivacalágu anucócanḍi,* do not think otherwise, i.e. don't be suspicious.

mariyáda, honour, respect. It must always be remembered that what every Indian lays most stress on is that he should be treated with *mariyáda,* honour, respect, consideration; also *marydáda.*

mariyevaḍu? who else? (masculine).

mariyevate? who else? (feminine). With the negative and the last vowel lengthened these words mean no one; *mí vanṭi ṣactimantuḍu lócamló mariyevadú lédu,* there is no such energetic person in the world as you.

mariyocaḍu, another man.

mariyocate, another woman.

mariyocaṭi, another thing.

marmamu, secret, secrecy, secret parts. Skt. *marmam viḍichi cheputánu,* I will reveal the secret; *amma puṭṭillu ménamáma vadda cheppin aṭṭu ní marmam antá yerigina ná vadda ní goppa cheppucócu,* like the man who told his maternal uncle what his mother's birthplace was, don't boast to me who know all your secrets; *vál̥la marmálú rahasyálú alóchanalú telusuconi,* knowing all their secrets and plans; *marmam antá ná chétuló v'unn appuḍu ná vadda gaḍusutanapu máṭalu cheppac anḍi,* don't talk clever to me who know all the details of the plot; *mantrasáni mundara marmamu dáchin aṭṭu,* like hiding the secret parts from the midwife.

marohaḍu, marohaṭi, another man, another thing; for *marocaḍu, marocaṭi. maró,* another; short for *marocaṭi; maró mucca,* another word; *maróḍu,* another man.

marri, banyan tree. *prayánicuḍu: í marri cheṭṭu yenni yéndlad anḍi? grámasthuḍu: renḍu vandala yenimidi yél̥lu. prayánicuḍu: mícu lecca inta sarigá yeṭlá telisind anḍi? grámasthuḍu: nénu í v'úrici vachchi yenimid él̥l aindi; appaṭici cheṭṭu renḍu vandala yénḍla nunchí und annáru.* Wayfarer: How old is that banyan? Villager: 208 years. Wayfarer: How do you know the exact figure? Villager: I came here 8 years ago; I was then told it had been here 200 years.

martabu, closed, settled (of an account, usually). Hindustani. *sabha martabu cheyyanḍi,* dismiss the meeting.

martyamu, mortal. Skt. *martya lócam* is earth as opposed to heaven.

martyuḍu, a mortal.

maru-, prefix meaning 'again'. *marumóta*, echo; *marumáṭa*, contradiction.

marugu, privacy, concealment. *tama marugu tsochchinánu*, I have invaded your privacy; or have sought shelter with you.

marugudoḍḍi, privy.

marugugóḍa, screen.

marugupaḍuṭa, to disappear.

maruguparatsuṭa, to hide something.

maruguperaḍu, courtyard where the privy is.

maruguṭa, to be hidden.

maruguṭa, to get used to; same as *maraguṭa*.

maruguṭa, to boil (intr.). *uḍucuṭa* is commoner.

maruguzzu, dwarf; also *maraguzzu*. *dirkha cáyuni bhuzamula mída cúrtsunna maruguzzuváni vale*, like a dwarf sitting on a giant's shoulders.

marulamandu, love potion. Skt. *marulu*, desire.

marumáṭa, contradiction; from *maru*, again; also *márumáṭa*.

marumóta, marumróta, echo, from *maru*, again, and *mróyuṭa*, to resound; also *márumóta*.

marunáḍu, the day after. *á marunáḍu*, the day after that.

marupu, forgetfulness. *ḍácṭaru: nic ém bádha? rógi: nácu marupu yeccuv aind andi; adi poyyé-ṭ-aṭṭu mand iyyaṅḍi? ḍácṭaru: istá gáni mundugá ná fízu antá iyyi.* Doctor: What's your trouble? Patient: Forgetfulness; can you give me a drug to cure it? Doctor: I will, but first my full fees, please.

marusaṭi, next. *marusaṭi dinamu*, next day.

marutsuṭa, to forget; also *maratsuṭa* and, commonly, *marachipóvuṭa*; *mai marutsuṭa* (to forget the body) is to lose consciousness.

maruvu, privacy; same as *marugu*.

maryáda, respect, honour, compliments; same as *mariyáda*. *manaló manacu maryádalu yémiṭi?* why compliments among ourselves?

maṣacamu, mosquito. Skt. Used only in books for *dóma*.

masaluṭa, to wander; to boil over (of water).

masálá, spices. Hindustani. *masálá poḍi*, curry powder.

maṣánamu, burial-ground, for Skt. *ṣmaṣánamu*.

mashácattu, survey (of land). Hindustani; an old revenue term.

mashálchi, lamp-lighter. Hindustani. Our revenue offices still have a mashálchi who lights lamps and sweeps and so on and counts below the peons and is paid from contingencies and does not get a pension.

mashi, ink. Skt. Used only in books; *yinci* is what we say.

mashṭu, grounds (of liquor).

masi, black, dirt. Skt. *mashi*, ink. *masi vadalan anduna núti daggira snánam chésinánu*, I went to the well and had a bath to get rid of the dirt.

masídu, mosque. Hindustani.

maṣúchi, small-pox. Skt. *maṣúchica matstsalu*, pock-marks.

mat-(mad-, man-), prefix meaning 'my'. Skt. *matcatha*, my story; *maddásulu*, my servants; *mannámamu*, my name.

mata, religion (in compounds). Skt., from word meaning opinion (religion is an opinion). *matadharmaddáyamulu* means religious endowments.

matabhrashṭuḍu, an apostate.

matalabu, purport. Hindustani. *arji matalabu* is the purport of a petition.

matamu, religion. Skt. *mana matam bódha chéyistú v'unḍa valenu*, we must teach our religion (note *mana*; this does not apply to conversion, but only to teaching those who are already of your religion).

matasambandhamaina, connected with religion; e.g. *matasambandhamaina criyalu*, religious ceremonies.

matábhimánuḍu, pious. Skt., from *matam*, religion, and *abhimánam*, love.

matácháryuḍu, head of sect. *matácháryulaina y'ilácá putstsuconi y'í durachâram mánpaddánici yémaina pani chésté bág unḍunu*, it would be a good thing if the bishops took notice of this bad use and did something; *pradhána* *matáchḁ́ryuḍu* translates metropolitan or primate.

matántaramu, conversion.

maṭhamu, monastery. Skt.

mati, mind, intellect. Skt. *canḍlu cheripiná dévuḍu mati y'ichchin aṭṭu,* just as God gives increased faculties to the blind; *gati lén ammacu, mati léni moguḍu,* a helpless woman and a foolish husband; *nácu mati pótú v'unnadi,* I am getting bewildered.

matibhrama, confusion of mind. Skt. *matibhrama yettuṭa* is to become of unsound mind.

matibhrashtuḍu, weak of mind. *donganu puṭṭinchinaváḍu matibhrashtunu puṭṭintsaca mánadu,* He who created rogues does not omit to create dupes.

matihínuḍu, fool.

matiléni, matimálina, matipóyina, foolish. *matimálina máṭalu,* foolish words.

matimantuḍu, sensible man.

matimpu, estimate. Hindustani. A revenue term for crop-estimate, &c.

matintsuṭa, to estimate, appraise.

matstsa, mole, stain. *maśúchica matstsalu,* pock-marks.

matstsaramu, malice, envy. Skt.

matstsu, sample.

matstsu, love-philtre.

matsyamu, fish. Skt. Used in books for *chépa.*

mattamu, intoxicated. Skt.

maṭṭamu, level.

maṭṭe, toe-ring; also *meṭṭe.*

maṭṭi, earth, mud.

mattu, intoxication. *tági mattugá v'unnáḍu,* he drank himself unconscious; *íyanacu y'illu bailudérin appuḍu y'inta mattu léḍu,* he was not so drunk when he left the house.

maṭṭu, measure. *maṭṭu mitamu lédu,* no end to it; *maṭṭu maryáda lénіváḍu,* no moderation or modesty; *maṭṭu mira vaddu,* do not go too far.

maṭṭucu, up to, only. *gráma sarihaddu maṭṭucu,* up to the village limit; *prastutam maṭṭucu,* only for the present.

mauḍhyamu, stupidity. Skt. *múḍhuḍu,* stupid.

maunamu, silence. Skt. (*muni*). There is a famous mauna svami, or silent ascetic, at Kuttálam. *maunam dharintsuṭa* is to keep silence; *maunam ardh angicáramu,* silence is half consent.

maurkhyamu, stubbornness. Skt. (*múrkhuḍu*).

-mayamu, suffix meaning 'composed of'. Skt. *jalamayamaina,* composed of water, aqueous; *agnimayamaina,* igneous; *vájmayamu,* composition (literary); *chinna cathala vájmayamu telugunacu cottadi,* the short story is a novelty in Telugu literature.

mayila, impurity; a way of spelling *maila.*

mazará, hamlet of a revenue village; a revenue term.

mazá, taste, refinement. Hindustani.

mazucúru, mazcúru, aforesaid. Hindustani.

mazúri, wages of a day-labourer, cooly. Hindustani.

mazúru, a cooly. Hindustani.

má, our (not including persons addressed, which is *mana*).

má, short for *maha,* great. Skt. *mábágu,* very good.

máchicáyalu, gall-nuts.

máḍa, half a pagoda (an obsolete gold coin).

máḍci, manner. *cheppina máḍci,* in the manner said. Used in books for *cheppin aṭlu.*

mádhyámica, middle, adj. from *madhya. mádhyámica páṭhásálalu,* middle schools.

mádiga, the cobbler caste. The málas and mádigas are the two pariah castes in the Telugu country; each thinks itself higher than the other; the mádigas, besides working in leather, beat drums, and no religious ceremony or marriage is complete without them; the male form is *mádigaváḍu,* the female *mádigadi. mádiga malli, camsáli yelli,* cobblers say 'again', goldsmiths 'another day' (Malli and Yelli are also common female names); *mádigaváḍi álu ainá, máḍé cálici cheppu léḍu,* though she is a cobbler's wife she has no shoes to prevent her feet being scorched (the cobbler's wife is the worst shod).

mádigapalle, madiga hamlet; madigas are, of course, not allowed in the village, and have to live in a hamlet apart.

mádiri, way, manner, sample. *rógi: ná zabbu cudurtsa galará? ḍácṭaru: mí zabbu mádiri zabbulanu cudurtsa-ḍamló nácu pratyéca sámarthyam undi; í mádiri rógam galavárici nénu iravai yéndlu mand ichchinánu,* Patient: Can you cure my disease? Doctor: Certainly; I am specially expert in curing your kind of disease; I have treated patients with that kind of disease for 20 years on end.

máḍtsuṭa, to scorch. *vánḍla puṭamu máḍchinádu,* he burnt their refining vessel (i.e. spoilt their scheme); *váḍu mukhamu máḍtsu connáḍu,* his brow turned black (he frowned); *caḍupu máḍchi,* starving.

máḍuṭa, to be scorched, to be distressed. *mádigaváḍi álu ainá, máḍé cálici cheppu lédu,* a shoemaker's wife and a smith's mare are always the worst shod; *mému y'íláguu bhójanam lécunḍá yenta sépu máḍamu?* how long are we to be famished for want of food? (when the servants delay serving dinner); *váni moham máḍi póyindi,* he was crestfallen; *máḍuchecca* is the crust of burnt rice.

máfu, cancellation. Hindustani. This is the word ryots use when they want the Collector to remit the land-tax.

máfuchéyuṭa, to cancel.

mágáni, irrigated land.

mághamu, February–March, the 11th Telugu month.

máhátmyamu, greatness. Skt., from *mahátma,* great soul; *Ráma máhát-myamulu* are the deeds or miracles of Rama.

mála, garland. Skt. *japamála* is a rosary.

mála, pariah. The malas and madigas (cobblers) are the two Telugu pariah castes; each thinks itself superior to the other and they will not share a well or food; *málaváḍu* is the masculine form, *máladi* or *mála-sati* the feminine; *mála* as an adjective is also used to mean vile; *málatulasi* is the wild basil, *mála déga,* the lesser hawk. *bráhmanulaló nallavánni, mála-laló yerravánni namma rádu,* beware of a dark brahmin and a fair pariah.

málacari, garland maker. Skt.

málacúḍu, polluted food, defilement in general. *ná cóḍalu cápuránici vach-china tarváta y'inṭló vaṭṭi málacúḍu,* it is all defilement since my daughter-in-law came into the house.

málacútalu, Billingsgate.

málapalle, pariah hamlet; the pariahs are, of course, not allowed in the village, and have a ghetto to themselves outside.

málaprabhutvamu, the pariah (i.e. English) government. *mála prabhut-vam cávaḍam chéta anni nirbhandhálé; aḍḍamainaváḷḷú tsaduvucóvaḍamé; aḍḍamaina váḷḷu v'udyógálu cheyya-ḍamé; yevarini cásta tiṭṭa valla cádu; coṭṭa valla cádu; y'í páḍu calicálam yeppuḍu pótundó!* because we are cursed with a foreign Government we are coerced on every side; any one may study; any one may hold appointments; we must not abuse any one; we must not beat any one; oh Lord, when will this bad time come to an end!

málati, jasmine. Skt.

máli, gardener; from Skt. *mála,* garland.

málica, garland. *japamálica* is a rosary.

málimi, affection, familiarity. *pilla-váḍu ná daggira málimi ainádu,* the boy took to me.

-málina, negative affix, '-less'. *siggu-málina,* shameless; *yerucamálina,* ignorant; *diccumálina,* helpless (having no quarter to turn to); *carunamálina,* merciless.

málísu, grooming. Hindustani.

málísu chéyuṭa, to rub a horse down.

máma, father-in-law; also short for *ménamáma,* maternal uncle; *pinamá-ma* is the younger brother of one's father-in-law; *peddamáma,* the elder brother; you will naturally add *gáru* in speaking of your own father-in-law.

mámiḍi, mango; the wild mango is *aḍavimámiḍi,* the graft mango *anṭu-mámiḍi.*

mámiḍicáya, unripe mango fruit.

mámiḍicheṭṭu, mango tree.

mámiḍipanḍu, mango fruit.

mámsamu, meat. Skt. *góvu mámsam tinéváru prabhutvánici vachchina taru-*

váta y'ikha yélá autund anḍi? what do you expect when people who eat cow's meat are in power? *casáyiváḍu méca mámsam ammutáḍu, nívu nara mámsam ammutú v'unnáu; váḍu yeccaḍanó puṭṭina paṣu mámsamu vicrayistáḍu; nívu caḍupuna puṭṭina ṣiṣu mámsamu vicrayistú v'unnáu; ní vyápáramu canṭé váḍidé manchidi,* the butcher sells goat's meat, you human flesh; he sells cattle-flesh born anywhere, you child's flesh born in the womb; his is a better trade than yours (infant-marriage).

mámsáṣanuḍu, flesh-eater. Skt., from *mámsam* and *aṣanam,* food.

mámúlu, custom; the customary bribe. Hindustani. *sommu cósam cádu cán anḍi, vaca sári manam vadili peḍité, idé mámúl ai, répu sommu paṭṭintsu cuni veḷḷé marivacaḍu cúḍá tanacé rá valen anṭáḍu; idi yeppuḍú huzúr gumastácé rávaḍam mámúl anḍi,* it isn't for the money's sake; but if once we drop it, that will become customary, and to-morrow some one else will claim it; this is a perquisite which always goes to the head-quarters clerk. *Lacshmayya: vaidyuḍu cheppina pracáram pathyam putstsu cunṭ unnává? Rangayya: putstsucunṭúné unnánu; cáni í madhya ácal aité, pathyam putstsu coni, mámúlu annam cúḍa tinnánu.* Smith: Are you dieting according to the doctor's prescription? Jones: Yes, but if I feel hungry, I take my usual food besides the diet.

mánabhangamu, disgrace. Skt., from *mánam,* honour, and *bhangam,* breach.

mánajaru, manager, especially an office manager. English; also *ménéjaru. gumástá: mánajaru veyyi rúpayilu cá chésháḍu; pustacamló yém ani vrásédi? incó gumástá: chillara khartsul ani ráyi.* Clerk: The manager has made away with Rs. 1,000; what does one enter in the ledger? Another clerk: Write it under petty cash.

mánamu, honour, modesty. Skt. *mánamu póyina venuca práṇam enducu?* what is life without honour? *ná mánamu daccintsu, ná mánamu nilupu,* preserve my honour.

mánanashṭamu, dishonour, defamation. *ḍiféméshan anṭé mánanashṭam,* it is the nearest Telugu word for 'legal defamation'; an offence under section 500 of the Indian Penal Code, under which many cases are filed, since the Telugus often defame one another.

mánasamu, mind. Skt.

mánasica, mental.

mánasintsuṭa, to consider. Skt.

mánava, human. Skt. *mí y'inṭici vachcheḍu chinnadánini strí rúpamuna vachchina bhágyadévatanugá bhávimpa valenu gáni, sámánya mánava bhámnigá bhávimpa cúḍadu,* you must regard the girl who has come to your house not as an ordinary human being but as the Goddess of Prosperity in the form of a woman.

mánavacóṭi, the world of men; from *mánava,* human, and *cóṭi,* crore, host.

mánavadharmamu, humanity. *itarulu páḍautú v'unṭé tsústú v'úrucóvaḍam mánava dharmam cádu,* humanity requires that we should not look on while others go to the devil.

mánavantuḍu, an honourable man. Skt.

mánavati, a modest woman. Skt.

mándyamu, torpor. Skt.

mánica, a grain measure, four to the cuntsam, 16 to the toom. *máṭa ghanamu, mánica pitstsa,* big words, small measure.

mánicyamu, jewel, very common figuratively. *cuppaló mánicyamu,* a diamond on a dunghill; *mánicyamvanṭiváḍu,* a jewel of a man.

mánipintsuṭa, mánpintsuṭa, to put a stop to; causative of *mánpuṭa*; *á vivdham mánpintsa valen ani nénu y'iccaḍacu vachchinánu,* I came here to stop that marriage.

mánipóvuṭa, to stop, cease. *mánipóyina punḍu maḷḷi répin aṭṭu,* like ripping up old sores.

mánó-, prefix meaning 'mind', 'heart'. *mánovallabhuḍu,* dear to my heart.

mánpuṭa, to stop (transitive). *mana saddácháramunu mánpi vésindru,* they stopped our good custom.

mánu, tree, wood. Tamil *maram.* The common word is *cheṭṭu,* but *cheṭṭu* also means a shrub. *cheṭṭu ai vanganidi* *mánu ai vanguná?* if it won't bend as a shrub, will it bend as a tree? (a stubborn boy is not likely to make a yielding man); *mánu pandlu mánu cindané rálutavi*, the tree's fruit falls under the tree (you will get what you deserve); *yéṭi dari mánici yeppudú chalanamu*, unsafe as a tree on the river brim.

mánupu, stopping. *caruvu mánupu panṭa, miḍatalu mánupu manṭa*, crops check famine, flame locusts.

mánushamu, honour. Skt. *mánushamunacu nilichi*, clinging to honour; *mánushamu daccintsuconuṭa*, to preserve one's honour.

mánushyamu, humanity, manliness. Skt.

mánuṭa, to cease, stop, give up. *caḍupuló v'unn amma canaca mánuná, vanḍin amma tinaca mánuná?* will the pregnant woman stop without giving birth or the woman who has cooked without eating? *chésina pápam cheppité mánunu*, confession removes sin; *tennisu pravínuḍu: nannu paricsha chesháru gadá, ná vaḷḷu yeṭlá v'unnadi? ḍácṭaru: nícu viṣránti cá valenu; connáḷḷu tennisu mánuconi, rózú cálé-jici veḷḷutunḍu, nimmalistundi.* Tennis champion: You have examined me, doctor, how about it? Doctor: You require rest; give up tennis for a bit and attend college daily.

mányamu, gift land, especially land gifted to brahmins; *sarvamányamu* is such land free of tax; *arthamányamu*, paying half the tax; *mányálú maḍulú*, ground and glebe.

mápu, haze, dirt. *mápaṭi yenḍa*, evening sun; *yenḍamávulu*, mirage.

máracamu, exchange.

máráḍuṭa, to contradict, chat back; from *máruṭa*, to exchange.

márchivéyuṭa, to change; more common than simply *mártsuṭa*.

márdavangá, softly, sweetly. Skt., connected with *mrüduvu*.

máréḍu cheṭṭu, Bengal quince. *máréḍu samasta abhishtamulan itstsunu*, the Bengal quince will grant you all your wishes.

márgamu, way. *peddamanishi: ní pér émi? nuvvu yevari pillaváḍivi? báluḍu: míru canuccó valen anṭé renḍu márgál unnai. peddamanishi: yémiṭivi? báluḍu: míru úhintsuconḍi, léca póté vichárintsanḍi.* Gentleman: What's your name? Whose child are you? Boy: If you want to find out there are two ways. Gentleman: What are they? Boy: Guess or inquire. *bharta: cáfi chéyyaḍánici iravai márgál unnai. bhárya: nác enducu chepputáru á sangati! bharta: váṭiló nuvvu occaṭi nértsucunná nácu tsálunu.* Husband: There are twenty ways of making coffee. Wife: Why do you say that? Husband: If you can learn one of them, that will do.

márgaṣiramu, the 9th Telugu month, December–January. Skt. *márgaṣira másamunacu mámiḷḷu púsunu*, mangoes flower in Margasiram.

márgasthuḍu, wayfarer. *míru vastár ani y'í rózuna y'iravaimandi márgasthulanu basa doracad ani cheppi pampi vésinánu.* (Hotel-keeper): Hearing you were coming I have shut the door to-day on twenty travellers.

Mári, goddess who gives cholera, small-pox, &c. *magaḍu vallan ammanu, Márí valladu*, Mari will shun the woman who is shunned by her husband. *mahámári* is cholera.

-mári, suffix meaning 'one who does'. *mandulamári*, poisoner; *munḍalamári*, womanizer.

márjálamu, cat. Skt. Used for *pilli* in books.

márpu, change.

mártsuṭa, to change (transitive). *gáraḍiváḍu: ní cheyyi teru; ní cattini gaḍiyárangá márchánu tsútsucó. ocaḍu: nizamé. gáraḍiváḍu: gaḍiyáránni maḷḷi cattigá márustánu tsúḍu. ocaḍu: nácu catti accara lédu, gaḍiyáramé cá valenu.* Conjurer: Open your hand; see, I have changed your knife into a watch. Stranger: True. Conjurer: See, I will change the watch into a knife again. Stranger: No, thank you, I prefer the watch.

máru, time, other, again; from *máruṭa*, to change. *ocamáru*, once; *í máru*, this time; *palumáru*, often; *mummáru*, three times; and what the auctioneer says is *mummáṭici. . . . yeḍala ná péru*

máru péru peṭṭu, my name is not John Smith if . . . .
márubéramu, barter, retail trade.
márudastúri, feigned handwriting.
márugá, instead.
márumaruvu, second marriage.
márumáṭa, reply, contradiction. *nívu márumáṭa yémi cheppa vaddu*, don't answer back; *márumáṭáḍacunḍá nénu cheppé nítulu vinanḍi*, hold your tongue and listen to my maxims.
márumogamu, averted countenance.
márumróta, echo.
márumróyuta, to echo. *parvata guhalu márumrógin aṭlu*, like the echo from mountain caves.
márumúlamu, in a corner. *y'í y'inṭici v'unna lópam allá idi v'úrici chivaranu conchem márumúlagá v'unnadi*, the only drawback about this house is that it is at the end of the village and rather out of the way.
márupalucuṭa, to contradict.
máruṭa, to change (intransitive). *rágá rágá mári póyi*, changing little by little.
márutalli, stepmother. *máṭalu má talli máṭalu, peṭṭu márutalli peṭṭu*, motherly words and stepmotherly feeding.
márutamu, wind. Skt. Used in books for *gáli*.
márutáḷamu, false key.
máruvéshamu, disguise.
márváḍi, marvadi, the Jew of India. *ocaḍu: márváḍílu ḍabbu khartsu peṭṭarú; bháryanu tísucu rávaḍánici tappa incó panici tama úḷḷacu póru. incóḍu: accaḍa nunchi ippuḍu cottagá vastunna váḷḷu canipinchár ém? ocaḍu: railu khartsu lécunḍá v'unḍaḍánici ippuḍu iccaḍé puṭṭut unnáru.* Smith: Marvadies won't spend money, they won't go home except to fetch their wives. Jones: Have there been any new arrivals among them? Smith: No, to save railway fares they are now being born here.
másamu, month. Skt. The Telugu is *nela*, but *másam* is just as common.
máshṭaru, master, especially schoolmaster. English; also *méshṭaru*.
másicamu, monthly.
másina, másipóyina, dirty. *másipóyina baṭṭalu*, dirty clothes.
máta, mother. Skt. for *talli*; *mátápitalu*, father and mother, for *tallidanḍrulu*.
máṭa, word, command, promise, affair, concerning. *aushadhamu máṭa smaranacu vachchi*, remembering about the medicine; *ní máṭa cheppa lédu*, he did not mention you; *idi véré máṭa*, this is another affair; *rendó máṭa lédu*, there is no alternative; *áme tirigi vastunnadé máṭa telisi*, knowing she would come back; *máṭa tappa lédu*, he kept his promise; *véṭucu véṭu, máṭacu máṭa*, a blow for a blow, a word for a word; *máṭa vinuṭa*, to obey; *veyya máṭal éla?* in a word; *ná máṭa véru, ní máṭa véru*, we don't agree; *vánici nácu máṭalu lévu*, we are not on speaking terms; *cadapaṭi máṭa yémi?* what was the result? *máṭalacu paṭṭucunṭé viḍavaḍu*, once he starts talking he never stops; *ad eccaḍi máṭa!* what nonsense! *máṭalu ráni biḍḍa*, a child that has not yet learnt to speak; *vánici máṭa ságutundi*, he commands respect; *máṭalacu mátramu pedaricamu lédu*, nominally he is well off; *áyana máṭacu yeduru lédu*, his word is law; *máṭa itstsuṭa*, give one's word; *áḍadáni máṭa níḷḷa múṭa*, a woman's word is a water bundle; *máṭacu máṭa tegulu, níḷḷacu nátsu tegulu*, words and weeds choke streams and speech; *máṭalacu Malli, panici Yelli*, in words a Malli, in deeds a Yelli. Malli and Yelli are women's names, but *malli* also means again and *yelli* to-morrow. (His Miss Bud never becomes a Mrs. Blossom.) *máṭalu cóṭalu dáṭutavi, cáḷḷu caḍapa dáṭa lévu*, his words breach forts, his foot does not pass his threshold (great boaster, little doer); *víl erigina máṭa, cíl erigina váta*, a word in season, a brand in reason; *evari cúḍu tinṭé vári máṭal áḍ dli*, he who pays the piper calls the tune.
máṭalamári, chatterbox.
mátangamu, elephant. Skt. Used only in books for *yénugu*.
máṭavinuṭa, to obey.
mátámahi, maternal grandmother. Skt.
mátámahuḍu, maternal grandfather. Skt.

PLATE IV

The Vitalrao Temple at Hampi (Vijayanagaram), Bellary district, the ruined capital of the Ándhra Empire

(Photo. D. T. Bak and Sons, Hospet)

mátápitalu, father and mother. Skt.

máṭimáṭici, again and again. *púrvam oca dhanavantuḍu sariramu ninḍa ratna-khachitamulaina svarnábhara-namulanu dharintsuconi vidhini baḍi (= vembaḍi) póvuts unḍagá, bidaváḍ ocaḍ átanini vembaḍinchi, nagalanu tsúchi, máṭimáṭici namascarimpa n'á-rambhinchenu, á dhanicuḍ átanini tsúchi 'ná nagalaló nén édiyu nic iyya lédí, yendunac aṭlu chéyutsunáv?' ani y'aḍi-genu. 'á nagalu nác accara lédu; míru nannu nagalanu tsúḍan ichchinaru ganuca, namascáramulu chésinánu; mírunu tsútsuconi santóshintsuṭayé cáni, nagala valana vér oca prayójanamunu ponda tsálaru; míru nagalanu cápáḍu conuṭacai yentayu ṣrama paḍuts un-náru; nác á ṣrama y'accara lécayé santóshamu labhintsuts unnadi; mícunu nácu gala vyatyásam idiyé.' y'ani váḍu badulu cheppi póyenu,* once a Dives was going along the street wearing all over the body gold ornaments set with jewels. A poor man following him, seeing the jewellery, began to bow again and again. Dives, seeing him, said: 'I shan't give you any of my jewels; why do you do like that?' The poor man replied: 'I don't want the jewels; I am bowing to you to thank you for letting me see them; you too have no other use for the jewels except to look at them and be pleased; you are at any amount of trouble to preserve the jewels; I get my pleasure without that trouble; that is the difference between you and me.'

máṭláḍuṭa, to speak, to engage, be-speak (a cart or taxi). *strí: ná penimiṭi nidraló máṭláḍut unṭáru, váric émainá mand istára? vaidyuḍu: mand accara lédu; pagaṭi púta áyananu svéchchagá máṭláḍan iyyanḍi.* Woman: My hus-band talks in his sleep, can you prescribe? Doctor: No medicine is necessary; let him talk freely in the day-time. *ocaḍu: Lacshmayyani tsústé nácu záli véstundi. incóḍu: yenducu? ocaḍu: Lacshmayya yéḍu báshalu nértsuconnáḍu, chésucunna peḷ-ḷám ataḍini occa máṭ ainá máṭláḍan iyyadu.* Smith: I pity Brown. Jones: Why? Smith: Brown has learnt seven languages but his wife won't let him talk a word of any of them.

mátra, pill. *ná chéti mátra vaicunṭha yátra,* (quack speaking) the pill in my hand will take you to heaven (take my pill and you go up the hill).

mátramu, only, as much as. *tóchina mátram sambhávana ivva vatstsunu,* you may give as much as you think fit to the brahmins.

matráná, as soon as; short for *mátra-muna. cheppina mátráná,* as soon as he spoke.

máṭrú-, prefix meaning 'mother'. Skt. *mátrúbhásha* is one's mother tongue; *mátrúbhúmi,* one's motherland; *má-trúhatya,* matricide.

-mátruḍu, affix meaning 'of the measure of'. *manushya mátruḍun aina nácu,* to me, being only of human measure.

mátsacamma, woman of masculine appearance, virago.

mátsaryamu, malice. Skt.

máṭu, time. *ocaḍu: nannu racshintsa pócanḍi; nácu niḷḷaló munigi tsáva valen ani v'unnadi. incóḍu: incó máṭu tsáva vatstsuné; né ninnu niḷḷaló nunḍi paici tístán anṭé, meḍal y'istáru.* Suicide: Don't save me, I want to die. Rescuer: You can die another time; if I pull you out now, I shall get a medal.

máṭuvéyuṭa, to tinker, solder. *máṭu* is the menstruum used by the tinker.

mávatuḍu, mahout (elephant driver). Skt.

máváḍu, my son, my servant.

mávánḍlu, mávâru, my husband, my people. *yenducu yéḍustáu rá, pillaváḍá, anṭé, yellunḍi mávánḍlu coṭṭutár annáḍ aṭa,* when they said, 'why are you crying?', boy, he answered, 'my people are going to thrash me after to-morrow' (crying before you are hurt).

mávi, mango. Used in books for *mámiḍi.*

mávi, after-birth.

máya, illusion; in philosophy it is the phenomenal world; in common talk it is deceit and conjuring, deceitful. *dáni máya máṭalu palumáru vinṭû* *v'unḍaḍam chéta, dáni valaló paḍi, nela dinamula nunchi dánni bahirangangáné v'untsuconnáḍ aṭa*, he is said to have listened often to her cajoleries, to have fallen into her net, and to have been openly keeping her for the last month.

máyacuḍu, rogue, deceiver.

Máyadévi, Nature, regarded as a goddess. Skt.

máyalamári, conjurer.

máyaláḍi, deceitful woman.

máyópáyamu, trick. Skt., from *máya* and *upayam*, trick, means. *lópala sáramléni alpagnyánulu chésé máyópáyálu y'iláganṭivé*, such are the jejune manœuvres of ignorant people; *micu yeccaḍa rünam puṭṭaca póté, amma meḍaló cásula péru yédó máyópáyam chési putstsucó léru?* if you can't raise the wind otherwise, can't you by some trick get hold of your mother's gold necklace?

máyuṭa, to be effaced. *tana néram mási póvuṭacai*, to efface her fault. *másina* is dirty.

meccuṭa, to gobble.

meḍa, neck. *pillaváni meḍacu bangárapu canṭé y'ainanu lédu*, my boy hasn't even a gold necklace round his neck; *vancara meḍa*, wry neck.

medaḍu, brain. Skt. *médhá*.

meḍalu, medal. English.

meḍaluṭa, to stir, often in conjunction with *cadaluṭa*. *cadala medalacunḍá mantsamu mída nemmadigá parunnáḍu*, he lay on the bed quietly without moving; *vréḷḷu cadaltsutsu, nóru medaltsutsu*, moving his fingers and his lips (pretending to play and sing).

mejáriṭi, majority. English. *manam andaramú miṭingucu veḷité mejáriṭi manadé autundi*, if we all go to the meeting we shall have the majority.

mejisṭréṭu, magistrate. English. *Lacshmayya: yémi manishiv oi! yevariṭó cheppacunḍá má doḍḍló nunchi póṭávu? Vencayya: nénu ippuḍu manishini cánu, benchi mejisṭréṭu ainánu; jágrata!* Smith: Ho there, man! going through my yard without saying anything to any one? Jones: I am not a man now, I am a Bench Magistrate; careful!

melacuva, watchfulness, being awake. *í chevuḍuló piḍugulu paḍutú v'unná nácu nidra melacuva rádu*, I am so deaf that if thunderbolts fall I shan't wake.

melaguṭa, to move about among. *vayassuló v'unna sundara purusha madhyamuna sadá melagutsu*, always moving about among handsome young men.

-melasi, mixing; this implies a verb *melayuṭa*, but *melasi* is the only part used and only in *calasi-melasi*, mixing and mingling.

meligonuṭa, to get entangled.

mella, squint. *í chinnadánidi mella cannu*, this girl squints; *gruḍḍiló mella*, it is better to squint than be blind (half a loaf is better than no bread; the lesser evil).

mella, mellani, soft, gentle, low, slow.

mellagá, slowly, gently, softly, low. *naucaru: ayyá! míru conchem mellagá máṭláḍanḍi, má yazamánaḍu tsaduvucó léca v'unnáḍu. ocaḍu: aṭlága! inni yéḷḷu vachchiná tsadavané lédá? nácu aidu sanvatsarálacé tsadavaḍam vatstsuné.* Servant: Sir, please speak a little lower; my master can't read. Stranger: Indeed! At his age! Why, I could read when I was five. *mellagá* is what you say to your driver when you want him to go slow.

menḍu, much. *calla pasiḍici cánti menḍu*, false gold glitters most.

menḍugá, greatly.

mentulu, fenugreek.

meppintsuṭa, to persuade, please; from *metstsuṭa*, to praise.

meppu, praise. *sévacuḍu yazamánula nimittamai yenta pani chésiná vánici meppu canupaḍaḍu*, a servant won't get praised however much work he does for his masters.

meppuṭa, to praise.

meraca, high ground. *padavanu íḍchi meracanu vésináru*, they beached the boat.

meracapallamulu, ups and downs.

merapu, lightning.

meratsuṭa, merayuṭa, to flash, as lightning. *merayuts unnadi*, it lightens.

merica, the particles which resist the pestle or remain in the sieve; often used figuratively. *í pillaváḍu clásuló merica*, this boy is the pick of the

class; *í ḍicshanariló mericala vanṭi máṭalu mátramé v'unnai*, this dictionary contains only choice words (all rare and pedantic words having been sifted out).
merugu, brightness. *míru atanici ṣástrálaló merugulu cheppa valenu*, teach him gems from the shastras.
merugupurugu, fire-fly, glow-worm.
merugutómuṭa, to burnish.
meṭica, snap (of fingers). *mogunni tsúchi meṭicalu virichinadi*, she snapped her fingers at her husband.
meṭlu, steps, stairs, stops on the lute, sandals. *meṭlu diguṭa* is to come downstairs; *nénu vínecu y'iravai múḍu meṭl anṭé, ná chellelu muppai renḍ anṭundi*, I say there are twenty-three stops on the lute, my sister maintains there are thirty-two.
metstsatagina, laudable.
metstsuṭa, to praise; with dative, to be pleased with; *metstsuconuṭa* is commonly used for to praise; *rázu mechchinadi máṭa, mogaḍu mechchinadi Rambha*, the right advice is that which the king praises, the right wife is the woman praised by her husband; *yazamáni: nuvvu má y'inṭló iravai yéḷḷa paṭṭi pani chést unnáu; ní panici mechchánu. naucaru: mechchi yém chéstár anḍi? yazamáni: ica nunchi ninnu naucarugá tsúḍaca, má cuṭumbamló ocanigá tsúštám; andu chéta níc ica mída jítam iyyamu.* Mistress: You have been working in our house for twenty years; we are pleased with your work. Servant: What are you leading up to? Mistress: In future we won't look upon you as a servant, but as one of the family, and pay you no wages.
meṭṭa, high ground, dry cultivation. *meṭṭanu v'unna yénugu, pallána v'unná yénugé*, an elephant is an elephant whether he stands on high ground or low (greatness transcends circumstances). The opposite of *meṭṭa*, high ground, is *pallam*, low ground; the opposite of *meṭṭa*, dry cultivation, is *mágáni*, wet cultivation. *meṭṭanu* means by land as opposed to by sea or canal.
metta, mettani, soft, fine. *catti mettani lédu, atta manchi lédu*, there is no softness in a sword or sweetness in a mother-in-law; *mettagá dantsuṭa* is to pound fine; *á gadiló v'unna dushṭunni velupalici y'íḍtsuconi vachchi mettagá dantsa valenu*, pull out the scoundrel in that room and give him a good thrashing; *ná págá mettagá vésucuni cúrtsóvaḍam*, to sit on my turban and squash it.
metta, pad, bedding. *metta náḷḷu póyinavi, chetta náḷḷu vachchinavi*; our mattress-days have gone and our straw days have come (we have come down in the world).
meṭṭe, toe-ring; also *maṭṭe*.
meṭṭinillu, a woman's own house (her husband's), as opposed to *puṭṭinillu*, the house she was born in, her father's house; it means the house you tread on as opposed to the house you were born in.
meṭṭu, step, stair; *meṭlu*, stairs, staircase.
meṭṭuṭa, to tread.
metucu, grain of boiled rice, a morsel. *ilágu bhójanam lécundá yenta sépu máḍamu? mému sommu y'ichchéṭ appuḍu pendarálé metuculu paḍa véyan accara léda?* (to innkeeper) how long are we to be famished? when we have paid our money can't we even have our morning grains of rice? *mingaḍánici metuculu lévu, cáni misalacu sampangi níne*, an oiled moustache, but no morsel to eat (a famished fop).
méca, goat. *méca vanni puli*, a tiger the colour of a goat (a wolf in sheep's clothing); *jítamú batyamú lécundá tóḍélu mécalu cástán annaṭṭu*, like the wolf offering to watch the goats without pay or perquisite.
mécapótu, he-goat.
mécu, nail, stake, peg. *ḍéra méculu*, tent-pegs.
méḍa, house with upper story (a terraced-roof house is *midde*; in the old days no one was allowed to flaunt a *méḍa* or a *midde* without special permission from the raja). *rája bhárya méḍa yeccité cummariváḍi cóḍalu guḍise yeccinadi*, the potter's daughter-in-law climbed to the top of the hut when she saw the king's wife walking on the palace roof (aping the great).

médara, basket-making caste; they also make mats. *médara tsápa*, a bamboo mat; *médaravāḍu*, a basket-maker or mat-weaver.

médhavi, a man of parts, a wit. Skt., from *médha*, intellect. *médhavulaina ní vale*, a genius like you.

méḍhramu, penis. Skt.

méḍicarra, plough-shaft; *méḍi* or *méḍitóca*, plough tail.

méghamu, cloud. Skt. *ácáṣamu mégham paṭṭindi*, the sky has clouded over; *súrya ciranamula véḍimi chéta, samudramulónú nadulalónú maḍugula-lónú v'unḍé níru áviri rúpangá paici léchi, vaca tsóṭa cúḍuconi, paini gáliló méghangá yérpaḍi, baruvu yeccuv ain appuḍu níru cinda paḍutundi*, the water of the sea, rivers, and lakes rises in the form of steam through the heat of the sun's rays, unites in one place in the upper air, forms clouds, and when they are heavy water falls down.

méjesṭréṭu, magistrate. English; also *mejisṭréṭu, majisṭréṭu*.

méjóḍu, stockings. Hindustani.

mélamu, fun. *mélamáḍuṭa*, to make fun.

méḷamu, music, band of dancing girls. Skt., from root meaning uniting.

méli, fine. *méli musugu*, a fine veil.

méli, mélu, upper, higher. *mélugóḍa* is top-wall or rampart.

mélu, good, prosperity, better advantage. *antya nishṭhuramu canná, ádi nishṭhuramé mélu*, harshness at the beginning is better than at the end (say no at once). *cíd enchi mél entsa valenu*, count the advantages, after calculating the disadvantages (do not be unduly optimistic); *caḍapaṭa chinnadi peddad ai, y'inta cálamunacu ná tapamu phalinchenu gadá ani santósha paḍeḍu dinamulu vatstsun appaṭici, daivamu ná mélunu tsúchi, órva léca, y'inṭici nátó cápuramu chéya vachcheḍu lópalané dánini ná páliṭi Yama dúta-nugá márchi vésináḍu*, at last after an age of hope deferred, when I thought of recompense and reward for protracted mortification of the flesh, and the joyful day had arrived, God cast a jealous eye on my bliss, and sent in her place a spiteful changeling to live with me; *yeppaṭi mélu appaṭicé*, benefits are soon forgotten (then only the ever benefit).

mélucaṭṭu, canopy.

mélucolpuṭa, to waken.

mélucólu, waking.

méluconuṭa, to be awake, wake up. *nidra póyina vánini lépa vatstsunu, mélucunna vánini lépa lému*, you can wake a sleeper, not a person who is awake already (none so blind as those that won't see).

méluvarta, good news.

mému, we, not including those spoken to; *manamu* includes them.

ména-, prefix denoting cognate relationship.

ménabáva, elder male first cousin through a female, being a father's sister or mother.

ménacóḍalu, cognate niece.

ménalluḍu, cognate nephew.

ménamaradalu, younger female cognate first cousin.

ménamaridi, younger male cognate first cousin.

ménamáma, mother's brother. *ocaḍu: mí ménamáma villu vrásin appuḍu ninnu gnyápacam peṭṭuconnáḍá? incóḍu: peṭṭucunnáḍu, anducané nác ém ichchi pó lédu*. Smith: Did your uncle remember you when he wrote his will? Jones: He did, and that's why he left me nothing.

ménaricamu, cognate relationship, marriage among cognates. Every woman considers that a girl of her family has a right to marry her son; boys are thus forced to marry maternal first cousins or nieces whom they dislike, and the plots of many Telugu novels are based on this bad custom.

ménatta, aunt who is either the wife of a maternal uncle or a father's sister.

ménavadine, elder cognate first cousin (female), i.e. daughter of a *ménatta* being older than yourself.

ménéjaru, manager. English; also *menéjaru, manajaru*.

mépari, feeder; from *méputa*, to graze, feed.

mépintsuṭa, to graze, active; to tend cattle; causal of *méputa*.

méputa, to graze, tend cattle.

méra, limit, distance, range. *tsúpu méra dúramló,* just within sight; *méra míri,* passing the limit.

méra, a village fee. This was the fee paid to village officers, menials, and artisans; the British Government abolished it and pay village officers and menials a monthly wage; the artisans do not now work for meras or even for their inams but charge like artisans everywhere else; status has given place to contract.

Méru, Mount Meru; a mythological golden mountain on which Brahma sits surrounded by rishis.

méshamu, ram. Skt. A book word for *poṭṭélu.*

méshṭaru, schoolmaster. English. *peddamanishi: yenducu yéḍust unnáu? báluḍu: nénu podduṭi nunchi áḍu conṭ unnánu; ivváḷa ṣucravâram ani teliyaca, ṣanivâram ani, áḍu cunṭ unnánu; ippuḍu nácu ṣucravâram ani cheppäru; méshṭaru coḍatáḍ émó ani yéḍust unnánu.* Gentleman: what are you crying about? Boy: I have been playing from the morning, not knowing to-day was Friday and thinking it was Saturday; now they have told me it is Friday; I am crying because I expect my schoolmaster to give me a thrashing.

méstri, foreman. English, from master.

méta, fodder; from *méyuṭa,* to graze; *méta caranamu,* a village karnam for graft.

méṭi, chief, leader. *méṭi* is also the transliteration of the English mate and denotes, e.g., the cook's matey we always employ.

méyuṭa, to graze. *ávu chéniló mésté, dúda gaṭṭuna mésuná?* if the cow gets down into the rice field to graze, will the calf be content to stay on the bank?

miccili, much, very. *góḍalu miccili paḍipóyinavi,* the walls are much ruined; *miccili rahasyamugá,* very secretly.

miḍata, grasshopper, locust. *caruvu mánapu panṭa, miḍatalu mánapu manṭa,* crop to stop famine and flame to stop locusts; *agniló miḍata paḍḍ aṭṭu,* like the grasshopper that jumped into the fire (to put it out).

midde, terraced house; once a sign of nobility; ordinary people were not allowed to build terraced houses.

miḍi, pride, projecting, bounding. *miḍipanḍlu,* projecting teeth; *miḍigruḍlu,* goggle-eyes; *miḍisipáṭu,* bounce, insolence.

migata, balance, surplus.

migilchichéyuṭa, to save.

migilina, remaining. *ṭicharu: miló yendarici svargánici pódám ani v'undi? unnaváḷḷu chétul ettanḍi. (Rámayya tappa migilina vidyárthul andaru chétul ettäru.) ṭicharu: nicu ishṭam lédá? Rámayya: ishṭam lédu, scúlu vadali peṭṭagáné má amma inṭici ramm annad anḍi.* Teacher: How many of you want to go to heaven? Those who want to, raise your hands. (All the rest of the boys except Ramayya raise their hands.) Teacher: You don't want to go to heaven? Ramayya: No, mother told me to come straight back home from school. *Lacshmayya tánu chinn appuḍu yuddhamló tsúpina sáhásam gurinchi upanyásamló goppagá cheppuṭ unḍenu. sabhacuḍu: yuddham antá míré chésté migilina sainyam antá yém chésind anḍi?* Lakshmayya is holding forth at a lecture on his prowess in war in his youth. Voice from the audience: When you did everything what was there for the rest of the army to do?

migula, excessive.

migulamáṭalu, impertinence. Impertinent words are described as excessive words in the South Indian languages. *adhicaprasangam* is another similar expression for impertinence; *migula máṭalu rán istú v'unnáu,* you are impertinent.

migulanáḍuṭa, to reproach.

migultsuconuṭa, to save. *yagnyamu nimittamu yáchinchi, árjinchina sommuló nunḍi migultsuconna áru vandala rúpáyalunu pilladáni tanḍri mogamuna tagula peṭṭi, mund entó sukha paḍa valen ani conḍ anta ḍ̤ató áru sanvatsarámula pillanu caṭṭu connánu,* I went round collecting alms for a burnt sacrifice, sacrificed six hundred rupees from the money saved to an earthly father, and with heaven-aspiring hopes of future bliss united myself in wedlock's bond with a child of six.

miguluṭa, to remain over. *máṭalu miguluṭa* is to be impertinent; *máṭalu migulabócu,* do not be impertinent.

mimmu, you (accusative).

mimmulanu, you (accusative).

minacarintsuṭa, to blink. *yémiyu tótsaca minucarintsuts unḍenu,* he was blinking in confusion.

minahá, deduction, remission. Hindustani. An old revenue term for a deduction from the land-tax, &c.

minaháyamu, exception. Hindustani.

minaháyintsuṭa, to reduce. Hindustani. To reduce the land-tax, &c.

minaminaláḍuṭa, to sparkle.

minapa, made of black gram (*minumulu*).

minḍaḍu, lover, master. Skt. *góchipátala ráyuḍu dongala minḍaḍu,* Mr. Clout Ragamuffin is master of thieves.

minguṭa, to swallow; also *mrinuguṭa. duhkhamu minguṭa,* to swallow one's grief; *guḍi mingéváḍici guḷḷó dévuḍu vaṭravaḍiyam cadá?* the image in the temple is a black gram bun to the being that swallows the temple; *conḍa mingévánici gópuram aḍḍamá?* a temple tower is nothing to the being that swallows a hill; *míru nannu mingi vésturu,* you would swallow me whole, i.e. you would go wild with anger.

minnalli, flea; a bounding bug, from *midi,* bounding, and *nalli,* bug.

minnu, sky; the genitive is *minṭi. minnu vanca tsûtsu álóchinchi,* looking towards the sky and taking thought; *minnu-mannu* is heaven and earth; *minnutsúlu,* offspring of the sky, is the wind; *cannu yerranainá, minnu yerranainá, cáraca mánadu,* red eye, red sky, mean storms; *cannulu yerra chési,* making your eyes red, means getting angry.

minnumuttuṭa, to reach the skies (as cheers, *jayaghóshamulu*).

mintsuṭa, to surpass. *rája putrula andarini minchi,* surpassing all the king's sons; *ilágu talacu minchina véshálu vésté tsûchina váru nalugurú navvutáru,* people will laugh seeing her dressed up to the ears like that; *ítacu minchina lótú, góchici minchina dáridryamú lédú,* when you are out of your depth in water, or when you are reduced to your loin-cloth, what further depths are there?

minucu, a glimmer.

minucuminucumanuṭa, to flash, twinkle, glitter.

minugupurugu, fire-fly.

minumulu, black gram (*phaselus mungo*), a small leguminous plant with edible grain; cakes, &c., are made of the flour.

mirapacáyalu, chillies (*capsicum annuum*).

mirási, a hereditary tenure. Hindustani. This is specially applied to a hereditary option to take up waste land in a village, and to hereditary offices; *mirási udyógam* is hereditary office; *mirásivartana,* hereditary allowance.

miriyálu, pepper. *magani tala mída miriyálu nûrust unnadi,* she grinds pepper on her husband's head (of a vixen).

mirumiṭlu, dazzle. *bhayamu chéta canulu mirimiṭlu cáni,* eyes dazzled by terror.

mirumiṭluconuṭa, to be dazzled.

misamisaláḍuṭa, to glitter; e.g. the flash of youth.

misha, pretext. *í misha mída,* on this pretext; *í misha peṭṭi,* putting forward this pretext; *viváham ané misha mída,* on pretence of marriage.

mishanéri, missionary. English.

missal, hereditary right of a village officer. *missal carnamu,* titular karnam.

mitamu, limit, limited, moderate. Skt. *mita janamutó,* with a moderate retinue; *mitamuléni* or *amitamaina* is unlimited; *mitangá tágité déhánici bahu manchidi,* a moderate use of alcohol is good for the health; *mitamu tappité amrütam ainá vishamé,* exceed the limit and nectar will be poison.

miṭháyi, sweets. Hindustani. *chedipóyina páta miṭháyi,* stale spoilt sweetmeats.

miṭhunamu, couple. Skt. *miṭhuna carmánubhavamu léni vidhavalu,* widows who have to do without the function of coupling (*miṭhuna carmam* is copulation).

miti, limit. Skt., same as *mitamu*.
mitratvamu, friendship. Skt.
mitrudu, friend. Skt.
mitta, high ground, mound, high. *mittapallamulu*, ups and downs; *mitta pandlu*, projecting teeth; *mitta madhyánamu*, high noon.
mitta, false, hypocritical. *mitta védántamulu*, false scriptures.
mí, your.
mícu, to you. You have is *mícu unnadi*.
mída, on, after that. *úru mída núru paddá, caranamu mída cásu padadu*, the karnam will never pay a pie of the village taxes; *chittamu Şivuni mída, bhacti cheppula mída*, his mind is on Siva but his inmost thoughts on the shoes he left outside the temple; *muddái: ná mída tsálá mandi ádhára padi v'unnáru; vállа pai daya tsúpintsandi; méjistrétu: yevaruvállu? ní pillalá? muddái: ná pillalu cádu, pólisuvállu.* Accused: There are many dependent on me, have mercy. Magistrate: Who are they? Your children? Accused: No, the police. *ica mída* means in future; *pani mída pani*, task after task; *máta mída máta*, word upon word; *ná mída cópam chési*, getting angry with me; *mída dévaravári chittamu*, after that as the Collector pleases.
mídata, after. *ica mídata*, in future; *atu mídata*, after that; *váru póyina mídata*, after they had gone.
mídati, subsequent; *á mídati panulu*, the subsequent works.
mídi, upper, higher, on (adjective). *góda mídi pilli* is the cat on the wall; it is a proverbial expression for sitting on the fence.
mídimiccili, mídumiccili, very much, all the more, on the contrary.
mídugá, by, past. *nénu váni y'inti mídugá vachchänu*, I came past his house.
mígada, cream.
mígálu, instep; from *mída* and *cálu*, foot.
mímámsa, discussion. One of the six Hindu philosophical systems. *védamunacu artham unnadá lédá y'anna mímámsa*, a discussion whether the Vedas have any meaning or none at all.
míru, you; plural of *nívu*, which is only used familiarly; *tamaru* is still more distinguished, and the Collector's peons prefer to refer to him not as *míru*, or even *tamaru*, but as *Dévara*. when will God start on tour? Does God desire us to pack?
míruta, to transgress, pass. *ádu mírina padutsu*, a girl who has passed the age (of puberty); *lá míruta*, to transgress the law.
mísamu, mísamulu, mísálu, moustache. *oca chétitó mísamu vadivéyutsu, rendava chétitó bozza nimurucontu, Şri Rájá váru prevéşintsuts unnáru*, one hand twisting his moustache, the other rubbing his belly, the Zamindar steps in.
míta, lever, latch, bar. *uricoyyi míta* is the gallows lever; *bónu míta* is the mouse-trap bar.
mítingu, meeting. English. *y'í v'úllo panicimálina vállu condaru bógam méláluv'unda cúdad ani vádálu chési, mítingulu chéstú v'unnár ata; manam cúdá mítingulu chési vállacu garva práyaşchittam chétámu*, some worthless people in this town are arguing that nautches should not be allowed and holding meetings, so they say; let's hold meetings too and take them down a peg or two.
mítuta, to fillip, touch (an instrument). *góta mítité poyyé panici goddali yenducu?* why an axe for what can be done with a fillip?
mívádu, your son. *A: mívádu pókhiríla sahavásam cúdi parama pókhiri ai póyinádu. B: mávádu pókhiri ani yevaru cheppucógá nén eppudu vina lédé; vádu dípálu pettina taruváta tsaduvémó vád émó cáni yeppudu gummam dáti vidhuló adugu pettadu. A: mívádu tappacundá pókhiri; míru cheppinché mála tsaduvu compa tístú v'unnadi.* Orthodox Brahmin: Your son has become a great rogue by association with rogues. Enlightened Brahmin: First I have heard of it; he never goes out after dark but studies his books and so on. Orthodox Brahmin: Undoubtedly he is a rogue; the pariah (English) education you are giving him will pull your house about your ears.

mléchchha, barbarous, foreign, heathen. To the Hindu all foreign races are lesser breeds without the law, and the British Government is a *mléchchha* or barbarous government; all foreign words are *mléchchhapu máṭalu* or barbarisms; all foreign religions are heathen. Two can despise.

mocamu, face, for *mogamu, mukhamu*; *mocam tsáṭu vési inṭló v'unḍi,* hiding your face in your house.

mocca, young plant, seedling; short for *molaca*.

moccadamá, affair. Hindustani. *cindi corṭu tírpu cévalam úhala mída moccadam ai v'unnadi,* the Lower Court's judgement is all an affair of conjectures.

moccalamu, stubbornness; from Skt. *mushcaram*.

moccazonna, Indian corn. *zonna* is the large millet which resembles Indian corn.

moccu, vow; also *mroccu*. *ápati mocculu, sampati cunṭhlu,* vows in ill-fortune, reviling in good fortune (the devil was ill, the devil a monk would be; the devil was well, the devil a monk was he).

moccuṭa, to vow; also *mroccuṭa*. *tsúḍa tsuṭṭamú, mocca daivamú lédu,* no relation to see, no god to vow to (abandoned by all); *cóṭi vélpalacu moccuṭa,* to vow to all the ten million gods.

modalaina, &c.

modalu, beginning, root, source, capital. *cheṭṭu modalu,* root of tree; *chevi modalu,* lower flap of ear; *váḍu modalé manchi váḍu cáḍu,* to begin with he is not a good man; *vaḍḍí modalú,* interest and principal; *modalanṭá,* from the root; *modaṭici mósamu, lábhánici gudduláṭa,* fighting for the profits after the capital is lost.

modaluconuṭa, modalupeṭṭuṭa, to begin. *nishcáranamugá tiṭṭa modalu peṭṭinár émi?* why have you started scolding without reason?

modaṭa, at first.

modaṭi, the first.

modaṭinundiyu, from the beginning.

moddu, block, stupid, blunt. *cheviṭimuddá!* you deaf adder! *moddu lágu yenta sépaṭici ná baṭṭalu tísu coni ráv émi?* how long are you going to be about bringing my clothes, blockhead? *ní mogamuna pedda moddulu peṭṭa valenu,* blocks should be laid on your face (I should like to see you nailed up in your coffin); *yeddu vale tini, moddu vale nidra póyin aṭṭu,* eating like a bullock and sleeping like a block.

moga, end. Skt., from *mukham*. *vídhi mogacu vachchéṭ appaṭici,* when he got to the end of the street.

Mogaláyi, Mogul. Hindustani. Applied commonly to Hyderabad.

mogamóṭamu, partiality; also spelt *mokhamáṭam* and in other ways; *mokhamáṭam lécunḍá cheppaḍam dharmam,* it is right to speak without partiality.

mogamu, face. Skt. *mukhamu*; also *mugamu, mohamu. mimmalni tsúchi y'istáru gáni, y'itarula mogam tsúchi vaccarú y'ivva lédu,* they will pay subscriptions if they see you (the Collector) but not for any one else's face; *váni mogam máḍi póyinadi,* his face fell; *á chinnadi mogamu chinna putstsuconadi,* the child looked crest-fallen.

mogatanamu, manliness. *y' induló ní mogatanam telustundi,* we shall see whether you are a man or not.

mogaváḍu, male, man, husband; also *magaváḍu*. *áḍaddáni chéti arthamú, mogaváni chéti biḍḍá bratacadu,* money in a woman's hand, a child in a man's, won't thrive.

mogga, bud.

mogguṭa, to bend. *taḍisi gáni guḍise caṭṭaḍu, táci gáni moggaḍu,* a man won't build himself a hut till he is drenched or stoop till he has hit his head.

moguḍu, husband. *moguḍi tala mída miriyálu núrin aṭṭu,* grinding pepper on your husband's head (ticking him off).

mohamu, face; vulgar for *mukhamu*. *váḍi moham manḍa,* may fire consume his face, is a common expletive; *ní moham lá v'unnadi* is a vulgar way of expressing contempt (like your face, face to you).

Moharamu, Muharram, the 1st Muhammedan month; the festival on the first ten days of it which is an occasion for brawls between Hindus and Muhammedans.

mohari, gold mohur. Hindustani. Old gold coin of rupee weight worth Rs. 16.

moharu, seal. Hindustani; but say *sílu* to your peons.

mokhamal, velvet; also *makhamalu*. Hindustani.

mokhásá, village held on service tenure. Hindustani. *mokhasas* still exist though service is not rendered.

mokhásadáruḍu, holder of a *mokhasa* village.

mola, loin, waist; *disamola* is totally naked.

molabilla, the metal bit on the female infant's loin-string.

molaca, a sprout; *molaca navvu* is a budding smile.

molacaṭṭu, molatáḍu, waist-band, loin-string; also *moltáḍu, moltráḍu*.

molatsuṭa, to sprout. *cumpaṭló támara molichin aṭṭu,* like a lotus sprouting in a saucepan (when two Sundays meet).

molavéyuṭa, to sow.

mona, point, front, headland; *monatsannu* (breast-point) means nipple.

monagáḍu, ringleader. *táné mahá monagáḍan ani prati mahávádi anucunṭu v'untáḍu,* every extremist agitator looks upon himself as a born leader.

monḍemu, trunk (of body), stump.

monḍi, maimed, crippled, stubborn, close-fisted. *léni v'uḍári canṭé caliguna monḍi mélu,* a rich miser is better than a lavish pauper. *monḍi tóca yeddu,* a bobtailed bull; *monḍic ettina vánḷanu yevaru yémi chéstáru?* you can do nothing with obstinate people. *monḍari, monḍicatte,* a stubborn man; *monḍitanamu,* stubbornness.

monna, day before yesterday.

monnamanánicimonna, only the other day.

monnamonna, just. *monna monna chinna y'udyógamulaló pravéṣinchina vár andaru manasu vachchin aṭṭu sampádinchi, bháryalacunu biḍḍalacunu déhamu ninḍa nagalu diga véyuts unnáru,* men who have just placed their foot on the first rung of the official ladder pile up money at their good will and load their wives and children with jewellery.

monnaṭi, last. *monnaṭi samvatsar ádi,* last New Year's day.

moppe, fool. *moppecu múreḍu nóru,* a fool has a wide mouth.

moppu, misfortune. *appu moppu,* debt is damnation.

mora, cry; word constantly used in petitions. *má mora álacinchi,* listening to our cry.

morapeṭṭuṭa, to cry out.

morri, defect, broken edge; used e.g. of the defective edge of the moon in an eclipse. *grahanam paṭṭi chandruniló conchemu morri póyi v'unnadi,* as the eclipse came on the moon's edge appeared broken; *morri pedavi* is a hare-lip; *morri chevi* a cropped ear.

moruguṭa, to bark. *dongalu coṭṭina áru másamulacu cuccalu moriginavi,* six months after the burglary the dogs began to bark; *yénugunu tsúchi cuccalu morigin aṭṭu,* like dogs barking at an elephant; *cucca véshamu vésté, moragacunḍá valla cáḍu,* if you disguise yourself as a dog you needs must bark. *Lacshmayya: mí cucca moragaḍam chéta má ammáyi sangítam páḍu cóvaḍánici vílu léca póyinadi. Vencayya: mí ammáyé mundugá morigindi.* Smith: My daughter's singing was stopped by your dog barking. Jones: It was your daughter that barked first.

mosali, crocodile. *Góddávari nadiló n'unḍeḍu mosallac enta tala birasó, dínic anta tala birusu,* she is as thick in the head as a Godavari crocodile; *mócshánici vasté mosali yettucu póyindi,* he came (to the river) for salvation and a crocodile carried him off.

mosamosaláḍuṭa, to giggle; onomatopoeic.

mostaru, kind, sort, way. *cotta mostarugá,* in a new way; *vyápára vishayamu yeṭlá unnadi?* how is business? *oca mostarugá zaruguts unnadi,* middling.

moṭima, pimple.

moṭṭamodaṭa, at the very first.
mottamu, total, multitude. *mottapu vyayamu,* the total expenditure; *mottamu chéyuṭa,* to total up; *cóti mottamu,* a herd of monkeys.
mottucóḷḷu, lamentations.
mottuconuṭa, to beat oneself, lament. *mottucunaṭṭé v'unnadi,* it is deplorable.
mottuṭa, to beat.
movvu, shoot of palm, plantain, &c.
moyyuṭa, to carry; same as *móyuṭa,* which is commoner. *mosuguveḷḷa, mosugupónu,* are expletives (may he be carried to his grave!).
mócarintsuta, to kneel. *nénu mócarintsucuni cúrtsunnán ani míru bhrama paḍḍ aṭṭ unnáru,* you seem to be surprised at my squatting on my knees.
mócálu, knee. *mócálibanṭi,* knee-deep. *caligité cáḷḷu muyyi, léca póté mócáḷḷu muyyi,* wear your dress to your feet if you can afford it, if not, to your knees.
mócáluchippa, knee-cap.
móchanamu, deliverance, salvation. Skt.; same as *mócshamu.*
mócheyyi, elbow. *móchéti pótu,* poke with the elbow. *attavári inṭi sukhamu, móchéti debba vanṭidi,* the joys of the mother-in-law's house are like a blow on the elbow.
mócshamu, deliverance, salvation. Skt. It is the deliverance from the bonds of sense, life in the absolute.
móḍugu, bastard teak (*butea frondosa*).
móduṭa, to beat. *í yelucanu tsáva móduḍu,* beat this rat to death.
móḍutsuṭa, to close, fold.
móhamu, love, especially sexual. *ná mída móhamu,* her infatuation for me; *móha páṣálu,* the bonds of love; *dabbu cósam tappa nizam chéta Ṣásturlagári mída nácu yémí préma léca póyiná, áyana vadda n'unn appuḍu léni móham tetstsu peṭṭucunṭánu,* though I care for Mr. Shastri only for money and have no love for him, when I am with him I feign passion for him.
móhintsuṭa, to love.
mómóṭa, pity, partiality; another form of *mogamóṭamu.*
mómu, face; another form of *mogamu.*
mópudala, imputation, charge.
mópuṭa, put down. *peṭṭe bhúmi mída mópi,* laying the box on the ground.
móputa, to impute; *árópintsuṭa* is another common word for this.
mósagáḍu, deceiver, swindler.
mósamu, deceit, harm. *cunṭic ullásam y'inṭici mósam,* mischief is the cripple's joy. *anéca vidhála mósálu chési, dhanam sampádinchi, jívanam chéstu v'unnánu,* I used to make my living by various kinds of swindles.
mósapóvuṭa, to be cheated, disappointed.
mósaputstsuṭa, to cheat.
mosévádu, he who carries. *mósévánici telusunu cáviḍi baruvu,* he who carries the yoke knows its weight (the wearer knows where the shoe pinches).
móta, load; *mótayeddu* is a pack-bullock.
móṭa, mote (irrigation water-wheel); *móṭabána* is the large bucket used on the mote.
móṭa, stupid, rough. Skt., from *múḍha. móṭa dunnapótá!* you buffalo! *móṭacu cópam muccu mída,* the rough man shows his anger on his nose.
mótárubanḍi, móṭabanḍi, móṭucáru, móṭáru, motor-car. English. *Lacshmamma: mí áyana mótárubanḍi contáḍ aṭé. Vencamma: anducané yatnam chést unnáru. Lacshmamma: móṭáru peṭṭédánici illu caṭṭist unnárá? Vencamma: mótárubandi cheḍi póté bágu cheyyaḍam yeṭlágó, banḍi talacindul aité yém cheyyál enó telipé pustacam coni tsaduvut unnáru.* Mrs. Smith: I hear your husband is buying a car. Mrs. Jones: He is thinking of it. Mrs. Smith: Is he building a garage? Mrs. Jones: He has bought a manual to find out how to repair it and what he is to do if it goes to pot. *Lacshmayya: í mótárucáru mícu yeṭṭá vachchindi? Vencayya: láṭariló. Lacshmayya: mí nambaru gelichindi cábólu? Vencayya: nénu láṭariló ḍabbu peṭṭa lédu, láṭari yérpáṭu chésindi néne.* Smith: How did you get this car? Jones: In a raffle. Smith: Your number won, I suppose? Jones: No, I ran the raffle.
móṭu, obstinate, stupid, rough. *áme*

pillanu mótugá yettucunnadi, she handles the child roughly.

mótubarí, mótuparí, substantial, well-to-do. Hindustani. *mótubarí rayitu,* a substantial farmer.

móvu, shoot of palm, plantain, &c.; also *movvu.*

móyuṭa, to carry, convey. *buṭṭa mósucuni veḷḷadánici nénu manushyulanu tísucuni vastánu,* I will go and fetch men to carry the basket off; *andarú andalamu yeccité, mósévárn yevaru?* if all get into the palanquin, who will there be left to carry it? *gandha poḍi mósé gáḍide vale,* like a donkey carrying sandal-powder (incongruity).

mránu, tree; also *mánu* and more commonly *cheṭṭu.*

mringuṭa, to swallow; also *minguṭa. tondaragá mringi,* swallowing in haste; *nóṭiló vrélu peṭṭuconi guṭacalu mringutsu,* putting his finger in his mouth and gulping down.

mroccu, vow; same as *moccu.*

mroccuṭa, to vow; same as *moccuṭa. mí cáḷḷacu mroccutánu,* I beseech you; *míru dévuḷḷ ani ráḷḷacú carralacú mroccutáru,* you make vows to stones and sticks which you take for gods.

mróta, ringing sound. *santsulaló gallu-gallumani rúpáyala mróta vinutsunduṭa chevula panḍuvu cádá?* what a delight to the ears is the ring of rupees jingling and jangling in their bags.

mróyuṭa, to resound, to ring.

mrüduvu, soft, mild, gentle. Skt. *mrüdu-madhura* are often combined; *mrüdumadhura gáḍpulu,* delicious breezes; *mrüdupu tappina,* discourteous; *ilá mrüduputappina máṭalu máṭáḍutú v'unṭé pillaváḷḷanu asalé máṭládan iyyanu,* if you boys use such ungentle words I won't allow you to talk at all.

mrügamu, animal. Skt. *mrügéndruḍu,* the king of beasts; *mrügácshi,* gazelle-eyed.

mrügaya, the chase. Skt.

mrüsha, false. Skt.

mrüti, death. Skt.

mrüttica, mire. Skt. Used metaphorically. *paniló yémí lábham? mrüttica,* no profit in that; a rotten business.

mrüttica, earth, soil. Skt. *ṣóna mrüttica parama pávanam ainadi,* red earth is very holy.

mrütuḍu, dead man. Skt. *mrütula yocca bhályal andarú tarváta svarga lócánici vachchi, bhartalató svarga sukham anubhavistár anna sangati ṣástrálanu baṭṭi mícu telisé v'unnadi gadá?* don't you know that according to the scriptures the wives of the dead follow them to heaven and enjoy heavenly bliss with them? *jívan mrütuḍu, mrüta jívuḍu,* the bad man is a living corpse, the good man still lives after death.

mrütyudévatalu, the gods of death, furies. Skt. *mana páliṭici mrütyudévatalu vale póg ainavi,* they have gathered like furies around us.

mu-, prefix meaning 3; *mummáru,* 3 times; *muppática,* three-quarters; *muccáni,* ¾ anna; *muccálu,* 3 legs; *muccáru,* 3 seasons.

mucca, piece. *renḍu muccalu vrástánu,* I will write a line or two; *nálugu yengili y'Inglíshu muccalu tsaduvu cóvaḍamtóṭé voḷḷ erugaca púrv ácháránní, peddalini dúshistáru,* once they have learnt a few defiling fragments of English they are so puffed up that they revile old customs and their elders; *ocaṭé debba renḍé muccalu,* one blow two pieces (to settle a matter at one blow).

muccammi, nose-ring. From *muccu,* nose, and *cammi,* wire.

muccálu, ¾. From *mu,* 3, and *cálu.*

muccáni, ¾ anna, 9 pies. From *mu,* 3, and *cáni.*

muccidi, snipe; but they say *ishnappu*; *muccidi* is from *muccu,* beak. The Italian for snipe, *beccacina,* is also the beak-bird.

muccónamu, triangle. From *mu-,* 3, and *cónamu,* angle. Commonly used of the whipping triangle.

muccu, nose, beak, tip. *tummité poyyé muccu yennáḷḷu v'unḍunu,* a nose that goes when you sneeze isn't much good; *muccu tsochchi canṭló pravéṣinchéváḍu,* he would go into your eye through your nose (a very clever fellow); *muccu chinna, muttemu pedda,* big pearl for small nose; *garuḍa muccu,*

Roman nose (eagle's beak); *tsappidi muccu*, snub nose; *daggité nilavani muccu, tummité nilutsundá?* will a nose that can't stand coughing stand sneezing?

muccubocca, nostril.

muccuchíduṭa, to blow the nose.

muccudúlamu, bridge of nose; from *muccu*, nose, and *dúlamu*, beam.

muccupoḍi, snuff; from *muccu*, nose, and *poḍi*, powder.

muccurandhramu, nostril; from *muccu*, nose, and *randhramu*, hole.

muccutáḍu, bullock's nose-string. *muccutáḍu léni yeddu, munḍa penchina biḍḍa ocaṭi*, there is no holding a widow's child or a bullock without a nose-string.

muchchelu, slippers.

muchchéváḍu, man of the Muchi caste, book-binders, paper cutters, makers of toys, saddles, &c.

muchchi, the office menial of the Muchi caste; he pastes and binds and cuts out envelopes and sews up files.

muchchilica, deed. Hindustani. A revenue term used especially of the counterpart of the *patta.*

muctasamgá, briefly, in brief. Hindustani.

mucti, salvation. Skt. A religious term from *muctam*, released, liberated.

muctyáru, agent. Hindustani. An old word for agent who has not a pleader's *sanad*; also *mukhtyáru.*

mudaliáru, a Tamil Sudra caste.

mudará, remission, discount. Hindustani. An old revenue term for remission of the land-tax or water-rate.

muḍata, wrinkle; also *muḍuta*. *gaḍḍam antayu tella paḍinanu déhamunan occa muḍuta y'ainanu léca póyindi*, though his beard is white he has not a wrinkle.

mudda, morsel, lump. *péda muddalu*, lumps of dung; *váru taḍisi mudda aináru*, they are soaking wet; *netturu muddugá n'unnadi*, caked blood; *venna mudda*, pat of butter.

muddáḍuṭa, to caress; from *muddu*, kiss; to kiss is *muddupeṭṭuconuṭa* or *muddiḍuconuṭa.*

muddáyi, the accused in a criminal case. Hindustani. *méjisṭréṭu: firyádi muddáyi coṭṭucunṭé tsúchává? sácshi: tsúchánanḍi. méjisṭréṭu: coṭṭacunḍá nuvvu yémi chéya lédá? sácshi: cheyya léd anḍi. méjisṭréṭu: yendu chéta? sácshi: nénu tsuṭṭa tágutunnán anḍi.* Magistrate: Did you see the accused beating the complainant? Witness: Yes. Magistrate: You did not try to stop him? Witness: No. Magistrate: Why not? Witness: I was smoking.

muḍḍi, rump. *gollavádá, gollaváḍá, dhányam eccaḍa v'unnad anṭé, gorre muḍḍiló y'unnad anṭáḍu*, shepherd, shepherd, where is the grain? In my sheep's rump, he will say (the utility of manure); *tana muḍḍi cáca póté Cáṣi dácá décam annáḍu*, he said, you may slide to Benares if you like so long as it is not on my rump; *dípamu muḍḍi cinda chícaṭi*, under the lamp it is dark; *áḍuvánḍla muḍḍi tsuṭṭú tirigéváḍu*, a poodle-faker.

muddiḍuconuṭa, to kiss; from *muddu*, a kiss.

muddu, kiss, darling, pet. *cáci pilla cácici muddu*, the crow's chick is the crow's darling (*all'orsa paion belli i suoi orsacchini*, to the she-bear the bear-cubs seem pretty); *muddulamúta* is a bundle of charms; *cuccanu muddu peṭṭu cunṭé múṭ ellá tega nácutundi*, kiss a dog and it will lick your whole face. *á biḍḍa muddugá unnadi*, that is a sweet child.

muḍḍuḍu, idiot.

muddupeṭṭuṭa, to kiss. *ámecu donga-tanamugá muddu peṭṭu cunnáḍu*, he stole a kiss from her.

muddutungaramu, signet ring (pet ring); from *muddu* and *ungaramu*, ring.

muddúmutstsaṭa, pleasant things, darlings. *míru muddúmutstsaṭa bágá yeragaru; chinna pillalacu peḷḷi chésté v'undé sogasu pedda pillalacu chésté v'unḍadu*, you don't understand the charm of child-marriages; the marriage of young children is much more elegant than the marriage of older children (defence of child-marriage).

muḍi, knot. *peṭṭuṭa* or *véyuṭa* is to make a knot; *vippuṭa* to undo one; *í muḍi rádu; adi zárumuḍi cádá? cádu, gaṭṭi muḍi*, this knot won't come undone; isn't it a slip-knot? no, a firm knot.

mudi, ancient. *mudi mánu chéva,* an old tree has a firm core (a brave heart in an old body).

mudicáḻḻaváḍu, knock-kneed man.

mudimi, decrepitude.

mudira, seal, stamp, print. *ivi Hayidrábádu mudira vésina rúpáyilu,* these rupees are of Hyderabad mintage; *í y'uttaramu mída Peddápuram mudira v'unnadi,* this letter bears the Peddapur stamp.

mudiyuṭa, to grow old. *mudisi muppuna,* in old age.

mudra, seal, signet-ring, sign, brand. Skt. *Tátácháryula mudra bhujamu tappina vípu tappadu,* if Tatachari's brand misses your shoulder it won't miss your back. (Tatachari was a priest who branded his disciples.)

mudrapodutsuṭa, mudravéyuṭa, to seal, brand.

mudrácsharaṣála, printing press; from *mudra, acsharam,* letter, and *ṣála,* hall.

mudrintsuṭa, to seal, print; *mudrimpabaḍinadi,* printed. *atstsuvéyuṭa* is also to print.

mudritamu, sealed.

muḍupu, purse, offering in money or jewels. *á muḍupu chellinchi dévatánugraham pondinadi,* you have obtained God's favour by that gift.

muduruṭa, to ripen. *mícu vayassu mudirindi,* you are of a ripe age; *ippuḍ á sangítapu pitstsa munapati canṭenú yábhai reṭlu yeccuva mudiri póyindi,* his mania for music has ripened fifty times as much now.

muḍuṭa, to touch; more commonly *muṭṭuṭa.*

muḍuta, wrinkle; also *mudata.*

muḍutsuṭa, to tie, bend, fold. *muḍutsuconuṭa* is especially to twine flowers into the hair; *manchi puvvulu techchi y'ichchinanu, oca náḍ ainanu mutstsaṭa tíra nénu tsútsuts unḍagá coppuló muḍutsucóvu,* although I bring you nice flowers you never think of sating the yearning of my eyes by twining posies in your hair.

mufassalu, up country, provincial. Hindustani.

mugamu, face; also *mukhamu, mogamu, mohamu, mómu. mukhamu* is the most correct form; *moham* is the usual colloquial form.

mugatáḍu, bullock's nose-rope. *munda penchina biḍḍa, mugatáḍu léni yeddutó samánam,* a child brought up by a widow is like a bullock without a nose-rope.

muggu, a pattern made with flowers or in powder especially in front of a house, a magic circle. *muggulu* can be seen in front of any Hindu house in the morning; *mugguló cúrtsunḍa peṭṭi, mantrálu cheppi,* putting him in a magic circle and repeating charms.

mugguru, three persons. *mugguru áḍaváru cúḍité paṭṭa pagalé tsuccalu poḍustavi,* if three women get together the stars come out in broad daylight.

mugimpu, termination.

mugintsuṭa, to finish. *dácṭaru vind ichchenu; vindu samáyamló tana rámachilaca canabaḍacunḍá tera aḍḍamu peṭṭenu. vachchina atithulaló ocaḍu ganṭala coddi máṭláḍut unḍenu; áyana muginchina pimmaṭa chilaca teraló nunchi iṭlá anenu: 'mí náluca tsúpintsanḍi',* a doctor gave a dinner-party and covered up his parrot with a curtain so that it could not be seen; one of the guests talked by the hour together; when he had finished the parrot said from behind the curtain: 'please put out your tongue'.

mugiyuṭa, to finish (intrans.). *Lacshmayya: nénu rachinchina náṭacam yeṭlá v'unnadi? sukhamgá mugisindá lédá? Rámayya: náṭacam áḍaḍam mugisina tarváta tsúḍa vachchinaváḻḻu sukha paḍḍáru.* Lakshmayya: How did my play go? Did it end up well? Ramayya: After it was all over the audience felt more comfortable.

muhúrtamu, time in astrology. Skt. Used commonly for auspicious time; you go to your astrologer to fix an auspicious time for a marriage, journey, &c.

mukhadácshinyamu, complaisance; from *mukham,* face, and *dácshinyam,* grace.

mukhalacshanamu, feature. Skt.

From *mukham*, face, and *lacshanam*, sign. *bhárya: ná mída mícu préma v'unnadá? bharta: ná mukhalacshanálanu nuvvu tsadavi tsúḍu. bhárya: nácu tsaduvu rádu gá, yeṭlá tsadivédi?* Wife: Do you love me? Husband: Read my features and you will see. Wife: But how can I? I don't know how to read.

mukhamu, face, direction. Skt. The usual colloquial form is *mohamu*; other forms are *mogamu*, *mugamu*, *mónu*; compounds such as *mukhamandalamu*, face-orb, are common in books; *mukham eruganiváḍu*, a stranger; *áḍadáni mukham eruganiváḍu*, a man who has not known woman; *náná mukhálá pári póyinárn*, they ran away in all directions; *pustacamunacu nalu mukhála veticinánu*, I have hunted high and low for the book; *á rúcalanu váni mukhamu mída páravéyi*, throw the money in his face; *váḍi mukham váḍic émi telusu?* what does he know? *svadéṣánici pó vál ani mukham váchi v'unnánu*, I am homesick (*Heimweh* takes the form of a swollen face in the Telugu country); *í panici darakhástulu nálu mukhamula nunchi vachchi paḍuts unnavi*, applications for this post are pouring in from all directions; *aṣudhamu mída ráyi vésté mukham anta chindutundi*, throw a stone into dirt and you will dirty your own face (stirring up mud); *vellacila parundi v'ummi vésté mukhamu mída paḍutundi*, if you lie on your back and spit upwards the spittle will fall on your face (proverb of blasphemy; whoso casteth a stone on high casteth it on his own head, Ecclus. xxvii. 25; the Italians have both these proverbs; *chi contro Dio gitta la pietra in capo gli ritorna*, the stone you throw against God falls back on your head; *chi sputa in su lo sputo gli torna sul viso*, if you spit up the spittle comes back on your face); *mukhamantapamu*, entrance porch to a temple.

mukhamukhi, face to face. *nannu mukhamukhi tsúḍa lécundá n'unnáḍu*, he cannot look me in the face.

mukharíti, complaisance. *úricé mukharíti cósam annánu*, I only said it to please you.

mukhaṣála, entrance hall.

mukhastuti, flattery (praise to your face). *míru v'úricé nannu mukhastuti chéstú v'unnáru*, you are simply flattering me; *y'idi tama mundara mukhastuti cósam ané máṭa cádu sumanḍí; nénu y'idi nizamgá tricarana ṣuddhigá cheppé máṭa*, this is not said to flatter you but in all sincerity of thought, word, and deed.

mukhtyáru, agent. Hindustani. An old word for an agent who is not a qualified pleader but appears before officers with a power of attorney from a party to proceedings.

mukhavarchassu, brilliance of face, beautiful complexion.

-mukhuḍu, affix meaning 'of' or 'belonging to' a face. *sumukhuḍugá*, graciously; *durmukhuḍai y'unḍi*, looking cross; *parámukhuḍai*, turning his face away.

mukhyamainaváḷḷu, the important people. *atithi: vindu tsálá bágá zarigindi, nénu yeppaṭici marachi pónu. yazamáni: mukhyamainaváḷḷu yevaḷḷú varsham valla rá léd ani nácu tsálá vichárамgá v'undi.* Guest: An excellent dinner, I shall remember it all the days of my life. Hostess: I am sorry all the important people were kept away by the rain.

mukhyamu, important, chief. *adi mukhyamu*, that is the chief point; *idi mukhyamu cádu*, this is not important.

mukhyamugá, chiefly.

mukhyuḍu, a leader.

mulle, bundle of money, purse. *múṭá mullé*, bag and baggage; *váḍi múṭá mullé dótsucu póyinárn*, they robbed him of all he had (his bundle and his purse).

mullócamu, the three worlds, the universe; being earth, heaven, and hell.

mullu, thorn. Used also of a spur, of the hand of a watch and the sting of a bee or wasp. *ná déham ippuḍu munḍla mída paḍucon aṭṭ unnadi*, I feel as if I were lying on thorns. *Lacshmayya cóṭu venuca mullu gutstsuconenu; yevarainá tístár émó n'ani oca mailu cúḍa naḍichenu; chivaracu ocaḍu canipinchenu.*

Lacshmayya: ayyá! ná cóṭu venuca muḷḷu gutstsu cunnai, conchem tísi peṭṭ anḍi, díni cósam mailu dúram vachchănu. Ocaḍu: adi saré gáni, cóṭu tísi vésté nuvvé tísu cunéváḍivi gá? Lakshmayya got some thorns in his coat behind; he walked a mile to find some one to pick them out; at last he met some one. Lakshmayya: Sir! I have got some thorns behind in my coat; would you mind picking them out? I have walked a mile for the purpose. Stranger: That's all very well, but couldn't you take off the coat and pick them off yourself?

mulucóla, goad.

muluguṭa, to groan; also *múluguṭa.*

mummáru, three times; *mummáṭici* for the third time, at auctions.

mumpu, immersion.

mun-, prefix meaning 'before', 'in front'.

munaga (*Hyperanthera moringa*), a sort of horse-radish; proverbially a weak plant. *nénu paṭṭindi munaga comma cádu, chinta comma,* it is no broken reed I rely on; *váḍu munaga cheṭlacu nichchenalu véstunnáḍu,* he plants ladders against munaga plants (a diminutive man).

munaguṭa, to dip; also *múnuguṭa. yevari niḷḷaló váru munuga valenu,* every one must bear his own cross.

munasabu, munsiff. Hindustani. An official with judicial functions. *gráma munasabu* is the village magistrate, *distriċṭu munasabu,* a civil judge of the lowest grade.

munḍa, widow, wretch; from Skt. *munḍam,* shaven, lopped. *munḍa coḍucé coḍucu, rázu coḍucé coḍucu,* a widow's son and a king's son are sons (i.e. are spoilt); *múlan unna musali munḍa lévadu,* even the old widow sitting in the corner won't get up for him; *muccutáḍu léni yeddu, munḍa penchina biḍḍa, ocaṭi,* a bullock without a nose-string and a widow's son are beyond control.

munḍácoḍucu, ordinary term of abuse like *lanjacoḍucu,* whoreson, widows being supposed to be often of bad character.

munḍalamári, whoremonger.

munḍamóyuṭa, to become a widow; *munḍamósina* is used as an expletive; *dáni munḍamósina sommu, munḍamósina carralu,* damned money, damned sticks; 500 *rúpáyilacu ammucunna ní cúturu munḍamósi múla cúrtsundi,* the daughter you sold for Rs. 500 has become a widow and sits in the corner; *coḍucu bág unḍa vale, cóḍalu munḍamoyya vale,* health to my son, widowhood to my daughter-in-law (the illogical curse of the mother-in-law).

mundara, in front, before. *mundara pallamu, venuca miṭṭa,* ditch before, bank behind (a dilemma); *mundaraci vasté goyyi venaccu póté nuyyi,* if you go forward a pit, if you go back a well (another dilemma, out of the frying-pan into the fire).

mundaṭa, before.

mundaṭi, first (adjective).

munḍlacanche, prickly-pear fence; from *mullu,* thorn, and *canche,* hedge.

munḍlapandi, porcupine; from *mullu,* thorn, and *pandi,* pig. Also *édupandi.*

munḍlapoda, thistle.

mundu, before, in front, in future. *mundu poyyé Mutarácharánni, venuca vachché Bóyavánni, paccanu vachché Paṭrátivánni namma rádu,* beware of the Mutarasa in front, the Boya behind, and the Patrati beside you (all more or less criminal castes); *mundu pani mundu chéya valenu,* you must first do what is first to hand.

mundugá, first (adverb). *gumástá: nácu jítam tsálad anḍi. vartacuḍu: níc ippuḍu yém y'istunnámu? gumástá: yém iyyaḍam léd anḍi, mundugá paricsha chéstám anṭé úrice pani chéstunnán anḍi. vartacuḍu: aité vachché nela nunchi renḍintalu chést álé.* Clerk: My pay isn't enough. Merchant: What are we giving you now? Clerk: Nothing, you said you would try me first and I am working for nothing. Merchant: Then we will double your pay from next month.

munduvenuca, causes and consequences; *munduvenuca tsúḍaca* or *álóchintsacunḍá* is used of rash resolves.

mungári, the first crop. Used in the Ceded Districts of the first dry crop or season (sown with the south-west monsoon); the second crop is *hingári*.

mungi, mongoose. *tsaduvu cóvaḍánici badulugá tóṭa gummam vadda mungi lágu pácutú v'unnává?* crawl along near the garden wall like a mongoose, would you, instead of studying?

mungili, courtyard; from *mundu*, *cala*, and *illu*; the genitive is *mungiṭi*. *mungiṭi nidhánam* is a windfall (treasure in the courtyard).

mungópi, fretful, peevish; from *mun*, in front, and *cópamu*, anger.

mungurulu, front curls; from *mundu* in front, and *curulu*, curls.

muni, hermit. Skt.

muni, point, tip.

municóla, point of goad.

munimanamuḍu, great-grandson.

munimanamurálu, great grand-daughter.

munishi, munshi. Hindustani. Originally clerk, now language teacher.

munjeyyi, wrist; from *mun*, in front, and *cheyyi*, hand. *munjéti cancanácu addamu cá valená?* do you want a glass to see the bracelet on your wrist?

munnáḷḷu, three days. *munnáḷḷ unṭe murici tsuṭṭamu*, in three days one's relations outstay their welcome (are dirt; the Italians have a proverb, *pesce e ospiti puzzano in capo a tre giorni*, fish and guests stink after three days).

munnáluca, tip of tongue.

munníru, ocean. A book word.

munnu, before. *intacu munnu*, before this.

munnúru, 300. *munnúru ṣikhal ainá cúḍa vatstsunu gáni, múḍu coppulu cúḍa rádu*, 300 pairs of trousers may get together, but 3 skirts cannot (*ṣikha* is the male top-knot, *coppu* the woman's).

munta, small pitcher or pail. *tsallacu vachchi munta dátsu conn aṭṭu*, like coming to beg milk and hiding the pail (beating about the bush); *munt eḍu pálacu mutyam anta chémiri*, sour milk the size of a pearl to a pailful of milk (to curdle it); *cathacu cáḷḷu lévu, muntacu chevulu lévu*, a story without legs and a pot without handles (nothing you can catch hold of).

muntsuṭa, to dip, to immerse.

munuguṭa, to dip, to be immersed, to bathe, to sink. *tá valachinadi Rambha, tá muniginadi Ganga*, the woman he loves is a Rambha, the water he bathes in the sacred Ganges (all his geese are swans; Rambha is the courtesan of the gods); *duhkha samudramló munigi póvuṭa*, to be drowned in a sea of sorrows; *naṭṭ éṭa puṭṭi munigin aṭṭu*, like the coracle sinking in midstream (a breakdown in your enterprise).

munumunu, at the very first.

munupaṭi, former.

munupu, before. *coṭṭuca munupé yéḍustáv ém anṭé, mundu coṭṭu pótáv ani yéḍustán ann aṭṭu*, why do you cry before you are hurt? Because it won't be long before I am hurt, said the boy.

munzúru, eaves; from *mundu*, in front, and *tsúru*, border, eaves.

muppadi, muppai, 30, *mu*, 3, ×*padi*, 10.

muppática, ¾; *mu*, 3, ×*pática*, ¼.

muppáu, ¾; *mu*, 3, ×*páu*, ¼.

muppáula, ¾ rupee; *mu*, 3, ×*páula*, quarters.

muppu, danger. *daivam é vélac, evaric, é vidhamugá muppu peṭṭunó, yevaricini teliyadu*, no one can tell what day, by whom, and in what way providence will endanger him.

muppu, old age. *mudisi muppuna*, in ripe old age.

murici, dirt. *munnáḷḷ unṭe murici tsuṭṭamu*, relations stink after three days' stay; *má abbáyi paṭṭu baṭṭa nénu áru nelalacu vaca paryáyam v'utucutánu, appuḍu dáníló nunchi nálugu cuntsála murici póyi jiḍḍu nillalló térutundi*, I wash my boy's silk cloth (silk is always *ceremonially* clean) once in six months and four pints of dirty grease rise to the top of the water.

muricicáluva, drainage channel as opposed to irrigation channel (*panṭa cáluva*).

murugulu, bangles.

muruguníḷḷu, drainage water, stagnant water. *muruguniḷḷa cálva* is a drain; *murudóva* is a dirty, muddy road.

muruguṭa, to rot, to decay. *cálu tannité*

murigédi gummiḍi cáya, cálu tannité perigédi putstsa cáya, trample on a pumpkin and it rots; trample on a water-melon and it flourishes.

muruvu, beauty, grace.

musalayya, old man.

musaláme, old woman.

musaláyana, old gentleman.

musali, musalidi, old, old woman.

musalitanamu, old age. *musali* is only of persons; *páta* of things.

musaliváḍu, old man.

musalmánu, musalman. Hindustani.

mushṭi, fist. Skt. The Telugu is *piḍicili.*

mushṭi, alms; also used as an expletive. *mushṭici bailudérináru,* they have gone out to beg; *mushṭi sambandham, y'í sambandham tappi póté nénu répu y'í páṭici mí chinnadánici y'inta canṭe manchi sambandham tisucu vastánu,* if this wretched marriage goes to pot, I will arrange another for your girl by this time to-morrow; *lantsálu putstsu coni, bágu paḍuṭa canṭé, mushṭi yettu cóvaḍam v'uttamam,* it is better to beg than to take bribes; *mushṭi nálu rúpayilu,* wretched four rupees.

mushṭi yettuconuṭa, to beg.

musimusi (navvuṭa), (to laugh) aloud; onomatopoeic.

mustábu, kit, dress. Hindustani. *mír andaru y'iḷḷacu veḷḷi mustáb ai ranḍi,* all go home and dress.

musugu, veil. *mogamu ninḍa musugu vési coni,* completely veiling his face; *álágu tala ninḍa musugu vésu coni dongavánni vale tala vantsu coni pári póvuts unnáv ém ayya?* what are you running away for like a thief with your head hanging down and completely covered?

musurumúti, peevishness.

musuruṭa, to swarm. *bellamu v'unḍé tsóṭa y'ígalu musurut unnavi,* flies swarm where jaggery is.

mutaca, coarse. *í mutaca chiretó nénu yélágu vastánu?* how can I come in this coarse dress? *boṭléruváḍu manam y'ichchina praṣastamaina sanna biyyam yeccaḍanó dáchi, yeccaḍivó mutaca biyyam vanḍi peṭṭi, doragáritó tahaṣṣíludáru ilágaṇṭi páḍu biyyam pampinchináḍ ani cheppinḍáḍ aṭa.* (Collector's butler, not having received the usual gratification) the butler is said to have hidden the A-1 fine rice we supplied somewhere, and served coarse rice he got from somewhere, and to have said the tahsildar sent such bad rice.

muṭhá, kind of estate. Hindustani. Originally a subdivision of a district; continued in some cases to descendants of the administrators.

mutstsaláḍuṭa, to converse pleasantly.

mutstsaṭa, pleasant conversation, pleasure, wish, longing. *mutstsaṭa tíra nénu tsútsuts unḍagá puvvulu coppuló muḍutsucóvu,* you won't tie flowers in your hair to sate the longing of my eyes; *nác entó mutstsaṭ ainadi,* how pleased I was; *muddú mutstsaṭá* is 'pleasant things' or 'darlings'.

mutstsaṭagá, pleasant. *í illu bahu tamáshágá v'unnadi, tsuṭṭú tóṭalu yenta mutstsaṭagá v'unnavi,* a wonderful house with pleasant grounds around it.

mutstsaṭagutsundi, is pleasant (with dative).

mutstsaṭapaduṭa, to desire, to be enamoured of.

mutstsaṭintsuṭa, to converse pleasantly. *Lacshmayya gurinchi abhinandana sabha zarigenu; sabhádhyacshul agu Vencayya Gáru í ritini mutstsaṭinchiri; Lacshmayyagáru paráyi grámam vár ainá mana v'úḷḷó iravai sanvatsarála nunchí unṭú, mana grámábhivrüddhicai páṭu paḍut unnáru, áyananu mana v'úri samádhilóné púḍchéṭ aṭṭu Bhagavantuḍu anugrahintsu gáca!* there was a congratulatory meeting in honour of Lakshmayya; Mr. Venkayya, who presided, congratulated him as follows: Mr. Lakshmayya belongs to another village, but he has lived here twenty years and done much for us and may God grant that he be buried in our village!

muṭṭachepputa, to hand over, to assign; from *muṭṭuṭa,* to touch, and *chepputa,* to tell; tell him to touch.

muṭṭaḍintsuṭa, to besiege.

muttaida, married woman.

muttarátsa, muttarasa; a caste, originally feudal retainers, now of bad reputation.

muttavatalli, great-grandmother.
muttáta, great grandfather; from *mu*, 3, and *táta*, grandfather. *moguḍu dánici muttáta lágu v'unḍaḍam chéta, alág anṭár ani siggu paḍi, á munḍa coḍucunu múla cúrtsó peṭṭi, svéchchhagá tirugutú v'unnadi*, as her husband is like a great-grandfather to her she is ashamed of people saying this, and leaves the old blighter in a corner and wanders freely about.
mutte, stone of fruit.
muttemu, pearl; also *mutyamu*.
muṭṭicállaváḍu, knock-kneed man.
muṭṭinadi, received (touched); the usual word in receipts for money.
muṭṭintsuṭa, to light; causal from *muṭṭuṭa*, to touch.
muṭṭu, defilement by contact, menses; from *muṭṭuṭa*, to touch; *muṭṭuváḷḷu* are untouchables (pariahs); *anṭa muṭṭu* is dirt and defilement; but *panimuṭlu* and *coramuṭlu* mean tools (things you touch for your work).
muṭṭucólu, siege.
muṭṭuṭa, to touch, to receive, to attack; *muṭṭuconuṭa* is to besiege. *nácu rúpáyilu muṭṭa lédu*, I did not touch (i.e. receive) the rupees; *vánini sarpamu muṭṭinadi*, a serpent touched (i.e. bit) him; *ulli muṭṭanidi vásana rádu*, if you had not touched the garlic, your fingers would not be smelling; *núru rúpáyalu ménéjaru gárici prati nela muṭṭa vatstsunu*, Rs. 100 (in bribes) may touch (reach) the manager every month; *ṣúdrulu modalainaváḷḷu muṭṭu cunṭé, maila paḍutám ani, dúranga tolugutáru*, if you touch sudras, &c., we shall be defiled, they say, and move to a distance. Also *muḍuṭa*.
mutyamu, pearl. *munteḍu pálacu mutyam anta chémiri*, a pearl of sour to a pailful of fresh milk (to curdle it); *yéṭi avatala mutyamulu táṭi cáyal ant ési ann aṭṭu*, the pearls on the other side of the river are as large as palm fruit (exaggerating when you can't be checked).
mutyapu chippa, oyster.
muvva, small bell; usually worn on the ankles, e.g. by postal runners, to scare away snakes; by dancing-girls to make a tinkling, &c.
muvvísamu, $\frac{3}{16}$; from *mu*, 3, and *vísamu*, $\frac{1}{16}$.
muzará, remission, discount. Hindustani. A revenue term for remission of land-tax or water-rate, and a business term for discount. *nácu y'ichchina dániló nunchi nícu chilli gavva muzará rádu*, I won't give you a farthing discount.
múca, crowd, troop. *varici váca, doracu múca*, the stream for the rice, the troop for the baron (what is rice without water or a baron without retainers?); *pedda múcanu venṭa peṭṭuconi vastú v'unnáru*, they are coming with a big crowd after them; *múca míḍa*, in the lump.
múcuḍu, earthen platter.
múḍava, third.
múḍha, stupid, superstitious. Skt. *múḍha viṣvásamu*, superstition.
múḍhatvamu, stupidity, superstition. Skt. *lócamló anéculu múḍhatvam chéta rógálu vachchin appuḍu mandu véyintsaca dayyál ani, bhútál ani, yéḍustú, snánálu chéyinchi, taḍi baṭṭalu caṭṭinchi, debbalù coṭṭinchi, tinḍi peṭṭaca, máḍchi, munta pogalu vési braticéváḷḷanu cúḍá tsampi véstáru*, in this world many people out of superstition give no medicine when diseases come, but thinking them due to devils and spirits, cry, and order baths, and have wet cloths put on, and have the patient beaten and starved and burning pots applied, and so kill the patient.
múḍhuḍu, stupid, superstitious person. Skt.
múḍintulu, three times as much. *ikha múḍintalu janam vrúddhi ainá, mana déṣamló panṭa manacu sari póyi, itara déṣálacu cúḍá yegumatí cheyya vatstsunu*, even if the population were to increase threefold, the crops of our country would suffice and leave a surplus for export.
múḍó, third; same as *múḍava*.
múḍu, three.
múḍumpáṭica, $1\frac{3}{4}$.
múḍuncálu, $3\frac{1}{4}$; *múḍuncálu ganṭa*, a quarter past three.
múḍunnara, $3\frac{1}{2}$.
múḍureṭlu, thrice.
múḍusárlu, three times.

múḍuṭa, to happen, to end. *ciḍu múḍun ani,* thinking a misfortune would happen; *iṭuvanṭi dushcáryálaló pravéṣisté yé ciḍu múḍacunḍa v'úricé pótundá yémiṭi?* if you enter into such a course of wickedness you won't get off without some evil happening; *vánici áyuvu múḍinadi,* his days are ended.

múga, dumb. *múgaváḍu* or *múcuḍu,* a dumb man.

múguṭa, to swarm, to crowd; also *musuruṭa, musuruconuṭa.*

múla, corner, use. *í múla tirigagáné má y'illu,* our house is just round the corner; *idi yé múlacu vatstsunu?* what is the use of this? *márumúlanu,* hidden in a corner; *múla y'illu,* a corner house; *múlan unḍéváni yéla mungiṭici y'íḍustáu?* why pull the man in the corner into the courtyard? (i.e. leave quiet men alone); *paṭṭanamu nálugu múlalanu tirigi,* wandering over all four corners of the town.

múlabandu, clamp.

múlachchhédamu, cutting at the root. Skt.; from *múlam,* root, and *chhédam,* cutting.

múladhanamu, capital. Skt.; from *múlam,* root, and *dhanam,* money. *lacsha rúpáyila múla dhanam gala campéníváru,* a company with a lakh of rupees capital.

múlaguṭa, to groan; also *múluguṭa. tiyyagá tiyyagá rágamu, múlagagá múlagagá rógamu,* practise and practise and your singing will get better, groan and groan and your illness will get worse.

múlamu, root, source, origin. Skt. Used of source of a book, source of a river, root of a quantity in mathematics, and so on. *nadi múlamu, rúshi múlamu, strí múlamu vichárintsa rádu,* you must not inquire into the source of a river or the origin of a rishi or a woman; *sammúlamugá* is root and branch; *samúla náṣanam ainadi,* ruined root and branch.

múlamugá, by means of. *y'í páḍu jvaram múlamugá gáni léca póté, y'í v'udayánna Dhavileṣvaram nénu svayangáné veḷḷi v'unḍunu,* if it wasn't for this beastly fever I would have gone to Dauleshvaram myself this morning.

múlapurushuḍu, first ancestor in a pedigree. Skt.

múlaṣanca or **múlavyádhi,** piles.

múládháramu, cause. Skt. *í ghóra pátacamulac ellanu mana cul ácháramu múl ádháram ai y'unnadi,* our caste customs are the original cause of these horrible sins; *lócálu yéḍ ani telucóvaḍam yógábhyásánic allá múl ádháramu,* knowledge that there are seven worlds is the basis of all yogi practice.

múluguṭa, to groan; also *múlaguṭa. inṭló dhanamu múlugutú v'unnadi,* the money is lying idle in the house; *noppi peṭṭi múlugutú,* groaning in pain.

múpu, shoulder; *bhuzamu* is commoner.

múpuramu, bullock's hump.

múra, cubit. *patti chéló v'unḍagáné, Pólici múḍu múḷḷu, nácu áru múḷḷu ann aṭṭu,* like the man who said 3 cubits for *Poli* and 6 for *me* while the cotton was still in the field (counting your chickens before they are hatched). *moppecu múr eḍu nóru,* a fool has a wide mouth.

múrchha, swoon. Skt.

múrchhapóvuṭa, to faint; also *múrchhilluṭa. yeluca tsávucu pilli múrchhapóná?* will the cat faint at the rat's death?

múrchhatéruṭa, to recover from a swoon. *múrchha téri céca véyutsunnadi,* she recovered from her swoon and screamed.

múrchhilluṭa, to faint; also *múrchhapóvuṭa. conṭa sépatici nénu múrchhillitini,* I fainted for a while.

múrkhamatamu, fanaticism. Skt.

múrkhatvamu, obstinacy. Skt. *múrkhatvam cheyya rádu,* you must not be obstinate; *intamandici ilá telustú v'unḍagá y'í tellaváḷḷacu y'í múrkhatvam yémayya?* when the facts are so well known to so many people why are the white men so obstinate in denying them? (such facts as that an eclipse is due to a monster biting the moon).

múrkhuḍu, obstinate man. Skt.

múrti, form, incarnate. Skt. *múrti conchem ainá, círti vistáramu,* small in form, great in fame; *idi vara dácá* *tama khyáti vinṭú rávaḍamé cáni yeppuḍú darṣanam mátram cheyya lédu; y'ippuḍu tama múrtini tsústé nénu vinnadánici y'ippuḍu tsúchinadánici sari póyinadi*, hitherto I had only been hearing of Your Honour's fame but had never had the joy of seeing you; now that I have seen Your Honour's form I see it equals Your Honour's fame (in some such words do people sometimes try to flatter the Collector). *trimúrti* is the trinity; *ataḍu nyáya múrti*, he is justice incarnate; *áme saundarya múrti ai y'unḍenu*, she was beauty in person; *Crüshnamúrti*, the god Krishna.

múrtibhavintsuṭa, to become incarnate. Skt. *lócamulóni cápatyam antayu múrtibhavinchi áyana rúpamuna avatarinchinadi*, all the world's fraud became incarnate in his shape.

múshacamu, mouse, rat. Skt. Book word for *yeluca*. *múshacéndra turanguḍu* is Gaṇeṣa (he whose steed is the mouse).

músiconuṭa, to close; middle form of *múyuṭa*; say *músicó* for shut, not *muyyu*; *nóru músicó*, shut your mouth; *talupu músicó*, shut the door.

múta, lid.

múṭa, bundle. *áḍaddáni máṭa niḷḷa múṭa*, a woman's word is a bundle of water (*la donna è mobile*); *y'iddaru cúliváḷḷu moyya léni múṭalanu polamló nunchi paṭṭu coni vachchi y'inṭi cáḍa vappaginchéránni*, I used to carry from the fields bundles that two coolies could not have lifted and take them to the house; *múṭá mullé*, bag and baggage; *váḍi múṭá mullé dótsucu póyinaru*, they stripped him of all he had; *nívu prayánamunacu múṭa mulle caṭṭu cona valenu*, you'll have to pack for the journey.

múti, mouth, face; but the ordinary word for 'mouth' is *nóru* and for 'face' *mugam*. *múti mída coṭṭu*, slap him on the mouth; *ná máṭacu yeduru cheppité múti paḷḷu v'úḍé lágu tannutánu*, if you contradict me I will kick you till the teeth in your mouth are loose; *vancara múti*, wry mouth. The word is contemptuous like German *Maul* for *Mund*.

mútramu, urine. Skt. Urinal would be *mútra visarjana sthalam* in Sanskritic Telugu; in ordinary Telugu there is no word (because there is no such thing). *yerr áu mútramunu, tell áu gómayamunu, patsts áu pálunu, nili áu perugunu, nall áu neyyunu pancha gavyamulu*, the five dairy products (*gavyam* is from root *gó*, cow) (required for the expiatory ceremony, *práyaṣchittam*) are the urine of a red cow, the dung of a white cow, the milk of a green cow, the curds of a blue cow, and the clarified butter of a black cow (I confess that I have never seen either a blue cow or a green one; the passage nevertheless is a translation of a text in the Smritis, Holy Scriptures); *malamútramu* is faeces and urine.

mútraputitti, bladder.

múyuṭa, to shut, to cover. *caligité cáḷḷu muyyi, léca póté mócáḷḷu muyyi*, if you can, cover your feet; if you can't, your knees (cut your coat according to your cloth); *reppalu músiyu múyaca*, with half-closed eyelids; *chésina tappu músi peṭṭina dágund?* murder will out.

múzaváni, oral.

myávu, mew (of a cat). *pilli myávu anuts unnadi*, the cat mews; the *v* is not pronounced. So also *ávu*, cow, is pronounced *áu* and *pávuram*, pigeon, *páuram*.

N

na, negative prefix. Skt. *lábha vishayamai ásti nástí y'ani sandéhintsuṭacu avacáṣam unnadi,* if we consider the profit, it will be a trifle or nothing at all; *ásticuḍu* is a theist, *násticuḍu* an atheist; *ippuḍu násticula élubaḍiló v'unnámu,* we are now under the rule of unbelievers.

-na, affix or case ending meaning 'in', 'on', 'at'. *grühamuna,* in the house, *vanamuna,* in the forest. Used in books and with Sanskrit words for *-ló*; *grühamuna* = *inṭló*; *vanamuna* = *aḍaviló*.

nacalu, copy. Hindustani. *nacalirúpam,* aping. *dorala nacali rúpamlató tayáru cávaḍamu goppa ghanatagá bhávinchi y'ippuḍu antá boṭléru véshálu vést unnáru,* they think it a great achievement to ape Europeans, but all they suceed in is looking like their butlers; *nacalí chéshṭalu,* imitative actions; *mana nacalí chéshṭalu tsúchì doralu navvutáru,* Europeans only laugh at us for imitating them.

nacaluvráyuṭa, to copy.

nacanacaláḍuṭa, to feel distressed and hungry; the plight of the unfed. *cucca tinḍi léca nacanacal áḍuts unnadi,* the dog is starving; *panṭalu póyi tinḍi sarigá léca póvuṭa valla, janulu nacanacal áḍuts unnáru,* the crops having failed, the people are in great distress.

nacca, jackal. *concunacca,* the timid jackal, is the fox. *naccalu yerugani boccalú, nágulu yerugani puṭṭalú v'unnavá?* are there holes the jackal does not know or ant-hills the snake is not familiar with? *nacca yeccaḍa, Déva lócam yeccaḍa?* where is the jackal, where is Heaven? (i.e. not in the same place; what is Heaven to the jackal?).

naccadósacáya, wild cucumber.

naccajittulu, jackal-tricks (monkey-tricks).

nacca-naichyamu, fawning servility. *váḍi nacca-naichyamu tsústé nácu asahyamu,* his fawning attitude disgusts me.

naccuṭa, ~~to~~ prowl, ~~to~~ crawl, to hide oneself.

nacshatramu, star. *lacsha nacshatramul ainá vaca chandruḍu cádu,* one moon is more than hosts of stars; *báluḍici talli nacshatrálu tsúpist unḍenu; intaló nacshatram ocati ráli paḍenu; talli: ad émitó telisinadá? báluḍu: dévuḍu nippu pulla veligist unnáḍu.* A mother is showing her boy the stars; meanwhile a star falls. Mother: Do you know what that is? Boy: God lighting a match. *panchángamulu póté nacshatramulu póná?* if you have mislaid your calendar, you still have the stars.

naḍa, naḍaca, walking, a trip. *cáli naḍacanu,* on foot; *naḍa pinuga,* a walking corpse; *paḍava múḍu naḍalu vachchinadi,* the boat has made three trips.

naḍabávi, step-well; the common wells with steps down; the people go down the steps and wash and spit and then take drinking-water home; the use of these wells leads to guinea-worm, hook-worm, cholera, &c., but they remain very popular.

naḍapintsuṭa, to make to walk, to conduct (a business, &c.); causative of *naḍatsuṭa,* to walk.

naḍapuṭa, to make to walk, to conduct; causative of *naḍatsuṭa,* to walk; also *naḍupuṭa. railu naḍapuváḍu,* the engine-driver of a train; *óda naḍapuváḍu,* the captain of a ship; *grantham naḍupuváḍu,* a leader (*grantham* is used here in the sense of business); *Gándhi gáru naḍaputéné cángres vári granthamu naḍust undi,* the Congress can work if Gandhi is there to direct it; *nyayamu naḍapuṭa* is to execute justice.

naḍata, conduct, the common word for 'conduct', 'behaviour'. *durnaḍata* is bad conduct; *ní durnaḍata chéta nícu promóshanu cádu,* you can have no promotion as your conduct is bad; *manchi naḍata galigi, praja séva chésinandulacu, doratanamu váru nícu y'í birudul ichchi bahúcarintsuts unnáru,* as your conduct and public service are good the Government has bestowed these honours on you; *áyana naḍata manchidi cádu*, his conduct is not good.

naḍatsuṭa, to walk; also *naḍutsuṭa. á pillācáya tappaṭ aḍugulu véyutsu naḍutsuts unnáḍu*, that child still totters when it walks.

naḍava, entrance (of house), porch, entrance-hall. *naḍavaló panḍuconnáḍu*, he slept in the porch; *A: yevvaró lópalici vatstsuts unnáru; váciṭlo cheppulu tsappuḍ agutsunnadi. B: lópala mír émó pani mída ūnnaṭṭ unnáru; occa sári naḍavalóci vachchedará. A: vatstsuts unnánu.* A: Some one is coming in, I hear a footstep on the threshold. B: Are you busy in there, Mr. A? Could you come into the hall a minute? A: Coming.

naḍayáḍuṭa, to roam; from *naḍa*, walking, and *áḍuṭa*, to play, to move.

naḍḍi, small of back. *naḍḍi viraga poḍichináḍu*, he gave him a blow that broke his back.

nadi, river. Skt.

naḍi-, prefix meaning 'middle'. *naḍicálamu*, the time between ploughings (the idle time for the ryots); *naḍiréyi*, midnight; *naḍicaṭṭu*, waist-band; *naḍivrélu*, the middle finger; *naḍivayasu*, middle age; *naḍivídhiló*, in the middle of the street.

naḍicaṭṭu, waist-band, girdle. *molatráḍu* is the waist thread worn by Hindus; *naḍicaṭṭu* is a belt.

naḍimi, middle.

naḍiréyi, midnight. Used in books.

naḍipintsuṭa, to make to walk, to conduct, to let one have free of cost; causative of *naḍutsuṭa. pillacáyani naḍipinchindi*, she made the child walk; *chénu vánici naḍipinchánu*, I let him have a field free of rent; *nénu ná máṭa naḍipistánu*, I will keep my word.

naḍivrélu, middle finger; also *naḍivélu*.

-naḍuma, affix meaning 'middle'; *inaḍuma*, presently, lately; *ánaḍuma*, meanwhile.

naḍuma, between. *naḍuma vachchináru*, they interposed; *naḍuma máṭláḍuṭa*, to interrupt.

naḍumu, waist, hip, loin. *vánici vrüddhápyamu chéta naḍumu vangi póyinadi*, he is bent double with age; *nácu naḍumu benicinadi*, my hip is sprained; *í gurramunacu naḍumu paḍḍadi*, this horse is gone in the loins.

naḍumucaṭṭuconuṭa, to gird up the loins, to take a vow of chastity. *andaru nadumu caṭṭuconi, manacu tóḍapaḍi, mana ṣatruvula mída dhvajam etta valenu*, all must gird up their loins, join us, and raise the banner against our enemies.

naḍupuṭa, to make to walk, to manage, to conduct, to steer; causative of *naḍutsuṭa. nyayamu naḍupuṭa*, to execute justice.

naḍutsuṭa, to walk, to move, to work; also *naḍatsuṭa. upanyásacuḍu: prapanchamló manac enni sangatulu teliyavu, nác inta varacu railu yeṭla naḍustundó tinnagá teliyadu. sabhicuḍu: oca anā ichchi railu ticceṭṭu conucconṭé telustund ayya?* Lecturer: How many things there are in the world we don't know; I don't properly understand yet how the railway works. Voice from the audience: Can't you find out by spending one anna on a railway ticket?

nafaru, personal. Hindustani. *nafaru zamín* is personal security (law term).

naga, jewel; more common in the plural *nagalu*, jewellery. The common object of female desire and the common subject of theft. *donga mantsam cinda pácut unḍenu. bharta (bháryató) yém év? nuvv'á mantsam cinda savarist unnáu? donga: nénu donganu; mí bhárya vanṭi mída nagalu y'idi varacé tísucunnánu, mantsam cinda peṭṭeló yém unnavó ani tsúst unnánu; paḍucondi.* A thief is crawling under the bed. Husband (to wife): Ho there, is that you tidying under the bed? Thief: I am a thief, I have already removed the jewellery that was on your wife and am now seeing what there is in the box under the bed; turn over and go to sleep.

nagadu, cash. *nagadu lecca*, cash-account.

nagaramu, town. Skt. *nagaramu* is larger than *paṭṭanamu*. The gradation is *palle*, hamlet, *úru*, village, *paṭnam*, town, *nagaram*, city.

nagaru, palace.
nagavu, laugh; more commonly *navvu*.
nagnamu, naked. Skt. Used in books; usually *disamola*.
naichyamu, baseness. Skt., from *néchamu*. *naccanaichyamulu* is cringing, fawning.
naipunyamu, skill. Skt., from *nipunam*.
naisargicamu, natural. Skt., from *nisargam*. *pinnala canṭé peddalacu buddhi hetstsaguṭa naisaragicamu*, it is natural for the old to be wiser than the young.
naivédyamu, oblation, wave offering. Skt. *má avva Vignéṣvara púja chésuconi naivédyam peṭṭindi*, my grandmother adored the Belly God and placed an oblation before him; *angaṭló bellamu guḷló lingánici naivédyamu*, offering the jaggery in the bazaar to the lingam in the temple (liberal at some one else's expense).
nakhamu, nail. Skt.
nakha-mukhálu, every corner. *nakhamukhálu yenta vedaciná ná v'ungaramu canupintsa lédu*, I have searched every corner for my ring but could not find it; *áme 'donga' 'donga' ani cécalu véyagá janulu nakha-mukhála nuṇḍi parugetticoni vachchiri*, she cried 'thief' 'thief', and the people ran up to her from all directions; *í y'inṭló nakha-mukhálanu dómalu vyápinchi y'unnavi*, there are mosquitoes all over this house.
nakhaṣikhaparyantamu, to the top of the nails, i.e. all over. Skt., from *nakham*, nail, *ṣikha*, top, and *pariyantam*, up to. *nakhaṣikhapariyantamu páratsúchi*, looking him up and down.
nalabhai, 40; also *naluvadi*, *nalubadi*.
nalagacoṭṭuṭa, to pound, to crush, to bruise. *váni nalagagoṭṭináru*, they thrashed him; *ná cheyyi nalaga coṭṭu connánu*, I bruised my hand.
nalagatroccuṭa, to tread down.
nalaguta, to be crushed, to be bruised, to be trodden, to become familiar. *á dóva bágá nalaga lédu*, not a well-trodden path; *páṭham atanici naligindi*, a well-worn lesson; *váru zagaḍam áḍaga nénu naligi póyinánu*, they quarrelled and I was crushed; *váru naligi póyináru*, they were in reduced circumstances. See also *naluguṭa*.
nalatsuṭa, to crush; also *nalipivéyuṭa*, *nalutsuṭa*.
nalguru, four people, several people, the public. *nalguru peddamanshulu cheppina pracáramu ráji aindmu*, we made up our quarrel on the advice of several respectable persons. See also *naluguru*.
nali, illness.
nalipivéyuṭa, to crush.
nalla, black. *sabhádhipati: í rózu upanyásam ichché áyana Américá déṣasthuḍu; áyana tólu tellanid aind ayana hrüdayam mana valé nallanidé; andu chéta míru ṣraddhagá vina valen ani córut unnánu.* Chairman: to-day's lecturer is an American; but though his skin is white his heart is as black as ours; so listen to him with attention.
nalla-mandu bhayi, an opium eater, a lazy man (from *bhái*, brother. Hindustani). *China váḷḷu vaṭṭi nallamandu bhayi-gáḷḷu*, the Chinese are great opium eaters.
nallachíma, black ant.
nallaguḍḍu, pupil of eye.
nallamaddi, a tree (*terminalia alata*).
nallamandu, opium, the black poison; *tellamandu*, the white poison, is arsenic.
nalli, bug; *minnalli*, the bounding bug, is the flea.
nalu-, prefix meaning 4; *naludicculu*, all round; *naldéṣalu*, all sides; *naluvadi*, 40.
nalubadi, 40. Same as *nalabhai*, *naluvadi*.
nalugu, a pasty ointment, sometimes highly perfumed, used by Indians in their oil baths.
nalugu-peṭṭuta, to rub on such ointment on ceremonial occasions. *nalugu-páṭalu*, the songs which ladies sing on such occasions; *nalugu-peṭṭe samayamuló maryádalu sarigá zaruga léd ani peḷḷivárici cópam vachchinadi*, the bridegroom's relations are offended and say that there was no proper exchange of courtesies when the ceremony of the ointments was on.
nalugupiṇḍi, ointment; from *naluguṭa*, to be crushed, and *piṇḍi*, flour.
naluguru, four persons, some persons,

the public. *míru smartula naluguri y'illacu veḷḷi bandóbastu cheyyanḍi*, go to some Smarta houses and make arrangements; *naluguritó pátu Nárá-yana*, do at Rome as the Romans do; *naluguriló tala yeṭṭuṭa*, to hold up one's head in public. See also *nalguru*.

naluguṭa, to be crushed; same as *nala-guṭa*. *ná tsocca naligi póyindi*, my coat is rucked up; *ninḍá vádaḍamu chéta naligina pustacamu*, a well-thumbed book; *ná voll anta naligi póyindi*, my whole body is bruised; *idi bágá naligina páṭhamu*, this is a most familiar lesson.

nalugutroccuṭa, to tread down. *pairu nalugutrocci*, treading down the crop.

nalumukhála, in all directions. *nénu pustacamunu nalamukhála veticindnu*, I have hunted high and low for the book.

naluputa, to crush.

nalutsuṭa, to crush; same as *nalatsuṭa*.

nalusu, particle. *canṭiló nalusu*, mote in the eye.

naluvadi, 40; *nalabhai* is commoner.

naluvanḍru, 40 persons; also *nalubadi mandi*.

namaluṭa, to chew. *cherucu típi ani véḷḷató namala vatstsuná?* can the sugar-cane be chewed to its roots just because it is sweet? (greediness); *namala cúdani náricéḷamu*, a hard nut to crack (in Telugu to chew; *náricéḷam* is Skt. for *cobbari*, coco-nut).

namascarintsuṭa, to salute (with folded hands). Skt. *namas*.

namascáramu, a salute (with folded hands). Skt. *namas*.

nambaru, number. English. *Lacsh-mayya: í móṭaru cáru mícu yeṭla vachchindi? Vencayya: láṭariló. Lac-shmayya: mí nambaru gelchindi cábólu. Vencayya: nénu láṭariló ḍabbu peṭṭa lédu; láṭari yérpátu chésindi néné*. A: How did you get that car? B: In a raffle. A: I suppose you drew the lucky number. B: No, I took no ticket; I ran the raffle. In this example the English words lottery, motor-car, number, are the only words that would or could be used; they are chaste and pure Telugu; *ná nambaru coṭṭésiri*, they dismissed my suit (or case); suits and cases are known by their numbers.

namdá, saddle-pad.

nammacadóshamu, criminal breach of trust; a law term.

nammacamaina, trustworthy. *tsálá nammacamaina cheruvu*, a very trust-worthy tank (sure to hold water in the irrigation season).

nammacamu, belief, trust, confi-dence. *Lacshmayya: tallidanḍrula gundlu coḍuculacu sancramistav ani vamṣa páramparyapu siddhántamló mícu nammacam unnadá? Vencayya: gaṭṭigá v'undi; ná ḍabbu antá allágé vachchindi*. A: Do you believe in the transmission of qualities from parents to children on the heredity principle? B (firmly): All my money came to me that way.

nammica, belief.

nammintsuṭa, to make a person believe in you. *namminchi gontu cósinádu*, he acquired his confidence and cut his throat (ruined him).

nammuṭa, to believe, to trust. *navvé áḍadánní, yéḍché mogavánní namma rádu*, don't trust a woman when she laughs or a man when he cries. *cáṭici póyina carananni namma rádu*, don't trust a karnam even when he has gone to the pyre (he will have left his lying accounts behind); *váḍu tsachchináḍ ani ghaṭṭigá nammu*, you may rest assured he is dead; *mému ní dayanu nammu cunnámu*, we counted on your kindness.

namóḍu, entry (in a book). Hindu-stani; also *namózu*.

namóná, sample, form (for official reports, &c.). Hindustani; also *namúná*.

namrata, humility, modesty. Skt., from *namram*, bowed. *namrata na-ṭintsutsu*, registering humility; *oca saundaryamu mátramé cádu, dínici namrata, sugunasampatti, vidya sama-sta sadguṇamulu v'unnavi*, it is not only beauty she had, but modesty, a procession of all the virtues, a galaxy of talents.

nana, bud. *nanaleṭṭuṭa*, to bud.

nanabóḍi, a budding girl. Used in books.

nandanavanamu, temple garden (where flowers and basil are grown for the services). Skt. Properly Indra's pleasure-garden.

nanga, weevil.

nanganáchi, minx, jade.

nanja, irrigated land. Hindustani. The Tamils still use *nanjai*, contrary *punja* (dry land). The Telugu words in use are *pallam* and *meraca*, *nanja* and *punja* being nearly obsolete.

nannu, me; accusative of *nénu*.

nannúru, 400.

nanzu, any lingering disease, e.g. beri-beri, dropsy.

napunsacuḍu, eunuch. Skt. *napunsacuḍici Rambható yémi prayójanam?* what use is the Heavenly Harlot to a eunuch? *bógamváḷḷanu v'untsu conna váḷḷu v'untsucóni váḷḷanu napunsacul ani, parihásam chéstáru,* those who keep dancing-girls deride those who don't as eunuchs.

nara-, prefix meaning 'human'. Skt. *narahatya* is murder, *narabali* human sacrifice.

nara, grey (of hair); also *nerasina*. *nara ventrucalu,* grey hair; *narapagaḍḍam,* grey beard.

narabali, human sacrifice. Skt.

naracamu, hell. Skt. *naracamu mana cósamu yeduru tsústu v'unṭundi,* hell's jaws are gaping for us.

naracuṭa, to cut; also *narucuṭa*. *góṭa chiduma taginadi goḍḍanṭa naracuṭa,* to fell with an axe what you could nip with the nail.

narahantucuḍu, murderer. Skt.

narahatya, murder. Skt. *narahatya dósham,* charge of murder; *í bhútavaidyulanu paṭṭuconi narahatya chésin anducu śicshisté bágá v'unḍunu,* it would be well to arrest these witch-doctors and punish them for murder.

naramánsabhacshacuḍu, cannibal. Skt., from *nara,* human, *mámsam,* flesh, and *bhacsham,* food.

naramu, nerve. *váni chétici naralu lévu* (he has no nerves in his hand) means he is a very liberal man; 'nerveless' has not this meaning in English.

narayuṭa, to turn grey (of hair); *nerayuṭa* is commoner.

narucuṭa, to cut to fell (a tree); also *naracuṭa*.

naruḍu, human being. Skt.

nashṭamu, loss. *ṭennisu áṭaló banti áṭagáni talacáyacu tagilenu. áṭagáḍu: banti tagili ná talacáyi boppi caṭṭindi, iṭla áḍaḍam anyáyam. précshacuḍu: acramam 'ém 'und ayya? indácaṭi nunchi tsúst unnánu; miru áḍuṭ unn appuḍu talacáyi upayógintsané lédu, andu ché debba tagilité mátram émi nashṭam?* At tennis a player was hit on the head. Player: I have got a lump on the head from a ball hitting me on it; I claim a let. Onlooker: What difference did it make, Sir? I have been looking on all the time and you have not used your head at all; what harm did it do you? *nénu nashṭamló pani chéstunnánu,* I am working at a loss.

nashṭapaduṭa, to suffer. *panṭa léca mému tsála nashṭapaḍinámu,* we have lost a lot through the failure of our crops.

naśimpu, destruction.

naśintsuṭa, naśinchipóvuṭa, to be destroyed. *í sénal anniṭini tísi vési, bráhmala chéta mahá mantrálu japam chéyisté, śatruvul anta vacca debbaló naśinchi pór anḍi?* why keep all these armies? you can get all your enemies destroyed at one stroke by having mantrams said by brahmins; *varnáśrama dharmálu samúlam naśistavi,* religion will be destroyed root and branch.

nasyamu, snuff. Skt., from *násica,* nose. *pogácu condaru nasyamugá chési muccuna píltsuts unnáru,* some make tobacco into snuff and sniff it up.

naṭanamu, dancing, cunning behaviour, fraud.

naṭintsuṭa, to act, to pretend. Original meaning 'to dance'. *nidra pótu v'unn aṭṭu naṭistu v'unṭánu,* I will pretend to be asleep; *áyana léca póté nácu prapanchamé léd ann aṭṭugá naṭistu v'unḍaḍam chéta, caṭṭu conna bháryacaina y'inta préma, y'inta viśvásamu v'undad ani, ná vishayamai áyana andaritónu ślághinchi cheputú v'unṭáru.* (Dancing-girl speaking): Because I pretend that he is all the world to me, he praises me to every one as having more love and faithfulness than a wedded wife; *itarul inṭici vachchin appuḍ ainá biggaragá máṭáḍaca ná* *yeḍala inta bhacti tsúpi, pati púja chéyutsunn aṭṭu paicaina naṭintsutsu rávé*, when a stranger comes please don't raise your voice; please look at me with some sort of dutifulness and please make believe at least that you are a devoted wife; *lópala nácu váḷḷa mída gontuca cáḍici cópam v'unná, paici yémi yerugani váni vale naṭistánu*, though I am choking inwardly with anger against them, I will pretend outwardly to know nothing; *paici mahá bhrütyuḍu lágu naṭistáḍu*, he is outwardly very servile.

natstsa-chepputa, to convince. *míru yenta ḍabbu khartsu chési, yendaru goppa goppa váḷḷanu tsúchiná, dora-tanamu várici natstsa-cheppa léca póyináru*, though you have spent a great deal of money in waiting upon some of the bigwigs you could not convince the Government.

natstsuta, to trust (*nammuta* is commoner), to like. *nívu nácu natstsina pillavu*, you are the girl of my own heart; *pilla natstsa léd ani váḍu peḷḷi chésucón antunnáḍu*, the boy says that he cannot marry a girl he does not like.

natta, snail, shell-fish.

naṭṭa-, prefix meaning 'in the middle'. *naṭṭaḍavilo*, in the heart of the forest; *naṭṭanaḍi*, the very middle; *naṭṭ éṭa puṭṭi munigin aṭṭu*, like the coracle sinking in midstream (a breakdown in business).

nattagulla, shell (of a fish, snail's shell). *nattagullal anni vaca révuna, mutyapu chippal anni vaca révuna*, all the common shells will be on one bank and all the oyster-shells on another (birds of a feather flock together).

naṭṭanaḍuma, in the very middle.

natti, stammer.

nattiváḍu, stutterer.

nattuta, to stammer. *nénu Telugu máṭláda bóté conchemu nattut undi*, my Telugu is a bit halting; *upanyásacuḍu madhya madhya nattutú vach-chináḍu*, now and then the speaker had to stop short in the middle of his speech.

naṭuḍu, actor. *váḍu abhinayintsa léni naṭuḍu*, he is an actor who can't act.

nauca, boat. Skt. *naucalu* is used in the newspapers for 'navy' for want of a better word; *samudra nauca*, a sea-going ship.

naucari, service. Hindustani. *váni coḍucunu ná vadda caṭṭubaḍi naucarici v'unchináḍu*, he articled his son to me. To enter a service is *naucari chéruṭa*.

naucaru, servant. Hindustani. *yazamani: nuvvu má y'inṭló iravai yéḷḷa baṭṭi pani chestunnáu; ní panici mech-chánu. naucaru: mechchi yém chéstár andi? yazamani: ica nunchí ninnu naucarugá tsúḍaca ná cuṭumbamló ocanigá tsústám, andu chéta níc ica mída jítam iyyamu.* Mistress: You have done us good service for twenty years. Servant: And therefore, ma'am? Mistress: And therefore we will, in future, not look upon you as a servant but as a member of the family and give you no wages. *Rámayya: mí cotta naucaru yeṭlá pani chést unnáḍu? Sómayya: ippaṭici nálugu chimni glásulu baddalu coṭṭáḍu, oca gaḍiyáram ákhar aindi; tsála cashṭa paḍi pani chéstáḍu.* A: How is your new servant working? B: So far his score is four lamp chimneys and one clock; he is very hard-working. *naucaru: mícu naucaru cá valen ani yevaró cheppité vach-chänu. peddamanishi: má y'inṭló pani antá má váḷḷé chésu conṭáré. naucaru: aṭlá aité nénu tappacunḍá iccaḍé v'unṭánu, untsu conḍi.* Servant: Some one said you wanted a servant. Gentleman: In this house we do all the work ourselves. Servant: Then that just suits me, take me on; *jítamu léni naucaru cópamu léni dora*, a master who gives his servant no wages must keep his temper.

nava-, prefix meaning 9. Skt. The Telugus are fond of enumerating kinds of anything as the 3 worlds, the 9 jewels. The alphabet book for children contains the list of *navaratnamulu*, the 9 jewels (diamond, ruby, &c.); *navarandhramulu*, the 9 holes (of the body); *navadhányamulu*, the 9 grains (rice, wheat, &c.), and so on. *navarátri* is a great festival in September or October continuing for 9 nights, also commonly known as the Dasara.

navalu, novel. English.
navaminádu, 9th day; the 9th lunar day after either the full moon or the new moon. *mahar-navami,* the great Navami festival during the Dasara from *maha,* great, and *navami.*
navamu, new. Skt.
navana, ninth.
navanavaláḍuṭa, to prosper, to appear fresh. *í cúragáyalu navanavaláḍutu v'unnayi,* those vegetables are quite fresh; *bágá vicasinchi navanavaláḍutu v'unna puvvulu coyyi,* pick out fresh blooming flowers.
navanágarículu, people of the new civilization, i.e. the English-educated. *y'í navanágarículu máṭalu nammi, mósa póyi, sadácháramulanu míru mánpa púnucunṭé nindala pál ai pótáru.* Believing these modernizers and being taken in by them you try and put a stop to good old customs and incur blame; *navanágarícula cuyuctula nammi mír evvarunu ṣúdrula vidyac angícarimpa cúdaḍu,* you must not believe the fallacies of the modernists and admit sudras to learning (of course, education should be confined to brahmins).
navábu, nabob. *navábu Sátulla Khán avva náṭidi,* of the days of Queen Anne; *náḍu v'unṭé navábu sáyebu, annamu v'unṭé amíru sáyebu, bida paḍité facíru sayebu, tsasté píru sáyebu,* if a Muhammedan has land he is a Nabob, if he has enough to eat an Amir, if he is poor he is a Fakir, when he dies he becomes a Pir.
naváru, broad tape. Hindustani. The tape they lace on bed frames. *í mantsamunacu naváru nésináru,* this cot is laced with tape; *í mantsam mída yevaru paḍu có cúdaḍu; dínidi páta naváru tegi pótundi,* no one should sleep on that bed; its old tape would break.
navínamu, new. Skt.
navvé, laughing, smiling. Aoristic participle of *navvuṭa,* to laugh.
navvintsuṭa, to be laughed at, to amuse; causal of *navvuṭa,* to laugh. *naluguri chéta navvintsu cóvaḍam nácu ishṭam lédu,* I don't care to be a common laughing stock.
navvu, laugh, laughter, laughing, smiling. *navvu nálu ganḍála nashṭacári,* laughter brings many dangers with it; *nádi yeppuḍu navvu mogamé,* mine is always a smiling face.
navvuláṭa, fun. *navvac anḍi, idi navvuláṭa vyavaháram cádu, idi mukhyamaina cáryam,* don't laugh; there is nothing to laugh at; it is important; *nénu navvaláṭac annánu,* I said it in jest.
navvuṭa, to laugh. *navva cheppéváḍu cheḍa cheppunu, yéḍava cheppéváḍu brataca cheppunu,* the advice which makes you laugh may bring you to ruin, the advice which makes you cry may save you; *poṭṭa checcal ayyéṭ antagá navvuṭa,* to laugh fit to split your sides; *paṭṭa léca paccuna navvináḍu,* he could not contain himself and burst out laughing. *Lacshmayya: podduna ná peḷḷám mída cópam vachchi tiṭṭánu. Vencayya: áviḍecu ní mída cópam rá lédá? Lacshmayya: rá lédu, navvindi. Vencayya: yendu chéta? Lacshmayya: nén inta dhairyam tetstsu coni cóp paḍḍ anducu santóshinchindi.* Smith: I lost my temper with my wife this morning and called her names. Jones: Did she lose her temper too? Smith: No, she laughed. Jones: Why? Smith: She was so pleased at my having had spunk enough to get angry; *navvé áḍadánni, yéḍché mogavánni namma rádu,* beware of a laughing woman and a weeping man.
nayamu, cheap.
nayamu, kindness, virtue, luck, improvement. Skt. *néḍu conchem nayam ainadi,* rather better to-day; *nayabhayamulu,* fair and foul; *vánici nayamugá n'unnadi,* he is better.
nayanamu, eye. Skt. Used in books for *cannu.*
nazaráná, homage-gift. Hindustani. If in money it is usually Rs. 1,116 or Rs. 116; hence *núta padaháru* is an honourable figure.
ná, my.
nábhi, navel. Skt. The Telugu word is *boḍḍu.*
nácu, to me; dative of *nénu.*
nácuṭa, to lick. *teḍḍu náci v'upavásamulu mánpin aṭṭu,* stopping the fast by licking the ladle.

nádamu, sound. Skt. *pátacuḍu: monna. Góclé háluló nénu páḍité ná nádam yeṭlá vyápinchindó canipeṭṭává? snéhituḍu: adi svéchchagá vyápintsaḍánici tsálamandi léchi póyináru.* Singer: Did you notice how my voice carried in the Gokhale Hall the other day? Friend: Yes, many got up and went away to give it free scope.

náḍamu, the hoof of a horse.

náde, shuttle.

nádhuḍu, lord, husband. Skt. *práṇa-nádhuḍu,* lord of my life is what women call their husbands in books; *muni-nádhuḍu,* saint.

nádi, mine (that which belongs to me).

náḍi, vein, pulse. Skt. *váni náḍi tsuchánu,* I felt his pulse; *náḍi bahu vaḍigá coṭṭu cunṭu v'unnadi,* the pulse is very quick.

náḍu, day, ago; *dinam* and *rózu* are other common words for 'day'. *oca náḍu vindu, vaca náḍu mandu,* feast one day and medicine the next; *yen náḷḷ aindi?* how long ago? *nálug énḍla náḍu,* four years ago.

náḍu, country, district. *náḍu v'unṭé navábu sáyebu,* if a Muhammedan has a district he calls himself a Nabob; *túrpu náḍu,* the eastern districts; and by this the Godavari people mean those of Vizag and Ganjam, to whose inhabitants they refer contemptuously as *túrpuváḷḷu*; the easterners come to work in the Godavari district in the harvest season; *ichché Muricináṭi-várici abhyantaram léca póte, putstsu-cónaḍánici Velindṭivárici yémi abhyantaram v'unṭundi?* if the Blackshire people have no objection to giving in marriage, what objection should the Whiteshire people have to taking? The usual word for country is *déṣam*; for district *disṭricṭu* or *jillá*; the usual word for foreign countries is *síma.*

-náḍu, -náṭinunchi, affix meaning 'when', 'at the time of'; from *náḍu,* day; *chinnáḍu,* when he was young; *ṭátanáḍu,* in his grandfather's time; *tanḍrináṭinunchi,* from the time of his father; *ánáḍu,* at that time.

nágabali, fourth day of marriage ceremony; also *nágavalli.*

nágadáḷi, prickly-pear; also *nágatáḷi.*

nágajemudu, the milk-hedge, a sort of cactus.

nágali, plough. *nágaṭicarru* is ploughshare and *nágaṭiduppa,* ploughstock.

nágamu, serpent; especially cobra. Skt.; also *nágu.* Telugu, *pámu. nága-cancanuḍu* is Siva because he wears a bracelet of snakes; *nágatáḷi,* prickly-pear is presumably so called because it harbours snakes; *nágalócamu,* serpents' world, is the underworld; *nágéndruḍu* is the King of Snakes.

nágarícata, civilization. Skt., from *nagar,* town; like our urbanity.

nágarícuḍu, a civilized man, a cultivated man, a polished man, a gentleman. Skt. *navanágariculu* are the English-educated reformers.

nágatáḷi, prickly-pear; also *nágadáḷi.*

nágavalli, betel-vine. Skt. The Telugu is *támbúlamu.* See also *nágabali.*

nágavalli, fourth day of marriage ceremony. Skt. So called because betel is distributed on that day.

nágéndruḍu, King of the Nagas. Skt. The Nagas are fairy-snakes.

nágu, snake, cobra. Skt.; same as *nágamu.*

náḷamu, horseshoe; but *láḍam* is commoner. Plural *náḷḷu.*

nálgava, fourth.

nálgu, four, some; also *nálu, nálugu.*

náli, mean work. *cúlináli,* hard and low work, drudgery.

nálica, tongue; also *naluca, nálice. nálica, nálica, vípucu debbalu téca,* tongue, tongue, bring not blows on my back.

nálimutstsu, hypocrite, traitor.

náḷḷu, days, period; plural of *náḍu,* day. *au páḍé náḷḷu, aiṣvaryamé náḷḷu, barre páḍé náḷḷu bhágyamaina náḷḷu,* make hay while the sun shines (the good days are those when the cow and she-buffalo give milk). Also plural of *náḍi,* vein; *náḍu,* country; and *náḷamu,* horseshoe. *náḷḷu véyuṭa,* to shoe.

náluca, tongue; also *nalica, nálice. ná náluca púchinadi,* my tongue is sore; *conḍanáluca* is the uvula; *conḍanálucacu mandu vésté, unna náluca úḍi póyin aṭlu,* pulling out your tongue to give medicine to the uvula (the remedy is worse than the disease).

nálugési, four at a time.

nálugu, four, several. Four only of things; four qualifying a personal noun is *naluguru* or *nálugumandi*, never *nálugu*. Indefinitely *nálugu* means several. *cécalató y'inṭi mída penculu nálugu yegiri póyinavi*, various tiles on the roof flew off at the noise (in this sense it may be postponed to the noun qualified, but need not be); *nálugu tiṭṭuṭa*, to do a bit of cursing; *nálugu coṭṭi aidu nimishálu* is 4.5 by the clock.

náluguretlu, four times.

-náma, suffix meaning 'document'. Hindustani. *rájináma*, document of composition; *carárunáma*, document of agreement.

námaca, námacach, námacártha-maina, nominally. Skt., from *námam*, name. *námaca zamindárudu*, a zamindar only in name.

námacaranamu, naming ceremony, corresponding to christening.

námadhéyamu, name. Skt. When you ask some one what his name is, you say *námadhéyam* rather than *námam*.

námamu, name. Skt.; same root as the English 'name' and probably also as the English 'know'; name was what a person was known by; Latin *nomen*, Greek *onoma*, German *Namen*; one of the most widely diffused of roots. *peddalu mícu Máyáchárlagárini sarthaca námam peṭṭinúru*, your elders gave you a very suitable name when they called you Proteus (cf. old John of Gaunt and gaunt in being old; *autó gar se dei prométheós hotó tropó tésd ecculisthései technés*; or the Collector's confidential note on the character of a tahsildar, Mr. A. Devasahayam: God help us); *péru* is the common word, but even *péru* is not always idiomatic for name. What is the name of that hill? is *á conḍa yém anṭáru?* or *yém anṭáru á conḍa?*

námamu, a cattle disease.

námamu, caste-mark; *panganámamu* is a Vaishnavite mark.

námarúpa, name and form, the phenomenal world (philosophy). Skt.

námóshi, shame. Hindustani.

nánabeṭṭuṭa, nánavéyuṭa, to lay out to soak, to delay. *manamu pánam chéyu nútiló carralu nánavéstáru*, they lay logs to soak in our drinking-water well (Telugus are not particular about material contamination of drinking-water; only about ceremonial contamination).

náná, several. Skt. *náná rúpamaina*, protean; *nánámukhála*, in several directions; *házaru várantu vastund émó-n ani náná mukhála pári póyináru*, thinking an arrest warrant was issuing they absconded in several directions.

nánáṭici, day by day; from *náḍu*, day.

nánemu, coin. *táluca gumásthála chétulaló venḍi nánemulu rúpam aina divy aushathamu paḍina pacshnamuna*, if a panacea in the shape of silver coins falls into the hands of the Taluk clerks.

nánna, father; for *náyana*. To this word you must always add *gáru* to show the respect due to a father if you are addressing him; more familiar than *tanḍri* but not slang like 'dad' or 'pater' or 'governor'; exactly equivalent to the Italian *babbo*. *nánnató v'unnadi lédani cheppum'ani, lénidi v'unnad ani cheppum'ani, abaddhálu nérputú v'unnáu*, you teach your child to lie to his father and say that what is is not and what is not is (a common fault of Telugu mothers). *ṭícharu: leccalaló inni tappulu occaḍavu yeṭlá chéṣávu? báluḍu: nénu occaḍane cád anḍi, má nánna cúda calisi cheṣáḍ anḍi.* Teacher: How did you manage to make so many mistakes in your sums all by yourself? Boy: I wasn't all by myself; father helped. *ṭícharu: ninna madhyánam scúlucu rá léd émi? báluḍu: má nánnanu saracasucu tísucu pó valasi vachchind anḍi.* Teacher: Why didn't you come to school yesterday afternoon? Boy: I had to take my father to the circus.

nántsuṭa, to soak, to wet.

nánuṭa, to soak, to become wet; commonly, with the auxiliary, *nánavéyuṭa*.

nára, fibre, bark. *ráta nára tiṣin aṭṭu*, like taking bark off a stone; *zanapa-nára pítsu vale gaḍḍamu*, oakum beard.

náraca, hellish. Skt.; adjective from *naracam*, hell.

nárachíra, bark garment supposed to be worn by sages.

Náraduḍu, Nárada, the Hindu Orpheus, inventor of the lute; appears in all the plays as a jeering personage, who makes mischief.

nári, náricurupu, guinea-worm.

nárinjacáyi, orange.

nárinjacheṭṭu, orange tree.

náru, seedling; also *mocca*. *nárumaḍi*, seed-bed; also *ácumaḍi*. *níru v'unṭé náru v'unḍa valenu*, if there be water, there must be seedlings.

nása, nose. Skt. The Telugu is *muccu*. Also *násica*.

násamani, nose-jewel. Skt.

náṣamu, náṣanamu, destruction. Skt. *magaváḷḷa náṣánici yeccaḍá áḍaváḷḷu cáranam*, women are everywhere the cause of men's ruin.

násápuṭamu, nostril; also *mukhu-randhramu*.

násica, nose. Skt. The Telugu is *muccu*; also *nása*.

násiluṭa, to be ruined. Skt.

násti, nullity, atheism. Skt. word meaning 'it is not'. *y'Inglishu tsaduvu cunna váḷlacu sarvam násti*, the English-educated are all atheism.

nástica, atheistical. Skt. *íyana nástica vádálu chéstu v'unnáḍu*, he is using atheistical arguments; *yédó nástica v'upanyásam chéstár aṭa*, they say he is going to deliver some atheistical lecture.

násticata, atheism; also *násticyamu*. Skt.

násticuḍu, atheist. Skt. *ippaṭiváḷḷu y'Inglishu tsaduvu coni násticul ai, puránamulu prámánamulu cáv antáru*, the English-educated having become atheists deny the authority of the Puranas; *ippuḍu násticula yélubaḍiló v'unnámu*, we are now under a régime of unbelievers.

násticyamu, atheism; also *násticata*. Skt.

náṭacamu, play (drama). Skt. *Lacsh-mayya: nénu rachinchina náṭacam yeṭlá v'unnadi? sukhangá mugisindá lédá? Rámayya: náṭacam áḍaṭam mugisina tarváta tsúchi vachchina váḷḷu sukha paḍḍáru*. Smith: How about my play? Did it go off well? Jones: The spectators were very pleased when it was over. *náṭuḍu: nénu náṭa-camló tsachchi pótu v'unn appuḍu précshaculu yeṭlá yéḍcháró tsúsává? snéhituḍu: dánici cáranam émiṭó telu-suná? náṭuḍu: yémiṭó nuvvu cheppu. snéhituḍu: nuvvu nizamgá tsáva léd ani.* Actor: Did you see how the audience cried when I died on the stage? Friend: Do you know why? Actor: Tell me. Friend: Because you did not really die.

náṭacaṣála, theatre. Skt. *ṭícharu: pápam cheyyani váḷḷu yeccaḍici pótáró mícu telusuná? báluḍu: teliyad auḍi. ṭícharu: nénu chepputánu canuccondi; accaḍa yeppuḍu sangítam páḍut unṭáru: nátyam chést unṭáru; chitramaina dípálu velugut unṭayi; suvásanalu vast unṭai; adi yeccaḍó cheppanḍi. báluḍu: náṭacaṣála*. Teacher: Do you know where those who don't sin will go? Boy: No, Sir. Teacher: I will tell you, guess; a place where they always sing and dance and where there are wonderful lights and fragrant odours; where is that? Boy: The theatre.

náṭici, on that day, from that time; from *náḍu*, day. *renḍ éḷḷa náṭici ippaṭi munchi siddham cheyy ál éná?* were two years not enough for preparation? *oca nela náṭici í césu tísuconṭánu*, I will take up that case to-day month.

náṭinunḍi, since that time; from *náḍu*, day.

náṭiváru, the people of that time.

nátsu, weed in water (*vallisneria octandra*). *máṭacu máṭa tegulu, níḷḷacu nátsu tegulu*, words and weeds choke speech and stream.

náṭu, country-made; from *náḍu*, country. *náṭumandu*, country-gun-powder; *náṭu márgamura*, by the road; also *náṭuna*. *jala márgamuna álasyam agun ani náṭuna vachchinánu*, I came by the road as the water-route is slow.

náṭupuramu, up country, the mu-fassal. *náṭupuránici póyindru*, they have gone up country.

náṭupurapuvánḍlu, up-country folk.

náṭuṭa, to plant, to fix in, to transplant. *náṭina pairucu nashṭamu lédu*, trans-planted crops never fail; *ná máṭalu váni cheviló mulucul ai náṭenu*, my words pierced his heart; *idi şil acsharam vale ni manassuló náṭuconi v' unṭundi*, this will remain indelibly inscribed on your mind.

nátyamu, dancing, nautch. Skt.

náva, ship. Skt. The Telugu is *óḍa*; the newspapers usually say *nauca*, as *yuddhanauca* for battleship.

návicuḍu, sailor, steersman. Skt.

náyacamu, leadership. Skt. *bahu náyacam, bála náyacam, strí náyacam*, the leadership of many, of minors, or of women leads to misfortune [Woe to thee, O land, when thy king is a child (Eccles. x. 16)].

náyacuḍu, leader, naick, chief, baron, hero. Skt. *náṭacamló allar autundi. mánéjaru: yendu chéta? náṭuḍu: náyacuḍu yuddhamló tsáva valasi v'unṭé, tsavacunḍá nilutstsuné unnáḍu; précshaculu navvut unnáru. mánéjaru: báci v'unna jitam ippuḍu istán ani cheppu.* Row at the play. Manager: What's it all about? Actor: The leading part ought to have died in battle but won't die and is still standing; the audience is laughing. Manager: Tell him I will at once give him his arrears of salary.

náyana, father, my dear Sir. Fathers being deservedly beloved, this word is also used as a term of endearment. *tanḍri: nénu tsachchipóyina tarváta, nuvvu yém chestávu? coḍucu: mí náyana póyina tarváta nuvvu yém cheşávó nénu adé chéstánu. tanḍri: aité nuvvu bágupaḍavu.* Father: What will you do when I am dead? Son: What you did when your father died. Father: Then you won't do well; *náyaná; yémi viparítam!* my dear Sir! what a remarkable thing!

náyantaṭanéné, by myself, alone by myself.

náyantâṭanénu, I myself.

náyuḍu, the caste title of several Sudra castes (in high position).

názaru, sheriff, the sheriff's department. Hindustani. The sheriffs collectively in the civil courts are called the nazar.

názúcu, fine, delicate. Hindustani.

negaḍuṭa, to increase, to spread. *grámam negaḍi casba aindi*, the village grew into a head-quarters town (e.g. Bezwada).

neggintsuṭa, to cause to succeed; causal of *negguṭa*. *á pani nénu neggintsa lénu*, I can't get it through; *induló mana prayójacatvam canaparichi mana pantam neggintsu có valenu*, we must show our dexterity and get our way.

neggu, success. *yélágu neggucu vastánu?* how shall I succeed?

negguṭa, to thrive, to succeed.

nela, month; also *másam*. *adugó anṭé áru nelalu*, there it is, he says, and it takes six months before you get it; *múḍu nelalacu veḷḷutánu*, I shall go in three months; *nelanelacu*, every month.

nelacolpuṭa, to establish.

nelavanca, half moon.

nemali, peacock; also *nemili*. *nemali canṭa níru cárité véṭacáḍici muddá?* is the hunter moved by the peacock's tears?

nemaru, the cud.

nemaruvéyuṭa, to chew the cud. *gorrelu nemaruvésé jantuvulu*, sheep are ruminants.

nemmadi, quiet, in good health. *itaḍu bahu nemmadigánu vinayangánu máṭláḍutú v'unnáḍu*, he talks very quietly and submissively.

nemmadi, peace. *nemmadibhangam* is a law term for breach of the peace

nemmadiparatsuṭa, to tranquillize.

nerasu, particle, flaw; *canṭi nerasu*, mote in the eye; same as *nalusu*. *nerasulu vedaci paṭṭuta tsála télica*, it is very easy to detect flaws; *nívu nerasulu vedaci paṭṭuconi ácshépana chéstávu*, you are picking out trifles to find fault.

neravértsuṭa, to accomplish.

neravéruṭa, to be fulfilled, to succeed. *ní abhishṭamu síghramugáné neravéruṭundi*, your wish will soon be fulfilled; *cáryam yenta síghramugá neravérité anta manchidi*, the sooner the better.

nerayuṭa, grow grey (of hair). *gaḍḍálu mísálu nerasina musaliváḷḷu*, grey-bearded and grey-haired old men.

neriya, crack.

neṭica, knuckle. *neṭica virutsuṭa*, to snap the fingers; *mogamuna neṭicalu virichi*, snapping her fingers in his face.

netti, head; *tala* is the ordinary word,

netti and *burra* other words; also *talacái*. *nett ecci*, raising the head (in pride); *netti múṭacu suncam aḍigin aṭṭu*, demanding toll for a head-load. (Head-loads are free still or charged with a nominal amount under the forest rules.)

netturu, blood; also *ractam* (there are at least two words for most things in Telugu). *vánici netturu viréchanamul autsunnavi*, he passes blood; *váni muccu venta netturu cárinadi*, he bled at the nose; *netturu-sparṣagalaváru* is blood-relations.

neyyi, ghee (clarified butter). *bhacshyamulu uḍucu nétilo vésté tsumyi manṭunnavi*, if you put sweetmeats into boiling ghee they will fizzle; *nyáyádhipati: nuvvu ḍabbu iyya léca póté, cammani neyyi poyyum ani yenducu aḍigáu? muddáyi: ḍabbu yeṭlágu iyya lédu ganuca manchi neyyi yenducu tísu có rád ani aḍigãnu*. Judge: If you could not pay, why did you ask for best ghee? Accused: As I was not paying, I might as well have the best; *néti cunḍa néla peṭṭi, vaṭṭi cunḍa v'uṭṭi mída peṭṭéváḍu*, like the man who put the pot of ghee on the ground and the empty pot on the sling (absent-mindedness).

-né, emphatic suffix made up of euphonic *n* after a vowel and *é*, emphatic particle. *váḍu veḷḷagáné*, as soon as he went away.

né, for *nénu*, I. *nénu veḷḷutánu* becomes in rapid speech *né veḍatá*.

néḍu, to-day, from *náḍu*, day.

néla, ground, soil, land, floor.

nélacoṭṭu, cellar; from *néla*, ground, and *coṭṭu*, store-room.

nélapálu, level with the ground. *peddalu cheppina dharmamul anní nélapál autavi*, the virtues taught by our elders are all abandoned.

nélaréḍu, the lord of the land, king.

némintsuṭa, to appoint. Skt., for the commoner *niyamintsuṭa*.

nénu, I, but *ná déhamu*, my body, or *ná manasu*, my mind, is often the equivalent of I; the Telugus are proud of using these circumlocutions and consider our failure to do so to be due to our inferior psychological insight.

néraca, involuntarily, unawares, not on purpose; from *nértsuṭa*. *néraca chésinánu*, I didn't do it on purpose; *nérchi néraca chésina pani*, an act committed unconsciously.

néradu, don't know how to, won't, can't; from *nértsuṭa*. *araché cucca carava néradu*, barking dogs don't bite.

néramu, crime; the common word, e.g. for those enumerated in the Indian Penal Code.

néramugala, criminal; used as a law term to translate 'criminal' in such expressions as criminal breach of trust, for which the stock expression of our Government translator is *néramugala nammaca dóshamu*; an expression which I warrant that the Telugu man in the street would never have thought out for himself.

nérani, the ignorance which comes from not having learnt. *páḍa nérani*, inability to sing, not having learnt to sing.

nérasthuḍu, a criminal.

néréḍu, a tree (*ardisia humilis*), sort of rose-apple. *jambu néréḍu* is *eugenia jambos*, of which we eat the fruit.

nérpintsuṭa, to cause to teach. A double causative, the steps being *nértsuṭa*, to learn, *nérpuṭa*, to teach, *nérpintsuṭa*, to cause to teach.

nérpu, skill, cleverness. *ṣástrulugáru ninnaṭi dinam Yélúru paḍava yecci Dhavaḷéṣvaram míduga y'í rózuna Piṭhápuram veḷḷutár ani ninna sayancálam vrüttánta patricaló tsadivinánu; tsadivi yémi chesinán anuconnávu? nérpu tsúḍu; vacca máṭu tappacunḍá darṣanam ichchi ghanta sép aina má grüham pávanam chési, vacca páṭa páḍi maḷḷi veḷḷa valasinad ani v'uttaram vrási, mana naucarla chétic ichchi, tellaváru zámuné banḍiní manushyalaní Dhavaḷéṣvaram pampinchinánu*, I read in the paper that the Shastri was going to get into the canal-boat at Ellore and go to-day to Pithapuram via Daulesh-varam; what do you suppose I did? See how clever I was: I wrote a letter saying that he must sanctify my house just for an hour by coming to it and sing one song, and gave it to my servants, and sent a bullock-cart and men to Dauleshvaram at dawn.

nérpuṭa, to teach; causative of *nértsuṭa*, to learn. *chépa pillacu y'ita nérpa valená?* have young fish got to be taught to swim? *tátacu dagga nérpa valená?* teach your grandmother how to suck eggs (your grandfather how to cough).

nértsuṭa, to learn. *váḍu ónamálu nérpuconuts unnáḍu*, he is learning his A, B, C (the letters *o*, *na*, and *ma* correspond to our *a*, *b*, *c*). *manamaḍu nértsucunn aṭṭu avvacu durada tírin aṭṭu*, the boy learnt his lesson by scrawling on his granny's back and at the same time relieved her itching (killing two birds with one stone); *tsaduvu nérchina ḍḍadánitónu, vanṭa nérchina magaváḍitónu yevvaru v'ópa léru*, a woman who has learnt to read, a man who has learnt to cook, are past bearing. *bharta: cáfí cheyyaḍánici iravai márgál unnai. bhárya: nác enducu chepputáru á sangati? bharta: váṭiló nuvvu occaṭi nértsu cunná, nácu tsálunu.* Husband: There are twenty ways of making coffee. Wife: Why do you say that? Husband: If you learnt one, I should be satisfied.

nérugá, straight. *á dóvanu nérugá pó valenu*, go straight along that road; but *tinnagá* is commoner in the Circars.

néstamu, friendship; but *snéhamu* is commoner.

néṭa, weaving. Also abl. of *néḍu*, to-day.

néticunḍa, pot of ghee; *néti* is the genitive of *neyyi*, ghee. *néticunḍa néla petti, vaṭṭi cunḍa v'uṭṭi mida peṭṭéváḍu*, putting the pot of ghee on the ground and the empty pot in the sling (instead of doing the reverse, proverb of absent-mindedness).

nétigúna, jar of ghee. *nétiguna chéta púni nichchena yeccin aṭṭu*, like going up the ladder with a jar of ghee in one's hands (rather a difficult thing to do).

néṭirátri, to-night; *néṭi* is the genitive of *néḍu*, to-day.

néṭisamácháramu, to-day's news.

nétramu, eye. Skt. The Telugu is *cannu*, but *nétramu* is also used in books, especially in compound words like *nétrótsavamu* (*nétra* and *utsavam*, festival); *nétraparvamu*, feast for the eyes; *nétrábhinayamu*, acting with the eyes.

néyamu, friendship; probably corrupt Skt. from *snéham* or *nyáyam* or a mixture of the two.

néyi, ghee; for *neyyi*, which is commoner.

néyuṭa, to weave, to lace, to thatch. *mantsamu néyuṭa*, to lace a bed with tape; *gaḍḍi néyuṭa*, to thatch with grass; *gaḍḍi nésina*, thatched. The root is one of the most universal: Skt. *nah*, join together, spin; Greek *neo*; Latin *necto*; German *nähen*, to sew; our own words 'connect', &c., derived from the Latin; Tamil *núl*, Telugu *núlu*, Greek *néma*, thread, are probably from the same root; so probably is our needle, German *nadel*, old Norse *nál*, Greek *nétron*, spindle, and so on.

ni-, negative prefix. Skt. Becomes *nir*, *nish*, *nis*, in composition.

nibadhamu, bound, restricted. Skt.

nibadhi, indubitable, certain. *váḍu bratucuṭa nibaddhi lédu*, it is not certain he will live.

nibandhanamu, agreement, condition. Skt.

nibandhintsuṭa, to bind, to restrain. Skt. *bind* and *bandh*, Skt., are the same root; so also *binden*, German. *bandhu*, relation, comes from this root and probably Greek *pentheros*, father-in-law.

nicaramu, net profit or balance or weight. *nicaram rábaḍi*, net income; *nicaramu bangáru*, net weight of the gold.

niccachchi, force, strictness. *váḍu tsála niccachchi manishi*, he is a very strict man.

niccamu, truth, certainty; *nizamu* is commoner for 'truth' and *mișchayamu* for 'certainty'.

niccaníluguṭa, to strut proudly, a reduplicated word from *niccuṭa* and *níluguṭa*, which both mean to strut.

niccapeṭṭuṭa, to prick up, to cock. *gurramu chevulu nicca peṭṭindi*, the horse pricked up its ears.

niccapoḍutsuṭa, to protrude, to bristle.

paici nicca poḍutsu coni v'unna dirkha rómumulu, thick bristling hair.

niccuṭa, to protrude, to strut. *niccupótu* is a proud man, a popinjay.

nicétanamu, house. Skt. Used in books for *illu* but less commonly than another Skt. word *grüham*, which is also used in common talk.

nichchena, ladder. *néti gúna chéta púni nichchena yeccin aṭṭu*, like going up a ladder with a firkin of ghee in your arms (a perilous undertaking); *cheṭṭu yeccinchi nichchena tísin aṭṭu*, like making a man climb a tree and then taking the ladder away (a low-down trick); *ácáṣánici nichchena véṣéváḍu*, he would plant a ladder to heaven (an ambitious man). Rung of a ladder is *nichchena meṭṭu*.

nicshépamu, treasure. Skt. *peṭṭinavánici telusunu nicshépamu*, the man who buried the treasure knows where it is; *dhana nicshépamu*, treasure of coins.

nidarṣanamu, example, proof. Skt. Usually in the sense of proof; *drüshṭánṭam* is commoner for 'example'; *amógha nidarṣanalu*, conclusive proofs; *granthanidarṣanam*, proof from the Book (Scripture).

nidánamu, source. Skt. *sukha anubhavamunacu nidánamulaina paṭṭanamulu*, towns, sources of comforts.

nidánamu, patience. *strilaló nidánamu taccuva*, women have little patience; *nidánamugá guri tsútsucó valenu*, aim carefully.

nidánintsuṭa, to ponder. *conta sépu nannu nidáninchi tsúchi*, pondering for a time and looking at me.

nidhi, treasure, often used metaphorically. Skt. *vivécanidhi*, storehouse of wisdom. *itaḍu sangitamu n'andu nidhi*, he is a treasure of song (a good singer).

nidhinicshépamu, hidden treasure. Skt.; a reduplicated word like *niccaniluguṭa* and many others.

niḍivi, length.

nidra, sleep. Skt. *gáḍhanidra*, deep sleep; *sukhanidra*, healthy sleep. *nidra póyinavánini lépa vatstsunu gáni, mélu cunna vánini lépa lému*, you can wake a man who is asleep but not one who is awake (none so blind as those that won't see); *ácali ruchi yerugadu; nidra sukham erugadu, valapu siggu yerugadu*, hunger knows not taste, nor sleep comfort, nor lust shame; *pagaṭi máṭalu panici chéṭu, rátri máṭalu nidracu chéṭu*, words by day spoil work, by night, sleep.

nidrabhangamu, interruption of sleep.

nidraléputa, to awaken.

nidramattu, drowsiness.

nidrapaṭṭaca, not being able to sleep.

nidrapaṭṭuṭa, to get to sleep. *Lacshmayya: nácu rátri nidra paṭṭadu, mandu putstsu có v'ále. Vencamma: pilla yéḍupu chéta nácunu nidra paṭṭadu, nác é mand istáró?* Smith: I can't sleep at night, I must take medicine. Mrs. Smith: I can't sleep at night for the child yelling; what soporific will you give me?

nidrapótu, sluggard.

nidrapóvuṭa, to go to sleep. *ocaḍu: Lacshmayya tsála kharidugala parupu connáḍu. incóḍu: háyagá nidra paṭṭinda? ocaḍu: paṭṭa lédu, dáni kharidu talutsu cunṭé digulu vési, Lacshmayya rátri antá nidra pó lédu.* Smith: Brown has bought a very expensive mattress. Jones: Did he sleep well on it? Smith: No, he was worried thinking about its price and could not sleep; *railu végangá pót unḍenu, Rámayya nidra pót unḍenu. Sómayya: yémayya, ní bhárya láuti manishá? Rámayya (cáḷḷu nalupu conṭu) aunu, aité yémi? Sómayya: railuló nunchi cinda paḍḍadi. Rámayya: aité golusu lági, banḍini ápi veyya léca poyindu? ṭicceṭlu ná bhárya daggira unnavi, tisucó valenu*, the train was moving fast and Smith was asleep. Jones: Ho, Sir, was that stout woman your wife? Smith (rubbing his eyes): Yes, what about it? Jones: She has fallen out of the train. Smith: Why didn't you pull the communication cord? She's got the tickets; I must get them from her.

nidratetsuṭa, to get sleepy.

nidratíyuṭa, to take a few winks. *parunḍi vaca nidra tísi*, lying down and getting a little sleep.

niḍuda, long. *niḍuda panḍlu,* long teeth; *niḍuda sirójamulu,* long tresses.
niḍupu, length.
nigarvamu, not proud. *íyana nigarva chúḍámani,* he is a jewel of modesty.
nigá, nighá, observation. Hindustani. *nigáló,* under observation; a common police term.
nighanṭuvu, dictionary. Skt. A *nighanṭu* is an *Indian* dictionary, that is a museum of antiquity and rarity, and if you commit it to memory you are a Pandit. Pandit speaking: *yédi nighanṭu? diccu málina nighanṭu samayánici smaranacu rádu; iṣvar anugraham valla gnyápacam vachchindi; néḍu ná páliṭa daivam unnáḍu*; '*lulayó mahishó váhadvishat cásara saribách*'. Where's the lexicon? I can't remember the damned lexicon just when I have need of it; by God's grace I have remembered; God is with me to-day. *lulayó, mahishó, váhadvishat, cásara, saribách*: these are all Skt. words for buffalo; any one who tries to learn them is a *dunnapótu* if he is only trying to learn Telugu.
nigiḍintsuṭa, to extend.
nigrahamu, disfavour. Skt., opposite *anu-graham,* favour; also rejection; *indriya nigrahamu* is continence.
niguḍtsuṭa, to extend, to emit. *tsúpu niguḍchi,* extending your gaze; *nittúrpu niguḍchi,* emitting a sigh.
niguḍuṭa, to stretch.
niguru, embers. Also *nivuru.*
nihatuḍu, slain. Skt.
nija, one's own. Skt. Used in books for *tana. nija grühamu,* one's own house.
nilabaḍuṭa, to stand, to stop, from *nilutsuṭa* and *paḍuṭa.*
nilacaḍa, steadfastness, in the long run. *nizamu nilacaḍa mída telusunu,* truth will come out in the long run; *nilacaḍa léni váni máṭa niḷḷa múṭa,* unstable as water he shall not excel (his word is a bundle of water); *máṭa nilacaḍa galaváḍu,* a man of his word.
nilayamu, house. Skt. One of the various book words for *illu.*
nilápaninda, calumny, more commonly *nirápaninda.*
nilipipaṭṭabaḍḍina, defined. This is one of the words our Telugu translator has had to make up; he uses it to translate 'defined' as a law term; it is quite intelligible, meaning 'it is caught, stopped'.
nilipivéyuṭa, to stop (transitive).
nilipiyunḍuṭa, detention. This is a word the Collector has to make up when he issues his notification about rate of detention for vehicles; it is quite intelligible, meaning 'being kept stopped'.
nilupuṭa, to stop (transitive); causal of *nilutsuṭa. máṭa nilupuconuṭa* is to keep one's word. *ocaḍu: Lacshmayya máṭa nilupu n'untáḍu. incóḍu: nilupucóca yém chéstáḍu? atani máṭa yevarici cávale?* Smith: Jones keeps his word. Brown: What can he do but keep it? Nobody wants it.
nilutsócu, don't stand (imperative). *talupu vadda nilutsócu, végiram lópalici rá,* don't stand by the door, come in (visitors have often to be encouraged to come in; they slink round corners; peons encourage this because they hope for a tip for showing the visitors in).
nilutsuṭa, to stand. *nilutsunḍaḍánacu zágá doricité, cúrtsunḍaḍánacu appuḍé dorucutundi,* get a place to stand in and you will soon get a place to sit in (it is the first step that counts).
niluva, remainder. *ná daggira yábhai rúpáyalu niluva v'unnavi,* I have Rs. 50 left.
niluvaníḍa, shade to stand in, last resource. *niluva níḍa, paṭṭa comma lécunḍá v'unnáḍu,* he has no shade to stand in or branch to catch hold of (he is at the end of all his resources).
niluvapaḍuṭa, to stand.
niluvapeṭṭuṭa, to establish.
niluvasaracu, stock.
niluvu, stature.
niluvugoṭṭamu, standpipe, such as they have in municipalities which have a water-supply.
niluvuṭaddamu, full-length looking-glass, from *niluvu,* stature, and *addam,* glass, *ṭ* added euphonically.
nilvalekha, balance-sheet.
nilviyunna, outstanding.
nimishacavi, improvisator. Skt.
nimishamu, minute. Skt.
nimittamu, for, because of; from Skt.

word for 'cause'. *ní nimittamu zám nunchi sabhavár andaru niricshist unnáru,* the whole meeting has been waiting for you for two hours (politicians in India always keep their meetings waiting to show what great men they are); *uppu nimittam póyindi,* she has gone for salt; *andu nimittam,* on that account, *darṣana nimittamai póyinánu,* I went to pay a visit.

nimmacáyi, lime (unripe). *nimmacáyalu uppu cáramuló úra véyuduru,* limes are pickled in salt.

nimmacheṭṭu, lime tree.

nimmalangá, gently, quietly, well (of health). *Lacshmayya: mic ippuḍu nimmalangá unnadá? Vencayya: nác émi? Lacshmayya: intacu mundu míru tsála sépu múligáré. Vencayya: nénu sangíta páṭacuḍi n'anḍi.* Smith: Feeling better? Jones: Why, what's the matter with me? Smith: You've been groaning for a long time. Jones: Sir, I am a singer.

nimmalinṭsuṭa, to get better, be quiet. *ocaḍu: ávacáya calupucuni, cáḷḷu músuconi tinṭu unnáv ém? incóḍu: zabbu nimmalinché varacu ḍácṭaru gáru nannu ávacáyanu caḷḷaló tsúḍa vadd annáru.* Smith: Why do you eat with your eyes shut when you're mixing pickle with your food? Jones: The doctor told me not to look at pickle till I was well again.

nimmapanḍu, lime (ripe). *nimmapanḍla rasamutó atani panḍlu pulisinavi,* he has set his teeth on edge by sucking limes.

nimnajátulu, depressed classes. Skt. A newspaper word from Skt. *nimna,* deep.

nimpádi, gentle, quiet. *nimpádiga cheppu,* don't raise your voice.

nimuruṭa, to stroke. *oca chétitó misamu vaḍi véyutsu, renḍava chétitó bozza nimurutsu, Srí Rázu gáru pravéṣintsuts unnáru,* twisting his moustache with one hand and stroking his stomach with the other, the zamindar comes in.

ninádamu, sound, note. Skt. A book word for *tsappuḍu.*

ninda, blame. Skt. The common word for blames it does not follow that if a word is Skt. it is not common; in fact most common words are Skt.

ninḍa, fully, filling, complete, of the contents, not the receptacle. The bad mistake is usually made of translating this word 'full'; the Telugu for 'full' is *ninḍu.* The construction of *ninḍa* is nominative of contents, genitive of receptacle. It is the common word to denote the idea of full, which is however, envisaged from a different side than in the European languages. *vanṭi* (*vanṭi* is the genitive of *oḍalu,* body) *ninḍa cantulu bailu dérutu v'unnavi,* boils are coming out all over his body; *caḍupu ninḍá tinnáru,* they ate their bellyful; *illu cálut unḍenu, nippu árput unḍiri. yazamáni: ayyá dánini racshintsanḍi, venṭané racshintsanḍi, oca másam ainá ninḍa lédu. nippu árpéváḍu; ammá, lópala tsúṣánu, pilla léd anḍi. yazamáni: pill émiṭ ayyá? nippu árpéváḍu: dénini racshintsam annadi? yazamáni: ná goḍugunu, dánini coni másam ainá cá lédu.* The house was burning, they were putting the fire out. Mistress of the house: Save it, save it quickly, it is not one full month yet. Man extinguishing the flames: Madam, I looked inside, there is no child. Lady: What child? Man: What did you want us to save? Lady: My umbrella, it isn't even a month since I bought it. *biḍḍacu déhamu ninḍa nagalu diga véyuts unnáru,* they load their infant with jewellery; *caḍupu ninḍá gárelu tinṭé, vanṭi ninḍá jvaramu,* a bellyful of cakes and a body full of fever; *váḍu ninḍá garvi,* he is a very proud man.

nindintsuṭa, to vilify. *upanyásacuḍini andarú nindist unḍiri, ataḍini samarthintsaḍánici ocaḍu léchenu. ocaḍu: upanyásacuḍu oca tsóṭa ichchina upanyásam incó tsóṭa ivvaḍu. incóḍu: iyyac ém? yeccaḍa cheppiná ocaṭé upanyásam. ocaḍu: ainá oca tsóṭa guddina balla incó tsóṭa guddaḍu; telusuná?* Every one was reviling the lecturer, Smith stood up for him. Smith: The lecturer never repeats his lecture in different places. Jones: What? Wherever he lectures, it is the same lecture. Smith: May be, but it's never the same table he thumps.

nindu, full, from *ninduța*, to be filled. *nindu cunda tonacadu*, the full pot does not spill (a half-empty pot or mind is easily overturned, the mind full of wisdom is steadfast).

ninduța, to be filled, to be full. *cadupu ninditė gárelu chédu*, the full belly scorns cakes; *cheruvu ninditė, cappalu chérutavi*, when the tank fills the frogs foregather; *cadupu nindina béramu*, bargaining with a man with his belly full (he will drive a hard bargain).

nindyamu, blameworthy.

ninna, yesterday. *ninna rátri*, last night; *ninna cuppá, nédu áḷḷu*, yesterday the heap, to-day the winnowed grain (*áḷḷu* is another form of *aricelu* (*paspalam scrobiculatum*), the proverb is like our 'grown up in a night'); *ninna v'unnaváru nédu léru*, all flesh is grass; *ninnați nunchi zabbugá undi nácu*, I have been ill since yesterday.

ninnu, you, accusative of *nivu*.

nintsuța, to fill (transitive), causative of *ninduța*.

nippanțuța, to be set on fire. *ocadu: ní tsuțțala ducánanici nipp anțu connad ani vinnánu; antá tagalabadi póyindá yémiți? incódu: tsuțțalu mátram cála lédu.* Smith: I hear your cigar shop got on fire; was everything burnt? Tobacconist: Everything except the cigars.

nippați, unleavened bread. *pindi yentó nippați anté*, the bread will vary with the flour (payment by results).

nippu, fire. *compa nipp peți léchipotánu.* (Wife speaking): I will set the house on fire and run away; *nippu chésinádu*, he struck a light; *vár iddarici nippu niḷḷugá n'unnadi*, they agree like fire and water (cats and dogs); *nippu cottité rendu aunu gáni, niḷḷu cottité rendu auná?* you can separate fire but can you separate water? (of inseparable intimacy); (Italian proverb *tra moglie e marito non mettere un dito*, do not put a finger between husband and wife); *nippu muțțanidi cheyyi cáladu*, don't play with fire; *nippuló poralinchin ațlu manasu paritapintsuța*, to grieve as though rolling in the fire (in an agony of grief); *ácháryuni talachi nippuló cheyyi pețțité cáladá?* put your hand in the fire with your priest in your mind and won't it burn?

nippupulla, match; also *aggipulla* from *aggi*, fire, corruption of Skt. word *agni*. Telugu has two common words for fire just as it has for blood (*netturu* and *ractam*) and most other common things, if it has not three as *nádu, rózu*, and *dinamu* for day.

nipuṇuḍu, expert. Skt.

nipunumu, skill, dexterity. Skt.

nir-, negative prefix. Skt.; also *ni-* and *nish-* and *nis-* (according to the laws of composition).

nir-, intensitive prefix. Skt.

niracshara, illiterate. Skt. *vádu niracshara cucshi*, he is a dunce.

nirancușamu, irresponsible. Skt. It does not really mean this in Sanskrit—it means unrestrained—but it is the word that politicians have invented to express their objection to our government; they call it *nirancușádhicáramu*, irresponsible government. (It is a newspaper word and was used when I was trying the leader of the Guntur No-Tax Campaign in 1922. I turned to the Police Inspector who was prosecuting, and said: 'Do you understand what the accused is saying? What is *nirancușádhicáramu*?' The Inspector, a Telugu, said he had no notion, and I had to explain the word to him. Such are many of the words used in the leading articles in Telugu newspapers to translate English words for which there is no real equivalent in Telugu; you can only understand these leading articles if you know English well and some Sanskrit.)

nirantaramu, endless. Skt. *Gópu: nuvvu vrásina 'nirantara sanchásram' ané vyásam yém aindi? Rámuḍu: á vyásánni nénu yenni patricalacu pampinchiná ná daggiracé vachchindi. Gópu: adi cúda nirantara sanchásram chéstu v'unnadi cábólu.* Smith: What has happened to your essay on perpetual motion? Jones: I have sent it to any number of papers but it always comes back to me. Smith: Does perpetual motion too, I suppose.

nirantaráyamu, unimpeded. Skt.

niraparádhamu, innocence. Skt.

niraparádhuḍu, innocent. Skt.

nirarthacamu, vain, useless. Skt.

nirarthacuḍu, useless person. *arthamu léni váḍu nirarthacuḍu,* a man without money is useless (a man without oof is not worth a spoof).

niraṣanamu, foodless. Skt. See also *nirádháramu.*

nirasintsuṭa, to refute, to reject, to deny. Skt. *idi vidhavá viváhamû yenta spashṭamugá nirasintsuts unnadó tsúḍu,* see how clearly this refutes the arguments for widow remarriage.

niratamu, eager, always. Skt. *niratánna dánamu* is daily alms; *niratánna pradánam chéta áme círti déṣam anta vyápinchindi,* her never-failing charity spread her fame all over the country.

nirácarana, scorn. Skt.

nirácarintsuṭa, to despise. Skt. *nív anta dínatvamutó chésina prárthananu nénu nirácarintsa lédu,* I have not despised the prayer you made with such humility.

nirácshépamu, without objection, unexceptionable. Skt. *análu paisalu senṭlu cúḍa vési nirácshépanga leccalu v'untsutánu,* I will keep accounts unexceptionably down to annas, pies, and cents.

nirádarana, contempt. Skt.

nirádháramu, groundless, helpless. Skt.

niráháramu, foodless, fasting. Skt. See also *niraṣanamu.*

nirápaninda, slander, blame; also *nilápaninda. nícu nirápaninda rácunḍá,* so that blame should not attach to you.

niráṣa, despair. Skt.

niráyudhamu, disarmed. Skt. *ní chétuló vaca carra v'unna manam niráyudhulamai vachchinámu,* you have a stick in your hand; we have come unarmed.

nirbandhamu, compulsion, insistence, complimentary insistence. Skt. *dina dina cramamugá nirbandhamu yeccuva cága,* the insistence becoming more and more daily; *mír intagá nirbandha parustú v'unnáru ganuca mír ann aṭṭé cán iyyanḍi,* have it your own way as you insist so much; *induló cá valasin anta nirbandham v'unnadi,* it is all compulsion.

nirbandhaparatsuṭa, nirbandhapeṭṭuṭa, to insist. *nannu véyi vidhamula nirbandha peṭṭinadi,* she pressed me in a thousand ways.

nirbandhintsuṭa, to compel. Skt.

nirbhayamgá, fearlessly.

nirbhayamu, without fear.

nirbhágyamu, unhappiness. Skt.

nirbhágyuḍu, unhappy man, wretch (often a term of abuse). Skt. *i y'iddaru canyalaló yevarin ainá y'i nirbhágyuḍici viváham ané misha mída bali peṭṭe-ṭ-aṭṭ aité ná mannassu bahu khéda paḍutundi,* I shall be very grieved if either of these girls is sacrificed to that wretch on the pretext of marriage; *yenducu panici ráni nirbhágyulu,* worthless wretches.

nirdayata, unkindness.

nirdayuḍu, cruel man. *nívu nirdayudavu; nícu ná mída nizangá préma v'unn' aṭṭ aité nátó álá pôṭláḍi v'undavu,* you are a cruel man; if you really loved me you would not have quarrelled with me like that.

nirdéṣamu, command. Skt.

nirdharintsuṭa, to determine. Skt.

nirdhâníyamu, fit to be settled. Skt.

nirdháramu, nirdháranamu, ascertainment, decision. Skt.

nirdháritamu, settled, determined. Skt.

nirdháryuḍu, a determined man. Skt.

nirdóshamu, without blame. Skt.

nirdóshatvamu, innocence.

nirdóshi, innocent man. *andaru nannu nirdóshi anucunṭáru,* every one will think me innocent.

nirdóshuḍaina, innocent; plural *nirdóshulaina. nirdóshulaina ná coḍuculu ná dósham chéta vachchina jádyam chéta mugguru varusagá pôyináru,* my innocent boys died, three of them one after the other, of the illness that I got through my sins.

nirdhóshurálu, innocent woman.

niríeshintsuṭa, to wait for. *ní nimittam zám nunchi niríeshist unnámu,* we have been waiting a couple of hours

for you; *áyana cósamé niricshistu v'unnánu,* it's he I am waiting for.
nirlacshyamu, disregard, disrespect. *naucarlu y'ílá nirlacshyangá máṭláḍutu v'unṭé nénu sahintsa lénu,* I won't stand the servants talking so disrespectfully.
nirlajjamu, shameless. Skt.
nirmalamu, pure. Skt. (free from impurity, *malam*).
nirmánamu, manufacture, production. Skt.
nirmúlamu, eradication, uprooting. Skt.
nirmúlamugá, root and branch. Skt.
nirnayamaina, settled, defined. Skt.
nirnayamu, decision, settlement, resolution at a meeting. Skt. Chairman of meeting: *í nirnayam écavácyangá niṣchayimpa baḍ aṭṭu vrásinánu,* I have written that this resolution was carried unanimously.
nirnayamugá, definitely. Skt.
nirnayintsuṭa, to settle, to determine, to allot, to declare, to arrange. Skt. *manishi vaccanṭici artha rúpáyi tsoppuna nénu bhójanánici nirnayinchinánu,* I settled for dinner at half a rupee a head.
nirnítamu, fixed. Skt.
niródhamu, interdiction, check. Skt.
niródhintsuṭa, to obstruct, to stop up, to debar. Skt. *nyayamaina márgamuna niródhinchi,* stopping up the proper road.
niru, very. *niru péda,* very poor; for *tsála,* hardly used except in this phrase. *nirupédacu pennidhi tsandamu,* like treasure-trove to the pauper. *niru* also means 'past' in composition as in the next word which stands for *niru-yéḍu.*
niruḍu, last year. *niruḍu sanvatsaram mámúluló vacca rúpáyi taccuva vachchind ani nénu y'ichchin dácá chélu yenḍi póyiná gidd eḍu niru vadili peṭṭináḍu cáḍu,* he (the overseer) would not let a pint of water into the parched fields on the pretext that there was a rupee short in his last year's customary bribe.
nirutsahamu, joyless. Skt.
nirúpamanamu, matchless, incomparable. Skt.
nirúpintsuṭa, to ascertain, to investigate. Skt. Used in the newspapers.
nirvachanamu, definition. Skt.
nirvachintsuṭa, to define. Skt.
nirvahanamu, management. Skt.
nirváhacuḍu, manager. Skt. *campinici miru cárya nirvahaculugá v'unḍa lédá?* weren't you business manager to the company?
nirváhanacarta, manager. Skt.
nirvánamu, eternal annihilation and that is eternal bliss. Skt. *mana pariṇáma siddhántánusáramugá manushyuḍu Nirvánánni pondaḍánici mundugá yéḍu lócálaló avatarintsa valenu,* according to the Scriptures man must pass through seven worlds to reach Nirvana.
nirvédamu, renunciation. Skt.
nirvédintsuṭa, to renounce. Skt.
nirvicháramu, without sorrow. Skt. *ica nénu nirvichárangá v'unḍa vatstsunu,* I need be in no anxiety in future.
nirvighnamu, unobstructed. Skt. *mém upadéṣinchina mantram nirvighnamugá phalintsunu gáca,* may the charm we have initiated you into work without obstruction.
nirvivádamu, unquestioned. Skt.
niṣáni, mark of illiterate person. Hindustani. Most of our witnesses cannot sign; their mark in the form of a cross used to be taken; now it is a thumb impression.
niṣchalamu, immovable. Skt.
niṣchayamu, resolution, certain. Skt. *maranamu niṣchayamu,* death is certain; *íme niṣchayamunu tippuṭacu samarthuḍu gáca,* not able to shake her resolution; *niṣchayamgá y'íme santóshadayinigá v'unnadi,* she is certainly a cheerful person.
niṣchayintsuṭa, to resolve. Skt. *í nirnayam écavácyangá niṣchayimpa baḍ aṭṭu vrásinánu,* I have written that this resolution has been passed unanimously.
niṣchéshtuḍu, niṣchéshtituḍu, not able to move, inanimate, lifeless, taken aback, aghast. Skt. *atadu niṣchéshtituḍai chitrapu paṭamu lágu v'unn appuḍu, nívu veḷḷi paṭṭu có valenu,* when he is lying inanimate like a picture, go up and catch hold of him.
niṣchitamu, settled. Skt. *niṣchita tátparyamu,* a settled opinion.
nishcaḷancamu, spotless, clear, unquestionable. Skt.

nishcapaṭamu, guileless. Skt.
nishcapaṭi, a guileless man.
nishcarsha, determination. Skt.
nishcarshintsuṭa, to determine. Skt.
nishcáranamugá, careless, without rhyme or reason, unnecessarily. Skt. *nishcáranangá y'ilá álasyam cheyyaḍam nácu y'ishṭamgá v'unḍadu,* I can't stand that sort of unreasonable delay; *nénu buddhi hínuni ai nishcáranangá manchi máṭal áḍa valasinaḍánici badulugá tagavul áḍinánu,* I was a fool and quarrelled unreasonably instead of speaking fair; *vaşyaushadhamu ichchedan ani y'oca véru chétiló peṭṭi bairágiváḍu, nishcáranamgá nálugu rúpáyalu yettu coni póyináḍé gáni, mandu gunamu conchemaina agapaḍi, adi náṭó mogam ichchi máṭáḍuṭa y'ainanu léca póyenu,* the other day a wandering friar said he would give me an aphrodisiac and put some root in my hand and made off with the four rupees I squandered on him; for all the virtue of the herb she would not open her lips or favour me with a single word.
nishcramintsuṭa, to disappear. Skt. The ordinary stage direction *exeunt omnes* is *andarunu nishcramintsuts unnáru.*
nishédhamu, nishiddhamu, prohibited. Skt. *samudra yánamu nishiddham ani telisinaváḍ ainanu,* though I know that sea voyages are prohibited (they are forbidden to Brahmins by Scripture).
nishédhintsuṭa, to prohibit. Skt. *strí punarvivádham nishédhintsun ani,* saying the second marriage of women is prohibited (it is among Brahmins); *şúdrulacu vidya manchidaina pacshamuna manapúrvulu dáni nishédhinturu?* if education were good for Sudras, would our ancestors have prohibited it?
nishpacshapátamu, impartiality (not taking a side). This common compound, for some unexpected reason, is not given in the ordinary dictionaries.
nishpacshapátuḍu, an impartial man, a fair man. *Lacshmayya: nénu nishpacshapátunni. nénu tappu pani chésiná, dánici vichára paḍutánu; incóḷḷató ná tappu chepputánu. Vencayya: mí daggira rahasyam dágadu cábólu.* Smith: I am a very fair-minded man. If I have done wrong, I feel remorse and confess. Jones: I suppose you can't keep it secret.
nishphalamu, fruitless. Skt. *váni prayatnamulu nishphalamulai póyinavi,* his attempts ended in smoke.
nishprayójanamu, useless. Skt.
nishṭha, austerity. Skt. A religious term.
nishṭhuḍu, austere man. Skt.
nishṭhuramu, harsh. Skt. *antya nishṭhuramu canná, ádini nishṭhuramé mélu,* severity at the beginning is better than severity at the end (it is better to say no at once); *nizam áḍité nishṭhuramu,* truth is bitter. (*Il n'y a que la vérité qui blesse.*)
nişíthamu, night. Skt. A book word for *rátri.*
nişşabdamu, noiseless. Skt. *iccaḍa nişşabdamugá v'unnadi, sukhamgá nidra pó vatstsunu,* there is no noise here; I can go to sleep comfortably.
nişşancamu, without hesitation. Skt.
nissandéhamu, without doubt. *nissandéhamugá canapaḍutu v'unnadi,* of course I can see it; *induló manchi illálu tahaşşíludáru gári bhárya várini racshinshinadi; pedda manushyula vishayamuló mariyoca vidhamugá zaraginchina pacshamuna nútiló paḍedan ani áme gaṭṭi paṭṭu paṭṭa baṭṭi gáni, léni yeḍala nissandéhamugá pantulugári maradal í páṭi—cárágrúhamu pravéşinchinadé,* that worthy matron the Tahsildar's wife, saved her; by threatening to throw herself into the nearest well if he acted otherwise towards a respectable family, she got a hefty hold on him; otherwise the Pantulugaru's sister-in-law would have been locked up—not a doubt of it.
nişşéshamu, completely (without remainder). *nálugu lankhandlató rógam nişşeshamai pótundi,* the disease will completely vanish after a few fasts.
nitstsalamu, motionless. Skt. *nişchalamu.*
niṭṭúrpu, sigh; from *níḍu,* long, and *úrupu,* breath.
nittúrtsuṭa, to sigh.
nityamu, always, continual, everlasting. Skt. *nitya hómam* is daily Mass;

nitya carmamu, daily service; *alpa vidya, visham nityam*, little knowledge is a daily poison; *nannu goppavánnani nityamu stuti chéstu v'unṭáru*, they will always praise me as a great man; *nityamu mí sangítamtó ná chevulacu vindu chéyanḍi*, give me a continual feast of song; *váni aḍangalu nityamu mí y'inṭici vastú pótú v'unnáru*, his female relations are always in and out of your house; *nityamaina paralóca sukhamulu*, the everlasting felicities of the next world.

nivarti, doing away with, divesting. Skt. *daridra nivarti aguṭacu*, so that poverty may be done away with.

nivartintsuṭa, to do away with. Skt.

niváranamu, doing away with, warding off. Skt. *dévatalam aina mávi ṣilá caṭṭina déhálu ganuca, má ṣaríralacu rógálu sócavu; amrüta pánam chéta mác anni niváránam autavi; amrüta pánam chéta tsávu lén appuḍu rógálu yeccaḍa nunchi vastavi?* as we are gods and have imperishable bodies, disease cannot attack us; nectar drinking wards off everything from us; as nectar drinking does away with death, where are diseases to come from? *andarící santánam caligi, janam abhivrüddhi autu v'unṭé, y'í bhúmi mída panḍé panṭa vá‍ḷḷa tinḍici tsálaca, caruvulu vachchi, andarú tsáva valasi vastundi; bógamváḷḷanu v'untsu cóvaḍam chéta, peḷḷánici santánam calugaca, janam taccuva póyi, iṭuvanṭi goppa ápaddálu nivāranam autundi*, if every one has issue the population will increase so much that the crops will not suffice to feed it, and famines will come, and every one will have to perish; by keeping dancing-girls, and our wives having no issue, the population will diminish and such calamities will be avoided (a simple and congenial method of birth-control).

nivárintsuṭa, to do away with, to ward off, to stop, to relieve, to avert. *calahamu nivárintsuṭa*, stopping turmoil.

nivásamu, dwelling, a house. Skt. *accaḍa nivásam aináru*, they dwelt there; *ṣásvita nivásamu* is what our Telugu translator uses to translate domicile (law).

nivási, inhabitant. Skt.

nivásintsuṭa, to live in. Skt.

nivédanamu, offering, oblation. Skt. *míru vachchi dévata nivédana chésténé cáni dánic annam peṭṭa valla cádu*, we can't give her food unless you come and make offerings to God. The form *naivedyamu* is commoner.

nivédica, report. Skt. The newspaper word for an official report.

nivédintsuṭa, to make known, to report.

nivéṣanasthalamu, house site. Skt.

nivuṟu, embers. Also *niguru*.

nivvera, astonishment.

nivveraganduṭa, nivverapaḍuṭa, to be astonished. *nivverapaḍi végiramu máṭa ráca taḍabaḍutsu '-é-é-émiṭidi?'*, astounded he stammered in confusion 'Wh-wh-what is this?'

nivverapáṭu, astonishment.

niyamamu, precept of religion. Skt. *ippaṭivár anni niyamamulanu cramamugá naḍapaca póvuṭa chéta vyabhichár ádi dóshamulu caluguts unnavi*, because the precepts of religion are not being strictly followed adultery and other sins prevail; *yécádaṣi vratam niyamangá zarapa valenu*, the 11th day of observance (a fast) must be observed as prescribed by religion.

niyamintsuṭa, to designate, to appoint. Skt.

niyamitamu, ordered, appointed. Skt.

niyógamu, order. Skt.

Niyógi, secular Brahmin. Skt. Brahmins are either Vaidikis (clergy) or Niyogis. There is not much difference at the present day except that Niyogis are allowed to smoke and Vaidikis are not supposed to. Both classes are equally anxious for Government jobs.

niyógintsuṭa, to command. Skt.

nizamaina, true, real. Skt. *ná nizamaina péru*, my real name. *doragáru: nuvvu cheppina sangatul anni nizamé gadá? í rúpáyi tísu có. ocaḍu: nizamaina cáca póyiná rúpáyi kharídu canna yeccuva sangatulé cheppānu.* Englishman: The things you have said are all true, aren't they? Here's a rupee for you. Stranger: Even if they aren't all true I have said more than a rupee's worth of things.

nizamáḍuṭa, to speak the truth.

nizamu, truth, true, real. *cómaṭi nizamu,* the shopkeeper's truth (which is the opposite); *nizamu nílacaḍa mída telusunu,* truth comes out in the long run; *nizam áḍité nishṭhuramu,* truth is unpalatable; *níḷḷu pallam erugunu, nizam dévuḍ erugunu,* water knows its level and God the truth; *báluḍu: nánna, manam í prapanchamuló itarulacu saháyam chéyaḍánicé v'unnám ani ṭicharu cheppäḍu. tanḍri: á sangati nizamé. báluḍu: aité itarul enduc unnáru?* Boy: Daddy, teacher said we are on this earth to help others. Father: That's true. Boy: Then what are the others on earth for? *ocaḍu: nácu scúlu anṭé ishṭam lédu. incóḍu: yendu chéta? ocaḍu: nizam cheppin anducu máshṭaru oca sári nannu coṭṭädu. incóḍu: aṭuvanṭi durabhyásam nícu taruváta póyindá?* Smith: I don't think much of school. Jones: Why? Smith: I got thrashed at school for telling the truth. Smith: You have lost that bad habit since? *ocaḍu: Lacshmayya caṭhinamaina manish allé (valé) unnáḍu. incóḍu: yeṭlá telisindi? ocaḍu: atani canḍlu tsústé telustundi; cuḍi cannutó ataḍu guḍḍu tappacunḍá nannu tsústé nácu bhayam ésindi (vésinadi). incóḍu: cuḍi cannu glásu cannu, nizam cannu cádu.* Smith: Jones looks a fierce man. Brown: How do you make that out? Smith: When he fixes me with his right eye without moving the pupil he terrifies me. Brown: His right eye is a glass eye, not a real eye.

ní, your; from *nívu,* you (second person singular).

níchamu, low, base, vile. Skt. *aṭuvanṭi níchapu pani nácu cheppaḍam mícu dharmam cádu, nénu mí guruvu n'anna máṭa gnyápacam v'unnadá? guruvucu maryáda cheyya valenu,* it is not right in you to ask me to do that menial service; remember I am your guru; you must respect your guru; *dhaniculu tama biḍḍalanu nícha séva-cula vaṣamuna viḍichi peṭṭi y'úracunḍuru,* rich people leave their children to the care of menials.

níchata, baseness. Skt.

níchuḍu, vile creature. Skt. *Lacshmayya: Rangaḍu occa rúpáyi badulu iyyam anṭé ivvan annáru; inta canṭé níchulu unṭárá? Rámayya: nénu unnánu.* Smith: I asked Jones to lend me a rupee and he refused; is there a viler wretch in the world? Brown: Yes, there's me.

nícu, to you; dative of *nívu,* you (second person singular).

níḍa, shade, shadow. *yeddu yenḍacu lága, dunnapótu níḍacu lága,* the bullock pulled towards the sun, the buffalo towards the shade (an ill-matched pair; no two heads were ever made the same); *tana níḍa tanatóné v'unṭ unnadi,* a man can't get rid of his shadow (or the consequences of his actions).

nídi, yours. *móṭáruváḍu: yémayyá, í róḍḍu antá nídé anuconi nadustáv ém ayyá? báṭasári: í banḍi antá nídé anuconi tólutáv enduc ayyá?* Motor-driver: Why do you walk as if the whole road were yours? Pedestrian: Why do you drive as if the whole car were yours?

nílacanṭhuḍu, Siva, the blue-throated. Skt., from *nílam,* blue, and *canṭham,* throat; hence the common name *Nílakanṭha.*

nílacheṭṭu, indigo plant.

nílamandu, indigo.

nílamu, blue. Skt.

Nílámbaruḍu, Balaram or Saturn. Skt., from *nílam,* blue, and *ambaram,* sky.

níḷḷáḍuṭa, to be brought to bed (of women). *puṭṭinṭici veḷḷi níḷḷáḍi,* she went to her parents' house and was brought to bed.

níḷḷu, water. The singular is *níru,* but the plural is much more common just as it is for grains; the Telugu says wheats, not wheat, because he thinks of it as a collection of grains; and waters, not water, because he thinks of it as a collection of drops; when it is one drop he has in mind as *cannu níru,* tear, he uses the singular. *áḍa-dáni máṭa, níḷḷa múṭa,* a woman's word is a bundle of water (*souvent femme varie*); *yevari níḷḷaló váru munaga valenu,* every one must bathe in his own water (bear his own troubles); *nippucú níḷḷacú v'uṇḍé snéhamu*, agreeing like fire and water (cats and dogs); *yazamanurálu: idi varac unna tsóṭu nunchi yenducu vadali vachchdu? dádi: váḷḷa pillalacu níḷḷu poyya léd ani tisivésár anḍi. bálica: amma, í manishi cudurtsu cóvé, nácu háyagá v'unṭundi.* Mistress: Why did you leave your last place? Nurse: They complained I did not wash the children enough and sent me away. Little girl: Mummy, take her on, I shall be comfy. *pólísu canisṭébilu: iccaḍa snánam cheyyaḍánici vílu lédu, veḷḷi pó. ocaḍu: nénu snánam cheyyaḍam lédu, níḷḷaló munugut unnánu.* Constable: Bathing is prohibited here, get out. Bather: I am not having a bathe, only a dip. *paḍavaváḍu: ayyó, yevaró manishi níḷḷaló paḍḍáḍu. strí: áyana ná penimiṭé, áyananu manishi anaca peddamanishi ani anu; maryádagá máṭláḍu.* Canal-boatman: Help, some man has fallen into the water. Woman: It's my husband; don't say man, say gentleman; keep a civil tongue in your head. For 'climate' use *níḷḷu*. This climate tells upon me is *í úri níḷḷu nácu zabbu chést unnavi* (the water of this place makes me ill).

nírasamu, weakness. Skt.

nírasuḍu, weak man, pauper.

níraipóvuṭa (*nír-ai-póvuṭa*), to be melted (by pity, &c.). *ninnu tsúḍagáné ná gunḍe níraipóyinadi*, my heart melted at the sight of you.

níru, water, more common in the plural, but *canníru*, tear; *cottaníru*, flood; *nírucásu*, the coin given to Brahmins at holy bathing-places; and the singular is used in compounds generally, *nírucóḍi*, waterfowl, *níṭidayyamu*, water-sprite. *níru níru vancané párut unnadi*, water runs to water (birds of a feather flock together); *níḷḷu múṭa caṭṭin aṭṭu*, like tying water in a bundle (a difficult job); *níru pallam erugunu, nizamu dévuḍ erugunu*, water finds its level on earth and lies their level in heaven; *parugetti pálu trágé canṭé, curtsonḍi níru tráguṭa mélu*, it is better to sit and drink water than to have to run for milk; *grámamló dastu chési delṭa syuparinṭenḍenṭu mokhánni pósténé cáni polálalóci vacca tsucca níru rádu*, unless I collect the money to grease the irrigation overseer's palm, not a drop of water will flow into the fields; *cannula níru peṭṭuṭa* is to cry; *nírucaṭṭuṭa* is to irrigate (with dative).

nírubugga, bubble; also *níṭibuḍḍa*; *déhamu nírubugga vanṭidi*, the body is like a bubble in the water (all flesh is grass).

nírucáci, water-crow.

nírucásu, alms given at sacred bathing-places, especially sacred rivers like the Godavari at the festival which comes every twelve years.

nírucávi, reddish. This is not a compound of *níru*, water, but of an old word *niru*, meaning 'slight'. *nírucavi dhóvati*, a soft-tinted dhoty.

nírucóḍi, waterfowl.

nírucucca, otter; the water-dog.

nírulli, onion.

nírupandi, porpoise; the water-pig.

níṭi-, prefix meaning 'water', genitive case of *níru*. *níṭidayyamu*, water-spirits; *níṭipámu*, water-snake; *níṭi sarafará*, water-supply.

níti, morals, maxims of morality. Skt. *nívu y'anni nítulu chepputávu gáni*, you are all moral maxims; *váḷḷa mída cópa paḍa cunḍa v'undaḍamu, váḷḷacu léni póni panulu cheppa cunḍa v'undaḍamu, modalaina grüha nítulu bódha chéstánu*, I shall inculcate household moral maxims as that you should not get angry with your servants or impose ridiculous tasks on them; *yevadaina vacaḍu á cálamló munḍanu v'untsu cunṭé, pedda manushyulu yevarú vánni marydda cheyyaca póvaḍam chéta, bhayam caligi taccinaváḷḷ andarú níti caligi v'undéváru*, at that time if any one kept a whore he was slighted by all respectable men, and all the rest for fear of that remained moral.

níṭibuḍḍa, water-bubble; also *nírubugga*.

nítihínuḍu, nítimálinaváḍu, an immoral man.

nítimantuḍu, a moral man.

nítipárudala, irrigation; from *níru*, water, and *páruṭa*, to flow.

níṭu, straight; *níṭugá póté,* if you go straight.

níṭu, elegance, neatness.

níṭucáḍu, a fop.

níṭucatte, a belle.

níṭuparatsuṭa, to make neat.

níṭutanamu, prettiness, neatness.

nívu, you; second person singular; intimate or contemptuous; *míru* is polite; *tamaru,* respectful; *dévara, svámi, máprobhó,* obsequious.

noccu, dint, tooth of a saw or wheel, dimple.

noccuṭa, to squeeze, to wring, to crush, to emphasize. *pillaváḍi gontuca nocci póyindi,* she wrung the child's neck; *ṣirastádáru gárici mí mída cópamé; paici manchi máṭalu cheputu v'unná, samayam doricité mimmalni yendulónainá paṭṭuconi gaṭṭigá nocci veyya valen ani tsústu v'unnáḍu,* the sheristadar is angry with you; outwardly he will speak you fair but he is lying in wait to trap you and squeeze the life out of you; *nocci chepputánu,* I say emphatically.

noga, cart-pole.

noppi, pain. *tági, cinda paḍi, dorlutu v'unn appuḍu sukhamugáné cana paḍinanu, tarváta déhamu noppi chési duhkham ani telistundi,* to get drunk and fall down and roll about may seem jolly at the time but wait till you feel cheap afterwards; *báluḍu: nánna; paḷḷa vaidyuḍi shápuló* (shop) *nénu yéḍava lédu. tandri: nuvvu buddhimantuḍavu; í rúpáyi tísu có; noppi tsála puṭṭindá? báluḍu: vaidyuḍu shápuló léḍu; yeccaḍicó veḷḷáḍu.* Boy: Daddy, I didn't cry at all at the dentist's. Father: Good boy, here's a rupee for you; did it hurt much? Boy: The dentist wasn't there; he had gone out.

noppintsuṭa, to hurt (transitive). *váni manassu noppintsacu,* don't hurt his feelings.

nosalu, forehead. *nosalu chemaṭa cárchi,* by the sweat of one's brow; *nosaṭa vrásina máṭa tappa galadá?* can what is written on the forehead fail to come true? (your fate is supposed to be written in the sutures of your skull). There are many variations of this, e.g. *dévuḍu nosaṭa vrási peḍité yédi tappadu; brahma dévuḍu váḷḷa nosaṭa álá vrási peṭṭináḍu,* it is Brahma, the Creator, who did the writing on their foreheads; *brahma vrásina vrálu tirugund,* will Brahma's writing fail?; *nosaṭa vrásina vrálu canná núr énḍlu chintinchina yémi lédu,* a 100 years' hard thinking will not alter your fate. See also *nuduru.*

notstsuṭa, to feel pain, usually in the middle form *notstsuconuṭa*; but *nochchi póyináru,* they were in reduced circumstances; *í máṭala valla váni manassu nochchindi,* these words cut him to the heart.

nómu, vow. *móchéti nómu chési Lacshmi Dévi aiṣvaryavanturálunnú suvásiniyunnú ainadi cád anḍi?* did not the goddess Lakshmi become rich and fragrant by making a vow on her knees? *míru nómulu vratálu v'upavásálu chéstáru; mému av anní pichchi ani mánivéstámu,* you perform vows and penances and fasts; we think that all insane and do nothing of the kind; *núru nómulu vaca rancutó póvunu,* one slip cancels a hundred vows.

nóráḍuṭa, to utter. *vánici yeṭlá nór áḍenó!* how could he say such a thing!

nóreṭṭuṭa, to raise the voice, to protest. *yéḍustu v'untávu, ippuḍu cánicalálu vachchinavi, yémi nór etta valla cádu,* wretch, it is a bad time for you, you can't raise your voice any more; *vappucóvaḍam chéta nénu y'ica nór ettaḍánici valla cádu,* as I agreed I can't protest any more; *váḍu maḷḷí nór ettacunḍá tagina samádhánamu cheppinánu,* I gave him his quietus, shut him up.

nóru, mouth, but sometimes to be translated voice. *nóru manchid aité y' úru manchidé,* if you keep a civil tongue in your head, you will find people civil to you; *adhyacshacuḍu: mana sangham gavarnaru gári daggirici rdyabáram pampints ále; inducu tagina sabhyul evaró cheppanḍi. sabhyuḍu: aiduguriniṁ pampintámá? adhyacshuḍu: aṭlágé pampintámu; Rámayyanu cúḍa váḷḷaló chérustámá? sabhyuḍu: chértsa vatstsunu gáni Rámayya nóru terava cunḍá v'unḍé sharatu mída pampintsa vatstsunu.* Chairman: Our committee has to send a deputation to the Governor; say who are suitable members. Member: Are we sending five? Chairman: Yes; shall we include Ramayya? Member: Yes, on condition that Ramayya does not open his mouth. *strí: ayyó pápam, chépa ní táḍucu tagulucuni tsachchi póyindi. chépalu paṭṭéváḍu: dáni telivi taccuvacu nén ém chésédi? adi nóru músu cuni v'unḍi, nénu peṭṭina yeranu tinaca póté, braticé v'unḍédi.* Woman: Oh dear, the poor fish has got itself caught and is dead. Fisherman: What am I to do, Lady, if the fish is so foolish? It had only to keep its mouth shut and not swallow my bait and it would be alive still; *nóru musucó* is shut your mouth; *nóru zári* is slip of the tongue; *y'inta varacu nénu y'í sangati vacca piṭṭató cheppa lédu; ajágratagá v'unn appuḍu y'ippuḍu máṭala parácuna mí daggira nóru zári paici vachchindi,* I had not told even a little bird; but now in a careless moment the words came out by a slip of the tongue; *nóṭamáṭaráca,* unable to speak; *nóṭiló áḍutsunnadi,* I have it at the tip of my tongue; *pedda nóru chéyuṭa,* to shout and storm (the Italian *fare la voce grossa,* make a big voice, more nearly translates it); *váni nóru manchidi cádu,* he is a foul-mouthed fellow; *andari nóḷḷaló n'unnadi,* it is in every one's mouth; *váni nóṭa nuvvu ginza nánadu,* an oil-seed won't melt in his mouth (he lets everything out; can't keep a secret); *rája purushulacu vanda rúpáyal ichchi, vári nóḷḷu caṭṭinámu,* we gave the police Rs. 100 to keep their mouths shut.

nóruléni, dumb. It does not mean without a mouth, but without a voice. The ordinary word for dumb is *múga.*

nóṭísu, notice. English. To put up a notice is *nóṭísu caṭṭuṭa*; to give notice is *nóṭísitstsuṭa*; *má plíḍaru mícu nóṭísu istáru,* you will get a lawyer's notice, is good Telugu.

nótsuconuṭa, middle form of *nótsuṭa,* to take a vow; used in the sense of to be able, to bring yourself to do something. *padimandiló tirugaṭacu nótsuco lédu gadá?* couldn't you bring yourself to move in society? *poruguváḷḷa inṭló vivá̀ham aina, veḷḷi véḍuca tsúḍaḍánici nótsucó lédu gadá?* couldn't you manage to go to the neighbours' houses when there is a marriage on to see the fun? *nénu inta mátrapu máṭal ainanu nótsu cóca pótini,* I could not go so far even in words.

nótsuṭa, to take a vow.

nóṭu, note (bank-note). English. *í nóṭu tísuconi rúcal immu,* please change this note for me.

nóṭubuccu, note-book. English. Every constable knows what a note-book is; he has one himself; every schoolboy knows it too. *vidhyárthi: ayyá, ná nóṭubuccu mída míru ráṣind émiṭó teliya léd anḍi. ṭicharu: ní dastúri tinnagá teliyaḍam léd ani ráṣánu.* Schoolboy: Sir, I can't read what you have written in my note-book. Teacher: I wrote that your handwriting is illegible. In a book I have found the paraphrase '*chinna súchica pustacamu*', little noting book.

nu, you. Short for *nuvvu,* the common form of *nívu.*

nuduru, forehead; also *nosalu.* There are two words for most things in Telugu, if not three.

nuḍuvuṭa, to say. There are half a dozen words for 'to say' in Telugu; *chepputa* is the most common.

nulaca, cord; especially the cord used for lacing the bottom of cots; probably connected with *núlu,* thread, and *néyuṭa,* to weave; *nulacamantsam,* a ticken cot.

nuli, a twist.

nuligonuṭa, to be twisted.

nulimivéyuṭa, to twist. *meḍa nulimivéyuṭa* is to twist the neck of.

nunchi, nunḍi, from, along. *nela nunchi y'iccaḍa y'unnánu,* I have been here a month; *nann nunchi vaca nalli y'ainanu tsávadu,* I don't even kill bugs; *yeccaḍanunchi?* whence? *ciṭicíló nunḍi tsútsutsu,* looking out of the window; *vídhi nunchi* may mean from the street or along the street; *paṭṭa pagalu vídhiló nunchi veḷḷutu v'unṭé nénu caḷḷárá tsúchinánu,* I saw him with my own eyes going along the street in broad daylight.

nunupu, smooth. *dúrapu conḍalu nu-*

nupu, distant hills are smooth (distance lends enchantment to the view).

nurugu, foam. *samudrapu nurugu*, foam of the sea.

nuvvu, you; common colloquial form of *nívu* (second person singular).

nuvvu, gingelly, an oil-seed plant (*sesamum orientale*), used almost always in the plural *nuvvulu*; a very common crop; in the other Dravidian languages it is *yeḷḷu*, in Hindi it is *til*; known to Anglo-Indians as gingelly, til, or sesamum; til is Skt. in origin; gingelly is Arabic. *nuvvulu panḍiná, tsóḷḷu panḍiná, rayitu cheḍadu*, the farmer will not be ruined if his gingelly or ragi yields (it is an uncertain crop); *nuvvu chénucu núru teguḷḷu*, gingelly is exposed to countless blights; *unḍévádu ulava, veḷḷévádu nuvvulu tsalla valenu*, if you mean to stay (in the village), sow horse-grain; if you mean to go, sow gingelly.

nuyyi, a well. The common word in the Circars; elsewhere they say *bhávi*. *tádu tsálaca póté nuyyi púdtsum ann aṭṭu*, like ordering the well to be filled when the rope was found short (cutting off your nose to spite your own face); *mundarici vasté goyyi venaccu póté nuyyi*, pit in front, well behind (caught between two fires); *áme nútiló níḷḷu tóduts unnadi*, she is drawing water from the well; *má peraṭló vaca nuyyi tistámu*, we shall sink a well in our back yard; (chagrined Indian women throw themselves down wells or threaten to); *cáryamu chéyaca póyina yedala nútilónó gótilónó paḍi tsachedan ani bhárya paṭṭu paṭṭi cúrutsunna taruváta, yenta manchivádunu lóbaḍaca yémi chéya galaḍu?* when his wife sat tight and stuck to 'if you don't square the business, I will drown myself as sure as eggs are eggs', what could a poor man, however honest, do but yield? (Indian husbands are apt to be weak with their wives.)

núgu, down. *núgu mísamulu*, down on the lips.

núlu, cotton thread; probably same root as *néyuṭa*, to weave. *núlu canḍe*, ball of thread.

núne, gingelly oil; probably compounded of *nuvvu*, gingelly, and *neyyi*, ghee; it is *yenna* in all the other Dravidian languages and *tél* in Hindi.

núrtsuṭa, to thresh (grain). A threshing-floor is *caḷḷamu*.

núru, 100. *úri mída núru paḍḍá, caranamu mída cásu paḍadu*, you may levy 100 pagodas from the village but the karnam won't pay a groat; *núṭici peṭṭi cóṭici goriginchévádu*, sweating a crore to feed a hundred (the slave-grinding philanthropist); (money speaking) *núru ayyé varacu nannu cápáḍité, núru aina venuca ninnu cápáḍutánu*, as the penny remarked, save one hundred of me and then I will save you; *núru cáculaló vaca cóyila yémi cheyya galadu?* a swan among geese (one cuckoo among a hundred crows, what can it do?); *núru-mandi guḍḍivánḍlu pógai vaca páḍu nútiló paḍḍ aṭṭu*, 100 blind men assembled and then fell into the first ruined well (there is no safety in numbers if all are helpless); *núru mandi monḍi chétula vánḍlu pógai vaca goḍḍu gédenu pálu pitaca léca póyinádru*, 100 men without fingers could not milk a barren buffalo (impossibilities cannot be conquered by numbers); *núru máṭalu vaca vrátacu y'iḍu cávu*, 100 words are not equal to one document. There is another word, *vanda*, for 100. 200 is either *innúru* or *renḍu vandala*. 100 persons is *núrumandi* or *vandamandi*. The Skt. for 100, *ṣata*, is used in compounds.

núruráyi, grindstone.

núruṭa, to grind. *moguḍi tala mída miriyálu núrin aṭṭu*, like grinding pepper on your husband's head (ticking him off).

nútanamu, recent. Skt. *nútanamugá* is in common use for 'recently'.

núṭapadaháru, 116. 116 and 1,116 are the numbers of coins that used to be given as presents by a feudatory to his chief; they are still considered honourable numbers for a present or fee.

núyi, a well; more commonly *nuyyi*; gen. *núti*.

nyáyamu, justice. Skt. *idi nyáyamá anyáyamá nívu cheppu*, ask yourself whether this is just; *Lacshmayya*,

Vencayya iddaru annadammulu; tanḍri villu vrási tsachchi póyenu; villu pracáram ásti pantsu cóḍánici póṭláṭa vachchenu; annadammul iddaru Mallayyanu madhyavartigá peṭṭu coniri. Mallayya: ná tírpu idi; Lacshmayyacu ástini cherisagangá pantsaḍánici adhicáram ichchänu. Lacshmayya: nyáyam chéṣäru. Mallayya: tana y'ishṭam vachchina bhágam tánu tísucóḍánici Vencayyaccu adhicáram ichchänu. Vencayya: nyáyam cheṣäru. Tom and Bill were brothers. Their father died leaving a will. They could not agree about the division of the property under the will and asked John to arbitrate. John: This is my decision: I have given Tom power to divide the property. Tom: A Daniel come to judgement. John: I have given Bill power to choose which of the two shares he will take. Bill: A Daniel come to judgement; *yéca cacshi vimarṣa mida tirmánam cheyyaḍam nyáyam cádu*, it is not just to give a decision on the examination of one party (*audi alteram partem*).

nyáyamu, like. Skt. *chandra chacóra nyáyamugá n'unnáru*, they are like the moon and the partridge (the partridge is supposed to make love to the moon; billing and cooing).

nyáyasabha, law court. Skt. Used for *córṭu* in books.

nyáyaṣástramu, law. Skt. Used for *lá* in books.

nyáyasthánamu, law court. Skt. Used for *córṭu* in books.

nyáyavádi, lawyer. Skt. Used for *plíḍaru* in books.

nyáyádhipati, judge. Skt. Used for *jaḍji* in books.

nyúnata, defect. Skt.

nyúspéparu, newspaper. English.

O

oca, one, a. There are various forms of this in speaking and even writing; when euphonic *v* is prefixed, the *o* is usually changed to *a*, *vaca*; the *c* is reduplicated for emphasis; *occa* and *vacca* are emphatic; *ó* is used for short as in *nív ó paryáyam veḷḷi rá*, come here a moment and in this instance *oca* is rather 'a' than 'one' (it is not true to say, as is usually said, that the Dravidian languages have no articles); one person (male) is *ocaḍu*, female *ocate*, neuter *ocaṭi*; and these words have the same variations, *occaḍu* for emphasis, *vacaḍu* and *vaccaḍu* for euphony; *occaḍi sampádyamu padimandi pálu*, one wage-earner to ten dependants; *oca náḍu vindu vaca náḍu mandu*, a day's feasting and a day's physicking; *occa abaddhamu cammaḍánacu veyyi abaddhálu cá valenu*, one lie draws a thousand after it; *oca cantsána tini vaca mantsána paḍu conéváru*, they shared cup and cot; *ocari calimici yéḍisté vaca cannu póyindi, tana lémici yéḍisté marivaca cannu póyindi*, he lost one eye weeping at others' weal and the other weeping over his own woe; *oca v'úrici veyyi dóvalu*, there are a thousand roads to any village; *occa cheyyi taṭṭité tsappuḍu auná?* can you clap with one hand? *oca dafá*, one time, once (the auctioneer begins with *oca dafá*).

ocaḍu, one man; dative *ocanṭici*. *Í naḍuma ná vale vaṭṭi máṭala chétané cácunḍa, anubhavamu chéta cúḍá, nén upadéṣinchina védántamunu cheppa gala paḍutsu ṣástri y'ocaḍu pravéṣinchin anduna, padi nelala nunḍi nác udvásam ainadi*, recently a boy fresh from school, a divinity student, who, unlike me, has gained an insight into spiritual truth beyond that which mere book learning can give, from the experience of a life-time, ousted me ten months ago.

oca máru, once. The auctioneer will say *oca máru, renḍu márlu, mummáṭici*, once, twice, three times (going, going, gone).

ocanigá, as one; also *ocaṇṇigá*. *ninnu cuṭumbamló ocanigá tsústámu*, we will look upon you as one of the family.

ocanoca, some or other. *ocanoca paṭṭanamuló*, in some town or other; *ocanoca tsóṭa*, in some place or other.

ocappuḍu, occasionally.

ocarivenucavacaru, in succession.

ocaru, people; plural of *ocaḍu*. *ocaru yém anduru?* what will people say? *váru ocaru mém ocaramu*, we keep ourselves to ourselves; *mém ocaramé y'adi chéṣámu*, alone we did it; *ocarini y'iddarini tsampiténé cáni vaidyuḍu cáḍu*, a doctor is no doctor till he has killed one or two.

oca sári, once. *buggal occa sári muddu peṭṭucon istárá?* will you let me kiss your cheeks? the literal meaning of *occa sári* is here 'once', but it is really an entreaty 'come let me'. (In the idiomatic *einmal* the Germans have the exact equivalent; *lassen Sie mich einmal Ihre Wangen küssen*.)

ocate, one (female) person.

ocaṭé, one (emphatic), it is all the same. *níc i alancárálu v'unná léca póyiná vacaṭé*, it is all the same whether you have these adornments or not; *andaru vacaṭé*, they are a close confederation (thus if you suggest that a corrupt policeman or overseer should be exposed and got rid of, the answer is 'they are all one', meaning that the next man would be as bad); *ocaṭé debba, rendé muccalu*, one blow, two pieces (settle the thing at once one way or the other).

ocaṭi, one (neuter) thing.

ocaṭinnara, $1\frac{1}{2}$.

ocaṭinpática, $1\frac{1}{4}$; also *ocaṭimbática*.

ocaṭuva, the first.

ocavéḷa, perhaps.

ocavéḷaite, supposing.

occa, one; emphatic form of *oca*.

occaḍu, one man; emphatic form of *ocaḍu*. *occaḍi sampádyamu padimandi pálu*, the wage-earner has nine dependants to keep (this is only a slight exaggeration and is to be remembered when the Indian Famine Code, which provides very low wages for workers, is criticized; add on the dependants' allowances, also provided by the Code, and you may get two or three times as much).

occocca, one by one. *occocca ráyi tístú v'unṭé conḍ ainá tarugutundi*, remove stone by stone and the hill itself will melt away (little strokes fell great oaks). Hills in the Telugu country are mostly composed of stones, this is illustrated by another proverb, *dúrapu conḍalu nunupu, daggira vasté ráḷḷa gunḍlu*, distant hills are smooth, if you come near they are heaps of stones; and by the British Tommy's description of Bellary: What's Bellary? Two heaps of road-metal.

occoccappuḍu, sometimes. *í bádha tsústé v'occoccappuḍu déham viḍisté bágá v'unṭund ani tóstundi*, in view of the agony I suffer I sometimes think it would be well to shuffle off this mortal coil.

oḍalu, the body; more common in the forms *oḷḷu, voḷḷu, vaḷḷu*; gen. *onṭi, vonṭi, vanṭi*. *oḍalu váchi*, swollen with pride. *oḍalu vanchi pani cheyyuṭa*, to work with heart and soul. (Telugu has many words for the body as for most common things; the Skt. words *ṣaríramu* and *déhamu* are also very common. *ná voḷḷu* and *ná déham* are often used where we say simply 'I'; which the Telugus think connotes greater precision of thought on their part. *á máṭalacu voḷḷu manḍi*, angered at these words.)

oḍambaḍica, agreement; from *paḍuṭa* with euphonic change of *p* to *b*; with euphonic *v* prefixed it becomes *vaḍambaḍica*.

oḍambarutsuṭa, to persuade; from *parutsuṭa* with euphonic change of *p* to *b*. *purusha véshamu vésu con aṭṭu áme oḍambarachi*, persuading her to put on a man's clothes.

odda, near to; more usually *vadda*. (*odda, vadda, daggira* are used where we omit the nearness. The Telugus are proud of this, just as they are of the use of *ná voḷḷu* for *nénu*, as indicating their greater precision of thought; they say *ná y'oddici vachcháru*, 'they came to near me', while we say simply 'they came to me'; *inṭi y'odda n'unnáḍu*, he is at home; *ná y'odda lédu*, I haven't it on me.)

oḍḍánamu, a gold or silver belt worn by women.

oḍḍu, shore, bank. *yéṭi v'oḍḍu chénu*, a field on the river-bank (a precarious situation).

oḍḍuṭa, to lay, to set. *chevi oḍḍuṭa*, to lend an ear. See also *ogguṭa*.

oḍi, lap, pocket formed by tying the lap-cloth up to the girdle. *oḍiló cúrtsunḍuṭa*, to sit on the lap as the king's little boy does in the Telugu play; *oḍiló vésuconuṭa*, to put some one in your pocket as the Sheristadar does the Collector (but *oḷló* would usually be said for short); *oḍicaṭṭuṭa*, to gird one's loins, to brace oneself to, to lower oneself to, the gradation of ideas is (1) tying up the front part of the cloth to the girdle, (2) preparing to receive in the fold of the cloth, (3) preparing oneself for; *nénu dáni máṭa vinani yeḍala tappaca cheppin anta paniyu chéyunu; dánin eṭlu viḍichi peṭṭi úracunḍá galanu? pratyacshamugá pápa cáryamunac étlu oḍigaṭṭa nértunu?* If I refuse to listen to her she will carry out her threat without fail; how can I abandon her to her fate? On the other hand, how can I brace myself to the deliberate perpetration of a crime? (a Tahsildar speaking whose wife has threatened to drown herself if he refuses a bribe).

oḍuguṭa, to get out of the way. *y'í múlanó oḍigi y'unḍu*, get out of the way into the corner (but when you want a bullock-cart to get out of the way of your car you say *tappucó*).

oḍupu, dexterity, ingenuity; becomes *vaḍupu* with euphonic *v* prefixed. *váḍu mahá vaḍupugá daga chéstáḍu*, he cheats very ingeniously.

ogartsuṭa, to gasp, to pant. *ogarpu*, panting.

ogguṭa, to apply. *chevi ogguṭa*, to lend an ear; also *oḍḍuṭa*; *tenniscu tala ogguṭa*, apply your head to tennis, play with your head; *chevi y'oggi y'álacintsutsu*, applying the ear to listen; *chevi v'oggi páṭa vina modalu peṭṭináḍu*, he began to lend his ears and listen to the song.

oi, form of address, usually affixed; also spelt *óyi*; this is neither honorific nor contemptuous; *oré*, *-rá* are the contemptuous terms, *-anḍi*, *dévara*, *svámi*, *ayya*, honorific; in addressing a ryot, begin *yémoi* and put another *-oi* at the end of your sentence; but if he is old, you may say *táta*, grandfather, instead, and if he is young you may say *tammuḍu*, younger brother; that is, if you are in a good temper, as you should always be.

oḷlu, body; short form of *oḍalu*.

olluṭa, to live in harmony, to fancy, to like; used especially in the negative and the negative compound *ollacapóvuṭa*. *álini ollanivánici cúraló uppu yeccuva y'ainad aṭa*, a man who does not like his wife complains there is too much salt in the curry; *inca áḍa n'ollanu*, shan't play any more.

olucapóyuṭa, to pour out, to spill. *áme pálu olaca pósindi*, she poured out (or she spilt) the milk.

olucipóvuṭa, to be spilt.

olucuṭa, to be spilt or shed (as tears). *pálaló pantsadáre v'olicin aṭṭu*, like sugar spilt into milk (luck upon luck).

olutsuṭa, to peel, to rob. *y'í chacracéḷi araṭi panḍu ná cósam teppinchináva? míru tsálá manchiváru, ani Asistenṭu Calecṭaru gáru y'olutsuconi tinuts unnáru*, saying, 'did you bring that sugar-plantain for me; thank you very much', the Assistant Collector proceeds to peel and eat it; *dáni meḍaló púsá buṭrá olutsu cunnár émi carmamu? id eccaḍi anyáyamu?* was it right to peel the very necklace off her neck? Unheard of injustice!

onarintsuṭa, to perform, to do. Book word for *chéyuṭa*. *chéyuṭa* is eschewed in books as being 'common'; the books say *onartsuṭa*, *onarintsuṭa*, or *cávintsuṭa* for 'to do'. These are not Skt. words but have the merit from the pedant's point of view of never being used in conversation. We never say 'proceed' for 'go' in talking, but our Telugu clerks, following their own bad traditions, write 'the Collector will proceed to camp' for 'the Collector is going into camp'.

onartsuṭa, to do. A book word.

onḍonḍa, one by one, continuously. A book word for *cramacramamgá* from *onḍu*, which is a book word for 'one'.

onḍorulu, each other.

onḍu, one. A book word for *oca*.

onḍu, sediment. *vánic émi chéṭu cálam vachchindó cáni prodduné Góddávari v'onḍu niḷḷaló munchi tetstsucunna ná panché tsúchi, cávalisté nídi mayala baṭṭa annáḍu,* at the sight of my cloth, which I had washed in the silt-laden waters of the Godavari, the wretch had the impertinence to say: 'Well, yours is a defiled cloth, if you like.' Also *onḍumannu, onḍrumaṭṭi. onḍuniḷḷu,* flood-water.

onduṭa, to obtain; same as *ponduṭa* with the initial *p* dropped.

onṭari, alone, single. *onṭaricamu,* privacy, solitude; *onṭaricatte,* a lone woman; *onṭaricáḍu,* a solitary man; *onṭarigá,* by oneself, in solitude.

onte, camel.

onṭeddu banḍi, cart drawn by a single bullock.

onṭi, one. *onṭi púṭa,* a single meal; *onṭiganṭa,* one o'clock; *onṭigá,* alone; *onṭiváḍu,* a single person, a lone man; *onṭivánici yama bádhé cáni, sédyamu cádu,* single-handed farming is not farming at all but hellish torture.

onṭu, a share.

onṭuṭa, to fit.

oppachepputa, to hand over charge; also *vappacheppuṭa.*

oppaginta, handing over; also *vappaginta.*

oppagintsuṭa, to hand over; also *vappagintsuṭa.*

oppintsuṭa, to assign, to obtain approval. *sarcáruvárunu oppintsuṭacu tsála ṣrama ainadi,* we had much difficulty in getting the approval of Government.

oppu, fitness, grace, airs. *vanḍa léni ammacu v'oppulu menḍu, té léni ayyacu tinḍi menḍu,* women who can't cook give themselves all the more airs, men who can't earn anything have the biggest appetites; *tappá y'oppá,* right or wrong.

oppucólu, consent, confession.

oppuconuṭa, to agree, to confess. With euphonic *v* prefixed it becomes *vappuconuṭa. ṣástrapramánam vappucóvaḍam chéta nénu y'ica nór ettaḍánici valla cádu,* as it is admitted by the Scriptures I cannot raise my voice against it any longer (e.g. the Scriptures are said to say thou shalt not make Brahmins angry and I acquiesce in this dictum though what the Scriptures actually say is that a Brahmin's wrath is sharper than Vishnu's disk).

oppudala, delivery.

oppuṭa, to become (one), to beseem, to agree, to confess, to deliver. *adi nícu oppuná?* does this conduct become you? *oppa chepputa* is to hand over charge.

ora, scabbard, case, sheath, ring of clay. *orala nuyyi* is well made of rings of baked earth; *talagaḍa ora* is a pillow-case; scabbard of sword and violin-case are also *ora*; it means anything that fits close on another thing.

oragallu, touchstone.

oraguṭa, to slant, bend back. *paḍava origindi,* the boat slanted over; *origi paḍináḍu,* he fell down aslant; *oragudindu* is a pillow to lean against; *yédó conchem bhaya vési venucac originánu,* I was startled and receded.

orapu, touch, fine. *orapu ducci* is light ploughing; *orapuḍu* or *varapuḍu ráyi* is a touchstone.

oratsuṭa, to touch with the touchstone.

orupuḍu ráyi, touchstone. *camsáli bangáramu orupuḍu ráti mída v'orachi tsúchi adi yenimidó vanne bangáram ani cheppináḍu,* the goldsmith tested the gold on a touchstone and said it was eighteen carats.

osaguṭa, to bestow; a book word. *itstsuṭa* is too 'common' for the literary men; in talking you never use anything else; in writing they never use it at all, being convinced that it would not be 'chaste' to do so; so they use *osaguṭa* which is not a Skt. word but has the advantage of being rare and noble; they say *muddosaguṭa* for 'to kiss' in books, instead of *muddu peṭṭuṭa* or *muddiḍuconuṭa.*

-ottamuḍu, affix meaning 'Excellent'. Skt., for *-uttamuḍu* in composition with words ending in *-u.* I merely note the form here under *o* because it is so common and the beginner would not find it in other dictionaries under *o.*

ottigilluṭa, to shrink, to step aside. *praccacu ottigilli,* shrinking aside.

oṭṭu, oath, curse. *nidra paṭṭité oṭṭu,* I'll be damned if I was asleep; *váḍu* *sárá tágan ani oṭṭu peṭṭu connáḍu*, he swore off arrack; *monna mém andaramu máṭláḍu conun appuḍu strílató rahasyamu cheppa cúḍad ani, máló n'ocaran anagá dáni nizamunu paricshintsa valen anu uddéṣamutó, yevaritónu cheppan ani oṭṭu peṭṭintsu coni, mahá rahasyam ani nénu caḍuputó n'unn aṭṭu ná bháryató cheppinánu*, the other day we were all talking together when some one said, we must keep our secrets from women; and with the idea of putting the matter to the test, I told my wife under the seal of secrecy, and bound her by oath to tell no one, that I was big bellied. (There are always at least two words in Telugu for common things; for oath, besides *oṭṭu*, there is *pramánam*.)

ottu, thick. *ottugá n'unna sasyamulu durbalamul agun aṭlu*, as crops sown too thick are weak.

ottucágitamu, blotting-paper; from *ottuṭa*, to press.

ottuḍu, crowding, squeezing.

oṭṭupeṭṭuconuṭa, to take an oath.

ottuṭa, to press, to squeeze, to blot.

oyyáramu, beauty, bloom. A book word; but Telugu and not Skt. I have not heard it used in conversation.

Ó

ó, one; short for *oca*. *ó paryáyam y'ilá ranḍi*, come here a minute.

ó, *o*, vocative. *ó gorrepilla Dévuḍá*, O Lamb of God (O son of a sheep, God; as the missionary hymn-book translates).

ó, the -th, turning cardinal numbers into ordinals. *áró*, the sixth; there is another equally common form for this, *-ava*; *árava* is also the sixth.

ó, dubitative affix; these one-vowel affixes of Telugu are very neat and brief: *-á* interrogative, *-é* emphatic, *-ó* dubitative; so at tennis *ouṭá?* is it out? *ouṭé!* it is indeed out! *ouṭó!* it may be out; the mere lengthening of final vowels for emphasis or in a series to denote 'and' is also a brief and neat feature of Telugu; *nénú* is emphatic I; *nénú nívú* is you and I; *-ó* also neatly and briefly takes the place of our 'or other' in such expressions as 'somewhere or other' which is *yeccaḍanó*, some one or other, *yevvaró*; *-ó* can be added to any part of the verb, *vasté*, if he comes, *vasténó* in case he should come (one Telugu word for five English).

óḍa, ship. *váḍu óḍaló nunchi samudramuló paḍináḍu*, he fell overboard; *pogayóḍa* (smoke-boat) is a steamboat.

óḍadonga, pirate.

óḍagoṭṭuṭa, to defeat. *mí ṣacti nácu telisi póyindi; mimmalni nénu nimishamló v'óḍagoṭṭa galanu*, I have gauged your strength; I can defeat you in a minute.

ódártsuṭa, to comfort. *nannu y'í pracárangá nívu v'odártsaḍánici prayatnam cheyyaḍam yentamátramú bágá v'unnadi cáḍu*, it is quite wrong to try and console me like that.

Óḍhramu, Orissa.

Óḍhruḍu, an Uriya.

óḍintsuṭa, to defeat.

óḍipóvuṭa, to suffer defeat. *nívu nácu v'óḍipóyináu*, you have suffered defeat at my hands; *Hiṭlaru gáru Hinḍenuburgu gáritó póṭi chési y'óḍi póyináru*, Hitler was defeated in his contest with Hindenburg.

óḍu, defeat.

óḍu, cracked. *cheruvu óḍu, úru páḍu*, a crack in the tank is ruin to the village. *cásta óḍ anṭé cantsam antá óḍu*, if there is a crack in the vessel they will say it is all cracked (the exaggerations of slander); *áḍa léca maddel óḍ ann aṭṭu*, a bad workman finds fault with his tools (the bad dancer says the drum is cracked).

óḍuṭa, to lose (be defeated). *áṭa óḍináḍu*, he lost the game; 'he lost' would be *óḍi póyinaḍu*. Also to shrink; *mogamóḍuṭa* is to be diffident, ashamed.

óhó! óhóyi! hullo!

óhóhó! álas!

óli, money given to bride's parents. The European dowry system is reversed here sometimes, and money given for the bride instead of with the bride; this is also called *canya ṣulcam*, maiden tax. *óli taccuva ani guḍḍidánni penḍláḍiṭé nelacu múḍu aválu*, thinking he would save on the bride-price by marrying a blind girl he found she cost him three kilnfuls of pottery a month (*cunḍal anní pagala coṭṭind aṭa!* they say she broke all the pots!).

ómcáramu, syllable *ÓM*, amen. The syllable *ÓM* is sacred and denotes the Trinity in a mystic symbol of Three in One (*A, V, M. Aditi, Varuṇa, Mittra*); amen may be connected, but *óm* always comes at the beginning, not the end; you begin a prayer with *óm*, also a book, also the alphabet.

ónamálu, the alphabet, A B C; these are the three syllables with which the syllabic alphabet begins, *óm*, with which you must begin everything, and *namach*, salutation; *váḍu ó, na, málu nértsu conuts unnáḍu*, he is learning his A B C; *yéḍisin aṭṭé v'unnadi; nícu pani chéta cádu, yémi chéta cádu; i vishayamló nívu y'incá v'ónamála cáḍ ané v'unnávu*, it is something to cry over; you are no good at this or anything else; in this business you are still at your A B C.

ópica, patience.

ópicachéyuṭa, ópicapeṭṭuṭa, be patient. *míru conchemu sépu v'ópica peṭṭin aṭṭ aité*, if you will be patient for a little; *conchem v'ópica chési canipeṭṭi v'unḍu*, have a little patience and wait; *nela dinálu v'ópica chésté sommu dákhalu chésu cunṭámu*, if you will be patient for a month we will pay up.

ópuṭa, to bear, to be patient. *ópanivárici vadd annaváre tallidanḍrulu*, those who can't stand work look upon those who say don't work as their father and mother; *vanṭa nérchina magaváḍitónú tsaduvu nérchina áḍadánitónú v'ópa rádu*, there is nothing more intolerable than the man who has learnt to cook or the woman who has learnt to read; *ópanivádu córinadi, onṭani-váḍu áḍinadi lédu*, there is nothing which the impatient will not demand, nothing which the unsuited will not say.

óra, edge. *óra canṭa tsúchi*, looking from the corner of the eye.

óragá, ajar. *talup óragá chési*, setting the door ajar.

óratsúpu, sidelong glance.

óréi, óri, sirrah! form of address to servant or other inferior; this is at the beginning; at the end you add on *-rá*.

órpu, patience.

órutsuṭa, órtsuṭa, to be patient, to stand up against. *óristé Órugallu paṭnam autundi*, with patience Orugal will become a city; *balavantamugala n'indryamula ḍhácac órtsutacu abalal entaṭivárù?* how can you expect weak women to withstand the onset of the senses?

órva, patience, tolerance. *tsúchi v'órva lér anḍi*, if they see it they can't stand it.

órvalénitanamu, órvami, impatience, intolerance. *má cálapu váḷḷalo y'iṭuvanṭi v'órvalénitanamú, fitúricórutanamú yémi lév anḍi; váḷḷ órvalénitanamú tsúché Daivam y'ippaṭiváḷḷacu yenta goppa v'udyógálu chésiná appalaló munigi yéḍustú v'unḍéṭ aṭṭu chéstú v'unnáru*, in our time there was none of this intolerance and desire to fight; seeing their intolerance (of bribe-taking) God has plunged the present generation in debt, however big the offices they hold.

ósí! form of address to a woman (younger than yourself). *bharta: ósí! ósí! oca sári daggiracu vachchi cheviló máṭa cheppedanu vini pó. bhárya! sari! sari! mí nóṭic astamánamu 'ósí, ósí' anna máṭacu visugu lédu.* Husband: My good girl! my good girl! come here a bit and let me whisper something in your ear. Wife: O gracious me! Don't you get sick of girling me my good girl all the blessed day?

óṭi, broken. *óṭicunḍa*, a broken pot.

óṭu, loss, defeat; same as *óḍu*.

óṭupátu, defeat.

óṭupóvuṭa, to be defeated; same as *óḍipóvuṭa*.

-óyi, form of address to equal; also *-oi, -oyi*.

P

pablícu, public. English. *Subbárau: áḍavállani yémí cheyya cunḍá v'uru-cunṭú v'unḍagá magavállanu ágnya peḍité ságutundá? Virabhadruḍu: áḍavá!!u vyabhichariste mátramu tsústú yevaru v'úrucom'annáru? áláṭi vá!!a-nu nalugurini y'inṭlo nunchi ve!!a coḍité taccina vá!!acu buddhi vachchi tinnagá v'unṭáru. Subbárau: áḍavá!!u chésédi rahasya crütyam; adi pablículóci tísu-coni vasté samsárálu cúli póvá?* SubbaRao: Can we leave the women alone and order male morals only? Virabhadrudu: Who tolerates female adultery? Turn a few of them out of their houses and the rest will learn wisdom and keep straight. SubbaRao: What the women do is secret; won't our families be ruined if that is made public?

pacapacanavvuṭa, to giggle, to guffaw. onomatopoeic.

pacca, side, direction; from *paḍuta,* short for *paḍaca*; *paccagá tólu,* also *pracca,* drive on the side; *iru paccalu,* both sides. *Óbí, Óbí, nívu vaḍlu dantsu, nénu paccalu yegara véstánu.* Lazy man: You do the pounding, Obi, and I will shake my sides (pretending to pound).

pacca, paccaduppaṭi, bedding, bed-sheet. *paccaló v'utstsa póse vá!!acu murici baṭṭalu, pílicalu cáca póté v'uti-cina tella maḍatalu pacca vésucunṭára?* Will you put clean sheets from the wash as a bedding (for infants) who make water on their bedding instead of dirty cloths and rags? See also *parupu.*

paccamu, side. Skt. *pacca,* side, is Telugu from *paḍuṭa,* but *paccanu,* side, is corrupt Skt. from *pacsham. tsuṭṭapaccamulu* means kith and kin.

paccapanḍlu, the side teeth.

paccaparuguna, in a trice.

paccayemuca, rib; from *pacca,* side, and *emuca,* bone.

paccayillu, next door; from *pacca,* side, and *illu,* home. *vaḍu mácu pacca y'inṭi porugu,* he is our next-door neighbour.

paccá, real, solid, permanent. Hindustani; spelt *pukka* in English; pukka buildings are opposed to temporary sheds; a pukka Sahib means a real gentleman; the opposite is *cachcha,* spelt *cucha* in English.

pacháru, walk, airing, constitutional. Hindustani. *bhójanam chési pacháru chéstú v'unḍagá,* I was taking a walk after dinner.

pachchecádu, swindler. Skt.

pachchemu, swindling. Skt.

pachchepáḍu, swindler, robber, gipsy.

pachcheputanamu, swindling disposition. Skt.

pachchepuváḍu, swindler, robber, gipsy. Skt.

pachchi, green, raw, fresh, arrant, used of unripe fruit, green firewood, a raw sore, an arrant rogue, a fresh colour. *idi pachchi abaddhamu,* that is a downright lie; *pacchi vishamu* is rank poison; *pachchi pulusu* is uncooked sauce.

pacshacuḍu, partisan. Skt. from *pac-sham,* side; also *pácshicuḍu.*

pacshamandu, on the side of, if. Skt.: *á pacshamandu,* in that case; *iṭlu cheppé pacshamandu,* if he says so; *śúdrulacu vidya manchid aina pacsha-ṅuna, mana púrvulu dánin éla nishé-dhinturu?* If learning were good for Sudras, why did our ancestors forbid it them?

pacshamu, side. Skt. *Vaishnava pac-shamu avalambinchina tarváta,* after taking sides for Vaishnavites; *púrva-pacshamu,* refutation, objection.

pacshamu, fortnight. Skt. *nén á rú-colu vaca pacshamuló vyayamu péṭṭi-nánu,* I ran through that money in a fortnight.

pacshapátamu, taking sides, partiality. Skt., from *pacshamu. sádhya-mainanta maṭṭucu nivu pacshapátamu lécundá naḍutsu cunṭéné cáni, palleṭúl-lálóni caraṇálu rahitulu v'úrucun aṭṭu paṭna vásálalóvá!!u zaḍisi v'úrucóru,* unless you show as much impartiality as possible you won't get town people to acquiesce out of fear like the karnams and ryots of rural villages.

pacshapáti, partial person.
pacshaváyuvu, paralysis.
pacshi, bird. Skt. *pacshi lágu yegaraḍánici nácu reccalu lévu,* I have no wings to fly like a bird (as the Collector replied to the Accountant-General when asked with reference to a T.A. Bill what was the distance as the crow flies); *pacshi mída guri peṭṭi mrügamunu vésinaṭṭu,* he shot at a bird and killed a beast; (beggars often compare themselves to birds); *nénu pacshi vanṭi váḍanu,* I am homeless.
pacshicuḍu, partisan; also *pacskacuḍu, pácshicuḍu.*
pacvamu, maturity. Skt. *áme rajasval ayyé pacvamuló n'unnadi,* she is fast growing into a woman.
pada, go, come; also *padamu.* A colloquial imperative of *póvuṭa*; *padará,* come along; *padavé,* go along.
paḍaca, bed, lying down; from *paḍuconuṭa,* to lie down. *iccaḍa paḍaca chésinaváru,* those who lay here.
paḍacagadi, paḍacayillu, bedroom. *viluva chíral ichchinanu marunáṭicé chimpi véyudavu gáni, occa rátri y'ainanu paḍaca gadilónici caṭṭuconi rávu,* I buy valuable cloths and the next day they are all in shreds and tatters and you don't deign to come into our bedroom decked with them.
padacamu, locket, pendant; also *paṭacamu.*
padaconḍu, 11 (eleven).
paḍaga, hood of snake. *pámu paḍaga yettinadi,* the snake raised its hood; *váḍu cóṭici paḍag ettináḍu,* he has reached the millionaire stage.
paḍagoṭṭuṭa, to knock down, to talk over; from *paḍa,* fall, and *coṭṭuṭa,* to strike. *nannu máṭala chéta paḍa coṭṭa valen ani tsúchináḍu,* he tried to talk me over.
padaháru, 16 (sixteen).
paḍamara, west; from *paḍuṭa,* to fall.
paḍamaṭi, western. *paḍamáṭi gáli,* the west wind; *paḍamaṭillu,* the west room; *paḍamaṭidora,* lord of the west (Varuṇa).
padamu, go, come; also *pada.* A colloquial imperative of *póvuṭa. padamanṭé mundugá vachchinánu,* they said come along and I stepped forward.
padamu, foot, word, phrase, high station. Skt. *chchí, chchí, ṣástram telisinavánini nénu v'unṭú v'unḍagáne ná mundara padálici iṭuvanṭi apárthálu chéstu v'unnávu?* good God, you dare to give such wrong meanings to Sanskrit words before me, a Pandit? *unnata padamu* means high station in life.
padamúḍu, 13 (thirteen).
paḍatróyuṭa, paḍaḍóyuṭa, paḍatóyuṭa, to push down; from *paḍuṭa,* to fall, and *tróyuṭa,* to push.
paḍava, boat. *Rájamahéndravaramu nunchi vachché paḍavalu pannenḍu ganṭal aiténe cáni rávu,* the Rajamundry canal boats do not get in till noon.
paḍavaváḍu, boatman. *paḍavaváḍu: ayyó! yevaró manishi níḷḷaló paḍḍáḍu; strí: áyana ná perimiṭé, áyananu manishi anaca peddamanishi ani anu; maryádaga máṭláḍu*; Boatman: Man overboard! Woman: That is my husband; say gentleman, not man; keep a civil tongue in your head.
paḍavaitsuṭa, to lay down.
paḍavéyuta, to throw down.
padavi, path, place, high station. Skt. Like most Sanskrit words it has various meanings; *tarugani padavi* is a worn track; *unnata padavi* is high station.
padárthamu, article, substance, thing. Skt. Quite a common word for thing; *vastuvu* is even commoner.
paddemu, verse. Skt. Corrupt for *padyam.*
paddhati, manner. Skt. Like most Skt. words it has several other meanings, but this is the meaning in Telugu.
paddhenimidi, padenimidi, 18 (eighteen).
paddu, item, entry, account. *y'iv anni ní paddulóne véstánu,* I will put all this down to you; *áyana paddu mana pustacamló yeccintsu có vatstsu,* you may put his entry down in our book; *paddu veyyaḍánici cágitam chétic icchi,* giving the paper to make the entry; 'other item wet' is a revenue expression for land which is not in the registered wet list, and 'item' is a translation of *paddu.*
padépadé, repeatedly; from *padi,* ten.

padi, ten (of things). *paḍisemu padi rógála peṭṭu,* one cold is as bad as ten other illnesses. Ten (of persons) is *padimandi.*

paḍi, a measure; ⅛ maund, 120 tolas; used chiefly to measure grain, and it may be either heaped or struck.

paḍide, clothes hired from washerman. *nívu paḍidecu tetstsu cuni vésu cunna y'í baṭṭalu tsúste y'í v'úllo ninnu yevaḷḷú bídavád ani anumána paḍaru lé,* no one will suspect you of being poor in those clothes you have hired from the dhoby (this pleasing custom of the washerman hiring out your clothes unbeknown to you is peculiar to the East; hence there is no word for it in the European languages).

padihéḍu, 17 (seventeen).

padihénu, 15 (fifteen).

padilamu, caution. *illu padilamu,* take care of the house.

padilamugá, carefully. *míru sommu padilamugá pampinchinárá?* have you sent the money carefully?

padimandi, 10 people, several people. *occaḍi sampádyamu padimandi pálu,* one earns and ten share (a truth in India: your clerk or peon will have 10 idle dependants to keep); *á cálamuló bógamváḷḷa y'inṭici veḷḷité yevaraina tsúchi pótár émó'n'ani siggu chéta rahasyamugá veḷḷévári; í cálamló andarú tsústé, gauravam ani, báhátamugá paṭṭa pagalé padimandini venṭa peṭṭuconi marí véṣyala y'inṭici veḷḷutú v'unnáru,* once if a man went to a nautch girl's house he would go secretly, ashamed that any one should see him; now they go in broad daylight accompanied by several persons and taking pride in every one seeing them.

padintalugá, tenfold. *ní ṣatruvu chéyu ciḍunacu padintalugá nívu mélu chéya valenu,* for the evil your enemy does you return tenfold good.

paḍipóvuṭa, to fall down.

padireṭlu, ten times.

paḍisemu, cold in the head. *paḍisemu padi rógála peṭṭu,* a cold in the head is ten diseases in one.

padiyava, 10th (tenth).

padmamu, lotus. Skt. One of the numerous Skt. words for lotus and perhaps the commonest. Padma is the goddess Lakshmi and a common female name.

padmásanamu, sitting like a lotus, i.e. cross-legged. Skt. form *padmam,* lotus, and *ásanam,* seat. *váḍu padmásanamu vésucu cúrtsunnáḍu,* he is sitting cross-legged.

padnálugu, 14 (fourteen); also *padnálgu, padunálugu.*

paḍucaṭillu, bedroom; from *paḍuconuṭa,* to lie down, and *illu,* house, apartment.

paducondava, 11th (eleventh); also *padacondava.*

paḍuconuṭa, to lie down, go to bed. *cúrtsunḍi paḍu có valenu,* sit before you lie (first creep, then go; look before you leap).

paḍugu, woof.

paduguru, ten people. Same as *padimandi.*

padunaidu, 15 (fifteen); also *padihénu.*

padunu, season. *adun erigi sédyamu, padun erigi pairu veyya valenu,* till in season, sow in season.

paḍupu, prostitution; *paḍupu cúḍu,* food gained by prostitution.

paḍupudi, prostitute. *paḍuputanamu,* prostitution.

paḍuṭa, to feel, to be, to happen, to fall, to bear, to take, to be caught, to be informed, to be killed, to pass, to be paralysed, &c. This is a very general verb, it turns any noun into a verb of feeling as *bhayapaḍi,* feeling fear; added to the root of a verb it forms the passive voice as *coṭṭapaḍuṭa,* to be beaten. *yéru yenni vancalu póyiná samudramulóné paḍa valenu,* however many twists the river takes, it must fall into the sea at last (the weariest river winds somewhere safe to sea); *peṭṭité tinṭáru, gáni tiṭṭité paḍévári léru,* if you lay food before people they will eat it, if you treat them to abuse they won't bear it; *tanḍri: má váḍici inṭici lecca iyya póc anḍi. ṭícharu: yenduchéta? tanḍri: railu daggira nunchi inṭiciráváḍanici yenta sépu paḍutundi ani míru lecca isté, máváḍu veḷḷi vachchéṭ appaṭici scúlu ṭayam* (time) *aipóyindi, váḍici y'í rózu páṭhálu póyindi.* Father: Don't give my boy home sums to do. Teacher:

Why? Father: You gave him a sum to do about how long it takes to go from the station home, and when he had gone and come school-time was up and he lost his lessons for the day. *á y'illu paḍinadi*, that house has fallen in (or down); *á valaló nálugu pacshulu paḍinavi*, four birds were caught in the snare; *pallamu paḍinadi*, a hollow has formed; *naluguru paḍipóyináru*, several people were killed; *vánici purugulu paḍinavi*, he passed worms; *vánici cuḍi cheyyi paḍinadi*, his right hand is paralysed; *venuca paḍináru*, they retreated; *á matamuló paḍináḍu*, he embraced that religion; *pérupaḍina*, celebrated; *nácu vachchina ápadacu váḍu aḍḍa paḍináḍu*, he saved me from a misfortune; *vár iddaricini paḍadu*, they don't get on together; *bávilo manchi niḷḷu paḍinavi*, good water gushed into the well; *vánitó paḍa lénu*, I can't stand the man; *vittanam incá paḍa lédu*, sowing has not been done yet; *rúcalu uricé paḍi y'unnavi*, the money is lying idle; *á samsáramu ná nettini paḍinadi*, that family is left on my hands; *á nashṭam ná tala mída paḍinadi*, the loss fell on me; *tala crindula paḍuṭa*, to be swelled-headed (topsy-turvy); *baiṭa paḍinadi*, it transpired.

paḍutsu, young, a girl. *paḍutsula cápuram puḍacala manṭa*, a houseful of girls is like a fire of twigs (similarity of the noises); *á chinnadi yevar áḍa paḍutsó yevarici teliyadu*, no one knows whose daughter that girl is.

paḍutsuconuṭa, to prostitute oneself. *áme paḍutsu coni tinṭunnadi*, she is on the town.

paḍutsutanamu, youth. *paḍutsutanamló v'unḍaḍam chétanu, alaváṭu paḍaḍam chétanu vaca paṭṭuna mána lécunḍá v'unnámu*, we can't give it up all at once, being young and accustomed to it.

padyacávyamu, verse. Skt.

padyamu, a verse. Skt.

paga, enmity. *idi ná pagavánic ainá cá rádu*, may this not happen even to my enemy; *má paga tírtsu cunṭéne gáni ná manassucu viṣránti v'unḍadu*, unless I satisfy my malice I shall not be at rest.

pagaḍamu, coral. Corrupt Skt.; the Skt. is *praváḷam*.

pagalacoṭṭuṭa, to break in pieces; also *pagulacoṭṭuṭa*.

pagalu, day-time. *rátrimpagalu*, night and day; *paṭṭapagalu*, broad daylight; *pani léni Mallayya pagalu nidra pótú ávalist unḍenu. Mallayya: ippuḍu coṭṭinavi nálugu ganṭal éna? Sómbéri: nénu vina lédu; incá cássépu v'unṭé, gaḍiyáram maḷḷi ganṭa coḍutundi; appuḍu lecca peṭṭa cúḍadú? ippuḍ ém tondara?* Unemployed Smith was yawning sleepily in the day-time. Smith: Was it four o'clock that struck just now? Weary Willie: I did not hear; wait a bit and the clock will strike again; can't you wait to count? What is the hurry now?

pagaṭi, by day; adjectival form of *pagalu. pagaṭi máṭalu panici chéṭu, rátri máṭalu nidracu chéṭu*, day words spoil business, night words sleep; *pagaṭi dongalu*, daylight thieves; *pagaṭi veḷa*, day-time; *strí: ná penimiṭi nidraló máṭláḍut unṭáḍu; váric émaina mand istárá? vaidyuḍu: mand accara lédu, pagaṭi púṭa áyananu svéchchhagá máṭláḍan iyyanḍi*; Woman: My husband talks in his sleep, can you give him any medicine for it? Doctor: No medicine is necessary; let him talk in the day-time.

pagaváḍu, enemy. *aḍaváḷḷu bahu gayyáḷi váḷḷu; bhárya rávaḍam ané ápada pagaváḍic ainá córa cúḍadu*, all women are shrews: you should not wish even your enemies the calamity of marriage.

paggamu, rope.

pagulacoṭṭuṭa, to break (transitive).

pagulaṭa, paguluṭa, pagilipóvuṭa, to break, to be broken. *gunḍelu pagili*, broken-hearted; *ní máṭala valla ná caḍupu pagili pótu v'unnadi*, your words break my heart (but the Telugus prefer to say break my stomach).

pahará, guard. Hindustani; also *párá*.

pai, upper, outer, subsequent. *paicappu*, upper covering (roof); *paipanulu*, further works. *dinamula pai dinamulu gaḍachi póvuts unḍenu*, day after day passed.

paibaḍuṭa, to fall upon, to attack, to drive; also *paipaḍuṭa. dánici andarunu* *paibaḍuduru*, all fall on this in their eagerness.

paicamu, cash. Originally a small coin, but now used generally for cash.

paicappu, roof. The ordinary dictionaries do not give this word, one of the commonest in the language.

paici, up, outwardly; dative of *pai. itarul inṭici vachchin appuḍ ainá biggaragá máṭáḍaca ná yeḍala inta bhacti tsúpi, pati púja chéyutsunn'aṭṭu paic ainá naṭintsutsu rávé*, when a stranger comes, please don't raise your voice, please look at me with some sort of dutifulness and please make believe at least to be a dutiful wife; *cheṭṭu coṭṭi paici tetstsu conn aṭṭu*, cutting a tree so that it falls on oneself (bringing troubles on oneself); *paici manchiváḷḷugáné canapaḍutú v'unnáru*, outwardly they seem to be good people.

paigá, besides, moreover.

paiguḍḍa, upper cloth. *yevari paiguḍḍa vánici baruvé*, it's one's own upper cloth that weighs on one (every one has his own troubles, *à chacun son fardeau pèse*).

paimáyishi, survey. Hindustani; the word is now obsolete, *sarvé* being used instead; but we still refer to the old survey records as the paimash records.

paina, above, on, further, next; also *paini. paina cheppu*, go on, please; *mimmu sicshinchévaḍu paina unnáḍu*, there is One above who will punish you; *paina chéya valasinadi yémi?* what is to be done next? *cott appucu póté, páta appu paina paḍḍadi*, when he went for the new loan, the old debt fell upon him (the creditor took occasion to ask for it).

painamu, journey. Skt. Corrupt for *prayánamu. yeddu léni sédyam, tsaddi léni painam*, farming without bullocks is like travelling without provisions.

paini, above, on, further, next. Same as *paina*; *paini cheppina*, aforesaid.

painṭu, point, appointment. English. Used very frequently of a point in law.

paipaḍuṭa, to fall on. *paipaḍḍa máṭa, maḍi paḍḍa niḷḷu pótavá?* will a word that has fallen on you or water that has fallen on a banked field escape? (some dirt will stick).

paira, cool breeze. *paira tólité pratti phalintsunu*, if the cool wind blows (in the north-east monsoon) cotton will yield well.

pairu, crop. Commonest in the plural *pairlu. adanu tappina pairunnu, musalivádni biḍḍalu ocaṭi*, crops out of season are like old men's children.

paisa, small coin, 3 pies or 1 pice. *bhánchót, má chétilo vacca paisa paḍa lédu*, blackguard, I haven't got even a farthing out of it.

paiṭa, cloth thrown over female breast. *má cóḍalu daggira nunchi veḷḷin appuḍu paiṭa congu tagalin aṭṭu anumánam caligi maḷḷí snánamu chésinánu*, suspecting I had been touched by the hem of my daughter-in-law's upper cloth as I passed her, I took another purifying bath; *Crüshṇuḍu Rádha paiṭanu tolaginchináḍu*, Krishna removed Radha's breast-cloth.

paityamu, bile. Skt. *iv anní paitya hárapu vastuvul aṭa*, these are all said to be articles of diet that remove bile.

paiváru, paiváḷḷu, those above, superior authorities. *prașna: yémi cáraṇam lécunḍa paiváḷḷu mátram v'úricé baratarapu chéstára? zavábu: veticéváḷḷacu anní cáraṇálé canapaḍatavi*; Question: Will our superiors dismiss us without any reason? Answer: Those who want to find a reason will always find one.

paivilásamu, address (on a letter). *í y'uttaramunacu paivilásamu vráya lédu*, there is no address on this letter.

palaca, plank, wooden slate, board, slab. *Lacshmayya: idi cavi tsani póyina illu; a sangaté ráti palaca mída checcāru. Vencayya: nénu tsachchi póté inṭi velapala yémani rástáru? Lacshmayya: 'ṭuleṭu' ani rástáru*; Smith: There is a slab on this house to show a poet died in it. Jones: If I die will they put up anything on the house? Smith: Yes, a board with 'To Let' on it.

palatsani, thin, poor; also *palutsani*.

palavarintsuṭa, to talk in one's sleep. *rátriḷḷu nidraló cúḍá sangítamu gurinché palavaristú v'unṭáru*, he will talk in his sleep too at nights about music; *á rátri má pillaváḍu tellavárina dácá* *palavaristúné vachchinádu; mantsam mída paḍi y'iṭu aṭu v'úricé dorlinádu*, my boy was talking in his sleep that night and rolling this way and that on his bed till dawn.

paláná, paláni, such and such. Hindustani.

palástri, plaster. English.

paláyanamu, flight. Skt. Used only in books.

palicintsuṭa, to cause to speak; causative of *palucuṭa*, to speak.

pallaci, palanquin.

pallamu, low ground, irrigated land. *meraca pallam*, high and low land; *pallapu panṭa*, an irrigated crop; *níru pallam erugunu, nizamu Dévuḍ erugunu*, water finds the low ground, God the truth.

pallaṭi, somersault. Hindustani; also *palṭi*.

paḷḷavaidyuḍu, dentist; from *paḷḷu*, teeth, and *vaidhyuḍu*, doctor. *báluḍu: nánna: paḷḷavaidyuḍi shápuló nénu yéḍava lédu. tanḍri: nuvvu buddhimantuḍavu, i rúpái tisu có; noppi tsála puṭṭindá? báluḍu: vaidhyuḍu shápuló lédu, yeccaḍicó veḷḷäḍu*; Boy: I did not cry at the dentist's. Father: Sensible boy, here's a rupee for you; did it hurt much? Boy: The dentist wasn't there; he had gone somewhere.

pallavi, chorus (in songs); burden of a song. Skt.

palle, palli, small village, hamlet. Skt. Greek *polis*; also the ending of innumerable place-names, e.g. *Banganapalli*. The ending in Constantinople is the same. *Málapalli* is the pariah hamlet outside the village.

paḷḷemu, plate, tray (metal). *paḷḷem ninḍa bucca*, a trayful of scent.

palleṭúru, small village. *oca prayáṇicuḍu: manam dáṭi vachchina úru palleṭúr ainá, dípálu bágá velugutú unn aṭṭ unnai. renḍó prayáṇicuḍu: dípalu cávayya, iḷḷu cálut unnai*; First traveller: Though the village we have passed is a small village, the lamps are burning well. Second traveller: It is not lamps, sir, it is the houses on fire.

palli, small village; also *palle*.

pallu, tooth; plural *paḷḷu*. *pedimacu minchina pallu, pramidacu minchina vatti*, a tooth beyond the lip, a wick beyond the lamp (proverbial expression for impertinence); *á mandahásamu sogasu tsuchinával á paḷḷu y'igalintsaḍamé?* did you observe the beauty of the smile, the grin of the teeth? See also *pandlu*.

palṭi, somersault. Hindustani; also *pallaṭi*.

palu-, prefix meaning 'many'. *paluguru*, several persons; *palumáru*, often.

palucarintsuṭa, to accost; from *palucuṭa*, to speak.

palucu, a word.

palucuṭa, to speak.

paluguru, several people.

palumáru, often.

palutsa, palutsana, thinness.

palutsagá, thin (adverb). *majjiga ninḍá palutsagá n'unnadi*, the buttermilk is very thin.

palutsani, thin, contemptible, slighting (adjective). *palutsani paluculu*, slighting words; *áme palutsani manishi*, she is a poor creature.

palutsapaḍuṭa, to become thin.

pamparapanasa, pomelose (*citrus decumana*).

pampintsuṭa, to send. *adhyacshuḍu: mana sangham gavarnaru gári daggirici ráyabáram pampintsálé; inducu tagina sabhyul evaró cheppanḍi. sabhyuḍu: aidugurini pampintáma? adhyacshuḍu: aṭlágé pampintámu; Rámayyanu cúḍá váḷḷaló chérustámá? sabhyuḍu: chértsa vatstsunu gáni Rámayya nóru teravacunḍá v'unḍe sharatu mída pampintsa vatstsunu*; Chairman: We have to send a deputation to the Governor; please suggest suitable persons. Member: Do we send five? Chairman: Yes; shall we include Ramayya? Member: By all means include Ramayya, but on condition that he does not open his mouth. See also *ampuṭa, pampuṭa*.

pampu, sending, order.

pampuṭa, to send; to send away; also *ampuṭa, pampintsuṭa*. *oca pracaṭanalo y iṭlá v'unḍenu; 'má daggira aidu rúpáyala vastuvulu conucconé váḷḷacu córu tagilinchédi ocaṭi, sigareṭlu cálchéd i incocaṭi bahumánamgá istám'; Lacshmayya aidu rúpáyala vastuvulacu árḍaru pampenu, váṭitó páṭu oca chila,* *oca nippu pulla pampiri*; an advertisement ran: Whoever orders Rs. 5-worth of goods from us will get as a present something to hang his coat on and something to light his cigarettes with: Lakshmayya sent an order for Rs. 5-worth of things and got a peg and a match. *ocaḍu : sarcasucó nipp'anṭu cundanḍi. incóḍu: sarcasulo nippu mingévāḍ unnáḍu, váḍici caburu pampité sari*; Smith: The circus is on fire. Jones: They have a fire-eater in the circus, it will be enough to send word to him. *Lacshmayya: ni bháryanu viṣránti cósam puṭṭ'inṭici pampäva? Vencayya: panpänu; nizam ém anṭé nácé viṣránti cá valasi aṭlá chéṣänu.* Smith: Have you sent your wife to her mother for a rest? Jones: Yes; but to tell the truth, it is because *I* was in need of a rest.

pana, sheaf.

panasacheṭṭu, jack-fruit tree.

panasatonalu, jack-fruit pips; *panasatonala miṭhāyi* is a sweet made of jack-fruit pips.

pancha, five. Skt. Used in Telugu as a prefix in Skt. compounds.

panchabhútamulu, the five elements. Skt.

panchacalyáni, a dark horse with white marks, a piebald.

panchagavyamu, the five things derived from the cow. Skt. *gavyamu* is from *góvu*, cow. The five products are milk, butter, ghee, urine, and dung (*pálu, perugu, neyyi, panchitam, péḍa*); you have to eat them all to purify yourself from certain pollutions.

panchami (*náḍu*), fifth lunar day. Skt.

panchamuḍu, pariah. Skt. A man of the fifth class; that is below the four castes.

panchâpátramulu, five cups used in worship. Skt.

panchapráṇamulu, the five vital spirits of the body. Skt.

pancháṇamu, the five artisan castes. Skt. The five castes are carpenter, blacksmith, brazier, goldsmith, stonecutter.

pancháṅgamu, calendar. Skt. So called because it specifies five things, viz. the lunar day, *tithi*, the weekday, *váram*, the sign in which the moon is, *nacshatram*, the conjunction of the planets, *yógam*, and the horoscope, *cáraṇam*; *pancháṅgamulu póté nacshatramulu pótavá?* if you have lost your almanac have you lost the stars? (i.e. you can work out the almanac again from the stars); *ácáṣa pancháṅgamu*, a sky calendar (a fanciful tale).

pancháṇulu, mechanic, crafts. Skt. The five crafts mentioned under *pancháṇamu*.

panchâyati, jury of five. Skt.

pancháyatídáruḍu, member of a jury of five. Skt.

panche, man's lower cloth. *i rúpáya putstsuconi vaca panche conucconḍi*, take this rupee and buy a lower cloth.

panchéndriyabaddhuḍu, the sensual man. Skt., from *pancha*, five, *indriyam*, organ, and *baddhuḍu*, bound.

panchéndriyamulu, the five organs. Skt. form *pancha*, five, and *indriyamu*, organ. The five organs are the eye, ear, nose, tongue, and skin (*nétra, carna, nasa, jihva, tvaccu* in Sanskritic Telugu).

panchipeṭṭuṭa, to divide.

panchitamu, urine. *góvu alpácha-manam chéstú v'unḍagá veḷḷi tócato netti mída tsallu coni, panchitam lópa-licí putstsu conṭé mari puṇyam*, you acquire much merit by going up to a cow when it is making water, shaking the urine on your head with the tail and drinking it down (I have never actually seen this done but there is no doubt that it is exceedingly meritorious).

panchivéyuṭa, to divide, to deal. *chiṭlu panchi vésináḍu*, he dealt the cards.

pancti, a row, especially at meals; from Skt. *pañcti*. *pancti-bhójanam* is a dinner in which guests sit in a line (the usual arrangement); *caḍa panctini*, end of the row, the lower seat.

panda, a term of abuse. Used chiefly in compounds. *piricipanda*, a dirty coward; *tinḍipanda*, a dirty glutton.

panḍáculu, ripe leaves or betel.

pandemu, a bet. *váḍu tana gurramunu ná gurramutó pandemucu vadalináḍu*, he raced his horse against mine; *iddariló abaddham yevaru tvaragá calpinchi chepputáró, váru pandem gelichéṭ aṭṭu nirnayinchiri. Lacshmayya: Chennapatnamló anagánagá oca pedda manishi v'unḍévádu. Vencayya: aité nuvvé pandem gelichánu, nénu inta canna yeccuva abaddham cheppa lénu.* Smith and Jones bet on which would tell the biggest lie first. Smith: Once upon a time there was a gentleman at Madras. Jones: You have won the bet, I can't tell a bigger lie than that; *tánu yenta ainá tina galan ani Lacshmayya pandem vésenu; Lacshmayya conta tini tsálinchenu. Vencayya: anta tina léd ém? pandemló óḍi poyinánu. Lacshmayya: podduna míru parícsha chésin appuḍu bágané tinṭini, ippuḍu yendu chétanó ácali mandaginchindi.* Smith laid a bet as to how much he would eat; having eaten some, he stopped. Jones: You could not eat it all; then you have lost the bet. Smith: When you tried me this morning I ate well, now for some reason or other I have lost my appetite.

pandi, pig. *aḍavipandi* is a wild boar, *munḍlapandi* a porcupine. *nandi anṭé nandi, pandi anṭé pandi,* if he says it's a bull it is a bull, if he says it is a pig it's a pig (*sic volo sic jubeo, sit pro ragione voluntas*); *pandici yélará panníru ginḍi ?* what can a pig do with a bottle of rose-water? *pandi gurgurintsuts unnadi,* the pig grunts.

pandicoccu, a large rat, bandicoot. *pandi-coccu* means pig-dog (*cucca*); our Anglo-Indian word 'bandicoot' is a corruption of it.

pandili, shed, pandal; also *pandiri.* Our Anglo-Indian 'pandal' is derived from this.

pandintsuṭa, to cause to ripen; causative of *panduṭa.*

pandiri, shed, pandal; also *pandili.*

panḍitammanyuḍu, person who thinks himself learned, conceited man. Skt.

panḍituḍu, learned man, pandit, professor. Skt. Our Anglo-Indian word 'pandit' is derived from this; *pantulu,* teacher, and *pantulu,* caste affix, are connected. *Telugu svalpamugá vachchinaváḍu Símaló goppa panḍituḍ anipintsu conunu,* a smatterer in Telugu passes for a professor of it in England. *Calecṭaru: méghálu samudramlóci veḷḷi níllu tágutú v'unḍagá mír eppudainá tsúchinárá? pámarulu cheppa valasina máṭa panḍitulai v'undinní míru cúḍá viṣvasistár émi? panḍituḍu: ayyó: ná máṭa nammaca póté nénu yémi cheppunu?* Collector: Have you ever seen the clouds going to the sea and drinking water? Do you mean to say that a Pandit like you believes these silly stories of the vulgar? Pandit: If you will not believe me, what can I say? (I fear the natural science of the Telugu Pandit is all myth.)

panḍlu, teeth; plural of *palu*; also *paḷḷu. páḍindé páḍará páchi panḍla Dásari,* sing again what you have sung, Dasari with dirty teeth.

panḍlu, fruits; plural of *panḍu. nimma panḍla rasamutó atani panḍlu pulisinavi,* his teeth were set on edge with lime juice; *báluḍu: nánná, aṭlá v'unnáv ém? tanḍri: tirigi, tirigi, vachchänu, cálú cheyyi cadilintsa lénu. báluḍu, aṭlágá? nuvvu techchina mámiḍi panḍl anni nénu tinnánu, nuvvu nannu coṭṭa lévu gá.* Boy: Father, what is wrong? Father: I have been wandering about so long that I can't move hand or foot. Boy: That so? I ate all the mangoes you brought; you won't be able to beat me.

panḍommidi, 19 (nineteen).

panḍrenḍava, 12th (twelfth); more commonly *pannenḍava.*

panḍrenḍu, 12 (twelve); more commonly *pannenḍu.*

panḍu, fruit. *panḍu zári páלaló paḍḍ aṭṭu,* like the fruit slipping into the milk (happy-go-lucky).

panḍuconuṭa, to lie down, to go to bed. *jvaramutó panḍu connáḍu,* he is laid up with fever; *atani vartacam antá panḍuconnadi,* his business is asleep.

panḍuḍu, eunuch. Skt.; also *napunsacuḍu.*

panḍuga, festival; also *panḍuvu. cannula panḍuga* is a sight for sore eyes; *nityamunu cannula panḍugá dhanamunu tsútsutsunḍu sukhamunu minchina sukhamu mari yém unnadi ?* what greater pleasure is there than always having money to look at? So also *chevula panḍuga*, a feast for the ears (e.g. good music); *ill alucagáné panḍuga y'agună?* does smearing the house (with cow-dung) constitute a feast? (this is supposed to make the house very clean and pure but it is only the prelude to feasting; the proverb means putting the cart before the horse).

pandum, ten tooms; from *padi*, ten, and *túmu*. A toom is four cuntsams; ten tooms is about 150 bushels; ten tooms of land is about nine acres.

panḍuṭa, to ripen, to yield a crop. *dunnaca tsallité, coyyaca panḍinadi*, sown unploughed it yielded unreaped (means that if you don't plough before you sow, you are not likely to get any harvest).

panḍuvu, festival. Another form of *panḍuga*.

pangalacomma, forked branch; *pangandmam* is the forked caste-mark Vaishnavites wear on their foreheads; *pangalacarra* is a forked stick.

pani, work, use, thing, shaving. *panici rádu*, it is no use; *panici vastundi*, it is useful; *panici vachché pillacáya*, a promising boy; *ní pani paṭṭistánu*, I will settle your hash; *atani pani tírchináru*, they did for him; *atani pani tsúst unnánu*, I am looking after his business; *iccaḍa níc émi pani?* what's your business here? *manchi pani*, good; *pani mída unnáḍu*, he is busy; *aina panici chintinchéváḍu alpa buddhi galaváḍu*, it is silly to grieve over the past (crying over spilt milk); *pagaṭi máṭalu panici chéṭu, rátri máṭalu nidracu chéṭu*, daylight words spoil business, night words sleep. *ocaḍu: í áfísu panulacu bádhyata galavár' evaru? gumástá: nácu bágá teliyad anḍi; yédainá lópam vasté mátram nanné andaru tiṭṭutáru*. Smith: Who is responsible for the work of this office? Clerk: I don't well know; all I know is that if anything goes wrong all blame me. *peddamanishi: inni cathalu cheppáu, ní goppa cheppu cunnáu; anniṭlónu nuvvé gelichin aṭṭu cheppáu; nícu chéta cáni pani v'unṭé cheppu; dánini nénu chéstánu. garvapótu: ná bácílu chelintsa lén anḍi, mír á pani cheyy anḍi*. Gentleman: You have told many stories; you have boasted; you say you have always won in everything; if there is anything you can't do, tell me and I will do it. Boaster: I can't pay my debts, you may do that for me. *naucaru: mícu naucaru cá valen ani yevaró cheppité vachchánu. peddamanishi: má y'inṭló pani antá má váḷḷé chésu conṭáré. naucaru: aṭlá aité nénu tappacunḍá iccaḍé v'unṭánu, untsucondi*. Servant: I hear you want a servant. Gentleman: In our house we do all the work ourselves. Servant: Then I will certainly take the job; please give it me.

panicaṭṭe, female servant, maid; feminine of *paniváḍu*.

panicheyyuṭa, to shave (to do the work).

panicimálina, paniciráni, useless. *iláganṭi panici málina praṣnalu yeppuḍú aḍugabócu*, never ask such silly questions.

panicivatstsuṭa, to be useful. *tana Ṣirashtádári y'iccaḍa yémainá panici vastund émó tsútámu*, we will see whether his Sheristadarship is any use to him here. *vidyárthi: vidyárthulacu cá valasina baṭṭalu iccaḍa dorucutavá? angaḍiváḍu: áḍucóḍánici panici vachchévá, tsaduvu cóḍánici panici vachchévá?* Student: Have you any clothes here useful to students? Shopman: Useful to play in or useful to work in?

paniléni, without work, unemployed. *paniléni mangali pilli tala goriginád aṭa*, the workless barber shaved the cat, they say.

panimuṭlu, tools.

panipáṭalu, toil and moil. *panipáṭalu lécunḍá v'úricé sómarigá cúrtsunḍi*, lazily sitting idle without doing any work.

paniváḍu, workman, servant. The feminine of this is *panicaṭṭe*.

panjaramu, cage. *áyana monna vacca césuló palleṭúru nunchi vachchina sácshici bódha chéséṭ appaṭici sácshyam antá váciṭló panjaramló v'unna chilucacu cúḍá vachchindi*, when he was tutoring a rustic witness the other day in the evidence he was to give in court, the parrot in the cage at the gate learnt it all by heart; *panjaramuló chiccuconi chiluca vale*, like a parrot in a cage; *cácini techchi, panjaramuló peṭṭité, chiluca vale palucuná?* put a crow in a cage and will it talk like a parrot?

pankhá, punkah. Hindustani. *rátri nénu ná bhárya paḍucunnappuḍu nívu mácu pankhá visara valenu*, at night when my wife and I go to bed you must pull the punkah for us.

pannenḍu, 12 (twelve); composed of *padi*, ten, and *renḍu*, two.

panniddumu, twelve tooms; composed of *padi*, ten, *iru*, two, and *túmu*, a measure of four cuntsams; so twelve tooms is forty-eight cuntsams, about 180 bushels.

panníru, rose-water. *pandici yélará panníru gindi?* What is the use of a bottle of rose-water to a pig? *bhárya: nénu yenta doḍḍa y'illálu aité n'émi? lénipónivádu mogunni coṭṭédánni ani nácu péru techchináru; mí múlangá ná doḍḍatanam antá búdidaló pósina panníru ai póyindi.* Wife: What if I am a good housewife? A worthless husband has got me the reputation of being in the habit of beating him and through you all my goodness has become like rose-water poured into mud (my name has become mud).

pannu, tax. *vrütti pannu*, profession tax.

pannugaḍa, scheme, device. *ad antá Bráhmalu tama ádhicyam niluvaḍánici pannina pannugaḍa*, that is all a device of the Brahmins to maintain their superiority.

pannuṭa, to contrive. *tánu pannina valaló táné paḍḍáḍu*, he has fallen into a trap of his own contriving; *manam y'iddaramú álochintsucuni yédó pannindm ani anumána paḍutáḍu*, he will suspect us two of having plotted something together.

panṭa, crop, harvest; from *panḍuṭa*, to ripen. *caruvu mánpu panṭa, miḍatalu mánpu manṭa*, the crop stays the famine and flame the locust; *panṭa penṭaló, páḍi púriló*, the harvest is in the manure, the milk in the grass; *yerra bhúmi panṭa, oca náṭi vanṭa*, a red soil crop yields but one day's food.

pantamu, wager, resolve, object. *mana caḷḷa mundara puṭṭina monnaṭi pillavāḍu pantam paḍité, pillaváḍici buddhi cheppi adamáyintsaca, váḍi pantam negginchi, pedda manishi máṭa nirácarintsaḍam dharmam ané tóchindá?* When a boy born before our eyes makes a resolve is it right to let him have his way and disregard the word of a grown man instead of teaching the boy sense and admonishing him? *induló mana prayójacatvam canaparichi, mana pantam neggintsu có valenu*, we must show our ability and attain our object.

panṭe, whirl on which weavers wind their thread.

pantsabangálamu, rout. *polísuváru vachchi dongalanu pantsa bangálamugá tarimi vésináru*, the police came and put the thieves to flight.

pantsadára, sugar. Skt. *pálaló pantsadára v'olicinaṭṭu*, like sugar dropped into milk (luck upon luck).

pantsapaḷi, arcade, verandah.

pantsuṭa, to divide; most commonly used in the compound *panchipeṭṭuṭa*.

pantulu, teacher; corrupt Skt. for *panḍituḍu*; also a Brahmin caste-affix.

pappáyapanḍu, poppoy; a common fruit appreciated by Europeans but despised by the natives of the country; also *bobbáyapanḍu*.

pappu, pulse, porridge, any split pulse or kernel. Any sort of pulse used for curry, but most commonly dholl (red gram), which is the more nutritious part of the diet of Brahmins and prisoners in jail. *á márázu vadda á pappu uḍacadu*, no use trying it on with that Maharaja; *badamcáyulu péḍu coḍité pappu canupintsunu*, shell almonds and the kernel appears.

para-, prefix meaning 'other'. Skt. *dánici para purushuḍ anṭé gaḍḍi paracató samánam*, she does not care a straw for any man but me.

paraca, trifle, blade of grass. *gaḍḍiparaca* is a blade of grass. I don't care a bit is *nácu gaḍḍi paracató samánam*.

parada, screen, purdah. Hindustani. What gosha ladies keep behind.

paradéṣamu, foreign country. Skt.

váḍu paradéṣam and unnáḍu, he is abroad.

paradéṣasthuḍu, paradéṣi, foreigner. Skt.

paradhyánamu, reverie, absence of mind. *paradhyánam chéta vélu tega cósucunnánu*, I cut my finger absent-mindedly.

paragaṇá, district, purganah. Hindustani. Obsolete; a common word in the old records, and the newspapers still write Madhya Paragaṇdlu, the Central Provinces.

paralócamu, other world, i.e. heaven. Skt. Opposed to *ihalócamu*, this world. *manacu dhanamu ṣaṣvatamu cádu, déhamulu ṣáṣvatamulu cávu, nityamaina paralóca sukhamulu vichárintsu có valenu*, wealth is perishable, our bodies are perishable; we must seek the eternal joys of the next world; *paralóca gátracu póyenu*, he died (gone to the next world).

parama, excellent, best. Skt. Common in compounds; *paramánanda-bharituḍu*, full of immense joy.

paramandu, beyond the grave; the opposite is *ihamandu*, on this side of the grave.

paramánamu, paramáná, firman. Hindustani. A grant or letter from the Moghul Government or other kings and rulers of that time; also *farmána*.

paramánandamu, great joy. Skt. *á dinam á mahánubhávuni darṣanamu chési, dyana séva chéta paramánandam pondi, crütárthuṇṇi autánu*, on that day I will visit that Great Man, do him homage and be full of joy; *mátó sambandham chésucóvaḍam mícu y'ishṭamgá v'unnadá? paramándamugá v'unnadi*, would you care for a marriage union with us? I should be delighted.

paramánnamu, rice-pudding, milk-rice. *váḍu paramánnamu zurrutsunnáḍu*, he is sipping the milk-rice.

paramárthamu, highest truth, highest object of life. Skt. *aṭuvanṭi várici canyádánamu cheyyaḍamé cévalamú paramártham; tama vanṭi paṇḍitulaina Mahánubhávulac evaricó tappa y'í cálicálamló paramártha chinta lédu*, to give a virgin to such people is the *summum bonum*; in this Iron Age only great pandits like you care for the *summum bonum*.

paramátmuḍu, supreme being. Skt., from *parama*, excellent, and *átma*, soul; the Highest Soul.

parampara, series, succession, tradition. Skt. *anéca ṣatábdamula varacu sadguru parampara Craistava matamun andu galadu*, Christianity has had a series of good teachers for many centuries; *má guru paramparaló intaváḍu lédu*, in the series of teachers we have had there is none equal to him; *vári bratucu duhkha paramparató ninḍi unḍenu*, their life was full of a series of sorrows.

paramu, foreign, other; *para* is a common prefix meaning 'other', as in *paradéṣi*, foreigner.

parangá, in the guard of. *madhyavartula parangá untsu*, put it in the custody of arbitrators.

parangi, feringhee, French, European, Eurasian; now usually applied to Eurasians.

parapara, noise of tearing; onomatopoeic. Sound of tearing cloth or paper.

parapati, credit. *nácu parapati bhangamu chéya talachináru*, they tried to destroy my credit; *parapati sanghamulu*, co-operative credit societies.

parapu, bed, bedding.

parasparamu, mutual. Skt. *parasparánurágamu*, mutual love; *paraspara viródhamu*, mutual enmity.

Paraṣurámuḍu, Parasurama, a West Coast hero; *Paraṣuráma cshétramu*, Malabar. *illu Paraṣuráma príti y'ainadi*, the house was burnt.

paratantramu, dependence on others. Skt. Opposite of *svatantram*, independence. *svatantramu svarga lócamu, paratantramu práṇa sancaṭamu*, independence is heaven, dependence a life of grief.

paratsuṭa, to cause; the word is itself a causal (from *paḍuṭa*) and is used as an auxiliary to form causals. *aṭanca-paratsuṭa*, to cause obstruction, to obstruct; *bhéda paratsuṭa*, to distinguish; *sammati paratsuṭa*, to obtain consent, to persuade; *teliya paratsuṭa*, to make known.

paratsuṭa, to spread (intransitive).

paravaṣamu, being carried away by, transported, ecstasy. Skt.

paravaṣuḍu, one who is carried away, transported. Skt. *móhaparavaṣuḍai*, carried away by love; *santóshaparavaṣuḍai*, in an ecstasy of joy.

paraválédu, it does not matter; from Hindustani *paravá*, regard, respect; also *pharválédu*. *peddamanishi: banḍiló nunchi mí tammuḍu cinda paḍacunḍá paṭṭucó. báludu: paravalédu; váḍu paḍḍá inṭló nác incó tammuḍu unnáḍu lenḍi.* Gentleman: Catch your little brother and stop him falling out of the cart. Boy: It doesn't matter, I have another little brother at home; *bhárya: mana ammáyini penḍli chésucuné váḍu yeṭlánṭiváḍu? bharta: anucúlamainaváḍé. bhárya: tsaduvu gáni, ḍabbu gáni léd aṭé. bharta: léca póyiná parválédu, atanic evaru tsuṭṭálu léru lé; mana ammáyi sukha paḍutundi.* Wife: What sort of a fellow is the bridegroom you have chosen for our girl? Husband: Quite suitable. Wife: They say he has neither education nor money. Husband: It doesn't matter if he hasn't; he has no relations, so our girl will be happy; *cásucu dóva lédu, núṭici paravá lédu*, no way to a penny but careless of pounds.

parábhavamu, defeat. Skt.

parábhavintsuṭa, parábhavaparatsuṭa, to defeat, to dishonour. Skt. *atithini parábhavinchitini*, I have dishonoured my guest.

parácramamu, heroism. Skt.

parácu, oversight, inattention. *parác 'untsaca vinu*, listen with attention; *tsaṭáluna lépin anduna parácu máṭalu vachchinavi*, as he was suddenly roused, his words came unawares.

parácuna, unawares. *ajágratagá v'unḍi y'ippuḍu máṭala parácuna mí daggira conchem nóru jári vachchindi*, I was careless just now and the words slipped out by oversight.

parácupaḍuṭa, to be inattentive, to forget. *rája: í sanvatsaram sarcáru peshcashu póga mana Samsthánam mída yenta lábham vachchind anḍi? crindaṭi nelaló míru cheppináru gáni parácu paḍḍámu. diván: tamaru álagu parácu paḍaḍamé dharmam anḍi; adi mahárázu chihnamu.* Zamindar: deducting the Government peshcash what was the revenue of our estate this year? You told us last month, but we have forgotten. Diwan: Such forgetfulness is beseeming to Your Honour; it is a sign of nobility.

parádhínamu, dependence, alien possession. Skt., from *para*, other, and *adhínam*, possession. *parádhínam* (or *paratantram*) *prána sancaṭam*, dependence is misery. *má sottu antá parádhínam ai póyinadi*, all our property has been alienated.

parádhínuḍu, a dependant.

parájayamu, defeat. Skt.; also *apajayamu*.

parájitamu, conquered. Skt.

parámarṣa, care, inquiry. Skt. *vár andarni mír yeṭlá parámarṣa chéstáró sumanḍi?* How will you manage to look after them all?

parámarṣintsuṭa, to investigate.

paráriyaguṭa, to abscond, to be out of view (of criminals). From Hindustani *parári* or *pharári*, absconded.

paráyaṇamu, devotion to. Skt.

paráyi, strange, foreign, unrelated. Corrupt form of Skt. *para*. *paráyiváḷlu*, other people; *paráyi chinnadi*, a girl who is no relation; *Lacshmayya gurinchi abhinandana sabha zarigenu; sabhádhyacshuḍ agu Vencayya gáru í rítini mutstsaṭinchiri. Lacshmayyagáru paráyi grámam vár ainá, mana v'úḷlo iravai sanvatsarála nunchi unṭú mana gramábhivrüddhicai páṭu paḍut unnáru; áyananu mana v'úri samádhilóné púḍchét aṭṭu Bhagavantuḍu anugrahintsu gáca*, at a complimentary party to Smith the chairman spoke as follows: Though Mr. Smith belongs to another village, he has lived twenty years in our village and worked for its progress; may God grant that he be buried in our cemetery! *nénu paráyiváḷlató sahavásamu cheyyanu*, I hold no commerce with strangers (keep myself to myself).

pari-, prefix meaning 'around', fully, completely. Skt.

paricaramu, tool.

PLATE V

The Lotus Mahal, a Hall of Audience of the Andhra Emperors at Hampi (Vijayanagaram), Bellary district, the ruined capital of the Andhra Empire

(Photo. D. T. Bak and Sons, Hospet)

paricaramu, examination, investigation. Corrupt Skt. for *paricsha*.
paricarintsuṭa, to examine, to investigate. Skt.
paricharintsuṭa, to attend, to serve. Skt.
paricharuḍu, attendant, guard. Skt.
parichayamu, familiarity. Skt. *nácu Véda vishayamuló viṣésha parichayamu lédu,* I am not very familiar with the Vedas; *nácu Peddápuramló mí anna gáritó moṭṭa modaṭa parichayam caliginadi,* I first struck up a friendship with your brother at Peddapur; *ati parichaya avagnyata,* familiarity breeds contempt.
paricháramu, service, attendance. Skt.
parichárica, female attendant. Skt.
parichchédamu, section of book. Skt.
paricimpuṭa, to examine, investigate. Skt., corrupt for *paricshintsuṭa*.
paridhi, circumference. Skt.
pariganintsuṭa, to calculate. Skt.
parigettuṭa, to run; also *parugettuṭa. Lacshmayya: ná peḷḷani carra tísuconi coṭṭänu, nannu coṭlo peṭṭi tálam veyyanḍi; polisusarjenṭu: coṭṭité tsachchipóyindá? Lacshmayya: tsáva lédu, nannu coṭṭa ḍánici parigettuconi vastunnadi.* Smith: Please lock me up, I have beaten my wife with a stick. Police Sergeant: Did you kill her? Smith: No, she is running after me to beat me.
parigrahaṇamu, acceptance. Skt.
pariharintsuṭa, to remove, to reject. Skt.
parihasintsuṭa, to mock. Skt.
pariháramu, removal. Skt. This is used as a legal term for relief, redress. *Hiṭlaru gárici Jarmaní nashṭa pariháramulanu chellintsuṭa asalé ishṭamu lédu,* Hitler does not want Germany to pay indemnities at all.
parihásacuḍu, jester. Skt.
parihásamu, ridicule, jesting. Skt. *parihásamunacu idi samayamu cádu,* this is not a time for jesting; *mír émi parihásamugá máṭáḍutsunnáru,* you are joking about something; *nén úraca parihásamunac annánu,* I was only joking.
parijanamu, suite, train of followers. Skt. Also *parivâramu*.
parimaḷamu, perfume. Skt.
parimaḷintsuṭa, to be fragrant. Skt.
parimáṇamu, limit, measure. Skt. In law *cáládvadhi parimáṇamu* is period of limitation.
parimiti, limit. Skt.
parinamintsuṭa, to be transformed. Skt.
pariṇayamu, marriage. Skt. *viváham, penḍli,* are commoner words.
parinámamu, transformation. Skt.
paripari, sundry. *pariparividhálugá,* in all sorts of ways.
paripálana, paripálanamu, government, rule. *Hiṭlaru gáru mantrulai paripálanádhicáramu vahintsutsó,* if Hitler becomes minister and takes up the government.
paripálintsuṭa, to rule.
paripúrṇamu, very complete. Skt. *paripúrṇánugraham,* complete grace.
parishattu, assembly, congress. Skt.
parishcarintsuṭa, to settle. Skt.; also *pharishcarintsuṭa. á caḍupulo v'unna pillacu yémi istávó cheppu; ippuḍu béramu parishcarintsu cunḍámu,* say what you will give for the child in that womb (as a future wife) and we will strike the bargain at once.
parishcáramu, settlement, also *pharishcáramu. incá béram parishcáram cá lédu,* the bargain is not settled yet; *í miṭingulóné pharishcáram cán iyyanḍi,* let us settle it at this meeting.
pariṣílana, examination. Skt. *leccala pariṣílana,* adjustment of accounts.
pariṣílintsuṭa, to investigate. Skt.
pariṣódhana, inquiry. Skt.
pariṣódhintsuṭa, to inquire. Skt.
pariṣrama, diligence. Skt.
pariṣuddhamu, very pure. Skt.
pariṣuddhi, purity. Skt.
paritapintsuṭa, to grieve. Skt. *ná manassu paritapintsutsunnadi,* I am in sorrow.
paritápamu, grief. Skt.
parityajintsuṭa, to abandon. Skt. *sarva bhógamulu parityajinchi,* abandoning all pleasure.
parityájamu, relinquishment. Skt.
parivartamu, exchange, transfer. Skt.
parivartana, turning back. Skt.
parivâramu, suite, retinue. Skt. Also *parijanamu*.

pariyáchacamu, jesting. Skt. *pariyáchacam áḍutú v'unnáru*, you are joking; *nénu v'úrici pariyáchicánici annánu*, I was only joking.

paricsha, trial, examination. Skt. *tennisu pravíṇuḍu: nannu paricsha chéşáru gadá, ná vaḷḷu yeṭlá v'unnadi? ḍácṭaru: nicu viṣranti cá valenu, connáḷḷu tennisu mánuconi rózú caléjici veḷḷut unḍu, nimmalistundi.* Tennis champion: You have examined me; how goes it? Doctor: You want rest, go to college for a few days and give up tennis and you will soon be all right.

paricshacuḍu, examiner.

parmaná, firman, letters patent; also *paramaná, farmana.*

parṇaṣála, leaf hermitage. Skt., from *parṇam*, Skt. for leaf, and *ṣála*. Used in Purána stories.

parócshamu, imperceptibility, absence. Skt. *ná parócsham andu cheppina máṭalu nácu tácavu*, I am not affected by what is said in my absence.

parra, bog.

parṭílu, parties (legal). English. The common word for parties in a case; also *párṭílu.*

parugettuṭa, to run. *parugetti pálu táge canṭe cúrtsunḍi níru trdguṭa mélu*, it is better to sit and drink water than to have to run to get milk. *ocaḍu: yeccaḍici parugettut unnáu? incóḍu: nácu pillan istán anna máma gári daggirici, áyana diváḷ ain aṭṭu telisindi. ocaḍu: áyana chicculu tírustává? incóḍu: nénu tírtsanu, áyana cúturini peḷḷi chesucón ani cheppaḍánici veḷḷut unnánu.* Smith: Where are you running? Jones: To the father of the girl I was engaged to; I hear he is bankrupt. Smith: Are you going to help him? Jones: Not I, to break off the engagement.

parugu, a run, pace of a horse. *chétan aité na parugu calusu conḍi, nénu léḍi lágu parugettutánu*, catch me if you can, I run like a deer; *manchi parugugala gurram*, a horse with good paces; *banḍi vacca paruguna tóluconi vachchinánru*, they drove the carriage without stopping.

parulu, others, neighbours. Skt. *parulapálaina*, alienated, having become the property of others. *y'í vacca róz aina parulanu áḍi pósu cóvaḍam máni veyyanḍi*, stop abusing your neighbours at least for a day.

parunḍapeṭṭuṭa, to put to sleep.

parunḍuṭa, to lie down, to go to sleep.

parupu, bedding. *ocaḍu: Lacshmayya tsála kharidu gala parupu connáḍu. incóḍu: háyigá nidra paṭṭindá? ocaḍu: paṭṭa lédu, dáni kharidu talutsu cunṭé digulu vési Lacshmayya rátri antá nidra pó lédu.* Smith: Brown has bought a most expensive mattress. Jones: Does he sleep well on it? Smith: No, he stays awake all night worrying about the cost. See also *pacca.*

parutsuṭa, to cause. Same as *paratsuṭa*, an auxiliary verb, used to change nouns, adjectives, &c., into verbs; *áṭancaparutsuṭa*, to raise objection; *drüḍhaparutsuṭa*, to establish; *bhédaparutsuṭa*, to distinguish.

parutsuṭa, to spread, to scatter.

paruvu, dignity. *yeruvu sommu paruvu chéṭu*, he who goes a-borrowing goes a-sorrowing; *länṭaru paruvu cósam gáni, veluturu cósam lédu*, a lantern for dignity, not light; *paruvu taccuv ani*, thinking it beneath your dignity; *paruv ichchi paruvu tetstsu có*, give respect and get respect; *paruvúpratishṭhá*, dignity and decorum.

parvamu, division, a certain festival. Skt. *parvamu* is properly a knot in a cane, a joint, a division, and so comes to be said of divisions of the year and month and festivals at these divisions; *nétraparvamu* is a feast for the eyes.

parvatamu, mountain. Skt.

paryantamu, up to. Skt. *nakha ṣikhá paryantamu*, to the tips of one's nails, i.e. all over.

paryavasánamu, result. Skt. *idi zagaḍamuló paryavasánam ainadi*, it resulted in a quarrel.

paryáyamu, time, occasion. Skt. *nív ó paryáyam veḷḷi rá*, go and come for once; *í renḍu paryáyamula nunḍi jvaramu baiṭa cáyaḍamu lédu*, these two times the fever did not come out.

pasandu, exquisite. Hindustani. *pasandu anṭu mámiḍi panḍlu*, exquisite graft mangoes; also *fasandu.*

pasaru, sap. *pasaru purugu* is the sap worm, a green caterpillar.

paşchattápamu, repentance. Skt. *paşchattápam caligi nizamgáné ni naḍata tinna chésu có*, repent and reform.

paşchattápapaḍuṭa, to repent. *ataḍu tala vantsuconi paşchattápapaḍutú v'unnáḍu*, he is hanging his head and repenting.

paşchima, western. Skt. *paşchima khandamu* is the western continent, Europe; *paşchima vidya* is western knowledge, the civilization of Europe.

paşchimamu, west. Skt.

pasi, young. *pasibiḍḍa* is an infant.

pasiḍi, gold. *calla pasiḍici cánti menḍu*, false gold is bright (all is not gold that glitters); *bangáramu* is commoner.

pasimi, yellow. *pasimi cháya*, yellow complexion.

pasipaṭṭuṭa, to scent. *cundéṭini cuccalu pasi paṭṭinavi*, the dogs got scent of the hare.

pasitanamu, infancy.

pastáyintsuṭa, to regret. Hindustani.

pasupu, saffron, yellow. *pasupú-cuncamú*, saffron and rouge, means a married woman's pin-money because these are the cosmetics no Indian woman can do without; the saffron is to make her face yellow, the rouge to make her lips red.

paşuşála, cattle-shed. Skt.

paşuvu, animal, especially cattle. Applied to human beings it means stupid; *paşujanamu* means the brute mob; *paşupráyuḍu*, a brutish man; *nívu vaṭṭi paşupráyaḍavugá v'unnáu*, you are a blockhead.

patacamu, locket.

patacáru, long pincers.

paṭamu, picture. Skt.; also *chitra paṭamu*; the word originally meant cloth; *gálipaṭamu* is a paper kite; *chitracárulu tama paṭála cinda santacam chéstáru yenducu? paṭánici modal édó, chivar édó, tsúchévál̤lu telusu códánici*, why do painters sign their pictures? So that people may know which is the top and which is the bottom; *i granthamuló bommalu paṭamulu unnavi*, this is an illustrated book.

patangi, kite (toy, not bird). *nívu patangi yegara veyya galavá?* can you fly a kite? also *gálipaṭamu.*

paṭapaṭa, crashing, grinding; onomatopoeic. *cannul erra chési panḍlu paṭapaṭa corucutsu*, glaring and grinding his teeth (in anger).

paṭá, bark (of tree); also *paṭṭá*.

patáca, flag. Skt.

pathamu, path, way. Skt.

paṭhanamu, reading. Skt.

paṭhanamuchéyuṭa, to learn by heart.

paṭhintsuṭa, to read. Skt.

pathyamu, diet. Skt. *Lacshmayya: vaidyuḍu cheppina pracáram putstsu cunṭ unnává? Rangayya: putstsu cunṭúné unnánu, cáni y'i madhya ácal aité pathyam putstsu coni, mámúlu annam cúḍa tinnánu.* Smith: Are you taking the diet the doctor ordered? Jones: Yes, but sometimes when I am hungry I take my usual food as well as the diet.

pati, husband. Skt. *patipúja* is the worship which a woman owes to her husband. *itarul inṭici vachchin appuḍu biggaragá máṭáḍaca ná yeḍala inta bhacti tsúpi pati púja chéyutsunnaṭṭu paicaina naṭintsu*, when people come to the house don't talk loud, make some show of devotion to me and outwardly at least pretend to be a dutiful wife.

paṭica, alum. Skt. *adi paṭica podumu*, this is alum powder.

paṭicabellamu, sugar-candy.

paṭima, cleverness, skill, vigour. Skt. *pillacáya telivi galaváḍé cáni vácpaṭima taccuva*, he is a clever boy but does not speak out properly.

pativrata, good wife, devoted. Skt. *nénu v'untsucunnadi mahá pativrata sumanḍi, nénu vacca dinam léca póté adi y'inṭló tinnagá annam tinadu*, the woman I keep is devoted to me, if I am not there she does not eat properly; *nén enta musalitanamló penḍli y'áḍinanu, mana Sómidévi vanṭi pativrata mariyocaṭé lédu sumí*, though I was an old man when I married there is no more devoted wife than our Somidevi.

paṭla, at, about, towards. *tsuttupaṭla*, the neighbourhood; *inṭipaṭla*, at home; *i paṭla*, in this respect. *muddáyi: ná mída tsálámandi ádhára paḍi* *v'unnáru; váḷḷa paṭla daya tsúpintsanḍi. mejisṭréṭu: yevaruváḷḷu? ní pillalá? muddáyi: ná pillalu cádu, polisuváḷḷu.* Accused: I have many dependent on me, show pity to them. Magistrate: Who do you mean? Your children? Accused: Not my children, the Police.

paṭnamu, town. Skt.; also *paṭṭanamu. óristé Orugallu paṭnam autundi,* patience and Oragal will become a town.

patni, lawful wife. Skt., from *pati,* she who has a husband.

patramu, leaf of a book, document. Skt. *á patramu mída mugguru sácshi vráḷḷu chésináru,* three persons attested the document; *pustacamunu tísi patramulu tiruga véyutsu,* taking a book and turning the leaves; *ichchévánici patramu vaddu,* the generous man requires no bond (the willing horse needs no spur).

patri, leaves used in worship. *bhacti léni púja patri chéṭu,* adoration without devotion only wastes the sacred leaves.

patrica, newspaper. Skt. *patrica* is properly any paper; *bahishcára patricalu* are letters of excommunication. *Gópu: nuvvu vrásina 'Nirantara Sanchàram' ané vyásam yém aindi? Rámudu: á vyásamu nénu yenni patricalacu pampinchiná maḷḷí ná daggaricé vachchindi. Gópu: adi cúḍa nirantára sanchàram chést unnadi cábólu.* Smith: What happened to your essay on 'perpetual motion'? Jones: I sent it to all the papers but it always came back to me. Smith: I suppose it is doing perpetual motion.

patricalaváḍu, journalist. *patrica ménéjaru: míru má patricacu aḍvartaizumenṭu yémaina istárá? mí vyápáránici tsála lábham vastundi. vartacuḍu: nén émi iyyanu, ponḍi; patricalaváḷḷu vasté rán iyya vadd ani má banṭrótutó cheppäné; váḍu ninnu yeṭlá rán ichcháḍu? ménéjaru: a banṭrótunu tísi veyyanḍi, banṭrótu cá valenu ani má patricaló aḍvartaizu cheyyanḍi; tappacunḍá dorucutáḍu.* Newspaper Manager: Will you advertise in my paper? It will boom your business. Merchant: I won't give you any advertisement; get out; I told my peon not to let any newspaper man in; how did he let you in? Manager: Dismiss him and advertise for another in my paper; you will get one without fail.

patricádhipati, editor of a newspaper.

patstsa, green, yellow; also *patstsani. ácupatstsa* is leaf green; *pasupupatstsa* is saffron green, that is yellow; *tellapatstsa,* light green; *chilacapatstsa* (colour of the green parrot), bright green; *patstsa bangáru,* yellow, i.e. pure, gold; *patstsagá v'unḍuṭa,* to prosper; *porugu patstsagá v'unṭé poiló níḷḷu pósucun aṭṭu,* like the man who poured water on his own hearth because his neighbour was doing well (biting off your nose to spite your neighbour's face).

patstsa, emerald.

patstsagaḍi, grass. *patstsagaḍi* is fresh grass as opposed to *yenḍugaḍi,* dried straw (not hay); hay is not made in India except by the Army department.

patstsaḷḷu, chutneys. *patsaḷḷu úragáyalu annamuló ruchini puṭṭinché vastuvulu,* chutneys and pickles are relishes.

patstsani, green, yellow. Same as *patstsa.*

patstsapoḍutsuṭa, to tattoo.

paṭṭa, bark of a tree, also *paṭá, paṭṭá.*

paṭṭa-, prefix meaning 'full', as *paṭṭapagalu,* broad daylight; *paṭṭabailu,* bare as a bone; *atirahasyam paṭṭabailu,* Tom Noddy's secret.

paṭṭa, patta, the ryot's land slip from which he can see what the extent and assessment of his holding is; it is not a title-deed or muniment of title, but a simple memorandum; in Estates it is something more, though not even a lease deed, because the Zamindar and ryot are supposed to exchange documents, *patta* and *muchilica,* and the ryot is supposed to accept the *patta*; but there is no question of contract; we are still in India in the stage preceding contract, the stage of status; and the Zamindari ryot has occupancy right, that is status, and cannot be given notice to quit; he is not a tenant.

paṭṭadáruḍu, the holder of a patta, landholder.

paṭṭamu, gold fillet tied on forehead at coronation. Skt.

paṭṭanamu, town. Skt. Same as *paṭnamu*.

paṭṭapagalu, broad daylight. *moguḍú peḷḷámu paṭṭapagalu máṭáḍutáru*, the husband and wife talk to one another by daylight (a very dreadful thing to do, only to be done in the privacy of the alcove).

paṭṭapudévi, queen; from *paṭṭamu*, coronation fillet, and *dévi*, divine woman.

paṭṭapuṭénugu, the royal elephant (the one the Raja rides).

paṭṭaráni, uncontrollable; from *paṭṭuṭa*, to catch. *paṭṭaráni ágrahamu*, uncontrollable anger.

paṭṭá, bark (of a tree, not a dog).

paṭṭábhishécamu, coronation. Skt., from *paṭṭam*, coronation fillet, and *abhishécam*, annointing.

paṭṭácatti, broadsword.

paṭṭe, tape.

paṭṭeda, necklace. This is a necklace made of small square plates. *peḷḷámu meḍaló v'unna paṭṭeḍa coṭṭi tisu coni póyi tácaṭṭu peṭṭináḍu*, he removed the necklace from his wife's neck and pawned it.

paṭṭemantsamu, tape cot.

paṭṭi, list. 'Budget' would be *áddáya vyayamula antsana paṭṭi*.

paṭṭi, according to.

patti, cotton; the plant; the product is *dúdi*. *chéló patti v'unḍagáné, Pólici múḍu múḷḷu, nácu áru múḷḷu ann aṭṭu*, three cubits of cloth for Poli and six for me, as he said when the cotton was still on the field (counting your chickens before they are hatched).

paṭṭintsuṭa, to settle; to besmear oneself; causal of *paṭṭuṭa*. *ní pani paṭṭistánu*, I will settle your hash; *putted ámudamu paṭṭintsu coni porláḍiná, anṭéḍé anṭunu gáni, anṭanidi anṭadu*, though a man besmear himself with a candy of castor oil and roll, only what sticks will stick, what won't stick won't (a fatalistic proverb); *vánini yegatáḷici paṭṭinchináru*, they made him their laughing-stock.

paṭṭu, grip, hug, support, scene in a play, plaster, prejudice, purpose, severity, stress, handle, side, passage in book. *bhallúcapu paṭṭu* is a bear's hug; *yuddhapu paṭṭu* is a battle scene in a play; *adi talacu paṭṭu peṭṭu coni panḍuconnadi*, she went to bed after plastering her head; *paṭṭu vadalaḍu*, he won't relinquish his purpose; *paṭṭu viḍupu telisinaváḍu*, a man who knows when to be severe and when to be lenient; *cútapaṭṭu*, the distance a shout will carry; *várici carmamuló paṭṭu lédu*, they lay no stress on ceremonies; *paṭṭu ivvacunḍá*, without giving a handle; *tsálamandi áyana paṭṭu áyiri*, many went on his side. In the plural, *paṭlu*, feats, as *jeṭṭipaṭlu*, wrestling feats; and places, as *tsuṭṭupaṭlu*, neighbouring places; and also cramp, which is *paṭlu*; *yeluca yenta yéḍchiná pilli paṭṭu vadaladu*, however much the rat cries, the cat will not let go her hold; *paṭla* means round about.

paṭṭu, silk.

paṭṭucáru, tongs.

paṭṭucomma, support (branch to hold). *niluva níḍa, paṭṭa comma lécunḍá n'unnáḍu*, he has no shade to stand in, no branch to lay hold of (he is at the end of his tether).

paṭṭuconuṭa, to catch hold of, to arrest. *gurram paṭṭucó*, hold the horse; *puli mísamu paṭṭu coni v'uyyála úgin aṭṭu*, swinging from a tiger's whiskers (a rash form of sport); *cálu paṭṭu coni lágité, tsúru paṭṭu coni véláḍéváḍu*, a fellow who will cling to the eaves if you try to haul him out by the leg (a bore or toady you can't get rid of). *peddamanishi: banḍiló nunchi ní tammuḍu cinda paḍacunḍá paṭṭucó. báluḍu: paravá lédu, váḍu paḍḍá, inṭló nác incó tammuḍ unnáḍu lenḍi.* Gentleman: Catch hold of your little brother so that he does not fall out of the cart. Boy: If he does fall it doesn't matter; I have another little brother at home. *bharta: nuvvu úḷḷó lén appuḍu dongala tsappuḍu aindi, parugettu coni meṭlu digi cindici vachchánu. bhárya? dongalanu paṭṭucunnárá? bharta: dongalu inṭi cappu mida niltsunnáru, andu chéta vílu paḍa lédu.* Husband: While you were out I heard the noise of thieves and ran down the steps. Wife: Did you catch the thieves? Husband: No, they were on the roof.

paṭṭudala, perseverance.

paṭṭuna, close, at one time. *í paṭṭuna*, now; *oca paṭṭuna*, at one go; *canche paṭṭuna*, along the hedge.

paṭṭupaṭṭuṭa, to insist. *cáryamu chéyaca póyina yeḍala nútilónó gótilónó paḍi tsachchedan ani bhárya paṭṭu paṭṭi cúrutsunna taruváta, yenta manchi-váḍunu lóbaḍaca yémi chéya galaḍu?* the best of men will yield if his wife sits and insists that she will throw herself down a well if he does not do what she wants.

paṭṭupurugu, silk-worm.

paṭṭusále, silk-weaver.

paṭṭuṭa, to catch, to be formed, to affect, to take (time), to fit, to hold, to cost, to do anything with zeal. *inṭi donganu y'íṣvaruḍú paṭṭa lédu*, God himself cannot catch the thief in the house; *yerranu tsúpi chépanu paṭṭin aṭṭu*, show the bait and catch the fish; *viḍuvum anṭé pámucu cópam, paṭṭum anṭé cappacu cópam*, you will displease the snake if you say let go, you will displease the frog if you say hold on (it is hard to please all parties); *á commanu téne tuṭṭe paṭṭindi*, a honey-comb has formed on that branch. *Lacshmayya: nácu rátriḷḷu nidra paṭ-ṭadu, mandu putstsu có válé. Ven-camma: pilla yéḍupu chéta nácunnu nidra paṭṭadu, nác ém mand istáró?* Smith: I can't sleep at night; I must take a drug. Mrs. Smith: I can't sleep at night for the child crying, what drug will you give me? *ḍabb unna váḷḷu munḍalanu v'untsu cunṭé madya mícu mácú yémi paṭṭindi?* if those who have the money to do so keep loose women, how does it affect you and me? *í murugu ná chétici paṭṭadu*, this bracelet does not fit my wrist; *váḍu nindá sépu úpiri paṭṭa lédu*, he cannot hold his breath long; *chépaṭṭuṭa* (take by the hand) is to marry; *cheyyipaṭṭuṭa* (take the hand) is to assault a woman indecently; *cáḷḷu paṭṭuṭa* is to massage the legs; *á boccaló ná cheyyi paṭṭadu*, my hand will not go into that hole; *mandu rógánni paṭṭa lédu*, the medicine has not taken effect; *ginza paṭṭé samayamu*, the time when the ear is forming; *nálugu dinamulu paṭṭunu*, it will take four days; *manishi paṭṭé mátramu*, only just large enough to hold (or admit) one man; *aidu rúpá-yilu paṭṭunu*, it will cost five rupees; *múḍu gajálu paṭṭunu*, it will take three yards; *yevari paṭṭité váru cheppuduru*, ask any one you like and they will say so; *idi chéyuṭacu vánic émi paṭṭinadi?* what possessed him to do this? *paṭṭi cheppité á pillavánici tsaduvu bágá vatstsunu*, if you teach sedulously, the child will learn well. Added to nouns *paṭṭuṭa* simply forms a verb, as *anavá-lupaṭṭuṭa*, to recognize; *tuppupaṭṭuṭa*, to rust; *accarapaṭṭuṭa*, to be necessary; *covvupaṭṭuṭa*, to get fat; *paṭlupaṭṭuṭa*, to get cramp; *nácu zalubu paṭṭinadi*, I have caught cold.

paṭutvamu, vigour. *tátagárici paḷḷu v'úḍi póyanavi, indriya paṭutvamu póyinadi, chevulu tinnagá vinabaḍavu, tsúpu tinnagá canabaḍadu, tala vanu-cutsú v'unnadi*, grandfather's teeth are loose, the vigour of his organs is gone, his ears don't hear right, his eyes don't see right, his head trembles; *ṣaríra paṭutvamu*, vigour of body.

pau, a quarter. Hindustani. *muppau* is three-quarters.

paula, a quarter anna. Hindustani. *muppaula* is three-quarter annas.

pauramu, pigeon; also *páruvamu*. The blue rock pigeon is called the black pigeon in Telugu, *nalla pauramu*; the green pigeon is *patstsa pauramu*.

pauramu, belonging to a town. Skt., adjectival form of *pura*. *pauralócamu* is the townsfolk.

paurashamu, manliness, courage, prowess. Skt., from *purusha*, man. *má rázu culamló v'unḍé paurasha-munnú abhimánamunnú míru álóchin-tsacunḍá mátláḍutú v'unnáru*, you forget our Kshatriya prowess and pride when you speak like that.

paurashaṣáli, hero.

pauráṇamu, appertaining to the Puranas. Skt.

pauráṇicamu, mythological. *Pau-ráṇicuḍu*, a Puranic exegist.

paurnama, full moon day. Skt., from *púrna*, full.

paurôhityamu, office of priest. Skt., from *purôhita*, priest.
paurudu, citizen.
pautri, granddaughter. Skt.
pautrudu, grandson (son's son only). Skt.
pavanamu, air, wind. Skt. A book word for *gáli*.
pavitramu, pure, holy. Skt.
payaru, crop; another way of spelling *pairu*.
payata, woman's cloth; another way of spelling *paita*.
páca, shed. *sthalam v'unté gurránni pácaló catti veyyi*, if there is room tie up the horse in the shed.
pácamu, cooking. Skt. It also means an author's style, as *drácshapácamu*, the grape style (ornate) and *cadalipácamu*, the banana style (soft and easy).
páchi, dirt, slime. *cond anta chicatigáné léchi, lópali páchi anta chésédánni*, I used to get up in the pitch dark and clear up all the messes inside; *pádindé pádará, páchi pandla Dásari*, sing again foul-toothed Dasari (proverb of dirty religious impostor).
páchica, die. *páchicalu tísu cu rá, vacca áta vétámu*, bring the dice and we will have a throw.
páci, female sweeper, toty (scavenger).
pácivádu, male sweeper, scavenger.
pácshicamu, partiality, from *pacshamu*. Skt. *mír occa nimishamu pácshica vrüttini vidumu*, give up your role of partiality for a minute.
pácshicudu, partisan; also *pacshacudu*.
pácuta, to crawl; also *prácuta*. *nívu chíma lágu prácutávu, végiram nadichi rá lév émi?* you are creeping like an ant, can't you hurry up? *adugó góda mída mála balli prácutú v'unnadi*, look, there is a pariah lizard crawling on the wall (an orthodox Brahmin has to take a bath if he sees a pariah in the street or a lizard on a wall).
pádaipóyina, ruined, from *pádu*, *auta*, and *póvuta*.
pádamu, foot. Skt. Also a foot in metre, but longer than our foot, one quarter of a Skt. stanza (*padyamu*); *pádaracshandlu*, foot-protectors, is a distinguished term for shoes. Obsequiousness makes frequent reference to the foot of the patron, thus, *tama pádala samukhánacu ná cumárunni techchi oppagist unnánu*, I deliver my son to the presence of Your Honour's feet; *tama pádala vadda*, in Your Honour's Presence; *tama pádala şaranu tsochchinánu*, I have crept under the protection of your feet.
pádapamu, tree. Skt. A book word for *chettu*.
pádarasamu, quicksilver. Skt.
pádauta, to get spoilt. *mejistrítu: nuvvu mótáru bassulu cottu cunn appudu tsuchává? sácshi: tsúchán andi. mejistrítu: cáranam émi? sácshi: bassulu rendu occa manishini y'eccintsu cóḍánici póti paddai, andu chéta cottu coni pád ainai.* Magistrate: Did you see the bus collision? Witness: Yes, Your Honour. Magistrate: What was the cause? Witness: The two buses were fighting over one passenger, so collided and got smashed up.
pádi, milk. Especially used in the expression *pádiau*, a cow in milk; the ordinary word for milk is not *pádi* but *pálu*. *panta pentaló v'unnadi, pádi púriló v'unnadi*, the harvest is in the manure, the milk in the grass. *Lacshmayya: santána niródhánni gurinchi upanyásam zarugutund ata, pódám, vastává? Vencayya: nénu ránu, má paşuvulacu santána niródham accara lédu, pádi und áli.* Smith: I hear there is a birth-control lecture on, we are going, will you come? Jones: No Sir, I don't want birth-control for my cattle, I want milk; *tallini tsúchi pillanú, pádini tsúchi barrenú, tisu có valenu*, look at the mother before you take the daughter; at the milk before you buy the she-buffalo.
pádi, bed (of flowers, &c.); also *pádu*.
pádiri, padre. Italian through English; a priest, any missionary.
pádu, waste, cursed, desolation, spoilt, ruined, bad. *unté v'úru, póté pádu*, inhabited it is a village, abandoned a desolation; *pádu v'úlló pogidévâru léru, nácu néne pogudu contán annád ata*, there is only myself to praise me in a ruined village, so he said (proverb of a man blowing his own trumpet);

ikha nén í pádu praṣnalacu zavábu cheppa lénu, I can't answer any more of these rotten questions; *boṭléruváḍu manam y'ichchina praṣastam aina sanna biyyam yeccaḍanó dáchi, yeccaḍivó mutaca biyyam vanḍi peṭṭi, doragáritó tahaṣṣiludáru iláganṭi páḍu biyyam pampinchináḍ ani cheppináḍ aṭa,* the butler (not having received his mamul from the Tahsildar) is said to have hidden the A 1 fine rice we sent and served up coarse rice and told the gentleman: 'This is the sort of bad rice the Tahsildar supplies'; *páḍu nuyyi* is a disused well; *páḍ ai póyindi,* is the usual way of saying it is spoilt or ruined.

pádu, garden bed; also *pádi.* It is a smaller plot than *maḍi,* which is used for the nursery plot from which paddy is transplanted; *curagáyala pádulu,* vegetable plots.

páducalu, sandals. Skt., from *pádamu,* foot.

páḍuchéyuṭa, to spoil, to ruin. *áṭ anta páḍu chésináru,* they have spoilt our whole game.

páḍupaḍuṭa, to go waste, to be spoilt, ruined. *bógamdánni v'untsucóvaḍam valla anni dóshálé; chinn appaṭi nunchi tallidandrulu penchina déham páḍ autundi,* &c. The ill results of keeping dancing-girls are manifold; the body your parents carefully reared is spoilt, &c.

pádushá, emperor. Hindustani; same as *pasha.*

páḍuṭa, to sing. *páḍindé páḍará, páchi panḍla Dásari,* sing your song again, Dasari of dirty teeth (proverb of ignorant religious impostor); *váḍu áḍinadi áṭa páḍinadi páṭa,* dancing to some one's tune (his word is law). *ṭícharu: pápam cheyyanivállu yeccaḍici pótáró nícu telusund? báluḍu: teliyad anḍi. ṭícharu: nénu chepputánu canucondi; accaḍa yeppuḍu sangítam páḍut unṭáru, nátyam chéstunṭáru, chitramaina dipálu velugut unṭavi, suvásanalu vast unṭai; avi yemiṭó chep-panḍi. báluḍu: náṭaca ṣálaló.* Teacher: Do you know where those who commit no sins go? Boy: No sir. Teacher: I will tell you, guess; there they are always singing and dancing and beautiful lights shine and fragrant odours come; say what that is? Boy: The theatre. *Lacshmayya: mí cucca moragaḍam chéta má ammáyi sangítam páḍucóḍánici vilu léca póyindi. Vencayya: mí ammáyi mundugá morigindi.* Smith: My daughter can't sing for your dog's barking. Jones: Your daughter barked first.

páḍuṭa, to bid at an auction.

páḍyami, first day after full moon. Corrupt Skt. for *prathama,* first.

págá, turban.

pála, on the side; ablative of *pálu. má pála galaḍu Dévuḍu,* God is on our side.

pálaci, palanquin. Hindustani.

pálacuḍu, protector. Skt., from *pálintsuṭa.*

páladádi, wet nurse; from *pálu,* milk, and *dádi,* nurse.

pálai, a prey to; from *pálu,* share; *parula pálaina,* having become a prey to others; *cácula pálainavi,* they have become a prey to crows; *appula pálai,* full of debts.

pálapaḷḷu, milk teeth.

pálapiṭṭa, jay. (*boracias indica.*)

pálegáḍu, poligar. A poligar is a person owning a palem or small fortified town; they were numerous especially in the Ceded Districts and had to be suppressed. There are still a few descendants who use the title.

pálemu, a poligar's fortified town, a barony, a village. The word is still found in place-names, usually at the end, but in *Palamcottah* in the Tamil country in the beginning; for the Tamil country was also cursed with poligars.

páléru, farm servant, agricultural labourer.

páḷi, edge, point, tip, nib. *váḍu calamunacu páḷi peṭṭináḍu,* he pointed the (quill) pen; *cárna páḷi* is the tip of the ear; *khaḍga páḷi,* the edge of the sword.

pálicápu, partner, farm servant.

pálintsuṭa, to govern, to cherish. Skt. *préma anu dharmamu yocca janma dinamugá Crishṭmas pálintsa baḍunu gáca,* may Christmas be cherished as the birthday of the religion of love!

pálipóvuṭa, to turn pale, to sink away.

cshíninchi, déham anta pálipóyi ná bhárya, a wife all wasted and sunk away.

páliṭi, in respect of, belonging to; from *pálu*, share. *ní páliṭi daivamu*, your good angel; *vádu ná páliṭici yamuḍu*, he has been a fiend to me; *y'iviḍa yauvana purushula páliṭi mrütyu dévatagá v'unnadé*, she is an angel of death to young men; *daivamu ná mélunu tsúchi órva léca y'inṭici nátó cápuramu chéya vachcheḍu lópalané dánini ná páliṭi yama dútanugá márchi vésináḍu*, destiny, jealous of my good fortune, sent a spiteful changeling in her place to live with me.

pálu, share. *cúlici vachchi pálici máṭláḍin aṭṭu*, like the man who came for hire and then asked for a share (impudence). *pálauṭa* is to become the share, that is the prey, of some one or something. *vocaḍi sampádyamu padimandi pálu*, one earns and ten share; *lóbhi sommu dongaváḍi pálu*, the miser's property falls to the thief; *doralu y'ichchina pálu canná dharani y'ichchina pálu mélu*, the earth gives a more liberal share than the Government. (False: the ryot's portion is really much more than the Government calculates it is.)

pálu, milk. *íta cheṭṭu cinda pálu tágina, callé anṭáru*, drink milk under a date-tree and they will say you are drinking toddy (you are judged by appearances or by the company you keep); *pálé cuḍichi rommé guddináḍu*, drinking the milk and striking the breast (untrue to your salt); *vádu cági tsallárina pálu*, he has sown his wild oats; *talli y'ainá yéḍavanidí pál ivvadu*, even the mother, unless the child cries, will not give milk; *panḍu zdri pálaló paḍḍ aṭṭu*, like the fruit that fell into the milk (happy-go-lucky); *pála puṭṭité mátramu mélu gunamu calugunâ?* milk-bred is not always well-bred (milk-bred = high-bred); *pálu pósi penchiná pámu caravaca mánadu*, feed the serpent on milk and it will bite you just the same (the viper nourished in the bosom); *parugetti pálu trágé canṭé cúrtsunḍi níru tráguṭa mélu*, it is better to sit and drink water than to have to run for your milk; *pálalo paḍḍa balli láguna*, like a lizard in a pail of milk (in difficulties); *cherucu pálu* is sugar-cane juice; *marri pálu*, juice of the banyan; *pálavanṭi*, like milk, means guileless; *pálavanṭi manasu*, a simple heart; *pálacaḍali* or *pála-velli* is the sea of milk of Hindu mythology; *Páléru*, a well-known river of South India, is Milk River; *pálau* is a milch cow.

pálupóvuṭa, to be divided or decided; from *pálu*, share; *émiyu pálupóca*, not being able to decide about anything; *Hariṣchandruḍu yémiyu n'álóchana pálupóca nivveragandi;* Hariṣchandra, not knowing what to do and being greatly afraid; *nác émi chéyaṭacunu pálu póc unnadi*, I don't know what to do, I cannot make up my mind.

pámarulu, the vulgar. Skt. *pámaralu cheppa valasina máṭa panḍitul ai v'unḍinní míru cúḍá viṣvasistár émi?* will a Pandit like you believe these vulgar errors? *samastamú telisinavâru pámurala vale míru y'ilágé ṣelav istár émi?* Will an encyclopaedia of knowledge like you talk like the vulgar in these matters? *pámarulu v'upayóginché sámányapu máṭalé v'upayógisté má pánḍityamú, má ádhicyamú yémiṭ anḍi?* if we use the same words as the vulgar where is our scholarship, where is our superiority?

pámpu, a bed; short for *pánupu*. Used also of flower-bed, tank bed.

pámu, snake. *téḷlalló conḍi, pámulaló paḍaga*, sting in scorpions, hood in snake (the acme of wickedness); *pámu cáḷlu pámunac eruca*, only a snake knows where its feet are; *pamutó chelimi, cattitó sámu*, friendship with a snake, playing with a sword (a dangerous game); *pálu pósi penchiná, pámu caravaca mánadu*, though you feed a snake on milk that will not prevent it biting you (nourishing a viper in your bosom); *cáni cálamucu carré pámu autundi*, when your luck is out your stick will turn into a snake; *yé puṭṭaló yé pám unnadó yevarici telustundi?* who can tell what snake is in what hole? *pámu busa coṭṭuts unnadi*, the snake hisses.

pámulavádu, snake-charmer.

pánacamu, a drink. Skt. *pánacamló pulla lágu aḍḍam vatstsuṭa,* to get in the way like a twig in your drink.

pánamu, drinking. Skt. *annapánádulu* is food and drink.

pánḍityamu, scholarship. Skt., from *panḍita,* scholar, pundit. *mádi panḍita sampradáyam ganuca pánḍityam canapadaḍánici cásta máramúla máṭa prayóginchinánu,* as we have a tradition of scholarship I used a rather out of the way word to show my scholarship.

pánigrahanamu, nuptials. Skt.; from *páni,* hand, and *grahanam,* clasping. *pánigrahanam chéyuṭa,* to marry; *á chinnadi ná daggiracu vachchi nannu viváham chésucóvaḍánici vappucunn appaṭici, míru anumati y'ichché dáca pánigrahanam cheyyáḍánici nén angicarintsa lédu,* though the girl came to me and agreed to marry me I did not agree to the nuptials being performed until you had given your consent.

páníyamulu, drinkables. Skt. *bhacshyamulú, páníyamulú,* eatables and drinkables.

pánupu, bed; also *pámpu*; used of a couch, a bed of flowers, bed of a tank, &c. (just like our bed). *nénu ná pánupu mída sukha nidra chéyuts unḍagá,* as I was sleeping happily on my bed.

pápa, child. *dánici biḍḍa pápulu léru,* she has neither chick nor child; *canu pápa* is the child in the eye, the pupil.

pápacáryamu, sinful act.

pápamu, sin; as an exclamation, oh dear; also *ayyó pápamu!* Skt. *pápamu punyamu* are often used together for good and evil; *atanni gurinchi pápamu punyamu renḍu yeruganu,* I know nothing whatever about him; also simply, *yé pápam eraganu,* I know nothing whatever about it. *pápamu, váru paḍináru,* oh dear, they have fallen down; *á chinnavánni coṭṭacu, pápamu,* for shame! don't beat the boy; *chésina pápamu cheppité mánunu,* confession removes sin; *váḍu pápamunacu vaḍi caṭṭucunnáḍu,* he fell into sin; *agrajanma racshaṇam andu bonca vatstsunu; y'induló veyyi abaddhál áḍiná punyam vastundi gáni, pápam yentamátramu rádu,* you may lie to save a Highborn (i.e. a Brahmin); if you tell 1,000 lies for that you will gain merit and it is no sin at all; *cuccanu tsampina pápamu, guḍi caṭṭiná pódu,* building a temple will not wipe out the sin of killing a dog. *bhárya: míru annam páréstē cuccacu peṭṭa valasi vastundi. bharta: pápamu, anta manchi cuccacu nívu vanḍina annam peḍité adi mátram cheḍi pódú?* Wife: If you leave the food, it will have to be given to the dog. Husband: Dear me, you wouldn't give such a good dog the food you have cooked? It would be the death of him.

pápata, parting (of hair). *áme pápata tísucunṭ unnadi,* she is parting her hair.

pápátmuḍu, sinner. Skt., from *pápam,* sin, and *átma,* soul; also *pápi, pápishthuḍu.* The feminine is *pápatmurálu.*

pápi, sinner. Skt. *cévala pápi y'agu váni pápamu manac éla?* what is to us the sin of that complete sinner?

pápishṭhi, sinful; more used as an expletive, beastly, bloody. Skt. *néḍu yeṭuvanṭi pápishṭhi rátri gaḍapinánu,* I have passed a beastly night; *pápishṭhi télu yeccaḍa nunchi vachchináḍó cáni tsaṭuccuna chiṭicina vél anta poḍichindi,* a beastly scorpion suddenly came out from I don't know where and stung me on the little finger.

pápósulu, slippers. Hindustani.

pápuṭa, to deliver; causative of *páyuṭa.* *pápuconuṭa* is to get rid of.

pára, spade.

páramparayamu, in series, hereditary. Skt., from *parampara. páramparyamugá anubhavinché bhúmi,* land that has come down from father to son; *vamṣa páramparyapu siddhántam* is heredity principle.

páramu, shore. Skt. It properly means the other or farther shore.

párana, eating after a fast. Skt. *oca náḍu dhárana, vaca náḍu párana,* one day fasting, one day breaking fast (of precarious livelihood).

párapoyuṭa, to pour off.

páratantryamu, dependence. Skt., from *paratantram.*

páratsútsuṭa, to view.

páravaşyamu, ecstasy. Skt.

páravéyuṭa, to throw away.

pára, watch, watching, guard. Hindustani.

páráváḍu, sentinel.

páráyanamu, devout reading. Skt. *pustacála gadilóci veḷḷi Purána páráyanamu chésucunṭánu,* I will go into the library and read the Puranas.

párcu, park. English. *dádi: ammá, pilla párculó tappi póyinadi. yazamánurálu: accaḍa pólisuváḷḷ unṭáru, váḷḷató cheppa lédá? dádi: cheppänu; cheppa baṭṭé pilla nídi cád ani pólisu stéshanu tísucu póyinàru.* Nurse: Madam, the child got lost in the park. Mistress: There are constables there, didn't you tell them? Nurse: I did and they said the child isn't yours and took it to the station.

páripóvuṭa, to run away. *mír inṭa léca póyiná, intaló penḍlámu n'evvarunu yettuconi páripóru lenḍi,* you needn't think that if you go out some one will come along and run away with your wife.

páritóshacamu, reward, donation.Skt.

párínata, expert knowledge or skill. Skt.

párínuḍu, one who has expert knowledge or skill. Skt. *sacala ṣástra párínuḍu,* a man who has mastered all science; *mí vanṭi parópacára párinulu,* a person like you skilled in all the arts of hospitality.

párṣvamu, side. Skt. *iru párṣvamulu y'anduna,* on both sides.

párṭilu, parties. English. Especially parties in a civil case. *pliḍaru ḍabbu lágaḍḍnici párṭila vadda anni ṭacculu canaparatsa valenu,* pleaders must use every trick to draw money out of their clients.

párudala, a flow.

páruṭa, to flow, to creep, to run on. *páré chíma tsappuḍu vinéváḍu,* a man who can hear an ant crawl; *á tóṭacu í níḷḷu páravu,* that water does not reach this garden; *váni manasu dáni mída páruts unnadi,* his thoughts run on her; *níḷḷu párani yéru,* a dry river bed.

páruvamu, pigeon; pronounced, and also sometimes spelt, *pauramu.*

Párvati, Siva's wife. Skt.

páṣamu, bond. Skt. *mohapáṣálu,* the bonds of love; *pápapáṣamu,* the bond of evil; *páṣápṭacamu,* the eight bonds —wife, child, wealth, cattle, vehicle, land, house, friend; *páṣacaruḍu* is a thug. Thugs used to get behind their victims and throw a *páṣam* (cord) round their necks and throttle them.

páṣchátya, western. Skt.

páshánamu, poison, arsenic. Skt. *tella páshánamu,* the white poison, is arsenic. The Skt. word means 'stone' and is used for *ráyi* in books.

páta, old (of things); old (of persons) is *musali. coṭṭa vinta páta róta,* fresh news delights, stale disgusts; *páta donga vacca rózuna doraca mánadu,* the old thief will be caught some day; *mangali páta, tsácali cotta,* choose a new washerman but your old barber; *páta banjaru,* old waste, is a revenue term.

páṭa, song; from *páḍuṭa,* to sing; *váḍu áḍinadi áṭa, páḍinadi páṭa,* his word is law.

-páṭa, suffix meaning 'manner'. *ippáṭa,* in this way.

pátacamu, sin. Skt. *panchapátacamulu,* the five sins, are: killing a Brahmin, stealing gold, drinking alcohol, dishonouring one's teacher's wife, and associating with those guilty of these sins; a very limited Pentalogue, 'framed from the Brahmin teacher's point of view.

páṭacuḍu, singer. *Lacshmayya: míc ippuḍu nimmaḷangá unnadá? Vencayya: nác émi? Lacshmayya: intaca mundu míru tsála sépu múligáré. Vencayya: nénu páṭacuḍin anḍi.* Smith: Feeling better? Jones: Why, what's the matter with me? Smith: You were groaning for a long time. Jones: I am a singer.

pátáḷamu, hell. Skt. *pátáḷaganga,* the river that runs through hell.

páṭhacuḍu, reader, lecturer. Skt.

páṭhamu, reading, lesson. Skt. *adi mácu ivála páṭham,* that is our lesson for to-day; *stótrapáṭhálu chéyuṭa* is to recite some one's praises.

-páṭi, suffix indicating 'extent'. *ipáṭi tsálunu,* that will do; *ipáṭici,* by this time; *yépáṭi rúcalu?* how much money?

pática, quarter of a hundred, 25.

Lacshmayya: má tammuḍici pátic éḷḷu. Vencayya: iruvai yéḷḷ ani nátó cheppāḍé. Lacshmayya: aidu sanvatsaramulu vachchin dáca váḍici banṭlu lecca peṭṭadam rá lédu. Smith: My brother is 25. Jones: He told me himself he was 20. Smith: He did not learn the abacus till he was 5.

páṭigá, in bad part, little by little; also *páṭipáṭigá. nén úraca parihásamunac annánu; i máṭalu páṭigá paṭṭa bócu,* I only spoke in jest; you must not take it ill.

páṭimpu, regard, care.

páṭintsuṭa, to have regard for. *ahitul áḍina téne máṭalu páṭimpité háni vatstsunu,* harm will come of paying attention to the honeyed words of evil-doers.

páṭipáṭigá, little by little; also *páṭigá.*

páṭivratyamu, wifely dutifulness. Skt., from *pati,* husband.

pátramu, character in a play. Skt. *pátramula y'andu varnimpa baḍina gunamulu,* the qualities the dramatist gives to his characters.

pátramu, utensil, vessel. *pátrasámánlu,* household utensils; *palatsani pairu pátraḷḷu ninḍunu,* a thin crop fills the grain-bins (don't sow too thick).

pátramu, worthy. Skt. *cshétram erigi vittanamu; pátram erigi dánamu,* seed to the soil known to be good, gifts to those known to be worthy.

pátrata, worthiness. Skt.

pátruḍu, deserving of, liable to. Skt. *danḍanacu pátrul airi,* they became liable to punishment; *mí dayacu pátrunni cávaḍam nimittam,* to deserve your favour.

páṭu, fall, distress, labour, ebb, part; also a suffix turning words into nouns. *nénu paḍa valasina páṭl anniyu paḍḍānu;* I drained the cup of misery to the dregs; *yé páṭu tappiná sápáṭu tappadu,* whatever labour is neglected meals won't be; *oca pracaṭanaló y'iṭlá v'unḍenu: 'má daggira aidu rúpáyala vastúvulu conucconévāḷḷacu cóṭu tagilinchédi ocaṭi, sigareṭlu cálchédi incóṭi bahumánamgá istámu.' Lacshmayya aidu rúpáyala vastúvulacu arḍaru pampenu. Váṭitó páṭu oca chíla, oca nippu pulla pampiri.* An advertisement ran: 'any one who buys Rs. 5-worth from us will get as a present something to hang his coat on and something to light his cigarettes with'; Smith ordered Rs. 5-worth; with them he got a nail and a match. *cudurupáṭu* is a settlement; *diddupáṭu,* a correction; *ontaripáṭuna,* alone; *ápáṭuna,* whereupon; *panipáṭulu,* jobs; *páṭlamári,* a drudge; *váru paḍé páṭlu,* the distresses they suffered; *reppapáṭu,* wink (fall of eye-lid); *mana bálicalacu vidyató páṭu sangítam cúḍá cheppintsa valenu,* we must make music part of the education of our girls; *várthaca daşaló viváhamu chésiconnavárici páṭl eccaḍanu ilágunané y'unḍunu. 'álu cád adi vrál' anna sámeta nác ippuḍ anubhavamunacu vachchindi,* this is what comes of taking a wife in one's old age; the old saying 'ill-mated ill-fated' has come home to me.

páṭupaḍuṭa, to work hard. *páṭupaḍi sampádinchi,* earning his living by honest labour; *á mahá purushulu, lócanni v'uddharintsaḍánici páṭu paḍutú v'unṭáru,* those great men are working hard to reform the world.

páṭupeṭṭuṭa, to plant, to fix, to bury. *moccalanu páṭupeṭṭuṭa* is to plant plants; *gunzanu páṭupeṭṭuṭa,* to fix a post.

páṭuṭa, to bury, to plant.

pávanamu, pure. Skt. *néḍu sudinamu, ná janmamu pávanam áyenu!* O happy day that has purified all my life!

pávu, pávula, pávuramu, pedantic ways of spelling *pau, paula, pauramu.*

páya, division, branch of a river, from *payuṭa.*

páyacaṭṭu, newly reclaimed land. Hindustani. An old revenue term.

páyacári, a temporary occupier of land. Hindustani.

páyikhána, latrine. Hindustani.

páyuṭa, to divide, to abandon.

peccanḍru, many people.

peccu, many. *peccu máruḷu,* many times; *peccu máṭal élá?* why so many words?

peda, bad, wrong. *peda mogamu peṭṭuconi,* making a wry face; *peda chevula peṭṭuta,* turn a deaf ear; *pedadári,* the wrong road; *peḍarthamu,* the wrong sense; *áḍaváḷḷu nálugu muccalu nérva-*

ḍamtóṭé paruvú maryádá anní marachi póyi, peda yuctulu pannutáru, as soon as women study at all they lose all respect for you and are at their tricks.

pedavi, lip. *péddváni cópamu pedavici chéṭu*, a poor man's anger only spites his own lip; *pedavula sandu nunchi chiru navvu bailudérutú v'unnadi*, a smile appears between the parted lips.

pedda, big, old, elder. *chinna pámu n'ainá, pedda carrató coṭṭa valenu*, though a snake be small take a big stick to him. *tanḍri: parícsha márculu tsústé, andari pillala canna nuvvu ákharuna unnáu. báluḍu: vayassuló néné pedda.* Father: From the examination marks it would seem you were last of the lot. Boy: In age I stand first. *pedda manishi oca chinna roṭṭe, inco pedda roṭṭe chétuló putstsuconenu, annadammul aina iddaru báluru canupinchiri. peddamanishi: míló yevaru manchiváḷḷó canuccunṭánu ranḍi. anna (pedda roṭṭe tísuconi tinṭú): ayyá, má tammuḍé manchiváḍ anḍi*, a gentleman holding a big loaf and a small loaf in his hands showed them to two boys, who were brothers. Gentleman: I will find out which of you two boys is the better boy, come along. Elder boy (taking the big loaf): Sir, my younger brother is the better boy.

peddabáṭu, goose. *báṭu* is a duck.

peddacápu, headman of a village. *cápu* is a ryot; *peddacápu* the head ryot.

peddadi, old woman.

peddalu, old people, our elders, ancestors. *peddalató váḍu, petarulató pondu*, don't argue with the old or keep company with ghosts.

peddamanishi, gentleman. *ippuḍu pedda manishi taraha bottigá pótú v'unnadi*, the race of gentlemen is dying out; *nénu cheyyaca póté 'yémoi peddamanishi' anu*, if I fail to do it, you are at liberty to say, 'I thought you were a gentleman'. *plíḍaru: muddáyi tiṭṭina tiṭl anni spashṭamugá cheppu. firyádi: nénu cheppan anḍi, pedda manushyula yeduṭa cheppa cúḍanav anḍi. plíḍaru: aité mejisṭréṭu gárici rahasyamgá cheppu.* Pleader: Tell us plainly the words of abuse the accused used. Complainant: I can't, Sir, they are not words I could repeat before gentlemen. Pleader: Never mind, tell the magistrate secretly. *Lacshmayya: ná daggira manchi cucca unḍédi, adi dongal evaró peddamanushyul evaró tsappuna gurtinchédi, dongalanu mátram carichédi. Vencayya: á cucca y'ippuḍ ém aindi? Lacshmayya: nannu caravaḍam chéta inṭló nunchi veḷḷa coṭṭänu.* Smith: I used to have a good dog which knew at once whether a man was a thief or a gentleman and only bit thieves. Jones: What has happened to that dog? Smith: It bit me, so I got rid of it.

Peddamma, goddess of poverty.

peddamma, maternal aunt, older than mother; also *pettalli*.

peddanáyana, paternal uncle, older than father; also *pettanḍri*.

peddapuli, tiger. *inṭló y'ígapuli, baiṭa peddapuli*, at home a spider, a tiger abroad; *peddapuli yedaṭan ainá paḍa vatstsunu gáni, nagarivári yedaṭa paḍa rádu*, a palace official is worse to come across than a tiger.

peddaricamu, greatness, old age.

peddaváḍu, old man. *nívu chinnatanamuló páṭupaḍi tsaduvu conaca póté, peddaváḍavai vichárapaḍuduvu*, a wasted youth means a sorrowful old age.

pedima, lip; more usually *pedavi*. *pedimacu minchina pallu, pramidacu minchina vatti*, a projecting tooth, a wick standing out of the oil-lamp (i.e. a proud person, a person with nostrils at 90° elevation).

peduṭa, to put, a form of *peṭṭuṭa*.

pellagintsuṭa, to pull out. *jilléḍu cheṭṭu pellaginchi, dáni véru gandham vrásté, télu cuṭṭiná pótundi*, if you pull up a swallow-wort and rub on the juice from its roots a scorpion bite will go.

peḷḷáḍuṭa, to marry. *áviḍenu cottagá peḷḷáḍindi ná ménamáma*, she is the woman my uncle recently married. Also *penḍláḍuṭa*.

peḷḷámu, wife. *Lacshmayya: ná peḷḷáni carra tísuconi coṭṭänu, nannu coṭló peṭṭi táḷam veyyanḍi. pólísu sarjenṭu: coṭṭité tsachchi póyindá? Lacshmayya: tsáva lédu, nannu coṭṭaḍánici parigettu cuni vast unnadi.* Smith: I took a stick and beat my wife; lock me up.

Police sergeant: Did you kill her? Smith: No, she is running after me to beat me. *Lacshmayya: podduna ná peḷḷámu mída cópam vachchi tiṭṭänu. Vencayya: ávideçu ní mída cópam rá lédá? Lacshmayya: rá lédu, navvindi. Vencayya: yenduc ani? Lacshmayya: nén inta dhairyam tetstsu coni cóppaḍḍ anducu santóshinchindi.* Smith: This morning I got angry and swore at my wife. Jones: Didn't she get angry? Smith: No, she laughed. Jones: Why? Smith: At my having the courage to get angry. She was pleased.

peḷḷi, marriage.

peḷutsu, brittle.

pempu, greatness, increase, rearing, nourishing.

pempuchéyuṭa, to enlarge. *illu pempuchéyintsa valenu*, you must enlarge the house.

pempuḍu, tame, adopted, adoption. *pempuḍu tanḍri*, adopted father; *pempuḍu comáruḍu*, adopted son; *pempuḍu bátu*, tame duck; *pempuḍu chiluca*, pet parrot.

pen-, prefix meaning 'great'. *penchiluva*, the great rock snake; *penchícaṭi*, pitch darkness; *penchemaṭa*, profuse perspiration; *penturumu*, full tresses; *pennidhi doricina pédavánini vale paramánandabharitulai*, rejoicing with great joy like a poor man who has found a great treasure.

penagonuṭa, to be twisted. *bhayamunu siggunu penagona*, with mixed feelings of shame and fear.

penaguláḍuṭa, to struggle; also *penaguṭa*.

penaguláṭa, a struggle.

penaguṭa, to struggle; also *penaguláḍuṭa*.

penamu, frying-pan, grid, cauldron. *cherucu penam* is the great cauldron sugar-cane juice is boiled in.

pence, penci, saucy. *í v'úḷḷó scúlu curravâḷḷu bhayamú bhactí lécunḍá ná mundara penci zavábu saváḷḷu véstáru*, the schoolboys of this town have no fear or respect and put saucy questions to my face.

pencetanamu, sauciness.

pencu, tile. *cécalató y'inṭi mída penculu nálugú yegiri póyinavi*, some tiles flew off the roof with the shouting; *y'iṭic ámulú, penc ámulú, peḷḷi pandiḷḷú modalainaváṭi bápatu cá valasin anta v'unṭundi*, he makes as much as he (municipal manager) wants out of brick-kilns, tile-kilns, and marriage pandals (i.e. issuing licences for them).

pencuṭillu, tiled house.

pendalacaḍa, early in the morning; also *pendaláḍa, pendaráḷé*.

penḍalamu, yam.

pendaláḍa, early in the morning; also *pendalacaḍa, pendarálé*.

pendarálé, early in the morning; also *pendalacaḍa, pendaláḍa*.

penḍe, rafter. *nén entó ní mída préma chéta dévat árchanac ani, y'inṭinṭa tirigi, nityamunu manchi puvvulu techchi y'ichchinanu, prati dinamunu inṭi munzúru penḍeló peṭṭiṭé cáni, yeccaḍainanu mutstsaṭa tíra nénu tsútsutsunḍagá coppuló muḍutsu cóvu*, I go about from house to house all out of love of you collecting nosegays for the gods, so I say, and give them you, and then you stick them up in some rafter in the gable and never think of sating the yearning of my eyes by twining posies in your hair.

penḍláḍuṭa, to marry, from *penḍli*, marriage, and *áḍuṭa*, to perform.

penḍlámu, wife; also *peḷḷámu*. *talli caḍupu tsútsunu, penḍlámu vípu tsútsunu*, the mother will look to his stomach, the wife to his back (to see what he is bringing home for her); *dongaváḍi penḍlámu yeppuḍú munḍamópé*, the thief's wife is a perpetual widow.

penḍli, marriage, plural *penḍlinḍlu, peḷḷilu*. *penḍli sandaṭló boṭṭu caṭṭa marichiváḍaṭa*, like the man who forgot to put on the ring in the marriage bustle; *penḍlic edigina pilla*, a marriageable girl. *bhárya: yevarainá bádha paḍut unṭé mícu váḷḷa cashṭam yeppuḍaina tírchárá? bharta: tírtsac émi? ninnu penḍli chésu coni cashṭálanu tírtsa lédá?* Wife: Have you ever relieved any one in distress? Husband: Didn't I relieve you of all distresses when I married you?

penḍlicoḍucu, penḍlicumáruḍu, bridegroom.

pendlicúturu, bride.

pendlindlu, marriages. Irregular plural of *pendli*; also *pellilu*.

penimiti, husband. *stri: ná penimiti nidraló mátládut untádu, váric émainá mand istárá? vaidyudu: mand accara lédu, pagati púta áyananu svéchchagá mátládan iyyandi.* Woman: My husband talks in his sleep; can you give him any medicine for it? Doctor: No medicine is necessary; let him talk freely in the daytime.

penta, manure. *panta pentaló v'unnadi,* the harvest is in the manure; *penta mída panta, manta mída vanta,* manure cooks crops. *paicamu pancti y'andu, culamu penta y'andu,* money takes its seat at meals and caste is thrown on the dung-hill (said of rich people who think themselves above caste rules).

pentsuta, to rear, to enlarge, to foment, to grow, to indulge, to feed, to train, to increase. *calahamu penchinádu,* he fomented the quarrel; *gaddamu pentsuta,* to grow a beard; *duhkhamu pentsuta,* to indulge one's grief; *pálu pósi penchiná pámu carava mánadu,* though you feed a snake with milk that won't stop it's biting; *sarcasucu tandricoduculu velli vachchiri. tandri: cótulu, cuccalu, simhalu, peddapululu, cúdá anta anucuvagá unté, nuvvu nénu cheppin atlu vin accara lédá? coducu: váti mádirigá nannu cúdá penchité atlágé vintánu,* father and son went to the circus and on the way back the father said: Monkeys, dogs, lions, tigers, all being so obedient, shouldn't you obey me? Son: Train me as well as they are trained and I will obey; *induló béramu léd ani modata cheppinánu; malli mátládité vanda rúpáyalu pentsutánu cáni, taggintsanu,* I said from the beginning there was no bargaining: if you say any more I will add another Rs. 100, but I will take off nothing.

penu, great.

peradu, back-yard. *perati chettu manducu rádu,* the back-yard tree is no good for medicine (familiarity breeds contempt).

perucuta, to pull out. *náluca peruc-coni tsachchenu,* he pulled out his own tongue and killed himself (cut off your nose to spite your own face); *ní grudl úda pericedanu tsúdu,* I will tear your eyes out.

peruguta, to grow. *peruguta viruguta coracé,* you grow only to be broken (*tout passe, tout casse, et, hélas, tout se remplace*); *bidatanamu modati nundiyu tanaló putti perigi,* born to poverty.

Perumállu, Vishnu. *ló guttu Perumállacu yeruca,* God knoweth the secrets of the heart.

pesalu, green gram (*Phaseolus radiatus*), a pulse; the genitive is *pesara*.

petapeta, crashing; onomatopoeic.

petarulu, ghosts. Corrupt Skt., from *pitrulu,* fathers. *peddalató vádu, petarulató pondu,* don't argue with elders or be familiar with ghosts.

petishanaru, petitioner. English; also *pitishinaru*.

petishanu, petition. English; also *pitishanu*.

petrólu, petrol. English. *ná mótáru bandici petrólu ai póyindi,* I have finished the petrol in my car.

petstsu, skin of fruit, rind.

petstsu, surplus. *paipetstsulu,* incidental profits.

petstsuperuguta, to grow great.

petta, hen.

pettalli, maternal aunt, older than mother; also *peddamma*.

pettanadárudu, respectable farmer, a village elder.

pettanamu, age, authority, strolling (being an occupation of old age); from *pedda. télucu pettanam isté, tellavárlu anta podichinad ata,* the scorpion was given power and they say it stung till morning. *bharta: nícu inti pettanamu cá valená? bhárya: accara lédu, dabbu ná chétic ist unté tsálunu.* Husband: Do you want to run this house? Wife: No, all I want is the money. *úri vembadini pettanamulacu bailu dérindu?* have you been for a stroll about the town?

pettandári, influence in a village. (To village headman) *nálugu vandala néta répatiló mí grámam mída vasúlu cheyya sádhanam tsúdu, ní pettandárí tsútámí,* see you raise Rs. 400 from your village by hook or by crook to-day or to-morrow; we shall see what influence you have there.

pettanḍri, paternal uncle, older than father; also *peddanáyana*.

peṭṭe, box; also compartment in a railway carriage, pillar-box, petrol tin, &c. *peddamanishi: nannu cshamints anḍi; ná gaḍiyáram yevaró yettu coni poyinár ani mícu ninna ripórṭu cheṣánu; inṭici veḷḷéṭ appaṭici peṭṭelóné canipinchindi. pólisu inspecṭaru: yém lábham? mému donganu paṭṭu coni cóṭló peṭṭämé.* Gentleman: I beg to be excused; I reported to you yesterday that my watch had been stolen; on going home I found it in a box. Police Inspector: No good, we caught the thief and have him in the lock-up. *nannu áḍaváḷḷa peṭṭiló yeccinturu*, you may put me in the ladies' compartment.

peṭṭintsuṭa, to cause to be placed, to supply; causative of *peṭṭuṭa*, to put.

peṭṭu, a blow, supply, time. *cóla léni peṭṭu, táḍu léni caṭṭu*, a rodless blow, a cordless tying. This is inscribed on a rock in Ganjam near an inscription of Asoka's with the English translation 'we govern by soul force'. *paḍisemu paḍi rógála peṭṭu*, a cold in the head is a blow from ten diseases at once; *peṭṭu tsuṭṭamu, poguḍu bhágyamu*, repasts collect relations, flattering brings fortune; *pégu tsuṭṭamá? peṭṭu tsuṭṭamá?* blood kin or dinner kin? *ná peḷḷámu pedda peṭṭuna yéḍchindi*, my wife cried for a long time; *máṭalu má talli máṭalu, peṭṭu márutalli peṭṭu*, motherly words and stepmotherly catering.

peṭṭubaḍi, capital, money advanced or laid out. *praṣna: peṭṭubaḍi anṭé yémiṭi? zavábu: nícu paḍi rúpáyalu app ichchán anucó, aḍi peṭṭubaḍi. praṣna: cúli anṭé yémiṭi? zavábu: á paḍi rúpáyalu rábaṭṭu cóḍam cúli.* Question: What is Capital? Answer: Supposing I lend you Rs. 10 that is your capital. Question: What is Labour? Answer: Getting those ten rupees back will be labour.

peṭṭuconuṭa, to wear, to give, &c. Middle form of *peṭṭuṭa*, to put; it means to put to one's own use, but there are many derivative meanings of which 'to wear' is only the commonest. *coḍucunacu tana tanḍri péru peṭṭuconnáḍu*, he gave his son his father's name; *yé mukhamu peṭṭuconi máṭláḍunu?* has he the face to speak?

peṭṭuṭa, to put, to place, &c. A very common general word much used as an auxiliary and to form verbs from nouns. *cannula níru peṭṭuṭa* is to weep; *vanca peṭṭi*, making the excuse; *pillalu peṭṭuṭa*, to bear young; *viḍichipeṭṭuṭa*, to give up; *guḍlu peṭṭuṭa*, to lay eggs; *áṣapeṭṭuṭa*, to give hopes; *ámecu núru rúpáyala sommu peṭṭináḍu*, he gave her jewellery worth Rs. 100; *annamu peṭṭuṭa*, to serve food; *cávali peṭṭuṭa*; to put a guard; *bobbalu peṭṭuṭa*, to yell; *bádhapeṭṭuṭa*, to torture; *canipeṭṭuṭa*, to wait; *chéṭlu peṭṭuṭa*, to plant trees; *guripeṭṭuṭa*, to take aim; *caṭhina pathyamu peṭṭináḍu*, he put him on strict diet; *ducánamu peṭṭuṭa*, to open a shop; *góḍapeṭṭuṭa*, to build a wall; *cúḍapeṭṭuṭa*, to amass; *parunḍapeṭṭuṭa*, to put to bed; *anḍánacu peṭṭina sommu ápadacu aḍḍam vastundi*, jewels worn for adornment come in useful in adversity; *peṭṭiṭé tinṭáru gáni, tiṭṭiṭé paḍéváru léru*, they will eat food you put before them but not stand abuse you lay on them; *peṭṭinavánici telusunu nicshépamu*, the man who buried the treasure knows where it is; *annamu péṭṭinavár illu, cannamu peṭṭa vatstsuná?* can you burgle a house where they fed you? *Lacshmayya: ní tópí nácu aḍḍangá v'unnadi; nénu múḍu rúpáyal ichchi ṭicceṭṭu connánu, ní tópí tísténé gáni nácu náṭacam canipintsaḍu. Vencayya: nénu iravai rúpáyalu peṭṭi ninnané y'í tópí connánu, áṇini andarû tsúḍa vaddá?* Smith: Your hat is in my way; I paid Rs. 3 for my ticket; unless you remove your hat I can't see the play. Jones: I spent Rs. 20 on that hat yesterday, I want every one to see it. *ocaḍu: mí áfísuló gumástá pani khálí aind ani vinnánu, nác ippistárá? mánéjaru: álasyam aindi, valla cádu. ocaḍu: yevaricainá ichchárá? mánéjaru: iyya lédu; nuvvu iravai sanvatsarála cinda darakhástu peṭṭiṭé ichché-*

vádin émó, nicu vayassu mudirindi. Applicant: I hear there is a clerk's vacancy in your office; will you give it to me? Manager: Too late. Applicant: Have you given it to some one else? Manager: No, if you had put in your application twenty years ago you might have got it. You are a bit long in the tooth. *ocaḍu: márváḍilu ḍabbu khartsu peṭṭaru, bháryanu tísucu rávaḍánici tappa, incó panici tama úḷḷacu póru. incóḍu: accaḍi nunchi cottagá vastunna váḷḷu canipintsar émi? ocaḍu: rayilu khartsu lécunḍá v'unḍaḍánici ippuḍu iccaḍé puṭṭut unnáru.* Smith: The Marvadies won't spend money; they don't go home except to fetch their wives. Jones: Why are none to be seen who have recently come from their homes? Smith: They now get themselves born here to save railway expenses.

peyya, heifer.

péca, warp.

péca, pécu, pack (of cards). English. *pécáḍuṭa* is to play at cards. *chíṭla péca áḍutú cúrtsuni,* sitting and playing cards.

péchi, responsibility, trouble. Corrupt form of *púchi. induló nívu maḷḷí yémí péchí peṭṭa cúḍadu,* you need not trouble yourself any further.

péda, poor. *cúṭici péd aité, culánici pédá?* poverty is not loss of caste (it is in Europe, but it is not in India, wherein there is Indian superiority); *nirupéda,* very poor.

péḍa, cow-dung. *Hinduvulu au péḍató inḍlu alicedaru,* Hindus smear their floors with cow-dung; *péḍaniḷḷu, pénníḷḷu,* cow-dung-water.

péḍapurugu, beetle.

pédaricamu, poverty.

pédaváḍu, poor man. *caligin ayya gáde tiseṭ appaṭici, pédavánici pránamu póyinaḍi,* before the rich man had opened his bins the poor man had died; *pédaváni cópamu pedavici chéṭu,* a poor man's anger only bursts his own lips.

péḍu, chip, wicker. *íta péḷla peṭṭe* is a box made of chips of palm-wood, i.e. a wicker box; *veduru péḷla buṭṭa* is a wicker basket made of bamboo splinters.

péducoṭṭuṭa, to split, to shell. *bádancáyalu péḍucoṭṭiṭé pappu canupintsunu,* if you split almonds, the kernels will appear.

pégu, bowel. *pégu tsuṭṭamá, peṭṭu tsuṭṭamá?* a blood relation or a dinner relation? *vaidyuḍu: nênu y'í madhya goppa ápareshanu cheṣánu. snéhituḍu: dénici cheṣáru? vaidyuḍu: oca úpiri tittini, pégunu, cósi veyya valasi vachchindi. snéhituḍu: rógi y'ippuḍu yeṭlá v'unnáḍu? vaidyuḍu: yeṭlá v'unḍédi yémiṭi? appuḍé tsachchi póyináḍu.* Doctor: I have just performed a big operation. Friend: What operation? Doctor: I had to remove a lung and a bowel. Friend: How is the patient now? Doctor: What has that to do with it? He died on the spot.

pélápana, chatter, nonsense; also *prélápanalu. iṭuvanṭi pélápanalu pélacu,* don't talk such nonsense; *iṭuvanti pichchi pélápanalu pélaca nóru músucó,* shut your mouth and don't talk nonsense.

pélica, rag.

péltsuṭa, to fry, to heat, to fire (a gun).

péluṭa, to go off (of a gun). *tupáci péla lédu,* the gun did not go off.

péluṭa, to chatter; also *préluṭa. iṭuvanṭi pélápana pélutú v'unṭé nácu pichchi yetti, vaḷḷu teliyaca yémainá chési pótánu, léchipó,* go away, you are driving me mad with your chatter and I shall do something dreadful.

pému, rattan. *nívu pému alla galavá?* can you plait rattan?

péna, pen. English.

pénníḷḷu, dung-water, from *péḍa,* dung; also *péḍaniḷḷu.* This is a very purifying article. (Old Brahmin woman speaking): *mávàru vidhiló nunchi vachchéṭ appaṭici yedurugunḍá chembedu pénníḷḷu calupucuni veḷḷi, mída pósi, ṣuddhi aina taruváta mari lópalici rán istánu,* I don't let my men-folk into the house till I have mixed a potful of dung-water, poured it over them, and so purified them.

pénu, louse, plural *pélu. ná cuccacu pélu paḍuṭú v'unṭavi,* my dog is full of lice.

pépara, a large bittern, common on the Telugu lakes and tanks.

péparu, newspaper. English. *yenducu péparlu tsadavaḍam? yém undi péparuló?* what is the use of reading the newspapers? What is there in the newspapers?

pérantamu, woman's visit to another woman at marriages and feasts; tittle-tattle. *nívu piluvani pérantamu chéya rádu,* never be unbidden guest on festive occasions; *mimmalin andarini pérantánici pilustú v'unnánu,* I bid you all welcome to our house for the show.

pérconuta, to call, to recount; from *péru,* name.

pértsuta, to string together, to pile.

péru, name. *péru pratishthalu,* name and fame. *cadupuló bidda cadupulóné v'undagá coducu péru Sómalingam,* naming the child before it is born, counting your chickens before they are hatched; *hásyam péru petti nannu anta máta anadam mícu bhávyam éná?* is it right to say such things to me on the plea that it is a joke? *ninnu sukhamugá bratucan ichchina yedala ná péru máru péru pettu,* my name is not A. B. if I let you live in peace. *peddamanishi: ní pér émi? nuvvu yevari pillavádivi? báludu: míru canuccó valen anté rendu márgal unnai. peddamanishi: yémitivi? báludu: míru úhintsu condi, léca póté vichárintsandi.* Gentleman: What is your name? Whose son are you? Boy: If you want to know there are two ways of finding out. Gentleman: What are they? Boy: You may guess or you may inquire. *ní pér evaru?* is as common as *ní pér émi?*

péruconuta, to curdle.

pérupettuta, to set to curdle.

péshcashu, the fixed tax paid by the holder of permanently settled estate. Hindustani. *rázu: í sanvatasaram sarcáru péshcashu pógá mana samasthánam mída yenta lábham vachchiná andi? Crindati nelaló míru cheppináru cáni parácu paddámu. diván: tamacu alágu parácu padadamé dharmam andi; adi Mahárája chihnamu.* Zamindar: What was our net profit on the estate this year after paying the peshcash? You told me last month but it has escaped our memory. Diwan: It is right for such things to escape Your Excellency's memory, it is a sign of high nobility.

péshcáru, an old term for a Revenue Inspector. Hindustani.

péta, suburb, ward, town; very common as the end of the name of a town or word: as *Sómpéta, Arundelpéta.*

pétanapettuta, to attempt. Used in books.

phalacamu, shield. Skt.

phalamu, fruit, profit; also *phalitamu.* Skt. *chettu vésinavád ocadu, phalam anubhavinchinavád ocadu,* one man plants the tree, another enjoys the fruit (*sic vos non vobis*). *phalasáyamu,* produce.

phalavrücshamu, fruit-tree. Skt. *nácu phalavrücshamulu v'unna udyánavanam vacati v'unnadi,* I have an orchard.

phaláháramu, lunch, any light meal. Skt., from *phalam,* fruit, and *áháram,* food. *Lacshmayya: nénu sandhya vártsucuné véla nannu phaláháranici pilavadam Mallayyacu dharmam éná? Vencayya: nuvvu sandhya vártsav ani Mallayyacu telusunu. Lacshmayya: telisiná, nénu sandhya vártsután ani anucódam dharmam cádá?* Smith: Was it nice of Brown to call me to lunch when I was saying my prayers? Jones: He knew you don't say your prayers. Smith: Even if he did, ought not he to have supposed I would be saying my prayers?

phaláni, so-and-so. Hindustani. *phalánivádi pellámun ani mushti yettuconi bratucutundi,* she lives by begging, saying she is so-and-so's wife.

phalintsuta, to be fruitful, to succeed. Skt. *mí córica tappacundá phalistundi,* your wish will doubtless be fulfilled; *mém upadéşinchina mantramu nirvighnamugá phalintsu gáca,* may our charm conquer all obstacles and prove successful; *paira tólité pratti phalintsunu,* a cool breeze brings a good cotton crop.

phalitamu, profit; also *phalamu.* Skt. *cashthé phalí,* profit after work. *cheppin attu chési phalitam yémi zarugutundó tsútámu,* if we act accordingly let us see what we shall gain.

pharavalédu, it doesn't matter. Usually spelt *paraválédu.*

pharishcáramu, decision. Skt. Usually spelt *parischcáramu. adde mátládi pharishcáram cheyyi,* settle the rent.

phasandu, beauty, nice. Hindustani. Usually spelt *pasandu*.
phasanduchéyuṭa, to prefer. *áyana dínini phasandu chésináḍu*, he thought this the nicest.
phálgunamu, the twelth lunar month, March.
picca, calf (of leg). *ná picca balam tsúpa valenu*, I must show my turn of speed.
pichchettuṭa, to go mad. *pichch ettin aṭṭu tiruguts unnáḍu*, he is running amok.
pichchi, pitstsa, mad, wild (of vegetable kingdom), bad (of money, weights, and measures). *pichchi mámiḍi*, wild mango; *pichchi rúpáyi*, a bad rupee; *pichchiv́ána*, useless rain; *pichchi yettuṭa*, to go mad; *nícu pichchi yettinadá yémi?* have you gone mad?
pichchica, sparrow; also *pitstsuca*. *pichchica mída Brahmástramá?* a thunder-bolt to kill a sparrow?
pichchiváḍu, pitstsaváḍu, madman. *pichchivánici lócam anta pichchi*, the madman thinks the whole world mad.
picilipiṭṭa, bulbul.
piḍaca, cow-dung cake.
pidapa, after. *pidapa chénu*, after crop.
piḍi, handle, fist, hilt.
piḍiceḍu, fistful, handful. *prititó peṭṭinadi piḍiceḍe tsálunu*, a handful is enough if given with love; *yeruca piḍiceḍu dhanamu*, acquaintance is a fistful of money.
piḍicili, fist, grasp. *piḍicili paṭṭuṭa*, to clench the fist.
piḍicóla, plough handle.
piḍiguddu, piḍigruddu, fisticuff.
piḍugu, thunderbolt. *í chevuḍiṭló piḍugulu paḍutú v'unná nácu nidra melacuva rádu*, with this deafness even if thunderbolts fall I shall not wake; *piḍugu vanṭi vartamánam vachchindi*, the news came like a thunderbolt.
piḍutsuṭa, to squeeze. *piṭṭa gontuca piḍutsu*, wring the bird's neck, to be said to your peon when he picks up a snipe you have wounded.
piḍuzu, tick.
pilaca, a young shoot, small root, end of tuft of hair. *í gáḍidalini zuṭṭu pilaca paṭṭuconi y'íḍchi veyyi*, catch this ass by his pigtail and push him out.
pilipintsuṭa, to send for; causative of *piluṭa*, to call.
pilla, the young of any animal including man, a girl, small. *cóḍipilla* is a chick; *cuccapilla*, puppy; *mécapilla*, a kid; *pillalu galaváḍanu*, I am a parent, is a common expression in petitions intended to excite sympathy; *pilla parvatamu* is a small hill, hillock; *pilla dúlamu*, a small beam; *pilla cáluva*, a small channel; *tallini tsúchi pillaní, páḍini tsúchi barrení, tísu có valenu*, choose a girl by her mother, a she-buffalo by its milk; *pilla galaváḍu pillacu yéḍisté, cáṭiváḍu cásucu yéḍchináḍu*, when the father cried for his child, the sexton cried for his money; *puli pilla puli pillé, méca pilla méca pillé*, cub is cub and kid is kid. *ocaḍu: nícu Lacshmayyacu sambandham émiti? incóḍu: nác istán anna pillanu Lacshmayyac ichcháru.* Smith: What's your relationship to Brown? Jones: They gave him the girl they promised me. *illu cálut unḍenu, nippu árput unḍiri. yazamáni: ayyó, dánini racshints anḍi, venṭané racshints anḍi; oca másam ainá ninḍa lédu. nippu árpéváḍu: amma, lópala tsúchánu, pilla léd anḍi. yazamáni: pill emiṭ, ayyá? nippu árpéváḍu: dénini racshintsam annadí? yazamáni: ná goḍugunu, dánini coni másam ainá cá lédu.* The house was burning, they were putting out the flames. Lady of the house: O save it, save it quickly, it isn't a month old. Man putting out the fire: Madam, I looked inside, there is no child there. Lady: Who said anything about a child? Man: What did you ask us to save? Lady: My umbrella. It isn't a month since I bought it. *ocaḍu: Rámayya ishṭam vachchina pillanu peḷḷi chesu cunṭé sari poyédi. incóḍu: atanu inca yenducu brahmachárigá v'unnáḍu? ocaḍu: yé pilla chésucóḍánici ishṭa paḍa lédu.* Smith: Brown would be satisfied to marry any girl he liked. Jones: Why is he still a bachelor? Smith: He hasn't liked to marry any girl.
pillacáya, small boy, child. *pillacáyalacú, piṭacáḷḷacú tsali lédu*, children and stool-legs don't feel the cold.

pillagalavádu, person having children; common in petitions.

pillagróvi, flute.

pillavádu, boy, child. *ticharu: oca cutumbamló talli, tandri pillavádu unnár anucó, yentamandi autáru? báludu: iddaru. ticharu: yetlá? báludu: pillavádini talli yettu cuntundi cábatti.* Teacher: In a family there are father, mother, and child, let us suppose; how many does that make? Boy: Two. Teacher: How two? Boy: Because the mother will hold the child in her arms. *Lacshmayya: mí pillavádu ná mída ráyi visiri vésinádu. Vencayya: adi mícu tagilindá? Lacshmayya: tagala lédu. Vencayya: aité vésinavádu mávádu cádu.* Smith: Your boy threw a stone at me. Jones: Did it hit you? Smith: No. Jones: Then it wasn't my boy.

pillavrélu, little finger.

pilli, cat. *adda góda mída pilli,* a cat on the cross wall (of persons sitting on a fence, double-dealers); *elucacu pilli sácshi,* the cat a witness in the rat's case (interested evidence for the prosecution); *paniléni mátsacamma pilli piticinad ata,* they say when the virago had nothing else to do she milked the cat; *pittá pittá póru pilli tírchin attu,* like a cat settling a dispute between birds (the cat settled it by eating them both); *pilli candlu músu coni, pálu tágutunnu yevarú yerugar ani yentsucon attu,* like the cat who shut her eyes and thought no one could see her drinking the milk (burying your head in the sand); *pillici chelagátamu, yelucacu prána sancatamu,* the cat frisks, the rat dies; *pilli brahma hanta,* kill a cat, kill a Brahmin; *pilli córáduts unnadi,* the cat purrs; *pilli myávu anuts unnadi,* the cat mews.

pillicúna, kitten.

pilupu, a call.

pilutsuta, to call. *prasna: yémi talupu vadda yenta sépu pilichinanu palicinávu cávu? cécalu vési vési gontuca baddalai póyinadi. zavábu: nénu lópala yémó pani sandadiló unnánu, mí pilupu nácu vinabada lédu.* Question: How long am I to bawl at the door without getting any answer? I have burst my lungs with shouting. Answer: I was bustling about inside, I didn't hear you call. *Lacshmayya: nácu ninnati nunchi zabbugá undi. Vencayya: vaidyudini pilichédá? Lacshmayya: jantu vaidyudini pilipintsu. Vencayya: yenducu? jantu vaidyudu yémi canuccó galadú? dáctaru prasna vésté jantuvulu zavábu cheppavu gadá. Lacshmayya: zavábu cheppavu cábatté, jentuvaidyulu prasnal adagacundá rógam canipetta galaru.* Smith: I have been ill since yesterday. Jones: Shall we send for the doctor? Smith: Send for the vet. Jones: Why? What can the vet find out? Animals can't answer questions. Smith: Just so, as animals can't answer questions, the vet has to diagnose the disease without asking questions. *pólisu súparintendentu: atlá poyyé manishini pilu. cánstébilu: áyana manishi cád andi, Sub Inspectar-ugár andi.* Police Superintendent: Call that man who is passing. Constable: That's not a man, that is the Sub Inspector.

pimmata, after.

pina, young; also *pinna.*

pinatalli, mother's younger sister or wife of father's younger brother: aunt; also *pinnamma, pinni.*

pinatandri, father's younger brother, uncle; also *pinnayya.*

pinchanu, pension. English. *pinchan sipáyi,* pensioned sepoy; this is what would be *said*; in a book they might write *upacára vétanam ondi vachchina óca vrüddha bhatudu*—seven words instead of two; *ippudu pinchhan putstsu coné muppai yéll ainadi,* it is thirty years since he took his pension.

pinchhamu, peacock's tail.

pindamu, sacred cake. Skt. It is the oblation that is made to deceased ancestors.

pindamu, embryo. *venuca Condalrdu Pantulu gáru sirastádári chésin appudu garbhálaló pindálu adiri póyévi,* when Kondalrau Pantulu was Sheristadar the foetuses in the womb would tremble.

pindá, sacred cake, same as *pindamu. príti léni cúdu pinda cútiló samamu,* food given without love is like food offered to the dead.

pindári, marauder. It is a Mahratta word for mounted freebooters who used to harry the Telugu country.

pinde, berry.

pinḍi, flour, oil-cake used for manure and for feeding cattle. *pinḍi dra pósin aṭlu vennela cáya tsochchenu*, the moonlight shone like outspread flour; *pinḍi yentó nippaṭi anté*, the cake will be according to the flour (payment by results); *vánini pinḍi pinḍigá danchinádru*, they beat him to a jelly; *pinḍi yeruvucu samánamu*, margosa oil-cake is equal to cattle-manure.

pinḍivanṭalu, cakes.

pinḍuṭa, to press out, to wring.

pingáni, crockery. Mahratta.

pinje, tuck, fold. *í baṭṭalu pinjelu peṭṭu*, fold these cloths.

pinna, young; also *pina*. *pinnapeddalu*, old and young; *pinnaváḍu*, boy; *pinnadi*, girl.

pinnamma, aunt, being mother's younger sister; also *pinatalli*, *pinni*.

pinnatanamu, childhood.

pinnayya, uncle, father's younger brother; also *pinatanḍri*.

pinni, aunt, same as *pinnamma*, *pinataḷḷi*.

pippalamu, pepul tree. Skt.

pippali, pepper. Skt.

pippi, refuse, what is left after you squeeze a fruit, &c. *mí vádamuló vaṭṭi pippiyé, cáni sáram émiyu lédu*, there is no juice in your argument, only refuse.

pirangi, cannon, from *firangi*, Frank. European because the French first introduced artillery.

pirici, cowardly. *pirici banṭucu tummu ástha*, the cowardly soldier will long for a sneeze (as an excuse for stopping); *nádi vaṭṭi pirici svabhávam*, I am a natural coward (as Brahmins will not be ashamed to say).

piricitanamu, cowardice.

piriciváḍu, coward.

piriconuṭa, to twist.

pirralu, buttocks.

piryádu, complaint. Hindustani; same as *firiyádu*.

pisaru, trash, trifle, pinch (e.g. of snuff). *pisaranta lédu*, not an atom.

piśáchamu, ghost, demon.

pisidigoṭṭu, pisinigoṭṭu, miser.

pisṭólu, pistol. English. *donga: ní ḍabb antá istává? léca póté pisṭólutó cálustá? peddamanishi: pisṭólu isté ḍabb antá istá. donga: ḍabbu tisuconi pisṭól icchináḍu. peddamanishi: ná ḍabbu nác istává lécapóté pistólató cálcheda? dongá: ḍabb iyyanu, pistólulú mandu gáni, gundu gáni lédu, nác ém bhayam lédu.* Thief: Give me all your money or I shoot. Gentleman: If you give me your pistol I will give you all my money. The thief takes the money and gives the pistol. Gentleman: Will you give me back my money or shall I shoot? Thief: I won't give the money back. The pistol is not loaded. I am not afraid.

pisucuṭa, pisuguṭa, to squeeze, to massage, to knead. *ná cáḷḷu pisugu*, massage my legs.

pita, father. Skt.

piṭishanu, petition. English; also *peṭishanu*.

pitrárjitamu, acquired by our fathers, ancestral property.

pitrü-, prefix meaning 'ancestral'. *pitrüdévatalu*, ancestral deities; *mátrü-pitrü-bhacti lécunḍá*, without reverence for father or mother; *pitrü-hatya*, parricide.

pitstsa, mad, false (of measures, &c.). *máṭa ghanamu, mánica pitstsa*, big words, short measure; *punyánici puṭṭ eḍ isté pitstsa cuntsam ani pícul ḍḍin aṭṭu*, like complaining of short measure when you have been given a candy gratis (looking a gift-horse in the mouth).

pitstsuca, sparrow; same as *pichchica*.

piṭṭa, bird. *vaca piṭṭató cheppa lédu*, I didn't tell even the birds; *piṭṭa conchem, cúta ghanam*, a little bird with a big cry (much cry, little wool); *piṭṭá piṭṭá póru pilli tírchin aṭṭu*, like the cat that settled the quarrel between the two birds (by eating them both).

pittamu, bile. Skt.

pitucuṭa, to squeeze out, to milk. *pál anniṭini pitucu conḍuru*, they squeeze out all the milk.

pitúri, raid, rebellion, plot, conspiracy. Hindustani; same as *fitúri*.

pículáḍuṭa, to wrangle, to squabble.

pículáṭa, squabble. *váḍu pículáṭa manishi*, he is a quarrelsome man.

píce, pipe, reed used in blowing musical instruments. *gontupíce*, wind-pipe.

pícuṭa, to pull out, to tear out. *náluca 'pícu coni tsachchenu*, he tore out his own tongue and killed himself (bite off your nose to spite your own face).

píḍa, pain, trouble. Skt.

píḍacala, nightmare. *vánici ninna rátri píḍacala vachchi, rommu aḍatsu coni póyi, y'úpiri salapa lédu*, last night he had a nightmare and oppression on the chest and could not breathe.

píḍintsuṭa, to trouble, to plague. Skt.

píḍitamu, afflicted. Skt.

pílicalu, rags. *pílicala guḍḍa caṭṭucunnáḍu*, he wore a ragged cloth.

píltsuṭa, to suck up, to inhale. *nasyam píltsuṭa*, to take snuff.

pínugu, corpse.

pípá, cask.

píru, pir, Muhammedan saint (when he is dead). *náḍu v'unṭé Navábu Sahébu, annamu v'unṭé Amíru Sahébu, bída paḍité Facíru Sahébu, tsasté Píru Sahébu*, if a Muhammedan has land he is a Nawab, if he has enough to eat he is an Amir, if he is poor he is Fakir, if he is dead he is a Pir.

píta, crab.

píṭa, stool; from Skt. *píṭham*. *pillacáyalacú píṭa cáḷḷacú tsali lédu*, children and stool-legs do not feel the cold.

píṭhamu, stool, seat of a svami. *píṭhasṭhuḍu* is one who has the distinction of sitting on a stool, i.e. a svami; most people in India sit on the ground.

píṭhica, preface. Skt.

pítsu, coir or other fibre. *zanapa nára pítsu vale gaḍḍamu*, a beard like hemp fibre.

plíḍaru, pleader. English.

poccati, *poccaṭi-ráḷḷu*, the stones or lumps of earth on which the boiler rests on the Indian hearth; fire-dogs. *váru poccaṭi-ráḷḷa ritigá n'unnáru*, as inseparable as fire-dogs (as thick as thieves).

poccili, navel. *poccili tsúlu*, the offspring of the navel, is Brahma.

poccipóvuṭa, poccuṭa, to blister, to come out (like a boil), to transpire. *ná nóru poccinadi*, my mouth is sore; *mém á pani yenta rahasyamgá zaraginchinámu, yéláginanó conchemu paici poccinadi*, we worked as secretly as possible, but somehow something transpired.

poccu, blister.

poda, bush.

poḍa, appearance, form. *váḷḷa poḍa canapaḍḍ appuḍu*, when they appeared; *dánici ná poḍa cana paḍina trátsu pámunu tsúchin aṭl unḍenu*, when she caught sight of me it was as though she saw a cobra.

poḍacaṭṭuṭa, to appear. *paitya chalanam ain aṭṭu nischayamgá poḍa caṭṭutú v'unnadi*, it seems to be certainly a bilious attack.

poḍamuṭa, to arise.

podarillu, arbour; from *poda*, bush, and *illu*, house. The *r* is euphonic.

poddu, sun, time. *báreḍu poddu yeccin appuḍu*, when the sun was a fathom high; *renḍu gaḍiyala poddu unḍagá*, there being two hours of daylight; *tsála poddu póyinadi*, it is very late; *poddu poḍichenu*, the sun rose; *poddu cruncenu*, the sun set; *poddu putstsuṭa*, to pass the time.

podduna, in the morning; from *poddu*, sun; also *produnna*. *peddamanishi: yenducu yéḍust unnáu? báluḍu: nénu podduṭi nunchi áḍucunṭ unnánu; ivváḷa Ṣucravár̥am ani teliyaca Ṣanivár̥am ani anucunṭ unnanú. ippuḍu nácu Ṣucravár̥am ani cheppäru; mésṭaru coḍatár émó n'ani yéḍust unnánu.* Gentleman: Why are you crying? Boy: I have been playing since the morning; I didn't know it was Friday, I thought it was Saturday; now they have told me it is Friday I am crying because I am afraid teacher will beat me.

poḍi, powder, snuff; also *poḍumu*.

poḍibarine, snuff-box.

poḍugaina, poḍugáṭi, tall, long. *ocaḍu: Lacshmammacu poḍugáṭi ventrucul unnai. incóḍu: tanḍri dvára vachchináya? ocaḍu: tanḍrici baṭṭa talé. incóḍu: baṭṭa tala ainá, sórálanu tayáru chési ammutáḍu*, Smith: Mrs. Brown has very long hair. Jones: Does she get it from her father?

Smith: He is bald. Jones: Though he is bald he sells eels. *ocaḍu: Lacshmayya inta chinna uttaram ráséd éla? incóḍu: Lacshmayya poṭṭiváḍ ani nuvvu yeragavá? ataḍu poḍugáṭi uttaram yeṭla ráya galaḍu?* Smith: How is it Brown writes so short a letter? Jones: Don't you know Brown is short? How could he write a long letter?

podugu, udder. *podugu cósi pálu tágin aṭṭu,* like cutting the udder to drink the milk (killing the goose that lays the golden eggs).

poḍugu, height, length. *poḍugu loḍugu,* tall and weak; the opposite is *poṭṭi gaṭṭi,* short and strong.

poduguṭa, to set (precious stones). *ittaḍini podigité ratnánici yémi lópam?* though you set it in brass the precious stone will shine just the same.

poḍumu, powder, snuff, dust; also *poḍi. tarimiḍi paṭṭin appuḍu rálina poḍum cúḍá v'úrice pó lédu,* he did not even waste the dust that came off the lathe; *oca chiṭice poḍumu véi,* give me a pinch of snuff.

podupu, thrift.

poḍupu catha, riddle.

poḍupu máṭa, taunt.

poḍutsuṭa, to pierce, to sting, to set a seal, to rise (of the sun, &c.), to poke. *télucu pettanam isté tellavárlu anṭa poḍichinadi,* when the scorpion was given power it went on stinging till morning; *mudra poḍutsuṭa,* to seal; *yéru póṭu poḍichinadi,* the tide has risen in the river; *tsalipandiṭi cunḍalacu túṭlu poḍichin aṭlu,* like making holes in the pots in a water-pandal (wanton mischief).

poga, smoke, steam. *pogayóda* is a steamship; *pogabanḍi* a railway engine; *pogatsuṭṭa* a cheroot.

pogaḍta, praise.

pogaḍuṭa, to praise. *í páḍu v'úḷḷó pogiḍéváru léru, nácu néné poguḍu conṭán annáḍ aṭa,* there is no one to praise me in this deserted village, so I praise myself, he said; *míru nannu v'úrice poguḍutu v'unnáru,* you are paying me empty compliments.

pogaru, pride. *mana tálucáló caranálu mahá pogar ecci v'unnáru,* the karnams of our taluk are full of pride; *pogar anatsuṭa* is to reduce pride; *córṭuló cúḍá vyájyálu véyinchi, vári pogaru anatsanḍi,* reduce their pride by bringing cases against them in the courts (this is the origin of many false cases in India).

pogarubótu, proud or vain man. *váḍu pogarubótu vedhava,* he is a conceited ass.

pogarubótutanamu, pride.

pogatsuṭṭa, cigar.

pogatsúrúṭa, to be smoked.

pogayóḍa, steamship; from *poga,* steam, and *óḍa,* ship.

pogácu, tobacco; from *poga,* smoke, and *ácu,* leaf.

poguḍu, flattery. *peṭṭu tsuṭṭamu, poguḍu bhágyam,* relations will flock for food, flattery brings fortune.

poguluṭa, to grieve.

poi, hearth; also written *póyi* or *poyyi. nícu múrchha póvaḍam y'ishṭangá v'unn aṭṭ aité, lópalici póyi, poi cáḍa nippulónó niḷḷalónó múrchcha pó,* if you want to faint go inside and faint near the hearth in fire or water.

polamu, field. *nénu má guruvu gári tsaduvu conéṭ appuḍu doḍḍi tavvi, sanvatsárinici cá valasina cúralu panḍinché váḍini; y'iddaru cúliváḷḷu moyya léni múṭalanu polamló nunchi paṭṭu coni vachchi y'inṭi cáḍa vappaginchévánni; marri áculu cósi techchi vistaḷḷu cuṭṭévánni; y'inṭló panul anni néné chésevánni; áyana anugraham vachchi, tírubadigá v'unn appuḍu renḍu muccalu cheppévádu; voccocc appuḍu adí lédu,* when I was reading with my guru I used to dig in his garden and provide vegetables for the whole year; I used to bring from the fields loads two coolies could not carry; I used to cut banyan leaves and stitch leaf platters; I did all the house-work; when he deigned and had leisure he would teach me a verse or two; sometimes not even that.

poliméra, inter-village boundary.

pollu, empty (of ears), worthless. *súdrunacu engili y'annamunu, chinigina baṭṭalunu, pollu dányamunu, jírnamulaina duppaṭulanu iyya valenu,* the proper gift to a Sudra is bad rice, torn clothes, grain with empty ears, worn-out sheets (whereas of course a Brahmin should have the best of everything. This is a text from the Hindu scriptures).

polusu, fish-scale. *vádu chépanu polusu poyyéṭ aṭṭu cadiginádu,* he washed the scales off the fish.

pommu, go; imperative of *póvuta*; *pó* is commoner, but *pomm* is used for euphony before a vowel. *úru pomm anṭundi, cádu ramm anṭundi,* (when you are going to die) the village says 'go', the graveyard says 'come'.

pon-, prefix meaning 'golden'; from *ponnu,* gold. Tamil. *pombaṭṭu,* cloth of gold.

ponaca, rattan grain-basket. *ponaca végiram alli peṭṭinánu,* I quickly put together a grain-basket.

ponaráruṭa, to be fine, to be agreeable. Used in books.

ponchivunduṭa, to lie in lurk. *Cóyaváḷḷu ponchi v'unḍi, níḷḷu méghamulu tágaḍánici cunḍalaló dúri, níḷḷu tágutú v'unn appuḍu, tsaṭucunna múta vési, cunḍa cinda manṭa peṭṭi, méghalanu vanḍu cuni tinṭáru,* the Koyyis (Godavari Agency hill tribe) lie in lurk for the clouds, and when the clouds come to drink and get into their pots and are drinking they suddenly put lids on them and put fire under the pots and cook the clouds and eat them (the physics of the Godavari Brahmins are somewhat mythological).

pondica, fitness, intercourse. *á daya dácshinyal émi, á máṭa pondica yémi!* what grace and elegance, what curious felicity of phrase!

pondu, intercourse; also sexual intercourse. *peddalató vádu, petarulató pondu,* disputing with the old, keeping company with ghosts (things to be avoided); *alancarintsu coni vachchi, dípamu veluturuna páḍutú v'unṭé, dáni mogam anta cantacu marinta andamugá canapaḍutú v'unḍédi; taruváta dáni pondu yenta sukhamugá v'unṭundó uni buddhi puṭṭind aṭa,* he was attracted first by the dancing-girl's beauty as she sang, richly adorned, in the light of the lamps; then he is said to have longed for the joys of sexual intercourse with her.

ponduṭa, to get. *avamánamu pondináḍu,* he incurred disgrace; *nashṭamu pondináḍu,* he incurred loss. Also *onduṭa.*

pongu, bubbling over, overflowing with joy, eruption of measles or chicken-pox (*taṭṭammavári pongu*).

ponguṭa, pongiporluṭa, to bubble over. *esaru pongi pótunnadi,* the rice-water is boiling over; *ní santósham anta pongi porli pótú v'unnadi,* you are bubbling over with joy.

ponnu, gold. *bangáramu* is commoner; this is the Tamil word.

pontsu, crouch, lurking. *yelucacu pilli pontsu vésin aṭṭu,* like a cat crouching for a rat; *pontsunḍé donga,* eaves-dropper.

pontsunḍi tsútsuṭa, to lie in wait.

pontsunḍi vinuṭa, to eavesdrop.

pontsuṭa, to lurk.

pora, layer, fold, film over the eye, cataract. Strata of soil or the skins of an onion are *poralu. nívu canṭici poralu tíya galavá?* can you couch the eye?

porabáṭaina, mistaken.

porabáṭu, mistake. *móṭáru banḍi cóḍi míduga póyi, dánini tsampenu. draivaru: ná valla porabáṭu zarigindi, mí cóḍi tsachchi póyindi, í padi rúpáyalu tísu coni yevaritó ripórṭu cheyya bócu. grámasthuḍu: cheppanu lenḍi, íca nunchi nénu cóḷḷanu eccuvagá pentsut unṭánu, míru í dóvana veḷḷut unḍandi,* a car goes over a fowl and kills it. Driver: My mistake, I have killed your fowl; here's Rs. 10, and make no report. Villager: I won't report it; in future I shall keep more fowls, and hope you will be coming this way.

poraca, blade of grass; commonly *paraca.*

poracacaṭṭa, broom.

poraláḍuṭa, porli porli unḍuṭa, to roll over, to overflow. *á callu cunḍa porli porli unnadi,* that toddy-pot is flowing over.

poralintsuṭa, to roll over. *máṭa porlinchináḍu,* he changed his statement; *nippuló poralinchin aṭlu manasu paratapintsuṭa,* to grieve as if rolling in fire.

porambócu. Hindustani. Waste or reserved land. Technically in the revenue department it is not used of waste land but only of land reserved for the common use of the villagers;

but the public use it of any uncultivated land.

porapaḍuṭa, to be mistaken. *bhárya: micu ná mída púrva préma lédu, nénu vanṭa chést unṭé míru tsústú úrucunṭáru. bharta: nuvvu porapaḍut unnáu, nuvvu vanṭa cheyyaḍam modalu peṭṭin daggira nunchí, ní mída préma marinta eccuv aindi, vanṭaváḍi khartsu taggi póyindi,* Wife: You do not love me as before, you let me do all the cooking. Husband: You are mistaken; since you began cooking my love for you has grown stronger; I save the cook's wages.

porapáṭu, mistake; same as *porabáṭu.*

porláḍuṭa, to roll. *puṭṭeḍ ámudamu paṭṭintsu coni porláḍiná, anṭédé anṭunu gáni, anṭanidi anṭadu,* though a man smear a candy of castor oil over himself and roll, only what sticks will stick, what won't stick won't (fatalistic proverb).

porluṭa, to roll, to bubble, to cross, to tup (animals). *porli, porli,* bubbling over; *poṭṭélu gorrenu porlinadi,* the ram tupped the ewe.

porugu, vicinity. *porugiḷḷu,* the next house; *iruguporugulu,* neighbours; *poruguváḍu,* the man next door. *porugu patstsagá v'unṭé poyiló niḷḷu pósucun aṭṭu,* like the man who put out his own hearth-fire because his neighbour prospered (envy). *Rangaḍu: í yéḍu mícu varsham bágá curisindá? Rámuḍu: curisindi gáni, má poruguváḍici eccuva varsham paḍḍadi. Rangaḍu: ad eṭlá? Rámuḍu: váḍici ná canṭé eccuva bhúmi v'undi.* Smith: Did you get good rain this year? Jones: Yes, but my neighbour got more. Smith: How so? Jones: He's got more land.

porugúriváḍu, man from next village. *úriváḍici cáṭi bhayam, porugúriváḍici níṭi bhayam,* the villager is afraid to walk through the graveyard, the man from the next village is afraid to walk through the tank (he does not recognize the graveyard and does not know how deep the tank is).

posagintsuṭa, to persuade; causal of *posaguṭa.*

posaguṭa, to get on together. *várici várici posaga lédu,* they don't get on; *manam y'iddaramu vacca y'inṭló v'unḍaḍam posagadu,* we cannot get on together in one house.

poṭapoṭa, gushing, swelling; onomatopoeic, of drops, tears, &c.

poṭlamu, packet.

poṭṭa, belly. *vaṭṭi máṭala valla poṭṭalu púḍutavá?* words don't fill the belly; *vindu bhójanamló oca báluḍu tsálá tinṭ unḍenu. peddamanishi: inca tina bócu, ajírnam chéstundi; inta chinna caḍupuló anta annam yeṭlá paṭṭindi? báluḍu: ná poṭṭa baiṭici canapaḍéṭ anta chinnadi cád anḍi.* At a feast a boy ate a lot. Gentleman: Don't eat any more, you will get indigestion. How can you get so much food into so small a stomach? Boy: My belly is not as small as it looks from outside. *nívu poṭṭa baddal ayyéṭ aṭṭugá cheḍa tinnáu,* you have eaten till your belly bursts; *núru rúpáyalu Bráhmala poṭṭa peṭṭi páḍu chésináru,* they have wasted a hundred rupees on filling the bellies of Brahmins.

poṭṭa, unopened ear of grain. *poṭṭacu puṭṭ eḍu níru,* a bushel of water for each ear of paddy. This proverb illustrates the erroneous view of the Telugus that paddy can never have too much water. If they have water to spare, they always spoil their paddy by using too much.

pottamu, book; for *pustacamu.*

poṭṭélu, ram.

poṭṭi, short. *poṭṭi gaṭṭi,* short and strong; the opposite is *poḍugu,* tall, long; *poḍugu loḍugu,* tall and weak.

poṭṭipótarázu, King Little. *poṭṭipótarázu coluvu* is a proverbial expression for a court which has a bad time of it, as the little king found fault with his retinue whatever it did. If they went behind him he complained they were treating him as a pariah; if they went in front he complained they were trying to show superiority to him; if they went by his side he complained they were claiming equality with him.

poṭṭiváḍu, short man. *poṭṭiváḍici puṭṭ eḍu buddhulu,* short men are full of sense.

poṭṭu, husk, scale. *poṭṭu poṭṭugá,* in

scales; *á rógi ṣaríram poṭṭ údi pótundi*, the patient's skin comes off in scales.

pottu, friendship, having in common. *póru nashṭam, pottu lábham*, quarreling means loss, friendship means profit; *pottula magaḍu puchchi tsachchenu*, the joint husband died of neglect; *vídhulu andarici pottu*, the streets are free to all (but pariahs are not allowed in Brahmin streets); *sarculu pottuna connáru*, they made a joint investment in merchandise.

poyi, poyyi, hearth; also *poi. poyyi áristé bandhuvulu, cuccalu cústé caruvu*, a singing hearth portends relations, a barking dog a famine; *poyyi v'údin ammacu bocc eḍ ainá daccadá?* won't she who blows the fire get a mouthful? *porugu patstsagá v'unṭé poyiló níḷḷu pósu conn aṭṭu*, he put out his own fire to spite his neighbour's face; *caṭṭe vanca poyyi tirustunnadi*, the hearth takes the bend out of a stick (i.e. the funeral pyre, and nothing else, will make a crooked man straight).

poyya, poyyé, bad. *poyyé cálam* is a common expression for a bad time. *nícu poyya cálam vachchinadi*, your bad time has come; *alá abaddhálu cheppaḍánici í gumástálacu yémi poyyé cálam vachchindi?* what devil has been at these clerks to make them tell such lies about me?

póca, areca nut, taken with betel. *aḍacattilóni póca*, like a nut between the nippers (between anvil and hammer); *rúca léni váḍu póca cheyya lédu*, a man without oof is not worth a spoof. The *tamalapáculu*, betel leaves, and *póca checcalu*, bits of areca nut, together are called *támbúlam*.

pócaḍa, going; verbal noun of *póvuta*. *vána rácaḍa, prána pócaḍa yevarici teliyadu*, the coming of rain, the going of life, are known to no one. *pócalu* is used of evil ways.

pócillamári, fop, affected puppy, minx.

póciri, blackguard, lewd fellow of the baser sort, obscene. In the plural, *póciḷḷu*, it also means whims, naughtiness. *nívu yé póciḷḷu póyiná, caḷḷu peṭṭu cuni tsútsu v'unṭánu*, I will keep my eyes open whatever tricks you are up to. *póciri máṭa* is an obscene word.

pócu, don't; from *póvuṭa*, to go, more often *bócu*.

póḍimi, thrift, wealth, comfort. *magapóḍimi yeruganidi*, a girl who has not known man.

pógá, besides; from *póvuṭa*, to go. *tamacu cá valasinavi póga migilinavi basa digina y'inṭiváḷlacu y'ichchi véstáru*, (clerks at Jamabandi) leave the remains of the supplies (besides what they want for themselves) to the friends who put them up.

pógauṭa, to collect; from *pógu*, heap. *téne v'unna tsóṭa y'ígalu póg'autavi*, flies collect where honey is.

pógottuṭa, to drive away, to lose; from *póvuṭa*, to go, and *coṭṭuṭa*, to beat. *Crístu tana pránamun ichchi mana pápamulanu pógoṭṭináḍu*, Christ gave his life and drove away our sins; *bhárya cópam pógotti ṣántunni chéstundi*, a wife drives away our anger and makes us mild. *pólísuváḍu: abbáyi yéḍava bócu, mí inṭicé tísucu pótunnánu. baluḍu: ná cósam nénu yéḍavaḍam lédu, má amma cósam yéḍust unnánu, má amma nannu yeppuḍu pógottu có lédu*, Policeman: Don't cry, little man, I will take you straight home. Boy: I am not crying for myself but for my mother. She has never lost me before.

pógu, heap, stack, crowd.

pógu, thread, ring. *muccupógu*, nose-ring. *pógu* by itself is a male earring.

póguchéyuṭa, to collect. *manam tellavárагaṭla léchi, y'inṭinṭici tirigi, baṭṭal anni pógu chésinámu*, (dhoby speaking) we got up early, went from house to house, and collected all the clothes.

póle, like.

pólica, imitation, resemblance, simile. *Lacshmayya: itani v'upamanálu vinṭé nácu gunḍelu pagulutú v'unnavi. Vencayya: viḍi páḍu pólicalu tsúsṭé nácu tala noppi véstu v'unnadi*, (lecturer making comparisons) Smith: I am fed up with this man's comparisons. Jones: His tiresome similes give me a headache; *váḍu coḍḍiló antá tanḍri pólica*, he is his father in miniature.

pólina, like.

póliyunna, identical.

pólísu, police. English.

pólísucanishṭébulu, pólísuváḍu, policeman. English. *Pólísusṭéshanu* police-station. English. *nívu pólísu-sṭéshanucu veḷḷi végiram vaca canishṭé-bulunu tísu cuni rá*, go to the police-station and fetch a constable quickly; *y'í v'úḷḷó y'intamandi pitstsaváḷḷu báhátangá tirugutú v'unṭé, paṭṭu có cunḍá pólísuváru yémi chéstu v'unnáru?* why are the police allowing so many lunatics at large in this village? *meji-sṭrétu: maḷḷí vachcháválá? ná vadda íca midata rá vadd ani nénu cheppa lédá? donga: míru cheppär ani cheppiná, vinacunḍá pólísu váḷḷu nannu aresṭu chési tísucu vachchár anḍi*, Magistrate: Back again? Didn't I tell you never to let me see your face again? Thief: Though I told the police you had said that, they wouldn't listen and arrested me and brought me here; *mótárubanḍi pólísuvánini samípintsuts unḍagá lópala cúrtsunna bhárya y'oca vaipucunu, bharta y'incoca vaipucunu chétulu tsú-pinchiri. pólísu consṭébilu: mír iddaru cheri y'oca dárini veḷḷa talatsu connárá?* as the motor-car approached a policeman the wife put out her hand on one side, the husband on the other. Constable: Are you two thinking of going different ways?

pólucarra, carriage pole. English 'pole' and Telugu *carra*, stick.

póluṭa, to be fit, to be like.

pólutsuṭa, to compare.

póni, like. Short for *pólina*. Used in books.

póni, participle of *póvuṭa*, to go; used as a negative; *lénipóni*, not existing, fictitious.

póní, let it go; from *póvuṭa*, to go, and *itstsuṭa*, to give; very common in the sense of 'go on'. *vachchéd ellá ráni, poyyéd ellá póni,* let things come and let things go; *póni, ḍabbu póté póyindi,* never mind, if the money is gone it is gone; *póni*, (to bandyman) drive on; *póni* or *póniddu* (to objector), very well.

póráḍuṭa, to fight.

póráni, where you should not go, forbidden. *póráni tsóṭlacu póté, ráráni nindalu ráca mánavu,* if you go where you shouldn't, you will get blame you would wish to avoid.

póru, strife. *póru nashṭam, poitu lá-bham*, you lose by fighting and gain by friendship; *piṭṭá piṭṭá póru pilli tírchin aṭṭu*, like the cat settling the birds' strife (by eating them both).

póruṭa, to strive.

póshacuḍu, patron.

póshanamu, support, patronage.

póshintsuṭa, to support, to patronize. *voḷḷu dátsucócunḍá pani chési, sampá-dinchi, andarini póshistánu,* I will not spare myself but work and earn money and support them all.

pósṭu, post. English. *yazamáni: utta-rálu pósṭuló véṣává? naucaru: véṣán anḍi, aité mír oca porabáṭu chéṣáru, aná chíṭi anṭintsa valasina uttaránici renḍ anála chíṭi anṭincháru, renḍ análu an-ṭintsa valasina dánici aná chíṭi anṭin-cháru. yazamáni: aité nuvvu yém chéshávu? naucaru: aḍresulu coṭṭ ési, oca dánidi incó dáni mida vráṣánu.* Mistress: Did you post the letters? Servant: Yes, but you made a mistake, you put a penny stamp on the one that required twopence and a twopenny stamp on the one that required a penny. Mistress: What did you do? Servant: I struck off the addresses and exchanged them.

póté, unless; from *póvuṭa*, to go.

póté, less (in subtraction); from *pó-vuṭa*, to go.

póté, if it goes. *udyógam purusha lac-shanam, adi póté, avalacshanam,* office makes the man, if he loses it he loses his honour.

póté, if it isn't. *unṭé v'úru, póté páḍu,* the people make the village, if they aren't there it is a ruin.

póṭi, competition. *Hiṭlaru gáru caḍa-china adhyacshuni-yennicalaló Hin-ḍembúrgu gáritó póṭi chési y'óḍi póyi-náru,* Hitler stood against Hindenburg at the last presidential election and was defeated; *renḍu bassulu occa mani-shini yeccintsu có ḍánici póṭi paḍḍai,* two buses competed for one passenger.

póṭi, like; from *póli*; short for *pólina*, resembling. *nápóṭi váḍu*, a man like me.

póṭigáḍu, rival.

póṭláḍuṭa, to quarrel. *iddaru pillalu póṭlaḍut unḍiri. peddamanishi: úru-conḍi, yenducu póṭláḍutáru? modaṭi* *pilla: ní cósamé. peddamanishi: ná cósam póṭláṭa yenducu? modaṭi pilla-váḍu: nícu gáḍidec unna telivi ainá léd ani váḍ anṭé, nénu v'und annánu; andu chéta póṭláṭa vachchindi.* Two boys were quarrelling. Gentleman: Keep quiet, what are you fighting about? First boy: About you. Gentleman: How about me? First boy: He said you hadn't even the brains of an ass, I said you had; that is what the quarrel was about; *áulú áulú póṭláḍité, légala cáḷḷu virugutavi*, when the cows fall out the calves' legs are broken (when the great fall out the poor suffer).

póṭláṭa, quarrel.

póṭu, blow, flow. *górutsuṭṭu pai rócaṭi póṭu*, the blow of a pestle on a corn; *cappacu cáṭu, Brahmanunici póṭu lédu*, frogs can't bite, Brahmins don't fight; *venacacu veḷḷité tannu, mundu vasté póṭu*, a kick if you go back, a blow if you come forward; *catti póṭu tappiná, calam póṭu tappadu*, the pen is mightier than the sword (the sword may miss but the pen doesn't).

-pótu, suffix turning other parts of speech into personal nouns (masculine). *tágubótu*, drunkard; *tinḍibótu*, glutton; *vadurubótu*, chatterbox.

pótu, male of animals, birds, insects, plants; tom. *énubótu*, male buffalo; *mécapótu*, ram; *pótuṭiga*, male fly; *pótuṭénugu*, male elephant; *pótutáḍu*, male palm-tree; *pótupilla*, any young male animal; *pótupilli* (or *ganḍupilli*), tom-cat.

póṭupáṭu, ebb and flow.

póvuṭa, to go; also a negative auxiliary; also to be lost. *pai paḍḍa máṭa, maḍi(mída) paḍḍa niḷḷu pótavá?* a word let fall against your honour, water let flow over the field, will not be without effect; *ataḍ ém ai póyináḍu?* what has become of him? *váḍu dánitó póyináḍu*, he has had sexual intercourse with her; *Lacshmayya: nénu ivváḷa renḍu tsóṭlacu póyinánu. ná goḍugu renḍó tsóṭa póyi v'unṭundi. Vencayya: modaṭi tsóṭané póyind émó? Lacshmayya: accaḍa pódu, modaṭi tsóṭa nác adi doricindi*, Smith: I went to two places to-day, I must have lost my umbrella in the second of them. Jones: Why not in the first? Smith: It was in the first I picked it up. *vaidyuḍu: gumpul unna tsóṭici pó vaddu, ní árógyam cheḍi pótundi. rógi: póca póté ná vrütti ságad andi. vaidyuḍu: ní vrütti yémiṭi? rógi: jébu dongatanam*, Doctor: Don't go into crowds, it will ruin your health. Patient: My profession requires me to go into crowds. Doctor: What is your profession? Patient: Picking pockets. In the above example, *póvaddu* is 'don't go', *cheḍi pótundi* is 'will go', 'be lost', *póca* is the negative, 'not going', and *póté* is the negative auxiliary and means 'unless'. *nác ém ichchi pó lédu*, he has given me nothing; *aṭuvanṭi durabhyásam nícu póyindá?* have you lost that bad habit? *tsachchi póyináḍu*, he died; *báci téri* (or *téli*) *pótundi*, the debt will be cleared; *rúpáyi póyindi*, I have lost a rupee; *accaḍici póḍámu*, let us go there; *váni tanḍri póyina taruváta*, after his father's death; *vána póyina taruváta*, when the rain had stopped; *pustacamu póyinadi*, the book is lost; *váni canḍlu póyinavi*, he has lost his eyesight; *chillulu póyina chembu*, a leaking mug; *paḍinṭiló nálugu póté áru*, four from ten is six; *vráya póté vadd annáḍu*, when I was about to write he told me not to; *á góḍa paḍi póyinadi*, the wall has fallen down; *rácapóyenu*, he did not come; *vachchina dóvané pótundi*, lightly come, lightly go (it goes the way it came); *iyyapóvuṭa*, to offer; *veḷḷipóvuṭa*, to go away.

póyina, last (month, year); lost. *póyina váramu*, last week; *póyina canṭici mandu vésté v'unna cannu v'úḍtsu coni póyinadi*, when he applied a remedy to his lost eye he lost the other (throwing good money after bad).

póyuṭa, to pour, with many derivative meanings. *cheṭṭu peṭṭinaváḍu niḷḷu poyyadá?* when you have planted a tree won't you water it? *pálu pósi penchiná pámu caravaca mánadu*, a snake will bite you though you pour out milk for it (a viper nourished in the bosom); *nácu vaḷḷ antá chemaṭa pósindi*, I was all of a sweat; *vánici y'incá ammavávru póya lédu*, he has never had small-pox; *catta pósindru*, they built a bank; *ácu pósindru*, they transplanted rice; *góda petti maduru pósinádu*, he built a wall with a coping over it; *utstsa póyuta* is to make water; *vada-póyuta* is to strain rice; *uripóyuta* is to cast a noose; *ná usuru pósuconnádu*, he injured me; *chinnadi vánici nillu póst unnadi*, the girl is giving him his bath; *amé chetlacu nillu póst unnadi*, she is watering the shrubs; *bitstsam etti potta pósucunt unnádu*, he fills his belly by begging.

pra-, prefix meaning 'great', 'very'. Skt.

prabalamu, very strong. Skt. *idi bahu prabalamaina pitstsa*, a violent form of madness; *prabala pramánam tsúputánu*, I will give a strong proof.

prabalintsuta, to swell, to increase.

prabandhacarta, prabandhacárudu, author, prose writer. Skt. *oca-noca Húna vachana prabandhacárudu*, a certain European prose writer (Hun is applied to Europeans as being barbarous).

prabandhamu, book. Skt.; the common word is *pustacamu*.

prabba, rattan; also *pému*. *yéti varadacu vangi y'unna prabba tígalu mélu pondunu, yeduta nilichi y'unna máculu chétu pondunu*, rattan twigs which yield to the flood survive, trees which stand up to it are destroyed.

prabha, light, radiance. Skt. Used in books.

prabhanjanamu, wind. Skt. Used in books for *gáli*.

prabhavamu, birth. Skt. Used in books. *janmamu* is the common word.

prabhátamu, dawn. Skt.; from *prabha*, light.

prabhávamu, might, majesty, dignity, power, merit. Skt. *nívu y'inta tsaduvu tsaduvucunná, nícu y'incá guptá dána prabhávamu bódha pada lédu*, though you are so learned you have not yet learnt the merit of hidden gifts.

prabhubhacti, loyalty. Skt.; from *prabhuvu*, lord, and *bhacti*, devotion.

prabhudróhamu, treachery.

prabhutvamu, power, sovereignty. Skt.

prabhuvu, lord, king. Skt. But a Collector is even more than this to his peons; he is a *náprobhó*, great lord. The feminine is *prabhvi*.

prabódhamu, wisdom, great intellect. Skt. Used in books.

pracaranamu, chapter of book. Skt.

pracatana, notification, advertisement. Skt.

pracatintsuta, to notify, to advertise. Skt.

pracándamu, trunk (of tree). Skt.; the common word is *bóde*.

pracáramu, pracáramugá, accordingly. Skt. *á pracáram chésinádu*, he acted accordingly. *Lacshmayya, Vencayya iddaru annadamulu; tandri villu vrási tsachchi póyenu; villu pracáram ásti pantsu códánici pótláta vachchenu; annadammul iddaru Mallayyanu madhyavartigá pettu coniri. Mallayya: ná tírpu idi, Lacshmayyacu ástini cheri sagamugá pantsadánici adhicáram ichchánu. Lacshmayya: nyayam cheşáru. Mallayya: tana y'ishtam vachchina bhágam tánu tísucódánici Vencayyacu adhicáram ichchánu. Vencayya: nyayam cheşáru.* John and Richard Doe were two brothers; their father made his will and died; there was a dispute about dividing the property according to the will; the brothers chose Roe as arbitrator. Roe: I decide that John is to divide the property in two parts equally. John: A Daniel come to judgement. Roe: I give Richard power to choose whichever part he likes. Richard: A Daniel come to judgement.

pracáşamu, light, splendour. Skt.

pracáşintsuta, to shine. Skt.

pracca, side; also *pacca*.

prachandamu, fierce. Skt.

prachára, propagandist. Skt.

pracháramu, custom, propaganda. Skt. The word means 'going' in Skt.; it has been taken up by the newspapers to translate propaganda.

prachchhanamu, private. Skt. Used in books. *rázu Smittanu máru pérító vachchi y'Inglandu déşamunu prachchhanna vrüttini pravéşinchenu*, the king entered England incognito under the name of Smith.

pracrütamu, present. Skt. *pracrüta cáryamu*, the present business.

pracrüti, nature, the world. Skt. Temperament (in medicine).

pradacshinamu, circumambulation. Skt. Used of walking round a temple, &c.; you have to walk round by the right (*dacshinam*).

-pradamu, suffix meaning 'giving'. Skt. *sukhapradamu,* health-giving; *jayapradamu,* giving victory.

pradarṣanamu, show, exhibition. Skt. *pradarṣana ṣála* is an exhibition room; *chitra vastu pradarṣana ṣála* is a paraphrase for museum; *pradarṣana polamu* is a translation of demonstration field.

pradéṣamu, place. Skt.

pradhánamu, chief. Skt. *pradhánamaina acshépana,* the principal objection; *váriló pradhánamaina vánini pilu,* call the chief man amongst them; *ippuḍ anniṭicini ḍabbu pradhánamu,* money is now the all-in-all.

pradhánamu, betrothal. Skt. *ná cumartenu Crüshnunici pradhánamu chésinánu,* I have betrothed my daughter to Krishna.

pradhánanamantri, Chief Minister. Skt. A compound adopted by the newspapers when the post of Chief Minister, Madras, came into existence.

pradhánavimarṣana, examination-in-chief. Skt. A compound adopted by the Telugu translator to Government when he had to translate this legal term.

pradháni, the queen in chess. Skt.

pradóshamu, evening. Skt.

pragnya, intelligence. Skt. *ní pragnya tsútámu,* we will test your intelligence. *pragnyavantuḍu* means a man of parts.

pragnyalu, boasts. Skt. *Uttara cumára pragnyalu,* the boasts of Uttara. This was Virata's son, who offered to attack the Kurus in the Mahabharata, but his courage failed him.

prahasanamu, mirth, a farce. Skt.

praháramu, blow. Skt.

prahlódamu, great joy. Skt.

prajá, people. Skt. In Telugu *prazalu*; *prajá* is used in the Skt. proverb, *yadhá rájá tadhá prajá,* as the king, so the people.

prajápati, Lord of Men, the Creator, Brahma; also his spiritual sons, such as Vasishtha.

prajvalintsuṭa, to burn, to shine. Skt. A book word.

prakhyáti, fame. Skt.

praḷayamu, destruction. Skt. A book word. Used in philosophy of periodic world-destruction, cosmic regression.

pralápamu, prattle, nonsense. Skt. *strílu cámam jéyintsa lér anna máṭa unmatta pralápamugá n'unnadi,* that women cannot conquer their lust is lunatic chatter.

pramadamu, joy. Skt. Used in books. *pramadavanamu,* pleasure-grounds.

pramattamu, very drunk. Skt. Used in books.

pramádamu, accident, danger. Skt. *iddaru vartacamló bhágasthulugá chéri láyaru chéta dastavézu vráyinchiri. láyaru: incá vaca vishayam chérts ále. modaṭi vartacuḍu: yémiṭadi? láyaru: divála zarigité gáni, agni pramádam vasté gáni, yémi cheyy'ál énó vráya lédu. renḍó vartacuḍu: á sandarbhamló lábham cheri sagangá pantsu có valen ani ráyanḍi.* Two business partners are having a deed drawn up by a lawyer. Lawyer: We must add one thing. First merchant: What? Lawyer: We must provide for the contingency of bankruptcy or accident by fire. Second merchant: In those cases we will share the profits equally; *pramádacara sthiti,* dangerous condition.

pramánamu, proof, rule, standard of truth, authority. Skt. *manacu Ṣástramu pramánamu,* the Shastras are our standard of truth; *nénu ṣruti smrüti pramánalató amóghamaina vádam chéstánu,* I will advance a conclusive argument from the scriptures; *Puráṇálu parama pramánálu,* the Puranas are the best authority; *inta canṭenú prabala pramánamu tsúputánu,* I will produce an even stronger proof; *pratyacsha pramánamu,* ocular demonstration.

pramánamu, oath. Skt. This is the common meaning of *pramánam* in Telugu. The court oath is: *dévun yedaṭa nizam chepputánu, anta nizam chepputánu, abaddhamu cheppanu,* I will tell the truth, the whole truth and nothing but the truth, so help me God.

pramida, oil-saucer of the primitive lamp.

pramódamu, joy. Skt. Used in books and newspapers.

pramódintsuṭa, to rejoice. Skt.

pramóshanu, promotion. English.

pramṣári nóṭu, promissory note. English.

pramukhuḍu, leader, chief man. Skt.

pranayamu, love, friendship. Skt. *pranayacópamu*, lovers' quarrels.

prapanchamu, world. Skt. *áyana léca póté nácu prapanchamé lédu*, he is all the world to me; *prapancham anta páḍai póyindi*, the whole world is out of joint; *váni bháryayé vánici prapancham*, his wife is all-in-all to him; *báluḍu: nánná, manam í prapanchamuló ittarulacu saháyam chéyaḍánice v'unnám ani ṭicharu cheppáru. tanḍri: á sangati nizamé. báluḍu: aité itarul enduc unnáru?* Boy: Father, teacher said we were in this world to help others. Father: Quite true. Boy: Then what are the others there for? *upanyásacuḍu: prapanchamlóc ellá goppa upanyásacul evaru? sabhicuḍu: nénu chepputá gáni, mí pér evaró cheppanḍi.* Lecturer: Who is the greatest lecturer in the world? Voice from the audience: I did not catch your name. *ḍácṭaru: í prapanchamló má vanṭi vaidyulac endaró ṣatruvul unṭáru. rógi: incó lócamló incá yeccuvamandi ṣatruvul unṭáranḍi.* Doctor: Physicians like myself have so many enemies in this world. Patient: More in the next, doctor.

praphulla, blooming. Skt.

prasacti, topic. Skt.

praṣamsa, topic, mention. Skt.

praṣamsintsuṭa, to mention. Skt.

prasangamu, conversation. Skt. *miló míru chésu cunna prasangam antá nénu bágá vinnánu*, I overheard all your conversation; *y'í prasangam ikha tsálintsu*, stop that talk.

prasangintsuṭa, to hold forth.

prasannamu, clear, bright. Skt.

prasarintsuṭa, to extend. Skt.

praṣastamu, excellent. Skt. *praṣastamaina sanna biyyam*, a fine rice.

prasavamu, parturition, confinement. Skt. *rátri prasavam ai*, having been confined in the night.

prasavavédana, throes of childbirth.

prasádamu, food presented to a god and then distributed (there is much contention as to who should get the *prasádam* first). Skt.

prasádintsuṭa, to bestow, to vouchsafe. Skt. *áme bhartacu ṣubhamulu prasádintsuṭacu Bhagavantuni prártinchenu*, she prayed God to vouchsafe blessings to her husband; *púrvamu unna Y'Iṣvaruḍé y'ippuḍ unnáḍu, púrvalac ichchina buddhiné y'ippaṭivárici prasádinchi y'unnáḍu*, the old God still exists, he bestows on the present generation the same intelligence as he bestowed on those of old.

prasiddhi, renown. Skt.

praṣna, question. Skt. *praṣna véyuṭa* is to ask a question. *nannu v'úricé praṣnalu vési bhrama peṭṭacanḍi; míru yábhai praṣnalu vési nénu abaddham áḍanu*, do not try and confuse me by asking questions; if you ask me fifty questions I will not speak anything but the truth. The *a* is the indefinite vowel. The pronunciation is nearer to 'presna'.

praṣnintsuṭa, to question. Skt.

prastávamu, mention. Skt.

prastávintsuṭa, to mention. Skt.

prastutam, prastutamuló, at present, present, for the present. Skt. The pronunciation is nearer to 'prestutam'. *vári vádamu prastut amṣamunacu antaga sambhandinchin aṭlu cana baḍadu*, their argument seems to be irrelevant to the present question; *prastutamuló aidu vandala rúpáyala maṭṭucu khartsu cá valenu*, for the present we must incur expenses up to Rs. 500.

pratápamu, glory. Skt.

prathamamu, first. Skt. *prathama bhárya*, first wife; *mana prathama darṣana samayam*, the first time I saw you.

prati, every, opposite. *prati dinamu*, every day; *praticacshi*, the opposite party; *prativádi*, defendant; *pratyécamu*, one by one; as a prefix *prati* may be said to denote substitution, opposition, reflection (*pratibimbamu*, reflection, *pratidhvani*, echo).

prati, copy. *í granthamu aidu vandala pratulu atstsu paḍḍavi*, 500 copies of this book have been printed.

pratibandhacamu, pratibandhamu, hindrance. Skt.

pratibandhintsuṭa, to hinder. Skt.

pratibimbamu, reflection. Skt.

pratibimbintsuṭa, to reflect. Skt.

pratibimbitamu, reflected. Skt.

praticacshi, opposite party. Also *pratipacshamu*.

praticáramu, praticríya, recompense, retaliation. Skt., giving back what you get. *praticáram osaguṭa*, to give compensation; *ippuḍé dánici tagina praticriya cheyya valenu*, we must take revenge at once for that; *váru chésina dánici praticáramu chésináḍu*, he paid them in their own coin.

praticúlamu, inconvenient, adverse. Skt. Opposite of *anucúlamu*, convenient. *praticúlamaina gáli*, an adverse wind; *tamaru má prayatnánici anucúlangá chepputárá, praticulangá chepputárá?* will you speak for or against our proposal?

pratidánamu, exchange. Skt.

pratidhvani, echo; also *pratimóta*. Skt.

pratidinamu, every day. Skt.

pratignya, vow, determination. Skt. *tanḍri pratignya vinn aṭṭ aité nícu yenta vichâristávó*, how you will grieve if you hear of your father's decision.

pratima, image. Skt. *yóga nidra chéta chitrapu pratima lágu ai pótáḍu*, in Yogi-sleep he will become like a statue.

pratimóta, echo; also *pratidhvani*. Skt.

pratinidhi, representative. Skt. The usual newspaper word for elected persons. Parliament or Legislative Council is *janapratinidhisanghamu* (assembly of persons elected by the people). *Rája Pratinidhigáru* is the Viceroy.

pratipacshamu, the opposite party. Skt. Also *praticacshi*.

pratipacshuḍu, opponent. Skt.

pratipadamu, synonym. Skt.

pratipádanamu, ascertaining. Skt.

pratipálanamu, protecting. Skt.

pratipálintsuṭa, to protect. Skt.

pratiphalamu, requital. Skt. In legal language it means consideration in a contract. *má y'uttama pratiphalamu vári crütagnyataló*, in their gratitude is our great reward.

pratishṭha, reputation. Skt. *bógamdánni v'untsucóvaḍamé pratishṭha gánu, v'untsucóca póvaḍam apratishṭha gánu yentsa baḍutú v'unnadi*, it is considered reputable to keep a dancing girl, disreputable not to; *paruvúpratishṭhá*, dignity and decorum.

prativácyamu, answer. Skt.

prativádamu, defence. Skt.

prativádi, defendant. Skt. Plaintiff is *vádi*.

pratícshintsuṭa, to expect. Skt. *andtha yuvatul indriya nigrahamu chési, pativratugá unḍa galudur ani, manam yeṭlu praticshimpa galamu?* how can we expect young women without husbands to control themselves and remain chaste?

pratsurintsuṭa, to publish. Skt.

pratti, cotton; also *patti*. This is the cotton plant or uncleaned cotton; cleaned cotton is *dúdi*.

pratyacsha, perception (philosophy).

pratyacshamu, perceived, manifest, distinct. Skt. *nácu dévata pratyacshamu ainadi*, a god stood revealed before me; *í prántamulaló mahá cheḍḍa dongalu v'unnár ani nénu vinna sangati pratyacshangá nácé anubhavam aindi*, what I have heard that these parts were full of bandits has become manifest experience; *í caliyugamuló mantra mahimalu pratyacshamugá cana baḍuná?* will the power of charms become manifest in this iron age? *pratyacsha pramánamu*, ocular demonstration.

pratyécamu, private, separate, special. Skt. *rógi: ná zabbu míru cudurtsa galará? vaidyuḍu: tappacunḍá cudurustánu; mí zabbu mádiri zabbulanu čudartsaḍamuló nácu pratyéca sámarthyamu undi; í mádiri rógamu galavárici nénu iravai yénḍlu mand ichchänu.* Patient: Can you cure my disease? Doctor: Without fail; I have special skill in curing your kind of disease; I have been giving medicine to patients suffering from that sort of disease for the last twenty years. *manacu mátramé pratyécamgá y'i gadi máṭláḍinánu; iccaḍacu renḍóváru ráru*, we have engaged this room for our private use; other people can't come into it.

pratyécintsuṭa, to separate. Skt.

pratyupacáramu, a return of favours. Skt.
pratyuttaramu, rejoinder.
praudha, grand. Skt. *praudha vácyamulató,* with grand words.
pravahintsuṭa, to flow. Skt.
pravartana, conduct. Skt. *pravartana valla ná yógyata mícu cana parustánu,* I will show you my worth by my conduct.
pravartintsuríti, demeanour.
pravartintsuṭa, to conduct oneself. Skt. *itanu y'ikha yeppuḍú peddala y'odda avidhéyatagá pravartintsaḍu,* he will never behave badly again towards his elders.
pravádamu, rumour. Skt.
praváhamu, flow. Skt.
pravéṣamu, entry. Skt. *grühapravéṣamu* is a house-warming on first entrance to a house; *amma grüha pravéṣamu, áyya smaṣána pravéṣamu,* when the bride entered the house the bridegroom entered the tomb; *mícu Mimámsaló bágá pravéṣam v'unnadi cadá?* you are well acquainted with the Mimansa, are you not? *á dora vadda nácu pravéṣamu lédu,* I am not on terms of private acquaintance with that Collector.
pravéṣapeṭṭuṭa, to enter for. *Rámu: mí pilla yé paniló pravéṣa peṭṭuṭáru? Gópu: pólísu pani. Rámu: yendu chéta? Gópu: váḍu yeppaṭicainá pólísula chétulaló chicca valasinaváḍé?* Smith: What trade are you entering your boy for? Jones: The police. Smith: Why? Jones: The police are sure to get hold of him some time.
pravéṣintsuṭa, to enter. Skt. The ordinary word in stage directions.
pravínata, skill. Skt.
pravínuḍu, expert. Skt. *tennisu pravínuḍu: nannu paricsha cheṣáru gadá, ná vaḷḷu yeṭlá v'unnadi? ḍácṭaru: mícu viṣránti cá valenu; conndáḷḷu tennisu mánuconi, rózu cálejici veḷḷut unḍu, mimmalistundi.* Tennis expert: You have examined me, what about it? Doctor: You want rest; stop playing tennis for a few days, be going to college daily, and you will get well.
prayatnamu, attempt. Skt.
prayánamu, journey. Skt. *léḍici léchinadé prayánamu,* the deer has only to get up to be ready for a journey; *répu nénu prayánam,* I shall be on the move to-morrow.
prayánicuḍu, traveller, passenger. Skt.
prayásamu, exertion, fatigue, difficulty. Skt.
prayásapaḍuṭa, to try hard, to suffer. Skt.
prayógamu, use. Skt. *upayógam* is commoner. *vishaprayógamu,* use or administration of poison; *yécavachana prayógamu,* to use the singular instead of the plural form of address (*nívu* instead of *míru*); from *éca,* one (Skt.). *prayógamu* is also used of bewitchment by charms.
prayógintsuṭa, to use.
prayójacatvamu, cleverness. Skt. *induló mana prayójacatvam canaparchi, mana pantam neggintsu có valenu,* we must show our ability and attain our object.
prayójanamu, use. Skt.
prazalu, people. Skt. *janalu* and *prazalu* are the common words for the people in general, subjects, the community. *prastuta vyavahárамuló mác émaina avamánamu taṭasthinchina yeḍala, má cuṭumbam antayu yéca cálamun andu caṭṭa caṭṭuconi Góḍávariló ḍiga valasinadé gáni, prazalaló tala yettu coni bratuca valasina váramu cámu,* if in this matter any disgrace befall us, we one and all with one accord would seek a common annihilation in the waters of the Godavari; we are not of a race to live when we can no longer raise our heads among the people. The first *a* in *prazalu* is the indefinite vowel and the pronunciation is nearer to 'prezalu'.
prácambhamu, beginning. Skt. *árambhamu* is commoner.
prácáramu, cincture of temple, &c. Skt.
práchínamu, ancient. Skt. *práchína sadáchárамulu,* good old customs.
prácuṭa, to crawl; also *pácuṭa.* *mellagá góḍa dári nunḍi práci póvuts unnáḍu,* he was creeping quietly along the wall.
pránamitruḍu, pranasnéhituḍu, bosom friend. Skt.
pránamu, life. Skt. *pránamu mídici*

vachchindi, in danger of life; *canṭha gata pránamugá v'unnadi*, life has reached the throat, life is nearly gone; *pránamutó paṭṭu coniri*, they caught him alive; *ná pránamu póyiná*, though it cost me my life; *prána sancaṭamu*, mortal peril; *prána snéhamu*, bosom friendship; *prána dánamu chésináḍu*, he spared their lives; *vána rácaḍa, prána pócaḍa, yevarici teliyadu*, no one can say when the rain will come or life will go; *yevari pránamu várici tipu*, life is sweet to all; *mánamu póyina venuca, pránam enducu?* what is life without honour? *pránamu v'unḍé varacu bhayamu lédu*, while there is life, there is hope; *vánini tsúchin appuḍ ella dánici pránamu léchin aṭṭu*, when she sets eyes on him she seems to live again; *jagatpránamu*, the world's life, is the air; *jagatpránamunacu yógya sthánam aina vellaḍi tsóṭlacu ráca, illu cadalaca póvuṭa chéta, mana áḍaváḷḷu itara játi strila vale balamugá v'unḍaru*, as our women do not come into the life-giving open air and do not move out of the house, they are not as strong as the women of other nations; *ḍabbú pránánacú lance*, money and life are linked; *ná pránamu tísináḍu*, he bored the life out of me; *nén idi vinagáné ná pránamu talladillinadi*, when I heard it my heart was in my mouth; *dáni mída pránamulu úḍustáḍu*, he dotes on her.

pránanáthuḍu, lord of my life, i.e. husband or lover; also *pránéşuḍu, pranéşvari*.

pránatyágamu. Skt., from *pránamu*, life, and *tyágam*, abandonment.

pránéşuḍu, pranéşvari, lord of my life, i.e. husband or lover; also *pránanáthuḍu*.

prántamulu, region, neighbourhood. Skt. *í prántamulaló mahá cheḍḍa dongalu v'unnáru*, this neighbourhood is infested with terrible brigands.

prápanchicamu, worldly. Skt., from *prapañcham*. *prápanchica sukhamulu*, worldly joys.

prápintsuṭa, to obtain, to happen to one. Skt. *nic ippuḍu í durdaşa prápinchindi*, this calamity has now befallen you.

-práptamu, affix meaning 'fraught with', 'in store'. Skt. *hánipráptamu*, fraught with evil; *cheraşála práptam autundi*, prison is in store; (beggar speaking) *tamaru goppa dharmátulé, mí sommu nácu práptam unnadi*, you are a generous lord, your money is my portion.

prápu, prop. Skt. *mí prápu v'unṭé mému yenta pan ainá chéstámu*, we can do anything with your support.

prárabdhamu, destiny. Skt.

prárambhintsuṭa, to begin. Skt. *Mádrasu prántamula y'andu agashṭu nelaló varshamulu prárambhintsunu*, the rains set in around Madras in the month of August.

prárthana, prayer. Skt. *mishanari: mí prárthana sphuṭangá cheppanḍi, nácu occa mucc ainá vinipintsaḍam lédu. vidyárthi: mému Dévuḍini prárthist unnámu gáni, mimmuni cád anḍi.* Missionary (to boy saying prayers): Speak up, I can't hear a word. Pupil: I am saying my prayers to God, Sir, not to you.

prárthintsuṭa, to pray. Skt. *mic í buddhi sthirangá v'unḍéṭ aṭṭu ná ishṭa daivamunu nityamú prárthistú v'unnánu*, I daily pray God to keep you of this mind.

práta, old. *páta* is more common.

prátachcálamu, early morning. Skt. (The *ch* is pronounced as in Scotch or German *loch*.)

prátachsnánamu, early morning bath. Skt. *prátachsnánálu* are part of the every-day ritual of the orthodox; *aṭani billagóchi yémi? prátachsnánálu yémi? vibhúti pinjica yémi? Bráhmana bhacti yémi?* he does not dress properly or put on proper caste marks or take early baths or revere Brahmins.

práyamu, time of life. Skt. *lé práyamu*, the age of blooming.

-práyangá, -práyuḍu, affix meaning 'like'. Skt. *paşupráyuḍu*, a brutish man; *manchi níḷḷa práyangá yécaruvu peṭṭa valenu*, pour out (your discourse) like flowing water.

práyaşchittamu, penitence, expiation. Skt. *tagina práyaşchittam chéstánu*, I will do proper expiation (e.g. if I go to Europe or touch a pariah);

ataḍu bálya viváhálu, canyá ṣulcálu cúḍad ani vádistú v'unṭáru, andu chéta atanici tagina práyaṣchittam chéyintsa valen ani manavál̤l̤ andaru álóchinchi svámulavárító cheppinámu, he goes about arguing against child marriage and saying girls should not be sold, and for that we all considered he should do penance and we spoke to the Svami. One form of *práya-ṣchittam* is consuming the five products of the sacred cow, including the urine and faeces.

précshaculu, audience, from Skt. word 'to see'. *naṭuḍu: náṭacamló allari autunnadi. mánéjaru: yendu chéta? naṭuḍu: náyaculu yuddhamló tsáva valasi v'unṭé tsávacunḍá nintsuné un-náru, précshaculu navvut unnáru. mánéjaru: báci v'unna jitam ippuḍé istán ani cheppu.* Actor: They are making a row in the theatre. Manager: What about? Actor: The leaders ought to have died in the battle, but did not die and are standing up and the audience is laughing. Manager: Tell them I will pay up their arrears of salary at once. *naṭuḍu: nénu náṭa-camló tsachchi pótu v'unn appuḍu, précshaculu yeṭlá yéḍcháró tsúchává? snéhituḍu: dánici cáranam émiṭó telu-suná? naṭuḍu: yémiṭó nuvvu cheppu. snéhituḍu: nuvvu nizangá tsáva léd ani.* Actor: When I died in the play did you notice how the audience wept? Friend: Do you know why? Actor: No, tell me. Friend: Because you had not died in earnest.

prélápanalu, chatter, nonsense; also *pélápanalu.*

préluṭa, to prattle; also *péluta. ataḍ inṭa n'unn anta sépu calacala áḍutsu, navvutsu, prélutsu, svargamuló v'unn aṭṭ unḍunu,* all the time he is in the house she is one burst of merriment and laughter and prattle.

préma, love. Skt. *bhárya: mícu ná mída púrva préma lédu.* Wife: You don't love me as once you did. *ocaḍu: mí mukham oca vaipuna yet-tugá v'unnadi; ṣástra pracáram tsústé mícu mí pillala mída préma yeccuva v'unnad anna máṭa. incóḍu: á sangati nácu teliyadu; má pillaváḍu rái vésté, mukhánici tagili, yettugá v'unnadi.* First Hindu: Your face is higher one side than the other; according to the Scriptures that bump denotes philo-progenitiveness. Second Hindu: I know nothing about that; I have a bump on one side of my face because my boy threw a stone at me and hit me. *bhárya: ná mída mícu préma v'unnadá? bharta: ná mukha lacshaná-lanu nuvvu tsadivi tsúḍu, telustundi. bhárya: nácu tsaduvu rádu gá, yeṭlá tsadivédi?* Wife: Do you love me? Husband: Read my features and you will see. Wife: Unfortunately I can't read.

préracuḍu, instigator.

prérépana, incitement. Skt.

prérépintsuṭa, to incite. Skt.

prétamu, corpse, ghost. Skt.

priyamu, dear (in all senses). Skt. *avi tsála priyam,* that is very dear; *ṣushca priyamulu, ṣúnya hastamulu,* vain cajoleries, empty hands.

priyarálu, priyuḍu, darling. *o pri-yarálá!* O my darling girl; *calaha-priyuḍu,* one who delights in quarrels.

príti, love. Skt. *prítipúrvacangá,* lovingly; *prítitó peṭṭinadi piḍic eḍé tsálunu,* a handful is enough if given with love (better a dinner of herbs where love is than a stalled ox with hatred thereby); *príti léni cúḍu pinḍá cúṭiló samamu,* food given without love is no better than an offering to the dead.

proddu, sun, time, early; also *poddu. yenta proddu v'unḍagá léchina Tum-magunṭa vaddané tellavárinadi,* how-ever early he got up it was always dawn by the time he reached Tumma tank.

prodduna, in the morning. *í dinamu prodduna,* this morning; *prodduné léchi,* getting up early.

proddupóvuṭa, to get late (the sun is low). *proddupóyindi, lópalici veḷu-dámu ranḍi,* it is late, let's go in; *tsála proddu pótu v'unnadi,* it is getting very late.

prodduputstsuṭa, to pass the time; also *prodduzaruguṭa. bógamvál̤l̤ató prodduputstsutú v'unḍadam,* to pass the time with dancing-girls.

proddutiruguḍupuvvu, sunflower; the flower that turns its face to the sun (the Italian *girasole* (turning to the sun) also means sunflower; and our Jerusalem artichoke is derived from *girasole*).

prodduzaruguṭa, to pass the time; also *prodduputstsuṭa. manac andarici khuláságá proddu zarigéṭ aṭṭu chéstundi*, she makes the time pass charmingly for all of us.

pródbalamu, instigation. Skt.

própózu, proposal. English.

prótsáhamu, encouragement. Skt.

prüthvi, prüthivi, earth. Skt. *váḍu prüthvici báramu*, he is a burden on the earth. *pedavi dáṭina máṭa prüthivi dáṭunu*, the word that has passed the lip will pass over the earth.

puccili, inside of cheek; the adjective *pucciṭi* means nonsensical (cf. tongue in one's cheek).

puccilinta, gargling.

pucciṭintsuṭa, to gargle; from *puccili*, inside of cheek.

pucciṭipuránamu, old wife's tale. *i pucciṭi puránál anni nácu telusunu*, I know all these old wife's tales; *idi puciṭi puránamu*, that is a cock-and-bull story.

puchchi, rotten, decayed; from *putstsuṭa. puchchi purugulu*, rot and worms.

puḍaca, bit of stick, especially in the funeral pyre. *purrenu puṭṭina buddhi puḍacalató gáni pódu*, the funeral pyre alone will change the skull one is born with (character is unchanging); *púchicapuḍaca*, grass and twigs (of anything trifling).

puḍisili, handful. *puḍiseḍu biyyamu*, handful of rice; *góvu alpachámánam chéstu v'unḍagá veḷḷi, tócató netti mída tsallu coni, panchiṭam múḍu puḍisiḷḷu lópalici putstsu cunṭé punyam*, you gain much spiritual benefit by going up to a cow when it is making water, sprinkling the urine over the head with the help of its tail, and drinking three handfuls thereof.

pulacarintsuṭa, to tingle, to bustle. *míru chésina ghóra crütyamu ná ṣaríramu pulacarintsuts unnadi*, I bristle with horror at your cruel deed; *antóshamu paṭṭa tsálaca déham antayu pulacarintsuts unnadi*, I tingle all over with inexpressible joy; *atanini tsústé nácu déham pulacaristú v'unnadi*, I quiver with fear at sight of him.

puli, tiger; *peddapuli* is the tiger; *chiruta puli*, the panther, *ígapuli* (fly-tiger), the spider. *idugó puli anṭé, adugó tóca ann aṭṭu*, 'tiger', said one. 'I see his tail', said the other (of people telling tall stories); *méca vanne puli*, a goat-coloured tiger (wolf in sheep's clothing); *puli náci viḍichin aṭṭu*, like the man who was licked by the tiger and got away (marvellous escape); *puli paccanu zóriga v'unn aṭṭu*, like a gad-fly on a tiger; *puli mísamulu paṭṭu coni, v'uyyála v'úgin aṭṭu*, like swinging on a tiger's whiskers (a dangerous thing to do); *puli cánḍrintsuts unnadi*, the tiger roars.

puli, acid; used chiefly in compounds as *pulihóru*, rice acidly dressed; *pulicápu*, tamarind water (used to clean brass).

puliyuṭa, to turn sour, to set on edge. *nimma panḍla rasamutó atani panḍlu pulisinavi*, his teeth were set on edge with lime juice.

pulla, dun-coloured, acid.

pulla, bit of stick, firewood. *cannu tagilé pullanu canipeṭṭu vaddá?* keep a look-out or you will get something in your eye (beware of enemies); *pánacamuló pulla lágu*, like a bit of stick in your drink (an inconvenience); *pullala cinda sagam tumma chéṭlu póyinavi*, half our babul trees have gone for firewood; *nippu pulla* is a match.

pullari, pasture tax, from *pullu*, grass. This has been abolished long ago except in some zamindaries.

pullu, grass; *patsagaḍḍi* and *casavu* are commoner.

pulusu, acid sauce, from *puli*, acid; *pulusu cúra*, sour curry; *ocanici y'iguru cúra y'ishṭamu, ocanici pulusu cúra y'ishṭamu*, one man's meat is another man's poison.

pun-, prefix meaning 'male'. Skt.

punach-, punar-, punas-. Skt. prefix meaning 'again'.

punachpravéṣamu, re-entry. Skt.

punarjanmamu, second birth. Skt.

punarjáricbéyuṭa, to reissue. Skt.

punarnirmánamu, reorganization. Skt.

punarsrüshti, second creation. Skt.

punaruddháranamu, resurrection, restoration. Skt. *Hindu matam punaruddháranam cheyyaḍánici manam andaramu y'iccaḍici vachchinámu,* we have all come here to restore the Hindu religion.

punarvichárana, punarvimarşa, re-investigation, re-trial. Skt. Used as a legal term. *í dáva Hai Córṭu vári valla punarvicháranacu pampa baḍḍadi,* the High Court has remanded this suit for re-trial.

punarviváhamu, second marriage. Skt. *míru strílacu punarviváhamulu cúḍav anduru; avi léca póté ghóra crütyamulu mana strílaló zaruguts unnavi.* Remarriage of women is strictly forbidden among us; it is because of this prohibition that daily horrors occur among us (infanticides, &c.).

punassandhánamu, marriage consummation ceremony. Skt. It means bringing together again.

punádi, foundation. *ippuḍu manam venṭané jágrata paḍi, má mata punádi balaparisténé cáni, antá cheḍi pótundi,* unless we take care and strengthen the foundations of our religion, it will all go to ruin.

punḍu, ulcer, sore. *ná gontu punḍuga v'unnadi,* I have a sore throat; *yeddu punḍu cácici muddá?* is the bullock's ulcer tender to the crow? (of unsympathetic persons); *máni póyina punḍu maḷḷi répin aṭṭu,* like ripping up old sores.

-pungavamu, affix meaning 'excellent'. Skt. *munipungavuḍu,* a venerable hermit.

punistrí, married women; from Skt. *punyastrí.*

punja, dry land (as opposed to irrigated land (*nanja*)). Hindustani. In the Tamil country these terms are still used; in the Telugu country they are nearly obsolete and *meṭṭa bhúmi,* high land, *palla bhúmi,* low land, are used instead.

punta, path; the wide cattle paths of Telugu villages, especially in the deltas.

punṭi, oblique case of *punḍu,* sore. *punṭiló purugulu gulagulal áḍuts unnavi,* the worms are crawling over the sore.

puntstvamu, virility. Skt.

punugu, civet. *punugu tsaṭṭamu pinḍin aṭṭu,* like squeezing an empty civet bag (getting blood out of a stone).

punyacshétramu, place of pilgrimage. Skt.

punyamu, virtue, merit. Skt. *púṭacúḷḷamma punyam eragadu,* innkeepers have no conscience; *punyamú purushárthamú,* virtue and manliness. *bitstsagáḍu: ayyá, oca cáni dharmamu cheyyanḍi, mícu punyam vastundi. dhanicuḍu: nuvvu buddhi cá valen ani aḍugu gáni, ḍabbu aḍaga bócu. bitstsagáḍu: mí daggira léni dánini nén eṭlá aḍigéd anḍi? unnaḍánné aḍigán anḍi.* Beggar: Sir, give me a copper, you will have your reward. Dives: Ask for sense not money. Beggar: How can I ask you for what you haven't got? I asked you for what you have. *guḍḍiváḷḷacu cunṭiváḷḷacu dánam chésté punyam vastund aṭa.* They (the Europeans) say that charity to the blind and the lame is meritorious (whereas of course only charity to Brahmins is really meritorious).

punyánici, for love, gratis. *nácu pustacamu punyánici ichchináḍu,* he gave me the book gratis; *punyánici puṭṭ eḍ isté pitstsa cuntsam ani póṭláḍin aṭṭu,* like the man who got a ton of corn for nothing and complained that the measure was false (looking a gift-horse in the mouth).

punyastrí, virtuous woman, married woman. Skt. Vulgarly *punistrí.*

punyátmuḍu, virtuous man.

punzu, cock. *mana dóra punzu bahu bágá póṭláḍindi sumanḍi,* to be sure our brown cock fought very well.

puppi, decay, rot. *puppi panḍlu,* decayed teeth.

puramu, city. Skt. Many city names end in pur as Berhampur, Chatrapur.

purascarintsuṭa, to revere. Skt.

purácrütamu, done in the former life. Skt. *purácrüta carmam anubhavintsaca tíradu,* you cannot escape the consequences of the acts of former lives.

puráṇamu, myth, purana. Skt. The

word means old stories; the old story-books of the Hindu religion; some people still believe these strange legends; though *y'ippaṭi váḷḷu Y'Inglishu tsaduvu coni násticulu purá-ṇamulu pramánamulu cáv anṭáru*, the present generation of atheists who have studied in English say that the puranas are not God's word.

puri, grain-basket. It is a large basket made of straw and mud.

puricolpuṭa, to incite.

puripeṭṭuṭa, to twist.

puriṭiníḷḷu, churching, ceremony of ablution after childbirth, from *puruḍu*. *mícu puriṭi niḷḷ eppuḍu?* when is your churching?

puróhituḍu, priest, especially family priest. Skt.

purre, skull. *purrenu puṭṭinadí puḍa-calató gáni póḍu*, character is unchanging (what is born with the skull will go only with the funeral pyre; the reference is to the lines of fate Brahma writes on the forehead).

puruḍu, childbirth. *áme puruḍu pósi-nánu*, I attended her in childbirth.

purugu, worm. *purugupaṭṭina*, worm-eaten.

purusha, of a man. Skt. *udyógam purusha lacshanam*, service makes the man (Government service is much more highly thought of in India than in England).

purushántaramu, generation, lifetime. Skt. *peddamanishi: i gaḍiyáram oca purushántaram varacu pani chés-tund ani cheppi ichchávu, appuḍé ági póyinadi. ammévádu: míru gaḍiyáram conn appuḍu zabbugá canipinchàru; andu chéta aṭla cheppänu.* Gentleman: You guaranteed me this watch would last my lifetime when you sold it me; it stopped at once. Shopkeeper: When you bought it you looked ill; that is why I said that.

purushárthamu, manliness. Skt. *punyamú purushárthamú*, virtue and manliness.

Purushóttama, The Supreme Spirit. Skt.

purushuḍu, man, husband. Skt. *puṭṭina y'inndḷḷacu purushuḍu yagnyam chésináḍu*, after many years the man performed the sacrifice (better late than never).

pushcalamu, abundant, excellent. Skt. Used in books.

pushcaramu, a river bathing festival held once in twelve years. Skt. The Godavari Pushcaram at Rajahmundry is the most famous of these festivals in the Telugu country. As many as a million pilgrims come to have their sins washed away. *doragáru: tamaru vinnár émó; y'í pushcara mahatyam nácu cásta selav istárá?* Collector: You will know about the glories of the Pushcaram; could you tell me something? *Bráhmanuḍu: nénu yé mahatyamú vina lédu; pratyacshamgá canapaḍé mahatyam cheputánu, cáva-listé vinanḍi. mana v'úḷḷó Vódhrulu múcalu múcalugá vachchi, murici guḍ-ḍalató mulagaḍam chéta, Gódávari jiḍḍu téri, nallagá Yamuna nadi autú v'unnadi; níru cásulu paṭṭe Bráhmanu-lacu dhana lábham calugutú v'unnadi; myúnisipalvárici cá valasin anta penṭa bhágyam calugutú v'unnadi; vídhul anniṭici chinna cáluvaloló muccu músu có valasina parimaḷam yeccuv autú v'unnadi; baḷḷu vistáram vastú pótú v'unḍaḍam chéta tólu canṭracṭarlacu santósham yeccuva autú v'unnadi; bazáruló vastuvulu priyam cávaḍam chéta pédalacu santósham taccuva autú v'unnadi. idi nácu telisina pushcara mahatyam.* Brahmin: I have not heard of any glories, but I can tell you what I have seen; the Vadras of our town come in crowds and bathe in their dirty clothes and made the Godavari like glue and as black as the Jumna. The Brahmins who take money for reciting charms make a profit; the municipality gets all the dung it wants; the street drains become more offensive than ever; the toll contractors rejoice because so many carts come and go; the poor are sad because the price of commodities goes up in the market; these are all the glories of the Pushcaram that I know of.

pushpamu, flower. Skt.

pushṭi, strength. Skt.

pushyamu, a lunar month. Skt. About January.

pustacamu, book; also business book. Skt. *gumástá: mánéjaru veyyi rúpáyilu cá chéṣáḍu, pustacamló yém ani vrásédi? incó gumástá: chillara khartsul ani ráyi.* First clerk: The manager has made away with Rs. 1,000. What does one write in the books? Second clerk: Put it down to sundry expenses.

puste, marriage locket. A small disk of gold worn round the neck by married women. *ná peḷḷámucu puste tappa mari yémi lédu*, my wife has no jewellery except her marriage token; *talli meḍaló pustalu tempu coni parugetté allari pilla váḷḷa vale*, like wild boys who cut off their mother's marriage tokens and run away.

puṭa, page (of a book). Skt.

puṭamu peṭṭuṭa, to heat a metal, to calcine a drug; from Skt. *puṭamu*, calix, hoof.

putravatsalyamu, affection for one's children. Skt.; from *putruḍu*, son, and *vatsalata*, affection. *vatsalata*, again comes from *vatsam*, breast.

putri, daughter. Skt.

putruḍu, son. Skt. *putrasantánamu léni*, without issue.

putstsacaya, wild melon. *putstsacăya donga anṭe, bhuzamu taḍimi tsútsu connáḍ aṭa*, like the man who felt his shoulders when some one called 'melon-thief' (giving one[illegible]).

putstsu, rotten.

putstsuconuṭa, to take. *Se*[illegible]*tstsuconuṭa*, to take leave, is the usual phrase used by a visitor on the termination of an interview. The word is used in all the senses of the English 'take'. *Lacshmayya: nácu rátriḷḷu nidra paṭṭadu, mandu putstsucó valenu. Vencamma: pilla yéḍupu chéta nácu nidra paṭṭadu, nác ém mand istáró?* Husband: I can't sleep at nights, I must take medicine. Wife: I cannot sleep for the child crying, what medicine am I to take? *vrüddhuḍu: ná manamaḍu mí áfisuló pani chést unnáḍu, váḍini míru yerugudurá? mánéjaru: yerugudunu, í madhyané míru tsachchi póyinár ani selavu putstsuconi veḷḷáḍu.* Old man: My grandson works in your office. Do you know him? Manager: Yes, he has just gone on leave on the ground that you had died.

putstsuṭa, to take, chiefly used as verbalizing affix; *podduputstsuṭa* is to kill time; *mósaputstsuṭa*, to cheat; *chinnaputstsuṭa*, to disgrace.

putstsuṭa, to rot, to decay. *pottula magaḍu puchchi tsachchenu*, the shared husband died of neglect.

puṭṭa, ant-hill, especially the large ant-hills made by white ants, which often harbour snakes. *yé puṭṭaló yé pám unnadó yevarici telustundi?* who knows what snake is in what ant-hill? *puṭṭa mannu vésté bhúmi pandunu*, white ant earth is a good manure (the earth of the white ant; ant-hills is also used as a top dressing for tennis-courts).

puṭṭi, candy, the usual large grain measure. The putti is twenty tooms, but as the toom varies the putti varies too. It is usually about ten hectolitres and will weigh about a ton. *punyánici puṭṭ eḍ isté pitstsa cuntsam ani pòṭláḍin aṭṭu*, like the man who was given a ton of grain gratis and complained it had been measured with a false measure (looking a gift-horse in the mouth); *poṭṭiváḍici puṭṭ eḍu buddhulu*, little men have tons of sense.

puṭṭi, the big basket used, e.g. on the Tungabhadra, as a ferry-boat; coracle. *naṭṭ éta puṭṭi munigin aṭṭu*, the coracle sinking in mid-stream.

puṭṭillu, the house you were born in, especially of women, who are always going to their *puṭṭillu* on some excuse or another; also *puṭṭinillu. Lacshmayya: ní bháryanu viṣránti cósam puṭṭinṭici pampăva? Vencayya: pampănu, nizam ém anṭé nácé viṣránti cá valasi aṭlá chéṣánu.* Smith: You have sent your wife to her mother's house for a rest? Jones: Yes, but to tell you the truth it was *I* that required a rest. *í y'úru calarácu puṭṭillu*, this town is a hot-bed of cholera; cholera is endemic in this town; *puṭṭinṭi péru*, maiden name.

puṭṭináḍu, birthday. *puṭṭináḍi buddhi pudacalaló cáni póḍu*, the mind a man was born with will last him till the pyre.

puṭṭinillu, the mother's house as opposed to *meṭṭinillu*, the mother-in-law's house (of women only).

puṭṭinstuṭa, to create, to cause to come into existence; causative of *puṭṭuṭa*, to be born, used also of such things as the creation of false documents; *donganu puṭṭinchinavádu, matibhrashṭunu puṭṭintsaca mánadu*, God that created rogues, did not fail to create dupes.

puṭṭubhógi, born rich (born with a silver spoon in his mouth).

puṭṭuca, birth.

puṭṭumatstsa, birth-mark.

puṭṭumúga, born dumb.

puṭṭupápa, albino.

puṭṭuṭa, to be born. *incó janmánici mí y'inṭló cucca'n ai puḍatánu*, at a rebirth I will be born as a dog in your house (gratitude). *cáranamu léca cáryamu puṭṭadu*, no effect without a cause; *pála puṭṭité mátramu, mélu guṇamu calugunā?* is everything made of milk good? *puṭṭani biḍḍacu péru peṭṭuṭáḍu*, he names the unborn child (counting your chickens before they are hatched); *puṭṭi buddhi yerigina tarváta*, all my life long; *nácu puṭṭi buddhi yerigina tarváta nác iṭuvanṭi y'adbhutam eppuḍunu calaga lédu*, so extraordinary a thing has never happened to me all the years of my life. *Lacshmayya: nuvvu samudra prayánam chéṣává? Vencayya: chéṣánu gáni, nácu visugu puṭṭindi. Lacshmayya: yendu chéta? Vencayya: oca ala tsústé anni alalú aṭlágé v'unnai, bhédam émi lédu.* Smith: Have you made a sea-voyage? Jones: Yes, but I got bored. Smith: Why? Jones: Because when you have seen one wave you have seen them all; they are all just alike. *cottaváḍu: í v'úḷḷó goppaváḷḷu yevarainá puṭṭárá? grámasthuḍu: nácu telisinanta varacu y'iccaḍa ṣiṣuvulé puṭṭutárandi, goppa váḷḷu puṭṭa lédu.* Stranger: Were any big people born in this place? Native: As far as I know only babies are born here, not big people.

puvvu, flower; also *pushpamu*; also *pú*; plural *puvvulu, púlu. púlavána*, a slight shower; *puvvilu*, Cupid's bow; *puvvuladanḍa*, flower garland.

pú, flower; same as *puvvu. púgutti*, nosegay.

púchi, responsibility. Hindustani. Also *púchí*.

púchica, grass of which brooms are made. *púchicapuḍaca*, grass and twigs (rubbish); *mana sommu púchicapuḍaca ainanu putstsuconi yerugadu*, he won't take a brass farthing from us.

púchicaṭṭu, broom.

púchí, responsibility. Hindustani; also *púchi. mícu peḷḷi cúturini sampádintsaḍapu púchí nádi*, I will take it on myself to find you a bride. *munisibu: mar émi parvá lédu, yélágó vacalágu vasúl autavi; caranam mída cásu paḍadu; nádi púchí*, village Munsiff (to Karnam): it doesn't matter, somehow or other the money will be collected; however much has to be collected the Karanam never pays anything; it is I who am responsible.

púchícaṭṭu, security bond, recognizance.

púḍtsuṭa, to fill up. *táḍu tsálaca póté nuyyi púḍtsum ann aṭṭu*, like the man who ordered the well to be filled up when the rope would not reach (he got cross with the well).

púḍuṭa, to be filled. *vaṭṭi máṭala valla poṭṭalu púḍutavá?* will words alone fill bellies?

púja, worship. Skt. *chésina Ṣiva pújalu, cheppévi abaddhálu*, what he performs is worship of the Lord, what he says is lies; *bhacti léni púja patri chéṭu*, worship without devotion is a waste of the sacred leaves.

pújacuḍu, worshipper, priest. Skt.

pújaliḍuṭa, to adore.

pújári, priest. Skt.

pújintsuṭa, to worship. Skt.

pújitamu, adored.

púladanḍa, flower garland. *cóti chéti púladanḍa*, a flower garland in a monkey's paw (pearls before swine).

púnica, attempt.

púnuṭa, to exert oneself for, to lend oneself to. *v'úrice álóchisté cáryam lédu, panici púna valenu*, thinking about it is no use, you must put your shoulder to the wheel; *ḍabbu cósam lóbhinchi y'iṭuvanṭi acárya carandnici púnucunṭé míru apacírti pál ai pótáru*, you will be disgraced if you lend yourself to evil for money.

púranamu, filling. Skt. Usually *púrnamu*.

púrá, full. Hindustani (no connexion with the preceding word). *púrá nashṭam*, total loss (as of a crop).

púréḍu, quail.

púri, grass, but *gaḍḍi* is commoner. *panṭa penṭaló v'unnadi, páḍi púriló v'unnadi*, the harvest is in the manure, the milk in the grass.

púripuḍaca, blade of grass.

-púritamu, affix meaning 'filled'. Skt.

púriṭiḷḷu, thatched house; from *púri*, grass, and *iḷḷu*, house; the *ṭ* is euphonic.

púrnamu, filling, what fills (such as stuffing).

púrnima, full-moon day. Skt.

púrti, complete. Skt. *púrti cáninḍi*; finish it; *púrti rózulu*, complete days, is a law term for clear days.

púrva, previous, former. Skt. *micu ná mida púrva préma lédu*, you do not love me as before; *púrvacálapu manushyulu*, old fogies; *púrvajanmamu*, former birth.

-púrvacamaina, affix meaning 'according to'. *buddhipúrvacamaina*, intentional; *vrátapúrvacamaina*, in writing; *vinayapúrvacamaina*, humble.

-púrvacamgá, -púrvamgá, affix turning nouns into adverbs. *santóshapúrvacamgá*, joyfully; *prítipúrvacamgá*, lovingly.

púrvamu, formerly. Skt.

púrvapacshamu, answer to an argument. Skt. Used as a legal term for written statement.

púrvácháramu, old customs. Skt. Especially of the traditions of the Hindu religion and caste system. *púrváchárinní peddalinní dúshistáru*, (modern people) revile old customs and their elders.

púrvicuḍu, ancestor. Skt.

púrvulu, ancestors. Skt.

púsa, bead, vertebra. *catha antayu púsa guchchin aṭṭu cheppinááḍu*, (the witness) told the whole tale as if he was threading beads (with the ease which results from careful tutoring); *puṭṭani biḍḍacu púsalu caṭṭin aṭṭu*, like tying beads on an unborn child (counting your chickens before they are hatched).

púsayemuca, backbone.

púṭa, time, especially of the number of times a day a meal is taken, so that *púṭacúḍu* means boarding, and *púṭacúḷḷamma* a woman who keeps a boarding house; *pagaṭipúṭa* is day-time, *rátripúṭa*, at night.

púta, smearing, coating, from *púyuṭa*, to smear.

púta, blooming; from *pútsuṭa*, to flower. *ní níti vrúcshamu púta paṭṭutundi*, your tree of goodness is putting out flowers.

púṭacúḷḷamma, woman who keeps a restaurant; she has notoriously no conscience. *púṭacúllamma punyam eragadu*, the innkeeper knows not virtue; the word is compounded of *púṭa*, time, *cúḍu*, food, and *amma*, woman; *púṭacúṭillu*, restaurant; also *vanṭacúṭillu*.

pútsuṭa, to blossom, to flower. *púchina púll ellá cáyal aité bhúmi paṭṭaḍánacu sthalamu unḍadu*, if all the flowers that blossom turned to fruit there would be no room left on earth.

púyintsuṭa, to have smeared or laid on; causative of *púyuta*. *inṭici sunnam púyintsuṭa* is to have one's house white-washed.

púyuṭa, to lay on, to smear, to anoint. *chaccara púta púsina vishamu*, poison covered with sugar (sugared words).

pyásu, pass (in an examination). English. *cástalési váḷḷu biyyélu (B.A.) pyás ai, v'udyógalóci vachchi, v'udyogála vakharé cheḍa coṭṭi véstu v'unnáru*, one clerk in the office who has passed the B.A. is enough to ruin the whole office (unpassed clerk speaking, and meaning that graduates will neither take bribes nor allow others to take them).

R

-ra, sirrah; affix of address to inferiors; it is usually written *-ri* (*óri*), but is pronounced *-ra*.

racamu, sort, kind. Hindustani. *cotta racam vāḷḷa mundara lantsálu putstsucuné vāḷḷanu dúshistú míru Ṣrí Ranga nítule selav istáré!* you are uttering moralities and reviling bribe-takers before people of the new sort.

rachaṇamu, composition (literary). Skt.

rachintsuṭa, to compose (a book). Skt. *Lacshmayya: nénu rachinchina náṭacam eṭlá v'unnadi? sukhamgá mugisindá lédá? Ramayya: náṭacam ḍḍaḍam mugisin taruváta tsúḍa vachchina vāḷḷu sukha paḍḍāru.* Smith: How about the play I composed? Didn't it end well? Jones: Yes, after the play was over the spectators were happy.

racshacuḍu, protector. Skt.

racshaṇamu, protection. Skt. *svaracshaṇārthamu* is a legal term; for the purpose of self-defence. *upanyásacuḍu: tsaḍuvu cheppéṭ appuḍu pillalanu yeppuḍú coṭṭa cúḍadu; nénu ṭícharugá unna iravai sanvatsarálaló occa sári cúḍá coṭṭa lédu. sabhicuḍu: occa sári cúḍá coṭṭa lédú? upanyasacuḍu: vidyárthulu nannu coṭṭa vachchin appuḍu svaracshaṇārtham mátram coṭṭānu.* Lecturer: A schoolmaster should never descend to corporal punishment; I never did in the twenty years I was a teacher. Voice from the audience: What, not once even? Lecturer: Oh! I did it in self-defence when the boys attacked me. *pádaracshalu*, feet-protectors, means shoes.

racshanu, demon. Skt. *rácshasi* is commoner.

racshintsuṭa, to protect, to save. Skt. *illu cáluts unḍenu, nippu árput unḍiri. yazamáni: ayyó dánini racshintsanḍi, venṭané racshintsanḍi; oca másam ainá ninḍa lédu. nippu árpévaḍu: amma, lópala tsúṣánu, pilla lédanḍi. yazamáni: pill émiṭ ayyá? nippu árpévaḍu: dénini racshintsam annadi? yazamáni: ná goḍugunu, dánini coni másam ainá cá lédu.* The house was on fire, they were putting the fire out. Lady: Save it, Oh save it at once; it is not even one month old! Fireman: Madam, I looked inside, there is no child there. Lady: Who said anything about a child? Fireman: What were we to save? Lady: My umbrella; it isn't a month since I bought it.

ractamu, blood. Skt. Common, another common word being *netturu; racta sambandhamu* is a legal term for consanguinity; *racta sparṣa galaváḍu* is a blood-relation.

raddu, cancellation, repeal, abrogation. Hindustani.

radduchéyuṭa, raddupartsuṭa, to cancel, to repeal, to abrogate.

ragilintsuṭa, to kindle.

raguluṭa, to take fire; usually in the middle form *raguluconuṭa*.

rahadári, highway, passage, passport. Hindustani. *í diccu málina baḷḷa rahadári múlanga monna caṭṭintsu cunna má vídhi arugul anni váránici renḍu sárlu paḍi pótú v'unnavi,* owing to the passage of these infernal carts the pials we have recently put up in our street all fall down twice a week. *rahadári bangáḷa* is a travellers' bungalow; *rahadári paḍava,* passenger-boat (especially on the Godavari canals).

rahasyamu, secret. Skt. *yémi rahaṣyam vachchinadi?* what is your last new secret? *ati rahasyam, paṭṭa bailu,* a public secret. *Lacshmayya: nénu nishpacshapátini; nénu tappu pani chésiná, dánici vichára paḍutánu, incóḷḷato ná tappu chepputánu. Vencayya: mí daggira rahasyam dágadu cábólu.* Smith: I am an impartial man. If I do wrong I am sorry and confess. Jones: Can't keep a secret, I suppose.

-rahitamu, affix meaning 'without'. Skt. *vidyárahituḍu*, devoid of learning; *cashṭarahitamu*, without troubles; *yuctirahitamaina y'í váḍálu manam* *vina rádu*, we should not listen to such senseless arguments.

railu, railway, train; also *rayilu*. English. *railu cadala pót unḍenu, gárḍu prayánicuḍini yetti railulóci tósenu; taruváta sṭéshanuló gárḍu banḍi daggirici vachchenu. gárḍu: mícu nénu yenta upacáram chéṣánó grahinchárá? nénu yeccintsaca póté mícu railu tappi poyyédé, nácu yémaina bahumánam ippintsanḍi. prayánicuḍu: nénu rail eccaḍánici rá lédu; railuló uttaram veyyaḍánici vachchánu; míru railulóci toyyaḍam valla maḷḷi iccaḍa nunchi má v'úru veḷḷa valasi vachchindi, ḍabbu danḍuga aindi*, the train was starting, the guard lifted up a passenger and shoved him into the train; at the next station the guard came up and said: Have you understood what I did for you? If I had not shoved you into the train you would have lost it. Are you going to give me anything? Passenger: I did not come to get into the train but to post a letter on it; now I have to find my way back at my own cost.

railvé, railway. English. *upádhyáyuḍu: ná salahá avalambintsanḍi; míru anni vishayáḷḷó mundugá v'unṭe bágu paḍutáru. vidhyárthi: má nánna venuca v'unná pedda jítam tetstsu cunṭ unnáḍ anḍi. upadhyáyuḍu: mi nánnac émi pani? vidhyárthi: railvé gárḍu pani*. Teacher: Take my advice and always be first in everything. Pupil: My father gets a big salary for being always behind. Teacher: What is his profession? Pupil: Railway guard.

raitu, peasant proprietor. Hindustani; also *rayitu*.

raituvári, by peasant proprietorship. The ryotvari system is the system by which Government collects its tax direct from the peasant instead of through a zamindar, who was originally a mere middleman but who has now developed into a land-owner.

rajani, night. Skt. Used in books for *rátri*.

rajasvalauṭa, to attain puberty (of girls). Skt. *rajasval ainadi*, she has attained puberty; *a chinnadi y'incá rajasvala cá ledu*, that girl has not yet attained puberty; *áme rajasval ayyé pacvamuló n'unnadi*, she is fast growing into a woman.

ramanintsuṭa, to be beautiful, to be charming. Skt.

ramárami, about, more or less, on an average.

Rambha, the heavenly courtesan. *tá valachinadi Rambha, tá muniginadi Ganga*, the woman he loves is Rambha, the river he bathes in is the Ganges (of people proud of their possessions); *Rambhanu minché vaca bhógastrí*, a courtesan surpassing Rambha; *dévatul andaru Rambha, Ménaca modalaina váḷḷanu v'untsucó lédá?* do not the gods keep Rambha, Menaca, and other courtesans? *napunsacuḍici Rambha yémi prayójanam?* what is the use of Rambha to a eunuch?

rammu, come, imperative of *vatstsuṭa*. *úru pomm anṭundi, cádu ramm anṭundi*, the village says go, the burning ground says come (death is near).

rampacáḍu, sawyer.

rampamu, saw. *rampapu cóta gáḍu*, sawyer.

ranamu, battle. Skt.

raṇamu, a bad ulcer, for *vraṇamu*; *punḍu* is commoner.

ranarangamu, battle-field. Skt.

rance, bellow. *yeddu rance véyuts unnadi*, the ox bellows.

rancu, adultery. *núru nómulu oca rancutó póyinavi*, one act of impurity has wiped out a hundred of penance; *idi ná peḷḷánici yevaritónó rancu caṭṭindaṭa*, she is said to have accused my wife of adultery with some one.

rancumunḍa, whore, adulterous widow. *osé rancumunḍa!* you bitch! *yentó ṣrótriyulam ani cheppu conutsu, mi vanṭi sómayazula péḷḷavḍré y'iṭuvanṭi rancumunḍala chéta lacsha vattula vratamulu modalainavi chéyinchi, sancóchimpaca hastóḍacamulu putstsu coni, mundugá bhójanamunacu siddha paḍuduru*, for all your pretence of piety and your high-sounding ecclesiastical titles, you are ready to perform for adulterous widows rites and ceremonies for the souls of their departed husbands, and without a moment's hesitation let them lave your hands and place your repast before you.

rancupóvuṭa, to commit adultery.

ranḍa, widow, a term of abuse. Skt. *ósí pádu randa? níc émi chéṭucálam vachchindé?* dirty bitch, what mischief are you up to now? *ranḍa vivāhálu,* widow marriages (a thing most shocking to the orthodox).

randhramu, hole. *rómarandhramu* is a pore (hair-hole).

ranḍi, come (plural); imperative plural of *vatstsuṭa*. *peddamanishi (fónuló): ḍácṭaru gáru, má pillavāḍu súdi 'mingāḍu, venṭané ranḍi. ḍacṭaru naucaru: ḍacṭarugáru inṭlo léru, sáyantránici gáni ráru; appaṭi dácá águtára, léca póte súdi y'ippuḍé ca valená?* Gentleman (on the phone): Doctor, my child has swallowed a needle, come at once. Doctor's Servant: The doctor is not at home, he won't come till the evening; can you wait till then or do you want the needle at once?

rangamu, battle-field, scene (in a play). Skt. *rangabhúmi,* battle-field; *rangasthalamu,* lists.

rangu, colour, paint.

ranjacuḍu, one who causes joy.

ranjintsuṭa, to delight, to gladden.

rappintsuṭa, to summon; causative of *vatstsuṭa,* to come.

rappu, darning. Hindustani.

rapputíyuṭa, to darn.

rasamu, flavour, emotion. Skt. Six flavours are recognized: *tipi,* sweet; *pulusu,* sour; *vagaru,* astringent; *uppu,* salt; *cáramu,* pungent; *chédu,* bitter. *cóparasamu* is angry passion; *dayárasamu,* the spirit of love. There are six flavours but nine emotions—lust, courage, pity, astonishment, merriment, timidity, austerity, wrath, gentleness (*ṣánṭarasamu*). *anna rasamu canna ádarana rasamu mélu,* the flavour of welcome is better than that of food.

rasamu, mercury. Short for *padarasamu.* *diccu málina vaidyuḍu savāyi rógánici mandu y'imm anṭé, rasam peṭṭaḍam chéta, cáḷḷu paḍi póyinavi,* the infernal doctor gave me mercury as a medicine for venereal disease and I cannot move my legs.

raṣana, a woman's girdle. Skt. A book word.

rasavargamulu, condiments.

rasábhásamu, inelegant, bad taste, common, vulgar. Skt. *rasabhásamugá máṭláḍuṭa* is to speak inelegantly, vulgarly.

rasi, pus.

rasicatvamu, elegance, refinement. Skt. *mí daggira yémaina rasicatvam v'unṭé bógamvaḷḷaló v'unḍé sáram mícu telusunu,* if you had any breeding you would understand the point in keeping dancing-girls (in India it is the mark of a gentleman to keep a dancing-girl just as in Europe royalties were expected at one time to have mistresses).

rasicuḍu, a man of taste, an elegant. Skt.

rasíḍu, receipt. English.

raṣmi, beam (of the sun), splendour. Skt. *púrvapu raṣmi, gauravamu niluputú v'unnámu,* we maintain our ancient pride and splendour.

rastá, road. Hindustani.

rathamu, chariot, especially the chariots of the gods and festival car. Skt. *ratham y'i vídhi nunchi veḷḷé véla cá vachchindi,* it is time the festival car came along this street.

rathótsavamu, car festival. Skt., from *rathamu,* chariot, and *utsavam,* procession.

rati, coitus. Skt.

ratnamu, jewel. Skt. There are nine gems—*navaratnamulu*: pearl, emerald, diamond, coral, sapphire, agate, ruby, chrysolite, cat's-eye; *strīratnamu* is a jewel of a woman; *ratnam ittaḍini podigité ratnánici yémi lópamu?* the jewel shines as bright though set in brass; *ratnál anní vaca tsóṭa, nattagullal anní vaca tsóṭa,* gems will all be in one place, so will snails (birds of a feather flock together).

ratstsa, highway, public place, place of meeting. *inṭa gelchi ratstsa geluva valenu,* command at home before you command abroad.

ratstsabanḍa, ratstsamánu, the stone seat or tree where the village assembles; also *ratstsatsáviḍi,* if there is a building.

rauluconuṭa, to take fire; also *raguluconuṭa, ravuluconuṭa.*

rautu, trooper. Skt.

rava, particle, pellet (e.g. of a shot-gun cartridge), small brilliant; also *ravva.*

ravanta, ravvanta, ever so little. *émi y'ấşcharyamu! ravanta sahấyamu chésina pacshamuna padi véla rúpáyalan ichchedam anna Síramvári vyavahấramulóné guḍḍi gavva putstsu cóca venuca şicsha vésinaré!* what a wonder! when we offered ten thousand rupees in the Siramvaru's case for ever so little help he would not take a single farthing and gave judgement against them.

ravána, dispatching (goods, letters). Hindustani.

ravídu, broker's commission, brokerage. Hindustani.

ravuluconuṭa, to take fire; same as *raguluconuṭa, rauluconuṭa.*

ravva, pellet; also *rava.*

ravva, ill-fame, bad name. *penimiṭi ágnyá mírinán ani vaṭṭi ravva nác enducu?* why should I get a bad name by transgressing my husband's orders? *nannu v'úrice ravva peṭṭaḍamé cáni, míru manchí-cheḍḍá yerugaru,* it is only to give me a bad name, you don't know right from wrong.

rayitu, peasant; same as *raitu,* so also *rayiti bhúmi, rayituvári* for *raitibhúmi, raituvári.*

-rá! appellative affix added to the verb, especially in the imperative in addressing inferiors; to call an inferior say *óré!*

rá-, prefix meaning 'royal'. Short for *rája. rácumáruḍu,* prince; *rátsúli,* royal issue.

rá! come! Imperative of *vatstsuṭa;* also *rammu;* plural *ranḍi.*

rá, to come, an infinitive of *vatstsuṭa,* and in fact much commoner than *vatstsuṭa.* For 'don't come' say *rávaddu,* not *vatsuvaddu;* for 'I cannot come' say *rálénu,* for 'I thought of coming' say *rátalachinánu.*

rábaḍi, income, what comes in; from *rá,* to come; also *vatstsubaḍi.*

rábandu, vulture; from Skt. *rámabandhu.*

rábaṭṭuṭa, to recover, to obtain; from *rá,* to come, and *paṭṭuṭa,* to take. *remishanula zábitá tayáru chéyintsaḍamló cá valasin anta sommu rábaṭṭa vatstsunu,* in making up the remission list you can knock off any amount of money.

ráca, rácaḍa, coming. Verbal noun of *rá,* to come. *vána racaḍa, práṇa pócaḍa, yevarici teliyadu,* no one can foretell the coming of rain or the going of life; *rácalu póculu* is a common expression for comings and goings, traffic, movement.

rácási, demon (female). Skt. A corrupt form of *rácshasi.*

rácshasi, female demon. Skt. Commonly used of any disagreeable woman, like English 'vixen'; *rácshasi buṭṭa* simply means a large basket.

rácshasuḍu, male demon. Skt. *Lancaló puṭṭinavár ella rácshasulé,* all born in Lanka are Racshasas (coming of a bad stock).

rádu, doesn't come; negative third person single of *rá,* to come. *cucca vasté ráyi doracadu, ráyi doricité cucca rádu,* if the dog comes the stone is not handy; if the stone is handy, the dog won't come.

rádu, must not, don't; negative imperative from *rá,* to come. *vípu mída coṭṭa vatstsunu, caḍupu mída coṭṭa rádu,* beat on the back, don't beat on the belly (punish me but don't touch my pay).

rádu, does not come (to him) in the sense of he does not know; this is the common way of saying I don't know, I don't speak. I don't speak English is *nácu Y'Inglishu rádu. ocaḍu: áru bháshalu máṭláḍut undani chilucanu ammitivi, dinici occa máṭaina rádu, yenta mósam cheṣáu. incóḍu: tondara paḍa bóc anḍi, nidánintsanḍi; yeppuḍú miré máṭláḍutunṭé, chilacacu sávacáşam eccaḍidi?* Smith: When you sold me the parrot you said it spoke six languages; it doesn't know even a word; you cheated me. Jones: Steady on. When you talk the whole time yourself, how can the parrot get a word in? *bhárya: ná mída mícu préma v'unnadá? bharta: ná mukha lacshaṇálanu nuvvu tsadivi tsúḍu telustundi. bhárya: nácu tsaduvu rádu gá* *yeṭlá tsadivédi?* Wife: Do you love me? Husband: Read my features and you will see. Wife: But as I can't read, how am I to read your features?

rágamu, tune. Skt. *tiyyagá tiyyagá rágamu, múlagagá múlagagá rógamu,* practice and patience will give you the tune, by moaning and groaning you will make yourself ill.

rágala, predestined (that which must come). *Rágala Ṣani Rámêṣvaramu póyiná tappadu,* you will not escape the predestined calamity though you go to Ramesvaram on pilgrimage.

rágamu, affection. Skt. more common in the compound *anurágamu.*

rágálu, screams.

rágálupeṭṭuṭa, to scream. *rágálu peṭṭi yéḍtsutsunnádi,* she is crying and screaming.

rágárágá, little by little.

rági, copper.

rágulu, the grain *rági,* a small millet (*Cynosurus coracanus*). Tamil. In the Circars this is *tsóllu. Ragi* is only used where Telugu is mixed with Tamil as in Madras and Chittoor.

ráhityamu, deficiency. Skt. *dóshará-hityamu,* faultlessness.

Ráhuvu, the demon Rahu, whose head (cut off by Vishnu) pursues the sun and the moon and causes eclipses. *ráhu cálamu,* inauspicious time.

rái, stone; usually spelt *ráyi. aṣud-dhamu mída rái vésté mukhána paḍu-tundi,* throw a stone into mire and the mire will fly into your face.

rája, king. Skt.; but the title is usurped by any moderate land-owner and is given by government to any large one either personally or as a hereditary title; ruling chiefs are usually distinguished as His Highness the Raja or Maharaja; the old use is preserved in the Skt. proverb *yadhá rájá tadhá prajá,* as the king, so his people; *qualis rex talix grex.* Also *rázu.*

rájabhatuḍu, king's servant, policeman.

rájabhágamu, the land-tax (the king's share of the produce).

rájadháni, king's head-quarters, capital town. Skt.

rájadróhamu, high treason. Skt.

rájagrühamu, palace. Skt.

rájahatya, regicide.

Rájapratinidhi, the Viceroy.

rájarázu, king of kings. Skt. Also *rárázu.*

rájaṣrí, form of address, especially on letters, which must be addressed *Mahárája Raja Ṣri,* Holy Emperor and King, but it means no more than Esquire or even Mr.

rájatvamu, royalty. Skt.

rájavídhi, the king's highway. Skt.

rájádhicáramu, sovereignty. Skt.

ráji, compromise. Hindustani. *ráji chéyuṭa* is to compound (in law).

rájínámá, deed of compromise or resignation. Hindustani. *rájínámá itstsuṭa* is to resign an office.

rájípaduṭa, to be reconciled.

rájíparatsuṭa, to reconcile. *várini rájíparichináḍu,* he composed their quarrel.

rájyamu, government, kingdom, public province. Skt. *rájya tantramu* is public policy; *adhinivéṣa rájyamulu* is the ordinary newspaper word for Dominions (of the British Empire).

rájyángamu, public department. Skt.

ráléḍu, has not come, did not come (neuter). *ṭícharu: ninna madhyánam scúlucu rá léd émi? baluḍu: má nán-nanu sarcasucu tísucu pó valasi vach-chindanḍi.* Teacher: Why didn't you come to school yesterday afternoon? Boy: I had to take my father to the circus.

ráléḍu, did not come, cannot come (masculine).

ráḷḷagani, quarry; from *ráyi,* stone, and *gani,* mine.

ráḷḷu, plural of *ráyi,* stone. *dúrapu conḍalu nunupu, daggirici poté ráḷḷu gunḍlu,* far hills are smooth, if you go close rocks and stones (distance lends enchantment to the view). *ráḷḷu* is also slang for rupees.

-rálu, feminine affix corresponding with masculine *-ḍu. racshassuḍu,* a male demon; *racshassurálu,* a female demon; *manamaḍu,* grandson; *mana-marálu,* granddaughter.

ráluṭa, to drop down. *panḍ ocaṭi ná cáli samípamuna rálindi,* a fruit fell near my feet; *í caruvuló janamu yenḍ* *áculu rálin aṭṭu ráli póyinadi*, in this famine the people dropped like dead leaves; *ní paḷḷu rála coṭṭuṭánu*, I will knock your teeth out; *mánu panḍlu mánu cindané rálutavi*, a tree's fruit falls under it.

Ráma, Rámuḍu, Ráméchendruḍu, Rama, the hero of the 'Ramayana'. *Rámuni vanṭi rázu v'unṭé, Hanumantuni vanṭi banṭu appuḍé v'unṭáḍu*, like master like man (when there is a king like Rama there will be a servant like Hanuman).

rámabandhu, vulture. Skt. Commonly *rámbandu* or *rábandu*.

rámachilaca, parrot. *ḍácṭaru vind ichchenu, vindu samayamló tana rámachilaca canabaḍacunḍá tera aḍḍamu peṭṭenu; vachchina atiṭhulaló ocaru ganṭala coddi máṭláḍut'unḍiri; áyana muginchina pimmaṭa, chilaca teraló nunchi iṭla anenu 'mí náluca tsúpintsanḍi'*, a doctor gave a dinner-party; he covered his parrot up with a curtain so that it should not be seen; among the guests there was one who talked for hours on end; when he had finished the parrot remarked from behind the curtain: 'Please put your tongue out.'

Rámarájyamu, Rama's rule or kingdom, i.e. a particularly good government.

Rámaráma, alas (Rama is invoked in trouble).

Rámavácyamu, God's truth (Rama's word). *tahaṣṣiludáru gári vácyamu Ráma vácyamu, vári nóṭi nunḍi vachchina máṭacu tirugu lédu*, the Tahsildar's word is as the word of God; the word that proceeds from his mouth will surely be fulfilled.

Rámáyanamu, the 'Ramayana' (epic poem). Skt. *tsadivédi Rámáyanamu, paḍagoṭṭévi dévasthálalu*, what he reads is the 'Ramayana', what he destroys temples (piety professed but not practised); *Rámáyanam antá vini, Rámuḍici Síta yémi cá valenu aḍigin aṭṭu*, like asking what relation Sita was to Rama after hearing the whole of the 'Ramayana'. (He that telleth a tale to a fool speaketh to one in a slumber; when he hath told his tale, he will say, what is the matter.)

rámbanḍu, vulture; from Skt. *rámabandhu*.

ráni, queen, proprietrix; *ránivásamu*, zenana. Skt.

rán'í', let it come; from *rá*, to come, and *itstsuta*, to give. *vachchéd ellá rán i, póyyéd ellá pón i*, let what is to come, come, and let bygones be bygones.

ráṇintsuṭa, to shine. Skt.

rárázu, king of kings. Skt. Also *rájarázu*.

ráshṭramu, realm, province. *bhásha-prayucta ráshṭramulu* is the newspaper expression for linguistic provinces.

rási, having written; for *vrási*.

rási, heap, from Skt. *ráṣi*.

ráṣi, constellation, sign of the zodiac. Skt.

rásipóyuṭa, to heap up.

ráta, writing. For *vráta*. *í ráta teliyacundá v'undi*, this writing is illegible.

ráta, ráti, of stone; inflexional forms of *ráyi*, stone. *ráta nára tísin aṭṭu*, like taking the bark off a stone; *púrvam vale ráti ganulaló peṭṭi áḍinché rázul unṭé, víḷḷu y'iṭla anṭár anḍi?* Would (the Svarajists) talk like this if as of old there were kings who put rebels into stone presses and squeezed them?

rátibanḍa, rock.

rátigunḍevádu, a hard-hearted man.

ráṭnamu, spinning-wheel. Skt. (Mr. Gandhi's panacea for India's ills.)

rátri, night. Skt. *tana talupu tisi, porug inṭici peṭṭi, rátri antá cuccalu tólutú cúrtsun aṭṭu*, he took his own door and put it on his neighbour's house, and spent the night driving away the dogs (charity begins at home). *ocaḍu: Lacshmayya tsálá kharídu gala parupu connáḍu. incóḍu: háyigá nidra paṭṭindá? ocaḍu: paṭṭa lédu, dáni kharídu talutsucunṭé digulu vési Lacshmayya rátri antá nidrapó lédu.* Smith: Jones has bought a very expensive bed. Brown: Does he sleep soundly on it? Smith: No, he lies awake all night worrying about what it cost him. *váḍ artha rátram andu vachchináḍu*, he came at dead of night.

rátrimpagalu, night and day. *míru*

rátrinpagaḷḷu pani páṭalu léca y'illu paṭṭucuni vadalaru, you sit indoors day and night doing nothing; *rátrimpagalu cashṭa paḍi nértsuconnánu,* I studied hard night and day.

rátsa, royal, public, adjective of *rája. rátsa pínugu tóḍu léca tsávadu,* a king will not die alone (will involve others in his ruin).

rátsacáryam, public affair. Skt.

rátsacomáruḍu, prince. Skt. *rátsacomárita,* princess.

rátsacurupu, rátsapunḍu, carbuncle.

rátsuṭa, to rub.

rávaddu, don't come.

rávale, rávalenu, must come. *yazamáni: nénu tsálá máṭalu máṭládanu, oca vélu cadilisté nuvvu venṭane rávale. cotta naucaru: nénu tsalá maṭal áḍan anḍi, nénu talacáyi adiste rán ani míru anucónḍi.* Mistress: I won't say much: if I move a finger you must come at once. New Servant: I don't speak much either; if I shake my head that means I am not coming.

rávatstsunu, may come.

rávi, the pipal tree (*ficus religiosa*).

rávintsuṭa, to summon; causative of *rá,* to come.

ráyabáramu, ráyabháramu, embassy, deputation. Skt. *ráya* stands for *rája. mana sangham Gavarnar-gári daggirici rayabáram pampints ále,* our association must send a deputation to the Governor.

ráyabári, ráyabhári, ambassador. Skt.

ráyi, stone; also *rái. cucca vasté ráyi doracadu, ráyi doricité cucca rádu,* when the dog comes the stone is not there, when you find a stone the dog has gone; *loḍa loḍa loḍamanṭú mangalamló ráḷḷu pósi véyinchin aṭlu Arava goḍava máṭláḍut unṭáru,* they talk the Tamil noise which is like pouring stones tup-tup-tup into an earthenware dish. *Lacshmayya: mí pillaváḍu ná mida ráyi visiri véṣáḍu. Vencayya: adi mícu tagilindá? Lacshmayya: tagala lédu. Vencayya: aité vesinaváḍu máváḍu cádu.* Smith: Your boy threw a stone at me. Jones: Did it hit you? Smith: No. Jones: Then it wasn't my boy that threw it. *cáchina cheṭṭucu ráḷḷa debbalu,* it is the laden tree that stones are thrown at.

ráyuṭa, for *vráyuṭa,* to write. *ṭícharu: ní dastúri bottigá bág unḍa lédu; bágá ráyaḍam nertsucó. báluḍu: bágá rásté mícu tappul anni canipistav anḍi.* Teacher: Your handwriting is bad, learn to write a better hand. Boy: If I write well you will see all my mistakes.

rázu, king. Skt., same as *rája. dhairyamu léni rázu, yóchana léni mantri,* if the king has no courage his minister can have no policy; *rázu yentó dharmam anté,* the people will reflect the qualities of the king.

rázuṭa, to take fire. *paic ém annanu, manasuló vánici cópamu rázutsuné y'unnadi,* though he says nothing his anger has taken fire within; *poyi rázadu,* I cannot keep the pot boiling.

recca, wing. Properly a bird's wing, but used analogically, like the English word, of other things, such as the wing of a door, the shoulder-blade, &c. *pacshi lágu yegaraḍánici nácu reccalu lévu,* as the officer replied to the Accountant-General's audit slip asking him to state the length of his march as the crow flies (I am not a crow); *reccalu virigina pacshi vale v'unnáḍu,* he is like a bird with broken wings (helpless).

reḍḍi, caste suffix, village headman. The Reddies are a farming caste, which supplies many village headmen.

rellu, reed.

renḍava, renḍó, second, other. *renḍóváru,* others; *manacu mátramé pratyécangá y'í gadi máṭláḍindámu, iccaḍacu renḍóváru ráru,* we have engaged this room; others can't come in.

renḍintalu, double.

renḍu, two. *danḍulóci póté renṭló vacaṭi,* if you go to war it will be one of the two (defeat or victory).

renḍureṭlu, twice.

renḍu sárlu, two times.

reppa, eye-lid. *reppa váltsaca,* without winking, staring.

reppapáṭu, wink.

-reṭlu, suffix meaning 'times', '-fold'. *múdureṭlu,* three times, threefold; *padireṭlu,* tenfold.

reṭṭimpu, twice as much.
reṭṭintsuṭa, to double, to repeat, to ingeminate.
ré, night, short form of *rátri, réyi.*
réca, row, stripe. Skt.; also *rékha.*
récu, petal of a flower, thin metal plate. *venḍi récu,* silver plate; *inupa récu,* iron plate; *puvvu tsúchi ánanda paḍu vánici á puvvucu yenni récul unnavi anu vichárana paṭṭadu,* the flower lover will not inquire how many petals a flower has.
régaḍa, clay. *vána níḷḷu régaṭi néla paḍi manchi níḷḷ annu,* rain-water falling on clay will be drinkable.
régu, a tree, the jujube (*Zizyphus jujuba*), the Indian long plum.
régupanḍu, Indian long plum.
réguṭa, to be excited, to be angry.
rékha, row, stripe. Skt.; also *réca.*
reṇuvu, atom, grain (e.g. of sand). Skt.
répacaḍa, early in the morning. Used in books.
répu, to-morrow (first meaning is dawn, but not now used of dawn). *répu ané rózu v'unnadá?* is there such a day as to-morrow? (to-morrow never comes).
répumápu, day and night. *áviḍa répómápó svargánici veḷḷe bharta cósam prati nimisham yeduru tsústú v'unnadi,* she is looking forward every minute to a husband who may go to heaven any night or day.
répuṭa, to excite, to irritate; causative of *réguṭa. máni póyina punḍu maḷḷí répin aṭṭu,* ripping up old sores.
rétsuṭa, to excite, to rouse, to set on; causative of *réguṭa;* also *répuṭa.*
réṭu, rate. English. *modaṭi vartacuḍu: chinnatanamlóne nácu sukhangá unḍedi. renḍo vartacuḍu: nácu sukhangá unḍédi, ardha réṭucu railulo prayáṇam cheyyaḍánici víl ayyédi.* First merchant: I had a happy childhood. Second merchant: So had I, I could travel half-price.
révu, ford, strand, port, landing-place. *dongalu tólina goḍḍu yé révuná dáṭiná vacaté,* what ford the thieves took the ox by is all the same. *Lacshmayya sṭímaru yecci nidrapóyenu; tellavárin tarváta Lacshmayya: sṭímaruló prayáṇam chésté nidra paṭṭadu, vántulu veḷḷutav ani nannu bhayam peṭṭár anḍi, nác émí ibbandi caluga lédu. sṭímaru adhicári: sṭímaru inca révu vadili peṭṭa lédu; injanu cheḍi póte bágu chést unnáru.* Smith went on board and slept, at dawn he remarked: they say you can't sleep on a steamer; they frightened me about seasickness, but I wasn't sick. Ship's Officer: The steamer has not left the landing-place; the engine got out of order and we are repairing it. *tsáci révu* is the dhoby's washing-ground (from *tsácali,* washerman; they wash on the bank of a river or tank).
réyi, night; also *ré, rátri.*
réyimpagaḷḷu, night and day. *Yélinavárici réyimpagaḷḷu vacaṭe,* day and night are alike to God.
-ricamu, suffix meaning 'state', like English '-hood'. *cannericamu,* virginity; *tsuṭṭaricamu,* relationship; *ménaricamu,* cousinhood (by the mother's side; the most favoured marriage is that with a cousin on the mother's side).
ricábu, stirrup. Hindustani.
ricárḍu, record. English. *ricárḍu chéyuṭa,* to record.
ricárḍu-pícaru, the record-keeper; from record, English, and *pícuṭa,* to pull (contemptuous).
rictamu, empty. Skt. *rictahastamu,* empty hand; *Briṭishuváru Mahátmuni ricta hastamulató pampinchinária,* the British sent Mr. Gandhi away empty-handed.
rimánḍu, remand. English. Of remands to jail.
rimishanu, remission. English. Of remission of taxes.
ripéru, repair. English. Of repair of buildings and roads and such things.
ripórṭu, report. English. Of reports to the police and such things.
risṭu, wrist. English. Of wrist-watches (*risṭu gaḍiyáramu*) and such things.
ritstsa, amazement, horror.
rivázu, custom. Hindustani.
rivvuna, suddenly; onomatopoeic.
rizalyúshanu, resolution. English. Of resolutions at a meeting.
ríti, way, manner. Skt.
roccamu, cash. *dínici aruvu béramu*

lédu, roccamu cummarintsa valenu, no credit, you must fork out cash.

roda, noise.

rommu, chest, bosom. *rommu pagilina* is broken-winded; *rommu taṭṭu conutsu,* beating his breast.

rompa, cold (in the head). *vāḍici rompa paṭṭinadi,* he has caught cold; also *paḍisemu.*

ronḍi, paunch. *ná ronṭini rupáyi,* the rupee I have on me (money being tied in the cloth near the paunch).

rotstsu, mud, foulness. *vídhulu rotstsu paḍi padi rózulu naḍavaḍḍánici valla aindi cádu,* the streets being befouled for ten days we could not walk in them; *rotstsu campu* is a foul smell.

roṭṭa, twig.

roṭṭe, roṭṭi, bread, loaf. Hindustani. *peddamanishi oca chinna roṭṭe, incó pedda roṭṭe chétuló putstsuconenu; annadammulaina iddaru báluru canupinchiri. peddamanishi: mílo yevaru manchiváḷḷó canuccunṭánu randi. anna (pedda roṭṭe tísu coni tinṭu) ayyá, má tammuḍé manchiváḍ andi.* A gentleman with a small loaf and a big loaf in his hands saw two boys who were brothers and said: 'I will now see who is the better boy.' Elder brother (taking and eating the big loaf): 'my little brother is the better boy'; *roṭṭe taguvu cóti tírchinadi,* the monkey settled the bread dispute (between two birds by eating the bread himself).

roṭṭelaváḍu, baker.

royya, prawn.

rócali, pestle. *rócaṭici chiguru paṭṭin aṭṭu,* like a rice-pounder budding (like a pig flying); *górutsuṭṭu pai rócaṭi pótu,* the blow of a pestle on a corn; *rótlo burra peṭṭi rócaṭi debbacu zaḍisin aṭṭu,* like the man who put his head in the mortar and was then afraid of the blow of the pestle (getting cold feet after starting); *ácali yettutundi, attagárá, anṭé, rócali mingavé, cóḍalá, annadi aṭa,* when she said, Mother-in-law, I am hungry, she answered, Daughter-in-law, eat the pestle.

ródanamu, lamentation. Skt. *araṇya ródanamu,* lamentations in the jungle (wasted efforts); *mí araṇya ródanam vinéváru yevaru?* you are wasting your breath; no one will listen to you.

róḍḍu, road. English. *móṭáruváḍu: yémayya i róḍḍu antá nídé anuconi naḍustáv émayya? báṭasári: i banḍi antá nídé anuconi tolutú v'enducayyá?* Motor driver: Why do you walk as if the whole road belonged to you? Pedestrian: Why do you drive as if the whole car belonged to you?

rógamu, illness. *tiyyagá tiyyagá rágamu, múlagagá múlagagá rógamu,* try and try and you will get the tune, moan and groan and you will get ill; *paḍisemu padi rógála peṭṭu,* a cold in the head is ten illnesses in one. *rógi: ná zabbu míru cudurtsa galará? vaidyuḍu: tappacunḍá cudurustánu; mí zabbu mádiri zabbulanu cudurtsaḍamló nácu pratyéca sámarthyam undi; i mádiri rógam galavárici nénu iravai yénḍlu mand ichchánu.* Patient: Can you cure my disease? Doctor: Without doubt, I have patients whom I have been treating for twenty years for the same sort of illness as yours. *oca ḍácṭaru: mí jayánic émi cáraṇam anḍi? rendo ḍácṭaru: rógi yém córité á pracáram cheyyaḍánici vappucunṭánu.* First doctor: To what do you attribute your success? Second doctor: I always humour my patients and let them do what they like.

rógishṭi, ailing.

rólu, mortar. *rótlo burra peṭṭi rócaṭi debbacu zaḍisin aṭṭu,* putting your head in the mortar and then being frightened by the pestle; *rólu caruvu yeragadu,* the mortar knows not famine (there will always be some grain to pound in it).

rómamu, hair. Skt. *paici niccapoḍutsuconi unna dírkha rómamulu,* thick hair sticking up; *róma randhramu* is a pore.

róshamu, anger. Skt. *róshaṁn vachchi,* getting angry.

róta, disgust. *cotta vinta páta róta,* fresh news pleases, stale news disgusts; *róta paḍindnu, róta caligindi, rósi y'unnánu,* I was disgusted.

róyuṭa, to be disgusted with.

rózá, rose. English; also *guládi,* which is Hindustani. There is no Telugu word for 'rose'.

rózu, day. Hindustani. *dunné rózulaló déṣam mida póyi, cóta rózulaló coḍavali paṭṭu coní vachchináḍ aṭa,* like the man who wanders around in the ploughing days and comes along with his sickle at harvest. *sabhádhipati: í rózu upanyásam ichché áyana América déṣasthuḍu, áyana tólu tellanid ainá, áyana hrüdayam mana vale nallanidé; andu valla míru ṣraddhagá vina valen ani córut unnánu.* Chairman: To-day's lecturer is an American; though his skin is fair, his heart is as black as ours; so I beg you to listen to him with attention.

rózuṭa, to pant. *cucca yenḍalo rózuts unnadi,* the dog is panting in the sun.

rubburólu, grinding mortar.

rubbuṭa, to grind.

ruchi, taste. Skt. *ácali ruchi yerugadu,* hunger knows not taste (hunger is the best sauce); *vachchí ráni máṭalu ruchi, v'úri v'úrani v'úragáya ruchi,* half-spoken words (childish prattle), and half-pickled vegetables are pleasant; *burracu vaca guṇamu, jihvacu vaca ruchi,* no two heads and no two palates are made alike, tastes differ; many men, many minds (or, as the Italians say, *tante teste tanti cervelli,* there is a different brain in every head).

ruchigá, tasty.

ruchintsuṭa, to be tasty.

ruchitsútsuṭa, to taste.

Rucmini, Krishna's wife (one of them).

rudduṭa, to rub.

Rudra, a name of Siva (the oldest name; the one used in the Rigveda, where Siva is only an adjective meaning gracious).

rudrabhúmi, burning or burial ground. Rudra is a name of Siva.

rudrácsha cheṭṭu, the bastard cedar (*elaeocarpus ganitrus*).

rudrácshalu, rosary (made from the seeds of the bastard cedar).

ruḷḷuveyuṭa, to rule. English. *y'í cágitamunacu ruḷḷuvéi,* rule this paper.

rumálu, handkerchief. Hindustani.

runamu, debt. Skt.; also *rünamu. Lacshmayya: nén ippuḍu yém bádha paḍut unnánó renḍu acshardḷḷó cheppu. Vencayya: cámam. Lacshmayya: cádu, rüṇam.* Smith: Tell me in one syllable what I am now suffering from. Jones: Love. Smith: No, debt.

rusumu, a customary fee. Hindustani. An old revenue term: village officers and Government officers used to get *rusums* which have all, alas, been abolished; some Zamindars still manage to extract *cancherusumulu,* pasture fees.

ruvvuṭa, to throw. *yecci pói, paṭṭi, tsúchi, digivachchi ráḷḷa ruvvin aṭṭu,* like the man who climbed the tree and felt the fruit and then came down and threw stones.

ruzuvu, proof. Hindustani. *vaca véḷa ná mida firyádu chési ruzuvu parichiná, sva samracshanártham chésinán ani cheppi tappintsu cunṭánu,* if he brings a case against me and proves it, I shall plead the right of self-defence and get off.

rú, contraction for *rúpáyi,* used in accounts.

rúca, two annas silver coin, more commonly called *béḍa*; money in general. *rúca lénivaḍu póca cheyya léḍu,* the man without a sixpence is not worth an areca nut; *tana conguna v'unna rúcá, tana caḍupuna v'unna biḍḍá, panici vastáru,* the coin in your cloth, the child of your begetting, will be of use to you.

rúḍhamu, certain. Skt.

rúḍhamugá, ruḍhigá, certainly. *Rangaḍu: mánéjaru gáru lópala lér ani nícu rúḍhigá telusuná? naucaru: lér ani áyané cheppär anḍi, áyana máṭ anṭé nícu nammacam léda?* Smith: Can you say for certain the manager is not in? Servant: It was himself that said he was not in: would you doubt his word?

rúḍhíparatsuṭa, to authenticate (legal).

rúlu, a rule. English; plural *rúlsu,* very common of Government rules, &c.

rúpamu, shape, beauty. Skt. The word, like Latin *forma,* means both shape and beauty. *rúpa yauvanamu,* beautiful youth; *rúpavati,* a beautiful woman; *márurúpamu,* disguise; *nizarúpamu,* real shape; *nijarúpamu,* own shape; *rúpahínuḍu,* ugly.

rúpáyi, rupee; from Skt. *rúpya*, silver.
rúpumáputa, to blot out, to destroy. Skt., from *rúpamu*, shape, and *máputa*, to destroy. *páṣacarula bádhalu rúpumápa badinavi*, thuggism has been destroyed.
rünadata, rünapradáta, creditor. Skt.
rünamu, debt. Skt. *rüna-ṣéshamu, vrana-ṣéshamu, agni-ṣéshamu v'untsa cúdadu*, leave no remains of a debt, a sore, or fire. *Lacshmayya: ní máta nilupu cunnáve. Vencayya: yém máta? Lacshmayya: padi rúpáyalu badul isté mi rünam ennatici tírtsu có lén ani venuca annáu; ippatici tirtsacundáne undi, máta chellintsu cunt unnáu.* Smith: You have kept your word. Jones: What word? Smith: If I lent you ten rupees you would always be in my debt is what you said; you haven't paid me back; you are keeping your word. *rünamu chéyuta* is to make a debt; *rünamu tírtsuta*, to pay a debt; *rünagrastudu*, deep in debt; *rünavimuctudu*, clear of debt.
rüshi, Skt. *ṛṣi*, rishi, sage, great wise man. Those most often named are Bruhaspati, the Gods' teacher, Narada and Vasishtha. *samsáramu tyájinchi, adavulaló canda múl ádulu tiné rüshulu sahitamu strila valaló padi, várici dásul ai, tirugutú v'unde várani cheputú v'undaga, uppu pulusu tini, samsáramuló padi coṭṭucuntú v'undé y'itaralacu cámamu jayintsadánici ṣacyam autundá?* when great wise men who have abandoned their family and live in the jungle on roots are said to have fallen into the snares of women and to have become their slaves, will it be possible for ordinary men living a family life and eating food seasoned and sauced, to conquer their desires? *rüshi múlamu, nadi múlamu vichárimpa rádu*, do not inquire the source of a rishi or a river (even now the Hindu sages, such as the Maunasvámi, Silent Sage, of Courtallum, must not be asked where they came from or why they took their vows); *maharshi*, a great rishi; *saptarshulu*, the seven sages.
rütuvu, season. Skt. There are six seasons of two months each: (1) *vasantamu*, spring; (2) *vésavi* or *gríshmamu*, the hot weather; (3) *varshamu*, the rainy weather; (4) *ṣarattu*, the sultry weather; (5) *hémantamu*, the dewy weather; (6) *tsali* or *ṣiṣiramu*, the cold weather, but they may also be differently given, thus: *peddamanishi: sanvatsaramló yenni rütuvul unnái? vidhyarthi: ṭennisu-rütuvu, phuṭbálu-rütuvu ani rendu.* Gentleman: How many seasons are there in the year? Student: Two, the tennis season and the football season.

S

sa-, prefix meaning 'with'. Skt. *sacuṭumbamugá*, with all one's family; *samúlamugá náṣam aináru*, they were ruined, root and branch; *sayuctamu*, reasonable.
sababu, reason, ground. Hindustani. *nívu cheppina sababul anni nácu cúdá panici vastavi*, all your arguments would be equally useful to me; *nícu v'uttaramé rá lédu? sádháranamgá v'uttarálacu zavábu vráyanivárú cheppé sababu y'idé*, the letter did not reach you at all? that is the usual excuse of those who don't answer letters.
sabbu, soap. English. *tahaṣṣiluddáru: boṭléru y'í tálúca yeccadá doracani suvásana gala sabbu dorasáni gárici cá valen aṇṭádu; asádhyamaina córicalu córité yeccada té galamu? yenta manchi vastuvulu techchiná manchivi cáv aṇṭádu; putstsuconna vastuvúlacu sommu y'ivvadu. gumástá: yevari mamúḷlu váḷlacu y'ivvaca póte anni ilágaṇṭi tanṭálé vastavi.* Tahsildar: The butler says the lady wants scented soap which can't be had in this taluk at all; how can we satisfy impossible wishes? However good the articles are that we supply, he says they are no good; he does not pay for what he takes.

Clerk: If you don't give every one his perquisites such troubles are bound to come.

sabha, assembly. Skt.

sabhápati, sabhádhyacshuḍu, chairman of a meeting. Skt. *Lacshmayya gurinchi abhinandana sabha zarigenu; sabhádyacshul agu Vencayya gáru í rítini mutstsaṭinchiri: 'Lacshmayya gáru paráya grámam vár ainá, mana v'uḷḷó iravai sanvatsarála nunchi unṭú, mana grámabhivrüddhicai páṭu paḍut unnáru; áyananu mana v'úri samádhilóné puḍchéṭ aṭṭu Bhagavantuḍu anugrahintsu gáca.'* A meeting was held in honour of Smith. Jones, being Chairman, spoke as follows: 'Though Mr. Smith is a stranger he has lived in our village for twenty years and worked for its welfare; we pray God that he may be buried in our cemetery.'

sabhicuḍu, sabhyuḍu, member of assembly. Skt. *Lacshmayya tánu chinnappuḍu yuddhamuló tsúpina sáhasamunu gurinchi upanyásamló goppagá cheppuṭ unḍenu. sabhicuḍu: yuddham antá míré chésté migilina sainyam antá yémi chésind anḍi?* Captain Bragg was boasting in a lecture of his valour in the wars. Voice from the audience: When you did everything what did all the rest of the army do?

sabjacṭu, subject. English. Telugu colloquial language is commonly interlarded with English words. Thus: *vivâhála gurinchi leccheru má sósayiṭílo tsadavaḍánici vrást unnánu; leccheru y'í sáyancálánici cá valenu ganuca míru vachchinadi tsúḍacundá vrásucunṭ unnámu; í sabjacṭu mída manam discassu chétámu,* I am writing a lecture on marriage for our society; I was busy writing and did not see you coming as the lecture is required for this evening; let us now discuss the subject.

sacala-, prefix meaning 'all'. Skt. *sacaladharmasvarúpulaina,* the embodiment of all charity.

sacilintsuṭa, to neigh.

sacuṭumbamugá, with all one's family. Skt. *Bhímarázu gáru sacuṭumbamugá Cáṣí yátra veḷḷina sangati míru vinnáru cádá?* you have heard, haven't you, that Mr. Bhimarazu has gone on pilgrimage to Benares with all his family?

sad-, prefix meaning 'good'. Skt., also *sat-, saj-, san-,* according to euphonic requirements. *sadácháramu,* good custom; *sadupáyamu,* good use, good expedient; *sadbhacti,* true religion; the opposite is *dur-, dush-,* bad.

sadaru, aforesaid. Hindustani.

sadasyamu, meeting (of Brahmins at wedding functions). Skt. *cómaṭi Cannayya gári inṭló sadasyam véḷa minchi pótundi,* it is getting late for the wedding at merchant Cannayya's house.

sadá, always. Skt. *sundara purusha madhyamuna sadá melagutsu,* always moving among handsome men.

sadácháramu, good custom. Skt., from *sad-,* good, and *achâram,* custom; the opposite is *durácháramu,* bad custom; *crüta yugam náṭi nunchi vastú v'unna sadácháram y'ippuḍu mána valen aṭa!* they pretend we should give up a good custom that has come down to us from the Golden Age!

saddu, noise, sound. Corrupt Skt. from *ṣabdam.*

sadguṇamu, good quality. Skt. *Inglishu baḷlalo tsaduvu cunévaḷḷ antá vaṭṭi ṣunṭhalu, váḷḷacu tsaduvu vachchina cáni vinayádi sadguṇamulu paṭṭu paḍavu,* those who study in English schools are just blockheads; they get some education but have not the good qualities of obedience and so on.

sadupáyamu, good expedient. Skt. *janula cashṭha nishṭhuralu telisina váḷḷu callecṭárlu v'unṭe lábham v'unnadi gáni, carcóṭaculu v'unṭé prazalacu yémi sadupáyam lédu,* the people profit from Collectors who know their difficuties, but if Collectors are hardhearted, they do not know where to turn.

sadvamṣamu, of good family. Skt.

sadvartanamu, of good conduct. Skt. The opposite is *durvartanam,* bad conduct; *ná baḷlo tsaduvucuné pillaváḷḷanu nénu vaccoccaṇṇi rózucu dazanu debbal ainá coṭṭa cunḍa viḍichi peṭṭanu; andu chéta váḷḷacu yenta vidhéyata!*

yenta bhayamu! yenta sadvartana! I don't let the boys in my school off with less than a dozen a day; what obedience! what fear! what good conduct!

sadyógamu, good fortune. Skt.

sagamu, half, also *sakham* in common talk; *santóshamu sagam balamu,* joy is half one's energy. *upanyásacuḍu: mí v'úḷḷó sagammandi buddhi hínullai unnáru. sabhicuḍu: iṭlá dúshinchin anducu míru cshamápaṇa córiténe cáni mému vadali peṭṭam. upanyásacuḍu: aṭlágé córutánu, sagammandi buddhi hinulu cár anṭánu, mícu sammatam éná?* Lecturer: Half the people of your village are fools. One of the audience: We won't let you off without an apology for that insult. Lecturer: I apologize; half of you are not fools; are you satisfied?

sagaṭu, average; also *sarásari.* Hindustani. *ippuḍu manacu vachchina lábhamlo nálugó vantu ménéjarugárunnu, múḍu vantulu taccina camíshanarlunnu putstsucunṭú v'unḍaḍam chéta sagaṭu mída ménéjarugárici yeccuva, camíshanarlacu taccuva muḍutú v'und ani vír antá cheputú v'unnáru,* all the (municipal) commissioners are complaining that while the manager is to get one quarter of the (illicit) profits and the commissioners three-quarters, on an average the manager touches more and the commissioners less.

saggubiyyamu, sago; from English (Malay) *sago* and *biyyam,* rice.

sagótruḍu, belonging to the same *gótra* or clan. Skt.

saha-, prefix meaning 'with'. Skt. *sahacáruḍu,* co-operator (working with); *sahagamanamu,* suttee (going with her husband); *sahajamu,* born with; *sahódaruḍu, sahajuḍu,* brother; *sahapanctibhójanamu,* eating together (in one line); *sahapáṭhi,* fellow student; *sahódari* or *sódari,* sister.

sahacári, accomplice. Skt. *sahacárula parapati sanghamulu,* co-operative credit societies (my munshi invented this term for them for a pamphlet on co-operation we wrote together in 1901, and it has stuck); *í durmárgamló mému cúḍá sahacárinigá v'unnámu,* we also are accomplices in this crime (coining Skt. expressions).

sahagamanamu, suttee. Skt. *saha,* with, and *gamanam,* going (departing this life with one's husband). *vénniḷḷacu v'órvan amma sahagamanamu chéstán annadaṭa,* the woman who could not stand hot water said she would do suttee (and be burnt alive); (orthodox Brahmin speaking): *sahagamanam cheyyan iyyaru gadánḍi? ammavárini álóchintsacunḍá Gódavarini caṭṭi vésináru gadánḍi? Devatalané y'ilá chésé váḷḷacu manushyul' anṭé lacshyam lédu; Brahmanula mányálacu pannulu caṭṭináru,* don't they say they won't allow suttee? Have they not ventured to dam Goddess Godavari? People who treat Gods so care nothing for men; they tax Brahmin land. (To build the great dam (three and three-quarter miles) across the Godavari at Dowlaishvaram was thought impious, and when it was undertaken the Brahmins prophesied that the Goddess would never allow herself to be dammed; it was still more impious to impose a quit-rent on the inams of Brahmins.)

sahajamu, natural, innate. Skt. *Rudramúrti y'andu sahajamugá iṭṭi vicára guṇamulu éviyu lévu,* Rudramurti hasn't these queer qualities by nature.

sahajuḍu, brother; also *sahódaruḍu.*

sahanamu, patience. Skt. *anta sahanam vahintsa galaḍá?* can he have so much patience?

sahasra, 1,000. Skt. Used in Skt. compounds; the common word is *veyyi. sahasra mukhamulu gala Ṣéshuḍu,* Seshudu, who has 1,000 faces.

sahavásamu, association. Skt. *nénu yenta tsaduvucóca póyiná, tsaduvu cunna váḷḷato sahavásam cheyyaḍam chéta nácu conchem manchi chedda telusunu,* though I have not studied much, by associating with those who have, I have learnt to distinguish good and evil to some extent; *paráyiváḷḷató sahavásamu cheyyanu,* I hold no commerce with strangers.

sahá, even, also. Skt.

saháyamu, help. Skt. *nácu dóvaló*

saháyamu chicca lédu, I got no assistance on the way; *dravyasaháyamu*, pecuniary assistance.

sahétucamugá, with good reason. Skt., from *sa*, with, and *hétuvu*, reason.

sahintsuṭa, to endure, to stand. Skt. *naucarlu y'ílá nirlacshyangá máṭláḍutú v'unṭe nénu sahintsa lénu*, I can't stand servants talking so disrespectfully; *nénu y'í avamánam sahintsévánni cánu*, I am not a man to stand that insult.

sahitamu, also. Skt. *mívanṭi peddalu sahitam*, even old people like you. *sayitamu* is another form.

sahódari, sister. Skt. The Telugu words are *acca* and *chellelu*, elder and younger sisters. *sódari* for short.

sahódaruḍu, brother; also *sahajuḍu*. Skt. The Telugu words are *anna* and *tammuḍu*, elder and younger brothers.

saicilu, bicycle. English. *tanḍri: paricsha pyás aité nícu baisicilu coni peṭṭután anṭini; ainá tappáu; tsaduvacunḍá yém chéstáu? coḍucu: saicilu toccaḍam yeṭlágó nértsuconnánu.* Father: I promised you a bicycle if you passed, but you have failed; what will you do without education? Son: Anyway I have learnt how to ride a bicycle.

saiga, sign. Corrupt Skt. from *sangnya*. *pomm ani saiga chéyutsu*, making him a sign to go; *yémiyó saigalu chésiconnuts unnáru*, they are making some signs to one another.

sainica, military. Skt., from *séna*, army. *sainica sancshóbham*, mutiny.

sainicuḍu, soldier. Skt., from *séna*, army.

sairaṇa, patience. Skt. A book word.

saitamu, also. Skt.; same as *sahitamu*.

saitsuṭa, to endure. Skt.

sajívamu, alive. Skt., from *sa*, with, and *jívam*, life. *váru sajívulai y'unnáru*, they are still alive.

sajjana, good people. Skt., from *sad*, good, and *janam*, people.

sakhamu, half; same as *sagamu*.

sakhi, female friend. Skt.

sakhuḍu, male friend. Skt.

sakhyamu, friendship. Skt.

salaga, a certain fee. An old revenue term for one of the customary fees, which have been abolished.

salahá, advice. Hindustani. *vaca clayinṭutó cheppina salahá*, advice given to a client. *upádhyáyuḍu: ná salahá avalambints'anḍi; míru anní vishayáḷḷó mundugá v'unṭe, bágu paḍutáru. vidyárthi: má nánna venuca v'unná, pedda jítam tetstsu cunṭunnáḍ anḍi. upádhyáyuḍu: mí nánnac émi pani? vidhyárthi: railvé gárḍu pani.* Teacher: Take my advice and always be to the fore in everything and you will do well. Pupil: My father is always at the back but he gets good pay? Teacher: What's his job? Pupil: Railway guard.

salasala, simmering, rustling. Onomatopoeic.

salámu, salaam. Hindustani.

sallápamu, talk. Skt.

sallápintsuṭa, to talk. Skt.

salupuṭa, to do, to perform; not so common as *cheyyuṭa*. In books they prefer *onarintsuṭa*. *úpiri salupuṭa* is to draw breath.

sam-, prefix meaning 'with', 'much', 'very'. Skt. *sampúrṇamu*, very full; *sampríti*, great affection; *samyuctamu*, joined with.

samacaṭṭuṭa, to try.

samacshamu, presence. Skt.

samacúrtsuṭa, to cause. *Daivamé samacúrchin appuḍu*, when God Himself has brought it about.

samamu, like, level. Skt. *yénugacu cálu viragaḍamu, dómacu recca viragaḍamu samamu*, the loss of a wing to a mosquito is as bad as the loss of a leg to an elephant; *príti léni cúḍu pinḍa cúṭitó samamu*, food given without love is no better than the cake offered to the dead.

samamuchéyuṭa, to level.

samanjasamu, right, proper. Skt. A book word.

samanvitamu, joined together. Skt. Used in books and newspapers.

samaramu, battle. Skt.

samarpaṇa; reverent offering. Skt. *á pustacál anniṭini agnihótruḍiki samarpaṇa chésté nácu yentó santóshamga v'unṭundi*, I shall be very pleased if you offer all those books to the God of Fire.

samarpintsuṭa, to offer reverently. *váḷḷa vadda ḍabbu putstsu coni páda* *púja samarpinchinávu*, you have taken money from them and done them reverence. Properly to offer something to a God, *samarpintsuṭa* is used of any humble and reverent offer and also as a legal term it is used to translate to assign.

samarta, female puberty.

samartáḍuṭa, to attain female puberty. *mí rendó chellelici samartáḍina dáca peḷḷi cheyyacuṇḍá atté v'untsanḍi*, keep your second sister unmarried till she has attained puberty.

samarthata, ability. Skt.

samarthintsuṭa, to succeed, to achieve. Skt.

samarthuḍu, a clever man, competent. Skt.

samashṭi, the whole. Skt. *samashṭi ṣásanóllanghanamu*, collective civil disobedience.

samastamu, all. Skt.

gnyapti y'atithci mari y'unṭunnadi rózulu y'anni
satcáram ṣri Rájá samastam chésina y'andu,

the guest will remember all the years of his life all the kindnesses of the Raja; in the above example *anni*, all, the common word, is used with *rózu*, the common word for 'day', and *samastam*, all, the Skt. word, with the Skt. word *satcáram*. The example is a literal translation of two lines of Homer on hospitality into Telugu hexameters. There is no Telugu translation of Homer, but the example illustrates how easy it would be to translate Homer into Telugu in the original metre.

samasthalamu, level land, a plain. Skt., from *samam*, level, and *sthalam*, place.

samasyamu, problem. Skt. The word properly means a poetical problem, but is commonly used in newspapers to translate problem in politics.

samayamu, occasion, time. Skt. *samayam ain appuḍu*, when an opportunity comes.

samayóchitamu, seasonable. Skt., from *samayam*, occasion, and *uchitam*, suitable; *samayóchitamaina máṭa* is a word in season; *samayóchitangá máṭláḍuṭa*, to speak appropriately to the occasion; *samayóchitangá nimishamló catha calpinchi nívu boncutaú*, you have made up a lie for the occasion on the spur of the moment.

samayuṭa, samasipóvuṭa, to be destroyed. Skt. *coddi coddiga tisté conḍa cúḍá samasi pótundi*, bit by bit even a mountain can be removed.

samácháramu, affair. Skt. Thus you say to a petitioner: *yémi samácháramu?* what is it all about?

samádhánamu, peace, satisfaction, a treaty. Skt. *váḍu maḷḷí nór ettacuṇḍá tagina samádhánamu cheppinánu*, I gave him such satisfaction that he could not raise his voice any more.

samádhánapaḍuṭa, to make peace, to compromise.

samádhánaparutsuṭa, to reconcile.

samádhi, grave, cemetery. Skt. *dáyanu mana v'úri samádhilóné púḍchéṭ aṭṭu Bhagavantuḍu anugrahintsu gáca!* May God grant that he be buried in our village!

samádhi, contemplation, religious meditation. Skt. *mému tapassamádhi nimittamu Himádrici póyedamu*, we will go to the Himalayas for penance and religious meditation.

samájamu, assembly, association. Skt.

samájicuḍu, member of association, congregation, and the like.

samánamu, like, equal. Skt. *manamu taccuva varṇamula váritó samánulamá?* are we on a level with persons of the lower castes?

samápti, end, conclusion. Skt. For instance, the end of a book or chapter.

samárádhánamu, worship, religious services. Skt. *míru lantsálu putstsuconi Bráhmalacu santarpaṇalú samárádhánálú chéstár ani vinaḍam chéta, mí mída v'unna cópam chéta, Dora y'iláguna chésinaḍu*, the Collector treated you like that because he was angry hearing that you took bribes and spent them on Brahmins and their ceremonies.

samávéṣamu, meeting. Skt. Common in newspapers.

sambaḷamu, wages. Skt. The Tamil expression. In Telugu *jítamu* is commoner.

sambandhamu, relevancy, connexion,

alliance by marriage. Skt. Common in all these senses, especially the last. *cudirina sambandhamu cheḍi póté, maḷḷí manchi sambandhamu rádu*, if the marriage arranged does not come off, it will not be possible to get another good alliance.

sambandhintsuṭa, to be connected.

sambhavamu, origin.

sambhavintsuṭa, to happen. Skt.

sambháshaṇa, conversation. Skt.

sambháshintsuṭa, to converse.

sambhávana, alms to Brahmins. Skt., properly honour, gift of honour.

sambhávintsuṭa, to honour.

sambhógamu, sexual intercourse. Skt. *hína játi sambhógamu* (with low caste persons) is specially reprehensible.

sambhógintsuṭa, to have sexual intercourse.

sambhramamu, flurry, confusion. Skt.

sambhramintsuṭa, to be confused.

samétam, samétu, even. Skt. *nalugurilóci velladánici siggubáṭugá v'unḍi, ataḍu sabhalóci yeccaḍici tambúlánici samétam veḷḷéváḍu cáḍu*, afraid to hold up his head in public he never went to a meeting or even to take betel with any one; *zamindárlu samétu nannu gauravam chést unnáru*, even Zamindars treat me with courtesy; *scúluló tsaduvu cuné pillacáyucu samétu adi telusunu*, every schoolboy knows that; *nácu chinnappuḍu samétu chícaṭ anṭé bhayam*, I have been afraid of the dark from my childhood.

samharintsuṭa, to kill, to destroy. Skt.

samháramu, killing, destruction. Skt.

samidha, sacrificial fuel. Skt.

samishṭi, undivided. Skt. *samishṭi cuṭumbamu*, undivided family; *samishṭi múladhanacampení*, joint-stock company.

samisipóvuṭa, to be destroyed; from Skt. *ṣamayuṭa*, to perish, and Telugu *póvuṭa*. *cúrtsunḍi tinṭu v'unṭe conḍa cúḍá samasipótundi*, if you sit at it you can eat even a mountain.

samiti, assembly. Skt.

samípamú, near. Skt. *áyána samípamuna*, near him; *samípa várasulu*, the nearest heirs.

samípintsuṭa, to approach. Skt. *móṭáru banḍi pólisuvánini samípintsuts* *unḍagá, lópala cúrtsunna bhárya y'oca vaipucunnu, bharta y'incoca vaipunacu chétulu tsúpinchiri; pólisu cánsṭébilu: mír iddaru cheroca dárini veḷḷa talatsu connárá?* a car was approaching a policeman and the wife put out her hand one way, the husband another. Constable: You are thinking of parting company?

samjáyashi, explanation, information; also *samujáyashi*. Hindustani. The ordinary word for explanation demanded of erring officials. *nizam dáchi vési tappu samujáyashi istáru*, they conceal the truth and give a false explanation.

sammatamu, agreed to. Skt. *upanyásacuḍu: mí v'úḷḷó sagammandi buddhi hínullai unnáru. sabhicuḍu: iṭlá dúshinchin anducu míru cshamápaṇa córiténe cáni mému vadali peṭṭam. upanyásacuḍu: aṭlágé, córuṭánu. sagammandi buddhi hínulu cár anṭánu, mícu sammatam éná?* Lecturer: Half the population of the town are fools. Voice from the audience: We won't let you off without an apology for that insult. Lecturer: I beg pardon, I will say half are not fools. Do you concur?

sammati, consent. Skt.

sammatintsuṭa, to consent. Skt.

sammánamu, respect. Skt.

sammánintsuṭa, to respect. Sk.

samme, league, strike. Skt. From the meaning 'league' comes the meaning 'league to get higher wages', hence a strike.

sammeṭa, large hammer.

sampada, sampannata, wealth. Skt. *guṇasampada* means wealth of virtue; *má balamu vári sampadaló*, our strength is in their prosperity, as Queen Victoria proclaimed.

sampangi, the champak (gold flower). Skt. (*michelia champaca*).

-sampannuḍu, affix meaning 'endowed with', 'possessed of'. Skt. *sishṭachárasampannulaina* means old fogyish; *satsaháyasampannuḍu*, a very helpful person; *mahaṣactisampannuḍu*, having great power.

sampati, prosperity. Skt. *ápati mocculu, sampati cunṭhlu*, vows in adversity, revilings in prosperity (to the

Gods; the Devil was sick, the Devil a monk would be).

sampatti, endowment, possession. Skt. *suguṇa sampatti*, possession of good qualities.

sampádacuḍu, one who acquires. Skt.

sampádanamu, acquisition, earnings; also *sampádyamu*. Skt. *váni sampádana váni khartsunacu sarigá sari póyinadi*, he just makes both ends meet.

sampádintsuṭa, to acquire. Skt.

sampádyamu, acquisitions, earnings; also *sampádanamu*. Skt. *occadi sampádyamu, padimandi pálu*, one earner to ten dependants—a very common state of things in India.

sampradáyamu, doctrine, custom, practice. *sampradáyamu telisina gáni ṣástramu teliyadu*, knowing the doctrines is not knowing the Scriptures.

sampratinsuṭa, to discuss, to examine. Skt. Used in newspapers.

sampráptamu, obtained. Skt. *váru chésina chicaṭi tappunacu phalamugá sampráptamulaina garbhamulu*, swollen wombs obtained as the fruit of erring in the dark; *ṣástra viṣvásamu cheḍina pacshamuna, déṣamunac enni y'anarthamulaina sampráptamulu agunu*, unbelief will bring disaster.

sampúrnamu, complete, perfect, end. Skt. End of a book, finis, is *sampúrnamu*.

samracshacuḍu, guardian, protector. Skt.

samracshana, protection. Skt.

samracshintsuṭa, to protect. Skt.

samrüdhi, opulence. Skt. Used in blessings; a Brahmin will (on payment) wish you: *áyurárógya putrapautra dhana canaca vastu váhana samrüdhir astu* and so on, all Skt. words for long life, health, progeny, and prosperity.

samsargamu, union, intercourse. Skt.

samṣayamu, doubt. Skt. *níc álaganṭi samṣayamu yenducu caligindi?* why did you have that suspicion? *sandéhamu* is commoner. *samṣayáspadamaina manushyulu*, suspicious characters; *samṣayátmuḍu*, suspicious.

samṣayintsuṭa, to doubt.

samsára, the phenomenal world (philosophy). Skt.

samsáramu, family, wife. Skt. *samsáramu lénivádu*, a man without wife and family; *samsáramu naḍipintsuṭa*, to support a family; *ippuḍu samsárulé bógamváḷḷa canṭe yeccuvagá járatvam chéstú v'unnáru*, nowadays family women are more licentious than dancing-girls; *sarva-jan-ádaraṇíyamaina sangítam véṣyala pálu chéyaca, samsára strílu dánini tama pálu chésuconi, bhartalanu santósha peṭṭi, grühamulanu svargatulyamulugá cheyyaḍánici dánni v'upayógistáru*, if married women, instead of leaving music, which gives universal pleasure, to dancing-girls will take it up themselves, they will give pleasure to their husbands and use it to make home heavenly.

samsári, householder. Skt.

samscarintsuṭa, to reform; in religion, to hallow. Skt.

samscáramu, reform. Skt. The usual word when you are talking of social reform, political reform, religious reform. In religion a sacrament. *Hindu sampradáyamló viváhamu samscáramu*, the Hindu doctrine is that marriage is a sacrament.

samsthánamu, estate. Skt. Now used commonly of Zamindars' estates; the old meaning was state, province. *nácu tama samsthánamló pani y'ippistám annáru*, you (the Zamindar) said you would give me a job on your estate.

samsthápanamu, establishing. Skt.

samuchitamu, suitable. Skt.

samudáyamu, joint, common. Skt. *samudáyapu-pani* is a communal purpose; *samudáyapu-nela*, common land.

samudáyintsuṭa, to comfort. Skt. *pillaváḍu viḍuvacunḍá yéḍustú unnáḍu; míru vacca paryáyam yettu coni veḷḷi samudáyintsanḍi*, (Wife to husband), The child is crying without stopping; suppose you take it up and soothe it for once in a way.

samudramu, sea. Skt. *yéru yenni vancalu póyina samudramulóne paḍa valenu*, even the weariest river winds somewhere safe to sea; *samudránici yétamu vésin aṭṭu*, like trying to pump out the sea; *samudramu y'ída vatstsunu gáni, samsáramu y'ída rádu*, you may ride the waves but be thrown by your wife. *Gangaḍu: nuvvu samudra prayáṇam chéṣává? Rangaḍu: chéṣánu gáni nácu visugu puṭṭindi. Gangaḍu: yenduchéta? Rangaḍu: oca ala tsústé, anni alalu aṭlágé v'unnáyi, bhédam yémí lédu.* Smith: Have you made a sea-voyage? Jones: Yes, but it disgusted me. Smith: Why? Jones: If you have seen one wave, you have seen all; there is no difference.

samuḍu, an equal. *váḍu nító samuḍu,* he is on an equal footing with you.

samujáyashi, explanation. Hindustani. More commonly *samjáyashí.*

samukhamu, presence. Skt. Used commonly in the exordium to petitions; petitions are addressed to 'the Collector's presence'.

samúhamu, crowd, multitude. Skt.

samúlamugá, with its roots. Skt., from *sa,* with, and *múlamu,* root. *Brahmaṇícamu bhrashṭam ai pótundi, varnáṣrama dharmálu samúlamu naṣistu v'unnavi,* Brahmanism is going to the dogs, caste sanctities are being destroyed root and branch.

samvatsaramu, year. Skt. Usually pronounced 'sanvatsaramu'.

samvádamu, discussion. Skt.

samyamamu, self-control. Skt.

samyógamu, union, association. Skt.

samyucta, joint, united. Skt. *Samyucta Ráshṭramulu* is the newspaper rendering of United Provinces.

sanámuḍu, namesake. Skt., from *sa,* with, and *náma,* name. *váḍu ná sanámuḍu,* he is my namesake.

sanátana, eternal, ancient. Skt. *sanátana dharma,* the eternal duties (prescribed by the Hindu religion). *áyana Teluguló vráya tala peṭṭenu. sanátamugá vatstsuts unna déva bhdshalóné unḍa valenu, gáni Teluguló vráyuṭacu yé vidhamugá sádhyam agunu?* he has chosen to write in Telugu. We must write in the eternal speech of the gods (Sanskrit). How can you write in Telugu?

sancalanamu, addition (in arithmetic). Skt.

sancalpamu, resolution, providence. Skt. *míru sidha sancalpulu, anni mí y'ishṭa pracáramé zariginavi,* you are a real Providence, everything happens according to your wish.

sancalpintsuṭa, to resolve, to decree (as Providence does). Skt. *veyyi rúpáyalu peṭṭi Tirupatiló dévuḍi guḍici dacshina gummánici venḍi récu chéyintsa valen ani sancalpintsu connánu.* I have resolved to place a silver plate of the value of Rs. 1,000 on the southern door of the God's Temple at Tirupati.

sancaramu, mixing, defilement. Skt. *varṇa sancaramu* is mixing of castes (very abominable according to the Hindus); *sancara bhásha,* an impure language; *táme cácunḍa culam várin andarini sancarulunu chési,* defiling not only themselves but the whole caste.

sancaṭamu, difficulty, trouble, affliction, venereal disease. Skt. *svatantramu svarga lócamu, paratantramu práṇa sancaṭamu,* independence is heaven, dependence mortal affliction; *sancaṭálu tagilintsu coni,* suffering from venereal disease.

sancela, fetter. Corrupt Skt. from *srünkhalam.* The plural is *sanceḷḷu.*

sancétamu, rendezvous, secret sign. Skt. *sancétácsharamulu* means a cipher-code.

sancharintsuṭa, to wander. Skt.

sancháramu, travel, wandering, motion. Skt. *Gópu: nuvvu vrásina 'Nirantara Sancháramu' ané vyásam ém aindi? Rámuḍu: á vyásamu nénu yenni patricalacu pampinchiná maḷḷi ná daggaricé vachchindi. Gópu: adi cúḍa nirantara sanchdramu chést unnadi cábólu.* Smith: What has happened to your essay on 'Perpetual Motion'? Jones: I sent it to all the papers but it has always come back to me. Smith: Perpetual motion, in fact.

sanchi, sack, purse, bag. *santsulaló gallugallumani rúpáyala mróta vinutsunḍuṭa chevula panḍuvu cádá?* is not the jingle-jingle of rupees in their bags a delight to the ears?

sanchica, pamphlet. Skt. (One number of a newspaper or a magazine.)

sancluptamu, abridged. Skt. *sancluptamu chéyuṭa,* to abridge.

sancóchamu, hesitation. Skt. *nic á*

sancócham accara lédu, you need not hesitate for that.

sancóchintsuṭa, to hesitate; also *sandéhintsuṭa.* Skt.

sancramintsuṭa, to enter on, to pass on, to make transit (of stars). Skt. *talli-dandrula guṇálu coḍuculacu sancramintsun ani vamṣa páramparyapu siddhántamló nícu nammacam unnadá?* do you believe in the qualities of parents passing on to their sons according to the heredity theory?

sancshépamu, summary, abridgement. Skt.

sancshóbhamu, agitation. Skt. *crotta crotta márpulu valana déṣa sancshóbhamu calugunu,* constant changes lead to agitation; *sainica sancshóbhamu,* mutiny.

sancu, chank, conch. Skt. *ṣankham.* Used to make a noise in temple worship. The Madras Government, following in the wake of native rulers, Portuguese, and Dutch still fishes for them at Tuticorin; there is a Government Bulletin on chanks.

sandaḍi, mob, shindy, bustle. *pendli sandaṭlo boṭṭu caṭṭa marichináḍ aṭa,* like the bridegroom who in the marriage bustle forgot the ring; *nénu lópaḷa yémó pani sandaḍilo unnánu, ní pilupu nácu vinabaḍa lédu,* I was busy inside and did not hear you call.

sandarbhamu, circumstance, juncture. Skt.

sandarṣanamu, seeing, sight. Skt.

sande, sandecaḍa, sandevéḷa, evening, in the evening. Skt., from *sandhya. sande chícaṭi,* twilight; *sandevártsuṭa,* to recite the daily prayers (Brahmins).

sandéhamu, doubt; also *sandiyamu.* Skt. Leader writers in the newspapers, laying down the most questionable propositions, always end their sentences *sandéhamu lédu,* there is no doubt.

sandéhapaḍuṭa, to doubt, to be suspicious. *mana y'inṭici yevarainá ná cósam vachchin' appuḍu canṭabaḍutú v'unṭe sandéha paḍi connáḷḷu vaca manishini cávali v'unchináḍu,* if he saw any one coming to our house for me he was suspicious and put a woman to watch me.

sandéhintsuṭa, to hesitate; also *sancóchintsuṭa.* Skt.

sandéṣamu, message. Skt.

sandhánamu, reconciliation. Skt. *nícu má Manóranjinitó sandhánam caluga cheyyaḍánici nénu saháyam cheyya tsálanu,* I cannot help you to a reconciliation with our Manoranji.

sandhi, treaty, peace, peacefulness. Skt. *sandhi* is the watchword, but not always the practice, of the Indian National party.

sandhya, twilight (morning or evening). Skt. *sandhyádi criyalu,* morning or evening ceremonies or acts; *sandyasnánamu,* morning or evening bath.

sandhyavandanamu, matins or vespers. Skt.

sandhyavártsuṭa, to perform matins or vespers; also *sandevártsuṭa. Lacshmayya: nénu sandhyavartsucuné véḷa nannu palaháránici pilavaḍam Mallayyacu dharmam'éna? Vencayya: nuvvu sandhyavártsav ani Mallayyacu telusunu. Lacshmayya: telesiná nénu sandhya vartsután ani anucóḍam dharmam cádá?* Smith: Was it considerate of Jones to invite me at prayer-time? Jones: He did it just because he knows you don't say your prayers. Smith: Though he knew that, ought he not to have considered I was saying my prayers?

sandiyamu, doubt. Skt. *sandéhamu* is commoner.

sandu, interval, opening, cleft, fissure, lane, opportunity. Skt. *véḷḷasandu* is the space between two fingers; *sanditstsuṭa* is to give room or opportunity for; *sandulu gondul antá veticináḍu,* he hunted in every nook and cranny; *sandu tsúchi tsorabadináḍu,* he waited for an opportunity and rushed in.

sangaḍi, pair, especially a double dugout canoe made of two hollow palmtrunks tied together. The single canoe is *dóne.*

sangamamu, coming together, confluence, sexual intercourse. Skt. *sangama dóshamu* is venereal disease.

sangamu, union, confluence. Skt. *nadí-ságara sangama sthalamu* is the place where a river falls into the sea;

nadula sangamu is the confluence of rivers.

sangaramu, war, battle. Skt.

sangatamu, joined. Skt.

sangati, thing, fact, that. Skt., from *sangatam*, joined; 'the fact that' is also *sangati; atadu tsani póyina sangati teliya lédu*, I did not know of the fact of his death; *Bhímarázu gáru sacuṭumbamugá Cáṣi yátra veḷḷina sangati nívu vinnávu cádá?* haven't you heard that Mr. Bhimarazu has gone to Benares with his whole family? *Lacshmayya: ninnu gurinchi anéca sangatulu vinnánu. Vencayya: ainá nuvvu ocaṭi ruzuvu cheyya lévu lé.* Smith: I have heard several things about you. Jones: Anyway you can't prove a single one of them. *ḍacṭaru: mí áyana vishayamai nácu áṣa lédu. bharta: nácu incá práṇam unnadi, bhaya paḍa bócu. bhárya: míru úrucóndi; ḍacṭarugárici anni sangatulu telusunu, bhár̥am antá áyana mída véstám.* Doctor: I have no hopes for your husband. Husband: There is life in the old dog yet, don't be afraid. Wife: Hold your tongue; the doctor knows everything; we will put the whole burden on him. *bharta: cáfi cheyyaḍánici iravai margálu v'unnai. bharya: nác enducu chepputáru á sangati? bharta: váṭiló nuvvu occaṭi nértsucunná nácu tsálunu.* Husband: There are twenty ways of making coffee. Wife: Why do you tell me that? Husband: I shall be satisfied if you learn one of them.

sanghamu, association, society. Skt. Used commonly to translate 'society' in such phrases as 'the welfare of society'.

sanghaṭanamu, happening. Skt. *daiva sanghaṭanamulu míru vicharintsa valasina pani lédu*, it is not for you to investigate the happenings of fate; *má Ratisundarici mícu viváham sanghaṭana cheyyaḍánici yenni páṭlaina paḍutánu*, I will do my very best to bring off your marriage with our Ratisundari.

sanghaṭintsuṭa, to happen. Skt.

sangítamu, song, music. Skt. *báluḍu: accayyacu sangítam peṭṭe coni peṭṭáu gadá? nácu baisicilu coni peṭṭu. tanḍri: baisicalu yenducu? báluḍu: accayya sangítam modalu peṭṭagáné nénu baicicilu yecci yeccaḍicaindveḷḷi pótánu.* Boy: You have given my sister a musical-box, buy me a bicycle. Father: Why a bicycle? Boy: So that I can get on it and ride away when she starts her music.

sangnya, sign, gesture; also *saungnya, saiga.* Skt.

sangóru, half share of crop; short for *sagamcóru.*

sangrahamu, abstract. Skt. The word properly means 'putting together', so compilation, précis. *sangraha námamu* is what our Government translator uses for the Short Title of an Act.

sangrahintsuṭa, to compile, to summarize. Skt.

sangrámamu, war, battle; also *sangaramu.* Skt.

sankhya, figure, numeral. Skt.

sanmánamu, honour. Skt.

sanmánascuḍu, right-minded. Skt.

sanmárgamu, the good way. Skt. A Tahsildar being urged to take a bribe by his wife says (*tanaló*): *ayyó, nén iṭuvanṭi y'acramamunac eṭlu lóbaḍunu? í rácshasin eṭlu sanmárgamunacu dimpa galugudunu;* (*biggaragá*): *nív enni cheppinanu rája cárya vishayamulaló ní máṭa vinanu; manacu dhanamu ṣáṣvatamu cádu, déhamulu ṣáṣvatamulu cávu, nityam aina paralóca sukhamunu vichárintsu có valenu* (aside): My God! how am I to yield to so base a temptation? How am I to turn the she-devil to ways of righteousness? (Aloud): Whatever you may have to say, I must abstain from discussing matters of public interest with you; the goods of this world are perishable; our bodies are perishable; the everlasting felicity of the next world should occupy our thoughts.

sanna, sannani, thin, fine. *sanna biyyam* is fine rice as opposed to *mutaca*, coarse.

sannadu, grant, patent of nobility, &c. Hindustani. For instance, the *sanads* given to Zamindars at the permanent settlement.

sannáhamu, preparations. Skt. *sannáhamu chéyuṭa*, to make ready.

sannicallu, currystone, the stone on which condiments are rubbed.

sannidhánamu, vicinity, presence. Skt. Used in the same way as *sammukhamu* of One's Honour's presence in petitions and so on.

sannihitamu, near. Skt. *sannihita gnyáti* is a near relation; *vánici cálamu sannihitam ainadi,* his time is near.

santa, fair, market, shandy; from Skt. *santhá.*

santa, recitation from Vedas. Skt. *nícu tsaduvu rádu ganuca Véda páṭhacula lágu santa cheppucó,* as you can't read, repeat after me like the Veda reciters.

santa, near. Same as *chenta.*

santacadáru, signatory; opposed to *niṣánidáru,* marksman.

santacamu, signature. *chitracárulu tama paṭála cinda santacam chéstáru; yenducu? paṭánici modal édo chivar édo tsúchéváḷḷu telusu cóḍanici,* Why do artists sign their pictures? So that people can see which is the top and which is the bottom.

santana, joining, agreement. Skt.

santarpaṇamu, feast given to Brahmins. Skt. It is a religious duty to feast Brahmins and give them presents. *mí ṣacti coladi renḍú vandalacó, múḍu vandalacó Bráhmalacu santarpaṇa chési, mícu tóchina mátram sambhávana y'ivva vatstsunu,* feed 200 or 300 Brahmins according to your means and then give them each a present to the amount you think fit (they don't get much as a rule, one rupee, half a rupee, four annas).

santasamu, joy. Skt. A less commoner form of *santósham.*

santatamu, constant, continual. Skt. *santatamuna,* constantly.

santati, santánamu, progeny. Skt. *nácu santánam calaga léd ani yetti poḍichináḍu,* he jeered at me for having no children. *Lacshmayya: santána niródhánni gurinchi upanyásan zarugut und aṭa, pódam, vastává? Vencayya: nénu ránu, má paṣuvulacu santána niródham accara lédu, mácu yeppuḍu páḍi und-áli.* Smith: There is a birth-control lecture on, will you come to it? Dairy-farmer: Not I, I don't want my cattle to exercise birth-control, I want milk.

santápamu, affliction. Skt. One of the very numerous words for grief.

santápintsuṭa, to grieve. Skt.

santóshamu, joy. Skt. *santóshamu sagam balamu,* joy is half one's strength (a cheery heart goes all the way, a sad tires in a mile-a); *chevvácu póyina ammacu yenta vyasanamó, doricin ammacu anta santóshamu,* the lady who found the ear-pendant was as happy as the lady who lost it was sad (it is an ill wind that blows no one any good). *ócaḍu: Rámayya yenducu anta santóshangá unnáḍu? incóḍu: móṭaru banḍi tsaucagá connáḍu. ocaḍu: nuvvu yenducu inta santóshangá unnávu? incóḍu: nácu paniciráni móṭáru banḍini Rámayyacu anṭa caṭṭänu.* Smith: Why is Brown so happy? Jones: He has bought a car cheap. Smith: Why are you so happy? Jones: I foisted a worthless car on Brown. *santósham* is the common way of saying thanks, please, &c.

santóshapaḍuṭa, to feel pleasure, to thank.

santóshapeṭṭuṭa, to please.

santóshapúrvacamgá, willingly. *yentamátram abhyantaram lédu, santóshapúrvacamgá y'istánu,* no objection at all, I will give it willingly.

santóshintsuṭa, to rejoice. *Lacshmayya: podduna ná peḷḷám midá cópam vachchi tiṭṭänu. Vencayya: áviḍecu mí mída cópam rá lédu? Lacshmayya: rá lédu, navvindi. Vencayya: yenducani? Lacshmayya: nén entó dhairyam tetstsuconi cóppaḍḍ anducu santóshinchindi.* Smith: I got angry with my wife this morning and called her names. Jones: Didn't she get angry with you? Smith: No, she laughed. Jones: Why did she laugh? Smith: She was so pleased at my summoning up courage to get angry.

santushṭamu, pleased (adjective). Skt.

santushṭi, pleasure. Skt.

sanuguṭa, to grumble. *váḍu yeppuḍú yédo sanuccuntú v'unṭáḍu,* he is always mumbling something; *nívu v'onṭariga y'iccaḍa yémi chéstu v'unnávu? mámúlu pracárangá níló nívu sanuccunṭú* *v'unnává yémiṭi?* what are you doing here all alone; grumbling to yourself as usual?

sanvatsaram, year. Skt.; also *samvatsaramu. Lacshmayya: sanvatsaram cindaṭa tísu conna bácini venṭane iyyamani ninnu ákhari sári aḍugut unnánu, ica mída aḍaganu. Rámayya: ica mída aḍagan ann'anducu nácu tsálá santóshamu.* Smith: This is the last time I ask you for the money I lent you last year. Jones: Thanks: I am glad to hear it. *ocaḍu: conni sanvatsarála cindaṭa ní vale nácu gaḍḍam v'unḍédi; adi bág unḍa léd ani canucconi, dánni tísi véṣánu. incóḍu: conni sanvatsarála cindaṭa ní vale nácu mukham unḍédi, adi bág unḍa léd ani canucconi, dáni tísi védám anṭé vílu léca póyindi, andu chéta gaḍḍam penchänu.* Smith: I had a beard like yours some years ago; thinking it was best off, I took it off. Jones: I had a face like yours some years ago; not being able to take it off, I grew a beard. *peddamanishi: sanvatsaramló yenni rütuvul unnai? vidhyarthi: tennisu rütuvu, phuṭbálu rütuvu ani renḍu.* Gentleman: How many seasons are there in the year? Student: Two, the tennis and the football seasons.

sanvatstsarádi, New Year's Day. Skt., from *sanvatsaram*, year, and *ádi*, beginning.

sanyasintsuṭa, to renounce the passions. Skt. *váḍu sanyasinchináḍu*, he bade adieu to the world.

sanyásamu, asceticism. Skt.

sanyási, ascetic, hermit. Skt. *turaca vídhiḷo sanyási bhicsha*, a *sanyási* going to a Muhammedan street for alms (a bad choice).

sanyásintsuṭa, to renounce the passions. Skt. *sanyasintsuṭa* is commoner.

saphalamu, successful. Skt., from *phalam*, fruit. *ná janmamu saphalam ainadi*, my life has borne fruit; *ná córica saphalam ainadi*, my wish has been fulfilled; *ná púrva janma punyamu saphalam ainadi*, the merit acquired in a former birth has borne fruit.

sapinḍudu, person with common male ancestor. Skt. Also *gnyáti*. The *pinḍa* is the funeral cake such persons eat together on the anniversary of the common ancestor's death; the connexion is not observed beyond the seventh generation.

sapláyi, supply. English. Used especially of camp supplies to officials and any other more or less compulsory supplies. *myúnisipal camishanarlac andarici dípálalóci tsamuru sapláyi chésé váḷḷamu*, we used to supply oil for their lamps to all the municipal commissioners.

saptam, seven. Skt. The Telugu is *yéḍu*. *saptami* is common in the sense of the seventh day of the lunar month; *saptarshulu*, the seven Rishis; *saptasamudramulu*, the seven seas.

sarabhasamu, haste. Skt. Used in books.

saracu, any merchantable commodity. *sarucu* in talk.

saracu, heed, regard.

saracuchéyuṭa, to have regard for.

saradá, fondness, interest. Hindustani, from Skt. *ṣraddha*. *tsúḍa valen ani saraddá v'unṭe,* if you care to see.

saradáru, sirdar, leader. Hindustani, from Skt. *ṣaradhari*.

sarafará, supply. Hindustani. *níṭi sarafará*, water supply.

sarafaráchéyuṭa, to supply. Hindustani.

sarambi, ceiling. Malay.

sarangu, head boatman, boatswain. Hindustani.

sarasamgá, sarasamaina, cheap. *sarasamaina dhara*, a cheap rate.

sarasamu, sarasamaina, charming, jocular. Skt., meaning 'juicy'. *sarasamu virasamé*, joking causes breach (a joke never gathers an enemy but often loses a friend); *idi sarasamgá v'unnadi*, that's very funny; *itaḍu nátó sarasál áḍutú v'unnáḍu*, he is laughing at me; *sarasál áḍaḍam árambhinchináḍu*, he began to joke.

sarassu, lake. Skt.

sarasuḍu, amiable or excellent man. Skt. *míru sangítamló sarasulu*; *dánni grahistáru*, you are very good at music, you understand it.

sarasurálu, amiable woman. Skt.

Sarasvati, the goddess of learning.

sarábu, shroff, money-changer, cashier. Hindustani. Also *shardbu.*

sarásari, average, on an average; also *sagaṭu. paddulanu sarásari chei,* average up the figures; from *sari-sari,* equal: *anni sarásarini yentacu istáu?* what will you sell them for at a flat rate?

sarcasu, circus. English. *ocaḍu: sarcasucu nipp anṭu cund anḍi. incóḍu: sarcasuló nippu mingévḍḍ unnáḍu; váḍici caburu pampité sari.* Smith: The circus is on fire. Jones: Send for the performer who eats fire.

sarcáru, government. Hindustani. *sarcár udyógam,* an official post.

sarchi, search. English. *muddái: nénu yém ettu coni poyinán ani míru anumána paḍuṭ'unnáru? pólisu inspecṭaru: gurram, banḍi. muddái: aité nannu sarchi cheyyanḍi, nácu bhayam lédu.* Accused: What do you suspect me of having stolen? Police Inspector: A horse and carriage. Accused: Then search me, I am not afraid.

sarculu, goods, merchandise. Hindustani.

sarcyúṭu, circuit. English. Used of the Governor's or Collector's tours.

sardi-chepputa, to arrange.

sarduconuṭa, to arrange oneself.

sarduṭa, to arrange.

saré! all right, right oh!; also the same. Emphatic of *sari. rátri ainá saré, pagal ainá saré,* it's all the same whether it is day or night.

sari, equal, end, right. Skt. *sadrüsach. sariléni máṇicyamu,* a matchless gem; *á vamṣamu itanitó sari,* his line ends with him; *nela sarici,* at the end of the month; *saricániváḷḷu,* people who are not our equals; *saricánipani,* improper behaviour; *aṭanici sari léḍu,* he has no equal; *idi sari cádu,* this is not right; *cáviḍi yenni vancalu pótén émi, y'illu chérité sari,* it's all right if the yoke reaches the house however many bends it may have made on the way; *gázulu béramu bhójanánici sari,* glass bangle-trade is a bare subsistence; *ninn alla nácu déhamu sari lédu,* I felt poorly all yesterday.

saricisari, tit for tat. *saricisari chesináḍu,* he paid them in their own coin.

sarigá, gold lace. Skt. *sarig antsu chira,* a woman's cloth with gold hem.

sarigá, correctly, equally. *renḍu pallacilu sarigá vatstsut unnavi,* the two palanquins were coming on abreast.

sarihaddu, boundary.

saripaḍuṭa, to suit, to fit, to be enough. *mícu saripaḍité untsuconḍi,* keep it if it suits you; *biyyam saripaḍi póyindi,* the rice is finished; *míru nácu sakham vantu vadali peḍiténé cáni saripaḍadu,* it won't be enough unless you leave me half.

saripóvunaṭṭi, corresponding, fitting.

saripóvuṭa, to correspond, be reconciled, to fit, be equal. *avi mícu saripótavi,* these will suit you, fit you. *nivu tiṭṭinaddnicini, nénu coṭṭinaddnicini saripóyindi,* the thrashing I gave you was only fair payment for your taunts; *váni sampádane váni khartsumacu sarigá saripóyindi,* he just makes both ends meet.

sariputstsuṭa, to equalize.

sarisamánamu, equality.

sarisari, all right.

saritsútsuṭa, to collate, to compare and correct.

sariyaina, equal, proper, level.

saróvaramu, pond. Skt. Used in books.

sarpamu, serpent. Skt. One of the few words which English and Telugu derive from a common source. *China désamuló cúḍá ghóra sarpamu vachchi paṭṭucunnad ani bhérilu váyinchi, ganṭalu coṭṭi, dánni bedara coṭṭadánicai pedda dhvani chéstáru.* (At eclipses) in China also they think a great serpent has caught the sun and beat their drums and gongs to frighten it away.

sarucu, an article for sale; also *saracu.*

sarva, prefix meaning 'all'. Skt. *sarvasámagri,* all one's household goods; *sarvasvatanturálai,* being a very independent woman; *sarvajanasámányamaina haccu,* public right.

sarvabhaumatvamu, empire. Skt., from *sarva,* all, and *bhúmi,* earth.

Sarvabhaumuḍu, the All-Ruler; the newspaper word for the King-Emperor.

sarvacaḷáṣála, university. Skt., from

sarva, all, *calá*, art, and *ṣála*, hall. Also *viṣvavidyálayamu*.

sarvadá, always.

sarvagnyátnamu, omniscience. Skt.

sarvagnyuḍu, omniscient. Skt.

sarvasvamu, entire property. Skt.

sarvatra, everywhere. Skt.

Sarveṣvaruḍu, Lord of all, the Almighty. Skt.

sarvóttamamamu, best of all. Skt., from *sarva*, all, and *uttamam*, excellent. *váru peddalu ganuca, andarú varu cheppina pracáram naḍutsu cunṭé sarvóttamamugá v'unṭundi*, as he is an old man it is most excellent for all to take his advice.

sasácalyamugá, fully. *ní charitram anta sasácalyamugá vinipimpumu*, let us hear your whole story from beginning to end.

sasi, beauty, health, good. *sasémirá?* what is the good of it? An expression applied to an obstinate man.

sasigá, in good health. *ámecu ollu sasigán unḍa lédu*, she wasn't well.

sasyamu, crop. Skt.

sat-, prefix meaning 'good'. Skt. *satsvabhávamu*, good character; *satcáramu*, kind treatment.

satcarintsuṭa, to treat kindly. Skt.

satcáramu, kind treatment. Skt. *atithi satcáramu pondi*, having received hospitality;

gnyapti y'atithci mari y'unṭunnadi rózulu y'anní

satcáram ṣrí rája samastam chésina y'andu:

are two Telugu hexameters which mean that the guest will remember the Raja's hospitality all the days of his life; *y'atithi satcáramu nénu maravanu*, I shall not forget this hospitality.

sati, virtuous woman. Skt. This is the source of the English word suttee.

satpravartana, good conduct. Skt.

satramu, caravanserai, choultry. Skt. *annaṣatramu* is a choultry where food is given as well as lodging.

satsángatyamu, keeping company with the good. Skt. *satsángatyamu ṣubhacáryam*, good company makes a festival.

satsvabhávamu, good character. Skt.

satti, power, vigour, a goddess; from Skt. *ṣacti*, power.

sattu, pewter.

sattuva, power, vigour, strength; from Skt. *satvam*, strength. *nácu vanṭló sattuva v'unṭénú, y'i renḍu chétulú tsallagá v'unṭénú*, if my strength holds out and these two arms keep strong; *mí chétiló sattuva lédu*, you have no strength in your arms; *yeruvu sattuva chétavennu tísu*, the strength of manure fills the ears.

satvamu, existence, essence. Skt.

satyamu, truth. Skt. *satyágraha*, truth-grasping, is Mr. Gandhi's name for civil disobedience though the connexion is not obvious. *Satya Harischandruḍu* is a proverbially truthful person like Washington who could not tell a lie; *satyayugamu*, the golden age.

satyasandhata, great truthfulness.

satyasandhuḍu, a very truthful man.

satyavantuḍu, a truthful man. The feminine is *satyavati*.

sau-, prefix meaning 'good'. Skt. It is an adjectival form of *su-*, good; as in *saubhágyamu*, good fortune, from *subhagamu*.

saubhágyavati, good wife, used as a title of address to married women, especially on letters. Skt. *nívu saubhágyavativi cammu*, may you become a happily married wife.

saucumáryamu, delicacy. Skt., from *sucumáramu*.

saudhamu, palace. Skt. Used in books.

saukhyamu, health, comfort. Skt., from *sukham*, health. *í y'inṭló nácu saukhyamu lédu*, I am not comfortable in this house; *nícu ollu saukhyamugán unnadá?* are you well?

saumyamu, mild. Skt.

saundaryamu, beauty. Skt., from *sundaram*, beautiful.

saungnya, sign. Skt.; also *sangnya*. *má váḷḷacu saungnya chéstánu*, I will make a sign to my people.

saushṭhavamu, beauty, excellence. Skt., from *sushṭhu*. Used in books.

savaramu, false hair used by women.

savaraṇa, correction; e.g. in a schoolboy's exercise.

savaraṇachéyuṭa, to correct.

savarimpu, correction.

savarintsuṭa, to correct.

savati, co-wife. Corrupt Skt. from *sa*, with, and *patni*, wife.
savatibiḍḍa, stepchild. *tana cheyyi cálutund ani savati biḍḍa chétitó caliga peṭṭinad aṭa*, she stirred with the step-child's hand so as not to burn her own (getting some one else to take the chestnuts out of the fire for you).
savaticoḍucu, stepson.
savaticúturu, stepdaughter.
savatitalli, stepmother. *ná savatitalli nácu tinnagá annam peṭṭa cunḍá máḍustú, adi ná mélu cósamé n'ani cheppédi*, my stepmother used to starve me and say it was for my good.
savá, quarter. *savásēru*, a weight of 30 tolas ($\frac{1}{4}$ vise, $\frac{1}{32}$ maund); about $\frac{3}{4}$ lb. *saválacsha* is a lakh and a quarter; *saválacsha granṭhamu*, a book of a lakh and a quarter, means an endless quarrel; from Skt. *sa-pádamu*, and a quarter.
saválu, cross-questions. Hindustani. *í v'úḷḷó scúlu curraváḷḷu mahá pogar ecci bhayamu bhacti lécunḍá ná mundaré penci zavábu, saváḷḷu véstáru*, the schoolboys of this place are insolent and without fear or respect put saucy questions and cross-questions in my presence.
savárí, riding, palanquin. Corrupt Skt. from *svári*. *gurrapu savári*, riding a horse; *á pillaváḍu gurrapu savári bágá chéya galaḍu*, that boy has a good seat.
saváyi, saváyirógamu, venereal disease.
savistaramugá, at length. Skt. *á catha savistaramugá cheppu*, tell that story at length.
sayitamu, also. Skt. The Telugu is *cúḍá*. *sahitamu* is another form.
sayuctamu, reasonable. Skt. *váru cheppina máṭa sayuctamugán unnadi*, what they say is reasonable.
sazzalu, cumbu, the bulrush millet, from Skt. *sarjach* (*Holcus spicatus*). *zonnalu, sazzalu*, and *tsóḷḷu* are the three principal millets and the common food of the peasantry where rice is not to be had.
sácalyamu, the whole. Skt., from *sacalam*.
sácshát, very own, in person. Skt., from *sa*, with, and *acshi*, sight. *sácsháttu tammuḍu*, own brother; *sácshát Vishṇuvu*, Vishnu in person.
sácshátcáramu, manifestation (of a divinity). Skt.
sácshátcarintsuṭa, to manifest oneself. Skt.
sácshátcrütamu, made manifest. Skt.
sácshi, witness. Skt., from *sa-* and *acshi*, sight. *dongasácshi* or *abaddhapu sácshi*, the false witness, is a very common phenomenon. *antarátma sácshiga*, witness my conscience; *écasácshinacartavyamu*, a single witness won't do, is so burnt into the Hindu brain that all sub-magistrates flout the contrary thesis of our Evidence Act that no particular number of witnesses is required to any particular fact, and the Police produce two to each fact, not caring whether they were really there or not; that is immaterial; *elucacu pilli sácshi*, the cat a witness in the rat's case (interested evidence); *sácshi caḷḷu paṭṭu cóvaḍamu canná, vádi cáḷḷu paṭṭu có vatstsunu*, better cling to the complainant's feet than to the witness's eyes.
sácshyamu, evidence. Skt. *cómaṭi sácshyamu*, the merchant's evidence. This refers to a story about how a merchant, wishing to please both sides, said the fore-part of a horse looked like the Muhammedan litigant's and the hind-part like the Hindu's.
sácu, excuse. *yédainá pani cheppité y'í paní á paní v'unnad'ani v'úricé sáculu cheputáru*, whatever we tell them to do, they make the idle excuse of some other work to do.
sácuṭa, to maintain, to bring up; more commonly *pentsuṭa*. *cúḍú guḍḍá aḍagaca póté, biḍḍanu sácin aṭṭu sácutánu annáḍ aṭa*, don't ask for food and clothes and I will bring you up like my own child.
sádaru, issued. Hindustani. Of an order or proclamation. *sádaru cheyuṭa*, to issue.
sádá, plain, ordinary. Hindustani. *paṭṭu chíra vippi sádá chíré caṭṭu cunnánu*, I have taken off my silk dress and put on my plain one.
sádhacabádhacamulu, pros and cons.

sádhacabádacamulanu púrvamugá vimarşinchi telisi cóca chévrálu chéyanu, I won't sign till I have considered all the pros and cons.

sádhacamu, means, contrivance, practice, exercise. Skt. *dhairyam sarvatra sádhacam*, courage is the means to all ends (fortune favours the brave); *pillavánici leccalaló bágá sádhacam chéyinchinádu*, he gave the boy good practice in accounts.

sádhanamu, means, contrivance; variant of *sádhacam*, but more commonly used.

sádharaṇamu, usual, ordinary. Skt.

sádharaṇamugá, sádharaṇamgá, usually.

sádháraṇuḍu, ordinary person. *sádháraṇula caḍupuna cúḍá goppavdru puḍutáru*, great men are born also from ordinary wombs.

sádhimpu, taming, conquering. Skt. *attagári sádhimpu*, a mother-in-law's taming of her daughter-in-law.

sádhintsuṭa, to tame, to master, to get the better of. Skt. *ávida yé pani talapeḍité, á pani sádhistund ani nácu nischayamgá nammacam v'unnadi*, I am firmly convinced she will carry through anything she takes it into her head to do; *tinḍi tinacunḍá veḷḷi nannu sádhistárá yémiti?* (Wife to husband): Do you think you will master me by going away without your food? *anduló yenta somm aina khartsu peṭṭi rahitu gáḍida coḍuculanu sádhintsanḍi* (Zamindar speaking): Spend what you like but get the better of those whoreson ryots.

sádhu, sádhuvu, a devotee, saint, virtuous man; also *sádu*. Skt. The first meaning of the word is 'tame'. The feminine is *sádhvi*, virtuous woman. *sádhutvamu* is used of linguistic correctness.

sádhyamu, possible. Skt. (same root as *sádhintsuṭa*).

sádu, tame, saintly; same as *sádhu*.

sáducheyuṭa, to tame. *gayyáḷini sáduchéyuṭa*, the taming of the shrew.

sáfu, fair copy. Hindustani.

ságacoṭṭuṭa, to hammer out, from *ságuṭa*, to go on, and *coṭṭuṭa*, to beat.

ságanampuṭa, to speed a traveller, to expel, to send about one's business, from *ságuṭa*, to go on, and *ampuṭa*, to send. *nénu várini úru velapala dáca ságan ampi vachchinánu*, I saw him out of the town; *ninnu gurrapu coraḍátó tsáva coṭṭi má y'inṭló nunchi ságan amputánu*, I will horsewhip you within an inch of your life and drive you out of the house; *á taruváta Khádar Sáhébu niyyógul andarini melligá ságan ampi, gaḍḍála Sahébulan andarini afisuló dúrchináḍu*, after that Khader Sahib (a new Deputy Collector) sent all the Niyyogi Brahmin clerks little by little about their business and brought bearded Muhammedans into the office.

ságaramu, ocean. Skt. It is used in flowery compounds such as *sukhaságaramu*, ocean of joy; *duhkhaságaramu*, ocean of grief.

ságatíyuṭa, to draw out.

ságilabaḍuṭa, to fall prostrate.

ságipaḍuta, to go ahead. *míru sági paḍanḍi, nénu vembaḍiné vastú v'unnánu*, you go ahead, I shall be coming behind.

ságubaḍi, cultivation; the usual word in 'I live by cultivation' and so on.

ságumánamu, suttee; corrupt form of Skt. *sahagamanamu*.

ságuṭa, to go on, to begin, to proceed, to get on. *dáni córica cona ságinadi*, her wish is fulfilled; *cheppa ságinadi*, she went on to say; *idi lécunḍá nácu ságadu*, I can't get on without it; *atani máṭa sága lédu*, his word was of no effect.

sáhasamu, daring. Skt. *sáhasa cáryamunacu diguṭa*, to venture on a daring deed; *mana şúratvamú sáhasamú lócánici velláḍi cá valenu*, our heroism and daring must be revealed to the world; *Lacshmayya tánu chinnappuḍu yuddhamló tsúpina sáhasamu gurinchi upanyásamló goppagá cheppuṭ unḍenu. sabhicuḍu: yuddham antá míré chésté migilina sainyam antá yémi chésind anḍi?* Colonel Smith was boasting in a lecture of his daring deeds in the war when he was young. Voice from the audience: What was there left for all the rest of the army to do?

sáhasintsuṭa, to dare. Skt.

sáháyyamu, help. Skt. Usually *saháyamu*.

sáhébu, sahib. Muhammedan. Hindustani. *nádu v'unṭé Navábu Sáhébu, annamu v'unṭé Áminu Sáhébu, bida paḍité Facíru Sáhébu, tsasté Píru Sáhébu,* if a Muhammedan has land he is a Nawab, if he has enough to eat an Amir, if he is poor a Fakir, when he is dead a Pir (saint).

sáhityamu, scholarship, erudition. Skt.

sáhucáru, sowcar, banker, rich merchant. Hindustani.

sála, hall. Corrupt Skt. from *ṣála. nátaca sála* is theatre; *tan•asála,* mint; *cherasála,* prison; *colupusála,* audience hall.

sálagrámamu, sáligrámamu, a stone which represents Vishnu. Skt. Dancing-girls and sometimes other girls are married to this stone in token that they will not take an earthly husband, just as nuns are married to Christ. *Vivâham cáca munupu Bráhmaṇa strí samartáḍité, culamváru Gangaló diga valen ani, dánni tappintsucóvaḍánici, váru tama comártenu araṭi cheṭlacu sáligrámálacu y'ichchi, viváham chési, tappintsucunṭáru,* if a Brahmin girl attains puberty before she is married her fate is to be drowned; to save her, her parents will give her in marriage to a plantain tree or idol-stone.

sále, sáli, weaving. Corrupt Skt.

sálegúḍu, spider's web. *nénu sálegúṭló paḍḍa y'íga lág aináu,* I am like a fly in a spider's web.

sálepaṭṭu, cobweb.

sálepurugu, spider, the weaving insect; also *igapuli,* the fly-tiger.

sáleváḍu, weaver.

sálgujastá, last year. Hindustani, from *sálu,* year.

sálucu, per annum. Hindustani.

sáluva, shawl. Hindustani; also *ṣáluva.*

sámagri, things, household goods. Skt.

sámarthyamu, skill. Skt. *atanni oḍa coṭṭagala sámarthyam mí daggira v'unn•dani nácu telusunu,* I know you can beat him.

sámánu, things, luggage. Hindustani.

sámányamu, ordinary. Skt. *sámányamulaina guṇamulu,* common qualities.

sámányuḍu, common person.

sámeta, sámita, sámite, proverb. '*Alu cád adi vrál*' *anna sámeta,* the proverb which says 'Ill-mated, ill-fated'.

sámu, gymnastics, feats of strength, fencing.

sámuchéyuṭa, to practice acrobatics or gymnastics or to fence.

sána, whetstone.

sánacaṭṭuṭa, to grind (a knife), to polish (a gem).

sángatyamu, association. Skt.

sántamugá, to the end. Skt., from *sa,* with, and *antamu,* end. *sántamugá chittagintsanḍi,* listen to the end, please.

sápáṭu, food, a meal. *yé páṭu tappina sápáṭu tappadu,* any piece of work may be given a miss but not meals.

sáphalyamu, success. Skt., from *phalam,* fruit. *prayatna-sáphalyamu,* success in an undertaking.

sáramu, essence. Skt. *lópala sáram léni alpagnyánulu,* inwardly pithless men of little learning.

sárasyamu, elegance. Skt. *svaramló y'indácaṭi canṭé conchem sárasyam taccuvagá v'unn'aṭṭ unnadi,* there seems to be a little less refinement in the singer's voice than before; *sangítam vachchina váḷḷu bógam vaḷḷanu ádaristé anduló sárasyamé lédu,* there is no elegance in music-lovers paying court to dancing-girls.

sáravantamu, fertile. Skt.

sára, sáráyi, arrack, any spirits. Corrupt Skt. from *sáram* or *súrá. sárá dukhdṇamu,* arrack shop; *vánici sárá talac eccinadi,* the spirits have gone to his head.

sárámṣamu, issue (in law). Skt., from *sáram,* essence, and *amṣam,* subject.

sári, a time. *oca sári,* once. *núru sárulu vachchi, pilichi, tondara peṭṭinadi,* she came round a hundred times if she came once to worry me.

sárla, success. Used in books.

sárlá aguṭa, to be finished. Used in books.

sárláchéyuṭa, to make it right, to get it ready. Used in books. *iṭuvanṭi svalpa vishayamloné y'inta támasam vastú v'unṭe mundu nizangá ná y'andu tappitam v'unn appuḍu míru nannu yélágu sárlá chéstáru?* If you get cross over such a trifle, how shall we make it right again if I really do something wrong?

sárlápaḍuṭa, to prosper. *í peḷḷi sárla paḍadu,* this marriage won't come off.

sárḷáparatsuṭa, to get it done.

sárthacamu, efficacious, suitable. Skt. *sárthaca námamu,* a fitting or significant name.

sáshṭángamu, eightfold prostration. Skt., from *ashṭa,* eight, and *angam,* limb. It is the most humble of attitudes. *sáshṭánga namascáram,* salutation with the eight limbs; the limbs are the two hands, the two knees, the two shoulders, the breast, and the forehead; your petitioner in fact lies flat before you.

sáṭi, like. *ní sáṭi mánavulu,* men like you.

sátvicamu, amiability. Skt.

sátvicuḍu, an amiable man. The feminine is *sátvicurálu.*

sávacáṣamu, leisure. Skt. *tondara paḍa bócu, sávacáṣangá cheppa vatstsunu,* don't be in a hurry, you may speak in your good time; *alóchintsu cóḍánici nácu conchem cálam sávacáṣam y'ivvanḍi,* give me a little time to think; *répu sávacáṣangá unṭé cheputánu,* I will tell you to-morrow at leisure. *ocaḍu: áru bháshalu máṭláḍut und ani, chilucanu ammitivi, dínici occa máṭ' ainá rádu, yenta mósam chésáu. incóḍu: tondara paḍa bóc anḍi; yeppuḍu míre máṭláḍut unṭé chilacacu sávacáṣam eccaḍidi?* Smith: You sold me that parrot saying it spoke six languages and it does not know a word of any, you cheat. Jones: Steady on there; you talk all the time and don't give the bird a chance to get a word in. *sávacáṣa tega,* leisured class.

sávadhánamu, attention. Skt. *í sangati sávadhánangá alóchintámu,* we will consider the matter carefully; *ná y'upanyásamunu sávadhánangá vinanḍi,* listen carefully to my lecture.

sáviḍi, office-room, lodge, porch, &c., more usually *tsáviḍi.* The commonest use is of the village headman's office-room, in which touring officials often halt. *gadi lédu, sáviḍi lédu, vasárá lédu, curtsóḍánic ainá sthalam lédu,* there is no room, no lodge, no verandah, no place to sit even.

sáyamu, help. Skt. Short for *saháyuma.*

sáyancálamu, evening. Skt.

sáyantramu, evening. Skt. *peddamanishi (fónuló): ḍacṭaru gáru, má pillaváḍu súdi mingáḍu, venṭane ranḍi. ḍácṭaru naucaru: ḍácṭaru inṭló léru, sáyantránici gáni ráru, appaṭi dáca águtára léca póte súdi y'ippuḍé cá valená?* Gentleman at the phone: Doctor, my child has swallowed a needle. Can you come at once? Doctor's Servant: The doctor is not at home; he won't be back till evening. Can you wait till then or do you need the needle at once?

scúlu, school. English. *ṭícharu: ninna madhyáhnam scúlucu rá léd émi? báluḍu: ná nannanu sárcasucu tísucu pó valasi vachchindi.* Teacher: Why didn't you come to school yesterday afternoon? Boy: I had to take my father to the circus.

scúluméshṭaru, schoolmaster. English. *scúluméshṭaru vidhyárthulacu bódhinchi dáni canṭenu yeccuva pani chéstáru; áyana monna vocca césuló palleṭúri nunchi vachchina sácshici bódha chését appaṭici, sácshyam antá váciṭló panjaramló v'unna chillucacu cúḍá vachchindi,* he (a pleader) works harder than any schoolmaster; the other day by the time he had taught a rustic witness what he was to say, a parrot in a cage in the hall had learnt the whole deposition by heart.

segarógamu, gonorrhoea; from Skt. *ṣekha,* heat.

selaga, a customary fee or commission which used to be paid in grain.

selavitstsuṭa, to be pleased to say. The literal meaning is to give permission or an order. When eminent persons speak to you they are giving you orders or permission to drink in their words. The Collector never speaks, he gives orders. A clerk will say to him: *á sangati antayu nén erugudunu, tamaru véré selav iyyan accara lédu,* I know all that, your Honour need not trouble to be pleased to explain; which is polite in form though rude in substance.

selavu, permission, leave, holiday. In Madras Telugu the word is also used for expense (Tamil). *vésangi selavulu*, the summer holidays. *ayyá! émi selavu?* sir, what are your orders?

selavuputstsuconuṭa, to take leave. The polite way of saying, please go away, is *selavu putstsucóndi*, take leave, and the polite way of saying, I am off, is *selavu putstsu cunṭánu*, I will take leave.

senagalu, Bengal gram, a pulse. Corrupt Skt. (*Ciccer arietinum*). *aité árica, cácunṭé candi, dunni tsallité senaga*, if arica millet fails, there will be red-gram (sown with it); if both fail, plough in and sow Bengal gram.

senṭu, cent. English. Acres and cents (*yécaramulu, senṭlu*) are now the common land measures.

sessu, cess. English. Used of the cesses on the land revenue (what the French call *centimes additionels*).

seṭṭi, merchant caste man. Corrupt Skt. from *sréshṭhi*. *cómaṭi* is commoner.

séda, fatigue. Corrupt Skt. from *svédach*. Used in books.

sédyamu, cultivation; also *vyavasáyamu, ságubaḍi*. *bápana sédyam batyapu chéṭu*, Brahmin tillage is waste of wages.

sémanti, chrysanthemum. Skt. *chémanti* is commoner.

séna, army. Skt.

sénádhipati, army commander. Skt. from *séna*, army, and *adhipati*, commander.

sépu, time. *tsálá sépaṭi nunchi*, from a long time; *conta sépu*, some time; *inta sépaṭici rá lédu*, all this time he has not come.

séri, home-farm. Hindustani. The original meaning was rent-free land; now used of land reserved by a Zamindar for himself.

séru, seer. Hindustani. A weight and measure now standardized to the metric standard, 1 litre and 1 kilo; also *ṣéru*.

sétubandhanamu, closing by a dam or causeway. Skt. *gata jala sétubandhanamu*, making the dam when the water is past (locking the stable door after the horse is stolen).

Sétupati, lord of the causeway. Skt.; a title of the Raja of Ramnad, feudal lord of Ramesvaram and Adam's bridge.

sétuvu, causeway. Skt.

séva, service, worship. Skt. *tírthaséva*, pilgrimage; *yécánta séva*, solitary adoration.

sévacuḍu, servant. Skt. *jítamu putstsu conuṭa chétan upádhyáyulu sévacul aguts unnáru, vétanam itstsuts unḍuṭa chéta vidhyárthulu prabhuvul aguts unnáru*, the teachers (in European schools) become servants by taking pay, the pupils their masters by paying fees. (The old Hindu relationship of *guru* and *ṣishya* was of course a finer one.)

sévintsuṭa, to serve, to worship, to take, administer to oneself (medicine, a drink).

sévyamu, venerable. Skt.

sévyuḍu, a venerable man. Skt.

shahá, check at chess.

sharatu, contract, condition. Hindustani. *sharatucu bhangam* is the legal term for breach of contract.

shará, note, remark. Hindustani.

sharábu, shroff, cashier. Hindustani; also *sarábu*.

shashṭhi, sixth. Skt. The sixth day of the lunar fortnight is *shashṭhi náḍu* or simply *shashṭhi*.

shashṭi, sixty. Skt. *ránigári shashṭi sanvatsara rájya pálanótsavamu*, the Queen's diamond jubilee.

shat, 6 (six). Skt. The Telugu is *áru*; *shat* is used in compounds.

shatpadamu, six-footed. Skt. Epithet of bee in verse and literary prose. *dushṭa shatpadam*, as Sakuntala in the play remarks of the big black bee that annoys her—troublesome six-footer.

shatrasamulu, the six flavours. Skt. The six flavours are *tîpi*, sweet; *uppu*, salt; *chédu*, bitter; *cáram*, pungent; *pulusu*, sour; *vagaru*, astringent.

shábash! good! Hindustani. The common exclamation of approval and applause; also *ṣabas!*

shápu, shop. English. *Lacshmayya: mícu vrüdhápyam vachchiná, mí zuṭṭu yenta nallagá v'und andi? Vencayya: ninna né shápuló connánu*. Lakshmayya: Though you are old your topknot is nice and black. Vencayya: I bought it in a shop yesterday.

shicári, shooting. Hindustani.

shicáru, walking or riding or an airing. Hindustani.

shicarupóvuṭa, shicaruveḷḷuta, to go for a walk or ride or airing. *manam phalaháram chési tsallapáṭu véla tsalla gáliló háyigá shicáru bailudérudámu,* we will take tiffin and then go comfortably for a walk in the cool of the evening. *ocaḍu: Guruvayya bóṭló shicárucu niḷḷaló paḍináḍu vinnává? incóḍu: pápam, anta lávâṭiváḍu chinna bóṭló prayáṇam chésté munigi póḍu? pedda stímarló prayáṇam chesté bág unḍédi.* Smith: Jones went for an airing in a boat and fell into the water, did you hear? Brown: Oh dear! so stout a man could not help it in a small boat; he ought to have chartered a large steamer.

sibbandi, band of irregulars, establishment, retinue. Hindustani. *vári y'inṭlo aravaimandi sibbandi v'unnadi,* his house establishment consists of sixty persons.

siddhamu, ready. Skt.

siddhamugá, in readiness, actually.

siddhapaḍuṭa, to be or to get ready.

siddhaparutsuṭa, to make ready.

siddhasancalpulu, a magician. Skt. *míru siddhasancalpulu, anni mi y'ishṭa pracáramé zarugutavi,* you are a regular magician, everything happens according to your will; *tama córica amóghangá siddhistundi; siddhasancalpulu Yélinaváru talatsucóvaḍamú cáca póvaḍamu cúḍánándi?* your wishes are inevitably fulfilled; Your Worship having the attributes of Providence what you think cannot but happen.

siddhántamu, maxim, proof, principle, theory, astrology. Skt. *Ṣástra pramáṇálaló cávalisté nénu siddhántam chéstánu,* I will prove it from Scripture if necessary; *monnaṭi dinamu manam andaramunu chéri, álóchinchi, strílató rahasyamu cheppa cúḍad ani siddhántamu chési conna náḍé, nén inṭici veḷḷina tarváta ná bháryató nénu caḍuputón unnán ani rahasyamugá cheppitini; máru máṭ áḍaca nimishamló namminadi, ammalaccalató maḷḷi cheppinadi,* all of us the other day were talking together about the maxim that women should not be trusted with secrets; well, when I got home I told my wife as a great secret that I was with child and she swallowed it without a word and went and told all the other women; *vamṣa páramparyapu siddhántamu* is the hereditary principle; *manushyulu cótuḷḷó nunchi vachchár 'ani siddhántam,* the theory that men are descended from monkeys.

siddhánti, astrologer. *manam oca illu caṭṭucó valen annatsó manac ishṭamaina távunanu samayamainanu caṭṭucónaca, múrkha siddhánti cheppina távunanu muhúrtamunanu caṭṭucona valasinavâramu agutsunnámu,* when we want to build a house we don't build it at the place and time we want to, but have to build at the place and at the auspicious time settled by a stupid astrologer; *nuyyi travvintsucó talatsuconnatsó mana manassu vachchina y'anucúlamaina távuna travvintsuconaca, múrkha siddhánti tsúpina múlanu travvintsucona valasina váramagutsunnámu,* when we want to dig a well we don't dig at what we think a convenient place but have to dig it in the corner pointed out by a stupid astrologer; *mana biḍḍacu penḍli chéya talatsuconnatsó manac anucúluḍugá çanabaḍu varuni nirnayinchi, vél aina cálam andu viváhamu chéyaca, múrkha siddhánti peṭṭina muhúrtamu n'andu, yeppuḍó pravartana chéta cácapóyinanu, janma patramu chéta n'ataḍu manchiváḍ anna varunic ichchi, penḍli chéya valasina váramagutsunnámu,* when we think of marrying our girl, instead of marrying her to a boy we have fixed on ourselves as being suitable, and performing the ceremony at a time convenient to us, we have to perform it at a time fixed by a stupid astrologer and give the child to a boy found to be good by his horoscope, not by his conduct; *manam oca y'úrici pó talatsuconnatsó, manacu tíricayaina samayamuna bailudéraca, múrkha siddhánti cheppina dinamun andunu váramun andunu prayáṇamu cá valasina váram aguts unnámu,* if we think of going to some village, instead of starting when we have leisure, we have to travel the week and day a stupid astrologer tells us to; *manamu cshauramu chéyintsucó talatsuconnatsó manac avacáṣamugá v'unna nádu chéyintsuconaca múrkha siddhánti cheppina tithi váramula y'andé tala gorintsucó valasinaváram agutsunnámu*, when we are thinking of getting our heads shaved, instead of choosing a time convenient to us, we have to be led by the nose by a stupid astrologer who fixes the day; *manamu crotta baṭṭanu caṭṭucó talachinatsó, cávalasin appuḍu caṭṭuconaca, múrkha siddhánti telisina dinamunu váramunu vatstsu varacunu véchi y'unḍa valasinaváram agutsunnámu*, when we are thinking of putting on a new cloth, instead of putting it on when it becomes necessary, we wait for a stupid astrologer to indicate the day and week; *véyéla? manamu crottagá bhárya vadda parunḍa talatsuconnanu, grühamuna pravéṣimpa talatsuconnanu, rógamunacu mandu putstsucó talatsucunnanu, múrkha siddhántiyé manacu cála nirnayamu chéya valenu*, finally, if we are thinking of going to bed for the first time with a wife, or of giving a house-warming to a new house, or of taking medicine for an illness, it is the stupid astrologer that must fix the time for us.

siddhi, success, effect. Skt. *dáni siddhi vishayamai nácu sandéhamu lédu*, I have no doubt of success; *súrapána siddhulu*, the effects of drinking nectar.

siddhintsuṭa, to accomplish. Skt.

siddhuḍu, a sage, magician. Skt. You can acquire powers over nature by meditation and penance and thus a sage becomes a magician; *mantrasiddhuḍu*, a man who exercises supernatural powers by means of charms.

siḍi, hook, especially the hook used in the hook-swinging ceremony; a hook was passed through the sinews of the back and men were swung round from a beam in honour of Póléramma; the British Government does not permit Póléramma to be so honoured now; this is a source of complaint. *ippuḍu bottigá siḍulu póyinavi cádanḍi? sahagamanam cheyyan iyyaru gadánḍi? ammavárini álóchintsacunḍá Gódávarini caṭṭi vésináru gadánḍi?* haven't they altogether abolished hook-swinging? and won't allow suttee at all? and dammed the Godavari without caring for the Goddess? (Such are among the major faults of the British Government.)

sifársu, recommendation. Hindustani.

siga, the female topknot. Corrupt Skt. from *sikha*, top.

sigareṭṭu, cigarette. English.

siggu, shame. *ácali ruchi yerugadu, nidra sukham erugadu, valapu siggu yerugadu*, hunger knows not flavour, nor sleep comfort, nor lust shame; *áṣa siggu yerugadu, nidra sukham erugadu*, avarice knows no shame, drowsiness heeds not comfort; *áháram andu, vyavahára m andu, siggu paḍa cúḍadu*, you must not be shy at victuals or business.

siggubáṭugá, shy. *nalugurulóci veḷḷaḍánici siggubáṭuga v'unḍi*, being shy of going into company.

siggulachéṭu, shameful. *alá anaḍam siggulachéṭu*, it is shameful to speak so; *iṭuvanṭi sabhaló v'unṭe siggumálinaváḷḷu v'unṭáru gáni, mánavanṭiváḍu v'unḍaḍu*, if you have such meetings they will be attended only by shameless people, not by an honourable man.

siggupaḍuṭa, to be ashamed.

siggupáṭu, shyness.

simhamu, lion. Skt. *cavisimhamu*, a noble poet; *simhasvapnam*, lion-dream, means the elephant's dream of a lion, a dreadful apprehension; *simhamu garjintsuts unnadi*, the lion roars.

simhadváramu, the lion-gate, the front gate of a palace. Skt. Palace portals are often adorned by stone lions.

Simhaḷadvípamu, Ceylon; also *Simhaḷadéṣamu, Lanca, Singaḷamu.*

simhásanamu, the lion-throne. Skt. Thrones are often supported by sculptured lions.

Sindhuvu, the Indus. Skt.; also sea in books. *Sindhuṣayanuḍu*, Indus couched, is an epithet of Ṣiva.

sinduramu, vermilion. Skt.

Singaḷamu, Ceylon; also *Simhaḷadéṣamu, Simhaḷadvípamu.*

singáramu, adornment. Corrupt Skt. for *ṣrüngáramu*.
singárintsuṭa, to adorn. Corrupt Skt. for *ṣrüngárintsuṭa*.
sinimá, cinema. Greek through English.
sipáyi, sepoy. Hindustani.
sirá, ink. Hindustani. *masi* from Skt. *mashi* is the more correct word and *inci*, from the English, the more common.
Siri, Lakshmi, the goddess of wealth.
sistu, land-tax. Hindustani.
síla, nail, peg; also *chíla*.
sílamanḍa, ankle; also *chilamanda*.
síma, district, country, foreign country, especially England. *síma boggu*, coal.
símacóḍi, turkey (the foreign fowl).
símasunnamu, chalk (the foreign lime).
sínu, scene. English. *naṭuḍu: vindu sínuló nácu nizangá bhójanam phalahárálu peṭṭints óle. mánéjaru: aṭlá aité tsávu sínulo nuvvu nizangá tsachchi pótává?* Actor: You must give me real food in the banquet scene. Stage Manager: Then will you really die in the death scene?
sísamu, lead. Corrupt Skt. from *sírshacam. venḍi sísamu* is pewter; *nalla sísamu*, black lead.
sísá, bottle. Hindustani. *í suvásana yocca mostaru tsústé y'idi yeccaḍidó paṣchima khandam nunchi sísálaló digumati aina amúlya parimaḷangá tóstú v'unnadi gáni, mana déṣapudigá tótsaḍam lédu*, judging by the fragrance it would seem to be a precious scent brought in bottles from the western continent and not country scent.
Síta, Síta, Rama's wife. *Síta puṭṭaḍam Lancacu chéṭucé*, Síta was born for Ceylon's ruin; *Sítárám árpaṇamugá chésina dánamu*, a gift in the sacred names of Síta and Rama.
sítacócachiluca, butterfly. It means the fly which has the colours of Síta's skirt.
sítáphalamu, the custard-apple. Anaother variety is called the *ráma-phalamu*.
smaraṇamu, memory. Skt.
smarintsuconuṭa, to recollect.
smaṣánamu, burial or burning-ground. Skt.; properly *ṣmaṣánamu*.
smáracamu, consciousness. Skt. *smáracam tappeṭ aṭṭu*, so as to lose consciousness.
smártuḍu, Smarta Brahmin. Skt. One of the main doctrinal and sub-caste sects of the Brahmins. They follow Sankara and worship Vishnu and Ṣiva equally.
smrüti, memory, the Books of the Law. The Smrütis are Scripture; they are the books of Tradition, and more especially the law books. *Ṣrutis*, Revelation, and *Smrütis*, Tradition, are often mentioned together; *Smrütulac aparthálu chéstáru, Smrütulacu tama y'ishṭanusáramugá artham chéstáru; Ṣrutismrütulaló vyabhichárам cúḍad anṭé dánici bógamváḷḷanu cúḍá v'untsu có rád ani artham aṭa*, they misinterpret the Prophets; they interpret the Law as they like; they pretend that the prohibition of adultery in the Law and the Prophets extends to keeping dancing-girls.
snánamu, bath. Skt. *balavanta Mágha snánamu*, forced bathing in January (a disagreeable duty); *snánamu cheyyaḍam vanṭi subhram cósam aṭa*, (Europeans) say bathing is for bodily cleanliness, a wrong notion; it is of course a religious rite. Brahmins bathe to remove pollution after seeing a pariah, if a lizard falls off the wall, &c. *bind ettuconi sagham dúram vachchéṭ appaṭici y'iravai gajála dúramló málaváḍu canapaḍi, niḷḷu naḍi vidhiló pára pósi, váṇṇi nálugu tiṭṭi, maḷḷi venucacu Góddávarici veḷḷi, snánamu chési, niḷḷu tetstsu cunnánu*, I took up my pitcher, but before I had gone half-way a pariah appeared; I poured away the water in the middle of the street, gave him a piece of my mind, went back to the Godavari, bathed, and again filled my pitcher.
snéhamu, friendship. *nippucu niḷḷacu v'unḍe snéhamu*, the friendship of fire and water (cats and dogs); *avivécitó snéhamu canná vivécitó viródhamu mélu*, enmity of the wise is better than friendship with the foolish; *ocaḍu: rúpáyi badulu istává? incóḍu: istá gáni andu valla mana snéhánici bhangam ayyéṭ aṭṭ aité iyyanu. ocaḍu: mana*

iddarici snéhamu lédugá. Smith: Will you lend me a rupee? Jones: Yes, but not if it is to affect our friendship. Smith: We are not friends.

snéhituḍu, friend. *cheḍi snéhituni y'inṭici veḷḷa vatstsunu gáni chelleli y'inṭici veḷḷa cúḍadu,* when you are ruined your friend will take you in but your sister won't; *ocaḍu: nuvvu vídhiló zári paḍité snéhitulu léva tíṣárá? incóḍu: lédu, cáḷḷ antá caḍu comm ani, na mída sabbu mucca paḍéṣáru.* Smith: When you fell down in the street did your friends help you to your feet? Jones: No, they threw a piece of soap at me and told me to clean myself.

sogasaina, beautiful.

sogasu, beauty. Corrupt Skt., from *sukham. yeccuva sogasugá cana paḍa-ḍánici y'í véḷa áviḍe duvvu cóvaḍam-lónu tóḍucóvaḍamlónu v'unnadi,* she is combing and titivating herself to improve her looks; *álá cheppiténe cáni cathaló sogasé v'unḍadu,* there won't be any beauty in the story unless you tell it that way; *chinna pillalacu peḷḷi chésté v'unḍe sogasu pedda pillalacu chéste v'unḍadu,* the marriage of small children is much more beautiful than the marriage of big ones—an argument in favour of child-marriage.

sogasucáḍu, a beau, a gallant; the feminine is *sogasucatte.*

sommariluṭa, to faint.

sommu, money, jewellery. *lóbhi sommu dongaváḍi pálu,* the miser's money falls to the thief; *andánacu peṭṭina sommu ápadacu aḍḍam vastundi,* jewellery worn for beauty comes in useful when times are bad; *nácu peṭṭu conna manchi sommu lédu,* I have no decent jewellery to wear; *yeruvula sommulu baruvu chétu, tiyyá peṭṭá típula chéṭu, váṭiló vocaṭi póté appula chéṭu,* borrowed jewels are a burden, a trial to put on and off, a disaster if one is lost.

sompu, elegance.

sona, white of egg, milk of milk-hedge.

sonta, own; corrupt for *svanta.*

sora, shark.

sorugu, drawer of a table, &c.

soṭṭa, dint; also *tsoṭṭa.*

sottu, property; corrupt form of *satvam.*

sócuḍu, contagion. *sócuḍu nivárana chéyuta* is to disinfect.

sócuḍugala, contagious.

sócuṭa, to touch, to be contaminated, to catch a contagion. *díni mída yenḍa sócuts'unnadi,* it is exposed to the sun; *gáli sócacunḍá unnadi,* it is not exposed to the wind; *maila sócin appuḍu manam tappacunḍá snánam cheyya valenu,* if we are touched by anything defiling we must without fail take a bath; *ná bháryacu graham sóci yenni vidhála vadali pón appuḍu múḍu náḷḷaló cudirchináḍu,* when my wife was touched by a demon and we had tried every means and she could not get rid of it, he cured her in three days.

sódari, sister. Skt.; from *udaram,* womb, and *sa-,* with.

sódaruḍu, brother. Skt.; from *udaram,* womb, and *sa-,* with. *sódarulamu cámu,* we are not brother and sister.

sódá, search. Hindustani; from Skt. *sódhana,* the usual word for police searches. *nénu yémi putstsu có lédu, cávalisté ná baṭṭalu sódá tsúḍu,* I have taken nothing, search me if you want to.

sóde, fortune-telling. Corrupt Skt. for *chódyam.*

sódecatte, female fortune-teller.

sóla, a measure, one-sixteenth of a cuntsam.

sóluṭa, to faint. *nácu múrchha vachehéṭ aṭṭu v'unnadi—ani sólutsunnadi,* saying: 'I feel faint', she swooned away; *parupu mída sóli,* sinking on to my couch.

sóma, moon-plant juice, nectar. Skt.

sómari, lazy.

sómaripótu, lazy beast. *óri sómaripótá, inta sépaṭi dácá yeccaḍici veḷḷináu ra?* (to a servant) Lazybones, where have you been all this time?

sómaritanamu, laziness.

sómavváramu, Monday. Skt.; from *sóma,* moon. *aité ádivváram, cácunṭé sómavváram,* if Sunday won't do, Monday will.

sómayáji, a Brahmin title meaning the sacrificer.

sómuḍu, the moon. Skt. *chandruḍu* is commoner; moonlight is *vennela.*

sópánamu, steps. Skt. Used in books for *meṭlu.*

spanji, sponge. Even the writers of natural history text-books cannot think of a Skt. equivalent. There is no Telugu word.

sparṣa, touch. Skt. *ractasparṣamu*, blood relationship; *jalasparṣamu*, making water; *á sparṣa sukham valla svargam doricin aṭṭu santóshinchi*, rejoicing at the heavenly delight of that contact.

sparṣéndriyamu, sense of touch. Skt.

spashṭamu, plain, clear. Skt. *spashṭamugá cheppu*, speak clearly.

sphaṭicamu, crystal. Skt.

sphóṭacamu, pustule. Skt. Commonly of small-pox pustules; small-pox is *masúchicamu*, but *sphóṭacamu* is sometimes used. *ná bháryacu sphóṭacamu vachchenu*, my wife has contracted small-pox.

sphuraṇamu, quivering; used chiefly of an idea occurring in the mind. Skt. *sphuraṇacu vatstsuṭa* is simply to occur to one; also *sphurintsuṭa*.

sphurintsuṭa, to occur to one. Skt.; also *sphuraṇacu vatstsuṭa*.

sphuṭamu, clear. Skt. *mishanari: mí prarthanálu sphuṭangá cheppanḍi; nácu occa mucca ainá vinipintsaḍam lédu. vidhyárthi: mému Dévuḍini prárthist unnámu gáni, mimmunu cád anḍi*, Missionary: Speak your prayers plainly, you are not letting me hear a word. Pupil: We are praying to God, not to you.

sprüha, wish, hope. Skt. *nisprühulai* is 'without hope'; *intalóṇe sprüha tappi póyinadi*, meanwhile I lost hope.

sprüṣata, touch. Skt.

sravanti, river. Skt. Used in books. *sravintsuṭa* is also used in books for 'to flow'.

srávamu, flow. *pravâham* is commoner. Both are Skt.

srüshṭamu, created. Skt.

srüshtamu chéyyuṭa, to create, i.e. to forge, a document or evidence; a common word and practice; also *srüshṭintsuṭa*.

srüshṭi, creation. Skt.

srüshṭintsuṭa, to create, to fabricate, to forge. Skt.; often used of making evidence come into existence; also *srüshtamu chéyyuṭa*.

stambhamu, pillar, post. Skt. *Lacshmayyacu drüshṭi mándyamu unḍenu, chícaṭlo pótú unṭe occa lánṭaru stambhamé múḍu stambhálugá canipinchenu. Lacshmayya: i muḍinṭiló nizamaindi nácu tagalacunḍá v'unṭe bág unḍunu.* Lacshmayya was half-blind; when he was walking in the dark one lamp-post looked to him like three, and he remarked: 'I hope I shan't knock against the real one of those three lamp-posts'; *aḍusuló náṭina stambhamu*, a post planted in the mud (uncertainty).

stambhimpuṭa, to stop dead (transitive). *nénu viḷḷanu yógadrüshṭitó tsúchi stambhimpa chéstanu*, I will stop them by the power of the human eye.

stambhintsuṭa, to stop dead (intransitive).

stámpu, stamp. English.

stanamu, woman's breast. Skt.; also *tsannu, cuchamu*.

sṭéshanu, railway station. English. *railvé inspecṭaru: mí ṭicceṭṭu yéd andi? Lacshmayya (jébul anni vetici): ayyó canupintsa léd anḍi. inspecṭaru: maḷḷi tsúḍ anḍi, canipistundi, mí vishayamai nácu bhayam lédu. Lacshmayya: mícu bhayam lédu gáni nácu bhayangá v'undi; nén é sṭéshanuló diga valenó ṭicceṭṭu tsústéné gáni teliyadu.* Ticket Collector: Ticket please. Lakshmayya (searching all his pockets): Dear me, I can't find it. Ticket Collector: Look again; you will find it, I am not afraid. Lakshmayya: You may not be, but I am; without my ticket I don't know what station I have to get out at.

sthairyamu, steadiness. Skt., from *sthiramu*.

sthalamu, place, space. Skt. *culam erigi tsuṭṭamu, sthalam erigi vásamu*, choose your wife from people you know, your house in a place you know; *púchina púll ella cáyal aité, bhúmi paṭṭaḍánacu sthalamu n'unḍadu*, if all flowers became fruit there would not be space on earth for them all; *ṣilă bhógam, sthalábhógam, narabhógam cána rávu*, you cannot tell what will become of a stone, a place, or a man (the stone may become an idol, the place a temple, the man a saint).

sthalapuráṇamu, the legend of the

place. Skt. Most ancient temples have such legends.

sthánamu, place, position. Skt. *tana balimi canná sthána balimi mélu,* it is the power of the place rather than the power of the man.

sthánicamu, local. Skt. *sthánica prabhutvamu,* local government; *sthánica cúṭamu,* local board.

sthápacuḍu, founder. Skt.

sthápana, founding, establishment. Skt.

sthápintsuṭa, to found. Skt.

sthápitamu, established. Skt.

sthirachittuḍu, firm-minded. Skt.

sthiramu, firm. Skt. *sthira drüshṭitó tsútsuṭa,* to stare; *mic í buddhi sthirangá v'unḍeṭ aṭṭu chéya valen ani ná y'ishṭa daivamunu nityamu prárthistú v'unṭánu,* I will daily pray my favourite God to keep you firmly of this mind.

sthirapaḍuṭa, to be confirmed, to be ascertained. *vádu tagina varuḍ ain aṭṭu sthira paḍité,* if we find for certain that he is a suitable bridegroom.

sthiraparatsuṭa, to confirm, to ratify.

sthirata, firmness, confirmation.

sthirásti, immovable property. Skt., from *sthira,* firm, and *ásti,* property. The usual legal and business term; *charásti* is movable property.

sthiti, state, condition. Skt. *bhústiti* has two meanings, the state of things on the ground (a survey term) and landed property.

sthitigalaváḍu, sthitimantuḍu, a man of property.

sthitigatulu, one's circumstances. *ippuḍu ná sthitigatulu mícu purṇangá telisinavi cadá,* now you know all my circumstances in full.

stimitamu, dull, better (in health). *dhara stimitamugán unnadi,* the market is dull; *atani oḷḷu stimitamugán unnadi,* he is a little better. The idea is that the disease is going.

sṭímaru, steamer. English.

stótramu, praise. Skt. *idi stótram cádu, v'inna nizamló nénu sahasránṣam ainá cheppa lédu,* this is no flattery, I have not said a thousandth part of the truth.

strí, woman. Skt. *bála náyacam, bahu náyacam, strí náyacam,* the rule of many or of a boy or a woman; *rüshi múlamu, nadi múlamu, strí múlamu,* the origin of a Rishi, a river, or a woman. These proverbs indicate that the monstrous regiment of women is no more appreciated in India than in Europe, and that you should not inquire too closely about a woman's early days.

stríbuddhi, woman's wit. Skt. This is not usually, as with us, a complimentary expression; it means feeble wit. *stríbuddhi praḷayántacamu,* woman's wit is fatal in the long run.

strídhanamu, married woman's personal property. Skt. It is a legal term and means the jewellery, pin-money, &c., given to a bride by her parents as distinguished from the dowry; paraphernal property, to use the Latin expression.

strílingamu, the feminine gender. Skt.

stuti, praise. Skt. *ná y'andali vátsalyam chéta mír uricé nannu stuti chést unnáru,* you are only praising me without good cause out of partiality.

stutintsuṭa, to praise. Skt. *ataṇṇi veyyi nóḷḷa stutistú v'unṭáru,* they praise him with a thousand mouths.

stutyamu, laudable. Skt.

su- ,prefix meaning 'good'. Skt.; as common in Skt. and Telugu compounds as *eu* in our Greek compounds. So our woman's name Eudoxia will be *Suprasiddha* in Telugu; euphony will be *suṣrávyamu,* and so on.

subédáru, subadar. Hindustani. The word has fallen in dignity. A subadar under the Moguls governed a province; he is now a non-commissioned officer in the army.

Subhadra, Krishna's sister, who married Arjuna.

subhagamu, good fortune. Skt.

subhagavati, a happy woman.

subhaguḍu, a happy man.

subhicshamu, subhicshata, affording easy means of subsistence. Skt. *subhicshamaina déṣamu,* a cheap or fertile country. *púrva cálamun andu pencuṭ inḍlu tsúḍa baḍini pallela y'andu sahitamu divya bhavanamulunu méḍalunu létsuts unḍuṭayé, déṣamu yocca y'ippaṭi subhicshatanu, sampannatanu* *ghóshintsuts unnadi*, palaces and mansions rising in villages which in the old days did not boast a tiled house proclaim our present prosperity.

sucrütamu, good deed. Skt.

sucrütátmuḍu, philanthropist. Skt., from *su*, good, *crüt*, deed, and *átma*, soul.

sucumáramu, comely, youthful, delicate. Skt. *ávide mahá sucumári, moguḍu áviḍenu y'inṭló yémí pani cheyyan'iyyadu*, she is very delicately reared, her husband won't let her do any housework.

suḍati, woman (the one with good teeth). Skt. One of a great number of similar words for woman used only in books.

sudda, pipe-clay. From Skt. *suddha*, pure.

suddamu, clean. Skt.; also *ṣudhamu*.

suddi, pure; from Skt. *ṣuddhi*.

suddichéyuṭa, to purify, to clean.

sudha, nectar. Skt.

suḍi, whirl, curl; used especially of curls in a horse's hair which are supposed to be 'good marks', lucky signs.

suḍigáli, whirlwind.

sudinamu, a lucky day. Skt. *mí darṣanam cávaḍam néḍu sudinam, má grüham pávanam aindi*, your visit sanctifies the day and purifies my house.

sugandhamu, fragrance. Skt.

Sugrívuḍu, Rama's ally who led the bears. Skt.

sugunamu, good character. Skt. *suguṇa sampadiyé goppa araṇamu*, the best dowry is character.

suhrüdayuḍu, good-hearted. Skt.

sujanulu, good people. Skt. *tama vanṭi sujanulanu tsúḍaḍam chéta nácu bahu santóshangá v'unnadi*, it is a great pleasure to me to see good people like you.

sukhajádyamu, venereal disease. Skt.

sukhamu, comfort, health, happiness, delight. Skt. *mí tandri sukhangá unnáḍá?* is your father well? *sukham* is contrasted with *duhkham*, sorrow, and *cashṭam*, trouble; *adi mícu duhkhamé cáni sukham entamátramu cádu*, that is no joy at all to you but sorrow; *ácali ruchi yerugadu, nidra sukham erugadu*, hunger needs no sauce, sleep no feather bed; *cashṭa sukhálu renḍu cávaṭi cunḍalu*, troubles and joys are like the two pots swinging on the yoke (they alternate), or, as the Italians say, *questa ruota sempre gira, chi è lieto e chi sospira*, the wheel of fortune is always going round; *modaṭi vartacuḍu: chinnatanamlóne nácu sukhangá unḍédi. rendo vartacuḍu: nácú sukhangáné unḍédi, artha réṭucu railuló prayáṇam cheyyaḍánici vil ayyédi*. First Merchant: I was happy when I was a boy. Second Merchant: So was I, I could travel half-price by rail; *ducci coddi panṭa, buddhi coddi sukhamu*, yield is proportionate to tillage as happiness to wisdom; *sukhápadamu* (*sukhamu* and *ápada*, misfortune), weal and woe.

sukhapaḍuṭa, to prosper, to be happy.

sukharógamu, venereal disease; also *sukhajádyamu, sukhasancaṭamu*. Skt.

sukhasancaṭamu, the afflictions of pleasure (that is, venereal disease). Skt.

sulabhamu, easy, accessible. Skt. *bhactasulabhuḍu*, accessible to worshippers. *ḍácṭaru: ivváḷa podduna nuvvu sulabhamgá daggut unnává? rógi: tellavárlú sulabhamgá daggaḍam abhyásam chéṣán anḍi*, Doctor: Were you coughing easily this morning? Patient: I have practised easy coughing in the morning.

sulabhaparatsuṭa, to facilitate.

sulóchanamu, spectacles. Skt. *sulóchanamula ẓóḍu*, a pair of spectacles; *sulóchana gúḍu*, spectacle case.

sultánu, sultan. Hindustani.

suluvu, easy. Skt.

suma, sumí, my good Sir! Really! The derivation is from *tsútsuṭa*, to see. *bágá álóchintsa valenu sumanḍi*, my good sir, we must think it well over.

sumanascuḍu, good-natured. Skt.

sumati, a sound mind, a wise heart. Skt.

sumáru, about, there, or thereabouts. Hindustani.

suncamu, toll; from Skt. *ṣulçam*.

suncésalamu, the tiger-bean tree, a large tree with white flowers, common in Bellary.

sundaramu, beautiful. Skt.

sundari, a pretty girl, any girl or woman.

sunna, dot, circlet, cipher, nothing; from Skt. *şúnyam*.

sunnamu, lime; from Skt. *chúrṇam*. *vélu cósu conná sunnamu peṭṭadu*, though you cut your finger he won't give you a bit of lime to stop the bleeding.

sunnapubaṭṭí, lime-kiln.

sunnapucáyi, the small box in which the lime which Indians take with their betel is kept.

sunni, powder. *minapa sunni* is black-gram flour.

suprasiddhamaina, very famous. *Rájamahéndravaramuna gala déválayamulaló Cóṭişvarálayamu suprasiddhamainadi*, of the Rajahmundry temples the Kotisvara temple is the most celebrated.

suprasiddhulaina, very distinguished (of persons). Skt.

sura, nectar. Skt.

suracshitamu, safe. Skt.

suralu, divine beings. Skt. *sura yocca mahima suralac ainá dur-avagáhamé*, even the gods find it difficult to realize the great qualities of nectar.

surúpamu, beautiful. Skt. *rúpamu* (like the Latin *forma*) means both form and beauty. *curúpi yémi chéstunnáḍ anṭé surúpál anni lekha peṭṭut unnáḍu*, when he asked what the ugly man was doing, he was counting up the handsome ones.

sushṭu, well, happy. *sushṭugá unnáḍu*, he is in good health.

suşrávyamu, melodious.

susti, laziness, delay. Hindustani.

suta, daughter. Skt. Used in books.

sutarámu, utterly. Hindustani. *sutarámu panici rádu*, no use at all.

sutte, hammer. *sutte mundá, cáru mundá?* which came first, the hammer or the tongs? (the chicken or the egg?).

sutuḍu, son. Skt. Used in books for *cumáruḍu, coḍucu*.

suvarnamu, gold. Skt. *suvarṇa cásulu*, gold coins.

suvásana, good smell. Skt. *suvásana gala sabbu*, scented soap.

suvásini, housewife, married woman. Skt.; from *su*, good, and *vásam*, house.

súchacamu, hint, indication; also *súchana*. Skt. *şubha súchacamu*, a good omen.

súchana, hint; also *súchacamu*. Skt. *í máṭala súchana mícu telisindá?* do you understand the hint conveyed?

súchica, index. Skt.

súchintsuṭa, to hint, to indicate.

súcshmabhójanuḍu, a small feeder (feminine *súcshmabhójini*).

súcshmamu, subtle. Skt. *súcshma crimulu* is the word invented to translate bacteria; *súcshma buddhi* is subtle intellect; *súcshmamaina pani*, delicate work; *vaca súcshmam*, a subtle point; *nénu álóchinchina v'upáyam mahá súcshmam ainadi*, the contrivance I thought of is very subtle.

súdanṭuráyi, magnet.

súdi, needle. Corrupt Skt. *ácali ácáşam anta, gontuca súdi bezzam anta*, appetite sky-high, throat a needle's eye (great ambition and small abilities, biting off more than you can chew); *cammara vídhiló súdulu ammin aṭṭu*, like selling needles in the blacksmiths' street (carrying coals to Newcastle).

súryuḍu, sun. Skt. The heat or light of the sun is *y'enḍa*.

súṭigá, straight, duly. *nosaṭici súṭigá ráyi vésinḍáḍu*, he threw a stone straight at his forehead; *cáci vale súṭigá póté*, as the crow flies.

sútradháruḍu, the manager in a play; the person who pulls the strings behind the scenes.

sútramu, thread. Skt.; especially a sanctified thread; *mangalasútramu*, the thread by which the *táli* is tied to the bride's neck.

sútramu, a rule in grammar, &c., derived from the meaning 'thread' (like the German *Richtschnur*); the idea is that of a guiding thread.

sútramu, contrivance; also derived from the thread idea; *capaṭasútramu* is a device of deception; *jalasútramu* is a water contrivance or machine; *tyága sútramu* is a means of renunciation.

sva-, prefix meaning 'self'. Skt.

svabhávamu, natural disposition. Skt. *plíḍaru: muddáyi dongatanam chése svabhávam galavaḍ énd? sácshi: yenta sommanḍi?* Pleader: Has the accused a natural disposition to commit theft? Witness: For what amount, Sir?

svabhávasiddhamaina, natural. Skt. *svabhávaviruddhamu,* unnatural.
svabuddhi, one's own desire. Skt. *svabuddhi chéta,* of one's own accord.
svacapólacalpitamaina, self-invented. Skt. *capólamu* means cheek; invented to your own cheek; used of a false story, *catha.*
svacáryamu, one's own business. Skt. *svacárya dhurandharuḍu, svámi cárya vanchacuḍu,* clever in his own business, a cheat in his master's.
svachchamu, pure. Skt. *veli anṭé telupu arthamu, anagá svachchamainavár ani tátparyamu, í deṣamuló svachchamaina Bráhmaṇulu yevaraina v'unṭe Velináṭiváré cáni marivacaru cáru; mí Muricináṭiváḷḷu yenducu panicimálina nirbhágyulu; veli* means 'white', that is to say, it gives the meaning of pure; if there are any pure Brahmins in this country it is the Velináti ones; your Muricináties are worthless scoundrels.
svacíyamu, one's own, private. Skt.
svadéṣabhacti, patriotism. Skt.
svadéṣamu, one's own country. Skt. *svadéṣa* is the usual adjective for national, patriotic, home-grown, Indian-made, and so on.
svadéṣastuḍu, a fellow countryman, a native, a patriot.
svadharmamu, one's own particular duty. Skt.
svahastamu, one's own hand. Skt. *svahastapálacuḍu,* one who rules by his own hand, of his own authority.
svahatya, suicide. Skt.; also *átmahatya.*
svajanulu, one's own people. Skt. *míru andarini svajanánni chériste, mí tarváta vachchinaváḍu váḷḷ andarici cshavarálu chéstáḍu,* if you introduce no one but your own caste-people into the office, your successor will shave them all off.
svajáti, of one's own mind, nation, or caste. Skt. *svajátivairi,* an enemy of his own people (a friend of every country but one's own).
svalpamu, small, trifling. Skt. *bhárya: míru chinnappuḍu yeṭṭi svalpa córicanainá chellistán anéváru. bharta: nizamé, svalpamaina córicanu córutáv émón ani y'inta cálam nunchi canipeṭṭucu v'unnánu,* Wife: When you were young you said you would fulfil my smallest wish. Husband: True, I have been waiting for a small wish ever since; *svalpa jítamu,* a small pay; *svalpa dúramu,* a short distance; *svalpa cáryamu,* a trifling matter of business.
svanamu, sound. Skt. Used in books.
svantamu, one's own. Skt. *svantánici conuconnáḍu,* he bought it on his own account.
svantamugá, in person. *svantamugá vachchináḍu,* he came in person.
svaparipálana, self-government. Skt.
svapnamu, dream. Skt.
svaprayójanamu, self-interest, one's own advantage. Skt.
svaprayójanaparatvamu, selfishness. Skt. *svadharmam aina Bráhmaṇa sévanu parityajintsuṭa valana, Ṣúdrulac ihalóca hániyu, paralóca hániyu sambhavintsunu, idi nénu Ṣúdrulu nishcáraṇamugá svadharmamumu gauravimpaca chedi povuts unndré y'anna záli chéta vári cshémamu coracu chepputs unnáné, cáni svaprayójanaparatvamu chéta cádu,* harm will come to Sudras in this life, harm in the next life, if they abandon their peculiar duty, which is to serve Brahmins. I say this out of compassion for the Sudras, to prevent them being unnecessarily ruined by not holding their special duty in honour. I say it for their good. I do not say it out of a selfish regard for the interest of Brahmins.
svaracshaṇárthamu, in self-defence. Skt.; from *sva,* self, *racshaṇam,* protection, and *arthamu,* for. *upanyásacuḍu: tsaduvu cheppeṭ appuḍu pillalanu yeppuḍú coṭṭa cúḍadu, nénu ṭicharugá unna iravai sanvatsarálaló occa sári cúḍá coṭṭa lédu. sabhicuḍu: occa sári cúḍá coṭṭa lédá? upanyásacuḍu: vidhyártulu nannu coṭṭa vachchin appuḍu svarachshaṇártham mátram coṭṭánu.* Lecturer: A teacher should never strike the boys; in the twenty years I was a teacher, I never struck a boy once. Voice from the audience: Really, never once? Lecturer: When the pupils came to attack me, I only struck them in self-defence.

svaramu, voice, note. Skt. A false note is *apasvaramu*; *svaramu* is the usual word for the singing voice.

svargamu, svargalócamu, heaven. Skt. *svargasthulairi*, he has gone to heaven, is the usual way newspapers announce a death; *svatantramu svargalócamu, paratantramu práṇa sancaṭamu*, independence is heaven, dependence is tribulation of the spirit. *báluḍu: ammá, ná chelli svargamló nunchi cindici vachchindá? talli: aunu náyaná. báluḍu: anta manchi tsóṭuló nunchi iccaḍacu yenducu vachchindi?* Boy: Did my little sister come down from heaven? Mother: Yes, dear. Boy: Why did she leave so good a place to come here?

svargatulyamu, like heaven. Skt. *cárágrühamulu svargatulyamugán unnay ani inspecṭarujanaralugáru vivarinchiri*, the Inspector General (of Prisons) makes out that his jails are like heaven.

svarnamu, gold. Skt. *svarṇacáruḍu* is a book word for *camsáli*, goldsmith.

svarúpamu, real form. Skt. Common in the expression in petitions *dharma svarúpulaina tamaru*, Your Honour who is the image of justice.

svasamrachshaṇa, self-defence. Skt. *vaca véḷa ná mída firyádu chési ruzuvu parichiná svasamracshaṇárthaṃ chésinán ani cheppi tappintsu cunṭánu*, even if he brings a case against me and proves it, I shall get off by pleading self-defence.

svasthachittuḍu, sane. Skt. Of sound mind.

svasthamu, good health, sound condition. Skt. *mí manassu svasthamugá lén aṭṭu canapaḍutú v'unnadi*, your mind does not seem to be in sound condition.

svasticamu, an auspicious object. Skt.

svatahágá, of itself, naturally, personally. Skt. *yé buddhi ainá yevarici várici svatahága puṭṭa valenu gáni, y'itaruḷu nérpité yémátram nilustundi?* sense is innate, if others teach it you, will it last? *calecṭaru gáru svatahágá vachchináru*, the Collector came in person (*svayamugá* is commoner in this sense).

svatantramu, right, independence. Skt. *yevari vastuvu váru manasu vachchin aṭṭu chésu cóvaḍḍánici prativárici svatantram unnadi*, a man may do what he will with his own.

svatantrintsuṭa, to act out of one's own head. Skt. *mana y'ishṭam putstsucócunḍá peddaváḷḷu svatantrinchi, tama y'ishṭam vachchinaváḷḷanu manacu caṭṭi peḍutú v'unṭé*, if our elders tie us up in marriage to any one they like out of their own heads without consulting us.

svatassiddhamu, natural. Skt. *svatassiddhamugán unḍé bádhyata*, a natural right.

svayampácamu, cooking for oneself. Skt. You may give a guest, especially if not of your own caste, food to cook for himself. *svayampáci*, one who cooks for himself.

svayamugá, in person, of one's own accord. Skt. *áyana svayamugá vachchiri*, he came in person; an automatic machine is *svayamugá ádé yantramu*.

svayamvaramu, self-choice. Skt.; especially of a princess choosing a husband for herself.

svayancrütamu, brought on oneself. Skt. *janulu svayancrüt áparádhamu valana caligina anarthamulanu bailu putstsuṭac ishṭamu lédu*, people do not care to disclose the misfortunes they have brought on themselves by their own fault.

svábhávicamu, natural. Skt.; from *svabhávam*, natural disposition. *svábhávicamaina andam*, natural beauty; unnatural is *asvábhávicamu*.

svádhicáramu, one's own right. Skt.

svádhicyamu, arrogance.

svádhínamu, possession, powers. Skt.; from *adhínam*. *mana svádhínam unnadi*, it is in our possession.

svágatamu, welcome. Skt.

svámi, lord. Skt. Used as a term of address to superiors and especially to priests. *Svámulaváru* is the Right Reverend, the head of a sect or monastery.

svámibhacti, devotion to a master or priest. Skt.

svámidróhamu, treason. Skt.

svámidróhi, traitor. Skt.

svámyamu, ownership, form of government. Skt. *prajasvámyamu* is the newspaper word for democracy; *sarva svámyamulu,* all rights.

svánubhavamu, personal experience. Skt.; from *anubhavam,* experience. *id antá nénu svánubhavam chéta cheputú v'unnánu,* I say all this from personal experience.

svárthamu, self-interest. Skt.; from *sva* and *arthamu,* interest. *svárthaparuḍu,* a selfish man; *svárthaparatvamu,* selfishness.

svárjitamu, self-acquired. Skt. *nádi svárjitam nícu bhágam yeṭlá vastundi?* mine is self-acquired property, how have you a right to a share? In the Hindu undivided family every male shares, but the lawyers get out of this by saying that their property is self-acquired, not hereditary.

svátantryamu, independence, freedom. Skt.

svéchchha, freedom. Skt.; from *sva* and *ichchha,* wish. *áyana yeccaḍicainá v'úricé veḷḷi rágáné, nénu á rózulaló marinta svéchchhagánú khuláságánú unṭánu,* when my husband goes away for a bit, I am more free and happy during those days; *svéchchhaváṇijyamu* is the newspaper term for free trade; *váṇijya racshana paddhati* is what they say for protection (Skt. translations of English terms).

svícarintsuṭa, to make one's own, to embrace or adopt. Skt. Not a technical term for adopting a son but rather for adopting a faith or condition of life. *dattu tísuconṭa* is to adopt a son.

svícáramu, entering or embracing a new condition of life, accepting, adopting. Skt. *putrasvícáramu* is used for adopting a son, and *svícrüta putruḍu* for an adopted son; *áṣrama svícáram* is adopting asceticism, becoming a hermit.

Ṣ

ṣabas! good! encore! Hindustani. An interjection of applause; also *ṣhábash!*

ṣabdamu, sound. Skt. *ṣabdam iḍuṭa,* to give tongue.

ṣabdaṣástramu, phonetics. Skt.

ṣacamu, era. Skt. *Cristu ṣacamu,* the Christian era; the era of a particular king, e.g. *Vicrama ṣacamu, Ṣálivàhana ṣacamu.*

ṣacaṭamu, vehicle. Skt. The bishop, in chess.

ṣacti, energy. Skt. It is used specially of the female vital energy and Ṣacti is a name of Parvati, wife of Ṣiva. *ocaḍu: má prayáṇála valla manushyuḍilóni ṣactul anní baiṭacu vastavi. incóḍu: nizamé, nénu samudram mída prayáṇam chést unṭe nác á sangati telisindi. ocaḍu: yém zarigindi? incóḍu: nénu tinna annam antá baiṭacu veḷḷi póyindi.* Smith: All the forces of humanity are brought out by distant travel. Jones: True, I learnt that on my voyages. Smith: What happened? Jones: All the nourishment I had put into myself came out.

ṣacunamu, omen (from flight of birds). Skt. *náḍu ṣacunálu gikhundálu lacshyam cheyyaca bailudérum ani cheḍa pórináḍu,* he strongly urged me to set out (on a journey) without paying any attention to omens and auspices.

ṣacuntamu, bird. Skt. Only used in books for *piṭṭa, pacshi.*

ṣacyamu, possible. Skt.

ṣaiṣavamu, infantile. Skt.; from *ṣiṣuvu. ṣaiṣava críḍalu,* childish sports; *ṣaiṣavadaṣa,* infancy.

ṣaityamu, cold. Skt.; from *sítamu. ṣaityópachàramulu,* refreshments; from *ṣaityamu* and *upachàramu,* ministering.

Ṣaivamu, Sivite; adjective of Siva. Skt.

Ṣaivuḍu, worshipper of Siva. Skt.

ṣancintsuṭa, to doubt, to hesitate. Skt.

ṣancitamu, doubtful. Skt.

Ṣani, Saturn (planet and god), bad luck. Skt. Ṣani is the god of misfortune. *ná cáli Ṣani! nénu accaḍici poyinánu,* the bad luck of my legs took me there; *rágala Ṣani Ráméṣvaramu* *póyiná tappadu,* a pilgrimage to Ramesvaram will not save you from the predestined evil.

şaniṭari-inspecṭaru, Sanitary Inspector. English. *míru nálugu rúpáyilu şániṭari-inspecṭaru chétuló peḍité, yevvaru á sangati cadipéváré léru,* put a few rupees in the Sanitary Inspector's palm and no one will move in that matter.

şanivááramu, Saturday. Skt. The day of Şani, Saturn.

şankhamu, chank, conch. Skt. A shell used as a trumpet in temple worship. The British still fish for them at Tuticorin like their predecessors, the Hindu Rajas, the Portuguese, and the Dutch.

sapanamu, şapathamu, oath, curse. Skt. *şapathamu* is the commoner of the two forms.

şapintsuṭa, to curse. Skt.

şaradrütuvu, şarattu, autumn (the two months between the monsoons). Skt.

şaramu, arrow. Skt. A book word for *bánamu.*

şaraṇamu, refuge. Skt.

şaraṇálayamu, orphanage. Skt.; from *şaranam* and *álayam,* abode.

şarattu, autumn; same as *şaradrütuvu.*

şaristádáruḍu, the Collector's head clerk or Sheristadar. Hindustani; also spelt *şirastadáruḍu.*

şaríramu, body. Skt. The Telugus refer to the body where we omit it; how are you? becomes *mí şaríramuló yeṭl unnadi?* how is it with your body?

şaríırapaṭutvamu, bodily vigour. Skt.

şarírasukhamu, bodily health. Skt.

şaşamu, hare. Skt. A book word for *chevulapilli* (the cat with ears); *şaşi* is a word for the moon because the marks on the moon are supposed to look like a hare.

şaşirékha, horn of the moon. Skt.

şastamu, excellent. Skt.

şastramu, surgeon's knife. Skt.

şastravaidyamu, surgery. Skt.

şataguṇamu, one hundredfold. Skt. *satamu,* 100.

şatamánamu, bridal locket. Skt. This, more commonly known as *tálibottu,* is what is tied round the bride's neck at the marriage ceremony and a married woman always wears it; it corresponds with our ring.

şatamu, 100. Skt. The Telugu words are *núru* and *vanda.*

şatapadi, centipede.

şatavrüddhu, centenarian. *şatavrüddhu, y'incá ḍyanacu yevvaru pillan istáru?* who will give his daughter in marriage to a centenarian like him?

şatruḍu, şatruvu, enemy. Skt. *şatrucóṭiló chéri póyináru,* he has joined our enemies; *ataḍu mana şatrupacshamlóváḍu,* he belongs to the party of our enemies; *ḍácṭaru: í prapanchamló mávanṭi vaidyulac endaró şatruvul unṭáru. rógi: incó lócamló incá eccuvamandi şatruvul unṭár anḍi.* Doctor: Doctors, like us, have many enemies in this world. Patient: More in the next, doctor.

şatrutvamu, enmity. Skt.

şauchamu, purity. Skt. from *şuchi.*

şauryamu, heroism. Skt.; from *şura.*

şavamu, corpse. Skt. *ocaḍu: ippaṭi peḷḷillaló tsappuḍé lédu. incóḍu: nizamé ippaṭi cálamló peḷḷilla canṭé şavála v'úrégimpulé bágá v'unṭai.* Smith: There is no noise at weddings nowadays. Jones: True; funeral processions are now better than weddings.

şayanamu, resting. Skt. *şayanagrühamu* is a bedroom.

şayanintsuṭa, to rest. Skt.

şayya, bedding. Skt. *púşayya* is a flower-bed, bed.

şábásu! bravo! Hindustani. Anglo-Indians write it *shabosh.*

şácamu, vegetable. Skt. The Telugu is *cúra. şácavratamu,* fasting by abstinence from vegetables.

şácunamu, augury, science of divination. Skt.; from *şacunam,* bird.

şákha, branch, sect, department. Skt. *sarásari şákha,* direct branch of descent; *sainica şákha* is the newspaper word for Army Department; *mana şákhaváru,* people belonging to our sect.

şála, hall. Skt. Much used in compounds, as *gurrapuşála,* stable; *ayudhaşála,* armoury; *mudrácsharaşála,* printing-press; *ṭancaşála,* mint.

-şáli, affix meaning 'having'; forms adjectives. Skt. *buddhişáli,* sensible;

dhairyaṣáli, brave; *anubhavaṣáli*, experienced.

ṣáluva, shawl. Hindustani.

ṣáná, much. *tsálá* is commoner.

ṣancshan, sanction. English. Commonly used of official orders of sanction. *núṭa yabhai rúpáyalu ṣáncshan cheyinchinúru*, Rs. 150 has been sanctioned; *peṭíshan miṭinguló peṭṭinchi, arugulacu sáncshan ippinchináru*, they got a petition put in at the municipal meeting and got the pials sanctioned.

ṣántamu, mild, meek, patient, tranquil. Skt. *níshcáranangá cópapaḍaca conchem sépu ṣántamu vahintsandi*, don't get angry without cause, but be patient for a bit; *ducci dunnité bhúmici ṣántamu*, ploughing soothes the soil.

ṣántapaḍuṭa, to become calm. Skt.

ṣánti, mildness, meekness, patience, rest, tranquillity. Skt. The watchword of the Svarajists. *dáhaṣánti*, quenching thirst.

ṣántintsuṭa, to be patient, to be pacified, to get better. Skt. *míru conchem sépu ṣántintsandi*, be patient for a little.

ṣántiparatsuṭa, to pacify, to calm.

ṣántuḍu, a calm man. Skt. *aṭani ṣántuṇṇi chéstánu*, I will pacify him; *yenta ṣántuḍic ainá yélá cópam rácunḍá v'unṭundi?* enough to try the patience of a saint.

ṣápamu, curse. Skt. *á ṣápal anní vacca araṭi pandu cósama?* all those curses for one plantain?

ṣárίra, ṣáríracamu, bodily. Skt.; from *ṣaríram*.

ṣásanamu, order, deed, inscription, law. Skt. Gifts of land to temples, &c., were commonly inscribed in the old days as *ṣilaṣásanálu*, stone inscriptions, or *támraṣásanálu*, copper-plate inscriptions; *maranaṣásanamu* is a will, *dánaṣásanamu* a deed of gift; *ṣásanamu* is also the word now used to translate Acts of the Legislature.

ṣásananirmáṇasabha, legislative council. Skt. The assembly that settles the law.

ṣásanóllanghanamu, civil disobedience. Skt.; from *ṣásanam*, law, and *ullanghanamu*, disregard; the newspapers have invented this word to translate the Congress's 'civil disobedience', which phrase is English in language and origin.

ṣásintsuṭa, to command, to punish, to enact. Skt.

ṣásti, punishment. Skt. *dínici tagina ṣásti ainadi*, she has been suitably punished (she has had her dose); *daivamu nác aparádhamu chésina vánḍlacu bágá ṣásti chésináḍu*, God avenged me on my enemies.

ṣástracáruḍu, writer of Shastras. Skt. *áḍadani chéti arthamu, magaváḍi chéti biḍḍá nilavad ani cheppina ṣástracáruḍu anta verriváḍ éna?* was the Shastra-writer who said that property was not safe with a woman, or a child with a man, such a lunatic?

ṣástramu, science, art. Skt. *vedánta-ṣástramu*, theology; *vaidyaṣástramu*, medicine; *dharmaṣástramu*, jurisprudence; *silpiṣástramu*, architecture; *alancáraṣástramu*, rhetoric; *nítiṣástramu*, ethics; *gaṇitaṣástramu*, arithmetic; *vyácaraṇaṣástramu*, grammar; *tarcaṣástramu*, logic; *ṣástragnyánamu*, knowledge of the Shastras. *occaḍu: mí mukham occa vaipuna yettugá v'unnadi, ṣástra pracáram tsústé mícu mí pillala mída préma yeccuva v'unnad anna máṭa. incóḍu: á sangati nácu teliyadu, má pillaváḍu rái vésté mukhánici tagili váchchi yettugá v'undi.* Phrenologist: That bump on one side of your face denotes philoprogenitiveness according to science. Smith: I know nothing of that: it is a swelling due to my boy throwing a stone at my face.

ṣástri, doctor of science, especially theological science. Skt. *ṣástrulu* in the plural is a common title of learned Smarta Brahmins.

ṣáṣvatamu, eternal. Skt. *ṣáṣvata nivásam* is the lawyer's term for domicile. *í lócamuló v'unn anta cálamu ṣáṣvatanga varthilluduru gáca!* may he prosper continually all the time he is on this earth! *manacu dhanamu ṣáṣvatam cádu, déhamulu ṣáṣvatamulu cávu, nityamaina paralóca sukhamulu vichárintsu có valenu*, the goods of this world are perishable, our bodies are perishable, the everlasting felicities of the next world should occupy our thoughts; *míru tsúpina páṇḍityánici tagina péru micu ṣáṣvatangá labhinchindi*, you have gained an immortal name by your scholarship; *batucul ennáḷḷu? bhágyál ennáḷḷu? círti ṣáṣvatamu gáni*, how long are our days? how lasting our riches? but fame is eternal.

ṣáyiru, sáyiru, sair, transit duty. Hindustani. The old transit duty long since abolished. The word is common in the old records.

Seṭṭi, Chetty, merchant, a caste title. A Tamil word. The Telugu is *cómaṭi*. *lábhamu lénidi Ṣetti yéṭa paḍaḍu*, if there is no profit to be got, the Chetti won't venture into a river; a variant is *ádayamu lécané Ṣetti varada póḍu*, without hope of gain the Chetti won't face the flood.

ṣémushi, intellect. Skt.

ṣéru, seer. Hindustani; also *séru*. It is now metrically standardized as the Indian kilo; also a measure equal to one litre.

ṣéshamu, residue, remnant. Skt. *rüna ṣéshamu, vraṇa ṣéshamu, agni ṣéshamu v'untsa cúḍaḍu*, do not spare the remnants of a debt, a sore, or fire; *aṣéshamu*, all.

ṣéshintsuṭa, to remain over. *ṣéshinchina sommu*, the balance; *ṣéshinchinaváru*, the rest of the people.

Ṣéshuḍu, Ṣésha, the king of serpents. Skt. Vishnu sits on Sésha who lies under the earth and supports it; he has 1,000 heads. *dénini sahasra mukhamulu gala Ṣéshuḍ ainanu varṇimpa tsáladu*, even the 1,000-headed Sésha could not describe it; *Garuḍáya lessá anṭé, Ṣéshdya lessá ann aṭṭu*, when he said 'How d'ye do, Garuda', Garuda had to answer, 'How d'ye do, Sesha' (of impertinent familiarity). *Ṣéshayya* is a common name for men.

ṣibiramu, encampment, camp. Skt.

ṣicastu, ruined. Hindustani.

ṣicsha, punishment, especially imprisonment. Skt. *caṭhinamaina ṣicsha* is imprisonment with hard labour; *lantsam ichchéváḷḷu firyádu chésu córu, firyádu chésu cunna ruzuvu partsaḍam mahá cashṭam; yeduru firyádu chésina váḍicé ṣicsha autundi*, those who give bribes will not complain; if they do, proof is extremely difficult; a countercharge will be made, and it is they that will be punished; *ménéjaru: abaddhálu áḍut annáu, inducu ṣicsha yémiṭó telusuná. naucaru: yém anḍi? ménéjaru: conta cálam aina tarváta ninnu úḷḷacu pani mída pampistánu*. Manager: You tell lies, do you know what is the punishment for that? Employee: What is it, Sir? Manager: After a bit we will send you on a round of the towns. *ṣicshartha-maina pannu*, penal assessment.

ṣicsha, discipline. Skt. *bála ṣicsha*, the teaching of children.

ṣicshintsuṭa, to punish. Skt.

ṣicshituḍu, one who is trained or punished.

ṣikha, ṣiga, crest. Skt. The crest of a bird, a mountain, &c.; the tuft of hair left at the top of the head when it is shaved. *andité ṣikha, andacunṭé, cáḷḷu paṭṭu coné váḍu*, the tuft if he could reach it, if not, your feet (an impudent but servile person); *abbité ṣiga, abbaca póté cáḷḷu* is a variation of the same proverb: he will take you by the hair if he can; if not, he will fall at your feet.

ṣikharamu, peak; also *ṣrüngamu*. Skt.

ṣikhámani, the finest gem in a diadem. Skt. The crest gem.

ṣila, stone. Skt. The Telugu is *ráyi*. *ṣilábhógam, sthalabhógam, narabhógam cána rávu*, you can never tell what a stone, a place, or a man may turn out (may become an idol, a garden, a king).

ṣilácsharamu, stone inscription. Skt. from *ṣila*, stone, and *acsharam*, letter. *idi ṣilácsharam vale ní manassuló náṭu coni v'unnadi*, this is inscribed on your memory as on a stone.

ṣilpamu, handicraft. Skt.

ṣilpi, artisan. Skt. *silpaṣástramu* is architecture.

ṣiramu, ṣirassu, head. Skt.

ṣirasávahintsuṭa, to obey. Skt. The idea is of placing the written order on your head and bowing in token that you will carry it out. *dévuḍaina cáni Bráhmaṇa vácyam anṭé sirasá vahistáḍu*, though he be a God, if a Brahmin is mentioned he will act in submission to the command.

şiraschchédamu, decapitation. Skt.
şirastádári, office of Sheristadar.
şirastádáruḍu, Sheristadar or Collector's head clerk, a very important person. Hindustani. In the early days of British rule the Sheristadar for all practical purposes was the Collector. Even now the Collector is popularly supposed to be in his pocket; he is usually a Brahmin. *mícu tappacunḍá Şirastádári autundi; idi yenta calicálam aina Brahmaṇa vácyam v'úricé pódu,* you will certainly be a Sheristadar one day; bad as times are the Brahmin still counts for something; *Conḍalráu Pantulu gáru şirashtádári chésin'appuḍu garbhálaló pinḍálu adiri póyévi,* when Mr. Kondalrao Pantulu held the office of Sheristadar the foetuses in the wombs trembled with fear. Also spelt *şaristádáruḍu.*
şirójamu, hair. Skt.
şirómaṇi, gem worn on the head. Skt.
şishṭamu, disciplined, obedient. Skt.
şishṭácháramu, an established rule of conduct. Skt. *Şishṭáchára viruddhamgá naḍutsu cunṭé pápam vastundi,* it is sin to transgress the rules of our faith; *ati bálya viváhálu şástránicinni şishṭácháránicinni cévalam virudhamgá vádam chést unnáru,* they argue that infant-marriage is contrary to the books of the law and tradition.
şishṭuḍu, pious, observant of traditional rules of conduct. Skt. *nívu cheppinadi şástraviruddham aguṭa chéta, céval unmatta pralápamulu, ní máṭalu pramána buddhigala má vanṭi şishṭul angicarinpa taginavi cávu,* your discourse being contrary to scripture and all clotted nonsense, orthodox people like us must shut our ears to it.
şishyuḍu, disciple. Skt. *şishyulacu yeppuḍu guruvu cheppé máṭala y'andu bhacti vişvásálu v'unḍa valenu,* disciples must always accept the teacher's words with devotion and faith; *guruvucu tagga şishyuḍu,* a disciple worthy of his teacher (a proverbial expression which indicates popular contempt for the system of theological apprenticeship).
şişira rütuvu, the cold weather. Skt. more usually *tsali cálamu,* one of the six seasons. The others are *vasantam,* spring; *vésari,* summer; *varsham,* the rains; *şarattu,* early autumn; and *hémantam,* late autumn.
şistu, land-tax. Hindustani.
şişuhatya, infanticide. Skt.; from *şişuvu,* infant, and *hatya,* slaying.
şişutvamu, infancy. Skt.
şişuvu, infant. Skt. *cottavádu: í v'úḷḷó goppaváḷḷu yevaraina puṭṭárá? grámasthuḍu: nácu telisin anta varacu iccaḍa şişuvulé puṭṭutár anḍi, goppaváḷḷu puṭṭa lédu.* Stranger: Have any big people been born in your village? Villager: So far as I know only infants are born, not big people.
şithilamu, decayed. Skt.
Şiva, the god Siva. Skt. *chésévi Şiva pújalu, cheppévi abaddhálu,* his acts are Siva worship, his words lies.
şivalingam, the phallus representing Siva. Skt.
Şivalócamu, Siva's heaven. *şivalócamu ponduṭa,* to die (a Saivite expression).
şivamu, inspiration, possession (by a demon). Skt.
Şivarátri, the great Siva festival. Skt. Siva's night; the festival comes off in *Mágha* (February to March).
şiváru, hamlet.
şiyáyi, besides, extra. Hindustani.
Şivuḍu, Siva. *Şivun ágnya lénidi chima cuṭṭadu,* without Siva's orders an ant will not bite you.
şícu, sick. English.
şíghramu, quick. Skt. *síghrangá* is the usual word for 'quickly'.
şílata, şíla, disposition, character. Skt. *suşílayaina,* of good disposition; *durşílayaina,* of bad disposition.
şírshamu, head. Skt. *şírsha* is commonly used in the sense of chief, main. *şírshica,* heading.
şítacálamu, winter, the cold weather. Skt.
şítalamu, şítamu, cold. Skt. *şítóshnamulu* (*şítamu* and *ushnamu*), heat and cold, climate.
şlághaníyamu, praiseworthy. Skt.
şlághintsuṭa, to praise. Skt.
şlócamu, a Sanskrit verse. Skt.
şmaşánamu, burning-ground. Skt. *amma grüha pravéşamu, áyya smaşána*

pravéşamu, the bride enters the house, the bridegroom the tomb (unlooked-for calamity).

şonţhi, dry ginger. Skt. *şunţhi.*

şóbha, lustre. Skt.

şóbhanamu, happy, auspicious, especially of marriages. Skt. *şóbhanamu chéyuţa* is to complete a marriage.

şóbhintsuţa, to shine. Skt. *má nérpu şóbhistundi*, my learning shines.

şócamu, grief. Skt. *şócópaşamana lékha* is a letter of condolence (*upaşamintsuţa*, to alleviate).

şócarnamulu, lamentations. Skt.

şóchaníyamu, lamentable. Skt. *Jarmaniló pradhána mantrul agu Brüningu gáru prabhutvam í samayamuna rájináman íya valasi vatstsuţa migula sóchaníyam*, it is very distressing that just at this time Brüning, the Chief Minister of Germany, should have to resign.

şócintsuţa, to grieve. Skt.

şódhana, investigation. Skt.

şodhintsuţa, to investigate, to search. Skt. *váni paţţu coni şódhimpagá*, when he was arrested and searched.

şósha, drying up, fainting. Skt. *vaţţi cantha şósha*, you are only making your throat dry, i.e. wasting your breath.

şraddha, diligence. Skt. *atithici şraddhábhactulató svayangá v'upacháram chésinádu*, he personally attended on his guest with diligence and devotion; *nénu şraddhagá v'unnánu*, I am all attention.

şrama, toil, trouble. Skt. *déhaşrama* is exercise.

şramapaduţa, to be in difficulties; also to take pains. Skt.

şramapeţţuţa, to give trouble.

şravanamu, ear, hearing. Skt. Used in Skt. compounds. *şravanéndriyamu* is the sense of hearing; *dúraşravana dúradarşanádi şactulu*, the faculties of hearing and seeing at a distance, &c. (supposed to be acquired by yogies).

şráddhamu, funeral rite. Skt.; from *şraddha*. *Sráddhadévuḍu* is Yama, the god of death.

şránti, rest, peace. Skt. More commonly *vişránti.*

şrávanamu, fifth lunar month, about July to August. Skt.

şréni, line, row. Skt.

şréshţhamu, excellent. Skt.

şréshţhuḍu, excellent man. Skt.

şréyascaramu, prosperous, auspicious, beneficial. Skt. *bógamváḷḷu rávaḍam vadhúvarulacu bahu şréyascaramu*, the attendance of dancing-girls at a marriage brings prosperity to the bridal pair; *Bráhmana dúshana nicu şréyascaram cádu*, the Brahmin's curse will bring you bad luck.

şréyassu, prosperity, good. Skt. *mí şréyassu córi cheppinánu*, I spoke for your good.

şrí, holy, blessed. Used commonly as an honorific prefix. Skt. Properly *Şrí* is a name of Lakshmi, wife of Vishnu and goddess of wealth. *Mahardája Rája Şrí* takes the place of our esquire in addresses on letters. The nationalists call their leaders *şríjut*. Rajas will be addressed as *Şrí Rája*. Gods and goddesses are all *Şrí*. *góvu léni v'úḷḷó goḍḍu gédé Şrí Mahá Lakshmi*, in a village where there are no cows the barren buffalo is a blessed goddess of wealth.

şrígandhamu, sandal wood. Skt.

şrímantuḍu, wealthy man. Skt.

şrímat, His Reverence. Skt.

şrímukhamu, pastoral letter. Skt.

şrírastu! good fortune! Skt.

şrótriyamu, a benefice. Skt. A village conferred on learned men. Shrotriyams are now held by any one as these villages were enfranchised long ago and are in the market.

şrótriyuḍu, a learned Brahmin. Skt.

şrüngamu, peak; also *şikharamu*. Skt.

şrüngáramu, adornment, beauty, gallantry. Skt. *şrüngáravati* is a belle; *şrüngáracávyamu* is belles-lettres; *şrüngáravanamu* is a pleasure-park; *mahámahópádhyayuluváru şrüngáranáyaculugá cana paḍutu v'unnáru, panḍitul eppuḍu mahá raşiculu gadá*, you look like a great scholar and a leader of fashionable society; scholars are very fashionable people; *yémí lén ammacu yéḍpula şrüngáramu, caligin ammacu caḍupula şrüngáramu*, what her fat belly is to the rich woman, that her lamentations are to the poor woman (her pride and joy); *lóna vicá-*

ramu, baiṭa ṣrüngáramu, fair without, foul within (a whited sepulchre).

ṣrüngárintsuṭa, to adorn. Skt.

ṣruti, revelation, the Vedas. Skt.

ṣrutismrütulu, the scriptures. Skt. *smrütiṣrutulaló vyabhicháram cúḍad anṭé dánici bógamváḷḷanu cúḍá v'untsu có rád ani artham aṭa,* they pretend that when the scriptures forbid adultery they forbid the keeping of dancing-girls; *nénu ṣrutismrüti pramánálaló amóghamaina vádam chéstánu,* I will produce an unanswerable argument founded on Scripture.

ṣubhacáryamu, festival occasion, especially a marriage. Skt. *subhacáryamulaló cúḍá bógamváḷḷa chéta páḍintsaḍam, áḍintsaḍam bottigá máni veyya valenu,* we must altogether stop dancing and singing by nautch-girls even on festive occasions.

ṣubhalékha, ṣubarékha, letter announcing a marriage or any festivity. Skt.

ṣubhavárta, good news. Skt.

ṣubhramu, clean. Skt. *snánamu cheyyaḍam vanṭi ṣubhram cósam aṭa!* they (Europeans) think baths are taken for bodily cleanliness! (the true doctrine, of course, is that they are religious ceremonies).

ṣubhramuchéyuṭa, to clean.

ṣuchi, purity. Skt.

ṣuclapacshamu, the fortnight of the moon's increase. From Skt. *ṣuclamu,* white; the opposite is *bahuḷa pacshamu* or *crüshṇa pacshamu.*

ṣucravávaramu, Friday. Skt.

ṣucruḍu, the planet Venus. Skt.

ṣuddhamu, pure, downright, utter, perfect. Skt. *nívu ṣuddha dongavu,* you are a downright thief; *ṣuddha abaddhamu,* an utter falsehood.

ṣuddhántamu, seraglio. Skt.

ṣuddhi, purification. Skt.

ṣuddhichéyuṭa, to purify. *déha ṣuddhi chéyuṭa,* to thrash.

ṣuddhigá, purely, completely. *tricaranaṣuddhigá,* absolutely (complete in 3 ways, thought, word, and deed).

ṣuddhuḍu, a pure or holy man. Skt.

ṣulcamu, toll, duty. Skt. *canyáṣulcamu* is the toll taken of parents when they marry off daughters.

ṣunacamu, dog. Skt. The Telugu is *cucca,* and *ṣunacam* is never used in speaking, but children are made to learn the word at school.

ṣunṭha, blockhead. Skt. *á sunṭhalu chési dushprayatnálu yeppaṭici cána ságavu,* the knavish tricks of those blockheads will always fail; *ataḍu vaṭṭi sunṭha,* he is an utter blockhead.

ṣushcamu, dry, vain, empty. Skt. *ṣushca priyamulu, ṣúnya hastamulu,* vain cajoleries, empty hands.

ṣuṣrúsha, service. Skt. *ippaṭiváḷlacu guruṣuṣrúsha bottigá lédu,* the present generation has given up service to the teacher.

ṣúdruḍu, sudra, the lowest caste. Skt.

ṣúla, throbbing or racking pain. *paccaṣúla,* stitch in the side; *caḍupuṣúla,* colic.

ṣúlamu, dart, stake, Ṣiva's trident. Skt. *chevici ṣúlamu vale sóci,* penetrating my ear like a stake; *manasuló ṣúlamu vale náṭu coni,* planted in my mind like a stake; *Vishnudévuḍici chacramunnu, Ṣivuḍici ṣúlamunnu, Indrunici vajrayudhamunnu,* Vishṇu's disk, Ṣiva's trident, and Indra's thunderbolt.

ṣúnya, the Buddhistic void, which neither is nor is not.

ṣúnyamu, empty, void of. Skt. *ṣushca priyamulu ṣúnya hastamulu,* vain cajoleries, empty hands (fair words butter no parsnips); *ṣúnyahastuḍu,* empty-handed.

-ṣúnyuḍu, affix meaning 'void of'. *dayáṣúnyuḍu,* without mercy; *gnyánaṣúnyuḍu,* devoid of knowledge; *vivécaṣúnyuḍu,* a boor.

ṣúratvamu, heroism. Skt. *árambha ṣúratvam,* daring at the outset, it is the first step that counts.

ṣúruḍu, hero. Skt. *árambhaṣúruḍu,* a good starter (and poor finisher).

ṣvásacóṣamu, lung. Skt., from *ṣvásamu,* breath, and *cóṣamu,* sheath. *úpirititti* is commoner.

ṣvásamu, breath. Skt. The common word is *úpiri.*

ṣvétamu, white. Skt. The common word is *tella. ṣvéta-* is used in composition: *ṣvétacushṭhuvu,* leprosy; *Ṣvétádri,* the White Mountain (the Himalayas); *Ṣvétapatramu,* the White Paper.

T

tabbibbu, flurry, agitation.
tabucu, tray.
tacarâru, dispute. Hindustani.
taccaḍa, scales. Telugu. Large scales such as those used in the Treasury to weigh rupees by the thousand.
taccina, remaining; from a verb *taccuṭa* which is seldom used. *taccinaváru ráni lópam v'unḍadu*, the rest won't fail to come.
ṭaccu, trick. Thug is derived from this; they had nasty tricks of sandbagging and garrotting.
taccuva, defect, less, too little. The opposite is *eccuva*. The *v* in both words is usually pronounced as a *w*. *telivi taccuva, acali yeccuva*, the bigger the appetite, the less the sense.
taccuvapaḍuṭa, to fall short.
tacshanamu, at once. Skt. *vári daggira paregettu coni tacshaṇam tísuconi rávalenu*, run and fetch him at once. The derivation is from *tat*, that, and *cshaṇam*, instant.
tad-, prefix meaning 'that'. Skt. *tat*. *tat* becomes *tad* before vowels, *d*, &c., *taddinamu*, commemoration day; *tadanuguṇamgá*, according to that.
taḍabaḍuṭa, to be confused, to stagger, to flutter.
taḍabáṭu, fluttering, confusion.
taḍaca, matting, frame, hurdle made of strips of bamboo, &c.; also *taḍica*. Anglo-Indians use the word in the form of *tatty*. *tappula taḍaca* is a confused mass of mistakes; *taḍaca léni y'inṭló cucca dúrin aṭṭu*, as a dog enters a house without a *tatty* (screen used as door).
tadanantaramu, after that.
tadanuguṇangá, according to. *ní taribítu chéta nénunnu tadanuguṇangáné máṭalu chepputánu*, I will speak according to your tutoring.
taḍavu, delay.
taḍavuṭa, to grope; also *taḍumuṭa, taḍuvuṭa*.
tadá, then. Skt. Used in books.
tadárabhyá, from that time. Skt. Used in books.

taddinamu, the day of commemoration of one's ancestors. Skt.
tadécadhyánamu, reverie. Skt., from *tat*, that, *éca*, one, and *dhyánam*, meditation; *váḍu tadécadhyánamugán unnáḍu*, he is in a reverie.
taḍi, damp. *taḍi guḍḍalató gontuca tega cóstáḍu*, he will cut a man's throat with a damp cloth (hidden malice).
taḍica, *tatty*, same as *taḍaca*. *áḍadi boncité góḍa peṭṭin'aṭṭu, mogaváḍu boncité taḍica caṭṭin'aṭṭu*, a woman's lies are built like a wall, a man's are mere matting.
taḍipeṭṭuconuṭa, to wet; also *taḍipintsuṭa, taḍupuṭa*. *áme canṭa taḍi peṭṭu connadi*, she melted into tears.
taḍipintsuṭa, to wet; also *taḍipeṭṭuconuṭa, taḍupuṭa*.
taḍisi, wet. *taḍisi gáni guḍise caṭṭadu, táci gáni moggadu*, a man won't build a hut till he is wet through or stoop till he has hit his head; *battal anni taḍasi mudd ainavi*, my clothes got soaking wet.
taḍisipóvuṭa, to get wet.
taḍiyuṭa, to be wet.
taḍumuṭa, to grope, to hesitate. *taḍumucócundá sabhaló manchi niḷḷa práyangá yécaruvu peṭṭa valenu*, I must pour out words at the meeting without hesitation like a stream of water; same as *taḍavuṭa, taḍuvuṭa*.
taḍupuṭa, to wet.
taḍuvuṭa, to grope. *chicatiló taḍuvuconutsu*, groping in the dark; same as *taḍumuṭa, taḍavuṭa*.
tagalabaḍuṭa, to be burnt. *ocaḍu: mí tsuṭṭala ducáṇánici nipp anṭu connad ani vinnánu; anta tagalabaḍi póyindá yémiṭi? incóḍu: tsuṭṭalu mátram cála lédu*. Smith: I hear your cigar shop got on fire; was everything burnt? Jones: Everything except the cigars.
tagani, unfit, not fitting, improper; negative from *taguṭa*, to be fit.
tagaramu, tin.
tagaramu, tagaru, ram. Skt. The Telugu is *poṭṭélu*. *conḍató tagaru*

pótláḍin aṭṭu, a ram butting a mountain (conceit).

tagavu, dispute.

tagavuláḍuṭa, to quarrel.

tagádá, quarrel, dispute. Hindustani. *induló tagádá peṭṭac ayyá, chinna paddu*, do not dispute that, it is a small item.

tagga, fit, worthy. Short for *tagina*. *guruvucu tagga sishyuḍu*, a disciple worthy of his master.

taggintsuṭa, to degrade, to debar.

tagguṭa, to decrease, to fall in price.

tagilina, struck, wounded. *tagilina cálé tagulutundi*, it is always the wounded foot that gets struck.

tagilintsuṭa, to fasten, to hang on, to entangle. *oca pracaṭanaló y'iṭlá v'unḍenu: 'má daggira aidu rúpáyala vastuvulu conuconévdḷḷacu cóṭu tagilinchédi ocaṭi, sigareṭṭu cálchédi incóṭi bahumánamga istánu.' Lacshmayya aidu rúpáyila vastuvulu árḍaru pampenu; vaṭitó páṭu oca chíla, oca nippupulla pampiri*, an advertisement ran: 'Purchasers of Rs. 5 worth of goods will get as a present something to hang their coats on and something to light their cigarettes with. Lakshmayya sent an order for Rs. 5 worth of goods and got with them a nail and match; *nannu á paniló tagilinchiri*, they entangled me in that business; *vánici sancelalu tagilinchiri*, they fixed fetters on him; *rógamu tagilintsuconuṭa*, is to contract a disease.

tagina, tagga, fit, worthy. *ádhyacshuḍu: mana sangham gavarnarugári daggirici ráyabáram pampints ále, inducu tagina sabhyul evaró cheppanḍi. sabhyudu: aidugurini pampintáma? adhyacshuḍu: aṭlágé pampintámu; Rámayya cúḍá vádḷḷaló chérustáma? sabhyudu: chértsa vatstsunu gáni, Rámayya nóru teravacunḍá v'unḍé sharatu mída pampintsa vatstsunu*. Chairman: Our association has to send a deputation to the Governor; say who will be fit representatives. Member: Shall we send five? Chairman: Yes, shall we include Ramayya? Member: By all means, but on condition that he keeps his mouth shut; *gantacu tagina bonta*, like saddle, like quilt (contemptuous); *guruvucu tagga ṣishyuḍu*, like teacher, like disciple. *taginanta* means enough.

tagulapaḍuṭa, to burn (intransitive); also *tagulupaḍuṭa*.

tagulapeṭṭuṭa, to set on fire; also *tagulupeṭṭuṭa*.

tagulaveyyuṭa, to set on fire. *yéru dáṭi teppa tagala vésin'aṭṭu*, to burn one's boat after crossing the stream.

tagulubaḍi, expense.

tagulupaḍuṭa, to burn (intransitive); also *tagulapaḍuṭa*.

tagulupeṭṭuta, to set on fire; also *tagulapeṭṭuṭa*.

taguluṭa, to touch, to have happen to one, to get on fire, to be incurred, to be found, to be wounded, to be struck, to be entangled. *tagilina cálé tagulutundi*, it is always the wounded foot that gets struck; *miru y'áme valaló taguluconnáru*, you have been entangled in her net; *tennisu átaló banti áṭagáni talacáyacu tagilenu. átagáḍu: banti tagili ná talacáyi boppi caṭṭindi, íṭla áḍaḍam anyáyam. précshacuḍu: acram ém und ayyá? indácaṭi nunchí tsúst unnánu; míru áḍut unn appuḍu talacáyi upyógintsané lédu; andu ché debba tagilité mátram émi nashṭam?* A ball hit a tennis-player on the head. Player: I have got a lump on the head from the ball hitting it, it is not fair that I should go on playing in that condition. Spectator: Where is the unfairness? I have been watching you all the time and you have never used your head at all, so what harm has the blow on the head done you? *Lacshmayya: mí pillaváḍu ná mída ráyi visiri vésáḍu. Vencayya: adi mícu tagilindá? Lacshmayya: tagala lédu. Vencayya: aité adi vésinaváḍu máváḍu cáḍu*. Smith: Your boy threw a stone at me. Jones: Did it hit you? Smith: No. Jones: Then it was not my boy that threw it. *inṭici nippu tagilindi*, the house is on fire; *iccaḍa gáli tagulutsunnadi*, we get the breeze here; *debba tagilindi*, it is wounded, is what we say when, e.g. we wound a snipe; *tagala lédu*, I have missed it.

taguṭa, to be fit, to suit, to suffice, to be right. *aṭlu cheyya tagundá?* is that a proper thing to do?

tahataha, agitation; onomatopoeic.

tahássíludáruḍu, Tahsildar. Hindustani. Officer corresponding with a sub-prefect; his charge is a taluk.

tailamu, oil, ointment. Skt., from *ṭila*. *taila yantramu*, oil pump.

tala, head. *prazalaló tala yettuconuṭa*, to raise our heads in society; *tala nindá musugu vésuconi*, with your head all muffled up; *talalu bóḍul aité, talapulu bóḍulá?* their heads are clean-shaven, but are their thoughts clear? (*Vémana*); *talá tócá léni catha*, a story without head or tail; *talári págá talató tírutundi*, a Talayari's hate does not end till he gets your head; *tong'unna ṣuncárini tala múṭa dimpum ann aṭṭu*, like the man who asked the sleeping toll-keeper to help him put down his head-load (a silly thing to do as he might have walked through without paying); *ná tala tirugutsunnadi*, my head swims; *vánici sára talac eccinadi*, the spirits have gone to his head; *talabirusu*, stubborn (rough in the head).

talacaṭṭu, the cedilla at the top of some of the Telugu letters.

talacáya, head-piece, head.

talacindugá, head downwards, upside down, in disorder. *moṭárubanḍi talacindul aité*, if your car is out of order; *nénu pustacam talacindulugá tsadava galanu*, I can read a book upside down.

talacuminchina, above one's head. *talacu minchina vyayam chési*, spending up to one's ears; *talacu minchina véshálu vési*, dressed up to one's eyes.

talagaḍa, pillow. *vacca duppaṭi talagaḍá tisúconi rá*, bring a sheet and pillow.

talaguḍḍa, turban.

talanoppi, headache. *nácu conchem talanoppi vachchi vaidyuni pilipinchinánu*, I got a little headache and sent for the doctor. *ḍácṭaru: nícu tala noppi yeccaḍa vachchindi? vidyárthi: baḷḷó.* Doctor: Where did you get your headache. Boy: At school.

talapaḍuṭa, put in one's head. *áviḍa yé pani talapadité á pani sádhistundi*, she will succeed in anything she undertakes.

talapága, turban.

talapeṭṭuṭa, to take into one's head. *tarváta yémi zárigindó yémiṭo maḷḷi dáni zóli tala peṭṭaru*, afterwards they won't take it into their heads to concern themselves again with what happened.

talapu, thought. *atuvanṭi talapulu pápa hétuvul ani tóchi*, thinking that such thoughts would lead to sin.

talatsuṭa, to think. *tán unḍédi dágili gunṭa, talachévi méḍa máligalu*, living in a pit and dreaming of palaces; *tán ocaṭi talisté, daivamu ocaṭi talachinadi*, man proposes, God disposes.

talatala, glittering, onomatopoeic.

talaticca, sauciness.

talatóca, head or tail. *talatóca léni catha*, a story without head or tail.

talatrippu, giddiness. From *tala*, head, and *trippuṭa*, to turn.

talayári, talavari, talári, village policeman. *dága póyi talári y'inṭló dúrináḍ aṭa*, like the man who went to hide and got into the policeman's house (ran into the lion's mouth).

talá, per head. *talá vaca rúpáyi ichchi*, give them a rupee a head.

talladilluṭa, talladintsuṭa, to be agitated, to quiver. *dánici yémainá háni chéyun émó ani ná hrüdayam talladillutsunnadi*, my heart is agitated lest some harm befall her; *támaráculó níḷḷu talladinchin aṭṭu*, like a drop quivering on a lotus leaf (precarious position).

talli, mother. *ṭícharu: occa cuṭumbamló tallí, tandrí, pillavádú unnár annucó, yentamandi unṭáru? báluḍu: iddaru. ṭícharu: elágu? báluḍu: pillavádini talli yettu cunṭundi cábaṭṭi.* Teacher: Suppose there is a family consisting of father, mother, and child, how many does that make? Boy: Two. Teacher: How so? Boy: The mother carries the child in her arms; *talli caḍupu tsútsunu, penḍlámu vípu tsútsunu*, the mother will look at her son's belly, the wife at his back (to see what he has brought back for her); *talli tsálu pillacu tapputsunnadá?* as is the mother, so is the daughter; *talli daivamu, tanḍru dhanamu*, a mother is a divinity, a father is a treasure; *tallini tsúchi pillanu tísucó valenu*, look at the mother before you take the daughter; *talli léni pillá ulli léni cúra*, a motherless child is curry without onions.

tallidanḍrulu, parents; from *talli*, mother, and *tanḍri*, father. *tallidanḍrula guṇálu coḍuculacu sancramistav anna vamṣa páramparyapu siddhantamuló mícu nammacam unnadá?* do you believe in the heredity theory of sons inheriting qualities from their parents?

tallitalli, maternal grandmother; also *ammamma, tátamma*.

tallivéru, tap-root.

talugu, halter (for cattle). *gédenu coni talugunacu lógudumá?* when we buy a she-buffalo shall we draw back for the halter?

talupu, door. *tana talupu tísi, poriginṭici peṭṭi, rátri antá cuccalu tólutú cúrtsunn aṭṭu*, like the man who took his door off the hinges and gave it to his neighbour and spent the night chasing the dogs away (charity begins at home).

tama, your (honorific); the gradation is *ní, mí, tama*.

tamala, betel.

tamalapácu, betel-leaf. Chewed with areca-nut and lime; offered to guests and then called *támbúlamu*.

tamamu, darkness. Skt. Used only in books.

tamaru, you (honorific). The gradations are *nívu, míru, tamaru*.

tamassu, darkness. Skt. Used only in books or of abstract things like *múḍhatvatamassu*, the night of ignorance.

ṭamaṭama, tom-tom, the noise of the drum; onomatopoeic. *ḍappu putstsuconi ṭama ṭamá vésé mádigaváḍitó cheppu*, tell the tom-tom Mádiga to take his drum. Tom-toming is the usual method of publication of orders or announcements in India, and it is the Mádiga caste (cobblers) who are the town-criers in the Telugu districts.

tamásha, wonder, spectacle, fun. Hindustani. *yémi zarugutundó tamáshá tsúdám ani vachchinánu*, I have come to see the fun; *tamáshá anuṭa*, to say in jest.

tamásháváḍu, funny person. *íyana bahu tamásháváḍugá cana paḍuṭú v'unnáḍu*, he looks a very funny person.

tambura, a kind of guitar, from *tanti*, string, and *burra*, shell.

tammi, lotus.

tammuḍu, young brother. *ávalintacu annadammul unnáru gáni, tummucu tammuḍainá léḍu*, a yawn has younger and elder brothers (*annadammul* = *anna*+*tammulu*), a sneeze not even a younger brother (you sneeze once and get it over, but one yawn draws another after it).

tana, his, her, their (reflexive). *tana níḍa tanalóne v'unṭunnadi*, a man's shadow always accompanies him (i.e., the fruit of his actions); *Táḷḷapácavári cavitvamu conta, tana paityamu conta*, part he stole from Tallapacu, the other part is rubbish (bile).

tanakhá, mortgage. Hindustani.

-tanamu, affix denoting quality: -ness, -ty, -tion, -ment. *doratanamu*, sovereignty, *manchitanamu*, goodness.

tanantaṭatáné, tanacutáné, of one's own accord. *tanantaṭatáné rá valenu*, he must come of his own accord.

ṭanaṭana, clanging, onomatopoeic. *ṭanaṭanam ani binde tsappuḍu chéyutsu*, the metal jar clanging.

tanaváḍu, one's own relation, casteman, &c. *vaḍḍinchéváḍu tanaváḍu aité caḍa banṭin cúrtsunná vaccaṭé*, it is all the same where your seat is so long as the waiter is your man; *tana váru lótucu títuru, cániváru caḍacu títuru*, your own people will try and drown you, strangers will draw you to the bank.

ṭancaṣála, mint.

tanḍélu, head boatman, tindal. Hindustani.

tanḍri, father. *váḍu tanḍri atstsu*, he is the image of his father; *durmárgamunacu tanḍri baddhacanu*, idleness is the root of all evil; *talli daivamu, tanḍri dhanamu*, you turn to your mother for divine love, and to your father for money; *á tanḍri coḍucu cáḍá*, his father's son; *talli tsanipóté tanḍri pinatanḍritó samánamu*, if the mother dies the father becomes an uncle (his fondness diminishes).

tangéḍu (*cassia auriculata*), a common shrub with a yellow flower. It is used by tanners to tan leather. *púchina ṭangéḍu,* the tangeḍu in full blossom (of prosperity).

ṭangu, ṭanguváru, horse's girth.

tanikhí, investigation. Hindustani.

tanivi, satisfaction. *tanivi tíra máṭláḍináḍu,* he talked till he was satisfied (he had his say).

tannu, kick.

tannuṭa, to kick, to trample on. *nálugu tannulu tannudunu,* I will give him a kick or two; *nénu vacchi, nálugu tanni, vídhilóci genṭi vésinánu,* I came along and kicked him out into the street. *ṭícharu: ní cóṭucu yenni gunḍíl unnai? báluḍu: aidu. ṭícharu: nénu nálugu tísu cunṭé yém autundi? báluḍu: má nánna tantáḍu.* Teacher: How many buttons are there on your coat? Boy: Five. Teacher: if I take four away, what then? Boy: My father will kick you. *cálu tannité murigédi gummuḍi cáya; cálu tannité perigédi putstsa cáya,* trample on a pumpkin and it decays; trample on a water-melon and it flourishes.

tanṭá, trouble. *tanṭá yémi v'unnadi?* what's the trouble? *nácu sthalam lécą nénu tanṭálu paḍutú v'unnánu,* I am in difficulties for want of room (I am boxed up); *mí bágu cósamai nén enni vidhamulagánainá tanṭálu paḍinánu,* I have taken any amount of trouble for your good.

tanṭálamári, troublesome, vicious. *tanṭálamári gurramunacu táṭi paṭṭé gorapam,* for the vicious horse a curry comb of palmyra-splinters.

tanti, tantri, wire. Used also, like our wire, of a telegram.

tantramu, device, scheme, policy, plot. Skt. The newspapers use *rájyatantramu* for public policy; *má peḷḷi végiram cácunḍá v'unḍaḍánici yédó tantram zurugutú v'unnadi,* some plot is going on to delay our marriage.

taṇucubeṇucu, glittering; onomatopoeic.

tanuvu, body. Skt. *oḷḷu, ṣaríram, déham* are commoner.

tapamu, tapassu, penance. Skt. *caḍapaṭa chinnadi peddad ai y'inta cálamunacu ná tapamu phalinchenu gadá y'ani,* when at last the girl grew up and I thought of recompense and reward for protracted mortification of the flesh.

tapaṣṣáli, tapasi, a recluse, ascetic. Skt. *i madhya tappaṣṣálulu taccuv ai mahimalu conta cálamu nunḍi canapaḍacunḍá unnavi,* miracles have decreased with the number of ascetics.

tapá, ṭapál, the post, especially an official's post-bag. Hindustani. *ṭapá dvára teliya chéstánu,* I shall inform you by post. The word originally meant a stage on the postal route.

tapábanṭrótu, postman. *adugó ṭapábanṭrótu v'uttaram tísu cuni vachchináḍu,* see the postman has brought a letter.

tapintsuṭa, to do penance.

tappa, except, besides. Properly 'missing out' from *tappuṭa,* to miss out. *nácu canipeṭṭu coni unḍuṭa tappa véré pani lédá?* I have something else to do besides hanging about here.

tappaca, unfailingly, certainly.

tappacunḍá, without doubt, certainly. *tappacunḍá váru má pacshamgáné vádistáru,* they will undoubtedly argue on our side. *naucaru: mícu naucaru cá valen ani yevaró cheppité, vachchänu. peddamanishi: má y'inṭló pani antá máváḷḷé chésu conṭáré. naucaru: aṭla aité nénu tappacunḍá iccaḍé v'unṭánu, untsucónḍi.* Servant: I heard you wanted a servant and have come along. Gentleman: My womenfolk do all the work themselves. Servant: Then I shall certainly stay; engage me.

tappáy'oppá, right or wrong. *tappáy'oppá y'ani vimarṣinchi telisicóca chévrálu cheyanu,* I shan't sign till I have made sure it is correct.

tappintsuṭa, to extricate; in the middle voice 'to escape'. *práṇamu tappintsuconi vachchänu,* I have escaped with my life.

tappipóvuta, to escape. *tappipóyina,* defaulting.

tappitamu, mistake. *aṭuvanṭi commishanarlanu veyyaḍam gavarnamenṭu tappitam,* it is Government's fault to appoint such (municipal) commissioners. (But, now that they are elected, the people are still dissatisfied.)

tappu, fault, mistake. *ná tappu,* my mistake; *tappulataḍaca,* a mass of mistakes; *tappudári,* the wrong road; *tappu máṭal áḍuṭa,* to be delirious; *tappulu, veticeváḍú tandri; oppulu veticéváḍu órva léni váḍu,* the man who seeks out your faults is a father to you; the man who pays you compliments is your enemy; *tappulénivánṇi uppuló veyyum annáḍ aṭa,* they say he said: 'put the man who has no faults in the Salt' (the Salt Department has a reputation for harshness and finding fault with the best of subordinates); *tappulénivéru dharaṇiló léru,* there is none without a fault; *tappú v'oppú Daivam erugunu; pappú cúḍú Bápaḍ erugunu,* God knows right and wrong, the Brahmin, rice and dholl; *Dásari tappu danḍamutó sari,* the Dasari has only to fold his hands to be forgiven (there is a play upon words here, *danḍamu* meaning also punishment). *Lacshmayya: nénu nishpacshapátini, nénu tappu pani chésiná dánici vichára paḍutánu; incóḷḷato ná tappu cheppu-tánu. Vencayya: mí daggira rahasyam dágadu cábólu.* Smith: I am a fair-minded man, if I make a mistake I am sorry and confess it. Jones: I suppose you can't keep a secret.

tappu, tappuḍu, mistaken, false. *tappusácshyam* is false evidence.

tappuconuṭa, to get out of the way. *tappucó,* get out, is what you say to people obstructing the way.

tappuṭa, to miss. *dinam tappi dinámu,* every other day; *yé páṭu tappiná sápáṭu tappadu,* whatever is missed it won't be meals; *rá gala ṣani Ráméṣ-varamu póyiná tappadu,* though you go on pilgrimage to Ramesvaram, the fated misfortune will not miss you; *talli tsálu pillacu tapputs unnadá?* will the daughter lose the mother's track? (as is the mother, so is the daughter); *adi vánici tappadu,* he is in for it.

tapsílu, particulars. Hindustani. An account word.

tarabítu, teaching, tutoring, coaching. Hindustani. *míru ṣishyunṇi bahu bágá tarabítu chesinár anḍi,* you have taught your disciple very well; also *taribítu.*

tarafu, on behalf of. Hindustani. *vári tarafuna máṭáḍaḍamunacu vach-chinánu,* I have come to represent them.

taragati, grade, rank, class. Skt. *renḍava taragati ṭicceṭṭu,* a second-class ticket. Class in a school, but that is more commonly *clásu.*

tarahá, sort, species. Hindustani. *ippuḍu peddamanishi tarahá bottigá pótú v'unnadi,* gentlemen as a species are dying out altogether; *viváham aina taruváta peddamanishi tarahá chértsu cunnáḍu,* after marriage he turned respectable (*il se rangea*).

tarahágá, like, in the fashion of. *váḍu dorala tarahágá tala cattirintsu cun-náḍu,* he had his hair cut in European fashion; *í paráchicálu manivési y'ikha manam peddamanishi tarahágá máṭlá-ḍuḍámu,* let us talk like gentlemen, not slaves.

taraluṭa, to set out, to move; causative *taralintsuṭa,* to cause to move, to remove, to set going; also *tarluṭa, tarlintsuṭa.*

-taram, the comparative affix. *sat-yamu canṭé sréshṭamainad édiyu lédu, asatyamuna canṭé tívrataram ainad incocaṭi lédu,* there is nothing more excellent than truth or more dire than untruth; *taram* is often omitted as in the first half of the above example; *canṭé,* than, which is literally 'looking at', by itself supplying the comparison.

taramu, class, sort.

taramu, generation. *tarataramula nunḍi,* generation after generation.

taramu, possible. *cámamu jayintsa-ḍánici yevari taram autundi?* who can conquer lust?

tarangamu, wave. Skt. Used in books for *ala.*

taravánṇi, sour rice water.

tarcamu, logic. Skt. *atanici conchemu vyácaraṇamu, tarcamu, alancáraṣá-stramu cúḍá telusunu,* he knows some grammar, logic, and rhetoric.

tarcaṣástramu, science of logic. Skt.

tarcaṣástri, logician. Skt.

tari, time. Skt. *ittari,* now; *oca tari,* once.

taribítu, teaching. *nénu páṭhaṣála peṭṭi, mimmaln andarini taribitu chésténé cáni, míru y'í lócamló guḍḍi gavvac ainá panici ráru,* unless I set up a school and train you all, you won't be worth a dud farthing in this world; also *tarabítu.*
tarimíḍí, lathe.
tarimiveyuṭa, to drive away. *míru sádhyamain anta varacu pedda paricshalan ichchina várini tarimi véstú, mí bandhuvulacé v'udyógálu y'ippistú v'unnáru,* you drive away those who have got good degrees as far as possible to make room in the offices for your relations; *váṇṇi vídhilóci tarimi vésináru,* they drove him into the street.
tarjani, index finger. Skt.
tarlintsuṭa, to set going; also *taralintsuṭa.*
tarlivatstsuṭa, to set out to come. *peḷḷicoḍucuváru tarlivastáru,* the bridegroom's party have started.
tarliveḷḷuṭa, to set out to go.
tarluṭa, to set out; also *taraluṭa.*
tartsugá, often.
tarugu, discount, wastage, brokerage; same idea as in the English 'tare and tret'. *taragari* is a broker.
taruguṭa, to be worn away, to be finished. *vanne tarigi y'unna ná mukhamu,* my worn-out complexion; *taragani padavi,* a well-trodden path; *dúramu tarugacunnadi,* the way is coming to an end; *occocca ráyi tóstú v'unṭé, conḍ ainá tarugutundi,* remove stone by stone and even a mountain will be removed; *dóva taraga lédu,* the way does not become shorter; *yenta vrásinanu y'í ḍicshanari tarugacunḍá v'unnadi,* though I have written such a lot this dictionary is not finished.
tarumuṭa, tarumuconipóvuta, to pursue.
taruṇamu, opportunity. Skt.
taruṇi, a young girl. Skt. Used in books.
taruváṭa, tarváta, after. *á tarváta,* after that; *ná tarváta,* after me; *tarváta catha,* the next story.
tarzumá, translation. Hindustani. You *can* say *bháshántaramu* (Skt.) but you don't. *ocaḍu: nénu gáraḍi chést unṭé tsúchéváḷḷu navväru. incóḍu: yendu chéta? ocaḍu: nénu cheppé máṭalu aravamlóci tarzumá cheyyaḍánici ocaḍini cudurtsu cunṭé, váḍu á máṭalu tinnagá cheppaca, gáraḍi yeṭlá chéstánó cúḍá cheppaḍam modalupeṭṭäḍu; á sangati nácu chivaracu gáni teliya lédu.* Smith: The spectators laughed when I was doing conjuring tricks. Jones: Why? Smith: I had engaged a man to translate my remarks into Tamil; he translated them all wrong and also explained how I did the tricks. I did not find out till it was all over.
tat-, prefix meaning 'that'. Skt. *tatcálamu,* at that time; *tatpúrvamu,* before that; *tacshanamu,* at that instant.
taṭapaṭa, bing-bang; onomatopoeic. *chétuló ḍabbu léca venuca mundu ṭaṭapaṭá y'istú v'unnánu,* though I had no money I kept giving it out right and left, bing-bang.
taṭasthamu, taṭasthuḍu, near, present, neutral. Skt.
taṭastintsuṭa, to happen. Skt., from *taṭastham,* near, present.
taṭataṭa, thump-thump; onomatopoeic. Used, e.g. of the heart.
taṭácamu, tank, pond. Skt. The common word is *cheruvu.*
tatáluna, suddenly.
tatcálica, tatcálamaina, coeval.
tathatá, fact of being what it is, *sicceitas* (philosophy). Skt.
tathá, so. Skt. *yathá rájá tathá prajá,* as the king so the people; *yathá bíjam tathácuram,* as the seed so the sprout.
tathástu, so be it! amen! Skt.
tathyamu, truth. *tavvagá tavvagá tathyam télutunnadi,* dig and dig and the truth will out.
tatimma, the rest.
taṭṭa, small flat basket.
taṭṭamma, the goddess of measles, measles.
tattarapaḍuṭa, be agitated.
tattarapáṭu, agitation.
taṭṭu, direction, side. *a taṭṭuna pó,* go that side; *midi taṭṭu,* the upper side; *cindi taṭṭu,* the lower side.
taṭṭu, a pony, small horse (Anglo-Indian *tat*).

taṭṭuṭa, to touch, to clap, to knock, to strike. *occa cheyyi taṭṭité tsappuḍu auná?* will there be any sound if you clap with only one hand? (union is strength, or, it takes two to make a quarrel); *talupu yavaró taṭṭuts unnáḍu,* some one is knocking at the door; *rommu taṭṭuconutsu,* striking his chest; *i v'upáyam divyangá v'unnadi, idi y'idi varacu ná buddhici taṭṭinadi cádu,* a very good idea, it had not struck me.

tatvamu, the real, real nature or constitution. Skt. (*ṣaríra*)*tatvam,* constitution (of the body). *tellaváḷḷu mámsamu roṭṭe tinṭáru ganuca váḷḷa tatválacú mana tatválacú tsálá bhédam v'unṭundi,* as white people eat meat and bread there is much difference between their constitution and ours.

tauḍu, bran; also spelt *tavuḍu. tavitici vachchina cheyyé dhanamucu vastundi,* the hand that steals bran will steal money.

tavva, a small measure of capacity, a pint, two solas. *tanacu aina tavveḍu tauḍu v'unṭé, ácaṭi véḷacu aragintsa vatstsunu,* if you have even a pint of bran of your own you will have something to eat when you are hungry; *pitstsa tavva,* a false pint measure.

tavvintsuṭa, to get dug; causal of *tavvuṭa.*

tavvuṭa, to dig. *conḍa tavvi yelucanu paṭṭin aṭṭu,* to dig up a mountain to catch a rat; *tavvagá tavvagá tathyam télutunnadi,* dig and dig and the truth will come out.

tá, he himself. *tá valasinadi Rambha, tá muniginadi Ganga,* his woman is Rambha, his river is the Ganges; *tá cheḍḍa cóti vanam ella cherichinadi,* one bad monkey ruins the whole grove (one sickly sheep infects the flock).

tábédáruḍu, subordinate. Hindustani. *lantsálu putstsu cóné Tahassíludárunni tsústé tábédárlacu ishṭangá v'unḍadu,* his subordinates do not look with a favourable eye on a Tahsildar who does not take bribes.

tábélu, tortoise, turtle.

tácaṭṭu, mortgage, pawning, *tákhaṭṭu.* Hindustani. *peḷḷámu medaló v'unna paṭṭeḍa coṭṭi tísu coni póyi tácáṭṭu peṭṭináḍu,* he pawned the necklace off his wife's neck.

ṭáci, a talky. English.

tácintsuṭa, to apply; causative of *tácuṭa,* to touch.

tácí, stitch. Hindustani. *cuṭṭu* is the Telugu word.

tácu, tácuḍu, contact, touch.

tácuṭa, to touch. *praṣna: turucaváḍu muṭṭu cunnanduc ainá práyaṣchiṭṭam v'unḍa valená? accara lédá? zavábu: manam yenni mátl ani práyaṣchiṭṭálu chéṣu cunṭámu; á móṭa munḍá coḍuculu táca vadd anṭé mánutárá?* Question: Must you not do penance if you touch even a Muhammedan? Answer: How often are we to do penance? If you tell those rough blackguards not to touch you will they abstain from doing so?

táḍu, cord, rope; also *tráḍu. cóla léni peṭṭu, táḍu léni caṭṭu,* a blow without a rod, a bond without a rope (the methods of civilized governments or a calamity coming unawares); *táḍu tsálaca póté nuyyi púḍtsum' ann aṭṭu,* the rope being too short he (lost his temper and) ordered the well to be filled up.

tágubóṭu, drunkard.

tágubóṭutanamu, drunkenness.

táguḍu, drinking. *peddamanishi: venaca ninnu tsúchin'appuḍu táguḍu alaváṭu léd ani cheppité nácu santósham vachhindi. ippuḍu ninnu tsústé tági v'unnanducu vicháram véstunnadi. táginaváḍu: mícu vicháram vésté, nác ippuḍu santóshamgá v'unnadandi.* Gentleman: When I saw you before and you told me you were not in the habit of drinking, I was happy. Now, seeing you drunk, I am sorry. Drunken man: But *I* am happy now, Sir.

táguṭa, to drink. *poduguu cósi pálu tágin aṭṭu,* cutting the udder to drink the milk; *tága nérani pilli bórlá tósu connad aṭa,* the cat which could not drink upset (the pot); *tsuṭṭa táguṭa,* to drink a cigar, is to smoke it; *tsuṭṭa tágutává?* try a cheroot; also *tráguṭa.*

tákhídu, order. Hindustani. A nearly obsolete word, but the orders issued from the Taluk office are still called takids.

táḷamu, lock. The key which unlocks it is called *chevi*, its ear, or *cheyyi*, its hand.

táḷamu, cymbal, time in music (which is taken from the cymbal). *cannulu músiconi, táḷamu véyutsu, tala y'útsutsu*, shutting his eyes, beating time, nodding his head.

táḷamupaṭṭuṭa, to be angry, to be in a rage. *íyana ná táḷam paṭṭistáḍu*, he will catch it from me; *yemainá anṭé tiragabaḍi mana táḷamu paṭṭaḍánici tsústáru*, if we say anything they will turn and try and make us angry.

táḷapuchevi, táḷapucheyyi, key, from *táḷam*, lock, and *chevi*.

táli, táliboṭṭu, bride-locket, the small piece of gold which the bridegroom ties round the bride's neck; corresponds with our wedding ring. (A woman will never part with her *táli* and young magistrates are advised not to seize it in payment of a fine, especially if the lady is a political offender.)

tálimi, patience, endurance. *tálimi tannú cátsunú, yederini cátsunú*, patience will save you and your opponent (don't lose your temper in a dispute). *déha-tálimi*, stamina.

táḷḷu, plural of *táḍu*, rope, and of *táḍi*, palmyra.

táltsuṭa, to wear. *garbhamu táltsuṭa* is to conceive a child.

táḷuṭa, to bear. *cshudbháḍacu táḷa léca*, not being able to bear the pangs of hunger.

táḷuṭa, to stop, to shut up. *táḷu, yevvaró vastu v'unnáru*, shut up, some one is coming.

tálúcá, taluk. Hindustani. The old Muhammedan division of the Zilla or District, which we have retained.

tálúcu, belonging to. Hindustani.

támara, lotus. *támaráculó níḷḷu talla-ḍinchin aṭṭu*, shaking like a drop on a lotus leaf (on the edge of a precipice).

támara, ringworm.

támasamu, dullness, darkness, peevishness, obscurantism. Skt. *iṭuvanṭi svalpa vishayamlóni támasam vastú v'unṭé*, if you get peeved over so small a matter; *idi cévala támasa vachanamu*, that is sheer obscurantism.

támasintsuṭa, to delay, to dawdle. *oca nimisham támasintsa rádu*, you must not delay a minute.

támbúlamu, betel and areca-nut folded ready for chewing. Skt. This is offered at all functions. *peddamanu-shyula nalugurini támbulánici pilu-stánu*, I will ask some respectable persons to *támbulam* (for a discussion or some affair); *vamanamu cácunḍá n'unḍuṭacu gánu támbúlamu vésucun-nánu*, I took betel to stay my stomach.

támé, by themselves. *cherucu v'unḍé tsóṭici chímalu támé vastavi*, ants will come of themselves to a place where there is sugar-cane.

tánamu, place. Corrupt Skt. for *sthá-namu*.

ṭáná, police station. Hindustani; also *ṭháná*.

ṭánádárudu, station-house officer. The bailiffs employed by zamindars are also called *ṭáṇédárs*.

tánḍavamu, dance. Skt. *praḷaya tánḍavamu*, Siva's death dance.

táné, himself (emphatic). *tana cáḷḷacu bandálu táné tetstsu con aṭṭu*, like the man who brought the fetters for his own legs; *tánu tummi táné ṣatáyushu anuconna*, he sneezed and blessed himself (*ṣatáyushu*, 100 years of life).

tántricamu, apocryphal. Skt. The Tantras are the Hindu Apocrypha.

tánu, himself. *tánu mingédi, tananu mingédi tsútsu có valasinadi*, see first whether you can swallow him or he you (don't hit a man bigger than yourself); *tánu ocaṭi talisté, Daivamu ocaṭi talichinadi*, man proposes but God disposes.

tápamu, sorrow. Skt.

tápasuḍu, ascetic. Skt. The feminine is *tápasi*.

tápi, bricklaying.

tápíváḍu, bricklayer, mason.

tápu, top. English. Used especially of the deck of canal boats.

tárasilluṭa, tárasintsuṭa, to approach, to encounter. *Dévatalu Rác-shasulanu tárasillin appuḍu mahá yuddhamu sambhavinchinadi*, where the Gods encountered the Demons there was a great war; *strílu tárasinchin appuḍu purushuḍi manassu yenta gaṭṭid* *ainá caragaca mánadu*, when women approach the stoutest male heart will melt.

táratamyamu, comparative, merit, difference. Skt., from *tara*, the more, and *tana*, the most. *várivári táratamyamulac arhamugá tagina mariyádalu chési*, giving them honours in proportion to their respective merits; *y'ippuḍu scúḷḷaló tsaduvu cuné váḷḷacu bottigá vinaya vidhéyatalú pinnápeddá táratamyálu lévu*, schoolboys of the present generation have no modesty or manners and make no difference between old and young.

táríkhu, date (in the month). Hindustani.

tártsugá, often; properly *taratsugá*.

tárumárugá, upside down; onomatopoeic. *yuddh ánantaramu árthica paristhitulu tárumár aina pimmaṭa*, when the economic situation was upset after the war.

táta, grandfather. You will say *tátá* in addressing any old man. *tátacu daggu nérpa valená?* must you teach grandfather to cough? (teach your grandmother to suck eggs).

tátamma, grandmother; also *ammamma, tallitalli*.

táṭácu, palm leaf.

tátcálicapu, transitory. Skt., from *tat*, that, and *cálamu*, time.

táṭicheṭṭu, palmyra. *táṭ eccé vánni yendácá yegasana toyyunu?* how far can you push up a man who is climbing a palmyra? (You can only give him a start, he must do the rest for himself.)

táṭinára, coir.

tátparyamu, opinion, meaning. Skt.

tátsu, cobra. But people always say *ṭáṭsupámu*, cobra-snake, and not simply *tátsu*. *tala vaca táṭsupámu ṭsampinár'ani cúliváḷḷac andarici páulá y'ippisté váḷḷu santósha paḍuṭáru*, if we give all the coolies four annas a head for every cobra they kill they will be delighted.

távaḷamu, necklace, rosary. *tulasi púsala ṭávaḷamulu vésuconi*, wearing necklaces of basil beads.

távi, fragrance. *púvuló távi*, like the fragrance in a flower.

távu, place.

táyittu, amulet.

tázácálamu, postscript; from Hindustani *tázá*, new.

teccoṭṭuṭa, to break off; from *teguṭa*, to break, and *coṭṭuṭa*, to beat; also *tegacoṭṭuṭa, tegagoṭṭuṭa*.

teḍḍu, oar, paddle, wooden spoon. *teḍḍu v'unḍagá cheyyi cálṭsu conn aṭṭu*, like the man who burnt his fingers when he had a ladle.

tega, sect, class; from *teguṭa*, to be cut. *sávacáṣa tega*, leisured class; *lócamló v'undé janul anḍaru mósa puchchéváru, mósa póyéváru ani renḍu ṭegalugá v'unnáru*, the whole world is divided into two classes, those who cheat and those who are cheated; *inṭamanḍi y'inni tegalaváru vacca tsóṭa y í pracárangá samávéṣam cávaḍam ṭsústé Hinḍuvulaló v'undé aicamatyamu mari yevariló cúḍá lén aṭṭu spashṭam autú v'unnadi*, this gathering together of men of so many sects in one place proves the incomparable unity of the Hindus (but perhaps the existence of so many sects proves them to be incomparably fissiparous).

tegacóyuṭa, to cut off, to cut. *cheppulu chinnani cálu tega cósu có vatstsuná?* will you cut your feet off because your shoes are too tight? *curchí cálu checca póyi paradhyánam chéṭa vélu tega cósu cunnánu*, I cut my finger absentmindedly when I went to pare the leg of a chair; *taḍi guḍḍalató gontuca tegacostáḍu*, he will cut your throat with a wet cloth (professing non-violence).

tegagoṭṭuṭa, to break off; from *teguṭa*, to break, and *coṭṭuta*, to beat; more commonly shortened to *teccoṭṭuṭa*.

teganammuṭa, to sell off. *ní bhárya vanṭani v'unna guḷḷalu tegan ammi mélam peṭṭandí*, sell your wife's trinkets and engage a nautch-party (for the wedding); *mányálú maḷḷú tegan ammi*, selling off ground and glebe.

tegintsuṭa, to dare. *teginchí venacacu póyin'anta televitaccuva lédu*, there is no greater folly than to go back after having dared.

tegulu, blight, rot, disease. *máṭacu máṭa ṭegulu, níḷḷacu nátsu tegulu*, word upon word rots speech as weed upon weed chokes the pond. Commonly used of an outbreak of plague.

tegulugonṭu, an invalid.

teguṭa, to be broken, burst, or cut. When a tank bursts or breaches that is *teguṭa*.

teguva, daring. *teguva Dévendra padavi*, daring leads to heaven (revenge is sweet).

telaga, a sudra caste.

telica, gingelly; more commonly *nuvvulu*, a field crop. Oil is made of the seeds and sold as best Lucca oil after being refined in Europe.

telicapinḍi, oil-cake. Used to feed cattle.

telicaváḍu, oilmonger.

telifónu, telephone. English.

telisiconuṭa, to find out.

telivaina, intelligent.

telivi, intelligence. *telivi tacuva, ácali yecuva*, the less the intelligence, the more the appetite.

telivicáḍu, a sensible man; the feminine is *telivicaṭṭe*.

teliviléni, telivimálima, stupid.

telivitaccuva, stupidity. *strí: ayyó pápam chépa táḍucu tagulu cuni tsachchi póyindí. chépalu paṭṭéváḍu: dáni telivitaccuvacu nén ém chésédí? adi nóru músu cuni v'unḍi, nénu peṭṭina eranu tinaca póté bratici v'unḍédī.* Woman: Oh, the poor fish, it has caught itself on your line and died. Fisherman: I am not to blame for its stupidity; it had only to keep its mouth shut and not swallow my bait and it would still be alive.

teliyachéyuta, to inform.

teliyuṭa, to become plain, to be known, to perceive, to be understood. *cannulu teliyuṭa* is to see with the eyes; *cannulu teliyaniváḍu*, a man whose eyes do not perceive, a blind man; *chicatiló pillici cannulu teliyunu*, a cat sees in the dark; *nícu telisindá?* or simply *telisindá?* do you see? is constantly said in conversation or in giving orders to make sure the other party has understood; *telisé varacu Brahma vidya, telisté cúsu vidya*, before you are expert, a recondite science, when you know, nothing simpler (practice makes perfect); *anni telisinaváḍú léḍu, yémi teliyaniváḍu léḍu*, there is no one who knows everything, no one who knows nothing. *coṭṭaváḍu: í v'úḷḷó goppaváḷḷu yevarainá puṭṭārá? grámasṭhuḍu: nácu telisinanta varacu y'iccaḍa ṣiṣuvulé puṭṭutárandí: goppaváḷḷu puṭṭa léḍu.* Stranger: Have any big people been born in this village? Villager: As far as I know people are born little here, not big.

tella, white.

tellapóvuṭa, to turn pale. *tellapóyi alá tsustáv émi?* Why have you turned pale and look this way?

tellavári, next morning; from *tellaváruṭa*, to dawn.

tellavárigaṭla, tellavárагaṭla, tellavárigaṭṭa, tellavárétappuḍu, tellaváruzámuna, tellavárlu, at dawn. *musugu vésuconi bógamdáni y'intici veḷḷi, vidhiló yevvarú lécunḍá tsúchi, lópala pravéṣinchi, maḷḷi tellavárigaṭṭa chicati v'unḍagáné y intici vachchi, chéréváḍu*, he used to disguise himself and look around to see there was no one in the street before entering the dancing-girl's house and come away home at dawn before it was light; *télucu peṭṭanam isté tellavárlú anṭa poḍichinaṭa*, when the scorpion was given supremacy it went on stinging till dawn; *tellavárагaṭla léchi*, getting up at dawn.

tellaváru, white men, Europeans. This translates our own expression; but they often think of us as red rather than white.

tellaváruṭa, tellavárintsuṭa, to dawn. *Lacshmayya sṭímaru yecci nidra póyenu. tellavárin tarvátá Lacshmayyá: sṭímaruló prayánam chésté nidra paṭṭaḍu, vántulu veḷḷutav aní nannu bhayam peṭṭär andí, nác émi ibbandi caluga lédu. sṭímaru adhicári: sṭímaru incá révu vadalipeṭṭa lédu; injanu cheḍipoté bágá chéstunnáru.* Smith got on board and went to sleep; at dawn he remarked: They frightened me with stories about seasickness and not being able to sleep on board, but I have suffered no discomfort. Ship's officer: The steamer has not left the shore. The engine went wrong and they are repairing it.

Telugu, the Telugu language, also Tenugu, probably derived from Dravidian *ten*, south; the language of the south. *tanḍri: ní heḍḍumásṭaru nácu vrásina uṭṭaramuló ní naḍata manchidi cádu, leccalu rávu, Inglishu rádu, charitra tsadavaḍu, Telugu anta canna rádu, ani vrásáḍu, aité tsaduvu mánéi; incá ḍabbu danḍuga yenducú? vidhyárthi: nánná, y'í uttaránni incóḍu yevarainá vrási heḍḍumásṭaru santacam peṭṭāḍ émó canuccó.* Father: From your head master's report I see that your conduct is not good, arithmetic bad, you know no English, history neglected, Telugu worst of all. Better give up studying, it is only a waste of money. Schoolboy: Daddy, find out whether some one else did not write the report and put the head master's signature to it.

telupuṭa, to make known; causal of *teliyuṭa.*

temaḍa, phlegm.

temma, damp.

tempari, bold, rash man. *atanu mukham tsústé ataḍu khúnilu chésé temparigá canapaḍḍáḍu,* to judge from his face he seemed a bold, murderous villain; *aṭuvanṭi temparivádító póṭláḍité nácé paruvu taccuv ani nénu nóru músu coni v'urucunnánu,* thinking it beneath my dignity to quarrel with such a rash man, I held my tongue and did nothing.

tempu, boldness, rashness. The derivation is from *teguṭa,* to break.

tempuṭa, to break.

ṭenca, stone of a fruit.

tenigintsuṭa, to turn into Telugu.

ṭennisu, tennis. English. *peddamanishi: samvatsaramló yenni rütuvul' unnai? vidhyárthi: ṭennisu rütuvu, phuṭbálu rütuvulu renḍu.* Gentleman: How many seasons are there in the year? Student: Two, the tennis season and the football season.

tentsuṭa, to break, to snap off.

-tentsuṭa, affix meaning 'going'. Added in the form *dentsuṭa* to other verbs in the literary language. *arudentsuṭa, tsanudentsuṭa, égudentsuṭa,* and so on simply mean 'to go', or, shall we say, 'to repair' or 'to proceed'? One rule of the literary language is never to use common words like 'to go' or 'to do'; you say to proceed or to perform.

Tenugu, Telugu; the older form of the word.

teppa, raft. *yéru dáṭi teppa tagala vésin aṭṭu,* like burning the raft after crossing the stream; *teppateralagá,* at full speed; *cuppateppalagá,* abundantly.

teppintsuṭa, to send for, to get; causal of *tetstsuṭa.*

tera, curtain, screen. *talli: náṭacam yeṭlá v'unnadi? báluḍu: tsálá bág' unnadi, dípálu, teralu adbhutangá v'unnavi. talli: mí nánna anta bág' unḍa léd annáru; madhya madhya mátramé bág unnad annáré. báluḍu: nizamé, anducané cábólu, madhya madhya nánna baiṭacu póyi, santóshistú lópalici vachchéváḍu.* Mother: How was the play? Boy: Excellent, the lights and curtains were wonderful. Mother: Your father did not find it so good, he said it was only good at intervals. Boy: Yes and I suppose it was because he went out at the intervals and came back happy.

teragu, way, manner; also *teravu.*

teraluṭa, to boil over; also *terluṭa.*

teratsápa, sail of a ship; from *tera,* screen, and *tsápa,* mat.

teratsuṭa, to open, to unfasten. *nóru teravacunḍá* is without opening one's mouth.

teravu, way, manner; also *teragu.*

terluṭa, to boil over; also *teraluta.*

tetstsuṭa, to bring, to earn. *cheṭṭu coṭṭi, paici tetstsu conn aṭṭu,* like cutting a tree and bringing it down on one's own head; *nálucá, nálucá, debbalu vípucu técé,* tongue, tongue, do not bring blows on my back; *váḷḷa ḍabbu váḷḷu pádu chésu cunṭú v'unnáru gáni mimmalan émí temm anaḍam lédu,* they waste their own money and don't ask you to contribute anything; *léni móham tetstsu peṭṭu coni,* affecting a love he did not feel; *té léni ayyacu tinḍi menḍu,* the less a man earns the more he claims to eat.

té, bring; imperative of *tetstsuṭa*. *teginchi dánam chéstánu, té rá, piḍiceḍu annam ann aṭṭu,* I will be bold to make a gift, bring hither a handful of rice, sirrah. The negative of *té* is *téca*, don't bring.

técu, teak tree.

téḍa, difference.

tédi, date (in the month).

téjassu, lustre. Skt. *ná tanḍri Súrya bhagavánulu; ataḍu pradóshacálamuna Brahma svarúpuḍunnu, madhyáhnamuna Ṣiva svarúpuḍunnu, sáyancálamu Vishṇu svarúpuḍunnu autáḍu; átanni téjassu yém anucunnáu?* my father is the blessed Sun; in the morning he takes Brahma's form, in the afternoon, Siva's, in the evening Vishnu's; how does his lustre strike you?

télagilluṭa, to rise to the top.

télagoṭṭuṭa, to set afloat; from *téluṭa*, to float, and *coṭṭuṭa*, to strike.

télavéyuṭa, to open (the eyes) wide.

télica, easy; from *téluṭa*, to float.

télintsuṭa, to cause to float, to achieve. *lálinchi télinchi,* fondling and caressing.

télipóvuṭa, to come out safe. *Bhímaráu Pantulu gári maradali vyavaháramuló yémó upadravamu vatstsun annuconnámu, tuḍac émiyu lécunḍá iṭṭé télipóyinadé,* we thought there was some danger in that matter of Bhima Row Pantulu's sister-in-law; as it turned out she got off scot free.

télu, scorpion. *pápishṭi télu yeccaḍa nunchi vachchinadó cáni, tsaṭuccuna chiṭicina vél anṭa poḍichindi,* a blasted scorpion springing suddenly from nowhere stung my little finger; *télucu puṭṭi tsalipurugu ain aṭṭu,* like a black ant born of a scorpion (this is an uncomplimentary expression); *télucu pettanamu isté tellavárlu anṭa poḍichind'aṭa,* they say that when supremacy was given to the scorpion it stung till morn; *téllaló conḍi pámulaló paḍaga,* the sting in scorpions, the hood in snakes (the greatest villain of the lot); *cuṭṭina télu gunavanturálu, cúsin amma cucca munḍa,* the scorpion that stung is a good-natured woman, the woman who blurted is a dirty bitch.

télupáruṭa, to arise, to be born.

téluṭa, to float, to come out, to result. *yé samudramuló paḍa vésiná télunu,* it will float in any sea (i.e. always come up smiling); *á paḍava conchemu lótu niḷḷalón ainá télutsunnadi,* that ship draws very little water.

téma, damp.

téne, honey. *téne máṭalu,* honeyed words; *téne v'unná tsóṭa y'igalu póg autavi,* flies will collect where there is honey; *ténela gúḍu* is a hive; *ténepaṭṭu,* honeycomb.

ténéṭiga, téniga, bee. *téneṭiga zum cáramu chéyuts unnadi,* the bee hums.

teníḷḷu, téníru, tea (the brew). English.

ténṭsuṭa, to belch. Belching is not considered disgusting, but a sign that you have enjoyed your food and a matter of congratulation. The conduct of a European judge who had his court cleared and fumigated when a vakil belched in it was not approved.

ténupu, a belch; also *tépu*.

tépa, time. *oca tépa,* once; *tépatépacu rúpái,* a rupee each time.

tépu, a belch; also *ténupu*.

téra, gratis. *téra gurramu, tangéḍu barice,* a switch for the borrowed horse (you don't spare him).

téra, clearness.

térapáratsútsuṭa, to stare. *tellapóyi nácési gudlagúba lágu térapáratsúchi,* turning pale and staring at me like an owl.

téri, térina, fully.

téruṭa, to become clear, to escape, to recover. *téruconuṭa,* in the middle mood, is to recover from illness.

térutsuṭa, to clarify, to console.

téṭagá, clearly.

téṭaparatsuṭa, to make clear, to explain.

téyácu, tea-leaf, from English 'tea' and *acu*, leaf.

ṭháná, police station. Hindustani.

ṭhánádáruḍu, station-house officer.

ṭicáṇá, trace, resource. *tinḍi ṭicáṇá lecunḍá,* without food or shelter; *záḍá ṭicáná lédu,* there is no trace of him anywhere.

ṭiceṭṭu, ticket. English. *Lacshmayya: mí ṭópi nácu aḍḍangá v'unnadi. múḍu* *rúpáyal ichchi ticceṭṭu connánu; mí tópi tísténe gáni nácu náṭacam canipintsaḍu. Vencayya: nénu iravai rúpáyalu peṭṭi ninnané y'i ṭópi connánu; dánici andaru tsúḍa vaddá?* Smith: Your hat is in my light. I have paid Rs. 3 for my ticket. If you don't remove your hat, I can't see the play. Jones: I paid Rs. 20 for that hat only yesterday; should not every one look at it?

tilacamu, beauty-spot, acme. *naditilacamu,* the prettiest of rivers.

tilalu, gingelly (an oil-seed crop), sesamum. Skt. The Telugu is *nuvvulu. tilách pápa hard,* sesamum removes sin (if given as a gift to a brahmin). (*ch* as in 'loch'.)

timingilamu, a fabulous great fish, Leviathan.

timiramu, darkness. Skt. Used in books.

timmiri, numb. *cálu timmirigá v'unnadi,* my leg has gone numb.

tinḍi, food. *cáṭici cáḷḷu tsátsuconi, tinḍici cheyyi tsáchéváḍu,* when his legs were stretched towards the tomb, his hand was still stretched towards food (greedy to the last breath); *tinḍici chéṭu, nélacu baruvu,* a waste of good food, a burden on the earth; *tinḍici Timmarázu, panici Pótarázu,* the Monkey King at food, the Buffalo King at work (he eats till he sweats and works till he freezes); *té léni ayyacu tinḍi menḍu,* the man who earns nothing eats all the more.

tinḍipanda, tinḍipótu, glutton.

tinipintsuṭa, to give to eat. *dévuḍ ittsuné gáni tinipintsuná?* God gives us our daily bread but He does not put it into our mouths.

tinnagá, straight, properly. *munḍalu tinḍi tini, tinnagá unḍa léca, canḍa cávaramuna cannu cánaca y'iláguna cáni panulu chéyuduru,* widows who live on the fat of the land will grow randy, and wanton, and forsake the narrow path. *vidhyárthi: ayyá, ná nóṭubuccu mída míru rásind émiṭó teliya léd anḍi. ṭícharu: ní dastúri tinnagá teliyaḍam léd ani rásánu.* Student: Sir, I can't read what you have written in my note-book. Teacher: I wrote that your handwriting is not legible.

tinuṭa, to eat. *debbalu tinuṭa,* to eat blows, is a common expression for to get a beating; *lantsálu tinnuṭa,* to take bribes; *gaḍḍi tinuṭa,* to eat grass, means to make a beast of oneself; *annamu tinṭára, gaḍḍi tinṭárá?* are you men or beasts? *vanḍin anna tinaca mánuná?* will the cook not eat? *caḍupu ninḍá tinṭé, vanṭi ninḍá jvaramu,* a bellyful of food means a bodyful of fever; *tinṭé cadala lénu, tinaca póté meḍala lénu,* if I eat I can't move, if I don't eat I can't stir; *tinṭé gáni ruchi teliyadu, digité gáni lótu teliyadu,* you can't tell the taste without eating or the depth without getting in; *tinna cucca léni póté, canna cucca cáḷḷu viraga coṭṭin aṭṭu,* like the man who broke the legs of the dog that happened to be there when he could not find the dog that had eaten the food (the innocent suffering for the guilty); *tsaddi tinn'amma magani y'ácal erugadu,* the woman who has had her cold rice does not realize her husband's hunger; *tánu yenta ainá tina galan ani Lacshmayya pandem vésenu, Lacshmayya conta tini tsálinchenu. Vencayya: antá tina léd ém? pandemló ọḍi póyindu. Lacshmayya: podduna nénu parícsha chésin appuḍu bágáné tinṭini, ippuḍu yendu chétanó ácali mandaginchindi.* Smith made a bet he could eat any amount; after he had eaten something he gave up. Jones: Why haven't you eaten it all? You have lost your bet. Smith: This morning when you tested me I ate well; now for some reason or other my appetite is reduced. *vindu bhójanamló oca báluḍu tsálá tinṭ unḍenu. peddamanishi: inca tina bócu, ajírṇam chéstundi; inta chinna caḍupuló anta annam yeṭlá paṭṭindi? báluḍu: ná poṭṭa baiṭici canapaḍéṭ anta chinnadi cád anḍi,* a boy ate a great deal at a feast. Gentleman: Don't eat any more, you will get indigestion; how did you get so much food into so small a belly? Boy: My stomach isn't so small as it looks from outside; *lantsam pantsam tinaḍam udyóga dharmam,* to take bribes is an official duty; *connavádḍé tinnavádu*, he who buys eats (he who pays the piper calls the tune); *tinna y'inṭi vásálu yennévádu*, counting the beams in the house in which you have eaten. This refers to a story of a man who made a false claim to a house and showed knowledge of every detail of it in court.

tippalu, difficulties. *tippala paḍuṭa*, to be in difficulties; *tippalu peṭṭuṭa*, to throw difficulties in the way.

tippivéyuṭa, to turn (active), to reject. The usual word for to reject a petition, turn down a request.

tippuṭa, to turn, to whirl, to send back; also *trippuṭa*, causative of *tiruguṭa*. *ill ecci corivi tippin aṭṭu*, like the man who climbed the roof and whirled a fire-brand about (misdirected energy); *banṭrótulunu v'úricé tipputú v'unnáru*, they send the peons back empty-handed.

tiragabáṭu, rebellion; from *tiruguṭa*, to turn; also *tirugabáṭu, tirugabaḍi*.

tiragali, hand-mill; also *tirugali*.

tiragapaḍuṭa, to rebel; also *tirugupaḍuṭa*.

tirascarintsuṭa, to scorn. Skt.

tirascáramu, scorn. Skt.

tirigi, again; from *tiruguṭa*, to turn.

tirigitirigi, round and round.

tiru-, prefix meaning 'holy'. Tamil, from Skt. *ṣri*. *tirucolanu*, a sacred tank; *Tirupati*, the sacred town.

tirugabaḍi, tirugabáṭu, mutiny. *mícu pani ápaca póyin aṭṭ aité tirugubáṭu néram cinda ṣicsha autundi*, if you don't stop work it will be mutiny and will be punished as such; *sipáyilu doratanamu vári mída tirugabaḍi*, the Sepoy mutiny; also *tiragabáṭu*.

tirugali, hand-mill; also *tiragali*.

tirugavéyuṭa, to turn over.

tirugu, tirugudala, tiruguḍu, a turn; in the plural *tiruguḷḷu*, difficulties. *vyádhi tirugudalagá v'unnadi*, the illness is on the turn; *brahmástránici tirugu lédu*, there is no turning the thunderbolt.

tirugubótu, a rambler, vagrant.

tiruguḍupuvvu, sun-flower; the flower that turns towards the sun. (The Italians also call the flower the sunturner, *girasole*, whence the English Jerusalem artichoke.)

tirugupaḍuṭa, to rebel. *vádu yazamáni mída tiruga baḍḍádu*, he flew in the face of his master; also *tiragapaḍuṭa*.

tiruguṭa, to turn, to rove. *vánici oḷḷu tirigindi*, his body turned, means he got giddy or sick; *á máṭa ná nóṭlo tiragadu*, I can't get my tongue round that word; *náluca tiragadu*, my tongue does not turn, means I have a difficulty in speaking, e.g. Telugu; *sácshini tiraga tíyuṭa* is to tamper with a witness; *hunḍi tirigipóyindi*, the bill was dishonoured; *tiraga marigina cálu, tiṭṭa marigina nóru, v'úracunḍavu*, wandering feet and reviling tongue will not stop quiet; *tala tiruguts unnadi*, my head swims.

Tirupati, famous place of pilgrimage. *Tirupati pógáne Turaca dásari auná*, will a pilgrimage to Tirupati turn a Muhammedan into a Dasari? *Tirupati mangalavádu*, the Tirupati barber, is proverbial, because he is the only one there and a very haughty man. The temple is at Tirumalai, a hill above Tirupati, six miles away. *tiru-* is corrupt for Skt. *ṣri*, holy.

tiryagjantuvu, animal (including birds and snakes). Skt. (Having the face down, unlike man.)

tithi, date (lunar). Skt.

titti, bellows, bag. *colimi tittulu*, blacksmith's bellows.

tiṭṭu, word of abuse. *aḍḍamaina tiṭlu tiṭṭinádu*, he cursed me all he knew; *talanoppi chéta bádha paḍuts unḍagá upacáramunacai mand iyya vachchina pedda manushyuni batimálucó valasinadi pógá, nishcáranamugá tiṭṭa modalu pettinár émi?* (Wife to jealous husband): Instead of going down on your knees before a kind gentleman who came to give me medicine and take away my headache, you have gone out of your way to insult him; *tiṭṭi tsachinavádu lédu, dívinchi braticinavádu lédu*, cursing never killed any one, blessings never brought any one to life; *tiṭṭité gálici pótavi, tinṭe lóga potavi*, abuse is scattered in the wind, food goes inside; *peṭṭité tinṭáru gani, tiṭṭite paḍevaru léru*, if you hand over food people will take it from you, but if you hand out abuse no one will take it from you. *ocaḍu: áfisu panulacu bádhyata galavár evaru? Gumástá: nácu bágá teliyad anḍi; yédaina lópam vasté mátram nanné andaru tiṭṭutáru.* Smith: Who is responsible for the business of this office? Clerk: All I know is that if anything goes wrong they all blame me.

tivásí, carpet. Hindustani. *óri, peddamanushyulu vachchinâru, végiramu tivásí tísucu rá,* ho there, some gentlemen have come, bring a carpet quickly (for them to sit on).

tiyya, tiyyani, sweet. *tiyyani rógamulu, cammani mandulu v'unnavá?* are there sweet illnesses and delicious medicines?

tiyyadanamu, sweetness. *angita vishamu, munnálucanu tiyyadanamu,* poison in the palate, sweetness on the tip of the tongue (the cajoleries of an enemy).

ṭícálu, vaccination.

ṭícáluvéyuṭa, to vaccinate.

ṭícharu, teacher. English.

tícshṇamu, heat. Skt. *tícshṇamulaina súrya ciraṇamulu,* the scorching rays of the sun.

tíga, creeper, tendril. *tígecu cáya baruvá?* is the gourd too heavy for the creeper?

típi, típu, sweet, sweetness, love. *praṇála mída típi,* love of life; *cheruca típi ani viḷḷató namala vatstsuná?* should you chew the sugar-cane to the root, just because it is sweet? (greediness); *yevari práṇamu várici típu,* life is sweet.

típu, anguish. *yennó vrandlu cósinánu gáni, ná vranam anta típu léd ann aṭṭu,* like the surgeon who said 'of all the boils I have cut, my own was the most painful'.

tíramu, shore, bank. *Góddávari tíramu,* the bank of the Godavari.

tírá, finally. *tírá chellinchenu,* he paid the last instalment; *tírá peḷḷi siddham ayyéṭ appaṭici,* when the wedding was at last ready.

tírchivéyuṭa, to defray, to pay off.

tírica, leisure. *tírica chicaca,* not finding leisure.

tírina, finished, settled; part. of *tíruṭa.*

tírmánámu, decision. *oca cacshi vimarṣa mída tirmánam cheyyaḍam nyáyam cádu,* it is not just to decide after hearing only one side.

tírpu, decision, especially of a court. *Lacshmayya, Vencayya iddaru annadammulu. tanḍri villu vrási tsachchi póyenu. villu pracáram ásti pantsu cóḍánici póṭláṭa vachchenu; annadammul iddaru Mallayanu madhyavartigá peṭṭu coniri. Mallayya: ná tírpu idi, Lacshmayyacu ástini cherisagangá pantsaḍánici adhicáram ichchänu. Lacshmayya: nyáyam cheṣáru. Mallayya: tana y'ishṭam vachchina bhágam tánu tísu cóḍánici Vencayyacu adhicáram ichchinánu. Vencayya: nyáyam chéṣáru.* Lacshmayya and Vencayya were two brothers; their father died leaving a will; a dispute arose about the division of the property under the will; the two brothers appointed Mallayya as arbitrator. Mallayya: My decision is that Lakshmayya divides the property into two equal parts. Lakshmayya: A Daniel come to judgement. Mallayya: And that Venkayya chooses whichever of the two parts he prefers. Venkayya: A Daniel come to judgement.

tírpuchepputa, tírpuvéyuṭa, to adjudicate.

tírthamu, water, sacred water, a sanctuary, salvation. Skt. *tinḍici vachchináva, tírthanacu vachchináva?* have you come to see the sanctuary or to get food (as a pilgrim or a beggar); *ṣankhuló pósté tírthamu, penculó pósté niḷḷu,* in a conch holy water, in a pot fresh water.

tírthayátra, pilgrimage.

tírthícarintsuṭa, to sanctify.

tírtsuṭa, to finish, to settle, to satisfy, to assuage, to set right, to discharge (a debt). *archévâré gáni, tírchévâru léru,* there are comforters indeed but no one who entirely consoles us; *córica tírtsu cóca,* not being able to satisfy a desire. *ocaḍu: itarulu páḍ autú v'unṭe tsústú v'úrucóvaḍam mánava dharmam cádu. incóḍu: dharmam cáca póte bhú bháram anta míru tírustárá? ocaḍu:*

tírtsa galiginá, tirtsa léca póyina, sádhyamaina anta maṭṭucu prayatnam cheyyaḍam manac andaracú vidhi. Smith: To look on while others are being ruined is not my idea of duty. Jones: Though it is not your idea of duty are you going to take the whole burden of the world on yourself? Smith: Whether we can set the whole world right or whether we can't, it is the duty of all of us to try to as far as possible. *bhárya: yevaraina bádha paḍut unṭé míru váḷḷa cashṭam yeppuḍainá tírchárá? bharta: tírtsac ém? ninnu penḍli chésu coni ní cashṭálanu tírtsa léda?* Wife: Have you ever assuaged another's ills? Husband: My dear, what did I do when I married you? *Lacshmayya: ní máṭa nilupu connávé. Vencayya: yém máṭa? Lacshmayya: padi rúpáyalu badul isté, ní rüṇam yennaṭici tírtsu có léd ani venuca annáu, ippaṭici tírtsacunḍáne unḍi, máṭa chellintsu cunṭ unnávu.* Smith: You are a man of your word. Jones: How so? Smith: When I lent you ten rupees you said you would never be able to clear your debt to me; you have not cleared it yet; you have kept your word. *cópamu tírtsuṭa,* to wreak one's anger; *dáhamu tírtsuṭa,* to quench one's thirst; *váni pani tírchináru,* they settled his hash.

tírubaḍi, leisure. *nénu tírubaḍigá v'unn appuḍu,* when I am at leisure.

tíruṭa, to be finished, to result, to be assuaged, to be satisfied, to be settled (of a debt). *caḍupu vasté cané tíra valenu,* after you have conceived you must end by bringing forth; *tanivi tíra máṭláḍináḍu,* he went on talking till he was satisfied (he had his say out); *nácu tíradu,* it won't suit me; *pápa phalamun anubhavimpaca tírunà?* will one's sins not find one out? *mutstsaṭa tíruta,* to satisfy one's desire; *ní púrácrüta carmam anubhavimpaca tíradu,* you will not escape the results of the actions of former lives; *báci tíripótundi,* the debt will be settled; *rácunṭé tíradu,* you must positively come; *veḷḷaca tíradu,* I can't possibly stay away.

tírvájásti, water-rate charge. Hindustani. A revenue term for the water-rate levied when a wet crop is grown on dry land.

tísiconipóvuṭa, to take. *tísconipó* or *tíscupó* is 'take' in the imperative.

tísiconivatstsuṭa, to bring. *tísconirá* or *tíscrá* is 'bring' in the imperative.

tísiconuṭa, to take away. *ṭicharu: ní cóṭuci yenni gunḍíl unnai. báluḍu: aidu. ṭicharu: nénu nálugu tísu cunṭé yém autundi? báluḍu: má nánna tanṭáḍu.* Teacher: How many buttons are there on your coat? Boy: Five. Teacher: Take one away and what do we get? Boy: Kicks from my father. *appu y'ichchinaváḍu bágu córunu, tísiconnaváḍu cheḍa córunu,* creditors wish you well, debtors wish you ill.

tísipóvuṭa, to dry up, to fall away. *oḷḷu tísipóyindi,* he has fallen away in flesh; *yéru tísipóyindi,* the river has gone down.

tísivéyuṭa, to take away, to send away; *tísei* is take away; the auxiliary may also be reduplicated and the word become *tísései*; *naucarlanu tísi vésináḍu,* he discharged the servants; to discharge a debt is *tírtsuṭa*; a gun, *cáltsuṭa*; duties, *nirvirtintsuṭa*; urine, *viḍutsuṭa. atani prárthana tísi veyya léca,* not being able to refuse his prayer.

tísiyunḍuṭa, to be open. *talupu tísi unnadi,* the door is open.

tíṭa, itch. *tíṭa paṭṭinaváḍu gócuconṭáḍu,* if you have an itch you will scratch.

tívramu, hot, keen, dire. Skt. *tívra cópam,* deep anger; *tívra védana,* smarting pain; *asatyamuna canṭé tívramainadi incocaṭi lédu,* there is nothing more terrible than untruth; *Bráhmala cópam Vishṇu Dévuni chacramu canṭenu tívram aindi,* the wrath of Brahmins is more to be feared than Vishnu's disk.

tíyani, sweet.

tíyani, not open, shut; negative participle of *tíyuṭa.*

tíyintsuṭa, to get removed; causal of *tíyuṭa.*

tíyuṭa, to remove, to open, to subtract, to subside, to pull, to dig, to be removed, to draw back. One of the most useful words in the language (transitive and intransitive). *tanavdru lótucu tituru, cánivdru caḍacu tituru,* his own people will pull him down, his enemies will draw him to the bank; *tiyyagá tiyyagá rágamu,* practise and practise and you will learn how to sing; *yéru tísindi,* the flood subsided. *Lacshmayya: cóṭu venuca muḷḷu gutstsu conenu; yevarainá tístár émón' ani oca mailu naḍichenu; chivaracu ocaḍu canipinchenu. Lacshmayya: ayyá, ná cóṭu venuca muḷḷu gutstsu cunnai; conchém tisi peṭṭanḍi; díni cósam mailu dúram vachchänu. ocaḍu: adi saré gáni, cóṭu tisivéste nuvvé tísu cunévááḍivigá?* Lacshmayya got some thorns into his coat behind, and walked a mile looking for some one to pull them out for him, and at last saw some one. Lachsmayya: Sir. I have got thorns into my coat behind, would you mind pulling them out? Stranger: All right, but why didn't you take your coat off and pull them out yourself? *calupu tiyani maḍi, Dévuḍu léni guḍi,* an unweeded field is like a temple without the god; *nuyyi tíyuta,* to sink a well; *sáne tíyuṭa,* to whet; *pálu tíyuṭa,* to milk; *góḷḷu tíyuṭa,* to cut your nails; *táḷamu tíyuṭa,* to unlock; *vácili tíyuṭa,* to open the front door; *viḍi tíyuṭa,* to draw apart; *jvaramu tísindi,* the fever has gone down; *venuca tíyuṭa,* to draw back.

tocca, rind, peel. Corrupt Skt. for *tvaccu.*

toccuḍibanḍi, bicycle; from *toccuṭa,* to tread, and *banḍi,* vehicle; but *saicilu* is commoner.

toccuṭa, to tread. *tóca toccina pámu láguna léchináḍu,* he sprang up like a snake whose tail has been trodden on.

toḍa, thigh. *toḍapuṭṭuvu* is a Vaisya, because Vaisyas were born of the Creator's thigh.

toḍigintsuconuṭa, to wear, to put on. *nénu gázulu toḍigintsu cunṭe, adi gázulu toḍigintsu cunṭundi, nénu coppuló puvvulu peṭṭu cunṭe adí puvvulu peṭṭu cunṭundi, nénu rangu chira caṭṭu cunṭe, adí caṭṭu cunṭundi,* if I put on glass bangles so does she, if I put flowers in my hair so does she, if I put on a coloured sari so does she.; also *toḍuguṭa.*

toḍuguṭa, to wear, to put on; also *toḍigintsuconuṭa. yeccuva sogasugá canapaḍaḍánici y'ivéḷa ávide duvvucóvaḍamlo toḍuccóvaḍamlónu cúḍá v'unnadi,* to make herself look nicer she has combed her hair and dressed herself with particular care.

tolacari, beginning of the rainy season. *tolacari vána,* the opening rain.

tolacarintsuṭa, to start raining (of a season).

tolagintsuṭa, to remove; causal of *tolaguṭa,* to recede.

tolaguṭa, to recede, to step aside. *talupu daggara nunḍi praccacu tolaguts unnáḍu,* he steps aside from near the door; *venucacu tolaguts unnáḍu,* he recedes.

tolliṭi, former, first; also *tonṭi tolu.*

tolutsuṭa, to bore, to perforate, to carve; *coyya tolutsu purugu* is the death-watch insect which bores into wood.

tombadi, tombhai, ninety. *tombhai tommanḍuguru póg ai tólu chiraga poḍichinḍru,* ninety-nine joining together only inflicted a skin wound (a cowardly mob).

tommanḍuguru, nine persons.

tommidava, ninth.

tòmmidi, nine.

tona, pip. *panasa tonalu,* jack-fruit pips.

toṇacuṭa, to spill. *ninḍu cunḍa toṇacadu,* the full pot will not spill.

tonḍa, chameleon. *tonḍa mudiri v' úsaravelli ain aṭṭu,* vice grows with age (an old chameleon is called *úsaravelli*).

tonḍamu, elephant's trunk. Skt. *Bráhmanuni cheyyé yénuga tonḍamú v'úracunḍavu,* an elephant's trunk and a brahmin's hand are never still.

tondara, hurry, trouble; all hurrying is looked upon as vexation in the East. *prayáṇamai tondaranu marichi póyinánu,* I forgot in the hurry of the journey.

tondarapaḍuṭa, to be in a hurry, to be in difficulties. *ocaḍu: áru bhásḥalu maṭládut und ani chilucanu ammitivi. dínici occa máṭ ainá ráḍu; yenta mósam chésáu! incóḍu: tondara paḍa* *bóc anḍi, nidánints anḍi, yeppuḍu míré máṭlaḍut unṭé chilacacu sávacáṣam eccaḍidi?* Smith: You sold me this parrot saying it spoke six languages. Why, it does not speak at all. What a swindle! Jones: Don't be in such a hurry, be patient. When you are always talking yourself, what chance has the parrot?

tondarapáṭu, hurry, troublesomeness.

tongitsútsuṭa, to peep, to peer.

tonguṭa, to lie down, sleep. *tongunna suncari, tala múṭa dimpum ann aṭṭu,* like asking the sleeping toll-keeper to help you put down your head-load (let sleeping dogs lie); *mí vyavaháram anta tongunṭundi,* your whole affair will be set at rest.

tonnúru, 900.

tonṭi, first, former; same as *tolliṭi. tonṭi múrti,* the original shape.

torra, tree-hollow.

toṭla, cradle; also *toṭṭi.*

toṭrupáṭu, dismay.

toṭṭi, cistern, tub, tank-bed, cradle.

-tó, -tóḍa, ablative case ending, meaning 'with'. *nannu dayató tsúḍu,* look on me with favour; *atanitó manavi chesinánu,* I represented it to him (to speak to is to speak with in Telugu).

tóca, tail. *á pilla talli tóca,* that child is the shadow of its mother (always after her); *tóca troccina pámu valé,* like a snake whose tail has been trodden on (very cross); *idugó puli anṭé adugó tóca ann aṭṭu,* like the man who said here is the tiger's tail when the other man said here is the tiger (capping a story); *tóca tentsu cuni pári póvuṭa,* to run away with your tail between your legs; *nénu yeccaḍacu veḷite accaḍic allá tóca lágu venṭa tirugutú v'untáv émi?* why do you follow me about like my shadow? *inca váḍu tóca áḍimpadu,* he won't wag his tail any more (will keep quiet).

tócatsucca, comet. The star with the tail (*tóca*).

ṭócubéṛamu, wholesale; retail is *chillarabéramu*; retail shop, *chillara dukhánam.*

tóḍaguṭa, to be with you. *íṣvaruḍu mícu tóḍagunu gáca,* God be with you.

-tóḍané, affix meaning 'as soon as'. *váru vachchinatóḍané,* as soon as they came.

tóḍapuṭṭinaváḍu, brother. One born together with you.

tóḍélu, wolf. *gorre yéḍisté tóḍélucu vicháramá?* will the sheep's cries move the wolf? *jítamu batyamu lécunḍá tóḍélu mécalu cástán ann aṭṭu,* like the wolf offering to guard the goats without pay or allowances; *tóḍéṭini gorrela cáya peṭṭin aṭṭu,* like putting the wolf to guard the sheep; *tóḍélu cúyuts unnadi,* the wolf howls.

tóḍi-, prefix meaning 'joint', 'fellow'. *tóḍicóḍalu,* fellow daughter-in-law.

tóḍpáṭu, help, sympathy.

tóḍu, buttermilk used to curdle milk.

-tóḍu, affix meaning 'I swear by'. *nítóḍu,* I swear by you.

tóḍu, accompaniment, convoy. *rátsa pínugu tóḍu lécunḍá tsávadu* king's corpse does not lack convoy (there is a superstition that when a king dies some one else dies to keep him company).

tóḍupaḍuṭa, to help, to sympathize.

tóḍuṭa, to draw up water, to bale.

tóla, goldsmith's weight, a little less than half an ounce. The rupee weighs one tóla and the gold mohur (Rs. 16) weighed one tóla. Rupees and gold mohurs were once hammered cubes of metal, not coins.

tólintsuṭa, to have driven; causal of *tóluṭa,* to drive.

tólivéyuṭa, to drive away.

tólu, skin, leather, complexion. *nalla tólu,* a dark skin; *yerra tólu,* a fair skin; *cheppulu toḍugu connavánici lócam anṭá tólutó cappa paḍḍ aṭṭu tóstundi,* to the man who wears shoe-leather all the earth seems to be covered with leather (he does not feel the heat of the earth as the bare-footed do); *ná chétici tól údinadi,* I have skinned my hand; *goḍḍuváḍu goḍḍuc éḍchináḍu, tóluváḍu tóluc éḍchináḍu,* the cattle-dealer cried for the beast and the hide-dealer cried for the hide (it's an ill wind that blows no one any good). *sabhádhipaṭi: í rózu upanyásam ichché áyana Americá déṣasthuḍu, áyana tólu tellanid' ainá áyana hrúdayam mana valé nallanidé.* Chairman: To-day's lecturer is an American; though his skin is white his heart is as black as ours.

tólucágitamu, parchment.

tóluṭa, to drive, to drive away, to blow (of wind). *tana talupu tísi, poruginṭici peṭṭi, rátri antá cuccalu tólutú cúrtsun aṭṭu,* like the man who lent his neighbour his front door and spent the night driving dogs away (charity begins at home); *dongalu tólina goḍḍu yé révuna dáṭiná vacaté,* it is all the same what ford the stolen ox passed; *paira tólité, prati phalintsunu,* if the north-east monsoon blows cool, the cotton crop will be good.

tóluváru, leather strap.

tómuṭa, to rub, to clean, to scrape, to scold. *pani cheyyam ani tómi tómi, vépucu tinṭú v'unnáḍu,* he says we do no work and scrapes and roasts and eats us up.

tópará or **tópaḍá,** a horse's nose-bag. Hindustani.

ṭópí, hat.

tópu, grove.

tóranamu, festoon (of leaves). They hang these leaf festoons over the door or gate on festive occasions, at the travellers' bungalow when the Collector comes, and so on.

tósivéyuṭa, to push away, to dismiss, to reject. *Daivamu tana nammina várini tósi véyaḍu,* God will not reject those who trust in Him; *ná máṭa tósiveyyacu,* don't reject my advice.

tósuconipóvuṭa, to push into, to bite into. *ungaramu bigutu chéta canḍalónici tósu coni póyinadi,* the ring being tight has bitten into the flesh.

tóṭa, garden.

tóṭacúralu, garden vegetables (those of which the leaf is eaten; the others are *cáyacúralu* or *cúragáyalu*).

tóṭamáli, gardener.

tóṭapani, horticulture.

tóṭi, pariah, sweeper.

tótsacunḍayunḍuṭa, not to be able to think, to be at sea. *vánic eṭú tótsacunḍá y'unnadi,* he is at his wits' end.

tótsuṭa, to be thought, to seem, to occur to one. *Gópu: ivvála ná goḍugunu renḍó sthalamuló marachi póyin aṭṭugá tóstundi. Rámuḍu: oca véḷa modaṭi sthalamulóné marachi póyindv émó? Gópu: lédu, modaṭi sthalamulóné nácu á goḍugu doricindi.* Gopu: I think I must have lost my umbrella in that second place. Ramudu: Perhaps you lost it in the first place. Gopu: No, that 's where I first picked up that umbrella.

tóyuṭa, to push; also *tróyuṭa.*

tráguṭa, to drink; more commonly *táguṭa.*

trásu, scales for weighing.

trétayugamu, the second or silver age. Skt. *crütayugam* is the golden age; *caliyugam* the present degenerate age.

tri-, three. Skt. *tricálamu,* the three times, morning, noon, and night. *Trinétruḍu,* the three-eyed God, Siva; *tricaranaṣuddhigá,* in thought, word, and deed.

tricónamu, triangle. Skt.

Trimúrti, Three in One, the Hindu Trinity.

trippuṭa, to turn; same as *tippuṭa.*

tróyuṭa, to push; also *tóyuṭa.*

trünacarintsuṭa, to despise, not care two straws. Skt., from *trünam,* straw. *návanṭi goppa y'inṭi biḍḍanu trünacarintsaḍam micu dharmam cádu,* it is not right for you to treat with contempt the scion of a noble stock like myself.

trünamu, a straw. Skt. The Telugu is *gaḍḍi paraca. trünapráyamu,* worthless; *trünamu Méruva, Méruva trünamu,* (a good man) looks upon the gift of a straw as the gift of Mount Meru, (a bad man) looks upon the gift of Mount Meru as the gift of a straw; *míru chevulu coyyaḍam anṭé trünapráyamugá v'unnadi,* I don't care two straws for your threat to cut my ears off; *nénu pránamulanu trünapráyamugá viḍuva galanu,* I could sacrifice my life with the utmost indifference.

trunguṭa, to be broken; also *tunguṭa.*

trünicáramu, contempt. Skt., from *trünam,* straw, and *cáram,* act.

truntsuṭa, to break (trans.), to break off, to break to pieces; also *tuntsuṭa.*

truppu, rust; more usually *tuppu.*

trüptamu, satisfied. Skt.

trüpti, satisfaction. Skt. *má cshémamu vári trüptiló,* our welfare is in their contentment, as Queen Victoria proclaimed.

trüptigá, satisfactorily. Skt.

trüshna, thirst. Skt. *svarája trüshna,* the longing for home-rule.

trütíyamu, third. Skt. *múḍó, múḍava* in Telugu.

tsabucu, whip; also *tsaucu.*

tsabucucheṭṭu, casuarina tree; also *tsaucu.*

tsacca, nice, straight, pretty.

tsaccachéyuṭa, to repair.

tsaccagá, nicely. *Lacshmayya: má ammáyi tsaccagá sangitam páḍutundi, cávalisté vina vatstsun ani peṇḍlicoḍucutó cheppanḍi. Vencayya: peṇḍlicoḍucu chevuḍu, andu chéta mí ammáyi páḍiná atanu bhaya paḍaḍu.* Smith: My girl sings nicely; tell the proposed bridegroom he may hear her if he likes. Jones: The man is deaf; so even if she sings he won't be frightened.

tsaccali, arm-pit.

tsaccani, pretty. *conchem mukham mudurugá v'unná y'ime y'ippaṭicini tsaccanidigáné v'unnadi,* though she is somewhat mature of feature she is still quite pretty.

tsaccaparutsuṭa, to put straight.

tsaccapeṭṭuta, to set right, to finish. *dípamu v'unḍagáné tsacca peṭṭu có valasinadi,* put things straight while the lamp is there (make hay while the sun shines).

tsaccatanamu, beauty. *dáni tsaccatanamu varṇintsaḍánici Brahmac ainá ṣacyam cádu,* she is of indescribable beauty.

tsaccápóvuta, to go straight away, to make off. *nénu sṭimaru vaddacu veḷḷéṭ appaṭici vacca tamáshá zarigindi; ticceṭṭu putstsu coni, a tamáshá tsúchi maḷḷi vaddám ani, y'iṭṭe avatalici veḷḷéṭ appaṭici, sṭimaruváḷḷu sṭimaru tísu coni tsaccá póyináru; rivenyú v'udyógasthula cósam canipeṭṭu coni v'unṭú, ná nimittam yenducu canipeṭṭu coni unnáru cáró váḷḷa pani nénu répu paṭṭistánu,* when I went to the steamer a show started; I took my ticket and said I would see the show and come back; but when I got back the steamer people had taken the steamer away and made off; when they wait for revenue officials, they would not wait for me and I will settle their hash for them to-morrow.

tsaccávatstsuṭa, to come straight.

tsaccera, sugar.

tsacciliginta, tickling. *tsacciliginta peṭṭuṭa,* to tickle.

tsaccuchéyuṭa, to chop up. *ní talacáya renḍu tsacculu chéstánu,* I will split your head in two.

tsachchipóvuṭa, to die. *tanḍri: nénu tsachchi póyina tarváta nuvvu yém chéstáu? coḍucu: mí náyana póyina tarváta nuvvu yém cheṣávo nénu adé chéstánu. tanḍri: aité nuvvu bágu paḍavu.* Father: What will you do when I die? Son: What you did when your father died. Father: Then you won't do well.

tsadara, a small mat to sit on.

tsadaramu, square. Skt. *tsadarapu maiḷḷu,* square miles.

tsadarangamu, chess. Skt., from *tsadaram,* square, and *rangam,* battlefield. Check is *shaha,* the king is *rázu,* the queen *mantri,* the castle *yénuga,* the bishop *ṣacaṭam,* the knight *gurramu,* the pawn *banṭu.* Chessmen are *balamu,* force.

tsaddannamu, tsaddi, tsalḍi, cold rice; from *tsalidi,* cold thing. *cheppinabuddhi, caṭṭina tsaddi nilavadu,* advice and cold rice will not keep; *tsaddi y'annamu tinn amma magani y'ácal erugadu,* the full belly does not believe in hunger.

tsadivintsuṭa, to get something read; causal of *tsaduvuṭa,* to read; specially used of the recital of the presents at a wedding; hence *tsadivimpulu,* wedding presents.

tsadunu, level.

tsadunuchéyuṭa, to level.

tsaduvari, student.

tsaduvu, learning, education, lecture. *tsálu, tsálu, ní tsaduvu tsálintsu,* enough, enough, stop your lecture.

tsaduvucheppuṭa, to teach.

tsaduvuconuṭa, to study. *oca tsaduvuconna Sómayazulu,* a Somayaji who has studied, an educated Somayaji.

tsaduvuṭa, to read. *tsadivédi Ramáyaṇamu, paḍa coṭṭédi dévasthalálu,* what he reads is the Ramayanam, what he knocks down temples; *tsaduva vésté v'unna mati póyindi,* set to learn he lost the little sense he had before. *majistréṭu: nuvvu vantena mída ati tondaragá móṭaru pón istunnáv ani chhárji vachchindi. accaḍa ganṭacu padi maiḷḷa canna yeccuvagá pó cuḍad ani noṭísu caṭṭáru, tsadava lédá? draivaru: ayyá, nénu 30 maiḷḷu tsoppuna banḍi naḍuput unṭe, noṭísu yeṭlá tsadava galan anḍi?* Magistrate: You are charged with excessive speed over a bridge. There is a notice up not to drive more than 10 miles an hour. Didn't you read it? Driver: How could I read the notice when I was going 30 miles an hour?

tsalava, coolness, bleaching. Clothes newly washed or bleached are also called *tsalava.*

tsaldi, cold rice; also *tsalidi, tsaddi, tsaddannamu.* It is the usual breakfast, cold food left over from the night before.

tsali, cold. *nácu tsali paṭṭinadi,* I felt a chill.

tsalicálamu, the cold weather, winter.

tsalichíma, black ant; also *tsallachima*; it means the cold-ant and is so called because it is not so fierce as the red ant (cold means kind, friendly in Telugu). *puli caḍupuna tsalichíma puṭṭuná?* the black ant wasn't born a tiger cub.

tsalijvaramu, ague.

tsalimiḍi, rice with flour and sugar.

tsalivéndramu, tsalipandili, water pandal. These are opened in the hot weather on roads by private charity or the local boards. *tsalipandiṭi cunḍalacu tūṭlu poḍichin aṭlu,* like making holes in the pots in a water pandal (a dirty trick).

tsalla, curds and water. *tsallacu póyi munta dátsaḍam yenducu?* why hide your pot when you have come for curds? (why beat about the bush?).

tsallagá, coolly, gently, healthily. *mí amma caḍupu tsallagá,* may your mother's womb be cool! is a common expression of felicitation. (India being a hot country, coolness is pleasant, friendly, blessed.)

tsallani, cool, kind. *tsallani prabhuvu,* a kind master.

tsallapaduṭa, to cool off.

tsallapáṭu, coolness. *tsallapáṭuvéḷa* is the cool of the evening. *tsallapáṭuvéḷa tsalla gálilò háyagá shicáru bailudérutámu,* we will set out for a comfortable stroll when the fresh breeze comes out in the evening.

tsallártsuṭa, to cool (active). *nívu cópam tsallartsucó valenu,* cool down, please.

tsalláruṭa, to cool down. *véḍi tsallárité,* when it has cooled down; *annamú cúralú tsalláripóvaḍam,* rice and curry getting cold; *váḍu cági tsallárina pálu,* he has sown his wild oats.

tsalluṭa, to sprinkle, to sow. *dunnaca tsallité, coyyaca panḍinadi,* sow without ploughing and you will be saved the trouble of reaping.

tsaluva, cold, bleaching, one's washing; also *tsalava.*

tsaluvachéyuṭa, to bleach.

tsampintsuṭa, to have some one killed; causative of *tsampuṭa.*

tsampuṭa, to kill; causative of *tsatstsuṭa,* to die. The auxiliary, *véyuṭa,* is commonly added, even in reduplicated form; kill the snake is *pámunu tsamp és éi. ocarini y'iddarini tsampiténe cáni, vaidyuḍu cáḍu,* a doctor is no doctor till he has killed one or two; *yevvaró pillanu cani, tsampivési rátri véḷa mana gummamunac edurugá vídhiló páravésináru,* the dead body of a new-born child was exposed in the street opposite my front door last night.

tsamuru, oil. *dípála cantrácṭaru vadda nelacu y'intani mámúlu putstsucóvaḍamé cácunḍa, y'inṭici cá valasina tsamur antá váḍi daggira putstsu cunṭáru,* they not only get a monthly commission from the lighting contractor but all the oil they require for household use.

tsanavu, familiarity; also *tsanuvu. tsanavari,* familiar, favourite.

tsanca, arm-pit. *tsanca múṭaló peṭṭu conna yábhai rúpayalu,* the fifty rupees in the bundle under my arm-pit; *yéru yéḍ ámaḍa v'unḍagáné, chira vippi tsanca peṭṭu coni póyin aṭṭu*, like the woman who took off her cloth and put it under her arm when she was still seven leagues from the river (Indian women strip or raise their one cloth to go through a river); *tsancacarra* is a crutch.

tsandamu, way, manner. *nirupédacu pennidhi tsandamuna*, like treasure-trove to a pauper.

tsandá, contribution, subscription. Hindustani.

tsandádáruḍu, subscriber.

tsandávéyuṭa, to subscribe. *tsandálu vési caṭṭindi adi andari haccunnu*, a building constructed by public subscription belongs to the public.

tsandugá peṭṭe, trunk, chest. Hindustani.

tsanipóvuṭa, to die; also *tsachchipóvuṭa*. This word is from *tsanuṭa*, to go.

tsanníḷḷu, cold water; contraction of *tsali níḷḷu*.

tsannu, breast. *tsannupálu* is human milk; *táḷḷacu talanu tsanḍlu, mécalacu meḍanu tsanḍlu*, palms have teats (*spadices*) on their heads, goats have teats (wattles) on their necks.

tsannucona, tsannumona, tsannumuccu, nipple.

tsanṭipilla, suckling.

tsanuṭa, to go. Used in books for *póvuṭa* and *veḷḷuṭa*, often in the compound form *tsanudentsuṭa*. Also used in the sense of to be right or proper; *tsanadu*, it is not right.

tsanuvu, familiarity. *tsanuvugá póvuṭa* is to frequent; *inṭa tsanuvugá tiruguts unnáḍu*, he is at home in the house; *magaváḍu daniṭó tsanuvugá máṭlaḍutu*, a man talking familiarly with her. Also *tsanavu*.

tsappani, insipid. *tsappani pathyamu*, plain diet; *tsappani níḷḷu*, insipid water.

tsappaṭa, slap, clap. *tsappaṭlu coṭṭuṭa* is to clap one's hands. Also *tsappaṭlu tsaratsuṭa*.

tsappiḍi, insipid, flat, snub. *tsappiḍi muccu* is a snub nose, *tsappiḍi pirudula chinnadi*, a thin-flanked girl.

tsappuḍu, noise. *tsappuḍu cácunḍa mellagá pravéṣinchináḍu*, he entered quietly without making any noise; *yevvaró lópalici vatstsuts unnáḍu, váciṭiló cheppula tsappuḍ aguts unnadi*, there is some one coming, I hear a footstep on the threshold.

tsaratsuṭa, to clap, to strike. *tsappaṭlu tsaratsuṭa*, to clap one's hands; *ché yetti tsarava póyin aṭṭugá midici veḷḷi*, attacking with raised hand ready to strike.

tsari, precipice.

tsarupu, a slap, clout. *iṭuvanṭi matimálina máṭalu yeppuḍú anacunḍá netti mída vacca tsarupu tsarutuná?* shall I give you a clout on the head to stop you talking such nonsense?

tsaṭáluna, suddenly.

tsaticila, tsatigila, flat (of the human body). *tsaticila cúrtsóvaḍam* is to sit with your legs stretched out flat and not tucked under you; *tsaticila paḍuṭa* is to fall flat.

tsaṭramu, frame; also *tsaṭṭamu*. *í paṭamulacu tsaṭramulu veyya lédu*, these pictures have not been framed.

tsaṭráyi, rock; from *tsaṭṭu*, rocky, and *ráyi*, stone.

tsatstsuṭa, to die. Usually, with the auxiliary, *tsachchipóvuṭa*. *atta tsasté cóḍalu yéḍchin aṭṭu*, like the daughter-in-law crying at her mother-in-law's death (hypocrisy); *ichéváṇṇi tsústé tsachchéváḍaina létsunu*, at the sight of one who gives men will rise from the dead; *tsachchinaváḍu yéḍisté ráḍu*, the dead won't come back for crying.

tsaṭṭamu, frame, law. We also talk of laws being framed. *punugu tsaṭṭamu*, civet bag or gland.

tsaṭṭi, earthenware dish (chatty).

tsaṭṭu, rocky. *tsaṭṭu mannu* is hard earth.

tsaṭṭutananu, stubbornness, a rock-like temperament.

tsauca, cheap. *Lacshmayya: nénu ninna tsauca cáfi hoṭalucu póyindnu. Vencayya: andu valla lábham caligindá? Lacshmayya: accaḍa cáfi andcé y'ichchäru, gárelu anácu nálugu ichchäru, anni tsauca, vachchéṭ appuḍu yevaridó cotta goḍugu cúḍa tísucu vachchänu.* Smith: I went to a cheap coffee hotel yesterday. Jones: Did you save much? Smith: The coffee was an anna, the buns four an anna, everything cheap, and, moreover, I got away with some one's new umbrella.

tsauci, customs or toll shed.

tsaucu, whip; also *tsabucu*.

tsaucu, casuarina; also *tsabucu*.

tsauḍu, salt land. Land in the Madras Presidency is often rendered uncultivable by excess of salt. *vána niḷḷu régaṭi néla paḍi manchi niḷḷ aunu, tsaviṭi néla paḍi y'uppu niḷḷ aunu gadá!* when rain falls on clay it will be drinkable water, when it falls on salt land it will be salt water.

tsavatitalli, stepmother; more usually *savatitalli*.

tsavi, taste.

tsaviṭi, fourth lunar day. *tsaviti náḍu*.

tsaviṭi néla, salt land. *tsaviṭi* is the oblique case of *tsauḍu*.

tsavuca, cheap; a way of spelling *tsauca*.

tsácalaváḍu, man of the washerman caste; the feminine is *tsácaladi*. *tellagá puvvu lágu tsácalidi v'utici techchina baṭṭa caṭṭu coni,* wearing a cloth fresh as a flower from the wash.

tsácali, washerman, dhoby. *uticévánici gáni tsácali v'utacaḍu,* the dhoby won't beat the clothes except for the man who drubs him (*utucuṭa*, to wash clothes, consists chiefly in beating clothes on a stone); *mangali páta, tsácali cotta,* choose an old barber and a new dhoby (you want vigour in a dhoby whose work is trying to break stones with clothes, and experience in a barber).

tsácirévu, the place near the river or tank where dhobies wash clothes.

tsáḍílu, slanders. *tsáḍílacóru* is a slanderer.

tsála, tsálá, much, many. *Lacshmayya: míc ippuḍu nimmaḷamgá v'unnadá? Vencayya: nác'émi? Lacshmayya: inta munducu míru tsálá sépu muligáré? Vencayya: nénu sangíta paṭacuḍin anḍi.* Smith: Feeling better? Jones: There is nothing the matter with me. Smith: You were groaning for a long time. Jones: I am a singer by profession. *Lacshmayya: cempula aḍḍige tísina tarváta ní peḷḷám yeṭla v'unnadi? Vencayya: tsálá santóshinchindi, renḍu nelalu dácá tsála aṇacuvagá v'unḍinadi. Lacshmayya: á pimmaṭanó? Vencayya: pimmaṭa yeppaṭi manishi aindi.* Smith: How was it with your wife after you bought her the ruby locket? Jones: She was very pleased; for two months she was very submissive. Smith: And after that? Jones: She became the same as before.

tsálaca, tsálanu, not able; negative forms of *tsáluṭa*, to suffice. *telisicó tsálaca póyiri,* they were not able to understand; *ana tsálanu,* I can't say.

tsálavaracu, at great length. *calecṭarutó ní vishayamuló tsála varacu cheppinánu,* I pleaded your cause at great length with the Collector.

tsálintsuṭa, to stop; causative of *tsáluṭa*, to suffice. *ní adhica prasangam tsálintsu,* enough of your impertinence; *sabha tsálintámu,* let us dissolve the meeting; *ní tsálintsu,* stop your lecture.

tsálu, sufficiency; also imperative of *tsáluṭa*, to be enough.

tsálu, row, furrow, trace, stream, features, ploughing. *í tsáluna,* in this manner; *talli tsálu pólica,* resemblance to his mother in his features; *tsálupugá,* in a line; *talli tsálu pillacu tapput unnadá?* will the child lose its mother's track? *pattici padi tsáḷḷu, ámudacu áru,* cotton wants ten ploughings, castor wants six.

tsálunu, it is enough, that will do; the negative is *tsáladu,* not enough. *bharta: cáfí cheyyaḍánacu iravai margálu v'unnai. bhárya: nác enducu chepputáru á sangati? bharta: váṭiló nuvvu vaccaṭé nértsucunná nácu tsálunu.* Husband: There are twenty ways of making coffee. Wife: Why do you tell me that? Husband: If you will learn *one* of them that will be enough for me.

tsáluṭa, to suffice. *táḍu tsálaca póté, nuyyi púḍtsum ann aṭṭu,* like the man who ordered the well to be filled up when the rope was found to be too short; *prítitó peṭṭinadi piḍicedé tsálunu,* a dinner of herbs where love is. In the negative *tsáluṭa* means usually not to be able, but not always. *gnyápacamu tsáladu,* I don't remember;

buddhi tsáladu nícu, you have no sense; *jítamu vyayamulacu tsáli tsálaca*, the salary sufficing and not sufficing (just covering expenses). The Italians have the same idiom, *sí e no che basta*, yes and no whether it is enough.

tsámalu, one of the common millets (*panicum mitraceum*). *dómulu paḍité tsámalu panḍunu*, if mosquitoes swarm the tsama millet will yield well.

tsámanatsáya, light complexion. It is a light brown or straw colour; the other complexions of Indians are *nallani*, black, and *yerrani*, red to yellow.

tsápa, mat, sail. If you have no chairs, you fetch a mat for visitors to sit on. *tahaṣṣiludáru gáru mana y'inṭici vachchedam'annáru; mému intacu munupu iccaḍa vésiconi cúrtsunna pedda tsápa yém ainadé?* Mr. Tahsildar said, 'We are coming to your house.' Where is the big mat which was spread here and on which we were sitting just now?

tsápacoyya, mast. *yé gálici á tsápa yettin aṭṭu*, setting your sail according to the wind.

tsápu, a length, e.g. of cloth.

tsápuṭa, to extend. *vaidyuḍu cheyyi tsústáru, mí cheyyi vacca máṭu tsápanḍi*, the doctor will feel your pulse, hold your hand out.

tsára, stripe, streak. *tsárala chíra*, a striped sari; a tiger's stripes are *tsáralū*.

tsáṭimpu, proclamation.

tsáṭintsuṭa, to proclaim.

tsátsuṭa, to stretch (transitive), to stretch out. *cheyyi tsátsuṭa*, to stretch out the hand; *cheyyi tsáchi puttsuconi*, stretching out the hand and taking; *cáṭici cáḷḷu tsátsuconuṭa*, to stretch your legs to the grave is an expression for an old or dying person; *cáṭici cáḷḷu tsátsuconi, tinḍici cheyyi tsachéváḍu*, he stretched his legs to the grave and stretched out his hand for food (greedy till death).

tsáṭu, screen, covering. *á conḍa tsáṭu ainadi*, that hill intercepted the view.

tsáṭucu, aside. *tsáṭucu pilichi*, calling a person aside.

tsáṭuna, covertly, behind. *peṭṭe tsáṭuna doricindi*, it was found behind the box.

tsáṭuṭa, to proclaim.

tsáviḍi, lodge, hall; also *chávidi*, now used generally of the village headman's office where he sits to collect the taxes and where officials put up when they go to the village. *cachéri-tsávidi* is the room in which a well-to-do person receives; *tsávaṭi máṭalu* is town-talk.

tsávu, death. *yeluca tsávucu pilli múrchha póvuná?* will a cat faint at a mouse's death? *nácu tsávugá v'unnadi*, I feel like death.

tsávubiḍḍa, still-born child; also *caḍupuló tsachchina biḍḍa*.

tsáya, hue, complexion, direction, grain of wood. *tsámanatsáya*, light complexion; *ná chéti tsáyanu veḷḷu*, go where I am pointing; *coyyatsáya*, the grain of wood.

tsáyavéyuṭa, to colour, to dye.

ṭsh-. The following words have already been given under *csh-*, that being the usual transliteration. But the pronunciation, even of pandits, is *ṭsh-*. They are all Sanskrit words. The Tamil pronunciation is also *ṭsh-*.

ṭshama, patience. Skt.

ṭshamápaṇa, forgiveness. Skt. *nácu bahu vichárangá v'unnadi, nénu ṭshamápaṇa véḍucunṭánu*, I am very sorry, I beg pardon; *nénu chésina aparádham cheppinaṭṭ aité nénu venṭané ní cáḷḷa mída paḍi ṭshamápaṇa córuc unṭanu*, if you will tell me what I have done wrong I will at once fall at your feet and beg pardon.

ṭshamintsuṭa, to pardon. Skt. *ṭshamintsa valenu*, please forgive me.

ṭshaṇamu, instant. Skt. *nénu veḷḷi sahávam tísuconi ṭshaṇamló vastánu*, I will go to fetch help and be back in an instant.

ṭshatamu, wound. Skt. Used in books for *gáyamu*.

Ṭshatriya, the Kshatriya or warrior caste. Skt., from verb for 'to strike'.

ṭshauramu, shaving; also spelt *ṭshavaramu*; the ordinary words for shaving are *pani chéyuṭa, goruguṭa*, but this also is common, especially in a figurative sense. *nívu andariní svajanánni chéristé ní taruváta vachchinaváḍu váḷḷ andarićí ṭshavarálu chéstáḍu*, if you put in all your caste-men the man who comes after you will shave them all.

ṭshayarógamu, consumption. Skt., from *ṭshayamu*, wasting away.
ṭshámamu, famine. Skt. *caruvu* is the Telugu word.
ṭshánti, patience. Skt.
ṭsháramu, salt. Skt. A book word for *uppu*.
ṭshátramu, Kshatriya's duty. Skt.
ṭshémamu, health, happiness. Skt.; ordinary word in inquiring after health, &c. *yógaṭshémamulu vichárintsuṭa* is to make such usual inquiries.
ṭshétragaṇitamu, geometry. Skt.
ṭshétramu, place of pilgrimage. Skt.
ṭshétramu, field. Skt. *ṭshétram erigi vittanamu, pátram erigi dánamu*, sow seed to suit the field, give charity to the deserving.
ṭshínamu, decline, decay. Skt. *ṭshína daṣaló n'unnámu*, we are on a downhill course; *áyushṭshínamu*, the decline of age; *dhana ṭshínamu*, decrease of wealth.
ṭshínintsuṭa, to waste away. Skt. *benga peṭṭuconi adi á dinamu canna á dinam ṭshíninchi déham antá pálipóyi*, in her distress she wasted away day by day and grew pale.
ṭshíra, milk. Skt. Book word for *pálu*.
ṭshóbha, grief, trouble. Skt. One of the numerous words for grief; the shade of meaning is 'agitation'. *santshóbhamu*, agitation; *chittaṭshóbhamu*, trouble of mind; *jailuló yenta ṭshóbha paḍḍáḍu*, what distress he felt in jail! *ṭshóbhapeṭṭuṭa* is to distress, to trouble; *chinnadánni nannu nishcáraṇangá y' ílágu ṭshóbha peṭṭaḍam canṭé crúra crütyam lócamló yédí v'unḍadu*, there is nothing more cruel in the world than to oppress a poor girl like me in this way.
ṭshóbhintsuṭa, to be distressed. Skt.
ṭshudha, hunger. Skt. Book word for *ácali*, used in compounds such as *ṭshudbádha*, pains of hunger.
ṭshudra, petty, low, trifling. Skt. *manam ṭshudrálu páṭigá paṭṭa rádu*, we should not pay attention to trifles.
tsoccá, tsoccái, shirt, coat, tunic. *ṭícharu: pillulacu tsáli yeṭla veyyacunḍá unṭundi? av émainá tsoccái toḍu cunṭavá? baṭṭa cappu cunṭavá? báluḍu: yémandi, pillini tsúda léda?* Teacher: How do cats protect themselves against cold? Do they wear coats or wrap themselves in clothes? Boy: Have you never seen a cat?
tsoppa, millet straw; rice straw is called dry grass, *yenḍa gaḍḍi*.
tsoppintsuṭa, to insert, to force in.
tsoppuna, according to, at the rate of. *áru rúpáyala tsoppuna*, at the rate of Rs. 6; *munupaṭi alaváṭu tsoppuna*, according to the previous custom.
tsora, shark.
tsorapaḍuṭa, to enter. *dongalu lópala tsora paḍi nannu nimushamuló dótsu cuni pó vatstsunu*, thieves may force an entrance and rob me in an instant.
tsorava, entrance, familiarity, forwardness. *nénu tsorava chési vacca muddu peṭṭu cunṭánu*, I will be so forward as to snatch a kiss; *anna tsoravé gáni acshara tsorava lédu*, well fed, ill taught.
tsoravachéyuṭa, to take courage (to do something).
tsotstsuṭa, to enter, to enter upon (an undertaking), to begin. *acáryamunacu tsotstsuṭa*, to enter upon a path of sin; *cáya tsotstsuṭa*, to begin to shine; *ṣaraṇu tsotstsuṭa*, to take refuge.
tsoṭṭa, dint; also *soṭṭa, noccu*.
-tsó, affix meaning 'if' or 'when', from *tsóṭu*, place. *tanayulu lénitsó*, in case there are no sons.
tsóḷḷu, one of the millets, commonly called *ragi* (*panicum paludosum*).
tsóṭu, place. *cherucu v'unḍé tsóṭici chímulu támé vastavi*, ants come of themselves to where there is sugar-cane; *téne v'unna tsóṭa, y'ígalu póg autavi*, flies collect where there is honey. *báluḍu: amma, ná chelli svargamló nunchi cindici vachchindá? talli: aunu, náyana. báluḍu: anta manchi tsóṭulo nunchi iccaḍacu yenducu vachchindi?* Boy: Mother, did my little sister come down from heaven? Mother: Yes, dear. Boy: Why did she leave such a good place to come here?
tsucca, drop, star, round caste-mark worn on the forehead (*tsucca boṭṭu*); omen. *turacalu coṭṭagá tsuccac edurá?* do you bother about omens when the Muhammedan is on the war-path?
tsuccáni, helm.

tsulacanagá, tsulággá, easily, lightly. *tsulággá tsútsuṭa* is to despise.

tsulacani, light, easy.

tsundi! look here! from *tsútsuṭa*, to see.

tsunḍu, scurf.

tsuntsu, projection, ledge, balcony in architecture. *tsuntsu múti véyuṭa*, to pout.

tsunyi, fizzing; onomatopoeic. *bhacshyamulu uḍucu nétiló vésté tsunyi manṭunnavi*, if you put cakes in boiling ghee they will fizz.

tsurucu, active, smart, energetic, diligent. *á tahaṣṣiluddáru tsurucugár pani chéstáru*, that Tahsildar is an energetic officer; *manam andarú pani tsurucugá cheyya valenu*, we must all work diligently. *Ráma: Chennapaṭnamló tsurucaina vartacuḍu occarú canipintsaru. Gópu: aṭlánṭiváḷḷu jailuló unṭár anḍi, cávalisté accaḍa tsúḍa vatstsunu.* Smith: There seem to be no smart merchants in Madras. Jones: Yes there are, but they are in jail; if you want to you can see them there.

tsuṭṭa, cigar, any roll; from *tsuṭṭuṭa*, to roll. *tsápa tsuṭṭa*, a rolled-up mat. To smoke a cigar is *táguṭa* (to drink it). *tsuṭṭa tágutává*, try a cheroot. *méjisṭríṭu: firyádini muḍḍái coṭṭut unṭe tsúchává? sacshi: tsúsán anḍi. méjisṭríṭu: cottacunḍá nuvvu yémi cheyya lédá? sácshi: cheyya léd anḍi. méjisṭríṭu: yendu chéta? sácshi: nénu tsuṭṭa tágut unnán anḍi.* Magistrate: You saw the accused beating the complainant? Witness: Yes, Sir. Magistrate: Did you do anything to stop him? Witness: No, Sir. Magistrate: Why not? Witness: I was smoking a cigar.

tsuṭṭamu, relationship, relations. *tsúḍa tsuṭṭamu, mocca daivamu lédu*, no relations to visit, no God to worship (utterly destitute, on his beam ends, down and out). *Lacshmayya: Mallayya nícu tsuṭṭam éna? Vencayya: dúrapu tsuṭṭamu. Lacshmayya: tsálá dúramá? Vencayya: dúramé, ná náyanacu padimandi coḍuculu, Mallayya andaricanná peddaváḍu, nénu ákharu váḍini.* John: Is Tom any relation to you? Bill: A distant relation. John: Very distant? Bill: Yes, my father has ten sons; Tom is the eldest and I am the last.

tsuṭṭaricamu, relationship.

tsuṭṭálu, relatives. *caliginavánici andarú tsuṭṭálé*, all are relations to the man of property. *bhárya: mana ammáyini penḍli chésu cunéváḍu yeṭlánṭi váḍu? bharta: anucúlamaina váḍe. bhárya: tsaduvu gáni ḍabbu gáni léd aṭé. bharta: léca póyiná parvá lédu, atanici yevaru tsuṭṭálu léru lé, mana ammáyi sukha paḍutundi.* Wife: What sort of a man is the son-in-law you have chosen? Husband: Quite suitable. Wife: They say he has neither education nor money. Husband: If he hasn't it doesn't matter, he has no relations at all; our girl will be happy.

tsuṭṭu, anything round. *talatsuṭṭu* is a turban, *górutsuṭṭu* a whitlow.

tsuṭṭu, around, round about. *tsuṭṭu dári*, a roundabout way.

tsuṭṭuconuṭa, to coil. *cáḷḷanu tsuṭṭuconna pámu caravaca mánuná?* will a snake coiled round your legs not bite? (or a dependant not wangle?).

tsuṭṭupaṭla, neighbourhood. *í tsuṭṭupaṭla tsálá y'iḷḷu dorucutavi*, there are many houses in this neighbourhood; *á conḍa mídan eccité, tsuṭṭupaṭla tsálá dúramu bágá canipints unnadi*, that hill commands an extensive view.

tsuṭṭupaṭlaváru, neighbours. *mí cécalató y'i tsuṭṭupaṭlaváḷḷac andarici méḷucuva vachchindi*, your yells have woken up all the neighbours.

tsuṭṭuta, to roll, to surround, to go round, to knot. *págá tsuṭṭuṭa* is to roll up a turban; *dóva tsuṭṭu coni veḷluts unnadi*, the road winds round.

tsuvaca, tsuvva, withe, fishing-rod.

tsuvve, of course, you see; short for *tsúḍave*, you see.

tsúḍa, to see. A form of *tsútsuṭa*, to see.

tsúḍu, glance; from *tsútsuṭa*, to see; also *tsúpu*.

tsúlu, conception. *álu lédu, tsúlu lédu, coḍucu péru Sómalingam*, no wife, no conception, but he has given his son the name of Somalingam (counting your chickens before they are hatched)

tsúpintsuṭa, to show; causal of *tsútsuṭa*, to see; also *tsúpuṭa*.

tsúpu, sight, look, glance; also *tsúḍu*.

mi abhiprâyamu mi maṭala canṭé y'ippuḍu mi tsúpulé nácu bágá cheputú v'unnavi, your looks tell me your opinion better than your words; *tsúpu méra dúramló*, within eyeshot; *cindi tsúpulu*, downcast looks.

tsúpuḍuvélu, forefinger.

tsúpuṭa, to show; also *tsúpintsuṭa*. *cótici addam tsúpin aṭṭu*, like showing a looking-glass to a monkey (persistently offering what is disliked).

tsúra, dust, soot. *pogatsúra*, soot.

tsúru, eaves. *yénugu dáhamucu tsúru niḷḷá?*, will the droppings from the eaves quench the thirst of an elephant? *nén entó ní mída préma chéta dévat archanac ani y'inṭ inṭá tirigi nityamunu manchi puvvulu techchi y' ichchinanu, prati dinamu inṭi muntsúru penḍeló peṭṭiṭé cáni, yocca náḍ ainá mutstsaṭa tíra nénu tsútsuts unḍagá coppuló muḍutsu cóvu*, I go about from house to house all out of love of you collecting nosegays for the Gods, so I say, and give them you, and then you stick them up on a rafter in the eaves and never think of sating the yearning of my eyes by twining posies in your hair; *cálu paṭṭu coni ládité tsúru paṭṭu coni véláḍéváḍu*, haul him out by the legs and he will cling to the eaves (difficult to shake off, a limpet).

tsútsuṭa, to see, to perceive, to look. It is used of all the senses. *ruchi tsútsuṭa* is to taste, and *vásana tsútsuṭa* is to smell, but by itself it means 'to see'. *ichchévanni tsusté tsúchchéváḍ ainá létsunu*, even a dying man will get up at the sight of a person who has something to give. *májistréṭu: moṭáru bassulu coṭṭucunn appuḍu nuvvu tsúchává? sácshi: tsúchán anḍi. májistréṭu: cáraṇam émi. sácshi: bassulu renḍu occa manishi yeccintsu cóḍanici póṭi paḍḍai, andu chéta coṭṭuconi páḍ ainai*. Magistrate: Did you see the collision of the motor buses? Witness: Yes, sir. Magistrate: What was the cause? Witness: The two buses were competing for one passenger and collided and got smashed up. *naṭuḍu: nénu rázu vésham vésina náḍu andarú ná vaipé tsuṣáru. snéhituḍu: tsúsi yémi cheṣáru? naṭuḍu: ráḷḷu vésináru*. Actor: When I acted the king every one looked my way. Friend: What did they do next? Actor: They threw stones. *tamanu tsúḍa valen ani nácu anéca dinamula nunḍi abhiláshagá unḍenu*, I have been wanting to see Your Honour for a long time past.

tuccu, rubbish, trash, dirt. *i páta tuccu pustacam*, this dirty old book.

tuchchhamu, vile. Skt.

tuda, end, tip.

tudacu, finally; in the reduplicated form, *tuṭṭatudacu*, at the very end.

tudamuṭṭuṭa, to reach the end, to finish. *iccaḍitó ná prayaṇam tuda muṭṭindi*, I have reached the end of my journey.

tudiléni, endless.

tuḍupu, erasure.

tuḍutsuṭa, to wipe away, to erase, to sweep.

tuladúguṭa, to be heavy, to weigh against. *svadharmamu viḍichi sampadalató tuladúguṭa canṭé svadharmamu n'and unḍi tinḍici léca maranamun onduṭa ṣréyascaram*, weighing duty against wealth it is better to sacrifice even your food to duty and to die; *tula* is Skt. for balance. *tulábháramu* is the ceremony of weighing themselves against gold of the old Rajas. They weighed themselves in complete panoply and the gold was then coined and distributed among brahmins. A stone weighing-balance for this ceremony still exists at Hampi (Vijayamagaram, the ancient Andhra capital).

tulamu, weight of one rupee. Usually called *tóla*.

tulasi, basil. This is a sacred plant in India, and a pot of basil will be found in many houses. *tulasi vanamuló ganzái mocca molichin aṭṭu*, like a hemp plant in a basil garden (black sheep in the flock).

-tulyamu, affix meaning 'equal'; from Skt. *tula*, balance. *svargatulyamu*, heavenly; *práṇatulyamugá*, as dear as life.

tumma, the babul tree (*Acacia arabica*).

tummeda, black bee. The poets compare braided black hair to clusters of black bees.

tummu, sneeze. *ávalintacu annada-*

mul unnáru gáni tummucu tammuḍ ainá léḍu, yawning is one of a family, a sneeze has not even a younger brother (one yawn draws another after it).

tummuṭa, to sneeze. *tummité poyyé muccu yennáḷḷu v'unḍunu?* how long will a nose last than can't stand sneezing?

tumpara, tuppara, splutter, drizzle. *váḍu matáḍuté tumparlu paḍutavi*, he splutters in speaking; *tumpara paḍuts unnadi*, it is drizzling.

tumpiḷḷu, a shower.

tunaca, tunḍu, piece, bit; e.g. a piece of wood, crumb of bread. *rottelaváni canté, tunacalaváḍu ghanuḍu*, the crumb-beggar scores over the loaf-beggar (gets more in the end).

tunguṭa, to get broken; also *trunguṭa*.

tunṭari, scoundrel.

tunṭi, hip. *tunṭinoppi*, hip-pain, is lumbago.

tuntsuṭa, to break, to pluck up. *váḷḷa prayatnam molacalóne tunchi veyya valenu*, we must pluck up their attempt from the roots; also *truntsuṭa*.

tupáci, gun. *tupáci cáltsuṭa*, to fire a gun; *tupáci mandu*, gunpowder; *tupáci caḍupuna firangi puṭṭin'aṭṭu*, a canon born of a musket; the butt-end of a gun is *tupáci maḍama*, the barrel of a gun *tupáci goṭṭamu*.

tupánu, storm, cyclone. Hindustani.

tuppa, bush.

tuppara, drop, drizzle; same as *tumpara*.

tuppu, rust.

tuppuna, sound of spitting; onomatopoeic.

Turaca, Turk; so Muhammedan in general. *Tirapatici pógáné Turaca Dásari auná?* will going to Tirupati turn a Muhammedan into a Dasari? *Turaca vídhiló sanyási bhicsha*, a Sanyasi's alms in the Muhammedan street (he won't get any); *Turacalu léni v'úḷḷo Dúdéculaváḍu Sayyadu Miyyá*, in a village where there are no other Muhammedans a Dudecula (mongrel Muhammedan) will call himself Saiyed Miyya.

turangamu, horse. Skt. Used in books.

turruna, quickly, suddenly; onomatopoeic.

turupu, troop, trump (at cards). English. A club is *caḷávaru*, a spade *ispéṭu*, a diamond *daimanu*, a heart *arakhu*; all corruptions of the English words.

tuṭṭatudacu, last of all, reduplicated form of *tudacu*.

tuṭṭe, cluster. *ténetuṭṭe*, swarm of bees.

tuválu, towel. English.

tuvva, sandy soil. *tuvvana vésina yeruvu, bápanici pósina neyyi*, tuvva hungers for manure as a brahmin for ghee.

túguṭa, to weigh (intransitive).

túlamu, down. *hamsatúlamu*, eiderdown.

túlanáḍuṭa, to revile.

túli, brush, paint-brush. Nail-, hair-, and tooth-brushes, being foreign articles, are *brush*, pronounced *borusu*.

túluṭa, to reel. *sprüha tappipóyinadi, voḷḷu túlutú v'unnadi, caḷḷu tirugutú v'unnavi*, hope fails, I reel, I am dizzy.

túmu, a grain measure of about fifteen bushels.

túmu, sluice.

túnica, weighing.

túnicaráḷḷu, stones for weighing. These large stones are still used even in factories.

túnicavéyuṭa, to weigh.

túníga, dragon-fly.

túri, time. *oca túri*, once.

túrpu, east. *túrpuváḷḷu* to the people of Godavari are those of Viyagapatam and Ganjam, especially coolies who come from the east for the harvest.

túrupárapaṭṭuṭa, to winnow. *gáli vachchin appuḍu gadá túrpára paṭṭucó valenu*, winnow when the wind comes; *túm eḍu vaḍlu túrpára paṭṭéṭ appaṭici yédumu vaḍlu yelucalu tini póyinavi*, while he was winnowing one toom, the rats ate five.

túṭá, cartridge.

tútsuṭa, to weigh (transitive).

túṭu, hole. *tsalipandiṭi cunḍalacu túṭlu poḍichin aṭṭu*, like making holes in the water-pots in a water-shed (a dirty trick).

tvaragá, quickly.

tyajintsuṭa, to abandon.

tyágamu, renunciation. Used chiefly in compounds. *práṇatyágamu*, renunciation of life, suicide.

U

ubbasamu, asthma. *áyanacu v'ubbasabu daggu,* he has an asthmatic cough.
ubbu, swelling, haughtiness.
ubbuṭa, to swell. *adi nácu doricind ani vánici caḍup ubbuts unnadi,* he is envious (his stomach swells) at my getting that job.
ubhayamu, both. Skt. *ubhaya bhrashṭutvam v'Uppara Sanyásitvam,* both ways a ruin as Digger and Saint (low-caste people should not set up as Sanyasis).
ubusu, chat, amusement; also *úsu.*
ubusuputstsuṭa, to loiter, to trifle.
uccagá, sultry, close (of the weather); short for *uḍacagá,* from *uḍucuṭa,* to boil.
ucciribicciri, close, suffocating. *ucciribicciri ai daggutsu yenta sép áyása paḍenu,* he choked and coughed and was uncomfortable for a long time.
uccu, steel. *uccu róshamu,* great anger. *uccumutó cheyya baḍina y'andamagu peṭṭe,* a handsome steel trunk.
uccutíge, steel wire.
uchcharintsuṭa, to pronounce. Skt.
uchchárana, pronunciation. Skt.
uchchi, crown of the head.
uchchishṭamu, spittle, leavings. Skt. Used in books for *yengili.*
uchitamu, proper, gratis. Skt. *uchitavastrádulanu dharinchi,* properly dressed and equipped.
uchitamugá, gratis, properly.
ucti, expression. Skt. *cutsitóctigala,* ironical.
ud-, Skt. prefix connected with English 'out'; also *un-* and *ut-* in composition.
udacamu, water. Skt. *hastódacamu,* water for the hands; *úsara nélaló vésina pairu udacamu léni cheruvucu samánamu,* a salt-land crop is like a tank without water.
udagramu, mighty. Skt. Used in books.
udaramu, belly. Skt. Used in books. *udarapóshanamu,* belly-filling.
uḍata, squirrel; also *uḍuta. uḍata bhacti* is proverbial because the squirrel helped Rama to build Adam's bridge and Rama stroked it, and hence the squirrel's white marks; but another proverb regards the squirrel as meddlesome: *uḍatac élará v'úḷḷó pettananu?* what has the squirrel to do with running the village?
udayamu, morning. Skt. *rép udayána,* to-morrow in the morning.
udáharaṇamu, example. Skt.
udáharintsuṭa, to instance. Skt. *cávaliste pramána vachanálu v'udáharistánu,* if necessary I will quote Scripture texts.
udáramu, liberality. Skt.
udári, udáruḍu, a liberal man. Skt. *udáralacu lócam antayu cuṭumbamé,* liberal men make the whole world their family; *léni v'udári canṭé caligina monḍi mélu,* it is better to deal with stingy rich people than with lavish paupers.
udbhavintsuṭa, to be born, to arise. Skt.
uddéṣamu, intention. Skt.
uddéṣintsuṭa, intend. Skt. *vaca cáryam cheyya valen ani v'uddéṣintsucunṭé,* thinking of doing something.
uddharintsuṭa, to establish, to restore. Skt. *matamu uddharinchi,* restoring religion; *á maha purushuḍu lócamu v'uddharintsaḍánici tsústú v'unnáru,* that great man is attending to the restoration of the world.
uddháraṇamu, restoration. Skt. *jírna matóddháranamu cheyya valenu,* we must restore decayed religion.
uḍicintsuṭa, to boil (transitive); causative of *uḍucuṭa.* Also *uḍucapeṭṭuṭa.*
udrécamu, excess, passion. Skt. *áyana munupaṭi valené sangítam anṭé chevi cósu cunṭu v'unnádá? y'ippuḍ á v'udrécam yémainá tagginadá? lédá?* is he as mad on your music as he used to be, or has his passion for it declined at all? *nénu venṭané vachchi, yóga drüshṭitó tsúchéṭ appaṭici á v'udrécam antá póyi, nimushamló ṣánta paḍi póyináḍu,* I came at once and fixed him with a yogi look and the excitement immediately left him and he quieted down.
udrécintsuṭa, to increase.
uḍucuṭa, to boil; also to boil with rage

or envy. *uḍucupótu*, an envious wretch; *á pappu uḍucadu*, that porridge won't boil (that will cut no ice).

uḍuguṭa, to cease. *cámam uḍiginavádu*, a man past sexual desire.

uḍuguṭa, to wash (clothes). Also *utucuṭa*.

uḍumu, the iguana lizard. *uḍumucu renḍu nálicalu*, said of a double-tongued man; *uḍumu póyiná, cheyyi vasté tsálunu*, let the iguana get away, you are lucky if it does not take your hand with it.

uḍupu, a dress, suit.

uḍuta, squirrel; same as *uḍata*.

udvásamu, expulsion. Skt.

udyanamu, attempt, project. Skt.

udyánamu, park. Skt.; also *udyánavanam*. *phala vrücshamulu v'unna v'udyánavanam*, a park containing fruit-trees.

udyógamu, office, post in the public service. Skt. *lantsam pantsam tinaḍam udyóga dharmam*, to take bribes and perquisites is the privilege of office; *udyógam purusha lacshanamu*, office makes the man.

udyógasthuḍu, official.

uggamu, carrying cord. *néti chembu uggamu vési paṭṭuconi*, with a cord to carry his pot of ghee.

uggu, castor oil and mother's milk given to babies. *chinn appaṭi nunchi v'uggu pálató*, from one's infancy; *bharta: pillavádici rózu cüri cüri yéḍustú v'unḍagá nóṭici mirapacáya rási yeccuva annam peḍutáu; andu chéta v'údara poṭṭa periginadi. bhárya: nénu annam yeccuva peṭṭadam chéta v'údara poṭṭa cá lédu. míru játi vaidyam nammi, v'uggu prati rózu peṭṭan iyyaca póvaḍam chétanú, chinn appaṭi nunchi annam peṭṭan iyyaca, pálaló niḷḷu calisi póyintsaḍam chétanú, y'í v'údara poṭṭa vachchindi*. Husband: When the child yells you smear its lips with chilly and give it too much rice, and so it has a swollen belly. Wife: The swollen belly does not come from too much rice, but from your not believing in our traditional physic, stopping the uggu, not allowing rice to be given from the beginning, and insisting on milk and water.

ulavalu, horse-gram. *dolichos biflor*, the pulse we feed horses on in India; we boil it and it is then called *guggillu*; *ulavalu* is the crop or the seed; a plural form like all words for crops and grains in Telugu. *gurránici guggiḷḷacu séru v'ulavalu tsálunu*, two pounds of gram will be enough for the horse's mash; *vachchéṭ appuḍu ulava, poyyéṭ appuḍu nuvvulu*, when you take up land sow horse-gram; when you give it up, gingelly. This and similar proverbs refer to the value of horse-gram in improving land. It adds nitrogen to the soil.

uli, chisel.

ulicipaḍuṭa, to start up. *tsappuḍu vini v'ulicipaḍi*, starting up at a noise.

ullamu, heart. *hrüdayam* is commoner.

ullanghanamu, contempt. Skt. *ṣásanóllanghanamu*, contempt of law, is the newspaper word for civil disobedience.

ullanghintsuṭa, to despise; *ágnyan ullanghintsuṭa*, to disregard an order.

ullásamu, joy. Skt. *cunṭic ullásam y'inṭici mósam*, to annoy is the cripple's joy.

ulli, garlic; also *vellulli*; *nírulli* is onion. *ulli muṭṭanidi vásana rádu*, if you had not touched the garlic you would not have smelt; *ulli v'unṭé Malli vanṭalaccé*, garlic makes up for bad cooking; *talli léni pilla, ulli léni cúra*, a motherless child and onionless curry; *ulli padi tallulu peṭṭu*, a pinch of garlic is worth a pound of mothers; *ulligaḍḍacu panníru pósi campu máṇadu*, garlic will stink even if you pour rose-water on it.

ulucuṭa, to start up.

ulúcamu, owl. Skt. (owl is from the same root.) *guḍlagúba* is the common word.

ummadi, joint. *ummadigán unḍé*, held jointly; *ummadi bhúsvámi*, joint landholder; *ummadi gorre puchchi tsachchindi*, the joint sheep died of rot.

ummi, umminíru, spittle.

ummivéyuṭa, to spit. *vellacittalá parunḍi v'ummi vésté mukham mída paḍutundi*, if you spit when you lie on your back, your spittle will fall on your face (of people who spit against God, atheists; the Italians have the same proverb: *chi sputa in su, lo sputo gli torna su la faccia*, if a man spit upwards his spittle will fall back on his face).

uncintsuṭa, to try.
unḍa, ball. *miṭhái unḍalu,* sweet balls.
unḍrál̤l̤u, round cakes offered to the Gods.
unḍuṭa, to be, to remain, to stay. *nénu accaḍa padi dinamul unnánu,* I remained there ten days; *unḍan'i,* let it be; *mí tandri bágá unnáḍá?* is your father well? *répu dácá unṭárá?* will they stay till to-morrow? As in many other languages 'to have' is expressed by 'to be' with the dative, *nácu bhárya unnadi,* I have a wife.
ungaramu, ring. *ungarapu vélu* is the fourth finger; *ungarapu venṭrucalu,* curly hair; *ungarála chétitó muṭṭité noppi v'unḍadu,* a rap from a ringed finger causes no pain.
unici, existence. *Bhagavantuni y'unici,* the existence of God. From *unḍuṭa,* to be.
unicipaṭṭu, dwelling, from *unḍuṭa,* to be.
unmattamu, madness. Skt. *strílu cámamu jéyimpa lér anna sangati unmatta pralápamugán unnadi,* it is mad drivel to say women cannot conquer their lust.
unmúlamu, from the root. Skt., from *múlam,* root. *unmúlam chéyuṭa* is to root up, to eradicate; also *unmúlintsuṭa.*
unna, true; participle of *unḍuṭa,* to be. *unna máṭa anṭé v'ulic ésu coni vastundi,* truth startles; *unna máṭa cheppité v'úru achchi rádu,* if he tells the truth he will not prosper in the village.
unnadi, that which you have; from *unḍuṭa* with implied dative. *lénidánici póté, y'unnad úḍinadi,* seeking for what you haven't got, you lose what you have.
unnata, high. Skt. *unnata ásanamu,* a high seat; *unnata padamu,* high station.
unnaṭṭaité, if it be.
unnaṭṭi, situate.
unni, wool.
unṭé, if there is or are. *unṭé v'úru, póté páḍu,* if there are people it is a village, if they go, a desert.
untsuconuṭa, to keep; causative middle of *unḍuṭa,* in all senses, e.g. to keep a woman. *ocaḍu: anni cálálu manavi cávu, vána cálánici conchem untsu có váli. incóḍu: nénu untsu cunnánu. ocaḍu: yém untsu connávu? incóḍu: goḍugu.* Smith: All times are not good times, we must keep something for a rainy day. Jones: I have kept something. Smith: What? Jones: My umbrella. *naucaru: mícu naucaru cá valen ani yevaró cheppité vachchänu. peddamanishi: má y'inṭló pani anta mávál̤l̤é chésu conṭáré. naucaru: aṭlá aité nénu tappacunḍá iccaḍa v'unṭánu untsuconḍi.* Servant: I heard you wanted a servant. Gentleman: We do all our housework ourselves. Servant: Then I will certainly stay here, keep me.
unṭsuṭa, to place, to keep, to let be; causative of *unḍuṭa,* to be. *í máṭalu aṭṭé untsu,* leave off saying that; *tamaru daya untsa valasinadi,* keep favour.
upa-, Skt. prefix equivalent to 'and' connected with English 'up', 'above', 'over', German *auf, über, oben,* Greek *hypo,* Latin *super;* the Skt. *upari* is also used in Telugu in the sense of 'over and above'.
upabalamaina, auxiliary. Skt.
upabhógamu, enjoyment. Skt.
upacarintsuṭa, do good to. Skt.
upacáramu, benefit, service. Skt. *apacáric ainá v'upacáramu cheyya valenu,* only do good even to those who have injured you; *upacáramunacu póté apacáramu venṭané vachchinadi,* evil was at once returned for my good; *tala noppi chéta bádha paḍuṭs unḍagá, upacáramunacai mand iyya vachchina peddamanishini batimálu có valasinadi pógá, nishcáranamugá tiṭṭa modalu peṭṭinár émi,* (Wife to jealous husband) Instead of going on your knees to a kind gentleman who came to give me medicine and take away my headache, you have gone out of your way to insult him; *váḍ upacára buddhi galaváḍu,* he is an obliging man.
upacharintsuta, to befriend, to wait on. Skt.
upacháramu, kindness, service. Skt. *nénu vachchina bátasárlacu chésé v'upacháramló yémi lópam chéyanu,* I will not neglect my duty of hospitality to travellers.
upacramintsuṭa, to start on. Skt. *vádamunacu upacramintsuṭa,* to start on an argument.
upacrüti, aid, kindness. Skt. *nénu*

chésina i satcáramu mir onarchina upacrütici taginadi cádu, my hospitality does not sufficiently compensate your kindness.

upadéṣamu, teaching. Skt.

upadéṣintsuṭa, to teach. Skt. *mém upadéṣinchina mahá mantramu*, the great charm we have taught.

upadravamu, trouble, danger. Skt. *yémó upadravamu vatstsun anuconnámu*, we thought some danger was coming.

upaháramu, complimentary present. Skt.

upamánamu, comparison. Skt. *ocaḍu: náḍi yeppuḍu navvu mogamé; lópala yémi v'unná, paici i niḷḷu yélágu ṣántigá v'unnávó, nénu álágé v'unṭánu. incóḍu (tanaló): itani v'upamanálu vinṭé nácu gunḍelu pagulutú v'unnavi.* Bully: I always have a smile on my face. I am like still waters hiding dangers beneath. Coward (aside): His similes make my heart tremble with fear.

upaminṭsuṭa, to compare. Skt.

upanayanamu, the ceremony of investing a high-caste boy with the initiatory thread. *mágha másamlo má pillaváḍic upanayanam tala peṭṭinánu; váḍici yéḍ éḷlu vachchinavi; vaḍugu y'iḍu dáṭi póyinadi ganuca végiram upanayanam cheyyaca tappadu*, we propose to invest our boy with the thread in Magha; he is seven, and as the thread age is past we cannot postpone the ceremony. Also *vaḍugu*.

upanyásacuḍu, lecturer. Skt.

upanyásamu, lecture. Skt. *sabádhipati: i rózu upanyásam icché áyana Americá déṣasthuḍu, áyana tólu tellinad ainá, áyana hrüdayam mana valé nallanidé*, the gentleman who will deliver to-day's lecture is an American citizen; though his skin is white, his heart is as black as ours.

upapati, paramour. Skt.

upari, over and above. Skt. *upariraitu*, a tenant at will.

upasamanamu, alleviation. Skt.

upasamharintsuṭa, to get rid of, withdraw. Skt. Used, e.g., of withdrawing a resolution at a meeting.

upasamháramu, getting rid of, withdrawal. Skt.

upaṣamintsuṭa, to relieve, alleviate.

upasanghamu, sub-committee. Skt.

upaṣánti, relief. Skt.

upavasintsuṭa, to fast. Skt.

upavásamu, a fast, fasting. Skt. *teddu náci v'upavásamulu mánpin aṭṭu*, like licking the ladle by way of stopping the fast.

upavidhi, by-law. Skt. A technical term invented by the Telugu translator to Government.

upayógamu, use. Skt.

upayógintsuṭa, to use. Skt. *tennisu áṭaló banti áṭagáni talacáyacu tagilenu. áṭagáḍu: banti tagili ná talacáyi boppi caṭṭindi, iṭlá áḍaṭam anyáyam. précshacuḍu: acram ém und ayyá? indáciṭi nunchi tsúst unnánu, míru áḍutun appuḍu talacáya upayógintsané lédu.* At tennis a player was hit on the head by a ball and claimed a let. Onlooker: No let, I have been watching your play, you don't use your head at all.

upádhyáyuḍu, teacher. Skt. *upádhyáyuḍu yémi chéstunnáḍ anṭé abaddhálu vrási diddu conṭunnáḍ annáḍ aṭa*, when asked what the teacher was doing he said he was correcting his own misstatements.

upásacuḍu, worshipper. Skt. *Iṣvarópásaculu*, worshippers of Isvara.

upásana, worship. Skt.

upásintsuṭa, to worship. Skt.

upáyamu, means, device. Skt. There are four devices in politics: *sámamu*, gentle means; *dánamu*, bribing; *bhédamu*, sowing dissension; *danḍamu*, punishment. *upáyamu yeragani vánni v'úḷḷó v'unḍan ivva cúḍadu*, the man who knows no devices should be turned out of the village.

upécsha, neglect, contempt. Skt.

upécshintsuṭa, to neglect, to despise. Skt.

-upétamu, suffix meaning 'joined with'. Skt.

upódghátamu, preface, introduction. Skt.

uppani, salt; adj. of *uppu*. *uppani máṭa cheppi, tsappani máṭa cheppi*, by fair means or foul (saying a salt word or saying an insipid word).

uppara, the uppara caste. They do earthwork, make tanks, dig wells.

upparavāḍu, man of the uppara caste; feminine *upparidi*; *ubhaya bhrashṭutvam, v'upparasanyásitvam*, doubly useless like a well-digger turned friar (Jack of all trades and master of none).

upponguṭa, to swell, especially with joy.

uppu, salt. *appu léca póté v'uppu ganji mélu*, it is better to live on rice water and salt than to be in debt; *tappu léni vánni v'uppuló veyyum annáḍ aṭa*, put the blameless man into the salt (department). (The Salt Department are supposed to treat their officers badly.) *uppu tininaváḍu niḷḷu tágutáḍu*, if you eat salt you will drink water.

uppucáyi, pickle; *úracáyalu* is commoner.

uppumaḍi, salt pan.

uppurévu, salt factory.

upputéru, salt stream (there is a well-known *upputéru* in the Godavari District).

uri, noose.

uricolpuṭa, to incite. *atanitó póṭláḍaḍánici nannu nívu yenducu v'uricolpináu?* why did you egg me on to fight him?

urimránu, uristambhálu, gallows, from *uri*, noose, and *mránu*, wood, or *stambhamu*, post.

uritíyuṭa, to hang (a man). *nannu uritístáru, nícu nácu cúḍá renḍ ési v'úritáḷḷu canṭhánici bigiyaḍánici siddhangá v'unnavi*, they will hang me, there are two ropes ready for your neck and mine.

uriyuṭa, to ooze, to leak.

urlagaḍḍa, potato; also *síma dumpa*.

urrútalúguṭa, to totter; reduplicated form of *úguṭa*.

urucuṭu, to run, not common; *párugettuṭa* is the common word. *urucu v'urucum ané ná savaté cáni, tóḍu v'uricé ná savati yocatéyunnu lédú*, my fellows all say run, run, but not one will run with me (on to the funeral pyre at a suttee); *cómati pirici, coṭṭité v'urici*, a Komati is a skunk; hit him and he'll bunk.

urumu, thunder.

urumuṭa, to thunder. *urumuts unnadi*, it is thundering; *urimi tsútsuṭa*, to look thunder (look daggers).

ushnamu, heat. Skt. Especially of a hot day, hot weather. Also *úshmamu*.

usi, hiss; onomatopoeic; also *bussu*. *cuccalanu ná mída usi colpináḍu*, he set the dogs on to me.

usuru, life, breath, a sigh. *áḍadáni usuru tagalaca pódu*, a woman's sigh will not fail to strike; *usuru v'unṭé v'uppu ammuconi brataca vatsisunu*, while you draw breath you can live at least by selling salt.

usurupósuconuṭa, to cause sighs, to afflict. *áḍaváḷḷa cúṭló dummu pósi, váḷḷa v'usuru pósu cunṭé micu jayam cádu*, you will not win if you afflict women by pouring dust into their food (as the dancing-girls said when the Madras Government resumed their inams).

usúrumanuṭa, to say alas. *vánni nálugu tiṭṭi, váḍici váḍi jivánici v'usúrum anṭú*, giving him a piece of my mind and making him wish himself dead.

utaca, pivot. *talupu utaca mída áduts unnadi*, the door turns on a pivot.

utcrüshtamu, excellent. Skt.

utpalamu, blue lotus. Skt.

utpatti, production. Skt.

utpátamu, prodigy, catastrophe (as an earthquake). Skt.

utsahintsuṭa, to attempt. Skt.

utsavamu, festival. Skt. *nétrótsavamu*, a feast for the eyes; *í sáyancálam v'úlló v'utsavam zarugutundi*, there is a festival on in the town to-night; *ránigári shashṭi sanvatsara rájyapálanótsavamu*, the Queen's diamond jubilee (*shashṭi* is Skt. for 'sixty'; *rájya*, kingdom; *pálanamu*, ruling; *utsavam*, festival).

utsáhamu, perseverance, energy, merriment, joy. *nén íppuḍu utsáha sthitiló unna pacshamuna*, if I were now in a merry mood; *manadi manchi pani cádu, ganuca v'utsáham lécunḍá v'unnadi*, we are doing wrong and so have no zest for the work; *santósham póyindi, v'utsáham póyindi*, I have lost my peace of mind and joy in life.

utstsa, urine. *utstsapóyuṭa*, to make water.

utstsu, noose. *í v'utstsu y'itani chétulacu vési biginchinám anṭé, y'itaḍu manacu chiccin aṭṭé*, if we fasten this noose round his hands and pull tight he will be in our power.

utta, empty, simple. *uttagurramu*, a

riderless horse; *utta chevi canna, tátácu chevi mélu,* an ear with a palm-leaf in it (instead of an ear-ring) is better than an ear with nothing in it; *utta chétulu múra vésin attu,* like measuring empty hands (idle dreams); *utta godduc arupul eccuva,* the empty cow lows loudest (much cry and little wool); *utta goddu* is the barren cow, *utta gurramu* the riderless horse.

uttamamu, best. Skt. *rájóttamudu,* best of rajas; also reduplicated *uttamóttamamu* (*uttamu* plus *uttamu*), superlatively best.

uttappudu, generally (on simple occasions). *uttapudu léca póyina máne gáni, itarul intici vachchin appudaina biggaragá mátádaca, ná yedala inta bhacti tsúpi, patipúja chéyutsunn attu paicaina natintsutsu rávé,* never mind what you say when we are alone; when a stranger comes please don't raise your voice, please show me some sort of dutifulness, and please make believe at least that you are a devoted wife.

uttara, the twelfth lunar mansion. Skt. *uttara tsúchi yettu rá gampa,* when you see the sun in *uttara,* take up your basket to sow. (It is supposed to rain when the sun is in *uttara.*)

uttara, following after. Skt. *uttara bhágamu,* the next part; *uttara Rámáyanamu,* the sequel to the 'Ramayana'; *uttara sácshi,* attestor; *uttara cshanamu,* the next moment; *uttaracshanamuna,* immediately.

uttaracríyalu, obsequies. Skt.

uttarajanmamu, the next life. Skt.

uttaramu, the north. Skt. *Lacshmayya: uttara désam antá tirigindu gadá, Himavat parvatánni tsúsává? Vencayya: tsúda lédu, yendu chétac anté accada niltsunté mana chinnatanam baita padutundi.* Smith: You have travelled all over the north, have you seen the Himalayas? Jones: No, I did not want to feel my littleness.

uttaramu, letter. Skt. *yazamáni: uttarálu póstuló vésává? naucaru: vésán andi, aité mír oca porabátu chésaru; aná chíti antintsa valasina uttaránici rend anála chiti antincháru, rend análu antintsa valasina dánici, aná chiti antincháru. yazamáni: aité nuvvu yém chésávu? naucaru: adresulu cott ési oca dánidi incó dáni mída vrásánu.* Mistress: Did you post the letters? Servant: Yes, but you had made a mistake; you put a one-anna stamp on a letter that required two, and a two-anna stamp on a letter that required one. Mistress: What did you do? Servant: I crossed out the addresses and exchanged them.

uttarapratyuttaramulu, correspondence. *ippudu vánici nácu uttara praty'uttaramulu lévu,* I have no correspondence with him now; from *uttaramu,* letter, and *prati,* exchange.

uttarasácshi, attesting witness; from *uttara,* subsequent, and *sácshi,* witness.

uttaróttara, ever after; reduplicated form of *uttara,* subsequent.

uttaruvu, answer, order. Skt. *uttaravitstsuta* is to give an order; *uttaruvu chepputa* is to answer; *uttaruvitstsuta* also means to give leave to go; for in this country you terminate an interview by ordering your visitor off, and this he expects and won't go until you tell him to; it would not be polite.

utti, sling. *utti cattuconi úguládduta,* to put up a sling and swing; *uttichéda* is the cord on which a sling hangs (slings are often fastened to beams). *utti mída venna v'undagá v'úr ellá nétici dévuládan éla?* when there is butter in the beam-sling, why hunt all through the village for ghee? *úrantá tsuttálu, v'utti catta távu lédu,* the village is full of our relations but we have no place to hang up our sling; *néti cunda néla petti, vatti cunda v'utti mída pettévádu,* putting the ghee-pot on the floor and the empty pot on the sling (absent-mindedness).

uttipaduta, to start forth, be manifested, e.g. a passion.

utucuta, to wash, to beat; also *uduguta.* The washerman in India beats clothes. *uticé váru gáni tsácali v'utacadu,* the washerman won't wash for any one who does not beat him.

uvvilúruta, to water at the mouth.

uyyála, swinging cradle or bed. *uyyálaló pillani v'unchi v'úr alla veticin attu,* like putting a child in its cradle and searching for it all over the village.

Ú

-ú, cumulative affix. There is no 'and' in Telugu and the usual way to express it is to lengthen the vowel (*a, i, o, u*) at the end of words. *siggú bidiyamú paruvú pratisthá yémi lédu,* no shame or modesty or proper pride.
úca, husk (of rice).
úda, weeds. *varici vaca váná, v'údacu vaca váná?* is it one rain for grain and another for weeds? (God sendeth rain on the just and on the unjust).
úḍa, sucker (of trees, especially the banyan).
úda, údara, swollen. *údacaḍupu, údara poṭṭa,* pot-belly.
úḍa-, úḍi, prefix meaning 'out', from *úḍuta,* to slip out. *úḍagoṭṭuṭa,* to loosen; *úḍapaḍuṭa,* to slip out; *úḍapóvuṭa,* to fall out; *úḍapícuṭa,* to root out; *úḍatiyuṭa,* to take off (clothes, &c.); *úḍaperucuṭa,* to tear out; *ní gruḍlu úḍa pericedanu tsúḍu,* take care or I will tear your eyes out; *artha rúpáyi áyana chétiló peṭṭiténé cáni nacalu úḍipaḍadu,* the copy won't come out unless you put half a rupee into the clerk's hand; *conḍanálucacu mandu vésté, unna náluca úḍi póyin aṭṭu,* like your tongue falling out when you put medicine on your uvula (the remedy is worse than the disease).
údá, violet, or purple. Hindustani. *ná v'údá chira caṭṭucuni vastánu,* I will go and put on my violet cloth.
úḍugu, plant of the *alangium* species (*alangium Lamarckii* or *alangium decapetalum*). *úḍuga vittanamu vanṭiváḍu,* a man like an uduga seed, is a man who sticks to you like a leech; an udugu seed is supposed to reattach itself to the plant after it has fallen.
úḍupu, transplantation (of rice); *úḍupupolamu,* field in which transplanted rice is grown.
úḍuṭa, to slip, to be loosened. *ná máṭacu y'eduru cheppité, múti paḷḷu v'úḍé lágu tannutánu,* if they contradict me I will kick them till all the teeth in their mouths are loosened; *ná chétici tól úḍinadi,* I have skinned my hand; *léniddánici póté y'unnad úḍinadi,* to over-reach oneself and let slip what one has got trying to get something else.
úduṭa, to blow (to play on flute, to blow on horn, &c.). *commulu v'údi, ḍappulu váyinchi,* blowing on horns, beating drums.
úduṭa, to be swollen.
údutsuṭa, to sweep. *vidhulu údutsuconuṭa,* to sweep the streets; *penṭal údutsu,* sweeping away dirt.
úgintsuṭa, to swing (transitive).
úguláḍuṭa, úguṭa to swing (intransitive). *puli mísamulu paṭṭu coni v'uyyála v'úgin aṭṭu,* like swinging on a tiger's whiskers—a rash enterprise.
úha, thought, conjecture, idea. Skt. *nívu v'úhalu mahá bágá chéstáu,* you guess well. *mánéjaru: nuvvu yé bănculó paní chéyaca póyiná, ár énḍla anubhavam unn aṭṭu darakhástuló yenducu vráşávu? gumástá: míru úha galaváru cá valen anté nénu úhinchi vráşán anḍi.* Manager: When you have never worked in any bank, how did you come to write in your application of your six years' experience? Clerk: You advertised for men with ideas, so I wrote giving my idea.
úhimpabaḍina, presumptive; a term invented by our translation department to translate the legal term 'presumptive'.
úhintsuṭa, to think, to conjecture, to have an idea. Skt. *peddamanishi: ní pér émi? nuvvu yevari pillaváḍivi? báluḍu: míru canuccó valen anṭé renḍu márgál unnai. peddamanishi: yémiṭivi? báluḍu: míru úhintsucónḍi léca póté vichárintsanḍi.* Gentleman: What's your name? Who is your father? Boy: If you want to find out there are two ways. Gentleman: That is to say? Boy: You can guess or you can inquire.
únuṭa, to have, to take, to assume. *vér' úni,* taking root.

úpiri, breath. *áme biḍḍanu úpiri tiragacunḍá chési tsampinadi,* she smothered the child; *úpiri paṭṭité bozza ninḍuná?* can you fill your belly by holding in your breath? (inadequate measures); *úpiricuṭṭu,* stitch in the side; *vánici ninna rátri piḍacala vachchi, rommu aḍatsuconi póyi, y'úpiri salupa lédu,* last night he had a nightmare and oppression on the chest and difficulty in breathing.

úpirititti, lung.

úpuṭa, to shake, to cause to swing; causative of *úguṭa*. *tala úpuṭa,* to shake one's head; *zuṭṭu paṭṭuconi gaṭṭigá úpi,* seizing his pigtail and shaking it hard.

úra, in the village. *úra cunṭu, aḍavi léḍi,* lame in the village, an antelope in the jungle (a man who prefers shikar to work).

úraca, simply, only; also *úricé*. *nén úraca parihásamunac annánu, í máṭalu páṭigá paṭṭa bócu,* I only spoke in jest, you must not take it ill.

úraḍilluṭa, to be comforted, to be consoled.

úraḍintsuṭa, to comfort, to console; also *úrártsuṭa*.

úraṭá, rest, comfort. *manassucu conchem úraṭa caligi,* being somewhat consoled.

úravéyuṭa, to pickle.

úrártsuṭa, to console; also *úraḍintsuṭa*.

úrdhvamu, high. Skt. *úrdhva níti lócamu,* the higher moral sphere.

úrégimpu, procession, especially marriage procession.

úrégintsuṭa, to take in procession. *bráhmalaló chésé peḷḷiḷḷu yémi peḷḷiḷḷu? váṭi canṭé bommala peḷḷiḷḷainá manchivé. pálu tágé pasi pillalanu, baṭṭa vippi vésucu tirigé pasi bálunni, pallacíló peṭṭi, ḍumyi ḍumyim ani bájálató v'urégincheti, peḷḷi anṭáru,* what are brahmin marriages? Worse than dolls' marriages. Girls taken from the breast and unbreeched boys are put in palanquins and carried in procession to the tom-tomming of drums and they call that a marriage.

úréguṭa, to go in procession; from *úru,* village, *éguṭa,* to go.

úricé, gratis, simply, idly, only. *yazamánuḍu: nénu selavuló v'unnappuḍu yém chéṣáu? naucaru: úricé álóchistú cúrtsunnánu.* English master: What did you do while I was on leave? Indian servant: I simply sat and thought (but he might also answer, *úricé,* simply). *gumástá: nácu jítam tsálad anḍi. vartacuḍu: níc ippuḍu yém istunnámu? gumástá: yém iyyaḍam léd anḍi, mundugá paríksha chéstám anṭé, úricé pani chést unnán anḍi. vartacuḍu: aité vachché nela nunchi renḍintalu chéstálé.* Clerk: Sir, my pay is not enough. Merchant: What are we giving you? Clerk: Nothing, sir; you said you would try me first and I am working for nothing. Merchant: Very well, we must double your pay from next month.

úru, village, town. *í v'úrici á v'úr entó, á v'úrici í v'úr anṭé,* it is the same distance from village *A* to village *B* as from village *B* to village *A* (six of one and half a dozen of the other); *unṭé v'úru, póté páḍu,* with the people in it a village, without a desert; *úri mída núru paḍḍá, caranamu mída cásu paḍadu,* though the village be assessed at Rs. 100, the karnam will not pay a penny of it; *úr antá tsuṭṭálu, v'uṭṭi caṭṭa távu lédu,* the village is all relations, but I have no place to hang my sling; *prayánicuḍu: í v'úḷḷó occa ḍácṭaru cúḍá lédá? gramasthuḍu: léd anḍi. prayánicuḍu: yevaricainá pramádamaina zabbu chésté yémi chéstáḍu? grámasthuḍu: aṭlánṭiváḍu sahájamaina tsávu tsastáḍu.* Traveller: Isn't there even one doctor in this village? Villager: No, sir. Traveller: If any one gets dangerously ill what does he do? Villager: He dies a natural death. *aḍavi pandi chénu mésté, úr pandi chevi cósin aṭṭu,* like cutting the village pig's ear when the jungle pig ate up the field (vicarious punishment).

úrubinḍi, a chutney made of fried grain and chillies.

úrucáya, úrugáya, pickle. *patstsalú úrucáyalu annamuló ruchini puṭṭinché vastuvulu,* chutneys and pickles are condiments that give relish to rice.

úruconuṭa, to keep quiet, to be silent. *iddaru pillalu póṭláḍut unḍiri. pedda-*

manishi: úrucondi, yenducu pótláḍutáru? modaṭi pilla: ní cósamé. peddamanishi: ná cósam póṭláṭa yenducu? modaṭi pilla: nícu gáḍidec unna telivi ainá léd ani váḍ anṭé, nénu v'und annánu; andu chéta póṭláṭa vachchindi. Two boys were quarrelling. Gentleman: What are you boys fighting about? Stop fighting. First boy: We were fighting about you. Gentleman: How about me? First boy: He said you had not even the brains of an ass and I said you had, and we were fighting about that. *ḍácṭaru: mí áyana vishayamu nácu áṣa lédu. bharta: nácu incá pránam unnadi, bhaya paḍa bócu. bhárya: míru úrucondi, ḍácṭaru gáru anni sangatulu telusunu, bháram antá áyana mída véstám.* Doctor: There is no hope for your husband. Husband: While there is life there is hope. Wife: Hold your tongue, the doctor knows best; we will lay all the responsibility on him.

úruṭa, to soak, to sink in (as ink into paper). *nór úruṭa,* to water at the mouth; *adi mithâyi v'unḍalu yélágu mingutú v'unnádó, dánni tsústé ná nóru v'úṭal úrutú v'unnadi,* watching her put down those balls of sweet makes my mouth water.

úrupu, breath, sigh. *nittúrpu* is a big sigh.

úsaranéla, salt soil. *úsaranélaló vésina pairu, udacamu léni cheruvucu samánamu,* a salt-land crop is like a waterless tank.

úsaṟavelli, chameleon.

úshmamu, heat. Skt. Also *ushnamu.*

úsu, chat.

úsuláduṭa, to chit-chat.

úta, prop.

úṭa, sap, juice, spring, the common word for a spring of water.

útacóla, crutch; also *tsancacarra.*

útsuṭa, to shake, to cause to swing; causative of *úguṭa,* to swing. *tala v'útsutsu,* shaking his head.

V

v with *y*, *ṭ* and *n* are euphonic letters inserted between words to prevent vowels clashing. As words in Telugu commonly end in a vowel *v*, *y*, or *n* is commonly inserted before all words beginning with a vowel. In the Roman script an apostrophe can be inserted, in the Telugu disyllabic script this is not done. Hence in Telugu characters *unḍuṭa,* to be, is almost always disguised as *vunḍuṭa, yunḍuṭa,* or *nunḍuṭa,* with much confusion of mind to the beginner; *oca,* one, is much more commonly *vaca*; *ópica,* patience, becomes *vópica,* and so on. This is one of the many reasons for which I prefer to write Telugu in Roman characters.

vaca, vacaru, vacaṭé, a person or people, the same thing, euphonic forms of *oca, ocaru, ocaṭé. atta vacar inṭi cóḍalé,* the mother-in-law was once a daughter-in-law in some one's house; *vésinadé vaca gantu, viriginadé vaca cálu,* a leap leapt, a leg lost (first venture a loss); *yélinavárici réyimpagalu vacaṭé,* day and night are the same to God; *vaca paṭṭána mána lécunḍá v'unnámu,* we cannot stop all at once. The *c* in *vaca* is reduplicated for emphasis (*vacca*), *vaca* also means 'a' as well as 'one'. *vaca pilla* is 'a child' as well as 'one child'.

vacavéla, perhaps; same as *ocavéḷa.*

vacálatu, vacáltunáma, power of attorney. Hindustani. *conchem córṭu vyavahâram v'unḍagá micu vacáltunáma y'ivva valen ani vachchinánu,* having a little affair in court I have come to brief you.

vacca, one; emphatic form of *vaca. vacca piṭṭató cheppa lédu,* I didn't tell even the birds.

vacca, bit, especially a bit of areca nut. *gáḍida coḍucu Ráhugáḍu dévatalató cúrtsonḍi amrütam tágináḍu,* *á sangati Súryuḍú Chandruḍu veḷḷi cheppéṭ appaṭici Ṣrí Vishnumúrtiváru chacram dharinchi váḍi tala renḍu vaccalú chési vésindru*, that son of a donkey Rahu was drinking nectar with the Gods; the Sun and Moon reported it to Vishnu; Vishnu took his disk and cut Rahu's head in two. (This, of course, is the explanation of eclipses. Rahu has never forgiven the Sun and Moon and occasionally pursues them and tries to bite bits off them and if the Hindus did not religiously pray and fast and bathe when this happens he would very likely succeed. The Hindus have the great merit of saving us all from this disaster.)

vaccánintsuṭa, to relate. Skt.

vachanamu, speech, word, dictum, prose. Skt. *húna vachana prabandha-cáruḍu*, an English prose-writer. (The Telugus called us Huns long before we applied the opprobious epithet to the Germans.)

vachché, vachchedu, next; from *vatstsuṭa*, to come. *vachchedu váramu*, next week; *vachché nelaló*, next month.

vachchiráni, half-formed, inarticulate (coming and not coming). *vachchiráni máṭalu ruchi, v'úri v'úrani v'úrugáya ruchi*, sweet are the half-formed words of children, sweet are half-pickled vegetables.

vachintsuṭa, to say. Skt.

vacílu, attorney. Hindustani.

vacramu, crooked; *vacrócti* (*vacra ucti*) is an insinuation.

vacshamu, the chest, bosom. Skt. The common word is *rommu*.

vaḍacaṭṭuṭa, to strain, to filter.

vaḍacuṭa, to tremble. *venuca Condatráu Pantulugáru ṣirashtáḍári chésin appuḍu garbhálaló pinḍálu adiri póyévi, vacca céca vésté v'úḷḷó váḷḷ anta gaḍa gaḍa vaḍici baṭṭalaló alpamachánam chésucunéváru*, when Kondatrao Pantulu was sheristadar the unborn babies quivered in the womb and there was not a dry dhoty in the town if he did but raise his voice.

vaḍagallu, hailstone. *daridruḍu tala caḍaga póté vaḍagaḷḷa vána vembaḍé vachchindi*, when the poor man went to wash his head a hailstorm came upon him (it never rains but it pours); *vaḍagaḷḷu paḍutsunnavi*, it is hailing.

vaḍalintsuṭa, to get rid of; causative of *vaḍaluṭa*.

vaḍalipeṭṭuṭa, to get loose.

vaḍaltsuconuṭa, to get free from. *áyanamu vadaltsuconnánu*, I have got rid of that gentleman.

vadalu, loose; also *vadulu*.

vadaluṭa, to get loose, to let go. *jvaramu vadali póyinadi*, the fever went off; *cáḷḷu vadalunḍi*, let go my legs, as the Collector says to petitioners who throw themselves at his feet and cling to his legs.

vaḍambaḍica, agreement. Same as *oḍambaḍica*.

vadanamu, face. Skt. The common word is *mokhamu, mugamu*. *chandravadana* is moon-faced, but this refers to the brightness of the moon and not to its shape as with us.

vadanti, rumour. Skt. *nívu bíḍaváḍ aninní, bhuctici zaragaca y'iccaḍacu vachchináv aninní, vadanti véstánu*, I will spread a rumour that you came here a starveling pauper.

vadarubótu, chatterbox. *vadarubótá, ní adhica prasangam tsálintsu*, chatterbox, a truce to your impertinence; *nénu vadarubótu n'ani ná yazamánurálu nannu yeppuḍu tiṭṭutu v'unṭundi*, my mistress is always twitting me with being a chatterbox.

vadaruṭa, to chatter. *idi tellavári léchinḍi modaluconi rátri paḍucó póyin dácá v'úricé vadurutu v'unḍaḍamé cáhi pani yémi cheyyadu*, she does nothing but chatter from the moment she gets up till she goes to bed and does no work at all.

vaḍasáramu, entirely.

vadda, at. *inṭi vadda*, at home; *ná vadda lédu*, I haven't got it; also *oddu, voddu*.

vaḍḍana, serving up. *vaḍḍana cheyya vatstsunu*, you may serve dinner.

vaḍḍi, interest. Corrupt Skt.. for *vrúddhi*, increase; *vaḍḍici vaḍḍi*, compound interest; *vaḍḍi vyápáram*, money lending; *atanici vaḍḍi mánivéstánu*, I will let him off the interest.

vaḍḍintsuṭa, to serve (food). *vaḍḍinchéváḍu tanaváḍ aité, caḍa bantini curtsunna vaccaṭé,* so long as the waiter is your man it does not matter if you sit last in the row; *conchemu annamu vaḍḍistárá?* will you help me to some rice?

vaddu, don't want, don't; from *valayuṭa,* to be wanted. It is one way of saying 'no thank you'; *accara lédu* is another. *tondara cheyya vaddu,* don't worry me; *vinnavi anni viṣvasintsa vaddu, viṣvasinchinavi anni veli putstsa vaddu,* don't believe all you hear or repeat all you believe.

vaḍḍu, bank, shore; same as *oḍḍu. ippudu y'iscúḷḷalló tsaduvucuné móṭa munḍá coḍuculu zuṭṭ ainá taḍavacunḍa vaḍḍuna cúrtsonḍi snánálu chéséváḷḷanu mídimiccili veccirisṭár ayyá,* nowadays, sir, the whoreson boys that study in the English schools will sit on the bank without even wetting their pigtails and laugh heartily at us doing our ceremonial washings in the river.

vadha, murder. Skt. The usual word is the Hindustani *khúni.*

vadhintsuṭa, to kill. Skt. A literary word, the usual word is *tsampuṭa.*

vadhuvarulu, bride and bridegroom. Skt.

vadhuvu, woman, bride. Skt.

vadhyasthalamu, place of death. Skt. *vadhyasthalamunacu póvu márgamuna,* on his way to martyrdom.

vadhyuḍu, one condemned to death. Skt.

vaḍi, speed, time. *conta vaḍi,* a short time; *náḍi bahu vaḍigá coṭṭucuntu v'unnadi,* the pulse is very rapid.

vaḍicaṭṭuṭa, to strain, to filter; same as *vaḍiyacaṭṭuṭa.*

vadilipeṭṭuṭa, to let go, to release, to abandon. *répu mí cumáruḍu peddaváḍ ai mí códalini vadilipeṭṭi bógamdánni v'untsuconi, y'inṭló ḍabb antá páḍu chéstú v'unṭé, adi tappitam aunó cádó mícu bágá telustundi,* if your son grows up and abandons his wife for a dancing-girl and wastes all the money in the house, you will very soon come to understand whether it is wrong or not.

vadilipóvuṭa, to get away.

vadilivéyuṭa, to abandon.

vadine, elder sister-in-law and so an older brother's wife or daughter of a mother's brother or of a father's sister if older than oneself.

vaḍisela, a sling (to throw stones). In books *oḍisela.*

vaḍivéyuṭa, to twist. *oca chétitó mísamu vaḍivéyutsu, renḍava chétitó bozza nimuruconutsu, ṣrí rájáváru pravéṣintsutsunnáru,* my Lord Zamindar enters twisting his moustachios with one hand and stroking his stomach with the other.

vaḍiyamu, a savoury cake made of black gram and condiments.

vaḍlaváḍu, carpenter.

vaḍlu, rice in the husk, the rice crop; it is the plural of *vari.* Words for grains and crops are put in the plural in Telugu. *vaḍlu muttúm, pichchicalu ártúm,* three tooms of paddy and six tooms of sparrows (loss keeping pace with gain).

vaḍrangamu, carpenter's trade.

vaḍrangi, carpenter.

vaḍucuṭa, to spin.

vaḍugu, the thread ceremony; more commonly *upanayanamu.*

vadulu, loose. *vadulu panḍlu,* loose teeth.

vaḍyamu, a savoury cake made of black gram, chillies, &c., same as *vaḍiyamu.*

vaga, grief.

vagairá, etcetera. Hindustani.

vagaru, astringent; also *ogaru.*

vagarutsuṭa, to pant; *vagarustú parugettuconuṭa,* to run panting.

vahanamu, vehicle. Skt.

vahintsuṭa, to bear, to carry. Skt. *ná mída cárpanyamu vahistáḍu,* he bears ill-will against me; *conchem sépu ṣántam vahintsanḍi,* keep quiet for a little.

vaibhavamu, splendour. Skt., from *vibhavam. v'utsavam vaibhavamgá zarigindi,* the festival was conducted with splendour.

vaicalyamu, deficiency. Skt. *anga vaicalyamu,* being maimed; *chitta vaicalyamu,* deficiency in the heart or mind.

Vaicunṭhamu, Vishnu's paradise,

heaven. *ná chéti mátra, Vaicunṭha yátra*, my pill a pilgrimage to heaven (quack speaking). *arachétiló Vaicunṭham tsúputádu*, he offers heaven in the palm of his hand (another sort of quack, a sky-pilot).

vaidhavyamu, widowhood. Skt., from *vidhava*.

vaidicamu, vedic. Skt., from *véda*.

vaidicuḍu, a brahmin versed in the Vedas, a clerical brahmin as opposed to a niyogi, secular brahmin (there is not much difference nowadays, the clericals prefer Government employment to spiritual ministrations).

vaiḍúryamu, lapis lazuli. *vajravaiḍúryam*, diamond and lapis lazuli, are often coupled in descriptions as the height of brilliancy.

vaidyamu, art of medicine. Skt. root *vid*, to know.

vaidyaṣála, hospital. Skt., but every one says *áspatri*.

vaidyuḍu, physician. Skt. *ocarini y'iddarini tsampiténé cáni vaidyuḍu cáḍu*, a doctor is no doctor till he has killed one or two; *jantuvaidyuḍu*, veterinary doctor; *pallavaidyuḍu*, dentist.

vaidyuta, electrical. Skt., from *vidyuttu*, lightning; *vaidyuta dípam*, electric lamp; *vaidyuta tantrulu*, electric wires.

vaikhari, manner, mien. Skt.

vainamulu, particulars; corrupt Skt. for *vivaranumulu*.

vaiparítyamu, diversity. Skt.

vaipu, direction, side.

vairamu, enmity. Skt.

vairági, an ascetic. Skt.

vairágyamu, asceticism. Skt.

vairi, an enemy. Skt.

vaiṣákhamu, the second lunar month (about May). Skt.

vaiṣályamu, breadth. Skt.

vaishamyamu, inequality, enmity. Skt.

vaishnuvuḍu, Vaishnavite, follower of Vishṇu. Skt.

vaiṣyuḍu, merchant (third) casteman. Skt.

vaitṣuṭa, to throw, connected with *véyuṭa*.

vaiváhicamu, nuptial. Skt., from *viváhamu*, marriage. *vaiváhicamulu* are among the things which may proverbially be lied about; others are *prána vittamána bhangamu*, danger to life or property; in fact all is fair in love and war.

vajramu, diamond. Skt. *vajrapuṭ ungaramu*, diamond ring. *Lacshmayya: ná bhárya tsálá caṭhinamaina manassu caladi. Vencayya: áviḍenu santósha peṭṭaḍam yeṭla? Lacshmayya: vajram isté manassu cósucó pótundi.* Smith: My wife is a very hard woman. Jones: How is she to be made happy? Smith: Diamond cut diamond; give her a present of a diamond; *vajravaiḍúryam*, diamond and lapis lazuli, are two gems often mentioned together, presumably because the words begin with the same syllable; symbolic of brilliancy.

vajráyudhamu, Indra's thunderbolt. Skt., from *vajram*, adamant, and *áyudham*, weapon. Tvastar made it from the bones of Agastya.

vala, net, toils. *strí valaló paḍḍáḍu*, he fell into a woman's toils.

valadu, don't; longer form of *vaddu* and not so common.

valana, by means of; longer form of *valla* and not so common.

valapu, love, especially sexual love. *valapuverri*, madness of passion; *valapu siggu yerugadu*, lust knows no shame; *ní comártecu ná mída valapu caliginadi*, your daughter has fallen in love with me.

valapumandu, aphrodisiac, love-philtre.

valasa, emigration. *valasarájyamu*, colony.

valasina, wanted, necessary; from *valayuṭa*, also *cávalasina*.

valasinadi, must. The longest form of the word; other forms are *valenu, váli, áli, alá, valayunu*; you must come is usually *nívu ráváli*, but the other forms may also be used; *valasinadi* is more often past than present; *rá valasinadi*, you ought to have come; *cá valasinadi* means a thing required; *ivva valasinadi* a thing owed; *valasi vastundi*, ought to have.

valatsuṭa, to love; with dative. *nícu*

PLATE VII

Bezwada, the future capital of the Andhra State

(*Photo. Klein and Peyerl, Madras*)

valachi, loving you; *tá valachinadi Rambha, tá mugisinadi Ganga*, the woman he loves is a Venus; the river he bathes in is the Ganges (all his geese are swans).

valayamu, circle, boundary. Skt. *drügvalayamu*, horizon (sight-boundary).

valayuṭa, to be wanted; exceedingly common in the forms *áli, alá, valenu, valasinadi, váli*, which mean ought, must, should, and in the negative aorist *vaddu*, which means don't, don't want, no thank you.

vale, like. *cóti chéti pámu vale*, like a snake in a monkey's paw (the monkey is afraid but won't let go).

valenu, must, ought, should. *yevari níḷḷaló váru munaga valenu*, every one must bathe in his own water (bear his own cross), &c.; also *valasinadi*.

valla, convenience, possibility. *gúniváḍu paḍucuné valla gúnivánicé telusunu*, it is the hunchback who knows how he can most conveniently lie.

valla, by means of; in books *valana*.

vallabha, loved woman, mistress, wife.

vallabhuḍu, loved man, lover, husband.

vallacádu, vallalédu, it is not possible, can't be done; from *valla*, possibility, and the appropriate negative. *accaḍici pó valla lédu*, you can't go there; *adi valla cádu*, that is impossible; *idi lécunṭé gáni valla cádu*, I can't do without it; *nívu vasté gáni valla cádu*, your presence is indispensable; *cheppucóca valla cádu*, you cannot but say it; *cucca véshamu vĕsté moragacunḍá valla cádu*, if you disguise yourself as a dog you needs must bark (in for a penny in for a pound).

vallacáḍu, cemetery, place for burning or burying. The genitive, *vallacáṭi*, is used as an expletive. *vallacáṭi daggu nannu tsamputsunnadi*, this damnable cough will be the death of me.

vallacáni, vallamálina, impracticable; from *valla*, possibility, and negative participles. *tyanacu vallamálina chevuḍu*, he is impossibly deaf.

vallana, valle, rote, repetition.

vallanavéyuṭa, valle véyuṭa, to repeat by rote. *í vádam antá tarca pracarandlu vallinchin aṭṭu vallana veyyi*, learn this argument off by heart like a chapter in logic (philosophy is committed to memory in India; argument is not allowed).

vallapaḍuṭa, to be possible. *váḷḷanu sádhintsaḍánici valla paḍadu*, it is not possible to propitiate them.

vaḷḷu, body; a form of *oḍalu, voḷḷu*. *nácu vaḷḷ antá chemaṭa pósindi*, I sweated all over the body; *mandu mácu accara lécunḍá lankhánálu chésté vacca debbanu paḍi rózula náṭici vaḷḷu nimmalamgá v'unḍunu*, take no pills or potions but only fast and in ten days you will be all right again at a blow; *vánici vaḷḷu telisinadi*, he came to himself; *í dinamu nácu vaḷḷu sari lédu*, I am out of sorts to-day. (The Telugus bring in the body where we refer simply to ourselves; they don't say 'I am ill'; they say 'my body is ill'.)

valluṭa, to love. *magaḍu vallan ammanu Mári valladu*, the goddess of pestilence will not love the woman unloved by her husband (the bad penny always comes back again); *álini vallanivanici y'ílacúraló v'upputsáladu*, a husband who does not love his wife will say there is not enough salt in the food.

valutsuṭa, to peel, flay; also *olutsuṭa*. *váḍu bratici unḍagáné tólu valchi vésindru*, they flayed him alive.

vamanamu, vomiting. Skt. *vamanamu cácunḍá n'unḍuṭa gánu támbúlamu vésucunndnu*, I chewed betel to stay my stomach; more commonly *vánti* or *caccu*.

vamṣamu, family, lineage, race. Skt. *vamṣapáramparyamugá*, from generation to generation; *vamṣavrücshamu*, a family tree; *tsála goppa vamṣamló v'unnáḍu*, he is of very good family.

vamṣasthuḍu, descendant. Skt. *goppa vamṣasthuḍu*, a man of a great family. (A large family is *pedda cuṭumbam*.)

vanacuṭa, to tremble; same as *vaḍacuṭa*. *váḍu bháryacu gaḍagaḍa vanacutáḍu*, he is all of a tremble before his wife (a hen-pecked husband); *ná* *chétulu vanacutú v'unnavi*, my hands are trembling; *vazavaza vanucutsu*, trembling all over.

vanamu, forest, park, grove. Skt. *vanabhójanamu*, a picnic; *udyávanamu*, a pleasure park; *chintavanamu*, a tamarind grove; *tá cheḍḍa cóti vanam ella cherachin aṭṭu*, like one bad monkey infecting the whole grove.

vanaru, grief.

vanaruṭa, to grieve.

vanca, stream, watercourse; *vancas* are torrents dry most of the year and full only when it rains hard.

vanca, side, quarter, towards.

vanca, crooked; also *vancara*.

vanca, bend, twist. *yéru yenni vancalu póyiná samudramuloné paḍa valenu*, even the weariest river winds somewhere safe to sea.

vanca, excuse, exception. *yenta manchid ainanu yédó oca vanca peṭṭutáḍu*, he picks holes in everything however good it is; *vancalu peṭṭuṭa* also means to make excuses.

vancara, crooked; also *vanca*. *vancara meḍa*, a wry neck; *vancara múti*, a wry mouth; *vancara tincaramgá vaca v'uttaramu gócináḍu*, he scribbled a letter all upside down.

vancáya, brinjal, egg-plant (*Solanum melongena*). *yéṭló vancáyalu cástává anṭé, cástavi ann aṭṭu*, like saying yes when asked whether brinjals grow in rivers (time-serving).

vanchacuḍu, cheat. Skt.

vanchana, cheating. Skt.

vanchituḍu, person cheated. *buddhimantula valla buddhínulacu v'upacáram calugutundi ganuca, alpasankhyagala vanchacula valla adhicasankhyagala vanchitulacu v'upacáram calugutundi*, sensible people do good to senseless people and so good is done to the numberless cheated persons by the few cheats.

vanda, one hundred; also *núru*. Both are common.

vandanamu, salutation, thanks. Skt.

vandintsuṭa, to praise. Skt.

vanḍintsuṭa, to have food cooked; causative of *vanḍuṭa*.

vanḍuṭa, to cook. *caḍuputó v'unn amma canaca mánund, vanḍin amma tinaca mánundá?* will the woman who has conceived not bring forth, will the woman who has cooked not eat?

vangacheṭṭu, the brinjal plant (*Solanum melongena*). *prodduné léchi vanga cheṭlacu níḷḷu tóḍipóyyum anṭáḍu*, he tells me to get up early and water the brinjals; *yeccaḍanainá bává ana vatstsunu gáni, vanga tóṭa vadda bává ana cúḍadu*, call me brother anywhere except in the brinjal garden (where it might cost me something).

vangasamu, race, breed. Skt. *paśu játi vangasamu bágu chéyuṭa*, to improve the breed of cattle.

vangatíyuṭa, to pull down, to bend down. From *vanguṭa*, to bend, and *tíyuṭa*, to pull.

vangavarugu, dried brinjal.

vanguṭa, to bend (intransitive). *cheṭṭu ai vanganidi, mánu ai vangunḍ?* if it won't bend as a sapling will it bend as a tree? *Dharmapuriló dongalintsa pótú, Dhárváḍaló nunchi vanguconi póyináḍ aṭa*, the thief crouched all the way from Dharvar when he was going to steal at Dharmapur (conscience makes cowards of us all); *vánici vrüddhápyamu chéta naḍumu vangi póyinadi*, he is bent double with age.

vanita, woman. Skt. *vamṣam erigi vanitanunnu, vanne yerigi paṣuvununnu sampádintsa valenu*, choose your bride for breed, your cattle for beauty (a paradox for which there is something to be said).

vanne, hue, complexion, beauty. *méca vanne puli*, a tiger in the hue of a goat (a wolf in sheep's clothing); *vannecatte*, a beauty; *vannecáḍu*, a beau, a handsome man.

vanta, vexation, regret, grief.

vanṭa, in or on the body. Oblique form of *vaḷḷu*.

vanṭa, cooking. *vanṭa brahmanuḍu*, a brahmin cook; a despised but necessary person since brahmins cannot eat food cooked by any one except a brahmin; *penṭa mída panṭa, manṭa mída vanṭa*, cooking depends on the fire, cropping on manure.

vanṭacáḍu, cook (male); also *cusinivádu*, which is Portuguese.

vanṭacatte, cook (female).

vanṭacaṭṭelu, vanṭacherucu, firewood for cooking.

vanṭagadi, kitchen; also *vanṭayillu, vanṭaṣála*.

vanṭapúṭillu, restaurant; also *púṭacúṭillu*; in Madras they say *annasatramu*; but this in the Circars would mean a choultry in which meals are supplied free of charge.

vanṭara, alone; a form of *onṭari*. *vanṭaricáḍu*, a man alone; *vanṭaricatte*, a lone woman.

vanṭayillu, cook-house; also *vanṭillu*.

vantena, a bridge.

vanṭi, the genitive of *vaḷḷu*, body.

-vanṭi, affix meaning 'like', oblique form of *valé*, like. *ná vanṭi*, like me; *Rámuni vanṭi rázu v'unṭé, Hanumantuni vanṭi banṭu appuḍé v'unṭáḍu*, a king like Rama makes a servant like Hanuman (like master like man); *aṭuvanṭi*, such; *aṭuvanṭi* is added to nearly every adjective in public speeches to give the speaker time to think out his sentences.

vanṭillu, cook-house, kitchen; short for *vanṭayillu*.

vantsuṭa, to bend (transitive). *gúna vantsuconi cúrtsona vaddu*, sit up.

vantu, share, turn. *vári vant ai póyinadi*, their turn is over; *sagham vantu*, a half share.

-vantuḍu, affix meaning 'endowed with'. Skt. *dhairyavantuḍu*, brave; *vidyavantuḍu*, learned; *dhanavantuḍu*, rich.

vappachepputa, to hand over; a form of *oppuchepputa*.

vappaginta, handing over; a form of *oppaginta*.

vappagintapeṭṭuṭa, to hand over.

vappagintsuṭa, to hand over. *iccaḍané parunḍi répu mí y'illú vastuvulú vappagistánu*, I will sleep here and hand you over your house and things to-morrow.

vappuconuṭa, to agree; form of *oppuconuṭa*. *á chinnadi nannu viváham chésu cóḍánici vappuconnadi*, that girl agreed to marry me.

vara, scabbard; another form of *ora*. *oca varaló renḍu cattulu y'imaḍavu*, two swords won't go into one scabbard (there can't be two masters in one house).

vara, limit; used chiefly in the inflected forms *varaló, varacu*.

varacamu, rigorous imprisonment. *nícu varacam vésindá?* have you been sentenced to rigorous imprisonment?

varacu, till, by that time. *á varacé pári pói y'unnáru*, by that time they had run away; *idi varacu*, till now.

varada, flood. *varada vachchin appuḍu Góḍávariló snánam cheyyum anṭé buradá níḷḷ antáru*, (Europeans) call bathing in the Godavari when the floods come down bathing in muddy water. (Europeans of course have the strange idea that you bathe in order to get clean whereas bathing in the Godavari is a religious ceremony and washes your sins away.) *áḍáyamu lécané Ṣetti varada póḍu*, without hope of gain the Chetti will not face the flood.

varagalu, a kind of millet.

varahá, the gold coin known as the pagoda, in which accounts were kept till 100 years ago; it was a small coin worth three and a half rupees; the derivation of the word is from *varáham*, Skt. boar; the coin had a boar (Vishnu) on it. Three and a half rupees was only the value of an account pagoda in terms of account rupees; there were many kinds of pagodas and rupees in circulation: the Ikkeri and Canteroy pagodas were among the most common in South India. *ḍabbucu vachchina cheyyé varahácu vastundi*, the hand that reaches for a pie will reach for a pagoda (*qui vole un œuf vole un bœuf*, who steals an egg will steal an ox).

-varaló, affix meaning 'within' from *vara*, limit. *idi varaló*, before this; *ivaraló*, meanwhile.

varamu, boon. Skt. *Dévuḍu varam ichchiná pújári varam ivvaḍu*, though God grant the boon the priest refuses it.

varasa, row, series, relationship. *varasacu unnáḍu*, he is related; *varasa tappuṭa*, to commit incest; *varasajvaramu*, recurring fever. Also *varusa*.

varaṣulcamu, bridegroom tax. Skt.

This is the depreciatory term for the dowry system, which differs from ours in that the money is paid not to the husband but to his father, who 'sells' his son to your daughter; prices vary with marketable educational qualifications; a B.A., B.L., is worth quite a lot of money; it is said that when a new Indian member of the I.C.S. lands at Bombay he finds a sheaf of telegrams offering girls with a lakh of rupees; on the other hand, if you marry your daughter to an old widower, he has to pay you; and this is called *canyaşulcamu*, sale of a virgin.

varáhamu, boar. Skt. The boar is one of the incarnations of Vishnu.

varchassu, lustre. Skt. *mukha varchassu*, radiance of face; *áme mukha varchass ippaṭi canṭé tétagá mari yeppuḍu n'unḍa lédu*, she has never had a more brilliant complexion.

vardhanamu, increase, thriving.

vardhilluṭa, to prosper. Skt. *ní talli caḍupu tsallagá, nívu veyy éḷḷu vardhilla valenu*, blessings on your mother's womb, may you live and prosper for a thousand years.

vargamu, class. Skt. *ca-vargamu*, the class of guttural letters; *áptavargamu*, a band of friends; *bandhuvargamu*, kith and kin; *tama póshya vargamuló v'unnánu ganuca*, as I am in the class of your protégés.

vari, rice; usually in the plural *vaḍlu*; it is the grain, rice in the husk; husked rice is *biyam*. (The languages of the rice-growing countries make this distinction: the Italians say *riso* for *bíyam* and *risone* for *vaḍlu*, and Anglo-Indians supply the want of an English equivalent of *vaḍlu* by calling it *paddy*.) *varici vaca vánd, v'údacu vaca vánd?* is it one rain for grain and another for weeds? (God sendeth the rain on the just and on the unjust); *tirigité vari polam, tirigaca póté aḍavi polam*, bestir yourself, you have a paddy field; idle, and you have a jungle.

varigaḍḍi, straw; what cattle lie on in England and feed on in India. The Telugus, not knowing the difference, translate it 'hay'.

varintsuṭa, to choose, especially choose for spouse. Skt. *nizamaina préma chétané nannu varinchináḍu*, he has proposed to me out of true love.

varjintsuṭa, to abandon. Skt.

varjyamu, evil hour, unlucky time. Skt.

varnamu, caste. Skt. The first meaning of the word is 'colour'; caste prejudice and caste distinction are in origin colour prejudice and distinction, and *varnáşramadharma*, the duty of maintaining caste and religion, of which the Hindus are always prating, is the ideal of the Ku Klux Klan. The *ádhicyamu* or superiority of the brahmin lies in his colour, and logically the white man should be recognized by the brahmin as a being of a superior caste.

varnamu, description. Skt., especially literary description.

varnasancaramu, mixing of castes. Skt. This is a great sin and a great misfortune. *caliyugam aidu véla sanvatsarála cávachchindi, ikha varnasancaram autundi*, the iron age of five thousand years has begun; the next thing will be confusion of castes; *ná vanṭi v'uttama purushula grahachāram chéta mana déşánici mḷéchcha prabhutvam vachchi, bottigá varnasancaram autú v'unnadi*, to the misfortune of excellent persons like myself our country is afflicted by a Government of heathens and there is complete confusion of castes.

varnáşramadharmamu, caste and religious duty. Skt., from *varnam*, caste, *áşramam*, stage in the religious life, and *dharmam*, duty. *cula vrüttiló pravéşa peṭṭi varnáşramadharmam nilava peṭṭi mícu punyam vastundi*, put him into his caste profession and you have the merit of upholding religion; *míváḍu bráhmulacu dannam peṭṭaḍu, guḷḷóci veḷḷaḍu, scúḷḷóci veḷḷi vachchi baṭṭalu taḍisi snánam cheyyaḍu, sarigadá zandhyál ainá taḍavaḍu, varada vachchin appuḍu Gódávariló snánam cheyyum anṭé burada niḷḷ anṭáḍu, gómayam şuchi cád anṭáḍu; míru v'upécsha chésté bráhmanícam bhrashṭ ai pótundi, varnáşramadharmálu sammúlam naşi-

stavi, your son does not salute brahmins, he does not go to the temples, on returning from school he does not wet his clothes and bathe, nay, does not so much as wet his sacred thread; he says the Godavari is too muddy to bathe in when the floods come down; he says cow-dung is not clean; if you overlook this sort of thing brahminism will fall from its high estate, the decencies of caste, the order of the religious life will be destroyed from their foundation.

varnintsuṭa, to describe. Skt. *dáni tsaccatanam varnintsaḍánici Brahmac ainá ṣacyam cádu*, Brahma himself could not describe her beauty.

varshacálamu, the rainy season.

varshamu, rain, year. Skt. *atithi: vindu tsálá bágá zarigindi, nénu yeppuḍu marachi pónu. yazamáni: ainá mukhyamainaváḷḷu yevaḷḷú varsham valla rá léd ani nácu tsála vichára̍mgá v'undi.* Guest: The dinner went off very well. I shall never forget it. Hostess: Yes, but I am so sorry all the best people were kept away by the rain.

varshintsuṭa, to rain. *varshintsutsunnadi*, it is raining.

vartacamu, trade. Skt.

vartacanáva, merchantman (ship). Skt.

vartacuḍu, merchant. Skt.

vartamánamu, information, word. Skt. *vartamánamu* is also the present tense (the information tense). *vartamánam pampité váḍu y'inṭi cáḍa canapaḍa lédu*, we sent word to him but he was not at home; *banḍi cósam vartamánam pampintsuṭa*, to send for a bullock-cart.

vartamánapatrica, a newspaper. *Rámuḍu: Rámayya vartamánapatricaló vrástunṭáḍ aṭé. Gópuḍu: yendu chéta? manchi cágitálu doracacaná?* Smith: Jones is said to be writing on newspapers. Brown: Why? Can't he find good writing-paper?

vartanamu, conduct. Skt.

vartintsuṭa, to be, to act, to behave. Skt.

varuḍu, bridegroom. Skt. *penḍlicoḍucu* is the common word. *varaṣulcamu*, the price paid for a bridegroom (a girl does not get engaged; a bridegroom is obtained for her); *ná pedda cumártecu varuḍu cudirindáḍu*, a bridegroom has been arranged for my eldest daughter.

varugu, dried vegetables, fruit, or fish. *vanga varugu*, dried brinjals; *mámiḍi varugu*, dry mango paste.

varunamu, water. Skt.

Varunuḍu, Varuna, the Hindu sky and rain god. Skt.; probably the same word as the Greek *Ouranos*, Uranus, heaven. *var* is the surrounding light. In the 'Mahabharata' Varuna is the God of the ocean, lakes, and watercourses. Now Hindus pray to Varuna for rain.

varupuḍi ráyi, touchstone; properly *orapuḍu ráyi*.

varusa, series, row. Skt. Also *varasa*. *meṭla varusa*, a flight of steps; *y'iṭuca varusa*, a course of bricks; *pustacál anní balla mída varusagá peṭṭu*, put all the books in a row on the table; *ná coḍuculu mugguru varusagá póyinúru*, my three sons died one after the other.

varuvaḍi, a copy set for one. *guruvu peṭṭina varuvaḍi*, the copy the teacher set.

vaṣamu, power, overcoming. Skt. *atani vaṣamuló unnadi*, it is in his power; *inṭini tana vaṣamu chésuconnáḍu*, he obtained possession of the house; *ná punyá vaṣamu*, by my merit; *adi ná vaṣán unnádá?* is that in my power? *adrüshṭa vaṣam chéta nácu áviḍe v'unna tsóṭa telisindi*, I found out where she was by the power of fortune; *ná peddal andarú Daiva vaṣam chéta cálam chésináru*, by God's providence all my elders without exception died.

vasantamu, the spring. Skt. In full, *vasanta rütuvu*, the spring season. *vasanta rütuvu impu*, spring is pleasant. The Telugus have six seasons. The others are: *vésavi*, summer; *varsham*, the rains; *ṣarattu*, the dews; *hémantam*, the cold weather; *ṣiṣiram*, the chill weather.

Vasantuḍu, the God of spring.

vaṣaparatsuconuṭa, to get into one's power.

vasati, accommodation, convenience.

Skt. *nīḷḷavasati*, water convenience; *accaḍa nīḷḷavasati lédu*, good water is not easily procurable there.

vasatigrŭhamu, lodging-house. Skt.

vaṣaushadhamu, love-philtre. Skt., from *vaṣamu*, power, and *aushadhamu*, medicine (a medicine that will give you power over another person). *vaṣaushadham ichched ani y'oca véru chétiló peṭṭi monnaṭi bairágiváḍu nishcáranamugá nálugu rúpáyalu yettuconi póyináḍu*, the other day a wandering friar said he would give me an aphrodisiac and made off with the four rupees I squandered on him.

vasárá, verandah, balcony. *gadi lédu, sáviḍi lédu, vasárá lédu, cúrtsóḍánici ainá sthalam lédu*, there is no room, verandah, or balcony, or any place even to sit in.

vaṣicaranamu, overcoming. Skt.

vasintsuṭa, to dwell. Skt.

Vaṣishṭuḍu, the sage Vasishtha, proverbially not to be moved from his word. *váḍu cheppinadi Vaṣishṭha vácyamu*, what he says is a dictum of Vasishtha's (peremptory).

vasté, if you come; from *vatstsuṭa*. *venaccu veḷḷité tannu, mundu vasté póṭu*, if you go back you will be kicked, if you come on you will be hit (between the devil and the deep sea).

vastramu, cloth, dress. Skt. *caṭṭa vastramutó nannu techchindru*, they brought me along in the clothes I had on; *annavastrálu*, food and dress; *unnivastramu*, woollen cloth; *maharázulu tamaru vaca vastram daya chéyistár ani, tama çírti vini vachchinánu*, (Beggar speaking) Hearing of Your Honour's fame I came along, thinking that Your Honour might deign to give me a cloth.

vastupradarṣanamu, exhibition. Skt., from *vastuvu*, article, and *pradarṣana*, exhibition.

vastupradarṣanaṣála, exhibition hall, museum. Skt., from *vastuvu*, article, *pradarṣanamu*, exhibition, and *ṣála*, hall.

vastu-rúpamugá, in kind. Skt., from *vastuvu*, article, and *rúpamu*, form.

vastuvu, thing, article. Skt. *oca pracaṭanaló y'iṭlá v'unḍenu: 'ná daggira aidu rúpáyala vastuvulu conucconévāḷḷacu cóṭu tagilinchédi ocaṭi, sigareṭlu calchédi incóṭi bahumánamgá istám.' Lacshmayya aidu rúpáyala vastuvulacu arḍaru pampenu. váṭitó páṭu oca chila, oca nippupulla pampiri.* An advertisement ran: 'Customers who buy Rs. 5 worth of things will get as presents something to hang their coats on and something to light their cigarettes with.' Lakshmayya sent an order for five rupees and got one nail and one lucifer with the parcel.

vasuvu, gold. Skt. The common word is *bangáram*.

vasúlu, collection (of money, especially taxes). Hindustani.

vasúluchéyuṭa, to collect (money).

vaṣyamu, overpowered by. Skt., from *vaṣam*, power. *vinayam lócavaṣyamu, vidya rája vaṣyamu*, humility places the world in your power, learning places kings in your power (the meek shall inherit the earth); *pámula mantragáḍu tátsupámunu vaṣyam chésucuntáḍu*, a snake-charmer will get a cobra into his power.

vaṭamu, banyan tree. Skt. The Telugu word is *marricheṭṭu*.

vaṭra, round. Skt. The Telugu word is *gunḍrani*. *guḍi mingeváḍici guḷḷó Dévuḍu vaṭravaḍiyam*, to the man who swallows the temple the temple idol is only a round bun.

vatstsuṭa, to come. *náto cúḍá vachchináḍu*, he came with me; *vachché nelaló*, next month (in the coming month); *aṭlu chéyutsu vachchinánu*, I have been doing so all along (Italian has the same idiom, *vengo facendo*); *iṭlu chéya valasi vachchindi*, it became necessary to do so; *idi nácu teliya vachchindi*, it came to our knowledge; *á bhásha vánici vatstsunu*, he knows that language; *í biyyamu nela dinálacu vachchinavi*, this rice lasted a month; *vánic émi vachchinadi?* what became of him? *iyya manasu vachchindi*, I have a mind to give; *vánici buddhi vachchinadi*, he learnt sense; *vánici mísálu vachchinavi*, his moustache has sprouted; *biḍḍacu paḷḷu vachchinavi*, the child has cut its teeth; *idi ná práṇamunacu vatstsunu*, this puts my life in danger; *nóṭici vachchin aṭṭu tiṭṭináḍu*, he swore without restraint (whatever came to his mouth); *atani péru nácu rá lédu*, his name escapes me; *páṭhamu váníci rá lédu*, he hasn't learnt his lesson; *vachchéṣámu*, here we are (*vatstsuṭa* with auxiliary *véyuṭa*). The negative of *vatstsuṭa* (*rá*) comes from another root, which also forms the verbal noun *rávaḍamu*, coming, and the usual infinitive, *rá*. The third person singular of the aorist, *vatstsunu*, is the Telugu for 'may'. *rá vatstsunu* means 'you may come'. The word occurs very commonly in proverbs. The following are examples: *caḍupu vasté cane tíra valenu*, the swollen womb must needs bring forth; *vachchina dóvané pótundi*, it will go the way it came (lightly come, lightly go); *vachchina váḍu tsachchiná póḍu*, ill will ceases only with death (give a dog a bad name and hang him); *vachchinavárici varam istánu, rániváríci rái istánu*, a boon to those who come, a stone to those who lag (come to do homage); *vachchíráni máṭalu ruchi, úrí úraní úrugáya ruchi*, sweet are the words that come and don't come (half-formed words of children), sweet is the taste of the half-pickled pickle; *vachché cálamu canna vachchina cálam mélu*, the time that has come is better than the time that is still to come (the good old times); *ḍabbucu vachchina cheyyé varahácu vastundi*, the same hand that reaches for a penny will reach for a pound (*qui vole un œuf vole un bœuf*, he who steals an egg will steal an ox). *ocaḍu: í áfísu panulacu bádhyata galavár evaru? gumástá: nacu bágá teliyad anḍi; yédaina lópam vasté mátram nanné andaru tiṭṭutáru.* Client: Who is responsible for the work of this office? Clerk: I don't rightly know, sir; only when anything goes wrong every one abuses me. *méjistrétu: maḷḷí vachchavá? ná vadda ica mídata rá vadd ani nénu cheppa lédá? donga: míru cheppär ani cheppänu gáni vinacunḍá pólísuváḷḷu nannu arresṭu chési tísucu vachchär anḍi.* Magistrate: Here again? Did I not tell you not to come before me again? Thief: I told the police you said that, but they wouldn't listen, Your Honour, and arrested me and lugged me along. *bhárya: magaváḷḷacu yémainá chevilóo cheppité incó chevilóo nunchi ivatalici vastundi. bharta: áḍadánici yémainá cheppité renḍu chevulalóci póyi nóṭló nunchi baiṭici vastundi.* Wife: Say anything to a man and it is in at one ear and out at the other. Husband: Say anything to a woman and it is in at both ears and out at her mouth. *upanyásacuḍu: manushyulu cótuḷḷó nunchi vachchär ani siddhántam unḍi, mícu telusuná? sabhicuḍu: míru cótuḷḷó nunchi vachchär émó gáni mému má v'úḷḷó nunchi vachchám anḍi.* Lecturer: There is a theory that men have come from the monkeys. Do you know it? Voice from the audience: You may have come from the monkeys, we have come from our village. *grühasthuḍu: bhárya v'unṭé yenta cashṭam vachchiná marichi pó vatstsunu. brahmáchári: brahmácháríci asalu cashṭamé unḍaḍu gá.* Married man: If you have a wife, whatever troubles come you can forget them. Bachelor: A bachelor has no troubles. *ica Venugópalaráu Gáru vachchina n'andarunu vachchin aṭṭé*, if Mr. Venugopalarao comes too that will be about all the people we expect.

vatti, wick. *mainapu vatti*, a candle.

vaṭṭi, empty, simple, mere. *vaṭṭi máṭala valla poṭṭalu púḍutavá?* will empty words fill bellies? (many words will not fill a bushel; the Italian proverb is still closer: *il ventre non si sazia di parole*, words don't sate the belly); *vaṭṭi góḍa*, a blind wall; *vaṭṭi cáḷḷaló*, barefoot; *vaṭṭi gáli*, a barren wind (wind without rain); *vaṭṭiváḍu*, a simpleton.

vaṭṭipóvuṭa, to go dry (of cows).

vayasu, vayassu, age, time of life. Skt. *vayasu vachchina chinnadi*, a grown girl; *padi padaháru samvatsarála vayassuló v'unna peḷḷi ɔáni tóḍapuṭṭina paḍutsu*, an unmarried sister of sixteen or so; *naḍi vayasuló v'unna bála vidhavulu cáma bádhacu lóbaḍuṭa áṣcháryamá?* is it a wonder that young widows in the flower of their age should respond to the goad of desire? (*naḍi vayasu* does not mean middle age but the prime of youth, *vayasu* being usually applied rather to the earlier than to the later periods of life); *ocaḍu: mí áfisuló gumástá pani kháli aind ani vinnánu, nác ippistárá? mánéjaru: álasyam aindi; valla cádu. ocaḍu: yevaricainá ichchärá? mánéjaru: iyya lédu; nuvvu iravai sanvatsarála cinda darakhástu peṭṭité ichchévâḍin émó; nícu vayassu mudirindi.* Applicant: I hear there is a vacancy in your office. Will you get it for me? Manager: Too late, nothing doing. Applicant: Have you given it to any one else? Manager: No. If you had applied twenty years ago you might perhaps have got it. You are a bit long in the tooth now. *tandri: parícsha márculu tsústé andari pillala canṭé nuvvu ákharuna unnáu. báluḍu: vayassuló nénépedda.* Father: Judging by the examination marks you were last in everything. Boy: I stand first for age.

vayyamu, vain, useless.

váca, stream. *varici váca, doracu múca,* what the stream is for rice, the troop is to the baron.

vácabu, experience. Hindustani.

vácabu chéyuṭa, to make inquiries.

váccu, speech. Skt. Used chiefly in compounds. *vác-chamatcáramu,* eloquence; *vágdánamu,* promise (word-gift); *vácsarani,* the course of speech; *Vágdévi,* the Goddess of speech (Sarasvati); *vángmúlamu,* deposition; *vágdhaṭi,* readiness of speech.

vácili, entrance, hall, yard. The genitive is *váciṭi. illúvácili,* house and home (lock, stock, and barrel); *váciṭiló cheppula tsappuḍ agutsunnadi,* I hear the sound of clogs at the entrance; *donga váciṭa mantsamu vésin aṭṭu,* like sleeping in the thief's yard (double-crossing him); *illú vácilí cúḍḍá ammuconuṭa,* to sell up house and home.

váconuṭa, to say, to relate; a literary word for *chepputa.*

vácsahayam, recommendation (help by words). Skt. *maḷḷé míru lantsálu, lantsálu anṭáru; yémi acáryacaranamu? manam svatantrangá chéséṭ appuḍu putstsucunté tappitam gáni paini pani chésévâḍu Dora ain appuḍu vácsaháyam chési, lábham pondité, yémi tappu?* you are again saying bribe, bribe; when we were independent it was wrong to take anything, but when the superior is a European and you say a word to him and procure an advantage to the party, and make something out of it, what is there wrong in it? (the true cause of the lamented corruption of our Indian subordinates thus stands revealed).

vácyamu, sentence, dictum. Skt. *tahaṣṣiluḍáru gári vácyam Ráma vácyamu,* the tahsildar's word is as good as a promise from heaven; so also *Vaṣishṭha vácyamu,* an irrevocable word. *ṭícharu: renḍu áulu polamló v'unnadi; í vácyamló yém tappu unnádó canuccondi. báluḍu: renṭiló ocaṭi yeddu ai v'unṭund anḍi.* Teacher: There is two cows in the field; find the mistake in that sentence. Boy: One of the two will be an ox, sir.

váḍa, ship; a form of *óḍa.*

váḍa, row, street.

vádamu, argument. Skt. *mí vádamuló vaṭṭi pippiyé cáni, sáram émiyu lédu,* there is no force in your argument (all refuse and no juice); *mí vádamu paḍi póyindi,* your argument has failed.

vádi, plaintiff, prosecutor. *sácshi cáḷḷu paṭṭucóvaḍam canná, vádi cáḷḷu paṭṭucó vatstsunu,* fall at the prosecutor's feet rather than at the witness's.

váḍi, sharpness (of tools, &c.). *catti váḍá, calam váḍá?* is the pen or the sword sharper? (the pen is mightier than the sword).

vádintsuṭa, to argue. Skt.

vádu, dispute. Skt. *vachchina vádu tsachchiná póḍu,* a dispute once started will cease only with death.

váḍu, he.

-váḍu, affix denoting 'man'. *gurrapuváḍu,* horseman (groom); *tsácaliváḍu,* washerman. *telisinaváru,* the people who know; *máváru,* my people.

váḍuca, custom, use, practice. *paniló váḍuca paḍḍaváru,* skilled labourers; *váḍucavánḍru,* customers; *váḍucacu tetstsuṭa,* to bring into use.

váḍucagá, commonly.

váḍucaina, habitual.
váḍucapaḍuṭa, to be accustomed.
váḍuconuṭa, to use.
váḍudala, use, practice.
váḍupóvuṭa, váḍuṭa, to fade, to wither.
vádyamu, any musical instrument, instrumental music. Skt.
vágdattamu, promise (word-giving). Skt.
vágdánamu, promise (word-gift). Skt.
vágdhára, fluency, eloquence (word-flow). Skt.
vágmúlamu, deposition, witness's statement. Skt., from *vác*, word, and *múlam*, origin. Spelt *vángmúlam* but pronounced as above.
vágmúlamugá, orally.
vágrúpacamaina, oral. Skt., from *vác*, word, and *rúpam*, form.
váguṭá, to babble. *Inglishu nálugu muccalu vágutáḍu*, he babbles a few words of English; *úricé vágabócu*, don't babble at random; *nívu cávalasin anta sépu vágu*, babble away as long as you like; *miṭingulóci vachchi, nálugu muccalu vági, tsacca pótáru*, they will come to the meeting, babble a few words, and go away.
váhacuḍu, bearer, carrier (especially of corpses). Skt.
váhanamu, vehicle (especially of the Gods). Skt. *yeluca anacú, Vighnéṣvaruḍi váhanam anu*, don't say mouse, say Vighnesvara's vehicle.
váhyáḷi, excursion. Skt.
vájmayamu, composition. Skt., from *vác*, speech, and *mayam*, composed.
váḷa, day; vulgar for *véla*.
válacamu, deceit, pretences. *i válacam tsústé alluḍu vaṭṭi buddhihínuḍu lágu canapaḍutú v'unnáḍu*, seeing his pretences my son-in-law seems to be an absolute fool.
vále, váli, must; forms of *valenu*.
váḷḷa, their.
váḷḷu, they.
váltsuṭa, to bend, to drop (transitive). *reppa váltsaca tsútsuṭa*, to stare (to look without dropping the eyelids); *rátri antá cannulu váltsa lédu*, I did not get a wink of sleep all night.
válu, slope; but the slopes which we make down canal banks for the passage of cattle are always called *slópu*.
váluṭa, to bend down, to alight (especially of birds). *váluḍu comma*, a branch that hangs down; *váluproddu*, the morning or evening sun.
vámi, stack. *vámidoḍḍi*, stackyard; *gaḍḍivámi*, strawstack.
vána, rain. *varici vaca váná, v'údacu vaca váná?* is there one rain for rice and one for weeds? (God sendeth rain on the just and the unjust); *vána rácaḍa, prána pócaḍa, yevarici teliyaḍu*, no one can predict the coming of rain or the going of life; *yénupótu mída vána curisin aṭṭu*, like rain falling on a buffalo (pathetic contentment).
vánacálamu, the rainy season. *vánacálapu tsaduvu valla vidya rá néradu*, knowledge will not come by studying only in the rains (only when you are kept indoors, desultory study); *ocaḍu: anni cálálu manavi cávu; vánacáláni ci conchem untsucó valenu. incóḍu: nénu untsucunnánu. ocaḍu: yém untsucunnávu? incóḍu: goḍugu.* Doe: All times are not our own; we must keep something for a rainy season. Roe: I have. Doe: What? Roe: My umbrella.
vánchha, desire. Skt.
vánchhitamu, desired. Skt.
vánḍlu, vánḍru, forms of *váru*, they.
vángmúlamu, deposition; pronounced *vágmúlamu*. Skt.
váni, his; genitive of *váḍu*.
vánijyamu, trade. Skt. *vánijya racshana paddhati* is the newspaper expression for protection; *vánijya svéchcha paddhati*, free trade.
vánni, accusative of *váḍu*, he. *carra léni vánni gorre ainá carustundi*, even a sheep will bite a man without a stick. Also *vánini*.
vánti, vomiting. Skt. *vánti bhédi* (vomiting and purging) is cholera, but people usually say *cálárá* or *vishúchica*. *Lacshmayya sṭímaru yecci nidra póyenu. tellavárina tarváta Lacshmayya: sṭímaruló prayánam chésté nidra paṭṭadu, vántulu veḷḷutav ani nannu bhayam peṭṭár anḍi; nác émí ibbandi caluga lédu. sṭímaru adhicári: sṭímaru incá révu vadilipeṭṭa lédu; injanu cheḍipóté bágu chéstunnáru.*

Lakshmayya got on board a steamer and went to sleep. Next morning he said to a ship's officer: I was told I should not get a wink of sleep on board and should be sick; I have been perfectly all right. Ship's officer: The steamer has never left port; something went wrong with the engine and they are repairing it.

vántsuṭa, to bend (transitive); also *vantsuṭa.*

vápasu, returning, giving back. Hindustani.

vápasuchéyuṭa, to return, to refund.

váramu, váramu dinamulu, a week. Skt. In composition, a day of the week. *sómavváram*, Monday, &c.; *oca váramu dinamula anantaramu mánava smrüti vicrütam agun ani manacu telusunu,* we know that the human memory cannot be relied on for a week.

váranṭu, warrant. English. *itaḍu váranṭu mída paṭṭucunna manishini viḍipinchináḍu,* he rescued a man arrested on warrant.

vára satvamu, inheritance, hereditary right (e.g. the hereditary right of village officers).

várasu, heir. Hindustani.

várdhacamu, old age. Skt.; also *várdhaca daṣa, vrüddhatvamu, vrüddhápyamu.* The Telugu is *musalitanamu: várdhaca daṣaló viváhamu chésuconnavárici páṭl eccaḍanú i lágunané y' unḍunu,* such will always be the troubles of men who marry in old age.

-vári, affix meaning 'according to'. Hindustani. *ásámivári,* man by man, individually; *tálucavári,* by taluks.

vári, their; genitive of *váru.*

várici, to them; dative of *váru. yevaruváru,* every; *yevari pai-guḍḍa várici baruvé,* every man feels the weight of his own upper-cloth (has to bear his own cross).

várintsuṭa, to ward off, to forbid, to prevent. Skt.

várta, report. Skt.

vártamánamu, news, intelligence, information. Skt. Also *vartamánamu.*

vártamána patrica, newspaper. Skt. Also *vartamána patrica.*

vártsuṭa, to drain off (as water from rice); causative of *váruta. póyi mída cúra vési ganji vártsucunnánu,* I put the curry on the fire and drained off the rice-water. *sandhyavártsuṭa* is to say your prayers, because you let water through your fingers when you are saying them.

váru, they; other forms are *váḷḷu, vánḍru, vánḍlu. yevari váru,* every. *yevari níḷḷaló váru munaga vale,* every one must bathe in his own water (bear his own troubles).

váru, strap. *caḷḷepuváru,* rein; *ṭanguváru,* girth.

váruṭa, to flow off (as water from rice).

váruvamu, steed; a literary word for horse; the common word is *gurram.*

vásamu, residence. Skt. *ágnyáta vásamu,* incognito; *váni garbha vásamuló puṭṭinaváḍu,* the son of his loins; *culam erigina tsuṭṭamu, sthalam erigina vásamu,* marry where you know the family, build where you know the place; *saha-vásamu,* dwelling with, usually means intercourse, intimacy.

vásamu, rafter.

vásana, smell. Skt. *ulli muṭṭanidi vásana rádu,* if you had not touched garlic you would not have smelt; *annam pásina vásana coṭṭutsunndi,* the food smells rancid; *vidya vásana léca,* without a tincture of learning.

vásanatsútsuṭa, to smell (transitive).

vásanavéyuṭa, vásanacoṭṭuṭa, to smell bad.

vási, inhabitant. Skt. *vanavási,* a hermit (forest-dweller); *grámavásulu,* villagers.

vási, fame. Skt. *vásic eccuṭa,* to rise to celebrity.

vásintsuṭa, to inhabit. Skt.

vástavamu, truth. Skt. *míru cheppinad antá vástavam,* all you say is true.

vástavica, true. *matótpatti (útpatti,* origin) *vástavica cartalu,* the real originators of the religion.

vástuvu, house. Skt. *vástu ṣastriyamu,* architecture.

váta, branding (especially of cattle), tiger's stripe. *pulini tsúchi nacca váta peṭṭucon aṭṭu,* like a jackal wearing tiger's stripes (aping one's superiors).

váta, in or by the mouth; from *váyi,*

mouth. *Dévuḍu y'istáḍu gáni, vanḍi, várchi váta coṭṭuṭáḍá?* God gives us our daily bread, but He does not bake it for us or put it in our mouths (God helps those who help themselves, *chi s'aiuta Iddio l'aiuta*).

vátamu, air, wind. Skt. Used only in books and compounds like *vátarógam*, rheumatism (air in the joints); also *váyuva*.

vátavéyuṭa, to brand, to cauterize. *corru yerragá cálchi, váta vési, nippu cálutundó lédó tsúpistánu*, I will heat a plough-share red-hot, brand him, and show him whether fire burns or not.

váṭi, váṭici, váṭini, irregular cases of *váḍu*, he.

váṭi, oblique case of *avi*, those things.

vátsalyamu, parental love. Skt. *putravátsalyamu*, paternal affection; *ná y'andali vátsalyam chéta mir úricé nannu stuti chéstunnáru*, you only praise me out of paternal affection.

vátsuṭa, to swell. The Shastras say that the face and legs swell with any emotion (love, pride, appetite). *mahá vaḷḷu váchi*, swelling with pride; *cúṭici váchi unnáḍu*, he is ravenously hungry; *ocaḍu: mi mukham oca vaipuna yettugá v'unnadi; ṣástra pracáram tsústé mícu mí pillala mída préma yeccuva v'unnad anna máṭa. incóḍu: á sangati nácu teliyadu; má pillaváḍu ráyi vésté mukhámici tagíli váchi yettugá v'unnadi.* Doe: Your face is swollen on one side; according to Scripture that shows you have great love for your children. Roe: I don't know about that; as a matter of fact the swelling comes from my boy having hit me in the face with a stone.

vávi, consanguinity, legitimacy. *vávi varasá yémi lédu*, there is no observance of consanguinity; *á paḍutsunu penḍli áḍaḍamu vávi cádu*, a marriage within the prohibited degrees.

vávitappu, incest (consanguinity infraction).

váyi, mouth. There are two other words for mouth: *nóru* is commoner, *múṭi*, vulgar. *vátibhiyyamu*, the rice put in the mouths of the dead; *váticásu*, hush-money (money to stop the mouth); *míru vachché varacu mácu váta taḍi lédu*, our mouths were dry (with fear) till you came.

váyida, time for payment, adjournment; a common word in the courts. Hindustani.

váyintsuṭa, to beat (a drum). *maddela tinnagá váyintsu*, beat the drum properly; *commulu v'údi, ḍappulu váyinchi*, blowing the horns and beating the drums.

váyuvu, air, wind; also *vátamu*. Skt. *váyurmánamu* is the newspaper word for aeroplane. *váyuvunu paṭṭé mandu*, medicine for flatulency; *váyupathamu*, atmosphere (path of the air); *váyuvégi*, swift as the wind; *Váyudévuḍu*, the wind god; *vári ráca teliya paratsaḍánici, vári vadda nunchi y'i parimaḷam grahinchi, mundugá Váyudévuḍu dútagá vachchináḍu*, to inform us of their arrival the wind god has seized their perfumes and brought them to us as a messenger (fishermen approaching with cavidies of dried fish); *agnici váyuvu sahayam ain aṭṭu*, fanning the flames (the fire god and the wind god are special friends according to Scripture, and this phrase alludes to their friendship; Wind coming to the aid of Fire); *ṭícharu: fizical jágrafi yémiṭi? báluḍu: bhúmini gurinchí, váyuvunu gurinchí, samudránni gurinchí, anéca sangatul unnavi.* Teacher: What is Physical Geography? Boy: It contains various things about the earth, the air, and the sea.

veccasamu, excess, disgust. *veccasamulu*, disgusting words, obscenities.

veccasapaḍuṭa, to loathe.

veccili, hiccup. Skt. *hicca*.

veccirintsuṭa, to mock. Skt. *guḍḍu pillanu (cóḍipillanu) veccirinchin aṭṭu*, like the egg making faces at the chicken (pulling the leg of a superior, insubordination).

vecci-vecci, noise of sobbing; onomatopoeic. *vecci-vecci yéḍtsuṭa*, to sob.

vechintsuṭa, to spend.

veḍalpu, breadth.

veḍaluṭa, to go; the original form of the common *veḷḷuṭa*. *veḍalucoṭṭuṭa*, to drive out; *veḍalipóvuṭa*, to go away (but *veḷḷipóvuṭa* is commoner); *né veḍatá*, I will go, is what is actually *said*, rather than *veḍalipótánu* or *veḷḷipótánu*.

vedatsalluṭa, to scatter, to sow.

vedhava, widow; often used as a term of abuse (even of males and inanimate objects). Skt. *vidhava. Hinduvulaló pánici málinavádu anuṭacu vedhava anu máṭa paripáṭi ai póyinadi,* widow has become a regular term of abuse among Hindus for any worthless person. They will say to a beggar: *chhí vedhava, avatalici pó,* get out, you swine; *vedhava sambhávana,* a worthless gift.

vedhavaricamu, widowhood.

veduru, bamboo. *vedurugaḍa,* bamboo stick. The common big bamboo is called a *bongu.*

vegaṭu, nasty. Skt. *vicaṭuch. chevulacu vegaṭugá unnadi,* it sounds nasty.

vela, price.

velaga, wood-apple (*feronia elephantum*). The fruit is *velaccái. yénugacu velaccáyalu loṭaloṭa,* wood-apples go down an elephant's throat slick-slick.

velagala, valuable. *velagala jívaratnamu vaccaṭé tsálunu; chilipi ráḷḷu taṭṭ eḍu v'unná phalamu yémi?* of valuable gems one is enough; what profits a basketful of worthless stones?

velaléni, priceless.

velavela, pale.

velayáli, dancing-girl, courtesan; from *vela,* price. (Cf. Lat. *meretrix,* which also refers to the earnings of the profession.)

velayuṭa, to appear. *ráti banḍa mída tsaccagá malachina Ráma pádamulu velasi y'unnavi,* the imprint of Rama's feet appears clearly on the rock.

veli, outcasting. *máló veli ané máṭa lédu,* in our caste there is no such thing as excommunication.

velicila, supine; also *vellacila.*

veligintsuṭa, to light. *baluḍici talli nacshatrálu tsúpist undenu; nacshatram ocaṭi ráli paḍenu. talli: ad émiṭó telisindá? báluḍu: Dévuḍu nippu-pulla veligistunnáḍu.* A mother was showing the stars to her boy; a shooting star fell. Mother: Do you know what that was? Boy: God lighting a match.

veliparatsuṭa, velipeṭṭuṭa, veliputstsuṭa, to publish, to reveal, to divulge. *vinnav anní viṣvasintsa vaddu, viṣvasinchinavi anní veliputstsa vaddu,* don't believe all you hear or divulge all you believe; also *vellaḍi chéyuṭa, vellaḍintsuṭa.*

velivéyuṭa, to outcaste, to excommunicate. *manam andaramú chéri, víḷḷaló condarini culamló nunchi velivésté, andaru bágu paḍutáru,* it will be a good thing for all of us if we all join and turn a few of them out of caste.

veliyuṭa, to stop (especially of rain). *vána velisindi,* the shower is over.

vella, whiteness, white.

vellacila, vellacittala, supine, on your back. *vellacila parunḍi v'ummi vésté mukham mída paḍutundi,* lie on your back and spit at heaven and your spittle will fall back on your face (blasphemy recoils on the blasphemer). (The Italians have the same proverb: *chi sputa in su, lo sputo gli torna sul viso,* if you spit upwards your spittle falls back on your face.) *eccirintsa póyi vellacila paḍḍáḍ aṭa,* going up to mock and falling on your back (the biter bit).

vellaḍi, publicity.

vellaḍi chéyuṭa, vellaḍintsuṭa, to publish, to disclose; also *veliparatsuṭa, velipeṭṭuṭa, veliputstsuṭa.*

veḷḷagoṭṭuṭa, to drive out; from *veḷḷuṭa,* to go, and *coṭṭuṭa,* to beat.

vellani, white.

vellasunna, whitewash.

vellavéyuṭa, to whitewash.

vellipóvuṭa, to go away.

veḷḷivatstsuṭa, to go and come, to come back. *veḷḷivastánu,* I will come back (see you again), is the polite way of taking leave; *sarcasucu tanḍri coḍuculu veḷḷivachchiri. tanḍri: cótulu, cuccalu, simhalu, pedda pululu cúḍá anta anucuvugá unṭé, nuvvu nénu chep-pin aṭṭu vin accara lédá? coḍucu: váṭi máddirigá nannu cúḍá penchité, aṭlágé vinṭánu.* Father and son were coming back from the circus. Father: When monkeys, dogs, lions, and tigers too, are so obedient shouldn't you obey me? Son: If you train me as they are trained, I shall obey like them.

vellulli, garlic (the white onion).

veḷḷuṭa, to go. *venaccu veḷḷité tannu,*

mundu vasté póṭu, behind a kick, in front a stab (between the devil and the deep sea); *mánéjaru: yeccaḍici veḷḷut unnáu? gumástá: cshavaram chéyintsucoḍánici. mánéjaru: áfísu taimló yenducu veḷḷ ále? tarváta veḷḷa rádá? gumástá: áfísu ṭaimló nácu venṭrucalu perugutunṭai.* Manager: Where are you off to? Clerk: To get a shave. Manager: Why should you go in office hours? Can't you go after? Clerk: My beard grows in office hours. *póvuṭa* also means 'to go', but it has other meanings as well.

velluva, flood.

velugu, fence. The last part of Tinnevelly is the same word. *velugudaḍi,* fence; *veluguvéyuṭa,* to fence, to enclose.

veluguṭa, to shine. *oca prayánicuḍu: manam dáṭi vachchina úru palleṭ úr ainá dípálu bágá velugut unn aṭṭ ai. renḍó prayánicuḍu: dípálu cáv ayyá, iḷḷu cálut unnai.* First wayfarer: Though the village we have just passed is a small one, the street lamps seem to be burning bright. Second wayfarer: That's not lamps, Sir. The houses are on fire.

velupala, outside.

velupaṭi, extrinsic, outside (adjective).

veluturu, light. *länṭaru paruvu cósam gáni, veluturu cósam lédu,* (the municipal councillor) has a street lantern (opposite his house) for the glory of it, not for light.

vembaḍi, behind, through, around, with. *úri vembaḍini pettanamucu bailudérinánu,* I started for a stroll round the town; *ná vembaḍi vachchinádu,* he came with me; *úḷḷa vembaḍi tirugutsunnáru,* they wander from village to village; *ná chénu vembaḍi chénu,* the field that runs with mine; *dáni vembaḍi padyamu,* the next verse; *áyana póyina vembaḍiné,* directly after he went away.

vembaḍintsuṭa, to follow.

venḍi, silver. *Venḍiconḍa,* Kailasa (the silver mountain). Kuvera, god of wealth, lives there; at the entrance there is a golden gate and it is covered with lovely woods, rivers, lakes, and caves.

venna, butter. *venna mudda,* a pat of butter; *venna daggira untsuconi nétici taḍumuconn aṭṭu,* looking for ghee when you have butter (too lazy to melt the butter yourself); *venna peṭṭité minga léḍu, vélu peṭṭité carava léḍu,* give him butter he can't swallow it, give him your finger he can't bite it (of demureness: butter won't melt in his mouth). (The French *Saint-nitouche.*) *vennaló venṭruca tísin aṭṭu,* taking a hair out of butter (nothing easier, as easy as shelling peas).

vennela, moonlight; from *veluguṭa,* to shine, and *nela,* moon. *vennela,* light of the moon, and *yenḍa,* light or heat of the sun, are used in Telugu where we talk of the moon or the sun. They do not speak of a scorching sun or of a bright moon, but of scorching sunheat and bright moonlight. Sun and moon to them are rather gods than lights. *aḍavi cáchina vennela,* the moon shining in the jungle, is a common expression for wasted efforts; *chícaṭi connáḷḷu, vennela connáḷḷu,* the dark days are succeeded by the moonlight days, means much the same as our ''tis a long lane that has no turning'.

vennemuca, backbone, spine; from *vennu,* back, and *emuca,* bone.

vennu, back. *vípu* is commoner.

vennu, ear of corn; also *canci. mannu veḷḷacunḍá dunnité, vennu veḷḷacunḍá panḍunu,* if the ploughman does not throw up the soil well, the crop will throw out no ears.

vennupúsa, vertebra of the backbone; from *vennu,* back, and *púsa,* bead, joint.

venṭa, with, behind, following.

venṭabaḍuṭa, to follow; from *venṭa,* behind, and *paḍuṭa,* to fall, to be.

venṭané, at once. *dyananu venṭané dayya cheyyum ani cheppu,* tell (the visitor) to step in at once. *Lacshmayya: sanvatsaram cindaṭa tísuconna bácini venṭané iyyum ani ninnu ákhari sári aḍugutunnánu, ica aḍaganu. Rámayya: ica mída aḍagan ann anducu nácu tsála santósham.* Doe: I am asking you for the last time for the money you promised last year to pay back at once. Roe: I am pleased to hear you won't ask again. *yazamáni: nénu tsálá maṭalu máṭláḍanu; oca vélu cadilisṭé nuvvu venṭané rá vále. cotta naucaru: nénu tsálá máṭalu máṭláḍan anḍi; nénu talacái áḍisté rán ani miru anucondi.* Mistress: I am a woman of few words; if I move my finger that means you must come at once. New servant: I am a man of few words, madam; if I shake my head that means I shan't come. *ocaḍu: má césu yém aind anḍi? vacílu: nyáyam gelichindi. ocaḍu: aité venṭané appilu cheyyanḍi.* Client: What has happened in our case? Lawyer: Justice has been done. Client: Then appeal at once.

venṭa peṭṭuconuṭa, to take with one. *pedda múcanu venṭa peṭṭuconi vastú v'unnáru,* they are coming with a big crowd behind them.

venṭruca, hair. *venṭruca mátram,* I don't care a hang; *vennaló venṭruca tísin aṭṭu,* like removing a hair from butter (nothing easier).

venuca, after, behind. It also means 'before' (behind in time); the time before is *venucaṭi sári*; *venucaṭi sangatulu* means both former particulars and subsequent particulars. But 'behind' is the root meaning, and *venucaṭi cáḷḷu* can only mean 'hind legs'. *dinini ná venuca ná coḍuculu anubhavistáru,* my sons will enjoy this after me; *mundu venuca tsúchi vídhi dáṭa valenu,* look before and behind when you cross the road; *mundu venuca tsútsucunḍá,* not knowing which way to turn; *mundarici vasté goyyi, venaccu póté nuyyi,* pit in front, well behind (Scylla and Charybdis); *venaccu veḷḷité tannu, mundu vasté póṭu,* kick behind, stab in front (between the devil and the deep sea); *ná cóṭu venuca muḷḷu gutstsucunnai,* thorns have got into my coat behind.

venucala, behind; also *venucála.*

venucatíyuṭa, to draw back, to hold back. *rúpáyila cósam venuca tísté,* if you hold back because of the money.

venucála, behind; also *venucala. nénu mitó vastánu, vanucála má banduvulu cúḍá vastáru,* I will come with you; our relations too are coming behind.

veragu, amazement.

veragupaḍuṭa, to be amazed, to be bewildered.

verasi, total. *verasi núru rúpáyilu,* total one hundred rupees; *ikha panasa tonalacu nálug análu, araṭi paḷḷacu nálug análu, verasi yenimid análu rá valenu,* there are still four annas to come for jack-fruit pips and four annas for plantains, total eight annas.

veratsuṭa, to be afraid. *ná nóṭici verachi,* afraid of what I may say; *lócánici verachi,* afraid of what the world may say.

verri, madness, mad, silly. *verri veyyi vidhálu,* there are a thousand forms of madness; *verri paḍutsu,* a silly girl; *vélamverri,* auction madness (silly extravagance); *verri tala noppi,* a maddening headache; *verriváḍu,* a madcap; *yevari verri várici ánandamu,* every fool rejoices in his folly (fools laugh at their own sport. The French proverb is nearer; *à chaque fou plaît sa marotte,* every madman likes his hobby).

verribágulu, fool, simpleton. *musalaina verribágula váḍu lágu canapaḍuṭú v'unnáḍu,* the old man looks a bit mad.

verritanamu, madness.

verriváḍu, madman. *verriváḍi chéti ráyi,* a stone in a madman's hand (put not a naked sword in a madman's hand).

verriyáspaṭri, lunatic asylum (*áspaṭri* is the English 'hospital').

vetacuṭa, to search; also *vetucuṭa.*

vetstsamu, expense. Corrupt Skt. for *visarjanam. jamábandiló v'udyógasthuḷu vetstsála nimittam cómaṭlacu vrásé chíṭlu chitramgá v'untavi; yevaric á vastuvulu cá valenó yeccaḍa péru v'unḍadu; yevaric í chiṭlu vrásinárό á cómaṭi péru v'unḍadu; sari gadá cinda cávalasinavári dascat ainá v'unḍadu,* the orders officials write at jamabandi for their expenses are really quaint; they don't show for whom the things are wanted nor the name of the trader from whom they are ordered; they don't even bear the signature of the official who orders.

vetstsani, vetstsa, hot.

vetstsapeṭṭuṭa, to heat up.

vetstsapeṭṭuṭa, to spend; from *vetstsamu*, expense.

veṭṭi, unpaid labour. Corrupt Skt. for *vistich*. The unpaid labour of the hill-tribes in the Agencies is called *veṭṭi*. *veṭṭi chácirí*, unpaid drudgery.

veṭṭiváḍu, the lowest of the village menials, once a public slave; later he was given land for subsistence; now he is a paid servant of the Government; he is usually a pariah.

vetucuṭa, to look for. *adi yenta veticiná canapaḍadu*, I have hunted high and low for it but can't find it; *vetucupóyina tíga cáḷḷacu tsuṭṭuconnaṭṭu*, he found the creeper he was looking for twined round his legs (looking for what is in front of your nose).

veyéla ? why a thousand (words), in short; a common expression in newspapers when the writer can't think of any more arguments against British rule or whatever he is arguing about.

veyi, veyyi, a thousand; the plural is *vélu*. The word is also written *véyi*. *oca abaddhamu cammaḍánacu veyyi abaddhálu cá valenu*, a thousand lies are wanted to cover one (one lie makes many; in French *qui dit un mensonge en dit cent*, who tells one lie tells a hundred; in Italian, *una bugia tira l'altra*, one lie draws another after it). *verri veyyi vidhálu*, madness takes a thousand forms; *veyyi áulu galavárici vacaṭi tannuconi póté yémiṭi ?* if you have a thousand cows, it does not matter if one kicks (the rich man hasn't all his eggs in one basket).

veyyuṭa, an auxiliary verb; *véyuṭa* is the commoner form.

vécuva, dawn.

Védamu, Véda, the Veda or Hindu Bible. Skt., from root *vid*, to know. *Vissanna cheppinadi Véda*, what Vissanna says is gospel.

védana, pain; also *védhamu*. Skt.

véda ṣáṣtriyamu, the philosophical part of the Veda.

véda vácyamu, Scripture text. *guruvu nippu tsallagá v'unṭund anṭé tacshanam Véda vácyam lágu namma valenu*, if your religious teacher says fire is cold you must at once believe it as gospel truth.

védántamu, the Upanishads, which expound the Veda. *védántam upadéṣintsuṭa*, to expound the Upanishads; *védántamu* is also in particular the Advaita system.

védánti, expounder of the Upanishads or of the Advaita system.

védha, a learned man. Skt.

védhamu, pain; also *védana*. Skt.

védhintsuṭa, to torment. Skt.

védi, védíca, platform. *viváhavédica*, the platform on which bride and bridegroom sit at a marriage.

véḍi, heat, hot. *vénniḷḷu* is the usual term for hot water. *véḍilóné cáryam ságintsa valenu*, strike while the iron is hot.

véḍimi, heat.

véḍuca, display, show, joy. *ninḍá véḍucagá unḍevéru*, they were very merry; *ninḍá véḍucagá zarigindi*, it went off with much pomp.

véḍucapaḍuṭa, to be happy.

véḍuconuṭa, to beg, to entreat, to solicit; in fact, what petitioners do.

végamu, speed. Skt.

végiramu, quick. Skt. But *végiramugá* being too long, what is actually said is *bégi*. In books they write it at full length. *tahaṣṣíludárugáru mí y'inṭici vachchi mimmu pilutsucuni ramm annáru, végiramugá ranḍi*, the tahsildar is waiting at your house and told me to call you; come quickly, sir.

végirapaḍuṭa, to be in a hurry.

végirapáṭu, haste.

végu, véguváḍu, végulaváḍu, spy. *jágratagá v'unḍa valenu; itaḍu mana záḍa tiyyaḍánici pampinchina véguváḍ ai v'unḍa vatstsunu*, we must be on our guard; he may be a spy sent on our track.

véguṭa, to be fried; often used metaphorically, when it means to endure or to suffer.

véḷa, time, day. Skt. Vulgarly *váḷa*. *í véḷa* or *ivéḷa*, to-day; *ocavéḷa, vacavéḷa*, perhaps; *ganṭa véḷa*, one hour's time; *adi mácu iváḷa páṭham*, that is our lesson for to-day.

véḷacu, in time. *Hinduvulaló idi y'oca durácháram vistárangá v'unnadi; yeppuḍu véḷacu ráru*, the bad habit of never being in time is widespread among Hindus.

vélamu, auction. Hindustani. Vulgarly *yálam*. *vélamverri*, auction madness (extravagance); *váni sottunacu vélamu vachchinadi*, his property was brought to the hammer.

vélamu paḍuṭa, velamu véyuṭa, to sell by auction.

vélavéyuṭa, to hang (transitive).

véḷácólamu, ridicule. *i y'Inglishu tsaduvucunévâḷḷacu mamalni tsústé véḷácólanici v'unṭundi*, we are a laughing-stock to these people who have learnt English; *úricé míru véḷácólánic annáru?* is it only your joke?

véláḍuṭa, to hang, to dangle (intransitive). *veḷḷipomm anṭé tsúru paṭṭuconi véláḍin aṭṭu*, like hanging on to the eaves when told to go away (sticking like a leech).

véḷḷu, roots, plural of *véru*; or fingers, plural of *vélu*.

vélpu, god (of the minor sort). *cóṭi vélpulu*, the 10,000,000 minor gods; *vélpuṭdu*, the cow that grants all wishes.

vélu, thousands; plural of *veyyi*.

vélu, finger, toe; also *vrélu*, *boṭanavélu* is the thumb or great toe; *chiṭicini vélu* the little finger or little toe. *renḍu véla minchina*, two fingers better (than some one else); *vélu cósuconná sunnamu peṭṭaḍu*, he will not even give you a bit of lime for a cut finger (a heartless man); *ná vélu putstsuconi ná canné poḍichin aṭṭu*, using my own finger to poke me in the eye (turning the tables in an argument); *amarchinaḍánṭló attagáru vélu peṭṭinadi*, the mother-in-law put her finger into the dish the daughter-in-law had prepared (all the credit and none of the work); *véluviḍichina*, all but (separated by a finger); *manam andaramunu daggara bandhuvulamu; mí talligári ménatta y'alluḍu má ménamámagárici sácshátṭugá véluviḍichina ménatta coḍucu*, we are all near relations; your mother's aunt's son-in-law is my uncle's all but own aunt's son; *má ménamámagári saviti tallici vaca véluviḍichina pinatalli manamaḍini anṭáḍu*, he calls himself the grandson of my maternal uncle's stepmother's all but younger aunt.

véluṭa, to hang (intransitive); also *vréluṭa*.

vémchéyuṭa, to visit, to deign to come, to condescend to go. Skt. Short for *vijayam chéyuṭa*. *má inṭici vém chéstárá?* will you honour me with a visit? Also *vichchéyuṭa*.

véni, a channel. Skt. Used in books.

vénníḷḷu, hot water; from *véḍi*, hot, and *níḷḷu*, water. *vénníḷḷacu tsanníḷḷu, tsanníḷḷacu vénníḷḷu*, add cold water to hot, hot to cold (to get it just right); *vénníḷḷacú, vésangici yenta tsalava, nicú nácú anta tsalava*, the coolness (friendship) between us is that of hot water or the hot weather (we hate one another like poison). Heat not being pleasant in India, friendship and love are in Telugu metaphor not ardour but coolness. Our warm friendship is their cool friendship; may your mother's womb be cool, and similar expressions, are blessings; may you be hot is a curse.

vépa, the margosa or neem tree. *bápalu tappiná vépulu tappavu*, though the brahmin's word fail, the margosa will not (the flowering of margosas is supposed to mean that the harvest will not fail).

vépuṭa, to fry. *vépuconi tinuṭa*, to fry and eat is common in the sense of to harass or, as we say, to eat (he won't eat you); *tsaduvu lén appuḍé paṭṭa paggamulu léni strílu tsaduvu cúḍá unna yedala bottigá nett ecci magalanu vépuconi tinará?* when without education our women put the bit between their teeth, if they are once educated, they will throw their husbands outright and trample them beneath their feet (fry and eat them).

véré, apart, specially, more. *véré n'aḍagan accara lédu*, so much for that (I need not ask more questions; the problem does not merit discussion).

véroca, another.

véru, difference, other.

véru, root; plural *véḷḷu*. *cherucu típi ani véḷḷató namala vatstsuná?* because the sugar-cane is sweet, should you munch it root and all? (of greedy people; greediness bursts the bag).

vérupaḍuṭa, vérupóvuṭa, to go apart, to differ.

vérupáṭu, separation, difference, enmity.

vérupurugu, worm at the root. *níti vrücshánici vérupurugu lágu,* like a worm at the root of the tree of morality.

vérusenagalu, ground-nut. Used in the plural as usual with names of crops.

véruvérugá, separately, severally.

vésangi, vésavicálamu, summer, the weather inadequately known in South India as the HOT (April, May, June). One of the six *rütuvulu* or seasons lasting two months each. *vésavi* or *gríshmam* comes between *vasantam,* spring, and *varsham,* the rains; it lasts till the rains break some time in June.

vésaruṭa, to be wearied, to be disgusted. *visigi vésari,* worn out.

véshacáḍu, actor; from *vésham,* disguise.

véshamu, costume, disguise. Skt. *Crüshna vésham vésinádu,* he acted Krishna; *véshál anni grásálacé,* all garbs (occupations) are for a living; *cucca véshamu vésté, moragacundá valla cádu,* disguise yourself as a dog and you needs must bark (in for a penny in for a pound).

véṣya, dancing-girl, courtesan. Skt., from *véṣamu,* brothel. *véṣya móham,* venal love.

véṭa, the chase; *véṭacáḍu,* hunter; *véṭacucca,* hunting dog.

véṭanamu, wage. Skt. The ordinary words are *cúli* and *jítamu.*

véṭapótu, ram; also *poṭṭélu.*

véṭáḍuṭa, to hunt.

vétámu, let us do, throw, &c.; a common form of *véstámu,* from *véyuṭa. páchicalu tíscrá, vacca áṭa vétámu,* bring the dice and we will play a game.

vétsuṭa, to fry; metaphorically, to harass, to torment.

vétta, scholar. Skt., from root *vid,* to know. *itaḍu mahá ṣástravetta lágunané v'unnáḍu,* he seems to be a great scripture scholar; *manchi mantravetta,* a man with a good knowledge of charms and incantations.

véṭu, blow; from *véyuṭa. véṭucu véṭu, máṭacu máṭa,* a blow for a blow, a word for a word.

véṭuláḍuṭa, to come to blows, to fight.

véyi, thousand; more commonly *veyyi.*

véyintsuṭa, to cause to throw, &c.; causal of *véyuṭa.*

véyuṭa, to throw, to put, to shut, to plant; also an intensitive auxiliary; it is sometimes added twice. *lág-és-éi* means little more than *lágu,* but you will usually stimulate the punkah-puller with the longer form; it impresses him more; *talupu vései,* completely shut the door; *dánini chempa mída debba vésináḍu,* he slapped her cheek; *guḍḍanu balla mída vésináḍu,* he spread the table-cloth; *ráyi vésináḍu,* he threw a stone; *rátri antá nénu reppa véya lédu,* I did not close a lid all night; *múta véyi,* put the lid on; *gantalu véyuṭa,* to jump about; *jíni véyuṭa,* to saddle; *praṣna véyuṭa,* to ask a question; *lecca véyuṭa,* to do one's accounts; *vrási véyuṭa,* to write off one's accounts; *cúta véyuṭa,* to utter a cry; *gáli véstundi,* the wind blows; *cósivéyuṭa,* to cut off; *tósivéyuṭa,* to push away; *paḍavéyuṭa,* to knock down; *pandem véyuṭa,* to lay a bet; *tini véyuṭa,* to eat up; *chéséstámu,* we shall finish off; *vachéṣámu,* we have come, here we are; *cheṭṭu vésinaváḍ ocaḍu, dáni phalam anubhavinchinaváḍ ocaḍu,* one man plants the tree, another enjoys the fruit (*sic vos non vobis*); *vésindi vaca gantu, viriginadi vaca cálu,* one leap leapt, one leg broken (loss at first venture); *cucca véshamu vésté, moragacundá valla cádu,* disguise yourself as a dog and you needs must bark (in for a penny in for a pound); *áu oca léganu vésindi,* the cow has dropped a calf; *uttarálu pósṭuló vésává?* have you posted the letters? *Lacshmayya: ná peḷḷáni carra tísuconi coṭṭánu; nannu cóṭló peṭṭi táḷam veyyenḍi. pólisu sárjenṭu: coṭṭité tsachchi póyindá? Lacshmayya: tsáva lédu; nannu coṭṭaḍánici parugettuconi vastundi.* Lacshmayya: I took a stick and beat my wife; lock me up in your cell and turn the key. Police Sergeant: Did you beat her to death? Lacshmayya: No, she is running after me to beat me. *ocaḍu: Lacshmayyacu tsústé nácu záli véstundi. incóḍu: yenduçu? ocaḍu: Lacshmayya yéḍu bháshalu nértsuconnáḍu; chésucunna peḷḷám ataḍini occa máṭ ainá maṭláḍan iyyadu.* First Hindu: When I think of Lacshmayya I feel pity. Second Hindu: How so? First Hindu: Lacshmayya has learnt seven languages but the wife he has married won't allow him to speak a word in any of them.

vi-, prefix meaning (1) apart and (2) great. Skt.

vibhactamu, divided. Skt. *avibhacta* and *vibhacta cuṭumbamu* are an undivided and a divided family. *míru vibhactulá avibhactulá?* is your family divided or not?

vibhactuḍu, a divided member of a family. *ná tammuḍu nénu vibhactamulu,* my brother and I are divided.

vibhajanamu, division, allotment. Skt.

vibhajintsuṭa, to divide, allocate. Skt.

vibhavamu, wealth, grandeur. Skt. *vittamu coddí vibhavamu, vidya coddí vinayamu,* the wealthier the grander, the more learned the humbler.

vibhágamu, division, apportionment. Skt.

vibhágintsuṭa, to apportion. Skt.

vibhúti, white ashes with which Saivites smear themselves. From the Skt. in which the word means blessedness, omnipotence, &c. *míváḍu vibhúti peṭṭadu; monna búḍsula zóḍu toḍuccuni, mokhánni boṭṭu lécundá, paṭṭa pagalu vídhiló nunchi veḷḷutsu v'unṭé nénu caḷḷárá tsúchánu,* your boy does not plaster his face with ashes; the other day I saw him with my own eyes going down the street in full daylight with boots on and without a castemark on his face.

vicalamu, confused, defective. Skt. *vicalatvamu,* confusion; *vicalánguḍu,* a cripple; *vicalitamu,* decayed.

vicasintsuṭa, to flower, to blow, to bloom. Skt.

vicaṭamu, changed, deformed. Skt.

vicáramu, change, deformation, disease, ugliness. Skt. *cáma vicáramuló n'ai,* being deformed by lust; *lóna vicáram, baiṭa srüngáram,* fair without, foul within (a whited sepulchre).

vicásamu, flowering, blooming. Skt. *ní mukha vicásamu tsústé nácu santóshamgá v'unnadi,* I am delighted at the sight of the bloom on your face.

vichháragrastuḍu, plunged in grief. Skt., from *vichháram,* grief, and *grastuḍu,* swallowed in. *nénu mí cáḷḷa mída paḍi cshamápana córuçunṭánu; cábaṭṭi ná y'andu daya v'unchi vichháragrastuḍanai v'unna nannu santósha peṭṭa valen ani marí véḍucunṭú v'unnánu,* I fall at your feet and beg for forgiveness. Have mercy on me. I pray you raise this afflicted one from sorrow to joy.

vicháramu, sorrow. Skt. *gorre yéḍisté tóḍélucu vicháramá?* does the wolf grieve when the sheep cries? *peddamanishi: venuca ninnu tsúchin appuḍu, táguḍu alaváṭu léd ani cheppité, nácu santósham vachchindi; ippuḍu ninnu tsústé, tági v'unn anducu vicháram vést unnadi. táginaváḍu: mícu vicháram vésté, nác ippuḍu santóshamgá v'unnad anḍi.* Gentleman: When I saw you before and you told me you took nothing I rejoiced. Seeing you drunk now I feel sad. Drunken man: You may be feeling sad but I am feeling happy.

vichárana, investigation. Skt. The usual word for police investigations, judicial inquiries, and so on.

vichárintsuṭa, to inquire. The answer to petitioners is *vichháristánu,* I shall inquire. *peddamanishi: ní pér émi? nuvvu yevari pillaváḍivi? báluḍu: míru canuccó valen anṭé renḍu márgál unnai. peddamanishi: yémiṭivi? báluḍu: míru úhintsucondi léca vichárintsanḍi.* Gentleman: What is your name? Whose little boy are you? Boy: There are two ways of finding out. Gentleman: What two ways? Boy: Guess or inquire.

vichchéyuṭa, to pay a visit; short for *vijayam chéyuṭa;* also *vémchéyuṭa.*

vichitramu, wonder. Skt. *adi vichitramgá v'unnadi,* that is strange.

vicrayamu, sale. Skt. In common use.

vicrayintsuṭa, to sell. Skt. The commoner word is *ammuconuṭa*.
vicrūtamu, deformed. Skt. *vicrūta vigrahamu*, a deformed figure; *vicrūtamaina sanghaṭanamu*, a ludicrous situation.
vicrūṭi, deformed, deformation. Skt.
viḍanáḍuṭa, to abandon; from *viḍuṭa*. *nannu viḍanáḍi pó bócu!* do not abandon me!
viḍapaḍuṭa, to break loose.
viḍatíyuṭa, to pull apart.
viḍḍúramu, stubbornness, indiscipline. *ippuḍu í mála prabhutvam múlamgá anni viḍḍúrálu puḍutú v'unnavi*, every sort of indiscipline prevails now on account of this pariah Government.
vidéhamu, bodiless. Skt., from *vi-*, apart, and *déham*, body.
vidéṣamu, foreign country. Skt., from *vi-*, apart, and *déṣam*, country.
vidéṣi, foreigner. Skt.
vidhamu, way, sort, form. Skt. *verri veyyi vidhálu*, madness takes a thousand forms; *oca vidhamaina yuddhamu*, a sort of war; *nívu yenni vidhála cheppiná vinaḍu*, whatever you may say he won't listen.
vidhava, widow. Skt.; often used as a term of abuse; more commonly *vedhava*. *naḍi vayasuló n'unna vidhavalu cáma bádhacu lóbaḍuṭa áscharyamá?* is it any wonder if widows in the flower of their age yield to the goad of lust?
vidhavátvamu, widowhood. Skt.
vidhánamu, ordinance, rubric. Skt. *púja vidhánamu*, the order of religious service; *vidhi vidhánamu*, the dictates of duty; *gnyánópadéṣam(upadéṣam) onarchi, Ṣrí Crūshnuni mantram upadéṣinchi, á dévun áradhintsu pújá vidhánamunacu bhódhinchiri*, they gave him religious training especially in the Krishna rubric and service.
vidháyacamu, prescribed, one's duty. Skt., from *vidhi*, duty. *chésucunna bhárya curúpi ainá, múrkhurál ainá, mari yeṭuvanti lópam galadi ainá, yélaḍam vidháyacam*, it is one's duty to enjoy one's wedded wife even if she is ugly or stupid or has anything else wrong with her.
vidhéyata, obedience. Skt. *vidhéyatulú maryádulu anni nérpa valenu*, you must inculcate all obedience and manners.
vidhéyuḍu, an obedient man. Skt.
vidhi, prescribed duty, fate. Skt. *ocaḍu: itarulu páḍ autú v'unṭé tsúştú v'úrucóvaḍam mánava dharmam cádu. incóḍu: dharmam cáca póté bhúbháram antá y'ippuḍu míru tírustárá? ocaḍu: tírtsa galiginá, tírtsa léca póyiná, sádhyam ain anta maṭṭucu prayatnam cheyyaḍam manac andaracú vidhi.* First Hindu: It is not right in all humanity to acquiesce in others spoiling their lives. Second Hindu: It may not be right but are you going to shoulder the whole world's burden straight away? First Hindu: Whether we can or not it is the bounden duty of all of us to do our best. *vyddhici mandu v'unnadi gáni, vidhici mandu v'unnadá?* there is physic for fever but is there physic for fate? *váḍu chellintsaca vidhi léḍu*, he cannot choose but pay.
vidhiléca, without alternative. *áyana veḷḷina tarváta bógamváḷḷu vasté, madhya léchi póté bág unḍad ani, vidhi léca muḷḷalló cúrtsun aṭṭu cúrtsunḍéváḍu*, after he had gone to the nautch and the dancing-girls had appeared, thinking it would not be right to get up and go away in the middle, he could not but sit on like a man sitting on thorns.
vidhintsuṭa, to order, to prescribe, to inflict (a punishment). Skt. *Bráhmana séva chésucóvaḍam mí cula dharmamu; á pani mícu Brahma Dévuḍu vidhinchináḍu*, worship of brahmins is your caste duty ordained of God.
vidhuruḍu, widower. Skt.
vidhyuctamu, ordained. Skt., from *vidhi*, duty, and *ucti*, speech.
viḍi-, prefix meaning 'loose'. Separate, odd (of a pair), spare, single, unemployed, &c. *viḍimanishi*, a spare man, an unemployed man, a single man; *viḍimutyamulu*, loose pearls; *viḍipúsa*, an odd bead; *viḍikhanḍuva*, a single cloth (of cloths usually sold in pairs); *viḍiáculu*, loose leaves (not stitched); *viḍiménu*, naked.
viḍichipeṭṭuṭa, to release.

viḍidi, halt, halting-place.
viḍikháidá, simple (loose) imprisonment, as opposed to *caṭhinakhdidd,* rigorous imprisonment. These are the technical terms used in court.
viḍigá, loosely, separately, singly.
viḍipintsuconuṭa, to escape.
viḍipintsuṭa, to release.
viditamu, known. Skt. *vidituḍu,* a celebrity.
viḍiviḍigá, in severalty, separately.
viḍiyanáḍu, the second day after the full moon. Skt., from *dvitiya,* second, dropping the initial *d.*
viḍiyuṭa, to halt. *aranyamuló viḍisi unḍenu,* he had halted in the jungle.
viḍudala, release. Also in the legal sense; *viḍudala patram,* release deed.
viḍupu, release, almsgiving. *viḍupari,* a liberal man.
viḍuṭa, to quit. *í bádha tsústé voccocc appuḍu déham viḍité bágá v'unṭund ani tóstundi,* the pain sometimes makes me wish myself dead; *viḍuvum anṭé pámucu cópam, paṭṭum anṭé cappacu cópam,* say let go and you offend the snake, say hold on and you offend the frog (it is hard to please all parties).
viḍutsuṭa, to leave, to abandon, to stop, to give up, to let go, to let loose, to discharge. *vána viḍichenu,* the rain has stopped; *mûtramunu viḍichenu,* he made water; *dayyamu viḍichinadi,* the devil has left him; *chéniló dunu méya viḍichináḍu,* he let the cow loose to graze in the field; *áháramu viḍichináḍu,* he gave up eating; *pránamu viḍichináḍu,* he gave up the ghost; *bánamu viḍintsuṭa,* to discharge a firework; *cumártenu attagári y'inṭa viḍichináḍu,* he left his daughter with her husband (at her mother-in-law's house); *dinamu viḍichchina dinamu,* every other day (leaving out a day); *marmam viḍichi chepputánu,* I will say without reserve.
viḍuvacunḍá, without stopping, persistently.
vidúramu, very far. Skt., from *vi-,* very, and *dúram,* far.
vidúshacuḍu, jester, especially the jester in plays. *Séḍricu vidúshacuḍu v'unna Vamba,* Wamba, Cedric's jester.
vidvámsuḍu, a learned man. Skt.
vidya, learning. Skt. *abhyásam cúsu vidhya,* practice is an inferior (or easier) learning (practice makes perfect); *cóṭi vidyálu cúṭi coracé,* all arts are for a living; *vittamu coddi vibhavam, vidya coddi vinayam,* prosperity is proud, learning is lowly; *vinayam lóca vaṣyamu, vidya rája vaṣyamu,* the meek inherit the earth, learning subjects kings; *vidyágandhamu,* tincture of learning; *jana samányamu vidyágandhamu n'ondi, cannu terachina gáni, mana déṣamu manchi sthitici rá néradu,* our country cannot improve unless the common people get some tincture of knowledge and open their eyes; *ayyacu vidhyá lédu, ammacu garvamú lédu,* ignorant husband, ignoble wife; *vidyacu bhúshanamu vinayamu,* modesty is the ornament of learning.
vidyavantuḍu, learned man. Skt.
vidyálayamu, school. Skt., from *vidya,* learning, and *álayam,* home. The common words are *iscúlu* and *baḍi. páṭhaṣála* is another Skt. word in use.
vidyárthi, pupil, schoolboy, student. Skt. *vidyárthi: vidyárthulacu cávalasina baṭṭalu iccaḍa dorucutavá? angaḍiváḍu: áḍucóḍánici panici vachchévá tsaduvucóḍánici panici vachchévá?* Schoolboy: Do you sell clothes for schoolboys? Shopkeeper: Clothes to play in or clothes to work in?
vidyuttu, lightning. Skt. The common word is *nerupu.* This is used in coining new terms such as *vidyuchchacti* (*vidyuttu* with *ṣacti,* power) for electricity.
vigatamu, gone. Skt., from *vi-,* apart, and root *ga-,* to go. *vigatajívuḍu,* deceased; *vigatáṣuḍu,* in despair; *vigatapragnyuḍu,* witless.
vighátamu, impediment; also *vighnamu.* Skt. *dánici vighátamu taṭaschinchedu pacshamuna,* if any impediment occurs.
vighnamu, impediment; also *vighátamu.* Skt. *mana panici vighnam chéyuvár evvaru unḍaru,* there will be no one to interfere with our enterprise; *nénu y'í cáryánici vighnálu peḍutánu,* I will put obstacles in the way of it.

Vighnéṣvaruḍu, the God Ganesa. Skt. He is the god that removes *vighnálu*, hindrances; the belly god with an elephant's trunk; schoolboys are among his chief devotees; *eluca Vighnéṣvaruḍi váhanam*, Ganesa rides on a rat.

vignyána, the thinking subject, thought (in philosophy). Skt. In idealist philosophy *álaya* or *múla vignyána* is the original store of thought, *vipáca vignyána* developed thought.

vignyánamu, learning. Skt., intensitive form of *gnyánamu*.

vignyápanamu, petition. Skt. The common form is *vinnapamu*.

vigrahamu, figure, image, idol. Skt. *ívidedi bahu sundaramaina vigraham*, she has a very beautiful figure.

vihanganamu, bird. Skt. Used in books for *piṭṭa, pacshi*.

viharintsuṭa, to walk for pleasure or exercise. Skt.

viháramu, a walk for pleasure or exercise. Skt. *chiccucona chilucala vale svéchchá viháramunacu avacáṣam léca*, having, like a caged parrot, no chance of exercise.

vihitamu, prescribed. Skt., from *hitam*, right. *ṣástra vihitamaina*, prescribed by Scripture.

vihitamu, friendship. Skt., from *hitam*, good.

vihituḍu, friend. Skt.

-vihínamu, affix meaning 'without'. Skt., from *hínam*, abandoned. *buddhivihínuḍu*, witless; *vastravihínuḍu*, devoid of clothes.

vijayamu, victory. Skt. *Vijayanagaramu*, the old capital of the Telugus on the Tungabhadra is the town of victory.

vijituḍu, conquered. Skt. *vijiténdriyuḍu*, one who has conquered his senses (*indriyamulu*).

vijrumbhanamu, prosperity, bloom. Skt.

vijrumbhintsuṭa, to bloom, to flourish, to prosper. Skt.

vikhyáti, great renown. Skt. Intensitive of *khyáti*.

vilacshanamu, different, select, refined, handsome. Skt., from *lacshanamu*, quality.

vilambamu, delay. Skt.

vilapintsuṭa, to lament. Skt.

vilasitamu, shining. Skt. Used in books. *vivécavilasitamu*, shining with wisdom.

vilápamu, lamentation. Skt.

vilásamu, address on a letter; also *paivilásamu*.

vilásamu, dalliance. Skt.

vilóchanamu, seeing. Skt. A book word.

vilócintsuṭa, to see. Skt. A book word. *sulóchanamulu* (things for seeing well) is, however, the common word for spectacles.

villu, will (testament). English. *ocaḍu: mí ménamána villu vrásin appuḍu ninnu gnyápacam peṭṭuconnádá? incóḍu: peṭṭuconnáḍu; anducané nác ém ichchi pó lédu.* Doe: Did your uncle remember you when he wrote his will? Roe: He did; that's why he left me nothing.

villu, vilu, bow. *vill-ambulu*, bow and arrows.

vilucáḍu, archer.

viluva, price, valuable. *viluva chíra*, a valuable dress; *viluvagala*, valuable; *viluvaléni*, invaluable; *viluvanu baṭṭi*, ad valorem.

vimarṣa, examination. Skt. *oca cacshi vimarṣa mída tírmánam cheyyaḍam nyáyam cádu*, it is not just to decide after hearing one party (*audi alteram partem*).

vimarṣintsuṭa, to examine. Skt.

vimánamu, a god's car or chariot. *dévatalu ácáṣamuna ecci tirigeḍi rathamu*, the car in which the gods go about the sky. The newspapers use the word to translate 'aeroplane'.

vimóchanamu, liberation. Skt. Primarily a religious term referring to the liberation of the soul, but also used in other senses. *nácu bandha vimóchanam caligindi*, I have got rid of my bonds.

vimucti, liberation. Skt. *ná bádha vimucti chési nannu braticinchipáru*, you have freed me from my pain and given me new life; *cárágrüha vásulu bandha vimuctulugá chéya baḍiri*, the prisoners were released.

vimuctuḍu, one liberated. Skt. *mi*

vadda n'unna ḍabb antá y'í Svámi chétic ichchi pitrü rüna vimuctulu cá vatstsunu, by putting all the money on you into this svami's hand you may be relieved of your inherited load of sin.

vimukhuḍu, with averted face. Skt. It is the opposite of *abhimukhuḍu,* which means one with his face towards you, favourable.

vinayamu, humility. Skt. *itaḍu bahu nemmadigánu vinayamgánu máṭláḍutú v'unnáḍu,* he is speaking very gently and humbly; *vidyaçu bhúshanam vinayam,* modesty is the ornament of learning; *vinayam lóca vaṣyam, vidya rája vaṣyamu,* humility subdues the world, knowledge subdues kings. (Such is the Telugu proverb but in practice they try to persuade the wide-ruling kings of the I.C.S. by gifts, now restricted by the rules for the conduct of Government servants to those which grow on trees or flower plants; and by the same things, flowers and fruit rather than the humble and contrite heart, they try to persuade the gods (but *cuncta serviliter pro dominatione*).

viná, save, except, without. Skt.

vináṣamu, complete destruction. Skt. Intensified form of *náṣamu. vináṣa cálé, viparíta buddhi,* mad counsels go with calamitous times.

vináyintsuṭa, to except, to exempt. Skt.

vindu, banquet, feast, dinner-party. *vindu marnáḍu mandu,* physic after the feast; *vindú mandú múḍu púṭalu,* three doses and no more of medicines and meals (it is not polite to cadge more than three consecutive meals. The Italians have a similar proverb: *'ospite è come il pesce, in capo a tre giorni puzza,* fish and guests stink after three days); *vinducu piltsuṭa,* to invite to dinner.

vinici, hearing, from *vinuṭa,* to hear. *nácu aṭlá vinici,* I hear so.

viniyógamu, use. Skt. *upayógamu* is commoner.

viniyógintsuṭa, to use. Skt.

vinílamu, very black. Skt. Intensitive of *nílamu.* Used in books.

vinnapamu, petition. Corrupt Skt. for *vignyápanamu.*

vinódacaramu, pleasurable. Skt.

vinódamu, pleasure, amusement. Skt. *mí múlamgá mácu conta vinódam calugutú v'unnadi,* we get some amusement out of you.

vinta, a wonder, a marvel. *yenni vintal ainá puḍutavi,* any sort of marvel may happen; *cotta vinta, páta róta,* fresh news is a marvel, stale news disgusts.

vinuṭa, to hear, to heed. *chevulára vinuṭa,* to hear with one's own ears; *peddala máṭa vinu,* listen to the advice of your elders; *mí sambhásbana vini y'unḍunu gáni y'arthamunu grahimpa caligi y'unḍadu,* he may have heard your conversation without catching the meaning of it; *nívu mari yé máṭa cheppinanu vindunu gáni, í máṭa mátramu vinanu, ituvanṭi máṭalu yeppuḍunu nátó cheppa bócu,* I will listen to anything else you may have to say but of this I won't hear another word, never mention the subject again; *cani guḍḍi, vini chevuḍu,* eyes have they but they see not, ears have they but they hear not; *vinnavi anní viṣvasintsa vaddu,* don't believe all you hear; *ná máṭa conta vintárá?* will you just give me a hearing? *Lacshmayya: ninnu gurinchi anéca sangatulu vinnánu. Vencayya: ainá nuvvu ocaṭi ruzuvu cheyya lévulé.* Smith: I have heard lots of things about you. Jones: But you can't prove one of them. *Lacshmayya: má ammáyi tsaccagá sangítam páḍutundi; cávalisté vina vatstsunu ani penḍli coḍucutó cheppanḍi. Vencayya: penḍlicoḍucu chevuḍu, anduchéta mí ammáyi páḍiná atanu bhaya paḍadu.* Smith: My daughter sings nicely, perhaps her suitor would like to hear her; let him know. Jones: The suitor is deaf; so even if your daughter sings, that won't frighten him off.

viparítamu, odd, queer. Skt. *proddana mana vídhiló zarigina viparítam tsúchinárá?* did you see the strange thing that happened in our street this morning? *vináṣa cálé viparíta buddhi ann aṭlu, cheḍi póyé cálánici míc andarici y'iṭuvanṭi viparíta v'úhalu* *pudutu v'unnavi; y'í vedhava Y'Inglishu doratanam cáca póténá*, bad times mad ideas, as the saying is; in these bad times you all get such strange ideas; if it wasn't for this infernal British Government!

vipattu, misfortune. Skt. *Dévuḍu mana cuṭumbamunac émi vipattu techchi peṭṭut unnáḍó!* what a calamity God has inflicted on our family!

vipácamu, ripe. Skt. In the idealist philosophy *vipáca vignyánamu* is developed thought.

viphalamu, fruitless. Skt. *ná prayatnam viphalam aité*, if my enterpirse fails.

viplavamu, ruin. Skt.

vippuṭa, to open, to untie, to take off (clothes), to explain. *muḍivippuṭa*, to untie a knot; *cathanu vippuṭa*, to solve a riddle; *sangati vippi cheppináḍu*, he explained the matter; *paṭṭu chíra vippi, sádá chíré caṭṭucunnánu*, I have taken off my silk cloth and am wearing my ordinary cloth; *tsápa tsuṭṭa vippi arugu mída véyutsunnáḍu*, he is unrolling the mat and placing it on the pial.

vipruḍu, brahmin. Skt.

vipulamu, vast, ample. Skt. *vipulamugá varnintsuṭa*, to describe amply.

viracti, aversion, especially ascetic aversion, and so asceticism. Skt. *santánamu léni váni bratuc émi, bratuc ani vánici viracti puṭṭinadi*, thinking that life without children was no life, he began to feel aversion for life itself.

viragacátsuṭa, viragapanḍuṭa, to be in full bearing (of a tree) from *viraguṭa*, to burst. *á cheṭṭu viragacáchinadi*, that tree is in full bearing.

viragaḍa, release, relief; also *virugaḍa*, from *viraguṭa*, to be broken. *í jamábandí yeppuḍu viragaḍ autundó cáni, grámamló bahu allarigá v'unnadi; bantrótuvaḷḷu v'úri mída paḍi y'íḍigavánḷa iḷḷalónu, tsácalivánḷa y'iḷḷalónu dúri, cóḍipiṭṭalanú cúragáyalanú balavantamgá coṭṭi láccuni pótu v'unnáru; v'úr antá góla yetti labbuna moṭṭucunṭu v'unnáru*, village headman speaking:

Pray God we'll soon be rid of this cursèd Jamabandi
The pilfering Bantrotu and plundering Sibbandi;
The houses of the Tappers and Washers they invade, Sir,
The chickens and the stored-up comestibles they raid, Sir.
Great noise of women wailing, reviling, bosoms slapping,
From compounds comes of those who by washing live or tapping.

viraguṭa, to be broken, to burst; also *viruguṭa*.

virahamu, separation, love-sickness. Skt.

virahi, a separated lover (male). Skt.

virahini, a separated lover (female). Skt.

virahituḍu, devoid of. Skt. *ahancáravirahituḍu*, a person devoid of conceit.

virasamu, unpleasantness. Skt., from *vi-*, apart, and *rasamu*, flavour. *sarasamu virasamé*, joking causes unpleasantness.

virámamu, rest, remission, respite. Skt. *virámamu léni duhkha parampara*, a series of sorrows without respite.

viréchanamu, purging. Skt.

virichicaṭṭuṭa, to pinion, to tie a man's hands behind his back; from *virutsuṭa*, to twist, and *caṭṭuṭa*, to tie. *banṭrótalacu sangnya chéséṭ appaṭici váru piḍugul lágu atanni mída paḍi, atani cáḷḷú chétulú virichicaṭṭinárú*, I made a sign to the peons and they fell upon him like thunderbolts and pinioned his arms and legs.

virivigá, abundantly.

viriyuṭa, to blow (of flowers), to burst open, to be dishevelled (of hair). *níḷḷu tsallagáné sunnapu ráḷḷu virisinavi*, on being sprinkled with water the lime stones cracked; *tala viriya pósiconi chimpiri Búchi vale canapaḍuduvu*, you have shaken out your hair so as to make yourself look more like a shock-headed bogy than anything else (Búchi is the Frenchman Bussy, who once ruled the Northern Circars and is now a bogy to frighten children with).

viródhamu, enmity. Skt. In very common use. *avivécitó snéhamu canna vivécitó viródhamu mélu*, better a wise man as an enemy than a fool as a friend.

viródhanamu, contradiction. Skt.

viródhi, enemy. Skt.

virṓdhintsuṭa, to oppose.
virravíguṭa, to be proud; a duplicated form of *víguṭa*, but commoner than the parent form. *mundarici vachchi néṭi cálánici goppa sthitilóci vachchinámu; anta mátram chéta má venucaṭi sthiti marachi póyi virraviga rádu*, we have got on and to-day we have reached a high position; nevertheless we must not forget our former lowliness or puff ourselves up.
viruddhamu, incongruity. Skt.
virugaḍa, release, relief, rest; also *viragaḍa*. *Daivamá! inta nác í pór eppuḍu virugaḍa chésedavó?* Gracious Heavens! shall I never hear the last of it?
virugucoṭṭuṭa, to break in pieces; from *viruguṭa*, to break, and *coṭṭuṭa*, to beat.
viruguṭa, to break (intransitive), to burst, to be disgusted, to be spoilt. *araca arigité, gariṣe virugunu*, wear the share and the barn will burst; *vésinadé vaca gantu, viriginadé vaca cálu*, one leap leapt, one leg broken (the first venture lost); *dáni manasu virigi póyinadi*, she was disgusted; *pálu virigi póyinavi*, the milk curdled; *reccalu virigina pacshi*, a bird with broken wings.
virutsuṭa, to break, to snap, to twist; causative of *viruguṭa*. *neṭicalu virutsuṭa*, to snap the fingers; *ná mogamuna neṭica virichi*, snapping his fingers in my face; *simhamu tóca virutsuṭa*, to twist the lion's tail; *yemucalu virutsuṭa*, to break your bones, to take trouble over something.
virúpamu, ugly. Skt., from *rúpam*, shape; also, and more commonly, *curúpamu*.
viṣadamu, apparent, manifest. Skt. *viṣadamauṭa*, to become clear, to come to light; *yevaru gelchédí míc appuḍu viṣadam autundi*, you will then see who is going to win; *viṣadaparatsuṭa*, to make clear.
visagu, disgust; also *visugu*.
visanacarra, fan; from *visaruṭa*, to fan, and *carra*, stick.
visaricoṭṭuṭa, to fling, to throw, to dash; from *visaruṭa*, to throw, and *coṭṭuṭa*, to beat. *cunḍanu góḍa mída visaricoṭṭináḍu*, he dashed the pot against the wall.
visarivéyuṭa, to throw, to fling, to hurl.
visarjanamu, abandoning, renouncing. Skt. *ghaṭa visarjana chésináḍu*, he left the body (died).
visarjintsuṭa, to abandon, to renounce. Skt.
visaruṭa, to throw; also intransitive, to blow (as the wind), to spread (as scent, or as a famine); also, transitive, to brandish (a sword), to turn (a mill), to fan.
viṣálamu, broad, spacious. Skt. *á y'illu viṣálamugá n'unnadi*, that is a spacious house.
viṣálata, breadth, spaciousness. Skt.
viṣéshamu, detail, special, particular. Skt. *í vaidyunici hasta viṣéshamu*, this doctor has a skilful hand; *néḍ émi viṣéshamu?* what is there special today? *incá yémi viṣésham?* anything special? (as the Collector says when the interview has lasted long enough and it is time the visitor came out with the real object of his visit, which he always keeps for the end. He would like to add: *inta sépu tsampaca póté y'í máṭa moṭṭamodaṭané cheppa léca póyinárá?* could you not have said that at the very beginning instead of boring me to death all this time? but he only thinks it).
vishamu, poison. Skt. *chaccara púta púsina vishamu*, sugar-coated venom (of words); *nén anṭé vánici visham*, he hates me like poison; *vishajvaramu*, typhoid (malignant fever); *vishapuníru*, pus (poison water).
vishayamai, about. Skt., from *vishayamu*, object.
vishayamu, object, subject-matter. Skt. *í vishayamuló ninḍá vyayamu chésináḍu*, he spent much money on this.
vishayi, organ of sense. Skt.
vishádamu, dejection. Skt.
vishúchi, vishúchica, cholera. Skt., also *vántibhédi*, but more commonly *cálárá*.
visicintsuṭa, to disgust (transitive); causal of *visuguṭa*, to feel disgust.
visigi vésari, tired out; from *visuguṭa*, to be disgusted, and *vésaruṭa*, to be tired. *visigi, vésari, y'áṣa niráṣa chésu-*

coni, y'inti maḷḷi vatstsutsu, coming home dog-tired, hope having turned to despair.

vismayamu, surprise. Skt. *ḍscharyamu* is the usual word. *vismitamu*, amazed, dismayed; *vismituḍu*, one who is amazed, dismayed.

vispashṭamu, very clear; intensitive of *spashṭamu*.

viṣramamu, rest. Skt., from *vi-*, negative affix, and *ṣramamu*, exertion.

viṣrántamu, rest, end. Skt., intensitive of *ṣrántamu*, rest. *diganta viṣrántamu*, the ends of the world.

viṣránti, rest, end. Skt. *pani chésina tarváta viṣránti cá valenu*, rest is required after work (all work and no play makes Jack a dull boy); *ná paga tírtsucunṭé gáni ná manasucu viṣránti v'unḍadu*, my mind will not be at rest till I have revenged myself. *Lacshmayya: ní bháryanu viṣránti cósam puṭṭ inṭici pampärá? Vencayya: pampänu; nizam ém anṭé nácé viṣránti cá valasi aṭlá chéṣänu.* Smith: You have sent your wife to her mother's house for a rest? Jones: Yes, but to tell the truth, it was I that wanted a rest. *ṭennisu pravínuḍu: nannu paricsha chéṣáru gadá? ná vaḷḷu yeṭlá v'unnadi? ḍácṭaru: nícu viṣránti cávalenu; connáḷḷu ṭennisu mánuconi rózú cáléjici veḷḷut unḍu, nimmalistundi.* Tennis expert: You have examined me; how goes it? Doctor: You want a rest; give up tennis for a bit and be going to college every day and you will soon be as fit as a fiddle.

viṣrutamu, famous. Skt., from *vi-*, intensitive prefix, and *ṣrutam*, heard. *lócaviṣrutamu*, world-famous.

vistara, vistari, leaf-platter. Skt. The plural is *vistaḷḷu*. *marri áculu cósi vistaḷḷu cuṭṭutáru*, they will cut banyan leaves and sew leaf-platters; *yémiyu léni vistari yegiri paḍutsunnadi, anniyu v'unna vistari anigi v'unṭunndi*, the empty leaf-platter flutters about, the full stays where it is (the vanity of the empty-headed, the steadfastness of the learned).

vistáramu, extensive. Skt. *á chénuló y'ishnaplu vistáramgá v'unnai*, there are plenty of snipe in that field.

vistírnamu, area. Skt. The usual word for the area of a field, &c.

visugu, disgust, boredom. *yeppuḍu adé panigá cúrtsuni vráyaḍam anṭé, visugu vastundi*, to be always sitting and writing at the same work is boring. *bhárya: sari! sari! mí ṅóṭic astamánamu 'ósí, ósí' anna máṭacu visugu lédu?* Wife: Oh gracious me! don't you get sick of girling me my good girl all the blessed day? *Gengaḍu: nuvvu samudra prayánam chéṣává? Rangaḍu: chéṣánu gáni nácu visugu puṭṭindi. Gengaḍu: yendu chéta? Rangaḍu: oca ala tsûsté anni alalú aṭlágé v'unnai.* Smith: Have you been on a sea-voyage? Jones: Yes, but I got bored. Smith: Why? Jones: When you have seen one wave you have seen them all.

visuguṭa, to be disgusted, to be sick at heart. *prándlu visigi pótu v'unnavi*, I am sick at heart; *visigi vésari*, dog tired.

viṣva-, prefix meaning 'universal'; from Skt. *viṣvamu*, universe. *Viṣvasrüjuḍu*, the All-Creator, Brahma; *Viṣvanádhuḍu*, the Lord of All, Siva; *viṣvarúpamu*, multiform, existing in all forms; *viṣvavidyálayamu* is the newspaper word for university; the ordinary word is *cáléjí*, college.

viṣvasaníyamu, believable. Skt.

viṣvasintsuṭa, to believe, to trust. Skt. *vinnav anni viṣvasintsa vaddu*, don't believe all you hear; *pámarulu cheppa valasina máṭa panḍitulai v'unḍinní míru viṣvasistár émi?* will a pundit like you believe the things that are for the vulgar to say?

viṣvásamu, faith, trust. Skt. *cómaṭi viṣvasamu*, merchant's faith (an ironical locution); *caṭṭuconna bháryacu ainá y'inta prémá, y'inta viṣvásamú v'unḍadu*, even a wedded wife won't have so much love and faithfulness.

viṣvási, faithful person. Skt.

vitanḍamu, wrangling. Skt. Used in newspapers to translate 'controversy'.

vitantuvu, widow. Skt. *vedhava* is commoner.

vitathamu, false. Skt.

vitstsalaviḍigá, freely. *vitstsalaviḍigá putstsucóvaḍam*, taking bribes freely; *vitstsalavidigá tirugutú v'unnáru*, they are moving about freely.

vitstsucatti, a drawn sword.

vitstsuṭa, to come open, to open, to spread. *góḍa vichchinadi*, a crack has opened in the wall; *pámu paḍaga vichchinadi*, the snake has spread its hood; *cannu vichchi*, opening his eyes wide; *mogga vichchinadi*, the bud opened.

vittamu, property. Skt. *vittamu coddi vibhavam, vidya coddi vinayam*, property and pomp, learning and modesty go together; *vaivávicamul andu, prána vittamána bhangam andu bonca vatstsunu*, you may lie about marriage affairs and to save your life or property.

vittanamu, seed. *vittanamu vacaṭi vésté, mocca vacaṭi molatsunu*, sow the seed, you get the shoot (a chip of the old block); *cshétram erigi vittanam, pátram erigi dánam*, suit the seed to the soil, the meed to the merit; *vittanapu ginzalu*, seed-grain.

vittu, seed, testicle. *vittulu coṭṭuṭa*, to castrate; *cheṭṭu mundá, vittu mundá ann aṭṭu*, which came first, the tree or the seed, as the saying is.

viṭuḍu, paramour; feminine *viṭi, viṭurálu*. *véṣya viṭuni mida tanac enta préma v'unna cán í, talli máṭa mira rádu*, however much love a courtesan may have for her lover she must not disobey her mother; *viṭulacu póṭilu peṭṭi sampádinchédánini*, I used to make money by setting my suitors by the ears.

vivaramu, detail, specification. Skt.

vivaranamu, description, specification. Skt.

vivarintsuṭa, to describe in detail. Skt.

viváda, dispute. Skt. *vivádáspadamaina*, contentious (law). *vivádapaḍuṭa*, to quarrel.

viváhamu, marriage. The Telugu word is *penḍli* but *viváham* is just as common.

vivécamu, prudence. Skt.

vivéchanamu, discrimination. Skt. *vivéchana ṣacti*, reason.

vivéci, a prudent man. Skt.

vividha, various. Skt.

viyógamu, separation, especially of lovers and married couples. Skt. *bhartrüviyógamu*, separation from husband, of which the stock instance is Sita's; *bhárya viyógam aina tarváta*, after I lost my wife.

viyyancuḍu, co-father-in-law; a useful word which we express clumsily. *viyyálavàru*, the co-father-in-law people; *viyyamu*, connexion by marriage; *viyyancurálu*, co-mother-in-law; *áme nácu viyyancurálu*, (woman speaking) our children have married; *viyyamanḍuṭa*, to form a marriage connexion; *bógam mélamu peṭṭaḍánici viyyalaváru v'oppucóca póyin aṭṭ aité, vári sambandham chésucó vaḍḍ ani cheppinár aṭa!* he is said to have declared the marriage off if the other side did not engage a nautch-party for the occasion!

vícsha, sight; *vícshanamu*, seeing; *vícshitamu*, seen; *vícshintsuṭa*, to see, are Skt. words used in books for *tsútsuṭa* and derivatives.

vídhi, street. Skt. *cammara vídhiló súdul ammin aṭṭu*, like selling needles in blacksmith street (carrying coals to Newcastle); *turaca vídhiló sanyási bhicsha*, a (Hindu) sanyasi's alms in Muhammedan street (nothing doing). *Rámuḍu: Lacshmayyagári illu idéná? Dámuḍu: idi cádu. Rámuḍu: í vídhiló v'undá? Dámuḍu: undi. Rámuḍu: namber émiṭó cheppanḍi. Dámuḍu: inṭi gétu mída v'unṭundi, tsúḍanḍi.* Roe: Is this Mr. Smith's house? Doe: No. Roe: Is it in this street? Doe: Yes. Roe: Please tell me the number. Doe: It's on the gate; look and see.

víḍu, he (this man); *váḍu*, he (that man).

víḍuconuṭa, to abandon, to take leave. *víḍucólu*, taking leave to go (after a visit); *víḍupáṭu*, difference, decision.

víguṭa, to be proud. The reduplicated form *virravíguṭa* is commoner.

vílu, convenient. When the Collector refuses an interview he tells the peon to say: '*víl lédu*', it is not convenient. *míṭinguló Lacshmayya allari chéstú, upanyásam vinan ivvaca póyenu. antaṭiló sabhyalu Lacshmayyanu genṭi veyyum ani arachiri. upanyásacuḍu: vaddu, vaddu, accara lédu. pápamu Lacshmayya inṭi daggira aravaḍánici vílu lédu cábólu; anducané iccaḍa *arustunnáḍu.* At the meeting Lakshmayya was making a row and drowning the lecturer's voice; the audience shouted that he should be chucked out. The Lecturer: No, no, leave him alone. I suppose the poor man is not allowed to raise his voice at home; so he does it here.

vína, the stringed instrument of India, a sort of lute. Skt.

víni, his; genitive of *víḍu.*

vínu, ear. Skt. Used in books for *chevi. vínulára vinnánu,* I heard with my own ears; *ní vácyámrütamu ná vínulacu vinód onarintuv éni,* if you will delight my ears with your sweet words.

vípu, back. *vípu tsúpuṭa,* to show your back, to run away. *talli caḍupu tsútsunu, penḍlámu vípu tsútsunu,* the mother looks at his stomach, the wife at his back (to see what he is bringing her; if pockets were known, she would look through his pockets); *vípu mída coṭṭa vatstsunu gáni, caḍupu mída coṭṭa cúḍadu,* beat me on the back but not on the belly (punish me but don't touch my pay); *náluca, náluca, vípucu debbalu téca!* tongue, tongue, don't draw blows on my back!

víramu, heroic. Skt. *vírasvargamu,* the Elysium of heroes; *vírapátivratyamu,* stern chastity.

víru, they; plural of *víḍu.*

víruḍu, hero. Skt.

víryamu, heroism. Skt.

vísamu, one-sixteenth, a grain (jeweller's weight).

víse, viss; a weight of 120 tolas, one-eighth of a maund, about three pounds.

vísubaḍi, one of the earlier forms of ryotvari settlement.

víṭi, their; genitive of *ivi.*

vítsuṭa, to blow (of the wind); to spread (as scent); to wave (as hand); *vícho̱pu,* a whisk; hence the secretariat chobdars, whose original function was to whisk flies off His Excellency and the Honourable Members.

vocca, a form of *oca,* one; *voccappuḍu,* a form of *ocappuḍu,* sometimes.

voḷḷu, body; a form of *óḍalu. sprüha tappi póyinadi, voḷḷu túlutú v'unnaḍi,* she lost hope and reeled; *voḷḷ antá chemaṭalu paṭṭeṭ aṭṭugá parugettutú v'unnáḍu,* he was running all of a sweat; *yémi teliyaca nálugu yengili Y'Inglishu muccalu tsaduvucóvaḍamṭóté voḷḷ erugaca púrv ácháránni peddalini dúshistáru,* ignoramuses, who because they have learnt a few dirty scraps of English, revile, without knowing what they are doing, our old customs and their elders.

voppuconuṭa, to agree; same as *oppuconuṭa, vappuconuṭa.*

vódhrulu, the Vadderas, a caste that does earthwork, quarries stones, makes roads, digs wells and tanks; in fact, navvies; also called *oḍḍevánḍlu, vaḍḍevánḍlu, oḍḍiyalu.*

vópica, patience; a form of *ópica. ocaḍu: conchem ópica peṭṭu. incóḍu: vópica lédu, gipica lédu, pó!* First Hindu: A moment's patience. Second Hindu: Patience be blowed. Get out!

vóṭu, vote. English. *vóṭaru,* a voter. *míru Dévendruḍ ainá, nénu mícu vóṭu ivvan anḍi! abhyarthi; nénu Dévendruḍin aité ninnu í v'úḷḷó unḍan istáná?* Voter: If you were God Almighty I would not give you my vote. Candidate: If I were God Almighty do you think I would leave you alive in this place? (*dévendruḍu* is compounded of *Déva* and *Indruḍu*; *abhyarthi,* person who solicits, Skt., is a newspaper word for candidate.)

vranamu, boil. *yennó vrandlu cósinánu gáni, ná vranam anta típu léd ann aṭṭu,* like the surgeon who said 'of all the boils I have cut, my own was the most painful'.

vratamu, fast, vow. Skt. *écádasi vratálu,* the customary fast on the eleventh lunar day; *yécádaṣi vratam niyamgá zarapa valenu,* you must perform the eleventh day fast properly (it is a libel on Hindus to deny that they perform their religious duties without due observance of ritual and to compare them to the young girl of Thermopylae, who never did anything properly, though their punctiliousness is different from ours).

vratasthuḍu, one who makes a vow, votary. Skt.

vrálu, writing, handwriting; from *vráyuṭa,* to write; also *vráta*; *chévrálu* signature. *nosaṭa vrásina vrálu*, what is written on your forehead, your fate; *nosaṭa vrásina vrálu tappa galadá?* can you escape your fate? *nosaṭa vrásina vrálu canná núr éndlu chintinchiná yémi lédu*, you may think for a hundred years but you will get nothing more than is written on your forehead; *álu cád adi, vrálu*, no wife but the writing on the forehead (ill mated, ill fated).

vráluṭa, to alight (of birds); more commonly *váluṭa*.

vráta, writing, handwriting, fate; same as *vrálu*.

vrátaballa, writing-table.

vrátapani, drawing or painting, especially chintz.

vráyintsuṭa, to get written, drawn, or painted; causative of *vráyuṭa*.

vráyuṭa, to write, to draw, to paint; vulgarly *ráyuṭa*. *nácu tsávu vrásindi*, I am doomed to death (refers to the writing on the forehead); *vráta caranamu*, a curnam to write; *vráyagá, vráyagá caranamu, daggagá, daggagá maranamu*, write and write and you will end as a curnam, cough and cough and you will end as a corpse; *vrásévánni, cósévánni, gisévánni namma rádu*, beware of the man who writes (curnam), the man who cuts (butcher) and the man who taps (the palm for toddy); *iddaru vartacamló bághastulugá chéri láyaru chéta dastávézu vráyinchiri. láyaru: incá vaca vishayam chérts ále. modaṭi vartacuḍu: yémiṭ adi? láyaru: diváḷa zarigité gáni, agni pramádam vasté gáni, yém cheyy álenó vráya lédu. rendó vartacuḍu: á sandarbhamló lábham cheri sagangá pantsucó valen ani vráyanḍi.* Two merchants were having a partnership deed drawn up by a lawyer. Lawyer: There is one more particular to be entered. First merchant: What is that? Lawyer: I have not entered what happens in the event of bankruptcy or accidental fire. Second merchant: Oh, in that case write that we divide the profit equally. *vartacuḍu: Lacshmayya péra tsálá uṭṭarálu má y'inṭici vachchinai. Lacshmayya adresu mícu telusuná? gumástá: teliyadé. vartacuḍu: aité, Lacshmayyacu vrási canuccondi.* Merchant: Many letters for Lacshmayya have come to us. Do you know his address? Clerk: No, Sir. Merchant: Then write to Lacshmayya and find out.

vréláḍuṭa, to hang down, to dangle; also *veluṭa, véláḍuṭa*.

vrélu, finger; also *vélu. nóṭiló vrélu peṭṭuconi, guṭaculu mingutsu, dinam oca calpamugá gaḍuputsu, nénu tondara paḍina coladini pilladi y'iḍéruṭa venucacé póvutsu vachchenu*, I would lay my finger on my mouth and gulp and think every day that passed an age and the more I was in a hurry the longer it took the girl to bud into womanhood; *vrélu viḍichina ménamáma*, an uncle once removed; *yémainá vrélucu vrélu yeḍamé*, there is a space between every two fingers (no two are equally favoured); *nóṭló vrélu peṭṭuconi póyináḍu*, he went off with his tail between his legs (his finger in his mouth).

vréluḍu, hanging; from *vréluṭa*, to hang.

vréluṭa, to hang down, to dangle; also *vréláḍuṭa, véluṭa*, and *véláḍuṭa*.

vrücshamu, tree. Skt. The Telugu is *cheṭṭu. vamṣavrücshamu*, the family tree, pedigree. *idi tamaru peṭṭina vrücshamé*, I am a tree Your Honour planted (and therefore it is up to you to water me, i.e. give me promotion).

vrüddha, old (of persons not things). Skt. The Telugu is *musali*.

vrüddhatvamu, vrüddhápyamu, old age. Skt. The Telugu is *musalitanamu*; another Skt. word is *várdhacadaṣa. Lacshmayya: mícu vrüddhápyam vachchinanú zuṭṭu yenta nallagá v'undandi! Vencayya: ninna shápuló connánu.* Lakshmayya: How is it that your pigtail is so black though old age has come upon you? Venkayya: I bought it in a shop the other day.

vrüddhi, increase, progress. Skt. A word commonly in the mouths of reformers and politicians; also *abhivrüddhi. janabhivrüddhi*, increase of population as well as public progress; *vrüddhi* also means interest on money, but in this sense the corrupt form *vaḍḍi* is the form in common use; *hánivrüddhulu*, loss and gain, profit and loss; *dáni hánivrüddhulacu nénu unnánu*, I am answerable for all loss and gain.

vrüddhuḍu, old man. Skt. The Telugu is *musaliváḍu*; the feminine is *vrüddhángi* or *vrüddhurálu. nizamu vichárimpagá n'alpa cálánubhavamu galavár aguṭa chéta púrvam unḍinaváré tarváta n'unḍinavári canṭé chinna ani cheppa vatstsunu; paramparagá vatstsutsunna peccu taramulavári y' anubhavam cúḍá mana y'anubhavamutó chéruts unḍuṭa chéta, manamé viṣésha gnyánamégala vrüddhalamu cá valenu,* if you think it out the older generations have less experience than the younger and should really be called younger; our experience joined to the experience of the numerous intervening generations makes us older and more knowledgeable than they.

vrüṣchicamu, scorpion. Skt. The Telugu is *télu,* but the Skt. word is used for Scorpio, the zodiac sign.

vrüshamu, vrüshabhamu, bull. Skt. The Telugu is *yeddu*, but *vrüshabhamu* is used of the zodiac sign Taurus; *rüshivrüshabhamu,* the mighty Rishi. The Skt. words are also used of the vehicle of Siva, who is known as *Vrüshánca,* he whose emblem is a bull; *Vrüshabhadhvaja,* he who has a bull on his standard; the bull is a white one with a black tail and a golden girth; its hump is like the top of a snow mountain.

vrüṭha, vain, empty, useless. Skt. The Telugu is *vaṭṭi,* but *vrüṭha* and its variant *vyarthamu* are quite common. *nuvvu cágitánici occa vaipuné vrástú, tsálá cágitálu vrüṭha chéstunnáu,* you waste much paper by writing only on one side.

vrüttántamu, news, particulars. Skt.

vrüttántapatrica, newspaper. Skt.

vrütti, existence, livelihood, profession, manner. Skt. *prachhanna vrüttini,* secretly. *plíḍari vrütti bógam vrütti vocca mostarudi: véṣya viṭula vadda yenni ṭacculu canaparustundó, plíḍaru cúḍa ḍabbu lágaḍánici párṭíla vadda anni ṭacculu canapartsa valenu; idi v'udyóga dharmam,* the lawyer's and the courtesan's professions are of the same kind; the pleader is up to as many dodges to extract money from his clients as the courtesan is to extract it from her suitors; it is their professional duty; *yevari vrütti yevaru mánutáru? lantsampantsam tinaḍam v'udyóga dharmam auná cádá?* every one will stick to his profession, won't he? Isn't it the official's professional duty to take bribes and douceurs? *vaidyuḍu: gumpul unna tsóṭici pó vaddu, ní árógyam cheḍi pótundi. rógi: póca póté ná vrütti ságad anḍi. vaidyuḍu: ní vrütti yémiṭi? rógi: jébu dongatanam.* Doctor: Don't go into crowds or your health will be ruined. Patient: But if I don't my trade will be ruined. Doctor: What is your trade? Patient: Picking pockets. *ḍácṭaru: ní vrütti yémiṭi? rógi: nénu gharána manish anḍi. ḍácṭaru: aité nén ichchina mandu panici rádu, incó mandu putstsucó váli.* Doctor: What is your profession? Patient: I am a Man of Property. Doctor: In that case the medicine I prescribed is no good, you must take another medicine; *tama chitta vrüttici lóbaḍa valen ani nénu vachchinánu,* I have come to submit to your will.

vyabhicharintsuṭa, to commit adultery. Skt., from *vi-*, apart, and *abhichá ram,* wandering.

vyabhicháramu, adultery. Skt.

vyactamu, plain, manifest. *vyacti,* an incarnation, *vyactaparatsuṭa,* to make plain.

vyacti, individual. Skt., adj. *vyashṭi. samashṭi ṣásanóllanghanamu avyashṭi ṣásanóllanghanamugá márchi,* changing collective to individual civil disobedience.

vyactuḍu, a clever man, a man of the world; feminine *vyacturálu.*

vyadha, suffering, distress, agony. Skt. *strílu vidya léni hétuvu chéta, yuctáyuctamulu teliyaca, paṣutulyarándrai n'anduna gadá, purushulac iṭuvanṭi manó vyadhalu sambhavintsuts unnavi,* it is because our women are uneducated and are like beasts, not knowing right from wrong, that we Hindu men are made to suffer these agonizing conflicts of the mind (the speaker is a magistrate whose wife is urging him to take a bribe).

vyarthamu, useless, vain. Skt. *mí*

cálam vyartham putstsaḍam lédu gadá? I am not wasting your time, am I? (as the importunate visitor says to the Collector); *somm anta vyarthamai pótundi*, all the money is being wasted.

vyarthuḍu, a worthless man. *cuṭumba bháranamu chésicona léca vyarthuḍanai y'unnánu*, I am a poor creature who cannot support his family (as petitioners sometimes write in their petitions).

vyasanamu, sorrow. Skt. *míru nácu yémi saháyam cheyya léni sthitiló v'unn anducu nácu bahu vyasanamgá v'unnadi*, I am very sorry you can do nothing for me; *chevvácu póyin ammacu yenta vyasanamó, doricin ammacu anta santósham*, the woman who has found the ear-ring is as pleased as the woman who has lost it is sorry (it's an ill wind that blows no one any good).

vyatirécamu, contrary. Skt. *ágnyacu vyatirécamugá*, contrary to orders; *rivázu vyatirécamuga*, contrary to custom; *vyatirécárthacamu*, the negative form of the verb.

vyatyastamu, different. Skt.

vyatyásamu, difference. Skt. The usual word is *bhédamu. Y'Inglishu tsaduvucunna mí nágaricatacú, Y'Inglishu tsaduvucóni mávanṭi anágaricatacú, nácu yémi bhédam canapaḍadam lédu; nácu teliyaca aḍugutánu; pravartanaló yémi vyatyásam cheppanḍi*, I don't see any difference between the culture of you people who have studied English and the want of culture of people like us who have not. I ask in my ignorance; say whether there is any difference in our conduct.

vyavadhánamu, interval, delay. Skt. *incá sumuhúrtam vyavadhánamgá n'unnadi*, the auspicious moment continues to be delayed.

vyavaharintsuṭa, to use. Skt.

vyavahávamu, usage, business. Skt. *ácháram lédu, vyavahăram lédu*, no good usage or custom; *áháram andú, vyavahăram andú, siggu paḍa lédu*, modesty is out of place at meat or mart; *vyavahăram* is the ordinary word for business of all sorts; *rájacíya vyavahárálu*, public business; *córṭu vyavahăram*, litigation; *vyavahári*, a merchant, litigant.

vyavasáyamu, cultivation (of land). Skt. The ordinary word; in courts the occupation entered in the heading of a witness's deposition will usually be *vyavasáyamu*.

vyavasáyi, agriculturist. Skt.

vyavastha, rule, decree. Skt. *vyavasthitamu*, laid down, fixed.

vyayamu, expense. Skt. *áyamu telisi vyayamu*, ascertain your income before you spend (cut your coat according to your cloth); *tala minchina vyayam chéyuṭa*, to plunge over your head in expenditure, to be extravagant; *vyayamulu* is also used of public expenditure.

vyácaranamu, grammar. Skt. *atanici conchemu vyácaranamú, tarcamú, alancára ṣástramú cúḍá telusunu*, he knows some grammar, logic, and rhetoric too.

vyáculamu, grief. Skt. Used in books. *vyáculapeṭṭuṭa*, to afflict; *ná manasuna vyácula peṭṭináḍu*, he sorely grieved me.

vyádhi, illness. Skt. *vyádhici mandu v'unnadi gáni, vidhici mandu v'unnadá?* there are drugs for illnesses but are there drugs for ill fortune?

vyághramu, tiger. Skt. The Telugu is *pedda puli. purushavyághruḍu*, a noble man, a king among men.

vyájamu, pretence. Skt. *vyájócti*, innuendo, double entendre (*ucti*, speech); *vyájastuti*, sarcastic praise (*stuti*, praise).

vyájyamu, law suit. Skt. *vyájyam áḍuṭa*, to bring a suit; *vyájyagáḍu*, a contending party; *vyájyagánḍru*, the parties.

vyákhyánamu, commentary. Skt. *vyákhyáta*, a commentator.

vyámóhamu, inordinate love, lust. Skt., from *móhamu*.

vyápanamu, diffusion. Skt.

vyápáramu, business. Skt. *vaḍḍi vyápáramu*, money-lending business; *vyápári*, a business man; *vyápáram chéyuṭa*, to trade.

vyápintsuṭa, to spread, to pervade. Skt. *mana círti lócánic antá vyápintsa valenu*, our fame must spread all over the world; *páṭacuḍu: monna Góclé* *háluló nénu páḍité ná nádam yeṭlá vyápinchindó canipeṭṭává? snéhituḍu: adi svéchchagá vyápintsaḍánici gánu tsálamandi léchi póyináru.* Singer: When I sang in the Gokhale hall the other day did you notice how my voice filled the hall? Friend: Yes, a great part of the audience got up and went out so that it might spread more freely.

vyásamu, essay. Skt. *Gópu: nuvvu vrásina 'nirantara sanchâram' ané vyásam yêm aindi? Rámuḍu: á vyásánni nénu yenni patricalacu pampinchiná, maḷḷi ná daggiracé vachchindi. Gópu: adi cúḍá nirantara samchâram chéstunnadi cábólu.* Smith: What has happened to your essay on perpetual motion? Jones: It comes back to me every time I send it to a paper. Smith: In fact it is doing perpetual motion.

vyáyámamu, exercise. Skt. *Lacshmayya: nuvvu yém vyáyámam chéstáu? Vencayya: móṭaru cáruló yecci shicáru póṭunṭánu. Lacshmayya: ad ém vyáyámam? Vencayya: apáyam lécunḍá inṭici vachchin tarváta nácu santóshamgá v'unṭundi; andu valla nácu árógyam nilustundi; vyáyámam árógyánicé gá?* Lakshmayya: What exercise do you take? Venkayya: I go out for a drive in my car. Lakshmayya: What exercise is that? Venkayya: After I come back safe I am happy; happiness keeps me in good health; exercise is for health, isn't it?

Y

There are very few words in Telugu that begin with *y*, but as it is a common helcistic euphonic letter before vowels, especially *e*, many of the commonest words in the language are almost always pronounced, and written, with a *y* before them. Thus *y* is practically part of the word in *yeccaḍa*, where; *yeccili*, hiccup; *yeccuṭa*, to go up; *yeccuva*, more; *yeḍa*, towards; *yeḍala*, if; *yeḍama*, left; *yeḍamu*, space; *yeḍári*, desert; *yeddu*, bullock; *yedirintsuṭa*, to oppose; *yeduguṭa*, to grow; *yeduṭa*, opposite; *yega*, up; *yegaruṭa*, to fly; *yegatáḷi*, mockery; *yegumati*, export; *yella*, all; *yellappuḍu*, always; *yellunḍi*, the day after to-morrow; *yeluca*, rat; *yelugubanṭi*, bear; *yemuca*, bone; *yenabhai*, eighty; *yenḍa*, sunlight; *yenḍáca?* how far? *yenḍacálamu*, the hot weather; *yendaru?* how many persons? *yenḍipóyina*, dry; *yendu?* what? *yenducanṭé*, because; *yenducu?* why? *yendunu*, everywhere; *yengili*, spittle; *yenimidi*, eight; *yennaḍó*, some time or other; *yennaḍu*, always; *yennáḷḷu?* how long? *yenni?* how many, *yennu*, ear of corn; *yenta?* how much? *yentamandi?* how many persons? *yenupótu*, buffalo; *yeppuḍainá?* ever? *yeppuḍu?* when? *yera*, bait; *yeravu*, loan; *yerra*, red; *yeruguṭa*, to know; *yeruvu*, manure; *yesaru*, boiling water; *yeṭlá?* how? *yeṭṭidi?* of what kind? *yettu*, height; *yettuṭa*, to raise; *yeṭuvanṭi?* of what sort? *yevaḍó*, some one; *yevaḍu?* who? *yé?* what? *yéca*, one; *yécaramu*, acre; *yédainá*, any; *yédi?* which? where? *yéḍó*, some; *yéḍtsuṭa*, to cry; *yéḍu*, year; *yéḍu*, seven; *yélamu*, auction; *yélá?* how? *yélágaina*, in any way; *yélágu?* in what way? *yéláṭi?* of what sort? *yélinavâru*, the rulers; *yémaina*, anything; *yémani?* what? *yémi?* what? *yémoi*, sir; *yémó*, perhaps; *yénugu*, elephant; *yénúru*, five hundred; *yérparatsuṭa*, to arrange; *yérpáṭu*, arrangement; *yéru*, river; *yéruṭa*, to pick; *yétámu*, picottah; *yévi?* which? *táḍ eccévánni yendácá yegasana toyyunu?* how far up can you help a man who is climbing a palmyra? (in this example *eccé* does not become *yeccé* because it is preceded by a consonant but *endáca* becomes *yendáca* and *egasana* becomes *yegasana*. The Telugus in speaking English invariably put a *y* before words beginning with *e* and *ä* (English *a*) and usually before words beginning with *i* (English *e*); thus 'average' is written (in Telugu characters) *yévâréji* and pronounced *yäveréji*; apple becomes *yäpel*; Edward becomes *Yedward*; English becomes *Y'Inglishu*; school becomes *iscúlu* and snipe becomes *y'isnappu* because euphonic *i* (in addition to euphonic *y*) is inserted before initial *s* followed by another consonant.

The following are the few common words really beginning with *y*:

yagnyamu, burnt sacrifice. Skt.; also *yágamu*. *yagnyamu chésédi yedala svarga bhógamu calugunu*, if you perform a burnt sacrifice you will win heaven; *yagnyamu nimittam yáchinchi, árjinchina sommuló nunchi migultsuconna áru vandala rúpáyalunu pilladáni tandri mogamuna tagulapetti, mund entó sukha pada valen ani cond anta áṣató áru sanvatsaramula pillanu cattuconnánu*, I went round collecting for a burnt sacrifice, scraped together six hundred rupees, sacrificed it to an earthly father and with heaven-aspiring hopes of future bliss united myself in wedlock to a child of six; *yagnyálu modalaina punya cáryálu chési, svargánici vellíná accada Rambha modalaina Déva véṣyalató sambhógam éná, mari yémainá v'unnadá?* when you have performed sacrifices and other meritorious acts and have gone to heaven, do you or do you not obtain the favours of Rambha and the other heavenly courtesans? *canyan ichchi dabbu putstsucunté pápam unnadi cáni canyadánam chésté veyyi yagnyálu chésina phalam vastund ani ṣástrálu chepputú v'unnavi*, it is a sin to take money for a virgin but the Scriptures say that the free gift of a virgin brings as much merit as a thousand burnt sacrifices.

Yamudu, the Hindu Pluto, Lord of death. (He is also called *pitrürája* because he rules over our *pitrülu*, ancestors, and *dharmarája*, lord of justice. He is dreadful to look upon but his assembly hall shines like bright gold and there is neither sorrow there nor decrepitude, neither is there hunger or thirst and there are Elysian fields for the righteous, but there are also punishments for the wicked as drastic as those of Dante's Inferno: the sword-leaved forest, the boiling stream.) *yamacincarudu*, *yamadúta*, angel of death, fiend; *cadapata chinnadi peddad ai, y'inta cálamunacu ná tapamu phalinchenu gadá y'ani santósha padedu dinamulu vatstsun appatici, Daivamu ná mélunu tsúchi, órva léca, y'intici nátó cápuram chéya vachchedu lópalané dánini ná páliti yamadútanugá márchi vésinadu*, at last, after an age of hope deferred, when I thought of recompense and reward for protracted mortification of the flesh, and the joyful day had arrived, God cast a jealous eye on my bliss and sent in her place a spiteful changeling to live with me; *yamalócamu*, Yama's world, the abode of the dead; *yamaráshtramu*, Yama's realm.

yamuna, the river Jumna. Skt.

yantramu, machine, engine, device. Skt.; also *jantramu*. The first vowel is the indefinite vowel and the pronunciation is nearer to *yentramu*. *mém induló goppa yantramu chésinámu; cannu chedarun attugá occa sári núru cásulu tísiconi velli tahásṣiludárigári bhárya chétiló pósi, mácu míru tappa véré diccu léd ani, rendu cállunu pattuconnámu*, we engineered it most powerfully; we took a hundred sovereigns all at once to dazzle the tahsildar's wife and poured them into her palm and caught her by both legs and said: 'you are our only hope, our only refuge'.

yaṣassu, glory. Skt.

yathá, as. Skt. *yathá rájá, tathá prajá*, as the king, so his people (*quidquid delirant reges plectuntur Achivi*); *yathácramamugá*, *yathápracáramu*, *yathávidhigá*, as before, orderly, duly, properly; *pelli yémi y'ibbandi lécundá yathávidhigá zarigi póyindi*, the marriage was performed without a hitch and with ritual precision; *yathásthiti*, the previous condition, the *status quo ante*; a legal expression.

yatnamu, effort. Skt. More commonly *prayatnamu*. *Daiva yatnamu*, effort of Providence (the finger of God).

yauvanamu, youth. Skt. (*yuva*.) *yémi márina, y'ippatici ní rúpamu yauvana purushulanu vivahánic ácarshintsé lágumé v'unnadi gáni, marivaca* *vidhangá lédu*, though changed you are still personable enough to attract young men to marriage; *yauvanamló v'unnáḍu*, he is in the bloom of youth; *yauvanasthuḍu*, a youth; *yauvanavatti*, a girl.

yavacuḍu, a Greek (Ionian).

yavalu, barley; used in the plural like other names of grains.

yazamánuḍu, master, employer, husband. Skt. The feminine is *yazamáni* or *yazamánurálu*. *vanṭabráhmanuḍu vanḍina gárelanu mundugá tinṭ unḍenu; intaló yazamáni vachchenu. yazamáni: ninnu tsústé áṣcháryamugá v'undi. vanṭabráhmanuḍu: mimmunu tsústénu áṣcháryamgáné v' undanḍi, míru iccaḍici vastár ani nénu anucó lédu*, the brahmin cook was having a first go at the cakes he had cooked; meanwhile his mistress came along. Mistress: I am surprised at you. Cook: Not so surprised as I am at the sight of you, Madam; I never thought you would come here.

yábhai, fifty.

yáchintsuṭa, to beg. Skt. *yagnyamu nimittam yáchinchi*, begging money for a burnt sacrifice; *yémiṭo mácu tóchindi mém ichchinámu, taccinadi marivaca tsóṭa yáchintsanḍi*, we have given what we thought fit, beg the rest elsewhere; *yáchacuḍu*, beggar; *yáchanamu*, begging.

yádástu, memorandum, note. Hindustani. It is an old word for the memoranda Collectors and other officials addressed to their subordinates; now confined to the tahsildar's communications to village officers.

yágamu, sacrifice. Skt.; same as *yagnyamu. yága bhicsha cósam vacca sári déṣa sanchάram chési vastánu*, I will go about the country some time begging money for a sacrifice.

yálaculu, cardamoms. Vulgar for *élaculu*.

yálamu, auction. Vulgar for *vélamu, élamu*.

yámini, night. Skt. Used only in books.

yánamu, journey. Skt. *samudra yánamu*, sea voyage.

yápanamu, spending. Skt. *cálayápanamu*, waste of time.

yátana, anguish. Skt. Used in books.

yátra, pilgrimage. Skt. *ná chéti mátra vaicuntha yátra* (quack speaking): Take my pill and you will go up the hill; *Bhimarázugáru sacuṭumbamugá Cáṣi yátra veḷḷinάru*, Mr. Bhimarazu has gone on pilgrimage to Benares with all his family; *paralóca yátracu póyenu*, he has gone on pilgrimage to the other world.

yáva-, prefix meaning 'all'. Skt. *yávattu*, all, the whole; *yávachchactini v'upayóga parichi cárya sáphalyam chéstár ani nácu sampúrna viṣvásam v'unṭundi*, I am fully satisfied that you will put out all your strength and bring the matter to a successful issue; *yávajívanamu*, all one's life; *viváhamu chésucunévάru y'iddaru yávajívanamú vacarini míri vacaru, tirugacunḍámí, vacari cashṭa sukhamulacu vacaru autú, y'iddaru calasi vaccarugá v'unḍéṭ aṭṭu gánu, chésuconna conṭracṭu*, marriage is a lifelong contract not to be transgressed or gone back upon by either party to share joys and sorrows and to be two in one; *chinnatanamló viváham cheyyaḍam chéta bahu nashṭálu v'unnavi; anduló peḷḷicoḍucuc émainá y'ibbandi taṭasthinchina yeḍala, chinnadi yávajívanamú duhkha paḍa valasi vatstsunu*, there are many drawbacks to child-marriage; among them that if the bridegroom comes to any harm the girl has to sorrow all the rest of her life. (There are numerous words, suffixes, and affixes for 'all' in Telugu: *-allá, anta, -aṣéshamu, -ella, sacala, samasta, sarva, viṣva-, yáva-*; all persons is *andaru, yávanmandi*, &c.)

yédumu, five tooms (grain measure). For *aidu túmulu*.

yóchana, thought, idea, judgement. Skt. *dhairyamu léni rázu, yóchana léni mantri*, a king without courage, a minister at his wits' end.

yóchintsuṭa, to think, to consider. Skt.

yógamu, union, lucky juncture. Skt. *nénu mútilónó gótilónó paḍa valenu gáni nácu peḷḷádi bháryató sukhamgácápuram cheyyа valasina yógam lédu*, I am destined to come to a bad end and shall not have the luck to marry and live happily.

yógamu, ascetic magic. Skt. (You are supposed to acquire magical powers by asceticism, abstraction, and meditation, stopping the breath, taking up certain postures, looking at your navel, &c.; you obtain *yógadrüshṭhi*, spiritual insight, by these means and fall into *yóganidra*, supernatural sleep, can practise levitation, and so on. *yógi*, one who practises *yógam*; feminine *yógini*, *yógurálu*. *yógyábhyásamu*, practice of *yógam*. *ṣiṣhyuḍu: svámí! cannulu músiconi rüshiṣvaruni vale divya chacshussu chéta míru múḍu lócá mahatyálú mahá tsústú v'unnáru; mí ṣishyunni aina nácu míru tsúchidániló lava léṣam caṭácshinchi nannu crütárthunni chéstárá? yógi: óri ṣishyá! nívu y'incá yógyábhyásamló modaṭi avasthalóné v'unnáu; nívu incá gnyánabhódhacu arhuḍavu cávu.* Disciple: Your Reverence, you have shut your eyes and like a Lord Rishi are gazing with divine sight at the glories of the three worlds. Will your Reverence deign to reveal to your humble disciple any trifle and make him ever grateful? Yogi: You are, O disciple, still in the first stage of yogi practice and still unfit for the teaching of wisdom.

yógamu, worthy. Skt. *yógyata*, merit, competence. *chinnaváḍ ainá ní yógyata bahu doddadi*, you have an old head on young shoulders; *yógyatamaina*, competent; *yógyuḍu*, a worthy man; feminine *yógyurálu*. *yógyurálaina cannelacu y'iṭuvanṭi yémi teliyavu*, respectable girls know nothing of such things.

yójanamu, about eight miles; two ćos make an amada and two amadas a yojanam.

yóni, female organs of generation, vulva. Skt. *yónizulu* is womb-born as distinguished from *anḍajamu*, egg-born. The *yóni* is a Vaishnavite symbol, just as the *lingam* is a Saivite symbol.

yuctamu, joined, fit, proper. Skt. *yuctáyuctamulu*, right and wrong. *strílu vidya léni hétuvu chéta, yuctáyuctamulu teliyaca, paṣutulyaránḍrai n'anduna gadá, purushulac iṭuvanṭi manóvyadhalu sambhavintsuts unnavi*, it is because our women are uneducated and are like beasts not knowing right from wrong that we men are made to suffer these agonizing conflicts of the mind.

yucti, union, stratagem, scheme. Skt. (The Italian *combinazione*, combination, also unites these two meanings.) *ní yuctici santóshinchinánu*, I am pleased with your scheme.

yuddhamu, war, battle. Skt. *Lacshmayya tánu chinn appuḍu yuddhamló tsúpina sahásam gurinchi upanyásamló goppagá cheppuṭ unḍenu. sabhicuḍu: yuddham antá míré chésté, migilina sainyam yém chésind anḍi?* Lacshmayya was boasting in a lecture of all he had done in the wars in his youth. Voice from the audience: When you conducted the whole war yourself, what was left for the rest of the army to do?

yugamu, age (of the world). Skt. The four ages of the world according to the Hindus are the *crüta*, golden, *tréta*, silver, *dvápara*, brazen, and *cali*, iron. *nénu yeṭuvanṭi pápishṭi rátri gaḍapinánu; adi rátri cádu; ná páliṭici vaca mahávugam lágu canapaḍḍadi*, I passed a horrible night; not a night at all; it seemed a never-ending age; *yugálanáṭi Yudhishtharuḍu*, a Yudhishthara of the olden days (a bragadoccio). We are now supposed to have had 5,000 years of the iron age; *caliyugamu aidu véla samvatsarálu cá vachchinadi.*

yuva, young. Skt. *yuvarázu*, young prince, heir apparent; *yuvati*, a young woman.

yúnivarsiṭi, university. English. The Skt. compounds *sarva-calá-ṣála*, hall of all arts, or *viṣva-vidy-álayamu*, abode of all knowledge, may also be used.

Z

This letter is confused in the Telugu script with *j* and *jh*. It is also substituted in writing for *ts* for supposed euphony as in *zálunu*, it is enough, for *tsálunu*.

zabba, shoulder. Also *zebba*.

zabbu, weakness, illness, sluggishness.

zabbugá, ill. *peddamanishi: í gaḍiyáram oca purushántaram varacu pani chéstund ani cheppi ichcháu; appuḍé ági póyindi. amméváḍu: míru gaḍiyáram conn appuḍu zabbugá canipinchāru, anduchéta aṭlá cheppānu.* Gentleman: When I bought this watch you said it would last a lifetime: it stopped at once. Watchmaker: I only said that because you looked ill at the time. *vanṭló* is often added; *vanṭló zabbugá* (ill in the body).

zabbupaḍuṭa, to be ill.

zaḍa, plait (of hair or straw); also *jaḍa*.

zaḍipintsuṭa, to frighten. *nénu áviḍenu zaḍipintsa lédu, áviḍenu tsúchi néné zaḍusu cunnánu,* I didn't frighten her, it was I that was afraid when I saw her.

zaḍivána, storm of rain, heavy rain. *zaḍigádpu,* hurricane.

zaḍiyuṭa, to be afraid. *yénuganu yeccinaváḍu cucca cútacu zaḍiyaḍu,* a man on an elephant won't be afraid of a dog's bark; *róṭló burra peṭṭi rócaṭi debbacu zaḍisin aṭṭu,* like the man who put his head in a mortar and was then afraid of the blow of the pestle (rashness and afterthought bringing trouble on oneself); *zaḍiya valasina pani lédu,* there is no reason to be afraid; *tsappuḍucu zaḍisi,* afraid at the noise; *palleṭúḷḷalóni carandlú rahitulu v'úrucunn aṭṭupaṭna vásálaló váḷḷu v'úrucóru,* the placid contentment of village curnams and ryots will not be found among the inhabitants of towns who are not afraid of us; *manam tinnagá v'unṭé yevarici zaḍiyan accara lédu,* he who walks uprightly need fear no one (*chi non li fa non li teme,* no wrong no fear). The word is sometimes pronounced and written *jhaḍiyuṭa*.

zaḍupu, fear.

zaftu, zaftí, distraint. Hindustani.

zagaḍamu, dispute.

zagamu, world. Skt. Used chiefly in compounds. *zagamutalli,* the world's Mother, is Lakshmi; *zagarautu,* the world's knight; *zaganmóhini,* the world's sweetheart (the cinema anticipated, *vixere formosae ante Mariam Pickford*). Also *jagamu, jagattu*.

zagannádhuḍu, zagannádhuḍu, Juggarnaut, Lord of the world, the famous Puri Vishnu, under the wheels of whose car many found salvation in death; *zagam erigina bráhmanunici zandem élá?* the worldwise brahmin needs no sacred thread (good wine needs no bush).

zalacamu, water, a bath. Skt.; also *jalamu, jalacamu*.

zalaga, leech. The first *a* is the indefinite vowel and the pronunciation is nearer to *zelaga*.

zalleḍa, sieve.

zallintsuṭa, to sift in a sieve.

zallumanuṭa, to shudder, to thrill; also spelt *jhallumanuṭa*.

zalubu, cold in the head.

zalubuchéyuṭa, to catch a cold. *vánici zalubu chésindi,* he has caught a cold.

zama, collection of money, credit as opposed to debit (*khartsu*) in accounts. Hindustani.

zamacaṭṭuṭa, to credit. *yenta sommu vachchinádó canccunéváru yevaru? íyana daya talachi chiṭṭhánu yenta zama caḍité anta,* who is to know how much money has come in? You can only see what he has been pleased to credit in the day-book; *í paicamu ná péra zamacaṭṭumu,* please carry this to my credit.

zamábandi, jamabandi, the Collector's annual settlement of accounts with the ryots under the ryotvari system. Hindustani. As the land-tax was fixed long ago this is now an interesting but useless survival. The Collector only meets the village officers. The Collector used to travel with his whole staff and thereby an additional heavy tax was laid on the villages. *í zamábandi yeppuḍu viragaḍ autundó? anni y'ippuḍé vastavi. avatala, grámamló dastu chési Deltá Syúparinṭenḍenṭu mukhánni pósténé cáni polalóci vacca tsucca níru rádu. ivatala zamábandi khartsulu dastu cheyya valenu. górutsuṭṭu mída rócaṭi póṭu paḍḍ aṭṭu sarcáru cisti cúḍá y'ippuḍu vachchindi.* (Village headman speaking): Pray God we'll soon be rid of this cursèd jamabandi, the pilfering dalait-man and plundering sibbandi; and all the damned collections all come, the devil take 'em, a-hustling one another. First and most important, the Delta Superintendent must get his bribe unshorten'd. Suppose I pays a pie less than what he thinks I oughter, our fields of paddy won't get a single drop of water. I must get money too for the cursèd jamaband, Sir; and then on top of all comes the dashed sarcar demand, Sir.

zamákhartsu, income and expenditure, profit and loss, credit and debit. *zamákhartsu pustacamunu tísi patramulu tiruga véyutsu,* taking his ledger out and turning the pages.

zamí, zamídári, zamínu, zamíndári, landed estate. Hindustani. These are estates held on permanent as opposed to ryotvari tenure.

zamíndáruḍu, holder of a permanently settled landed estate. The feminine is *zamindárini. crindi tsúpulu tsúputsu, oca chétitó misamu vaḍi véyutsu, renḍava chetitó bozza nimurucontsu, zamindáruḍuváru pravéṣintsutsunnáru,* enter my lord zamindar with disdainful looks, one hand twisting his moustachios, the other hand stroking his stomach.

zammu, bulrush.

zanáná, zenana, harem. Hindustani; also *janáná.*

zancu, hesitation, fear. *zancu lécunḍa máṭláḍutánu,* I will speak without fear or hesitation.

zancuṭa, to fear, to hesitate, to shake. *nichchena zancutsunnadi,* the ladder is shaky.

zandemu, zandhyamu, sacred thread. The brahmins wear this; so do the artisans (goldsmiths, &c.) who call themselves Visva Brahmins. *áchárya vyavahárálu léca póté y'í brahmanícamu yenducu? meḷḷó zandhyálu yenducu? tísi cucca meḷḷó veyya rádu?* but for customary observances what is brahminhood? What are the sacred threads around our necks for? We might as well take them off and tie them on dogs' necks. *zagam erigina bráhmanunici zandem élá?* good wine needs no bush.

zanṭa, a pair.

zanṭinchi máṭláḍuṭa, to string words together, to jabber.

zanṭuṭa, to be strung together.

zanumu, the jute-plant.

zanupunára, jute fibre from *zanumu,* jute, and *nára,* fibre. *zanupunára pítsu vale gaḍḍamu,* a beard the colour of jute.

zaptí, distraint. Hindustani; also *zaftí, zaftu.*

zaptízavánu, bailiff.

zaraguṭa, zaruguṭa, to move, to pass, to happen, to go on, to be finished. *ani, zaragutsunnáḍu,* as he spoke he stepped forward; *bhuctici zaragaca,* not being able to manage for food; *váḷḷa lécunḍá v'utsavalu zaragavu,* without them festivals will not be properly conducted; *atithi: mácu ákharu vindu yeppuḍandi? peddamanishi: indácá zarigindé.* Guest: When is our last meal? Gentleman: The last is over.

zarapuṭa, zarupuṭa, to pass (time), to perform; causal of *zaraguṭa. yécádaṣi vratam niyamamgá zarapa valenu,* the eleventh day fast must be properly performed.

zari, gold or silver lace.

zarigintsuṭa, to conduct, to execute, carry on.

zarimáná, a fine. Hindustani; also *zulmána, jarimáná.*

zarugubáṭu, subsistence; also *zarugubaḍi.*

zarúru, urgent. Hindustani.

zata, a pair.

zatapaḍuṭa, to pair off, to agree, to unite. *vánici zatapaḍináru,* they joined him.

zaṭṭi, a contract. Hindustani. *dhányam zaṭṭi putstsucunṭáru*, they take grain contracts.

zaṭṭu, party, clique, team. *má zaṭṭuló coṭṭavá/ḷḷanu chértsucó cúḍadu*, we don't want new members in our party; *í v'úḷḷó pókhiríl andaru zaṭṭu v'unnáru*, all the blackguards in this village have formed a clique; *criceṭṭu zaṭṭu*, a cricket team.

zava, frame. *zavacaṭṭuṭa*, to frame. *zavadáṭuṭa*, to transgress, disobey.

zavábu, answer. Hindustani; also *javábu*. *yeduru zavábu*, back-chat.

zavábudárí, responsibility. Hindustani. *rúpáyici mátramé nénu zavábudárí chéstánu*, I will be responsible only for one rupee; *zavábuddárí pani antá náḍi*, I take the whole responsibility.

zavábudáríléni, non-liability. A legal term.

zavábudáruḍu, person responsible, surety. Hindustani.

zavábunivísu, zavábuvísu, clerk. Hindustani. This is an obsolete word. It is used in the old records of the clerks who wrote down the Collector's orders or replies (*zavábulu*).

zavánu, peon, bailiff, constable; also *javánu*. *zapti zavánu voḷḷ antá chemaṭulu paṭṭéṭ aṭṭugá parugettutú v'unnáḍu*, the bailiff comes running all of a sweat.

zavvanamu, youth. Corrupt Skt., cf. *yuva*. Also *javvanamu*.

zavvani, damsel. Also *zavarálu*, cf. *yuvati*. Also *javvani*.

zábitá, list. Hindustani. *rimishanarla zábita tayáru chéyintsaḍamló cávalasin anta sommu rábaṭṭa vatstsunu*, we can make quite a tidy sum when we come to prepare the remission list.

zábú, letter. Hindustani.

záḍa, trace, clue, track. *aḍugula záḍa*, footsteps; *víḍu tanḍri záḍagá n'unnáḍu*, he is cut on his father's pattern; *záḍagá cheppuṭa*, to supply a clue; *mí záḍa vetuccunṭú y'iccaḍici parugettucuni vachchinánu*, I have come running here on your tracks; *itaḍu vaca véla mana záḍa tiyyaḍánici pampinchina véguváḍai v'unḍa vatstsunu*, he may be a spy sent out to trace us.

záḍi, a jar.

záḍintsuṭa, to flap, to twit. *cóḍi reccalanu záḍintsutsunnadi*, the fowl is flapping its wings; *nénu vánini diṭṭamgá záḍinchinánu*, I ticked him off properly.

zágá, room, space.

zágáramu, vigil. *nénu pinugutó zágáram chésin aṭṭu tellavárin dáca mélucó lédu*, I can't lie awake till dawn like a man watching a corpse; *Dévuḍu gulḷalló dévuḷḷanu ráti bommal anṭáru; zágárálu chésté vaḷḷu zabbu chéstund anṭáru*, they (Europeans) call the gods in the temples stone images; they say keeping vigils is bad for the health.

zágárúcata, wakefulness.

zágu, delay.

zájicáya, nutmeg. Skt.

zála, fishing-net.

zálacarra, open-work in stone, tracery.

záli, pity, love. *vacílu: órí dongá, nénu y'ichchinadi cáca póté nícu y'incá ḍabb evaru istáru rá? gumástá: yevaru y'istárá? mí párṭílu y'istáru; váru mí svabhávam yeruguduru ganuca ná mída záli talachi yémaina y'istú v'unṭáru.* Pleader: Thief, if I don't give you money, who will? Pleader's Clerk: Who will give it? Why, your clients. They know your character and take pity on me and give me something or other. *pápam vínini tsústé nácu záli véstú v'unnadi*, I pity him; *itanici chevuḍu rávaḍam tsústé záli véstú v'unnadi*, I pity him for being deaf. *ocaḍu: Lacshmayya tsústé nácu záli véstundi. incóḍu: yenducu? ocaḍu: Lacshmayya yéḍu bháshalu nértsuconnáḍu. chésucunna peḷḷám ataḍini occa máṭ ainá máṭláḍan iyyaḍu.* First Hindu: I pity Lakshmayya. Second Hindu: Why? First Hindu: Lakshmayya has learnt seven languages but his wife won't let him get in a word in any of them.

zálu, stream, rivulet.

zálunu, it is enough for *tsálunu*.

záma, guava; also *jéma*.

zámíndáru, surety.

zámínu, bail, security. Hindustani.

adhicamaina záminu, additional security. In the Ceded Districts a ryotvari holding. They say *ná záminu*, my land, instead of *ná jiráyati*.

záminucaṭṭu, bail-bond.

zámu, watch (period of time). The day is divided into four watches. The first watch ends about 9 a.m., the second at noon, the third about 3 p.m., the last at sunset, the night is similarly divided. So *rendu zámulu* is midday or midnight; *tellavári zámuna* is the morning. Witnesses in court usually reckon time by zamus.

záríchembu, pot with a spout. Also written *jhárichembu*.

záruḍu, adulterer; also *járuḍu*. Skt. The feminine is *zárini, járini*, adulteress, prostitute. *zárinula vadda sangítam v'unḍaḍam chéta cula stríl adi níchamgá yenchi, sangitam nértsucóca póvaḍam valla purushulu sangíṭánic áşa paḍi véşyalu sangítánni purushulanu tama valaló paḍa vésucóvaḍánici sádhanamgá chésucóvaḍanni, taṭastham autú v'unnadi*, music being the province of prostitutes our women look upon it as low and won't practise it; and the men go to courtesans' houses after music and then fall into the net spread by the courtesans, who use music as a means of subjugation.

zárugóchi, slip-truss. It is supposed to be improper. *míváḍu mokhánni vibhúti peṭṭaḍu, zárugóchi peṭṭutáḍu; monna búḍsula zóḍu toḍucconi paṭṭa pagalu vídhiló nunchi veḷḷutú v'unṭé nénu caḷḷáré tsúchinánu*, your boy does not powder his face with ashes. He wears a slip-truss. The other day I saw him with my own eyes going down the street in broad daylight in boots.

zárumuḍi, slip-knot; from *záruṭa*, to slip, and *muḍi*, knot. *adi zárumuḍi cáḍá? cádu, gaṭṭi muḍi*, is that a slip-knot? No, a firm knot.

záruṭa, to slip; *zára viḍutsuṭa*, to let slip; *zárutundi*, it is slippery; *talacu záru debba tagilindi*, a glancing blow on the head; *buradaló cálu zári paḍḍáḍu*, he lost his footing in the mud; *cálu zárité tísucó vatstsunu gáni nóru zárité tísucó cúḍadu*, a slip of the foot may be recovered but not a slip of the tongue (*il vaut mieux glisser du pied que de la langue*).

záva, gruel.

zebba, shoulder. Sometimes written *zabba*. The vowel is indeterminate between *a* and *e*. *zabbapushṭi*, muscular strength. *zebbayemuca*, the shoulder-blade.

zelaga, leech; sometimes written *zalaga*, the vowel being indeterminate. Also *jelaga*.

zompamu, cluster of twigs or bamboos.

zonna, the great millet, *cholum* in Tamil and Anglo-Indian, *jowari* in Anglo-Indian Hindustani; for the grain the plural *zonnalu* is used. *moccazonna*, maize; *zonna* is a hardy crop. As the proverb says: *cshánamuna zonna, varshamuna vaḍlu*, paddy when there is rain, when there is none cholum.

zócoṭṭuṭa, to hush (a child).

zócyamu, connexion, business, interference, concern; also *zóli, jócyamu, áyana yé zócyamu caluga chésucócunḍá yevaru vachchiná, mâṭláḍutú, rüshi lágu yeppuḍu puranálu mundu peṭṭucuni tsaduvucunṭú cúrtsunṭáḍú*, he always sits reading with the Puranas in front of him like a rishi and has no dealings with any one who comes and talks; *míru zócyam caluga chésucóca pillavánni nénu penchin aṭṭ allá pentsan isté*, if you will mind your own business and leave the rearing of the child to me; *induló nácu zócyam lédu* is what the Collector says when petitioners bring a petition about a matter for the civil courts or the taluk boards; it is no concern of mine; *nívu yevari zócyamunacu véḷḷa cúḍaḍu*, keep yourself to yourself.

zóḍintsuṭa, to join, to clasp; from *zóḍu*, pair. *chétulu zóḍintsuṭa*, to fold the hands (as in *namascáramu*, salutation).

zóḍu, pair. *sancella zóḍu*, a pair of fetters; (*cheppula*) *zóḍu*, pair of pattens; (*sulóchanamula*) *zóḍu*, pair of spectacles.

zóli, concern, business, connexion; also *zócyamu*. *váni zólici pó vaddu*, have nothing to do with him; *adi ní zóli cádu*, that is no concern of yours; *ní zóli nác accara lédu*, I don't want to have anything to do with you; *á v'uttaram zóli manac enducu?* what have we to do with that letter? *á pitstsaváḍu ná zólici rádu lé*, I am not concerned with that lunatic; *ná zólici yevaru rá cúḍaḍu*, I won't have any one meddling.

zóríga, gadfly. *simhamu pacca zóriga unḍina mádiri*, like the gadfly near the lion (safety near the strong).

zóru, force, violence. *y'í déṣamuló ativáguḍuváḷḷa gaḍabiḍa zórigá v'unnadi*, the extremists are making much noise in this country.

zósyamu, astrology. Skt.

zósyuḍu, astrologer.

zó zó, hush hush; onomatopoeic.

zulmáná, fine. Hindustani; also *zarimáná, jarimáná. méjisṭréṭu zulmáná vésté Gavarnamenṭuvárici lábham calugutundi*, magisterial fines are Government revenue; *chhárji shiṭu chési padi rúpáyalu zulmáná véyinchináru*, they put in a charge-sheet and got a fine of Rs. 10 imposed.

zum, hum; onomatopoeic. *téneṭiga zumcáram chéyutsunnadi*, bees hum.

zunnu, honey-comb, cheese, any close-pressed article of diet. *pulizunnu*, tiger's milk cheese (an unobtainable luxury).

zurruṭa, to suck up. *váḍu paramánnamu zurrutsunnáḍu*, he is sucking up the milk-rice.

zuṭṭu, the top-knot worn by men; convenient to catch hold of in a fight. *zuṭṭu paṭṭi sommu aḍigináḍu*, he pressed him for payment (taking him by the hair); *zuṭṭu paṭṭuconi vanga tíyutsunnáḍu*, he has got him by the top-knot and is bending him down.

zúdamu, gambling. Corrupt Skt. for *dyútam. zúdamu, pánamu, asatyamu modalaina dushcáryamulu*, gambling, drink, untruthfulness, and the rest of the vices.

zúdamáḍuṭa, to gamble. *zúdamáḍi rózucu nálugu rúpáyalu gelustánu*, I win four rupees a day at games of chance.

zúdári, gambler.

zúlu, mane. The Anglo-Indian jool for horse-cloth is derived from this.

zúpuṭa, euphonic for *tsúpuṭa*, to show This is not misapplied euphony. Telugu is spoilt by its harsh *ts* and *ch*. Could anything be uglier than *tsútsutsu*, seeing, the present participle of *tsútsuṭa*, to see?

APPENDIX

Familiar phrases with the nearest equivalents in Telugu.

A

He is abroad, *vaḍu paradéṣam and unnáḍu.*

The food does not agree with him, *í tinḍi vánici giṭṭadu.*

Agreeing like cats and dogs, *nippucu niḷḷacu v'unḍé snéhamu.*

Alpha and omega, *ádyantálu.*

An anatomy (thin man), *gunṭanacca.*

An angel of death, *mrütyu dévata.*

My good angel, *ná páliṭi daivamu.*

Anno Domini, *ána.*

In the article of death, *maranávasthaló.*

Asking for trouble, *tongunna suncari tala múṭa dimpum annaṭṭu.*

B

Back-chat, *yeduru zavábu.*

Bag and baggage, *múta mulle.*

His bark is worse than his bite, *morigé cucca carava néradu.*

On his beam ends, *tsúḍa tsuṭṭamu, mocca daivamu lédu.*

Every one must bear his own cross, *yevari niḷḷaló váré munaga valenu.*

To make a beast of oneself, *gaḍḍi tinuṭa.*

Beating about the bush, *tsallacu vachchi munta dátsuconn aṭṭu* (hiding the pot when you have come for the buttermilk).

Don't believe all you hear, *vinnavi anni viṣvasintsa rádu.*

Benefits are soon forgotten, *yeppaṭi mélu appaṭicé.*

Better late than never, *puṭṭina y'innáḷḷacu purushuḍu yagnyamu chésináḍu.*

Between the devil and the deep sea, *venucacu veḷḷité tannu, mundu vasté póṭu.*

Between you and me, *y'í sangati mana y'iddariloné v'unḍa valenu sumí.*

Billing and cooing, *chandra chacóra nyáyamu* (the way of the partridge with the moon).

I haven't told a little bird, *vacca piṭṭató cheppa lédu.*

Killing two birds with one stone, *manamaḍu nértsucunn aṭlu, avvacu durada tírin aṭṭu* (like the boy who scratched his granny's back by writing his lessons on it). *éca criyá dvyarthacári.*

Birds of a feather flock together, *nattagullal anni vaca révuna, mutyapu chippal anni vaca révuna* (all the common shells on one bank, all the pearl oysters on another). *níru níru vancané párutundi* (water flows to water).

The biter bit, *eccirintsu póyi vellacila paḍḍáḍ aṭa* (went up to mock and fell on his back).

Biting off more than you can chew, *ácali ácáṣam anta, gontuca súdi bezzam anta* (hunger as high as heaven, a gullet the size of a needle's eye).

He looked black at me, *nannu tsúchi mukham máḍchináḍu.*

Blessed are the meek, *ahimsa parama dharmam.*

In the land of the blind the one-eyed man is king, *turucalu léni v'úḷḷó Dúdéculaváḍu Sahib Miyyá.*

His blood was up, *vánici váḷḷu manḍinaḍi.*

Blow upon blow, trouble upon trouble, *górutsuṭṭu pai rócaṭi póṭu* (the blow of a pestle on a whitlow).

A blow for a blow, *véṭacu véṭu.*

Great boaster, little doer, *máṭalu cóṭalu dáṭutavi, cáḷḷu caḍapa dáṭa lévu* (his words breach forts, his feet do not pass his threshold).

Burning your boats behind you, *yéru dáṭi teppa tagala vésinaṭṭu.*

A bolt from the blue, *adháttugá vachchina piḍugu.*

To bore to death, *pránamu tíyuṭa* (take one's life).

Born with a silver spoon in one's mouth, *puṭṭubhóghi.*

He who goes a-borrowing goes a-sorrowing, *yeruvu sommu paruvu chéṭu.*

A bragadoccio, *yugálanáṭi Yudhishtharuḍu.*

I haven't a brass farthing, *nácu guḍḍi gavva lédu.*

Brave heart in old body, *mudi mánu chéva* (the core of an old tree is sound).

Broad daylight, *paṭṭapagalu*.
A broken reed, *munaga comma*.
You brute! *paṣuprâyaḍavá!*
To bubble over with joy, *santósham anta pongiporli póvuṭa*.
He is busy, *pani mída v'unnáru*.
But me no buts, *ní cánulu ginulu dúramgá peṭṭu*.
Butter won't melt in his mouth, *venna peṭṭité minga léḍu*.
Let bygones be bygones, *poyyed·ellá pón í*.

C

Capping a story, *idugó pul anṭé adugó tóc annaṭṭu*.
I don't care a bit, *nác émi lacshyam lédu*.
A cat's paw, *savati biḍḍa cheyyi* (step-child's hand).
Like cats and dogs, *nippucu nílḷacu v'unḍé snéham* (the friendship of fire and water).
To rain cats and dogs, *cumbhapótagá curiyuṭa* (to rain pitchers).
Castles in the air, *gontemma córicalu*.
He will catch it, *tâḷam paṭṭistáḍu* (catch the cymbal).
Caught between two fires, *mundarici vasté goyyi, venaccu póté nuyyi* (a pit before, a well behind).
To rise to celebrity, *vásic eccuṭa*.
Charity begins at home, *tana talupu tisi, porigințici peṭṭi, rátri antá cuccalu tólutu cúrtsunn aṭṭu* (lent his neighbour his front door and spent the night chasing dogs away).
Cheese-paring, *tarimiḍi paṭṭin appuḍu rálina poḍum v'úricé pó lédu* (collecting the lathe shavings).
Taking the chestnuts out of the fire, *tana cheyyi cálutund ani, savatibiḍḍa chétitó caliya peṭṭinad aṭa* (thinking it would burn her own hand she made the stepchild put her hand in).
She has neither chick nor child, *dánici biḍḍapápulu léru*.
Stop your clack, *ní loḍaloḍa mánu*.
To clinch a bargain, *béram áḍuṭa*.
Clotted nonsense, *unmatta pralápamulu*.
No concern of yours, *ní zóli cádu*.
Cut your coat according to your cloth, *caligité cáḷḷu muyyi, léca póté mócáḷḷu muyyi* (cover your feet if you can; if not, your knees). *áyamu telisi vyayamu* (knowing your income your expenditure).
The cobbler's wife is the worst shod, *mádigaváḍi álu máḍi cálici cheppu lédu*.
He paid them in their own coin, *sarici sari chésináḍu*.
To come down in the world, *hína daṣacu vatstsuṭa. metta náḷḷu póyinavi, chetta náḷḷu vachchinavi* (mattress days are gone, straw days have come).
A great come-down, an anti-climax, *diviṭí cinda dípálu*.
He commands respect, *vánici máṭa ságutundi*.
Conceited ass! *pogarabótu vedhava!*
I count on your kindness, *mí dayanu nammucunnánu*.
Counting your chickens before they are hatched, *puṭṭani biḍḍacu péru peṭṭu-táḍu* (or *púsalu caṭṭin aṭṭu*), naming (or putting beads on) the unborn child. *álú lédu, tsúlú lédu, coḍucu péru Sómalingam* (no wife, no conception, but the child's name is Sómalingam). *chéló patti v'unḍagáné Pólici múdu múḷḷu, nácu áru múḷḷu annaṭṭu* (like the man who said three ells of cloth for Póli and three for me when the cotton was still on the field).
They can't put two coppers together, *váḷḷacu nálugu ḍabbulu yérucóvaḍam chéta cádu*.
You have got the credit, *nícu péru daccinadi*.
All the credit and none of the work, *amarchinaddánṭló attagáru vélu peṭṭinadi* (the mother-in-law put her finger into the dish the daughter-in-law had prepared).
To creep like an ant, *chíma lágu prácuṭa*.
He is crestfallen, *váni moham máḍipóyindi* (or *chinnapóyindi*).
Criticism is very easy, *nerasulu vedacipaṭṭuṭa télica*.
Crocodile tears, *atta tsasté coḍalu yéḍchin aṭṭu* (like the daughter-in-law crying at her mother-in-law's death).
Every man has to bear his own cross. *yevari paiguḍḍa várici baruvé* (every one's mantle is heavy to himself). *yevari níḷḷaló váru munaga vale* (every one has to bathe in his own water).

The crow thinks her own bird fairest, *cáci pilla cácici muddu.*

As the crow flies, *cáci vale sútigá póté.*

Crying before you are hurt, *coṭṭuca munupé yéḍtsuṭa.*

Crying over spilt milk, *aina panici chintinchévádu alpa buddhi galaváḍu.*

Much cry and little wool, *utta goḍḍucu arupul eccuva* (the barren cow lows loudest).

To pass current, *chelluṭa.*

D

To look daggers, *urimi tsútsuṭa* (to look thunder).

Dancing to his tune, *váḍu páḍinadi páṭa, áḍinadi áṭa.*

In mortal danger, *pránamu mídici vachchindi.*

A Daniel come to judgement, *Brüha-spiti.*

Any day will do, *aité ádivánam, cácunṭé sómavánam.*

Day or night; *répó mápó.*

Wishing himself dead, *jivánici v'usú-rum anṭu.*

Deep sleep, *gádha nidra.*

To run like a deer, *léḍi lágu parugettuṭa.*

In the seventh heaven of delight, *bramhánandamgá v'unnadi.*

Possessed by a devil, *dayyamu paṭṭina.*

Diamond cut diamond, *mani manitó coyya valenu.*

A diamond on a dunghill, *cuppaló mánicyam.*

Dignity and decorum, *paruvú pratish-ṭhá.*

Dignity and impudence, *yénuguni tsúchi cuccalu moriginaṭṭu* (like dogs barking at an elephant).

A dinner of herbs where love is, *prítitó peṭṭinadi piḍicedi tsálunu.*

Throw dirt and some will stick, *pai-paḍḍa máṭa, maḍi paḍḍa níḷḷu pótavá?* (the word let fall, the water let into the seed-bed).

Distance lends enchantment to the view, *dúrapu conḍalu nunupu* (distant hills are smooth).

Documentary support, *dastavézula ádhdramu.*

To go to the dogs, *bhrashṭai póvuṭa.*

Dog-tired, *visigi vésari.*

Let sleeping dogs lie, *tungunna suncari tala múṭa dimpum annaṭṭu* (like the man who asked the sleeping toll-keeper to give him a hand with his head-bundle).

Give a dog a bad name and hang him, *vachchina vádu tsachchiná pódu* (a bad name will stick to you till you die).

Down and out, *tsúḍa tsuṭṭamu, mocca daivamu lédu* (no relation to see, no God to call upon).

On a downhill course, *cshina daṣaló.*

He dotes on her, *dáni mída pránamulu viḍustáḍu* (he gives out his life on her).

The only drawback, *unna lópam allá.*

Dressed up to one's eyes, *talacu min-china véshálu vési.*

I gave him a good dressing down, *vánini diṭṭamgá záḍinchinánu.*

To be drowned in a sea of sorrows, *duhkha samudramló munigi póvuṭa.*

E

To set by the ears, *póṭilu peṭṭuṭa.*

Too many for an embassy, too few for an army, *góchici pedda, angavastra-mucu chinna* (big for a loin-cloth, small for a mantle).

Eyes have they but they see not, they have ears but they hear not, *cani guḍḍi, vini chevuḍu.*

Within eyeshot, *tsúpu méra dúramló.*

F

His face fell, *váni mocam múḍi póyindi.*

Fair and foul, fair means or foul, *nyáyabhayamulu* (fair words and threats). *uppani máṭa cheppi, tsappani máṭa cheppi* (saying salt words, saying insipid words).

Falling into your own trap, *yevaru travvucunna gótiló váré paḍḍaṭṭu.*

Falling out of the frying-pan into the fire, *mundara pallam, venuca miṭṭa* (precipice in front, cliff behind). *adi dummu* (dust) *idi cummu* (ashes).

Familiarity breeds contempt, *ati pari-chaya avagnyata* (Skt.). *peraṭi cheṭṭu mandacu rádu* (the tree that grows in your backyard is no good for medi-cine).

His father's son, *á tandri coḍucu.*

There is no one without faults, *tappulé-nivdru dharaṇiló léru.*

Do me the favour, *daya cheyyanḍi.*

Having no fear of God or man, *ihapardádulacu veraca.*

Feast one day, physic the next, *oca nádu vindu, oca nádu mandu.*

You could have knocked me down with a feather, *piḍuguvanṭi vartamánamu* (news like a thunderbolt).

A poor feeder, *súcshma bhójanuḍu.*

Sitting on the fence, *góḍa mídi pilli* (the cat on the wall).

A fig for . . ., *yéḍisinaṭṭé v'unnadi.*

The finger of God, *Daiva yatnamu.*

Pouring oil on the flames, *agniló ájyam* (Skt. for ghee) *pósinaṭṭu.*

The flame of passion, *cámagni.*

All flesh is grass, *déham nírubugga vanṭidi* (the body is like a water-bubble).

A fly in a spider's web, *sálegúṭló paḍḍa y'íga.*

A reproof entereth more into a wise man than a hundred stripes into a fool, *manchivánici máṭé mandu* (a word is medicine to a good man).

A fool's mouth calleth for stripes, *náluca, náluca, vípucu debbalu téca* (tongue, tongue, do not bring blows on my back).

Fools laugh at their own sport, *yevari verri várici ánandam* (every one's folly is pleasant to him).

(Famine) my foot, *cshámálu gímálu.*

Fortunatus's cap, *ívi mánu* (the tree that gives all one wishes).

Fortune favours the brave, *dhairyam sarvatra sádhacamu* (a Skt. proverb meaning 'courage is always a means of success').

They poked fun at him, *vánini yegatálici paṭṭinchináru.*

Your funeral, not mine, *yevari níḷḷaló váré munaga valenu* (every one must dip in his own water).

What a fuss! *yenta brahmándam!*

G

No gains without pains, *cashṭí phalí.* (A Skt. proverb meaning 'from labour fruit'.)

All his geese are swans, *tá valasinadi Rambha, tá munaginadi Ganga* (his sweetheart is a Rhamba, his river is the Ganges).

I can't get on without it, *idi lénidi nácu ágadu.*

They don't get on, *várici várici posaga lédu* (*ciṭṭadu*).

Looking a gift-horse in the mouth, *punyánici puṭṭeḍ isté pitstsa cuntsam ani pícul áḍin aṭṭu* (like the man who fought about the measure being false when they gave him a quarter of grain gratis).

Give a dog a bad name and hang him, *vachchina vádu tsachchiná pódu.*

Giving yourself away, *gummadicáyalu donga anṭé bhuzálu táné paṭṭi tsútsu-cunnáḍu* (feeling your own shoulders when pumpkin-thief is mentioned).

God sendeth rain on the just and on the unjust, *varici vaca váná, v'údacu vaca váná?* (is there one rain for rice and another for weeds?).

God knoweth the secrets of the heart, *lóguṭṭu Perumáḷḷacu yeruca.*

God's own country, *carmabhúmi* (India).

God's truth, *Ráma vácyam.*

A God-given opportunity, *daivicamgá labhinchina samayam.*

All is not gold that glitters, *calla pasiḍici cánti menḍu* (false gold glitters most).

The Golden Age, *crútayugamu.*

The good old times, *vachché cálamu canna vachchina cálamu mélu* (the past is better than the future).

It is all for your good, *id anta ni bágu cósamé.*

Good wine needs no bush, *zagam erigina bráhmanunici zandem élá?* (the experienced Brahmin needs no sacred thread).

To return good for evil, *apacárici upacáramu.*

Killing the goose that lays the golden eggs, *podugu cósi pálu tágin aṭṭu* (like cutting the udder to get at the milk).

What he says is gospel, *Vissanna cheppinadi Véda.*

Teach your grandmother to suck eggs, *tátacu dagga nérpa valená?*

In their gratitude is our great reward, *vári crútagnyataló má y'uttama pratiphalamu.*

On this side of the grave, *iham andu.*

A Gretna Green marriage, *Gandharva viváhamu.*

One foot in the grave, *cáṭici caḷḷu tsátsuconi* (stretching the feet towards the cemetery). *úru pomm anṭundi, cáḍu ramm anṭundi* (the village says 'go', the cemetery says 'come').

Grinding his teeth, *panḍlu paṭapaṭa corucutsu.*

Ground and glebe, *mányḍlú maḷḷú.*

I will be on my guard, *ná jágrata mida v'unṭánu.*

H

The play without Hamlet, *divvena tísina gúḍu* (the niche without the lamp).

Hand and glove, *chandra chacóra nyáyamugá* (like the moon and the partridge).

I don't care a hang, *nácu ventruca mátram* (the measure of a hair to me).

Hard words break no bones, *tiṭṭi tsachchinaváḍu léḍu* (no one yet died of hard words).

I will settle your hash, *ní pani paṭṭistánu.*

Make hay while the sun shines, *gáli vachchin appuḍu túrpára paṭṭucó valenu* (winnow when the wind comes).

No two heads are made alike, *burracu vaca gunamu.*

My head swims, *ná tala tirugutundi* (*tirugutsunnadi*).

It has gone to my head, *talac eccinadi.*

Without head or tail, *tala tóca léni.*

Burying your head in the sand, *pilli canḍlu músuconi pálu táguṭa* (the cat drinking milk with its eyes shut).

Heart of oak, *mudi mánu chéva.*

To work with heart and soul, *oḷḷu vanchi pani cheyyuṭa.*

To set one's heart on, *manassu paṭṭuṭa.*

A merry heart goes all the way, *santósham sagam balamu* (joy is half one's strength).

My heart was in my mouth, *ná pránamu talladillinadi.*

Better a dinner of herbs where love is than a stalled ox and hatred thereby, *prítitó peṭṭinadi piḍic eḍé tsálunu* (a handful is enough if given with love).

Herculean labours, *Bhagíratha prayatnamulu.*

Where shall I hide my head? *yé boccaló dúrutánu?*

Hidebound (conservative), *gaḍḍacaṭṭina* (*cansarvaṭivu*).

Hoist with your own petard, *yevaru travvucunna gótiló váré paḍḍaṭṭu* (like a man falling into a trap-pit he has dug himself).

By hook or by crook, *nyáyabhayamulugá.*

Putting the cart before the horse, *gurramu tócanu caḷḷemu peṭṭinaṭṭu* (like putting the bridle on the horse's tail).

House and home, *illúvácili.*

He has cleaned me out of house and home, *illu gulla ainadi.*

A house-warming, *grühapravéṣamu.*

Humble pie, *cuccina pénu* (a crushed louse).

Hunger is the best sauce, *ácali ruchi yerugadu* (hunger does not distinguish tastes).

To hunt high and low, *nalumukhála vetucuṭa.*

Holding with the hare and hunting with the hounds, *inṭivánni lépi donga chétici carra y'ichchin aṭṭu* (like waking the master and giving the thief a stick).

I

That will cut no ice, *á pappu uḍucadu* (that porridge won't boil).

Idleness is the root of all evil, *durmárgamunacu tandri baddhacamu.*

He is seriously ill, *atanici voḷḷu baluvugá n'unnadi* (his body is heavy).

To take a thing ill, *páṭigá paṭṭuṭa.*

He is the image of his father, *váḍu tanḍri atstsu.*

He is in for it, *adi vánici tappadu.*

The Iron Age, *caliyugamu.*

J

Jack of all trades and master of none, *ubhaya bhrashṭutvam y'upparasanyásitvam* (navvydom and halidom, Jack of two trades and master of neither; of a navvy turned sanyasi).

I will dust your jacket for you, *ní dummu duluputánu.*

To beat to a jelly, *pinḍi pinḍugá dantsuṭa* (to beat to a paste).

Job's comforters, *árchéváru gáni tírchéváru léru* (people who allay but do not assuage).

Justice incarnate, *Nyáyamúrti.*

K

Keep yourself to yourself, *yevari zócyamunacu veḷḷacu.*

We keep ourselves to ourselves, *pardyiváḷḷató sahavásam cheyyamu.*

To kick over the traces, *haddu míri pravartintsuṭa.*

Woe to thee, O land, when thy king is a child, *bahu náyacam, strí náyacam, bála náyacam* (the rule of many, of a woman, of a child).

Kith and kin, *tsuṭṭapaccamulu.*

L

Golden lads and lasses, *bangáru chinnaváḷḷu.*

It's a long lane that has no turning, *chícaṭi connáḷḷu vennela connáḷḷu.*

Laughing in his sleeve, *lólópala navutu.*

His word is law, *áyana máṭacu yeduru lédu* (there is no gainsaying him). *Nandi anṭé Nandi, pandi anṭé pandi* (if he says it is Siva's bull it is Siva's bull, if he says it is a pig it is a pig).

To give a leg up, *paici legatíyuṭa.*

On his last legs, *tsúḍa tsuṭṭamú, mocca daivamú lédu* (no relation to call on, no God to call upon).

To lend an ear, *chevi ogguṭa.*

The lesser evil, *guḍḍiló mella* (better squint than be blind).

One lie makes many, *oca abaddhamu cammaḍánacu veyyi abaddhálu cá valenu.*

To lie like a trooper, *yugála náṭi Yudhishṭharuḍu.*

Life is sweet to all, *yevari pránamu várici típu.*

While there is life there is hope, *pránamu v'unḍé varacu bhayámu lédu.*

What is life without honour? *mánamu póyina venuca pránam enducu?*

Though it cost me my life, *ná pránamu póyiná.*

It came to light, *baiṭabaḍinadi.*

Lightly come, lightly go, *vachchina dóvané pótundi.*

Falling into the lion's mouth, *dága póyi, talári y'inṭló dúrináḍ aṭa* (going to hide he got into the policeman's house).

Putting your head into the lion's mouth, *róṭló burra peṭṭuṭa* (putting your head into the mortar).

Half a loaf is better than no bread, *guḍḍiló mella* (better squint than be blind).

Lock, stock, and barrel, *illû vácili* (house and hall).

Long in the tooth, *vayasu mudirindi.*

A long-winded story, *Conḍavíṭi chéntráḍu* (Kondavidu well-rope, of a proverbially deep well like the well of San Patrizio at Orvieto).

Look before you leap, *illu caṭṭi tsúḍu, peḷḷi chési tsúḍu* (look before you marry or build). *cúrtsunḍi paḍucó valenu* (sit before you lie).

Looking a gift-horse in the mouth, *puṭṭeḍu punyánic isté pitstsa cuntsam ani pícul áḍin aṭṭu* (like disputing the measure when taking a gift of grain).

What bad luck! *id eccaḍi grahachâram!*

M

Her maiden name, *puṭṭinṭi péru.*

Man proposes, God disposes, *tán ocaṭi talisté, Daivamu ocaṭi talachinadi.*

A mare's nest, *gurrapu gúḍu.*

Like master like man, *Rámuni vanṭi Rázu v'unṭé, Hanumantuni vanṭi banṭu appuḍé v'unṭáḍu.*

One man's meat is another man's poison, *ocanici y'iguru cúra y'ishṭamu, ocanici pulusu cúra.*

Many men many minds, *burracu vaca gunamu.*

There is no medicine for a mind diseased, *manóvyádhici mandu lédu.*

The meek shall inherit the earth, *vinayam lóca vaṣyam.*

Milk from a stone, *atti púchinaṭṭu* (flowers from a banyan).

Crying over spilt milk, *gatamu gurinchi vichárintsuṭa.*

Money rules the world, *dhana múlam idam jagat* (Skt.). *dabbu prámánacu lancé* (money is the link of life).

Monkey tricks, *nacca-jittulu.*

Moral influence, *táḍu léni caṭṭu, cóla léni peṭṭu* (tying up without a rope and hitting without a missile).

Mortal peril, *prána sancaṭam.*

Making a mountain out of a mole-hill, *góranta v'unṭé conḍanta cheyyuṭa* (making a mountain out of a thing the height of a nail).

I shall move off to-morrow, *répu nénu prayánam.*

He has another move up his sleeve, *vánici vére yettu v'unnadi.*

Stirring up mud, *dṣuddhamu mída ráyi vésté.*

My name is mud, *búḍidaló pósina panníru ai póyinánu* (I have become like rose-water thrown on mud).

To muddle through, *gaṭṭeccintsuṭa* (to climb the bank).

N

Name and fame, *pérú pratisthalú.*

At dead of night, *artha rátramandu.*

A nod for a wise man, a rod for a fool, *manishic oca máṭa, goḍḍuc oca debba.*

None so blind as those that won't see, *nidra póyina vánici lépa vatstsunu, mélucunna vánici lépa lému* (you can wake a sleeper but not a man who is awake).

He hunted in every nook and corner, *sandulu gondulu antá veticináḍu.*

Cutting off your nose to spite your own face, *náluca pícuconi tsachchenu* (he tore out his own tongue and died).

Cutting off your nose to spite your neighbour's face, *porugu patstsagá v'unṭé poiló níḷlu pósucunaṭṭu* (like pouring water on your own hearth because your neighbour is doing well).

Looking for what is in front of your nose, *vetucupóyina tíga cáḷlu tsuṭṭuconn aṭṭu* (looking for a creeper twined round your legs).

Nothing doing, *Turaca vídhiló sanyási bhicsha* (a Sanyasi's takings in Muhammedan street).

O

He has sown his wild oats, *váḍu cágitsallárina pálu* (he has boiled and cooled his milk).

Ocular demonstration, *pratyacsha pramánamu.*

Old wife's tale, *pucciṭi puránamu.*

Olla podrida, *calagúra gampa.*

Once upon a time, *anagá anagá.*

P

Enough to try the patience of a saint, *yenta ṣántudic ainá yeṭlá cópam rácunḍá v'unṭundi?*

To throw pearls before swine, *pandici yélárá panníru ginḍi?* (rose-water before swine). *gáḍidecu pósina gandhi poḍi* (scent before an ass). *búḍidaló pósina panníru* (rose-water poured on mud). *cóti chéti púladanḍa* (a flower-garland in the hand of a monkey).

As easy as shelling peas, *vennaló ventruca tísinaṭṭu* (like drawing a hair out of butter).

The pen is mightier than the sword, *catti váḍá, calam váḍá?* (is the sword or the pen sharper?). *catti póṭu tappiná calam póṭu tappadu* (you may parry the thrust of the sword but not the thrust of the pen).

To the last penny, *vaca dammiḍi migultsucócunḍá.*

Without a penny to bless himself with, *bhuctici zaragaca. garbhadaridruḍu. caṭicadaridruḍu. púṭacúṭici gati lédu. vaṭṭi bitstsagáḍu.*

Robbing Peter to pay Paul; *cáculanu coṭṭi gaḍḍalacu vésinaṭṭu* (beating the crows and throwing to the kites).

The pick of the class, *clásuló merica.*

Like a pig flying, *rócaṭici chiguru paṭṭinaṭṭu* (like a pestle blossoming).

I don't care a pin, *nácu gaḍḍi paracató samánam.*

He who pays the piper calls the tune, *connaváḍé tinnaváḍu* (he who buys eats). *yevari cúḍu tinṭé vári máṭal áḍ áli,* you must obey the person whose food you eat.

Pitch dark, *conḍanta chícaṭi* (darkness as high as a hill).

A man of pith, *baláḍhyúḍu.*

No pleasing every one, *viḍuvum anṭé pámucu cópam, paṭṭum anṭé cappacu cópam* (if you say let go the snake is angry, if you say hold on the frog is angry).

Putting a man in your pocket, *jébuló vésuconuṭa.*

One man's meat is another man's poison, *ocanici y'iguru cúra y'ishṭamu, ocanici pulusu cúra.*

He hates me like poison, *nén anṭé vánici visham.*

A poodle-faker, *áḍavánḍla muḍḍi tsuṭṭu tirigéváḍu.*

You must positively come, *míru rácunṭé tíradu.*

What possessed him to do it? *idi cheyyuṭacu vánic émi paṭṭindi?*

I can't possibly stay away, *nénu veḷḷaca tíradu.*

Smoking in a powder magazine, *ill ecci corivi tippin aṭṭu* (getting on the roof and brandishing a fire-brand).

Practice makes perfect, *abhyásam cúsú vidya*, also *telisé varacu Brahma vidya, telisté cúsu vidya* (difficult when you don't know, easy when you do).

He pressed for payment, *zuṭṭu paṭṭi sommu aḍigináḍu* (seized him by the long hairs).

For our private use, *manacu pratyécamgá.*

Pros and cons, *sádhaca bhádacamulu.*

A providential opportunity, *daivicamugá labhinchina samayamu.*

Pulling your house about your ears, *compa tístu v'unnadi.*

He did it on purpose, *yerigi chésináḍu.*

A full purse never lacked friends, *caliginavárici andaru tsuṭṭálé.*

Purse pride, *dhana madamu.*

Putting the cart before the horse, *ill alucagáné panḍuga y'aguná ?* (smearing the house does not bring on the festival).

Q

Considering both sides of a question, *cíḍ enchi mél enchi.*

Keep it quiet, *gópyamgá n'unḍa valenu.*

'Quidquid delirant reges plectuntur Achivi', *yaṭhá rájá táṭhá prajá.*

'Quot homines tot sententiae', *burracu vaca gunamu.*

R

It never rains but it pours, *tala caḍaga póté vádagalla vána vembaḍé vachchinadi* (he went out into the rain to wet his head and a hail-storm came along).

Reaping where you have not sown, *dunné rózulaló désam mída póyi, cóta rózulaló coḍavali paṭṭuconi vachchináḍu.*

They are in reduced circumstances, *váru nochchi póyindru.*

To reel off, *yécaruvu peṭṭuṭa.*

The remedy is worse than the disease, *conḍandlucacu mandu vésté unna naluca úḍi póyinaṭṭu* (like the tongue coming out when medicine was applied to the uvula).

Revenge is sweet, *teguva Dévendra padavi* (revenge is very heaven).

The rich hath many friends, *caligina-várici andaru tsuṭṭálé.*

Right or wrong, *tappá y'oppá.*

He is always right, *Nandi anṭé Nandi, pandi anṭé pandi* (if he says it is Siva s bull it is Siva's bull, if he says it is a pig it is a pig).

Ripping up old sores, *máripóyina punḍu malli répinaṭṭu.*

Root and branch, *sammûlam* or *amûlágramugá.*

A roundabout way, *tsuṭṭudári.*

Running with the hare and hunting with the hounds, *inṭivánni lépi donga chétici carra y'ichchinaṭṭu* (waking his master and handing the thief a stick).

S

He had his say, *tanivi tíra máṭláḍináḍu.*

Every schoolboy knows, *scúluló tsaduvucunné pillacáyacu samétu adi telusunu.*

Scion of a great house, *goppa y'inṭi biḍḍa.*

To put the screw on, *zuṭṭu paṭṭi sommu aḍaguṭa* (to take by the hairs and demand money).

He puts the screw on, *váḍu maramécugáḍu.*

Between Scylla and Charybdis, *mundarici vasté goyyi, venaccu póté nuyyi.*

Between the devil and the deep sea, *mundara pallam, venuca miṭṭa.*

To be at sea, *Ntsacunḍá n'unḍuṭa.*

A word in season, *víl erigina máṭa.*

Happy is he who serveth not another's will, *svatantramu svargalócamu.*

To settle a matter at a blow, *ocaṭé debba renḍé muccalu* (one blow, two pieces).

A black sheep in the flock, *tulasí vanamló ganzái mocca* (hemp among the basil).

As well be hanged for a sheep as a lamb, *ḍabbucu vachchina cheyyi varahácu vastundi* (the hand that stretches for a pie will stretch for a pagoda).

Every one knows where his own shoe pinches, *gúniváḍu paḍucuné valla*

gúnivánici telusunu (the cripple knows how he can lie most comfortably).
Short and strong, *poṭṭi gaṭṭi*.
The taming of the shrew, *gayyáḷini sádu cheyyuṭa*.
Sick at heart, *pránam visigi pótu*.
A sickly sheep infects the flock, *tá chedda cóti vanam anta cherichinadi* (a bad monkey infects the grove).
A sight for sore eyes, *cannula panḍuga*.
There is no making a silk purse out of a sow's ear, *Gangaló munigité cáci hamsa autundá?* (will a crow become a swan by bathing in the Ganges?).
Your sin will find you out, *pápa phalamu anubhavimpaca tirundá?*
To sing a Te Deum, *jayabhéri véyuṭa* (to beat the big drum).
To sit on thorns, *muḷḷaḷḷó cúrtsunḍuṭa*.
Six of one and half a dozen of the other, *í v'úrici á v'úr entó, á v'úrici í v'úr anté* (it is as far from village A to village B as from B to A).
At sixes and sevens, *pani árumúḍ ai póyinadi* (at sixes and threes).
The skeleton in the cupboard, *inṭi guṭṭu*.
A slip of the tongue, *nóru zári* (my tongue having slipped).
A slow as a snail, *chíma lágu pácutáḍu*.
He comes up smiling, *yé samudramló paḍiná télunu* (he will float in any sea).
Snapping his fingers at me, *ná moga-muna meṭica virichi*.
A soldier of fortune, *áyudhópajívi*.
A Solon, *Brühaspati*.
He is a bit out of sorts, *váḍ émó y'idigá n'unnáḍu*.
Spare the rod and spoil the child, *debba Dévendra lócaṃ* or *danḍam daṣa gunam bhavét* (both Skt. proverbs often in the mouths of schoolmasters; they mean that boys are the better for a whipping).
We are not on speaking terms, *vánici nácu máṭalu lévu*.
I will show you a turn of speed, *picca-balam* (strength of calf) *tsúpistánu*.
Sponging, *atucula bratucu*.
Throwing in a sprat to catch a salmon, *íta ginza y'ichchi táṭi ginza lágéváḍu* (a date to catch a palm-fruit; the Indian date is worthless).
The willing horse needs no spur, *ich-chéváníci patram vaddu* (the man who is making a free gift does not require a document).
A man of standing, *ghardna manishi*.
The 'status quo ante', *yathá sthiti*.
Steady on, *tondara paḍa bócu*.
It is the first step that counts, *nilutsun-ḍaḍánacu zágá doricité, cúrtsunḍaḍá-nacu appuḍé dorucutundi* (as soon as you have found a place to stand you will find one to sit). *árambha ṣúrat-vam* (daring at the outset).
To stick like a leech (or limpet), *úḍuga vittanamu vanṭiváḍu* (a man who sticks like an uduga seed). *cálu paṭṭu-coni lágité, tsúru paṭṭuconi véláḍéváḍu* (when they pulled him away by the legs he clung to the eaves).
Locking the stable door after the horse has been stolen, *gata jala sétubandhan-namu* (damming after the flood has passed).
They come of a bad stock, *Lancaló puṭṭinavár ella rácshasulé* (all who are born in Lanka are demons).
Falling between two stools, *góchici pedda, angavastramucu chinna* (large for a loin-cloth, small for a mantle).
It will make a long story, *adi y'oca Bháratam agunu* (this will be as long as the Mahabharata).
The streets are free to all, *víḍhulu andarici pottu*.
To stuff oneself with food, *canṭhach-púrtigá bhacshintsuṭa* (to eat up to the neck).
Strike while the iron is hot, *véḍilóné cáryam ságintsa valenu*.
To pull the strings, *áḍintsuṭa*.
Sugared words, *téné máṭalu* (honeyed words). *chaccara púta púsina visham* (poison coated with sugar).
Sunlight puts out the fire, *diviṭi cinda dípamu* (the lamp under the torch).
A swan among geese, *núru cáculaló vaca cóyila* (one cuckoo among a hundred crows).
In the sweat of one's brow, *nosalu chemaṭa cárchi*.
What a swindle! *yenta mósam!*

T

His tail between his legs, *tóca ten-tsuconi*.
I will take it on myself, *nádi púchí*.

Tastes differ, *burracu vaca gunamu, jihvacu vaca ruchi* (every head has its character and every tongue its sense of taste).

Tears of joy, *ánanda báshpamulu.*

He that telleth a tale to a fool speaketh to one in a slumber; when he hath told his tale, he will say, what is the matter? *Rámáyanam anta vini, Rámuḍici Síta yémi cávalenu aḍigin aṭṭu* (when he had heard the whole of the 'Ramayana' he asked what relation Sita was to Rama).

At the end of his tether, *niluva nída paṭṭu comma lécunḍá* (no shade to stand in, no branch to catch hold of).

As thick as thieves, *poccaṭi ráḷḷu ritigá* (like two fire-dogs).

Set a thief to catch a thief, *donganu dongayé paṭṭa valenu.*

To thrash within an inch of his life, *tsáva coṭṭuṭa.*

To give a good thrashing, *lessagá coṭṭuṭa.*

Threatened men live long, *dina Indám veyy éndlu áyussu.*

To tick off, *diṭṭamgá zádintsuṭa* or *tala mída miryálu núruṭa* (to grind pepper on his head).

His time is near, *vánici cálam sannihitam ainādi.*

On the tip of my tongue, *nótló ádutsunnadi.*

To fall into the toils, *valaló paḍuṭa.*

Tom Noddy's secret, *ati rahasyam paṭṭa bailu.*

To-morrow never comes, *répu ané rózu v'unnadá?* (is there such a day as to-morrow?).

To strike a total, *verasi caṭṭuṭa.*

He fell into his own trap, *tánu pannina valaló táné paḍḍáḍu.*

Travellers' tales, *Cáśici veḷḷi gáḍide guddu techchinaṭṭu* (like coming back from Benares with a donkey's egg).

Trembling on the brink, *támaráculó niḷḷu talladinchinaṭṭu* (like water quivering on the edge of a lotus leaf).

Bringing troubles on oneself, *cheṭṭu coṭṭi paici tetstsuconnaṭṭu* (felling a tree and bringing it down on oneself).

To blow one's own trumpet, *goppalu cheppuconuṭa.*

God's truth, *Ráma vácyamu.*

Truth will out, *nizamu nilacaḍa mída telusunu.*

Truth is bitter, *nizam áḍité nishṭhuram.*

All dance to his tune, *váru áḍin alla áṭa, páḍin alla páṭa.*

A turn of speed, *picca balam.*

Turning the tables on me, *ná vélu putstsuconi ná canné poḍichinavá?* (did you take my own finger to poke me in the eye?).

It's a long lane that has no turning, *chícaṭi conndḷḷu, vennela connáḷḷu* (for some days it is dark, for some days moonlight).

To have two strings to one's bow, *aité árica cácunṭé candi* (millet if it sprouts, if not pulse; i.e. if you sow both in the same field you will get one or the other).

U

Union is strength, *occa cheyyi taṭṭité tsappuḍu auná?* (takes two hands to clap).

If anything untoward happens, *avacatavaca yémaina zarigité.*

Ups and downs, *meracapallamulu* or *miṭṭapallamulu.*

Ups and downs of fortune, *calimiḷémulu.*

Upside down, *talacindulagá.*

V

'Verbum sat sapienti', *manchivárici máṭé mandu.*

Empty vessels make the most noise, *piṭṭa conchemu, cúṭa ghanamu* (small bird making much noise).

A viper nourished in the bosom, *pálu pósi, penchiná, pámu caravaca mánadu* (a snake will bite though you feed it on milk).

A voice crying in the wilderness, *aranya ródanam.*

They lifted up their voices and wept, *golluna góla peṭṭináru.*

'Sic vos non vobis', *cheṭṭu vésinaváḍ ocaḍu, dáni phalam anubhavinchinaváḍ ocaḍu* (one man plants the tree, another enjoys it).

Vows made in storms are forgotten in calms, *ápati moccálu, sampati cunṭhlu* (vows in bad times, revilings in good).

W

Walls have ears, *gódalacu chevul unnavi.*

That won't wash, *á pappu uḍucadu* (that porridge won't boil).

Washington could not tell a lie, *Harischandruḍu áḍi tappanivádu.*

Water finds its own level, *níḷḷu pallam erugunu.*

His wedded wife, *caṭṭucona bhárya.*

He is wedded to that, *á panici chengu vésináḍu.*

When the devil was ill the devil a monk would be, when the devil was well the devil a monk was he, *ápat cálamuna mocculu, sampat cálamuna bútulu.*

Every why has a wherefore, *cáranamu lécunḍá cáryamu puṭṭaḍu.*

To get the wind up, *váta taḍi lédu* (a dry mouth), or *battalaló alpáchamánamu cheyyuṭa* (wet breeches).

It is an ill wind that blows no one any good, *goḍḍuváḍu goḍḍuc édchinḍu, tóluváḍu tóluc éḍchináḍu* (the cattle-dealer cried for his cattle, the hide-dealer cried for the hides). *chevvácu póyina ammacu yenta vyasanamó doricin ammacu yanta santósham* (the lady who found the ear-ring was as pleased as the lady who lost it was sorry).

Set your sail according to the wind, *yé gálic á tsápu yettu.*

Fair without, foul within, *lóna vicáramu, baiṭa srüngáramu.*

At one's wits' ends, *tótsacunḍá n'unḍuṭa.*

To give the wolf the wether to keep, *tóḍéṭini gorrela cáya peṭṭinaṭṭu.*

She is fast growing into a woman, *áme rajasval ayyé pacvamló n'unnadi.*

Many words will not fill a bushel, *vaṭṭi máṭala valla poṭṭalu púḍutavá ?*

Fair words butter no parsnips, *ṣushca priyamulu, ṣúnya hastamulu* (vain cajoleries, empty hands).

Bad workmen find fault with their tools, *áḍa léca, maddel óḍ annaṭṭu* (the bad dancer said the drum was broken).

He is all the world to her, *váḍé ámecu prapancham.*

The world's sweetheart, *jaganmóhini.*

The whole world has gone to the dogs, *prapancham anta páḍ ai póyinadi.*

To have come down in the world, *metta náḷḷu póyinavi, chetta náḷḷu vachchinavi* (the mattress days have gone, the straw days have come).

A worm at the root, *vrüicshánici véru purugu.*

To wreak one's anger, *cópamu tírtsuṭa.*

Y

All the years of one's life, *puṭṭi buddhi yerigina tarváta* (ever since I was born and reached the age of discretion).

Youth's a stuff will not endure, *cálach crídati gachchhatyáyuch* (a Skt. proverb meaning 'time sports, life goes').

PLATE VIII

Railway Bridge over the Canal, Bezwada

The Kistna Bridge, Bezwada

The Kistna Anicu, Bezwada